# FUTURES GUIDE
# 2023

## The Top Prospects For Every MLB Team and more

### Edited by Andrew Mearns

Smith Brickner, Marc Delucchi, Nathan Graham, Tyler Oringer, Jeffrey Paternostro, Grant Schiller, Jarrett Seidler, Ben Spanier, John Trupin, Eli Walsh, Brandon Williams, Matt Winkelman

Bret Sayre, Consultant Editor
Robert Au, Harry Pavlidis and Amy Pircher, Statistics Editors

Library of Congress Cataloging-in-Publication Data:
paperback
ISBN-10: 1950716996
ISBN-13: 978-1950716999

Project Credits
Cover Design: Ginny Searle
Interior Design and Production: Amy Pircher, Robert Au
Layout: Amy Pircher, Robert Au

Cover Photos
Front Cover: Gunnar Henderson. © Mitch Stringer-USA TODAY Sports

Baseball icon courtesy of Uberux, from https://www.shareicon.net/author/uberux

Manufactured in the United States of America
10 9 8 7 6 5 4 3 2 1

# Table of Contents

# Top 101 Prospects

by Jeffrey Paternostro, Jarrett Seidler, Nathan Graham and Ben Spanier

## 1.) Gunnar Henderson, SS/3B, Baltimore Orioles

Sam Miller once wrote that "we're each of us a single machine, and all the little parts of that machine thrive off each other in some way that brings them all up or down together." So what happens when those little parts work together to pull an already very good prospect skyward? Henderson provides the answer, as he jumped from "interesting power/speed shortstop with hit tool questions" to "the best prospect in baseball." Over the course of 2022, Henderson's power projection ticked up from plus to plus-plus. His bat-to-ball abilities improved from below-average to solid-average or even a touch higher. He not only started chasing less but began taking pitcher's strikes early in the count and fouling them off in two-strike counts. All of those micro improvements led to one macro outcome: He's an exponentially better hitting prospect now because he makes more contact and does a lot more damage when he does. After spending the bulk of 2021 at High-A, where he hit .230 with a 30% strikeout rate, Henderson torched both levels of the upper minors all spring and summer—much of that before he could legally drink—to the score of a .297/.416/.531 slash line. Called up to the show that never ends on the last day of August to bolster Baltimore's unexpected playoff chase, he ended the season hitting .259/.348/.440 at age 21 in the majors while falling just short of losing rookie eligibility. We don't expect him to leave the dirt at Camden Yards for a very, very long time.

## 2.) Jordan Walker, OF/3B, St. Louis Cardinals

Walker began the season as a 19-year-old in Double-A and posted a near-.300/.400/.500 batting line. If he doesn't have the most raw power in the minors he's within a shout of the top of the list. While he still hits the ball on the ground a bit too much to get his 80-grade pop into games consistently, he started lifting the ball more over the course of the 2022 season. Walker knocked more than half his home runs after July 1, and he tightened up his ability to make contact in the zone as well. Walker is listed at 6-foot-5 and 220 pounds and both those measurements look light nowadays, so he's going to deal with some swing-and-miss given how long it will take his arms to get the bat through the zone. He's officially grown off third base as well, spending most of the latter half of the season in the outfield. The Cards are trying him a bit in center field—and he's still an above-average runner—but right field might be his ultimate home, where he should slug enough to be a star. Walker enters the 2023 season as a 20-year-old on the cusp of the majors and one of the top prospects in baseball.

## 3.) James Wood, OF, Washington Nationals

One of the single most important skills for a hitting prospect is the ability to make contact within the strike zone. Scouts express this as "bat-to-ball," analysts as "Z-Contact" or its inverse, "In-Zone Whiff." Unlike for the majors, you can't go on our website or FanGraphs or Baseball Savant or anywhere else to find it comprehensively for minor leaguers (at least not yet), but it's incredibly important. It was considered Wood's major flaw out of the draft, except then he went to Low-A and displayed superior in-zone contact ability—both from an eye-scouting perspective and an analytical one—to most of the hitters surrounding him near the top of this list. Given that he already had among the highest power potentials in the entire minor leagues and makes solid swing decisions...well, he missed some time last year with knee and wrist injuries, but other than that there's not much to nitpick here. If the Juan Soto trade ends up working out for Washington, Wood will probably be the reason why.

## 4.) Francisco Álvarez, C, New York Mets

Álvarez is a short, wide backstop who was a fringy defender behind the plate before his offseason ankle surgery. He must really be able to hit, huh? Well, he's hit 51 dingers the last two seasons in the minors in just a shade over 200 games. Álvarez is plenty twitchy at the plate where he flashes plus-plus bat speed and raw power. He can get a bit pull-happy and has an expansive view of what he can hit hard, but he's been one of the youngest players at every minor-league stop and he's the first notable catching prospect to debut at 20 years old since Dioner Navarro. He's about as high-variance as you will find in a top-five prospect. If Álvarez can't catch, he's not athletic enough to play elsewhere in the field, and while he could hit enough to be a good designated hitter, we don't really rank future DHs this high. If he can stick behind the plate—and there has been some year-over-year improvement in his receiving—well, how many catchers out there are banging 30+ home runs?

## 5.) Elly De La Cruz, SS, Cincinnati Reds

De La Cruz has the best chance of any prospect to be a franchise-defining, face-of-baseball kind of superstar. He's an electric athlete, with a mix of fast-twitch movements, body control, size and speed, which is unparalleled across the minors. He has true top-of-the-line bat speed with surprisingly strong barrel control from both sides of the plate. If just *one thing* clicks a little bit more for him, he's going to be a superstar. But at present, he simply chases outside the zone way, way, **way** too much. Like, "as much as anyone in the majors but Javier Báez" too much—and that's against minor-league pitching. De La Cruz hasn't actually needed to improve his approach to perform yet—he hit .304 and slugged .586 last year, as neither High-A nor Double-A pitchers could actually exploit his love for swinging at breaking balls low and fastballs high, which speaks to the special nature of his bat. When and if that day comes, he'll either make the adjustment and become one of the best players in the game, or "what if Elly De La Cruz made average swing decisions?" will become a question we ask ourselves for decades to come.

## 6.) Corbin Carroll, OF, Arizona Diamondbacks

Carroll has recovered nicely from a shoulder injury that cost him almost all of the 2021 season. He posted a 1.000 OPS in the upper minors—despite a mere 29 full-season plate appearances previously—and added an .830 OPS in the majors at the end of 2022. Amarillo, Reno and Chase Field are three very nice places to hit mind you, and Carroll posted a pretty significant platoon split. If we nitpick further, his contact rates and exit velocities were just "fine," and he isn't the most natural center fielder despite good foot speed. Carroll also doesn't have a real weakness in his game; he's a potential 20/20 outfielder who should get on base and impact the game with his speed. He's the favorite for 2023 National League Rookie of the Year, and as likely to be a perennial above-average regular as anyone in the top 10 other than Henderson. All our nitpicks just mean he's the sixth-best prospect in baseball rather than the second.

## 7.) Anthony Volpe, SS, New York Yankees

"Anthony Volpe will have to be ___ to validate himself in view of [insert angsty Yankee fan's grievance with the organization here]" will never be an easy bar to clear, especially for a prospect who, despite his universally agreed upon global top-10 status, is a sum-over-parts type of talent. All of those parts are above-average or better, of course, which is what gives this Jersey guy a chance to be the Yanks' best first-round outcome since Aaron Judge. Volpe maintains his hit tool well even with a very modern swing designed to lift the

ball as much as possible, and his glove, arm and instincts make him a good shortstop who may profile more cleanly as a very good third baseman. He also generates additional value with his opportunistic baserunning and feel for the game. He'll be up sometime in 2023. So, an infielder who makes multiple All-Star games probably clears the bar. (Alright, who are we kidding? He needs to win a World Series.)

## 8.) Grayson Rodriguez, RHP, Baltimore Orioles

Rodriguez remains the best pitching prospect in baseball due to a combination of some major service time shenanigans and a minor lat injury. Oh, and the stuff. The stuff is really good. He came out dominating Triple-A as he has every other stop on the Orioles organizational ladder. He flashes five potential above-average pitches including a mid-90s—touching higher—fastball and a potential plus-plus change and slider. The curve and cutter are pretty good as well. Rodriguez didn't always have the breaking balls working for him consistently—especially post-injury—but his arsenal is so deep he can pick and choose what looks good on the menu from start to start. And when the full five-course Michelin-starred meal is on offer, he looks like a budding ace. His command is maybe a bit too far to the fringe side of average to project as a no. 1 starter quite yet, so look for Baltimore to have Rodriguez work on that in Norfolk for, oh, let's say the first three or four weeks of 2023.

## 9.) Jackson Holliday, SS, Baltimore Orioles

In a year's time, Holliday went from a projected second-round pick who might head to Oklahoma State to play for his uncle to the 1.1 pick and a spot atop a trio of brilliant emerging prospects named Jackson. As the pre-draft process unfolded, Holliday emerged late as the best prospect in the class, pairing incredibly advanced swing decisions with a tremendous feel for contact; his chase and zone-contact rates are just stupendous for his age, and we know in 2023 that's what drives a lot of hit tool development. Holliday has decent power projection too, and on top of it all he's likely to stick at shortstop from a talent perspective, although the Orioles have three other middle infielders on this list, so where everyone plays in 2025 is a ball still up in the air. Matt Holliday made seven All-Star teams and tallied over 40 WARP, so it's going to be quite an uphill climb for his son to become the best player at Christmas dinner. But it's possible.

## 10.) Jackson Chourio, OF, Milwaukee Brewers

Chourio might end up an interesting test case in the sometimes tense relationship between traditional eye-scouting and modern batted ball data. On one hand it is beautiful to watch him play—the Maracaibo, Venezuela native is a superior athlete who runs and throws well enough to stick in center long-term, and at the dish he showcases an explosive swing with advanced balance and torque designed to get as much power as he can out of his frame. On the other hand, that frame isn't huge, and there is room for improvement in both swing decisions and quality of contact. What can't be debated is Chourio's precociousness—the man was born in 2004 and dominated full-season ball as an 18-year-old (.324/.373/.600 at Low-A, .252/.317/.488 at High-A), drawing comparisons to Trout, Harper and Stanton. It remains possible that he blitzes Double-A and Triple-A in short order and ends the conversation before it can begin.

## 11.) Eury Pérez, RHP, Miami Marlins

The towering righty—now listed at 6-foot-8, and that might be short—kept climbing up the ranks by reaching Double-A a week before his 19th birthday and striking out 110 batters over 77 innings. Ho-hum, totally normal stuff. Pérez has a full four-pitch mix now and they're all pretty developed. His fastball easily sits in the mid-90s and regularly gets into the upper-90s; it doesn't have true bat-missing shape so it has induced more weak contact over swinging strikes, but it's still a decent fastball. He already had a breaking ball that flashed plus dating back to 2021, and he's more recently added a hard slider that is also going to be an above-average to plus offering. His changeup has also flashed huge in bursts, although he hasn't leaned on it a ton yet, and it's worth noting that Miami has shown elite skill at maximizing that particular pitch, sometimes at the MLB level. Pérez fills up the zone and gets both chases and whiffs. Overall, he has everything you could want in an elite pitching prospect short of an obvious 80-grade pitch. He only pitched four innings after the first week of August while battling a reported minor shoulder issue.

## 12.) Andrew Painter, RHP, Philadelphia Phillies

As good as Pérez is, he may not even have the best pure stuff for a teenage pitching giant who has already reached Double-A. Painter, who reached that level for a five-start end-of-season run (with a strikeout-to-walk ratio of 37:2), throws a tick or two harder than Pérez, regularly hitting triple-digits. And his heater *does* have carry and movement that misses bats up and out of the zone. Painter primarily throws two breaking balls off his fastball, a diving curve and a sweeping slider, both of which only have above-average visual properties but miss bats at plus to plus-plus levels. His changeup is lagging currently but should improve with additional use. Painter has yet to be challenged as a pro and, coming off one of the best modern minor-league pitching campaigns by a teenager, it's plausible he opens 2023 in the majors while still just 19.

## 13.) Marcelo Mayer, SS, Boston Red Sox

Mayer might have been the top hitting talent in the 2021 amateur class at the time of the draft, and 18 months or so later, he still only ranks behind James Wood. Drafting is an inexact science, but Mayer's talent isn't mere hypothesis at

this point. He hit for average and power across both A-ball levels and showed off enough faculty in the field that we are a bit more confident he sticks at shortstop than we were on draft day. Mayer may not end up with a true plus tool in his locker—although both hit and power have more than a puncher's chance—so his level-by-level progression will be important to watch. He will get to Double-A at some point in 2023, perhaps even starting there—pack layers for Portland in April, Marcelo—and his Eastern League performance will either stamp him as a top-10 prospect in baseball or reveal the cracks in the offensive tools.

## 14.) Jackson Merrill, SS, San Diego Padres

This has been one heck of a two-year rocketship ride. Merrill was largely unknown to amateur scouts entering the 2021 prep season, an obscure kid from suburban Maryland who hadn't done much on the showcase scene before the pandemic hit. A couple months before the draft, his name started being whispered about in hushed tones by the few who had seen him as one of the secret best prospects in the draft due to late physical and hit tool development. Then general managers started showing up in Severna Park, and it became clear he was going to go in the top few rounds of the 2021 Draft as a potential star two-way shortstop. Despite the lack of foundation, the risk-tolerant Padres ultimately popped him with the 27th pick. After looking the part in the complex after the draft, Merrill was a top priority follow coming into 2022, where he promptly displayed a preternatural feel for hard contact despite having little experience hitting off anyone better than Annapolis-area high school pitchers and missing a bunch of time with a wrist injury. He does hit the ball way too much on the ground at present, but it's his only analytic flaw—and perhaps the only thing stopping him from being the best prospect in baseball in a year's time.

## 15.) Ricky Tiedemann, LHP, Toronto Blue Jays

It will take a few years to suss out the player development effects from the lost 2020 pandemic season. One thing it did do was send some prep players—who may have broken out and become major draft prospects—to college. Tiedemann was one such arm, heading off to junior college and becoming a 2021 third-rounder, the Golden West Rustlers' highest draft pick since Keith Kaub in 1986. Tiedemann's velocity popped into the mid-90s by the time fall instructs rolled around and he spent 2022 blitzing three levels of the minors, whiffing almost 40% of the batters he faced. His slider was the big riser in 2022, while he held his velocity gains, giving him two potential plus-plus pitches with a pretty good change to boot. There's a bit more uncertainty with Tiedemann compared to the arms ahead of him. He tossed just 78 innings last year following a short JuCo season in 2021 and a lost season in 2020. But he's merely a year away from erasing those concerns, and if he does this will likely be the last time we get to rank him. So let's just get our marker down under the wire here: Tiedemann has a good shot to be a top-of-the-rotation lefty, anchoring the Blue Jays rotation with Alek Manoah for years.

## 16.) Curtis Mead, 3B/2B, Tampa Bay Rays

Curtis Mead is an extremely good hitting prospect, justifying an aggressive ranking despite a murky and not altogether encouraging defensive outlook. The guy just hits, slashing .305/.394/.548 at Double-A in 2022 and following it up with .278/.377/.486 in a brief Triple-A campaign. He hits the ball early, hits it often and hits it very hard. He has a longish swing but a quick bat, and a plus power outcome is well within reason. What position will he be playing? TBD. He is still primarily a third baseman, but his actions and arm there aren't great. In the past, it may have been tempting to stick him at second despite his limited athleticism, but the new shift rules will make that difficult. First base is his likely landing spot, and that'll do just fine if he keeps hitting. Oh, and he's from Australia. We meant to make a joke about that.

## 17.) Brett Baty, 3B/OF, New York Mets

At a glance, Baty's 2022—.315/.410/.533 in the high-minors with the Mets briefly entrusting him with a regular job in a desperate pennant race before he hurt his thumb—seems valedictory. Under the hood, there's some real concern. Despite occasional glimpses of progress, Baty has continued to hit the ball on the ground way more than you want an emerging power threat to do. In practice, that means although he already hits the ball harder than most major-leaguers and flashes 80-grade power when he does lift and drive it, it's hard to actually project him for 30+ homers in the majors without changes. Things aren't much clearer for him in the field; despite decent fluidity and a big arm, he's never displayed a consistently reliable glove at third, and his frame is on the larger side for the hot corner anyway. Recent developments in Flushing threaten to push him to the outfield—where he's made occasional forays already but needs more experience—if he remains a Met at all.

## 18.) Marco Luciano, SS, San Francisco Giants

The zeal of the convert has its limits. Luciano dropped stateside and onto prospect writers' radars just as minor-league exit velocity was becoming more widely available, and subsequently a factor in things like...well, this list. His second appearance on our Top 101—this is year four—noted his 119-mph home run in fall instructs. But after four years, Luciano is still in High-A, has yet to dominate a minor-league level and dealt with a back strain that cost him two months of the 2022 season. Perhaps that is a bit unfair. He had a great stretch in Eugene before the back injury, showing both mechanical and approach improvements at the plate. He's still playing shortstop everyday and faced only a handful of pitchers younger than him in the Northwest League. He's

stagnated a bit in recent years, but with tools like these—as John Darnielle once wrote—something here will eventually have to explode, have to explode.

## 19.) Diego Cartaya, C, Los Angeles Dodgers

Cartaya stands out on the diamond, both for his physical size and his ability to impact the baseball at the plate. He's always been viewed as a hit-first prospect since coming stateside in 2019, but he's made strides with the glove, becoming a passable receiver behind the plate. Despite his lack of foot speed, he has enough lateral quickness to block well and a strong enough throwing arm to keep opponents from running wild on the bases. The Dodgers also love the soft skills he displays, raving about his leadership and ability to handle a pitching staff. The defensive gains are a bonus, but the carrying tools remain with his bat. He has double-plus power and he does pretty well getting to it in-game, recognizing spin well and having a feel for the barrel. There's still plenty of polishing remaining before Cartaya is big league-ready, but if it all comes together he'll become a power-hitting backstop, a rare commodity in today's game.

## 20.) Kyle Harrison, LHP, San Francisco Giants

Harrison has an analytically friendly modern starting arsenal. He comes from a very low arm slot for a starting pitcher and primarily works off two pitches that play well from that angle. His fastball velocity and spin is just fine—yes, low- to mid-90s is "just fine" now—but it plays well and induces plenty of swings-and-misses up in the zone due to his slot and the deception of perceived rise. The fastball tunnels well with his out-pitch, a dastardly sweeping slider that he uses to beat batters around the edge of the zone. He also mixes in a changeup with above-average potential. Harrison could use some improvements in command, but his fastball/slider combination gives him top-of-the-rotation potential.

## 21.) Ezequiel Tovar, SS, Colorado Rockies

Tovar is as complete a shortstop prospect as you will find in the minors. He's the best shortstop glove thus far on our list, a polished present plus defender who does everything well in the field. He will hit for average, hit for power—Coors won't hurt on either account—and he's a heady baserunner, if only a solid runner. He was the second-youngest player in the majors when he debuted in September. So why isn't Tovar up with the top shortstop prospects above? Well, we think he will hit for average, but that average will be in the .270 range—in a vacuum; again, Coors—and he was overmatched by better spin at times in Double-A. He needs to fill out and get stronger—especially in his upper half—to tap into the present sneaky pop. We think these things will all happen, and he will be one of the youngest players in the National League again in 2023, where he might just put some pressure on Corbin Carroll for that Rookie of the Year crown. But they haven't happened yet.

## 22.) Evan Carter, OF, Texas Rangers

Amidst the never-ending story that is the Rangers attempting to develop a hitting prospect to preconceived expectations, Carter represents the possibility for an apotheosis of sorts. Unlike top Texas prospects from 101s past, Carter is not a player outfitted with speed, defensive skills and elite athleticism who needs simply to develop the most difficult of tools, the ability to hit, in order to become a star. It isn't that Carter doesn't possess those traits—he does, in spades. What differentiates him from the others is that there are indications in his offensive performance that he shares characteristics with the types of prospects who become successful big-league hitters. Carter is extremely selective at the plate and makes excellent swing decisions, producing rock-solid numbers (.287/.388/.476 at High-A Hickory) that earned him a late-season taste of Double-A as a 19-year-old. The frame is still a bit willowy and he doesn't currently hit the ball extremely hard, so pop may be the last tool to appear.

## 23.) Taj Bradley, RHP, Tampa Bay Rays

Like his org-mate Curtis Mead, Bradley has acquitted himself well in Triple-A and should expect to debut sometime in 2023. Once an overslot fifth-round prep, the now-21-year-old has pretty clearly been the top non-Shane Baz Rays pitching prospect since mid-2021, when he was striking out all comers in the lower minors with an analytically appealing mid-90s fastball, a killer cut/slider thing and a very good curve. At one point it was fun to discuss Bradley's future role —the Rays, creative or nickel-and-dime depending on your vantage, would certainly find an interesting way to deploy him, even if not as a strict starter or reliever. A year of dominance in the upper minors—he would boast a 1.70 ERA and 30.9% strikeout rate over 74⅓ Double-A innings before drifting a bit nearer to earth following the midseason promotion to Durham—made it clear that Bradley projects as a starting pitcher. The question now: Will his health hold up better than it has for other recent Rays power arms?

## 24.) Jordan Lawlar, SS, Arizona Diamondbacks

You could argue, as we did, that Lawlar was the best prep shortstop prospect in the 2021 draft class. While perhaps lacking the same upside with the bat as Mayer, he was the more advanced hitter and that bore out in their first pro seasons. Lawlar made it all the way to Double-A in his age-19 season, hitting .300 with power. He has less projection in his bat, though, and his propensity to swing-and-miss in the zone is a concern, underpinning a strikeout rate that's a tad higher than you'd like for a plus, but not elite offensive profile. Lawlar has also looked a bit more like a second baseman than a shortstop in the pros, with throwing being a particular issue—he's the second of three Diamondbacks first-round picks who've suffered horrible shoulder injuries

that you will encounter on this list. So no, we don't think he's the best prep prospect in his class anymore, but he's still a very, very good one.

## 25.) Daniel Espino, RHP, Cleveland Guardians

If we had run a Top 101 Prospects list in late-April 2022, Espino would've easily been in the top half-dozen, and perhaps even at no. 1 overall. For a few weeks there, he looked like the best pitching prospect in recent memory. Espino was nuking Double-A hitters with three offerings projecting in the plus-plus to 80-grade band: a fastball hitting triple-digits with killer characteristics, one of the best sliders in the entire minors and a distinct downer breaking ball. He struck out 35 in 18⅓ innings over his first four starts, and was headed toward having a big impact on the pennant race. Then he was shut down with a reported knee injury. He never got back into games, and by the summer the Guardians acknowledged he was battling shoulder soreness. Given that his huge jump in stuff was almost immediately followed by a barking shoulder, we certainly have significant concerns about sustainability and durability. But man, it's the best stuff on the list.

## 26.) Gavin Williams, RHP, Cleveland Guardians

Speaking of Guardians pitchers with latent medical concerns, we wrote last year that if Williams sustained the health and performance he showed during the 2021 college season, he'd very quickly be one of the top pitching prospects in the minors. Well, he more or less did, and here he is. This isn't the world's most complicated profile, and it's extremely Guardians in the way that they maximize every college pitching prospect possible. Williams throws strong characteristic mid- to upper-90s fastballs, plus some sliders, up in the zone, and everything else down. At present he leans most on his slider out of his secondary offerings, although his curveball is more consistent and he's also developing a useful changeup. He's had two clean, dominant seasons in a row, and the years where he was struggling with ineffectiveness and injury in the East Carolina bullpen are now long in the rearview mirror.

## 27.) Bobby Miller, RHP, Los Angeles Dodgers

You'll notice a theme as you read through the reports on Dodgers' pitchers on this list—they have power stuff with less than ideal command—and nobody fits that profile better than Miller. His four-seam fastball flirts with triple digits, has decent ride and holds its velocity deep into games. He'll even mix in an occasional sinking two-seamer to keep hitters honest. The breaking stuff, a 12-5 curve and power slider, both have the makings of knee-buckling offerings that can miss bats. Throw in the change, which has excellent velocity separation, and you have the repertoire of a front-line starter. He got hit a little harder than expected during his time in the hitter-friendly Texas League but looked more the part of top prospect after his late-season promotion to the PCL. While his command isn't great and he could use a bit more polish in the upper minors, Miller is another weapon the Dodgers can utilize down the stretch in 2023.

## 28.) Pete Crow-Armstrong, OF, Chicago Cubs

Part of the prospect haul the Cubs garnered in their 2021 selloff, PCA used his first healthy minor-league season to plant his flag as the top prospect in the organization. An intense competitor with a high motor, he's an excellent defender whose plus range and instincts will allow him to patrol center field in Wrigley for the foreseeable future. The defense and speed give him a reasonably high floor but it's the bat that will have him in future All-Star conversations. He's an intelligent hitter, always tinkering and making adjustments to maximize his simple, efficient swing. Exceptional bat control and speed make for plenty of loud contact off the bat. While he's never going to be a slugger, he added some physical strength while rehabbing a shoulder injury, and that led to an increase in the over-the-fence power last season. Crow-Armstrong should serve as a table-setter atop the lineup for the next competitive Cubs team.

## 29.) Noelvi Marte, SS/3B, Cincinnati Reds

Marte was a casualty of the Mariners going all in at the deadline in an attempt to end their long playoff drought. It worked out for them, but for Marte, joining the Reds meant being part of an organization deep in shortstop talent. Cincinnati sent him to the AFL to get some reps at third but he struggled there, committing six errors in just 20 games. It really doesn't matter where he winds up defensively—the bat is the calling card in the profile. He possesses double-plus raw power and he knows how to get to it in-game without sacrificing contact ability. His approach at the plate is advanced, especially for a young player, as he commands the zone well and punishes mistakes. The jump to Double-A can be daunting, and he's sure to be tested by the advanced arms of the Southern League this year, but his huge offensive upside gives Cincinnati something to dream on no matter where he lands defensively.

## 30.) Masyn Winn, SS, St. Louis Cardinals

Drafted as a two-way player, there's not a lot of talk about Winn returning to the mound now that his bat has taken a large step forward. He looked overmatched in his initial professional season, getting overpowered by High-A pitching. He spent the following offseason getting stronger and more physical, and the results showed it in 2022. Pitchers could no longer overwhelm him with velocity as he began to impact the ball with more frequency. His throwing arm from short is unrivaled and he's not too shabby with the glove either. Those tools, plus his quick hands and excellent range, will make him an everyday player at the six.

## 31.) Termarr Johnson, 2B, Pittsburgh Pirates

Maybe we can give the Pirates credit here—they didn't galaxy brain this one. The 2022 fourth overall pick is this high on the list for a reason: we have a reasonably high degree of confidence that he will attain a plus hit tool. Despite being vertically challenged as professional athletes go, Johnson is a strong kid with a quick bat who barrels the ball hard and with consistency despite interesting swing mechanics. He is also pretty advanced already for a prep bat—he did well (.275/.396/.450) in a late season assignment to the Florida State League and could open 2023 at High-A if the organization is so inclined. He is a second baseman through and through, which limits his upside a bit, but his hitting ability and potential above-average power output from the left side are star-quality at the keystone.

## 32.) Colson Montgomery, SS, Chicago White Sox

If it is possible to be an immediately successful first-round pick who already looks like a developmental win, yet at the same time be a bit underwhelming, Montgomery is pulling it off. He packs a plus hit tool projection, but nothing else really pops despite a surprisingly advanced profile for a prep hitter that should allow him to matriculate quickly. His plate approach is very good, and excellent barrel feel and an ability to pick up spin enabled him to dominate Low-A and hold his own in High-A as a 20-year-old, slashing .324/.424/.477 and .258/.387/.417, respectively, over a combined 369 plate appearances at those levels. His power hasn't really manifested yet (though there should be more in that large frame), and the defense certainly could be better. Athleticism is present but foot speed is not, so there will be limited ancillary value to round out the profile. In the end Montgomery will have to hit and hit for power, and we think he will.

## 33.) Druw Jones, OF, Arizona Diamondbacks

The no. 2 pick in the 2022 Draft, Jones is a phenomenal defender in center field already, following in the footsteps of his 10-time Gold Glove-winning father. He's a plus-plus runner and thrower who takes brilliant routes: he's really the total package out there. At the plate, he brings a classic, smooth swing and a lot of bat speed. His power projection is above-average, albeit geared for opposite-field power over pull power at the moment. We don't have any professional data at all on Jones, because he suffered a severe shoulder injury while taking swings after signing and before even getting into a complex game. (Along with the severe shoulder injuries Carroll and Lawlar suffered in 2021, that means all three top Arizona outfield prospects have missed many months recently with similar, unusual injuries. No, we don't know what's in the water there.) We'll see how his bat plays against pro pitching this summer.

## 34.) Zac Veen, OF, Colorado Rockies

Veen's sweet lefty swing and projectable frame will tick every box for your more traditional scouting eye. He's a plus runner who swiped 55 bags last year while only getting caught nine times. Sure, the stat line doesn't pop, and he struggled after a promotion to Double-A, but he was only 20 and his skill set is sure to blossom soon enough, right? Maybe! He'll show you plus raw pop at 5 PM, but he doesn't actually hit the ball in games harder than his org-mate Ezequiel Tovar (despite looking like he should) and he hits the ball on the ground far too often to make consistent use of his power, anyway. The speed that makes him such an effective base-stealer isn't quite enough to let him play center field. Veen's swing remains one to dream on, and he isn't that far off from boasting an impact power/speed combo and starting everyday in Coors, but we're still mostly dreaming at present.

## 35.) Triston Casas, 1B, Boston Red Sox

The December DFA of Eric Hosmer (we hardly knew ye) seems to all but guarantee that Casas will be manning first during the vast majority of this season's Red Sox games. We don't expect an easy learning curve. Boston's lineup is short on thump after losing a lot of their old homegrown talent, and cheap production from new homegrown talent will be vital. Casas actually hasn't hit as many minor-league homers as you think, massive 6-foot-4 frame notwithstanding, but the raw pop is in there and he exhibits traits consistent with a plus hit grade. Casas struggled in his September cameo last season, but a few more oppo shots over the Monster against Gerrit Cole should get him in good with the Fenway faithful.

## 36.) Mick Abel, RHP, Philadelphia Phillies

Abel had the slight misfortune of being drafted a year ahead of Andrew Painter, a player with roughly the same profile who has better stuff and is moving much faster. But there's absolutely nothing wrong with Abel, who is exactly where you want a prep first-round pitcher to be entering his age-21 season. He throws in the mid- to upper-90s with good but not elite fastball characteristics, getting a solid number of whiffs. His best pitch is his slider, which visually presents as plus-plus but doesn't induce an overwhelming amount of chase outside the zone because it doesn't tunnel ideally with the rest of his arsenal. His curveball and changeup are both consistently average. He throws strikes but sometimes nibbles too much. He's a fairly high probability mid-rotation starter. He's just not Andrew Painter.

## 37.) Brooks Lee, SS, Minnesota Twins

Lee might be the polar opposite of Zac Veen. He looks like he learned to swing a Louisville Slugger by watching a Rankin/Bass animation of Hunter Pence. But all Lee's ever done is hit baseballs and hit them hard, including posting a ludicrous .400 batting average in the tough environs of the Cape Cod League. He hit almost as well across his sophomore and junior seasons at Cal-Poly and kept on hitting after the Twins made him the ninth pick in last summer's draft. Lee is a bit barrel-chested for shortstop—although he's twitchier and more athletic than you'd think given the frame—but should fit just fine at third base, where he may hit .300 now and again. He should settle in as a perennial plus hit/plus power bat at the hot corner, and will have a plus-plus "funny Twitter clips of weird swings that end up as doubles in the gap" game if nothing else. Assuming that Twitter is still up and running by the time he reaches the majors, that is.

## 38.) Colton Cowser, OF, Baltimore Orioles

Cowser's about as good of a prospect as you'd expect the no. 5 pick two years ago to be, but the *shape* of his projected performance has changed fairly substantially since he was drafted. His plate discipline has been great for as long as he's been a relevant prospect, but the strong contact ability we projected at Sam Houston State and even in the lowest rungs of Baltimore's system wilted in 2022 as he went up the organizational ladder. Cowser piled up 174 strikeouts between High-A, Double-A and Triple-A, and if you don't swing a whole lot and run up that many strikeouts, it means you're swinging through an awful lot of hittable pitches in the zone (and probably taking a few too many, too). To his credit, he's lifting and driving the ball on contact more than expected, so his game power projection is trending up even as he's connecting less. On the opposite side of the ball, he now projects to stay in center and maybe even excel there: a surprise given that he seemed likely to move to a corner just a year ago. In all, he's gone from a contact-first corner masher to a three-true-outcomes center field archetype before he's even hit the majors. Prospects, man.

## 39.) Miguel Vargas, 3B/OF, Los Angeles Dodgers

Rough debuts haven't derailed Vargas in the past. While the sweet swinger has posted a .300-or-better average at five out of six stops over the last three minor-league seasons, he came out the gates professionally with a .115/.148/.154 line back in the Cuban National Series over eight games. At age 14. Compared to that, his .170/.200/.255 big-league debut isn't so sour. Vargas' intervening work has honed his swing to a fine point: it is short to the ball and stays in the zone a long time, covering all quadrants. He has solid-average power that plays up because of how frequently he makes contact. He's no hacker, though, walking at an above-average clip throughout the upper minors. A third baseman by trade, the Dodgers have moved Vargas all over defensively, including having him take balls at first, second and left. That forced versatility is more representative of how much they want his bat in the lineup than some sort of endorsement of his ability to handle all of these positions with aplomb. He's a capable defender at third, but his skills would likely shine most at first base.

## 40.) Royce Lewis, SS, Minnesota Twins

Lewis made his big-league debut last May, a spot start made necessary by Carlos Correa's brief trip to the IL. Now that Correa is a free agent, the (other) former first-overall pick may be back to reclaim the future that was once his. It's been a long time coming for the (still just) 23-year-old, who has had to battle through horrible issues with his swing mechanics and even worse injuries in order to even get to this point. He's filled out some and may eventually have to move off short, though he is fine there for now. More importantly, his elite bat speed has not been diminished, and his swing is correctly modulated to create power. Lewis even posted a Correa-like OPS+ of 145 over the tantalizing 40 at-bats he managed before going down with his second serious knee injury. Now, he just needs to do the one thing in the game that is more difficult than hitting—stay healthy—and the world is his.

## 41.) Sal Frelick, OF, Milwaukee Brewers

We all have aesthetic preferences when it comes to baseball players. You might like Rich Hill's big, arcing lefty curveball, the direct, no-nonsense violence of a Giancarlo Stanton laser beam to the opposite field, or Jazz Chisholm Jr., full stop. I'm sure there is an audience out there for Sal Frelick, too—the universe contains multitudes—but a hit-first, left field prospect with a good approach is not high on our list of favorite archetypes. We are fond of the occasional scouting platitude though, and Frelick embodies one of our favorite tautologies: "Hitters hit." Frelick hit .331 across three levels and looked like a potential future batting champ, short to the ball with good wrists able to drive the outside pitch the other way, and punish pitchers that challenged him inside. He picks his pitches well too, and while his home run totals might only go as high as a Spinal Tap amp, Frelick will be the perfect complement to a Brewers lineup that has been awfully reliant on the long ball the last few seasons.

## 42.) Emmanuel Rodriguez, OF, Minnesota Twins

A recurring question from our readership, paraphrased: Who on this list is most likely to take a jump into the top 10 next year? This is of course merely a disguised dynasty league question, but it provides a useful frame for this blurb. Our answer: Emmanuel Rodriguez. We don't know if he would have gotten there with a full, healthy season for Fort Myers—he missed the second half of the season with a torn meniscus—but early signs were pointing way up. Rodriguez was crushing the Florida State League as a 19-year-old, showing a remarkably disciplined approach and punishing anything in the zone. All five tools flashed in short bursts in 2022. The knee injury might force him to a corner—and that was a possibility regardless, despite good foot speed—but Rodriguez's potential impact with the bat is equal to those in the top 10 right now. And if you want to expand on our opening question even further, he's one of a small handful of prospects outside the top 20 who have a chance to be the best prospect in baseball someday.

## 43.) Tink Hence, RHP, St. Louis Cardinals

The Cardinals picked three times in the first 63 picks in the 2020 Draft and Hence is the *lowest*-ranked of the three; their next pick, outfielder Alec Burleson, came reasonably close to making this list himself. Suffice to say, that has a chance to be a legendary class even though it was only a five-round draft. St. Louis has been extremely cautious with Hence, keeping him in extended spring training for most of 2021 and then limiting him to a series of one-inning complex appearances that summer. His 2022 debut was delayed until mid-May, he pitched with a lot of extra rest and never even went five innings, so he only threw 56⅓ of them in the regular season. But when he was on the mound he was simply sensational, toying with Low-A hitters while showing plus-or-better projections on his fastball, breaking ball and changeup. He continued to shine in the Arizona Fall League, where he got classmate Jordan Walker to fly out in the Fall Stars Game. We have little idea if he can handle anything resembling a true starting workload, but the sky's the limit if he can.

## 44.) Adael Amador, SS, Colorado Rockies

The Rockies don't lack for interesting middle infield prospects. Amador is a couple levels behind Ezequiel Tovar, but has far more advanced bat-to-ball skills despite spending his entire 2022 season in A-ball. He's a switch-hitter with 70-grade bat speed who sprays hard line drives to the outfield seemingly at will. He walked more than he struck out last year, and while he doesn't really look to lift the ball now, at least average power is possible given how much hard contact he makes. The profile is bat-first (and maybe second and third). Amador is an above-average runner but a bit too aggressive on the bases at present, and his infield actions will likely force him to second base in the medium term. Still, the hit tool is a true carrying tool, and the 19-year-old has at least a plus one.

## 45.) Hunter Brown, RHP, Houston Astros

You may remember Brown from his scoreless 12th and 13th innings in the ALDS Game 3 marathon. The Astros called him up for a pair of early-September spot starts in place of Justin Verlander, and he pitched well enough in them to earn a lower-leverage spot in the playoff bullpen. He's able to carry mid- to high-90s with high spin as a starter or a reliever, although his movement profile is average so the pitch isn't a complete monster. His out-pitch is a plus-plus downer of a curveball that shows hard, late break. He also mixes in one of the hardest sliders you'll see, in the low- to mid-90s and overlapping some in the same velocity band as his fastball; some pitch classifications classify it as a cutter despite the slidery break. He rarely uses his changeup but has shown some ability to get whiffs with it, too. Brown is a higher-effort pitcher with mediocre command, and that could push him into a full-time bullpen role, although the Astros have been more malleable than most with pitching roles and are likely to give him every chance to start.

## 46.) Henry Davis, C, Pittsburgh Pirates

Davis is either too high or too low on this list, depending on who you ask. He is a catcher with obvious plus power (that's good) who might not be all that good at the finer points of catching (that's bad). The bat speed is elite and he hits the ball hard (that's good) but he tends to swing through too many pitches in the zone and struggled at Double-A—his .207/.324/.379 Altoona slash line contrasts dramatically with his .342/.450/.585 Greensboro output—amid an injury-riddled 2022 (that's bad). The massive upside inherent in his profile is still present, but so is the significant risk. His age-23 season will be an important one.

## 47.) Zach Neto, SS, Los Angeles Angels

The 2022 college hitter class was pretty deep at the top, but there wasn't really a clear, standout top option. Neto ended up the sixth college bat taken, going 13th overall. Perhaps he slid a bit due to the level of competition in the Big South conference, but Neto dominated there, hitting over .400 his sophomore and junior seasons for Campbell. Modern draft models tend not to see as big a gap between the Big South and the SEC as pundits might proffer, and Neto promptly hit .300 in his pro debut, most of which was spent in Double-A. Neto is likely to stick at shortstop all the way to the majors, and while it remains to be seen how much power he will generate with wood bats, everything else looks on target to make him a plus major league regular as soon as 2023.

## 48.) Oswald Peraza, SS, New York Yankees

After making a brief cameo in the playoffs that probably should have been less brief, Peraza seems the odds-on favorite to break camp as New York's (or in the event of a major trade, someone else's) starter at the six. The best infield defender in the org, he plays a stress-free shortstop and seems ready to contribute with the bat. A gap power guy who has been tapping into some over-the-fence pop, Peraza boasts very good in-zone contact rates and can be an above-average offensive producer despite pedestrian pitch selection abilities. Throw in some speed and baserunning ability and you've got a solid contributor at a premium position, something that every team needs.

## 49.) Cam Collier, 3B, Cincinnati Reds

Collier went down a road paved by Bryce Harper, getting his GED two years early and heading to a JuCo powerhouse in what should've been his high school junior season,

ultimately reclassifying for the draft a year before he'd have been eligible by graduating high school. Playing for Chipola College at age 17, Collier hit .333 with power, thereby breaking a bunch of draft model inputs that weigh age and college performance heavily. He then broke the models a little more with a cameo as the youngest player in recent Cape Cod League memory. Eligible for the 2022 Draft still four months shy of his 18th birthday, he slid down to the 18th pick and signed for a well above-slot $5 million bonus. Collier is a skills ahead of tools player right now, driven by bat-to-ball ability. While he's still very young and further physical growth is quite possible, he's not really hitting the ball that hard and his power projection is questionable at present. He's a suitable match for third base with the glove. He's likely to be one of the youngest players in full-season ball this year.

## 50.) Gavin Stone, RHP, Los Angeles Dodgers

A former small college bullpen arm, Stone followed up his breakout 2021 by becoming the most dominant pitcher in minor-league baseball last year. A large part of his success is due to his devastating changeup, which is quite possibly the best secondary pitch in the minors. It's a true bat-misser that tunnels well off of his mid-90s fastball. The slider also plays up from the change, breaking sharply glove-side and generating plenty of weak contact. He's proven himself to be a durable starter over the last two years, logging over 200 innings without missing any time due to injury. Stone might not have the upside of Bobby Miller, but he's very close and it's likely he gets a chance to make his debut in Los Angeles sometime in 2023.

## 51.) Griff McGarry, RHP, Philadelphia Phillies

A recurring theme of modern pitching prospect analysis is that everyone has great stuff now; at least every prospect a devoted fan is likely to know about. McGarry throws distinct four-seam and two-seam fastballs in the mid- to high-90s; the four-seamer gets whiffs up in the zone and the two-seamer has demon sinker properties and almost acts as a changeup at fastball velocity. His slider has taken a big step forward to become a potential out-pitch, overtaking a curveball that flashes plus itself, as his primary secondary offering. Yes, his changeup isn't much to look at, and yes, his command is still pretty spotty even if tremendously improved (he spent most of his college career walking around a batter an inning), but McGarry has the type of pitch mix where you kind of just have to ignore the bad parts and hope for the best. The Phillies tried him out of the bullpen late in the 2022 season in Triple-A in the hopes he could impact the pennant race. It didn't go great, so he might have less of an impact-reliever fallback than you'd think, given the profile.

## 52.) Tanner Bibee, RHP, Cleveland Guardians

Tell me if you've heard this story before: The Guardians drafted a command-first day-two college pitcher (in this case a 2021 fifth-rounder out of Cal State-Fullerton) with low-90s velocity, below-average stuff and no apparent projectability. By the end of his first full pro season, his velocity had jumped four or five ticks and he was striking out the world with a plus sweeping slider while still displaying pinpoint command and a usable change. Bibee struck out 167 batters last year in 132⅔ innings between High-A and Double-A after striking out 67 batters in 89⅔ innings in the Big West Conference the year before. There was just no way to see that coming, except that Cleveland keeps getting the same velocity and slider bumps out of the command-first college pitcher cohort year after year, a credit to their amateur acquisition and pitching development program alike.

## 53.) Marco Raya, RHP, Minnesota Twins

Modern pitching prospect evaluation is balancing ever more hellacious stuff—in this instance mid-90s heat with two potential plus-or-better breakers—against more conservative usage patterns. Raya had a barking shoulder in 2021 and only pitched into the sixth inning once in 2022. So there's an open question as to whether his stuff can hold up over longer stretches, especially since Raya is on the shorter and slighter side. On the other hand, we don't expect our major-league starters to throw much more than 150 innings in a season nowadays, and there are all sorts of roles you can carve out between starter and one-inning reliever. On the other, *other* hand, if Raya shows he can hold up as that 150-inning arm in 2023, he'll be one of the best pitching prospects around.

## 54.) Nick Nastrini, RHP, Los Angeles Dodgers

Once on the brink of quitting baseball due to the yips after thoracic outlet surgery, Nastrini has worked his way back, harnessing his electric stuff to become one of the top arms in a deep Dodgers system. His fastball easily sits in the mid-90s with some ride up in the zone and he pairs it well with a plus changeup. His breaking pitches both flash as future swing-and-miss offerings, with the sweeping slider currently ahead of the curve developmentally. It's a quality repertoire, nearly as good as both Gavin Stone's and Bobby Miller's, but Nastrini's command and control started off so poor that he massively improved in hitting his spots and still only got to fringe-average. Given the history of walks and injury, he still carries major bullpen risk.

## 55.) Endy Rodriguez, C/IF/OF, Pittsburgh Pirates

Not that the Steve Cohen Mets care, but they probably lost their end of the Joey Lucchesi trade. Rodriguez made himself an elite hitting prospect during the second half of the 2022 season—the April version of him would not have placed here—and he plays catcher (and second, first and left field).

Note that we didn't say he is a catcher—his receiving isn't great and his bat seems to be jolting him through the system more quickly than he can improve his skills behind the dish. We think he will ultimately be playing a lot of corner outfield, where his athleticism allows him to profile well. But listen, the man hits. The game power can get to plus, and a midseason stance adjustment has him tapping into an above-average hit tool. And he's a switch-hitter. How the Pirates manage the contradictions in his profile and where they see his ultimate defensive home are the questions we're keeping an eye on as Rodriguez begins 2023, likely at Triple-A.

## 56.) Dalton Rushing, C, Los Angeles Dodgers

It's very rare for a player selected outside of the first round to make the next winter's Top 101. When it does happen, it's usually at the bottom of the list, and it's usually a player who got pushed out because of bonus demands or similar weirdness. Rushing was last summer's 40th pick—the Dodgers' "first-rounder," but penalized 10 spots for luxury tax infractions, in fact—as a one-year college wonder who spent the early part of his career at Louisville stuck behind Henry Davis. After signing, Rushing blitzed the California League like he was playing The Show on rookie mode, hitting .404/.522/.740 in 30 games and walking as much as he struck out. We suspect his line would've been taken more seriously if he had hit a little *less*, because what he did was so absurd that it was easy to discount. The top-line average and power was underpinned by truly impressive batted ball data; nearly everything he hit was in the air and really freakin' hard. The Dodgers already have an embarrassment of catching riches between fellow former Louisville Cardinal Will Smith and Diego Cartaya, but that's why they're the Dodgers.

## 57.) Spencer Jones, OF, New York Yankees

Speaking of on-brand 2022 picks who probably should've gone earlier, the Yankees nabbed this super-sized exit velocity kingpin with endless Aaron Judge comps with the no. 25 pick. Once one of the top prep prospects for the 2019 Draft—as a left-handed pitcher—Jones honored his commitment to Vanderbilt and ended up giving up pitching when chronic elbow issues turned into Tommy John surgery. He finally got to focus on hitting and playing the outfield full-time in 2022 and exploded, hitting the ball as consistently hard as any player in the nation. He continued vaporizing baseballs in the Low-A Florida State League, spawning regular social media video threads of triple-digit exit velos, and he made a lot more contact than you'd expect for a behemoth swinging out of his shoes. If Jones continues to keep the swing-and-miss manageable...well, those Judge comps will get more pointed, even if they're impossible to live up to.

## 58.) Gordon Graceffo, RHP, St. Louis Cardinals

Graceffo started trending up almost immediately after he was drafted as a 2021 fifth-rounder out of Villanova—a jump in velocity to the mid-90s helped him post a 1.73 ERA in his pro debut and earn a mention in our Cardinals list that fall. The true breakout came last season as he tore his way through the Midwest League before finishing up the year with an impressive Double-A campaign. He has all the makings of a future major-league starter: a strong frame, an advanced changeup and the ability to pound the strike zone. Graceffo's track record of success is rather short and he needs to find a consistent breaking pitch—his slider is more promising than his curveball at the moment—but he's really close to earning starter's innings in St. Louis.

## 59.) Michael Busch, 2B, Los Angeles Dodgers

Busch was mostly a first baseman who moonlighted in the outfield in college, but the Dodgers pushed him up the defensive spectrum to second after drafting him in 2019. Despite being a major college first-rounder who has had success at every level, he's moved fairly slowly through the system, including beginning 2022 by repeating Double-A after spending a full and productive 2021 there. Busch doesn't do any one thing at an incredible level at the plate, but he hits the ball hard enough and makes good enough decisions to carry average bat-to-ball ability. The defense at the keystone isn't superb, but he should survive the elimination of the shift. He's ready for major-league time and likely to just be a good, solid bat who can stand at second or any corner.

## 60.) George Valera, OF, Cleveland Guardians

On the subject of baseball aesthetics, Valera's swing has long been a particular favorite of our staff. It's more outsider art than Rembrandt, the work of a true iconoclast, but the commercial viability is starting to come into question. The art world might love a shark in formaldehyde—just ask Steve Cohen—but in the prospect world we need some rigorous form under the bouts of postmodern improvisation. That is all to say, Valera didn't really make enough contact in the upper minors last year. The power looks effortless even when he doesn't completely square a pitch, but there are in fact more moving parts than a Collectif Scale installation. The in-zone swing-and-miss is a problem and drove his batting average down into the .250 range. Valera has a great approach and will do enough damage on contact that he can be a good major leaguer—even as a corner outfielder—if he doesn't give back anymore hit tool, but that last step up is the steepest. Still, we are excited to see Valera's magnum opus, *The Physical Impossibility of Whiff in the Mind of Someone Swinging*, when it comes to a major-league ballpark near you.

## 61.) Edwin Arroyo, SS, Cincinnati Reds

Arroyo broke out in the first half of 2022 as one of the youngest players in the Cal League. Drafted as a glove-first prep talent in 2021 by the Mariners, his bat has quickly caught up. Arroyo showed feel for contact from both sides of the plate and burgeoning pull-side pop. His slick glove was on display night in and night out, as well. Shipped off to Cincinnati—by way of Daytona—as part of the Luis Castillo return, Arroyo struggled a bit in his new digs. But that all adds up to a month of a bit more swing-and-miss, which you wouldn't even notice if it weren't a separate row on his player card. And that's before we get into how much of a pain it can be to focus on baseball when you've just moved across the country to a new organization. His overall line—.297/.368/.486 in Low-A, while playing most of the season at 18—and the top-notch live reports point to a true breakout, and Arroyo may have another gear if he can more consistently tap into his power.

## 62.) Garrett Mitchell, OF, Milwaukee Brewers

Speaking of tapping into power, Mitchell has now made it all the way to the majors without ever hitting more than eight home runs in a season—including his time with ping bats at UCLA—despite looking the part of a middle-of-the-order thumper. He's played more like a table-setter, using his elite foot speed on the bases and in the outfield. He's had durability issues throughout his pro career—an oblique injury cost him time in 2022—and his MLB debut featured a frightening amount of swing-and-miss. If he can iron that issue out with more reps, his hit tool, speed and defense should give him a fairly high floor as a regular center fielder. That's just an okay outcome for the 62nd best prospect in baseball, but we'll keep baking in that 10% chance he starts hitting home runs and becomes a real star.

## 63.) Jasson Domínguez, OF, New York Yankees

The discourse around "The Martian" has been going on for what feels like an interminable length of time, and likely will continue interminably, as Domínguez probably isn't too close to making his debut despite finishing 2022 at Double-A. No, he isn't Mickey Mantle, nor is he Mike Trout, and he might not even be Bryan Reynolds. He is, however, a very good prospect. He isn't as fast as you think, he's probably a corner outfielder and he doesn't hit the ball prodigiously hard, at least consistently. But when he does get into one the high-end exit velos are very nice, and his production at High-A and Double-A (.306/.397/.510 and .266/.374/.440, respectively) was impressive when factoring in his age—yes, he is still a teenager. Above-average big-league production is the likely outcome, even if it falls short of superstardom.

## 64.) Kevin Parada, C, New York Mets

The Mets got one of the best college players in the draft when Parada slid to the 11<sup>th</sup> pick. A draft-eligible sophomore, he slugged .700 for the Georgia Tech Ramblin' Wreck, following up on an almost-as-good freshman campaign. Parada has a bit of an unusual setup, starting with the bat pointed almost directly toward the ground, but he has good enough wrists to make it work and is strong enough to wring plus power out of the resulting swing. He's a two-way catcher, although the defensive skills aren't as loud as those at the plate, and we could list all the usual caveats about non-elite catching prospects and their potential offensive regression. But for now, let's just enjoy the potential plus outcome that Parada carries in his locker.

## 65.) Joey Wiemer, OF, Milwaukee Brewers

Major League Baseball tilts more and more toward the three true outcomes every year. A lot of that is due to spiking K-rates as pitching just gets better and better. But if you can hit enough home runs and generate enough wind energy to power a few Wisconsin counties, you'll find yourself in the lineup every day. That's the gambit Wiemer plays every time he steps up to the plate. He swings hard in case he hits it. He swings up, which means there are holes to exploit. But he also knows when not to swing, which means he can pile up walks—that *other* true outcome. It's a precarious balancing act. He's a pretty good runner and right fielder, but those are "nice to haves." The 30 home runs are the "have to have." Wiemer has that kind of power, and he was very good in Triple-A after scuffling a bit in the Southern League to start 2022.

## 66.) Robert Hassell III, OF, Washington Nationals

A former top-10 selection and one of the top prospect bats for San Diego, Hassell was a key piece in the deadline deal that sent Juan Soto to the Padres. In him the Nationals have an athletic, projectable player with a knack for finding the barrel and enough range and arm to hold down center field. His inability to generate much loft and weak exit velocities were concerning even before he suffered a broken hamate bone late in the season, but now the lack of hard contact is even more magnified. The contact ability, speed and defense give Hassell a relatively high floor, but unless he begins to impact the ball more consistently, the profile is going to lack high-impact upside.

## 67.) Miguel Bleis, OF, Boston Red Sox

Signed for $1.5 million out of the Dominican Republic a mere two years ago, Bleis is another name outside the top 20 who has a chance to be an elite prospect down the road. The complex-level stats were good, but keeping stats on the backfields seems a bit silly. The tools are even better: all five are checked off, including potential plus center field defense.

His swing decisions are ponderous at times, his approach too aggressive overall, but Bleis has that scout-friendly swing that marries power and contact and plays well analytically, too. He just has to get a bit better at picking which pitches to play with, which is only one of the toughest things in baseball to do.

## 68.) Elijah Green, OF, Washington Nationals

Green is the player with the highest variance on this list. You can find scouts who think he's a near-generational talent, the kind of athlete who comes into baseball once or twice a decade. If he hits their view of his reasonable upside, he'll be a future MVP because of his explosive bat speed, immense power potential, lightning speed and great swing. But you can find just as many others who think he's going to struggle to make it out of A-ball because of contact problems, the magnitude of which are unusual for such a high pick; he's pretty hopeless against velocity up in the zone at present, specifically. His in-zone contact woes are just brutal, and an anchor attached to any sort of hit tool projection. Green's whiff rates were alarming even against prep pitching, and he was basically a windmill at the complex after the draft. One of two things is going to happen here, probably pretty quickly: He's going to improve his bat-to-ball skills *a lot,* or he's going to start hitting for really low averages with a really high number of strikeouts.

## 69.) Coby Mayo, 3B, Baltimore Orioles

Have the Orioles cracked the code on hitting development? They keep getting huge gains out of all of their top hitting prospects, some rather unexpected. Mayo is a big, hulking corner prospect—currently a third baseman, maybe an outfielder or first baseman down the road—and he checks the boxes for traditional power projectability. He hasn't really had his huge breakout a la Gunnar Henderson yet, but he's pretty well-rounded at the plate for his experience and age—he reached Double-A at 20 after only playing 95 games between Low-A and High-A—with decent contact and discipline skills. Mayo's profile hasn't fully coalesced to a star projection quite yet, though the same could be said for Henderson just a year ago.

## 70.) Gavin Cross, OF, Kansas City Royals

Another top college bat—this one with bona fide major conference production—Cross is an advanced slugger who should move quickly through the minors and reach Kansas City as a good corner outfielder capable of hitting .280 and swatting 25+ bombs. The power may play a bit above that; he's strong and knows how to use the length and leverage in his swing to inflict maximum damage. The hit tool might come in a bit below that average, given his expansive view on what breaking balls he should be swinging at. Cross is perhaps a bit of a dull subject as a polished college offensive player of the Michael Conforto variety. That's still a player every team would love to have, even if every team doesn't have one.

## 71.) Cade Cavalli, RHP, Washington Nationals

On the flip side of all of the pitchers with ideal modern stuff who get more whiffs than it looks like they should is Cavalli, who is a 2010s scout's dream but who has induced consistently underwhelming swing-and-miss rates in the upper minors. Cavalli throws his fastball in the mid- to upper-90s and scrapes triple-digits, but with very generic movement. In the 2020s, fastballs in the 95–97-mph range with a little sink just don't generate elite whiff rates, even in Triple-A. Both his curveball and slider have flashed plus but don't get enough chases, with the curve lately further ahead, and his changeup flashes average. Cavalli is headed down the path of a frustrating but effective mid-rotation starter outcome where you always think he should be better based on the radar gun and visual movement. All of this comes with the caveat that he came down with shoulder soreness after his late-August debut and was never able to ramp back up before season's end—and that injuries were a recurring problem for him in college.

## 72.) Max Meyer, RHP, Miami Marlins

Meyer shares some of Cavalli's knocks in that the optics of his mid- to upper-90s fastball are better than their pedestrian underlying shape, which causes them to miss fewer bats than you'd otherwise think. Where Meyer excels is with his plus-plus slider, which has nuked hitters dating back to college and was continuing to obliterate them for a short time in the bigs. His changeup was also developing on schedule, but he blew out his elbow in the first inning of his second major-league start last July. Dating back to his college days, there have been concerns that Meyer's ultimate home would be in the bullpen, as he's a smaller pitcher with a high-octane fastball/slider combo. An elbow reconstruction is unlikely to quell those concerns. Given that he's going to miss most or all of the 2023 season on rehab, we'll likely be confronted with ranking him again next year.

## 73.) Ceddanne Rafaela, OF/SS, Boston Red Sox

The loyal rooters of New England might not want to hear it right now, but Rafaela may just be Boston's next homegrown fan favorite (and it will be many years before he hits free agency). The Curaçaon isn't a huge guy—listed at 5-foot-8 and probably closer to 150 than 200 pounds—but he is an excellent athlete with a smooth explosiveness to his game. His wiry strength and quick, loose stroke at the dish have him spraying liners gap-to-gap and should get him to average or slightly above game power at the highest level. He also has a hit tool that should reach average or better and is a quick and savvy baserunner. Rafaela plays a very cool center field and handles shortstop, too, with the potential to cover other spots around the diamond. The 21-year-old was a massive hit at High-A Greenville (.330/.368/.594) and adjusted well to Double-A breaking stuff following a June promotion (.278/.324/.500). Turbocharged Enrique Hernández might be in play.

## 74.) Jordan Westburg, IF, Baltimore Orioles

Westburg's offensive improvements in 2022 didn't get blared through a bullhorn like Gunnar Henderson's, but they were notable just the same. Previously showing a collection of mostly average tools as a high-floor college bat, Westburg traded off a bit of batting average for some real game power improvements—a more than fair bargain. He's started ratcheting up earlier in his swing, and while that's added to his whiff rates, he's gained bat speed, lift and pull-side pop. Westburg is also a versatile infielder who can move around second, third and short, giving you adequate to above-average defense wherever Henderson isn't playing that day. While he won't ever be first—or now perhaps even second—among Orioles infield prospects, he's no third banana.

## 75.) Jett Williams, SS, New York Mets

This has been said so much over the last year that it's a bit trite, but once more with feeling: If Williams—listed at 5-foot-8 and perhaps not even that tall—was 6-foot-2, he'd have been one of the top few picks in the 2022 Draft. (That anecdote should reinforce how specially the similarly statured Termarr Johnson's hit tool is viewed.) Instead, he's a short king who fell all the way to the Mets at no. 14. He had one of the best contact profiles in the draft class, a clear benefit to shorter levers that has been a noticeable industry trend recently, and has a surprising bit of pop for his size. We're listing Williams as a shortstop because the Mets announced him as a shortstop and that's where he played in the complex, but he's much more likely to be a second baseman or even a center fielder over the long haul—his arm doesn't project for the left half of the infield. Regardless of where he plays defensively, Williams projects as well as a natural hitter as you can without significant pro data to confirm.

## 76.) Oscar Colás, OF, Chicago White Sox

Colás may seem low here considering his strong second-half campaign at Double-A Birmingham and proximity to the majors. It is true that the now-24-year-old boasts wicked bat speed and massive power, and he seems a little less old for his levels when considering that he essentially took the prior two years off from professional baseball (2019 saw him take his at-bats in Cuba and Japan). Still, his swing decisions are not especially strong, and while he should provide solid defense, it will be in a corner, as he doesn't have enough speed or baserunning ability to add value around the edges.

We see him as someone who can impact the middle of the lineup with his left-handed power production, but relying on him as a starter from day one may be a risky proposition.

### 77.) Logan O'Hoppe, C, Los Angeles Angels

Last July, the Phillies traded O'Hoppe—a near-ready catching prospect totally and utterly blocked by J.T. Realmuto—for Brandon Marsh, the no. 44 prospect from 2021. It was a rare one-for-one trade of young players with considerable upside—Marsh might yet be a star because of his defense and how much damage he can do on contact. Meanwhile, O'Hoppe swatted 26 long balls between his two Double-A clubs, and he doesn't chase or miss within the zone all that much. He doesn't really have huge raw power potential, but he's getting to every bit of what he has under the lights. The Angels gave him a one-week trial run at catcher at the end of 2022, and he should take over the full-time gig from Max Stassi imminently.

### 78.) Tyler Soderstrom, 1B/C, Oakland Athletics

Even with the current selloff happening in Oakland, Soderstrom remains the top prospect for the Athletics. A hit tool-driven catcher when drafted 26th overall in 2020, it's likely he makes the move to first to get his near big league-ready bat in the lineup rather than develop behind the plate. His offensive skills are strong enough to handle the move down the defensive spectrum, with a combination of an advanced feel at the plate and the ability to hit for over-the-fence power. Take a look at the current depth chart for Oakland and you'll realize that not only is Soderstrom the best prospect in the organization, he might just be the best hitter at the major-league level as well.

### 79.) Nick Frasso, RHP, Los Angeles Dodgers

*I want you to know that I'm happy for you*
*I wish nothing but the best for you both*
*An older version of me*
*Does he throw a hundred like me?*
*Would he go down on an in-zone slider?*
*Does he pitch adequately?*
*And would he throw it zippy?*
*I'm sure he'd make a really excellent starter*

*Cause the stuff that you gave that we made*
*Wasn't able to make it enough for you to get pitch design, no*
*And every time you start Mitch White*
*Does he know how you told me*
*You'd make my sweeper slide?*
*Until my elbow died, 'til it died, but it's back alive*

*And I'm here to remind you*
*Of the mess you left when you traded me*

*It's not fair to deny me*
*Of the whiffs I bear that you gave to me*
*You, you, you oughta know*

### 80.) Owen Caissie, OF, Chicago Cubs

Maybe they wanted to see how he would handle advanced pitching, or maybe they thought spending spring in the upper Midwest would remind him of his Ontario home. Either way, the Cubs gave Caissie an aggressive High-A assignment to begin his age-19 season. He struggled early but looked more comfortable and more the part of slugging corner outfielder as the season progressed. He'll need to work on getting the ball in the air more consistently to take full advantage of his plus bat speed and physical strength. He's a fairly well-rounded hitter at the plate, showing a good amount of barrel control and a command of the strike zone. Defensively, the glove is improving and he has more than enough arm to handle right field. Caissie can get overlooked in the Cubs' vastly improved system, but he has the tools to become a middle of the order run producer for the next competitive team on the North Side.

### 81.) Kyle Manzardo, 1B, Tampa Bay Rays

You can find a lot of things Manzardo isn't—defensively gifted for one, as he's limited to first base. Of impressive stature, for another, as he's just 6-foot-1, 205 pounds. He only boasts average power, and his swing setup and mechanics can look frantic to the naked eye. But he's an absolute masher at the plate, and he does the one thing that matters most: *he hits*. He cranked out a .327/.426/.617 line between High-A and Double-A last year, and his ability to mash is grounded in tangible things he excels at. While Manzardo may never hit 115-mph moonshots, his swing constantly produces hard contact in the air. He doesn't chase terrible pitches, and he makes more than his share of contact. He just hits, even if absolutely none of it looks or seems right.

### 82.) Connor Norby, 2B, Baltimore Orioles

Speaking of college bats in strong drafting and development organizations getting to all of their power in games, Norby also has merely average raw power. Nevertheless, he socked 29 home runs last year across three levels, far exceeding any reasonable expectations. The rest of the profile has a ton of "average to above-average" attached—he projects in that band on his contact, swing decisions, overall hit tool projection and second base defense—and frankly his power will probably recede back into that area as well. It's worth noting that Baltimore is completely overloaded with middle infielders in their system and Norby is likely the weakest defender of the crop; he doesn't have the arm to play short and might end up in the outfield.

## 83.) Brandon Pfaadt, RHP, Arizona Diamondbacks

Pfaadt throws a pretty standard array of above-average pitches, but lacks a clear plus attribute other than command. His fastball ranges from the low-90s up to 95 on the regular, with enough spin and carry that it gets past more hitters at the top of the strike zone than you would expect. He pairs that with a solid sweeping slider, a change that flashes above-average but with less consistency, and a curveball. He has very good command and control, and while there's nothing in the arsenal that looks better than a 55-grade pitch, he should get enough chases and whiffs on the edges of the zone to become a mid-rotation starter.

## 84.) Mason Montgomery, LHP, Tampa Bay Rays

The modern version of a crafty lefty profile, Montgomery has an odd, extremely short arm path that creates significant visual deception. That lends both his low-90s fastball and changeup some baffling extra oomph, and the Texas Tech product struck out 171 batters in 124 innings mostly off those two offerings. Despite the strange-looking mechanics, he repeats his delivery very well and hits his spots. His arm action is less well suited for a breaking ball, and improvements in his slider would enhance things even further. The Rays are well known for maximizing swing-and-miss from oddball release points and arm actions—they love creating different looks on the arm clock—so Montgomery is a great match for his organization.

## 85.) Harry Ford, C, Seattle Mariners

Ford has a weird but neat grouping of outlier skills. He's one of the speediest catchers in affiliated baseball. His swing decisions are about as good as you're going to see out of a teenage hitter, which allow him to maximize average-to-above contact and power abilities. He hasn't caught a ton yet—the Mariners never made him catch two games in a row last year—but he graded out as an excellent framer in the 54 games in which he donned the tools of ignorance. He's a candidate to play elsewhere on the field if the position ends up holding his bat back, and his athleticism would provide more defensive options than a standard backstop's would. After posting a pretty representative .274/.425/.439 line at Low-A, he basically carried his parents' home country of Great Britain through World Baseball Classic qualifying last fall. Expect to see him as one of the featured players for a very fun British squad in the main tournament in March.

## 86.) Jace Jung, 2B, Detroit Tigers

The last and only other time Detroit picked 12th in the amateur draft they did pretty well, selecting future World Series hero Kirk Gibson. Jung has a long way to go to match Gibby's career, but he was one of the top college bats available last July. He features a profile that is entirely dependent on his ability to impact the ball at the plate. The setup is unconventional but the swing is quick and direct, making hard contact to all fields. He also displays an advanced approach, commanding the zone well, which helps him get to most of his plus-raw pop. Everything in the field is fringe-average at best, with his range, quickness and arm strength limiting him to somewhere on the right side of the infield and putting a ton of pressure on the bat.

## 87.) Wilmer Flores, RHP, Detroit Tigers

A 2020 undrafted free agent, Flores followed up his breakout in 2021 with an even more impressive sophomore campaign, striking out over 30% of opposing hitters and showing a much improved cutter/slider. The new breaker combines with his mid-90s fastball and above-average curve to give him a more complete repertoire. His stuff is quality, but not quite on par with the eye-popping, high-upside offerings that you might see featured by pitchers toward the top of the list. However, you won't find anyone in Detroit crying if Flores the Younger becomes a middle-of-the-rotation workhorse.

## 88.) Matt Mervis, 1B, Chicago Cubs

Another 2020 undrafted free agent with limited defensive skills and a slugging percentage that started with a three in his first professional season, Mervis was not on anyone's prospect radar to begin the season. However, getting away from pitcher-friendly Myrtle Beach and implementing a more disciplined approach helped unlock his immense raw pop and rocket him up the organizational ladder. There's more than just a slugger in the profile: He has enough bat speed to catch up to velocity and he's shown enough contact ability to keep his strikeout rate in an acceptable range. After missing out on José Abreu in free agency, the Cubs are willing to trot out Eric Hosmer at first base at the season's onset, but sooner than later Mervis should get a chance to provide consistent thunder to a lineup that desperately needs it.

## 89.) Edgar Quero, C, Los Angeles Angels

Not to be confused with Jeferson Quero, a pretty good Brewers catching prospect himself, Edgar torched the pitching in the Cal League as a 19-year-old, posting a .965 OPS. The switch-hitting backstop shows plus power and contact ability from both sides of the plate. Behind it, the arm and athleticism are strong assets, but his receiving is going to need work. That kind of fine glovework is a teachable skill, but Quero is a long way from being a major-league factor. This is a long-term value list though, and if he is even an average defender in time, his bat could make him one of the top five or so catchers in baseball.

## 90.) Andy Pages, OF, Los Angeles Dodgers

After punishing Midwest League pitching in 2021 and establishing himself as the top power-hitting prospect in the organization, Pages was tested this past season by the advanced pitching in Double-A. The slugging dipped, but he still managed an elite fly-ball rate and continued to post a very manageable 25% strikeout rate. Despite concerns about his hit tool, he still has two double-plus-graded tools in his pop and his cannon of an arm in the outfield, both which rank among the best in all of minor-league baseball. Pages might not be a perennial All-Star, but he's got what it takes to become an everyday corner outfielder.

## 91.) Jackson Jobe, RHP, Detroit Tigers

Jobe was the first prep pitcher taken in the 2021 draft, but back issues limited him to just 77 innings last season, and when on the bump his command came and went. He has the kind of stuff that, well, gets you drafted third overall. Jobe fires mid-90s heat that can beat batters up in the zone, backed by a potential plus-plus spin-monster slider that rips off late, two-plane break, leaving A-ball hitters flailing at air. The changeup is also developing apace, but everything was a little too hittable in 2022. Jobe has as much upside as the low-minors arms already effusively praised in these pages like Tink Hence and Marco Raya, but is a bit further behind at present with higher relief risk.

## 92.) Kyle Muller, LHP, Oakland Athletics

This year's "prospect fatigue" entry, Muller feels like he should have established himself as a frustrating mid-rotation starter or dominant late-inning reliever by this point. He's struck out a batter per inning in the majors, and it's not hard to see why. His fastball is mid-90s from the left side with good extension, and he features two bat-missing breaking balls. Muller is a very modern pitching prospect, but he was never able to outpitch his command and control issues and establish himself in Atlanta. A trade to Oakland for Sean Murphy puts him in a much better situation to get the ball every fifth day, so this will likely be the last time we rank him. And despite his major-league struggles, he was very good in Triple-A last year. Muller is one of many prospect arms that's a grade or so of command away from having top-of-the-rotation impact. He likely won't get to it, but again, he should be a good, if frustrating mid-rotation starter in Oakland.

## 93.) Jose Salas, IF, Miami Marlins

As we've remarked before in these pages, there are worse strategies than just filling the tail end of these lists with good shortstop prospects. Salas played a bit all over the infield in 2022, but spent the majority of his games at the six, and should be just fine there. And one of the advantages inherent in being a shortstop prospect is that you have a ways to slide down the defensive spectrum before it puts real pressure on your bat. Salas is a contact merchant at present, but hits the ball decently hard for a 19-year-old in A-ball. If he grows off shortstop he'll likely grow into enough power to balance it out, and he'll likely be an above-average defender wherever he lands. The one concern with Salas is that he may lack a carrying tool, but when infield prospects in this range of the list find one, they often end up much higher in a year's time.

## 94.) Casey Schmitt, 3B, San Francisco Giants

To prospect rankers, a great glove at third will get you as much attention as cinephiles give to the Best Art Direction Oscar, but Schmitt's defense might be the *Barry Lyndon* of this category. It ranks among the best in the minors. He tossed in 21 homers across three levels in 2022, and while the pop is mostly pull-side—and he struck out more as he went up the ladder—good third base defenders in this range can sometimes go Matt Chapman and then we don't get another chance to rank them.

## 95.) DL Hall, LHP, Baltimore Orioles

*DL Hall strides toward the Orioles mound*
*In his left arm great stuff can be found*

*Fastball and slider, plus is the word*
*Total package says starter the third*

*But then his pitches move far and wide*
*Walks are a problem we can't elide*

*DL Hall, inevitably then*
*Takes his free passes to the Camden bullpen*

## 96.) Connor Phillips, RHP, Cincinnati Reds

What do David Ortiz, Moises Alou, Jesse Orosco and Phillips have in common? All were included as the PTBNL in trades that shipped them away from their original teams. Phillips topped out in Double-A last year, so there's a long way to go before he's on the same level as his trade add-on counterparts, but the tools are apparent. It starts with his high-octane fastball. With plenty of life and high-90s velocity, he uses it up in the zone to generate plenty of awkward, late swings. The secondaries are inconsistent, but both his 12-to-6 curve and sweeping slider show signs of being plus future offerings. The effort in his delivery will likely keep him from ever having pinpoint command, but his athleticism should allow him to control his repertoire. There's a good deal of reliever risk in his profile but there's also a chance he puts it all together and becomes a front-line starter.

## 97.) Ken Waldichuk, LHP, Oakland Athletics

A crafty lefty who actually has good stuff, Waldichuk is one of the more distinctive arms to arise from the Yankees' pitching development lab. Sent over to Oakland as the centerpiece of last deadline's Frankie Montas deal, the former fifth-rounder runs his heater well into the mid-90s and throws one of those fashionable sweeping sliders along with a legit changeup that also gets more than its share of whiffs. Both secondaries offer a substantial speed differential from the fastball, and the deception created by his tall frame hurling those pitches from a low three-quarters slot doesn't make him any easier to square up. Waldichuk made his debut late in 2022, and there should be nothing but wide-open spaces in Oakland's rotation next season.

## 98.) Colt Keith, 3B, Detroit Tigers

Had it not been for a midseason shoulder injury, Keith might have climbed even higher on this list. He was in the midst of a breakout season at High-A, hitting for average and a newfound amount of power. Surgery was reportedly not required, and he showed no ill-effects upon his return to action in the Arizona Fall League, leading his Salt River squad in most offensive categories. He's still raw in the field and a bit stiff in his actions at third but should develop into an adequate defender as he garners more experience. He looked the part of a burgeoning power-hitting infielder in 2022 and we look forward to seeing if he continues to grow into the role next season.

## 99.) Junior Caminero, 3B, Tampa Bay Rays

Just stop dealing low, low-minors players to the Rays. Tampa flipped Tobias Myers to Cleveland rather than add him to the 40-man in the 2021-22 offseason and got back Caminero, who had spent 2021 in the Dominican Summer League. He got stateside complex time this past summer and was so good there that he was bumped to full-season ball as an 18-year-old. He kept hitting thereafter, and while he's going to have to move off shortstop—and is already playing a fair bit of third base—his lightning-quick bat and strong approach should get him over the hot corner's higher offensive bar in due time. We're not saying he's going to end up like Curtis Mead, but we're not *not* saying it either.

## 100.) Josh Jung, 3B, Texas Rangers

Our no. 1 prospect emphatically stamped that ranking in permanent ink with his major-league performance. Our no. 100 prospect homered in his first Rangers at-bat and then struck out in almost 40% of the subsequent ones. Jung has been snakebitten with injuries during his pro career, but had always hit when on the field…right up until they added a third deck to the stadiums. Now, if you are still eligible for one of these lists, your MLB time won't be a significant sample, but there were some warning signs in his gaudy Triple-A numbers, too. His contact rates and exit velocities are fairly pedestrian, and he chases a bit more than you'd prefer. Jung has improved a lot as a defender, but he's going to be a bat-first third baseman, and his bat isn't quite there yet.

## 101.) Alex Ramirez, OF, New York Mets

A seven-figure IFA signing in 2019, Ramirez has done just about everything you'd ask of that kind of prospect so far. He held his own in the Florida State League (or Low-A Southeast or whatever it was called for that one regrettable year) as an 18-year-old in 2021. He was better than that in 2022 and took the step up to High-A Brooklyn in stride. He hits the ball very hard, though not in the air as much as you'd like, and has a bit of a noisy swing with a bit too many whiffs in it at the moment. He's a good runner but a bit of a ponderous center fielder. He won't be able to legally drink when we lock the 2024 Top 101, in which he might rank 75 spots higher or not really be in consideration for. This list is—as our predecessors have always emphasized—a snapshot in time.

# Arizona Diamondbacks

## The State of the System:
Still talented at the top, Arizona's system suffers from a bevy of players who have not taken the necessary next step.

## The Top Ten:

**1** **Corbin Carroll** **OF**    OFP: 70    ETA: Debuted in 2022
Born: 08/21/00   Age: 22   Bats: L   Throws: L   Height: 5'10"   Weight: 165 lb.   Origin: Round 1, 2019 Draft (#16 overall)

| YEAR | TEAM | LVL | AGE | PA | R | 2B | 3B | HR | RBI | BB | K | SB | CS | AVG/OBP/SLG | DRC+ | BABIP | BRR | DRP | WARP |
|------|------|-----|-----|-----|-----|-----|-----|-----|-----|-----|-----|-----|-----|-------------|------|-------|-----|-----|------|
| 2021 | HIL | A+ | 20 | 29 | 9 | 1 | 2 | 2 | 5 | 6 | 7 | 3 | 1 | .435/.552/.913 | 113 | .571 | -0.4 | CF(7) 0.7 | 0.2 |
| 2022 | AMA | AA | 21 | 277 | 62 | 11 | 8 | 16 | 39 | 41 | 68 | 20 | 3 | .313/.430/.643 | 125 | .379 | 2.4 | CF(35) 1.1, RF(9) -0.9, LF(2) -0.1 | 2.1 |
| 2022 | RNO | AAA | 21 | 157 | 25 | 11 | 0 | 7 | 22 | 24 | 36 | 11 | 2 | .287/.408/.535 | 114 | .345 | 1.8 | CF(19) 2.1, RF(9) 0.1, LF(5) 0.3 | 1.4 |
| 2022 | AZ | MLB | 21 | 115 | 13 | 9 | 2 | 4 | 14 | 8 | 31 | 2 | 1 | .260/.330/.500 | 93 | .333 | -0.2 | LF(25) 1.2, CF(5) 0.3, RF(2) 0.4 | 0.4 |
| 2023 DC | AZ | MLB | 22 | 493 | 59 | 22 | 9 | 13 | 56 | 52 | 124 | 14 | 6 | .242/.336/.424 | 112 | .313 | -0.6 | CF 0, RF 0 | 2.2 |

*Comparables: Andrew Benintendi, Christian Yelich, Mookie Betts*

**The Report:** Five tools and a bag of chips. Carroll's 2022 was a massive reassurance coming off his shocking season-ending shoulder injury in 2021 on a swing so powerful that he still hit a home run. The kid from the same high school as Bill Gates won't likely be a billionaire by age 31, but he could be a National League MVP by then. His bat speed is impressive, as he rockets line drives with astounding frequency in an approach well-suited to take full advantage of his triple-happy home park. Carroll's over-the-fence power came on as he bulked up in the pros, as he was drafted on a more balanced profile that seemed likely to be led by true center field chops. Reports are more mixed now, though Carroll's foot speed remains strong enough to handle any outfield spot and in my own viewings I've not seen enough to shake him out of center.

Though his profile is strong enough to make him a favorite for NL Rookie of the Year in 2023, there are concerns to monitor. Whereas Carroll could get by in the minors on a patient approach that yielded free passes from overmatched arms, his contact rates were sometimes subpar, and he can swing and miss too often on hittable pitches. When he puts the next pitch into the gap on a line, that's no sweat, but that margin for error is significantly thinner against world-class pitching.

**OFP:** 70 / All-Star outfielder with five above-average tools

**Variance:** Medium. Carroll's future looks a bit different if he's an average center fielder versus a decent corner one, but this mostly comes down to if Carroll hits at merely a solid clip or a Silver Slugger one.

**Jesse Roche's Fantasy Take:** Carroll teased his immense fantasy upside in his debut, including a robust .240 ISO and a MLB-leading 30.7 feet/second sprint speed *and* 90-foot splits. It is true top-of-the-scale speed, and it plays on the bases. While his batted-ball data did not pop in the pros, he did register a well-above MLB average 50% hard-hit rate and 112-mph max and 105.8-mph, 90th-percentile exit velocity in Triple-A. Further, Carroll has a patient approach that resulted in a 15.2% walk rate in the minors. The chief concern, noted above, is the relationship between his approach and some underlying swing-and-miss, which could result in elevated strikeout rates. (No prospect is without a wart.) Regardless, Carroll is a potentially elite fantasy performer who could provide significant five-category production as soon as 2023.

**2** **Druw Jones** **OF**    OFP: 60    ETA: 2026
Born: 11/28/03   Age: 19   Bats: R   Throws: R   Height: 6'4"   Weight: 180 lb.   Origin: Round 1, 2022 Draft (#2 overall)

**The Report:** Abandon all shoulders, ye who enter here. The three men atop this list are the three most recent position players selected first in the MLB Draft by the Diamondbacks, and each has suffered a season-ending shoulder injury early in their minor-league career. For Jones, like Jordan Lawlar, it somewhat helpfully came in his draft year, shorting him only part of a season he likely would not have played heavily in regardless. Still, it means the analysis hasn't shifted much since last June.

That is to say Jones is a sure-fire center fielder, with graceful routes and range, a cannon for an arm, plus speed and, of course, the pedigree of his father Andruw being one of the greatest defensive center fielders in MLB history in the eyes of plenty of fans. Like dad, Jones is a five-tool talent, though the big concern will be on ensuring that his swing fosters enough consistent contact. As might be expected of the son of a big leaguer, Jones has more experience than the average prep against high-level competition, appearing in plenty of high-profile showcases. At his best, Jones is lofting the ball into the gaps and over fences, and he's demonstrated at least 55-grade power for just that purpose. Even with his injury, however, Jones is as "high-floor" as things can get for a toolsy prep outfielder; if he can simply find any niche as a hitter he'll have a long career thanks to his glove and speed on the bases. Odds are, he might fill several.

**OFP:** 60 / Gold Glove center fielder with enough pop to crack some All-Star games

**Variance:** Very High. Prep outfielder missing his first pro winter with injury. Even for a player scouts have known for years, that's a lot of uncertainty.

**Jesse Roche's Fantasy Take:** The above report may not wax poetic about Jones' lofty offensive ceiling because, in large part, it requires substantial projection. While he already flashes solid power, his broad-shouldered and high-waisted 6-foot-4 frame promises a lot more. Like many prep bats, Jones is not bereft of hit tool variance. However, his power-speed upside could legitimately approach 30/30 if he develops as many hope. As such, Jones arguably has the most fantasy upside in FYPDs.

## 3 Jordan Lawlar  SS    OFP: 60    ETA: Late 2024/early 2025

Born: 07/17/02   Age: 20   Bats: R   Throws: R   Height: 6'2"   Weight: 190 lb.   Origin: Round 1, 2021 Draft (#6 overall)

| YEAR | TEAM | LVL | AGE | PA | R | 2B | 3B | HR | RBI | BB | K | SB | CS | AVG/OBP/SLG | DRC+ | BABIP | BRR | DRP | WARP |
|------|------|-----|-----|----|----|----|----|----|-----|----|----|----|----|-------------|------|-------|-----|-----|------|
| 2022 | VIS | A | 19 | 208 | 44 | 9 | 4 | 9 | 32 | 27 | 48 | 24 | 4 | .351/.447/.603 | 120 | .437 | 1.0 | SS(37) -1.1 | 1.1 |
| 2022 | HIL | A+ | 19 | 130 | 31 | 8 | 2 | 3 | 17 | 16 | 33 | 13 | 1 | .288/.385/.477 | 109 | .382 | 3.6 | SS(27) -1.8 | 0.8 |
| 2022 | AMA | AA | 19 | 97 | 18 | 0 | 0 | 4 | 11 | 10 | 28 | 2 | 1 | .212/.299/.353 | 85 | .259 | 0.2 | SS(17) -0.2 | 0.1 |
| 2023 non-DC | AZ | MLB | 20 | 251 | 22 | 10 | 2 | 4 | 23 | 19 | 75 | 9 | 2 | .227/.291/.342 | 80 | .317 | 0.0 | SS 0 | 0.2 |

*Comparables: Heiker Meneses, Xander Bogaerts, Matt Dominguez*

**The Report:** After the annual Arizona top-position-player-pick shoulder injury (in his case, a torn left shoulder labrum) sidelined Lawlar in 2021, a mostly healthy 2022 concluded with a fractured scapula on the left side of his back from a hit-by-pitch in the Arizona Fall League. Though Lawlar should be all systems go for spring training, it's frustrating to see the big infielder sidelined once again.

When healthy, Lawlar is a dynamic player with 20/20 capabilities. His athleticism manifests in all aspects of his game, though his swing can occasionally drift into overwrought length and he's shown unsurprising struggles against quality offspeed for his age. He'll be 20 for the 2023 season, and Double-A should provide an ample test for his offensive development. Disappointingly, Lawlar has not always looked like the defender he was as a prep, with his arm strength fluctuating at times and seemingly diminished. Though his range remains excellent, consistent issues with his arm could push Lawlar to second base or broader utility work, which would place his contact development under stricter scrutiny.

**OFP:** 60 / Athletic power threat who fills in all over the field and makes hay on the basepaths

**Variance:** High. Lawlar's tools remain mostly top-notch, but there are real whiff worries, even with his youth.

**Jesse Roche's Fantasy Take:** Like Carroll and Jones above, Lawlar offers dynamic power-speed potential with some worrisome contact issues (and, of course, a past shoulder injury). Those contact issues became even more apparent during a brief late-season stop in Double-A (.212/.299/.353). Nevertheless, Lawlar's season was a resounding success, showcasing burgeoning power, solid plate discipline and huge speed. His promise of future 20/20 or better campaigns places him firmly in the fantasy top-10 conversation.

## 4 Brandon Pfaadt  RHP   OFP: 55   ETA: 2023

Born: 10/15/98   Age: 24   Bats: R   Throws: R   Height: 6'4"   Weight: 220 lb.   Origin: Round 5, 2020 Draft (#149 overall)

| YEAR | TEAM | LVL | AGE | W | L | SV | G | GS | IP | H | HR | BB/9 | K/9 | K | GB% | BABIP | WHIP | ERA | DRA- | WARP |
|------|------|-----|-----|---|---|----|----|----|------|-----|----|------|------|-----|-------|-------|------|------|------|------|
| 2021 | VIS | A | 22 | 2 | 2 | 0 | 7 | 7 | 40¹ | 29 | 5 | 1.6 | 12.7 | 57 | 40.0% | .267 | 0.89 | 3.12 | 94 | 0.4 |
| 2021 | HIL | A+ | 22 | 5 | 4 | 0 | 9 | 9 | 58 | 39 | 5 | 2.2 | 10.4 | 67 | 39.9% | .246 | 0.91 | 2.48 | 100 | 0.4 |
| 2021 | AMA | AA | 22 | 1 | 1 | 0 | 6 | 6 | 33¹ | 37 | 12 | 1.9 | 9.7 | 36 | 30.6% | .291 | 1.32 | 4.59 | 99 | 0.2 |
| 2022 | AMA | AA | 23 | 6 | 6 | 0 | 19 | 19 | 105¹ | 113 | 19 | 1.6 | 12.3 | 144 | 34.9% | .372 | 1.25 | 4.53 | 68 | 2.5 |
| 2022 | RNO | AAA | 23 | 5 | 1 | 0 | 10 | 10 | 61² | 47 | 9 | 2.0 | 10.8 | 74 | 29.8% | .270 | 0.99 | 2.63 | 102 | 0.3 |
| 2023 DC | AZ | MLB | 24 | 1 | 1 | 0 | 3 | 3 | 13.3 | 13 | 2 | 2.4 | 8.6 | 13 | 32.0% | .296 | 1.24 | 3.88 | 105 | 0.1 |

Comparables: Matt Bowman, Erik Johnson, Nick Nelson

**The Report:** The Diamondbacks have a rash of pitchers with intriguing profiles who don't *quite* add up to a slam=dunk starter but include many of the possible aspects of a performer. Pfaadt was the best of them this year, with a stellar season at Double-A Amarillo followed by decent numbers in the launching pad of Triple-A Reno. He gets outs with a three-pitch mix, combining a running fastball at 91-95 with a sharp, sweeping slider and a changeup that hovers around average. On days when the *cambio* is present, the well-built righty is exceptionally tough to square up for hitters, as Pfaadt has tightened up his arm action to remove some extra swing and length, leaving him with above-average command. Issuing few free passes and consistently spotting his slider off the plate, Pfaadt bolsters the sum of his parts, though as Jeffrey Paternostro saw, when Pfaadt is lacking that changeup, he looks decidedly more like a reliever. If it's all working, as it was most days in 2022, Pfaadt instead looks likely to capably eat up innings for the next several seasons.

**OFP:** 55 / no. 3 starter or strong multi-inning relief role

**Variance:** Medium. Pfaadt is knocking on the door of a big-league rotation debut, but the floor is comfortably above-average length from the pen.

**Jesse Roche's Fantasy Take:** Pfaadt, a standout in August, was the *only* pitcher on this list who came out of the Pacific Coast League (PCL) unscathed. Indeed, his 0.99 WHIP led the league for pitchers with 60+ innings under their belt. Given his hitter-friendly home parks, Pfaadt's 26.9% K-BB%–5th-best in the minors–is all the more impressive. While he may not have the loudest stuff, he has superb command, which allows him to regularly work outside the zone and elicit chase attempts. Pfaadt is not on the 40-man roster, and several other young arms that are will be vying for rotation spots, but he likely arrives at some point in 2023 and could surprise in all formats.

## 5 Deyvison De Los Santos  3B   OFP: 55   ETA: Late 2024/early 2025

Born: 06/21/03   Age: 20   Bats: R   Throws: R   Height: 6'1"   Weight: 185 lb.   Origin: International Free Agent, 2019

| YEAR | TEAM | LVL | AGE | PA | R | 2B | 3B | HR | RBI | BB | K | SB | CS | AVG/OBP/SLG | DRC+ | BABIP | BRR | DRP | WARP |
|------|------|-----|-----|-----|----|----|----|----|-----|----|----|----|----|-------------|------|-------|-----|-----|------|
| 2021 | DIA | ROK | 18 | 95 | 19 | 4 | 2 | 5 | 17 | 13 | 24 | 1 | 1 | .329/.421/.610 | | .415 | | | |
| 2021 | VIS | A | 18 | 160 | 26 | 12 | 0 | 3 | 20 | 13 | 43 | 2 | 0 | .276/.340/.421 | 95 | .374 | 1.0 | 3B(35) 5.8, 1B(1) -0.0 | 1.0 |
| 2022 | VIS | A | 19 | 349 | 43 | 18 | 2 | 12 | 67 | 22 | 84 | 4 | 1 | .329/.370/.513 | 98 | .404 | -1.4 | 3B(59) -3.2, 1B(14) -1.4 | 0.5 |
| 2022 | HIL | A+ | 19 | 166 | 24 | 9 | 0 | 9 | 33 | 7 | 54 | 1 | 0 | .278/.307/.506 | 103 | .365 | -2.8 | 3B(29) -1.6, 1B(7) 0.6 | 0.1 |
| 2022 | AMA | AA | 19 | 45 | 5 | 2 | 0 | 1 | 6 | 5 | 9 | 0 | 0 | .231/.333/.359 | 100 | .276 | 0.0 | 3B(6) -0.9, 1B(4) 0.3 | 0.1 |
| 2023 non-DC | AZ | MLB | 20 | 251 | 21 | 11 | 1 | 5 | 24 | 12 | 78 | 1 | 0 | .225/.267/.339 | 69 | .315 | -4.2 | 1B 0, 3B 0 | -0.7 |

Comparables: Vladimir Guerrero Jr., Hudson Potts, Ronald Acuña Jr.

**The Report:** Potentially the quickest swinger in the entire Arizona system, De Los Santos rounded out an impressive age-19 season rising from Low-A Visalia all the way to Double-A Amarillo, followed by a trip to the Arizona Fall League. His youth has been increasingly apparent at each stop, with the stocky infielder's max-effort swing yielding tape-measure tanks and plenty of clean energy through wind power on his whiffs. Both Double-A and the AFL offered serious reality checks, however the power De Los Santos displayed is some of the best in the minor leagues, in any system.

The D'Backs seem to be working on shortening his approach, with a once-floaty leg kick pared down to a more minute load, ideally allowing De Los Santos to make his swing decisions slightly later and still get above-average pop upon contact. But make no mistake, this is a bat-first profile with plenty of swing-and-miss risk. The righty whiffed 169 times in 630 plate appearances this year, and while he plays with effort at the hot corner, his range and arm are well below-average, making him likely to demand the more challenging role of a right-handed first baseman. As he is fairly maxed out physically, most development going forward will be mechanical and experiential, hoping to craft a future big-league approach to pair with his already-extant big-league power.

**OFP:** 55 / Above-average 1B clubbing 30+ home runs per year

**Variance:** Very High. This is the precipice for position players in Arizona's system. De Los Santos' age and whiff struggles make him a total flameout risk, but if he can keep making contact at higher levels, he could be a premier slugger within a few seasons.

**Jesse Roche's Fantasy Take:** With great power comes great whiffs, and De Los Santos is no exception. While he is capable of sending balls into the stratosphere, his typically aggressive approach and propensity to drive balls into the ground limit his damage. Meanwhile, his defensive and athletic shortcomings add even more risk to a generally risky profile. Ultimately, De Los Santos may be a one-tool (power) wonder. At least that one tool is very fantasy-friendly and can allow him to find MLB success (just look at Franmil Reyes for a time). Still, De Los Santos' hit tool and positional risk is enough to drop him out of the dynasty top 100.

## 6 Drey Jameson  RHP    OFP: 55    ETA: Debuted in 2022

Born: 08/17/97   Age: 25   Bats: R   Throws: R   Height: 6'0"   Weight: 165 lb.   Origin: Round 1, 2019 Draft (#34 overall)

| YEAR | TEAM | LVL | AGE | W | L | SV | G | GS | IP | H | HR | BB/9 | K/9 | K | GB% | BABIP | WHIP | ERA | DRA- | WARP |
|---|---|---|---|---|---|---|---|---|---|---|---|---|---|---|---|---|---|---|---|---|
| 2021 | HIL | A+ | 23 | 2 | 4 | 0 | 13 | 12 | 64$^1$ | 60 | 9 | 2.5 | 10.8 | 77 | 52.6% | .319 | 1.21 | 3.92 | 95 | 0.7 |
| 2021 | AMA | AA | 23 | 3 | 2 | 0 | 8 | 8 | 46$^1$ | 38 | 6 | 3.5 | 13.2 | 68 | 38.5% | .327 | 1.21 | 4.08 | 79 | 0.8 |
| 2022 | AMA | AA | 24 | 2 | 1 | 0 | 4 | 4 | 18$^2$ | 13 | 0 | 1.9 | 11.1 | 23 | 55.8% | .302 | 0.91 | 2.41 | 63 | 0.5 |
| 2022 | RNO | AAA | 24 | 5 | 12 | 0 | 22 | 21 | 114 | 139 | 21 | 3.3 | 8.6 | 109 | 48.2% | .351 | 1.59 | 6.95 | 101 | 0.6 |
| 2022 | AZ | MLB | 24 | 3 | 0 | 0 | 4 | 4 | 24$^1$ | 20 | 2 | 2.6 | 8.9 | 24 | 56.1% | .281 | 1.11 | 1.48 | 90 | 0.4 |
| 2023 DC | AZ | MLB | 25 | 5 | 5 | 0 | 16 | 16 | 77.7 | 79 | 8 | 3.3 | 7.8 | 67 | 48.5% | .307 | 1.38 | 4.10 | 107 | 0.5 |

*Comparables: Zach Plesac, Taylor Jungmann, A.J. Griffin*

**The Report:** Arizona's hardest throwing upper-minors arm, Jameson had a whale of a time in the Pacific Coast League in 2022 but still earned a big-league call-up late in the season. His four starts in the majors were quite encouraging, as the former Ball State standout hit triple-digits with his heater and generally showcased better command of his top-flight stuff under the lights of The Show. Though undersized for a starter at a generously listed 6-feet, Jameson's high-effort delivery helps him sit 95-97 as a starter, with significant run on his four-seam and a bit more sink on his sinker. His best out-pitch is a late-biting slider that he shows consistent ability to locate just off the plate glove-side to both lefties and righties. He'll throw a slightly more vertical curveball as well as a below-average changeup to complete the five-pitch mix, but the heaters and slider are often enough.

What holds Jameson back is that he will often give away at-bats with uncompetitive pitches, and has not always shown the ability to course-correct in-game. With a high-effort motion that can get tricky to repeat, his mechanics can put him in hot water as often as they can make him look unhittable. When he's forced to come into the heart of the plate, his heater is not quite a bat-misser despite its speed. At its best, he is starting it off the plate and running it back in for a strike against lefties, or starting it down the middle and running it in to saw off righties. When he cannot get either option working, Jameson can unravel quickly, and looks more like a reliever.

**OFP:** 55 / High K and BB no. 3/4 starter or high-leverage reliever

**Variance:** Medium. Jameson is already a big leaguer, and Arizona may decide to roll with him in their rotation to start 2022. He's perhaps the safest bet to have some positive role as a pro on this list, but between his size, motion and track record, he'll need to be a starter for a few years before folks fully trust him.

**Jesse Roche's Fantasy Take:** Liberated from the PCL, Jameson thrived in his brief MLB debut, allowing just four earned runs across four starts (1.48 ERA). Notably, his four- and two-seam fastballs found more success, with improved shape and strike-throwing. What makes Jameson such an intriguing fantasy arm (as well as his proximity) is his bat-missing slider that generated a 47% whiff rate in his debut. That said, he still infrequently throws his curveball or changeup for strikes which, along with his size, create very real long-term relief risk. Yet, Jameson enters 2023 with a rotation spot to lose, and he possesses enough upside to be rostered in most fantasy formats.

## 7  Ryne Nelson  RHP          OFP: 55          ETA: Debuted in 2022
Born: 02/01/98   Age: 25   Bats: R   Throws: R   Height: 6'3"   Weight: 184 lb.   Origin: Round 2, 2019 Draft (#56 overall)

| YEAR | TEAM | LVL | AGE | W | L | SV | G | GS | IP | H | HR | BB/9 | K/9 | K | GB% | BABIP | WHIP | ERA | DRA- | WARP |
|------|------|-----|-----|---|---|----|----|----|----|----|----|------|-----|----|------|-------|------|-----|------|------|
| 2021 | HIL | A+ | 23 | 4 | 1 | 0 | 8 | 8 | 39¹ | 21 | 3 | 3.2 | 13.5 | 59 | 29.5% | .240 | 0.89 | 2.52 | 85 | 0.6 |
| 2021 | AMA | AA | 23 | 3 | 3 | 0 | 14 | 14 | 77 | 66 | 13 | 3.0 | 12.2 | 104 | 38.0% | .312 | 1.19 | 3.51 | 89 | 0.8 |
| 2022 | RNO | AAA | 24 | 10 | 5 | 0 | 26 | 26 | 136 | 142 | 25 | 3.1 | 8.5 | 128 | 36.0% | .301 | 1.39 | 5.43 | 108 | 0.1 |
| 2022 | AZ | MLB | 24 | 1 | 1 | 0 | 3 | 3 | 18¹ | 9 | 2 | 2.9 | 7.9 | 16 | 25.5% | .156 | 0.82 | 1.47 | 104 | 0.1 |
| 2023 DC | AZ | MLB | 25 | 4 | 6 | 0 | 16 | 16 | 72.7 | 75 | 11 | 3.6 | 8.1 | 65 | 30.3% | .305 | 1.43 | 4.68 | 120 | 0.0 |

*Comparables: Joe Ryan, Zach Plesac, A.J. Griffin*

**The Report:** Like Jameson, Nelson got his big-league debut in 2022, with three starts late in the season. Like Jameson, Nelson had a solid line in his first taste of the bigs despite, taking a trip or three through the ringer trying to prevent runs in Triple-A Reno. The antithesis of Jameson in many ways, Nelson gets excellent extension on his over-the-top delivery. Last year, I referred to Nelson's motion as a "Powerpoint presentation" and it still retains those qualities, as though he is methodically aiming to tick each box for each stage of his delivery. However, that is not a full indictment, as Nelson's fastball command was a clear positive for him in 2022.

The baseline tool set is encouraging, with a mid-90s heater that sits around 94 mph and has almost pure backspin. He leaned on that heater heavily despite what seems to be two offspeed options in his breaking ball and slider. Nelson's curve is dramatically slower, in the upper-70s to pair off his heater, making for a 15-20 mph gap between his heater and all other offerings. Tightening up his slider, which sits and sweeps in the low-80s, to perhaps be thrown slightly firmer would help Nelson take some pressure off his heater. With a starter's build, it is imperative that Nelson's secondaries step forward to meet his fastball, as he did not display consistent confidence in either breaking ball nor his changeup in Reno or Phoenix.

**OFP:** 55 / no. 3/4 starter or long man

**Variance:** Medium. Nelson is not yet a sure-fire, big-league caliber starter by dint of his secondaries, but he'll get to learn on the job in 2023.

**Jesse Roche's Fantasy Take:** Nelson lives or dies on his fastball, including 69.6% usage in his debut. Early on this year, his fastball velocity was down, and he struggled mightily in the PCL. Then, as we entered the summer months, his fastball gradually ticked up. At its best, his fastball possesses elite carry, and, during his debut, it trailed only Nestor Cortes in vertical movement versus average among starting pitchers. If his secondary quality and command improve, Nelson could make an immediate fantasy impact this year.

## 8  Blake Walston  LHP          OFP: 55          ETA: 2023
Born: 06/28/01   Age: 22   Bats: L   Throws: L   Height: 6'5"   Weight: 175 lb.   Origin: Round 1, 2019 Draft (#26 overall)

| YEAR | TEAM | LVL | AGE | W | L | SV | G | GS | IP | H | HR | BB/9 | K/9 | K | GB% | BABIP | WHIP | ERA | DRA- | WARP |
|------|------|-----|-----|---|---|----|----|----|----|----|----|------|-----|----|------|-------|------|-----|------|------|
| 2021 | VIS | A | 20 | 2 | 2 | 0 | 8 | 8 | 43¹ | 34 | 4 | 3.5 | 12.5 | 60 | 43.7% | .303 | 1.18 | 3.32 | 86 | 0.6 |
| 2021 | HIL | A+ | 20 | 2 | 3 | 0 | 11 | 11 | 52¹ | 52 | 12 | 2.8 | 9.8 | 57 | 36.8% | .288 | 1.30 | 4.13 | 120 | -0.2 |
| 2022 | HIL | A+ | 21 | 1 | 0 | 0 | 4 | 4 | 17² | 13 | 0 | 3.6 | 13.8 | 27 | 48.7% | .333 | 1.13 | 2.55 | 81 | 0.3 |
| 2022 | AMA | AA | 21 | 7 | 3 | 0 | 21 | 21 | 106¹ | 115 | 16 | 3.3 | 9.3 | 110 | 34.0% | .345 | 1.45 | 5.16 | 83 | 1.6 |
| 2023 DC | AZ | MLB | 22 | 1 | 1 | 0 | 3 | 3 | 13 | 14 | 2 | 3.8 | 7.9 | 12 | 33.8% | .309 | 1.48 | 4.89 | 124 | 0.0 |

*Comparables: Tyler Viza, Gabriel Ynoa, Domingo Robles*

**The Report:** A rough welcome to Double-A marred Walston's trajectory this year, as his age-21 season was spent predominantly in the hitter-friendly haven of Amarillo. The new level required adjustments from the young southpaw, whose heater was no longer enough to keep hitters off balance. While Walston tends to be impressive early, his struggles tend to come later in games, unsurprising for a pitcher with his youth. His frame still suggests a workhorse capability, but at the moment his stuff tends to fade in later innings. Grant Schiller had him at 90-93 in an August outing with his sinker, and as Walston began to incorporate his slider more frequently later in the season, he found more success to somewhat salvage his numbers.

Walston's projectability comes in part from his 6-foot-5 frame, which has added some muscle but remains lean. He also commands a pair of potential above-average offspeed pitches, with the aforementioned slider sweeping almost exclusively, with little drop. Walston will use the pitch in all areas of the zone, tying up hitters on and off the plate at his best. This is Walston's best weapon against lefties and he used it against them with increasing impunity as the season went on. His fading changeup is enough of a threat to keep righties honest, which should allow Walston a future in the rotation if his command allows it. At some point he'll have to either revamp or ditch his loopy curveball, which can steal strikes on occasion but does not have the pace to miss bats consistently. On occasion he appeared to flash a firmer version of the pitch in 2022, though not with consistency. Unlike several of the other arms in the top tier of Arizona's system, Walston lacks the above-average velo to get away with subpar command, so while he typically controls his repertoire acceptably, it is brutal when he loses it. His current delivery provides deception as he hides the ball well, but he can close himself off at times as he lands, losing his release point and his effectiveness.

**OFP:** 55 / no. 3/4 starter or multi-inning reliever

**Variance:** Medium. Though this is a fairly "safe" profile as a likely back-end starter, Walston's youth and frame do still have the upside to spike further. His ranking here reflects the distance between his current self and that projection.

**Jesse Roche's Fantasy Take:** A potential back-end starter with a mediocre fastball presently going through the Amarrillo/Reno ringer is unlikely to drum up much fantasy hype, even with viable secondaries.

## 9 Slade Cecconi RHP  OFP: 50  ETA: 2024

Born: 06/24/99  Age: 24  Bats: R  Throws: R  Height: 6'4"  Weight: 219 lb.  Origin: Round 1, 2020 Draft (#33 overall)

| YEAR | TEAM | LVL | AGE | W | L | SV | G | GS | IP | H | HR | BB/9 | K/9 | K | GB% | BABIP | WHIP | ERA | DRA- | WARP |
|------|------|-----|-----|---|---|----|----|----|-----|-----|----|------|-----|-----|------|-------|------|------|------|------|
| 2021 | HIL | A+ | 22 | 4 | 2 | 0 | 12 | 12 | 59 | 53 | 5 | 3.1 | 9.6 | 63 | 43.8% | .310 | 1.24 | 4.12 | 101 | 0.4 |
| 2022 | AMA | AA | 23 | 7 | 6 | 0 | 26 | 25 | 129² | 139 | 22 | 2.2 | 8.8 | 127 | 38.5% | .313 | 1.32 | 4.37 | 81 | 2.1 |
| 2023 non-DC | AZ | MLB | 24 | 3 | 3 | 0 | 58 | 0 | 50 | 55 | 8 | 3.2 | 6.8 | 38 | 36.7% | .304 | 1.45 | 4.87 | 125 | -0.4 |

*Comparables: Dario Agrazal, Trevor Williams, Darren McCaughan*

**The Report:** In some ways, the trajectory of Arizona's many highly-touted or highly-drafted pitching prospects could be laid out like the lunar cycle. Pfaadt is a resplendent full moon, maximizing many of his tools towards a promising future. Jameson and Nelson are a bit off that, waxing or waning, but still providing plenty of light. On the other end of the spectrum, Bryce Jarvis is indistinguishable from another near-infinite gap between the stars. Like Walston, Cecconi occupies more of a half-moon, though he perhaps skews closer to a crescent than he'd hope. With a year of mostly full health to try and show how his radar-pleasing stuff could translate to professional success, Cecconi neither answered many questions nor wrote himself off entirely.

His fastball has yet to manifest as a consistent bat-misser, though he was more consistently back around 93-96 after an alarming drop late in 2021 where he was more consistently 90-93 following an elbow injury. Cecconi needs those extra ticks because hitters have continued to have reasonable success making contact with most of his offerings. His slider is still a plus pitch, and when he leans on it more earlier in counts it can help him rack up Ks, but the profile skews closer to a relief one. Both his curveball and changeup fluctuate between 45-55 given the day, but he needs both to be effective in the rotation as his deceptively hittable fastball should not be his primary offering. His control of his pitches showed signs of improvement this year, and he consistently placed the slider glove-side of the plate for putout pitches when he could get to two strikes. Cecconi still looks the part of a rotation stalwart in street clothes, but the 24-year-old is on his fourth year of hoping to take another step with his arsenal. This may simply be it.

**OFP:** 50 / no. 4/5 starter or slider-heavy reliever

**Variance:** High. Cecconi's stuff has vacillated up and down massively multiple times over the past few seasons.

**Jesse Roche's Fantasy Take:** *See* Walston, Blake, above.

## 10 Ivan Melendez CI  OFP: 50  ETA: 2025

Born: 01/24/00  Age: 23  Bats: R  Throws: R  Height: 6'3"  Weight: 225 lb.  Origin: Round 2, 2022 Draft (#43 overall)

| YEAR | TEAM | LVL | AGE | PA | R | 2B | 3B | HR | RBI | BB | K | SB | CS | AVG/OBP/SLG | DRC+ | BABIP | BRR | DRP | WARP |
|------|------|-----|-----|-----|----|----|----|----|-----|----|----|----|----|-------------|------|-------|------|-----|------|
| 2022 | VIS | A | 22 | 106 | 11 | 3 | 1 | 3 | 8 | 10 | 20 | 0 | 0 | .207/.349/.368 | 107 | .234 | -0.9 | 1B(14) -0.2, 3B(10) -0.4 | 0.3 |
| 2023 non-DC | AZ | MLB | 23 | 251 | 20 | 10 | 1 | 3 | 21 | 16 | 68 | 0 | 0 | .207/.273/.301 | 64 | .279 | -4.4 | 1B 0, 3B 0 | -1.0 |

*Comparables: Eric Campbell, Skyler Ewing, Brock Stassi*

**The Report:** Setting the standard for college slugging, Melendez clubbed 32 homers for the Longhorns in 2022, tops of any player in the BBCOR era, surpassing Kris Bryant's record. While that helped "The Hispanic Titanic" get selected 43rd overall in 2022, his first taste of pro ball provided a firmer test. Though a 107 DRC+ in 106 plate appearances is hardly devastating, Melendez is a college performer who should be expected to handle low-minors pitching and move quickly with his bat.

The Golden Spikes winner has a short, low load into an uppercut swing that typically meets the ball in front of the plate. It makes for a swing that typically avoids getting too long and allows Melendez to put consistent contact on the ball with authority. Melendez's strength is immense, and in contrast to De Los Santos–who at times seems to be swinging to chop a tree in half in a single blow–Melendez trusts that his consistent stroke will do damage. The trick, like De Los Santos, is that this is the hardest profile to crack the bigs with, as Melendez is even more statuesque in the field. Arizona gave him double-digit looks at third in an experiment that is at best described as ambitious.

**OFP:** 50 / second-division starter at 1B who DHs more than he plays elsewhere

**Variance:** Medium. Melendez will either hit enough to force his way onto a big-league roster or hit a wall quickly.

**Jesse Roche's Fantasy Take:** Melendez had a college season for the ages, hitting .387/.508/.863 with 32 home runs, all in a major conference no less. He has big raw power, makes consistent hard contact, regularly barrels up the ball, puts the ball in the air to all fields and has strong plate discipline. What's not to like? The offensive bar for his profile is high, but much of the same was said about Pete Alonso (also a second-round pick) so many years ago. Despite his so-so debut, Melendez should be a high-priority target outside the top 20 in FYPDs.

## Outside the Top Ten:

# 11 Blaze Alexander   SS

Born: 06/11/99   Age: 24   Bats: R   Throws: R   Height: 6'0"   Weight: 160 lb.   Origin: Round 11, 2018 Draft (#339 overall)

| YEAR | TEAM | LVL | AGE | PA | R | 2B | 3B | HR | RBI | BB | K | SB | CS | AVG/OBP/SLG | DRC+ | BABIP | BRR | DRP | WARP |
|---|---|---|---|---|---|---|---|---|---|---|---|---|---|---|---|---|---|---|---|
| 2021 | HIL | A+ | 22 | 389 | 60 | 16 | 3 | 10 | 38 | 44 | 126 | 17 | 4 | .218/.316/.372 | 94 | .314 | 3.8 | SS(86) -1.4 | 1.1 |
| 2022 | AMA | AA | 23 | 363 | 48 | 17 | 3 | 17 | 54 | 33 | 92 | 10 | 6 | .306/.388/.539 | 95 | .383 | -0.9 | SS(70) 0.7, 2B(11) 0.4, 3B(8) -0.1 | 0.9 |
| 2022 | RNO | AAA | 23 | 34 | 8 | 1 | 0 | 2 | 4 | 4 | 8 | 0 | 0 | .259/.412/.519 | 101 | .294 | 1.1 | SS(6) 0.7, 2B(1) 1.5, 3B(1) -0.2 | 0.4 |
| 2023 DC | AZ | MLB | 24 | 64 | 7 | 3 | 0 | 1 | 6 | 5 | 20 | 2 | 0 | .223/.293/.347 | 82 | .322 | -0.1 | 3B 0, SS 0 | 0.0 |

*Comparables: Matt Reynolds, Abiatal Avelino, Alex De Goti*

For years, it seemed Alexander's shortcomings at the dish would see his potential Gold Glove defense confined to grainy minor-league highlight reels. In 2022, however, a more physically developed Alexander demonstrated growth at the plate. Amarillo and Reno are launching pads, so his career-high 17 home runs should be evaluated with some skepticism, but as a fleet-footed baserunner with huge defensive chops, he doesn't need to slug a ton. He simply needs to justify a roster spot.

# 12 Justin Martinez   RHP

Born: 07/30/01   Age: 21   Bats: R   Throws: R   Height: 6'3"   Weight: 180 lb.   Origin: International Free Agent, 2018

| YEAR | TEAM | LVL | AGE | W | L | SV | G | GS | IP | H | HR | BB/9 | K/9 | K | GB% | BABIP | WHIP | ERA | DRA- | WARP |
|---|---|---|---|---|---|---|---|---|---|---|---|---|---|---|---|---|---|---|---|---|
| 2021 | VIS | A | 19 | 1 | 3 | 0 | 7 | 7 | 23 | 25 | 1 | 5.9 | 9.4 | 24 | 56.9% | .381 | 1.74 | 6.65 | 96 | 0.2 |
| 2022 | HIL | A+ | 20 | 1 | 2 | 1 | 13 | 0 | 27 | 21 | 1 | 4.7 | 14.7 | 44 | 49.1% | .385 | 1.30 | 2.67 | 79 | 0.5 |
| 2023 DC | AZ | MLB | 21 | 1 | 1 | 0 | 28 | 0 | 23.7 | 23 | 4 | 5.4 | 10.1 | 27 | 37.3% | .308 | 1.54 | 4.98 | 123 | -0.2 |

Signing for just $50,000 out of the Dominican Republic, Martinez is on the path to a big-league bullpen role. After returning from Tommy John surgery in mid-2021 which took away almost half of his 2022 season, Martinez rocketed up three levels in 2022, with an impressive upper-90s heater that touches triple-digits and overpowered hitters from High-A all the way up to Triple-A and the Arizona Fall League. His best secondary is a split-change that can flummox lefties with late bite and run, while his slider lags behind but can flash average. Even in a bullpen role, Martinez's command is suspect, and his double-digit walk rates are too much to stomach despite his bat-missing, but with more distance from his surgery and just 21 years of age, the athletic 6-foot-3 righty should be competing for a bullpen spot in Arizona in 2023.

# 13 Yu-Min Lin   LHP

Born: 07/12/03   Age: 19   Bats: L   Throws: L   Height: 5'11"   Weight: 160 lb.   Origin: International Free Agent, 2021

| YEAR | TEAM | LVL | AGE | W | L | SV | G | GS | IP | H | HR | BB/9 | K/9 | K | GB% | BABIP | WHIP | ERA | DRA- | WARP |
|---|---|---|---|---|---|---|---|---|---|---|---|---|---|---|---|---|---|---|---|---|
| 2022 | DIAR | ROK | 18 | 0 | 2 | 0 | 7 | 7 | 23 | 9 | 0 | 2.3 | 16.0 | 41 | 51.4% | .250 | 0.65 | 2.35 | | |
| 2022 | VIS | A | 18 | 2 | 0 | 0 | 7 | 7 | 33¹ | 31 | 2 | 4.3 | 13.5 | 50 | 31.5% | .408 | 1.41 | 2.97 | 84 | 0.4 |
| 2023 non-DC | AZ | MLB | 19 | 3 | 3 | 0 | 58 | 0 | 50 | 50 | 8 | 5.0 | 8.6 | 48 | 32.9% | .301 | 1.55 | 5.11 | 128 | -0.5 |

Though Arizona has slightly pared back Lin's heavy-twisting leg kick, the 2021 international amateur signee has looked every bit as promising as when the club inked him for a $525,000 bonus. The Taiwanese southpaw has a reasonably consistent motion that is impressive for his age, having just completed his age-18 season. At times he can fly open, and he saw some struggles with free passes in the California League, however he made up for it with 50 strikeouts in just 33 1/3 innings.

The 5-foot-11 lefty gets quality deception with what seems to be a low vertical approach angle on his upper-80s heater. He tunnels both a tight slider and sharp-biting changeup for mirrored movement profiles. Lin must add strength and velocity to remain a rotation consideration, but will be just 19 in 2023.

## 14 A.J. Vukovich 3B
Born: 07/20/01   Age: 21   Bats: R   Throws: R   Height: 6'5"   Weight: 210 lb.   Origin: Round 4, 2020 Draft (#119 overall)

| YEAR | TEAM | LVL | AGE | PA | R | 2B | 3B | HR | RBI | BB | K | SB | CS | AVG/OBP/SLG | DRC+ | BABIP | BRR | DRP | WARP |
|---|---|---|---|---|---|---|---|---|---|---|---|---|---|---|---|---|---|---|---|
| 2021 | VIS | A | 19 | 276 | 42 | 15 | 1 | 10 | 42 | 19 | 77 | 10 | 1 | .259/.322/.449 | 94 | .329 | -0.7 | 3B(53) -9.2 | -0.3 |
| 2021 | HIL | A+ | 19 | 124 | 13 | 4 | 2 | 3 | 20 | 3 | 28 | 6 | 3 | .298/.315/.438 | 108 | .367 | 0.0 | 3B(29) -0.8 | 0.4 |
| 2022 | HIL | A+ | 20 | 448 | 55 | 26 | 2 | 15 | 69 | 18 | 105 | 35 | 4 | .274/.308/.450 | 113 | .330 | 1.1 | 3B(76) -4.5, LF(10) -0.6, RF(10) 0.8 | 1.8 |
| 2022 | AMA | AA | 20 | 45 | 6 | 0 | 0 | 2 | 9 | 1 | 13 | 1 | 0 | .295/.311/.432 | 92 | .379 | -0.2 | LF(7) -0.3, 3B(4) -1.1 | 0.0 |
| 2023 non-DC | AZ | MLB | 21 | 251 | 21 | 11 | 1 | 5 | 24 | 10 | 68 | 7 | 2 | .225/.261/.342 | 67 | .294 | -0.9 | 3B 0, LF 0 | -0.4 |

*Comparables: Josh Vitters, Miguel Vargas, Manuel Margot*

Unlike De Los Santos and Melendez, Vukovich is a 3B/1B profile of a different breed. Sort of. The 2020 fourth-rounder has massive power that earned him a promotion to Double-A Amarillo at age-20, and hits most everything he squares up hard. The risk for the long-levered former Wisconsin prep is that he can often look overmatched, and his aggressive approach at the plate can lead to too many three-strike paths back to the bench and not nearly enough free passes. His low-OBP trajectory is a shame, because Vukovich's athleticism is striking, as the toolsy 6-foot-5 cheesehead swiped 36 of 40 bags between Hillsboro and Amarillo. His ultimate defensive home may be in the corner outfield, but he made strides at the hot corner and could carve out a passable, Alec Bohm-like existence with enough time to develop.

## 15 Wilderd Patino CF
Born: 07/18/01   Age: 21   Bats: R   Throws: R   Height: 6'1"   Weight: 175 lb.   Origin: International Free Agent, 2017

| YEAR | TEAM | LVL | AGE | PA | R | 2B | 3B | HR | RBI | BB | K | SB | CS | AVG/OBP/SLG | DRC+ | BABIP | BRR | DRP | WARP |
|---|---|---|---|---|---|---|---|---|---|---|---|---|---|---|---|---|---|---|---|
| 2021 | DIA | ROK | 19 | 30 | 2 | 1 | 1 | 0 | 1 | 0 | 9 | 0 | 2 | .250/.276/.357 | | .368 | | | | |
| 2021 | VIS | A | 19 | 132 | 18 | 2 | 1 | 2 | 8 | 5 | 49 | 6 | 3 | .210/.288/.294 | 69 | .338 | -0.6 | CF(26) -1.1, RF(5) 0.5 | -0.1 |
| 2022 | VIS | A | 20 | 338 | 54 | 16 | 2 | 8 | 42 | 23 | 84 | 54 | 7 | .290/.370/.440 | 94 | .377 | 7.0 | CF(59) 0.3, RF(10) 0.9 | 1.4 |
| 2022 | HIL | A+ | 20 | 80 | 14 | 5 | 0 | 1 | 11 | 4 | 25 | 13 | 2 | .288/.342/.397 | 80 | .426 | 1.2 | CF(19) 1.0 | 0.3 |
| 2023 non-DC | AZ | MLB | 21 | 251 | 19 | 10 | 1 | 3 | 21 | 12 | 85 | 12 | 4 | .218/.266/.307 | 62 | .329 | 1.9 | CF 0, RF 0 | -0.1 |

Patino's second run at full-season ball was significantly better than his first, though he still struggled to post clearly above-average numbers with a 94 DRC+ in Visalia in 338 plate appearances. It was nonetheless enough to earn a promotion to Hillsboro, where he struggled more acutely. Still as laden with tools and upside as most of the position players in this group, Patino is also still striving to stabilize his offensive profile, but his athleticism shone through with 67 stolen bases in 76 attempts. There's still enough here to hope on as a speedy corner outfielder, but with a profile based on singles and steals, there's a lot of risk that it never comes together.

## 16 Tommy Henry LHP
Born: 07/29/97   Age: 25   Bats: L   Throws: L   Height: 6'3"   Weight: 205 lb.   Origin: Round 2, 2019 Draft (#74 overall)

| YEAR | TEAM | LVL | AGE | W | L | SV | G | GS | IP | H | HR | BB/9 | K/9 | K | GB% | BABIP | WHIP | ERA | DRA- | WARP |
|---|---|---|---|---|---|---|---|---|---|---|---|---|---|---|---|---|---|---|---|---|
| 2021 | AMA | AA | 23 | 4 | 6 | 0 | 23 | 23 | 115² | 116 | 24 | 4.1 | 10.5 | 135 | 38.7% | .335 | 1.46 | 5.21 | 84 | 1.8 |
| 2022 | RNO | AAA | 24 | 4 | 4 | 0 | 21 | 21 | 113 | 103 | 11 | 3.6 | 8.2 | 103 | 44.1% | .295 | 1.31 | 3.74 | 90 | 1.3 |
| 2022 | AZ | MLB | 24 | 3 | 4 | 0 | 9 | 9 | 47 | 47 | 10 | 4.0 | 6.9 | 36 | 38.6% | .276 | 1.45 | 5.36 | 137 | -0.4 |
| 2023 DC | AZ | MLB | 25 | 2 | 2 | 0 | 6 | 6 | 32.3 | 35 | 5 | 4.2 | 7.7 | 28 | 38.3% | .315 | 1.55 | 5.21 | 130 | -0.2 |

*Comparables: Andrew Suárez, Ben Lively, Brett Oberholtzer*

The velocity bump has not returned for Henry, leaving the southpaw as an upper-80s to low-90s heater with a medley of offspeed pitches that are all just so-so. Although the 74th pick of the 2019 draft debuted in 2022, things went about as expected given his lack of bat-missing stuff. His low velocity forces him to nibble on the edges, while his middling secondaries do not afford him a swing-and-miss profile to dig out of holes if he falls behind. His changeup and slider do enough to keep hitters honest when he's locating well, but if his hectic delivery creates deception for hitters, it will need to pair with greater consistency for Henry to provide a no. 5/6 depth starter role between Arizona and Reno for the next few seasons.

## 17 Dominic Fletcher  OF

Born: 09/02/97   Age: 25   Bats: L   Throws: L   Height: 5'9"   Weight: 185 lb.   Origin: Round 2, 2019 Draft (#75 overall)

| YEAR | TEAM | LVL | AGE | PA | R | 2B | 3B | HR | RBI | BB | K | SB | CS | AVG/OBP/SLG | DRC+ | BABIP | BRR | DRP | WARP |
|---|---|---|---|---|---|---|---|---|---|---|---|---|---|---|---|---|---|---|---|
| 2021 | AMA | AA | 23 | 440 | 60 | 18 | 5 | 15 | 56 | 25 | 109 | 3 | 3 | .264/.314/.445 | 95 | .320 | 0.4 | RF(48) 1.7, CF(46) 0.8, LF(6) 2.1 | 1.6 |
| 2022 | AMA | AA | 24 | 142 | 28 | 6 | 2 | 7 | 34 | 13 | 25 | 4 | 2 | .346/.408/.591 | 106 | .385 | 0.5 | RF(18) 1.4, CF(6) -1.1, LF(2) 0.2 | 0.7 |
| 2022 | RNO | AAA | 24 | 449 | 70 | 29 | 8 | 5 | 38 | 42 | 88 | 5 | 6 | .301/.368/.452 | 99 | .369 | -5.4 | CF(74) 8.2, RF(21) 1.3, LF(4) 0.9 | 1.9 |
| 2023 DC | AZ | MLB | 25 | 64 | 7 | 3 | 1 | 1 | 6 | 4 | 13 | 1 | 0 | .233/.292/.353 | 77 | .286 | -0.1 | CF 0, RF 0 | 0.0 |

*Comparables: Mike Baxter, Henry Ramos, Danny Ortiz*

In a lost season where so many prospects debuted for Arizona, it was slightly surprising to not see Fletcher get at least a cup of coffee in his age-24 campaign. The undersized tri-positional outfielder posted decent numbers at the dish between both Amarillo and Reno, even considering their offense-friendly natures. It seems likely Fletcher gets a look in 2023, if only because the Diamondbacks don't seem likely to be contending and may as well see if he can fill a fourth-outfielder role. Slightly subpar speed puts a damper on the 2019 draftee's profile, as he isn't a natural base-stealing threat, putting pressure on a mature plate approach that nonetheless lacks serious home run pop.

## 18 Jorge Barrosa  CF

Born: 02/17/01   Age: 22   Bats: S   Throws: L   Height: 5'9"   Weight: 165 lb.   Origin: International Free Agent, 2017

| YEAR | TEAM | LVL | AGE | PA | R | 2B | 3B | HR | RBI | BB | K | SB | CS | AVG/OBP/SLG | DRC+ | BABIP | BRR | DRP | WARP |
|---|---|---|---|---|---|---|---|---|---|---|---|---|---|---|---|---|---|---|---|
| 2021 | VIS | A | 20 | 163 | 30 | 8 | 0 | 3 | 16 | 7 | 31 | 9 | 4 | .333/.389/.449 | 111 | .404 | 1.4 | CF(20) 2.0, LF(14) 1.5, RF(2) 0.1 | 1.3 |
| 2021 | HIL | A+ | 20 | 272 | 41 | 18 | 3 | 4 | 21 | 22 | 48 | 20 | 7 | .256/.332/.405 | 110 | .304 | -0.2 | CF(60) 6.5 | 1.9 |
| 2022 | HIL | A+ | 21 | 43 | 5 | 3 | 0 | 1 | 6 | 2 | 5 | 4 | 1 | .300/.349/.450 | 117 | .324 | 0.6 | CF(9) -0.0 | 0.2 |
| 2022 | AMA | AA | 21 | 510 | 85 | 30 | 2 | 12 | 51 | 65 | 80 | 22 | 11 | .276/.374/.438 | 113 | .314 | 1.5 | CF(87) 2.6, RF(15) 0.5, LF(6) -0.2 | 2.8 |
| 2023 non-DC | AZ | MLB | 22 | 251 | 21 | 12 | 2 | 3 | 21 | 20 | 41 | 9 | 3 | .228/.297/.329 | 79 | .266 | 0.2 | LF 0, CF 0 | 0.2 |

Similarly undersized like Fletcher, Barrosa has a more suspect offensive profile, but makes up for it with plus foot speed and strong defensive instincts. The soon-to-be 22-year-old signed for $415,000 out of Venezuela back in 2017 and has gone back and forth on switch-hitting, but has shown greater acuity for the craft in the past couple seasons. Grant Schiller picked him as his personal cheeseball at the end of this season, noting that Barrosa outperforms his tools with maximum-effort play and precocious pitch recognition. That manifested in a career-high 12.7% walk rate in Amarillo as a 21-year-old just three ticks below his strikeout rate, something that bodes well for a potential future fourth outfielder.

## 19 Jacob Steinmetz  RHP

Born: 07/19/03   Age: 19   Bats: R   Throws: R   Height: 6'5"   Weight: 220 lb.   Origin: Round 3, 2021 Draft (#77 overall)

| YEAR | TEAM | LVL | AGE | W | L | SV | G | GS | IP | H | HR | BB/9 | K/9 | K | GB% | BABIP | WHIP | ERA | DRA- | WARP |
|---|---|---|---|---|---|---|---|---|---|---|---|---|---|---|---|---|---|---|---|---|
| 2022 | DIAR | ROK | 18 | 0 | 7 | 0 | 11 | 7 | 24 | 28 | 1 | 7.5 | 10.1 | 27 | 50.0% | .415 | 2.00 | 7.87 | | |

At 6-foot-6 with some sense of where it's going, the lanky third-round pick from the 2021 draft was handled with unsurprising cautiousness in 2022, making just 11 appearances in the Arizona Complex League. This is pure projection, but his fastball-curveball combo was encouraging enough to lure him straight to the bigs. His fastball has been up to the mid-90s, and though he's likely half a decade from the bigs, his upside is worth keeping tabs on.

## 20 Manuel Pena  2B

Born: 12/05/03   Age: 19   Bats: L   Throws: R   Height: 6'1"   Weight: 170 lb.   Origin: International Free Agent, 2021

| YEAR | TEAM | LVL | AGE | PA | R | 2B | 3B | HR | RBI | BB | K | SB | CS | AVG/OBP/SLG | DRC+ | BABIP | BRR | DRP | WARP |
|---|---|---|---|---|---|---|---|---|---|---|---|---|---|---|---|---|---|---|---|
| 2021 | DSL DB1 | ROK | 17 | 222 | 30 | 5 | 2 | 4 | 30 | 26 | 46 | 17 | 7 | .253/.342/.361 | | .310 | | | |
| 2022 | DIAR | ROK | 18 | 128 | 25 | 3 | 3 | 4 | 28 | 10 | 30 | 4 | 1 | .284/.336/.466 | | .345 | | | |
| 2022 | VIS | A | 18 | 158 | 17 | 7 | 1 | 0 | 17 | 20 | 41 | 1 | 3 | .248/.344/.314 | 84 | .354 | -0.8 | 2B(26) -3.3, SS(8) -1.4, 3B(3) -0.2 | -0.4 |
| 2023 non-DC | AZ | MLB | 19 | 251 | 19 | 10 | 2 | 1 | 19 | 18 | 77 | 4 | 3 | .212/.273/.291 | 60 | .310 | -1.8 | 2B 0, 3B 0 | -0.7 |

Arizona gave Pena plenty of time at all three demanding infield positions over the past few seasons, though they leaned most heavily on the keystone in 2022. Signed out of the Dominican Republic for $1,200,000 in the 2021 signing period, Pena was the Diamondbacks' top bonus signee and has the profile to be a thumping infielder, albeit likelier at second or third than shortstop. His first taste of affiliated ball did not quite match that, however, as he did not hit a homer as an 18-year-old in his first 158 plate appearances at Low-A Visalia.

# Top Talents 25 and Under (as of 4/1/2023):

1. Corbin Carroll, OF
2. Gabriel Moreno, C
3. Druw Jones, OF
4. Alek Thomas, OF
5. Jordan Lawlar, SS
6. Geraldo Perdomo, IF
7. Brandon Pfaadt, RHP
8. Jake McCarthy, OF
9. Deyvison De Los Santos, 3B/1B
10. Drey Jameson, RHP

The best big leaguer of the three graduates listed above will likely be Thomas, whose major-league debut showed promise even as his bat lagged behind. The jack of all trades, master of none had a DRC+ of merely 81, but still showed his ability to impact the game with savvy baserunning and capable defense. The 25-year-old McCarthy made a similar impression, albeit in his sophomore season, showing bits and pieces of his toolsy kit, but ultimately performing like a second-division player or a quality fourth outfielder on a team overflowing with that profile.

Perdomo's performance was more troublesome, as the 22-year-old floundered offensively, failing to compensate for his meager power with the other aspects of his game. While the young infielder handles all infield positions well and uses his blazing speed ably, with one of the lowest average exit velocities in the game, he cannot afford to pop the ball up roughly once every 20 plate appearances. His abysmal BABIP of .243 should show drastic improvement for a player with his speed, but that can only happen if he affords himself a reason to run.

# Atlanta Braves

## The State of the System:

Three of last year's Atlanta Top 10 were key cogs for a 101-win team (and two of them placed 1-2 in Rookie of the Year voting). Six of last year's Atlanta Top 10 were traded for two core pieces for the 2023 team (and beyond). If you can be the worst system in baseball for all the right reasons, the 2023 Atlanta system makes a case. But either way it's a good thing they have almost an entire major-league lineup under control for a good while.

## The Top Ten:

### 1 Owen Murphy RHP    OFP: 55    ETA: 2025/2026

Born: 09/27/03    Age: 19    Bats: R    Throws: R    Height: 6'1"    Weight: 190 lb.    Origin: Round 1, 2022 Draft (#20 overall)

| YEAR | TEAM | LVL | AGE | W | L | SV | G | GS | IP | H | HR | BB/9 | K/9 | K | GB% | BABIP | WHIP | ERA | DRA- | WARP |
|------|------|-----|-----|---|---|----|----|----|----|---|----|------|-----|---|-----|-------|------|-----|------|------|
| 2022 | AUG | A | 18 | 0 | 1 | 0 | 3 | 3 | 7 | 5 | 0 | 7.7 | 12.9 | 10 | 62.5% | .313 | 1.57 | 7.71 | 119 | 0.0 |
| 2023 non-DC | ATL | MLB | 19 | 3 | 3 | 0 | 58 | 0 | 50 | 55 | 9 | 5.8 | 7.7 | 43 | 36.7% | .308 | 1.73 | 6.13 | 149 | -1.0 |

*Comparables: Charlie Neuweiler, Jake Woodford, Robert Gsellman*

**The Report:** A Chicago-area prep arm, Murphy showed off an advanced four-pitch mix as an amateur, bumping his stock into the first round despite being slightly undersized and from a cold weather background. It was more of the same in his pro debut, as Murphy showed off a potential plus fastball/slider combo backed by an average curve and change. His fastball sits in the low 90s—but has good life—and he could throw it by A-ball hitters while locating it to either side of the plate. His slider disappears late with plus two-plane action. Murphy doesn't always repeat his quick arm stroke consistently, so he can have bouts of wildness. He'll also need to improve the non-slider secondaries to settle in as a mid-rotation pitching prospect. We're confident he'll get there in short enough order, and there might be another level here if the offspeed stuff takes a jump.

**OFP:** 55 / no. 3/4 starter

**Variance:** High. Murphy is a cold-weather prep arm with two projectable major-league offerings and a limited pro track record.

**Jesse Roche's Fantasy Take:** Murphy may lack size, velocity or much projection, but he offers intriguing upside due to his athleticism, advanced arsenal, solid command and feel for spin. Should he happen upon a bit more velocity or improve his offspeed, which is never a given, he could explode up rankings. Murphy should be rostered in leagues with up to 300 prospects.

### 2 AJ Smith-Shawver RHP    OFP: 55    ETA: 2025

Born: 11/20/02    Age: 20    Bats: R    Throws: R    Height: 6'3"    Weight: 205 lb.    Origin: Round 7, 2021 Draft (#217 overall)

| YEAR | TEAM | LVL | AGE | W | L | SV | G | GS | IP | H | HR | BB/9 | K/9 | K | GB% | BABIP | WHIP | ERA | DRA- | WARP |
|------|------|-----|-----|---|---|----|----|----|----|---|----|------|-----|---|-----|-------|------|-----|------|------|
| 2021 | BRA | ROK | 18 | 0 | 1 | 0 | 4 | 4 | 8¹ | 4 | 2 | 10.8 | 17.3 | 16 | 33.3% | .200 | 1.68 | 8.64 | | |
| 2022 | AUG | A | 19 | 3 | 4 | 0 | 17 | 17 | 68² | 54 | 4 | 5.1 | 13.5 | 103 | 32.9% | .338 | 1.35 | 5.11 | 86 | 1.3 |
| 2023 non-DC | ATL | MLB | 20 | 3 | 3 | 0 | 58 | 0 | 50 | 46 | 8 | 5.2 | 8.9 | 49 | 32.2% | .285 | 1.50 | 4.81 | 121 | -0.3 |

*Comparables: Luis Patiño, Carlos Martinez, Jake Thompson*

**The Report:** Lest you think the well has run dry on breakout Atlanta prospects, Smith-Shawver has the foundation to make some big jumps up lists if he can rein in his command a bit in 2023. Drafted in the seventh round, but paid like a Day 1 arm, Smith-Shawver has early-round stuff for sure. The Texas prep already has a sturdy frame and a wicked fast arm with lively mid-90s heat to match. The secondaries are a bit rougher, but both his slider and change show promise. The breaker is the more advanced of the two, flashing bat-missing depth, but Smith-Shawver's command of the pitch can be inconsistent, and it often is a bit too easy to lay off. His sinking change is a bit firm at present, but has a clear above-average projection as well and may end up the better offspeed long term. His full-season debut went better than the top-line ERA would indicate, but his walk rate accurately captures the present strike-throwing issues. Smith-Shwarver has an uptempo delivery with an occasionally violent arm action, so he's unlikely to ever have a razor sharp command profile. His three-pitch mix might end up good enough that you don't really mind the occasional bouts of walks and general inefficiency.

**OFP:** 55 / no. 3/4 starter or late-inning reliever

**Variance:** High. Full-season ball was an aggressive assignment for Smith-Shawver, but the teenager missed plenty of bats. Still, he's a long way off from the majors and there is significant command and relief risk in his profile.

**Jesse Roche's Fantasy Take:** I attended Smith-Shawver's shortest start of the season on May 21 in Charleston. That day, he simply had no command, and his volatile command plagued him for much of the season, resulting in a 13% walk rate. Regardless, in a system bereft of much upside, he stands out, and his bat-missing potential is worth chasing in deeper dynasty formats.

## 3 JR Ritchie RHP     OFP: 55     ETA: 2026

Born: 06/26/03   Age: 20   Bats: R   Throws: R   Height: 6'2"   Weight: 185 lb.   Origin: Round 1, 2022 Draft (#35 overall)

| YEAR | TEAM | LVL | AGE | W | L | SV | G | GS | IP | H | HR | BB/9 | K/9 | K | GB% | BABIP | WHIP | ERA | DRA- | WARP |
|------|------|-----|-----|---|---|----|----|----|----|----|----|------|-----|----|------|-------|------|------|------|------|
| 2022 | AUG | A | 19 | 0 | 0 | 0 | 3 | 3 | 10 | 7 | 1 | 3.6 | 9.0 | 10 | 47.8% | .273 | 1.10 | 2.70 | 103 | 0.1 |
| 2023 non-DC | ATL | MLB | 20 | 3 | 3 | 0 | 58 | 0 | 50 | 55 | 9 | 5.2 | 7.7 | 43 | 34.9% | .312 | 1.68 | 5.97 | 146 | -0.9 |

*Comparables: Yoendrys Gómez, Roansy Contreras, José Soriano*

**The Report:** Atlanta doubled down on cold-weather prep arms in the 2022 draft, selecting Ritchie with the Comp pick they received from the Royals in the Drew Waters trade. The Washington state product has a polished arsenal for a high school arm, and he can run his fastball up into the mid-90s. The heater comes in at a tough angle from his lower arm slot, and each of his three offspeed pitches at least flash above-average. The slider is the most advanced as present, showing consistent short depth, but Ritchie also has feel for the changeup and curveball as well. At least one, probably two of his secondaries are getting to 55, and he is in and around the zone with everything. There isn't a clear plus swing-and-miss offering yet, but he has the foundation to be a good pitching prospect even if he ends up with just a collection of solid-average pitchers. Like Murphy and Smith-Shawver though, I suspect there's the potential for a breakout here with more time spent in Atlanta's pitching development program.

**OFP:** 55 / no. 3/4 starter

**Variance:** High. You can mostly C+P the text from Murphy and Smith-Shawver here. Ritchie has a bit more fastball velocity than Murphy, and a deeper, more polished arsenal than Smith-Shawver, but he has limited pro reps and has to find more consistency with his offspeed pitches.

**Jesse Roche's Fantasy Take:** Ritchie nearly received the same bonus as Murphy despite being drafted 15 picks apart. That should tell you something. Neither possess the upside typically associated with prep righties, but both have well-rounded arsenals and intriguing fastball traits (Murphy's shape versus Ritchie's angle/velocity). Ritchie should be rostered in leagues with up to 400 prospects.

## 4 Jared Shuster LHP     OFP: 50     ETA: 2023

Born: 08/03/98   Age: 24   Bats: L   Throws: L   Height: 6'3"   Weight: 210 lb.   Origin: Round 1, 2020 Draft (#25 overall)

| YEAR | TEAM | LVL | AGE | W | L | SV | G | GS | IP | H | HR | BB/9 | K/9 | K | GB% | BABIP | WHIP | ERA | DRA- | WARP |
|------|------|-----|-----|---|---|----|----|----|-----|----|----|------|------|-----|-------|-------|------|------|------|------|
| 2021 | ROM | A+ | 22 | 2 | 0 | 0 | 15 | 14 | 58¹ | 47 | 10 | 2.3 | 11.3 | 73 | 34.7% | .272 | 1.06 | 3.70 | 95 | 0.6 |
| 2021 | MIS | AA | 22 | 0 | 0 | 0 | 3 | 3 | 14² | 19 | 5 | 3.1 | 10.4 | 17 | 36.2% | .341 | 1.64 | 7.36 | 90 | 0.2 |
| 2022 | MIS | AA | 23 | 6 | 7 | 0 | 17 | 16 | 90² | 65 | 8 | 2.2 | 10.5 | 106 | 46.2% | .263 | 0.96 | 2.78 | 81 | 1.9 |
| 2022 | GWN | AAA | 23 | 1 | 3 | 0 | 10 | 9 | 48² | 43 | 10 | 3.0 | 7.2 | 39 | 45.1% | .246 | 1.21 | 4.25 | 100 | 0.7 |
| 2023 non-DC | ATL | MLB | 24 | 3 | 3 | 0 | 58 | 0 | 50 | 52 | 7 | 3.1 | 7.9 | 44 | 37.8% | .304 | 1.38 | 4.32 | 114 | -0.1 |

*Comparables: Domingo Acevedo, Andrew Heaney, Marco Gonzales*

**The Report:** The lone holdover from last year's Top 10, Shuster does mostly rise on the basis of list attrition, but his upper-minors performance was fine enough. If you want to try and find the seams on his polished lefty starter profile, Shuster may not have a swing-and-miss pitch in the majors. His changeup has always led the report, and if he's going to have a true plus pitch, the *cambio* will be the pick. It's certainly above-average, but it didn't always have consistent bat-missing fade in Triple-A. His slider has improved and is an average left-on-left weapon. It's not a huge breaker, but it comes from a tough angle for his fellow southpaws. Shuster's fastball remains in the low-90s, and he throws strikes with everything, but he might not garner enough swinging strikes to carve out a mid-rotation role in the majors.

**OFP:** 50 / no. 4 starter

**Variance:** Low. Shuster will go as far as the changeup will take him, and it's not a dominant swing-and-miss offering like, say, Gavin Stone's. The rest of the arsenal is perfectly adequate though, and he has a fairly high floor as some sort of back-end starter or long man.

**Jesse Roche's Fantasy Take:** Shuster's upside looks a lot like Tyler Anderson. It is not flashy, but it has fantasy value, particularly in deeper formats. Given his proximity, Shuster should be rostered in leagues with up to 300 prospects.

### 5   Cole Phillips   RHP    OFP: 50    ETA: 2026/2027
Born: 05/26/03   Age: 20   Bats: R   Throws: R   Height: 6'3"   Weight: 200 lb.   Origin: Round 2, 2022 Draft (#57 overall)

**The Report:** Atlanta went with three straight high school arms to start off their 2022 draft class, but the last of the group was the most traditional. Phillips is a 6-foot-3 Texas prep with some room to fill out and was already pumping mid-90s (and higher) heat during his senior season. He has a potential above-average power slider as well. Phillips likely would have gone a lot higher than the late second round, but he had Tommy John surgery last spring. I guess that's less traditional, but not exactly uncommon among 2022 pitching draftees. Phillips is likely to miss most of if not all of the 2023 season, as I imagine Atlanta will be fairly conservative here, despite his being on the older side for a high school arm.

**OFP:** 50 / Throw a dart somewhere between mid-rotation starter and middle relief

**Variance:** Extreme. Phillips is a prep arm with TJ. He already had an uptempo, high effort delivery, and there was relief risk in the profile before surgery.

**Jesse Roche's Fantasy Take:** While Phillips has intriguing arm strength, he is best left on watch lists until reports surface on the state of his stuff later this year.

### 6   Spencer Schwellenbach   RHP    OFP: 50    ETA: 2024/2025
Born: 05/31/00   Age: 23   Bats: R   Throws: R   Height: 6'1"   Weight: 200 lb.   Origin: Round 2, 2021 Draft (#59 overall)

**The Report:** Schwellenbach missed all of the 2022 season recovering from Tommy John surgery. In 2021 he won the John Olerud Award as college baseball's best two-way player, manning shortstop and touching the upper-90s out of the pen for the Huskers. Atlanta intends to stretch him out as a starter, but he had very little experience on the mound as an amateur and his elbow scar only ups the variance here.

**OFP:** 50 / Throw a dart somewhere between mid-rotation starter and middle relief

**Variance:** Extreme. Schwellenbach could see major gains in Atlanta's pitching development program given his lack of mound experience. He could be back to being just a hitter in 18 months.

**Jesse Roche's Fantasy Take:** While Schwellenbach has intriguing arm strength, he is best left on watch lists until reports surface on the state of his stuff early this year.

### 7   Darius Vines   RHP    OFP: 45    ETA: 2023
Born: 04/30/98   Age: 25   Bats: R   Throws: R   Height: 6'1"   Weight: 190 lb.   Origin: Round 7, 2019 Draft (#217 overall)

| YEAR | TEAM | LVL | AGE | W | L | SV | G | GS | IP | H | HR | BB/9 | K/9 | K | GB% | BABIP | WHIP | ERA | DRA- | WARP |
|------|------|-----|-----|---|---|----|----|----|------|-----|----|------|------|-----|-------|-------|------|------|------|------|
| 2021 | AUG | A | 23 | 2 | 0 | 0 | 8 | 8 | 36 | 24 | 3 | 2.5 | 12.0 | 48 | 51.8% | .256 | 0.94 | 2.25 | 66 | 1.0 |
| 2021 | ROM | A+ | 23 | 4 | 4 | 0 | 14 | 14 | 75 | 60 | 12 | 2.3 | 9.7 | 81 | 43.5% | .255 | 1.05 | 3.24 | 93 | 0.9 |
| 2022 | MIS | AA | 24 | 7 | 4 | 0 | 20 | 20 | 107 | 100 | 16 | 2.5 | 10.7 | 127 | 43.5% | .312 | 1.21 | 3.95 | 86 | 1.9 |
| 2022 | GWN | AAA | 24 | 1 | 0 | 0 | 7 | 5 | 33² | 29 | 1 | 3.7 | 7.8 | 29 | 42.0% | .283 | 1.28 | 3.21 | 98 | 0.5 |
| 2023 DC | ATL | MLB | 25 | 1 | 1 | 0 | 3 | 3 | 12.7 | 13 | 2 | 3.3 | 7.9 | 11 | 37.9% | .304 | 1.41 | 4.37 | 115 | 0.0 |

Comparables: A.J. Griffin, Tyler Wilson, Aaron Civale

**The Report:** A fairly unremarkable Day 2 college arm on draft day, Vines has spent the last couple seasons quietly breezing through every full-season level, missing bats with an above-average changeup. He looks unassuming on the mound too, a 6-foot-1 righty with a low-90s fastball that can be a bit too hittable when it's not skirting the edges of the zone. Vines often prefers to work backwards because of that and is willing to throw his change at any time in any count. It will miss bats due to how well it tunnels off the fastball, but you can sit on the *cambio* and it doesn't always have the consistent sink to get under bats when upper-minors batters were getting multiple looks at it. His slider is fringy, with late, short depth, but it also doesn't consistently miss barrels. Despite his smaller frame, Vines has a pretty easy delivery, logs innings and throws strikes. The quality of the major-league innings he fills, however, is yet to be determined.

**OFP:** 45 / Back-end starter or swingman

**Variance:** Medium. Vines' strikeout rate dipped a bit in his short Triple-A stint. It's not enough of a sample to be significant, but it does feel a bit like a harbinger. He might not have the swing-and-miss pitch to turn over a major-league lineup multiple times. Vines will have very fine margins once he lands in Atlanta, but he's very close to doing so.

**Jesse Roche's Fantasy Take:** Vines is on the 40-man roster so he likely arrives at some point in 2023 in some form. However, Ian Anderson and Bryce Elder almost certainly will receive rotation looks before him, and, as noted above, his upside is limited. As such, he likely can be safely left on waivers in nearly all formats.

## 8 Braden Shewmake  SS    OFP: 45    ETA: 2023

Born: 11/19/97  Age: 25  Bats: L  Throws: R  Height: 6'4"  Weight: 190 lb.  Origin: Round 1, 2019 Draft (#21 overall)

| YEAR | TEAM | LVL | AGE | PA | R | 2B | 3B | HR | RBI | BB | K | SB | CS | AVG/OBP/SLG | DRC+ | BABIP | BRR | DRP | WARP |
|---|---|---|---|---|---|---|---|---|---|---|---|---|---|---|---|---|---|---|---|
| 2021 | MIS | AA | 23 | 344 | 40 | 14 | 3 | 12 | 40 | 17 | 75 | 4 | 2 | .228/.271/.401 | 100 | .262 | -0.4 | SS(79) 5.3 | 1.5 |
| 2022 | GWN | AAA | 24 | 307 | 37 | 14 | 2 | 7 | 25 | 23 | 57 | 9 | 0 | .259/.316/.399 | 95 | .298 | 1.5 | SS(65) 1.9, 2B(9) -0.1 | 1.0 |
| 2023 DC | ATL | MLB | 25 | 96 | 9 | 4 | 1 | 2 | 9 | 5 | 22 | 2 | 1 | .219/.269/.332 | 67 | .272 | 0.2 | 2B 0, SS 0 | 0.0 |

*Comparables: Luis Marté, Luis Alfonso Cruz, Tzu-Wei Lin*

**The Report:** Shewmake never flashed particularly loud tools as an amateur or pro prospect, so the level-by-level performance was always going to be more closely scrutinized. His slugging percentage scraped .400 in 2021, but it came at the cost of bat-to-ball. He struck more of a balance in 2022, but the end result was a low-.700s OPS for the 24-year-old in Triple-A. Shewmake has a pretty simple swing that makes a fair bit of not-particularly-hard contact. He can drive pitches into the gaps now and again, but it's a hit-over-power profile and he only batted .259. He actually posted a bit of a reverse split, but that was most entirely BABIP-driven, as Shewmake struck out far more against fellow lefties, and struggled particularly staying in against spin. Defensively he still plays mostly shortstop, but while his range and throwing are fine, his hands and actions are a bit light for the six. I'd expect his major-league role will see him moving around the dirt a bit as his current offensive projection is a bit fringy for a starting role at any one spot.

**OFP:** 45 / Fifth infielder

**Variance:** Low. Shewmake should provide infield depth for Atlanta in 2023, contingent on a normal recovery from the knee injury that he suffered on a collision last August.

**Jesse Roche's Fantasy Take:** The Braves have little in the way of infield depth behind Ozzie Albies and Vaughn Grissom. Shewmake could carve out nominal fantasy value as an injury replacement at some point. That potentiality is not worth chasing.

## 9 Blake Burkhalter  RHP    OFP: 45    ETA: 2024 as a reliever, 2025 as a starter

Born: 09/19/00  Age: 22  Bats: R  Throws: R  Height: 6'0"  Weight: 204 lb.  Origin: Round 2, 2022 Draft (#76 overall)

| YEAR | TEAM | LVL | AGE | W | L | SV | G | GS | IP | H | HR | BB/9 | K/9 | K | GB% | BABIP | WHIP | ERA | DRA | WARP |
|---|---|---|---|---|---|---|---|---|---|---|---|---|---|---|---|---|---|---|---|---|
| 2023 non-DC | ATL | MLB | 22 | 3 | 3 | 0 | 58 | 0 | 50 | 51 | 8 | 4.2 | 7.8 | 43 | 36.2% | .298 | 1.50 | 4.96 | 126 | -0.4 |

**The Report:** Auburn's closer in 2022, Burkhalter filled up the zone and missed bats with a low-90s cutter. Atlanta drafted him in the second round and immediately signaled they wanted to lengthen him out as a starter. It's a bit of an odd profile in any role. He likes to throw his cutter more than his mid-90s fastball, and it's unclear if the fastball will maintain plus velocity when Burkhalter is stretched out. He has a changeup as well, but it's been used sparingly and has fringe projection. He's a shorter righty with an over-the-top slot that provides little extension on his pitches and he can struggle to consistently get his fastball down. Burkhalter's delivery also looks relieverish, perhaps because he was a reliever. It is a very good cutter, and the fastball can miss bats up in the zone, but he's an odd conversion candidate, especially given how fast he might move in the bullpen.

**OFP:** 45 / Back-end starter or setup reliever

**Variance:** Medium. I'm not arrogant enough to say Burkhalter can't start—we've seen too many Atlanta pitching development success stories recently—but it's not really a starter's arsenal at present, and I think there's a pretty good chance he ends up back in the bullpen by 2024.

**Jesse Roche's Fantasy Take:** If he looks like a reliever, pitches like a reliever and has mechanics like a reliever, he is probably a reliever.

# 10   Ignacio Alvarez   SS/3B      OFP: 45      ETA: 2025/2026

Born: 04/11/03   Age: 20   Bats: R   Throws: R   Height: 6'0"   Weight: 190 lb.   Origin: Round 5, 2022 Draft (#155 overall)

| YEAR | TEAM | LVL | AGE | PA | R | 2B | 3B | HR | RBI | BB | K | SB | CS | AVG/OBP/SLG | DRC+ | BABIP | BRR | DRP | WARP |
|---|---|---|---|---|---|---|---|---|---|---|---|---|---|---|---|---|---|---|---|
| 2022 | BRA | ROK | 19 | 51 | 11 | 1 | 1 | 1 | 5 | 7 | 6 | 4 | 0 | .279/.392/.419 | | .306 | | | |
| 2022 | AUG | A | 19 | 71 | 14 | 2 | 1 | 0 | 6 | 19 | 9 | 4 | 1 | .294/.493/.373 | 134 | .357 | 0.5 | SS(10) -0.9, 3B(5) -0.4 | 0.4 |
| 2023 non-DC | ATL | MLB | 20 | 251 | 21 | 10 | 2 | 2 | 19 | 24 | 47 | 4 | 2 | .213/.295/.297 | 72 | .260 | -2.2 | 3B 0, SS 0 | -0.3 |

**The Report:** Alvarez does two things very well already. He doesn't swing at balls, and he hits strikes. The 19-year-old is not going to expand the zone, and he has a very simple swing that is geared for contact. Alvarez can struggle to impact the baseball though, as he likes to extend and hit line drives to all fields, leading to some awkward contact if you can run in on his hands. And his strong knowledge of the strike zone can lead to a bit of passivity at the plate at times. OBP-driven profiles can struggle in the upper minors as by the time you get to Double-A, more pitchers can throw good strikes and challenge you to do damage. Alvarez does have a bit of gap power, but home runs are unlikely to be a huge part of his game. Defensively, he is perfectly fine at third base, and can probably fake short once a week for you, although his raw foot speed is below-average. Alvarez has a bit of an oddball set of skills of present, and I'm not entirely sure it all adds up to a major leaguer yet. But he will still be 19 when the 2023 season kicks off, so he has plenty of time to figure it out.

**OFP:** 45 / Bench infielder

**Variance:** Very High. I wouldn't be surprised if Alvarez struggles in Double-A, I also wouldn't be surprised if his weird profile works all the way up the ladder.

**Jesse Roche's Fantasy Take:** Statline scouts likely are all over Alvarez after his debut, but he has a very narrow path to fantasy utility given his limited power and speed. Are you hoping to discover the next Luis Arraez? I hope not.

## Outside the Top Ten:

# 11   Adam Maier   RHP

Born: 11/26/01   Age: 21   Bats: R   Throws: R   Height: 6'0"   Weight: 203 lb.

Maier is a bit of a mystery box. He barely pitched in college, losing almost two full seasons at the University of British Columbia to pandemic restrictions, and then after transferring to Oregon for the 2022 season, suffered a season-ending elbow injury after just three starts. All told, he tossed just 60 innings from 2020-22. The quality of the stuff is less of a mystery. Maier's fastball and slider both move. The low-90s heater has sink and run, while the slider is a power breaker. He has upside that fits alongside the top three arms in this system, but his arm health is a question and his recent track record on the mound is short.

# 12   Victor Vodnik   RHP

Born: 10/09/99   Age: 23   Bats: R   Throws: R   Height: 6'0"   Weight: 200 lb.   Origin: Round 14, 2018 Draft (#412 overall)

| YEAR | TEAM | LVL | AGE | W | L | SV | G | GS | IP | H | HR | BB/9 | K/9 | K | GB% | BABIP | WHIP | ERA | DRA- | WARP |
|---|---|---|---|---|---|---|---|---|---|---|---|---|---|---|---|---|---|---|---|---|
| 2021 | MIS | AA | 21 | 1 | 4 | 0 | 11 | 11 | 33² | 32 | 5 | 5.9 | 11.0 | 41 | 52.9% | .333 | 1.60 | 5.35 | 93 | 0.5 |
| 2022 | MIS | AA | 22 | 0 | 0 | 1 | 7 | 0 | 7 | 4 | 0 | 3.9 | 18.0 | 14 | 63.6% | .364 | 1.00 | 0.00 | 83 | 0.1 |
| 2022 | GWN | AAA | 22 | 2 | 0 | 2 | 24 | 0 | 27² | 26 | 2 | 5.2 | 10.7 | 33 | 52.9% | .353 | 1.52 | 2.93 | 86 | 0.6 |
| 2023 non-DC | ATL | MLB | 23 | 3 | 3 | 0 | 58 | 0 | 50 | 46 | 7 | 4.9 | 9.3 | 52 | 41.6% | .298 | 1.48 | 4.44 | 113 | -0.1 |

*Comparables: José Leclerc, Phillippe Aumont, Jeremy Jeffress*

Vodnik missed time with injuries and was converted to bullpen work in 2022, but despite being left off the 40-man and passed over in the Rule 5 Draft, he could contribute to Atlanta's bullpen as soon as this season. His fastball routinely reached the upper-90s in short bursts and his slider and change give him a couple different offspeed looks out of the pen. The change flashes above-average power sink and fade, but his command of the pitch isn't always where you'd want it. Meanwhile his slider isn't a real bat-misser, and can be a bit cutterish. Vodnik's arsenal isn't a traditional fit for the late innings, but he has a lot of fastball and has missed bats all the way up the ladder. He should be a useful major-league reliever in some capacity in short order.

## 13  Dylan Dodd  LHP
Born: 06/06/98  Age: 25  Bats: L  Throws: L  Height: 6'2"  Weight: 210 lb.  Origin: Round 3, 2021 Draft (#96 overall)

| YEAR | TEAM | LVL | AGE | W | L | SV | G | GS | IP | H | HR | BB/9 | K/9 | K | GB% | BABIP | WHIP | ERA | DRA- | WARP |
|------|------|-----|-----|---|---|----|----|----|----|----|----|------|-----|----|------|-------|------|------|------|------|
| 2021 | AUG | A | 23 | 0 | 1 | 0 | 3 | 3 | 11 | 10 | 0 | 2.5 | 11.5 | 14 | 38.5% | .385 | 1.18 | 4.91 | 92 | 0.1 |
| 2022 | ROM | A+ | 24 | 9 | 5 | 0 | 16 | 16 | 89 | 85 | 6 | 1.7 | 9.2 | 91 | 51.9% | .313 | 1.15 | 3.44 | 95 | 0.9 |
| 2022 | MIS | AA | 24 | 2 | 4 | 0 | 9 | 9 | 46¹ | 46 | 3 | 2.5 | 10.7 | 55 | 39.2% | .352 | 1.27 | 3.11 | 90 | 0.7 |
| 2022 | GWN | AAA | 24 | 1 | 0 | 0 | 1 | 1 | 6² | 5 | 1 | 1.4 | 9.5 | 7 | 22.2% | .235 | 0.90 | 4.05 | 122 | 0.0 |
| 2023 non-DC | ATL | MLB | 25 | 3 | 3 | 0 | 58 | 0 | 50 | 54 | 6 | 2.9 | 7.3 | 41 | 36.3% | .311 | 1.40 | 4.39 | 115 | -0.1 |

Yet another pitcher with a low-90s fastball and an advanced changeup, the gap between Dodd and Vines is a bit overstated by their respective ordinal rankings. A 23-year-old senior sign in the 2021 draft, he mixes his four pitches well and while there's nothing clearly above-average here, Dodd made it all the way to Triple-A in his first full pro season. He has at least an average change and slider, and moves his low-90s fastball around well enough that he can slot into the back of a rotation and give you a chance to win. It won't be dominant stuff, and there are fine command margins here—I don't doubt he will keep throwing strikes—but Dodd has flourished in the Atlanta system, and is perfectly cromulent back-end rotation depth.

## 14  Tyler Tolve  C
Born: 07/16/00  Age: 22  Bats: L  Throws: R  Height: 6'1"  Weight: 200 lb.  Origin: Round 17, 2021 Draft (#517 overall)

| YEAR | TEAM | LVL | AGE | PA | R | 2B | 3B | HR | RBI | BB | K | SB | CS | AVG/OBP/SLG | DRC+ | BABIP | BRR | DRP | WARP |
|------|------|-----|-----|----|---|----|----|----|-----|----|----|----|----|-------------|------|-------|-----|-----|------|
| 2021 | AUG | A | 20 | 92 | 12 | 3 | 2 | 2 | 10 | 6 | 28 | 2 | 0 | .294/.348/.447 | 90 | .418 | 0.5 | C(23) 0.3 | 0.2 |
| 2022 | ROM | A+ | 21 | 325 | 42 | 14 | 5 | 12 | 47 | 30 | 104 | 8 | 1 | .261/.338/.470 | 85 | .362 | 0.3 | C(68) 4.3 | 0.9 |
| 2023 non-DC | ATL | MLB | 22 | 251 | 22 | 10 | 3 | 4 | 23 | 16 | 91 | 2 | 1 | .228/.286/.350 | 78 | .356 | -3.4 | C 0, RF 0 | 0.0 |

Lest you think the well has run dry on Georgia scouting finds, Atlanta popped Tolve in the 17th round of the 2021 draft after he was a three-year starter for Kennesaw State. He showed off a polished receiving game in Rome, with soft, quiet hands around the edge of the zone. The throwing part of the catch-and-throw skills lags behind though. Tolve just doesn't get good carry from his arm, and High-A runners took advantage all season. At the plate, his swing is a bit length-and-strength, but there's above-average pop, and he can pull outer-half breaking stuff out. Breaking stuff down is a more troubling issue, and swing-and-miss is a short-and-long term concern. If Tolve can improve his work in the running game—and I think some of this is mechanical more than arm strength—he profiles as a traditional pop-and-glove backup catcher.

## 15  Jesse Franklin V  RF
Born: 12/01/98  Age: 24  Bats: L  Throws: L  Height: 6'1"  Weight: 215 lb.  Origin: Round 3, 2020 Draft (#97 overall)

| YEAR | TEAM | LVL | AGE | PA | R | 2B | 3B | HR | RBI | BB | K | SB | CS | AVG/OBP/SLG | DRC+ | BABIP | BRR | DRP | WARP |
|------|------|-----|-----|----|---|----|----|----|-----|----|----|----|----|-------------|------|-------|-----|-----|------|
| 2021 | PEJ | WIN | 22 | 66 | 10 | 1 | 0 | 1 | 5 | 12 | 23 | 0 | 0 | .098/.303/.176 | | .148 | | | |
| 2021 | ROM | A+ | 22 | 406 | 55 | 24 | 2 | 24 | 61 | 34 | 115 | 19 | 4 | .244/.320/.522 | 126 | .284 | -0.2 | RF(40) -2.2, CF(32) -4.0, LF(18) -0.9 | 1.9 |
| 2022 | MIS | AA | 23 | 66 | 6 | 1 | 1 | 2 | 9 | 6 | 18 | 2 | 0 | .236/.333/.400 | 98 | .297 | 0.6 | RF(12) -0.8, LF(1) -0.6, CF(1) -0.1 | 0.2 |
| 2023 non-DC | ATL | MLB | 24 | 251 | 23 | 11 | 2 | 6 | 26 | 17 | 83 | 6 | 2 | .215/.278/.354 | 78 | .307 | -1.4 | LF 0, CF 0 | -0.1 |

Franklin's 2022 season ended in April when a UCL tear necessitated Tommy John surgery. A mere 15-game showing in Double-A is not enough to give us a hint one way or the other if Franklin's max-effort, pull-happy swing will work in the upper minors. Franklin has potential plus game power and should be pretty good in a corner outfield spot, but he's already 24 and will have to make some hay when he's back on the field in 2023 to stay list-relevant.

## 16  Roddery Muñoz  RHP
Born: 04/14/00   Age: 23   Bats: R   Throws: R   Height: 6'2"   Weight: 210 lb.

| YEAR | TEAM | LVL | AGE | W | L | SV | G | GS | IP | H | HR | BB/9 | K/9 | K | GB% | BABIP | WHIP | ERA | DRA- | WARP |
|---|---|---|---|---|---|---|---|---|---|---|---|---|---|---|---|---|---|---|---|---|
| 2021 | AUG | A | 21 | 1 | 2 | 0 | 8 | 6 | 29² | 33 | 3 | 3.3 | 10.0 | 33 | 37.6% | .366 | 1.48 | 6.67 | 87 | 0.5 |
| 2022 | ROM | A+ | 22 | 8 | 4 | 0 | 19 | 19 | 89¹ | 85 | 9 | 3.7 | 10.6 | 105 | 47.0% | .319 | 1.37 | 4.03 | 85 | 1.4 |
| 2022 | MIS | AA | 22 | 0 | 0 | 0 | 3 | 3 | 11 | 12 | 3 | 4.1 | 11.5 | 14 | 45.5% | .310 | 1.55 | 9.82 | 98 | 0.1 |
| 2023 non-DC | ATL | MLB | 23 | 3 | 3 | 0 | 58 | 0 | 50 | 53 | 8 | 4.3 | 7.9 | 44 | 36.6% | .309 | 1.54 | 5.14 | 130 | -0.5 |

Munoz is in a similar spot to where Vodnik was at the end of 2021. Command and control haven't really been there for him as a starter, and while he has a big fastball, the secondaries are even rougher than Vodnik's. A move to the pen might be coming in 2023, where his fastball should sit in the upper-90s in short bursts, and hopefully his cutterish slider will round into a more consistent above-average shape.

## 17  Luis Vargas  RHP
Born: 05/02/02   Age: 21   Bats: R   Throws: R   Height: 5'11"   Weight: 196 lb.

| YEAR | TEAM | LVL | AGE | W | L | SV | G | GS | IP | H | HR | BB/9 | K/9 | K | GB% | BABIP | WHIP | ERA | DRA- | WARP |
|---|---|---|---|---|---|---|---|---|---|---|---|---|---|---|---|---|---|---|---|---|
| 2022 | AUG | A | 20 | 4 | 4 | 0 | 22 | 17 | 96 | 86 | 10 | 3.9 | 9.9 | 106 | 38.8% | .302 | 1.33 | 3.75 | 91 | 1.5 |
| 2023 non-DC | ATL | MLB | 21 | 3 | 3 | 0 | 58 | 0 | 50 | 56 | 9 | 4.6 | 7.2 | 40 | 34.1% | .308 | 1.63 | 5.75 | 142 | -0.8 |

To be honest, Vargas has already had more success as a starter in the minors than Munoz or Vodnik, but he also might not be able to avoid an eventual shift to relief. A shorter, stouter righty with a lot of effort in his delivery, Vargas has plus arm strength and consistently pops mid-90s with his fastball. His breaking ball and change don't do much more than flash at present, and his command of the slider will be a particular point for development. Vargas probably ends up in the bullpen by the time he hits the upper minors, but it's a lively fastball and sometimes a flash secondary becomes a sit secondary. He's one for the follow list.

## 18  Drake Baldwin  C
Born: 03/28/01   Age: 22   Bats: L   Throws: R   Height: 6'1"   Weight: 210 lb.

| YEAR | TEAM | LVL | AGE | PA | R | 2B | 3B | HR | RBI | BB | K | SB | CS | AVG/OBP/SLG | DRC+ | BABIP | BRR | DRP | WARP |
|---|---|---|---|---|---|---|---|---|---|---|---|---|---|---|---|---|---|---|---|
| 2022 | AUG | A | 21 | 101 | 13 | 3 | 0 | 0 | 6 | 18 | 22 | 1 | 0 | .247/.396/.284 | 97 | .339 | 0.1 | C(16) 1.2 | 0.4 |
| 2023 non-DC | ATL | MLB | 22 | 251 | 20 | 10 | 2 | 2 | 19 | 23 | 69 | 1 | 0 | .209/.290/.289 | 66 | .295 | -4.2 | C 0 | -0.4 |

Atlanta's third-round pick in the 2022 draft, Baldwin is another small college catcher who mashed against NCAA competition. His receiving skills are a bit more raw than Tolve's and despite hitting for big power in the Missouri Valley Conference, that hasn't translated into the pros yet. Baldwin has a loose swing, and swings hard with a good path for pop, but it's not super torquey and he feels like he will need a tweak at the plate to unlock any consistent game pop. He's a bit of a long-term project for a college catcher, but there might be a reward to go with the risk.

## Top Talents 25 and Under (as of 4/1/2023):

1. Ronald Acuña Jr., OF
2. Michael Harris II, OF
3. Austin Riley, 3B
4. Spencer Strider, RHP
5. Vaughn Grissom, 2B/SS
6. Mike Soroka, RHP
7. Ian Anderson, RHP
8. Bryce Elder, RHP
9. Huascar Ynoa, RHP
10. Owen Murphy, RHP

If Kolby Allard had shown a bit more promise in his first few shakes at the big league level, we might be looking at a 25U list first in my memory: a full sweep of big leaguers. Instead, Atlanta and their fans will have to settle for one of the most staggering collections of young talent in the sport and indeed in recent memory. Sure, Ozzie Albies turned 26 in January, but somehow Georgia's preeminent peaches will persevere.

The assembled nonet of list graduates above can be broadly grouped into two subsections: the four stars atop and the five solid role players/incomplete starters below. In deference to the superstar he's been at full health and the solid contributor he was last year, Acuña tops this list. A decline in the Venezuelan wunderkind's foot speed would have been expected, but the explosive young outfielder looked more rusty than physically compromised. That could read good or ill, as he continued hitting the ball as hard as anyone in baseball but struggled to elevate or barrel the ball. Riley had no such issues, erupting for his first All-Star selection and second-straight MVP also-ran campaign. The sturdy slugger won't likely add a Gold Glove to his collection, but so long as the April 2-born 26-year-old-to-be can keep swatting balls into The Battery district night, there won't be many complaints. Harris emerged on the heels of huge preseason helium and the 58th-overall prospect in the preseason Top 101 ripped through Double-A Mississippi straight into the NL East division champs' lineup. He came one big fly shy of a 20/20 debut in just two-thirds of MLB play, but his Rookie of the Year crown helps him pair with Acuña and Riley for one of the most imposing young tops of the order anywhere.

Strider rounds out the stars, and by WARP, none had a better year than the fiery young righty. His 51 DRA- was the best in baseball by a rather significant margin (min. 130 IP) though he was not fully workhorsed until late in the season as he transitioned out of the bullpen to terrorize the league (and the Rockies in particular, in one record-setting outing). His Dinelson Lamet impression has been virtuoso, through the way the compact righty will toggle his slider to vary it between a sweeping monstrosity and a hard-dropping power curve-type offering to pair with triple-digit heat.

In the stead of Dansby Swanson, Grissom may be overmatched. The defensively dependable Swanson does not have an exact heir in the 22-year-old Floridian, but his debut flashed a balanced toolkit at the plate highlighted by steady, quality contact which took advantage of a steady diet of fastballs over the plate. Grissom may be challenged more in 2023, but if he's hitting low in Atlanta's order it's hard to envision clubs eager to pitch around him with the aforementioned trio bearing down on them. None of Soroka, Anderson or Ynoa had the seasons they'd hoped for in 2022, with devastating injuries undercutting Soroka's second straight campaign. Now supposedly healthy, it's hard to imagine him recreating his 2019 eminence; however, in Atlanta's deep rotation he can be hidden and eased in with relatively minimal difficulty. That will of course rely on strides back in the positive realm from Anderson and Ynoa, who were shellacked by opposing hitters and their own bodies, respectively. Dips in velo and command, as Michael Ajeto pointed out in July, spelled corresponding drops in performance, as Anderson posted a 117 DRA- in 111.7 IP, a year anteceding his 88 DRA- in just a couple more starts. Ynoa bore an even greater pox, slipping as well from 2021 competence into a disappointing campaign primarily in Triple-A that culminated in a September trip to Tommy John station. Elder avoided quite such dire straits as he looked largely the same steady arm he was as a dominant force for Triple-A Gwinnett. More meandering than the overpowering stuff wielded by Ynoa, the groundball specialist weaved in and out of trouble on the edges of the zone, but will be a major test case for the efficacy of Atlanta's less defensively proven infield.

# Baltimore Orioles

## The State of the System:

The Orioles might be still tap dancing around what "liftoff" actually means and when it's happening, but their loaded farm system—once again among the best baseball—is ready to fire the booster rockets.

## The Top Ten:

**1** **Gunnar Henderson**  **SS/3B**          OFP: 70          ETA: Debuted in 2022

Born: 06/29/01   Age: 22   Bats: L   Throws: R   Height: 6'2"   Weight: 210 lb.   Origin: Round 2, 2019 Draft (#42 overall)

| YEAR | TEAM | LVL | AGE | PA | R | 2B | 3B | HR | RBI | BB | K | SB | CS | AVG/OBP/SLG | DRC+ | BABIP | BRR | DRP | WARP |
|---|---|---|---|---|---|---|---|---|---|---|---|---|---|---|---|---|---|---|---|
| 2021 | DEL | A | 20 | 157 | 30 | 11 | 1 | 8 | 39 | 14 | 46 | 5 | 1 | .312/.369/.574 | 108 | .404 | 0.8 | SS(20) 3.2, 3B(11) 0.2 | 1.0 |
| 2021 | ABD | A+ | 20 | 289 | 34 | 16 | 3 | 9 | 35 | 40 | 87 | 11 | 1 | .230/.343/.432 | 98 | .313 | -1.9 | SS(40) 4.2, 3B(23) -0.7 | 0.9 |
| 2022 | BOW | AA | 21 | 208 | 41 | 11 | 3 | 8 | 35 | 41 | 38 | 12 | 2 | .312/.452/.573 | 138 | .350 | 1.1 | 3B(27) 0.7, SS(18) 0.1 | 1.7 |
| 2022 | NOR | AAA | 21 | 295 | 60 | 13 | 4 | 11 | 41 | 38 | 78 | 10 | 1 | .288/.390/.504 | 110 | .374 | 1.3 | SS(32) -1.4, 3B(21) 1.1, 2B(6) 0.0 | 1.3 |
| 2022 | BAL | MLB | 21 | 132 | 12 | 7 | 1 | 4 | 18 | 16 | 34 | 1 | 1 | .259/.348/.440 | 96 | .333 | -0.5 | 3B(24) -0.5, SS(7) -0.2, 2B(3) -0.2 | 0.1 |
| 2023 DC | BAL | MLB | 22 | 550 | 57 | 25 | 4 | 14 | 50 | 60 | 149 | 11 | 4 | .239/.328/.394 | 107 | .316 | 0.1 | 3B -1, SS 0 | 1.9 |

*Comparables: Rafael Devers, Mookie Betts, Eric Hosmer*

**The Report:** Coming into the 2022 season, Henderson was a very good prospect, don't get us wrong. He was a back of the Top 101 guy, a pull-happy, power-hitting left-side infielder with some questions about his hit tool and swing decisions, and without a real track record in the upper minors. He ended 2022 in the majors, where he posted a near-.800 OPS in just enough at-bats to keep him eligible for this list—and the 2023 Rookie of the Year bonus draft pick. So what happened?

Jarrett Seidler outlined the reasons for his jump right before we crowned Henderson the number one prospect in baseball on our Midseason 50. The tl;dr: He continued to hit the ball hard in the upper minors, while narrowing the amount of pitches he swung at, and increasing his contact rate when he swung. That was good for a .950 OPS between Double- and Triple-A as a 21-year-old while playing a premium defensive position. After his major-league cup of coffee confirmed much of what he did in the minors, he remains the best prospect in baseball.

You could argue he doesn't have the most upside on this list. Names like Jordan Walker and Elly de la Cruz are perhaps more likely to win MVP awards. Henderson's hit tool is perhaps merely plus in the majors. He's a better fit at third, although he's capable of the spectacular play up the middle. He will get on base, lace plenty of doubles, flirt with 30 home runs now and again and be a better-than-the-sum-of-his-statline guy. He's the most likely player on these lists to be a plus regular for 10 years. And it's not like Henderson is low-upside. A .300 average and 30 bombs are in play if he makes a bit more contact in the zone like he did in the upper minors. And that can win some MVP awards after all.

**OFP:** 70 / All-Star at either shortstop or third base

**Variance:** Low. Henderson is only eligible for this list by 14 at-bats. He looked the part of a plus regular in the majors from day one and will be the betting favorite for American League Rookie of the Year.

**Jesse Roche's Fantasy Take:** Dynasty prospect 1B to Corbin Carroll's 1A, Henderson is a dynamic player with the potential to make an immediate fantasy impact across all five standard categories. Indeed, it is very reasonable to prefer him in both redraft and dynasty to Carroll. Henderson plays at an increasingly-shallow third base and he arguably carries less risk in both playing time and performance. During his stellar debut, he flashed plus power, a plus approach and solid speed. That said, he did suffer some in-zone swing-and-miss and had scary small-sample platoon issues (.130/.231/.217 versus lefties). There likely will be bumps in the road, but Henderson has substantial long-term upside with ".300 and 30 bombs" plus some steals as a potential peak outcome.

## 2 Grayson Rodriguez  RHP          OFP: 70          ETA: Should be Opening Day 2023, will likely be late April 2023

Born: 11/16/99   Age: 23   Bats: L   Throws: R   Height: 6'5"   Weight: 220 lb.   Origin: Round 1, 2018 Draft (#11 overall)

| YEAR | TEAM | LVL | AGE | W | L | SV | G | GS | IP | H | HR | BB/9 | K/9 | K | GB% | BABIP | WHIP | ERA | DRA- | WARP |
|---|---|---|---|---|---|---|---|---|---|---|---|---|---|---|---|---|---|---|---|---|
| 2021 | ABD | A+ | 21 | 3 | 0 | 0 | 5 | 5 | 23¹ | 11 | 2 | 1.9 | 15.4 | 40 | 42.5% | .237 | 0.69 | 1.54 | 69 | 0.6 |
| 2021 | BOW | AA | 21 | 6 | 1 | 0 | 18 | 18 | 79² | 47 | 8 | 2.5 | 13.7 | 121 | 37.8% | .252 | 0.87 | 2.60 | 83 | 1.4 |
| 2022 | NOR | AAA | 22 | 6 | 1 | 0 | 14 | 14 | 69² | 44 | 2 | 2.7 | 12.5 | 97 | 42.1% | .280 | 0.93 | 2.20 | 58 | 2.5 |
| 2023 DC | BAL | MLB | 23 | 6 | 5 | 0 | 19 | 19 | 93 | 74 | 11 | 3.5 | 10.9 | 113 | 37.0% | .281 | 1.18 | 2.98 | 85 | 1.6 |

*Comparables: Tyler Glasnow, Chris Archer, Archie Bradley*

**The Report:** The Orioles have the best position player prospect in baseball and they might still have the best pitching prospect as well. Like Henderson, you can argue Rodriguez shouldn't be eligible for this list, but a lat injury cut out a few months of his 2022 season. Before the IL stint, his power stuff was dominating Triple-A, as it has every other level of the minors. His fastball is one of the best around, featuring mid-90s velocity—touching higher—with the kind of ride that makes it an elite swing-and-miss pitch up in the zone.

Behind the potential 80-grade heat, Rodriguez throws four secondaries that all have at least plus potential. I prefer the slider, a mid-80s, big breaking tilt monster, that looks like the fastball until it takes a sharp left turn. The changeup is also advanced, with big velocity separation and good sink and fade. Rodriguez will bury it down and away to lefties, but can also toss it at their front hip to freeze them. His curve comes in a few ticks lower than the slider with more vertical action, but it's generally not commanded quite as well. He also added a low-90s cutter last year that has developed quickly although it tends to be used more sparingly than the rest of the arsenal.

That is *a lot* of stuff. Rodriguez doesn't even need this many weapons to be a well-above-average major-league starter, and when everything is cooking, he looks like an ace. Now let's quibble. He hasn't ever worked deep into games, even when healthy. This hasn't been an unusually conservative development track for a prep arm, but we don't know how sharp stuff looks when measured out over 6-7 innings a start, 150+ innings over a season. And he wasn't healthy in 2022, he had the aforementioned lat injury, and both his command and breaking balls looked a little rusty when he returned to the mound in August and September. These are minor quibbles all in all, but if he ends up more a mid-rotation starter than top, those might be the reasons.

**OFP:** 70 / no. 2 starter

**Variance:** Medium. Rodriguez is major-league ready and arguably has been since late 2021. The only question is how the stuff plays over the course of a full season, but the stuff is very, very good.

**Jesse Roche's Fantasy Take:** Rodriguez's repertoire depth and quality and imminent arrival set him apart from all other pitching prospects. At his best, he looks the part of a future front-of-the-rotation starter. Yet, his stuff can wax and wane. He'll enter the bigs on an up-and-coming team with a new-look, pitcher-friendly home park. In fact, Camden Yards went from 1st in park factor and home-run factor in 2021 to 24th in park factor and 26th in home-run factor in 2022. Pitching prospects are a risky demographic, and injury is an ever-present concern, but Rodriguez could find success right away, providing excellent ratios and plenty of strikeouts.

## 3 Jackson Holliday  SS          OFP: 70          ETA: Late 2025/2026

Born: 12/04/03   Age: 19   Bats: L   Throws: R   Height: 6'1"   Weight: 175 lb.   Origin: Round 1, 2022 Draft (#1 overall)

| YEAR | TEAM | LVL | AGE | PA | R | 2B | 3B | HR | RBI | BB | K | SB | CS | AVG/OBP/SLG | DRC+ | BABIP | BRR | DRP | WARP |
|---|---|---|---|---|---|---|---|---|---|---|---|---|---|---|---|---|---|---|---|
| 2022 | ORI | ROK | 18 | 33 | 6 | 1 | 0 | 1 | 3 | 10 | 2 | 3 | 0 | .409/.576/.591 | | .400 | | | |
| 2022 | DEL | A | 18 | 57 | 8 | 4 | 0 | 0 | 6 | 15 | 10 | 1 | 1 | .238/.439/.333 | 124 | .313 | -0.1 | SS(8) -0.4, 2B(4) 0.3 | 0.3 |
| 2023 non-DC | BAL | MLB | 19 | 251 | 20 | 10 | 2 | 2 | 19 | 25 | 52 | 2 | 1 | .212/.297/.295 | 71 | .269 | -3.2 | 2B 0, SS 0 | -0.4 |

*Comparables: Yasel Antuna, Michael De León, Wenceel Perez*

**The Report:** The first-overall pick in last summer's draft, Holliday was a riser up boards since the Fall 2021 showcases. Once in the pros he immediately looked like one of the best prospects in the game, showing off an incredibly advanced approach for his age, plus bat speed and the ability to do damage to all fields.

For low-minors players, I like to delineate between having a good eye and taking major-league at-bats. The former doesn't always play as well up the ladder—if you have a good eye at these levels, you can just keep the bat on your shoulder and draw walks. Holiday does the latter. He is fine being aggressive early in counts and comfortable working back from two strikes. He can hold up against breaking balls diving out of the zone, foul off stuff that catches a bit of plate. When he gets something to drive he has the kind of bat whip that can spray line drives from line-to-line. He can stay back on offspeed and drive it to the left-center gap, and should grow into 25+ home run power in time. He's a complete hitter, a plus hit/plus power shortstop who will be a nightmare for any pitcher who likes to nibble.

In the field, Holliday is an above-average defender at short with the kind of range you'd associate with a plus runner. His hands and actions are solid. His arm is plus when he needs it to be. Holliday can get a little loose with his throwing on the move, but there's little to quibble with in terms of his glove. He is a true two-way shortstop prospect and one of the top overall prospects in baseball despite his short pro track record.

**OFP:** 70 / All-Star shortstop

**Variance:** Medium. Holliday doesn't have much pro experience, but in those limited reps he looked like one of the best prospects in baseball and it's a high-floor skill set considering he only just graduated high school.

**Jesse Roche's Fantasy Take:** It is difficult not to fall in love with the above description of Holliday as "a plus-hit/plus-power shortstop" who "should grow into 25+ home run power in time." Oh, and he's "a plus runner." He has the potential to develop into a high-end five-category producer. The main draw at present, though, is his precocious hitting ability. Indeed, last spring, Holliday broke J.T. Realmuto's national high school record for hits. Further, in his brief debut between the complex and Low-A, he had an impeccable 12-to-27 strikeout-to-walk ratio. Given his advanced, well-rounded skill set, Holliday is in play to be the first player selected in upcoming FYPDs, and a top-20 overall dynasty prospect.

## 4   Colton Cowser   OF    OFP: 60    ETA: 2023

Born: 03/20/00   Age: 23   Bats: L   Throws: R   Height: 6'3"   Weight: 195 lb.   Origin: Round 1, 2021 Draft (#5 overall)

| YEAR | TEAM | LVL | AGE | PA | R | 2B | 3B | HR | RBI | BB | K | SB | CS | AVG/OBP/SLG | DRC+ | BABIP | BRR | DRP | WARP |
|---|---|---|---|---|---|---|---|---|---|---|---|---|---|---|---|---|---|---|---|
| 2021 | ORIO | ROK | 21 | 25 | 8 | 3 | 0 | 1 | 8 | 3 | 4 | 3 | 2 | .500/.560/.773 | | .588 | | | |
| 2021 | DEL | A | 21 | 124 | 22 | 5 | 0 | 1 | 26 | 22 | 19 | 4 | 2 | .347/.476/.429 | 124 | .418 | -1.1 | CF(16) -2.8, RF(4) 3.0 | 0.7 |
| 2022 | ABD | A+ | 22 | 278 | 42 | 19 | 2 | 4 | 22 | 45 | 79 | 16 | 1 | .258/.385/.410 | 112 | .374 | 4.2 | CF(41) -3.9, LF(12) -0.1, RF(3) -0.0 | 1.2 |
| 2022 | BOW | AA | 22 | 224 | 49 | 10 | 0 | 10 | 33 | 36 | 57 | 2 | 2 | .341/.469/.568 | 127 | .446 | -1.4 | CF(37) -0.2, RF(5) -0.1, LF(3) -0.1 | 1.3 |
| 2022 | NOR | AAA | 22 | 124 | 23 | 7 | 0 | 5 | 11 | 13 | 38 | 0 | 0 | .219/.339/.429 | 90 | .290 | 1.8 | CF(16) 1.3, RF(9) 0.2, LF(4) 1.1 | 0.6 |
| 2023 DC | BAL | MLB | 23 | 28 | 3 | 1 | 0 | 0 | 2 | 3 | 8 | 0 | 0 | .240/.334/.358 | 100 | .338 | -0.1 | CF 0 | 0.1 |

*Comparables: Josh Reddick, Steven Duggar, Zach Walters*

**The Report:** Cowser had kind of a weird year. He actually struggled at High-A early on, hitting for little power while both taking and swinging through too many hittable strikes. After getting more used to pro pitching, he exploded for two huge months in Double-A, earning a Triple-A cameo to end the season.

At his best, Cowser doesn't chase much at all outside the zone, and can cover most of the zone with a quick, compact swing. He flashes above-average power and can drop the barrel and turn on nearly anything. As hinted at above, his swing decisions can straddle the line of patient and overly passive, and he's shown a surprising amount of swing-and-miss in the zone for a player whose on-base skills will have to drive his offensive profile.

Cowser was widely seen as a likely corner outfielder coming out of the draft. But he played the vast majority of the time in center in 2022 and looked pretty competent out there.

**OFP:** 60 / On-base heavy first-division center fielder

**Variance:** Medium. Cowser is showing a different profile than he did as an amateur, with better defense and less bat-to-ball; that also increases the chances he might not hit.

**Jesse Roche's Fantasy Take:** Cowser's Double-A explosion (.341/.469/.568) behind a .446 BABIP hides some underlying concerns mentioned above. His borderline-passive approach coupled with generally average contact skills resulted in a boatload of strikeouts (27.8% K%). Further, he hit a disastrous .194/.324/.287 against left-handed pitchers. Strikeouts and platoon issues can be stomached, however, when a prospect mashes righties like Cowser does (.307/.432/.532). Ultimately, his plate discipline, emerging game power and even some speed make for a promising fantasy player, particularly in OBP formats.

## 5 Coby Mayo 3B    OFP: 60    ETA: 2024
Born: 12/10/01   Age: 21   Bats: R   Throws: R   Height: 6'5"   Weight: 215 lb.   Origin: Round 4, 2020 Draft (#103 overall)

| YEAR | TEAM | LVL | AGE | PA | R | 2B | 3B | HR | RBI | BB | K | SB | CS | AVG/OBP/SLG | DRC+ | BABIP | BRR | DRP | WARP |
|---|---|---|---|---|---|---|---|---|---|---|---|---|---|---|---|---|---|---|---|
| 2021 | ORIB | ROK | 19 | 84 | 17 | 6 | 0 | 3 | 13 | 11 | 13 | 6 | 0 | .324/.429/.535 | | .364 | | | |
| 2021 | DEL | A | 19 | 125 | 27 | 8 | 1 | 5 | 26 | 16 | 26 | 5 | 0 | .311/.416/.547 | 118 | .373 | 1.3 | 3B(27) -3.3 | 0.4 |
| 2022 | ABD | A+ | 20 | 288 | 50 | 16 | 2 | 14 | 49 | 27 | 62 | 5 | 1 | .251/.326/.494 | 142 | .275 | -1.6 | 3B(61) 3.2 | 2.3 |
| 2022 | BOW | AA | 20 | 145 | 21 | 4 | 0 | 5 | 20 | 12 | 50 | 0 | 0 | .250/.331/.398 | 92 | .365 | 0.5 | 3B(20) 1.1, 1B(2) -0.4 | 0.4 |
| 2023 non-DC | BAL | MLB | 21 | 251 | 23 | 11 | 1 | 6 | 26 | 17 | 66 | 2 | 0 | .221/.283/.356 | 81 | .284 | -3.7 | 1B 0, 3B 0 | -0.3 |

*Comparables: Josh Vitters, Blake DeWitt, Maikel Franco*

**The Report:** In a broad sense, Mayo is about where Henderson was a year ago. He flashes a broad base of skills—huge bat speed, decent feel for the barrel, solid approach, sometimes flashy defense at third—but he has not consistently coagulated everything into production yet. He could use some maximization on swing decisions and particularly pitch recognition, which Baltimore appears to be one of if not the best organizations at teaching; we think that would unlock his plus-plus power projection into games better. He's still pretty inexperienced despite having reached Double-A, with only 129 games above the complex.

Defensively, he's a gigantic kid with some reliability issues, so he could end up having to slide over to first base. That would put a lot more pressure on his bat.

**OFP:** 60 / First-division third baseman

**Variance:** Medium. Mayo still needs some things to come together.

**Jesse Roche's Fantasy Take:** The large 6-foot-5 slugger has only just touched the surface of his long-term power potential. What distinguishes Mayo from other hulking power hitters, however, is underrated bat-to-ball ability. So while his overall line last year (.247/.326/.456) may underwhelm, he has a ton of untapped hit-power upside. If I may be so bold as to say, there are shades of a young Austin Riley in Mayo.

## 6 Jordan Westburg IF    OFP: 55    ETA: 2023
Born: 02/18/99   Age: 24   Bats: R   Throws: R   Height: 6'3"   Weight: 203 lb.   Origin: Round 1, 2020 Draft (#30 overall)

| YEAR | TEAM | LVL | AGE | PA | R | 2B | 3B | HR | RBI | BB | K | SB | CS | AVG/OBP/SLG | DRC+ | BABIP | BRR | DRP | WARP |
|---|---|---|---|---|---|---|---|---|---|---|---|---|---|---|---|---|---|---|---|
| 2021 | DEL | A | 22 | 91 | 18 | 5 | 1 | 3 | 24 | 12 | 24 | 5 | 1 | .366/.484/.592 | 114 | .500 | 0.8 | 3B(11) -1.3, SS(8) -0.8 | 0.3 |
| 2021 | ABD | A+ | 22 | 285 | 41 | 16 | 2 | 8 | 41 | 35 | 71 | 9 | 4 | .286/.389/.469 | 114 | .372 | 0.5 | SS(40) 4.4, 3B(20) -2.1 | 1.6 |
| 2021 | BOW | AA | 22 | 130 | 15 | 6 | 2 | 4 | 14 | 14 | 32 | 3 | 0 | .232/.323/.429 | 96 | .282 | 0.3 | SS(21) 1.7, 3B(5) 0.0 | 0.5 |
| 2022 | BOW | AA | 23 | 209 | 32 | 14 | 0 | 9 | 32 | 26 | 57 | 3 | 0 | .247/.344/.473 | 113 | .310 | 1.6 | 2B(16) -1.8, 3B(16) 1.6, SS(13) -0.3 | 1.0 |
| 2022 | NOR | AAA | 23 | 413 | 64 | 25 | 3 | 18 | 74 | 44 | 90 | 9 | 3 | .273/.361/.508 | 113 | .318 | -1.2 | SS(41) -2.9, 2B(24) 0.8, 3B(21) -0.5 | 1.5 |
| 2023 DC | BAL | MLB | 24 | 95 | 10 | 4 | 0 | 2 | 10 | 8 | 25 | 1 | 1 | .232/.306/.364 | 94 | .304 | 0.0 | 3B 0, SS 0 | 0.2 |

*Comparables: Todd Frazier, Matt Reynolds, Jedd Gyorko*

**The Report:** Nowadays the "We have _____ at home" meme is practically ancient in internet terms, but Jordan Westburg is a decent approximation of "We have Gunnar Henderson at home." Now that's more than a bit of a backhanded compliment, but it is a compliment. Westburg struck out a little less and hit for a lot more power in 2022, and while his swing decisions aren't quite as good as the top prospect in baseball, he also crushed the upper minors. He has a pretty simple weight transfer, and an upper-body-heavy swing, but it's a strong upper body with commensurate plus raw power. Westburg pulled the ball more in the air this year, and good things (mostly) happened. He should get to most of his pop, settling in around 25 homers with plenty of doubles. He's lacked much more than average tools on past scouting reports, so real power development would be a game changer.

The extra pop has come at a bit of a cost though. Westburg will flash a bit more swing-and-miss in the zone than Henderson, and the good stuff diving down and out of the zone can tie him up too, but overall the strikeout rate shouldn't be too onerous. However, the fly-ball-heavy approach does lead to a lot of pop-ups among the big flies, so the hit tool may play more around average. Westburg should also get on base at a fair clip, and is serviceable at shortstop, more than that at second or third. The hot corner might be his best fit given the strong, accurate arm, but the defensive flexibility will be an asset if the Orioles want to keep Henderson as their mostly-everyday shortstop.

**OFP:** 55 / Above-average regular who can float around your infield spots

**Variance:** Low. I suppose there's a chance the hit tool is fringy or even below-average. You don't know until you know with these type of hitters, but there really isn't a weakness in Westburg's game overall, and the realistic floor here is something like a fringe regular.

**Jesse Roche's Fantasy Take:** Westburg quietly launched 27 home runs and led the organization in extra-base hits (69) last year. Where he'll stand in the infield is unclear, but, regardless, his power will play in all fantasy formats. Westburg also possesses enough contact skills and speed to not be a liability in non-power categories. Although he is far from the shiniest prospect in the system, he has legit fantasy upside, and he comfortably falls within the dynasty top 100.

## 7 Connor Norby 2B    OFP: 55    ETA: Late 2023

Born: 06/08/00   Age: 23   Bats: R   Throws: R   Height: 5'10"   Weight: 187 lb.   Origin: Round 2, 2021 Draft (#41 overall)

| YEAR | TEAM | LVL | AGE | PA | R | 2B | 3B | HR | RBI | BB | K | SB | CS | AVG/OBP/SLG | DRC+ | BABIP | BRR | DRP | WARP |
|------|------|-----|-----|----|----|----|----|----|-----|----|----|----|----|-------------|------|-------|-----|-----|------|
| 2021 | DEL | A | 21 | 126 | 17 | 4 | 1 | 3 | 17 | 21 | 28 | 5 | 3 | .283/.413/.434 | 113 | .352 | 0.3 | 2B(26) -0.1 | 0.6 |
| 2022 | ABD | A+ | 22 | 209 | 27 | 7 | 2 | 8 | 20 | 18 | 50 | 6 | 3 | .237/.311/.425 | 105 | .277 | 0.8 | 2B(40) -0.0, LF(3) -0.3, SS(1) -0.0 | 0.7 |
| 2022 | BOW | AA | 22 | 296 | 58 | 14 | 2 | 17 | 46 | 34 | 59 | 10 | 2 | .298/.389/.571 | 122 | .322 | -1.3 | 2B(56) 0.1, LF(7) -0.4 | 1.3 |
| 2022 | NOR | AAA | 22 | 42 | 7 | 2 | 0 | 4 | 7 | 3 | 5 | 0 | 1 | .359/.405/.718 | 120 | .333 | -0.2 | 2B(6) 1.1, LF(1) 0.2 | 0.3 |
| 2023 non-DC | BAL | MLB | 23 | 251 | 25 | 10 | 2 | 7 | 27 | 20 | 62 | 4 | 1 | .231/.300/.375 | 92 | .290 | -2.5 | 2B 0, SS 0 | 0.3 |

*Comparables: Nick Madrigal, Scott Kingery, Yung-Chi Chen*

**The Report:** We wrote last year that Norby had "sneaky pop" but struggled to lift the ball consistently. He started lifting the ball and, well, the pop is no longer sneaky.

Norby doesn't really have any obvious standout offensive tool, but he's above-average at most of the important stuff. His bat-to-ball is above-average. We're skeptical that his game power sticks in full, but it should be at least above-average. His swing decisions are above-average. He should hit for above-average offensive production—not superstar production, but a decent average and solid power.

Norby's likely going to be limited to the right side of the infield in pro ball, although he did play a handful of games in left field over the course of the season. Given that he already reached Triple-A in his first full pro season, he could arrive quickly.

**OFP:** 55 / Starting second baseman

**Variance:** Low. Norby has a pretty stable base of skills.

**Jesse Roche's Fantasy Take:** Norby led the organization with 29 home runs, 19 of which he hit over his final 54 games between Double- and Triple-A. His epic finish (.330/.406/.656) oversells his offensive upside. Nevertheless, if he develops above-average hit and game power tools, he will be a fantasy force, especially at light-hitting second base.

## 8 DL Hall LHP    OFP: 55    ETA: Debuted in 2022

Born: 09/19/98   Age: 24   Bats: L   Throws: L   Height: 6'2"   Weight: 195 lb.   Origin: Round 1, 2017 Draft (#21 overall)

| YEAR | TEAM | LVL | AGE | W | L | SV | G | GS | IP | H | HR | BB/9 | K/9 | K | GB% | BABIP | WHIP | ERA | DRA- | WARP |
|------|------|-----|-----|---|---|----|----|----|-----|----|----|------|------|-----|-------|-------|------|------|------|------|
| 2021 | BOW | AA | 22 | 2 | 0 | 0 | 7 | 7 | 31² | 16 | 4 | 4.5 | 15.9 | 56 | 59.3% | .240 | 1.01 | 3.13 | 80 | 0.6 |
| 2022 | NOR | AAA | 23 | 3 | 7 | 0 | 22 | 18 | 76² | 62 | 10 | 5.8 | 14.7 | 125 | 35.5% | .327 | 1.45 | 4.70 | 60 | 2.6 |
| 2022 | BAL | MLB | 23 | 1 | 1 | 1 | 11 | 1 | 13² | 17 | 0 | 4.0 | 12.5 | 19 | 46.2% | .436 | 1.68 | 5.93 | 89 | 0.2 |
| 2023 DC | BAL | MLB | 24 | 4 | 3 | 0 | 31 | 3 | 38 | 29 | 4 | 5.2 | 11.0 | 46 | 40.8% | .276 | 1.34 | 3.45 | 92 | 0.4 |

*Comparables: Josh Hader, Darwinzon Hernandez, Renyel Pinto*

**The Report:** Hall has been a prospect for so long that when he was drafted, jokes about both Orioles pitching prospects and the DL were still topical. He did finally make his MLB debut in 2022, and remains eligible for this list mostly because the Orioles shifted him to relief to help with the major-league pen during their late-season playoff chase. Ironically, his reliever risk—due to command and control issues—is the main thing that kept him from ascending to the ranks of the tippy-top pitching prospects during his minor-league career. Well, that and injuries, the most recent of which was a bout of elbow tendinitis which cost him most of 2021 and delayed the start of his 2022 season.

Hall showed the same power stuff from the left side in 2022, led by a fastball that can touch triple digits—but was more 95-97 even in the bullpen—from a tricky angle for hitters and with good extension. He doesn't always throw enough strikes with the ol' number one to turn over even minor-league lineups though. Hall has two above-average secondaries to back up the potential plus-plus fastball. His power slider sits in the mid-80s with a lot of sweep, and his improving changeup misses a fair bit of bats now. The change doesn't show a ton of movement, but he commands it arm-side better than the fastball and it tunnels well off the heater. Hall will drop in an average-ish curve on occasion as well. There's enough stuff to start, but he has just never thrown enough quality strikes—or strikes in toto—to make me confident that he's a long-term rotation piece in the majors.

**OFP:** 55 / no. 3/4 starter or second-division closer

**Variance:** Medium. Hall's major-league cameo is the only level he's thrown more than 10 innings at and had a walk rate under 10%. He misses enough bats that you can live with the walks—even as a starter—but they may limit his ability to work deep into games, even when he's going well. However, if he can somehow get to even below-average command—and stay healthy—he could end up more of a 2/3 starter. That kind of command jump happens far less frequently than we wishcast it though.

**Jesse Roche's Fantasy Take:** Hall's pure stuff is undeniable. Unfortunately, his command of said stuff is not. His minor-league career 13.3% walk rate has shown no real signs of improvement (14.2% in Triple-A last year). As such, Hall has about as much relief risk as any non-relief-only prospect. Granted, there is a chance–however slim–that he becomes the next Robbie Ray. It is that unlikely probability we're here to chase in fantasy.

## 9 Heston Kjerstad  RF    OFP: 55   ETA: 2024

Born: 02/12/99  Age: 24  Bats: L  Throws: R  Height: 6'3"  Weight: 205 lb.  Origin: Round 1, 2020 Draft (#2 overall)

| YEAR | TEAM | LVL | AGE | PA | R | 2B | 3B | HR | RBI | BB | K | SB | CS | AVG/OBP/SLG | DRC+ | BABIP | BRR | DRP | WARP |
|------|------|-----|-----|-----|----|----|----|----|-----|----|----|----|----|-------------|------|-------|------|--------|------|
| 2022 | DEL | A | 23 | 98 | 17 | 9 | 0 | 2 | 17 | 13 | 17 | 0 | 0 | .463/.551/.650 | 127 | .565 | -0.4 | RF(16) 0.4 | 0.6 |
| 2022 | ABD | A+ | 23 | 186 | 28 | 8 | 2 | 3 | 20 | 16 | 47 | 1 | 0 | .233/.312/.362 | 77 | .302 | 0.5 | RF(31) 1.8 | 0.3 |
| 2023 non-DC | BAL | MLB | 24 | 251 | 21 | 11 | 2 | 3 | 21 | 19 | 64 | 0 | 0 | .225/.291/.323 | 75 | .300 | -4.4 | RF 0 | -0.6 |

*Comparables: Jonathan Davis, Daniel Spingola, Kentrail Davis*

**The Report:** At 6-foot-3 and 205 pounds, the former second-overall pick (and Fall League MVP) is an intimidating presence in the box. Kjerstad uses an open stance with a leg kick and strong, quick hands. There is a bit of bat movement pre-pitch but Kjerstad drops his hands consistently and gets to balls all over the zone while pushing the ball to all fields. There is a lot to like here at the plate. At times, his swing can get a bit uppercutty, but the Orioles have shown a real knack for hitter development over these last few years, and I fully trust that this can be one of the better power swings in the minors come next season.

A main concern, however, is that the discipline and somewhat max-effort swings could lead to a less than stellar K-rate that only goes up as he rises the ranks. Sadly, this *could* be a what-could-have-been given the fact that he did miss out on some serious development time due to myocarditis after a bout of COVID-19, but it does seem that he has a real chance to be a plus corner outfielder in Baltimore. Yes, he is 23 years old and played no higher than High-A this year—where he struggled after torching Low-A, but the swing should really have both Orioles fans and their front office excited.

**OFP:** 55 / Above-average corner outfielder

**Variance:** High. Kjerstad's health issues make him a bit of an outlier prospect in terms of risk. It's great that he is back on the field, but he will be 24, hasn't seen the upper minors yet and there are swing-and-miss concerns. Well okay, outside of the age that's not that much of an outlier profile.

**Jesse Roche's Fantasy Take:** Kjerstad's power bat knocked me on my butt during the AFL Home Run Derby. (Well, to be clear, a gaggle of kids going after the ball felled me.) His power (and that of preteen kids) is very real. His swing-and-miss—aggravated by a tad aggressive approach—is also very real. How Kjerstad performs in Double-A after a disappointing showing in High-A will be telling. The hope for a 30-homer lefty slugger is still there, however remote it is.

## 10 Hudson Haskin  OF    OFP: 55   ETA: Late 2023

Born: 12/31/98  Age: 24  Bats: R  Throws: R  Height: 6'2"  Weight: 200 lb.  Origin: Round 2, 2020 Draft (#39 overall)

| YEAR | TEAM | LVL | AGE | PA | R | 2B | 3B | HR | RBI | BB | K | SB | CS | AVG/OBP/SLG | DRC+ | BABIP | BRR | DRP | WARP |
|------|------|-----|-----|-----|----|----|----|----|-----|----|-----|----|----|-------------|------|-------|------|-----------------------------------|------|
| 2021 | DEL | A | 22 | 254 | 44 | 13 | 1 | 5 | 33 | 22 | 60 | 17 | 5 | .276/.377/.415 | 108 | .362 | -0.8 | CF(39) -1.7, LF(11) -1.5, RF(3) 1.2 | 0.9 |
| 2021 | ABD | A+ | 22 | 109 | 15 | 6 | 2 | 0 | 9 | 10 | 18 | 5 | 2 | .275/.389/.385 | 114 | .342 | 0.5 | CF(23) 2.7, RF(2) -0.4, LF(1) -0.2 | 0.8 |
| 2022 | BOW | AA | 23 | 466 | 58 | 23 | 3 | 15 | 56 | 43 | 101 | 5 | 3 | .264/.367/.455 | 124 | .313 | -2.2 | CF(51) -0.9, LF(31) -0.1, RF(22) 1.1 | 2.4 |
| 2023 non-DC | BAL | MLB | 24 | 251 | 22 | 11 | 1 | 3 | 22 | 17 | 59 | 4 | 1 | .224/.293/.329 | 79 | .286 | -2.5 | LF 0, CF 0 | -0.1 |

*Comparables: Greg Allen, Donnie Dewees, Braden Bishop*

**The Report:** I should probably write a column about this one of these days, but two of the sea changes in the Orioles' draft evaluation and acquisition over the last few years have been (1) modeling college performance with less regard given to strength of conference or schedule, and (2) moving away from visual hit tool evaluation. (1) Haskin had a limited amateur track record at Tulane, due to being a draft-eligible sophomore and then losing most of that sophomore season to the pandemic. (2) He has rhythmic jitteriness pre-swing and then utilizes a big, hokey-pokey leg kick before basically twisting himself into a pretzel as he swings. Well, he mashed at Tulane, and has hit well enough at every minor league stop despite the fact that I'm not positive he's looking anywhere near the baseball at the point of contact. Baltimore is also fairly conservative with their college hitter tracks, so Haskin just reached Double-A in 2022 as a 23-year-old, and spent the whole season there despite a 124 DRC+. He marries the weird swing with a solid approach and while there aren't any clear plus tools here, nothing really dips below average and Haskin is an above-average runner whose—almost as awkward—loping strides eat up a lot of grass in the outfield.

**OFP:** 55 / Above-average outfielder

**Variance:** Medium. Haskin's still has some hit tool risk, as major-league arms are good at finding holes, and it won't take much more swing-and-miss to drop the hit and power tools to the wrong side of 50. That's still a major leaguer, but more of a bench outfielder than starter. But maybe most of this is me still struggling to shed my visual hit tool evaluation priors. If Haskins ends up with five 55s on the sheet, that's a plus regular in center.

**Jesse Roche's Fantasy Take:** No tool may stand out as plus for Haskin, but the sum of his parts could amount to a useful fantasy player.

## Outside the Top Ten:

### 11 Dylan Beavers OF

Born: 08/11/01   Age: 21   Bats: L   Throws: R   Height: 6'4"   Weight: 206 lb.   Origin: Round 1, 2022 Draft (#33 overall)

| YEAR | TEAM | LVL | AGE | PA | R | 2B | 3B | HR | RBI | BB | K | SB | CS | AVG/OBP/SLG | DRC+ | BABIP | BRR | DRP | WARP |
|---|---|---|---|---|---|---|---|---|---|---|---|---|---|---|---|---|---|---|---|
| 2022 | DEL | A | 20 | 77 | 13 | 7 | 2 | 0 | 13 | 12 | 11 | 6 | 1 | .359/.468/.531 | 122 | .434 | 0.0 | RF(9) 0.9, CF(6) -0.4 | 0.5 |
| 2023 non-DC | BAL | MLB | 21 | 251 | 20 | 10 | 2 | 2 | 20 | 21 | 66 | 6 | 2 | .222/.293/.312 | 73 | .305 | -1.5 | LF 0, CF 0 | -0.3 |

*Comparables: Alex Kirilloff, Rymer Liriano, Brett Phillips*

We continue in the modern dance school of hitting development with the Orioles' Comp-A pick in the 2022 draft. Beavers mashed at Cal-Berkeley despite a squatty, handsy, steep swing. His default setting can look like an emergency hack at times, but that belies really strong wrists and barrel control married with the ability to do real damage in the zone. Beavers power is more of the sneaky kind, which is a little concerning given he's ending up in a corner outfield spot—he's a solid runner, but will settle into the kind of foot speed better suited for left field I suspect—but he'll be yet another win for the old scouting tautology: hitters hit. He has more upside with the bat than Haskin, but proximity keeps him on just the other side of a very strong Top 10. I suspect he'd make just about any other system in baseball's.

### 12 Seth Johnson RHP

Born: 09/19/98   Age: 24   Bats: R   Throws: R   Height: 6'1"   Weight: 200 lb.   Origin: Round 1, 2019 Draft (#40 overall)

| YEAR | TEAM | LVL | AGE | W | L | SV | G | GS | IP | H | HR | BB/9 | K/9 | K | GB% | BABIP | WHIP | ERA | DRA- | WARP |
|---|---|---|---|---|---|---|---|---|---|---|---|---|---|---|---|---|---|---|---|---|
| 2021 | CSC | A | 22 | 6 | 6 | 0 | 23 | 16 | 93² | 86 | 7 | 3.2 | 11.0 | 115 | 48.0% | .336 | 1.27 | 2.88 | 89 | 1.4 |
| 2022 | BG | A+ | 23 | 1 | 1 | 0 | 7 | 7 | 27 | 23 | 4 | 3.7 | 13.7 | 41 | 31.0% | .352 | 1.26 | 3.00 | 89 | 0.4 |
| 2023 non-DC | BAL | MLB | 24 | 3 | 3 | 0 | 58 | 0 | 50 | 49 | 8 | 4.1 | 8.3 | 46 | 35.5% | .295 | 1.44 | 4.60 | 119 | -0.2 |

*Comparables: Garrett Richards, Chris Stratton, Rogelio Armenteros*

Despite having a top two or three system in baseball—check back in February if you want a more precise number—the Orioles would probably be merely above-average in terms of pitching prospect talent. Baltimore made a clever little move to help out with that, acquiring Johnson from the Rays as part of the Trey Mancini deal. Johnson had a breakout 2021 that got him into consideration for the 2022 Top 101, and was well on his way to making a Midseason 50 case before a UCL tear. He will miss most of, if not all, of 2023, and will be 25 years old before he's ready to conquer the upper minors, but he showed off a 70-grade fastball and two above-average breaking balls pre-surgery. You get that guy into your system even if you have to wait 18 months or so to see him on a mound.

# 13 Cade Povich LHP

Born: 04/12/00  Age: 23  Bats: L  Throws: L  Height: 6'3"  Weight: 185 lb.  Origin: Round 3, 2021 Draft (#98 overall)

| YEAR | TEAM | LVL | AGE | W | L | SV | G | GS | IP | H | HR | BB/9 | K/9 | K | GB% | BABIP | WHIP | ERA | DRA- | WARP |
|---|---|---|---|---|---|---|---|---|---|---|---|---|---|---|---|---|---|---|---|---|
| 2021 | FTM | A | 21 | 0 | 0 | 0 | 3 | 2 | 8 | 6 | 0 | 2.3 | 18.0 | 16 | 33.3% | .400 | 1.00 | 1.13 | 91 | 0.1 |
| 2022 | CR | A+ | 22 | 6 | 8 | 0 | 16 | 16 | 78² | 71 | 9 | 3.0 | 12.2 | 107 | 44.5% | .326 | 1.23 | 4.46 | 83 | 1.5 |
| 2022 | ABD | A+ | 22 | 2 | 0 | 0 | 2 | 2 | 12 | 4 | 0 | 1.5 | 11.3 | 15 | 45.8% | .167 | 0.50 | 0.00 | 86 | 0.2 |
| 2022 | BOW | AA | 22 | 2 | 2 | 0 | 6 | 5 | 23¹ | 21 | 5 | 4.2 | 10.0 | 26 | 39.4% | .267 | 1.37 | 6.94 | 88 | 0.4 |
| 2023 non-DC | BAL | MLB | 23 | 3 | 3 | 0 | 58 | 0 | 50 | 50 | 7 | 3.9 | 8.6 | 47 | 35.7% | .302 | 1.42 | 4.49 | 116 | -0.2 |

Comparables: Yohander Méndez, Rob Rasmussen, David Peterson

Another pitching prospect acquired at the trade deadline—this time from Minnesota for Jorge López—Povich does not have the same kind of plus stuff as Johnson. A pitchability lefty with multiple ways to get you out and a deceptive crossfire delivery to keep hitters off balance, Povich can get bad swings with a low-90s fastball, setting up both a slider and curve that can get swings and misses. Povich's curve is a 1-7 yakker in the mid-70s which can beat you down and out of the zone, but he snaps it off at times to spot it. The slider flashes better but is more inconsistent; the best are low-80s sweepers with enough depth to get under barrels. He will show a cutter a tick or two higher on the radar gun than the slider for a different look, and he has a potentially average change as well. It's all tied together by above-average command, but command is rarely a carrying tool, and Povich did get knocked around a bit in Double-A. Nevertheless he feels like a back-end starter prospect who overperforms that projection.

## Eyewitness Report: Cade Povich

**Evaluator:** Nathan Graham
**Report Date:** 07/08/2022
**Dates Seen:** 6/12/22
**Risk Factor:** High
**Delivery:** Extra-large frame with a slender, thin build; moderate growth remaining; Repeats his easy, balanced delivery well; 3/4 arm slot.

| Pitch Type | Future Grade | Sitting Velocity | Peak Velocity | Report |
|---|---|---|---|---|
| Fastball | 50 | 88-91 | 92 | Velocity currently sits in the average band for a lefty but will tick up a notch as he matures. He commands the fastball well to both sides and his natural arm-side run and ability to cut it help him stay off barrels. |
| Changeup | 50 | 80-84 | 85 | Currently the most advanced secondary. Replicates his arm action well. Fades away from hitters, eliciting weak contact. |
| Slider | 50 | 77-80 | 83 | Thrown slightly harder than the curve, but the two will blend together at times. When he gets it right it features 1-7 shape. Not a true swing and miss offering but will be an effective breaking pitch with continued development. |
| Curveball | 40 | 74-78 | 78 | Lacks feel, only mixed in a handful during my look mostly to steal a strike early in the count. |

**Conclusion:** Povich doesn't blow hitters away with premium stuff but he's more than just a typical soft-tossing, under-slot, college lefty. He displays knowledge of pitch sequencing and mixes his pitches well to keep hitters off-balance. With expected velocity gains for the fastball and continued development of the secondaries Povich profiles as a future back of the rotation starter.

## 14 Joey Ortiz SS

Born: 07/14/98 Age: 24 Bats: R Throws: R Height: 5'11" Weight: 175 lb. Origin: Round 4, 2019 Draft (#108 overall)

| YEAR | TEAM | LVL | AGE | PA | R | 2B | 3B | HR | RBI | BB | K | SB | CS | AVG/OBP/SLG | DRC+ | BABIP | BRR | DRP | WARP |
|------|------|-----|-----|-----|-----|----|----|----|-----|----|----|----|----|-------------|------|-------|------|-----|------|
| 2021 | ABD | A+ | 22 | 89 | 14 | 7 | 2 | 0 | 8 | 10 | 18 | 3 | 0 | .289/.382/.434 | 104 | .373 | 0.2 | SS(14) -0.3, 2B(5) 0.6, 3B(2) 0.3 | 0.4 |
| 2021 | BOW | AA | 22 | 67 | 11 | 2 | 0 | 4 | 9 | 6 | 14 | 1 | 0 | .233/.313/.467 | 113 | .238 | 0.8 | SS(6) -0.1, 2B(5) 0.3, 3B(2) 0.4 | 0.4 |
| 2022 | BOW | AA | 23 | 485 | 69 | 28 | 4 | 15 | 71 | 41 | 81 | 2 | 1 | .269/.337/.455 | 130 | .298 | -0.1 | SS(85) 5.2, 2B(21) 1.5, 3B(2) -0.1 | 3.7 |
| 2022 | NOR | AAA | 23 | 115 | 22 | 7 | 2 | 4 | 14 | 9 | 17 | 6 | 1 | .346/.400/.567 | 113 | .381 | -0.4 | SS(17) -1.3, 2B(5) 1.3 | 0.5 |
| 2023 DC | BAL | MLB | 24 | 129 | 13 | 6 | 1 | 2 | 13 | 8 | 23 | 2 | 0 | .229/.287/.342 | 80 | .266 | 0.0 | 3B 0, SS 0 | 0.1 |

Comparables: Brad Miller, Erik González, Matt Reynolds

The Orioles' 2020 fourth-round selection can be added to the ever-growing list of exciting middle-infield prospects in Baltimore. It is pretty clear Ortiz is an at least above-average shortstop, displaying clean and swift actions that along with an above-average arm make him a sure-fire candidate to stick at the position. However, it isn't just the glove that makes Ortiz intriguing.

Ortiz uses a slightly open stance with a bit of a leg kick. The front foot starts inside out, but ends up almost perfectly perpendicular to the mound as he does a really nice job of squaring up his entire lower half to the pitcher. The upper half is very relaxed as his hands start over the plate and seamlessly brings his hands back to then rip through the baseball. While Ortiz did hit 19 home runs, it's not a power swing by any means, but one that will generate some doubles and overall loud contact. Ortiz's .269 average and .337 on-base percentage seem like a realistic 75th-percentile type outcome, and if the power isn't merely a 2022 anomaly, Ortiz could be a Top 10 prospect in a system even as stacked as Baltimore's.

## 15 Max Wagner 3B

Born: 08/19/01 Age: 21 Bats: R Throws: R Height: 6'0" Weight: 215 lb. Origin: Round 2, 2022 Draft (#42 overall)

| YEAR | TEAM | LVL | AGE | PA | R | 2B | 3B | HR | RBI | BB | K | SB | CS | AVG/OBP/SLG | DRC+ | BABIP | BRR | DRP | WARP |
|------|------|-----|-----|-----|-----|----|----|----|-----|----|----|----|----|-------------|------|-------|------|-----|------|
| 2022 | DEL | A | 20 | 62 | 9 | 2 | 2 | 1 | 8 | 9 | 13 | 0 | 0 | .250/.403/.438 | 107 | .314 | -0.4 | 3B(9) 0.5 | 0.3 |
| 2023 non-DC | BAL | MLB | 21 | 251 | 20 | 10 | 2 | 3 | 20 | 17 | 67 | 1 | 1 | .206/.272/.298 | 62 | .279 | -3.8 | 3B 0 | -0.9 |

Comparables: Travis Denker, Jeimer Candelario, Jason Taylor

As an amateur, Wagner turned heads with his power. At Clemson, the third baseman showed an uber-open stance in which he basically leaned back on his hind leg pre-pitch, creating a powerful load moving his weight from his backside to his front foot. In his first taste of pro ball, that same stance and swing remained. While it might be a bit high effort—and one that can lead to Ks—Wagner boasts a true potential for above-average power. There is no question that he has the tools to be an MLB home run hitter, but he did have some issues making contact, striking out 19 times in 18 games in High-A Delmarva. The Orioles' PD staff, who have shown the ability to get the most of guys, might end up trying to adjust the bend in his back leg as it might be something that is actually slowing his overall swing process down. Though a few things can be cleaned up, there seem to be the very early makings of a 20+ homer third baseman here (but the hit tool needs to come along).

## 16 Jud Fabian OF

Born: 09/27/00 Age: 22 Bats: R Throws: L Height: 6'1" Weight: 195 lb. Origin: Round 2, 2022 Draft (#67 overall)

| YEAR | TEAM | LVL | AGE | PA | R | 2B | 3B | HR | RBI | BB | K | SB | CS | AVG/OBP/SLG | DRC+ | BABIP | BRR | DRP | WARP |
|------|------|-----|-----|-----|-----|----|----|----|-----|----|----|----|----|-------------|------|-------|------|-----|------|
| 2022 | DEL | A | 21 | 52 | 16 | 7 | 2 | 3 | 9 | 8 | 9 | 0 | 0 | .386/.481/.841 | 134 | .438 | 0.9 | LF(3) 0.2, CF(3) 1.0, RF(2) 0.1 | 0.6 |
| 2022 | ABD | A+ | 21 | 30 | 1 | 1 | 0 | 0 | 4 | 5 | 8 | 0 | 2 | .167/.300/.208 | 88 | .235 | -0.3 | CF(7) -0.1 | 0.0 |
| 2023 non-DC | BAL | MLB | 22 | 251 | 21 | 11 | 2 | 3 | 22 | 18 | 74 | 3 | 1 | .217/.282/.325 | 73 | .304 | -3.0 | LF 0, CF 0 | -0.4 |

Comparables: Matt Szczur, Edward Olivares, Kevin Smith

One of the potential value picks of the 2022 Draft, University of Florida alum Jud Fabian hit the ground running in his short stint in Delmarva, eventually coming back to Earth in High-A Aberdeen. It is an athletic frame where Fabian chokes up and causes really difficult at-bats for the opposing pitcher. Along with a good eye, Fabian shows plus bat speed and gap power to all fields with a two-handed, clean follow through. The former Gator flashes plus barrel control with a slightly open stance with an easy swing to old fields—a line drive swing with really quick wrists. At age 21, he probably has slightly more room to fill out, but the overall offensive profile is what to be most excited about here.

He's probably a Mark Canha type center fielder who profiles better in the corners. With slightly above average speed and real athleticism, Fabian is a very exciting prospect to watch for the Orioles.

## 17   Ryan Watson   RHP

Born: 11/15/97   Age: 25   Bats: R   Throws: R   Height: 6'5"   Weight: 215 lb.   Origin: Round 39, 2016 Draft (#1181 overall)

| YEAR | TEAM | LVL | AGE | W | L | SV | G | GS | IP | H | HR | BB/9 | K/9 | K | GB% | BABIP | WHIP | ERA | DRA- | WARP |
|---|---|---|---|---|---|---|---|---|---|---|---|---|---|---|---|---|---|---|---|---|
| 2021 | DEL | A | 23 | 3 | 1 | 1 | 11 | 3 | 33² | 24 | 2 | 1.9 | 10.7 | 40 | 46.1% | .256 | 0.92 | 2.14 | 100 | 0.3 |
| 2021 | ABD | A+ | 23 | 3 | 2 | 0 | 11 | 1 | 31 | 36 | 2 | 2.6 | 11.3 | 39 | 39.1% | .400 | 1.45 | 4.94 | 101 | 0.2 |
| 2022 | BOW | AA | 24 | 7 | 5 | 1 | 20 | 18 | 95 | 81 | 15 | 2.0 | 9.5 | 100 | 42.0% | .275 | 1.07 | 3.41 | 96 | 1.5 |
| 2022 | NOR | AAA | 24 | 0 | 0 | 0 | 7 | 0 | 12¹ | 8 | 1 | 5.8 | 5.8 | 8 | 50.0% | .189 | 1.30 | 3.65 | 112 | 0.1 |
| 2023 non-DC | BAL | MLB | 25 | 3 | 3 | 0 | 58 | 0 | 50 | 52 | 7 | 3.1 | 7.0 | 39 | 37.9% | .297 | 1.39 | 4.45 | 117 | -0.2 |

Watson was a NDFA out of Auburn in 2020, after three nondescript seasons in the Tigers' bullpen, and then a senior year cut off by the pandemic. The Orioles moved him into the rotation in 2022 and he thrived, winning the organization's Pitcher of the Year award. Watson has the repertoire to start, a full four-pitch mix, led by a heavy fastball in an otherwise-average velocity band, and a sharp, short mid-80s slider. He has some feel for the change, although it can be a little firm and flat, and he will pop a curve now and again around 80. It's usually to steal a strike against a lefty, but there's an interesting power slurve in there when the two breakers bleed together a bit. Watson moved back to the 'pen after a September promotion to Triple-A, likely for some of the same reasons as DL Hall, but also perhaps for innings management given his lack of starter's reps over the years. There's no reason not to roll him back out in the 2023 Tides rotation, as while the stuff doesn't overwhelm, Watson is a potential fourth starter.

## 18   Chayce McDermott   RHP

Born: 08/22/98   Age: 24   Bats: L   Throws: R   Height: 6'3"   Weight: 197 lb.   Origin: Round 4C, 2021 Draft (#132 overall)

| YEAR | TEAM | LVL | AGE | W | L | SV | G | GS | IP | H | HR | BB/9 | K/9 | K | GB% | BABIP | WHIP | ERA | DRA- | WARP |
|---|---|---|---|---|---|---|---|---|---|---|---|---|---|---|---|---|---|---|---|---|
| 2021 | FAY | A | 22 | 0 | 0 | 0 | 6 | 4 | 18¹ | 11 | 3 | 4.9 | 16.2 | 33 | 45.2% | .286 | 1.15 | 3.44 | 80 | 0.3 |
| 2022 | ASH | A+ | 23 | 6 | 1 | 0 | 19 | 10 | 72 | 57 | 9 | 5.4 | 14.3 | 114 | 46.2% | .318 | 1.39 | 5.50 | 79 | 1.4 |
| 2022 | BOW | AA | 23 | 1 | 1 | 0 | 6 | 6 | 26² | 17 | 7 | 6.7 | 12.1 | 36 | 35.6% | .192 | 1.39 | 6.07 | 92 | 0.5 |
| 2023 non-DC | BAL | MLB | 24 | 3 | 3 | 0 | 58 | 0 | 50 | 45 | 9 | 5.9 | 10.9 | 61 | 36.3% | .296 | 1.56 | 5.02 | 125 | -0.4 |

*Comparables: Angel Ventura, Nick Nelson, Brandon Bailey*

Another piece of the Trey Mancini deal—this one actually coming from the Astros—McDermott regularly bumps 95 from a high slot with good extension, backing it up with two distinct breaking balls that both can induce swing-and-miss. His approach to the strike zone might remind you of Jackson Pollock working with a firehorse, and he's likely a reliever when it all shakes out. However, his stuff moves in very effective—if not always consistent—ways and if McDermott can harness it a bit better in short bursts, he could be a late-inning weapon.

## 19   Samuel Basallo   C

Born: 08/13/04   Age: 18   Bats: L   Throws: R   Height: 6'3"   Weight: 180 lb.   Origin: International Free Agent, 2021

| YEAR | TEAM | LVL | AGE | PA | R | 2B | 3B | HR | RBI | BB | K | SB | CS | AVG/OBP/SLG | DRC+ | BABIP | BRR | DRP | WARP |
|---|---|---|---|---|---|---|---|---|---|---|---|---|---|---|---|---|---|---|---|
| 2021 | DSL OR1 | ROK | 16 | 154 | 18 | 8 | 0 | 5 | 19 | 19 | 32 | 1 | 0 | .239/.338/.410 | | .278 | | | |
| 2022 | ORI | ROK | 17 | 180 | 22 | 5 | 0 | 6 | 32 | 15 | 37 | 1 | 0 | .278/.350/.424 | | .322 | | | |

The Orioles have been more aggressive in the IFA market in recent years, and Basallo was one of the bigger names from their 2021 class. He came stateside at 17 and showed off potential big power, but struggles with his swing decisions, because he's a 17-year-old in the complex. He's also a 17-year-old catcher in the complex, which is not a cohort I usually rank, especially in a system this deep, but he has a strong arm and a solid frame back there. Basallo might grow off the position and he might not hit in full-season ball, but the upside here as a power-hitting backstop is worth a mention even in this system.

## 20  Darell Hernaiz  IF

Born: 08/03/01   Age: 21   Bats: R   Throws: R   Height: 6'1"   Weight: 190 lb.   Origin: Round 5, 2019 Draft (#138 overall)

| YEAR | TEAM | LVL | AGE | PA | R | 2B | 3B | HR | RBI | BB | K | SB | CS | AVG/OBP/SLG | DRC+ | BABIP | BRR | DRP | WARP |
|------|------|-----|-----|-----|----|----|----|----|-----|----|----|----|----|-------------|------|-------|------|-----|------|
| 2021 | DEL | A | 19 | 410 | 62 | 12 | 0 | 6 | 52 | 28 | 70 | 22 | 6 | .277/.333/.358 | 105 | .323 | -1.6 | SS(61) 9.1, 2B(19) 3.0, 3B(11) -1.7 | 2.3 |
| 2022 | DEL | A | 20 | 138 | 25 | 7 | 2 | 6 | 25 | 8 | 22 | 9 | 0 | .283/.341/.512 | 126 | .303 | 2.6 | SS(20) -2.1, 2B(7) 0.5, 3B(3) -0.4 | 0.9 |
| 2022 | ABD | A+ | 20 | 255 | 41 | 13 | 3 | 5 | 29 | 22 | 43 | 22 | 3 | .305/.376/.456 | 107 | .356 | -0.3 | SS(25) -1.9, 3B(18) 0.9, 2B(17) 1.5 | 1.0 |
| 2022 | BOW | AA | 20 | 59 | 6 | 1 | 0 | 1 | 8 | 5 | 16 | 1 | 1 | .113/.186/.189 | 90 | .135 | 0.4 | SS(13) -0.2 | 0.1 |
| 2023 non-DC | BAL | MLB | 21 | 251 | 20 | 10 | 1 | 3 | 21 | 13 | 54 | 7 | 1 | .218/.267/.314 | 64 | .270 | -1.2 | 2B 0, 3B 0 | -0.4 |

The Orioles' fifth-round selection in 2019 has an open stance with very relaxed hands and shows off really good bat speed. However, and a big "however," the bat speed was something that Hernaiz showcased far more in High-A and years prior as opposed to his very unfortunate Double-A cup of coffee. After a successful 92 games in A-ball, he got the call to the Eastern League, where he struggled tremendously for the last 13 games of the minor-league season. However, despite his rough end to the season, the jump in power (if only 12 home runs) was a very pleasing development to Hernaiz's game. He seemed to demonstrate more of a max-effort swing when getting to Bowie. Though a small sample size, his K-rate jumped from 16% in High-A to 27% in Double-A. Hernaiz has the tools in the field to stick at short but he is not much more than an average fielder at premier infield spot, so he will need to conquer the upper minors at the plate to make it as a major-league starter at the six.

## Top Talents 25 and Under (as of 4/1/2023):

1. Adley Rutschman, C
2. Gunnar Henderson, IF
3. Grayson Rodriguez, RHP
4. Jackson Holliday, SS
5. Colton Cowser, OF
6. Coby Mayo, 3B
7. Jordan Westburg, IF
8. Connor Norby, 2B
9. DL Hall, LHP
10. Heston Kjerstad, OF

The immense depth of the high minors and early debuting MLBers last year was the spark for a surprising run at competency. They saw debuts from several prospects, including Henderson and Kyle Stowers, but the jewel of course was Rutschman—even with an injury-delayed campaign that might have cost him a Rookie of the Year trophy. Still, he had a staggering first showing in The Show, handling Baltimore's pitching staff with aplomb while putting up immediate impact offensively. He's been expected to be a star behind the dish since draft day, and he's shown he's already exactly that.

# Boston Red Sox

## The State of the System:

Up-the-middle prospects with plus offensive potential are the main feature here, but the Red Sox are short on arms, and overall the system still remains on the shallow side.

## The Top Ten:

### 1 Marcelo Mayer  SS      OFP: 70      ETA: Late 2024/Early 2025

Born: 12/12/02   Age: 20   Bats: L   Throws: R   Height: 6'3"   Weight: 188 lb.   Origin: Round 1, 2021 Draft (#4 overall)

| YEAR | TEAM | LVL | AGE | PA | R | 2B | 3B | HR | RBI | BB | K | SB | CS | AVG/OBP/SLG | DRC+ | BABIP | BRR | DRP | WARP |
|---|---|---|---|---|---|---|---|---|---|---|---|---|---|---|---|---|---|---|---|
| 2021 | RSX | ROK | 18 | 107 | 25 | 4 | 1 | 3 | 17 | 15 | 27 | 7 | 1 | .275/.377/.440 | | .361 | | | |
| 2022 | SAL | A | 19 | 308 | 46 | 26 | 1 | 9 | 40 | 51 | 78 | 16 | 0 | .286/.406/.504 | 121 | .375 | 2.3 | SS(58) -0.5 | 1.8 |
| 2022 | GVL | A+ | 19 | 116 | 15 | 4 | 1 | 4 | 13 | 17 | 29 | 1 | 0 | .265/.379/.449 | 91 | .338 | 0.1 | SS(21) 2.3 | 0.5 |
| 2023 non-DC | BOS | MLB | 20 | 251 | 22 | 12 | 2 | 3 | 22 | 24 | 80 | 5 | 0 | .225/.306/.338 | 85 | .334 | -2.4 | SS 0 | 0.1 |

Comparables: Royce Lewis, J.P. Crawford, Bo Bichette

**The Report:** Mayer spent 2022 making a strong argument that he was actually the best prospect in the 2021 draft class. The SoCal shortstop may not have a loud, plus-plus carrying tool at present, but it's hard to nitpick his game, and he performed well at two A-ball levels as a 19-year-old despite dealing with a wrist sprain early in the season. Mayer has a very loose swing with good whip and plus bat speed. His swing plane can be a bit flat at times, but he hits the ball hard already, and even a bit more lift should get him into the 20-home run range. He does expand a bit against breakers down, and there's a bit more pull-side ground-ball contact than you'd prefer at present, but these are fairly manageable developmental issues, and the fundamentals of his swing and contact profile suggest at least an above-average hit tool.

Defensively Mayer's tools don't scream sure-shot shortstop, but he moves well enough laterally despite pedestrian run times, and his hands and actions are both fine enough for the premium spot on the dirt. His arm strength is merely above-average, but he gets the ball out quickly and accurately. This is a pretty dry report all in all for a prospect who will end up very high on this year's 101, but how many potential plus-hit/plus-power shortstops are there really? So our apologies for not waxing poetic and comparing his offensive game to Mahler's Fifth this time around.

**OFP:** 70 / All-Star shortstop

**Variance:** High. Mayer does need to clean up his swing decisions a bit as he faces better pitching. He may end up being a better fit at second base. That lack of a plus-plus tool can end up being lack of a plus tool if his offensive development falls short.

**Jesse Roche's Fantasy Take:** Mayer's swing, approach and burgeoning power are promising, but it's worth noting his aforementioned questionable swing decisions have resulted in a pedestrian contact rate for such a well-regarded hitter. He has been adept at stealing bases despite modest speed, including a perfect 17-for-17 last year. Mayer may not be as flashy as other top prospects, but his fantasy profile should be well-rounded and, if his hit/power tools develop as hoped, his offensive production could look awfully similar to Xander Bogaerts.

## 2 Triston Casas 1B    OFP: 60    ETA: Debuted in 2022
Born: 01/15/00  Age: 23  Bats: L  Throws: R  Height: 6'4"  Weight: 252 lb.  Origin: Round 1, 2018 Draft (#26 overall)

| YEAR | TEAM | LVL | AGE | PA | R | 2B | 3B | HR | RBI | BB | K | SB | CS | AVG/OBP/SLG | DRC+ | BABIP | BRR | DRP | WARP |
|---|---|---|---|---|---|---|---|---|---|---|---|---|---|---|---|---|---|---|---|
| 2021 | SCO | WIN | 21 | 97 | 19 | 6 | 0 | 1 | 11 | 17 | 18 | 0 | 1 | .372/.495/.487 | | .475 | | | |
| 2021 | POR | AA | 21 | 329 | 57 | 12 | 2 | 13 | 52 | 49 | 63 | 6 | 3 | .284/.395/.484 | 128 | .323 | -0.8 | 1B(73) -6.2 | 1.4 |
| 2021 | WOR | AAA | 21 | 42 | 6 | 3 | 1 | 1 | 7 | 8 | 8 | 1 | 0 | .242/.381/.485 | 107 | .280 | -0.4 | 1B(7) 0.0 | 0.1 |
| 2022 | WOR | AAA | 22 | 317 | 45 | 20 | 1 | 11 | 38 | 46 | 68 | 0 | 0 | .273/.382/.481 | 101 | .323 | 0.7 | 1B(63) -1.1 | 0.9 |
| 2022 | BOS | MLB | 22 | 95 | 11 | 1 | 0 | 5 | 12 | 19 | 23 | 1 | 0 | .197/.358/.408 | 114 | .208 | -0.8 | 1B(27) -1 | 0.1 |
| 2023 DC | BOS | MLB | 23 | 523 | 61 | 24 | 4 | 14 | 56 | 61 | 132 | 5 | 1 | .218/.318/.378 | 98 | .279 | -0.4 | 1B -1 | 0.7 |

*Comparables: Dominic Smith, Jon Singleton, Anthony Rizzo*

**The Report:** Casas has always been an easy elevator pitch as a prospect: a young-for-his-level, power-hitting first baseman, who wasn't just a one-dimensional slugger. However, once you pull up his player page, you might notice he's never posted a slugging line starting with a five at any full-season stop. The raw power isn't at issue. Casas has plus-plus pop at five o'clock, and showed the ability to drive the ball out of the park even using his wider, contact-oriented, two-strike stance. He's just really strong, and is able to generate loud lift without opening a major hole in his swing. His approach is solid, and while he might veer a bit Three-True-Outcomesy at times, swing-and-miss isn't a huge issue. So this should all work out fine offensively. He just hasn't really blown up yet, and I can't shake the nagging feeling he's "just" an .850-OPS first baseman. That's a fine regular, but it does feel like he should be more than that.

**OFP:** 60 / First-division first baseman, occasional All-Star

**Variance:** Medium. There's certainly an outcome where Casas is the linchpin of the next great Red Sox era, hitting .280 and socking 35 home runs in the middle of their order in perpetuity. There's also an outcome where he's #offensivethreat Triston Casas.

**Jesse Roche's Fantasy Take:** Casas' MLB debut was far from a success, but he displayed his massive power and disciplined approach. In fact, his chase rate (17.5%) was seventh-lowest among MLB players with as many plate appearances. Meanwhile, only Bobby Dalbec stands in Casas' way to a full-time role in 2023. Given his proximity and upside, he is a top-20 dynasty prospect who ranks even higher in OBP formats.

## 3 Miguel Bleis OF    OFP: 60    ETA: 2026
Born: 03/01/04  Age: 19  Bats: R  Throws: R  Height: 6'3"  Weight: 170 lb.  Origin: International Free Agent, 2021

| YEAR | TEAM | LVL | AGE | PA | R | 2B | 3B | HR | RBI | BB | K | SB | CS | AVG/OBP/SLG | DRC+ | BABIP | BRR | DRP | WARP |
|---|---|---|---|---|---|---|---|---|---|---|---|---|---|---|---|---|---|---|---|
| 2021 | DSL RSR | ROK | 17 | 136 | 17 | 6 | 1 | 4 | 17 | 12 | 25 | 7 | 4 | .252/.331/.420 | | .283 | | | |
| 2022 | RSX | ROK | 18 | 167 | 28 | 14 | 4 | 5 | 27 | 10 | 45 | 18 | 3 | .301/.353/.542 | | .394 | | | |

**The Report:** A seven-figure signing who highlighted the Sox 2021 IFA class, Bleis' stateside debut was nothing short of spectacular. He's a potential five-tool center fielder with a swing that marries pull-side lift with significant barrel time in the zone, so both plus hit and power tools are in play at his peak. Bleis is an aggressive hitter, especially early in the count, but his pitch recognition is advanced enough to do damage before he's down two strikes. But once he's there, the present swing decisions aren't so good that strikeouts won't be an issue for a bit. You will take that trade-off for now, especially when it comes with a potential above-average center fielder who can do damage on the basepaths as well.

**OFP:** 60 / Plus center fielder, occasional All-Star

**Variance:** Extreme. There are building blocks here for a future top-20 prospect, but Bleis will have to take the next step against full-season arms...and several more steps after that.

**Jesse Roche's Fantasy Take:** Bleis may still go under the radar in many fantasy leagues. Don't let that happen! His potential to develop into a plus-hit, plus-power and plus-speed prospect is akin to recent breakout Jackson Chourio. Also like Chourio, Bleis has an aggressive approach that leads to plenty of whiffs. Yet, the tools are so loud that we can forgive these foibles for now, especially for an 18-year-old prospect. Unlike Chourio, however, Bleis likely retains a reasonable acquisition cost and is only just entering top-100 lists. That will quickly change if he starts hot in Low-A next year.

## 4 Ceddanne Rafaela OF/SS      OFP: 60      ETA: Late 2023/Early 2024
Born: 09/18/00   Age: 22   Bats: R   Throws: R   Height: 5'8"   Weight: 152 lb.   Origin: International Free Agent, 2017

| YEAR | TEAM | LVL | AGE | PA | R | 2B | 3B | HR | RBI | BB | K | SB | CS | AVG/OBP/SLG | DRC+ | BABIP | BRR | DRP | WARP |
|------|------|-----|-----|-----|-----|-----|-----|-----|-----|-----|-----|-----|-----|-------------|------|-------|------|-----|------|
| 2021 | SAL | A | 20 | 432 | 73 | 20 | 9 | 10 | 53 | 25 | 79 | 23 | 3 | .251/.305/.424 | 110 | .288 | 1.6 | CF(52) 7.0, 3B(20) 0.8, SS(16) -0.3 | 3.1 |
| 2022 | CAG | WIN | 21 | 76 | 10 | 4 | 0 | 1 | 8 | 9 | 16 | 5 | 2 | .262/.368/.369 | | .333 | | | |
| 2022 | GVL | A+ | 21 | 209 | 37 | 17 | 4 | 9 | 36 | 10 | 51 | 14 | 2 | .330/.368/.594 | 110 | .409 | 0.1 | CF(32) -2.4, SS(9) -0.7, 2B(1) -0.2 | 0.6 |
| 2022 | POR | AA | 21 | 313 | 45 | 15 | 6 | 12 | 50 | 16 | 62 | 14 | 5 | .278/.324/.500 | 107 | .310 | -0.5 | CF(60) 5.0, SS(12) 1.5 | 1.8 |
| 2023 non-DC | BOS | MLB | 22 | 251 | 21 | 11 | 3 | 5 | 25 | 11 | 62 | 8 | 2 | .232/.274/.368 | 80 | .294 | -0.6 | 2B 0, 3B 0 | 0.2 |

*Comparables: Dalton Pompey, Teoscar Hernández, Brett Phillips*

**The Report:** One of the real breakout stories of 2022, Rafaela is already looking like a developmental win for the organization when considering his signing bonus and how his prospect trajectory looked as recently as 2021. He's a smaller guy with athleticism that plays big on both offense and defense. He's a plus baserunner on both speed and instincts who plays a good shortstop and an excellent center field with more than enough arm for both spots. Rafaela has a smooth explosiveness in his wiry frame that at the plate is expressed through a loose, quick stroke that plays gap-to-gap and generates more power than it looks like he should be able to. He's a very exciting player. The remaining questions are about the hit tool and general on-base ability. My main concern when I saw him at High-A was that he would be troubled by more advanced breaking stuff, but he actually managed to lower his strikeout rate following his promotion to Portland even as the batting average took a hit from BABIP regression. Rafaela really likes to swing and may never become a swing decisions king, but if he continues to adapt his pitch recognition he'll be a big-league contributor and possibly more.

**OFP:** 60 / Star center fielder who impacts the game with all five tools and can moonlight at shortstop

**Variance:** Medium. Hit tool uncertainties remain, but Rafaela's speed and glove should allow him to contribute even given lesser offensive production.

**Jesse Roche's Fantasy Take:** Few prospects started the season hotter than Rafaela, who launched six home runs over his first 11 games. While his pace cooled, his later-season performance actually engendered more confidence in his hit tool despite his aggressive approach (55% swing rate). Rafaela held his own in Double-A and improved his pitch recognition and, consequently, his contact and strikeout rates. The Red Sox added him to the 40-man roster this offseason, and he could make noise as soon as 2023 in MLB. Rafaela has legitimate 20/20 potential with the defensive acumen to secure playing time (unlike, say, Jarren Duran), and he is a borderline top-50 fantasy prospect.

## 5 Nick Yorke 2B      OFP: 55      ETA: Late 2024
Born: 04/02/02   Age: 21   Bats: R   Throws: R   Height: 6'0"   Weight: 200 lb.   Origin: Round 1, 2020 Draft (#17 overall)

| YEAR | TEAM | LVL | AGE | PA | R | 2B | 3B | HR | RBI | BB | K | SB | CS | AVG/OBP/SLG | DRC+ | BABIP | BRR | DRP | WARP |
|------|------|-----|-----|-----|-----|-----|-----|-----|-----|-----|-----|-----|-----|-------------|------|-------|------|-----|------|
| 2021 | SAL | A | 19 | 346 | 59 | 14 | 4 | 10 | 47 | 41 | 47 | 11 | 8 | .323/.413/.500 | 144 | .353 | -4.9 | 2B(66) 7.0 | 3.0 |
| 2021 | GVL | A+ | 19 | 96 | 17 | 6 | 1 | 4 | 15 | 11 | 22 | 2 | 1 | .333/.406/.571 | 116 | .407 | 0.3 | 2B(19) -1.0 | 0.4 |
| 2022 | GVL | A+ | 20 | 373 | 48 | 10 | 1 | 11 | 45 | 33 | 94 | 8 | 4 | .231/.303/.365 | 92 | .288 | -2.1 | 2B(68) 5.3 | 1.0 |
| 2023 non-DC | BOS | MLB | 21 | 251 | 22 | 10 | 1 | 4 | 22 | 17 | 62 | 3 | 2 | .226/.286/.330 | 75 | .293 | -2.7 | 2B 0 | -0.2 |

*Comparables: Heiker Meneses, Royce Lewis, Manuel Margot*

**The Report:** After a breakout 2021, Yorke scuffled in High-A during an injury-riddled 2022 campaign that saw his batting average deflate by almost 100 points. Some of his struggles can certainly be pinned on wrist and toe issues, but when on the field he tended to get a bit long with his swing, selling out for some of the surprising pull-side pop he found in 2021. Yorke was late on velocity more than you'd like given that he was drafted for his plus hit tool and gap-to-gap doubles pop, although he looked more like himself during his Arizona Fall League stint. Sometimes you just have a year, and he remains a potential above-average, hit tool-driven second baseman, but when you hit .220 we're going to look a bit askance at that hit tool until you start finding holes again. Yorke remains a fine second baseman, although one unlikely to add a ton of defensive value. His hands and actions are solid, the arm strength is a bit of an issue on double play turns and moving up the middle, but none of this matters if he doesn't resume scorching the ball in 2023.

**OFP:** 55 / Above-average second baseman

**Variance:** High. The injuries aren't a long-term concern, but the 2022 underperformance will remain in the back of our minds for a bit. There isn't much of a floor here if Yorke doesn't resume hitting in short order.

**Jesse Roche's Fantasy Take:** It is difficult to sugarcoat Yorke's poor season. Yes, injuries certainly played a part, but nearly every aspect of his offensive performance regressed. That said, Yorke still displays a savvy plate approach and flashes the ability to make impact contact to all fields. He remains a top-100 fantasy prospect, even though confidence in his future hit tool is waning.

## 6 Bryan Mata RHP

OFP: 55   ETA: 2023

Born: 05/03/99   Age: 24   Bats: R   Throws: R   Height: 6'3"   Weight: 238 lb.   Origin: International Free Agent, 2016

| YEAR | TEAM | LVL | AGE | W | L | SV | G | GS | IP | H | HR | BB/9 | K/9 | K | GB% | BABIP | WHIP | ERA | DRA- | WARP |
|---|---|---|---|---|---|---|---|---|---|---|---|---|---|---|---|---|---|---|---|---|
| 2022 | GVL | A+ | 23 | 0 | 1 | 0 | 3 | 3 | 9 | 6 | 1 | 6.0 | 15.0 | 15 | 50.0% | .294 | 1.33 | 4.00 | 88 | 0.1 |
| 2022 | POR | AA | 23 | 5 | 2 | 0 | 10 | 9 | 48² | 35 | 4 | 4.3 | 10.7 | 58 | 52.2% | .279 | 1.19 | 1.85 | 86 | 1.0 |
| 2022 | WOR | AAA | 23 | 2 | 0 | 0 | 5 | 5 | 23¹ | 19 | 0 | 5.8 | 11.6 | 30 | 54.5% | .345 | 1.46 | 3.47 | 83 | 0.5 |
| 2023 DC | BOS | MLB | 24 | 5 | 5 | 0 | 37 | 8 | 61 | 56 | 7 | 5.0 | 8.9 | 60 | 43.7% | .301 | 1.47 | 4.34 | 109 | 0.2 |

Comparables: Sean Reid-Foley, Joe Ross, Touki Toussaint

**The Report:** Mata's 2021 UCL tear delayed his ascension up Boston's organizational ranks, but he once again finds himself on the precipice of the majors entering 2023. Mata remains much the same pitcher post-surgery for good and for ill. His upper-90s fastball has both run and ride, and comes out pretty free and easy for 99. However, his command of the pitch remains below-average, and his quick arm action and three-quarters slot can often leave him under the ball and missing up with the heater. Mata's power slider can get up into the low-90s and flashes razorblade cut that gets under bats. He'll also throw a short, sweepier version of it to spot. His curveball is a 10-5 power roller with at least average projection, and his upper-80s change is a tick better than that when it has the good tumble. The stuff has never really been at issue for Mata; it's the strike-throwing which remains a problem. Command is the last thing to come back from Tommy John, or so they say, but Mata's was a 40 at best before going under the knife. Throw in an effortful delivery, and he may be best off missing bats and walking tightropes in the late stages of games.

**OFP:** 55 / no. 3/4 starter or late-inning reliever

**Variance:** Medium. Mata is coming off elbow surgery and profiles better in relief, but his stuff can be explosive in any role and he should be in play for 2023 innings in Fenway.

**Jesse Roche's Fantasy Take:** Mata is the type of pitching prospect who is perfect for the prompt: If you could pick any pitching prospect to have plus command, who would you pick? His nasty stuff and proximity make him an intriguing arm and a top-200 fantasy prospect, but his ultimate role is almost wholly dependent on command gains and reducing his unseemly 13% walk rate.

## 7 Mikey Romero 2B

OFP: 55   ETA: 2026

Born: 01/12/04   Age: 19   Bats: L   Throws: R   Height: 6'1"   Weight: 175 lb.   Origin: Round 1, 2022 Draft (#24 overall)

| YEAR | TEAM | LVL | AGE | PA | R | 2B | 3B | HR | RBI | BB | K | SB | CS | AVG/OBP/SLG | DRC+ | BABIP | BRR | DRP | WARP |
|---|---|---|---|---|---|---|---|---|---|---|---|---|---|---|---|---|---|---|---|
| 2022 | RSX | ROK | 18 | 43 | 5 | 3 | 0 | 1 | 6 | 7 | 4 | 1 | 0 | .250/.372/.417 | | .258 | | | |
| 2022 | SAL | A | 18 | 44 | 6 | 4 | 3 | 0 | 11 | 1 | 11 | 1 | 0 | .349/.364/.581 | 93 | .469 | 0.2 | 2B(4) 0.2, SS(3) -0.5 | 0.1 |
| 2023 non-DC | BOS | MLB | 19 | 251 | 18 | 10 | 4 | 2 | 20 | 13 | 66 | 2 | 1 | .217/.262/.314 | 60 | .293 | -3.3 | 2B 0, SS 0 | -0.8 |

**The Report:** The Red Sox went back to the SoCal prep shortstop well in the 2022 draft, grabbing Marcelo Mayer's travel ball teammate with their first pick. Romero doesn't have the same offensive upside, but he's an advanced, rangy defender at the six, with clean actions and a solid, accurate arm. At the plate, Romero prizes contact over power, but he has above-average bat speed, stays back well on offspeed, and keeps the barrel in the zone a good while, allowing him to drive pitches gap-to-gap. I suspect the power will play as doubles more than home runs, but there should be oodles of doubles to go with an above-average hit tool. Romero may not have the most upside of this year's prep class, but he's a high-probability regular at a premium position.

**OFP:** 55 / What if Mets-era Daniel Murphy were a cromulent shortstop?

**Variance:** High. Romero has only dipped his toe into the pros, and sometimes prep bats who look like they will hit, won't, and prep shortstops who look like they will stick, don't.

**Jesse Roche's Fantasy Take:** Romero has underrated fantasy upside with superb bat-to-ball skills, a quick bat and sneaky pop. It is even possible that pro instruction will coax out more game power. Regardless, Mets-era Daniel Murphy hit .288/.331/.424 over seven seasons. Take it and run!

## 8   Chris Murphy   LHP    OFP: 55    ETA: 2023

Born: 06/05/98   Age: 25   Bats: L   Throws: L   Height: 6'1"   Weight: 175 lb.   Origin: Round 6, 2019 Draft (#197 overall)

| YEAR | TEAM | LVL | AGE | W | L | SV | G | GS | IP | H | HR | BB/9 | K/9 | K | GB% | BABIP | WHIP | ERA | DRA- | WARP |
|------|------|-----|-----|---|---|----|----|----|----|---|----|------|-----|---|-----|-------|------|-----|------|------|
| 2021 | GVL | A+ | 23 | 5 | 3 | 0 | 14 | 14 | 68¹ | 62 | 17 | 3.0 | 10.7 | 81 | 38.8% | .281 | 1.24 | 4.21 | 103 | 0.4 |
| 2021 | POR | AA | 23 | 3 | 2 | 0 | 7 | 6 | 33 | 30 | 4 | 3.5 | 12.8 | 47 | 33.8% | .356 | 1.30 | 5.45 | 96 | 0.3 |
| 2022 | POR | AA | 24 | 4 | 5 | 0 | 15 | 13 | 76² | 46 | 6 | 3.6 | 10.7 | 91 | 35.9% | .229 | 1.00 | 2.58 | 94 | 1.3 |
| 2022 | WOR | AAA | 24 | 3 | 6 | 0 | 15 | 15 | 75¹ | 77 | 8 | 4.9 | 6.9 | 58 | 45.8% | .305 | 1.57 | 5.50 | 127 | 0.0 |
| 2023 DC | BOS | MLB | 25 | 3 | 3 | 0 | 20 | 5 | 34.3 | 37 | 5 | 4.3 | 7.6 | 29 | 35.6% | .313 | 1.54 | 5.11 | 126 | -0.2 |

*Comparables: Harrison Musgrave, Adam Scott, Jason Wheeler*

**The Report:** Murphy has had a bit of an up-and-down career as a pitching prospect. He first came to our attention after a velocity bump at the 2020 alternate site. Then his 2021 was marred by command and control issues—which have intermittently plagued him since college—but he got off to a strong start back in Double-A this past season. Murphy's fastball sits a little above-average on the stalker, but it plays above its velocity, garnering bad hacks as it bores in on righties from a tough angle. His change is a second plus pitch with swing-and-miss sink. He also offers two different breaking balls, but neither is consistently distinct or does more than bump average. Either can be slurvy at times, but he will flash a better curve here and there. If Murphy can get one of the breaking balls to a 50, he has a shot to be a solid starter, but he also dealt with control issues once again in 2022 after a promotion to Triple-A. The best option for the Sox might be to deploy him as a left-handed Garrett Whitlock type, but he should be a versatile weapon for their pitching staff as soon as this season, if he can throw good strikes.

**OFP:** 55 / A good Rays pitcher

**Variance:** Medium. If I had to pin him down on a role, I think Murphy is best suited to a 4-6 out fireman, but if he can harness some command gains and tighten up a breaking ball, mid-rotation starter is in play. Conversely, he hasn't flashed the kind of consistency in the minors that has you writing his name on your 26-man roster in permanent ink.

**Jesse Roche's Fantasy Take:** If he looks like a reliever, has a pitch mix like a reliever and has command issues like a reliever, then he is probably a reliever.

## 9   Roman Anthony   CF    OFP: 55    ETA: 2026

Born: 05/13/04   Age: 19   Bats: L   Throws: R   Height: 6'3"   Weight: 200 lb.   Origin: Round 2, 2022 Draft (#79 overall)

| YEAR | TEAM | LVL | AGE | PA | R | 2B | 3B | HR | RBI | BB | K | SB | CS | AVG/OBP/SLG | DRC+ | BABIP | BRR | DRP | WARP |
|------|------|-----|-----|----|---|----|----|----|-----|----|---|----|----|-------------|------|-------|-----|-----|------|
| 2022 | RSX | ROK | 18 | 40 | 5 | 2 | 0 | 0 | 7 | 4 | 4 | 1 | 0 | .429/.475/.486 | | .469 | | | |
| 2022 | SAL | A | 18 | 43 | 2 | 2 | 0 | 0 | 5 | 5 | 4 | 0 | 0 | .189/.279/.243 | 110 | .206 | 0.3 | CF(8) 0.8 | 0.2 |
| 2023 non-DC | BOS | MLB | 19 | 251 | 18 | 10 | 2 | 2 | 19 | 15 | 51 | 1 | 0 | .209/.262/.290 | 55 | .261 | -4.2 | CF 0 | -1.0 |

**The Report:** Anthony got first-round money in the second round as a potential power-hitting center fielder. His left-handed swing reminds me a bit of Josh Bell's, and while it's a bit early to say 30-home-run power is in play, Anthony is already quite strong and should add more good weight in his 20s. Upright and fidgety at the plate, he draws his hands back before unleashing a big-time cut. The present bat-to-ball is solid considering his age, experience and violence in the swing, and while there's little pro track record here on the hit tool, I think he'll consistently make enough good contact to get the power into games further up the org chart. Defensively, Anthony is fine in center field at present, but could grow off the position, and his arm is a better fit for left than right. But if the bat plays to projection, none but Anthony should conquer Anthony, and woe it be so to opposing pitchers.

**OFP:** 55 / Everyday center fielder

**Variance:** High. The tools are loud, but when it comes to prospect development—and certainly Roman Ant(h)onys—all strange and terrible events are welcome.

**Jesse Roche's Fantasy Take:** Anthony has the type of huge physical tools that fantasy managers crave. Further, his contact skills have steadily improved, and he posted an impressive 9.6% strikeout rate between the complex and Low-A in his debut. At the same time, however, Anthony ran up a 60.6% ground-ball rate and put up a miniscule .056 ISO. If he is able to somehow marry his raw power with his bat-to-ball ability, he could break out. Target Anthony as a late-round flier in FYPDs in leagues that roster over 400 prospects.

## 10  Matthew Lugo  IF    OFP: 50    ETA: 2024

Born: 05/09/01   Age: 22   Bats: R   Throws: R   Height: 6'1"   Weight: 187 lb.   Origin: Round 2, 2019 Draft (#69 overall)

| YEAR | TEAM | LVL | AGE | PA | R | 2B | 3B | HR | RBI | BB | K | SB | CS | AVG/OBP/SLG | DRC+ | BABIP | BRR | DRP | WARP |
|------|------|-----|-----|----|---|----|----|----|----|----|----|----|----|-------------|------|-------|-----|-----|------|
| 2021 | SAL | A | 20 | 469 | 61 | 21 | 3 | 4 | 50 | 38 | 94 | 15 | 4 | .270/.338/.364 | 104 | .335 | 0.5 | SS(93) 4.0, 2B(6) 0.9 | 2.2 |
| 2022 | CAG | WIN | 21 | 140 | 20 | 3 | 0 | 6 | 19 | 11 | 34 | 2 | 3 | .275/.360/.450 | | .329 | | | |
| 2022 | GVL | A+ | 21 | 512 | 76 | 25 | 10 | 18 | 78 | 35 | 100 | 20 | 7 | .288/.344/.500 | 102 | .330 | -1.3 | SS(73) 1.2, 3B(25) -2.4, 2B(7) -0.8 | 1.3 |
| 2023 non-DC | BOS | MLB | 22 | 251 | 20 | 11 | 2 | 3 | 22 | 13 | 63 | 4 | 1 | .227/.275/.335 | 72 | .296 | -2.5 | 2B 0, 3B 0 | -0.3 |

*Comparables: Ryan Brett, Vidal Bruján, Billy Hamilton*

**The Report:** Lugo had one of the more significant year-over-year improvements I saw this past season. With Low-A Salem in 2021, Lugo was lanky of frame and appeared to lack some coordination both in the field and at the plate. My High-A looks were much more encouraging—he's added good weight and now possesses an authoritative swing that consistently impacts the ball, thanks in part to an ability to cover the plate and pick up spin. He doesn't do a lot of walking or a lot of striking out, and the power is more gap than fence at present, so it's a sum-over-parts sort of profile. He's a better-than-solid defensive shortstop now, but has already been dabbling at third and could end up sliding over there if circumstance or further physical development dictate.

**OFP:** 50 / Everyday shortstop or third baseman

**Variance:** Medium. Has to prove he can produce against high-level pitching, as the other tools won't carry him.

**Jesse Roche's Fantasy Take:** Sum-over-parts players like Lugo often surprise in fantasy. He may lack a plus tool, he may be too aggressive and he may not be a power hitter. Yet, Lugo has just enough hitting ability, power and speed to be a potential impact player.

## Outside the Top Ten:

## 11  Brandon Walter  LHP

Born: 09/08/96   Age: 26   Bats: L   Throws: L   Height: 6'2"   Weight: 200 lb.   Origin: Round 26, 2019 Draft (#797 overall)

| YEAR | TEAM | LVL | AGE | W | L | SV | G | GS | IP | H | HR | BB/9 | K/9 | K | GB% | BABIP | WHIP | ERA | DRA- | WARP |
|------|------|-----|-----|---|---|----|---|----|----|---|----|------|-----|---|-----|-------|------|-----|------|------|
| 2021 | SAL | A | 24 | 1 | 1 | 2 | 13 | 2 | 31 | 21 | 0 | 1.7 | 13.4 | 46 | 67.1% | .288 | 0.87 | 1.45 | 67 | 0.8 |
| 2021 | GVL | A+ | 24 | 4 | 3 | 0 | 12 | 12 | 58¹ | 46 | 6 | 2.2 | 13.3 | 86 | 58.3% | .317 | 1.03 | 3.70 | 73 | 1.4 |
| 2022 | POR | AA | 25 | 2 | 2 | 0 | 9 | 9 | 50 | 36 | 6 | 0.5 | 12.2 | 68 | 53.3% | .263 | 0.78 | 2.88 | 71 | 1.4 |
| 2022 | WOR | AAA | 25 | 1 | 1 | 0 | 2 | 2 | 7² | 9 | 0 | 4.7 | 8.2 | 7 | 68.0% | .360 | 1.70 | 8.22 | 107 | 0.1 |
| 2023 DC | BOS | MLB | 26 | 1 | 1 | 0 | 5 | 5 | 21.7 | 21 | 2 | 2.5 | 8.4 | 20 | 45.9% | .306 | 1.23 | 3.37 | 92 | 0.3 |

*Comparables: Joey Lucchesi, Ben Braymer, Hiram Burgos*

Walter put up downright Petitish peripherals in Double-A—I mean Yusmeiro in this context, but that's also a slim walk rate—before being felled by a neck strain shortly after a promotion to Worcester. That's better than arm stuff—although he has a college TJ on his CV—but he likely would have made his major-league debut in 2022 had he stayed healthy. It's a bit of an odd profile. Walter's breaking ball might end up plus-plus; it's a nasty sweeper that turns late and just keeps going. The change is good enough to keep righties in check, although he doesn't always get it down and out of the zone. He'll need to lean heavily on those secondaries, as the fastball is very pedestrian. Walter sat around 90 in my look. In some starts, he's been more low-90s; other outings, upper-80s. The pitch has some sink and run, but the arm-side command isn't too fine. Walter might be able to just spam that breaking ball in a fair imitation of early-40s Rich Hill, but he'll be 26 himself on Opening Day 2023 and has barely thrown more pro innings than Hill did in 2021.

## 12   Ronaldo Hernández   C/DH

Born: 11/11/97   Age: 25   Bats: R   Throws: R   Height: 6'1"   Weight: 230 lb.   Origin: International Free Agent, 2014

| YEAR | TEAM | LVL | AGE | PA | R | 2B | 3B | HR | RBI | BB | K | SB | CS | AVG/OBP/SLG | DRC+ | BABIP | BRR | DRP | WARP |
|------|------|-----|-----|----|----|----|----|----|-----|----|----|----|----|-------------|------|-------|-----|-----|------|
| 2021 | POR | AA | 23 | 357 | 44 | 26 | 1 | 16 | 53 | 11 | 70 | 0 | 2 | .280/.319/.506 | 113 | .311 | -1.3 | C(61) 6.7, 1B(1) 0.3 | 2.4 |
| 2021 | WOR | AAA | 23 | 30 | 1 | 3 | 0 | 0 | 5 | 1 | 7 | 0 | 0 | .333/.400/.444 | 86 | .450 | -0.8 | C(5) -0.1 | 0.0 |
| 2022 | WOR | AAA | 24 | 439 | 50 | 27 | 0 | 17 | 63 | 21 | 92 | 0 | 3 | .261/.297/.451 | 98 | .295 | -0.4 | C(67) 4.4 | 1.5 |
| 2023 DC | BOS | MLB | 25 | 63 | 7 | 3 | 0 | 2 | 7 | 2 | 15 | 0 | 0 | .230/.273/.370 | 76 | .288 | -0.1 | C 0 | 0.1 |

*Comparables: Blake Swihart, A.J. Jimenez, Tomás Telis*

Hernández remains a pretty good catching prospect, but he's a very good illustration of two player development concepts. The first is prospect fatigue. We initially ranked Hernández on the 2018 Rays list. He was a high-upside catcher in the Appy League, with potential impact hit and power tools, but a long way to go defensively. Over the last five years he never really collapsed, but never really broke out either. He's just been hanging around team top 10s—first Tampa, now Boston—every year, but we haven't had anything particularly interesting to write about him in recent editions. That's due in part to the second concept: John Sickels' Young Catcher Offensive Stagnation Syndrome. Hernández hasn't ever been capital "B" bad at the plate, but he's seen his K-rate creep up, his quality of contact go down and his overall offensive profile now driven solely by his plus raw power. His glove has gotten there though. He's at least average in all facets of backstop play, and that plus the 15-20 home run potential as a regular arguably makes him Boston's best internal catching option. You just maybe hoped that sentence would carry more of an enthusiastic exclamation point in 2023.

## 13   Brainer Bonaci   IF

Born: 07/09/02   Age: 20   Bats: S   Throws: R   Height: 5'10"   Weight: 164 lb.   Origin: International Free Agent, 2018

| YEAR | TEAM | LVL | AGE | PA | R | 2B | 3B | HR | RBI | BB | K | SB | CS | AVG/OBP/SLG | DRC+ | BABIP | BRR | DRP | WARP |
|------|------|-----|-----|----|----|----|----|----|-----|----|----|----|----|-------------|------|-------|-----|-----|------|
| 2021 | RSX | ROK | 18 | 162 | 27 | 13 | 1 | 2 | 17 | 21 | 37 | 12 | 0 | .252/.358/.403 | | .330 | | | |
| 2021 | SAL | A | 18 | 52 | 5 | 3 | 1 | 0 | 8 | 3 | 8 | 0 | 0 | .224/.269/.327 | 113 | .268 | -1.4 | SS(8) 0.4, 2B(5) 0.6 | 0.2 |
| 2022 | SAL | A | 19 | 494 | 86 | 19 | 6 | 6 | 50 | 89 | 89 | 28 | 6 | .262/.397/.385 | 119 | .319 | 7.1 | 2B(57) -0.3, SS(31) 3.5, 3B(10) 0.5 | 3.6 |
| 2023 non-DC | BOS | MLB | 20 | 251 | 21 | 10 | 2 | 2 | 20 | 26 | 54 | 7 | 3 | .215/.302/.307 | 76 | .275 | -0.6 | 2B 0, 3B 0 | 0.0 |

*Comparables: J.P. Crawford, Jonathan Araúz, Ketel Marte*

Bonaci is a switch-hitting utility type with enough glove to stick at shortstop and enough pop from the right side to at least keep an eye on over the coming seasons. He's undersized and a little square, with a very busy pre-swing routine, but once he lets it rip he shows loose hands, a good approach and solid bat speed from the left side, although he tends to roll over on grounders more than you'd like. From the right side of the plate, his swing is a bit stiffer, with more lift but also more swing-and-miss, especially against stuff diving down. In the field, Bonaci checks all the boxes for above-average defense at three spots. He's rangy with good body control, quick transfer and actions, and a plus arm with good carry. If he can marry his two swings a bit more and settle in with average hit and power tools, there's low-end starter potential, but the most likely outcome is a good utility infielder.

## 14   Luis Perales   RHP

Born: 04/14/03   Age: 20   Bats: R   Throws: R   Height: 6'1"   Weight: 160 lb.   Origin: International Free Agent, 2019

| YEAR | TEAM | LVL | AGE | W | L | SV | G | GS | IP | H | HR | BB/9 | K/9 | K | GB% | BABIP | WHIP | ERA | DRA- | WARP |
|------|------|-----|-----|---|---|----|----|----|----|---|----|------|-----|----|-----|-------|------|-----|------|------|
| 2022 | RSX | ROK | 19 | 0 | 1 | 0 | 9 | 7 | 25 | 10 | 0 | 3.2 | 12.2 | 34 | 44.0% | .200 | 0.76 | 1.08 | | |
| 2022 | SAL | A | 19 | 0 | 1 | 0 | 4 | 4 | 10² | 10 | 1 | 9.3 | 13.5 | 16 | 33.3% | .391 | 1.97 | 3.38 | 103 | 0.1 |
| 2023 non-DC | BOS | MLB | 20 | 3 | 3 | 0 | 58 | 0 | 50 | 52 | 9 | 6.4 | 8.9 | 50 | 33.3% | .310 | 1.76 | 6.22 | 150 | -1.0 |

Signed in 2019, but unable to officially debut until 2021, Perales is quickly making a name for himself in a system rather thin on pitching prospects. An undersized righty with a bit of effort in his delivery, he sits mid-90s with his fastball, which also shows some pop at the top of the zone. Both of Perales' secondaries flash above-average already. His mid-80s curve can be a little flat, but he'll snap one off to the back foot off a lefty as well. His upper-80s change is a steep, sinking version, but the shape can vary and sometimes the *cambio* just runs like a firm two-seam. Perales' size and delivery may end up impediments to a long-term starter projection, but the stuff should fit just fine at the back of a rotation, with upside past that if the secondaries develop further.

## 15 Wikelman Gonzalez   RHP

Born: 03/25/02   Age: 21   Bats: R   Throws: R   Height: 6'0"   Weight: 167 lb.   Origin: International Free Agent, 2018

| YEAR | TEAM | LVL | AGE | W | L | SV | G | GS | IP | H | HR | BB/9 | K/9 | K | GB% | BABIP | WHIP | ERA | DRA- | WARP |
|------|------|-----|-----|---|---|----|----|----|-----|----|----|------|-----|----|------|-------|------|------|------|------|
| 2021 | RSX | ROK | 19 | 4 | 2 | 0 | 8 | 7 | 35 | 29 | 1 | 2.1 | 11.8 | 46 | 40.5% | .337 | 1.06 | 3.60 | | |
| 2021 | SAL | A | 19 | 0 | 0 | 0 | 4 | 4 | 17² | 13 | 1 | 4.1 | 10.2 | 20 | 34.8% | .279 | 1.19 | 1.53 | 106 | 0.1 |
| 2022 | SAL | A | 20 | 4 | 3 | 0 | 21 | 21 | 81¹ | 63 | 2 | 5.3 | 10.8 | 98 | 38.1% | .305 | 1.36 | 4.54 | 99 | 0.9 |
| 2022 | GVL | A+ | 20 | 0 | 0 | 0 | 4 | 4 | 17 | 13 | 0 | 3.2 | 12.2 | 23 | 42.1% | .342 | 1.12 | 2.65 | 88 | 0.2 |
| 2023 non-DC | BOS | MLB | 21 | 3 | 3 | 0 | 58 | 0 | 50 | 50 | 8 | 5.2 | 8.1 | 45 | 33.7% | .297 | 1.59 | 5.28 | 131 | -0.5 |

Comparables: *Jordan Balazovic, Emilio Vargas, Drew Hutchison*

Gonzalez's name was buzzy around list time last year, but his time spent at both A-ball levels in 2022 hasn't really clarified his long-term role. His fastball still consistently touches 95 and even a bit higher. It can hum right by hitters with its flat approach and garner late swings, but the 6-foot righty doesn't always hold the top-end heat later in outings. Gonzalez's curveball is a big 11-5 breaker in the upper-70s and shows good characteristics if also some inconsistency in both shape and location. His change is just sort of there at present—good velocity separation in the mid-80s, but flat with just a bit of wiggle. Gonzalez's 2022 wasn't a disappointment per se, but it wasn't a step forward either, and he remains more likely a reliever than starter for me. He and Perales are an interesting comparison point as shorter IFA righties, and while Perales might encounter the same struggles and scuffles in his age 20-season, I prefer his stuff slightly to Gonzalez's at present.

## 16 Eddinson Paulino   IF

Born: 07/02/02   Age: 21   Bats: L   Throws: R   Height: 5'10"   Weight: 155 lb.   Origin: International Free Agent, 2018

| YEAR | TEAM | LVL | AGE | PA | R | 2B | 3B | HR | RBI | BB | K | SB | CS | AVG/OBP/SLG | DRC+ | BABIP | BRR | DRP | WARP |
|------|------|-----|-----|-----|----|----|----|----|-----|----|-----|----|----|-------------|------|-------|-----|-----|------|
| 2021 | RSX | ROK | 18 | 133 | 25 | 16 | 4 | 0 | 13 | 15 | 21 | 5 | 2 | .336/.436/.549 | | .413 | | | |
| 2022 | SAL | A | 19 | 539 | 96 | 35 | 10 | 13 | 66 | 64 | 105 | 27 | 5 | .266/.359/.469 | 122 | .314 | 4.2 | SS(36) 1.8, 3B(34) 0.1, 2B(30) 1.5 | 3.7 |
| 2023 non-DC | BOS | MLB | 20 | 251 | 20 | 11 | 3 | 3 | 22 | 18 | 63 | 5 | 3 | .218/.281/.332 | 73 | .288 | -1.5 | 2B 0, 3B 0 | -0.2 |

Comparables: *Richard Urena, Royce Lewis, Javy Guerra*

Bouncing around the Salem infield (and outfield) with Bonaci, Paulino has a bit more thump in his bat, despite an average frame and average bat speed. His swing can be a bit top-hand dominant and there's additional swing-and-miss in the zone, but like Bonaci he has a solid approach and a ton of defensive flexibility. He's not quite as slick a fielder, but his above-average foot speed plays in center as well as the infield dirt, and if he makes enough contact further up the ladder, could be a fun four-day-a-week starter bouncing around defensive locales.

## 17 Blaze Jordan   CI

Born: 12/19/02   Age: 20   Bats: R   Throws: R   Height: 6'2"   Weight: 220 lb.   Origin: Round 3, 2020 Draft (#89 overall)

| YEAR | TEAM | LVL | AGE | PA | R | 2B | 3B | HR | RBI | BB | K | SB | CS | AVG/OBP/SLG | DRC+ | BABIP | BRR | DRP | WARP |
|------|------|-----|-----|-----|----|----|----|----|-----|----|----|----|----|-------------|------|-------|-----|-----|------|
| 2021 | RSX | ROK | 18 | 76 | 12 | 7 | 1 | 4 | 19 | 6 | 13 | 1 | 0 | .362/.408/.667 | | .396 | | | |
| 2021 | SAL | A | 18 | 38 | 7 | 1 | 0 | 2 | 7 | 2 | 8 | 0 | 0 | .250/.289/.444 | 113 | .269 | 0.3 | 3B(5) -1.3, 1B(2) 0.2 | 0.1 |
| 2022 | SAL | A | 19 | 415 | 48 | 29 | 3 | 8 | 57 | 37 | 67 | 4 | 1 | .286/.357/.446 | 116 | .329 | 1.0 | 3B(50) -3.8, 1B(34) 5.5 | 2.4 |
| 2022 | GVL | A+ | 19 | 106 | 12 | 1 | 0 | 4 | 11 | 11 | 27 | 1 | 0 | .301/.387/.441 | 87 | .387 | -2.2 | 1B(13) -1.1, 3B(9) -1.5 | -0.4 |
| 2023 non-DC | BOS | MLB | 20 | 251 | 20 | 11 | 1 | 3 | 21 | 15 | 63 | 1 | 0 | .220/.274/.319 | 68 | .287 | -4.2 | 1B 0, 3B 0 | -0.8 |

Comparables: *Miguel Vargas, Anthony Rizzo, Nolan Gorman*

Jordan doesn't turn 20 until just before Christmas—he re-filed to enter the 2020 draft as a 17-year-old—and hit surprisingly well for a teenager at two A-ball levels given his profile as a power-over-hit corner slugger. There wasn't noteworthy over-the-fence power in 2022, but he hit plenty of doubles. The traditional scouting maxim is that those turn into home runs as a prospect develops, but Jordan already cuts the figure of a hulking slugger at the dish, and his strength-based swing should be socking plenty of deep drives to left field. Said swing is also a bit stiff with fringy bat speed, so quality of contact has been an issue, even if pure swing-and-miss has been manageable. Jordan is passable at third for now, so there's a lot of moving parts in the ultimate projection here. As always, Double-A will clarify things.

## 18 Alex Binelas  CI

Born: 05/26/00   Age: 23   Bats: L   Throws: R   Height: 6'3"   Weight: 225 lb.   Origin: Round 3, 2021 Draft (#86 overall)

| YEAR | TEAM | LVL | AGE | PA | R | 2B | 3B | HR | RBI | BB | K | SB | CS | AVG/OBP/SLG | DRC+ | BABIP | BRR | DRP | WARP |
|------|------|-----|-----|-----|----|----|----|----|-----|----|----|----|----|-------------|------|-------|-----|-----|------|
| 2021 | BRWG | ROK | 21 | 27 | 4 | 0 | 0 | 0 | 2 | 5 | 6 | 1 | 1 | .286/.444/.286 | | .400 | | | |
| 2021 | CAR | A | 21 | 132 | 29 | 11 | 0 | 9 | 27 | 12 | 33 | 0 | 0 | .314/.379/.636 | 126 | .364 | 0.7 | 3B(20) -4.9, 1B(5) -0.4 | 0.3 |
| 2022 | GVL | A+ | 22 | 259 | 41 | 10 | 1 | 14 | 43 | 38 | 69 | 8 | 0 | .245/.355/.495 | 108 | .285 | 1.5 | 1B(29) -0.2, 3B(23) 0.5 | 1.1 |
| 2022 | POR | AA | 22 | 241 | 30 | 10 | 1 | 11 | 35 | 25 | 78 | 0 | 0 | .166/.254/.379 | 87 | .192 | 0.0 | 3B(40) -1.3, 1B(10) -0.3 | 0.1 |
| 2023 non-DC | BOS | MLB | 23 | 251 | 24 | 10 | 1 | 7 | 26 | 21 | 86 | 1 | 0 | .214/.284/.358 | 81 | .312 | -4.0 | 1B 0, 3B 0 | -0.4 |

*Comparables: Hunter Dozier, David Vidal, Brandon Wagner*

The big prospect piece in the Jackie Bradley Jr./Hunter Renfroe deal, Binelas is a TTO guy straight out of *Moneyball* central casting. A big dude currently splitting time between the infield corners, Binelas walks a lot, whiffs a lot and hits the ball very hard from the left side of the plate. Even with the swing-and-miss, he has a very advanced approach, and there should be more power coming if he can lift the ball with a little more consistency. After struggling upon his first exposure to Double-A pitching, he'll have to prove that he can make enough contact and salvage enough defensive utility to give his strengths a chance to play.

## 19 Cutter Coffey  SS

Born: 05/21/04   Age: 19   Bats: R   Throws: R   Height: 6'2"   Weight: 190 lb.   Origin: Round 2, 2022 Draft (#41 overall)

| YEAR | TEAM | LVL | AGE | PA | R | 2B | 3B | HR | RBI | BB | K | SB | CS | AVG/OBP/SLG | DRC+ | BABIP | BRR | DRP | WARP |
|------|------|-----|-----|-----|----|----|----|----|-----|----|----|----|----|-------------|------|-------|-----|-----|------|
| 2022 | RSX | ROK | 18 | 40 | 7 | 1 | 0 | 0 | 0 | 7 | 11 | 1 | 0 | .125/.300/.156 | | .190 | | | |

The Red Sox aggressively targeted up-the-middle prep talent early in the 2022 draft, spending the vast majority of the pool to ink Romero, Anthony and Coffey. Coffey has the lowest offensive floor of the three, as there are questions about his ability to make consistent contact, but he also clearly has the most electric bat speed and power potential of the trio of high school picks. He's also the least likely to stick up the middle, but his strong arm should play well at third base if the power plays up the ladder.

## 20 Andrew Politi  RHP

Born: 06/04/96   Age: 27   Bats: R   Throws: R   Height: 6'0"   Weight: 193 lb.   Origin: Round 15, 2018 Draft (#460 overall)

| YEAR | TEAM | LVL | AGE | W | L | SV | G | GS | IP | H | HR | BB/9 | K/9 | K | GB% | BABIP | WHIP | ERA | DRA- | WARP |
|------|------|-----|-----|---|---|----|----|----|-----|----|----|------|------|----|-----|-------|------|-----|------|------|
| 2021 | POR | AA | 25 | 6 | 9 | 0 | 21 | 15 | 75 | 77 | 11 | 4.6 | 10.7 | 89 | 40.6% | .328 | 1.53 | 6.36 | 100 | 0.6 |
| 2022 | POR | AA | 26 | 0 | 1 | 4 | 12 | 0 | 13¹ | 7 | 2 | 2.0 | 13.5 | 20 | 51.9% | .208 | 0.75 | 2.03 | 76 | 0.3 |
| 2022 | WOR | AAA | 26 | 4 | 0 | 4 | 38 | 2 | 56 | 38 | 4 | 3.1 | 10.1 | 63 | 43.4% | .258 | 1.02 | 2.41 | 77 | 1.4 |
| 2023 DC | BAL | MLB | 27 | 2 | 2 | 0 | 35 | 0 | 30 | 29 | 4 | 4.1 | 9.0 | 30 | 37.4% | .301 | 1.42 | 4.40 | 114 | -0.1 |

Politi was converted to a reliever towards the end of the 2021 season, and the new role suits him quite well. He sits in the mid-90s and works the fastball well down in the zone, using his upper-80s cutter in the same locations to get under barrels or generate ground-ball contact. Politi will pop an upper-70s curve at times as well to steal a strike, although it's a bit too slurvy to consistently induce whiffs. It's not the loudest late-inning profile, but Politi should be able to take over the seventh or eighth inning for the Sox as soon as this spring.

# Top Talents 25 and Under (as of 4/1/2023):

1. Marcelo Mayer, SS
2. Triston Casas, 1B
3. Brayan Bello, RHP
4. Miguel Bleis, OF
5. Ceddanne Rafaela, SS/OF
6. Nick Yorke, 2B
7. Bryan Mata, RHP
8. Mikey Romero, SS
9. Chris Murphy, LHP

10. Roman Anthony, OF

Things are tumultuous in the land of Dunkin' and pine trees, and there isn't quite a wave of youth ready to pick up the slack in Beantown. Of course, this is only Rafael Devers' first year not qualifying for this list; however, no young star has yet established himself as next in line behind the San Diego-bound Xander Bogaerts and the now-departed Killer B's outfield. Bello brings high heat and mid-rotation potential that is sorely needed for a club that was well below-average by DRA- as a rotation and a pitching staff overall. He can be pencilled into the 2023 rotation, though his workload may still need management. RHP Josh Winckowski is more likely to figure into the bullpen or a swingman role, as big leaguers had far more success against his out-pitch slider than opponents in Worcester.

# Chicago Cubs

## The State of the System:

This farm system should be better after trading Yu Darvish, Javier Báez, Anthony Rizzo, Kris Bryant, David Robertson and Scott Effross, but it is pretty good all in all.

## The Top Ten:

### 1 Pete Crow-Armstrong  OF          OFP: 60      ETA: Late 2024
Born: 03/25/02   Age: 21   Bats: L   Throws: L   Height: 6'0"   Weight: 184 lb.   Origin: Round 1, 2020 Draft (#19 overall)

| YEAR | TEAM | LVL | AGE | PA | R | 2B | 3B | HR | RBI | BB | K | SB | CS | AVG/OBP/SLG | DRC+ | BABIP | BRR | DRP | WARP |
|------|------|-----|-----|----|----|----|----|----|-----|----|----|----|----|-------------|------|-------|-----|-----|------|
| 2021 | SLU | A | 19 | 32 | 6 | 2 | 0 | 0 | 4 | 7 | 6 | 2 | 3 | .417/.563/.500 | 119 | .556 | 0.1 | CF(5) 1.6 | 0.3 |
| 2022 | MB | A | 20 | 183 | 39 | 5 | 3 | 7 | 27 | 22 | 33 | 13 | 4 | .354/.443/.557 | 121 | .415 | 0.7 | CF(32) 0.9 | 1.3 |
| 2022 | SB | A+ | 20 | 288 | 50 | 15 | 5 | 9 | 34 | 14 | 69 | 19 | 7 | .287/.333/.498 | 87 | .353 | 0.5 | CF(59) 1.7 | 0.6 |
| 2023 non-DC | CHC | MLB | 21 | 251 | 21 | 10 | 4 | 4 | 23 | 15 | 60 | 8 | 4 | .235/.288/.354 | 80 | .301 | 0.2 | CF 0 | 0.3 |

*Comparables: David Dahl, Brett Phillips, Jordan Schafer*

**The Report:** The significant shoulder injury suffered as a member of the Mets' organization in 2021 feels like a distant memory. PCA showed no ill effects, scorching the ball in pitching-friendly Myrtle Beach and earning an early summer call-up to High-A. It was at South Bend where he got his first taste of adversity in the professional ranks, struggling initially against older, more advanced pitching but eventually making adjustments to get back on track. The swing is violent, yet controlled, producing rocket line drives to all fields with his excellent barrel control. The knock on him post-draft was a lack of power in the profile but he added some muscle during the injury rehab and it's not inconceivable to project average over-the-fence pop. Defensively, he's double plus with the glove in center, covering tons of ground and making difficult plays look routine. The sudden teardown of the 2016 championship team was tough on Cub fans and losing Báez was an especially hard pill to swallow, but Crow-Armstrong becoming a star should help ease that pain.

**OFP:** 60 / Plus regular, occasional All-Star in center field

**Variance:** Medium. He only has one full season under his belt and is yet to face advanced pitching. However, the speed and defense give a high floor to the profile.

**Jesse Roche's Fantasy Take:** What a difference a swing change can make. Crow-Armstrong began tapping into legit power, knocking 16 home runs and a strong 14.8% HR/FB ratio, while maintaining superb contact skills. Meanwhile, he can fly, and his speed plays on the bases, including 32 stolen bases and 10 triples. His aggressive approach will be tested as he climbs the ladder, but all the ingredients are here for a five-category fantasy stud. Crow-Armstrong is a top-50 dynasty prospect.

### 2 Owen Caissie  OF          OFP: 55      ETA: Late 2024
Born: 07/08/02   Age: 20   Bats: L   Throws: R   Height: 6'4"   Weight: 190 lb.   Origin: Round 2, 2020 Draft (#45 overall)

| YEAR | TEAM | LVL | AGE | PA | R | 2B | 3B | HR | RBI | BB | K | SB | CS | AVG/OBP/SLG | DRC+ | BABIP | BRR | DRP | WARP |
|------|------|-----|-----|----|----|----|----|----|-----|----|----|----|----|-------------|------|-------|-----|-----|------|
| 2021 | CUB | ROK | 18 | 136 | 20 | 7 | 1 | 6 | 20 | 26 | 39 | 1 | 2 | .349/.478/.596 | | .500 | | | |
| 2021 | MB | A | 18 | 90 | 15 | 4 | 0 | 1 | 9 | 16 | 28 | 0 | 0 | .233/.367/.329 | 92 | .356 | -0.4 | LF(14) 0.7 | 0.2 |
| 2022 | SB | A+ | 19 | 433 | 57 | 21 | 1 | 11 | 58 | 50 | 124 | 11 | 6 | .254/.349/.402 | 94 | .350 | 3.8 | RF(77) 1.6, LF(22) -0.2 | 1.6 |
| 2023 non-DC | CHC | MLB | 20 | 251 | 21 | 10 | 1 | 3 | 21 | 21 | 77 | 2 | 1 | .218/.290/.316 | 73 | .315 | -3.3 | LF 0, RF 0 | -0.5 |

*Comparables: Dylan Carlson, Eric Jenkins, Jay Austin*

**The Report:** Despite his Canadian roots, Caissie struggled in the frigid early season in the Midwest League. He struggled out of the gate, posting a meager .122/.173/.163 slash line during the month of April, but like the weather, his bat began to heat up in May as he began to make more consistent contact. It was an aggressive assignment to place the then-teenager in High-A, but after the initial rocky start, he more than held his own against the older competition.

The raw power generated by his physical strength and plus bat speed is arguably the tops in the system, producing upper-echelon exit velocities. It's easy power to all fields but the in-game outputs have been muted by the fact that he hits the ball on the ground too much. There's always going to be some swing-and-miss to his game due to the length of his hack but Caissie shows a solid offensive approach and makes good swing decisions. In the field, there were improvements made over the course of the year. His routes became more efficient, combining with his solid instincts and plus throwing arm to give the profile of an average right fielder. There's still work to be done but if he can continue to unlock the pop, Caissie could turn into a middle-of-the-order masher on the North Side.

**OFP:** 55 / Power-hitting corner outfielder

**Variance:** High. There's not much utility outside of the bat and there's a risk that Caissie never fully taps into the raw power. If the swing stays flat and he produces 15-20 home runs instead of 25-30, he might just become a strong-side platoon bat.

**Jesse Roche's Fantasy Take:** Caissie bookended an otherwise successful season with bad looks in April and the AFL. Given his youth and aggressive assignments, he can be excused for these struggles. His huge power is worth chasing in dynasty formats with the promise of 25-30 home run potential. If he can manage his swing-and-miss, Caissie has substantial fantasy upside. He is a borderline top-100 dynasty prospect.

## Eyewitness Report: Owen Caissie

**Evaluator:** Nathan Graham
**Report Date:** 09/17/2022
**Dates Seen:** Multiple 2022
**Risk Factor:** High
**Physical/Health:** Extra-Large frame, thick build with plenty of natural strength.

| Tool | Future Grade | Report |
|---|---|---|
| Hit | 50 | Features an upright, slightly open stance with a minimal load and leg kick. There's above-average bat speed and barrel control. Swing can be long, making him susceptible to velocity on the inner half. Commands the zone well, is a patient hitter who doesn't chase often, and will use the entire field. There's always going to be some swing-and-miss but I also see additional hit tool development as he gains experience and will settle into a big league average hitter in the future. |
| Power | 60 | Plus bat speed and physical strength make for excellent raw power that can get out to any field. He's still learning how to get to it in-game, and as the swing decisions continue to improve it will produce 25-30 home runs per year during his peak. |
| Baserunning/ Speed | 50 | Has some sneaky athleticism, with above-average foot speed currently. Will settle into an average runner with maturity, not a base stealer but will not be a liability on the base paths. |
| Glove | 50 | Showed improvement over the course of the year as he continued to get reps in right field. Not a flashy defender and has just average range but shows solid instincts and takes efficient routes. Will work his way into becoming a major league average outfielder. |
| Arm | 60 | Strong arm, and shows good carry. More than enough to handle right field. |

**Conclusion:** A classic corner outfielder with a power bat and strong arm. It was easy to forget he was one of the youngest players in the league this year, he shows a patient, mature approach usually seen in those with more experience. There's room for growth in the bat that will come as he continues to get reps against advanced pitchers. When it does the power is going to blossom in-game giving Caissie a profile of a future middle-of-the-order run producer.

## 3   Matt Mervis   1B    OFP: 55    ETA: 2023

Born: 04/16/98   Age: 25   Bats: L   Throws: R   Height: 6'4"   Weight: 225 lb.   Origin: Round 39, 2016 Draft (#1174 overall)

| YEAR | TEAM | LVL | AGE | PA | R | 2B | 3B | HR | RBI | BB | K | SB | CS | AVG/OBP/SLG | DRC+ | BABIP | BRR | DRP | WARP |
|---|---|---|---|---|---|---|---|---|---|---|---|---|---|---|---|---|---|---|---|
| 2021 | MB | A | 23 | 289 | 38 | 11 | 1 | 9 | 42 | 36 | 66 | 6 | 0 | .204/.309/.367 | 106 | .236 | -0.5 | 1B(59) 6.6, 3B(1) -0.6, LF(1) -0.6 | 1.3 |
| 2022 | SB | A+ | 24 | 108 | 17 | 9 | 0 | 7 | 29 | 5 | 26 | 0 | 0 | .350/.389/.650 | 138 | .412 | 1.0 | 1B(27) 2.3 | 1.1 |
| 2022 | TNS | AA | 24 | 230 | 34 | 16 | 1 | 14 | 51 | 20 | 46 | 2 | 0 | .300/.370/.596 | 133 | .322 | -0.6 | 1B(36) 3.1 | 1.8 |
| 2022 | IOW | AAA | 24 | 240 | 41 | 15 | 1 | 15 | 39 | 25 | 35 | 0 | 0 | .297/.383/.593 | 134 | .294 | 0.5 | 1B(53) -0.7 | 1.6 |
| 2023 DC | CHC | MLB | 25 | 296 | 35 | 14 | 2 | 9 | 33 | 21 | 66 | 1 | 0 | .238/.302/.405 | 94 | .286 | -0.4 | 1B 0 | 0.3 |

*Comparables: Jared Walsh, Steve Pearce, Andrew Toles*

**The Report:** Mervis might end up the best undrafted free agent signed after the truncated 2020 draft. His 2021 pro debut in Myrtle Beach was a struggle—granted it's a tough place to hit—and a senior-sign first baseman slugging .367 in Low-A is widely going to be considered a non-prospect. That's the only time and place Mervis has struggled to hit though, and he promptly broke out in a big way in 2022, slugging over .600 this time around—knocking 42 home runs in 154 games across three levels and the AFL—generating a ton of power despite utilizing a fairly direct path to the ball. Now top-line production isn't everything, but that's very loud performance, even for a 1B/DH prospect. Mervis' underlying contact profile doesn't quite support that going forward—it's good, but not elite—but he's likely to settle in as a .280, 25-homer bat in the majors with the occasional 30-homer spike. Mervis is not going to contribute much with the glove, but for a bat-only prospect, it's a pretty swanky bat.

**OFP:** 55 / Above-average bopper

**Variance:** Low. Mervis is unlikely to hit for the kind of elite power that would make him a clear plus regular given the defensive limitations, but he's likely to hit enough to carve out at least a long-side platoon spot in your lineup.

**Jesse Roche's Fantasy Take:** Few prospects had as eye-opening a season as Mervis, traversing three levels and the AFL with an ISO approaching around .300 at each stop. Incredibly, he improved as he matriculated up the minors, with better plate discipline and more contact. As noted above, he doesn't quite measure up to his top-line performance, though "a .280, 25-homer bat in the majors with the occasional 30-homer spike" is a nifty fantasy player. Mervis is ticketed to open 2023 in Triple-A after the Cubs signed Trey Mancini and Eric Hosmer, but his bat will seemingly force its way into the lineup at some point. He is a top-50 dynasty prospect.

## 4   Hayden Wesneski   RHP    OFP: 55    ETA: Debuted in 2022

Born: 12/05/97   Age: 25   Bats: R   Throws: R   Height: 6'3"   Weight: 210 lb.   Origin: Round 6, 2019 Draft (#195 overall)

| YEAR | TEAM | LVL | AGE | W | L | SV | G | GS | IP | H | HR | BB/9 | K/9 | K | GB% | BABIP | WHIP | ERA | DRA- | WARP |
|---|---|---|---|---|---|---|---|---|---|---|---|---|---|---|---|---|---|---|---|---|
| 2021 | HV | A+ | 23 | 1 | 1 | 0 | 7 | 7 | 36¹ | 24 | 2 | 2.2 | 11.6 | 47 | 51.9% | .293 | 0.91 | 1.49 | 77 | 0.8 |
| 2021 | SOM | AA | 23 | 8 | 4 | 0 | 15 | 15 | 83 | 76 | 11 | 2.4 | 10.0 | 92 | 43.6% | .305 | 1.18 | 4.01 | 94 | 0.9 |
| 2021 | SWB | AAA | 23 | 2 | 1 | 0 | 3 | 2 | 11 | 10 | 0 | 4.1 | 9.8 | 12 | 41.4% | .345 | 1.36 | 3.27 | 99 | 0.2 |
| 2022 | SWB | AAA | 24 | 6 | 7 | 0 | 19 | 19 | 89² | 75 | 9 | 2.8 | 8.3 | 83 | 40.9% | .270 | 1.15 | 3.51 | 95 | 1.5 |
| 2022 | IOW | AAA | 24 | 0 | 2 | 0 | 5 | 4 | 20² | 17 | 1 | 3.5 | 10.0 | 23 | 47.2% | .308 | 1.21 | 5.66 | 96 | 0.3 |
| 2022 | CHC | MLB | 24 | 3 | 2 | 0 | 6 | 4 | 33 | 24 | 3 | 1.9 | 9.0 | 33 | 46.1% | .244 | 0.94 | 2.18 | 98 | 0.3 |
| 2023 DC | CHC | MLB | 25 | 8 | 7 | 0 | 51 | 15 | 96.3 | 96 | 11 | 3.1 | 7.9 | 84 | 42.8% | .303 | 1.34 | 4.00 | 103 | 0.6 |

*Comparables: Joe Ryan, A.J. Griffin, Kyle Hendricks*

**The Report:** The Cubs are reaping the benefits of another small southern college arm who broke out in the Yankees system. They acquired Wesneski at the deadline for Scott Effross and he entered their rotation at the end of the season. His Cubs debut went swimmingly, and showed off his big sweeping slider, which will be an out-pitch for him in the majors. Wesneski has a deep repertoire past that. There's nothing else plus, but he can show three different looks with the firm stuff: a four-seam, sinker, and cutter—all of which cluster 88-94 or so and have distinctly different movement—and he'll flash an average changeup as well. Mostly, it's all about keeping hitters off-balance until he can drop that low-80s, potential plus-plus sweeper on them. Wesneski commands his slider well, showing equal aplomb backdooring it to lefties or getting righties to chase it down and out of the zone. Given that the rest of the arsenal is pretty average—and his four-seam especially is nothing special—Wesneski is going to need to lean on his slider a lot in the majors, and he may have some frustrating nights when hitters aren't chasing it. Those nights won't be all that often though, as he is a major-league-ready mid-rotation starter *in toto*.

**OFP:** 55 / no. 3/4 starter

**Variance:** Low. Wesneski is likely to be in the Cubs' Opening Day rotation and likely to be a bit above-average above-average across the 160 or so innings he will toss this season. Health-permitting of course; he is a pitcher after all.

**Jesse Roche's Fantasy Take:** Wesneski, a dynasty standout in September, leans on the type of pitch in his slider that can *make* a pitcher in MLB. (Just look at what Justin Steele did with his slider last year.) How the rest of his arsenal holds up will determine his ultimate role. The additions of Jameson Taillon and Drew Smyly may squeeze Wesneski out of the rotation, unfortunately. Even without an immediate spot, he should receive a long look this year. Wesneski is a top-100 dynasty prospect.

## 5 Brennen Davis OF

OFP: 55    ETA: Late 2023/Early 2024

Born: 11/02/99   Age: 23   Bats: R   Throws: R   Height: 6'4"   Weight: 210 lb.   Origin: Round 2, 2018 Draft (#62 overall)

| YEAR | TEAM | LVL | AGE | PA | R | 2B | 3B | HR | RBI | BB | K | SB | CS | AVG/OBP/SLG | DRC+ | BABIP | BRR | DRP | WARP |
|------|------|-----|-----|-----|----|----|----|----|-----|----|----|----|----|-------------|------|-------|------|-----|------|
| 2021 | SB | A+ | 21 | 32 | 6 | 2 | 0 | 2 | 5 | 3 | 6 | 2 | 0 | .321/.406/.607 | 113 | .350 | 0.0 | CF(5) -0.3 | 0.1 |
| 2021 | TNS | AA | 21 | 316 | 50 | 20 | 0 | 13 | 36 | 36 | 97 | 6 | 4 | .252/.367/.474 | 105 | .344 | -1.0 | CF(33) 1.0, RF(29) -1.6, LF(8) 1.4 | 1.1 |
| 2021 | IOW | AAA | 21 | 68 | 10 | 3 | 0 | 4 | 12 | 11 | 15 | 0 | 0 | .268/.397/.536 | 113 | .297 | -0.9 | RF(9) -2.0, CF(4) -0.2, LF(2) 0.3 | 0.1 |
| 2022 | IOW | AAA | 22 | 174 | 16 | 6 | 0 | 4 | 13 | 23 | 52 | 0 | 1 | .191/.322/.319 | 87 | .258 | -1.4 | CF(14) -0.2, LF(13) 0.5, RF(12) -0.8 | 0.3 |
| 2023 non-DC | CHC | MLB | 23 | 251 | 24 | 11 | 1 | 6 | 26 | 20 | 81 | 2 | 1 | .220/.296/.356 | 86 | .316 | -3.3 | LF 0, CF 0 | 0.0 |

*Comparables: Daz Cameron, Dalton Pompey, Wil Myers*

**The Report:** After a lost season due to back issues keeping him off the field, and struggles in Triple-A on the field, Davis is a bit of a confounding prospect to rank. A healthy Davis is capable of flashing all five tools in center field, with the pop, run, glove and arm all grading out as true plus, but he's also struck out almost 30% of the time since reaching the upper minors. He did appear to be making some adjustments in 2021 that could pay dividends with the hit tool moving forward, but hit under .200 for Iowa in 2022. Some of that—perhaps a large part of that—can be chalked up to the back issues, but now you have an up-the-middle prospect with back issues. Davis also missed a fair bit of developmental reps in 2019 and 2020 due to a hand injury and the pandemic. He'll be 23 next season, which isn't that old, considering he's on the cusp of the majors, but it's not that young in prospect years either. A Triple-A prospect with this much variance in his profile is unusual, but Davis certainly fits that category.

**OFP:** 55 / Above-average outfielder

**Variance:** Very High. In a world without back problems, Davis might have been in the global top 10 about now. He might have also had the same swing-and-miss problems in the upper minors that we saw in 2021. He also now has recurring back problems, because a world without back problems is not the world we live in, much to the author's chagrin as well.

**Jesse Roche's Fantasy Take:** Back injuries, poor performance and scary contact issues are not a recipe for fantasy excitement. The same loud tools are likely there somewhere. A healthy Davis could quickly vault back into the dynasty top 50. Are you willing to bet on it?

## 6 Kevin Alcántara OF

OFP: 55    ETA: 2025

Born: 07/12/02   Age: 20   Bats: R   Throws: R   Height: 6'6"   Weight: 188 lb.   Origin: International Free Agent, 2018

| YEAR | TEAM | LVL | AGE | PA | R | 2B | 3B | HR | RBI | BB | K | SB | CS | AVG/OBP/SLG | DRC+ | BABIP | BRR | DRP | WARP |
|------|------|-----|-----|-----|----|----|----|----|-----|----|-----|----|----|-------------|------|-------|------|-----|------|
| 2021 | YNK | ROK | 18 | 31 | 5 | 1 | 0 | 1 | 3 | 4 | 8 | 2 | 0 | .370/.452/.519 | | .500 | | | |
| 2021 | CUB | ROK | 18 | 107 | 27 | 3 | 5 | 4 | 21 | 13 | 28 | 3 | 0 | .337/.415/.609 | | .443 | | | |
| 2022 | MB | A | 19 | 495 | 76 | 19 | 6 | 15 | 85 | 55 | 123 | 14 | 3 | .273/.360/.451 | 108 | .345 | 2.9 | CF(69) 5.7, RF(23) 0.5 | 2.5 |
| 2023 non-DC | CHC | MLB | 20 | 251 | 21 | 10 | 2 | 4 | 22 | 18 | 79 | 3 | 1 | .216/.278/.322 | 70 | .312 | -2.8 | CF 0, RF 0 | -0.4 |

*Comparables: Johan Mieses, Andrew McCutchen, Manuel Margot*

**The Report:** Alcántara's full-season debut went quite well, considering he spent most of the season as a 19-year-old, and Myrtle Beach is among the worst places to hit in the minors. A projectable, long-limbed power hitter acquired from the Yankees at the 2021 trade deadline, he has a shot to stick in center long term, and a cannon for an arm if he has to slide over to right field. He looks the part of—and takes cuts like—a future 30-home run hitter. His swing decisions however, often looked more like a 19-year-old seeing full-season arms for the first time. Like Davis, Alcántara checks off four of the five tools pretty effortlessly, but between some pitch recognition and swing plane issues, the hit tool will need some further development.

**OFP:** 55 / Above-average outfielder

**Variance:** Very High. Between the long limbs and an at-times stiff cut, swing-and-miss will probably always be somewhat of an issue for Alcántara. He has the kind of power potential that papers over higher K-rates, but for now it remains mostly in the realm of potential.

**Jesse Roche's Fantasy Take:** Even if he falls short of the 30-homer potential his frame presumably promises, he offers intriguing fantasy upside given his present power and speed. As noted above, however, Alcántara has plenty of underlying swing-and-miss given his long levers. There remains a long way to go, and a lot of risk, but his ceiling is so high that it is well worth chasing in dynasty formats. Alcántara is a top-100 dynasty prospect.

## 7 Cade Horton RHP    OFP: 55    ETA: 2025
Born: 08/20/01  Age: 21  Bats: R  Throws: R  Height: 6'1"  Weight: 211 lb.  Origin: Round 1, 2022 Draft (#7 overall)

**The Report:** Horton made a late charge up draft boards with his performance in the college postseason, and perhaps penned the best finishing notes since Shostakovich's Fifth with his 13-strikeout outing in the College World Series. A new power slider in the upper-80s was the key to his breakout, and it looked to be present-plus almost immediately. Horton's fastball is a power pitch as well, sitting mid-90s and touching higher. He was a two-way player for the Sooners and was coming off Tommy John surgery as a draft-eligible sophomore, so he doesn't have a long track record on the mound. So Horton might see larger gains in a pro development program than you would from a more advanced college arm. But the overall profile at the moment feels more like a good two-pitch reliever given his elbow surgery and high-octane delivery.

**OFP:** 55 / no. 3/4 starter or second-division closer

**Variance:** Medium. Horton's present fastball/slider combo gives him a reasonable floor in middle relief, health permitting.

**Jesse Roche's Fantasy Take:** At his best, Horton's high-spin, mid-to-upper-90s fastball and upper-80s wipeout slider match any pitching prospect in this draft class. Given his limited track record, Horton is a bit riskier than other college arms, though he arguably has the highest ceiling. He is a top-200 dynasty prospect.

## 8 Jordan Wicks LHP    OFP: 55    ETA: Late 2023/2024
Born: 09/01/99  Age: 23  Bats: L  Throws: L  Height: 6'3"  Weight: 220 lb.  Origin: Round 1, 2021 Draft (#21 overall)

| YEAR | TEAM | LVL | AGE | W | L | SV | G | GS | IP | H | HR | BB/9 | K/9 | K | GB% | BABIP | WHIP | ERA | DRA- | WARP |
|---|---|---|---|---|---|---|---|---|---|---|---|---|---|---|---|---|---|---|---|---|
| 2021 | SB | A+ | 21 | 0 | 0 | 0 | 4 | 4 | 7 | 7 | 0 | 3.9 | 6.4 | 5 | 37.5% | .304 | 1.43 | 5.14 | 117 | 0.0 |
| 2022 | SB | A+ | 22 | 4 | 3 | 0 | 16 | 16 | 66² | 66 | 5 | 2.3 | 11.6 | 86 | 45.1% | .363 | 1.25 | 3.65 | 69 | 1.8 |
| 2022 | TNS | AA | 22 | 0 | 3 | 0 | 8 | 8 | 28 | 24 | 5 | 3.5 | 11.3 | 35 | 50.0% | .284 | 1.25 | 4.18 | 83 | 0.5 |
| 2023 non-DC | CHC | MLB | 23 | 3 | 3 | 0 | 58 | 0 | 50 | 51 | 6 | 3.7 | 8.3 | 46 | 38.8% | .306 | 1.42 | 4.35 | 113 | -0.1 |

*Comparables: Luis Leroy Cruz, Nik Turley, Chris Reed*

**The Report:** Wicks went in the first round of the 2021 draft on the strength of a polished college arm resume and a potential plus-plus changeup. His 2022 went more or less how you'd expect, although he got off to a bit of a rough start after a midseason promotion to Double-A. His changeup is as advertised, with downright nasty sink and fade and 10+ mph of separation off the fastball. Wicks' fastball sits in a pretty average velocity band, but plays down a bit due to being a "control over command" pitch, at present. He has two breaking ball looks: a firmer slider that offers a tricky left-on-left look, and a big breaking mid-70s curve that has nice 1-7 shape, but shows a bit early to consistently generate chases. Wicks has a bit of a funky arm action, with a stab down and a quick move to a high slot. That adds a bit of deception, but does impact his ability to throw good strikes. As a lefty who throws a lot of changeups and doesn't generally overpower batters, he may be a bit susceptible to bouts of homeritis, but Wicks should be ready to slot into the middle of the Cubs' rotation by the end of this season.

**OFP:** 55 / no. 3/4 starter

**Variance:** Low. Wicks probably is more on the no. 4 side of the line for me given the rather unremarkable nature of his arsenal outside of the change, but it might be such a good changeup the rest won't matter.

**Jesse Roche's Fantasy Take:** Lefties with changeups like Wicks' and otherwise mediocre stuff carry sneaky fantasy upside even if they don't ultimately miss a ton of MLB bats (see Tyler Anderson). It is not the most compelling profile, though, and often can be safely left on waivers outside of leagues with up to 300 prospects.

## 9  James Triantos  3B       OFP: 50     ETA: 2025
Born: 01/29/03   Age: 20   Bats: R   Throws: R   Height: 6'1"   Weight: 195 lb.   Origin: Round 2, 2021 Draft (#56 overall)

| YEAR | TEAM | LVL | AGE | PA | R | 2B | 3B | HR | RBI | BB | K | SB | CS | AVG/OBP/SLG | DRC+ | BABIP | BRR | DRP | WARP |
|------|------|-----|-----|-----|-----|-----|-----|-----|-----|-----|-----|-----|-----|-------------|------|-------|-----|-----|------|
| 2021 | CUB | ROK | 18 | 109 | 27 | 7 | 1 | 6 | 19 | 7 | 18 | 3 | 3 | .327/.376/.594 | | .351 | | | |
| 2022 | MB | A | 19 | 504 | 74 | 19 | 6 | 7 | 50 | 39 | 81 | 20 | 3 | .272/.335/.386 | 112 | .315 | 3.2 | 3B(104) -6.5 | 2.0 |
| 2023 non-DC | CHC | MLB | 20 | 251 | 18 | 10 | 2 | 2 | 20 | 13 | 47 | 4 | 1 | .215/.264/.301 | 59 | .260 | -2.4 | 2B 0, 3B 0 | -0.8 |

*Comparables: Juan Yepez, Juremi Profar, Edilio Colina*

**The Report:** Triantos went right to full-season ball as a second-round prep pick, and a tough place to hit at that. His funky swing generated a few too many groundballs, and way too many pop-ups, but Triantos held his own on balance. That's not enough to keep him on the fringes of the Top 101, but it's something to build off of. He is developing defensively at the hot corner—while seeing some time at second and short as well—but he's going to need to hit all the way up the Cubs' organizational ladder and the early returns were a bit more muted than we expected. Triantos is never going to have traditionally loud corner-bat power numbers, so the hit tool will have to carry him. Considering how young he was compared to the rest of the Carolina League, and considering that the fundamentals of his swing are strong, we'd expect Triantos to bounce back some, if not break out in 2023.

**OFP:** 50 / Average infielder

**Variance:** High. Triantos is unlikely to offer much defensive value, so he will really have to hit. He's unlikely to hit for above-average power for a third baseman, so he will really have to hit. He also may really, really hit.

**Jesse Roche's Fantasy Take:** Triantos barely topped his home run total at the complex in 2021 (6) in nearly 400 more plate appearances last year (7). His compact stroke generates oodles of contact, but lacks much thump at present. On the bright side, Triantos swiped 20 bases last year, with a quick first step that bodes well for long-term stolen-base success. His bat-to-ball ability is so advanced for his age that he should still be rostered in leagues with 200+ prospects.

## 10  Ben Brown  RHP       OFP: 50      ETA: Late 2023/Early 2024
Born: 09/09/99   Age: 23   Bats: R   Throws: R   Height: 6'6"   Weight: 210 lb.   Origin: Round 33, 2017 Draft (#983 overall)

| YEAR | TEAM | LVL | AGE | W | L | SV | G | GS | IP | H | HR | BB/9 | K/9 | K | GB% | BABIP | WHIP | ERA | DRA- | WARP |
|------|------|-----|-----|-----|-----|-----|-----|-----|-----|-----|-----|------|-----|-----|------|-------|------|------|------|------|
| 2021 | JS | A+ | 21 | 0 | 0 | 0 | 4 | 2 | 12 | 12 | 2 | 5.3 | 10.5 | 14 | 46.9% | .333 | 1.58 | 7.50 | 90 | 0.2 |
| 2022 | JS | A+ | 22 | 3 | 5 | 0 | 16 | 15 | 73 | 53 | 7 | 2.8 | 12.9 | 105 | 43.0% | .291 | 1.04 | 3.08 | 88 | 1.0 |
| 2022 | TNS | AA | 22 | 3 | 0 | 0 | 7 | 7 | 31 | 33 | 3 | 3.8 | 12.8 | 44 | 40.5% | .395 | 1.48 | 4.06 | 91 | 0.5 |
| 2023 non-DC | CHC | MLB | 23 | 3 | 3 | 0 | 58 | 0 | 50 | 47 | 8 | 3.9 | 9.0 | 50 | 35.9% | .291 | 1.37 | 4.21 | 110 | 0.0 |

*Comparables: Akeem Bostick, Maikel Cleto, Dae-eun Rhee*

**The Report:** Brown has taken a fairly winding route to prospectdom since he was a cold-weather prep pick for the Phillies over a half-decade ago. He spent parts of five seasons in the low minors, earned a Tommy John scar right before a global pandemic, and finally broke out last year after a velocity jump into the mid-90s. Brown can touch higher than that too, and overpowered minor-league hitters with the ol' number one last year to the tune of a near-35% strikeout rate. He backs it up with two pretty average breaking balls, although his power slider will flash some bat-missing utility. Brown has a very uptempo delivery with some late arm effort, and between the not-so-distant elbow surgery and the command issues, might be best suited for late-inning relief work.

**OFP:** 50 / no. 4 starter or setup man

**Variance:** Medium. A bit more consistency with one of the breaking balls could get Brown into higher-leverage pen opportunities, but conversely the command might end up a half-grade or so short for what you'd prefer in the seventh or eighth inning.

**Jesse Roche's Fantasy Take:** Brown can miss bats in spades largely on the strength of his fastball. That is often a harbinger of good things to come. If his breaking balls and command continue to take steps forward, Brown could skyrocket up rankings. For now, he should be on your radar in leagues with up to 300 prospects.

# Outside the Top Ten:

## 11  Alexander Canario  OF
Born: 05/07/00   Age: 23   Bats: R   Throws: R   Height: 6'1"   Weight: 165 lb.   Origin: International Free Agent, 2016

| YEAR | TEAM | LVL | AGE | PA | R | 2B | 3B | HR | RBI | BB | K | SB | CS | AVG/OBP/SLG | DRC+ | BABIP | BRR | DRP | WARP |
|---|---|---|---|---|---|---|---|---|---|---|---|---|---|---|---|---|---|---|---|
| 2021 | SJ | A | 21 | 274 | 43 | 14 | 3 | 9 | 29 | 33 | 79 | 15 | 3 | .235/.325/.433 | 98 | .307 | 1.0 | LF(22) 1.9, RF(20) 0.3, CF(14) -1.3 | 1.0 |
| 2021 | SB | A+ | 21 | 182 | 19 | 6 | 1 | 9 | 28 | 10 | 46 | 6 | 5 | .224/.264/.429 | 106 | .248 | -1.7 | CF(26) 2.1, RF(18) 0.7 | 0.8 |
| 2022 | SB | A+ | 22 | 100 | 17 | 6 | 0 | 7 | 22 | 10 | 35 | 3 | 0 | .281/.360/.584 | 110 | .383 | -0.6 | RF(12) 0.6, CF(6) -0.8 | 0.4 |
| 2022 | TNS | AA | 22 | 350 | 51 | 18 | 2 | 24 | 61 | 36 | 91 | 17 | 3 | .248/.329/.552 | 117 | .269 | 0.0 | CF(54) 0.9, RF(22) -0.7, LF(6) 0.3 | 2.0 |
| 2022 | IOW | AAA | 22 | 84 | 16 | 2 | 0 | 6 | 14 | 13 | 21 | 3 | 0 | .231/.386/.538 | 115 | .231 | 0.2 | RF(7) 1.0, LF(5) -0.5, CF(4) -0.3 | 0.4 |
| 2023 DC | CHC | MLB | 23 | 61 | 7 | 3 | 0 | 2 | 7 | 5 | 18 | 2 | 0 | .219/.287/.385 | 87 | .288 | 0.1 | LF 0, CF 0 | 0.1 |

Canario would have been a lock to make the top 10 had he not suffered a devastating ankle and shoulder injury while playing in this past season's Dominican Winter League. The power came alive in the regular season with his 37 home runs topping the organization. The pop is generated by his strong frame and near-elite bat speed. He destroys fastballs but his pitch recognition is still an issue and his aggressive approach has him chasing too many breaking pitches out of the zone. Defensively, he can handle center in a pinch but his future home is in a corner. He's slated for a midseason return and while the Cubs are certain to ease him back with time in Iowa, a late-season call-up to Wrigley is a possibility. When it happens, if he can quickly prove that he can handle left-handed pitching, he could carve out a near-term role as a short-side platoon outfielder, with long-term upside well beyond that.

## 12  Daniel Palencia  RHP
Born: 02/05/00   Age: 23   Bats: R   Throws: R   Height: 5'11"   Weight: 160 lb.   Origin: International Free Agent, 2020

| YEAR | TEAM | LVL | AGE | W | L | SV | G | GS | IP | H | HR | BB/9 | K/9 | K | GB% | BABIP | WHIP | ERA | DRA- | WARP |
|---|---|---|---|---|---|---|---|---|---|---|---|---|---|---|---|---|---|---|---|---|
| 2021 | MB | A | 21 | 1 | 0 | 0 | 7 | 7 | 27 | 17 | 2 | 6.0 | 12.7 | 38 | 20.7% | .268 | 1.30 | 3.67 | 114 | 0.0 |
| 2021 | STK | A | 21 | 0 | 2 | 0 | 6 | 6 | 14¹ | 17 | 3 | 3.8 | 8.8 | 14 | 40.5% | .359 | 1.60 | 6.91 | 105 | 0.0 |
| 2022 | SB | A+ | 22 | 1 | 3 | 0 | 21 | 20 | 75¹ | 56 | 7 | 4.2 | 11.7 | 98 | 46.0% | .290 | 1.21 | 3.94 | 64 | 2.2 |
| 2023 non-DC | CHC | MLB | 23 | 3 | 3 | 0 | 58 | 0 | 50 | 49 | 8 | 5.1 | 9.2 | 51 | 33.9% | .301 | 1.55 | 5.13 | 128 | -0.5 |

Comparables: Luis Garcia, Oliver Ortega, Hector Perez

A little-known prospect when acquired from Oakland as part of the 2021 Andrew Chafin trade, Palencia garnered buzz this summer with his triple-digit fastball and much-improved secondaries. He doesn't have the classic starter's build but has added good weight and now possesses a strong, durable frame that should hold up to the rigors of pitching. The fastball jumps out of his hand, getting on hitters in a hurry and producing uncomfortable-looking at-bats. This past season also saw him rely more on a power slider rather than the curve used in the past. He's still developing feel for it but it sits in the low-90s with vertical break, and has the potential to be a true swing-and-miss pitch. A changeup that lags behind and command that can waver put some reliever risk in the profile but with the possibility of two double-plus offerings, Palencia has as much upside as any arm in the organization.

## 13  Miguel Amaya  DH
Born: 03/09/99   Age: 24   Bats: R   Throws: R   Height: 6'2"   Weight: 230 lb.   Origin: International Free Agent, 2015

| YEAR | TEAM | LVL | AGE | PA | R | 2B | 3B | HR | RBI | BB | K | SB | CS | AVG/OBP/SLG | DRC+ | BABIP | BRR | DRP | WARP |
|---|---|---|---|---|---|---|---|---|---|---|---|---|---|---|---|---|---|---|---|
| 2021 | TNS | AA | 22 | 106 | 11 | 4 | 0 | 1 | 13 | 21 | 22 | 2 | 0 | .215/.406/.304 | 127 | .281 | 1.0 | C(12) 0.7, 1B(2) -0.4 | 0.8 |
| 2022 | CUB | ROK | 23 | 44 | 4 | 0 | 0 | 2 | 4 | 7 | 13 | 0 | 0 | .216/.341/.378 | | .273 | | | | |
| 2022 | TNS | AA | 23 | 116 | 15 | 6 | 1 | 4 | 19 | 14 | 28 | 0 | 0 | .278/.379/.485 | 115 | .343 | -1.9 | | 0.3 |
| 2023 non-DC | CHC | MLB | 24 | 251 | 25 | 11 | 1 | 5 | 24 | 26 | 65 | 0 | 0 | .221/.316/.346 | 93 | .291 | -4.4 | C 0, 1B 0 | 0.2 |

Amaya returned to the field in July after 2021 Tommy John surgery and showed flashes of the kind of power that got him onto consecutive Top 101 lists. It's not overly effusive power, and there have always been hit tool questions. That of course doesn't matter if you're a catcher—hitting .250 with 15-20 home runs in a season with a solid glove makes you a true two-way threat. But Amaya spent most of the second half of the year as a designated hitter. Not all that surprising given he was recovering from Tommy John surgery on his throwing arm, but we'll need to see both the offensive and defensive skills on display in 2023 before he moves back into the conversation around top catching prospects.

## 14    Cristian Hernández   IF
Born: 12/13/03   Age: 19   Bats: R   Throws: R   Height: 6'2"   Weight: 175 lb.   Origin: International Free Agent, 2021

| YEAR | TEAM | LVL | AGE | PA | R | 2B | 3B | HR | RBI | BB | K | SB | CS | AVG/OBP/SLG | DRC+ | BABIP | BRR | DRP | WARP |
|------|------|-----|-----|----|---|----|----|----|-----|----|---|----|----|-------------|------|-------|-----|-----|------|
| 2021 | DSL CUBB | ROK | 17 | 191 | 38 | 5 | 1 | 5 | 22 | 30 | 39 | 21 | 3 | .285/.398/.424 | | .345 | | | |
| 2022 | CUB | ROK | 18 | 175 | 21 | 4 | 1 | 3 | 21 | 13 | 53 | 6 | 3 | .261/.320/.357 | | .365 | | | |

Signed for $3 million as the top name in the Cubs' 2021 IFA class, Hernández has now spent two seasons in the complex—one in the Dominican, one in Arizona. Since he hasn't had a loud statistical breakout, hit full-season ball or had his Bowman cards selling for six figures, he might be flying under the radar a bit as a shortstop prospect, especially in a beefed-up Cubs farm system. And yes, nothing from his summer in Mesa pops on the player card. You'd have hoped for more power from a player unfortunately nicknamed "Baby A-Rod" right around when he signed, but his high-end exit velocities are quite good. And despite a 30% K-rate, his overall contact profile doesn't have any glaring weaknesses especially when you consider his age. So you might be waiting a bit longer to see him in this organization's top 10, but given that Hernández was born the same week that *The Lord of the Rings: Return of the King* was released, patience can be a virtue (which also applies if you are sitting through a screening of the director's cut of *The Lord of the Rings: Return of the King*).

## 15    Jackson Ferris   LHP
Born: 01/15/04   Age: 19   Bats: L   Throws: L   Height: 6'4"   Weight: 195 lb.   Origin: Round 2, 2022 Draft (#47 overall)

Drafted in the second round out of IMG this past summer, Ferris is a tall, projectable lefty who can run his fastball up into the mid-90s and has a potential plus curveball backing up the heater. His delivery is a bit unusual, as it looks sort of like he's about to fall out of a rocking chair as he lets go of the ball, but he's in the zone with the fastball enough, and can start the breaker there as well. The track record for non-elite prep prospects has been sketchy for a bit, but Ferris has the kind of present and projectable profile that you look for in a potential future mid-rotation high school arm.

## 16    DJ Herz   LHP
Born: 01/04/01   Age: 22   Bats: R   Throws: L   Height: 6'2"   Weight: 175 lb.   Origin: Round 8, 2019 Draft (#252 overall)

| YEAR | TEAM | LVL | AGE | W | L | SV | G | GS | IP | H | HR | BB/9 | K/9 | K | GB% | BABIP | WHIP | ERA | DRA- | WARP |
|------|------|-----|-----|---|---|----|---|----|----|---|----|------|-----|---|-----|-------|------|-----|------|------|
| 2021 | MB | A | 20 | 3 | 4 | 0 | 17 | 17 | 65² | 32 | 6 | 5.2 | 14.4 | 105 | 30.9% | .252 | 1.07 | 3.43 | 81 | 1.4 |
| 2021 | SB | A+ | 20 | 1 | 0 | 0 | 3 | 3 | 16 | 10 | 1 | 3.4 | 14.6 | 26 | 51.6% | .300 | 1.00 | 2.81 | 76 | 0.4 |
| 2022 | SB | A+ | 21 | 2 | 2 | 0 | 17 | 17 | 63² | 33 | 3 | 5.2 | 14.0 | 99 | 41.8% | .252 | 1.10 | 2.26 | 77 | 1.4 |
| 2022 | TNS | AA | 21 | 1 | 4 | 0 | 9 | 9 | 31² | 24 | 5 | 9.4 | 11.9 | 42 | 35.1% | .275 | 1.80 | 8.24 | 127 | -0.1 |
| *2023 non-DC* | CHC | MLB | 22 | 3 | 3 | 0 | 58 | 0 | 50 | 42 | 7 | 6.6 | 11.6 | 65 | 33.2% | .299 | 1.58 | 4.92 | 121 | -0.3 |

*Comparables: Andrew Faulkner, Patrick Sandoval, Daniel Norris*

A plus changeup will get you plenty of outs in the low minors, just like it did for Herz during his breakout 2021 season. An over-slot prep arm nabbed in the eighth round of the 2019 draft, he utilized his *cambio* and funky delivery to generate plenty of awkward swings during his time in A-ball. His first taste of adversity came after a July promotion to Tennessee, where he found the advanced Southern League hitters less likely to chase and more adept at pouncing on low-90s fastballs left in the zone. The results were ugly, with 33 walks and 29 earned runs given up in just 31 innings. He's still young and will likely get a full year of Double-A in 2023 but he'll need to improve his control and find ways to stay off the barrel if he's going to find success in the upper minors and beyond.

## 17    Luis Devers   RHP
Born: 04/24/00   Age: 23   Bats: R   Throws: R   Height: 6'3"   Weight: 178 lb.

| YEAR | TEAM | LVL | AGE | W | L | SV | G | GS | IP | H | HR | BB/9 | K/9 | K | GB% | BABIP | WHIP | ERA | DRA- | WARP |
|------|------|-----|-----|---|---|----|---|----|----|---|----|------|-----|---|-----|-------|------|-----|------|------|
| 2021 | CUB | ROK | 21 | 2 | 4 | 0 | 12 | 11 | 51¹ | 48 | 3 | 2.5 | 9.5 | 54 | 48.6% | .319 | 1.21 | 3.33 | | |
| 2022 | MB | A | 22 | 9 | 3 | 0 | 15 | 14 | 66¹ | 57 | 3 | 1.9 | 10.2 | 75 | 53.2% | .321 | 1.07 | 2.58 | 76 | 1.6 |
| 2022 | SB | A+ | 22 | 4 | 0 | 0 | 11 | 8 | 51¹ | 29 | 1 | 2.1 | 8.2 | 47 | 50.8% | .217 | 0.80 | 1.05 | 93 | 0.7 |
| *2023 non-DC* | CHC | MLB | 23 | 3 | 3 | 0 | 58 | 0 | 50 | 54 | 7 | 3.3 | 7.0 | 39 | 40.3% | .310 | 1.46 | 4.67 | 120 | -0.3 |

A low-level signee out of the Dominican in 2017, Devers had put up solid numbers in his limited DSL and Rookie league stints but excelled this year, his first full season stateside. Despite his lack of prospect clout, his 1.91 ERA over two A-ball levels helped earn him Cubs' Minor League Pitcher of the Year honors. His fastball jumped a few ticks last offseason but still sits in an average velocity band. He does, however, locate it well and finds ways to keep it off the barrels of opposing hitters. He replicates the same arm speed as the fastball with his spin-killing changeup. It sits an easy 10 mph slower and generates plenty of weak contact. He'll mix in the occasional breaking pitch, but it currently lacks feel and is basically used to steal a strike. He's going to be challenged in 2023 by the advanced hitters of the Southern League and like all finesse pitchers, there's very little margin for error.

## 18  Moises Ballesteros  C/DH
Born: 11/08/03   Age: 19   Bats: L   Throws: R   Height: 5'10"   Weight: 195 lb.   Origin: International Free Agent, 2021

| YEAR | TEAM | LVL | AGE | PA | R | 2B | 3B | HR | RBI | BB | K | SB | CS | AVG/OBP/SLG | DRC+ | BABIP | BRR | DRP | WARP |
|---|---|---|---|---|---|---|---|---|---|---|---|---|---|---|---|---|---|---|---|
| 2021 | DSL CUBR | ROK | 17 | 187 | 22 | 10 | 0 | 3 | 25 | 31 | 24 | 6 | 1 | .266/.396/.390 | | .299 | | | |
| 2022 | CUB | ROK | 18 | 110 | 12 | 5 | 0 | 7 | 18 | 13 | 19 | 0 | 0 | .268/.355/.536 | | .268 | | | |
| 2022 | MB | A | 18 | 129 | 17 | 7 | 0 | 3 | 15 | 18 | 28 | 0 | 1 | .248/.349/.394 | 104 | .300 | -1.5 | C(18) -1.2 | 0.2 |
| 2023 non-DC | CHC | MLB | 19 | 251 | 20 | 10 | 2 | 2 | 20 | 19 | 78 | 2 | 0 | .212/.278/.303 | 65 | .310 | -3.5 | C 0, 1B 0 | -0.6 |

Comparables: Francisco Peña, Lana Akau, Ramón Flores

The Cubs' other major IFA signing in 2021, Ballesteros is more advanced than Hernández, making it all the way to full-season ball last year while showing advanced feel to hit for a teenager. He has a smooth left-handed swing that covers the zone well and there's some potential game pop down the line as well. Ballesteros is already pretty hefty and isn't the twitchiest defender behind the plate, so his defense will warrant monitoring further up the ladder, but the upside here is an everyday catcher who doesn't have to hide at the bottom of the lineup.

## 19  Javier Assad  RHP
Born: 07/30/97   Age: 25   Bats: R   Throws: R   Height: 6'1"   Weight: 200 lb.   Origin: International Free Agent, 2015

| YEAR | TEAM | LVL | AGE | W | L | SV | G | GS | IP | H | HR | BB/9 | K/9 | K | GB% | BABIP | WHIP | ERA | DRA- | WARP |
|---|---|---|---|---|---|---|---|---|---|---|---|---|---|---|---|---|---|---|---|---|
| 2021 | TNS | AA | 23 | 4 | 8 | 0 | 21 | 20 | 93 | 111 | 12 | 3.1 | 7.2 | 74 | 41.8% | .341 | 1.54 | 5.32 | 119 | 0.0 |
| 2022 | TNS | AA | 24 | 4 | 1 | 0 | 15 | 14 | 71² | 68 | 6 | 3.5 | 9.3 | 74 | 43.3% | .330 | 1.34 | 2.51 | 96 | 0.9 |
| 2022 | IOW | AAA | 24 | 1 | 2 | 0 | 8 | 7 | 36² | 31 | 4 | 1.7 | 9.1 | 37 | 46.1% | .276 | 1.04 | 2.95 | 88 | 0.7 |
| 2022 | CHC | MLB | 24 | 2 | 2 | 0 | 9 | 8 | 37² | 35 | 4 | 4.8 | 7.2 | 30 | 41.4% | .277 | 1.46 | 3.11 | 118 | 0.0 |
| 2023 DC | CHC | MLB | 25 | 4 | 3 | 0 | 32 | 3 | 39.3 | 44 | 6 | 3.7 | 7.2 | 31 | 40.2% | .317 | 1.52 | 5.05 | 125 | -0.1 |

Comparables: Alec Asher, Stephen Fife, Chase De Jong

I half-remember asking about Assad after a fairly solid stateside debut in 2016. As I hazily recall, I got back something along the lines of "physically maxed" and "strike-throwing over stuff." And sure enough, six years later he's still rather stocky and sits mostly in the low-90s with his fastball, while showing six different pitch looks, none of which really pop, but all of which can be effective enough. And after throwing 37 ⅔ effective enough major-league innings, Assad is in some ways less a prospect than he's ever been. But prospect lists are ultimately about major-league value, and he is ready to provide it.

## 20  Luke Little  LHP
Born: 08/30/00   Age: 22   Bats: L   Throws: L   Height: 6'8"   Weight: 220 lb.   Origin: Round 4, 2020 Draft (#117 overall)

| YEAR | TEAM | LVL | AGE | W | L | SV | G | GS | IP | H | HR | BB/9 | K/9 | K | GB% | BABIP | WHIP | ERA | DRA- | WARP |
|---|---|---|---|---|---|---|---|---|---|---|---|---|---|---|---|---|---|---|---|---|
| 2021 | CUB | ROK | 20 | 0 | 1 | 0 | 5 | 4 | 11 | 6 | 1 | 4.1 | 15.5 | 19 | 33.3% | .250 | 1.00 | 4.91 | | |
| 2022 | MB | A | 21 | 1 | 4 | 0 | 20 | 19 | 52² | 37 | 0 | 5.5 | 14.4 | 84 | 57.0% | .325 | 1.31 | 2.91 | 73 | 1.3 |
| 2022 | SB | A+ | 21 | 0 | 1 | 0 | 4 | 3 | 13 | 6 | 0 | 4.2 | 11.8 | 17 | 52.0% | .240 | 0.92 | 0.69 | 86 | 0.2 |
| 2023 non-DC | CHC | MLB | 22 | 3 | 3 | 0 | 58 | 0 | 50 | 45 | 6 | 5.2 | 9.8 | 55 | 40.0% | .296 | 1.48 | 4.46 | 113 | -0.1 |

Little got attention as a JuCo arm after popping 105 in...well, let's call it a controlled laboratory environment. That's, uh, premium velocity even in the 2020s, but he's settled more in around 95 as a starter in the Cubs' system. That's plenty of velocity even in the 2020s, especially when it comes way out in front from a 6-foot-7 lefty. The fastball—and everything else—doesn't come from the most fluid delivery, however, and Little's arm path tends to go every which way. Walks have been an issue, but his fastball/breaking ball combo misses plenty of bats, so if and when he does end up in the pen, the stuff will play.

## Top Talents 25 and Under (as of 4/1/2023):

1. Nico Hoerner, SS/2B
2. Pete Crow-Armstrong, OF
3. Owen Caissie, OF
4. Matt Mervis, 1B
5. Hayden Wesneski, RHP
6. Brennen Davis, OF
7. Kevin Alcántara, OF
8. Christopher Morel, UT
9. Cade Horton, RHP
10. Jackson Ferris, LHP

The Chicago Cubs spent more of their season fretting about the potential departure of Willson Contreras than being able to envision playoff contention, but the brightest spark of their season by the time October rolled around was Hoerner. While Nick Madrigal (age 26) had a disappointing, injury-squashed campaign, his compatriot in contact-dom put together the type of season that made the Cubbies feel it was time to dip their toe back into contention. While that toe won't likely get them all the way there, Hoerner's progression from likely second baseman to cromulent shortstop (who...will be playing second) while striking out at a numerical rate that would be easily accessible on cable TV has made him a column that a more robust big-league roster can be built upon. Although Morel carved more of a bench role in his debut season, the versatile Dominican showcased top-notch athleticism even as his rawness bled through into inconsistent defense, basestealing and pitch selection. The 24-year-old desperately needs to elevate the ball more consistently to make the most of his powerful, compact frame, but a bit more contact of any kind would likely do wonders as a starting block.

# Chicago White Sox

## The State of the System:

The White Sox system remains shallow, but it is at least improving at the top.

## The Top Ten:

### 1 Colson Montgomery SS    OFP: 60    ETA: 2024

Born: 02/27/02   Age: 21   Bats: L   Throws: R   Height: 6'4"   Weight: 205 lb.   Origin: Round 1, 2021 Draft (#22 overall)

| YEAR | TEAM | LVL | AGE | PA | R | 2B | 3B | HR | RBI | BB | K | SB | CS | AVG/OBP/SLG | DRC+ | BABIP | BRR | DRP | WARP |
|------|------|-----|-----|----|----|----|----|----|-----|----|----|----|----|-------------|------|-------|-----|-----|------|
| 2021 | WSX | ROK | 19 | 111 | 16 | 7 | 0 | 0 | 7 | 13 | 22 | 0 | 1 | .287/.396/.362 | | .375 | | | |
| 2022 | KAN | A | 20 | 205 | 31 | 12 | 1 | 4 | 26 | 26 | 42 | 0 | 1 | .324/.424/.476 | 125 | .402 | 1.3 | SS(41) 0.1 | 1.3 |
| 2022 | WS | A+ | 20 | 164 | 22 | 4 | 1 | 5 | 14 | 26 | 26 | 1 | 0 | .258/.387/.417 | 126 | .282 | -0.7 | SS(37) 0.6 | 1.0 |
| 2022 | BIR | AA | 20 | 52 | 5 | 1 | 0 | 2 | 7 | 2 | 15 | 0 | 0 | .146/.192/.292 | 99 | .156 | -0.3 | SS(14) -1.5 | 0.0 |
| 2023 non-DC | CHW | MLB | 21 | 251 | 21 | 10 | 2 | 3 | 21 | 21 | 53 | 0 | 0 | .222/.295/.319 | 76 | .278 | -4.3 | SS 0 | -0.4 |

*Comparables: Ian Desmond, Kaleb Cowart, Ramiro Pena*

**The Report:** The report on Montgomery prior to his full-season debut had him as a strong overall talent with a high level of polish considering he was a prep pick. He's backed that up with an excellent debut campaign, along the way displaying the tools that should carry him to the majors. Montgomery's most apparent and most important trait is a plus hit tool. In addition to a natural feel for the barrel despite his lengthy frame, he carries a surprisingly advanced and disciplined all-fields approach paired with an ability to recognize spin. The power projection is more above-average than plus, but he has some present strength and I think there's an extra gear in there if he's able to optimize it.

Montgomery isn't a stiff at short, but his actions can be disconnected at times. His arm is strong and the range, at present, is fine, but a slide over to third isn't out of the question. Montgomery dominated Low-A for half a season but was merely above-average following his promotion to the Sally League. He hit the ground running in 2022 and we are forecasting more of the same for 2023.

**OFP:** 60 / Plus shortstop with most of the production coming from the offensive side.

**Variance:** Medium. Montgomery still has to prove that he can perform in the upper minors, and there is a chance he will ultimately move to a less difficult spot on the dirt.

**Jesse Roche's Fantasy Take:** Montgomery has consistently received comps to Corey Seager due to his size, swing and, um, looks. His tools support the comps, even if he is hit over power right now. He floundered in the second half between High- and Double-A, hitting just .174/.281/.296 over his final 33 games. That cratering performance leaves a poor aftertaste on what was otherwise a wildly successful 20-year-old season. So while Montgomery may not develop into the next Corey Seager, he still is quite a promising hitter and a top-100 fantasy prospect with clear top-50 upside should his power emerge in games.

---

### Eyewitness Report: Colson Montgomery

**Evaluator:** Ben Spanier

**Report Date:** 07/07/2022

**Dates Seen:** several Apr, May, Jun

**Risk Factor:** Medium

**Physical/Health:** Tall, high-waisted, large frame with broad shoulders. Good athlete but movements aren't always fluid, especially in the lower body. Slight physical projection possible.

| Tool | Future Grade | Report |
|---|---|---|
| Hit | 60 | Fairly quiet, assured set-up with some rhythmic pre-pitch hand movement, slightly open stance with very small leg kick. Excellent barrel ability, very good plate discipline and approach, has ability to recognize spin/location and adjust, can use all fields. Has handled anything thrown at him at this level. |
| Power | 55 | Expecting power output to tick up on account of large, broad-shouldered frame with strength throughout, some physical projection, decent bat speed and leverage in swing. Seems to use contact-minded approach for the most part, but advanced plate discipline and pitch recognition bodes well for increased pop as he should be able to pick out pitches to turn on and drive when he desires it. He may very well get to a plus grade here, but not assuming it. |
| Baserunning/ Speed | 40 | Below-average runner already, might slow further as he continues to grow into his body. |
| Glove | 50 | Has enough range and arm to play an average shortstop, though upper and lower-body movements can be somewhat disconnected at times. Not always the smoothest, but generally makes the plays. Should handle third or second if he has to move off position. |
| Arm | 55 | Plays overhand or sidearm, plenty strong enough for any IF position. |

**Conclusion:** 60 OFP is based on well above-average offensive production for shortstop position, overall grade might get dinged slightly if move to 3B/2B proves necessary. While there is some negative variance re: the positional fit, there is positive variance depending on power output. Will be an impactful offensively-minded player regardless.

## 2 Oscar Colas OF    OFP: 55    ETA: 2023

Born: 09/17/98    Age: 24    Bats: L    Throws: L    Height: 6'1"    Weight: 209 lb.    Origin: International Free Agent, 2022

| YEAR | TEAM | LVL | AGE | PA | R | 2B | 3B | HR | RBI | BB | K | SB | CS | AVG/OBP/SLG | DRC+ | BABIP | BRR | DRP | WARP |
|---|---|---|---|---|---|---|---|---|---|---|---|---|---|---|---|---|---|---|---|
| 2022 | WS | A+ | 23 | 268 | 37 | 13 | 3 | 7 | 42 | 22 | 54 | 1 | 1 | .311/.369/.475 | 108 | .375 | -1.5 | CF(54) -4.0 | 0.6 |
| 2022 | BIR | AA | 23 | 225 | 39 | 9 | 1 | 14 | 33 | 14 | 54 | 1 | 2 | .306/.364/.563 | 122 | .355 | 0.7 | RF(32) 0.1, CF(12) -1.0 | 1.5 |
| 2022 | CLT | AAA | 23 | 33 | 5 | 2 | 0 | 2 | 4 | 2 | 12 | 1 | 1 | .387/.424/.645 | 79 | .588 | 0.2 | CF(4) 0.3, RF(2) -0.3 | 0.0 |
| 2023 DC | CHW | MLB | 24 | 482 | 50 | 19 | 3 | 11 | 50 | 29 | 134 | 4 | 2 | .225/.282/.352 | 77 | .298 | -0.7 | CF 0, RF 0 | -0.2 |

*Comparables: Adam Haseley, Andre Ethier, Anthony Webster*

**The Report:** There were quite a few shouts on White Sox Twitter for a Colas call-up in late summer, a reasonable request when considering that two of the primary Sox right fielders in 2022 came through the system as first basemen and the third was posting a well-below-average DRC+. Right field is the natural landing spot for Colas, both because of team need and because--though he is capable of handling center in a pinch—his speed and arm are average to above-average more than they are spectacular.

What is spectacular is the power, resulting from the merging of clear physical strength with wicked bat speed. The ball just carries differently when he makes solid contact—opposite-field liners sail past the outfielder for extra bases, pop-ups carry to the warning track. It's plus pop at least, and Colas really began tapping into it following a July promotion to Double-A—he hit 16 bombs in 58 games the rest of the way. I've been at least slightly worried about the hit tool and the strikeout rate does still run a bit high, but any approach or swing-and-miss issues have not put a damper on his ability to wreck the majority of opposing pitchers. There will likely be a learning curve against big-league breaking stuff, but Colas should finally be getting the call early next season.

**OFP:** 55 / Slugging corner outfield bat

**Variance:** Low. There is some hit tool risk but he should be able to make enough contact for the pop to play.

**Jesse Roche's Fantasy Take:** Colas' aggressive approach (55% swing rate) is concerning, but, as long as it is married with 70%+ contact rates and oodles of loud contact, it shouldn't be a detriment to his long-term success. With the MLB club starved for left-handed impact bats and corner outfield defense (see above), Colas could land an everyday role as soon as early 2023. Given his power potential and proximity, he is a top-100 fantasy prospect with underrated short- and long-term upside.

## 3  Bryan Ramos  3B   OFP: 55   ETA: 2024

Born: 03/12/02  Age: 21  Bats: R  Throws: R  Height: 6'2"  Weight: 190 lb.  Origin: International Free Agent, 2018

| YEAR | TEAM | LVL | AGE | PA | R | 2B | 3B | HR | RBI | BB | K | SB | CS | AVG/OBP/SLG | DRC+ | BABIP | BRR | DRP | WARP |
|---|---|---|---|---|---|---|---|---|---|---|---|---|---|---|---|---|---|---|---|
| 2021 | KAN | A | 19 | 504 | 64 | 23 | 6 | 13 | 57 | 51 | 110 | 13 | 4 | .244/.345/.415 | 103 | .295 | 1.4 | 3B(34) 1.1, 2B(25) -0.2 | 1.8 |
| 2022 | WS | A+ | 20 | 433 | 64 | 16 | 1 | 19 | 74 | 40 | 71 | 1 | 0 | .275/.350/.471 | 125 | .291 | 2.6 | 3B(86) -0.3 | 2.6 |
| 2022 | BIR | AA | 20 | 86 | 8 | 3 | 0 | 3 | 12 | 5 | 15 | 0 | 1 | .225/.279/.375 | 107 | .242 | -0.3 | 3B(10) 0.0, 2B(8) -0.2 | 0.3 |
| 2023 non-DC | CHW | MLB | 21 | 251 | 22 | 10 | 1 | 5 | 24 | 16 | 57 | 2 | 0 | .216/.277/.334 | 73 | .267 | -3.6 | 2B 0, 3B 0 | -0.5 |

Comparables: Josh Vitters, Maikel Franco, Blake DeWitt

**The Report:** He lacks some of the flash and fame of Colas—for the moment at least—but Ramos is four years younger than his org mate and only one level behind him. The 20-year-old's production was somewhat uneven. He jumped out to a scalding start at High-A Winston-Salem, but cooled down somewhat as the season wore on, and then struggled in a late-season cameo for Double-A Birmingham.

Ramos possesses clear plus pop to all fields, something that has been evident since his time with Low-A Kannapolis. What he was able to do this past season is tap into his latent hitting ability—for a young power hitter his swing is fluid and versatile, and he is able to move the barrel to pitches in all four quadrants of the zone. He is quick on inside heat, stays on breaking stuff and hits everything hard. He already has a large frame and has migrated around a bit defensively, but at present he can handle the hot corner with his average glove and strong arm. Next year he'll have to adjust to Double-A, but I think he'll manage it well.

**OFP:** 55 / Above-average power-hitting third baseman.

**Variance:** Medium. Ramos hasn't adjusted to Double-A pitching yet and might have to move off third base as he ages.

**Jesse Roche's Fantasy Take:** Ramos may be the most underrated fantasy prospect in this system. In fact, he was the *only* prospect in the minors last year under 21 years old all season with 18+ home runs (22) and a strikeout rate under 20% (16.6%). His blend of power and bat-to-ball ability is uncommon. Although he likely doesn't have high-end upside, Ramos is a top-200 fantasy prospect, and he projects to be a valuable long-term contributor, especially at an increasingly shallow third base.

## 4  Norge Vera  RHP   OFP: 55   ETA: 2024

Born: 06/01/00  Age: 23  Bats: R  Throws: R  Height: 6'4"  Weight: 185 lb.  Origin: International Free Agent, 2021

| YEAR | TEAM | LVL | AGE | W | L | SV | G | GS | IP | H | HR | BB/9 | K/9 | K | GB% | BABIP | WHIP | ERA | DRA- | WARP |
|---|---|---|---|---|---|---|---|---|---|---|---|---|---|---|---|---|---|---|---|---|
| 2021 | DSL WSX | ROK | 21 | 1 | 0 | 0 | 8 | 7 | 19 | 9 | 0 | 2.4 | 16.1 | 34 | 73.3% | .300 | 0.74 | 0.00 | | |
| 2022 | KAN | A | 22 | 0 | 2 | 0 | 8 | 8 | 24 | 12 | 1 | 5.6 | 13.1 | 35 | 51.0% | .229 | 1.13 | 1.88 | 82 | 0.5 |
| 2022 | BIR | AA | 22 | 0 | 0 | 0 | 3 | 3 | 8 | 5 | 0 | 13.5 | 13.5 | 12 | 37.5% | .313 | 2.13 | 5.62 | 119 | 0.0 |
| 2023 non-DC | CHW | MLB | 23 | 3 | 3 | 0 | 58 | 0 | 50 | 46 | 8 | 7.2 | 10.2 | 56 | 38.0% | .297 | 1.72 | 5.50 | 135 | -0.6 |

Comparables: John Simms, Joe Gardner, Brandon Bailey

**The Report:** It was nearly a year-and-a-half between Vera's signing day and his stateside debut, owing to injury issues and other concerns. This left plenty of time for the hype machine to get rolling, and for the most part the 22-year-old didn't disappoint. Vera stands 6-foot-4 with the ideal hurler's frame and owns a fastball that I've graded as a plus-plus. The pitch sat 94-96 on my looks, touching a couple ticks higher and explodes through the zone with the illusion of "rise."

Vera possesses more control than command at present, but his delivery is clean and he has shown feel for locating the fastball up, which is where it plays best. There is also some deception in his motion, which begins deliberately, but eventually leads to a last-second burst of a quick arm action out of a high slot. His main secondary is a true overhand curve that seemed sluggish in his first couple of starts but appeared more promising on my third look. The pitch shows great depth and at times sharp and late movement, projecting above-average and occasionally flashing plus, contrasting well with the number one when located at the bottom of the zone. The change is a show-me pitch at present, but it's improved command and consistent execution of the curve that will get Vera where he needs to go.

**OFP:** 55 / High-end but inconsistent third starter or sometimes dominant late-inning reliever

**Variance:** High. Vera still needs to make improvements in command and consistency of pitch execution.

**Jesse Roche's Fantasy Take:** Vera made his stateside debut this year and promptly ran up a 20.1% walk rate behind just 57% strikes across three levels. Not good. His fastball/curveball combo elicits whiffs, but he'll need to seriously improve his command and control to develop into an impact fantasy arm.

## 5 Cristian Mena  RHP     OFP: 55     ETA: 2024

Born: 12/21/02   Age: 20   Bats: R   Throws: R   Height: 6'2"   Weight: 170 lb.   Origin: International Free Agent, 2019

| YEAR | TEAM | LVL | AGE | W | L | SV | G | GS | IP | H | HR | BB/9 | K/9 | K | GB% | BABIP | WHIP | ERA | DRA- | WARP |
|------|------|-----|-----|---|---|----|----|----|------|----|----|------|------|----|-------|-------|------|------|------|------|
| 2021 | WSX | ROK | 18 | 1 | 4 | 0 | 13 | 12 | 48¹ | 69 | 8 | 3.9 | 11.5 | 62 | 48.6% | .442 | 1.86 | 7.82 | | |
| 2022 | KAN | A | 19 | 1 | 2 | 0 | 11 | 11 | 53² | 45 | 2 | 2.5 | 11.1 | 66 | 45.1% | .328 | 1.12 | 2.68 | 86 | 1.0 |
| 2022 | WS | A+ | 19 | 1 | 3 | 0 | 10 | 10 | 40² | 39 | 4 | 4.9 | 10.4 | 47 | 44.5% | .330 | 1.50 | 4.65 | 89 | 0.5 |
| 2022 | BIR | AA | 19 | 0 | 1 | 0 | 3 | 3 | 10 | 16 | 1 | 0.9 | 11.7 | 13 | 35.5% | .500 | 1.70 | 6.30 | 98 | 0.1 |
| 2023 non-DC | CHW | MLB | 20 | 3 | 3 | 0 | 58 | 0 | 50 | 54 | 8 | 4.1 | 7.8 | 44 | 35.5% | .310 | 1.53 | 5.09 | 129 | -0.5 |

*Comparables: Franklin Pérez, Luis Patiño, Francis Martes*

**The Report:** Another White Sox IFA arm with an overhand slot, Mena is smaller-framed than his teammate Vera but nearly as powerful. He is also three years younger while taking on roughly the same competition. He has what would have been considered a very modern pitching profile a year or two ago—high-spin fastball/curve combo that plays best when the heater is thrown up in the zone and the breaker is located down. Both pitches could end up plus for Mena but the curve is a safer bet to get there. The best version of the pitch is slurvy in a positive way—upper-70s to lower-80s with sharp vertical and horizontal action—but I've also seen him mix in a slower curve to steal called strikes against lefties. Most effective working glove-side and down, the hook gets whiffs against both lefties and righties. Mena's fastball is low-to-mid 90s at present, but plays well when located properly, and he has a feel for pitching that is ahead of his age. His numbers suffered a bit when the 19-year-old was promoted to High-A, but even there he was managing a healthy strikeout rate against older and more advanced bats. Look for Mena in this upcoming season to consolidate with command and changeup gains.

**OFP:** 55 / Mid-rotation starter or back-end reliever.

**Variance:** High. As a primarily two-pitch guy, Mena will need to continue to lock in his command

**Jesse Roche's Fantasy Take:** Mena was one of four pitching prospects who finished the season in Double-A at just 19 years old. The other three? Eury Pérez, Andrew Painter and Ricky Tiedemann. That is very good company. As noted above, Mena can spin it, and his curveball carved through lineups all year. Should he continue to improve his fastball's sitting velocity, he could truly break out next year.

## 6 Noah Schultz  LHP     OFP: 55     ETA: 2026

Born: 08/05/03   Age: 19   Bats: L   Throws: L   Height: 6'9"   Weight: 220 lb.   Origin: Round 1, 2022 Draft (#26 overall)

**The Report:** The White Sox shelled out almost $3 million to buy out Schultz's Vanderbilt commitment, and the lanky lefty immediately became the highest-upside arm in the South Side's system. A projectable 6-foot-9 skyscraper, he works from a low-three-quarters slot with a fastball he dials up to the mid-90s and a big, sweeping upper-70s slider that he can run right off the deck. Schultz also has reasonable feel for a low-80s change given his lack of experience on the mound. That lack of experience isn't just age-related though, as he's missed a lot of time on the mound as an amateur, to the point he was pitching in local summer ball to add some reps.

**OFP:** 55 / no. 3/4 starter or late-inning reliever

**Variance:** Extreme. There's plenty of ceiling to dream on here, but we'll need to see Schultz in pro ball to start making those dreams a prospect-ranking reality.

**Jesse Roche's Fantasy Take:** Schultz offers as much ceiling as height. As projectable as they come, he already flashes mid-90s velocity from a unique release point with a bat-missing slider. For those chasing lottery tickets with late-round FYPD picks, Schultz is a worthwhile gamble.

## 7 Peyton Pallette  RHP     OFP: 55     ETA: 2025

Born: 05/09/01   Age: 22   Bats: R   Throws: R   Height: 6'1"   Weight: 180 lb.   Origin: Round 2, 2022 Draft (#62 overall)

**The Report:** Another in the long line of 2022 college picks dealing with a recent UCL tear, Pallette missed all of his junior season after a preseason Tommy John surgery. You could certainly argue that the White Sox got a first-round talent in the second, as a healthy Pallette likely would have been one of the first college arms due to his lively fastball and high-spin curve. He is a shorter righty with limited college innings and an elbow scar, so we don't really know what even the medium-term forecast is for Pallette, but broadly speaking if the stuff comes back and he shows the ability to hold it deep into games across a pro season, he's a potential mid-rotation starter. Those questions may not get answered until 2024 though.

**OFP:** 55 / no. 3/4 starter or late-inning reliever

**Variance:** High. Pallette is coming off Tommy John surgery and didn't have consistently dominant performances in college. The fastball/curve combo is legit, but there's development work to be done.

**Jesse Roche's Fantasy Take:** The White Sox may have a type: pitching prospects with arm strength and high-spin curveballs. Pallette is firmly on brand with arguably the best curveball in the 2022 draft class. Outside the curve, however, he has a risky fantasy profile due to his size, pre-injury command, fastball shape and, of course, health.

## 8 Jose Rodriguez  MI      OFP: 50      ETA: 2024
Born: 05/13/01   Age: 22   Bats: R   Throws: R   Height: 5'11"   Weight: 175 lb.   Origin: International Free Agent, 2018

| YEAR | TEAM | LVL | AGE | PA | R | 2B | 3B | HR | RBI | BB | K | SB | CS | AVG/OBP/SLG | DRC+ | BABIP | BRR | DRP | WARP |
|------|------|-----|-----|-----|-----|-----|-----|-----|-----|-----|-----|-----|-----|-------------|------|-------|------|-----|------|
| 2021 | GDD | WIN | 20 | 66 | 5 | 1 | 1 | 1 | 13 | 4 | 10 | 2 | 0 | .226/.273/.323 | | .255 | | | |
| 2021 | KAN | A | 20 | 361 | 58 | 22 | 4 | 9 | 32 | 21 | 57 | 20 | 5 | .283/.328/.452 | 111 | .317 | 1.8 | SS(71) -8.9, 2B(3) 0.1 | 0.9 |
| 2021 | WS | A+ | 20 | 126 | 19 | 4 | 1 | 5 | 19 | 5 | 13 | 10 | 5 | .361/.381/.538 | 138 | .369 | -1.7 | SS(29) -4.0 | 0.4 |
| 2022 | BIR | AA | 21 | 484 | 75 | 21 | 6 | 11 | 68 | 38 | 66 | 40 | 10 | .280/.340/.430 | 106 | .308 | 3.7 | SS(53) -1.0, 2B(43) -0.4 | 2.0 |
| 2023 DC | CHW | MLB | 22 | 27 | 3 | 1 | 0 | 0 | 3 | 1 | 5 | 1 | 1 | .227/.272/.331 | 70 | .266 | -0.1 | 2B 0 | 0.0 |

*Comparables: Henry Alejandro Rodriguez, Domingo Leyba, Gavin Cecchini*

**The Report:** Rodriguez burst onto the prospect scene in 2021 thanks to impressive top-line stats that were driven primarily by prodigious hand-eye coordination and excellent bat speed. He was also swinging at nearly everything, which foreshadowed his struggles once he hit the upper minors. Rodriguez got off to a very slow start at Double-A this season but managed to rebound convincingly and finished with a very respectable line while playing in a difficult park for hitters. He still prefers to swing—he'll probably always prefer to swing—but he did manage to up his walk rate a bit in 2022 and continues to limit his strikeouts. A main concern going forward is whether he is selective enough to maximize his contact outcomes—his power output is limited despite consistently hefty swings, and he hits a lot of ground balls. Rodriguez has the required defensive tools for a premium spot, but hasn't always played the cleanest shortstop, and last season split his time between the two middle-infield positions. The contact/speed/potential for more power output keeps him intriguing.

**OFP:** 50 / Everyday middle-infielder driven by bat-to-ball, a sometimes-frustrating sparkplug

**Variance:** High. He's managed to mitigate some of the approach concerns, but they still exist.

**Jesse Roche's Fantasy Take:** Before a broken hamate bone ended his season in August, Rodriguez was on an absolute tear, hitting 10 (of his 11) home runs over his final 18 games. If he can tap more regularly into his sneaky pop, he has legit fantasy upside. Even if his power falls short, Rodriguez can be a source of batting average–he has consistently hit .280+ in the minors–and speed–he was 40-for-50 in stolen bases last year. Further, the White Sox recently added him to the 40-man roster, and he may debut at some point in 2023. Rodriguez should be rostered in leagues with up to 200 prospects.

## 9 Luis Mieses  RF      OFP: 50      ETA: 2024
Born: 05/31/00   Age: 23   Bats: L   Throws: L   Height: 6'3"   Weight: 180 lb.   Origin: International Free Agent, 2016

| YEAR | TEAM | LVL | AGE | PA | R | 2B | 3B | HR | RBI | BB | K | SB | CS | AVG/OBP/SLG | DRC+ | BABIP | BRR | DRP | WARP |
|------|------|-----|-----|-----|-----|-----|-----|-----|-----|-----|-----|-----|-----|-------------|------|-------|------|-----|------|
| 2021 | KAN | A | 21 | 225 | 31 | 12 | 1 | 6 | 41 | 13 | 33 | 0 | 0 | .305/.347/.463 | 114 | .329 | -0.4 | RF(38) -4.5, LF(15) -1.0 | 0.6 |
| 2021 | WS | A+ | 21 | 234 | 30 | 19 | 2 | 9 | 33 | 11 | 48 | 0 | 1 | .236/.278/.464 | 117 | .262 | -1.6 | LF(32) 1.2, RF(26) -5.6, CF(2) 1.2 | 0.8 |
| 2022 | WS | A+ | 22 | 451 | 54 | 34 | 0 | 12 | 72 | 24 | 72 | 0 | 0 | .281/.324/.448 | 102 | .313 | -2.5 | RF(88) 3.1, 1B(9) 0.6 | 1.6 |
| 2022 | BIR | AA | 22 | 102 | 12 | 5 | 0 | 3 | 16 | 4 | 20 | 1 | 0 | .299/.333/.443 | 103 | .351 | 0.8 | LF(13) 0.6, RF(6) 1.8, 1B(3) -0.6 | 0.6 |
| 2023 non-DC | CHW | MLB | 23 | 251 | 20 | 13 | 1 | 4 | 23 | 11 | 53 | 0 | 0 | .226/.266/.341 | 68 | .275 | -4.3 | 1B 0, LF 0 | -0.8 |

**The Report:** Mieses hit full-season ball in 2021 at age 20 and put up very decent numbers in Low-A, but scuffled after his promotion to Winston-Salem. However, he conquered High-A in 2022 and was very solid in his Project Birmingham cameo. For me the eye test sent mixed signals—Mieses has a pretty left-handed swing and consistently smashes the ball, but he doesn't walk much due to his chase-heavy, free-swinging ways and he hasn't yet hit the homers you'd expect despite a pull-heavy approach. Mieses lacks above-average athleticism at the plate, and I've seen the bat path as a bit grooved, but an ability to limit strikeouts and make hard contact in the zone gives him a chance to play an everyday role, if he can iron out some approach issues and find a way to tap into the latent pop.

**OFP:** 50 / Everyday right fielder

**Variance:** Medium. There are possible limitations on his hit tool and the power hasn't really shown up yet.

**Jesse Roche's Fantasy Take:** The White Sox exposed Mieses to the Rule 5 Draft. That should tell you something about his MLB-readiness, and no one bit. Despite his approach issues, Mieses has solid bat-to-ball ability with enough power to be on the fantasy radar in deeper dynasty leagues.

## 10 Sean Burke RHP

OFP: 50     ETA: Late 2023/Early 2024

Born: 12/18/99   Age: 23   Bats: R   Throws: R   Height: 6'6"   Weight: 230 lb.   Origin: Round 3, 2021 Draft (#94 overall)

| YEAR | TEAM | LVL | AGE | W | L | SV | G | GS | IP | H | HR | BB/9 | K/9 | K | GB% | BABIP | WHIP | ERA | DRA- | WARP |
|------|------|-----|-----|---|---|----|----|-----|------|-----|-----|------|------|-----|-------|-------|------|-------|------|------|
| 2021 | KAN | A | 21 | 0 | 1 | 0 | 5 | 5 | 14 | 9 | 0 | 6.4 | 12.9 | 20 | 43.3% | .321 | 1.36 | 3.21 | 92 | 0.2 |
| 2022 | WS | A+ | 22 | 2 | 1 | 0 | 6 | 5 | 28 | 24 | 3 | 3.9 | 10.0 | 31 | 30.9% | .318 | 1.29 | 2.89 | 114 | 0.0 |
| 2022 | BIR | AA | 22 | 2 | 7 | 0 | 19 | 19 | 73 | 72 | 11 | 4.1 | 12.2 | 99 | 44.8% | .361 | 1.44 | 4.81 | 83 | 1.4 |
| 2022 | CLT | AAA | 22 | 0 | 2 | 0 | 2 | 2 | 7 | 12 | 1 | 3.9 | 9.0 | 7 | 34.6% | .440 | 2.14 | 11.57 | 120 | 0.0 |
| 2023 DC | CHW | MLB | 23 | 1 | 1 | 0 | 3 | 3 | 12.7 | 13 | 2 | 4.9 | 8.5 | 12 | 35.8% | .300 | 1.54 | 5.10 | 128 | -0.1 |

*Comparables: Hunter Wood, Carson LaRue, Bryan Mitchell*

**The Report:** Burke dominated High-A to start his 2022 season, but continued to struggle with control and command across two subsequent promotions. Fairly compact in his delivery despite a filled-out 6-foot-6 frame, he pumps mid-90s heat in short bursts and pairs it with a big, diving spike curve in the upper-70s. He rounds out his four-pitch mix with a cutterish slider and the very occasional change. The fastball and curve are both above-average, but the heater can be a bit hittable in the fat part of the zone. The curve is a big breaker, but it can show a bit early and doesn't always get down and under bats when hitters offer. Burke got knocked around a bit in the upper minors, but if he can smooth out the command wobbles he profiles as a back-end starter.

**OFP:** 50 / no. 4 starter

**Variance:** Medium. Burke may not throw enough strikes, or enough good strikes to turn over a lineup multiple times, and the relief fallback here is more middle innings than high-leverage.

**Jesse Roche's Fantasy Take:** A pitching prospect without a potential plus pitch, with command and control issues, and without a high-leverage relief fallback is not the type of pitcher you should be targeting in fantasy.

# Outside the Top Ten:

## 11 Lenyn Sosa MI

Born: 01/25/00   Age: 23   Bats: R   Throws: R   Height: 6'0"   Weight: 180 lb.   Origin: International Free Agent, 2016

| YEAR | TEAM | LVL | AGE | PA | R | 2B | 3B | HR | RBI | BB | K | SB | CS | AVG/OBP/SLG | DRC+ | BABIP | BRR | DRP | WARP |
|------|------|-----|-----|-----|----|----|----|----|-----|----|----|----|----|-------------|------|-------|-----|-----|------|
| 2021 | WS | A+ | 21 | 353 | 45 | 19 | 1 | 10 | 49 | 14 | 77 | 3 | 4 | .290/.321/.443 | 98 | .349 | 0.4 | SS(64) 5.1, 2B(21) 1.2 | 1.6 |
| 2021 | BIR | AA | 21 | 121 | 10 | 5 | 0 | 1 | 7 | 2 | 28 | 0 | 1 | .214/.240/.282 | 77 | .273 | -0.2 | SS(20) 1.9, 2B(9) 0.8, 3B(4) -0.3 | 0.3 |
| 2022 | CAR | WIN | 22 | 170 | 18 | 9 | 1 | 2 | 15 | 14 | 36 | 0 | 0 | .272/.343/.384 | | .342 | | | |
| 2022 | BIR | AA | 22 | 289 | 47 | 10 | 2 | 14 | 48 | 21 | 40 | 0 | 0 | .331/.384/.549 | 136 | .340 | 1.5 | SS(35) 2.1, 3B(13) 0.8, 2B(9) 0.3 | 2.5 |
| 2022 | CLT | AAA | 22 | 247 | 30 | 12 | 0 | 9 | 31 | 18 | 43 | 3 | 4 | .296/.352/.469 | 108 | .331 | 0.3 | SS(33) 0.5, 2B(23) -0.6 | 1.0 |
| 2022 | CHW | MLB | 22 | 36 | 3 | 1 | 0 | 1 | 1 | 1 | 12 | 0 | 0 | .114/.139/.229 | 75 | .136 | 0.8 | 2B(6) 0.5, SS(5) -0.2 | 0.1 |
| 2023 DC | CHW | MLB | 23 | 60 | 6 | 2 | 0 | 1 | 6 | 3 | 12 | 0 | 1 | .225/.270/.340 | 72 | .266 | -0.2 | SS 0, 2B 0 | -0.1 |

*Comparables: Hanser Alberto, Miguel Andújar, José Rondón*

Sosa cleaned up the swing decision issues he had in A-ball in 2021, and started hitting for intriguing power in the upper minors last season. After hitting his way to the majors in the summer, he resumed chasing a bit too much during his two stints in the bigs. Sosa should smooth that issue out in time, but the power is more likely to be on the fringe side of average despite the gaudy 2022 home run totals, and he's a better fit for second than anywhere else on the dirt. He can play three spots and hit a bit, so that should make him a useful bench piece at least, and if he keeps some of those power gains against major league arms, he could be a useful starter for a few years.

## 12 Kohl Simas RHP

Born: 12/22/99   Age: 23   Bats: R   Throws: R   Height: 6'1"   Weight: 190 lb.   Origin: Undrafted Free Agent, 2021

| YEAR | TEAM | LVL | AGE | W | L | SV | G | GS | IP | H | HR | BB/9 | K/9 | K | GB% | BABIP | WHIP | ERA | DRA- | WARP |
|------|------|-----|-----|---|---|----|----|-----|------|-----|-----|------|------|-----|-------|-------|------|-------|------|------|
| 2021 | KAN | A | 21 | 2 | 0 | 1 | 10 | 0 | 18 | 9 | 1 | 2.0 | 11.5 | 23 | 41.0% | .211 | 0.72 | 1.50 | 88 | 0.3 |
| 2022 | KAN | A | 22 | 2 | 2 | 0 | 16 | 15 | 61² | 51 | 7 | 3.6 | 11.1 | 76 | 38.8% | .301 | 1.23 | 3.65 | 88 | 1.1 |
| 2022 | BIR | AA | 22 | 0 | 0 | 0 | 6 | 0 | 6¹ | 10 | 3 | 5.7 | 8.5 | 6 | 30.0% | .412 | 2.21 | 9.95 | 118 | 0.0 |
| 2023 non-DC | CHW | MLB | 23 | 3 | 3 | 0 | 58 | 0 | 50 | 53 | 8 | 4.3 | 7.4 | 41 | 34.3% | .301 | 1.55 | 5.22 | 132 | -0.6 |

Simas was a huge pop-up story early this season, dominating Low-A hitters with a set of skills generally unseen at that level. He has an above-average command projection of a legit four-pitch mix that is already very advanced. The fastball sits mostly low-90s but with heft and run, his low-80s slider has good late bite, and his change fades well and is effective against lefties.

Simas also pops a mid-70s curve for strikes as a change of pace. His stuff will get hit—the heater especially—if he is not on top of his location, but overall it's a refreshing profile and a nice find from an undrafted free agent. Simas was out from early June to early July with a forearm issue and upon his return pitched primarily in relief. In 2023 he will need to maintain health and prove that his stuff can withstand stiffer competition.

## 13 Jonathan Cannon   RHP

Born: 07/19/00   Age: 22   Bats: R   Throws: R   Height: 6'6"   Weight: 213 lb.   Origin: Round 3, 2022 Draft (#101 overall)

| YEAR | TEAM | LVL | AGE | W | L | SV | G | GS | IP | H | HR | BB/9 | K/9 | K | GB% | BABIP | WHIP | ERA | DRA- | WARP |
|------|------|-----|-----|---|---|----|----|----|-----|----|----|------|-----|----|------|-------|------|------|------|------|
| 2022 | KAN | A | 21 | 0 | 0 | 0 | 3 | 3 | 6¹ | 4 | 0 | 2.8 | 4.3 | 3 | 52.9% | .235 | 0.95 | 1.42 | 111 | 0.0 |
| 2023 non-DC | CHW | MLB | 22 | 3 | 3 | 0 | 58 | 0 | 50 | 57 | 8 | 4.5 | 6.9 | 39 | 36.5% | .313 | 1.64 | 5.78 | 143 | -0.8 |

*Comparables: Nicholas Padilla, Moises Lugo, Elvin Rodriguez*

Cannon had rather pedestrian numbers for the Georgia Bulldogs his junior year, but the addition of a cutter to his mid-90s fastball and average slider gives him a better chance to stick in a rotation over the long haul. He's a big-framed righty with an easy tempo and fairly compact delivery, who will fill up the zone with his whole arsenal. There's a somewhat limited ceiling here without a true swing-and-miss offering, but Cannon could move quickly given the now well-rounded repertoire and strike-throwing ability.

## 14 Jordan Sprinkle   SS

Born: 03/06/01   Age: 22   Bats: R   Throws: R   Height: 5'11"   Weight: 180 lb.   Origin: Round 4, 2022 Draft (#131 overall)

| YEAR | TEAM | LVL | AGE | PA | R | 2B | 3B | HR | RBI | BB | K | SB | CS | AVG/OBP/SLG | DRC+ | BABIP | BRR | DRP | WARP |
|------|------|-----|-----|-----|----|----|----|----|-----|----|----|----|----|-------------|------|-------|------|------|------|
| 2022 | KAN | A | 21 | 101 | 11 | 3 | 0 | 1 | 4 | 6 | 21 | 8 | 1 | .237/.290/.301 | 93 | .296 | 0.6 | SS(21) 2.0 | 0.5 |
| 2023 non-DC | CHW | MLB | 22 | 251 | 18 | 10 | 1 | 2 | 19 | 14 | 69 | 9 | 2 | .206/.257/.284 | 53 | .282 | -0.2 | SS 0 | -0.6 |

Taken from UC Santa Barbara in the most recent draft, Sprinkle carries some hit tool risk but appears to have been worth the fourth-round gamble. A smallish 5-foot-11, Sprinkle runs well and plays excellent defense at shortstop—he shows great range to both his left and right, and possesses a very good arm that he can manipulate up and down depending on what the situation requires. His twitchiness also manifests at the plate, where Sprinkle has a quick bat and a swing path designed to get all the pop he can out of his frame. He covers high, hard stuff without issue but seems to have a tougher time with spin down in the zone, and his pre-pitch mechanics may be excessively active. The White Sox might have something here if Sprinkle can get his timing right at the plate.

## 15 Yoelqui Céspedes   CF

Born: 09/24/97   Age: 25   Bats: R   Throws: R   Height: 5'9"   Weight: 205 lb.   Origin: International Free Agent, 2021

| YEAR | TEAM | LVL | AGE | PA | R | 2B | 3B | HR | RBI | BB | K | SB | CS | AVG/OBP/SLG | DRC+ | BABIP | BRR | DRP | WARP |
|------|------|-----|-----|-----|----|----|----|----|-----|----|-----|----|----|-------------|------|-------|------|------------------------|------|
| 2021 | GDD | WIN | 23 | 78 | 8 | 3 | 0 | 0 | 1 | 2 | 22 | 2 | 0 | .181/.244/.222 | | .260 | | | |
| 2021 | WS | A+ | 23 | 199 | 34 | 17 | 0 | 7 | 20 | 13 | 56 | 10 | 2 | .278/.355/.494 | 89 | .372 | 0.5 | CF(21) -1.5, RF(3) -0.4 | 0.2 |
| 2021 | BIR | AA | 23 | 100 | 14 | 3 | 2 | 1 | 7 | 3 | 27 | 8 | 4 | .298/.340/.404 | 81 | .409 | -0.2 | CF(26) 3.9 | 0.5 |
| 2022 | BIR | AA | 24 | 512 | 65 | 29 | 1 | 17 | 59 | 29 | 154 | 33 | 12 | .258/.332/.437 | 78 | .349 | 1.7 | CF(101) -0.5, RF(9) 0.5 | 1.2 |
| 2023 DC | CHW | MLB | 25 | 60 | 6 | 3 | 0 | 1 | 5 | 3 | 21 | 4 | 1 | .222/.274/.328 | 70 | .337 | -0.1 | RF 0 | -0.1 |

*Comparables: Darrell Ceciliani, Drew Ferguson, Braden Bishop*

I concluded last offseason's blurb on Céspedes by calling him high-variance and expressing that "we need to see the hit tool play against high-level pitching." In 2022 we saw him strike out in 30% of his plate appearances as a 24-year-old in Double-A. The jury might be allowed some additional time to deliberate, but a verdict is probably on its way shortly. There is still significant defensive utility here, so a future as a fourth outfielder buoyed by speed and pop is not unrealistic.

## 16 Wilfred Veras 1B

Born: 11/15/02   Age: 20   Bats: R   Throws: R   Height: 6'2"   Weight: 180 lb.   Origin: International Free Agent, 2019

| YEAR | TEAM | LVL | AGE | PA | R | 2B | 3B | HR | RBI | BB | K | SB | CS | AVG/OBP/SLG | DRC+ | BABIP | BRR | DRP | WARP |
|------|------|-----|-----|-----|-----|-----|-----|-----|-----|-----|-----|-----|-----|-------------|------|-------|------|-----|------|
| 2021 | WSX | ROK | 18 | 178 | 25 | 16 | 2 | 4 | 26 | 21 | 42 | 3 | 1 | .322/.416/.533 | | .421 | | | |
| 2022 | KAN | A | 19 | 433 | 58 | 19 | 2 | 17 | 67 | 27 | 118 | 5 | 0 | .266/.319/.454 | 95 | .332 | -2.1 | 1B(54) -3.2, 3B(19) 0.6 | 0.7 |
| 2022 | BIR | AA | 19 | 48 | 5 | 3 | 0 | 3 | 5 | 3 | 14 | 0 | 0 | .267/.313/.533 | 102 | .321 | -0.1 | LF(1) -0.0 | 0.1 |
| *2023 non-DC* | *CHW* | *MLB* | *20* | *251* | *21* | *10* | *1* | *5* | *24* | *11* | *89* | *1* | *0* | *.216/.259/.332* | *64* | *.322* | *-4.1* | *1B 0, 3B 0* | *-1.0* |

Veras is a right-handed hitter with limited positional utility. If that sounds familiar to White Sox fans, well, sorry. The 19-year-old is often listed as a third baseman but already is more likely to be written into a lineup at first base or DH, although he's adding left field to his résumé in winter ball, as well. However, he deserves a spot on this list thanks to his one carrying tool—his easy plus power plays to all fields. Veras uses a short stride and a low-effort swing, so he's not selling out to get to the pop, either. He slashed .267/.319/.454 in 433 Low-A plate appearances, overall acquitting himself very well in an aggressive assignment to full-season ball. He'll have to hit and hit for power to make it, but that isn't out of the question.

## Top Talents 25 and Under (as of 4/1/2023):

1. Luis Robert, OF
2. Andrew Vaughn, 1B/OF
3. Colson Montgomery, SS
4. Oscar Colas, OF
5. Garrett Crochet, LHP
6. Bryan Ramos, 3B
7. Norge Vera, RHP
8. Cristian Mena, RHP
9. Noah Schultz, LHP
10. Peyton Pallette, RHP

Despite a disappointing 2022, Chicago still enters 2023 with a young core struggling to fire on all cylinders simultaneously. Robert is as much a possible future MVP as any 24-year-old in the league, however, his injury-shortened campaign concluded a surprisingly power-sapped showing from him that will hopefully be rectified as he achieves full health with a wrist free of injury. His stardom, alongside 26-year-old Eloy Jiménez, is in many ways the fulcrum of this White Sox club's present and future.

Vaughn made his mark as an above-average bat as he'd long been expected to be; however, his slow-footed baserunning and butchering his way around the outfield made for a nearly unbearable defensive specter, combining for a ghastly -16 Outs Above Average in the outfield. With José Abreu now in Houston, Vaughn can finally return to first base where he belongs. Crochet missed the entire 2022 season with Tommy John, but he should align to be at full bore in 2023, wherein he may align once again for bullpen work in lieu of a starter's workload. That would likely be just fine, assuming a successful rehab, where Crochet has been one of the best young lefty relievers in baseball when healthy.

# Cincinnati Reds

## The State of the System:

Cincinnati acquired all manner of good prospects in their trade teardown—six of the top seven on this list are fairly recent trade pickups. Beyond that, they've done a nifty job with certain kinds of maximized-stuff pitchers and seem to be focusing on modern hit tool and power evaluations.

## The Top Ten:

### 1 Elly De La Cruz  SS    OFP: 70    ETA: Mid-2023

Born: 01/11/02    Age: 21    Bats: S    Throws: R    Height: 6'5"    Weight: 200 lb.    Origin: International Free Agent, 2018

| YEAR | TEAM | LVL | AGE | PA | R | 2B | 3B | HR | RBI | BB | K | SB | CS | AVG/OBP/SLG | DRC+ | BABIP | BRR | DRP | WARP |
|------|------|-----|-----|-----|----|----|----|----|-----|----|----|----|----|-------------|------|-------|------|-----|------|
| 2021 | RED | ROK | 19 | 55 | 13 | 6 | 2 | 3 | 13 | 4 | 15 | 2 | 0 | .400/.455/.780 | | .531 | | | |
| 2021 | DBT | A | 19 | 210 | 22 | 12 | 7 | 5 | 29 | 10 | 65 | 8 | 5 | .269/.305/.477 | 89 | .372 | -0.7 | 3B(28) 7.0, SS(20) 2.7 | 1.2 |
| 2022 | LIC | WIN | 20 | 101 | 19 | 4 | 2 | 1 | 14 | 16 | 27 | 9 | 4 | .286/.396/.417 | | .404 | | | |
| 2022 | DAY | A+ | 20 | 306 | 53 | 14 | 6 | 20 | 52 | 24 | 94 | 28 | 4 | .302/.359/.609 | 116 | .389 | 1.7 | SS(54) -0.2, 3B(14) 0.5 | 1.7 |
| 2022 | CHA | AA | 20 | 207 | 34 | 17 | 3 | 8 | 34 | 16 | 64 | 19 | 2 | .305/.357/.553 | 96 | .420 | 2.2 | SS(30) 1.3, 3B(10) 0.2 | 0.9 |
| 2023 DC | CIN | MLB | 21 | 194 | 21 | 9 | 3 | 5 | 23 | 10 | 65 | 12 | 3 | .245/.292/.420 | 93 | .355 | 1.0 | 3B 0, SS 0 | 0.5 |

*Comparables: Corey Seager, Javier Báez, Oneil Cruz*

**The Report:** If you ignore swing decisions, De La Cruz has the best hit/power/speed/defense projection combination in the entire minor leagues—and it's not even close. He has a quick, whippy swing that produces extraordinary bat speed from both sides of the plate. His in-zone contact rates are running well ahead of his strikeout rates (we'll get to that more in a minute). He hits the ball hard in the air, and hits more absolutely majestic dingers than anyone else in the minors. He's a plus-plus runner, bordering on 80-grade, even though he's huge. He has probably the best body control of any player in the minors. His defense at shortstop is rapidly improving, although half this list is composed of current shortstops, so he could end up elsewhere anyway.

De La Cruz's walk rates improved marginally in the minors last year; he walked 4.8% of the time in Low-A in 2021 and 7.8% of the time split between High-A and Double-A in 2022. But a lot of that is an artifact of opponents pitching around him because he demolished both leagues; he was thrown a lower percentage of strikes in 2022 than any other top prospect I've gathered plate discipline data for. His chase rate improved a little, but still remained very poor—hence all the strikeouts despite above-average in-zone contact.

It's likely that De La Cruz's plate approach is going to become a significant problem in either Triple-A or the majors, and for the first time in his stateside career he'll either make that adjustment—as you can see above, he's produced monster numbers despite chase rates in the high-30s so far, so there's been no real need to adjust—or he won't. We believe whether or not he can make that adjustment is going to be the difference in whether he wins MVP awards or is just a decent player who runs on-base percentages too low to be a star, or somewhere in between. We're optimistic that he will, and for whatever it's worth, everyone surrounding De La Cruz—including Reds folks, other teams' scouts and media who have dealt directly with him—absolutely raves about his mental skills.

**OFP:** 70 / He could be a future superstar. Not star. Super. Star.

**Variance:** Very High. There's a pretty good case for an 80/Extreme here because the reasonable upside cases are so strong.

**Bret Sayre's Fantasy Take:** So, how lucky do you feel? The characteristics of a half-decade plus of first-round value is there if he can make good enough swing decisions. The bright side is that even if he doesn't, you're still looking at a potential Adolis García type fantasy player—although García's 2022 season represents a high-water mark for someone with these skills. (Not that you'd shake your head at him being a top-20 player in a peak season.) The unfiltered four-category upside makes him an easy top-five dynasty prospect right now.

## 2 Noelvi Marte SS/3B    OFP: 60    ETA: 2024
Born: 10/16/01   Age: 21   Bats: R   Throws: R   Height: 6'0"   Weight: 216 lb.   Origin: International Free Agent, 2018

| YEAR | TEAM | LVL | AGE | PA | R | 2B | 3B | HR | RBI | BB | K | SB | CS | AVG/OBP/SLG | DRC+ | BABIP | BRR | DRP | WARP |
|---|---|---|---|---|---|---|---|---|---|---|---|---|---|---|---|---|---|---|---|
| 2021 | MOD | A | 19 | 478 | 87 | 24 | 2 | 17 | 69 | 58 | 106 | 23 | 7 | .271/.368/.462 | 123 | .326 | 4.1 | SS(92) -1.1 | 3.1 |
| 2021 | EVE | A+ | 19 | 33 | 4 | 4 | 0 | 0 | 2 | 2 | 11 | 1 | 0 | .290/.333/.419 | 95 | .450 | 0.4 | SS(7) 0.9 | 0.2 |
| 2022 | DAY | A+ | 20 | 126 | 12 | 4 | 0 | 4 | 13 | 17 | 23 | 10 | 3 | .292/.397/.443 | 112 | .338 | -0.1 | SS(23) 0.2 | 0.6 |
| 2022 | EVE | A+ | 20 | 394 | 62 | 19 | 0 | 15 | 55 | 42 | 84 | 13 | 6 | .275/.363/.462 | 115 | .321 | -1.0 | SS(81) -2.8 | 1.9 |
| 2023 non-DC | CIN | MLB | 21 | 251 | 23 | 10 | 1 | 5 | 24 | 20 | 59 | 6 | 3 | .228/.297/.342 | 83 | .289 | -1.1 | SS 0 | 0.2 |

*Comparables: Richard Urena, Willi Castro, Cole Tucker*

**The Report:** Marte has been a buzzed-about name since before he signed as an international free agent four-and-a-half years ago, and we're just now finally starting to zoom into a more granular understanding of the type of player he'll become. A lot of good things are still present in his profile. He's got a nice, loose swing. He makes a decent amount of contact now, especially for a player for whom bat-to-ball has been a past concern; he's cut down some on his leg action and that seemed to help his swing mechanics substantially. His approach is solid, and when he gets the right pitch he can pull and drive it.

But a carrying offensive tool has yet to clearly emerge for Marte. It might be his power, which has long projected for a plus-plus grade due to his physical strength and projectability, but his swing is more of a strength-in-levers over enormous-bat-speed construct. The underlying hit tool projection is fine, but nothing special. So if there's going to be something that carries his profile, it's going to be his power. But there's a little concern here too; his batted-ball data is pointing towards above-average-to-plus power potentially right now, not carrying power potential.

If he was a sure thing to stick at shortstop, this would all be fine, but between so-so agility and an inconsistent arm, he's no better than the fourth-best defensive shortstop on this list. The Reds had him play third exclusively in the Arizona Fall League—long his theorized future home—and he was atrocious there, enough that even though it was only 21 games, it raises some questions about whether that's a reasonable spot to project him to. Could he end up at an outfield corner? Second? First? Time will tell.

**OFP:** 60 / Good all-around starter, position TBD

**Variance:** High. The pressure on the offense will increase the further he slides down the defensive spectrum.

**Bret Sayre's Fantasy Take:** Typically, it would be okay to be a little apprehensive about a top prospect who gets traded prior to reaching the upper minors, but we are all just pawns in Jerry Dipoto's world. Marte is on the way to a five-category contributor future although, as noted above, it's more likely to be a sum-of-its-parts profile than we may have hoped. That said, his home park will help him get the most out of that power and 25-30 bombs a year might still be reasonable even if he doesn't max out from a tool perspective. Add a decent average and double-digit steals and you see why you don't want to let prospect fatigue get the better of you over the next year or so.

## 3 Cam Collier 3B    OFP: 60    ETA: 2026
Born: 11/20/04   Age: 18   Bats: L   Throws: R   Height: 6'2"   Weight: 210 lb.   Origin: Round 1, 2022 Draft (#18 overall)

| YEAR | TEAM | LVL | AGE | PA | R | 2B | 3B | HR | RBI | BB | K | SB | CS | AVG/OBP/SLG | DRC+ | BABIP | BRR | DRP | WARP |
|---|---|---|---|---|---|---|---|---|---|---|---|---|---|---|---|---|---|---|---|
| 2022 | RED | ROK | 17 | 35 | 7 | 1 | 0 | 2 | 4 | 7 | 6 | 0 | 2 | .370/.514/.630 | | .421 | | | |

**The Report:** Collier took a path towards pro ball that only Bryce Harper has taken in recent memory. Originally a top prep player for the 2023 draft class, he got his GED two years early and enrolled at Chipola College, a perennial junior college powerhouse. After hitting .333 against pitchers 2-4 years older there and making a brief sojourn into the Cape Cod League, he was then eligible for the 2022 Draft at just 17 years and seven months old; between being one of the youngest players in the draft and having a track record against reasonable collegiate pitching, Collier was an anomaly player-type in many draft models.

Collier's profile is currently driven by strong bat-to-ball ability and swing decisions for his age cohort, the vast majority of whom are either still in high school or in international complexes. Quality of contact was flagged to us as a finite concern, albeit with the caveat that he just turned 18 a couple months ago and is likely to add significant physical strength. He has a nice, quick swing and gets the barrel through the zone, and he might eventually develop more power and more pull in his swing as he gets older. Defensively, he's a polished third baseman with more than enough arm for the position.

**OFP:** 60 / First-division third baseman

**Variance:** High. He's a hit tool-driven player who has barely seen pro pitching yet; we'd like to have more data before crowning him.

**Bret Sayre's Fantasy Take:** There are concerns here from our perspective because there may just not be a ton of power or speed projection coming, but he's likely to hit for the most average of anyone on this list. If 25-homer power comes, he could be a Justin Turner-type corner infielder with future .300 seasons sprinkled in. He's an interesting case in FYPDs this offseason, and while he's a borderline first-rounder in standard formats, he becomes a very interesting points league target.

## 4 Edwin Arroyo SS    OFP: 55    ETA: 2025

Born: 08/25/03    Age: 19    Bats: S    Throws: S    Height: 6'0"    Weight: 175 lb.    Origin: Round 2, 2021 Draft (#48 overall)

| YEAR | TEAM | LVL | AGE | PA | R | 2B | 3B | HR | RBI | BB | K | SB | CS | AVG/OBP/SLG | DRC+ | BABIP | BRR | DRP | WARP |
|------|------|-----|-----|-----|----|----|----|----|-----|----|----|----|----|-------------|------|-------|------|--------|------|
| 2021 | RA12 | WIN | 17 | 65 | 6 | 3 | 0 | 0 | 2 | 6 | 14 | 1 | 0 | .250/.333/.304 | | .333 | | | |
| 2021 | MRN | ROK | 17 | 86 | 16 | 2 | 0 | 2 | 10 | 10 | 26 | 4 | 1 | .211/.337/.324 | | .295 | | | |
| 2022 | DBT | A | 18 | 109 | 16 | 6 | 3 | 1 | 16 | 9 | 31 | 4 | 2 | .227/.303/.381 | 80 | .318 | -0.1 | SS(25) 2.8 | 0.2 |
| 2022 | MOD | A | 18 | 410 | 76 | 19 | 7 | 13 | 67 | 35 | 90 | 21 | 4 | .316/.385/.514 | 106 | .386 | 3.1 | SS(84) 2.6 | 2.2 |
| 2023 non-DC | CIN | MLB | 19 | 251 | 20 | 10 | 3 | 3 | 22 | 14 | 70 | 6 | 2 | .230/.278/.340 | 73 | .314 | -1.5 | 2B 0, SS 0 | -0.2 |

*Comparables: Royce Lewis, Chris Owings, Addison Russell*

**The Report:** Arroyo played nearly the entire 2022 season as an 18-year-old in full-season ball, a fine accomplishment in its own right. While he has no especially standout offensive abilities, he did everything well as one of the youngest regular players in Low-A. He displayed adequate approach and bat-to-ball skills from both sides of the plate, as expected, but also unexpectedly displayed above-average power potential and a surprising amount of loud contact. He did struggle after the trade to Cincinnati, but all in all it was a very successful debut, even if the Dayton line wasn't so hot.

Where Arroyo really shines is on defense. He's a highly advanced shortstop and likely will end up as the best defender of all the infielders on the list. Arroyo has soft hands at the six and a shortstop-caliber arm.

**OFP:** 55 / Two-way starting shortstop

**Variance:** Medium. His ability to play short will get him to the majors.

**Bret Sayre's Fantasy Take:** It doesn't matter if he's playing half his games on the moon—a near-.900 OPS as a true 18-year-old in full-season ball is something worth paying very close attention to. Arroyo is the kind of prospect who may get overlooked a little in fantasy because he's a strong defensive player, but that glovework is going to get him a ton of reps to work through any struggles he might have at the plate at the highest levels. He's heady and fast enough for 30-plus steals and even just moderate contributions around that would make him a top-10 shortstop in time.

## 5 Connor Phillips RHP    OFP: 55    ETA: 2023

Born: 05/04/01    Age: 22    Bats: R    Throws: R    Height: 6'2"    Weight: 209 lb.    Origin: Round 2, 2020 Draft (#64 overall)

| YEAR | TEAM | LVL | AGE | W | L | SV | G | GS | IP | H | HR | BB/9 | K/9 | K | GB% | BABIP | WHIP | ERA | DRA- | WARP |
|------|------|-----|-----|----|----|----|----|----|-----|----|----|------|------|-----|------|-------|------|------|------|------|
| 2021 | MOD | A | 20 | 7 | 3 | 0 | 16 | 16 | 72 | 62 | 1 | 5.5 | 13.0 | 104 | 41.2% | .361 | 1.47 | 4.75 | 95 | 0.6 |
| 2022 | DAY | A+ | 21 | 4 | 3 | 0 | 12 | 12 | 64 | 39 | 5 | 4.5 | 12.7 | 90 | 46.5% | .279 | 1.11 | 2.95 | 96 | 0.8 |
| 2022 | CHA | AA | 21 | 1 | 5 | 0 | 12 | 12 | 45² | 48 | 3 | 6.7 | 11.8 | 60 | 28.7% | .378 | 1.80 | 4.93 | 125 | -0.2 |
| 2023 non-DC | CIN | MLB | 22 | 3 | 3 | 0 | 58 | 0 | 50 | 46 | 7 | 5.7 | 9.8 | 55 | 34.4% | .296 | 1.55 | 4.82 | 120 | -0.3 |

*Comparables: Nick Kingham, Jhoan Duran, Edwin Díaz*

**The Report:** Cincinnati has invested in analytic-friendly power arms as an organization, hoping that the overwhelming stuff pans out over command concerns. With the PTBNL spot in their March trade with Seattle, they got Phillips, one of the top pitchers in the minors with this archetype.

Phillips' stuff is enormous. He sits in the mid-90s and regularly touches the upper-90s with flat, riding movement and generates swings and misses up in the zone. He pairs a 12-to-6, upper-70s curve with a tilty, lower-80s slider that work well off each other; the curveball is ahead of the slider but both of them are trending towards the above-average-to-plus range. Even with only a nascent change, that's a bat-missing arsenal.

But his command and control are inconsistent at best, and too often poor—Phillips can't locate his breaking stuff on the edges when he has to, and that's led to elevated walk rates. If he can't hit his spots better and limit the walks as a starter, this would all play very well out of the bullpen, at least.

**OFP:** 55 / Mid-rotation starter or high-leverage reliever

**Variance:** High. He's a big arm with walk problems.

**Bret Sayre's Fantasy Take:** This is admittedly not my favorite profile and screams reliever, but the command/control issues can still plague him in the pen. If your league rosters 200-plus prospects, he's worth a flier on the chance that he can throw enough strikes to be an A.J. Burnett-type in the rotation or at least find someone to trust him enough for saves otherwise.

## Eyewitness Report: Connor Phillips

**Evaluator:** Nathan Graham
**Report Date:** 05/27/2022
**Dates Seen:** 4/29/22
**Risk Factor:** High
**Delivery:** Large frame with an athletic build, mild projection remaining. Utilizes a semi-windup, pitches from the 1B side of the rubber and features a slight crossfire action. 3/4 slot, quick arm, moderate effort in the delivery.

| Pitch Type | Future Grade | Sitting Velocity | Peak Velocity | Report |
|---|---|---|---|---|
| FB | 60 | 95-96 | 98 | Flat offering but stays off the barrel with some natural arm side run. Generates swing and miss by working high in the zone. Plenty of late life in the pitch makes for uncomfortable at bats for hitters. Phillips has the stamina to hold velocity deep into a pitch count but if used in short relief bursts could touch triple digits. |
| CB | 55 | 76-78 | 80 | 12-6 shape with good depth. Pairs well with the high octane, up in the zone fastball. Will steal a strike with it early in the count. Still developing fell for it, missed with it early in the start but as the game progressed it became sharp and generated several awkward swings. |
| SL | 50 | 82-83 | 85 | Inconsistent, currently gets left in the zone to often, but when he gets it right it shows potential to be an average major league pitch. 11-5 shape that sweeps out of the zone, away from right handed hitters. |
| CH | 0 | 78 | 78 | Only threw a couple in my look. |

**Conclusion:** Young and athletic, Phillips has potential to add to his already impressive arsenal. Effort in the delivery makes it unlikely he ever has pinpoint command, but the athleticism is there to control every offering. The high fastball and sharp curve combo would make him a powerful late inning arm but the developing slider will allow him to remain in a starting role.

---

## 6  Spencer Steer  IF   OFP: 55   ETA: Debuted in 2022

Born: 12/07/97   Age: 25   Bats: R   Throws: R   Height: 5'11"   Weight: 185 lb.   Origin: Round 3, 2019 Draft (#90 overall)

| YEAR | TEAM | LVL | AGE | PA | R | 2B | 3B | HR | RBI | BB | K | SB | CS | AVG/OBP/SLG | DRC+ | BABIP | BRR | DRP | WARP |
|---|---|---|---|---|---|---|---|---|---|---|---|---|---|---|---|---|---|---|---|
| 2021 | CR | A+ | 23 | 208 | 37 | 7 | 1 | 10 | 24 | 35 | 32 | 4 | 4 | .274/.409/.506 | 143 | .283 | 2.5 | 2B(28) 0.9, SS(7) -0.4, 3B(5) -0.6 | 1.9 |
| 2021 | WCH | AA | 23 | 280 | 45 | 11 | 2 | 14 | 42 | 20 | 73 | 4 | 0 | .241/.304/.470 | 99 | .274 | 0.6 | 3B(36) 2.4, 2B(18) 1.3, SS(8) -1.0 | 1.1 |
| 2022 | WCH | AA | 24 | 156 | 27 | 13 | 1 | 8 | 30 | 14 | 23 | 1 | 3 | .307/.385/.591 | 130 | .318 | -0.5 | 3B(17) 2.5, SS(9) -1.2, 2B(6) -0.0 | 1.1 |
| 2022 | STP | AAA | 24 | 232 | 39 | 10 | 1 | 12 | 32 | 28 | 43 | 2 | 0 | .242/.345/.485 | 119 | .248 | 0.3 | 3B(26) 0.0, 2B(15) 0.6, SS(4) 0.1 | 1.1 |
| 2022 | LOU | AAA | 24 | 104 | 14 | 7 | 0 | 3 | 13 | 9 | 23 | 1 | 0 | .293/.375/.467 | 100 | .364 | 0.5 | 3B(8) 0.2, SS(7) -1.2, 2B(5) -0.6 | 0.3 |
| 2022 | CIN | MLB | 24 | 108 | 12 | 5 | 0 | 2 | 8 | 11 | 26 | 0 | 1 | .211/.306/.326 | 87 | .269 | 1.1 | 3B(14) -0.3, 1B(9) 0.2, 2B(5) -0.3 | 0.2 |
| 2023 DC | CIN | MLB | 25 | 529 | 56 | 23 | 2 | 14 | 55 | 42 | 111 | 5 | 1 | .216/.294/.358 | 82 | .255 | -0.5 | 3B 0, 2B 0 | 0.2 |

Comparables: J.D. Davis, James Darnell, Taylor Ward

**The Report:** In evaluating Steer's swing, what sticks out is his ability to turn on the ball quickly despite a wide base and a noticeable leg kick. Other than that, the offensive profile is mostly showcased by his above-average discipline. Steer continued to show an ability to lift the ball this year—something that wasn't the case when he entered pro ball. Despite the 24 home runs he hit in the minors, Steer offers more of a line-drive swing with some gap power. As our own Nathan Graham pointed out, Steer does not have a carrying tool but does grade out as an average player pretty much across the board. However, given the improvements he has made, it remains to be seen whether that 5 hit tool or 5 power could jump to above-average.

Defensively, Steer is an average infield defender but not one who should be playing short. He will get the job done at first or third (and maybe second) but is far from anything more than a 5 at those spots. Without a doubt, Steer playing second base would make his bat more dangerous but given the crowd there with De La Cruz and Marte in the pipeline, the hot corner seems the most reasonable place for him.

**OFP:** 55 / Regular third or second baseman

**Variance:** Medium. He's performed at the upper levels of the minors and his skill set seems fairly stable, albeit with the power questions.

**Bret Sayre's Fantasy Take:** Give me the guy with a likely job and the home park that will get the most out of his weakest offensive tool. In deep mixed and NL-only leagues, Steer figures to be a bargain as his MLB stats were weak and there are better prospects coming in Cincy, but the playing time and broad base of skills should be there to hit .260 with 15 homers and a smattering of counting stats.

## 7  Christian Encarnacion-Strand  3B     OFP: 55     ETA: 2023

Born: 12/01/99   Age: 23   Bats: R   Throws: R   Height: 6'0"   Weight: 224 lb.   Origin: Round 4, 2021 Draft (#128 overall)

| YEAR | TEAM | LVL | AGE | PA | R | 2B | 3B | HR | RBI | BB | K | SB | CS | AVG/OBP/SLG | DRC+ | BABIP | BRR | DRP | WARP |
|---|---|---|---|---|---|---|---|---|---|---|---|---|---|---|---|---|---|---|---|
| 2021 | FTM | A | 21 | 92 | 17 | 2 | 2 | 4 | 18 | 5 | 26 | 2 | 0 | .391/.424/.598 | 101 | .526 | 0.2 | 1B(17) -0.5, 3B(4) 1.1 | 0.3 |
| 2022 | CR | A+ | 22 | 330 | 52 | 23 | 3 | 20 | 68 | 30 | 85 | 7 | 1 | .296/.370/.599 | 136 | .353 | 1.3 | 3B(55) -0.6, 1B(2) -0.2 | 2.3 |
| 2022 | CHA | AA | 22 | 148 | 13 | 6 | 1 | 7 | 29 | 6 | 38 | 0 | 0 | .309/.351/.522 | 105 | .376 | -1.0 | 3B(15) -0.8, 1B(12) -1.0 | 0.3 |
| 2022 | WCH | AA | 22 | 60 | 11 | 2 | 1 | 5 | 17 | 4 | 14 | 1 | 1 | .333/.400/.685 | 112 | .371 | 0.2 | 3B(8) 1.7 | 0.2 |
| 2023 non-DC | CIN | MLB | 23 | 251 | 25 | 11 | 2 | 7 | 28 | 14 | 72 | 1 | 0 | .247/.299/.400 | 97 | .328 | -3.9 | 1B 0, 3B 0 | 0.1 |

*Comparables: Nick Senzel, Ryan Braun, Vinnie Catricala*

**The Report:** This list has too much discussion about what's a carrying tool and long-term potential projections for players who aren't really there yet. So here's an easy one: Encarnacion-Strand's carrying tool is plus-plus game power. It's already there, as he hit 32 homers and slugged .587 last year. He hits the ball consistently hard and he lifts almost everything.

Uh, about everything else... well... Encarnacion-Strand has pretty bad chase issues, like De La Cruz. He does not have De La Cruz's knack for contact, speed or defensive profile. His bat-to-ball is fringe-average. He's not particularly fast. He's a third baseman now and possibly headed for first. So that's all not quite so good, and you need to hit a hell of a lot of homers to make up for all of that. But hey, he probably will.

**OFP:** 55 / Power-hitting first baseman

**Variance:** High. The lack of bat-to-ball could limit the hit tool.

**Bret Sayre's Fantasy Take:** If your league counts letters as a category, he's a slam-dunk first-rounder. If your league counts batting average, well...

The power is dreamy but the profile screams Bobby Bradley and sometimes, that guy hits enough to actually get to 30 homers a couple of times in the majors. Other times, he's just Bobby Bradley.

## 8  Sal Stewart  3B     OFP: 55     ETA: 2026

Born: 12/07/03   Age: 19   Bats: R   Throws: R   Height: 6'3"   Weight: 215 lb.   Origin: Round 1, 2022 Draft (#32 overall)

| YEAR | TEAM | LVL | AGE | PA | R | 2B | 3B | HR | RBI | BB | K | SB | CS | AVG/OBP/SLG | DRC+ | BABIP | BRR | DRP | WARP |
|---|---|---|---|---|---|---|---|---|---|---|---|---|---|---|---|---|---|---|---|
| 2022 | RED | ROK | 18 | 28 | 5 | 4 | 0 | 0 | 5 | 4 | 5 | 0 | 0 | .292/.393/.458 | | .368 | | | |

**The Report:** Your prototypical big offensive potential high school bat. Like Collier, he presents with higher-end bat-to-ball and swing decisions for his age cohort, although a bit less extreme—you might be sensing a trend in that the Reds took two of the most advanced teenaged hitters with their two first-round picks. Stewart has significant power potential as he adds strength and can already drive the ball with his quick, uppercut swing. There's a shot for a plus hit, plus power bat here.

Unlike Collier, Stewart doesn't excel on defense. He has limited agility and well-below-average speed, and he's likely to end up at first instead of third some day. That day might be sooner than later given that he might have to share the infield with Collier as early as this year. But the bat has the potential to play anywhere, even as a right-handed first baseman.

**OFP:** 55 / Regular corner infielder

**Variance:** High. This type of profile can go in many directions once wood bats come into play.

**Bret Sayre's Fantasy Take:** Stewart is one of my favorite prospects in FYPDs that are almost certain to go outside the top-20. He has the frame you want in a fantasy corner infielder and, as with almost all of these guys, there's a very friendly landing spot if/when he hits the majors. It'll be a long burn, but the potential for a .270 hitter with 25-plus homers is there.

## 9 Matt McLain  SS   OFP: 55   ETA: 2023

Born: 08/06/99   Age: 23   Bats: R   Throws: R   Height: 5'11"   Weight: 180 lb.   Origin: Round 1, 2021 Draft (#17 overall)

| YEAR | TEAM | LVL | AGE | PA | R | 2B | 3B | HR | RBI | BB | K | SB | CS | AVG/OBP/SLG | DRC+ | BABIP | BRR | DRP | WARP |
|------|------|-----|-----|-----|-----|-----|-----|-----|-----|-----|-----|-----|-----|-------------|------|-------|-----|-----|------|
| 2021 | DAY | A+ | 21 | 119 | 15 | 6 | 0 | 3 | 19 | 17 | 24 | 10 | 2 | .273/.387/.424 | 111 | .329 | 0.4 | SS(27) 1.3 | 0.7 |
| 2022 | CHA | AA | 22 | 452 | 67 | 21 | 5 | 17 | 58 | 70 | 127 | 27 | 3 | .232/.363/.453 | 129 | .300 | 2.5 | SS(74) -7.9, 2B(23) -1.3 | 2.3 |
| 2023 non-DC | CIN | MLB | 23 | 251 | 24 | 10 | 2 | 5 | 24 | 26 | 75 | 9 | 1 | .220/.309/.350 | 90 | .307 | -0.5 | 2B 0, SS 0 | 0.5 |

*Comparables: Kevin Smith, Héctor Gómez, Pat Valaika*

**The Report:** Last offseason, Jeffrey Paternostro wrote "McLain's advanced approach and compact swing makes him a tough out at the plate, and if any tool gets to plus, it might be hit." Fast-forward a season, and that compact swing has added some length and loft, as the infielder emphasized lifting the ball. This didn't manifest in a massive gain in fly-ball rate (42.1% to 44.6%), but the change in intent is readily apparent in the mechanics of his swing. This was good and bad for McLain, as he slugged 17 home runs in only 383 Double-A at-bats, but the trade-off was 127 strikeouts. He maintained his keen eye at the dish, but that represents an increase of eight percentage points in strikeout rate. It's possible that his adjustment to hunt for more power could backfire, though, as a lack of hit tool could sink the broader profile. If McLain can marry the two approaches, he could find himself as a legitimate top-of-the-order bat, thanks to his strong knowledge of the zone.

McLain has the prototypical athletic build and shows off plus wheels and the threat to steal 25 bases in a season *if* he does turn into a true regular. Defensively, given his athleticism and quick twitch, McLain grades out as an average shortstop and slightly above average second baseman.

**OFP:** 55 / OBP-first, table-setting middle infielder.

**Variance:** High. Athletic and disciplined, but can he find a way to balance out his hit and power tools with a somewhat new approach?

**Bret Sayre's Fantasy Take:** The talk about whether it's the average or power that'll play through when he gets to the majors is all fine and good, but let's not forget that McLain is a strong baserunner and a successful thief across all levels of the minors. So that means whether he's a .240/25 guy or a .270/15 guy, those numbers should come with 15-20 steals and make him a sneakily valuable fantasy infielder.

## 10 Andrew Abbott  LHP   OFP: 55   ETA: 2023

Born: 06/01/99   Age: 24   Bats: L   Throws: L   Height: 6'0"   Weight: 192 lb.   Origin: Round 2, 2021 Draft (#53 overall)

| YEAR | TEAM | LVL | AGE | W | L | SV | G | GS | IP | H | HR | BB/9 | K/9 | K | GB% | BABIP | WHIP | ERA | DRA- | WARP |
|------|------|-----|-----|-----|-----|-----|-----|-----|-----|-----|-----|------|------|-----|------|-------|------|-----|------|------|
| 2021 | DBT | A | 22 | 0 | 0 | 0 | 4 | 3 | 11 | 11 | 2 | 3.3 | 15.5 | 19 | 48.0% | .391 | 1.36 | 4.91 | 84 | 0.2 |
| 2022 | DAY | A+ | 23 | 3 | 0 | 0 | 5 | 4 | 27 | 16 | 1 | 2.3 | 13.3 | 40 | 47.3% | .278 | 0.85 | 0.67 | 76 | 0.6 |
| 2022 | CHA | AA | 23 | 7 | 7 | 0 | 20 | 20 | 91 | 84 | 7 | 4.1 | 11.8 | 119 | 43.4% | .360 | 1.37 | 4.75 | 80 | 1.9 |
| 2023 non-DC | CIN | MLB | 24 | 3 | 3 | 0 | 58 | 0 | 50 | 48 | 7 | 4.3 | 9.5 | 53 | 37.2% | .307 | 1.43 | 4.37 | 113 | -0.1 |

*Comparables: John Gant, Steven Matz, Sean Nolin*

**The Report:** Heading into the month of September, Abbott put forth a 5.70 ERA over 16 starts at Double-A and was struggling to find the zone with consistency. However, the delivery is repeatable and the stuff flashes that of a major-league pitcher. After a rocky couple of months, Abbott's potential was on full display to close out the season where he finished September with 16 scoreless innings, 21 strikeouts and three (!) walks. Prior to the close of the year we noted that given his professional approach and the very possible ability to clean up his fastball command, Abbott could and should continue his eye-popping K-rate. Well, he did just that and, with the fastball working in tandem with his plus curveball, the impressive lefty confirmed our inklings and dominated the month of September.

The fastball sits at 92-93 (t95) mph with life, but he struggled with command up until the last month of the season. The aforementioned plus curveball that is, at times, slurve-like in a good way, is one of the better breaking pitches in all of Minor League Baseball. The pitch is quite unique in that it works in different quadrants of the strike zone as a breaking pitch and is so diabolical because it comes out of a near-identical slot as the fastball. To complement his potentially above-average fastball and potentially plus-plus curveball, Abbott also has a slightly below-average changeup. Heading into 2023, the keys here will be if the UVA alum can keep his control and command of his fastball intact while also developing that third pitch.

**OFP:** 55 / Mid-rotation starter.

**Variance:** High. Control and command were all over the place in 2022, and lacking a true third pitch.

**Bret Sayre's Fantasy Take:** There's a little more to like from a fantasy standpoint with Abbott than there was Phillips simply because he's more likely to stick in the rotation. Of course, that only is the case because he can miss enough bats to strike out more than a batter per inning as well. There's not a ton of helium on Abbott, which makes him a nice watch list guy if you're in a medium-sized dynasty league. If he keeps the control gains from the end of 2022, jump on quickly.

## Outside the Top Ten:

### 11 Steve Hajjar LHP
Born: 08/07/00   Age: 22   Bats: R   Throws: L   Height: 6'5"   Weight: 240 lb.   Origin: Round 2, 2021 Draft (#61 overall)

| YEAR | TEAM | LVL | AGE | W | L | SV | G | GS | IP | H | HR | BB/9 | K/9 | K | GB% | BABIP | WHIP | ERA | DRA- | WARP |
|---|---|---|---|---|---|---|---|---|---|---|---|---|---|---|---|---|---|---|---|---|
| 2022 | FTM | A | 21 | 2 | 2 | 0 | 12 | 12 | 43² | 25 | 3 | 4.5 | 14.6 | 71 | 34.2% | .289 | 1.08 | 2.47 | 75 | 1.2 |
| 2022 | DAY | A+ | 21 | 0 | 1 | 0 | 2 | 2 | 7 | 4 | 0 | 7.7 | 12.9 | 10 | 21.4% | .286 | 1.43 | 6.43 | 108 | 0.0 |
| 2023 non-DC | CIN | MLB | 22 | 3 | 3 | 0 | 58 | 0 | 50 | 43 | 7 | 5.5 | 10.0 | 55 | 31.9% | .284 | 1.47 | 4.41 | 112 | -0.1 |

*Comparables: Brett Adcock, Logan Allen, Konnor Pilkington*

What if I told you that the third-best prospect in the Tyler Mahle deal was a lefty who ran huge whiff rates with four different pitches? Hajjar is your man. His low-90s fastball has the kind of tough movement that gets past hitters at the top of the zone. He has two high-spin breaking balls with distinct movement profiles. And none of those three are reputationally his best pitch; that's his changeup.

There are downsides, of course; as deep as this list is, a four-pitch lefty who is whiffing a ton of batters wouldn't be this low. Hajjar's command is inconsistent, which is probably partly mechanical due to an unusually upright release point and a pretty violent landing, and he had individual starts where he began walking the world. He had some shoulder problems over the course of the season, with two separate IL stints of significance, and only made two starts in the Reds org after the trade. All of this implies significant relief risk, basically.

### 12 Brandon Williamson LHP
Born: 04/02/98   Age: 25   Bats: R   Throws: L   Height: 6'6"   Weight: 210 lb.   Origin: Round 2, 2019 Draft (#59 overall)

| YEAR | TEAM | LVL | AGE | W | L | SV | G | GS | IP | H | HR | BB/9 | K/9 | K | GB% | BABIP | WHIP | ERA | DRA- | WARP |
|---|---|---|---|---|---|---|---|---|---|---|---|---|---|---|---|---|---|---|---|---|
| 2021 | EVE | A+ | 23 | 2 | 1 | 0 | 6 | 6 | 31 | 21 | 4 | 2.9 | 17.1 | 59 | 44.2% | .354 | 1.00 | 3.19 | 77 | 0.6 |
| 2021 | ARK | AA | 23 | 2 | 5 | 0 | 13 | 13 | 67¹ | 62 | 7 | 3.1 | 12.6 | 94 | 36.6% | .353 | 1.26 | 3.48 | 77 | 1.3 |
| 2022 | CHA | AA | 24 | 5 | 2 | 0 | 14 | 14 | 67¹ | 61 | 5 | 5.3 | 9.9 | 74 | 39.1% | .322 | 1.50 | 4.14 | 105 | 0.5 |
| 2022 | LOU | AAA | 24 | 1 | 5 | 0 | 13 | 13 | 55¹ | 53 | 4 | 6.0 | 8.0 | 49 | 31.9% | .302 | 1.63 | 4.07 | 127 | 0.0 |
| 2023 DC | CIN | MLB | 25 | 3 | 4 | 0 | 23 | 8 | 47.3 | 47 | 7 | 4.9 | 8.3 | 44 | 34.6% | .305 | 1.54 | 5.01 | 121 | -0.1 |

*Comparables: Charlie Leesman, Andrew Chafin, Adam Scott*

Acquired as the best prospect in the Jesse Winker/Eugenio Suárez trade just before the 2022 season, Williamson was quickly surpassed by the trade's player-to-be-named-later, Connor Phillips. The TCU product had quite a troubled season on a bunch of fronts, losing his ability to get whiffs in the zone or chases out of it, which led to mediocre strikeout totals and walk rates above five-per-nine at both levels of the high minors. His arsenal features a full assortment of average-ish stuff—a low-90s fastball that scrapes higher, a humpy curve, a cutterish slider and a changeup—and he simply couldn't get anything by better hitters with his wavering command. At times, all three secondaries have flashed and it's possible something jumps here, but we might be talking about "pick a second pitch and hope for a bullpen velocity jump" sooner than we originally thought.

## 13 Chase Petty RHP

Born: 04/04/03   Age: 20   Bats: R   Throws: R   Height: 6'1"   Weight: 190 lb.   Origin: Round 1, 2021 Draft (#26 overall)

| YEAR | TEAM | LVL | AGE | W | L | SV | G | GS | IP | H | HR | BB/9 | K/9 | K | GB% | BABIP | WHIP | ERA | DRA- | WARP |
|------|------|-----|-----|---|---|----|---|----|----|---|----|------|-----|---|-----|-------|------|-----|------|------|
| 2022 | DBT | A | 19 | 0 | 4 | 0 | 18 | 13 | 67² | 57 | 5 | 3.2 | 8.4 | 63 | 59.0% | .292 | 1.20 | 3.06 | 101 | 1.1 |
| 2022 | DAY | A+ | 19 | 1 | 2 | 0 | 7 | 7 | 30² | 27 | 2 | 2.1 | 9.7 | 33 | 43.5% | .301 | 1.11 | 4.40 | 95 | 0.4 |
| 2023 non-DC | CIN | MLB | 20 | 3 | 3 | 0 | 58 | 0 | 50 | 58 | 8 | 4.0 | 6.8 | 38 | 39.4% | .316 | 1.60 | 5.68 | 141 | -0.8 |

*Comparables: Spencer Adams, Tyler Danish, Jacob Turner*

The 19-year-old, 6-foot-1, 190-pound right-hander is the definition of a project. Petty displays impressive raw stuff, with a plus fastball and potentially plus slider, but there are so many questions revolving around his profile. The delivery is very high effort and a bit inconsistent, leading to hanging sliders and fastballs all over the zone. His slot varies and his arm motion is, at times, a bit whippy, causing some concern about durability when throwing 96 mph consistently at such a young age. Though he didn't walk too many this season, the lack of repeatability in delivery is a concern for command moving forward.

The good news here is that the slider is as tight and spinny, when on, as any slider you will see from a teenager in the minors. It is not commanded well, however, and comes from a different slot than Petty's fastball which could cause problems against better hitters. Right now, Petty is a power pitcher who mows down batters with pure stuff. As he faces better hitters, that isn't going to play. The fastball is a late-life riser that will torment opposing minor leaguers but, like his slider, needs to be fine tuned for consistency and command. His changeup lags behind the other two pitches and could get to average in time, but isn't there yet. Between the lack of a consistent third offering, challenges in command, and a need for more good weight, there are a lot of indicators pointing towards relief. That said, the Reds are going to be patient and continue to develop him as a starter even if it's a bit slower going. The waiting is the hardest part.

## 14 Jay Allen II CF

Born: 11/22/02   Age: 20   Bats: R   Throws: R   Height: 6'2"   Weight: 190 lb.   Origin: Round 1, 2021 Draft (#30 overall)

| YEAR | TEAM | LVL | AGE | PA | R | 2B | 3B | HR | RBI | BB | K | SB | CS | AVG/OBP/SLG | DRC+ | BABIP | BRR | DRP | WARP |
|------|------|-----|-----|----|---|----|----|----|-----|----|---|----|----|-------------|------|-------|-----|-----|------|
| 2021 | RED | ROK | 18 | 75 | 20 | 3 | 1 | 3 | 11 | 8 | 12 | 14 | 1 | .328/.440/.557 | | .362 | | | |
| 2022 | DBT | A | 19 | 299 | 48 | 13 | 2 | 3 | 21 | 40 | 73 | 31 | 6 | .224/.359/.332 | 106 | .305 | 1.2 | CF(71) 4.8 | 1.5 |
| 2022 | DAY | A+ | 19 | 84 | 13 | 1 | 2 | 0 | 8 | 4 | 19 | 12 | 4 | .230/.301/.297 | 90 | .304 | 1.8 | CF(16) -0.8 | 0.2 |
| 2023 non-DC | CIN | MLB | 20 | 251 | 19 | 10 | 2 | 2 | 19 | 17 | 74 | 14 | 4 | .206/.275/.290 | 62 | .295 | 2.5 | CF 0 | 0.0 |

*Comparables: Daniel Carroll, Carlos Tocci, Jonathan Mota*

In one of the least explicable promotions I can remember, the Reds pushed Allen—hitting .224/.359/.332 as a teenager in Low-A sandwiched around a month missed with an oblique injury—to High-A for the last month of the season. After flashing a power/contact/plate discipline profile in the complex post-draft in 2021...well, there's a reason we don't get *that* excited about small-sample complex ball gains, and Allen's 2022 is it. There wasn't much in the way of anything loud here except the speed (he stole 43 bases) and defense (he covers a lot of ground in center with a big arm). Allen still has a quick bat on video and doesn't chase an alarming amount, so parts of the underlying 2021 excitement still remain. But he's not driving the ball that much, his swing path is causing him to hit down on the ball, and he's not making the extremely high amount of contact you'd want to carry a speedy groundball profile; there's just not a lot to sustain high hit or power projections at this time. That said, there's also no enormous red flag here to say he's trending towards a bust and if it wasn't for the stock rollercoaster this would be a perfectly reasonable spot for a speedy 2021 second-round prep bat to be a year and a half out. It just looks like the complex gains didn't stick.

## 15 Carlos Jorge 2B

Born: 09/22/03   Age: 19   Bats: L   Throws: R   Height: 5'10"   Weight: 160 lb.   Origin: International Free Agent, 2021

| YEAR | TEAM | LVL | AGE | PA | R | 2B | 3B | HR | RBI | BB | K | SB | CS | AVG/OBP/SLG | DRC+ | BABIP | BRR | DRP | WARP |
|------|------|-----|-----|----|---|----|----|----|-----|----|---|----|----|-------------|------|-------|-----|-----|------|
| 2021 | DSL REDS | ROK | 17 | 188 | 38 | 8 | 10 | 3 | 33 | 24 | 32 | 27 | 5 | .346/.436/.579 | | .413 | | | |
| 2022 | RED | ROK | 18 | 154 | 32 | 7 | 2 | 7 | 21 | 25 | 41 | 27 | 4 | .261/.405/.529 | | .324 | | | |

Jorge has been incredibly productive in both the international and domestic complex leagues over the past two years, hitting a combined .309/.422/.558 with 54 steals in 89 games. A January 2021 international signing for a touch under a half-million dollars, Jorge has smaller levers (listed at 5-foot-10) and makes a very quick move on the ball with a simple, low-effort, uppercut swing. Other than speed, he does not have any obvious carrying tool offensively. While his contact, exit velocity and swing decision markers are all acceptable given his age, they're not standout, and his strikeout rate increased to 26.6% in the Arizona Complex League last summer, raising some hit tool concern. He's likely to be headed to Low-A in 2023 and will be a priority follow given his level of complex performance. (I imagine fantasy managers will be quite excited by his steal totals.)

## 16  Logan Tanner  C

Born: 11/10/00   Age: 22   Bats: R   Throws: R   Height: 6'0"   Weight: 215 lb.   Origin: Round 2, 2022 Draft (#55 overall)

| YEAR | TEAM | LVL | AGE | PA | R | 2B | 3B | HR | RBI | BB | K | SB | CS | AVG/OBP/SLG | DRC+ | BABIP | BRR | DRP | WARP |
|------|------|-----|-----|-----|----|----|----|----|-----|----|----|----|----|--------------|------|-------|------|---------|------|
| 2022 | DBT | A | 21 | 70 | 9 | 3 | 0 | 1 | 7 | 12 | 20 | 1 | 0 | .211/.343/.316 | 111 | .297 | -1.1 | C(14) 0.6 | 0.3 |
| 2023 non-DC | CIN | MLB | 22 | 251 | 20 | 10 | 1 | 2 | 19 | 21 | 92 | 1 | 0 | .204/.278/.288 | 63 | .331 | -4.0 | C 0 | -0.5 |

*Comparables: Dusty Ryan, Adrian Nieto, Armando Araiza*

Tanner was the Reds' second-round pick out of Mississippi State. Long a scout favorite for his huge arm strength and light-tower power potential, it's not actually clear that either his defense or game power is going to be a huge overall plus on a professional field. Tanner slugged just .425 in college with ping bats and .316 with wood in Low-A in 2022. Power *potential* is great, but it does need to show up in games, and his lagging hit tool and downward swing plane has been a significant limitation on his game power. And while he has howitzer arm strength, that doesn't actually necessarily translate to the overall nuances of catching defense, although he's shown potential there too. Tanner does have strong two-way catching potential if he can figure this all out, because there are a lot of plusses on the report.

## 17  Austin Hendrick  OF

Born: 06/15/01   Age: 22   Bats: L   Throws: L   Height: 6'0"   Weight: 195 lb.   Origin: Round 1, 2020 Draft (#12 overall)

| YEAR | TEAM | LVL | AGE | PA | R | 2B | 3B | HR | RBI | BB | K | SB | CS | AVG/OBP/SLG | DRC+ | BABIP | BRR | DRP | WARP |
|------|------|-----|-----|-----|----|----|----|----|-----|----|-----|----|----|--------------|------|-------|------|------------------------------|------|
| 2021 | DBT | A | 20 | 266 | 30 | 16 | 0 | 7 | 29 | 51 | 100 | 4 | 2 | .211/.380/.388 | 93 | .363 | 0.3 | RF(56) 3.0, CF(5) -0.3 | 0.9 |
| 2022 | DBT | A | 21 | 145 | 19 | 4 | 0 | 7 | 21 | 14 | 58 | 2 | 0 | .205/.297/.402 | 80 | .302 | 0.7 | RF(29) -1.2, CF(8) 0.0 | -0.1 |
| 2022 | DAY | A+ | 21 | 299 | 39 | 17 | 0 | 14 | 48 | 29 | 107 | 14 | 5 | .222/.311/.448 | 74 | .308 | -0.3 | CF(31) -0.7, RF(31) 0.1, LF(2) -0.4 | 0.1 |
| 2023 non-DC | CIN | MLB | 22 | 251 | 23 | 11 | 1 | 5 | 24 | 21 | 109 | 4 | 1 | .213/.286/.334 | 76 | .381 | -2.3 | LF 0, CF 0 | -0.3 |

*Comparables: Luis Liberato, Jamie Romak, Demi Orimoloye*

Hendrick, unlike Allen, has some major red flags. Since his pro debut in 2021, he's struck out over 37% of the time at the A-ball levels, just an absurd number even for a relatively inexperienced cold weather prep bat. Swing-and-miss has been a substantive concern on Hendrick dating back to well before the draft due to a grooved-yet-inconsistent swing (one that also causes excessive ground-ball contact), and he pairs it with moderate overall approach issues that manifest very severely against lefties. In summation, he just has not put the bat on the ball even close to enough as a professional. It's unfortunate, because when Hendrick does hit it, he can hit it a mile; he slugged .448 in High-A Dayton last year striking out as much as he did. There's still reasonable upside given his inexperience and ability to put a charge in the ball against righties, but the contact ability will need significant improvement or he's going to top out as a Quad-A platoon bat.

## 18  Joe Boyle  RHP

Born: 08/14/99   Age: 23   Bats: R   Throws: R   Height: 6'7"   Weight: 240 lb.   Origin: Round 5, 2020 Draft (#143 overall)

| YEAR | TEAM | LVL | AGE | W | L | SV | G | GS | IP | H | HR | BB/9 | K/9 | K | GB% | BABIP | WHIP | ERA | DRA- | WARP |
|------|------|-----|-----|---|---|----|----|----|------|----|----|------|------|-----|-------|-------|------|------|------|------|
| 2021 | RED | ROK | 21 | 0 | 0 | 0 | 4 | 4 | 7 | 3 | 0 | 1.3 | 16.7 | 13 | 40.0% | .300 | 0.57 | 0.00 | | |
| 2021 | DBT | A | 21 | 0 | 0 | 0 | 4 | 4 | 12² | 6 | 1 | 9.2 | 19.9 | 28 | 50.0% | .385 | 1.50 | 3.55 | 78 | 0.3 |
| 2022 | DAY | A+ | 22 | 3 | 4 | 0 | 17 | 17 | 74² | 25 | 3 | 7.1 | 14.7 | 122 | 42.6% | .198 | 1.13 | 2.17 | 78 | 1.6 |
| 2022 | CHA | AA | 22 | 0 | 2 | 0 | 6 | 5 | 26 | 21 | 3 | 8.7 | 10.7 | 31 | 34.9% | .300 | 1.77 | 4.85 | 120 | 0.0 |
| 2023 non-DC | CIN | MLB | 23 | 3 | 3 | 0 | 58 | 0 | 50 | 40 | 8 | 8.1 | 12.7 | 71 | 36.0% | .296 | 1.69 | 5.22 | 125 | -0.4 |

A 2020 fifth-rounder out of Notre Dame, Boyle has absolutely no sense of the strike zone, walking 84 in 100 2/3 innings between High-A and Double-A. But he's got a mid-to-upper-90s fastball with bat-missing action and a high-spin plus-plus curveball that makes batters look absolutely foolish when they swing at it. The Reds converted him from a college reliever to a starter, and let's be honest, it's very likely not going to stick with this inability to throw strikes. But he's a potentially dominant two-pitch reliever if and when he ever finds the strike zone.

## 19  Esmith Pineda   OF

Born: 11/13/04   Age: 18   Bats: R   Throws: R   Height: 5'10"   Weight: 183 lb.   Origin: International Free Agent, 2022

| YEAR | TEAM | LVL | AGE | PA | R | 2B | 3B | HR | RBI | BB | K | SB | CS | AVG/OBP/SLG | DRC+ | BABIP | BRR | DRP | WARP |
|---|---|---|---|---|---|---|---|---|---|---|---|---|---|---|---|---|---|---|---|
| 2022 | DSL REDS | ROK | 17 | 57 | 10 | 2 | 0 | 3 | 13 | 7 | 9 | 2 | 1 | .367/.456/.592 | | .405 | | | |

The rare Cincy-developed prospect who has some contact ability. Well, we think he does, at least—he hasn't actually played much or domestically at all yet. Pineda was an $800,000 signing out of Panama last January, six years after starring in the Little League World Series. He was touted as a hit-first outfielder when signing. He only took 57 plate appearances in the DSL (within Voros' Law range, certainly) before being shut down in late-June, but he hit .367/.456/.592. Basically, he made a lot of contact for three weeks in the DSL and hit the ball pretty darn hard, enough to get our attention. He's one to watch for potentially positive 2023 complex reports.

## 20  Victor Acosta   SS

Born: 06/10/04   Age: 19   Bats: S   Throws: R   Height: 5'11"   Weight: 170 lb.   Origin: International Free Agent, 2021

| YEAR | TEAM | LVL | AGE | PA | R | 2B | 3B | HR | RBI | BB | K | SB | CS | AVG/OBP/SLG | DRC+ | BABIP | BRR | DRP | WARP |
|---|---|---|---|---|---|---|---|---|---|---|---|---|---|---|---|---|---|---|---|
| 2021 | DSL PAD | ROK | 17 | 240 | 45 | 12 | 5 | 5 | 31 | 38 | 45 | 26 | 7 | .285/.431/.484 | | .345 | | | |
| 2022 | RED | ROK | 18 | 34 | 5 | 4 | 0 | 0 | 1 | 5 | 7 | 0 | 0 | .214/.353/.357 | | .286 | | | |
| 2022 | PAD | ROK | 18 | 131 | 17 | 3 | 2 | 2 | 11 | 16 | 30 | 5 | 7 | .243/.346/.360 | | .313 | | | |

Picked up for Brandon Drury at the trade deadline, Acosta was originally a seven-figure January 2021 signee in the Padres' system, considered one of the top players in that international class. He's hit a perfectly acceptable .265/.397/.431 across the two complex levels over the past two seasons. On the whole, he has neither shown major offensive holes nor any obvious standout abilities, although at present things seem to be trending power-over-hit and lefty-over-righty. The switch-hitter has a lot of bat speed and a solid swing from the left side, but his right-handed cut does not show the same ability at present, and he's badly struggled from that side of the plate so far. While he has the tools for the position, Acosta has been unreliable defensively at shortstop so far, fielding below .900 everywhere he's gone.

## 21  Allan Cerda   OF

Born: 11/24/99   Age: 23   Bats: R   Throws: R   Height: 6'3"   Weight: 203 lb.   Origin: International Free Agent, 2017

| YEAR | TEAM | LVL | AGE | PA | R | 2B | 3B | HR | RBI | BB | K | SB | CS | AVG/OBP/SLG | DRC+ | BABIP | BRR | DRP | WARP |
|---|---|---|---|---|---|---|---|---|---|---|---|---|---|---|---|---|---|---|---|
| 2021 | DBT | A | 21 | 276 | 42 | 14 | 4 | 14 | 42 | 31 | 85 | 1 | 7 | .242/.362/.524 | 110 | .311 | -1.5 | CF(63) -8.3 | 0.5 |
| 2021 | DAY | A+ | 21 | 87 | 15 | 8 | 1 | 3 | 13 | 10 | 20 | 1 | 1 | .273/.356/.519 | 104 | .333 | -0.2 | RF(11) -0.7, CF(8) -0.8 | 0.2 |
| 2022 | DAY | A+ | 22 | 249 | 38 | 13 | 1 | 13 | 31 | 42 | 91 | 3 | 3 | .219/.369/.488 | 104 | .320 | 0.0 | CF(38) 0.8, RF(16) -1.3 | 1.0 |
| 2022 | CHA | AA | 22 | 257 | 36 | 9 | 0 | 11 | 25 | 42 | 77 | 4 | 1 | .198/.350/.401 | 107 | .250 | 0.3 | RF(39) -0.7, LF(1) 0.1 | 0.8 |
| 2023 non-DC | CIN | MLB | 23 | 251 | 25 | 11 | 1 | 6 | 26 | 26 | 93 | 2 | 1 | .215/.310/.365 | 94 | .338 | -3.5 | LF 0, CF 0 | 0.2 |

*Comparables: Isiah Gilliam, Michael Hermosillo, Jamie Romak*

An extreme Three-True-Outcomes prospect. Cerda takes big, giant hacks at pitches, usually ones within the strike zone. Occasionally he makes contact. It often goes pretty far when he does. All tallied up, he hit .208/.360/.444 as a 22-year-old between High-A and Double-A; the truly concerning number is a 33% strikeout rate, and as you could probably guess, his zone contact numbers are pretty poor. The Reds, facing a bit of a 40-man crunch, pulled a "non-tender and immediately re-sign maneuver" with him in November to avert waivers but keep him in the system, and given that he would probably hit .150 in the majors right now, he wasn't exactly a risk to get Rule 5'd.

# Top Talents 25 and Under (as of 4/1/2023):

1. Elly De La Cruz, SS
2. Hunter Greene, RHP
3. Nick Lodolo, LHP
4. Noelvi Marte, SS/3B
5. Cam Collier, 3B
6. Edwin Arroyo, SS
7. Connor Phillips, RHP

8. Spencer Steer, IF
9. Christian Encarnacion-Strand, 3B
10. Sal Stewart, 3B

Cincinnati has one of the worst big-league rosters in MLB, but it is composed almost exclusively of players under the age of 30. Much of that talent is already detailed above or old enough to escape it here, including 26-year-old former Rookie of the Year Jonathan India; however, the top of their youthful rotation begat what should hopefully be another season dedicated to seeing many talented youngsters debut.

It's a testament to De La Cruz that a pair of likely present mid-rotation starters are supplanted from the first spot, but that's no slight to Greene nor Lodolo. Both posted laudable lines in 2022, with DRA- marks of 84 and 87 respectively and near-identical strikeout and walk rates in very healthy shape. Both players are also well-suited with such a strikeout-laden profile towards surviving in Great American Ball Park, where contact of even the more banal persuasion can end with a trip around the bases and an early stroll back to the dugout. A shoulder strain did cast a pall on Greene's potential Rookie of the Year candidacy, costing him nearly two months in the back half of the season, but he showed the ability to adjust as his constant triple-digit heat began being handled by big leaguers, leaning on his slider with greater frequency. Progression on a firm changeup as has been in vogue for many of the premier young fireballers league-wide would be extremely valuable, and his sophomore campaign will be one to watch with intrigue. Likewise, Lodolo has built a sturdy foundation for himself, with four pitches he utilized at double-digit rates to form a duo worthy of flipping over to on any given night. Perhaps, even, the foundation of the next competitive Reds team.

Worthy of highlighting despite failing to crack these rankings are two players who have surpassed rookie eligibility: righty pitcher Graham Ashcraft and utilityman Jose Barrero. Last year, Ashcraft slotted in just outside the Top-10, and he remains right around that same categorization. The stocky righty has a groundball-oriented repertoire, but was woefully unable to generate swings and misses in his first big-league season. Ashcraft's stuff is surprisingly hittable when a quick glance at the radar gun shows him pushing near triple-digits consistently, but the trouble has stemmed largely from his underwhelming secondaries. It's a good enough heater to have success even as a primary pitch, but Ashcraft won't be more than an innings-eater unless he has an offspeed breakthrough.

Barrero's big-league journey has been nothing short of an unmitigated disaster. Last year, I wrote "Struggles with contact at the dish were always going to be a question mark," and then he went out and struck out 76 times in 174 MLB plate appearances this year. Barrero has fallen a long way from his lofty ceiling as a young prospect ripping through the low minors, but the Cuban is still shy of his 25th birthday and moves well for how much power his swing packs. He's in perhaps the worst organization to get prove-it reps in the middle infield with, however, with a half-dozen talented players elbowing their way into the high minors and big leagues, hungry for a shot.

# Cleveland Guardians

## The State of the System:

Unsurprisingly, Cleveland's system is topped by right-handed pitching prospects who have gotten stuff jumps. It's then filled out by a seemingly endless list of interesting middle infielders and is one of the deeper organizations around overall.

## The Top Ten:

### 1 Daniel Espino   RHP       OFP: 60      ETA: Oh, 20 or so healthy starts from now

Born: 01/05/01   Age: 22   Bats: R   Throws: R   Height: 6'2"   Weight: 225 lb.   Origin: Round 1, 2019 Draft (#24 overall)

| YEAR | TEAM | LVL | AGE | W | L | SV | G | GS | IP | H | HR | BB/9 | K/9 | K | GB% | BABIP | WHIP | ERA | DRA- | WARP |
|------|------|-----|-----|---|---|----|----|----|-----|----|----|------|------|----|------|-------|------|------|------|------|
| 2021 | LYN | A | 20 | 1 | 2 | 0 | 10 | 10 | 42² | 34 | 2 | 4.9 | 13.5 | 64 | 48.4% | .352 | 1.34 | 3.38 | 68 | 1.2 |
| 2021 | LC | A+ | 20 | 2 | 6 | 0 | 10 | 10 | 49 | 30 | 7 | 2.9 | 16.2 | 88 | 31.1% | .280 | 0.94 | 4.04 | 58 | 1.6 |
| 2022 | AKR | AA | 21 | 1 | 0 | 0 | 4 | 4 | 18¹ | 9 | 4 | 2.0 | 17.2 | 35 | 20.7% | .200 | 0.71 | 2.45 | 71 | 0.5 |
| 2023 non-DC | CLE | MLB | 22 | 3 | 3 | 0 | 58 | 0 | 50 | 41 | 8 | 4.1 | 11.7 | 65 | 33.4% | .292 | 1.29 | 3.73 | 100 | 0.3 |

*Comparables: Matt Manning, Drew Hutchison, Mitch Keller*

**The Report:** Espino's profile took a jump in 2021 with a more streamlined delivery showing off a potential plus-plus fastball/slider combo. A consolidation season in 2022 would have been more than fine, but he found yet another gear, sitting 99 with a potentially elite slider and a curveball that flashed plus-plus. After four dominant starts for Akron in April, he hit the IL with tendonitis in his knee. Not ideal, but not a big deal in the grand scheme of things. Then he disappeared for months and it eventually came out that he was dealing with shoulder soreness. Very, very not ideal, and a much bigger deal. A second stuff jump followed by a barking shoulder is concerning, but more concerning is that Espino just didn't get back on a pro mound at any point in 2022. He looked like the best starting pitching prospect in baseball for a month, and he has the requisite development track to suggest this might not have been mere mirage or small sample size. But there's also a reason we used to close every risk section for every pitching prospect with "Also, he's a pitcher."

**OFP:** 60 / no. 3 starter

**Variance:** Very High. Espino doesn't fit neatly into an OFP given his injury-plagued, yet spectacular 2022. The stuff he showed last year was clearly top-of-the-rotation quality. He also showed it for 18 innings and immediately broke down. Four short, dominant starts might have gotten washed out by the rest of a season's worth of outings. It might have been the start of a breakout for the best pitching prospect in baseball. He might not be healthy in 2023, and we'll be talking about him like Forrest Whitley in a few years. He might start Game 2 of the playoffs for the Guardians in October. You know, maybe this should be extreme.

**Jesse Roche's Fantasy Take:** Espino could be this year's Spencer Strider. His fastball-slider combo is elite, and his strikeout potential is unrivaled among pitching prospects. Yet, he enters 2023 with a lot to prove—most importantly, his health. Espino is a top-five dynasty pitching prospect and, if he picks up where he left off, he could quickly ascend to the top with arguably the most fantasy upside.

## 2 Gavin Williams RHP     OFP: 60     ETA: 2023

Born: 07/26/99   Age: 23   Bats: L   Throws: R   Height: 6'6"   Weight: 255 lb.   Origin: Round 1, 2021 Draft (#23 overall)

| YEAR | TEAM | LVL | AGE | W | L | SV | G | GS | IP | H | HR | BB/9 | K/9 | K | GB% | BABIP | WHIP | ERA | DRA- | WARP |
|------|------|-----|-----|---|---|----|----|----|----|----|----|------|------|----|------|-------|------|------|------|------|
| 2022 | LC | A+ | 22 | 2 | 1 | 0 | 9 | 9 | 45 | 25 | 0 | 2.8 | 13.4 | 67 | 40.5% | .298 | 0.87 | 1.40 | 73 | 1.1 |
| 2022 | AKR | AA | 22 | 3 | 3 | 0 | 16 | 16 | 70 | 44 | 9 | 3.3 | 10.5 | 82 | 35.5% | .219 | 1.00 | 2.31 | 79 | 1.7 |
| 2023 non-DC | CLE | MLB | 23 | 3 | 3 | 0 | 58 | 0 | 50 | 46 | 7 | 4.1 | 9.1 | 51 | 34.6% | .290 | 1.37 | 4.20 | 110 | 0.0 |

*Comparables: Spencer Howard, Corbin Burnes, Dellin Betances*

**The Report:** Williams is no stranger to arm issues himself, dealing with several injury-plagued seasons at East Carolina before his 2021 season for the Pirates where he may have been the best pitcher in college baseball. He continued to be both healthy and dominant last year, striking out over 30% of the batters he faced in High- and Double-A. Williams' stuff isn't quite as loud as Espino's but it's chock-full of plus pitches. His fastball has generally sat mid-90s in the pros but it plays above the velocity as it shows good ride up in the zone and plays heavy below the thighs. And he can reach back for 98 or 99 when he needs it. It's a 70-grade fastball and Williams has two above-average breaking balls behind it. His mid-80s slider is inconsistent, but can flash plus two-plane break, while his curve has a bigger 11-6 bend, but given it's more mid-70s it doesn't always show as a true power breaker. Williams' change is a perfectly fine pitch that he sells more with arm speed than fade, but he's not going to need it much even if it reaches its average projection.

Obviously the broader health track record is concerning, but he's currently healthy. Wiliams also has a big, durable frame—one that logged 115 very good innings last year—and a delivery with no real red flags. You could certainly make an argument for Williams over Espino, as I'm far more confident that he's standing on a mound and striking out opposing batters in April 2023, but I'd like to see a little more consistent swing-and-miss out of the slider before I prefer him over the upside that Espino offers.

**OFP:** 60 / Mid-rotation starter

**Variance:** Medium. Williams is just about ready for the majors, just needs to stay healthy.

**Jesse Roche's Fantasy Take:** Williams' profile—fastball up, breaker down—is en vogue in MLB. His analytically-friendly fastball is the star of the show. How much success Williams has, however, likely hinges on further development of his secondaries. His size and stuff bear a resemblance to Logan Gilbert, though his present command falls well short. Williams is a top-50 dynasty prospect.

## 3 Tanner Bibee RHP     OFP: 60     ETA: 2023

Born: 03/05/99   Age: 24   Bats: R   Throws: R   Height: 6'2"   Weight: 205 lb.   Origin: Round 5, 2021 Draft (#156 overall)

| YEAR | TEAM | LVL | AGE | W | L | SV | G | GS | IP | H | HR | BB/9 | K/9 | K | GB% | BABIP | WHIP | ERA | DRA- | WARP |
|------|------|-----|-----|---|---|----|----|----|----|----|----|------|------|----|------|-------|------|------|------|------|
| 2022 | LC | A+ | 23 | 2 | 1 | 0 | 12 | 12 | 59 | 50 | 8 | 2.0 | 13.1 | 86 | 37.4% | .344 | 1.07 | 2.59 | 89 | 1.0 |
| 2022 | AKR | AA | 23 | 6 | 1 | 0 | 13 | 13 | 73² | 51 | 4 | 1.7 | 9.9 | 81 | 34.2% | .260 | 0.88 | 1.83 | 86 | 1.5 |
| 2023 non-DC | CLE | MLB | 24 | 3 | 3 | 0 | 58 | 0 | 50 | 49 | 7 | 2.9 | 8.2 | 46 | 33.5% | .295 | 1.30 | 3.97 | 107 | 0.1 |

*Comparables: Parker Dunshee, Erik Davis, Erik Johnson*

**The Report:** The Guardians' pitching development nowadays is just the "He can't keep getting away with it" GIF. Bibee was drafted as a fourth-year college arm with a pedestrian fastball who posted similarly pedestrian K-rates for the Titans. He did have a suite of polished secondaries and good command. Well, guess what? He now sits in the mid-90s and his slider has tightened up into a swing-and-miss pitch with 12-5 break that goes off a cliff on batters. Bibee offers a second breaking ball look, a more traditional, slower 12-6 curve, but his change is a third potential above-average offering. He moves it around well against lefties, chucking it to the front hip and working it back, or using its good, late fade to get whiffs. He'll double up with it as well. The stuff was backed up by the performance, utter dominance of High-A and Double-A in 2022, giving the Guardians another close-to-ready mid-rotation arm with upside past that.

**OFP:** 60 / no. 3 starter

**Variance:** Medium. Bibee only has a short track record of this kind of stuff and sometimes pitchers give back a bit of these kinds of velocity gains. Still, you can't argue with the development track record of the team or the concrete improvements of the player, and if we give Bibee full credit he is closer to a no. 2 starter than a no. 3.

**Jesse Roche's Fantasy Take:** Bibee throws strikes, lots of strikes, resulting in a miniscule 5.2% walk rate. At the same time, he also misses plenty of bats—placing fourth in K-BB% among pitching prospects with at least 100 IP. Bibee is a tad fly-ball prone, and his fastball sometimes operates best as a get-ahead offering than anything else, but he fits the modern Guardians' pitching dev philosophy to a tee. Remember, we were once skeptical of Shane Bieber as well. Bibee is a top-100 dynasty prospect.

## 4  George Valera  OF       OFP: 55      ETA: 2023
Born: 11/13/00   Age: 22   Bats: L   Throws: L   Height: 6'0"   Weight: 195 lb.   Origin: International Free Agent, 2017

| YEAR | TEAM | LVL | AGE | PA | R | 2B | 3B | HR | RBI | BB | K | SB | CS | AVG/OBP/SLG | DRC+ | BABIP | BRR | DRP | WARP |
|------|------|-----|-----|-----|----|----|----|----|-----|----|-----|----|----|-------------|------|-------|------|-----|------|
| 2021 | LC | A+ | 20 | 263 | 45 | 2 | 4 | 16 | 43 | 55 | 58 | 10 | 5 | .256/.430/.548 | 157 | .276 | 0.4 | RF(38) 3.1, CF(12) -0.8, LF(9) -0.5 | 2.8 |
| 2021 | AKR | AA | 20 | 100 | 6 | 3 | 0 | 3 | 22 | 11 | 30 | 1 | 0 | .267/.340/.407 | 93 | .357 | -0.4 | RF(10) 3.5, LF(8) 0.6, CF(4) -0.4 | 0.6 |
| 2022 | AKR | AA | 21 | 387 | 64 | 17 | 3 | 15 | 59 | 52 | 100 | 2 | 4 | .264/.367/.470 | 109 | .332 | -2.1 | RF(49) -0.2, LF(24) 0.9, CF(12) 2.3 | 2.1 |
| 2022 | COL | AAA | 21 | 179 | 25 | 8 | 0 | 9 | 23 | 22 | 45 | 0 | 0 | .221/.324/.448 | 106 | .248 | -1.0 | RF(21) 1.1, LF(13) 0.3 | 0.6 |
| 2023 DC | CLE | MLB | 22 | 63 | 7 | 2 | 1 | 1 | 6 | 7 | 18 | 1 | 0 | .224/.312/.364 | 93 | .308 | -0.8 | RF 0 | 0.0 |

Comparables: Jesús Sánchez, Carlos González, Michael Saunders

**The Report:** It's no secret that I love George Valera's swing, just check back through the archives of these Cleveland lists and you will see the overwrought metaphors it inspires. But while it might be as cool to look at as a 1950s Alfa Romeo, in the upper minors it was also about as reliable in practice as a 1950s Alfa Romeo. Simply put, Valera didn't make enough contact in the zone last year for us to project even an average hit tool. This was always a potential downside outcome, and while he doesn't chase at all and does pretty good damage when he does make contact, the risk of hit tool collapse against major-league stuff is concerning now. Also, Valera might not make quite enough loud contact for the swing-and-miss trade-off truly worth it. To be clear, he's still a good prospect. Even if he hits .240 in the majors the walks and power should be enough to carry an everyday corner outfield role. He's a better fit for left than right as his arm, while accurate, is merely above-average. He's stretched but playable in center, at least solid, maybe plus in a corner. It all should add up to a nice little regular.

**OFP:** 55 / Above-average corner outfielder

**Variance:** High. The hit tool and positional risks remain, and haven't really mellowed over the years.

**Jesse Roche's Fantasy Take:** Valera struck out, walked or hit a homer in 50.2% of his plate appearances last year. He is what we call a classic Three-True-Outcomes slugger. His minor-league production has been remarkably consistent as a .250-.260 hitter with .210+ ISO and HR/FB rates around 20%. Valera did just that last year, despite ongoing swing-and-miss concerns. Hey, Michael Conforto was a fine fantasy player for several years, particularly in OBP formats. That hope remains for Valera, though he'll still need to make more contact. He is a top-100 dynasty prospect.

### Eyewitness Report: George Valera

**Evaluator:** Jeffrey Paternostro
**Report Date:** 06/30/2022
**Dates Seen:** 6/14/22-6/17/22, 6/19/22
**Risk Factor:** High
**Physical/Health:** Average build, athletic frame, not notably physical, limited projection left

| Tool | Future Grade | Report |
|------|-------------|--------|
| Hit | 50 | Wide open, stooped over like an old timey baseball card photo, steps/dives in to close, waggly and rips it up through the zone with 70 bat speed, barrel control is better than you'd think, but still tops a lot of balls or swings over at his thighs, never expands, some incredible takes. Does damage on contact, but not enough maybe, super high variance hit tool, on-base should be solid though. Stays in well against lefties, can get him inside given how much he dives in |
| Power | 60 | Ball goes boom when he gets the barrel on it, and it's plus raw that plays line to line. Consistent hard contact although the top end exits are just "good." Approach should allow him to get to most of the raw. 25-home-run type bat with plenty of doubles to the left-center gap as well. |
| Baserunning/ Speed | 50 | Perfectly fine runner but violence in the swing means he's never going to pop big home to first. Not a base stealing threat but won't be station to station |
| Glove | 55 | Graded here as a left fielder, has played all three spots and saw in all three. Aggressive defender that tracks well in the gaps, straight line speed isn't ideal for center although he wouldn't kill you there and could handle a smaller outfield. |
| Arm | 55 | Accurate, solid, better fit for left than right. |

**Conclusion:** High variance, impact offensive corner outfielder. Under our old system would argue to 60/40 and he's more likely to be one of those than just an average regular. Potential impact on-base and slugging even in a corner, might hit .220. I know what I'm betting on here though.

## 5 Chase DeLauter  OF    OFP: 55    ETA: Late 2024
Born: 10/08/01  Age: 21  Bats: L  Throws: L  Height: 6'4"  Weight: 235 lb.  Origin: Round 1, 2022 Draft (#16 overall)

**The Report:** DeLauter is one of the more divisive top draft picks in recent memory, and maybe the most divisive college bat since Corey Ray. It's an oversimplification to say this is an analytics versus scouting split, as you can find plenty of scouts who had him as one the best college hitters in the draft. But yeah, both the top-line stats and underlying performance were incredible across his three years at James Madison, including a .437/.576/.828 line last spring before a broken foot ended his season early. That limited action included a rough series against Florida State, which was the best pitching DeLauter faced all year and did perhaps raise an eyebrow or two about how he might fare against better arms in the pro. He has a bit of an unorthodox swing, although in a very different way than Valera's. It looks stiffer than it is, but he isn't a huge bat speed merchant, and despite a good showing with wood in Cape Cod, some amateur scouts weren't sold on a true impact bat. DeLauter has an excellent approach and I'll buy above-average hit and power tools despite a swing less likely to send me into flights of purple prose. He's a good outfielder, but a better fit in a corner than center, so merely above-average offensive performance isn't going to stand out. Still, if the swing decisions and contact rates in the pros are even close to what they were in school, perhaps there's an impact offensive outcome here after all.

**OFP:** 55 / Above-average corner outfielder

**Variance:** Medium. Despite being a bit of a weird college prospect, the risk factors here are fairly normal and what you'd expect given a polished corner bat that might not have a plus offensive tool at the end of the day.

**Jesse Roche's Fantasy Take:** On paper, my oh my, DeLauter pops, with wild stats in college and on the Cape. Nevertheless, he had a lot to prove last spring and, well, he was unable to due to injury. As such, he is *the* premier mystery box of FYPDs. DeLauter is big, powerful and fast with massive upside if his performance translates to pro ball. Given his risk and potential reward, he is a borderline top-10 pick in FYPDs and a top-100 dynasty prospect.

## 6 Bo Naylor  C    OFP: 55    ETA: Debuted in 2022
Born: 02/21/00  Age: 23  Bats: L  Throws: R  Height: 6'0"  Weight: 205 lb.  Origin: Round 1, 2018 Draft (#29 overall)

| YEAR | TEAM | LVL | AGE | PA | R | 2B | 3B | HR | RBI | BB | K | SB | CS | AVG/OBP/SLG | DRC+ | BABIP | BRR | DRP | WARP |
|---|---|---|---|---|---|---|---|---|---|---|---|---|---|---|---|---|---|---|---|
| 2021 | AKR | AA | 21 | 356 | 41 | 13 | 1 | 10 | 44 | 37 | 112 | 10 | 0 | .188/.280/.332 | 82 | .255 | -0.5 | C(73) 7.1 | 1.1 |
| 2022 | AKR | AA | 22 | 220 | 29 | 12 | 2 | 6 | 21 | 45 | 46 | 11 | 3 | .271/.427/.471 | 122 | .333 | 1.3 | C(42) -0.9 | 1.3 |
| 2022 | COL | AAA | 22 | 290 | 44 | 14 | 2 | 15 | 47 | 37 | 75 | 9 | 1 | .257/.366/.514 | 113 | .306 | -1.5 | C(56) 7.2 | 1.8 |
| 2022 | CLE | MLB | 22 | 8 | 0 | 0 | 0 | 0 | 0 | 0 | 5 | 0 | 0 | .000/.000/.000 | 66 | | | C(4) -0.0 | 0.0 |
| 2023 DC | CLE | MLB | 23 | 197 | 20 | 8 | 2 | 4 | 18 | 20 | 51 | 4 | 1 | .207/.296/.346 | 82 | .268 | 0.0 | C 0 | 0.4 |

Comparables: Miguel Montero, John Ryan Murphy, Jarrod Saltalamacchia

**The Report:** Naylor had a nightmare 2021 season, hitting under .200 and striking out in almost a third of his plate appearances in Double-A. Now you can rightfully point out that he was a cold-weather catching prospect who lost a year of important reps to a global pandemic and then had to skip a level. And two of our hoarier cliches apply here: (1) Prospect Lists are a snapshot in time, and (2) player development is not linear. Naylor raised his batting average almost 100 points repeating the Eastern League and continued to hit after an early-season promotion to Triple-A. He got one last kick upstairs to the majors at the end of the season, completing one of the bigger prospect bounce-backs in recent memory.

Naylor has made major strides with his defense as well. He's got good hands and actions behind the plate, although he doesn't always sell the frame jobs as long as you'd like. He can be a bit awkward blocking balls and struggled with his transfers on throws when I saw him live—although his arm strength is fine, and his overall success controlling the running game suggests that was a blip. Naylor may never be the kind of plus defender Cleveland prefers behind the plate, but he's more than good enough to stick and has improved at the more teachable skills to the point that I wouldn't be shocked if there are more gains to come with the glove.

At the plate, Naylor tends to have a bit of a hitch and can struggle to deal with pitches on the outer half, as it appears almost as if he's casting a lure at them. He can drive the ball the other way even when he's late on stuff away, but too many of those pitches can get popped up over the tarp in left field. Naylor's approach is very advanced and there should be enough power and walks to buoy lower batting averages into an overall above-average—if not spectacular—offensive profile, which is plenty fine given his current catching skills.

**OFP:** 55 / Starting catcher

**Variance:** High. Naylor's strikeout and walk rates went in the wrong directions as soon as he wasn't repeating a level, and the swing might lend itself to enough suboptimal contact on top of that where he's sliding back towards the wrong side of .200 again in the majors. Conversely if he does keep hitting for enough power, any more improvements with the glove could move him into the upper echelon of major-league catchers given the scarcity of quality, two-way backstops.

**Jesse Roche's Fantasy Take:** Cleveland's top catchers since 2019 have been glove-first Austin Hedges and Roberto Pérez. This offseason, they signed–wait for it–glove-first Mike Zunino. How do you think this will work out in 2023? That said, Naylor could eventually buck the trend. His impressive blend of contact skills, plate discipline and power should generate a healthy OBP and solid .250/20 production with maybe even a few steals tossed in. That'll play at catcher. Naylor is a top-100 dynasty prospect.

## 7  Gabriel Arias  IF      OFP: 55      ETA: Debuted in 2022

Born: 02/27/00   Age: 23   Bats: R   Throws: R   Height: 6'1"   Weight: 217 lb.   Origin: International Free Agent, 2016

| YEAR | TEAM | LVL | AGE | PA | R | 2B | 3B | HR | RBI | BB | K | SB | CS | AVG/OBP/SLG | DRC+ | BABIP | BRR | DRP | WARP |
|------|------|-----|-----|-----|----|----|----|----|-----|----|-----|----|----|-------------|------|-------|------|-----|------|
| 2021 | COL | AAA | 21 | 483 | 64 | 29 | 3 | 13 | 55 | 39 | 110 | 5 | 1 | .284/.348/.454 | 101 | .351 | -1.1 | SS(82) 0.3, 3B(19) -1.9, 2B(9) -0.3 | 1.3 |
| 2022 | SAN | WIN | 22 | 110 | 9 | 4 | 0 | 1 | 5 | 5 | 28 | 1 | 1 | .202/.245/.269 | | .267 | | | |
| 2022 | COL | AAA | 22 | 323 | 46 | 9 | 0 | 13 | 36 | 25 | 78 | 5 | 1 | .240/.310/.406 | 95 | .279 | 0.6 | SS(43) 0.2, 3B(14) -1.2, 1B(10) -0.3 | 0.7 |
| 2022 | CLE | MLB | 22 | 57 | 9 | 1 | 1 | 1 | 5 | 8 | 16 | 1 | 0 | .191/.321/.319 | 90 | .267 | 0.1 | 3B(9) -0.4, 2B(3) -0.1, SS(3) -0.1 | 0.0 |
| 2023 DC | CLE | MLB | 23 | 161 | 16 | 7 | 1 | 3 | 16 | 10 | 45 | 1 | 1 | .210/.268/.332 | 70 | .277 | -0.2 | 3B 0, SS 0 | -0.2 |

*Comparables: J.P. Crawford, Luis Urías, Jim Pyburn*

**The Report:** The Guardians' middle-infield depth chart is more crowded than The Dead Rabbit on St. Patrick's Day, and Arias' early-season struggles—followed by a May hand injury—kept him from truly establishing himself in the majors in 2022. He bounced back and forth between Columbus and Cleveland after getting back on the field in late June, and added first baseman and outfielder's gloves to his locker. He was even the Guardians' starting first baseman for most of the ALDS, despite arguably being a better defensive shortstop than Amed Rosario. One thing Cleveland needs is hitters though, and Arias struggled at the plate in 2022. A lot of that can be chalked up to the hand injury, and he was quite good in Triple-A in 2021.

Arias seems like a weird choice out of the surfeit of Guardians infield options to end up the super-utility player that his 2022 portented. Perhaps a full-time spot at shortstop opens up if Cleveland chooses to deal Rosario entering his walk year. Sometimes a good problem to have ends up an actual problem for one of your prospects. And Arias doesn't have an obvious fit on the 2023 Guardians roster, but if the offensive tools play to the previous 5-hit/6-power projection—and we're somewhat confident a healthy Arias gets back there—they should be able to find a place in the lineup and in the field for his bat.

**OFP:** 55 / Above-average infielder

**Variance:** Medium. Arias showed a bit too much swing-and-miss in his various major-league call-ups, but he dealt with injuries, new positions and bouncing between Triple-A and the majors, so you can handwave some of the struggles. Still his stock is down a bit from last year even if the plus regular upside is still clearly present.

**Jesse Roche's Fantasy Take:** Arias' glove makes him a much better real-life than fantasy prospect. His suspect contact rate, aggressive approach and groundball-heavy batted-ball profile limit his offensive potential. Yet, he has amassed 880 plate appearances between Triple-A and MLB before his 23rd birthday. Some slack must be afforded. Arias has flashed 20+ homer power and some speed, and he should be rostered in leagues with over 300 prospects.

## 8  Brayan Rocchio  MI     OFP: 55     ETA: 2023

Born: 01/13/01   Age: 22   Bats: S   Throws: R   Height: 5'10"   Weight: 170 lb.   Origin: International Free Agent, 2017

| YEAR | TEAM | LVL | AGE | PA | R | 2B | 3B | HR | RBI | BB | K | SB | CS | AVG/OBP/SLG | DRC+ | BABIP | BRR | DRP | WARP |
|------|------|-----|-----|-----|----|----|----|----|-----|----|----|----|----|-------------|------|-------|------|-----|------|
| 2021 | LAG | WIN | 20 | 76 | 11 | 6 | 1 | 2 | 6 | 5 | 5 | 2 | 2 | .391/.440/.594 | | .403 | | | |
| 2021 | LC | A+ | 20 | 288 | 45 | 13 | 1 | 9 | 33 | 20 | 65 | 14 | 6 | .265/.337/.428 | 108 | .319 | 1.0 | SS(36) -1.4, 2B(16) 2.2, 3B(12) 0.3 | 1.3 |
| 2021 | AKR | AA | 20 | 203 | 34 | 13 | 4 | 6 | 30 | 13 | 41 | 7 | 4 | .293/.360/.505 | 112 | .350 | -1.1 | SS(43) 1.5, 2B(2) 0.2 | 1.0 |
| 2022 | AKR | AA | 21 | 432 | 62 | 21 | 1 | 13 | 48 | 42 | 81 | 12 | 6 | .265/.349/.432 | 114 | .302 | 2.9 | SS(51) -2.1, 2B(44) 4.0 | 2.4 |
| 2022 | COL | AAA | 21 | 152 | 21 | 6 | 0 | 5 | 16 | 12 | 21 | 2 | 3 | .234/.298/.387 | 112 | .241 | -0.1 | SS(26) -2.9, 2B(8) 0.5 | 0.4 |
| 2023 non-DC | CLE | MLB | 22 | 251 | 22 | 11 | 2 | 4 | 23 | 16 | 53 | 6 | 3 | .227/.286/.341 | 77 | .277 | -0.8 | 2B 0, 3B 0 | 0.0 |

*Comparables: Jorge Polanco, Adrian Cardenas, J.P. Crawford*

**The Report:** Rocchio followed up his 2021 power breakout with a bit of an uneven campaign in 2022. He's still wringing a fair bit of power out of his narrow, 5-foot-10 frame, but he sells out for pull-side fly ball contact with a longer swing and a lot of lift. Rocchio never gets cheated up there, but has enough barrel control to rip line drives and run into 15 or so home runs a year. The grip-it-and-rip approach can make the quality of contact suffer, and he can get a bit indecisive against offspeed, leading to a suboptimal batted-ball profile despite overall solid contact rates. Rocchio still hasn't found the ideal hit/power balance but, as he is now, should be around average with the stick.

Rocchio split his time between second and shortstop in 2022—in deference to the crowded middle-infield situation up and down the Guardians org—but is a sure-handed everyday shortstop with a plus arm. The glove is only above-average there, so you'd like a little more out of the bat to stamp him as a first-division regular at the six, and that's not even considering the other slick gloves ahead of him on Cleveland's depth chart.

**OFP:** 55 / Above-average shortstop

**Variance:** Medium. I do worry that Rocchio's aggressive, pull-happy approach may see him swing and miss a fair bit more in the majors, but he's consolidated the power gains in the upper minors, is a switch-hitter with little platoon split and a solid glove man at a premium position. That player usually vests his pension.

**Jesse Roche's Fantasy Take:** Rocchio has intriguing five-category potential, even though he likely never actualizes it. As stated above, he has solid bat-to-ball ability and enough pull-side pop to knock 15 homers, but his hit/power balance is off. Meanwhile, he has plenty of speed, but he is woefully inefficient stealing bases, including 14-for-23 last year. In some universe, Rocchio puts it all together and turns in a .280/15/20 force. Is it this one? Unlikely. Still, there is enough to like here in fantasy to edge him into the dynasty top 100.

## 9  Logan Allen  LHP     OFP: 55     ETA: 2023

Born: 09/05/98   Age: 24   Bats: R   Throws: L   Height: 6'0"   Weight: 190 lb.   Origin: Round 2, 2020 Draft (#56 overall)

| YEAR | TEAM | LVL | AGE | W | L | SV | G | GS | IP | H | HR | BB/9 | K/9 | K | GB% | BABIP | WHIP | ERA | DRA- | WARP |
|------|------|-----|-----|---|---|----|----|----|-----|----|----|------|------|----|------|-------|------|------|------|------|
| 2021 | LC | A+ | 22 | 5 | 0 | 0 | 9 | 9 | 51¹ | 37 | 3 | 2.3 | 11.7 | 67 | 44.1% | .296 | 0.97 | 1.58 | 80 | 1.1 |
| 2021 | AKR | AA | 22 | 4 | 0 | 0 | 12 | 10 | 60 | 40 | 9 | 2.0 | 11.4 | 76 | 28.8% | .238 | 0.88 | 2.85 | 96 | 0.5 |
| 2022 | AKR | AA | 23 | 5 | 3 | 0 | 13 | 13 | 73 | 58 | 9 | 2.7 | 12.8 | 104 | 39.0% | .316 | 1.10 | 3.33 | 79 | 1.8 |
| 2022 | COL | AAA | 23 | 4 | 4 | 0 | 14 | 14 | 59² | 64 | 8 | 4.4 | 11.0 | 73 | 37.3% | .354 | 1.56 | 6.49 | 101 | 0.8 |
| 2023 non-DC | CLE | MLB | 24 | 3 | 3 | 0 | 58 | 0 | 50 | 47 | 7 | 3.5 | 9.3 | 52 | 34.9% | .297 | 1.32 | 3.91 | 104 | 0.1 |

*Comparables: Marco Gonzales, TJ House, Kyle Gibson*

**The Report:** The last remaining Logan Allen in Cleveland's org, Logan Allen the Younger—soon to be an IPA from Market Garden Brewery—is on the cusp of his own major-league debut. The arsenal won't overwhelm you, as his fastball sits either side of 90. He will move it around well, and isn't afraid to try and work it inside to righties, so the pitch plays to average despite the velocity readings. Both his slider and changeup offer swing-and-miss looks, with the slide piece showing big 1-7 sweep that can get under bats as well. Allen will front-door it against righties or run it down and away from lefties. The change is the bigger platoon neutralizer though, a potential plus pitch with good sink. Allen has added a cutter recently for a firmer glove-side look, but he can struggle to get it consistently down. Allen checks every other crafty lefty box. He mixes the whole repertoire well and works at a Buehrlesque pace. He struggled in Triple-A where he was a bit more hittable and consequently nibbled a bit more, but assuming he can iron that out in 2023, he should be a cromulent major-league starter in short order.

**OFP:** 55 no. 3/4 starter

**Variance:** Medium. The Triple-A struggles were prolonged enough to be concerning given the pedestrian fastball and merely above-average command. This is always a pitching prospect profile with thin margins against the bigger boppers. Allen's secondaries do have more swing-and-miss characteristics—and he did continue to miss bats in the International League—than you usually find in the fourth-starter/pitchability-lefty type. So he's got that going for him.

**Jesse Roche's Fantasy Take:** Allen's limited fastball velocity caps his fantasy utility. It is true that an occasional pitcher who barely scraps 90 mph finds sustained success, but usually those arms have exceptional command. Allen does not. On the other hand, he has a now-lengthy track record of missing bats despite his limitations. Consequently, Allen is a rare soft-tossing lefty who may be fantasy-relevant, and he is a borderline top-200 dynasty prospect.

## 10   Angel Martinez   MI     OFP: 50     ETA: 2024

Born: 01/27/02   Age: 21   Bats: S   Throws: R   Height: 6'0"   Weight: 165 lb.   Origin: International Free Agent, 2018

| YEAR | TEAM | LVL | AGE | PA | R | 2B | 3B | HR | RBI | BB | K | SB | CS | AVG/OBP/SLG | DRC+ | BABIP | BRR | DRP | WARP |
|---|---|---|---|---|---|---|---|---|---|---|---|---|---|---|---|---|---|---|---|
| 2021 | LYN | A | 19 | 424 | 62 | 20 | 6 | 7 | 46 | 43 | 88 | 13 | 6 | .241/.319/.382 | 101 | .296 | -1.3 | 2B(49) 3.9, SS(32) -0.3, 3B(13) -0.3 | 1.5 |
| 2022 | LC | A+ | 20 | 331 | 46 | 17 | 3 | 10 | 27 | 40 | 58 | 10 | 6 | .288/.384/.477 | 121 | .330 | -2.3 | SS(50) -3.2, 2B(23) 0.1, 3B(4) -0.1 | 1.3 |
| 2022 | AKR | AA | 20 | 103 | 10 | 6 | 1 | 3 | 17 | 12 | 18 | 2 | 1 | .244/.356/.451 | 116 | .266 | 0.2 | 2B(19) -2.5, SS(4) 1.9 | 0.4 |
| 2023 non-DC | CLE | MLB | 21 | 251 | 21 | 11 | 2 | 3 | 22 | 20 | 52 | 4 | 2 | .222/.290/.335 | 77 | .273 | -2.2 | 2B 0, 3B 0 | -0.1 |

*Comparables: Jonathan Araúz, José Peraza, J.P. Crawford*

**The Report:** Yet another IFA middle infielder with a solid major-league projection. Like Rocchio, Martinez is a switch-hitter who generates surprising power out of a smaller frame. He gets his power with a bit more whippy bat speed and isn't as pull-happy, but does struggles more against offspeed. Martinez also shows near equal facility from both sides of the plate, although his right-handed swing is a bit more contact-oriented. He's aggressive if he gets something to hack at early in counts, but he knows the zone well and will work a walk or two. The offensive projection is a bit more stable than Rocchio's, although he lacks the same power upside if everything clicks. In the field, Martinez is more likely to settle in as a good second baseman than good shortstop, but like every other Guardians prospect he has a fair bit of experience at short and third as well.

**OFP:** 50 / Second-division regular or good fifth infielder

**Variance:** Medium. Martinez is gonna need to hit a bit more than the infielders ahead of him on this list given he's less likely to have significant defensive value. He scuffled a little in his first taste of Double-A, but I don't have a ton of long-term concern about the bat, even if he isn't the highest-upside hitter.

**Jesse Roche's Fantasy Take:** Martinez offers a little of everything: He makes contact, has enough pop to hit double-digit homers and he has some speed. Whether it is enough to (1) secure a MLB job likely at the keystone and (2) provide solid fantasy production is unclear. As noted above, "he isn't the highest upside hitter," though Martinez's well-rounded game places him within the dynasty top-200.

# Outside the Top Ten:

## 11   Justin Campbell   RHP

Born: 02/14/01   Age: 22   Bats: L   Throws: R   Height: 6'7"   Weight: 219 lb.   Origin: Round 1, 2022 Draft (#37 overall)

Campbell could have been purpose-built for the Guardians' pitching development. It was even a bit of a surprise that he slid to their second-round pick, but he perhaps wasn't as overpowering his junior year at Oklahoma State as he'd been the year before. He's a 6-foot-7 long-limbed righty with an advanced suite of secondaries and a fastball he can run into the mid-90s. Campbell has the Guardians' preferred higher slot and a bit of deception in his delivery to boot. Would anyone be shocked if he's sitting mid-90s next year, a tweaked slider sitting plus rather than flashing there and the same 60-grade change sitting in his back pocket? I won't be, but it hasn't happened yet, and we suggested similar kinds of breakouts for Guardian pitching prospects last year that didn't come to pass. Yes, we need to consider the player development apparatus more, but we also need to see some signs that development is happening first. So for now, let's say Campbell is a potential third or fourth starter and see where the chips fall from here.

## 12  Jaison Chourio  CF

Born: 05/19/05   Age: 18   Bats: S   Throws: R   Height: 6'1"   Weight: 162 lb.   Origin: International Free Agent, 2022

| YEAR | TEAM | LVL | AGE | PA | R | 2B | 3B | HR | RBI | BB | K | SB | CS | AVG/OBP/SLG | DRC+ | BABIP | BRR | DRP | WARP |
|---|---|---|---|---|---|---|---|---|---|---|---|---|---|---|---|---|---|---|---|
| 2022 | DSL CLER | ROK | 17 | 175 | 32 | 7 | 3 | 1 | 28 | 40 | 22 | 14 | 4 | .280/.446/.402 | | .324 | | | |

Yes, he's Jackson's younger brother. Yes, his DSL OPS was higher than Jackson's at the same age. No, you should not care about that. No, we are not predicting a similar breakout in 2023. Yes, you should already own him in your dynasty league. Yes, that constitutes the one and only piece of fantasy baseball advice I will give this year. No, I don't ever want to rank a foreign complex 17-year-old. Yes, his contact profile is so good already that he ends up this high in a good system.

## 13  Cody Morris  RHP

Born: 11/04/96   Age: 26   Bats: R   Throws: R   Height: 6'4"   Weight: 205 lb.   Origin: Round 7, 2018 Draft (#223 overall)

| YEAR | TEAM | LVL | AGE | W | L | SV | G | GS | IP | H | HR | BB/9 | K/9 | K | GB% | BABIP | WHIP | ERA | DRA- | WARP |
|---|---|---|---|---|---|---|---|---|---|---|---|---|---|---|---|---|---|---|---|---|
| 2021 | AKR | AA | 24 | 0 | 0 | 0 | 5 | 5 | 20 | 14 | 1 | 3.2 | 13.1 | 29 | 38.1% | .317 | 1.05 | 1.35 | 91 | 0.3 |
| 2021 | COL | AAA | 24 | 2 | 2 | 0 | 9 | 8 | 36² | 25 | 1 | 2.9 | 12.8 | 52 | 43.8% | .304 | 1.01 | 1.72 | 76 | 0.9 |
| 2022 | GUA | ROK | 25 | 0 | 0 | 0 | 3 | 3 | 6 | 4 | 0 | 0.0 | 13.5 | 9 | 46.2% | .308 | 0.67 | 0.00 | | |
| 2022 | COL | AAA | 25 | 0 | 0 | 1 | 6 | 3 | 15¹ | 5 | 2 | 3.5 | 17.6 | 30 | 45.5% | .150 | 0.72 | 2.35 | 59 | 0.5 |
| 2022 | CLE | MLB | 25 | 1 | 2 | 0 | 7 | 5 | 23² | 21 | 3 | 4.6 | 8.7 | 23 | 36.9% | .290 | 1.39 | 2.28 | 109 | 0.1 |
| 2023 DC | CLE | MLB | 26 | 7 | 6 | 0 | 48 | 10 | 75.3 | 64 | 10 | 3.6 | 10.2 | 86 | 37.0% | .284 | 1.24 | 3.42 | 94 | 0.9 |

*Comparables: Framber Valdez, Jefry Rodriguez, Domingo Germán*

When Morris has been healthy, he's been dominant. He just hasn't been healthy enough. His last two seasons have both started in July. A shoulder strain delayed his 2022 debut, but he quickly pitched his way to the majors and looked like the Guardians' fourth-best starter during his September outings. He snagged a bullpen spot for the Division Series as well, and while he may not start 2023 in the Cleveland rotation, if he starts the year healthy, he'll be on the major-league staff somewhere. Morris' changeup is an easy plus bat-misser, and his curve and hard cutter aren't too shabby either. The injury track record is concerning—and the fastball is pretty pedestrian despite regularly hitting 95—but when he has pitched, he's looked like an above-average pitcher of some sort.

## 14  Jose Tena  MI

Born: 03/20/01   Age: 22   Bats: L   Throws: R   Height: 5'11"   Weight: 190 lb.   Origin: International Free Agent, 2017

| YEAR | TEAM | LVL | AGE | PA | R | 2B | 3B | HR | RBI | BB | K | SB | CS | AVG/OBP/SLG | DRC+ | BABIP | BRR | DRP | WARP |
|---|---|---|---|---|---|---|---|---|---|---|---|---|---|---|---|---|---|---|---|
| 2021 | SCO | WIN | 20 | 75 | 16 | 6 | 1 | 0 | 9 | 10 | 10 | 2 | 1 | .387/.467/.516 | | .444 | | | |
| 2021 | LC | A+ | 20 | 447 | 58 | 25 | 2 | 16 | 58 | 27 | 117 | 10 | 5 | .281/.331/.467 | 102 | .355 | 1.6 | SS(81) -7.3, 3B(13) 0.3, 2B(11) 1.0 | 1.0 |
| 2022 | EST | WIN | 21 | 154 | 11 | 5 | 1 | 2 | 16 | 8 | 32 | 4 | 3 | .259/.301/.353 | | .312 | | | |
| 2022 | AKR | AA | 21 | 550 | 74 | 25 | 6 | 13 | 66 | 25 | 138 | 8 | 5 | .264/.299/.411 | 86 | .332 | 0.5 | SS(71) -0.4, 2B(47) -0.9 | 0.7 |
| 2023 non-DC | CLE | MLB | 22 | 251 | 20 | 10 | 2 | 4 | 22 | 12 | 66 | 3 | 1 | .221/.263/.328 | 63 | .292 | -2.8 | 2B 0, 3B 0 | -0.6 |

*Comparables: Willi Castro, Jorge Polanco, J.P. Crawford*

One more medium-power, slick-gloved infielder for the road. Tena is more likely to be the bench version of this kind of player as he is more aggressive at the plate and is looking to lift and pull to the point where the hit tool is more fringy than average. Tena is a perfectly fine shortstop: good on the backhand with rangy, smooth actions and a plus, accurate arm. However, it's not a good enough shortstop glove to carry the fringy offensive profile on its own. The defensive flexibility—he'd be plus at third or second—should make him a nice bench infielder, although you'd prefer he be a bit more leverageable. He's run reverse platoon splits the last two years.

## 15 Petey Halpin   CF
Born: 05/26/02   Age: 21   Bats: L   Throws: R   Height: 6'0"   Weight: 185 lb.   Origin: Round 3, 2020 Draft (#95 overall)

| YEAR | TEAM | LVL | AGE | PA | R | 2B | 3B | HR | RBI | BB | K | SB | CS | AVG/OBP/SLG | DRC+ | BABIP | BRR | DRP | WARP |
|------|------|-----|-----|-----|----|----|----|----|-----|----|----|----|----|----------------|------|-------|------|------------------------|------|
| 2021 | LYN | A | 19 | 246 | 34 | 14 | 6 | 1 | 18 | 21 | 50 | 11 | 9 | .294/.363/.425 | 101 | .376 | 0.4 | CF(29) 2.2, LF(17) 4.0 | 1.5 |
| 2022 | LC | A+ | 20 | 434 | 68 | 21 | 4 | 6 | 36 | 45 | 92 | 16 | 7 | .262/.346/.385 | 103 | .330 | 3.1 | CF(94) 0.6, RF(9) 0.8 | 2.5 |
| 2023 non-DC | CLE | MLB | 21 | 251 | 19 | 11 | 3 | 2 | 20 | 17 | 54 | 5 | 3 | .223/.283/.315 | 69 | .284 | -1.4 | LF 0, CF 0 | -0.3 |

*Comparables: Tyrone Taylor, Dustin Fowler, Gorkys Hernández*

Halpin didn't really take much of a step forward in 2022, but he also continued to hold his own against older competition. There was a bit of attrition in the offensive line, and a bit more swing-and-miss in the zone, which is concerning, but he continued to hit line drives and get on base. His swing shows off above-average bat and good whip and has always seemed just a slight tweak away from unlocking a bit more game power, but we are now at the point where there is a bit too much swing-and-miss without any kind of loud contact trade-off. Halpin stays prospect-list relevant for now, though as he is a potential above-average center fielder who shows off his plus wheels on the grass and can really go get it. That will buy him some time to find a bit more juice in the bat, but Double-A is always a stern test for this kind of profile. We'll have a much better idea of if he can be an average starter or if he's just a bench outfielder by next year's list.

## 16 Jake Fox   UT
Born: 02/12/03   Age: 20   Bats: L   Throws: R   Height: 6'0"   Weight: 185 lb.   Origin: Round 3, 2021 Draft (#95 overall)

| YEAR | TEAM | LVL | AGE | PA | R | 2B | 3B | HR | RBI | BB | K | SB | CS | AVG/OBP/SLG | DRC+ | BABIP | BRR | DRP | WARP |
|------|------|-----|-----|-----|----|----|----|----|-----|----|----|----|----|----------------|------|-------|------|--------------------------------|------|
| 2021 | IND | ROK | 18 | 49 | 10 | 1 | 0 | 0 | 6 | 6 | 9 | 7 | 0 | .405/.469/.429 | | .500 | | | |
| 2022 | LYN | A | 19 | 470 | 74 | 25 | 4 | 5 | 44 | 74 | 90 | 21 | 3 | .247/.381/.374 | 136 | .307 | 3.9 | 2B(61) 1.1, CF(31) 0.5, 3B(6) -1.3 | 3.9 |
| 2023 non-DC | CLE | MLB | 20 | 251 | 20 | 11 | 2 | 2 | 20 | 23 | 50 | 5 | 1 | .214/.293/.307 | 72 | .267 | -1.9 | 2B 0, 3B 0 | -0.2 |

*Comparables: Kelvin Melean, Reegie Corona, Hector Guevara*

Fox—the Guardians' third-round pick in 2021—was a prep shortstop who is now mostly splitting his time between second base and center field. The arm will limit him to the right side of the infield—at least in an everyday role—and while his routes on the grass are raw, the foot speed might make him a bit more valuable in the outfield. He's perfectly fine at second base mind you, and was perfectly fine at the plate in 2022 given the aggressiveness of the assignment. Once upon a time, Fox would have spent the summer wearing delightfully goofy jerseys in short-season Mahoning Valley. And at present, his swing doesn't really match his game. There's a big leg kick, a bit of a dippy hand path and a lot of medium-depth fly ball contact. Fox might grow into some game power, but he's better off focusing more on line drives in the meantime, as his swing left him failing to adjust to full-season breakers a bit too often.

## 17 Xzavion Curry   RHP
Born: 07/27/98   Age: 24   Bats: R   Throws: R   Height: 6'0"   Weight: 195 lb.   Origin: Round 7, 2019 Draft (#220 overall)

| YEAR | TEAM | LVL | AGE | W | L | SV | G | GS | IP | H | HR | BB/9 | K/9 | K | GB% | BABIP | WHIP | ERA | DRA- | WARP |
|------|------|-----|-----|---|---|----|----|----|------|----|----|------|------|----|-------|-------|------|------|------|------|
| 2021 | LYN | A | 22 | 3 | 0 | 0 | 5 | 5 | 25¹ | 12 | 1 | 1.4 | 13.5 | 38 | 27.5% | .220 | 0.63 | 1.07 | 72 | 0.6 |
| 2021 | LC | A+ | 22 | 5 | 1 | 0 | 13 | 13 | 67² | 53 | 10 | 1.6 | 10.6 | 80 | 30.9% | .261 | 0.96 | 2.66 | 91 | 1.0 |
| 2022 | AKR | AA | 23 | 5 | 3 | 0 | 13 | 11 | 69 | 56 | 9 | 2.5 | 10.4 | 80 | 31.7% | .275 | 1.09 | 3.65 | 102 | 0.9 |
| 2022 | COL | AAA | 23 | 4 | 1 | 0 | 12 | 10 | 53 | 50 | 9 | 3.9 | 9.2 | 54 | 36.2% | .287 | 1.38 | 4.58 | 103 | 0.6 |
| 2022 | CLE | MLB | 23 | 0 | 1 | 0 | 2 | 2 | 9¹ | 13 | 1 | 5.8 | 2.9 | 3 | 32.4% | .333 | 2.04 | 5.79 | 142 | -0.1 |
| 2023 DC | CLE | MLB | 24 | 3 | 2 | 0 | 22 | 3 | 30.3 | 31 | 5 | 3.1 | 7.7 | 26 | 31.7% | .297 | 1.37 | 4.38 | 116 | 0.0 |

*Comparables: Erik Johnson, Justin Grimm, Daniel Mengden*

Curry got knocked around a bit more in the upper minors—and during his major-league cameo—despite having a good ride on his fastball, as the fringy velocity and command meant it could be too hittable at times. His power slider is above-average though, and he might fare better in shorter bursts, where he can lean more heavily on his swing-and-miss secondary, as neither the curve or change have been anything to write home, or too much in this blurb, about.

## 18  Jhonkensy Noel  RF

Born: 07/15/01   Age: 21   Bats: R   Throws: R   Height: 6'3"   Weight: 250 lb.   Origin: International Free Agent, 2017

| YEAR | TEAM | LVL | AGE | PA | R | 2B | 3B | HR | RBI | BB | K | SB | CS | AVG/OBP/SLG | DRC+ | BABIP | BRR | DRP | WARP |
|------|------|-----|-----|-----|-----|-----|-----|-----|-----|-----|-----|-----|-----|------------------|------|-------|------|-----------------------------|------|
| 2021 | LYN | A | 19 | 162 | 36 | 10 | 1 | 11 | 40 | 7 | 27 | 2 | 1 | .393/.426/.693 | 148 | .421 | 0.3 | 1B(18) 0.8, 3B(13) 1.5 | 1.6 |
| 2021 | LC | A+ | 19 | 111 | 13 | 3 | 0 | 8 | 25 | 9 | 31 | 3 | 1 | .280/.351/.550 | 124 | .328 | -1.0 | 3B(17) 0.5 | 0.6 |
| 2022 | LC | A+ | 20 | 252 | 35 | 9 | 0 | 19 | 42 | 18 | 80 | 1 | 0 | .219/.286/.509 | 114 | .237 | -1.7 | 3B(24) -3.3, RF(17) -1.6, 1B(6) 1.3 | 0.6 |
| 2022 | AKR | AA | 20 | 278 | 43 | 16 | 2 | 13 | 42 | 30 | 63 | 2 | 0 | .242/.338/.488 | 119 | .271 | -1.5 | RF(33) 0.4, LF(16) -0.2, 1B(9) 0.3 | 1.5 |
| 2023 DC | CLE | MLB | 21 | 29 | 3 | 1 | 0 | 1 | 3 | 2 | 9 | 0 | 0 | .226/.281/.376 | 86 | .301 | -0.4 | RF 0 | 0.0 |

*Comparables: Jo Adell, Byron Buxton, Anthony Rizzo*

Noel made it all the way to Triple-A as a 20-year-old with his light-tower power intact every step of the way. He has a rather unusual setup at the plate, wide and squatty with basically all his weight on his back leg before lunging forward via a big leg kick. It all takes a while to get going, and it's a length and (a whole lotta) strength swing that is going to load up on all three true outcomes. Twenty-four more games at third base—and a fielding percentage of .854 therein—moved him off the hot corner for good, and he saw time at corner outfield and first base in 2022. First base is the more likely long-term home, which means he will have to keep banging 30 bombs every year, as there's not much bench utility if he's not starting.

## 19  Tanner Burns  RHP

Born: 12/28/98   Age: 24   Bats: R   Throws: R   Height: 6'0"   Weight: 210 lb.   Origin: Round 1, 2020 Draft (#36 overall)

| YEAR | TEAM | LVL | AGE | W | L | SV | G | GS | IP | H | HR | BB/9 | K/9 | K | GB% | BABIP | WHIP | ERA | DRA- | WARP |
|------|------|-----|-----|-----|-----|-----|-----|-----|------|-----|-----|------|------|-----|-------|-------|------|------|------|------|
| 2021 | LC | A+ | 22 | 2 | 5 | 0 | 18 | 18 | 75² | 64 | 10 | 3.4 | 10.8 | 91 | 39.7% | .300 | 1.23 | 3.57 | 88 | 1.3 |
| 2022 | AKR | AA | 23 | 3 | 7 | 0 | 21 | 21 | 88² | 75 | 14 | 4.6 | 9.3 | 92 | 34.7% | .269 | 1.35 | 3.55 | 108 | 0.8 |
| 2023 non-DC | CLE | MLB | 24 | 3 | 3 | 0 | 58 | 0 | 50 | 52 | 8 | 4.7 | 7.8 | 43 | 33.7% | .301 | 1.56 | 5.22 | 131 | -0.5 |

*Comparables: A.J. Schugel, Drew Anderson, Chris Ellis*

Lest you think every right-handed college arm the Guardians pick is guided by fate to a big stuff gain, Burns remains pretty close to the same pitcher he was when they drafted him out of Auburn in 2020. He missed plenty of bats in Double-A, owing to good extension on his low-90s fastball and a mid-80s slider that he can manipulate for razorblade movement or a bit slurvier sweep, but his uptempo delivery and mechanical upper half meant continued command and control wobbles. Just because the step forward hasn't happened doesn't mean it won't, but for now, Burns remains somewhere in the back-end starter/ good middle-reliever tier, depending on how you want to deploy him.

## 20  Doug Nikhazy  LHP

Born: 08/11/99   Age: 23   Bats: L   Throws: L   Height: 6'0"   Weight: 205 lb.   Origin: Round 2, 2021 Draft (#58 overall)

| YEAR | TEAM | LVL | AGE | W | L | SV | G | GS | IP | H | HR | BB/9 | K/9 | K | GB% | BABIP | WHIP | ERA | DRA- | WARP |
|------|------|-----|-----|-----|-----|-----|-----|-----|-----|-----|-----|------|------|-----|-------|-------|------|-------|------|------|
| 2022 | LC | A+ | 22 | 4 | 4 | 0 | 21 | 21 | 93 | 59 | 8 | 6.6 | 11.4 | 118 | 40.5% | .252 | 1.37 | 3.19 | 94 | 1.2 |
| 2022 | AKR | AA | 22 | 0 | 2 | 0 | 3 | 3 | 9¹ | 14 | 1 | 10.6 | 9.6 | 10 | 53.3% | .448 | 2.68 | 11.57 | 116 | 0.1 |
| 2023 non-DC | CLE | MLB | 23 | 3 | 3 | 0 | 58 | 0 | 50 | 50 | 8 | 7.3 | 9.7 | 54 | 36.6% | .314 | 1.82 | 6.13 | 146 | -0.9 |

*Comparables: Framber Valdez, Justin Steele, Aaron Miller*

Nikhazy dominated the SEC in 2021, working his way into the second round of the draft. He works off a low-90s fastball and a big yakker of a hook, but has struggled to throw strikes in the pros so far. He has a funky delivery and a bit of a stiff arm action which can lead to bouts of wildness with the fastball. When he can get into counts to unleash his big breaking curve though, he will be able to rack up strikeouts. It's never going to be a particularly tidy command and control profile, but Nikhazy will need to throw more strikes to pitch his way into the back of a major-league rotation. They say lefties figure it out later, I suppose, and the curve is intriguing enough to give him a bit of time.

# Top Talents 25 and Under (as of 4/1/2023):

1. Andrés Giménez, 2B/SS
2. Steven Kwan, OF
3. Triston McKenzie, RHP
4. Emmanuel Clase, RHP
5. Daniel Espino, RHP
6. Gavin Williams, RHP
7. Tanner Bibee, RHP
8. Oscar Gonzalez, OF
9. George Valera, OF
10. Tyler Freeman, IF

The surprising AL Central title winners rode a wave of youth to the top of the division, soaring past injury-wracked White Sox and Twins clubs to push a limping Yankees club to the brink in the ALDS. Between the current depth on the farm and the youth of the club's productive core, this year's Cleveland club should be no surprise as they contend once again. Even names unlisted above like outfielder Will Benson, utilityman Richie Palacios and southpaw Konnor Pilkington could be quality contributors.

The top of Cleveland's crop is as versatile as any quintet a club could hope to build around. Giménez was a 23-year-old revelation, hoovering up everything in range and many things outside of it defensively, while also taking a huge stride forward offensively. Giménez had flashed better abilities at times in the minors, but it'd always come at a cost. Power, but more whiffs, or contact, but meager pop. 2022 was a season of synergy. He was joined in a breakout by Kwan, whose season in many other years would have brought home Rookie of the Year hardware. A surprise contender amidst the expected frontrunners of Julio Rodríguez and Adley Rutschman, Kwan delivered as the type of profile often hardest to project for evaluators: an undersized, power-light spray hitter who walks consistently and strikes out rarely in the minors. For every Kwan, there are a dozen players whose repertoire does not translate, and yet Kwan's exceptional pitch selection and bat control have not fallen off against the best pitching in the world. That makes the Californian a delightful outlier, and perhaps the most impactful breakout for Cleveland this past season.

On the pitching side, last year I suggested McKenzie needed to get more out of his fastball to complement his excellent offspeed, and McKenzie did just that. His curveball remained a vital weapon, and he worked in the zone with both breaking balls more often, but the key step forward was an extra half-tick on his heater. It's tempting to say the four-seamer was markedly different, but much of what benefited the slender slinger was primarily better results, and a sensational defensive group behind him. Clase also relied heavily on that defense even despite his blistering triple-digit average heat. His cutter is something without true comparison in MLB, and helps him run one of the highest ground-ball rates in the bigs. Cleveland had Clase's back like few other relievers are privy to, but the truth is that Clase consistently saws hitters off and misses barrels enough to be one of the league's premier high-leverage solutions.

Gonzalez is a toolsy outfielder with ample power and a knack for contact that does not crack. Cleveland will have to settle for their 6-foot-4 right fielder being a solid hitter despite one of the most aggressive approaches in MLB. The variance is still wild here, but as he sees more big-league pitching, he could respond by shedding some less discerning taste buds or being offered an even more well-curated platter of pitches outside the zone that he cannot help but chase. Freeman might have been expected to be the more big-league ready hitter, but his 102 DRC+ in limited work to Gonzalez's 108 DRC+ suggests he was not nearly so far off the path despite lesser results. Freeman is an ideal bench player for this Cleveland club, with experience at shortstop, third and second base, and a low-whiff approach that is in keeping with the majority of his teammates. He's performed brilliantly at every minor-league level and seemed just as capable of putting the bat to the ball in the bigs. The question is whether he can take the step Kwan did and convert that contact and barrel control into consistent success despite next to no over-the-fence power.

# Colorado Rockies

## The State of the System:

This isn't a good system yet, but it continues to improve, especially on the position player side.

## The Top Ten:

### 1 Ezequiel Tovar  SS      OFP: 60      ETA: Debuted in 2022

Born: 08/01/01   Age: 21   Bats: R   Throws: R   Height: 6'0"   Weight: 162 lb.   Origin: International Free Agent, 2017

| YEAR | TEAM | LVL | AGE | PA | R | 2B | 3B | HR | RBI | BB | K | SB | CS | AVG/OBP/SLG | DRC+ | BABIP | BRR | DRP | WARP |
|------|------|-----|-----|-----|-----|-----|-----|-----|-----|-----|-----|-----|-----|-------------|------|-------|-----|-----|------|
| 2021 | SRR | WIN | 19 | 96 | 10 | 2 | 0 | 3 | 10 | 5 | 20 | 2 | 0 | .161/.219/.287 | | .167 | | | |
| 2021 | FRE | A | 19 | 326 | 60 | 21 | 3 | 11 | 54 | 14 | 38 | 21 | 4 | .309/.346/.510 | 132 | .320 | 2.5 | SS(64) 8.1 | 3.3 |
| 2021 | SPO | A+ | 19 | 143 | 19 | 9 | 0 | 4 | 18 | 3 | 19 | 3 | 2 | .239/.266/.396 | 115 | .252 | -1.0 | SS(32) -1.8 | 0.4 |
| 2022 | HFD | AA | 20 | 295 | 39 | 15 | 3 | 13 | 47 | 25 | 64 | 17 | 3 | .318/.386/.545 | 113 | .378 | 1.4 | SS(64) 0.9 | 1.6 |
| 2022 | COL | MLB | 20 | 35 | 2 | 1 | 0 | 1 | 2 | 2 | 9 | 0 | 0 | .212/.257/.333 | 94 | .261 | -0.1 | SS(9) -0.4 | 0.0 |
| 2023 DC | COL | MLB | 21 | 422 | 44 | 19 | 3 | 9 | 42 | 21 | 95 | 10 | 4 | .227/.276/.357 | 75 | .280 | -0.7 | SS -1, 2B 0 | -0.1 |

*Comparables: Carlos Correa, Xander Bogaerts, Starlin Castro*

**The Report:** Tovar followed up a breakout 2021 season in A-ball by hitting .300 with power in Double-A. This should have been a more challenging assignment for a prospect who hit just .239/.266/.396 during a month of High-A at-bats—and then struggled in Fall Ball—but whatever Tovar worked on over the winter paid dividends, as he showed all five tools at the six in 2022. He has a smooth stroke with an easy, rhythmic weight transfer. It's a line-drive swing with enough lift and bat speed to show sneaky present pop, even though he hasn't really filled out his 20-year-old frame. His eyes get a little wide on breakers down—something that major-league arms exploited in his brief cameo in Coors—so I'm not fully in on a plus hit tool here yet, but a context-neutral .270 and 15-20 bombs seems reasonable, with more in the tank with some refinement of his swing decisions.

Tovar is a slick shortstop who is just one tier below "competes for Gold Gloves." He's rangy without looking like it, as he just glides along the dirt and gets to more balls than you'd think given that his straight-line speed is only average. He checks every other box for a plus shortstop. He's good on the turn, his hands and actions are elevator-jazz smooth, he throws well on the run and his overall arm strength is solid for the left side. Tovar generally posted below-average or fringe run times for me, but other scouts had a few 4.25s in there. I assume he will settle in around average, but is an aggressive baserunner who will look to steal when he's on. He missed time over the summer with a groin injury and could use a month or two in Albuquerque to adjust to better-quality offspeed, but Tovar is likely to be the everyday shortstop for Colorado at some point next summer.

**OFP:** 60 / Plus, two-way shortstop

**Variance:** Low. Tovar wasn't exactly ready for the majors during his late September call-up, but he has handled an aggressive development track and just needs to smooth out some issues on offspeed pitches to be a good regular in short order.

**Jesse Roche's Fantasy Take:** The Rockies are a perpetual fantasy tease these days. The organization has failed to truly develop a prospect into a fantasy force since Nolan Arenado and Trevor Story. Seemingly, Tovar will receive a significant opportunity next year. But, we're talking about the Rockies here, and my ~~pessimistic~~ realistic expectation is that we'll see an aging veteran siphon off playing time from Tovar. Yet, "a context-neutral .270 and 15-20 bombs" from "an aggressive baserunner who will look to steal when he's on" is quite a fantasy player, especially when aided by Coors Field. Tovar is a top-20 dynasty prospect in standard formats (dinged in OBP formats) with even more fantasy value in formats that value proximity.

## Eyewitness Report: Ezequiel Tovar

**Evaluator:** Jeffrey Paternostro
**Report Date:** 06/30/2022
**Dates Seen:** 17x 4/2022-6/2022
**Risk Factor:** Med.
**Physical/Health:** Average frame, some room to fill out upper body further but should maintain most of his twitch/athleticism.

| Tool | Future Grade | Report |
|---|---|---|
| Hit | 55 | Even stance, rhythmic weight transfer with leg lift, never out of balance even when swinging over offspeed. Plus bat speed, looking to hit line drives. Can handle elite level velocity, struggles with better breakers down, but he's 20 and the approach is solid enough. Will hit it where it's pitched, doesn't get pull happy. Enough struggles with non-fastballs so far to keep it below plus, but should be a very solid hitter. |
| Power | 50 | Wants to be level and extend, prefers to work gap-to-gap, but will absolutely crush a mistake, average raw at present will get to solid-average as he fills out, should get to most of it. |
| Baserunning/ Speed | 45 | Low 4.3s for the most part, not a burner, but speed plays better laterally in the field than straight line base-to-base. Good, aggressive baserunner underway, and will get some steals. |
| Glove | 60 | Silky shortstop, glides in the field, has grown on me from 55 to true plus over the breadth of the looks. Smooth on the turn, actions and hands are plus, gets to more balls than you'd think given the foot speed. Good internal clock. Not super loud at the 6, but seems to make at least one plus defensive play a game. |
| Arm | 60 | Might be 55 arm strength and carry, but ability to get the ball out quickly and accurately from a variety of angles and on the move makes the throwing play up. |

**Conclusion:** Tovar is one of the youngest players in the Eastern League and while the lack of game experience shows through at the plate from time to time, he's a true two-way shortstop with offensive upside past the grades above. I wouldn't be shocked if he grows into more power than this, and even if the hit tool falls a little short, the defensive nous should make him a regular for a number of years.

## 2 Zac Veen OF          OFP: 60     ETA: 2024

Born: 12/12/01   Age: 21   Bats: L   Throws: R   Height: 6'4"   Weight: 190 lb.   Origin: Round 1, 2020 Draft (#9 overall)

| YEAR | TEAM | LVL | AGE | PA | R | 2B | 3B | HR | RBI | BB | K | SB | CS | AVG/OBP/SLG | DRC+ | BABIP | BRR | DRP | WARP |
|---|---|---|---|---|---|---|---|---|---|---|---|---|---|---|---|---|---|---|---|
| 2021 | FRE | A | 19 | 479 | 83 | 27 | 4 | 15 | 75 | 64 | 126 | 36 | 17 | .301/.399/.501 | 117 | .396 | -1.7 | RF(69) -0.2, LF(26) 2.2 | 2.6 |
| 2022 | SPO | A+ | 20 | 400 | 72 | 19 | 3 | 11 | 60 | 50 | 90 | 50 | 4 | .269/.368/.439 | 100 | .332 | 6.7 | RF(77) 3.3, LF(2) -0.1 | 2.6 |
| 2022 | HFD | AA | 20 | 141 | 12 | 4 | 0 | 1 | 7 | 14 | 42 | 5 | 5 | .177/.262/.234 | 71 | .253 | -0.7 | RF(33) -1.1 | -0.2 |
| 2023 non-DC | COL | MLB | 21 | 251 | 22 | 10 | 2 | 3 | 22 | 22 | 72 | 11 | 5 | .223/.296/.330 | 79 | .310 | 1.7 | LF 0, RF 0 | 0.2 |

*Comparables: Jorge Bonifacio, Justin Williams, Carlos González*

**The Report:** On the surface, Veen's performance in 2022 looks confirmatory of his top-prospect status. He got out of the gates in Spokane a touch slow, but heated up over the summer, earning a late-season promotion to Hartford. There, he scuffled, but not in an overly concerning way for a 20-year-old getting his first taste of the upper minors. The staff report on him described a player without a real weakness in his game, showing an all-fields approach with potential plus power. Veen is a plus runner who's a canny base thief, and he has about the sweetest lefty swing you will see.

However, that swing has produced fairly pedestrian underlying metrics. Veen's all-fields approach means he's in the big part of the ballpark too often. For a future corner bat—he's played almost exclusively right field despite the foot speed—he hits the ball on the ground an awful lot. And while he may have plus raw power, his in-game outputs are fairly average. So what exactly is the carrying tool here? This is of course all fixable, and many future plus bats have to go through these kinds of adjustments in the minors. But Veen hasn't yet, and that's worth keeping an eye on.

**OFP:** 60 / First-division outfielder

**Variance:** Medium There's a disconnect between what Veen looks like from behind home plate and what he's produced on the field. And he hasn't produced in the upper minors.

**Jesse Roche's Fantasy Take:** Veen stole 55 bases across 126 games between High- and Double-A, then 16 more in just 18 games in the AFL. Let that sink in for a second. It is uncommon for 6-foot-4 presumed sluggers to be such a threat to steal. Indeed, Veen's speed surprisingly drives his future fantasy value. As noted above, his power has not quite developed as expected, and there is an even further gap between his game and raw power. Despite his fantasy-friendly skill set, he comes with a lot of risk, especially after crashing and burning in Double-A. Regardless, Veen has incredible upside should the long-promised power finally arrive, and he falls squarely in the middle of the top 50 for dynasty.

## 3  Adael Amador  SS   OFP: 60   ETA: 2025
Born: 04/11/03  Age: 20  Bats: S  Throws: R  Height: 6'0"  Weight: 160 lb.  Origin: International Free Agent, 2019

| YEAR | TEAM | LVL | AGE | PA | R | 2B | 3B | HR | RBI | BB | K | SB | CS | AVG/OBP/SLG | DRC+ | BABIP | BRR | DRP | WARP |
|---|---|---|---|---|---|---|---|---|---|---|---|---|---|---|---|---|---|---|---|
| 2021 | RCK | ROK | 18 | 200 | 41 | 10 | 1 | 4 | 24 | 27 | 29 | 10 | 7 | .299/.394/.445 | | .331 | | | |
| 2022 | FRE | A | 19 | 555 | 100 | 24 | 0 | 15 | 57 | 87 | 67 | 26 | 12 | .292/.415/.445 | 122 | .312 | 4.3 | SS(108) -4.8, 2B(7) -1.4 | 3.1 |
| 2023 non-DC | COL | MLB | 20 | 251 | 22 | 10 | 1 | 3 | 21 | 24 | 40 | 5 | 3 | .217/.297/.313 | 76 | .252 | -1.2 | 2B 0, SS 0 | 0.0 |

*Comparables: Daniel Robertson, Brad Harman, Jake Hager*

**The Report:** Amador shined all year in Low-A, getting glowing reports on his hit tool from our whole Cal League contingent. The switch-hitter starts wide open with a fair bit of hand movement pre-swing, but once he gets going, there's plus-plus bat speed and he spits out hard line drives on anything close to the plate. Amador knows the zone well, too, walking more than he struck out in 2022. His swing is geared to go back through the origin—although he does have some pop from the left side—so this is a hit-over-power profile, but there might be a lot of hit.

Amador is an above-average runner who is an aggressive, if inefficient base stealer. The speed plays on the dirt though, and he has the arm and range for short, although the rest of the defensive tool set needs further refinement. He might end up at second base long-term, but wherever he winds up in the field, he'll look good as a classic no. 2 hitter.

**OFP:** 60 / Plus regular up-the-middle

**Variance:** Medium. The hardest thing to project is the hit tool, but Amador passes both the eye and metrics test so far.

**Jesse Roche's Fantasy Take:** Amador's blend of superb bat-to-ball ability, impeccable plate discipline and huge bat speed combine to make one helluva hitter. Among qualified batters in full-season ball, he had the third best walk-to-strikeout ratio (1.3). In addition, he has enough pop and speed to potentially provide sneaky five-category production. Regardless, Amador's hitting ability is the fantasy draw. He is a top-100 dynasty prospect and even more valuable in simulation formats like Scoresheet.

## 4  Drew Romo  C/DH   OFP: 55   ETA: Late 2024 / Early 2025
Born: 08/29/01  Age: 21  Bats: S  Throws: R  Height: 6'1"  Weight: 205 lb.  Origin: Round 1, 2020 Draft (#35 overall)

| YEAR | TEAM | LVL | AGE | PA | R | 2B | 3B | HR | RBI | BB | K | SB | CS | AVG/OBP/SLG | DRC+ | BABIP | BRR | DRP | WARP |
|---|---|---|---|---|---|---|---|---|---|---|---|---|---|---|---|---|---|---|---|
| 2021 | FRE | A | 19 | 339 | 48 | 17 | 2 | 6 | 47 | 19 | 50 | 23 | 6 | .314/.345/.439 | 121 | .348 | 1.2 | C(69) 13.1 | 3.2 |
| 2022 | SPO | A+ | 20 | 420 | 52 | 19 | 5 | 5 | 58 | 35 | 81 | 18 | 3 | .254/.321/.372 | 100 | .306 | 0.0 | C(57) 8.3 | 2.1 |
| 2023 non-DC | COL | MLB | 21 | 251 | 19 | 10 | 2 | 2 | 20 | 14 | 52 | 6 | 2 | .221/.268/.310 | 62 | .275 | -1.3 | C 0 | -0.3 |

*Comparables: Neil Walker, Austin Romine, Austin Hedges*

**The Report:** There was a fair amount of internal debate last offseason about whether Romo or Tovar was the better prospect, and both ended up just off the Top 101. But while Tovar jumped to Double-A and established himself as one of the top shortstop prospects in the game, Romo spent 2022 in High-A, fading badly in the second half and struggling to consistently impact the baseball. Now, he's a prep catching prospect, so he's going to have a slower burn than an infielder, and catching in the minors is a grind for anyone. While our Northwest League reports did note him wearing down late in summer, he only caught 57 games, and given his light usage behind the plate, it's difficult to hand-wave that as merely a young catcher tiring at the end of a long season.

Romo's glove still rates as well-above-average, garnering at least plus marks for both blocking and framing. At the plate, he makes good swing decisions, but a wide base cuts off much of his above-average raw power, and a contact-oriented stroke leaves him with exit velocities far off what you'd like at this point. There's more to unlock at the plate, and the defense will likely get him to the majors one way or the other, but Romo's 2022 is once again a reminder that catching prospects are weird.

**OFP:** 55 / Everyday, glove-first catcher

**Variance:** High. Romo is a prep catching prospect who struggled after a level jump. He hasn't worked close to a standard 100-game workload behind the plate yet, and while you could project both offensive tools at average-or-better, there's a lot of variance there as he moves up the ladder and spends more time decked out in the tools of ignorance.

**Jesse Roche's Fantasy Take:** Any time a prospect is pegged as a "glove-first catcher" it doesn't inspire much fantasy excitement. While there may be more to unlock with Romo, he has failed to hit for much power yet, including a paltry 4.4% HR/FB ratio last year. It'll only get tougher as he enters the upper minors.

## 5 Benny Montgomery CF    OFP: 55    ETA: 2025/2026

Born: 09/09/02   Age: 20   Bats: R   Throws: R   Height: 6'4"   Weight: 200 lb.   Origin: Round 1, 2021 Draft (#8 overall)

| YEAR | TEAM | LVL | AGE | PA | R | 2B | 3B | HR | RBI | BB | K | SB | CS | AVG/OBP/SLG | DRC+ | BABIP | BRR | DRP | WARP |
|------|------|-----|-----|-----|-----|-----|-----|-----|-----|-----|-----|-----|-----|-------------|------|-------|-----|-----|------|
| 2021 | RCK | ROK | 18 | 52 | 7 | 0 | 1 | 0 | 6 | 5 | 9 | 5 | 1 | .340/.404/.383 | | .421 | | | |
| 2022 | FRE | A | 19 | 264 | 48 | 20 | 3 | 6 | 42 | 21 | 71 | 9 | 1 | .313/.394/.502 | 93 | .429 | 0.5 | CF(44) -0.8 | 0.5 |
| 2023 non-DC | COL | MLB | 20 | 251 | 19 | 11 | 2 | 2 | 20 | 14 | 84 | 4 | 0 | .215/.270/.307 | 63 | .326 | -2.8 | CF 0 | -0.6 |

*Comparables: Albert Almora Jr., Drew Waters, Andrew McCutchen*

**The Report:** Injuries limited Montgomery to just 62 games in 2022. The top-line performance in the Cal League was solid considering he played the entire season as a 19-year-old, and he has toned down some of the extraneous motions in his swing—which was incredibly divisive when he was an amateur. It's not exactly quiet though, featuring a leg kick and a dippy little hitch in the hand path. Montgomery can hit the ball hard when he squares it up given his plus bat speed, but his trigger can lack fluidity and the quality of contact suffers for it. He hits the ball on the ground more often than not, and you can beat him inside with good fastballs, or leave him poking harmlessly at offspeed away. The speed and defense remain pristine despite the injuries, and if he can tap into some of his ample raw power, there's an above-average regular lurking the profile. But until he proves that herky-jerky swing can square better stuff, there's significant risk that he's merely a bench outfielder.

**OFP:** 55 / Above-average center fielder

**Variance:** High. I'm a soft touch for an unconventional stroke, but Montgomery doesn't consistently make his work yet.

**Jesse Roche's Fantasy Take:** Montgomery has as much fantasy upside as any prospect in this system due to his power potential and plus speed. Over his final four weeks, he hit .362/.455/.617 and closed the year on a 14-game hitting streak. His evolving swing remains a concern, however, meaning he remains a project. That said, Montgomery is an intriguing fantasy prospect who could quickly jump into the dynasty top 100 with further development.

## 6 Warming Bernabel 3B    OFP: 55    ETA: Late 2024/Early 2025

Born: 06/06/02   Age: 21   Bats: R   Throws: R   Height: 6'0"   Weight: 180 lb.   Origin: International Free Agent, 2018

| YEAR | TEAM | LVL | AGE | PA | R | 2B | 3B | HR | RBI | BB | K | SB | CS | AVG/OBP/SLG | DRC+ | BABIP | BRR | DRP | WARP |
|------|------|-----|-----|-----|-----|-----|-----|-----|-----|-----|-----|-----|-----|-------------|------|-------|-----|-----|------|
| 2021 | RCK | ROK | 19 | 86 | 18 | 5 | 0 | 6 | 31 | 5 | 12 | 5 | 1 | .432/.453/.743 | | .426 | | | |
| 2021 | FRE | A | 19 | 94 | 9 | 6 | 0 | 1 | 7 | 7 | 14 | 4 | 1 | .205/.287/.313 | 111 | .232 | -0.9 | 3B(17) 0.6 | 0.4 |
| 2022 | FRE | A | 20 | 300 | 52 | 19 | 0 | 10 | 54 | 29 | 39 | 21 | 6 | .317/.390/.504 | 127 | .336 | -1.1 | 3B(64) 1.8 | 2.1 |
| 2022 | SPO | A+ | 20 | 109 | 18 | 7 | 0 | 4 | 17 | 2 | 17 | 2 | 2 | .305/.315/.486 | 114 | .329 | 0.1 | 3B(25) -0.7 | 0.4 |
| 2023 non-DC | COL | MLB | 21 | 251 | 20 | 11 | 1 | 3 | 22 | 13 | 48 | 5 | 3 | .220/.267/.319 | 65 | .264 | -1.3 | 3B 0 | -0.5 |

*Comparables: Juan Silverio, Aderlin Rodríguez, Dustin Geiger*

**The Report:** Bernabel has been on my radar for a couple years now given his feel for hitting, and sure enough he posted a .300 batting average at both his A-ball stops in 2022. Like Amador, his partner on the left side of the Fresno infield for much of the season, Bernabel's swing is a bit noisy. He is handsy during his load and uses a big leg kick for timing. That should lead to some sync or adjustment problems, but he just makes good contact more often than not. While not really looking to lift and pull, Bernabel has a fair bit of pop already and should have at least average power to go with a plus hit tool. In the field, his work at third base is inconsistent at best. He has the arm strength for the position, and while he's not as hopeless there as his error total might suggest, he didn't always look comfortable. If he can get to even a gentleman's 45 at the hot corner, the bat should take care of the rest, but that's still a bigger "if" than you'd like at this point.

**OFP:** 55 / Bat-first, but above-average third baseman

**Variance:** High. I'm a soft touch for an unconventional stroke—and I think Bernabel's will work just fine—but there needs to be some positional/defensive value for him to be a good regular.

**Jesse Roche's Fantasy Take:** Now, "bat-first" is what we want to hear! He is an extremely aggressive hitter with solid bat-to-ball ability and enough quality contact to drive strong batting averages. However, Bernabel's swing-happy approach results in lots of swings outside the zone, some resulting poor contact and few walks. As such, he has far less value in OBP formats. Nevertheless, Bernabel is a top-200 dynasty prospect in standard formats given his batting-average upside.

## 7  Gabriel Hughes  RHP          OFP: 55          ETA: Late 2024
Born: 08/22/01   Age: 21   Bats: R   Throws: R   Height: 6'4"   Weight: 220 lb.   Origin: Round 1, 2022 Draft (#10 overall)

| YEAR | TEAM | LVL | AGE | W | L | SV | G | GS | IP | H | HR | BB/9 | K/9 | K | GB% | BABIP | WHIP | ERA | DRA- | WARP |
|------|------|-----|-----|---|---|----|----|----|----|---|----|------|-----|---|-----|-------|------|-----|------|------|
| 2023 non-DC | COL | MLB | 21 | 3 | 3 | 0 | 58 | 0 | 50 | 56 | 8 | 4.7 | 7.1 | 39 | 37.9% | .310 | 1.64 | 5.77 | 143 | -0.8 |

**The Report:** Hughes was a rarity in the 2022 college pitching class, as he threw a full, healthy season last year. A two-way player for much of his time at Gonzaga, the tall, sturdy righty works primarily off a mid-90s fastball and a power 12-6 slider. He can pop a four-seam up to miss bats or work down with the two-seam for ground balls. The slide piece has above-average potential, but can be a bit humpy at times. Hughes' change should end up with some utility, although it's pretty firm at present. Given the late acceleration and effort in his delivery, though, there'll be reliever risk in the profile until the fastball/slider combo proves good enough to turn over lineups.

**OFP:** 55 / no. 3/4 starter or late-inning reliever

**Variance:** High. Frankly, Hughes' delivery makes my elbow wince, but he held up in 2022 throwing over 100 innings between college and the pros. I still think it's better than a coin flip that he ends up in the bullpen given the current arsenal and delivery, but with this kind of arm speed, he might be a very good reliever.

**Jesse Roche's Fantasy Take:** Ignore the draft capital attached to Hughes in fantasy. He is a hard pass in upcoming first-year player drafts. Avoid Rockies pitching prospects, especially those with a reliever risk. End stop.

## 8  Yanquiel Fernandez  RF          OFP: 50          ETA: 2025
Born: 01/01/03   Age: 20   Bats: L   Throws: L   Height: 6'2"   Weight: 198 lb.   Origin: International Free Agent, 2019

| YEAR | TEAM | LVL | AGE | PA | R | 2B | 3B | HR | RBI | BB | K | SB | CS | AVG/OBP/SLG | DRC+ | BABIP | BRR | DRP | WARP |
|------|------|-----|-----|----|----|----|----|----|-----|----|----|----|----|-------------|------|-------|-----|-----|------|
| 2021 | DSL ROC | ROK | 18 | 202 | 29 | 17 | 0 | 6 | 34 | 22 | 26 | 0 | 0 | .333/.406/.531 | | .361 | | | |
| 2022 | FRE | A | 19 | 523 | 76 | 33 | 5 | 21 | 109 | 39 | 114 | 5 | 1 | .284/.340/.507 | 108 | .330 | -3.3 | RF(90) 0.9 | 2.1 |
| 2023 non-DC | COL | MLB | 20 | 251 | 20 | 11 | 2 | 4 | 22 | 13 | 72 | 1 | 0 | .216/.262/.330 | 64 | .294 | -4.2 | 1B 0, RF 0 | -0.9 |

*Comparables: Carlos González, Caleb Gindl, Justin Williams*

**The Report:** Fernandez is your classic right field prospect. He's projectable with present pop at the plate. There's plenty of runway to his swing, as he sets up high and wraps a bit, but plus bat speed with good whip allows him to catch up to and lift even better velocity. Although it's a power-over-hit profile due to fringe barrel control, Fernandez he should make enough hard contact to keep his batting averages in the .260 range. You might prefer your right field prospect to still be playing center field in A-ball. I hear ya. You would definitely prefer your right field prospect to be a better right fielder than Fernandez is right now. His foot speed is fine for a corner, and his arm is strong enough for the position. He is just a bit awkward and heavy-footed tracking and closing on balls. Routes and reads can be improved with reps of course, but he needs a fair bit of defensive development in addition to conquering the future challenges he'll face at the plate.

**OFP:** 50 / Average corner outfielder

**Variance:** High. The power stroke looks like it will play up the ladder, but Fernandez has a ways to go up said ladder, and if he ends up more of a 1B/DH type, you will be less enthused about penciling him into the lineup everyday.

**Jesse Roche's Fantasy Take:** Sign me up for a "power-over-hit" prospect who "should make enough hard contact to keep his batting averages in the .260 range" and potentially call Coors Field home. Like others on his list, Fernandez is a tad aggressive with so-so contact skills and too many balls on the ground. Yet, he possesses underrated fantasy upside, and very well could look like a .260 hitter with 20-plus homers when it is all said and done.

## 9 Jaden Hill  RHP     OFP: 50     ETA: 2025
Born: 12/22/99   Age: 23   Bats: R   Throws: R   Height: 6'4"   Weight: 234 lb.   Origin: Round 2, 2021 Draft (#44 overall)

| YEAR | TEAM | LVL | AGE | W | L | SV | G | GS | IP | H | HR | BB/9 | K/9 | K | GB% | BABIP | WHIP | ERA | DRA- | WARP |
|------|------|-----|-----|---|---|----|----|----|-----|----|----|------|------|----|------|-------|------|------|------|------|
| 2022 | RCK | ROK | 22 | 0 | 0 | 0 | 7 | 7 | 10¹ | 11 | 0 | 3.5 | 9.6 | 11 | 44.8% | .379 | 1.45 | 3.48 | | |
| 2022 | FRE | A | 22 | 0 | 0 | 0 | 3 | 3 | 7¹ | 7 | 0 | 2.5 | 17.2 | 14 | 38.5% | .538 | 1.23 | 2.45 | 78 | 0.1 |
| 2023 non-DC | COL | MLB | 23 | 3 | 3 | 0 | 58 | 0 | 50 | 49 | 8 | 4.2 | 8.8 | 49 | 36.2% | .296 | 1.44 | 4.67 | 120 | -0.2 |

*Comparables: Todd Van Steensel, Pedro Araujo, Phil Irwin*

**The Report:** A potential first-overall pick before Tommy John surgery a mere seven starts into his junior year at LSU, Hill made it back onto the mound towards the end of the 2022 season. The strengths and weaknesses remain the same as they were in college—not a surprise given the lack of pro innings in the interim—a fastball he can dial up into the high-90s with run, a six-plus change on the positive side of the ledger, poor command and a lack of a right-on-right glove-side option for the negative. How the breaking balls and strike-throwing progress in 2023 will tell us a lot more about whether Hill is a starter or reliever long-term, but he still may have the most upside of any arm in the Rockies system.

**OFP:** 50 / no. 4 starter or late-inning reliever

**Variance:** Extreme. Hill has a realistic plus ceiling as a starter or reliever. He's also pretty likely to be a reliever. He's also thrown 69 innings in the last four years. Not nice.

**Jesse Roche's Fantasy Take:** Avoid Rockies pitching prospects, especially those with a reliever risk. End stop.

## 10 Sean Bouchard  LF     OFP: 50     ETA: Debuted in 2022
Born: 05/16/96   Age: 27   Bats: R   Throws: R   Height: 6'3"   Weight: 215 lb.   Origin: Round 9, 2017 Draft (#266 overall)

| YEAR | TEAM | LVL | AGE | PA | R | 2B | 3B | HR | RBI | BB | K | SB | CS | AVG/OBP/SLG | DRC+ | BABIP | BRR | DRP | WARP |
|------|------|-----|-----|-----|----|----|----|----|-----|----|-----|----|----|-------------|------|-------|-----|-----|------|
| 2021 | HFD | AA | 25 | 381 | 58 | 30 | 3 | 14 | 46 | 33 | 101 | 8 | 4 | .266/.336/.494 | 104 | .336 | 0.1 | LF(37) 0.3, 1B(25) 2.0, 3B(9) -1.3 | 1.4 |
| 2022 | ABQ | AAA | 26 | 312 | 61 | 15 | 6 | 20 | 56 | 44 | 70 | 12 | 2 | .300/.404/.635 | 120 | .333 | 0.7 | LF(25) -0.2, 1B(21) 0.4, RF(18) 0.7 | 1.9 |
| 2022 | COL | MLB | 26 | 97 | 9 | 6 | 0 | 3 | 11 | 21 | 25 | 0 | 0 | .297/.454/.500 | 116 | .404 | -0.8 | LF(26) -1.5 | 0.3 |
| 2023 DC | COL | MLB | 27 | 185 | 21 | 9 | 1 | 5 | 19 | 18 | 51 | 5 | 1 | .206/.297/.361 | 85 | .270 | 0.4 | LF 0, RF 0 | 0.2 |

*Comparables: Scott Van Slyke, Tommy Pham, J.D. Martinez*

**The Report:** I saw a lot of Bouchard in 2021 in Hartford, and to be honest, I didn't take copious notes at the time. He was a polished, well-rounded, but overaged corner bat. The type that would be a perfectly fine bench outfielder if they were a bit better in center. He was always going to "make it" in the scouting parlance—especially in the Rockies' org—but I did not expect him to have the immediate major-league impact he did.

Bouchard looks broadly the same at the plate to me—a quiet, upper-body-heavy swing with solid bat speed and a little less barrel control than you'd like, but he can sting it when he makes contact. I do worry about that contact rate taking a bit of a dive once teams decide to throw him more offspeed, something that happened to a similarly athletic, overaged performer in Sam Hilliard, but Bouchard's swing is a little less stiff and the approach is a bit better, so perhaps he carves out that fine bench outfielder role after all.

**OFP:** 50 / Second-division outfielder

**Variance:** Low. Bouchard doesn't have much to give back on swing-and-miss if the league gets a book out on him after his early success, but he's a high-probability bench outfielder even if that's the case.

**Jesse Roche's Fantasy Take:** Bouchard opened a lot of eyes with an impressive debut after torching the Pacific Coast League. It is not all smoke, mirrors and the Coors Field/Albuquerque effect. Bouchard has solid power with enough contact skills and plate discipline to carve out a fantasy-relevant role. Unfortunately, the playing time may not be there with Kris Bryant, C.J. Cron, Charlie Blackmon and Randal Grichuk all returning.

## Outside the Top Ten:

### 11   Jordan Beck   OF

Born: 04/19/01   Age: 22   Bats: R   Throws: R   Height: 6'3"   Weight: 225 lb.   Origin: Round 1, 2022 Draft (#38 overall)

| YEAR | TEAM | LVL | AGE | PA | R | 2B | 3B | HR | RBI | BB | K | SB | CS | AVG/OBP/SLG | DRC+ | BABIP | BRR | DRP | WARP |
|------|------|-----|-----|----|---|----|----|----|-----|----|---|----|----|-------------|------|-------|-----|-----|------|
| 2022 | RCK | ROK | 21 | 57 | 9 | 5 | 0 | 1 | 10 | 8 | 11 | 0 | 0 | .306/.404/.469 | | .378 | | | |
| 2022 | FRE | A | 21 | 52 | 11 | 2 | 0 | 2 | 9 | 13 | 9 | 0 | 0 | .282/.462/.487 | 119 | .321 | 0.6 | RF(6) 0.4, LF(3) 1.1 | 0.4 |
| 2023 non-DC | COL | MLB | 22 | 251 | 21 | 10 | 1 | 3 | 20 | 23 | 76 | 0 | 1 | .210/.291/.301 | 72 | .305 | -4.3 | LF 0, RF 0 | -0.7 |

*Comparables: Mark Zagunis, Matt Joyce, Pedro Gonzalez*

A Rockies Comp pick in last summer's draft, Beck broadly fits with what they tend to target in college bats—a corner masher with a bit more defensive versatility than you'd expect. He generates plus-plus raw power and is reasonably short to the ball for a slugger. The swing does have some stiffness, and it's not amazing bat speed, so Beck can be a bit late on velocity away. I'd worry about swing-and-miss in the zone generally, given how much he's looking to lift. Beck fits best defensively in right field, but could sneak some time in all three spots if he maintains his athleticism in his 20s. He'll need to zero in on the pitches he can actually drive, and do damage when he swings, but there's enough power potential here—even before accounting for Coors—to project an everyday middle-of-the-order bat down the line.

### 12   Jordy Vargas   RHP

Born: 11/06/03   Age: 19   Bats: R   Throws: R   Height: 6'3"   Weight: 153 lb.   Origin: International Free Agent, 2021

| YEAR | TEAM | LVL | AGE | W | L | SV | G | GS | IP | H | HR | BB/9 | K/9 | K | GB% | BABIP | WHIP | ERA | DRA- | WARP |
|------|------|-----|-----|---|---|----|---|----|-----|----|----|------|------|----|------|-------|------|------|------|------|
| 2021 | DSL COL | ROK | 17 | 2 | 0 | 0 | 11 | 9 | 34² | 18 | 0 | 4.2 | 11.9 | 46 | 41.8% | .228 | 0.98 | 1.30 | | |
| 2022 | RCK | ROK | 18 | 2 | 1 | 0 | 7 | 5 | 26² | 13 | 0 | 1.4 | 13.5 | 40 | 49.1% | .245 | 0.64 | 2.36 | | |
| 2022 | FRE | A | 18 | 2 | 0 | 0 | 6 | 6 | 24² | 20 | 5 | 4.7 | 8.8 | 24 | 44.6% | .250 | 1.34 | 3.65 | 106 | -0.1 |
| 2023 non-DC | COL | MLB | 19 | 3 | 3 | 0 | 58 | 0 | 50 | 57 | 9 | 5.3 | 6.9 | 38 | 35.0% | .307 | 1.73 | 6.32 | 154 | -1.1 |

*Comparables: Robinson Ortiz, Shane Watson, Peter Tago*

A teenaged pitcher with arm speed to spare, Vargas is a bit of a developmental project at present. His mid-90s fastball plays below the plus velocity as it is control over command, and the pitch mostly just runs down barrels. He does have good touch and feel for an 11-6 breaker, although the shape can get a little loopy at times. His changeup has a chance to be at least average as well, although Vargas doesn't always replicate his arm speed and the fade is fringy at present. There's the outline of a three-pitch, mid-rotation starter in his profile, and Vargas spent all of last season as an 18-year-old. The Rockies, however, do not have a great track record with maximizing arms and he could be in the top 10 or well off this list when his 19th birthday rolls around.

### 13   Juan Brito   2B

Born: 09/24/01   Age: 21   Bats: S   Throws: R   Height: 5'11"   Weight: 162 lb.   Origin: International Free Agent, 2018

| YEAR | TEAM | LVL | AGE | PA | R | 2B | 3B | HR | RBI | BB | K | SB | CS | AVG/OBP/SLG | DRC+ | BABIP | BRR | DRP | WARP |
|------|------|-----|-----|----|---|----|----|----|-----|----|---|----|----|-------------|------|-------|-----|-----|------|
| 2021 | RCK | ROK | 19 | 109 | 20 | 3 | 0 | 3 | 11 | 15 | 21 | 5 | 4 | .295/.406/.432 | | .354 | | | |
| 2022 | FRE | A | 20 | 497 | 91 | 29 | 6 | 11 | 72 | 78 | 71 | 17 | 9 | .286/.407/.470 | 128 | .319 | -0.9 | 2B(102) 0.5, SS(4) 0.7 | 3.3 |
| 2023 DC | CLE | MLB | 21 | 63 | 6 | 3 | 1 | 1 | 5 | 6 | 12 | 0 | 0 | .219/.300/.323 | 79 | .267 | -0.1 | 2B 0, SS 0 | 0.0 |

*Comparables: Enmanuel Valdez, Tony Granadillo, Mookie Betts*

Brito is another young Rockies middle infielder who has performed in the low minors despite lacking in loud tools. His contact ability plays up due to good swing decisions, and while he won't hit for significant power outside of the friendly confines of Rockies affiliates, he'll hit the ball hard enough to keep opposing pitchers from challenging him too much. Defensively, he's limited to second due to his average speed and defensive tools, so he isn't an ideal bench infielder. Whether Brito can hit enough to be a useful second-division regular at the bottom of your lineup is an open question that won't get fully answered until the high minors, but he's certainly worth keeping an eye on.

## 14   Jackson Cox   RHP

Born: 09/25/03   Age: 19   Bats: R   Throws: R   Height: 6'1"   Weight: 185 lb.   Origin: Round 2, 2022 Draft (#50 overall)

Cox is a shorter, cold-weather, second-round prep righty. There's a lot of compounding risk in each subsequent adjective there, but his breaking ball was one of the better ones in the class, a high-spin hellion of a curve. He also sits mid-90s from a traditional three-quarters slot, but struggles to consistently throw strikes out of an uptempo, upright delivery. So yes, there's a lot of variance here—and Cox has yet to throw a pro pitch—but the breaker gives you something to dream on.

## 15   Sterlin Thompson   3B

Born: 06/26/01   Age: 22   Bats: L   Throws: R   Height: 6'4"   Weight: 200 lb.   Origin: Round 1, 2022 Draft (#31 overall)

| YEAR | TEAM | LVL | AGE | PA | R | 2B | 3B | HR | RBI | BB | K | SB | CS | AVG/OBP/SLG | DRC+ | BABIP | BRR | DRP | WARP |
|------|------|-----|-----|-----|----|----|----|----|-----|----|----|----|----|-------------|------|-------|-----|-----|------|
| 2022 | RCK | ROK | 21 | 61 | 9 | 3 | 0 | 1 | 6 | 2 | 16 | 1 | 0 | .273/.328/.382 | | .359 | | | |
| 2022 | FRE | A | 21 | 50 | 9 | 4 | 0 | 1 | 4 | 3 | 12 | 2 | 0 | .348/.380/.500 | 95 | .441 | 0.2 | 3B(11) -1.5 | 0.0 |
| 2023 non-DC | COL | MLB | 22 | 251 | 19 | 10 | 2 | 2 | 20 | 17 | 67 | 3 | 1 | .216/.274/.305 | 63 | .292 | -2.9 | 3B 0 | -0.8 |

A Rockies Comp pick in last summer's draft, Thompson broadly fits with what they tend to target in college bats—a corner masher with a bit more defensive versatility than you'd expect. Thompson didn't take the jump his junior year that some scouts expected, but he had a very nice season for the Gators while playing a fair bit of second base in addition to right field. The Rockies are giving him some run at third, and he's a passable infielder at present, but his likely major-league landing spot is in an outfield corner. Thompson has a bit less power and is a bit less pull happy than Beck—while a better all-around hitter—but I have similar concerns about his bat speed and in-zone whiff, especially when his noisy swing gets out of sync.

## 16   Ryan Rolison   LHP

Born: 07/11/97   Age: 25   Bats: R   Throws: L   Height: 6'2"   Weight: 213 lb.   Origin: Round 1, 2018 Draft (#22 overall)

| YEAR | TEAM | LVL | AGE | W | L | SV | G | GS | IP | H | HR | BB/9 | K/9 | K | GB% | BABIP | WHIP | ERA | DRA- | WARP |
|------|------|-----|-----|---|---|----|----|----|-----|----|----|------|------|----|------|-------|------|------|------|------|
| 2021 | RCK | ROK | 23 | 0 | 0 | 0 | 2 | 2 | 6¹ | 10 | 0 | 2.8 | 12.8 | 9 | 27.8% | .556 | 1.89 | 7.11 | | |
| 2021 | HFD | AA | 23 | 2 | 1 | 0 | 3 | 3 | 14² | 11 | 1 | 1.2 | 12.3 | 20 | 52.9% | .303 | 0.89 | 3.07 | 88 | 0.2 |
| 2021 | ABQ | AAA | 23 | 2 | 2 | 0 | 10 | 10 | 45² | 51 | 7 | 3.2 | 8.9 | 45 | 41.3% | .336 | 1.47 | 5.91 | 103 | 0.1 |
| 2023 DC | COL | MLB | 25 | 1 | 2 | 0 | 5 | 5 | 19.7 | 22 | 3 | 3.4 | 7.5 | 17 | 37.8% | .311 | 1.46 | 5.00 | 125 | -0.1 |

*Comparables: Josh Rogers, Chris Flexen, Trey Supak*

Rolison has been on the cusp of his MLB debut for two seasons now, but injuries have kept him off the bump in Coors, and off mounds entirely in 2022. His 2021 spate of injuries were hard luck, but last year, shoulder soreness turned into shoulder surgery. The former first-round pick had a fourth starter projection as recently as the 2022 edition of this list, but shoulder injuries are bad news, so we will have to wait and see how he looks in 2023.

## 17   McCade Brown   RHP

Born: 08/15/00   Age: 22   Bats: R   Throws: R   Height: 6'6"   Weight: 225 lb.   Origin: Round 3, 2021 Draft (#79 overall)

| YEAR | TEAM | LVL | AGE | W | L | SV | G | GS | IP | H | HR | BB/9 | K/9 | K | GB% | BABIP | WHIP | ERA | DRA- | WARP |
|------|------|-----|-----|---|---|----|----|----|-----|----|----|------|------|-----|-------|-------|------|------|------|------|
| 2021 | RCK | ROK | 20 | 0 | 0 | 0 | 4 | 3 | 8 | 10 | 2 | 3.4 | 10.1 | 9 | 43.8% | .381 | 1.63 | 6.75 | | |
| 2022 | FRE | A | 21 | 4 | 4 | 0 | 18 | 18 | 89² | 90 | 10 | 2.3 | 11.8 | 118 | 44.7% | .356 | 1.26 | 5.22 | 88 | 0.8 |
| 2023 non-DC | COL | MLB | 22 | 3 | 3 | 0 | 58 | 0 | 50 | 52 | 8 | 3.4 | 7.7 | 43 | 36.3% | .300 | 1.41 | 4.60 | 120 | -0.2 |

A third-round college pick who didn't pitch all that much at Indiana, Brown offers mid-90s heat and a swing-and-miss curveball careening down from his 6-foot-6 frame. The rest of the repertoire—a slider and change—aren't particularly noteworthy, and he doesn't consistently throw good strikes with the fastball. The breaker might be good enough to carve out a major-league relief role regardless, and there's some upside given the cold-weather profile and limited reps.

## 18 Case Williams   RHP

Born: 02/16/02   Age: 21   Bats: R   Throws: R   Height: 6'3"   Weight: 210 lb.   Origin: Round 4, 2020 Draft (#110 overall)

| YEAR | TEAM | LVL | AGE | W | L | SV | G | GS | IP | H | HR | BB/9 | K/9 | K | GB% | BABIP | WHIP | ERA | DRA- | WARP |
|------|------|-----|-----|---|---|----|----|----|-----|----|----|------|-----|----|------|-------|------|------|------|------|
| 2021 | FRE | A | 19 | 1 | 3 | 0 | 7 | 6 | 28¹ | 31 | 2 | 4.4 | 5.4 | 17 | 47.0% | .296 | 1.59 | 5.72 | 130 | -0.4 |
| 2021 | DBT | A | 19 | 2 | 5 | 0 | 12 | 11 | 47 | 45 | 7 | 6.3 | 6.5 | 34 | 33.8% | .270 | 1.66 | 5.74 | 156 | -0.6 |
| 2022 | FRE | A | 20 | 9 | 2 | 0 | 16 | 16 | 89² | 91 | 13 | 3.4 | 9.0 | 90 | 42.5% | .315 | 1.39 | 4.22 | 113 | -0.6 |
| 2022 | SPO | A+ | 20 | 2 | 2 | 0 | 6 | 6 | 32¹ | 39 | 6 | 3.1 | 9.2 | 33 | 31.1% | .340 | 1.55 | 5.57 | 121 | -0.1 |
| 2022 | HFD | AA | 20 | 0 | 1 | 0 | 1 | 1 | 6 | 6 | 1 | 1.5 | 18.0 | 12 | 8.3% | .455 | 1.17 | 6.00 | 94 | 0.1 |
| 2023 non-DC | COL | MLB | 21 | 3 | 3 | 0 | 58 | 0 | 50 | 60 | 9 | 4.5 | 6.3 | 35 | 31.8% | .317 | 1.70 | 6.22 | 153 | -1.1 |

The Rockies' fourth-round pick in 2020—then traded to and from Cincinnati in a classic Dipotosian gambit—is still a work in progress as a pitching prospect. His fastball can catch a bit too much plate, given that he sits low-90s. A bit more velocity might help set up his potential above-average curve, and he will need to find a bit more fade on the changeup as well. Williams has the breaker to miss some bats, but needs to firm up the fastball command and the rest of the arsenal to settle in at the back of a major-league rotation, or in the middle innings of a bullpen.

## 19 Joe Rock   LHP

Born: 07/29/00   Age: 22   Bats: L   Throws: L   Height: 6'6"   Weight: 200 lb.   Origin: Round 2, 2021 Draft (#68 overall)

| YEAR | TEAM | LVL | AGE | W | L | SV | G | GS | IP | H | HR | BB/9 | K/9 | K | GB% | BABIP | WHIP | ERA | DRA- | WARP |
|------|------|-----|-----|---|---|----|----|----|-----|----|----|------|-----|----|------|-------|------|------|------|------|
| 2021 | RCK | ROK | 20 | 1 | 0 | 0 | 4 | 2 | 8 | 5 | 0 | 1.1 | 12.4 | 11 | 70.6% | .294 | 0.75 | 1.13 | | |
| 2022 | SPO | A+ | 21 | 7 | 8 | 0 | 20 | 20 | 107² | 87 | 10 | 3.8 | 9.1 | 109 | 44.7% | .270 | 1.23 | 4.43 | 103 | 0.8 |
| 2022 | HFD | AA | 21 | 0 | 0 | 0 | 2 | 2 | 8 | 9 | 2 | 5.6 | 12.4 | 11 | 45.5% | .350 | 1.75 | 10.12 | 84 | 0.2 |
| 2023 non-DC | COL | MLB | 22 | 3 | 3 | 0 | 58 | 0 | 50 | 55 | 8 | 4.8 | 7.5 | 41 | 37.5% | .314 | 1.64 | 5.56 | 138 | -0.7 |

*Comparables: Eduardo Rodriguez, Daniel Camarena, Domingo Robles*

A long, lean, fastball/slider lefty with a bit of deception, Rock leans heavily on his mid-80s breaking ball, which shows sharp two-plane break and has above-average projection. His fastball sits low-90s, but there might be more in the tank either in short bursts or given more physical development. The fastball is merely around to set up the slider, as Rock doesn't have much command of or carry on the pitch. He will probably stay stretched out for another season as a starter in Hartford, but his eventual home will be working the middle innings out of the bullpen.

## 20 Gavin Hollowell   RHP

Born: 11/04/97   Age: 25   Bats: R   Throws: R   Height: 6'7"   Weight: 215 lb.   Origin: Round 6, 2019 Draft (#189 overall)

| YEAR | TEAM | LVL | AGE | W | L | SV | G | GS | IP | H | HR | BB/9 | K/9 | K | GB% | BABIP | WHIP | ERA | DRA- | WARP |
|------|------|-----|-----|---|---|----|----|----|-----|----|----|------|-----|----|------|-------|------|------|------|------|
| 2021 | FRE | A | 23 | 2 | 0 | 4 | 22 | 0 | 22 | 15 | 1 | 2.0 | 12.7 | 31 | 44.0% | .286 | 0.91 | 2.45 | 83 | 0.3 |
| 2022 | HFD | AA | 24 | 4 | 2 | 16 | 42 | 0 | 48² | 30 | 3 | 2.6 | 11.8 | 64 | 31.4% | .265 | 0.90 | 3.14 | 89 | 0.9 |
| 2022 | COL | MLB | 24 | 0 | 2 | 0 | 6 | 0 | 7 | 7 | 1 | 5.1 | 10.3 | 8 | 25.0% | .316 | 1.57 | 7.71 | 106 | 0.0 |
| 2023 DC | COL | MLB | 25 | 1 | 1 | 0 | 27 | 0 | 23.7 | 21 | 3 | 3.5 | 9.2 | 24 | 32.6% | .289 | 1.29 | 3.84 | 100 | 0.1 |

Hollowell made his major-league debut after a dominant season out of the Yard Goats bullpen. He's a very tall righty with a lower slot, creating extension on his high-spin, mid-90s fastball. He pairs it with a trendy sweeping slider with a ton of run. This is the kind of profile that can just die in Coors Field—or Albuquerque, where Hollowell is likely to start 2023—but the former Johnnie is the right kind of 95-and-a-slider arm for a modern MLB bullpen.

# Top Talents 25 and Under (as of 4/1/2023):

1. Ezequiel Tovar, SS
2. Zac Veen, OF
3. Adael Amador, SS
4. Drew Romo, C
5. Benny Montgomery, OF
6. Warming Bernabel, 3B
7. Gabriel Hughes, RHP

8.  Yanquiel Fernandez, OF
9.  Jaden Hill, RHP
10.  Elehuris Montero, 3B/1B

First things first: a hearty congratulations to Brendan Rodgers for at long last graduating off this list, having a reasonable enough season that nonetheless could not rescue the Rockies from the doldrums that observers from every angle but within seem able to perceive them mired within. It's far from ideal for a last-place club to feature so few young talents on their big-league roster.

Montero is the best of the few eligible non-prospects, narrowly graduating in 2022 with a difficult-but-not-wholly-disastrous debut. His 78 DRC+ in his first 185 plate appearances won't hack it as a corner bat. He'll have to hit far more to eclipse C.J. Cron at first or outdo Ryan McMahon's glove at third, though matching or exceeding whatever a 37-year-old Charlie Blackmon is capable of producing next year seems manageable. He also displaces Bouchard on this list who, while prospect-eligible, is already 26.

# Detroit Tigers

## The State of the System:

As Tank 2: Tank Harder commences, you'd prefer your farm system to be in better shape than Detroit's, as they lack both impact prospects at the top and depth overall.

## The Top Ten:

**1** **Jace Jung**  **2B**  OFP: 55  ETA: 2024
Born: 10/04/00  Age: 22  Bats: L  Throws: R  Height: 6'0"  Weight: 205 lb.  Origin: Round 1, 2022 Draft (#12 overall)

| YEAR | TEAM | LVL | AGE | PA | R | 2B | 3B | HR | RBI | BB | K | SB | CS | AVG/OBP/SLG | DRC+ | BABIP | BRR | DRP | WARP |
|------|------|-----|-----|-----|----|----|----|----|-----|----|----|----|----|--------------|------|-------|------|---------|------|
| 2022 | WM | A+ | 21 | 134 | 16 | 6 | 1 | 1 | 13 | 25 | 28 | 1 | 0 | .231/.373/.333 | 104 | .300 | -1.6 | 2B(27) 3.4 | 0.6 |
| 2023 non-DC | DET | MLB | 22 | 251 | 21 | 10 | 2 | 2 | 20 | 26 | 71 | 1 | 0 | .216/.302/.307 | 76 | .305 | -4.2 | 2B 0 | -0.4 |

*Comparables: Luis Alejandro Basabe, Max Moroff, Josh Johnson*

**The Report:** Drafting outside the top 10 for the first time in four years, Detroit used the 12th-overall pick to nab Jung, the Big 12 Player of the Year and one of the top college bats available. His setup at the plate is unconventional, upright with the bat starting at an odd angle, but his quick swing helps him make consistent loud contact. Offensively, he brings everything to the table that you would expect from an advanced, big conference bat, rarely expanding the zone and recognizing spin well. There's plenty of all-field power in the profile as well, generated by above-average bat speed and a compact, strong frame.

Despite the strength of his offensive game, Jung fell down draft boards due to the deficiencies with the glove. He's extremely limited in the field, showing below-average agility and range and lacking the arm strength for the left side of the diamond. It might not matter. Detroit will gladly accept the liabilities in the field if he can hit .270 with 25 home runs against big-league pitching.

**OFP:** 55 / Slugging second baseman

**Variance:** High. It's hit-or-bust for Jung. If the bat stalls out against advanced pitching or the power is just average, there's not much else to fall back upon.

**Jesse Roche's Fantasy Take:** So far, not so good for Jung, who struggled to impact the ball in his debut in High-A, mustering a paltry .101 ISO. As noted above, he'll really need to hit to carve out a big-league role given his defensive shortcomings. On a positive note, however, Jung did run up an 18.6% walk rate in his debut, after a 20% walk rate in his junior year. His plate discipline is arguably the best in the college class to go with solid contact skills and solid power to all fields. If he can develop into a ".270 with 25 home runs" hitter, that'll play quite nicely at second base. Still, Jung has more risk than your typical established college bat, which pushes him outside the dynasty top 100 and outside the first round in most FYPDs.

**2** **Wilmer Flores**  **RHP**  OFP: 55  ETA: Late 2023/Early 2024
Born: 02/20/01  Age: 22  Bats: R  Throws: R  Height: 6'4"  Weight: 225 lb.  Origin: International Free Agent, 2020

| YEAR | TEAM | LVL | AGE | W | L | SV | G | GS | IP | H | HR | BB/9 | K/9 | K | GB% | BABIP | WHIP | ERA | DRA- | WARP |
|------|------|-----|-----|----|----|----|----|----|------|----|----|------|------|----|-------|-------|------|------|------|------|
| 2021 | TIGW | ROK | 20 | 2 | 1 | 0 | 3 | 2 | 13 | 15 | 0 | 1.4 | 12.5 | 18 | 58.8% | .441 | 1.31 | 4.85 | | |
| 2021 | LAK | A | 20 | 4 | 3 | 0 | 11 | 11 | 53 | 47 | 1 | 3.7 | 12.2 | 72 | 52.4% | .368 | 1.30 | 3.40 | 99 | 0.6 |
| 2022 | WM | A+ | 21 | 1 | 0 | 0 | 6 | 5 | 19² | 14 | 2 | 0.9 | 16.0 | 35 | 57.9% | .333 | 0.81 | 1.83 | 67 | 0.5 |
| 2022 | ERI | AA | 21 | 6 | 4 | 0 | 19 | 19 | 83² | 67 | 8 | 2.3 | 10.2 | 95 | 45.7% | .280 | 1.05 | 3.01 | 89 | 1.6 |
| 2023 non-DC | DET | MLB | 22 | 3 | 3 | 0 | 58 | 0 | 50 | 49 | 7 | 3.3 | 8.3 | 46 | 39.9% | .297 | 1.35 | 4.17 | 110 | 0.0 |

*Comparables: Drew Hutchison, Matt Manning, Edwin Escobar*

**The Report:** After a breakout 2021, Wilmer Flores the Younger continued to dominate minor-league hitters in 2022. The 21-year-old struck out over 30% of the batters he faced at High- and Double-A, and showed enough improvement with his sliderish cutter—or, if you prefer, cutterish slider—that he is now a better-than-even bet to stick as a starter in the majors. The top line fastball/curve combo is still above-average. Flores' fastball sits in the mid-90s, runs true in a good way and is a swing-and-miss pitch up in the zone. His breaker is an 11-5 yakker in the upper-70s, that projects more 55 than 60 at present as it can start a little early and isn't always sharp enough to miss bats, although it gets plenty of weak contact down in the zone. Flores has a wide, sturdy frame and his delivery is pretty repeatable. He throws strikes and enough good strikes to project as a mid-rotation starter, although it's not the highest-upside profile you'll find.

**OFP:** 55 / no. 3/4 starter

**Variance:** Low. The stuff doesn't jump off the page, but Flores has had upper-minors success and displays a deep enough arsenal now to be a useful rotation piece of some sort. The reliever risk isn't non-zero, and I imagine the stuff would play up a little in short bursts, but there's a similarly narrow likely range of outcomes there running from good middle reliever to good seventh-inning guy.

**Jesse Roche's Fantasy Take:** What a difference a year makes! Flores' 2021 season ended with a disastrous showing in the AFL, where he ran up a 23.2% walk rate. This year, however, he began throwing far more strikes (5% more) and nearly halved his walk rate. Although his stuff may not pop, it is still quality, and his frame and delivery portends a potential workhorse if he can further develop a useful third offering. Still, Flores lacks "the highest-upside profile" and has more fantasy value in deeper formats.

## 3 Jackson Jobe  RHP   OFP: 55   ETA: 2025

Born: 07/30/02  Age: 20  Bats: R  Throws: R  Height: 6'2"  Weight: 190 lb.  Origin: Round 1, 2021 Draft (#3 overall)

| YEAR | TEAM | LVL | AGE | W | L | SV | G | GS | IP | H | HR | BB/9 | K/9 | K | GB% | BABIP | WHIP | ERA | DRA- | WARP |
|---|---|---|---|---|---|---|---|---|---|---|---|---|---|---|---|---|---|---|---|---|
| 2022 | LAK | A | 19 | 2 | 5 | 0 | 18 | 18 | 61² | 59 | 12 | 3.6 | 10.4 | 71 | 40.2% | .299 | 1.36 | 4.52 | 103 | 0.9 |
| 2022 | WM | A+ | 19 | 2 | 0 | 0 | 3 | 3 | 15² | 10 | 2 | 2.9 | 5.7 | 10 | 40.4% | .178 | 0.96 | 1.15 | 115 | 0.0 |
| 2023 non-DC | DET | MLB | 20 | 3 | 3 | 0 | 58 | 0 | 50 | 57 | 9 | 4.4 | 6.8 | 38 | 34.8% | .307 | 1.62 | 5.85 | 145 | -0.9 |

Comparables: Simeon Woods Richardson, Franklin Pérez, Francis Martes

**The Report:** If you prefer a higher-upside profile, here's Jackson Jobe. His first full pro season was heavily innings-managed, in part due to occasional back issues, but he missed plenty of bats in the Florida State League when he was on the bump. He can struggle to command his mid-90s fastball at times, but he can also overpower hitters when he elevates it. His high-spin slider maintains its plus-plus projection (although it's still a fair bit of projection), buzzsaw sweep and depth in the low-80s. Jobe uses it mostly to get glove-side chases and when he tries to start it arm-side, it can back up. He also has a mid-80s change that is firm, but can flash average fade.

Jobe feels a little down from this time last year, which might be a little unfair. His workload wasn't unusual given his age and experience level—Marco Raya and Tink Hence showed similarly big stuff in similarly short Florida State League outings—but Jobe also wasn't quite as dominant as those two. The combination of command wobbles and back soreness just makes him a bit riskier as a pitching prospect to me at this point in time.

**OFP:** 55 / no. 3/4 starter or late-inning reliever

**Variance:** Extreme. Volatility here isn't the worst thing in the world. If Jobe comes out throwing good strikes more consistently over 100+ innings, like Hence and Raya, he'll be among the best pitching prospects in baseball. He's also a 19-year-old pitching prospect with power stuff and an intermittently sore back. That's not the ideal cohort to find yourself in.

**Jesse Roche's Fantasy Take:** Jobe can really spin it. His slider regularly tops 3,000 rpm and its average spin rate would fall squarely within the top five in MLB. Unfortunately his command—as is often the case for teenage arms—comes and goes. The building blocks, however, are there for Jobe to develop to match his draft pedigree. Given his sizable upside, he is the top fantasy pitching prospect in this system, even if his risk is extreme.

## 4   Colt Keith    3B      OFP: 55      ETA: 2025

Born: 08/14/01    Age: 21    Bats: L    Throws: R    Height: 6'3"    Weight: 211 lb.    Origin: Round 5, 2020 Draft (#132 overall)

| YEAR | TEAM | LVL | AGE | PA | R | 2B | 3B | HR | RBI | BB | K | SB | CS | AVG/OBP/SLG | DRC+ | BABIP | BRR | DRP | WARP |
|---|---|---|---|---|---|---|---|---|---|---|---|---|---|---|---|---|---|---|---|
| 2021 | LAK | A | 19 | 181 | 32 | 6 | 3 | 1 | 21 | 30 | 39 | 4 | 1 | .320/.436/.422 | 117 | .422 | 1.4 | 3B(27) 3.3, 2B(14) -1.3 | 1.2 |
| 2021 | WM | A+ | 19 | 76 | 7 | 1 | 1 | 1 | 6 | 8 | 27 | 0 | 0 | .162/.250/.250 | 80 | .250 | 0.9 | 3B(15) 1.1, 2B(2) -0.4 | 0.2 |
| 2022 | WM | A+ | 20 | 216 | 38 | 14 | 3 | 9 | 31 | 22 | 42 | 4 | 0 | .301/.370/.544 | 138 | .343 | 1.6 | 3B(27) -2.0, 2B(13) 0.2 | 1.5 |
| 2023 non-DC | DET | MLB | 21 | 251 | 22 | 10 | 3 | 4 | 23 | 21 | 65 | 1 | 0 | .231/.299/.348 | 84 | .307 | -3.9 | 2B 0, 3B 0 | -0.2 |

*Comparables: Trey Michalczewski, Marcos Vechionacci, Eric Hosmer*

**The Report:** Keith was one of the few bright spots in the organization this year and in the midst of a breakout at West Michigan before an injured shoulder abruptly ended his time in High-A. Surgery was not required and no ill-effects were shown as he returned in time to garner some Arizona Fall League at-bats. Offensively, he displays an advanced approach, commanding the zone with his quick left-handed swing. The jump in production in 2022 can be attributed to Keith tapping into the power more efficiently. He's had the physical strength and bat speed since being drafted in 2020 but has begun to generate more loft in the swing, allowing for the pop to play more in-game. It's a nice mix of power and contact ability, making the bat strong enough to handle wherever he lands defensively. In the field, the arm is strong enough to handle the left side but the motions can be stiff. It's unlikely he ever wins a Gold Glove but with more experience, he should develop into a capable defender at third.

**OFP:** 55 / Solid starter at third base

**Variance:** Medium. We're fairly confident Keith will continue to hit but there could be some positive variance in the profile if the power develops more than expected.

**Jesse Roche's Fantasy Take:** Keith has yet to reach the upper minors and he has missed substantial time in each of the last two years. So while there is a lot to like in his fantasy profile, he still has a lot to prove. With that in mind, Keith could quickly ascend into the dynasty top 100 if he picks up where he left off in Double-A.

## 5   Justyn-Henry Malloy    LF      OFP: 55      ETA: 2024

Born: 02/19/00    Age: 23    Bats: R    Throws: R    Height: 6'3"    Weight: 212 lb.    Origin: Round 6, 2021 Draft (#187 overall)

| YEAR | TEAM | LVL | AGE | PA | R | 2B | 3B | HR | RBI | BB | K | SB | CS | AVG/OBP/SLG | DRC+ | BABIP | BRR | DRP | WARP |
|---|---|---|---|---|---|---|---|---|---|---|---|---|---|---|---|---|---|---|---|
| 2021 | AUG | A | 21 | 147 | 23 | 5 | 0 | 5 | 21 | 24 | 30 | 4 | 2 | .270/.388/.434 | 123 | .318 | -0.4 | 3B(31) -1.4, LF(1) -0.0 | 0.6 |
| 2022 | ROM | A+ | 22 | 320 | 51 | 16 | 0 | 10 | 44 | 47 | 73 | 3 | 0 | .304/.409/.479 | 126 | .376 | 1.0 | 3B(51) -1.9, LF(3) -0.6 | 1.6 |
| 2022 | MIS | AA | 22 | 238 | 35 | 11 | 0 | 6 | 31 | 43 | 60 | 0 | 0 | .268/.403/.421 | 113 | .354 | 0.9 | LF(51) -1.9 | 0.8 |
| 2022 | GWN | AAA | 22 | 33 | 5 | 1 | 0 | 1 | 6 | 7 | 5 | 2 | 0 | .280/.424/.440 | 116 | .300 | -1.4 | LF(7) 0.7 | 0.1 |
| 2023 non-DC | DET | MLB | 23 | 251 | 24 | 10 | 1 | 4 | 24 | 28 | 62 | 1 | 0 | .232/.322/.347 | 95 | .303 | -3.9 | 3B 0, LF 0 | 0.1 |

*Comparables: Tito Polo, Ramon Hernandez, Lorenzo Cain*

**The Report:** It's not even worth noting nowadays how good Atlanta is at scouting their backyard—just assume every breakout prospect in their system is local—but Malloy was indeed yet another scouting and development success story for them in The Peach State. A polished bat-to-ball merchant with a great approach at Georgia Tech, he got all the way to Triple-A in his first pro season. Malloy has added power from his college days, but it's come at the cost of some added bulk and stiffness, and he's moved from third base to left field, after some scouts thought he might be able to play some shortstop. He ticks all our boxes for a modern plus hit tool. He doesn't chase and didn't post a below-average zone-contact rate until his cup of coffee in Gwinnett. There's average power here as well, and while the total package is maybe just average in left field, if he can get back some of his defensive flexibility in Detroit, Malloy could be a useful regular in short order.

**OFP:** 55 / Above-average corner bat

**Variance:** Medium. Malloy made a smooth transition from the ACC to pro ball, and while it's not the most impactful offensive profile—especially in a corner—players with this kind of hit tool and approach are always welcome on your major-league roster.

**Jesse Roche's Fantasy Take:** A potential plus hitter with average power is a very fantasy-friendly profile. Whether Malloy gets to his power in games and whether his glove doesn't hinder his playing time are open questions. Even if his game power plateaus at 15 home runs, he could still provide fantasy value, particularly in OBP leagues (16.4% walk rate last year).

## 6 Joey Wentz LHP  OFP: 50  ETA: Debuted in 2022

Born: 10/06/97  Age: 25  Bats: L  Throws: L  Height: 6'5"  Weight: 220 lb.  Origin: Round 1, 2016 Draft (#40 overall)

| YEAR | TEAM | LVL | AGE | W | L | SV | G | GS | IP | H | HR | BB/9 | K/9 | K | GB% | BABIP | WHIP | ERA | DRA- | WARP |
|---|---|---|---|---|---|---|---|---|---|---|---|---|---|---|---|---|---|---|---|---|
| 2021 | LAK | A | 23 | 0 | 3 | 0 | 5 | 5 | 18² | 23 | 5 | 3.9 | 11.6 | 24 | 34.6% | .383 | 1.66 | 6.75 | 110 | 0.1 |
| 2021 | ERI | AA | 23 | 0 | 4 | 0 | 13 | 13 | 53¹ | 41 | 7 | 5.6 | 9.8 | 58 | 33.3% | .256 | 1.39 | 3.71 | 109 | 0.2 |
| 2022 | TOL | AAA | 24 | 2 | 2 | 0 | 12 | 11 | 48¹ | 37 | 6 | 3.7 | 9.9 | 53 | 39.3% | .267 | 1.18 | 3.17 | 86 | 1.0 |
| 2022 | DET | MLB | 24 | 2 | 2 | 0 | 7 | 7 | 32² | 23 | 2 | 3.6 | 7.4 | 27 | 40.4% | .228 | 1.10 | 3.03 | 111 | 0.1 |
| 2023 DC | DET | MLB | 25 | 5 | 6 | 0 | 27 | 13 | 70.3 | 70 | 9 | 4.5 | 8.0 | 63 | 37.5% | .297 | 1.49 | 4.45 | 118 | 0.0 |

*Comparables: Danny Duffy, Adalberto Mejía, Chris Archer*

**The Report:** Another year removed from his 2020 Tommy John surgery saw some minor improvement in Wentz's stuff and command. That's good. He also lost some mound time to a neck/shoulder issue. That's bad. His average four-pitch mix missed enough minor-league bats and kept enough major-league hitters off balance that we're a little more confident in the average starter projection we had last year. We're not bumping it up, although the slider/cutter has improved a fair bit and can get some swings-and-misses down in the zone, allowing Wentz to effectively change eye levels with his low-90s fastball up.

Wentz's plan is mostly to fill up the zone with those two offerings and hope the big outfield at Comerica generally keeps any wayward fastballs at the top of the zone from landing in the bleachers. His change shows average fade and is good enough against righties, and on occasion he will still pop off the big 1-7 curve that was his party piece as a prep. I do wonder if hitters will start squaring the fastball a little more second time around the league in 2023, but we are already at a point in this system where we are running low on both upside or surety, and Wentz has some upper-minors (and major-league) success under his belt at least.

**OFP:** 50 / no. 4 starter

**Variance:** Low. Wentz may be more of a fifth starter or swingman type if the HR-rate creeps up or the K-rate sinks down any further, but he's also third on the Tigers' starting pitching depth chart per Roster Resource, and it's not like those above or below him have been much better or much more durable. He'll get his turns as long as he's healthy, and is likely to be okay when he does.

**Jesse Roche's Fantasy Take:** With a rotation spot to lose, Wentz has some fantasy appeal in deeper leagues despite middling stuff and limited strikeout potential. Generally, however, he is better left only to leagues that roster well over 200 prospects and occasionally employed as a streaming option in favorable matchups.

## 7 Ty Madden RHP  OFP: 50  ETA: Late 2023

Born: 02/21/00  Age: 23  Bats: R  Throws: R  Height: 6'3"  Weight: 215 lb.  Origin: Round 1, 2021 Draft (#32 overall)

| YEAR | TEAM | LVL | AGE | W | L | SV | G | GS | IP | H | HR | BB/9 | K/9 | K | GB% | BABIP | WHIP | ERA | DRA- | WARP |
|---|---|---|---|---|---|---|---|---|---|---|---|---|---|---|---|---|---|---|---|---|
| 2022 | WM | A+ | 22 | 6 | 4 | 0 | 19 | 19 | 87 | 69 | 10 | 2.7 | 8.7 | 84 | 32.1% | .254 | 1.09 | 3.10 | 123 | -0.2 |
| 2022 | ERI | AA | 22 | 2 | 2 | 0 | 7 | 7 | 35² | 28 | 6 | 3.0 | 12.4 | 49 | 46.9% | .293 | 1.12 | 2.78 | 72 | 1.0 |
| 2023 non-DC | DET | MLB | 23 | 3 | 3 | 0 | 58 | 0 | 50 | 53 | 8 | 3.7 | 7.6 | 42 | 33.8% | .305 | 1.48 | 5.00 | 128 | -0.5 |

*Comparables: Adam Warren, Daniel Gossett, Shaun Anderson*

**The Report:** Madden's top line performance in 2022 was right in line with what you'd expect for a late-first round, major college arm pitching in High-A and Double-A in their first full pro season: plenty of strikeouts and an ERA right around 3.00. The stuff was more or less as advertised as well, with a fastball he can run up into the mid-90s, a slider that flashes above-average and three other secondaries he mixes in liberally. None of the secondaries do much more than scrape 50—with the cutter and change ahead of the curve—but Madden has a deep arsenal, and I think he's more likely to stick as a starter than I did this time last year. However, the fastball can be more low-90s at times, and the slider doesn't always get down and under barrels, so he might not end up with a true plus pitch in the arsenal.

Madden throws strikes from a medium tempo with a repeatable delivery, but he's control-over-command at present, especially with the heater. The five-pitch mix gives him plenty of options to turn over a lineup a couple times, but without a consistent swing-and-miss offering, he may not have a ton of impact as a starter or reliever.

**OFP:** 50 / no. 4 starter

**Variance:** Medium. Madden has been a little more homer-prone than you'd like and still isn't a lock to stick as a starter until he tightens up his command a bit more.

**Jesse Roche's Fantasy Take:** When repertoire depth is the primary argument for a pitching prospect, that is not a good sign for fantasy. Without a "true plus pitch" or "a consistent swing-and-miss offering," Madden simply lacks much fantasy upside, and, like Wentz above, should only be rostered in leagues that roster over 200 prospects.

## 8 Parker Meadows CF   OFP: 50   ETA: Late 2023/Early 2024

Born: 11/02/99   Age: 23   Bats: L   Throws: R   Height: 6'5"   Weight: 205 lb.   Origin: Round 2, 2018 Draft (#44 overall)

| YEAR | TEAM | LVL | AGE | PA | R | 2B | 3B | HR | RBI | BB | K | SB | CS | AVG/OBP/SLG | DRC+ | BABIP | BRR | DRP | WARP |
|---|---|---|---|---|---|---|---|---|---|---|---|---|---|---|---|---|---|---|---|
| 2021 | WM | A+ | 21 | 408 | 50 | 15 | 2 | 8 | 44 | 37 | 99 | 9 | 8 | .208/.290/.330 | 94 | .261 | 1.7 | CF(73) -2.0, RF(13) -0.8, LF(4) 0.1 | 1.0 |
| 2022 | WM | A+ | 22 | 67 | 16 | 4 | 1 | 4 | 7 | 4 | 18 | 0 | 0 | .230/.288/.525 | 126 | .256 | 1.0 | CF(12) -0.7, RF(1) -0.1 | 0.4 |
| 2022 | ERI | AA | 22 | 489 | 64 | 21 | 6 | 16 | 51 | 52 | 90 | 17 | 2 | .275/.354/.466 | 117 | .309 | 0.2 | CF(109) 2.2, RF(3) 0.9 | 2.7 |
| 2023 non-DC | DET | MLB | 23 | 251 | 21 | 10 | 2 | 4 | 22 | 19 | 59 | 4 | 1 | .212/.276/.322 | 69 | .267 | -2.6 | LF 0, CF 0 | -0.4 |

*Comparables: Juan Lagares, John Matulia, Luis Barrera*

**The Report:** Meadows finally took a step forward with the bat in 2022, tapping into more of his raw power and cutting down on the swings and misses. He uses a fairly simple weight transfer from a wide base, and—for lack of a better term—just swats at the ball. He has strong wrists, enough bat speed and everything looks a bit simpler at the plate than it has in the past. Meadows has cut his ground-ball rate as well and is looking to lift at the plate, although that can lead to swinging over or topping stuff sinking down and out of the zone. Despite the above-average walk rate, Meadows is up there looking to hack, but his pure volume of contact should produce around average hit and power tools.

Defensively, Meadows is an adequate center fielder—capable of the spectacular play—but that is more based on his plus foot speed than advanced outfield instincts. His speed plays on the bases as well, and while there isn't really an above-average tool here other than run—and still some risk in the hit—Meadows now looks the part of an average regular or good fourth outfielder on a first-division team.

**OFP:** 50 / Second-division outfielder

**Variance:** Medium. The combination of speed and ability to play all three outfield spots gives Meadows some MLB utility even if the offensive improvements don't carry forward.

**Jesse Roche's Fantasy Take:** Meadows was fantastic in the second half in Double-A, hitting .312/.390/.533 with nine home runs and eight stolen bases. His long-promised power-speed upside *may* have arrived. If his hit-power tools can develop to average to go with his plus speed, he would be an intriguing fantasy player who could flirt with 20/20 seasons. Yet, Meadows still cannot hit lefties (.196/.225/.336) and the quality of his contact is inconsistent. As such, he remains well outside the dynasty top 200 despite his Double-A success.

## 9 Dillon Dingler C   OFP: 50   ETA: 2024

Born: 09/17/98   Age: 24   Bats: R   Throws: R   Height: 6'3"   Weight: 210 lb.   Origin: Round 2, 2020 Draft (#38 overall)

| YEAR | TEAM | LVL | AGE | PA | R | 2B | 3B | HR | RBI | BB | K | SB | CS | AVG/OBP/SLG | DRC+ | BABIP | BRR | DRP | WARP |
|---|---|---|---|---|---|---|---|---|---|---|---|---|---|---|---|---|---|---|---|
| 2021 | WM | A+ | 22 | 141 | 25 | 6 | 1 | 8 | 24 | 13 | 36 | 0 | 0 | .287/.376/.549 | 127 | .342 | 2.1 | C(24) 5.0 | 1.5 |
| 2021 | ERI | AA | 22 | 208 | 24 | 3 | 3 | 4 | 20 | 9 | 62 | 1 | 0 | .202/.264/.314 | 82 | .272 | -0.3 | C(40) 5.5 | 0.8 |
| 2022 | ERI | AA | 23 | 448 | 56 | 22 | 3 | 14 | 58 | 45 | 143 | 1 | 0 | .238/.333/.419 | 97 | .335 | 0.7 | C(82) 11.9 | 2.4 |
| 2023 non-DC | DET | MLB | 24 | 251 | 22 | 10 | 2 | 4 | 23 | 17 | 84 | 0 | 0 | .216/.282/.329 | 74 | .320 | -4.4 | C 0 | -0.2 |

*Comparables: Óscar Hernández, David Rodríguez, Phil Avlas*

**The Report:** The first taste of Double-A baseball can be tough for even good prospects, and Dingler struggled badly in Erie after a midseason 2021 promotion. The top-line numbers were better his second time in Double-A, but he still struck out too much, and the underlying issue—struggles with offspeed moving away from him—will only be highlighted and underlined against better pitching. Dingler has a bit of a stiff swing and is looking to launch, which leads to him pulling off breaking stuff. He can do damage on contact—there's above-average bat speed and he's a strong kid—but he's going to need to tighten up the approach and swing decisions to hit enough to be an everyday backstop. The defense should get Dingler to the majors in some capacity though. He's on the larger side for a catcher, but is a good receiver who holds the edges of the zone well, and capably handles the running game on the strength of his plus arm.

**OFP:** 50 / Plus defender, bit of pop, second-division catcher

**Variance:** Medium. The offensive bar for catchers is low, and even if Dingler hits in the low-.200s with 10+ dingers, he'll play for a fair bit, but the offensive tools will only be tested more between now and the bigs.

**Jesse Roche's Fantasy Take:** Dingler has hit just .226/.312/.384 with *205* strikeouts (31.2%) over 157 games in Double-A over the last two years. Yikes! Although he may have a MLB future due to his glove, he likely has no fantasy utility outside of the deepest of leagues.

## 10   Cristian Santana   IF    OFP: 50    ETA: 2026

Born: 11/25/03   Age: 19   Bats: R   Throws: R   Height: 6'0"   Weight: 165 lb.   Origin: International Free Agent, 2021

| YEAR | TEAM | LVL | AGE | PA | R | 2B | 3B | HR | RBI | BB | K | SB | CS | AVG/OBP/SLG | DRC+ | BABIP | BRR | DRP | WARP |
|---|---|---|---|---|---|---|---|---|---|---|---|---|---|---|---|---|---|---|---|
| 2021 | DSL TIG | ROK | 17 | 216 | 40 | 12 | 2 | 9 | 27 | 30 | 46 | 12 | 7 | .269/.421/.520 | | .319 | | | |
| 2022 | LAK | A | 18 | 340 | 52 | 13 | 0 | 9 | 30 | 54 | 88 | 10 | 5 | .215/.379/.366 | 109 | .281 | 0.7 | SS(34) -2.5, 2B(29) 0.7, 3B(11) 0.1 | 1.2 |
| 2023 non-DC | DET | MLB | 19 | 251 | 21 | 10 | 1 | 3 | 21 | 22 | 78 | 4 | 2 | .206/.287/.302 | 70 | .300 | -2.0 | 2B 0, 3B 0 | -0.3 |

*Comparables: Yasel Antuna, Luis García, Jesus Lopez*

**The Report:** The Tigers broke their previous IFA bonus record to sign Santana in 2021, and he made his stateside debut in 2022 with an aggressive Florida State League assignment. He was overmatched much of the time and lacked the present physicality at the plate to do much damage when he did make contact. Santana has a nice rotational swing and the bat stays in the zone long enough that he makes a fair bit of contact on strikes. His chase rate on the other hand was a bit high, and the stroke breaks down against spin, but all in all it wasn't a disastrous season at the plate for the 18-year-old despite the low batting average. Santana will need to get bigger and stronger, which might eventually necessitate a move off shortstop—he's fine there at present, but just fine—and while the fundamentals of the swing are solid, the approach and swing decisions remain raw enough that you have to squint a bit to imagine an everyday player at this point.

**OFP:** 50 / Second-division middle infielder

**Variance:** Extreme. Santana struggled in his first taste of full-season ball, and there may not be impact offensive tools down the line.

**Jesse Roche's Fantasy Take:** As the youngest hitter in Low-A to start the season, Santana understandably struggled out the gate, resulting in a demotion to the complex in May. Upon his return in June, he held his own, hitting .240/.417/.408 over his final 61 games. Santana flashed some pop–108.9-mph max exit velocity–and some plate discipline–15.9% walk rate. With a pretty swing and a decent showing in Low-A at 18 years old, he remains intriguing enough to roster in leagues with over 200 prospects.

## Outside the Top Ten:

## 11   Izaac Pacheco   3B

Born: 11/18/02   Age: 20   Bats: L   Throws: R   Height: 6'4"   Weight: 225 lb.   Origin: Round 2, 2021 Draft (#39 overall)

| YEAR | TEAM | LVL | AGE | PA | R | 2B | 3B | HR | RBI | BB | K | SB | CS | AVG/OBP/SLG | DRC+ | BABIP | BRR | DRP | WARP |
|---|---|---|---|---|---|---|---|---|---|---|---|---|---|---|---|---|---|---|---|
| 2021 | TIGW | ROK | 18 | 125 | 16 | 4 | 2 | 1 | 7 | 18 | 43 | 1 | 0 | .226/.339/.330 | | .371 | | | |
| 2022 | LAK | A | 19 | 371 | 54 | 21 | 2 | 8 | 39 | 38 | 80 | 12 | 4 | .267/.342/.415 | 103 | .328 | -0.3 | 3B(63) 5.6, SS(18) 1.5 | 2.0 |
| 2022 | WM | A+ | 19 | 73 | 9 | 2 | 0 | 3 | 13 | 9 | 17 | 0 | 1 | .183/.274/.367 | 103 | .182 | -0.3 | 3B(15) -0.8, SS(2) -0.4 | 0.1 |
| 2023 non-DC | DET | MLB | 20 | 251 | 20 | 11 | 2 | 3 | 21 | 18 | 67 | 3 | 1 | .215/.275/.317 | 66 | .288 | -2.8 | 3B 0, SS 0 | -0.6 |

*Comparables: Trey Michalczewski, Josh Vitters, Brice Turang*

Pacheco was popped by the Tigers in the second round of the 2021 draft as a Texas prep shortstop with plus power potential. He's played mostly third base as a pro, not a huge surprise given his broad, 6-foot-4 frame. He's already hitting the ball pretty hard considering his age and level, and makes a downright precocious amount of contact in the zone. Pacheco's swing is muscley, not overly stiff, but can take a bit to get going, so when he squares something that catches too much plate, the ball can just take a leisurely path through the big part of the park. That's limited his over-the-fence pop so far, as has his propensity to chase outside the zone.

Pacheco is a perfectly fine third baseman with the requisite strong arm, but he's already on the larger side for the hot corner too, and isn't the twitchiest prospect in the field or at the plate, so the long-term defense merits watching. Still, he's only 19 and had a perfectly cromulent performance across two A-ball levels. If he can start generating more pull-side fly-ball contact, he might end up with middle-of-the-lineup game power, but for now he looks more like an average regular who hits sixth or seventh.

## 12 Reese Olson  RHP

Born: 07/31/99   Age: 23   Bats: R   Throws: R   Height: 6'1"   Weight: 160 lb.   Origin: Round 13, 2018 Draft (#395 overall)

| YEAR | TEAM | LVL | AGE | W | L | SV | G | GS | IP | H | HR | BB/9 | K/9 | K | GB% | BABIP | WHIP | ERA | DRA- | WARP |
|---|---|---|---|---|---|---|---|---|---|---|---|---|---|---|---|---|---|---|---|---|
| 2021 | WIS | A+ | 21 | 5 | 4 | 0 | 14 | 14 | 69 | 58 | 5 | 4.6 | 10.3 | 79 | 43.4% | .312 | 1.35 | 4.30 | 88 | 1.2 |
| 2021 | WM | A+ | 21 | 1 | 0 | 0 | 2 | 2 | 11 | 6 | 0 | 1.6 | 11.5 | 14 | 44.0% | .240 | 0.73 | 0.00 | 87 | 0.2 |
| 2021 | ERI | AA | 21 | 2 | 1 | 0 | 5 | 5 | 24² | 18 | 1 | 5.1 | 7.7 | 21 | 49.3% | .250 | 1.30 | 4.74 | 110 | 0.1 |
| 2022 | ERI | AA | 22 | 8 | 6 | 0 | 26 | 25 | 119² | 109 | 15 | 2.9 | 12.6 | 168 | 42.1% | .337 | 1.23 | 4.14 | 70 | 3.4 |
| 2023 DC | DET | MLB | 23 | 1 | 1 | 0 | 28 | 0 | 24 | 24 | 3 | 4.2 | 8.7 | 24 | 37.5% | .297 | 1.44 | 4.44 | 119 | -0.1 |

*Comparables: Robert Gsellman, Touki Toussaint, Raúl Alcántara*

Olson threw about 120 innings in Double-A as a 22-year-old, striking out just a smidge under a third of the batters he faced. Yet, his stuff can remain maddeningly inconsistent at times. His fastball will never be the star of the show here. It's a low-90s offering with a bit of two-seam action, but more run than sink. He will pop 95 now and again, but it can also slide down closer to 90 within the same outing.

His secondaries frustrate in a similar way. Olson's best changeups are clearly plus—mid-80s with late dive and fade. He can double up with it when it's looking sharp, and it's a true-swing-and miss pitch. Then a batter later, the change will be fringy and just sort of running down barrels. His slider can be a big sweeping low-80s offering—a potential 55—or it can bleed into the mid-70s, 12-6 curve in a slurvy sort of way. And when Olson wasn't striking out guys, the stuff was a bit more hittable than it really should be. He's likely to be a major leaguer, even as soon as 2023, but without more consistency in command and secondaries, he projects as a very frustrating back-end starter.

## 13 Dylan Smith  RHP

Born: 05/28/00   Age: 23   Bats: R   Throws: R   Height: 6'2"   Weight: 180 lb.   Origin: Round 3, 2021 Draft (#74 overall)

| YEAR | TEAM | LVL | AGE | W | L | SV | G | GS | IP | H | HR | BB/9 | K/9 | K | GB% | BABIP | WHIP | ERA | DRA- | WARP |
|---|---|---|---|---|---|---|---|---|---|---|---|---|---|---|---|---|---|---|---|---|
| 2022 | WM | A+ | 22 | 8 | 6 | 0 | 20 | 19 | 83¹ | 78 | 6 | 2.3 | 9.3 | 86 | 43.5% | .312 | 1.19 | 4.00 | 102 | 0.7 |
| 2023 non-DC | DET | MLB | 23 | 3 | 3 | 0 | 58 | 0 | 50 | 56 | 7 | 3.4 | 6.5 | 36 | 37.2% | .309 | 1.50 | 5.06 | 129 | -0.5 |

*Comparables: Bryan Evans, Robert Morey, Tyler Duffey*

An overslot 2021 third-round selection, Smith doesn't have electric stuff but found a way to get hitters out during his initial professional season. There's some deception in his delivery, helping his improving, mid-90s fastball play up. The breaking balls are inconsistent, sometimes blending together in shape but both the curve and slider show signs of becoming average offerings. He struggled throwing strikes during his time in the SEC but has become more consistent since being drafted. If the command and secondaries continue to improve, Smith could carve out a role for himself on the Tigers' staff.

## 14 Peyton Graham  SS

Born: 01/26/01   Age: 22   Bats: R   Throws: R   Height: 6'3"   Weight: 185 lb.   Origin: Round 2, 2022 Draft (#51 overall)

| YEAR | TEAM | LVL | AGE | PA | R | 2B | 3B | HR | RBI | BB | K | SB | CS | AVG/OBP/SLG | DRC+ | BABIP | BRR | DRP | WARP |
|---|---|---|---|---|---|---|---|---|---|---|---|---|---|---|---|---|---|---|---|
| 2022 | LAK | A | 21 | 113 | 19 | 5 | 1 | 1 | 13 | 10 | 29 | 7 | 1 | .270/.345/.370 | 92 | .366 | 2.9 | SS(14) 2.7, 2B(5) 0.7, 3B(2) 0.6 | 0.9 |
| 2023 non-DC | DET | MLB | 22 | 251 | 19 | 10 | 1 | 2 | 19 | 16 | 81 | 7 | 1 | .206/.264/.291 | 57 | .305 | -1.2 | 2B 0, 3B 0 | -0.6 |

*Comparables: John Santiago, Toby Thomas, Connor Kaiser*

The Tigers stuck with up-the-middle college performers in the second round of the 2022 draft, taking Graham in the second round. He destroyed baseballs his junior year at Oklahoma, posting a 1.058 OPS, but with a slightly higher K-rate than you might expect from that kind of offensive work in the Big 12. Graham is unlikely to hit for the same kind of power with wood bats, as his swing is geared more to staying in the zone. That kind of contact-oriented profile is fine if you make a lot of contact, but Graham has a very aggressive approach and chases out of the zone a concerning amount. He's a solid bet to stick at short given his footspeed and left-side arm, but I'm going to want to see a track record of hitting in the pros before I sign off on an everyday infield role for him.

## 15 Ryan Kreidler    IF
Born: 11/12/97   Age: 25   Bats: R   Throws: R   Height: 6'4"   Weight: 208 lb.   Origin: Round 4, 2019 Draft (#112 overall)

| YEAR | TEAM | LVL | AGE | PA | R | 2B | 3B | HR | RBI | BB | K | SB | CS | AVG/OBP/SLG | DRC+ | BABIP | BRR | DRP | WARP |
|------|------|-----|-----|-----|----|----|----|----|----|----|----|----|----|----|----|----|----|----|----|
| 2021 | ERI | AA | 23 | 388 | 67 | 15 | 0 | 15 | 36 | 32 | 119 | 10 | 4 | .256/.325/.429 | 96 | .341 | 3.2 | SS(88) -4.1 | 0.9 |
| 2021 | TOL | AAA | 23 | 162 | 28 | 8 | 0 | 7 | 22 | 24 | 39 | 5 | 2 | .304/.407/.519 | 108 | .374 | 2.4 | SS(35) -1.4, 3B(7) -0.6 | 0.7 |
| 2022 | TOL | AAA | 24 | 250 | 29 | 12 | 2 | 8 | 22 | 36 | 72 | 15 | 1 | .213/.352/.411 | 90 | .280 | 0.8 | SS(26) 3.6, 2B(12) 0.6, 3B(11) -0.4 | 0.9 |
| 2022 | DET | MLB | 24 | 84 | 8 | 1 | 0 | 1 | 6 | 6 | 22 | 0 | 1 | .178/.244/.233 | 81 | .231 | 0.6 | 3B(13) 0.3, SS(13) -0.7, 2B(2) 0 | 0.0 |
| 2023 DC | DET | MLB | 25 | 360 | 34 | 13 | 1 | 7 | 31 | 31 | 109 | 17 | 4 | .216/.293/.332 | 83 | .301 | 3.0 | 3B 0, SS 0 | 0.6 |

*Comparables: Yadiel Rivera, Brent Lillibridge, Chin-Lung Hu*

Kreidler couldn't repeat his 2021 success in Triple-A, dealing with a broken hand and groin injury that cost him a large chunk of the 2022 season. There's a little too much swing-and-miss to get either offensive tool past average, and he's a better fit at second or third than shortstop—Detroit rolled him out for a game in center field too. If he can bounce back in 2023 and continue to tap into his 2021 power gains, he should be a useful bench infielder who can start for you for a month here and there when someone else goes down with injury.

## 16 Wenceel Perez    2B/DH
Born: 10/30/99   Age: 23   Bats: S   Throws: R   Height: 5'11"   Weight: 203 lb.   Origin: International Free Agent, 2016

| YEAR | TEAM | LVL | AGE | PA | R | 2B | 3B | HR | RBI | BB | K | SB | CS | AVG/OBP/SLG | DRC+ | BABIP | BRR | DRP | WARP |
|------|------|-----|-----|-----|----|----|----|----|----|----|----|----|----|----|----|----|----|----|----|
| 2021 | LAK | A | 21 | 107 | 16 | 5 | 1 | 1 | 12 | 12 | 21 | 9 | 1 | .293/.383/.402 | 114 | .366 | 1.3 | 2B(21) 3.1 | 0.9 |
| 2021 | WM | A+ | 21 | 369 | 51 | 13 | 6 | 3 | 31 | 31 | 64 | 13 | 1 | .245/.313/.348 | 106 | .295 | 2.2 | 2B(59) -0.4, 3B(24) -2.7 | 1.3 |
| 2022 | WM | A+ | 22 | 236 | 35 | 13 | 5 | 9 | 38 | 27 | 38 | 13 | 1 | .286/.364/.529 | 138 | .309 | 0.1 | 2B(30) 0.2, 3B(7) 0.2 | 1.8 |
| 2022 | ERI | AA | 22 | 171 | 28 | 10 | 5 | 5 | 28 | 15 | 23 | 5 | 4 | .307/.374/.540 | 128 | .328 | -0.2 | 2B(30) -1.1 | 0.9 |
| 2023 DC | DET | MLB | 23 | 29 | 3 | 1 | 1 | 0 | 2 | 2 | 5 | 1 | 0 | .224/.285/.348 | 75 | .272 | 0.0 | 2B 0 | 0.0 |

*Comparables: Abiatal Avelino, Juan Lagares, Nick Madrigal*

Perez created some buzz in 2018 when, as a teenager, he hit .309 during a short, late-season stint in the Midwest League. It quickly faded the next year when he was overmatched by advanced pitching and struggled in the field at shortstop. Fast-forward to 2022, and in year four at West Michigan, things began to come together. He's always shown the ability to make contact but this past season he showed up stronger and began to drive the baseball more than ever before. In the field, he's been moved off the six and seems to have found a home at second, where the glove profiles as slightly above average. It's a relatively small sample size of success but he's still just 23, and now that he's been added to the 40-man roster, he could see big-league at-bats soon.

---

### Eyewitness Report: Wenceel Perez

**Evaluator:** Nathan Graham
**Report Date:** 08/01/2022
**Dates Seen:** Multiple 2019, 2021, 2022
**Risk Factor:** High
**Physical/Health:** Extra-Large frame, athletic, physically mature.

| Tool | Future Grade | Report |
|---|---|---|
| Hit | 50 | Perez has made significant mechanical changes since my first looks in 2019. He's closed the stance, removed much of the pre-swing noise, and incorporates his lower half much more efficiently. He's a competent switch hitter, showing solid bat-to-ball skills from both sides of the plate. The approach has improved greatly since his first season at West Michigan. He looks for pitches to drive now instead of the weak ground balls that plagued him early in his career. Spin recognition, once a weakness, has improved and he now shows the ability to jump on off-speed that gets too much of the plate. |
| Power | 50 | Good weight was added during the offseason as he added muscle and became a more physical player. The swing is still geared more for contact and lacks leverage but the physical strength and plus bat speed will produce plenty of doubles and an average amount of home runs. |
| Baserunning/ Speed | 50 | Slightly above-average foot speed, 4.16 clock home to first from the left side. Quick to accelerate, he'll steal the occasional base. Should settle in at average speed as he ages. |
| Glove | 50 | Lacks the range for shortstop but shows solid instincts in the field. Soft hands and quick transfers will make him a slightly above average defender at second base. |
| Arm | 40 | Lacks the arm strength for the left side of the diamond, which will limit him to second base. |

**Conclusion:** Perez came into West Michigan as a hyped prospect but quickly looked overmatched. Velocity would knock the bat out of his hands and he was often fooled by mediocre off-speed. He's come back this year in much better shape and actually looks like he has a game plan when he comes to bat now. He's hitting hard line drives to all fields now and shows the ability to adjust at the plate. The defensive liabilities will limit his ceiling but his offense should get him some major league at-bats in the future.

## 17 Danny Serretti  SS
Born: 05/07/00  Age: 23  Bats: S  Throws: R  Height: 6'1"  Weight: 195 lb.  Origin: Round 6, 2022 Draft (#177 overall)

| YEAR | TEAM | LVL | AGE | PA | R | 2B | 3B | HR | RBI | BB | K | SB | CS | AVG/OBP/SLG | DRC+ | BABIP | BRR | DRP | WARP |
|---|---|---|---|---|---|---|---|---|---|---|---|---|---|---|---|---|---|---|---|
| 2022 | LAK | A | 22 | 46 | 11 | 4 | 0 | 2 | 7 | 14 | 6 | 4 | 1 | .375/.565/.688 | 152 | .417 | 0.1 | SS(5) 0.1, 2B(4) -0.1, 3B(1) -0.0 | 0.4 |
| 2022 | WM | A+ | 22 | 46 | 9 | 4 | 0 | 0 | 4 | 6 | 11 | 1 | 1 | .289/.413/.395 | 99 | .407 | -0.1 | SS(10) 0.1 | 0.1 |
| 2023 non-DC | DET | MLB | 23 | 251 | 23 | 11 | 1 | 3 | 21 | 29 | 65 | 6 | 2 | .226/.323/.327 | 90 | .307 | -1.4 | 2B 0, 3B 0 | 0.4 |

A sixth-round senior sign in the 2022 draft, Serretti will go as far as his contact-oriented, switch-hitting prowess will take him, but it might get him there quickly. The Tigers pushed him all the way to Double-A in his first pro summer, and he never looked overmatched. His swing is a bit unorthodox, starting with very high hands, before dropping them into his load and looking to slash the ball the other way. Serretti tries to lift the ball a bit more from the right side, but power is unlikely to be a big part of his game. He does have an incredibly disciplined approach—which can border on passive early in counts—so he should run above-average OBPs even if the hit tool is merely average. The Tigers have played Serretti all around the infield so far, and his hands and actions are fine anywhere, but his range and arm fit best at second base. There isn't a ton of upside in the profile, but I can't help but bet on Serretti having a longer major-league career than you might expect just looking at the scouting report, even if it's mostly as a bench infielder.

## 18 Roberto Campos  OF
Born: 06/14/03  Age: 20  Bats: R  Throws: R  Height: 6'2"  Weight: 200 lb.  Origin: International Free Agent, 2019

| YEAR | TEAM | LVL | AGE | PA | R | 2B | 3B | HR | RBI | BB | K | SB | CS | AVG/OBP/SLG | DRC+ | BABIP | BRR | DRP | WARP |
|---|---|---|---|---|---|---|---|---|---|---|---|---|---|---|---|---|---|---|---|
| 2021 | TIGW | ROK | 18 | 155 | 20 | 5 | 0 | 8 | 19 | 17 | 41 | 3 | 0 | .228/.316/.441 | | .261 | | | | |
| 2022 | LAK | A | 19 | 448 | 52 | 26 | 5 | 5 | 50 | 40 | 97 | 7 | 3 | .258/.326/.385 | 93 | .326 | 1.6 | CF(67) -6.0, RF(28) -1.6, LF(8) -0.4 | 0.3 |
| 2023 non-DC | DET | MLB | 20 | 251 | 18 | 11 | 2 | 2 | 19 | 14 | 73 | 2 | 0 | .211/.261/.300 | 58 | .298 | -3.6 | LF 0, CF 0 | -0.9 |

*Comparables: Henry Ramos, Gorkys Hernández, Greg Golson*

Cristian Santana broke Campos' record for biggest IFA bonus, inked a mere 18 months before. Physicality is not an issue here, as Campos looks the part of a major-league corner outfielder at 19, and already posts major-league quality exit velocities. It comes at a cost though, as he has a long trigger with some bat wrap that can leave him late on even average fastball velocity. He also struggles to consistently lift the ball, meaning the raw power doesn't really play in games yet. Given that Campos is likely to end up in right field long-term, he'll need to show more with the bat in terms of both contact and approach to carve out an everyday corner outfield spot in the majors.

## 19   Carlos Marcano   RHP

Born: 07/08/03   Age: 19   Bats: R   Throws: R   Height: 6'2"   Weight: 150 lb.   Origin: International Free Agent, 2021

| YEAR | TEAM | LVL | AGE | W | L | SV | G | GS | IP | H | HR | BB/9 | K/9 | K | GB% | BABIP | WHIP | ERA | DRA- | WARP |
|------|------|-----|-----|---|---|----|---|----|----|---|----|----|----|----|----|----|----|----|----|----|
| 2021 | DSL TIG | ROK | 17 | 5 | 6 | 1 | 18 | 1 | 36 | 39 | 1 | 2.5 | 10.3 | 41 | 48.5% | .384 | 1.36 | 5.25 | | |
| 2022 | LAK | A | 18 | 3 | 3 | 2 | 29 | 0 | 42¹ | 47 | 2 | 3.8 | 8.7 | 41 | 50.4% | .341 | 1.54 | 4.68 | 104 | 0.6 |
| 2023 non-DC | DET | MLB | 19 | 3 | 3 | 0 | 58 | 0 | 50 | 60 | 8 | 4.7 | 6.2 | 34 | 37.5% | .320 | 1.73 | 6.19 | 152 | -1.1 |

The Tigers always seem to have a teenaged arm—already filled out physically—with advanced stuff at one of their low-minors affiliates every year. They used to swing through Norwich regularly: think Gio Arriera, Keider Montero and Jack O'Loughlin. None of them have really worked out as pitching prospects yet, but I have more of a soft spot for this profile than I should. Marcano is an 18-year-old A-ball reliever. He already has a solid, mature frame. There's a lot of arm speed, but late effort to generate it. His fastball can touch 95 but sits low-90s, showing occasional wiffle ball two-seam action. His low-80s slider has plus vertical action. There's a crude changeup. Marcano may eventually get stretched out as a starter, it's worth a punt given the stuff, but a good outcome here is a 95-and-a-slider guy. Still, if I am forced to go this deep in this system, I'm going to just start picking guys I like on gut feel. It's better than the alternatives.

## Top Talents 25 and Under (as of 4/1/2023):

1. Riley Greene, OF
2. Spencer Torkelson, 1B
3. Matt Manning, RHP
4. Akil Baddoo, OF
5. Jace Jung, 2B
6. Wilmer Flores, RHP
7. Jackson Jobe, RHP
8. Colt Keith, IF
9. Casey Mize, RHP
10. Kerry Carpenter, OF

Jeffrey said at the top that you'd prefer your system to look different given how long Detroit's been helping keep folks in the Twins, Guardians and White Sox organizations employed. It is in fact very much what you don't want. That's not to say Detroit's farm hasn't recently graduated talented players, but none have shown a clear brand of excellence at the big-league level.

Were it not for an ill-fated foul ball off his own foot, Greene would have had the chance to join a storied group of top prospects who made their clubs' Opening Day rosters. Instead, Greene joined the Tigers for just 93 games, looking rusty at times and overmatched at others, posting a mere 78 DRC+ in 418 plate appearances and whiffing a bit more than is tenable, especially if Greene struggles to get to his power despite strong exit velocities. The hopes of a fresh spring await the 22-year-old, who still projects to be an excellent corner outfield bat, but underwhelmed in his debut campaign.

A fresh autumn, winter, spring and summer might be best for Torkelson, whose 2022 was likely the most disappointing relative to expectations of any of the big name debut rookies. His .203 average and .319 slugging don't give you all the information, we've left those days behind analytically, and yet they do tell the story effectively enough. Nathan Graham (and most baseball analysts with eyes) called him the "best power-hitting prospect in the game" last winter, so why did he ISO in the same range as Josh Harrison, Jonathan Schoop, and Amed Rosario? His barrel rate was above-average, as were his hard-hit rate, walk rate and line-drive rate, and his plate discipline was solid. And yet, almost every time he took the bat off his shoulder, things went awry, with a particularly atrocious display on pitches over the heart of the plate. Tork's track record of hitting is too strong to discount him, but it has raised enough flags to slip behind Greene.

The overwhelming power arm that Manning flashed at times in the minors has not manifested in the pros, as injuries and ineffectiveness, as well as a fastball that's backed up from sitting 95 to a liveable-but-lesser 93-94 makes his projection more measured. Right-shoulder inflammation shut down Manning's season after two April starts, because he is a young Tigers pitcher, and though he returned to take 10 more turns, he did not quite do enough to pass Go and collect $100. The 6-foot-6 righty ran a passable 102 DRA- on the year, still struggling to miss bats and skirting disaster at times, but his best stride was a step forward with his slider. The pitch has overtaken his picturesque 12-6 curve as his best secondary, and he must now figure how to rein in his fastball command to let it work.

Baddoo's season also featured a trip to Triple-A Toledo, like each previously listed member here. His was, like Torkelson's, performance-based. Sure, his 2021 fell off after the hot start, and was at least somewhat over his skates but staying narrowly on balance. But the 22-year-old seemed in line to improve, or at least keep pace as a fleet-footed corner glove with plus range and defense enough to be platooned with or be a stout fourth outfielder. Instead, the Motor City vortex sucked him in as well, part of the worst offensive club in the league by a wide margin. Baddoo bounced back in Toledo, looking far more the multifaceted threat he'd been a year ago, but without major over-the-fence power, Baddoo is an ambush hitter who needs to land gap shots to thrive.

Mize crushingly underwent Tommy John surgery in June of 2022 after elbow discomfort in April that he couldn't shake. A.J. Hinch's disbelief in describing the specifically peculiar diagnosis—Mize's UCL was not actually torn, but still malfunctioning—is understandable, and highlights the grisly misfortune of the former Auburn ace. He maintains this spot out of respect for his reasonable pitch mix that hopefully bounces back post-surgery, but it could easily be 2024 when he next pitches in competitive games.

If you've made it this far, you deserve a treat, and for Tigers fans, Carpenter hopefully continues to be a pleasant surprise amidst a ghastly scene of top picks laid low left and right. The 562nd pick of the 2019 draft, snapped up in the 19th round from Virginia Tech, was the best rookie hitter on the Tigers in his 31-game tour through Michigan. His profile is mostly one-dimensional, slugging six big flies in 113 plate appearances, but darn it if that isn't exactly what he did at every level. Thirty-six homers between Double-A Erie, Triple-A Toledo and the bigs in 461 plate appearances is worth keeping an eye on, as was a .252/.310/.485 slash line. He may be a slugging corner bat who whiffs too much to stick, but that's not going to make or break this club. *Anything* is something.

# Houston Astros

## The State of the System

The Astros' system gets a bit of a bump from having actual Day 1 draft picks this year, but it remains thin overall and lacks the usual cadre of analytically-friendly arms in the Top 10.

## The Top Ten:

### 1 Hunter Brown  RHP     OFP: 60     ETA: Debuted in 2022

Born: 08/29/98   Age: 24   Bats: R   Throws: R   Height: 6'2"   Weight: 212 lb.   Origin: Round 5, 2019 Draft (#166 overall)

| YEAR | TEAM | LVL | AGE | W | L | SV | G | GS | IP | H | HR | BB/9 | K/9 | K | GB% | BABIP | WHIP | ERA | DRA- | WARP |
|------|------|-----|-----|---|---|----|----|----|------|----|----|------|------|-----|------|-------|------|------|------|------|
| 2021 | CC | AA | 22 | 1 | 4 | 1 | 13 | 11 | 49¹ | 45 | 6 | 5.3 | 13.9 | 76 | 45.5% | .379 | 1.50 | 4.20 | 96 | 0.4 |
| 2021 | SUG | AAA | 22 | 5 | 1 | 0 | 11 | 8 | 51 | 47 | 6 | 3.7 | 9.7 | 55 | 52.5% | .311 | 1.33 | 3.88 | 84 | 0.7 |
| 2022 | SUG | AAA | 23 | 9 | 4 | 1 | 23 | 14 | 106 | 70 | 5 | 3.8 | 11.4 | 134 | 54.3% | .271 | 1.08 | 2.55 | 67 | 2.7 |
| 2022 | HOU | MLB | 23 | 2 | 0 | 0 | 7 | 2 | 20¹ | 15 | 0 | 3.1 | 9.7 | 22 | 64.7% | .294 | 1.08 | 0.89 | 90 | 0.3 |
| 2023 DC | HOU | MLB | 24 | 9 | 7 | 0 | 53 | 15 | 108.3 | 90 | 10 | 4.1 | 9.1 | 109 | 51.3% | .276 | 1.28 | 3.13 | 86 | 1.6 |

*Comparables: Anthony Reyes, Robinson Tejeda, Chris Archer*

**The Report:** Our main concern about Hunter Brown last year—and the one that kept him from serious Top 101 consideration—was his well-below-average command. Well, it's still not even average—he walked over 10% of the batters he faced in Triple-A—but that may just not matter. It doesn't hurt that his curve—which was inconsistent in 2021, is now a drop-off-a-cliff plus pitch that batters beat into the ground when they aren't swinging over the top of it. Brown still has mid-to-upper-90s heat which is effectively wild, and it's a riding four-seamer featuring good extension. There's a cutterish slider and change as well, but he threw the heater and hook the majority of the time in the majors. Brown was dominant in his few relief appearances for the Astros at the end of the year and might settle into a shutdown multi-inning relief role, à la Collin McHugh on those late-2010s teams. While he doesn't check the usual boxes for a starting pitching prospect, the Astros always turn this type of arm into a surprisingly good rotation piece, don't they?

**OFP:** 60 / Another Astros pitcher who tosses 150ish innings with a low-3s ERA

**Variance:** Low. I do think there's an upper-bound limit of what Brown can do in a rotation given his bouts of inefficiency. He'd also be a very good reliever if he ends up settling in the pen due to organizational preference or need.

**Jesse Roche's Fantasy Take:** The Astros have recently turned prospects with command and repertoire-depth questions into high-end MLB starting pitchers in Cristian Javier and Framber Valdez. Given that recent success, it is an easy leap of faith to believe Brown will follow in their footsteps. Brown is far from a finished product despite his Triple-A success, but the org's track record and his raw stuff are a match made in heaven. He is a top-50 dynasty prospect and a borderline top-five fantasy pitching prospect.

## 2 Drew Gilbert CF    OFP: 55    ETA: 2024
Born: 09/27/00   Age: 22   Bats: L   Throws: L   Height: 5'9"   Weight: 185 lb.   Origin: Round 1, 2022 Draft (#28 overall)

| YEAR | TEAM | LVL | AGE | PA | R | 2B | 3B | HR | RBI | BB | K | SB | CS | AVG/OBP/SLG | DRC+ | BABIP | BRR | DRP | WARP |
|------|------|-----|-----|----|---|----|----|----|-----|----|---|----|----|-------------|------|-------|-----|-----|------|
| 2023 non-DC | HOU | MLB | 22 | 251 | 20 | 10 | 2 | 3 | 20 | 17 | 60 | 11 | 4 | .216/.277/.307 | 65 | .280 | 1.6 | CF 0 | 0.0 |

**The Report:** Gilbert's monster junior year with the Volunteers got him picked at the back of the first round by Houston. This was the Astros' first first-rounder in quite a few seasons and they took as big a swing as Gilbert does. He has a very loud collection of tools for a college outfielder. His aforementioned massive cuts are geared for pull-side lift and he has at least plus bat speed. Gilbert also has the foot speed to stick in center, and a plus-plus arm if he has to shift to right field down the road. If that sounds more like a top-half-of-the-first-round prospect than the back-half, well yeah, he probably should have been off the board well before the Astros picked. Now, Gilbert doesn't have the longest track record of this kind of production, and while his swing does generate hard contact, he's not the biggest dude. He's listed at 5-foot-9, and his longer swing while taking those kinds of rips should make you a bit concerned about his long-term hit tool projection—although contact was not an issue at any stop, amateur or pro, in 2022.

**OFP:** 55 / Above-average outfielder

**Variance:** Medium. Gilbert's shorter track record of performance injects some medium-term variance, but I also expect him to be on the Top 101 next year with an OFP a half-grade up. I guess that's a solid argument for doing it this year, but...

**Jesse Roche's Fantasy Take:** Gilbert can do it all: make tons of contact and tons of quality contact, exhibit strong plate discipline and flash plus raw power and plus speed. He flashed all his tools in his brief, injury-shortened debut (dislocated right elbow). The whole package is slightly similar to Alek Thomas, who was also underrated coming out of his draft.

## 3 Justin Dirden OF    OFP: 55    ETA: 2023
Born: 07/16/97   Age: 25   Bats: L   Throws: R   Height: 6'3"   Weight: 209 lb.   Origin: Undrafted Free Agent, 2020

| YEAR | TEAM | LVL | AGE | PA | R | 2B | 3B | HR | RBI | BB | K | SB | CS | AVG/OBP/SLG | DRC+ | BABIP | BRR | DRP | WARP |
|------|------|-----|-----|----|---|----|----|----|-----|----|---|----|----|-------------|------|-------|-----|-----|------|
| 2021 | FAY | A | 23 | 249 | 46 | 15 | 3 | 11 | 41 | 40 | 74 | 8 | 1 | .267/.402/.535 | 115 | .364 | 0.9 | RF(31) 1.6, LF(15) 0.9, CF(7) 2.0 | 1.8 |
| 2021 | ASH | A+ | 23 | 101 | 13 | 3 | 3 | 4 | 17 | 12 | 26 | 2 | 3 | .289/.386/.542 | 103 | .357 | -0.1 | RF(10) 2.0, CF(7) -0.7, LF(6) -0.2 | 0.5 |
| 2022 | CC | AA | 24 | 407 | 64 | 32 | 5 | 20 | 73 | 41 | 94 | 7 | 2 | .324/.411/.616 | 121 | .391 | 1.0 | CF(38) -2.1, LF(26) -0.4, RF(20) -1.5 | 1.7 |
| 2022 | SUG | AAA | 24 | 142 | 18 | 8 | 0 | 4 | 28 | 10 | 40 | 5 | 1 | .242/.305/.398 | 81 | .318 | -0.4 | RF(15) 0.9, CF(10) 0.4, LF(5) 0.4 | 0.2 |
| 2023 non-DC | HOU | MLB | 25 | 251 | 24 | 12 | 3 | 5 | 26 | 19 | 70 | 3 | 0 | .234/.304/.381 | 94 | .314 | -3.1 | LF 0, CF 0 | 0.2 |

**The Report:** Dirden might be the first Savannah Banana to make the majors, and that is just a small slice of the very meandering path he took to the doorstep of Minute Maid Park. A non-drafted senior sign out of Southeast Missouri State, injury and a pandemic limited his game reps as an upperclassman; while his 2021 line looks quite healthy, that was compiled as a 23-year-old at two A-ball levels. You might even look askance at his 2022 breakout: that .955 OPS came as a 24-year-old—that's just the math—and is heavily buoyed by his Double-A performance. And yeah, he sort of looks like a Quad-A slugger who 10 years ago would have have been the subject of a whole #FreeDirden campaign, replete with obnoxious *Fight Club* references. Meanwhile, scouty types would tell you his stiff swing won't work in the majors, and watch some games, nerd.

Well, we've all learned a few things since then. The sweeter the swing doesn't mean the sweeter the contact, and top-line upper minors stats aren't as important as batted-ball data. Dirden's hard-contact profile is good but not elite, but he can hit balls out from line to line, despite a swing path that would end up on Da Vinci's drawing room floor. He did struggle a bit more in Triple-A although that slash line overstates the underlying contact issues, and as awkward as it can look, Dirden does tend to get the barrel to the ball. It is fair to wonder if he is going to be a consistent 25+ home run bat to fill out the third of the three true outcomes, and he's likely to land in a corner, as he just doesn't have the high-end foot speed or canny routes of a true center fielder. If Dirden hits it won't matter, and we think he's an everyday bat even in a corner.

**OFP:** 55 / Above-average corner outfielder

**Variance:** Medium. Dirden handled Double-A, which was the first big test of this profile. The majors is the final one, outcome TBD.

**Jesse Roche's Fantasy Take:** Every once in a while, something clicks for an older, undrafted prospect in a big way and that prospect establishes himself as a MLB regular. That could be the case for Dirden. However, it is difficult to fit him in an outfield with Kyle Tucker and Yordan Alvarez at the corners, and he may spend all of 2023 in Triple-A. Dirden should be rostered in dynasty leagues with up to 400 prospects.

## 4  Colin Barber  OF    OFP: 55    ETA: 2024

Born: 12/04/00   Age: 22   Bats: L   Throws: L   Height: 6'0"   Weight: 200 lb.   Origin: Round 4, 2019 Draft (#136 overall)

| YEAR | TEAM | LVL | AGE | PA | R | 2B | 3B | HR | RBI | BB | K | SB | CS | AVG/OBP/SLG | DRC+ | BABIP | BRR | DRP | WARP |
|------|------|-----|-----|----|---|----|----|----|-----|----|---|----|----|-------------|------|-------|-----|-----|------|
| 2021 | ASH | A+ | 20 | 53 | 10 | 1 | 0 | 3 | 7 | 9 | 22 | 1 | 1 | .214/.365/.452 | 76 | .353 | 0.7 | RF(7) 0.5, LF(5) -0.5, CF(3) -0.8 | 0.0 |
| 2022 | ASH | A+ | 21 | 260 | 35 | 10 | 1 | 7 | 33 | 30 | 57 | 7 | 4 | .298/.408/.450 | 113 | .374 | -0.8 | CF(20) -0.3, RF(19) -0.7, LF(15) -1.6 | 0.8 |
| 2023 non-DC | HOU | MLB | 22 | 251 | 22 | 10 | 2 | 3 | 22 | 20 | 65 | 2 | 2 | .234/.306/.335 | 84 | .314 | -3.0 | LF 0, CF 0 | -0.1 |

Comparables: Danry Vasquez, Trayvon Robinson, Brandon Nimmo

**The Report:** Barber's got one of the most professional approaches in the Astros system. He employs a fundamental and solid all-fields left-handed swing that was more pull-centric in the past. He grades out as a solid-average hitter with average power who can confidently handle a corner outfield spot, while giving you a .275 batting average, plenty of walks and 20 homers at his peak. Like many in this list, Barber hasn't touched Double-A yet, but despite a significant shoulder injury in 2021, he bounced back strong and looked every bit as good as the Astros could have hoped in 2022.

**OFP:** 55 / Above-average corner outfielder

**Variance:** Medium. Despite a season-ending injury in 2021, Barber has multiple average-or-better tools and above-average plate discipline. He should be at least an everyday corner outfielder if he can stay healthy.

**Jesse Roche's Fantasy Take:** If not for lengthy injury absences the last two years, Barber likely would receive a lot more press. Indeed, his upside—"a .275 batting average, plenty of walks and 20 homers at his peak"--is significant. He just needs to stay on the field. Barber is a top-250 dynasty prospect.

## 5  Yainer Diaz  C    OFP: 50    ETA: Debuted in 2022

Born: 09/21/98   Age: 24   Bats: R   Throws: R   Height: 6'0"   Weight: 195 lb.   Origin: International Free Agent, 2016

| YEAR | TEAM | LVL | AGE | PA | R | 2B | 3B | HR | RBI | BB | K | SB | CS | AVG/OBP/SLG | DRC+ | BABIP | BRR | DRP | WARP |
|------|------|-----|-----|----|---|----|----|----|-----|----|---|----|----|-------------|------|-------|-----|-----|------|
| 2021 | FAY | A | 22 | 49 | 3 | 2 | 0 | 1 | 7 | 0 | 4 | 1 | 0 | .229/.224/.333 | 115 | .227 | 0.0 | C(5) 1.4, 1B(2) 0.2 | 0.4 |
| 2021 | LYN | A | 22 | 258 | 30 | 19 | 1 | 5 | 50 | 15 | 42 | 1 | 1 | .314/.357/.464 | 115 | .361 | -1.3 | C(36) 2.1, 1B(2) -0.2 | 1.3 |
| 2021 | ASH | A+ | 22 | 105 | 28 | 4 | 0 | 11 | 33 | 8 | 17 | 2 | 0 | .396/.438/.781 | 156 | .391 | -0.4 | C(12) -1.1, 1B(8) -0.1 | 0.9 |
| 2022 | CC | AA | 23 | 267 | 37 | 13 | 3 | 9 | 48 | 21 | 40 | 1 | 0 | .316/.367/.504 | 115 | .345 | 0.6 | 1B(26) 2.4, C(23) 1.5, RF(4) -0.2 | 1.7 |
| 2022 | SUG | AAA | 23 | 219 | 38 | 9 | 1 | 16 | 48 | 13 | 39 | 1 | 0 | .294/.342/.587 | 119 | .291 | 0.4 | C(27) -8.2, 1B(10) 1.0, LF(1) -0.1 | 0.6 |
| 2022 | HOU | MLB | 23 | 9 | 0 | 1 | 0 | 0 | 1 | 1 | 2 | 0 | 0 | .125/.222/.250 | 89 | .167 | | C(2) -0.0 | 0.0 |
| 2023 DC | HOU | MLB | 24 | 31 | 3 | 1 | 0 | 1 | 3 | 2 | 6 | 0 | 0 | .236/.280/.382 | 86 | .274 | -0.3 | C 0 | 0.0 |

Comparables: Kendrys Morales, Christian Walker, Conor Jackson

**The Report:** Diaz showed impressive skills with the bat in 2021, both before and after his deadline move to Houston. However, an overly aggressive approach at the plate—and fringy defense behind it—led us to write last year: "The swing is going to have to show out in Double-A before we really buy the bat as good enough to start." Diaz accepted this challenge and kept on swinging from his heels at just about everything. The results: A K-rate still under 20%, oodles of hard contact and a near-.900 OPS between Double- and Triple-A. Diaz's chase rate is still terrifying, and you wonder if he will be able to adjust once major-league pitchers realize you never need to throw him a strike. But he doesn't miss much in the zone, and hits the ball really, really hard when he makes contact, despite pretty pedestrian bat speed. He needs to lift the ball a bit more, but has the baseline skills for an above-average offensive outcome. Yeah, we're still not sure the batting average will do more than scrape .260—and we're pretty sure he won't walk much—but Diaz should hit for enough power to carve out an everyday spot in a major-league lineup.

Ideally, that'd be at catcher, but his receiving continues to be fringy at best, although he's twitchy with good arm strength. Diaz has played a bit of first base, where he hasn't looked great, and even a bit of corner outfield, where he likely doesn't have the foot speed to be even average. He's a weird fit for an org that has highly prioritized catcher defense—and especially the soft skills therein—but you'd think the Astros would be flexible enough to find some role for this kind of hitter.

**OFP:** 50 / Timeshare catcher, occasional DH, 10% better than league-average bopper

**Variance:** Low. The chase and ground-ball rates raise an eyebrow, and the fringy glove limits the upside, but Diaz crushed the upper minors in 2022 and will be ready to take major-league at-bats as needed.

**Jesse Roche's Fantasy Take:** Diaz hit .306/25 between Double- and Triple-A with strong batted-ball data to match, including a 106.2-mph, 90th-percentile exit velocity in Triple-A. As noted above, his aggressive approach and poor defense may be near-term roadblocks to his playing time. That said, he has rare offensive upside behind the plate, akin to Salvador Perez (excluding his 2020 and 2021 seasons). Diaz is a top-200 dynasty prospect.

## 6  Korey Lee  C/DH        OFP: 50        ETA: Debuted in 2022
Born: 07/25/98   Age: 24   Bats: R   Throws: R   Height: 6'2"   Weight: 210 lb.   Origin: Round 1, 2019 Draft (#32 overall)

| YEAR | TEAM | LVL | AGE | PA | R | 2B | 3B | HR | RBI | BB | K | SB | CS | AVG/OBP/SLG | DRC+ | BABIP | BRR | DRP | WARP |
|------|------|-----|-----|-----|----|----|----|----|-----|----|-----|----|----|-------------|------|-------|------|-----|------|
| 2021 | GDD | WIN | 22 | 71 | 8 | 2 | 0 | 1 | 6 | 9 | 19 | 1 | 0 | .258/.352/.339 | | .357 | | | |
| 2021 | ASH | A+ | 22 | 121 | 24 | 5 | 0 | 3 | 14 | 12 | 24 | 1 | 0 | .330/.397/.459 | 112 | .402 | -0.6 | C(20) -0.3, 3B(2) 0.3 | 0.5 |
| 2021 | CC | AA | 22 | 203 | 25 | 9 | 1 | 8 | 27 | 17 | 35 | 3 | 1 | .254/.320/.443 | 116 | .275 | 1.3 | C(38) -1.6, 3B(4) -0.1, 1B(3) 0.2 | 1.1 |
| 2021 | SUG | AAA | 22 | 38 | 2 | 4 | 0 | 0 | 4 | 2 | 9 | 0 | 0 | .229/.263/.343 | 83 | .296 | 0.1 | C(4) -0.5, 1B(2) -0.6 | -0.1 |
| 2022 | SUG | AAA | 23 | 446 | 74 | 20 | 2 | 25 | 76 | 36 | 127 | 12 | 1 | .238/.307/.483 | 93 | .281 | 2.1 | C(66) 5.8, LF(2) 0.1, 1B(1) -0.0 | 1.6 |
| 2022 | HOU | MLB | 23 | 26 | 1 | 2 | 0 | 0 | 4 | 1 | 9 | 0 | 0 | .160/.192/.240 | 77 | .250 | -0.2 | C(12) -1.2 | -0.1 |
| 2023 DC | HOU | MLB | 24 | 214 | 22 | 8 | 1 | 6 | 22 | 14 | 61 | 3 | 1 | .209/.265/.344 | 71 | .271 | 0.0 | C -11 | -1.1 |

*Comparables: Danny Jansen, Devin Mesoraco, John Ryan Murphy*

**The Report:** On a long enough timeline, every good, but not great, catching prospect eventually becomes a 40 hit prospect with a bit of raw pop that may or may not get fully actualized. Lee dominated the Pac-12 with the bat his junior year for the Golden Bears, showed flashes of true two-way catcherdom as a pro, got some Top 101 shortlist consideration and then inevitably hit .238 with a K-rate approaching 30% in Triple-A. John Sickels' elucidation of Young Catcher Offensive Stagnation Syndrome is almost 30 years old now, and baseball player dev seems no closer to a cure. Lee remains a solid defender, but not so good he can carve out a career just on his glove. It does give him a higher floor than Diaz, but he has the less dynamic bat among Houston 2022 catching debutantes. If Lee can get enough of his top-end power into games, he will be a very useful part of a catching tandem. But if the stiffness in his swing means too many Ks in the bigs, he might have to take another half-step forward with his defense to be rosterable as a twice-a-week backup.

**OFP:** 50 / Average catcher

**Variance:** Medium. If Lee can replicate his Triple-A line in the majors, he'd be a top-10 catcher in baseball. That's not all that common a development though, and he may not have a clear carrying tool if he doesn't get his strength- and leverage-based pop into games.

**Jesse Roche's Fantasy Take:** Overshadowed by Diaz's offensive breakout, Lee quietly had a *powerful* second half after this brief, ugly MLB debut. Over his final 40 games, he launched 15 home runs with a .327 ISO. Lee has legitimate power, with a strong 104.8-mph, 90th-percentile exit velocity in Triple-A. Still, his inconsistent quality of contact, aggressive approach and, as noted above, elevated swing-and-miss cast doubt on his ability to hit enough. His power is intriguing, though, and he should be rostered in deeper leagues.

## 7  Jacob Melton  CF        OFP: 50        ETA: 2025
Born: 09/07/00   Age: 22   Bats: L   Throws: L   Height: 6'3"   Weight: 208 lb.   Origin: Round 2, 2022 Draft (#64 overall)

| YEAR | TEAM | LVL | AGE | PA | R | 2B | 3B | HR | RBI | BB | K | SB | CS | AVG/OBP/SLG | DRC+ | BABIP | BRR | DRP | WARP |
|------|------|-----|-----|-----|----|----|----|----|-----|----|----|----|----|-------------|------|-------|------|-----|------|
| 2022 | FAY | A | 21 | 86 | 11 | 6 | 0 | 4 | 13 | 11 | 20 | 4 | 2 | .324/.424/.577 | 114 | .396 | -1.0 | CF(15) -0.3, RF(1) -0.0 | 0.3 |
| 2023 non-DC | HOU | MLB | 22 | 251 | 21 | 10 | 2 | 3 | 22 | 20 | 80 | 6 | 2 | .216/.287/.321 | 73 | .316 | -1.2 | CF 0, RF 0 | -0.1 |

*Comparables: Brian Goodwin, LeVon Washington, Derek Fisher*

**The Report:** In 2021, Melton was in the middle of a torrid sophomore season in Corvallis before shoulder surgery cut short his year. He showed no ill effects in 2022, hitting .360 with power for the Beavers. If you want to know why he lasted all the way to the late second round with that level of major college performance, a quick gander at his swing should clue you in. We are getting away from visual hit tool evaluation, but if you are an amateur scout who leans more that way, Melton is incredibly unorthodox. He stands about as open as you can while still having both feet in the batter's box and takes a big step in, as he starts a hitchy, pretty long swing. Even when he's ripping pitches pull-side, it never actually looks like he's in sync.

Hitters hit though, right?

Well, Melton ran a bit higher K-rate than you'd expect given the gaudy college numbers, and he doesn't move the barrel around the zone as well as you'd hope. Despite plenty of strength and bat speed, his swing plane may allow pro pitchers to get in his kitchen and get whiffs in the zone, or otherwise produce weak, topped contact. Melton has one of the highest-variance offensive profiles in this draft class for me, college or otherwise. Defensively, he's a little less volatile: an above-average runner, although not a burner, with a reasonable shot to stick in center, he'd likely be plus in a corner.

**OFP:** 50 / Second-division outfielder

**Variance:** High. Melton tests our newfound love of unorthodox swings, as he did seem to swing through a few more strikes in his pro debut than you'd expect. While he's certainly capable of raking his way up the ladder and into the three-hole in future Astros lineups, there's also not a real major-league floor if the swing gets exposed at higher levels of the minors.

**Jesse Roche's Fantasy Take:** Melton's college performance—.360/.424/.671 with 17 home runs and 21 stolen bases—is the type fantasy managers salivate over. His raw power and speed both resoundingly support his production. Will he be able to hit? Melton is a streaky, aggressive hitter with below-average contact rates and elevated ground ball rates. Regardless, his power-speed potential puts him on the fantasy radar in leagues that roster up to 300 prospects.

## 8   Pedro Leon   CF    OFP: 50    ETA: 2023

Born: 05/28/98   Age: 25   Bats: R   Throws: R   Height: 5'10"   Weight: 170 lb.   Origin: International Free Agent, 2021

| YEAR | TEAM | LVL | AGE | PA | R | 2B | 3B | HR | RBI | BB | K | SB | CS | AVG/OBP/SLG | DRC+ | BABIP | BRR | DRP | WARP |
|------|------|-----|-----|----|---|----|----|----|-----|----|---|----|----|-------------|------|-------|-----|-----|------|
| 2021 | GDD | WIN | 23 | 84 | 9 | 3 | 0 | 1 | 9 | 13 | 20 | 4 | 1 | .257/.381/.343 | | .347 | | | |
| 2021 | CC | AA | 23 | 217 | 29 | 7 | 1 | 9 | 33 | 25 | 67 | 13 | 8 | .249/.359/.443 | 101 | .339 | 0.3 | SS(41) -3.9, CF(9) 0.1 | 0.3 |
| 2021 | SUG | AAA | 23 | 75 | 11 | 2 | 0 | 0 | 2 | 14 | 23 | 4 | 2 | .131/.293/.164 | 77 | .211 | 0.2 | SS(7) -0.5, 3B(6) -1.2, CF(4) 0.4 | -0.1 |
| 2022 | SAN | WIN | 24 | 113 | 14 | 2 | 1 | 4 | 11 | 11 | 33 | 3 | 1 | .204/.286/.367 | | .254 | | | |
| 2022 | SUG | AAA | 24 | 504 | 71 | 27 | 3 | 17 | 63 | 71 | 145 | 38 | 18 | .228/.365/.431 | 97 | .306 | -5.0 | CF(53) 0.8, RF(33) -0.7, 2B(20) 1.4 | 1.0 |
| 2023 DC | HOU | MLB | 25 | 163 | 17 | 6 | 1 | 3 | 14 | 16 | 50 | 10 | 6 | .219/.308/.342 | 89 | .310 | -2.3 | CF 0, RF 0 | 0.0 |

*Comparables: Pat Valaika, Erik González, Deven Marrero*

**The Report:** When Leon debuted with the Astros org in 2021, he hadn't played meaningful competitive baseball in over two years. You'd expect an adjustment period, and he showed flashes of an intriguing power/speed combo with the ability to handle a couple premium defensive spots. But 2022 brought more of the same, and the ill here might outweigh the good. Leon still chases too much and doesn't make enough contact in the zone—or enough hard contact—to make up for this expansive an approach. When he dons an infield glove, he's more often playing second base than short, which is a better fit for him defensively, but he's unlikely to man either middle infield spot in the near term in Houston. They could use the outfield help though, and he can handle all three spots on the grass. Last year we hoped for more consistency from Leon, and we got it at the plate, but given the slide down the positional spectrum, his offensive tools might be a bit short for an everyday role now.

**OFP:** 50 / Second-division starter, bouncing around the diamond

**Variance:** Medium. Leon is close to major-league-ready on paper, but hasn't really hit in the minors, and we will be waiting a bit longer for any more progress at the plate, as offseason hernia surgery means he will get a late start to his 2023 season.

**Jesse Roche's Fantasy Take:** Leon is tooled up and on the cusp but remains raw in many ways. While he often generates loud contact—including a 108.1-mph, 90th-percentile exit velocity in Triple-A—he makes a lot of weak, auto-out contact. Further, his approach is both passive and expansive, resulting in a lot of strikeouts. Indeed, Leon is effectively a Three-True-Outcomes hitter with a home run, strikeout or walk in 46.2% of plate appearances. That'll play in fantasy, especially given his speed and penchant to run. Whether he'll receive, and run with, an opportunity given his current faults appears unlikely. Regardless, Leon has power-speed upside and enough proximity to warrant being rostered in leagues with up to 200 prospects.

## 9   Jayden Murray   RHP    OFP: 50    ETA: 2023

Born: 04/11/97   Age: 26   Bats: R   Throws: R   Height: 6'1"   Weight: 190 lb.   Origin: Round 23, 2019 Draft (#698 overall)

| YEAR | TEAM | LVL | AGE | W | L | SV | G | GS | IP | H | HR | BB/9 | K/9 | K | GB% | BABIP | WHIP | ERA | DRA- | WARP |
|------|------|-----|-----|---|---|----|---|----|-----|---|----|------|-----|---|-----|-------|------|-----|------|------|
| 2021 | BG | A+ | 24 | 7 | 1 | 0 | 12 | 12 | 57² | 30 | 5 | 1.6 | 8.3 | 53 | 45.7% | .171 | 0.69 | 1.72 | 89 | 0.8 |
| 2021 | MTG | AA | 24 | 1 | 2 | 0 | 8 | 8 | 38¹ | 21 | 6 | 1.6 | 10.1 | 43 | 38.0% | .176 | 0.73 | 2.82 | 89 | 0.6 |
| 2022 | MTG | AA | 25 | 8 | 2 | 0 | 16 | 15 | 76¹ | 65 | 9 | 2.7 | 7.7 | 65 | 51.1% | .257 | 1.15 | 2.83 | 98 | 0.9 |
| 2022 | CC | AA | 25 | 0 | 2 | 0 | 6 | 6 | 27¹ | 24 | 3 | 3.6 | 8.6 | 26 | 48.1% | .288 | 1.28 | 4.28 | 95 | 0.2 |
| 2023 non-DC | HOU | MLB | 26 | 3 | 3 | 0 | 58 | 0 | 50 | 53 | 7 | 3.1 | 6.9 | 39 | 40.0% | .302 | 1.40 | 4.49 | 117 | -0.2 |

*Comparables: Tejay Antone, Julian Merryweather, Trevor Richards*

**The Report:** The Rays and Astros have some overlap in terms of pitching development philosophy, so it's not too surprising that the Astros snagged Murray as part of their return for Jose Siri at the deadline. It's also not too surprising then that he is effective running his fastball up in the zone and up into the mid-90s. Murray works off the heater with a potentially average slider and change and throws strikes with all three pitches. He's on the shorter side for a right-handed pitching prospect, but has thrown around 100 innings each of the last two seasons without issue, and has no red flags of note in his delivery. Murray is not going to show you overwhelming stuff and could be a bit too hittable at times in the upper minors last year, but the arsenal is advanced as is the strike-throwing, so he profiles well as a near-horizon back-end starter.

**OFP:** 50 / no. 4 starter

**Variance:** Medium. The usual trials and tribulations await the no. 4 starter without a clear plus pitch. Murray will have fine margins for his command and secondaries against major-league batters and may not miss enough bats to stick in a rotation long-term.

**Jesse Roche's Fantasy Take:** A back-end starter without overwhelming stuff has nearly no chance to break into the crowded Astros rotation as anything more than a spot starter in the short-term. Murray likely shouldn't be rostered in most dynasty leagues.

## 10    Kenedy Corona   OF    OFP: 50    ETA: 2024

Born: 03/21/00   Age: 23   Bats: R   Throws: R   Height: 5'11"   Weight: 184 lb.   Origin: International Free Agent, 2019

| YEAR | TEAM | LVL | AGE | PA | R | 2B | 3B | HR | RBI | BB | K | SB | CS | AVG/OBP/SLG | DRC+ | BABIP | BRR | DRP | WARP |
|------|------|-----|-----|-----|----|----|----|----|-----|----|----|----|----|--------------|------|-------|-----|-----|------|
| 2021 | ZUL | WIN | 21 | 86 | 16 | 5 | 0 | 2 | 14 | 4 | 23 | 1 | 2 | .291/.341/.430 | | .389 | | | |
| 2021 | FAY | A | 21 | 224 | 30 | 12 | 1 | 2 | 22 | 14 | 53 | 19 | 7 | .244/.306/.343 | 91 | .318 | 0.3 | CF(22) 2.3, RF(19) 0.9, LF(16) 4.6 | 1.3 |
| 2022 | ZUL | WIN | 22 | 89 | 10 | 1 | 0 | 1 | 5 | 7 | 23 | 1 | 3 | .185/.247/.235 | | .241 | | | |
| 2022 | FAY | A | 22 | 188 | 32 | 9 | 1 | 9 | 30 | 21 | 43 | 8 | 2 | .261/.346/.491 | 121 | .298 | -0.1 | LF(16) 0.6, RF(10) 1.5, CF(7) -0.3 | 1.4 |
| 2022 | ASH | A+ | 22 | 279 | 56 | 15 | 3 | 10 | 37 | 28 | 63 | 20 | 6 | .290/.373/.498 | 107 | .353 | 1.4 | LF(21) 1.0, CF(20) 0.9, RF(15) -0.1 | 1.6 |
| 2023 non-DC | HOU | MLB | 23 | 251 | 20 | 11 | 1 | 4 | 22 | 16 | 70 | 8 | 3 | .213/.272/.320 | 68 | .289 | 0.0 | LF 0, CF 0 | -0.2 |

**The Report:** Unlike the other toolsy outfielders on this list, Corona is just 22 years old. The young Venezuelan outfielder has a fascinating profile—he possesses a ground-ball swing, hits the ball hard, is a plus runner and socked 19 home runs between Low- and High-A this year.

In 62 games at High A, Corona put forth a 48% ground-ball rate but used his plus speed and strength to put balls through the infield and—at times—over the wall. There is an effort to get the ball in the air and work the count, but he is still raw offensively and can improve on the lift in his swing, although he maximizes the damage when he does elevate his pitch. Regardless of the inconsistency in getting the ball up, there is a lot to like here.

Corona is a coach's dream: He runs really hard, can play all three outfield spots, and has some (not a ton) of room to fill out. While he isn't a head-turner, he's got tools across the board but his full offensive development will hinge on the consistency in which he can make hard fly ball contact.

**OFP:** 50 / Average corner outfielder or slightly below average center fielder

**Variance:** (Very) High. Corona has a short track record of hitting for power.

**Jesse Roche's Fantasy Take:** Interestingly, Corona hit just three of 10 home runs in High-A at hitter-friendly McCormick Field in Asheville. Without park-aided homers, his 2022 power outburst carries more weight. Corona has some underlying swing-and-miss, and his tools don't stand out, but he has interesting power-speed potential. It is the type of profile to scoop in deep formats to see how much of his A-ball production carries over to the upper minors.

# Outside the Top Ten:

## 11    Jaime Melendez   RHP

Born: 09/26/01   Age: 21   Bats: L   Throws: R   Height: 5'8"   Weight: 190 lb.   Origin: International Free Agent, 2019

| YEAR | TEAM | LVL | AGE | W | L | SV | G | GS | IP | H | HR | BB/9 | K/9 | K | GB% | BABIP | WHIP | ERA | DRA- | WARP |
|------|------|-----|-----|---|---|----|---|----|-----|----|----|------|------|----|------|-------|------|-----|------|------|
| 2021 | FAY | A | 19 | 2 | 2 | 0 | 6 | 3 | 18¹ | 7 | 1 | 2.5 | 18.7 | 38 | 52.0% | .250 | 0.65 | 0.49 | 54 | 0.6 |
| 2021 | ASH | A+ | 19 | 2 | 3 | 0 | 11 | 7 | 32 | 34 | 2 | 6.7 | 11.5 | 41 | 44.3% | .376 | 1.81 | 4.78 | 89 | 0.5 |
| 2021 | CC | AA | 19 | 0 | 1 | 0 | 3 | 1 | 7² | 8 | 0 | 4.7 | 12.9 | 11 | 47.8% | .348 | 1.57 | 5.87 | 79 | 0.1 |
| 2022 | CC | AA | 20 | 2 | 8 | 0 | 23 | 16 | 73² | 59 | 7 | 6.2 | 13.0 | 106 | 45.7% | .331 | 1.49 | 5.01 | 74 | 1.5 |
| 2023 non-DC | HOU | MLB | 21 | 3 | 3 | 0 | 58 | 0 | 50 | 44 | 7 | 5.8 | 10.3 | 57 | 38.8% | .292 | 1.51 | 4.58 | 115 | -0.1 |

Melendez is listed at 5-foot-8 (maybe in spikes), but can absolutely overpower hitters with a mid-90s fastball that comes with oodles of deception and ride. Texas League hitters often looked like they were swinging late through 99 against Melendez's heater, which comes from a true overhand slot. The secondaries are not as whiffy, although both his breaking balls will show some potential. Melendez's little downer 12-6 curve is the better present pitch but, although he will snap his slider off a bit too much, I might prefer it long-term as it hums a little more out of the hand, while still showing late dive. Melendez's fastball should be good enough on its own to earn some major-league per diems, but he has struggled with walks the last two seasons as a piggybacking starter, and might be best suited to just airing the fastball out in one- or two-inning bursts in medium-leverage innings.

# 12 Misael Tamarez   RHP

Born: 01/16/00   Age: 23   Bats: R   Throws: R   Height: 6'1"   Weight: 206 lb.   Origin: International Free Agent, 2019

| YEAR | TEAM | LVL | AGE | W | L | SV | G | GS | IP | H | HR | BB/9 | K/9 | K | GB% | BABIP | WHIP | ERA | DRA- | WARP |
|------|------|-----|-----|---|---|----|----|-----|------|----|----|------|------|-----|-------|-------|------|------|------|------|
| 2021 | FAY | A | 21 | 4 | 2 | 1 | 12 | 6 | 43 | 28 | 3 | 5.9 | 13.4 | 64 | 38.0% | .281 | 1.30 | 3.98 | 70 | 1.1 |
| 2021 | ASH | A+ | 21 | 2 | 1 | 0 | 7 | 7 | 33² | 30 | 4 | 2.7 | 10.4 | 39 | 34.1% | .310 | 1.19 | 3.48 | 99 | 0.3 |
| 2022 | CC | AA | 22 | 3 | 6 | 1 | 24 | 19 | 103¹ | 76 | 18 | 4.8 | 10.6 | 122 | 41.0% | .249 | 1.27 | 4.62 | 71 | 2.3 |
| 2022 | SUG | AAA | 22 | 1 | 1 | 0 | 4 | 4 | 18 | 6 | 2 | 7.5 | 10.0 | 20 | 40.5% | .114 | 1.17 | 2.50 | 98 | 0.1 |
| 2023 non-DC | HOU | MLB | 23 | 3 | 3 | 0 | 58 | 0 | 50 | 48 | 8 | 5.6 | 9.3 | 52 | 34.9% | .295 | 1.57 | 5.11 | 127 | -0.4 |

*Comparables: Robert Stephenson, Touki Toussaint, Matt Magill*

Another future relief arm who remained stretched out in 2022, Tamarez has a more traditional high-octane fastball/slider combo. The slider improved a fair bit year-over-year, showing more consistent firm, late tilt. The fastball still sits mid-90s as a starter, and might play at the upper end of that range in short bursts. It's still a lively bat-misser for Tamarez when it's around the zone, but if anything his control and command backslid in the upper minors last year. It's not an unfamiliar tale, eighth-inning stuff married to up-and-down control. He has a pretty easy delivery for the plus velocity, but there's a long and at-times scattershot arm action that leads to the strike throwing issues. You can be a major-league reliever nowadays while walking five per nine, but it's harder to be a good one without an elite swing-and-miss arsenal to back it.

# 13 Forrest Whitley   RHP

Born: 09/15/97   Age: 25   Bats: R   Throws: R   Height: 6'7"   Weight: 238 lb.   Origin: Round 1, 2016 Draft (#17 overall)

| YEAR | TEAM | LVL | AGE | W | L | SV | G | GS | IP | H | HR | BB/9 | K/9 | K | GB% | BABIP | WHIP | ERA | DRA- | WARP |
|------|------|-----|-----|---|---|----|----|-----|------|----|----|------|------|-----|-------|-------|------|------|------|------|
| 2022 | SUG | AAA | 24 | 0 | 2 | 0 | 10 | 8 | 33 | 32 | 2 | 6.8 | 9.8 | 36 | 47.4% | .326 | 1.73 | 7.09 | 94 | 0.3 |
| 2023 DC | HOU | MLB | 25 | 2 | 2 | 0 | 6 | 6 | 29.7 | 29 | 5 | 5.4 | 9.3 | 31 | 38.0% | .300 | 1.57 | 5.05 | 126 | -0.1 |

*Comparables: Manny Bañuelos, Tyler Skaggs, Alex Reyes*

*"We're so caught up in our everyday lives that events of the past, like ancient stars that have burned out, are no longer in orbit around our minds. There are just too many things we have to think about every day, too many new things we have to learn. New styles, new information, new technology, new terminology ... But still, no matter how much time passes, no matter what takes place in the interim, there are some things we can never assign to oblivion, memories we can never rub away. They remain with us forever, like a touchstone."*

*- Haruki Murakami, Kafka on the Shore*

The first year we ranked Forrest Whitley as a prospect, we ended every pitcher's risk factor with some variation on: "He's a pitcher."

Forrest Whitley returned from Tommy John surgery midseason. He still throws six pitches but now only his curve and change flash as potential plus. His fastball was still around 95, but he struggled mightily to throw strikes with it. This is all within a shout of average when you are only a year-plus removed from Tommy John surgery. But nothing has ever remained average too long for Forrest Whitley, pitcher.

# 14 Ryan Clifford   LF

Born: 07/20/03   Age: 19   Bats: L   Throws: L   Height: 6'3"   Weight: 200 lb.   Origin: Round 11, 2022 Draft (#343 overall)

| YEAR | TEAM | LVL | AGE | PA | R | 2B | 3B | HR | RBI | BB | K | SB | CS | AVG/OBP/SLG | DRC+ | BABIP | BRR | DRP | WARP |
|------|------|-----|-----|-----|---|----|----|----|-----|----|----|----|----|-------------|------|-------|-----|-----|------|
| 2022 | ASO | ROK | 18 | 50 | 8 | 3 | 0 | 1 | 5 | 12 | 16 | 2 | 0 | .222/.440/.389 | | .368 | | | |
| 2022 | FAY | A | 18 | 51 | 5 | 2 | 0 | 1 | 5 | 10 | 15 | 0 | 0 | .268/.412/.390 | 101 | .400 | -0.2 | LF(7) -0.6, 1B(2) 0.3, RF(2) 0.2 | 0.2 |
| 2023 non-DC | HOU | MLB | 19 | 251 | 20 | 10 | 2 | 2 | 19 | 22 | 94 | 0 | 1 | .208/.284/.294 | 65 | .345 | -4.3 | 1B 0, LF 0 | -0.9 |

*Comparables: Ramón Flores, Luigi Rodriguez, Danry Vasquez*

The Astros went well over slot to sign Clifford with their first pick on Day 3 of the draft. A prep bat from North Carolina—with the emphasis here on bat—he looks every bit of the 6-foot-3, 200 pounds listed on his player card. Power is going to be the calling card, as Clifford has a strength-over-bat speed swing—although be careful if you try to beat him inside—with a bit of length to the hand path and a near arm bar at the end of his load. It does generate real pop already, but I do wonder how much he will hit against better pitching without some swing tweaks, and given that he's already splitting time between first base and corner outfield, Clifford is really going to have to hit.

## 15 Miguel Ullola RHP

Born: 06/19/02   Age: 21   Bats: R   Throws: R   Height: 6'1"   Weight: 184 lb.   Origin: International Free Agent, 2021

| YEAR | TEAM | LVL | AGE | W | L | SV | G | GS | IP | H | HR | BB/9 | K/9 | K | GB% | BABIP | WHIP | ERA | DRA- | WARP |
|------|------|-----|-----|---|---|----|----|----|----|----|----|------|------|----|------|-------|------|-----|------|------|
| 2021 | DSL AST | ROK | 19 | 1 | 1 | 0 | 8 | 5 | 21¹ | 10 | 1 | 7.2 | 14.3 | 34 | 44.7% | .243 | 1.27 | 4.22 | | |
| 2022 | FAY | A | 20 | 2 | 2 | 2 | 22 | 11 | 72 | 39 | 3 | 6.9 | 15.0 | 120 | 40.5% | .281 | 1.31 | 3.25 | 74 | 1.8 |
| 2023 non-DC | HOU | MLB | 21 | 3 | 3 | 0 | 58 | 0 | 50 | 41 | 8 | 6.6 | 11.2 | 62 | 35.1% | .284 | 1.56 | 4.80 | 119 | -0.2 |

*Comparables: Joe Boyle, Bryan Abreu, Chris Anderson*

Perhaps a future "fringe Top 10 Astros prospect despite relief markers" like Melendez and Tamarez, Ullola is a couple levels behind them, has similarly mid-90s heat with good traits, perhaps slightly more projection on his two breaking balls, and is also a shorter righty with strike-throwing issues. If you have enough of these profiles in your system, there's a chance one of them takes a leap on the control and command side. Ullola has time on his side there, at least until he doesn't and he's the 12th-best prospect on the 2025 list as a 95-and-a-slider guy.

## 16 Kenni Gomez CF

Born: 05/14/05   Age: 18   Bats: L   Throws: R   Height: 5'11"   Weight: 185 lb.

| YEAR | TEAM | LVL | AGE | PA | R | 2B | 3B | HR | RBI | BB | K | SB | CS | AVG/OBP/SLG | DRC+ | BABIP | BRR | DRP | WARP |
|------|------|-----|-----|----|---|----|----|----|-----|----|---|----|----|-------------|------|-------|-----|-----|------|
| 2022 | DSL HOUB | ROK | 17 | 122 | 20 | 5 | 2 | 4 | 24 | 18 | 28 | 10 | 5 | .294/.402/.500 | | .366 | | | |

Signed out of Cuba for $775,000 last January, Gomez is a physically advanced outfielder who perhaps chased a bit too much in the Dominican complex but otherwise posted strong top-line and underlying numbers for his first taste of pro ball. The bat speed is intriguing and while again I will reiterate I don't love ranking the previous year's IFA class—even though they get actual game time now—Gomez is worth watching as a breakout candidate in a shallow system.

## 17 Zach Daniels OF

Born: 01/23/99   Age: 24   Bats: R   Throws: R   Height: 6'1"   Weight: 220 lb.   Origin: Round 4, 2020 Draft (#131 overall)

| YEAR | TEAM | LVL | AGE | PA | R | 2B | 3B | HR | RBI | BB | K | SB | CS | AVG/OBP/SLG | DRC+ | BABIP | BRR | DRP | WARP |
|------|------|-----|-----|----|----|----|----|----|-----|----|-----|----|----|-------------|------|-------|-----|-----|------|
| 2021 | FAY | A | 22 | 197 | 29 | 5 | 1 | 6 | 30 | 26 | 65 | 14 | 3 | .228/.345/.377 | 89 | .333 | 2.3 | CF(18) 0.3, LF(12) 3.4, RF(9) 0.9 | 1.0 |
| 2021 | ASH | A+ | 22 | 174 | 24 | 8 | 0 | 3 | 18 | 23 | 64 | 8 | 3 | .219/.339/.336 | 73 | .363 | 0.4 | RF(14) 1.0, LF(13) -1.7, CF(11) -0.4 | -0.1 |
| 2022 | ASH | A+ | 23 | 412 | 76 | 15 | 1 | 23 | 64 | 48 | 127 | 22 | 5 | .282/.371/.522 | 101 | .371 | 5.2 | LF(30) -1.4, CF(27) -0.3, RF(22) 0.6 | 1.8 |
| 2023 non-DC | HOU | MLB | 24 | 251 | 23 | 10 | 1 | 5 | 24 | 20 | 92 | 7 | 2 | .227/.297/.339 | 83 | .358 | -0.8 | LF 0, CF 0 | 0.1 |

The Astros deserve a ton of credit for taking Daniels in the 2020 draft. A fourth-round selection off a shortened board, Daniels was far from a sure-fire thing to be picked. With easily the top five loudest tools on the Cape in 2019, Daniels struggled to put a dent in his counting stats but absolutely showed off why he was worthy of a selection. The issue wasn't pitch recognition, it was whether or not he could make contact. There are still issues here, as he did strike out 127 times in 358 at-bats, but the ability to hit the ball hard and use his legs to beat out close plays makes Daniels as intriguing as any prospect in this system. The swing is certainly more compact than it was in college, and he seems to be able to catch up to velocity more often than he used to. Daniels is among the highest variance prospects around, as he could be an above-average outfielder or a fourth/fifth outfielder depending on his bat-to-ball improvements. He's best suited for the corner spots, despite being a plus runner as he still struggles to make consistent reads on difficult fly balls.

## Top Talents 25 and Under (as of 4/1/2023):

1. Yordan Alvarez, DH/OF
2. Cristian Javier, RHP
3. Jeremy Peña, SS
4. Hunter Brown, RHP
5. Drew Gilbert, OF
6. Bryan Abreu, RHP
7. Justin Dirden, OF
8. Colin Barber, OF
9. Yainer Diaz, C/1B
10. Korey Lee, C

The reigning World Series champions emphatically demonstrated they would not be fading into mediocrity, and despite yet another offseason with a star departing in Justin Verlander, Houston is once again the huge favorite for at least another AL West title banner and seems well-suited to defending their pennant and World Series throne ferociously thanks in heavy measure to the four young studs interwoven in the list above.

Yordan's playoff heroism was a fitting capper on a season that could have merited MVP honors had Aaron Judge not, well, you know. Alvarez was third among position players in WARP at 6.0 despite missing around 20 games and showcasing limited defensive value. His age-26 season offers the chance to build upon one of the most impressive first five offensive seasons of a career in MLB history (and really four, as he missed most of 2020). The worries about his knees and overall health will linger for as long as he continues missing time each year, but Alvarez has established himself as one of the league's best hitters, and the Cuban star may have even more yet to show.

Peña didn't hit the ground as explosively as Alvarez, as his hot start at the plate faded fast, big-time World Series performance notwithstanding. However, that still left the 25-year-old with a respectable 1.6 WARP debut campaign. Whether Peña builds on his 95 DRC+ at the plate is a question mark—his swing-and-miss issues and low-OBP approach do not quite align with his consistency of contact. But defensively, he seemed at least up to the task of manning shortstop in the majors, as he appeared to be an elite defender, in keeping with his scouting report. With a stellar but slightly more mortal pitching staff in Verlander's stead, Peña's glovework will likely have an even greater spotlight upon it in 2023.

That said, neither of the two pitchers included in this under-25 grouping are prone to relying on their defense to back them up. Abreu was arguably Houston's most dominant arm (min. 60 IP) with a microscopic 64 DRA- just ahead of Verlander (69), Ryan Pressly (69), and Javier (73). While Abreu has always had dynamite stuff, his weakness for free passes has previously held him back too much. With several options at his disposal, Abreu took a "Going On a Bear Hunt" approach to the problem, becoming one of the most unhittable bullpen arms in baseball with increased slider usage and an over-200 RPM jump in spin on the pitch, earning him a cartoonish 51.3% whiff rate on the pitch and rendering any errant baserunners moot consistently. Javier's ascension into a no. 2 or no. 3 starter was also key for Houston, who will rely on the young strikeout artist in particular to step into the void left by Verlander. The bat-missing ability of Javier's four-seam is nothing short of elite, as he's managed to wrangle his command of the pitch into the top half or even third of the strike zone with almost total consistency. This meant near-average walk rates paired with top-notch strikeout ability, adding up to one of the least-hittable arms in baseball. The undersized righty is still unlikely to post 180+ innings due to his trials with durability and efficiency, but in the innings he is out there, Houston would be better served with few other arms anywhere.

# Kansas City Royals

## The State of the System:

There's a lot of turnover on this year's Royals list after graduations at the top. The rest of the system hasn't exactly taken a step forward though, and there are some troubling signs, especially with pitching development.

## The Top Ten:

### 1 Gavin Cross  OF     OFP: 55    ETA: Late 2024

Born: 02/13/01   Age: 22   Bats: L   Throws: L   Height: 6'3"   Weight: 210 lb.   Origin: Round 1, 2022 Draft (#9 overall)

| YEAR | TEAM | LVL | AGE | PA | R | 2B | 3B | HR | RBI | BB | K | SB | CS | AVG/OBP/SLG | DRC+ | BABIP | BRR | DRP | WARP |
|------|------|-----|-----|-----|----|----|----|----|-----|----|----|----|----|-------------|------|-------|------|----------|------|
| 2022 | COL | A | 21 | 123 | 20 | 5 | 2 | 7 | 22 | 22 | 31 | 4 | 2 | .293/.423/.596 | 113 | .355 | -2.0 | CF(22) -0.5 | 0.2 |
| 2023 non-DC | KC | MLB | 22 | 251 | 23 | 10 | 2 | 4 | 23 | 23 | 81 | 4 | 1 | .224/.301/.341 | 83 | .330 | -2.3 | CF 0 | 0.1 |

*Comparables: LeVon Washington, Derek Fisher, Brian Goodwin*

**The Report:** After turning in a pair of monster seasons for the Hokies across his sophomore and junior years, Cross went in the top 10 of the draft to Kansas City. He's a potential plus-hit/plus-power outfielder who has good enough bat control and hand-eye coordination to make a bit of a longer and more leveraged swing work. The power may end up playing over the hit, as he can crush pitches in the down-and-in lefty happy zone, and drive the ball out to the opposite field when he gets extended away, while he did look vulnerable at times to better spin. Cross plays center field like a strong safety and may not have the pure foot speed to stick there all the way to the majors, but he should be comfortably above-average in a corner, and has the thump in his bat to hurdle the higher offensive bar.

**OFP:** 55 / Above-average outfielder

**Variance:** Medium. Cross is an advanced college bat and while his brief pro debut maybe sets the bar a bit too high, I expect he will make short work of minor-league pitching. There is a bit of a hitch and some length to the swing, and he's likely to end up in a corner spot, but I expect he will hit enough to be a regular of some sort.

**Jesse Roche's Fantasy Take:** Let's not get too excited about an advanced college bat crushing late-season Low-A pitching. Still, as detailed in July, Cross offers a fantasy-friendly hit-power profile with even a little speed for good measure. His future home park is not ideal, but he has enough pop to overcome its power-suppressing environment. Cross is a top-10 pick in upcoming FYPDs and a top-100 dynasty prospect.

### 2 Nick Loftin  CF     OFP: 55    ETA: 2023

Born: 09/25/98   Age: 24   Bats: R   Throws: R   Height: 6'1"   Weight: 180 lb.   Origin: Round 1, 2020 Draft (#32 overall)

| YEAR | TEAM | LVL | AGE | PA | R | 2B | 3B | HR | RBI | BB | K | SB | CS | AVG/OBP/SLG | DRC+ | BABIP | BRR | DRP | WARP |
|------|------|-----|-----|-----|----|----|----|----|-----|----|----|----|----|-------------|------|-------|------|-------------------------------|------|
| 2021 | QC | A+ | 22 | 410 | 67 | 22 | 5 | 10 | 57 | 42 | 60 | 11 | 2 | .289/.373/.463 | 122 | .323 | 1.6 | SS(47) -3.9, 2B(21) 1.0, 3B(11) -0.2 | 2.1 |
| 2022 | NWA | AA | 23 | 425 | 78 | 17 | 1 | 12 | 47 | 45 | 57 | 24 | 4 | .270/.354/.421 | 108 | .288 | 0.8 | CF(53) -1.4, 2B(19) -1.6, SS(6) 0.5 | 1.4 |
| 2022 | OMA | AAA | 23 | 168 | 26 | 7 | 0 | 5 | 19 | 10 | 41 | 5 | 2 | .216/.280/.359 | 89 | .259 | 0.3 | 3B(24) -1.9, CF(9) -1.4, LF(4) 0.5 | 0.0 |
| 2023 DC | KC | MLB | 24 | 62 | 6 | 3 | 0 | 1 | 5 | 4 | 11 | 2 | 1 | .220/.287/.320 | 74 | .261 | 0.0 | CF 0 | 0.0 |

**The Report:** Around midseason, it appeared that Loftin was on a fast track toward Kansas City, compiling solid numbers at Northwest Arkansas and earning an August promotion to the International League. It was there that the wheels fell off, the power evaporated and he began to expand the zone, causing the strikeout rate to spike. He began to look more like his former self during the final two weeks of the season, helping the overall Triple-A numbers to look more respectable. Chalk it up to just a bump in the road, or a rough patch in his first go against advanced upper-minors pitching. He's still an excellent defender, strong enough with the glove to handle shortstop but versatile enough to be plugged in at multiple other positions. He'll be back in Omaha for round two this spring and a rebound at the plate should make him part of the next wave of prospects to make their major-league debuts for the Royals.

**OFP:** 55 / First-division regular

**Variance:** Medium. The struggles against Triple-A pitching cause some concern, but his speed and defense give a high floor to the profile.

**Jesse Roche's Fantasy Take:** Loftin continues to fly under the fantasy radar despite a contact rate typically over 80% and speed that increasingly plays on the bases (29-for-35 in stolen bases). Indeed, his profile and frame are eerily reminiscent of Whit Merrifield, which is not an outcome outside the realm of possibilities. Loftin likely returns to Triple-A to open the season, and may not debut until his age-25 season in 2024 due to all the upper-level 40-man roster options ahead of him. An older debut would certainly fit the Merrifield comp...

## 3  Tyler Gentry  RF  OFP: 55  ETA: Late 2023/Early 2024
Born: 02/01/99  Age: 24  Bats: R  Throws: R  Height: 6'2"  Weight: 210 lb.  Origin: Round 3, 2020 Draft (#76 overall)

| YEAR | TEAM | LVL | AGE | PA | R | 2B | 3B | HR | RBI | BB | K | SB | CS | AVG/OBP/SLG | DRC+ | BABIP | BRR | DRP | WARP |
|------|------|-----|-----|-----|----|----|----|----|-----|----|----|----|----|-------------|------|-------|------|-----|------|
| 2021 | QC | A+ | 22 | 186 | 29 | 10 | 0 | 6 | 28 | 29 | 55 | 4 | 0 | .259/.395/.449 | 101 | .360 | -1.3 | RF(37) 1.3, LF(5) 0.2, CF(1) -0.2 | 0.6 |
| 2022 | QC | A+ | 23 | 152 | 22 | 6 | 1 | 5 | 23 | 20 | 39 | 2 | 2 | .336/.434/.516 | 126 | .447 | -0.9 | RF(27) 0.4 | 0.8 |
| 2022 | NWA | AA | 23 | 331 | 57 | 16 | 0 | 16 | 63 | 40 | 66 | 8 | 4 | .321/.417/.555 | 129 | .362 | -0.9 | RF(34) 1.8, LF(20) 0.6 | 3.2 |
| 2023 non-DC | KC | MLB | 24 | 251 | 25 | 10 | 1 | 5 | 25 | 23 | 64 | 2 | 1 | .235/.316/.361 | 95 | .305 | -3.4 | LF 0, CF 0 | 0.2 |

*Comparables: Alfredo Marte, Francisco Peguero, Evan Bigley*

**The Report:** Fully recovered from a knee injury suffered during the 2021 season, Gentry became Kansas City's breakout hitter of the year. Physical and strong, he's a classic right fielder, with a strong throwing arm and enough range to become an above-average defender. Offensively, improved swing decisions helped spur the offensive jump. The aggressive approach shown pre-draft at Alabama was toned down and he became more disciplined, more often getting to hitter's counts where he could do damage. He also tapped into more of his plus raw pop, adding more loft to the swing without sacrificing any of the contact ability. Early in the year he got a bit pull-happy but as the season progressed, he began to drive offspeed to the opposite field, where he's more than strong enough to put it over the fence.

**OFP:** 55 / Above-average corner outfielder

**Variance:** Medium. The track record of success is not long and being a corner outfielder puts plenty of pressure on the bat to continue to perform.

**Jesse Roche's Fantasy Take:** Gentry absolutely mashed all year long, including a particularly impressive 129 DRC+ and .234 ISO in Double-A. Power is certainly his carrying tool; however, improved approach and contact rates support a solid hit tool as well. That said, some underlying swing-and-miss and average bat speed bring some pause. Gentry is a top-200 dynasty prospect with underrated upside should his contact gains carry forward.

---

### Eyewitness Report: Tyler Gentry

**Evaluator:** Nathan Graham
**Report Date:** 07/08/2022
**Dates Seen:** 4/10/22
**Risk Factor:** Medium
**Physical/Health:** Extra large frame, strong build with a thick lower half; Physically mature.

| Tool | Future Grade | Report |
|---|---|---|
| Hit | 50 | Gentry utilizes an upright, balanced stance with a toe-tap for timing. He shows plus bat-to-ball skills and a solid command of the strike zone. Attacks in hitters counts, punishing mistakes, and recognizes spin well enough to not chase out of the zone. Average bat speed and some length in the swing leave him susceptible to high velocity. |
| Power | 60 | Plus raw power is generated by physical strength and natural loft in the swing. Very little is lost in-game due to the advanced approach shown at the plate. Hunts fastballs in hitters counts and is strong enough to put them over the fence to all fields. |
| Baserunning/ Speed | 40 | Average present runner, not a threat to steal but runs the bases well. Likely to settle in as below average as he ages. |
| Glove | 50 | Limited range, but shows good instincts in the field. Takes efficient routes, and will be an adequate defender. |
| Arm | 60 | Strong arm, throws show good carry, will be able to handle any outfield position. |

**Conclusion:** Aside from Bobby Witt Jr., recent Royals prospects certainly have a type. They tend to be older, more polished hitters who do everything well but lack loud tools. Gentry definitely fits this mold, likely to settle in at the major league level as an average hitter who hits with just enough power to be an average right fielder.

## 4  Frank Mozzicato  LHP     OFP: 55     ETA: 2025/2026

Born: 06/19/03   Age: 20   Bats: L   Throws: L   Height: 6'3"   Weight: 175 lb.   Origin: Round 1, 2021 Draft (#7 overall)

| YEAR | TEAM | LVL | AGE | W | L | SV | G | GS | IP | H | HR | BB/9 | K/9 | K | GB% | BABIP | WHIP | ERA | DRA- | WARP |
|---|---|---|---|---|---|---|---|---|---|---|---|---|---|---|---|---|---|---|---|---|
| 2022 | COL | A | 19 | 2 | 6 | 0 | 19 | 19 | 69 | 55 | 6 | 6.7 | 11.6 | 89 | 53.4% | .314 | 1.54 | 4.30 | 73 | 1.7 |
| 2023 non-DC | KC | MLB | 20 | 3 | 3 | 0 | 58 | 0 | 50 | 54 | 9 | 6.8 | 8.7 | 49 | 37.4% | .316 | 1.83 | 6.42 | 153 | -1.1 |

*Comparables: Robbie Ray, DL Hall, Grant Holmes*

**The Report:** Mozzicato and the Royals were always a bit of a weird fit of pitcher and player dev apparatus, and his first full year in the pros has been marked by fits and starts. He's flashing a viable changeup already—a pitch I saw him throw exactly once as a CT prep and it was late in a blowout. His fastball velocity still sits around 90, however, and he's struggling intermittently to throw strikes with the pitch. The Royals don't appear to have tweaked his mechanics much, although he does appear to have a bit more pronounced front leg lift and gets a bit lower at foot strike. He doesn't always seem to be comfortable with this new timing and can miss badly. His curveball is still an absolute demon, a real Charlezelbub if you will. It simply overpowers hitters in A-ball when he uncorks one. On balance, Mozzicato remains roughly the same pitching prospect he was at this time last year, which is a frustrating place to be for evaluation purposes. He's a year older—although he was a young draftee—and every year the velocity bump doesn't come, the less likely it ever does. He can still be a nice little pitching prospect throwing 90-91 with good secondaries—you can't teach this feel for spin—but Mozzicato seemed like a good candidate to take a big step forward as a prospect if paired with the right org.

**OFP:** 55 / no. 3/4 starter

**Variance:** High. The stuff missed bats in A-ball, but Mozzicato also walked almost seven per nine as he struggled to find the zone with his fastball. He remains about as far away from his projection as he was last year, but there's still a nice bit of upside here too if the gains start to come.

**Jesse Roche's Fantasy Take:** A prep projection arm without much present velocity or command should be left on waivers outside of the deepest formats.

## 5 Maikel Garcia  SS     OFP: 50     ETA: Debuted in 2022
Born: 03/03/00   Age: 23   Bats: R   Throws: R   Height: 6'0"   Weight: 145 lb.   Origin: International Free Agent, 2016

| YEAR | TEAM | LVL | AGE | PA | R | 2B | 3B | HR | RBI | BB | K | SB | CS | AVG/OBP/SLG | DRC+ | BABIP | BRR | DRP | WARP |
|---|---|---|---|---|---|---|---|---|---|---|---|---|---|---|---|---|---|---|---|
| 2020 | LAG | WIN | 20 | 60 | 10 | 3 | 1 | 0 | 7 | 8 | 12 | 0 | 1 | .314/.407/.412 | | .410 | | | |
| 2021 | LAG | WIN | 21 | 124 | 15 | 5 | 1 | 0 | 14 | 11 | 18 | 4 | 2 | .355/.410/.418 | | .419 | | | |
| 2021 | COL | A | 21 | 237 | 40 | 13 | 3 | 1 | 26 | 38 | 33 | 24 | 3 | .303/.409/.415 | 125 | .352 | 1.8 | SS(41) 4.3 | 2.0 |
| 2021 | QC | A+ | 21 | 243 | 38 | 8 | 4 | 3 | 24 | 24 | 40 | 11 | 3 | .281/.351/.396 | 113 | .331 | 0.7 | SS(48) -0.0 | 1.2 |
| 2022 | LAG | WIN | 22 | 250 | 48 | 13 | 5 | 4 | 33 | 46 | 31 | 10 | 2 | .323/.444/.498 | | .361 | | | |
| 2022 | NWA | AA | 22 | 369 | 63 | 24 | 1 | 4 | 33 | 41 | 60 | 27 | 3 | .291/.369/.409 | 111 | .345 | 1.7 | SS(78) 0.3 | 1.9 |
| 2022 | OMA | AAA | 22 | 186 | 41 | 10 | 0 | 7 | 28 | 17 | 42 | 12 | 5 | .274/.341/.463 | 106 | .322 | -0.3 | SS(39) -1.2 | 0.5 |
| 2022 | KC | MLB | 22 | 23 | 1 | 1 | 0 | 0 | 2 | 1 | 5 | 0 | 0 | .318/.348/.364 | 92 | .412 | -0.3 | SS(8) -0.1 | 0.0 |
| 2023 non-DC | KC | MLB | 23 | 251 | 22 | 11 | 2 | 3 | 22 | 20 | 44 | 9 | 3 | .237/.302/.336 | 84 | .281 | 0.4 | SS -1 | 0.3 |

*Comparables: Yamaico Navarro, Eugenio Suárez, José Rondón*

**The Report:** Garcia made it to the majors in 2022 and is likely to stick there for a good long while because he does a couple important things very well: (1) He's a good up-the-middle defender with above-average range and arm strength; (2) He makes good swing decisions, and when he does let it rip, he makes a lot of contact. Garcia might even have enough gap-to-gap pop to keep pitchers honest, although he's not the most physically imposing figure at the plate. That's ultimately going to determine which side of the "eight-hitter who can pick it and get on base a bit" versus "useful bench infielder" line he falls on. There may not be enough sting in the swing to scare off opposing arms from challenging him in the middle of the zone and daring him to try and line it over the second baseman's head. Garcia is a good runner but not the kind of burner who is going to beat out a lot of infield hits, so he will need at least doubles pop to be a viable everyday guy.

**OFP:** 50 / Second-division starter

**Variance:** Low. The speed and defense coupled with the bat-to-ball skills mean that Garcia will likely find a long-term home on the major-league bench even if he doesn't do enough damage on contact to start every day for you.

**Jesse Roche's Fantasy Take:** Garcia's potential offensive output may mirror, for example, Isiah Kiner-Falefa. In other words, he may flash fantasy utility at times, but generally will be at best a bench option in most formats. Without impact upside, Garcia should only be rostered in leagues with 400+ prospects.

## 6 Ben Kudrna  RHP     OFP: 50     ETA: 2025/2026
Born: 01/30/03   Age: 20   Bats: R   Throws: R   Height: 6'3"   Weight: 175 lb.   Origin: Round 2, 2021 Draft (#43 overall)

| YEAR | TEAM | LVL | AGE | W | L | SV | G | GS | IP | H | HR | BB/9 | K/9 | K | GB% | BABIP | WHIP | ERA | DRA- | WARP |
|---|---|---|---|---|---|---|---|---|---|---|---|---|---|---|---|---|---|---|---|---|
| 2022 | COL | A | 19 | 2 | 5 | 0 | 17 | 17 | 72¹ | 66 | 4 | 4.0 | 7.6 | 61 | 39.4% | .292 | 1.35 | 3.48 | 112 | 0.3 |
| 2023 non-DC | KC | MLB | 20 | 3 | 3 | 0 | 58 | 0 | 50 | 61 | 8 | 5.0 | 6.1 | 34 | 34.1% | .320 | 1.77 | 6.39 | 155 | -1.2 |

*Comparables: Eric Pardinho, Michael Soroka, Eduardo Rodriguez*

**The Report:** The Royals used most of their savings on Mozzicato's underslot deal to sign Kudrna in the second round. Strike-throwing was less of an issue for him in 2022—although he can overthrow a bit from his very downhill delivery—and both his slider and changeup flashed bat-missing potential, but only flashed. Kudrna's slider is the better of the two at present, showing above-average late depth. It can get a bit slurvy at times or run flatter, and often gets groundballs more than whiffs. His change has a little bit of wrinkle to it, flashing true fade, and he sells it pretty well for his experience level. Kudrna has less projection than Mozzicato and sits a couple ticks higher—with a bit more effort to get there—but it's not an overpowering fastball and the overall arsenal doesn't have analytically friendly characteristics. Nevertheless, the potential for three average-or-a bit-better pitches are present, and there's plenty of runway for further development.

**OFP:** 50 / no. 4 starter

**Variance:** Medium. Kudrna might have a bit more present in his profile than Mozzicato, but he's also a prep pitcher in A-ball without clear-cut plus stuff, so we will need to take it level-by-level here.

**Jesse Roche's Fantasy Take:** A prep arm with underwhelming stuff who did not miss many bats in Low-A (19.6% strikeout rate) should be left on waivers outside of the deepest formats.

## 7 Carter Jensen DH/C  OFP: 50  ETA: 2025

Born: 07/03/03  Age: 20  Bats: L  Throws: R  Height: 6'1"  Weight: 210 lb.  Origin: Round 3, 2021 Draft (#78 overall)

| YEAR | TEAM | LVL | AGE | PA | R | 2B | 3B | HR | RBI | BB | K | SB | CS | AVG/OBP/SLG | DRC+ | BABIP | BRR | DRP | WARP |
|------|------|-----|-----|-----|----|----|----|----|-----|----|-----|----|----|-------------|------|-------|-----|-----|------|
| 2021 | ROYG | ROK | 17 | 65 | 8 | 1 | 1 | 1 | 7 | 10 | 19 | 4 | 0 | .273/.385/.382 | | .400 | | | |
| 2022 | COL | A | 18 | 485 | 66 | 24 | 2 | 11 | 50 | 83 | 103 | 8 | 6 | .226/.363/.382 | 117 | .275 | -2.8 | C(46) 1.5 | 2.3 |
| 2023 non-DC | KC | MLB | 19 | 251 | 21 | 11 | 2 | 3 | 21 | 24 | 65 | 2 | 1 | .212/.293/.311 | 73 | .286 | -3.2 | C 0 | -0.1 |

Comparables: Chris Parmelee, Isael Soto, Jack Suwinski

**The Report:** The Royals stayed close to home with Jensen, who played high school ball about a half hour from Kauffman Stadium. The prep catcher cohort has a pretty terrible track record, although Kansas City has one of the more successful ones in recent years in MJ Melendez (granted he is playing a fair bit of outfield nowadays). Jensen broadly profiles similarly, a potential power-hitting backstop who needs some refinement in his overall defensive game, but who already has the requisite strong arm.

At the plate his swing isn't really quick-twitch, but he will make enough contact and can pull in and do damage on the inner half. Jensen is still a pretty good athlete overall and runs well for a catcher. His framing work is fine for his level of experience, but he can push pitches a bit at the edges and doesn't always hold a great target. His arm strength is plus but his throwing actions are a bit raw and he doesn't always get strong carry down to second. The outline of an everyday two-way catcher are here, but it's a much longer trip from the Carolina League to Kauffman than it was from Park Hill High.

**OFP:** 50 / Starting catcher

**Variance:** High. Jensen isn't a sure-shot catcher and he isn't a sure shot to hit enough. On the other side, he has the potential to be average at just about everything—maybe above with the pop—and that can add up to an above-average catcher.

**Jesse Roche's Fantasy Take:** Jensen spent all year in Low-A as the youngest qualified catcher and, while his overall numbers don't pop, he turned a corner in the second half. Since July 1, he hit .286/.440/.429 with more walks (51) than strikeouts (38). There is enough hit-power potential here to keep tabs on, particularly in two-catcher or deep formats. Yet: catchers, man.

## 8 Asa Lacy LHP  OFP: 50  ETA: Uh, 2024 maybe?

Born: 06/02/99  Age: 24  Bats: L  Throws: L  Height: 6'4"  Weight: 215 lb.  Origin: Round 1, 2020 Draft (#4 overall)

| YEAR | TEAM | LVL | AGE | W | L | SV | G | GS | IP | H | HR | BB/9 | K/9 | K | GB% | BABIP | WHIP | ERA | DRA- | WARP |
|------|------|-----|-----|---|---|----|----|----|----|----|----|------|------|----|-----|-------|------|-----|------|------|
| 2021 | QC | A+ | 22 | 2 | 5 | 0 | 14 | 14 | 52 | 41 | 5 | 7.1 | 13.7 | 79 | 33.0% | .346 | 1.58 | 5.19 | 81 | 1.1 |
| 2022 | ROY | ROK | 23 | 1 | 0 | 0 | 4 | 2 | 8 | 4 | 1 | 15.7 | 11.2 | 10 | 44.4% | .176 | 2.25 | 9.00 | | |
| 2022 | NWA | AA | 23 | 1 | 2 | 0 | 11 | 3 | 20 | 9 | 2 | 12.6 | 11.3 | 25 | 50.0% | .167 | 1.85 | 11.25 | 127 | -0.2 |
| 2023 non-DC | KC | MLB | 24 | 3 | 3 | 0 | 58 | 0 | 50 | 44 | 8 | 8.4 | 11.7 | 65 | 35.1% | .305 | 1.81 | 6.05 | 142 | -0.8 |

Comparables: Matt Krook, Edgar Olmos, Blake Taylor

**The Report:** Lacy was absolutely dominant for the Aggies and was considered one of the top arms, if not *the* top, in his draft class. But like his fellow college aces Max Meyer and Emerson Hancock, Lacy's pro career has been marred by injuries. Shoulder issues in 2021 and back troubles in 2022 have limited him to just 80 professional innings so far. They haven't been good innings either, as he's walked more than a batter per and saw his control completely collapse after his midseason return to the bump. Lacy seemed to be feeling his way through his delivery after a move to relief late in the year, and the slider and change still missed copious bats in short bursts when they were anywhere near the zone, but the control is a 20 at this point, especially with the fastball, which was "only" mid-90s. The arm talent is still there, but he needs a clean healthy slate in 2023.

**OFP:** 50 / Eighth-inning guy

**Variance:** Extreme. Lacy's pro track record of health and command—or lack thereof—might merit an NP if he wasn't a top amateur pitcher as recently as spring 2020. That isn't all that recent though, and 2023 will be a make-or-break season for him.

**Jesse Roche's Fantasy Take:** "Eighth-inning guy" with a 27.6% walk rate last year is not relevant in any fantasy format.

## 9 Cayden Wallace 3B   OFP: 50   ETA: 2025
Born: 08/07/01   Age: 21   Bats: R   Throws: R   Height: 6'1"   Weight: 205 lb.   Origin: Round 2, 2022 Draft (#49 overall)

| YEAR | TEAM | LVL | AGE | PA | R | 2B | 3B | HR | RBI | BB | K | SB | CS | AVG/OBP/SLG | DRC+ | BABIP | BRR | DRP | WARP |
|---|---|---|---|---|---|---|---|---|---|---|---|---|---|---|---|---|---|---|---|
| 2022 | COL | A | 20 | 122 | 15 | 7 | 3 | 2 | 16 | 12 | 22 | 8 | 1 | .294/.369/.468 | 112 | .353 | -1.8 | 3B(25) -0.2 | 0.4 |
| 2023 non-DC | KC | MLB | 21 | 251 | 19 | 11 | 2 | 2 | 20 | 16 | 53 | 7 | 2 | .214/.272/.306 | 64 | .268 | -0.9 | 3B 0 | -0.5 |

*Comparables: Kaleb Cowart, Colin Moran, Jovan Rosa*

**The Report:** A draft-eligible sophomore for the Razorbacks, Wallace was a major college performer with a knack for contact, but it remains to seen how much power he will hit for with wood bats. He's pretty level at the plate and generally works up-the-middle or to the opposite gap. There could be average power in there, but he will need to pull the ball in the pros a bit more to tap into it. At third base, he's a perfectly adequate defender, but does have to rear back a bit to get to the left-side arm strength, which can impact his accuracy. Wallace is a potential everyday bat, but he's also perhaps a tad riskier than you'd expect from a college prospect with those stat lines in the SEC.

**OFP:** 50 / Average third-baseman

**Variance:** High. Wallace has a strong college track record, but nothing really pops on the scout sheet, and I'd be a little worried about the bat playing at higher levels.

**Jesse Roche's Fantasy Take:** Potentially average offensive tools are rarely what fantasy managers seek out in FYPDs. Hence, Wallace is only a deep-league target outside the top 50.

## 10 Beck Way RHP   OFP: 50   ETA: 2024
Born: 08/06/99   Age: 23   Bats: R   Throws: R   Height: 6'4"   Weight: 200 lb.   Origin: Round 4, 2020 Draft (#129 overall)

| YEAR | TEAM | LVL | AGE | W | L | SV | G | GS | IP | H | HR | BB/9 | K/9 | K | GB% | BABIP | WHIP | ERA | DRA- | WARP |
|---|---|---|---|---|---|---|---|---|---|---|---|---|---|---|---|---|---|---|---|---|
| 2021 | TAM | A | 21 | 3 | 1 | 0 | 15 | 14 | 47 | 23 | 2 | 5.6 | 10.3 | 54 | 62.0% | .202 | 1.11 | 2.68 | 88 | 0.7 |
| 2021 | HV | A+ | 21 | 1 | 2 | 0 | 4 | 4 | 16¹ | 18 | 3 | 5.0 | 16.0 | 29 | 51.4% | .469 | 1.65 | 7.71 | 84 | 0.3 |
| 2022 | QC | A+ | 22 | 3 | 3 | 0 | 7 | 7 | 35² | 24 | 1 | 4.3 | 11.9 | 47 | 41.0% | .288 | 1.15 | 3.79 | 90 | 0.5 |
| 2022 | HV | A+ | 22 | 5 | 5 | 0 | 15 | 15 | 72¹ | 55 | 9 | 3.2 | 10.0 | 80 | 46.1% | .271 | 1.12 | 3.73 | 95 | 0.7 |
| 2023 non-DC | KC | MLB | 23 | 3 | 3 | 0 | 58 | 0 | 50 | 49 | 7 | 4.8 | 8.3 | 46 | 39.0% | .295 | 1.51 | 4.84 | 122 | -0.3 |

*Comparables: Pedro Fernandez, Jairo Heredia, Trey Supak*

**The Report:** Another Yankees arm from a directional Southern school—and the rare double directional at that—Way used his advanced fastball/slider combo to strike out plenty of batters in two different High-A leagues in 2022. His uptempo, effortful delivery combined with the two-pitch nature of his arsenal may point to a relief role long-term, but his mid-90s fastball has decent sink and run, and his slider shows hard depth as part of its two-plane action despite a low-three-quarters slot. Last year, Ben Spanier pegged the development of his changeup as a key, and it remains a bit firm in the upper-80s. You don't need a third pitch to be a starter—it's the 2020s after all—but Way will need a bit better command and a bit more consistency with the breaker to stick in a rotation regardless.

**OFP:** 50 / no. 4 starter or setup man

**Variance:** Medium. Beck's fastball/slider combo should have some major-league utility, but the ultimate role and overall upside are going to be limiting factors.

**Jesse Roche's Fantasy Take:** The Yankees know how to draft and develop two-plane sliders, and Way has a good one. Whether he'll throw enough strikes to stick as a starter, however, remains to be seen. Regardless, Way has intriguing, bat-missing stuff that could eventually make a fantasy-relevant impact.

## Outside the Top Ten:

### 11 Luca Tresh   C/DH

Born: 01/11/00   Age: 23   Bats: R   Throws: R   Height: 6'0"   Weight: 193 lb.   Origin: Round 17, 2021 Draft (#499 overall)

| YEAR | TEAM | LVL | AGE | PA | R | 2B | 3B | HR | RBI | BB | K | SB | CS | AVG/OBP/SLG | DRC+ | BABIP | BRR | DRP | WARP |
|------|------|-----|-----|-----|----|----|----|----|-----|----|----|----|----|-------------|------|-------|------|------|------|
| 2021 | COL | A | 21 | 39 | 0 | 1 | 0 | 0 | 5 | 4 | 11 | 0 | 0 | .143/.231/.171 | 93 | .208 | -0.3 | C(7) -1.2 | -0.1 |
| 2022 | QC | A+ | 22 | 347 | 48 | 15 | 1 | 14 | 54 | 41 | 85 | 3 | 3 | .273/.360/.470 | 127 | .332 | -0.5 | C(49) -5.0 | 1.6 |
| 2022 | NWA | AA | 22 | 106 | 16 | 4 | 0 | 5 | 14 | 13 | 25 | 1 | 0 | .253/.358/.462 | 112 | .295 | 0.2 | C(23) -3.9 | 0.1 |
| 2023 non-DC | KC | MLB | 23 | 251 | 23 | 10 | 1 | 5 | 24 | 20 | 69 | 1 | 0 | .219/.288/.334 | 78 | .291 | -4.1 | C 0 | -0.1 |

*Comparables: Luis Exposito, Carlos Santana, Sean Murphy*

A 17th-round selection in 2021, Kansas City doled out fourth-round money to entice Tresh to forgo his final year at NC State. After struggling during his brief post-draft debut, he rebounded nicely in 2022, hitting well enough to earn a late-season promotion to Double-A. Offensively, he controls the zone well and has enough physical strength and bat speed to produce above-average power numbers. There's still some room for growth in his catching skills but he possesses a strong throwing arm that helps to hold opposing runners in check. The tools are there for Tresh to be a future everyday backstop but with Salvador Perez and MJ Melendez getting the lion's share of the work at the big-league level, there's plenty of time for him to refine his skills in the upper minors.

### 12 Peyton Wilson   2B/CF

Born: 11/01/99   Age: 23   Bats: S   Throws: R   Height: 5'9"   Weight: 180 lb.   Origin: Round 2, 2021 Draft (#66 overall)

| YEAR | TEAM | LVL | AGE | PA | R | 2B | 3B | HR | RBI | BB | K | SB | CS | AVG/OBP/SLG | DRC+ | BABIP | BRR | DRP | WARP |
|------|------|-----|-----|-----|----|----|----|----|-----|----|----|----|----|-------------|------|-------|------|------|------|
| 2021 | ROYG | ROK | 21 | 41 | 7 | 3 | 1 | 1 | 7 | 5 | 10 | 2 | 2 | .219/.366/.469 | | .273 | | | |
| 2021 | COL | A | 21 | 46 | 6 | 3 | 1 | 0 | 1 | 4 | 10 | 5 | 0 | .231/.326/.359 | 106 | .300 | 0.4 | 2B(11) 0.3 | 0.2 |
| 2022 | QC | A+ | 22 | 390 | 60 | 16 | 3 | 14 | 44 | 41 | 97 | 23 | 2 | .268/.359/.456 | 107 | .335 | 2.5 | 2B(51) -3.3, CF(35) -2.3 | 1.8 |
| 2023 non-DC | KC | MLB | 23 | 251 | 22 | 10 | 2 | 4 | 23 | 19 | 69 | 8 | 1 | .229/.293/.339 | 80 | .311 | -0.9 | 2B 0, CF 0 | 0.1 |

*Comparables: Jemile Weeks, Devin Mann, Eric Sogard*

The tools aren't loud and the ceiling isn't high for Wilson, but he does everything well. Offensively, he makes plenty of loud contact from both sides of the plate with his quick, compact swing and has a sneaky amount of pop. Despite his lack of size, he's an excellent athlete, which allows him to be plugged in at multiple positions, seeing time in both the infield and outfield this season. It's not a very sexy profile, but Wilson sure feels like the type of prospect that the Royals will move quickly through the organization and allow him the opportunity to earn big-league at-bats.

### 13 Ben Hernandez   RHP

Born: 07/01/01   Age: 22   Bats: R   Throws: R   Height: 6'2"   Weight: 205 lb.   Origin: Round 2, 2020 Draft (#41 overall)

| YEAR | TEAM | LVL | AGE | W | L | SV | G | GS | IP | H | HR | BB/9 | K/9 | K | GB% | BABIP | WHIP | ERA | DRA- | WARP |
|------|------|-----|-----|---|---|----|----|----|------|----|----|------|------|----|------|-------|------|------|------|------|
| 2021 | COL | A | 19 | 1 | 2 | 0 | 9 | 9 | 31¹ | 32 | 2 | 4.9 | 8.9 | 31 | 48.3% | .353 | 1.56 | 4.31 | 95 | 0.4 |
| 2022 | COL | A | 20 | 1 | 7 | 0 | 23 | 23 | 77 | 83 | 7 | 4.7 | 8.3 | 71 | 49.6% | .342 | 1.60 | 5.38 | 110 | 0.4 |
| 2023 non-DC | KC | MLB | 21 | 3 | 3 | 0 | 58 | 0 | 50 | 58 | 8 | 5.2 | 6.9 | 38 | 38.2% | .320 | 1.74 | 6.12 | 149 | -1.0 |

*Comparables: Scott Blewett, Tyrell Jenkins, Shane Watson*

Hernandez is yet another young Royals pitching prospect who struggled in the Carolina League in 2022. He was kept on a fairly limited workload, and even within those shorter outings could struggle with holding the zone, but the stuff still looks solid enough: a good sinking fastball, an inconsistent-but-promising curveball and a developing change. The breaker can vacillate between a bit of a loopy 11-6 downer and more of an 11-5 slurvy thing, with the latter showing better bat-missing potential. Hernandez's delivery can be a bit mechanical and he sort of unfurls the ball from a three-quarters slot. That gives him a bit of deception, but it's not easily repeatable. The overall arsenal is a bit rawer than the prep arms ahead of him on the list, but his upside is within a shout of theirs.

## 14 Angel Zerpa  LHP

Born: 09/27/99   Age: 23   Bats: L   Throws: L   Height: 6'0"   Weight: 220 lb.   Origin: International Free Agent, 2016

| YEAR | TEAM | LVL | AGE | W | L | SV | G | GS | IP | H | HR | BB/9 | K/9 | K | GB% | BABIP | WHIP | ERA | DRA- | WARP |
|---|---|---|---|---|---|---|---|---|---|---|---|---|---|---|---|---|---|---|---|---|
| 2021 | QC | A+ | 21 | 4 | 0 | 0 | 8 | 8 | 41$^2$ | 32 | 2 | 1.7 | 11.4 | 53 | 44.2% | .297 | 0.96 | 2.59 | 83 | 0.8 |
| 2021 | NWA | AA | 21 | 0 | 3 | 0 | 13 | 13 | 45$^1$ | 51 | 7 | 3.8 | 10.7 | 54 | 47.6% | .370 | 1.54 | 5.96 | 88 | 0.5 |
| 2021 | KC | MLB | 21 | 0 | 1 | 0 | 1 | 1 | 5 | 3 | 0 | 1.8 | 7.2 | 4 | 40.0% | .214 | 0.80 | 0.00 | 117 | 0.0 |
| 2022 | NWA | AA | 22 | 2 | 5 | 0 | 13 | 13 | 64 | 70 | 7 | 3.0 | 9.7 | 69 | 46.5% | .354 | 1.42 | 4.36 | 81 | 1.0 |
| 2022 | OMA | AAA | 22 | 0 | 0 | 0 | 6 | 6 | 7$^2$ | 2 | 0 | 4.7 | 0.0 | 0 | 58.3% | .083 | 0.78 | 1.17 | 111 | 0.1 |
| 2022 | KC | MLB | 22 | 2 | 1 | 0 | 3 | 2 | 11 | 9 | 2 | 2.5 | 2.5 | 3 | 50.0% | .194 | 1.09 | 1.64 | 139 | -0.1 |
| 2023 DC | KC | MLB | 23 | 2 | 2 | 0 | 17 | 3 | 26 | 28 | 3 | 3.5 | 5.8 | 17 | 43.0% | .298 | 1.45 | 4.32 | 115 | 0.0 |

Comparables: Yohander Méndez, Daniel Norris, Adalberto Mejía

Zerpa performed well in his two big-league starts, but unfortunately a tear in his patella tendon abruptly ended his stint in Kansas City. When healthy, he commands his repertoire well, featuring a sinker, slider and changeup. He probably will require some additional time in Triple-A to ramp back up to a starter's workload but will eventually work his way back to a back-of-the-rotation profile.

## 15 Chandler Champlain  RHP

Born: 07/23/99   Age: 23   Bats: R   Throws: R   Height: 6'5"   Weight: 220 lb.   Origin: Round 9, 2021 Draft (#273 overall)

| YEAR | TEAM | LVL | AGE | W | L | SV | G | GS | IP | H | HR | BB/9 | K/9 | K | GB% | BABIP | WHIP | ERA | DRA- | WARP |
|---|---|---|---|---|---|---|---|---|---|---|---|---|---|---|---|---|---|---|---|---|
| 2022 | TAM | A | 22 | 2 | 5 | 0 | 16 | 15 | 73$^1$ | 72 | 11 | 2.3 | 11.5 | 94 | 51.3% | .333 | 1.24 | 4.30 | 88 | 1.6 |
| 2022 | QC | A+ | 22 | 1 | 3 | 0 | 8 | 7 | 32 | 58 | 3 | 3.1 | 6.2 | 22 | 39.7% | .466 | 2.16 | 9.84 | 139 | -0.3 |
| 2023 non-DC | KC | MLB | 23 | 3 | 3 | 0 | 58 | 0 | 50 | 59 | 8 | 3.5 | 6.4 | 36 | 37.3% | .315 | 1.57 | 5.51 | 139 | -0.7 |

Yes, there was a level jump involved, but it's perhaps a little too on-the-nose that a breakout Yankees Day 2 college arm immediately saw a huge dip in performance once he was shipped off to the Royals. Champlain's fastball is perhaps a bit above-average, but his two breaking balls both have plus potential. The stuff looked basically fine across both orgs, the results less so, and on balance, Champlain is likely best-suited to relief anyway.

## 16 Jonathan Bowlan  RHP

Born: 12/01/96   Age: 26   Bats: R   Throws: R   Height: 6'6"   Weight: 240 lb.   Origin: Round 2, 2018 Draft (#58 overall)

| YEAR | TEAM | LVL | AGE | W | L | SV | G | GS | IP | H | HR | BB/9 | K/9 | K | GB% | BABIP | WHIP | ERA | DRA- | WARP |
|---|---|---|---|---|---|---|---|---|---|---|---|---|---|---|---|---|---|---|---|---|
| 2021 | NWA | AA | 24 | 2 | 0 | 0 | 4 | 4 | 17 | 13 | 0 | 1.6 | 13.2 | 25 | 50.0% | .342 | 0.94 | 1.59 | 83 | 0.3 |
| 2022 | ROY | ROK | 25 | 0 | 1 | 0 | 7 | 7 | 19$^1$ | 29 | 1 | 1.9 | 12.1 | 26 | 36.2% | .491 | 1.71 | 5.12 | | |
| 2022 | NWA | AA | 25 | 1 | 3 | 0 | 9 | 9 | 39 | 51 | 7 | 3.9 | 6.9 | 30 | 42.4% | .352 | 1.74 | 6.92 | 135 | -0.6 |
| 2023 DC | KC | MLB | 26 | 1 | 1 | 0 | 3 | 3 | 12.7 | 14 | 2 | 3.1 | 7.2 | 10 | 38.1% | .311 | 1.43 | 4.63 | 123 | 0.0 |

Comparables: Jon Harris, Angel Sánchez, Austin Ross

The command is usually the last component to return after Tommy John surgery and that proved to be true for Bowlan in 2022. He struggled to hit his spots in his brief Texas League stint, unable to stay off barrels and giving up plenty of hard contact. He had jumped onto our radar pre-pandemic with his heavy, mid-90s fastball and plus command, and likely would have made his big-league debut in 2021 if he could have stayed healthy. Now that he's fully recovered, it's likely that he gets his shot in the Royals' rotation sometime this summer.

## 17  Andrew Hoffmann  RHP

Born: 02/02/00  Age: 23  Bats: R  Throws: R  Height: 6'5"  Weight: 210 lb.  Origin: Round 12, 2021 Draft (#367 overall)

| YEAR | TEAM | LVL | AGE | W | L | SV | G | GS | IP | H | HR | BB/9 | K/9 | K | GB% | BABIP | WHIP | ERA | DRA- | WARP |
|------|------|-----|-----|---|---|----|----|----|-----|----|----|------|------|----|------|-------|------|------|------|------|
| 2021 | AUG | A | 21 | 2 | 2 | 0 | 7 | 7 | 29² | 21 | 2 | 2.4 | 11.2 | 37 | 43.7% | .275 | 0.98 | 2.73 | 94 | 0.4 |
| 2022 | ROM | A+ | 22 | 7 | 2 | 0 | 15 | 15 | 80 | 63 | 9 | 2.4 | 10.1 | 90 | 46.6% | .277 | 1.05 | 2.36 | 91 | 1.0 |
| 2022 | NWA | AA | 22 | 2 | 4 | 0 | 9 | 9 | 39¹ | 50 | 5 | 4.6 | 6.9 | 30 | 31.8% | .354 | 1.78 | 6.64 | 147 | -0.9 |
| 2023 non-DC | KC | MLB | 23 | 3 | 3 | 0 | 58 | 0 | 50 | 53 | 8 | 3.8 | 7.2 | 40 | 35.9% | .302 | 1.49 | 4.95 | 127 | -0.4 |

*Comparables: Andrew Church, Cody Anderson, Alex Balog*

Dealt midseason to the Royals from Atlanta, it might be easy to write off Hoffmann's professional success to just a combination of a deceptive delivery and plus command but there's actually sneaky good stuff in the profile as well. The fastball has ticked up in velocity and it pairs well with his late-breaking slider and developing change. After dominating for the Braves' High-A squad, Kansas City sent him straight to the Texas League post-trade where he took his lumps, giving up plenty of hard contact while having his command take a step backwards.

## 18  T.J. Sikkema  LHP

Born: 07/25/98  Age: 24  Bats: L  Throws: L  Height: 6'0"  Weight: 221 lb.  Origin: Round 1, 2019 Draft (#38 overall)

| YEAR | TEAM | LVL | AGE | W | L | SV | G | GS | IP | H | HR | BB/9 | K/9 | K | GB% | BABIP | WHIP | ERA | DRA- | WARP |
|------|------|-----|-----|---|---|----|----|----|-----|----|----|------|------|----|------|-------|------|------|------|------|
| 2022 | HV | A+ | 23 | 1 | 1 | 0 | 11 | 10 | 36¹ | 21 | 3 | 2.2 | 13.4 | 54 | 47.9% | .257 | 0.83 | 2.48 | 82 | 0.6 |
| 2022 | NWA | AA | 23 | 0 | 5 | 0 | 8 | 8 | 32² | 42 | 6 | 4.1 | 8.0 | 29 | 56.5% | .360 | 1.74 | 7.44 | 118 | -0.2 |
| 2023 non-DC | KC | MLB | 24 | 3 | 3 | 0 | 58 | 0 | 50 | 51 | 7 | 3.9 | 7.7 | 43 | 40.6% | .296 | 1.45 | 4.70 | 120 | -0.3 |

*Comparables: Sam Howard, David Rollins, Mario Hollands*

The third acquiree from the Yankees in the Andrew Benintendi trade, Sikkema missed almost three full years of starts between the pandemic and various arm maladies. He's a three-pitch lefty, the most notable of which are a low-90s fastball he can spot glove-side to righties and a big-breaking slider. Sikkema also has a mid-80s change that he is developing more feel for, but it shows only fringe fade. If he can stay healthy, he has a shot at settling in at the back-end of the rotation, but fits better in the pen, where he has enough change to cross over and has shown some facility getting the sweepy slider under the bats of righties as well.

# Top Talents 25 and Under (as of 4/1/2023):

1. Bobby Witt Jr., SS/3B
2. MJ Melendez, C/OF
3. Vinnie Pasquantino, 1B
4. Gavin Cross, OF
5. Nick Loftin, UT
6. Nick Pratto, 1B
7. Michael Massey, 2B/3B
8. Tyler Gentry, OF
9. Frank Mozzicato, LHP
10. Drew Waters, OF

Given that the most common reader of this list will be Royals fans, I should not expect ages that surprise me to surprise the average person perusing these rankings. However, it was surprising to me to realize that lefy Kris Bubic and righty Max Castillo are the only 25U-eligible pitchers in a Kansas City system that has heavily prioritized pitching in their draft during this rebuild. Names like Singer, Keller, Lynch and Kowar have already aged out of this categorization, with only Singer establishing himself as yet as a consistent quality rotation arm. Kansas City signing Jordan Lyles and Ryan Yarbrough as upgrades is indicative of the troubles they've had in that realm.

Fortunately, their organization is blessed with one of the brightest young infielders in baseball. Witt was overshadowed in part by Julio Rodríguez and Adley Rutschman, as well as a stellar season league-wide for rookies, but his 20/30 season looked very much like a sign of things to come. He barreled the ball consistently, and even as he faded somewhat in the second half, he began making more consistent contact that should continue to be rewarded. The only point of real concern was with his glove, which graded out far worse than his reputation as a prospect. At -9 Outs Above Average at shortstop, even with an above-average arm, ranking 34th out of 37 qualified shortstops. His athleticism and mechanics have typically looked far superior, but it's an area of his game with a convention center's size of room for improvement.

Speaking of young players who had promising debuts undercut by devastatingly poor defensive performances, Melendez may be to blame for at least some of the pitching staff's struggles. The lanky, athletic lefty swinger showed promising power and patience at the plate, as well as some possible acuity for right field given his cannon of an arm. However, the heir to Salvador Perez he may not be, as Melendez was the second-worst pitch framer by OAA at -12, or -17.5 framing runs by BP's own metrics. Framing is a combination of technique and familiarity, and can often be a skill developed in the bigs by backstops, but it's again an ominous limitation for a player who is far more valuable as a viable catcher than a pure outfielder.

Pasquantino leapfrogged Pratto with his performance in 2022, but both players are exclusive 1B/DH types with immense power. Posting average exit velocities that put him as a contemporary of folks like Aaron Judge and Yordan Alvarez, as Ryan Boyer wrote in October, Pasquantino looks like nothing short of a first-division lefty slugger who handles lefty pitching decently and can contribute offensively in every facet of the game. Pratto by contrast seemed overmatched in his first big-league opportunity, displaying his as-expected Three-True-Outcome profile with far too many of the most negative of the extremes as he struck out 36.3% of the time. It's likely both players will get ample 1B/DH time, either in platoon with or in supplantation of an increasingly dismal Hunter Dozier.

Last is Waters, as well as honorable mention 2B/3B Michael Massey, both of whom had surprisingly strong big-league debuts that are tough to wholly buy. Waters whiffed a ton in 2022, running an 82 DRC+ despite a strong .803 OPS, in large part due to a lofty .353 BABIP only partially explained by his strong foot speed. While he ran into a few balls with authority, on the whole his contact quality fell far below league-average. Massey has none of Waters' raw athleticism, but he's been a consistent performer in the minors and can handle a utility role so long as he's not pressed into shortstop. The former University of Illinois standout has a simple, flat swing and above-average barrel control that does nonetheless come at the cost of power. A bench bat who can handle a challenging defensive position and put up respectable numbers at the dish isn't supremely exciting, but it does lengthen a Kansas City lineup that was well below-average last year.

# Los Angeles Angels

## The State of the System:

The Angels drafted a Top 101 prospect, traded for one and got one big breakout in the low minors. The rest of the system lags far behind as they continue to struggle to develop hitters.

## The Top Ten:

### 1  Zach Neto  SS          OFP: 60      ETA: Late 2023

Born: 01/31/01   Age: 22   Bats: R   Throws: R   Height: 6'0"   Weight: 185 lb.   Origin: Round 1, 2022 Draft (#13 overall)

| YEAR | TEAM | LVL | AGE | PA | R | 2B | 3B | HR | RBI | BB | K | SB | CS | AVG/OBP/SLG | DRC+ | BABIP | BRR | DRP | WARP |
|------|------|-----|-----|-----|-----|-----|-----|-----|-----|-----|-----|-----|-----|-------------|------|-------|------|------|------|
| 2022 | TRI | A+ | 21 | 31 | 2 | 0 | 1 | 1 | 4 | 4 | 4 | 1 | 0 | .200/.355/.400 | 113 | .200 | -0.3 | SS(6) -0.1 | 0.1 |
| 2022 | RCT | AA | 21 | 136 | 22 | 9 | 0 | 4 | 23 | 8 | 29 | 4 | 2 | .320/.382/.492 | 99 | .389 | -0.6 | SS(28) -0.3 | 0.3 |
| 2023 non-DC | LAA | MLB | 22 | 251 | 21 | 10 | 1 | 4 | 22 | 15 | 61 | 3 | 1 | .217/.274/.317 | 68 | .278 | -2.8 | SS 0 | -0.5 |

*Comparables: Jose Martinez, Luis Rengifo, Mauricio Dubón*

**The Report:** Neto made any questions about the quality of competition he faced at Campbell as an amateur irrelevant after a mere month in the Angels system. He dominated the Big South, hitting .400 each of the last two seasons, and then dropped right into Double-A and looked like one of the better *pro* prospects in the Southern League. He has a bit of an unorthodox swing, with one of the biggest leg kicks you will see, but is always on time and on the barrel, spraying hard line-drive contact. With two strikes, Neto tones everything down and becomes a pesky out. He's aggressive when needs to be, but will take his walks, and while the swing isn't geared for power at present, he should develop at least average pop to go with a plus hit tool.

Neto was a college shortstop who is actually going to stick there long term in the pros. He's a potential plus defender, rangy with good hands and actions. His profile may not have the most upside in the recent draft class, but Neto might be the quickest to the majors among significant 2022 draftees, and he's a good bet to be a plus regular once he gets there.

**OFP:** 60 / First-division shortstop

**Variance:** Low. Neto can hit and play an above-average shortstop. That will give him a high floor and the inside track to a long major-league career of some sort.

**Jesse Roche's Fantasy Take:** Small conference bats almost always have something to prove. Over two small samples, Neto has proved it in the Cape Cod League (.304/.439/.587) and, more importantly, in Double-A (.313/.380/.508). While he may lack the pure upside of other first-year players, Neto does everything well and could develop into a five-category producer capable of going .280/20/15. Plus, he is on a fast track to the majors, and the Angels have recently pushed draftees quickly (see Chase Silseth below). Neto's proximity and well-rounded production make him a top-100 dynasty prospect and a top-10 pick in FYPDs.

## 2  Logan O'Hoppe  C    OFP: 55    ETA: Debuted in 2022
Born: 02/09/00  Age: 23  Bats: R  Throws: R  Height: 6'2"  Weight: 185 lb.  Origin: Round 23, 2018 Draft (#677 overall)

| YEAR | TEAM | LVL | AGE | PA | R | 2B | 3B | HR | RBI | BB | K | SB | CS | AVG/OBP/SLG | DRC+ | BABIP | BRR | DRP | WARP |
|---|---|---|---|---|---|---|---|---|---|---|---|---|---|---|---|---|---|---|---|
| 2021 | PEJ | WIN | 21 | 100 | 19 | 8 | 0 | 3 | 17 | 21 | 15 | 3 | 1 | .299/.440/.519 | | .328 | | | |
| 2021 | JS | A+ | 21 | 358 | 43 | 17 | 2 | 13 | 48 | 30 | 63 | 6 | 3 | .270/.335/.459 | 124 | .294 | 0.2 | C(60) 3.9 | 2.5 |
| 2021 | REA | AA | 21 | 57 | 6 | 1 | 0 | 3 | 7 | 1 | 9 | 0 | 0 | .296/.333/.481 | 109 | .310 | -0.3 | C(11) -1.0 | 0.1 |
| 2022 | REA | AA | 22 | 316 | 48 | 11 | 1 | 15 | 45 | 41 | 52 | 6 | 2 | .275/.392/.496 | 142 | .289 | -0.1 | C(58) -0.6 | 2.4 |
| 2022 | RCT | AA | 22 | 131 | 24 | 3 | 0 | 11 | 33 | 29 | 22 | 1 | 2 | .306/.473/.673 | 167 | .288 | 0.1 | C(27) 2.2 | 1.7 |
| 2022 | LAA | MLB | 22 | 16 | 1 | 0 | 0 | 0 | 2 | 2 | 3 | 0 | 0 | .286/.375/.286 | 92 | .364 | -0.4 | C(5) 0.3 | 0.0 |
| 2023 DC | LAA | MLB | 23 | 250 | 29 | 9 | 1 | 7 | 26 | 23 | 48 | 3 | 1 | .220/.302/.358 | 91 | .251 | 0.0 | C -3 | 0.4 |

*Comparables: Wilin Rosario, John Ryan Murphy, Austin Romine*

**The Report:** The development path for cold-weather prep catchers can be a bit of a leisurely jog, but O'Hoppe kicked it into a full-on sprint in 2022, socking 11 home runs in 29 post-deadline games for Rocket City, which earned him a brief cup of coffee in Anaheim. The power is for real—he had sneaky raw even in the Penn League that has grown into full-throated plus pop in the intervening years. O'Hoppe drops his hands into his swing and fires off uppercut after uppercut, showing above-average bat speed. His barrel control isn't ideal, however, and the whole thing can look a bit stiff. He should make enough hard contact to get most of the plus raw power into games, even if his batting averages struggle to top .250. Defensively, O'Hoppe has developed into a perfectly adequate catcher. He's not the softest receiver or the most agile blocker, and his throwing is likewise very average. But O'Hoppe will stick there, and you won't really notice him for good or ill. You'll notice the dingers though. There's a Twitter account for them and everything.

**OFP:** 55 / Solid starting catcher

**Variance:** Low. O'Hoppe's 2022 performance overstates his offensive potential just a tad, but he should draw enough walks and drive enough extra-base hits to be an above-average major-league hitter and is basically ready now. There's no reason he shouldn't be the starting backstop for the Angels on Opening Day.

**Jesse Roche's Fantasy Take:** O'Hoppe displayed impressive power (.261 ISO), patience (15.7% walk rate) and contact (16.6% strikeout rate) skills at Double-A last year. As noted above, his epic late-season heater was nearly unrivaled among prospects. He ran a 47.1% fly-ball rate and 50.9% pull rate—which results in plenty of homers but few line drives and subpar BABIPs. That said, his offensive profile somewhat resembles Will Smith, if not more extreme given his pull tendencies. If his bat develops similarly, O'Hoppe will be one of the top fantasy catchers, even if he struggles to hit .250 while launching 20+ home runs. Meanwhile, he likely enters 2023 as the starting catcher. Don't overlook O'Hoppe in dynasty or redraft formats as he could immediately produce in an improved Angels lineup. He is a top-100 dynasty prospect.

## 3  Edgar Quero  C    OFP: 55    ETA: 2025
Born: 04/06/03  Age: 20  Bats: S  Throws: R  Height: 5'11"  Weight: 170 lb.  Origin: International Free Agent, 2021

| YEAR | TEAM | LVL | AGE | PA | R | 2B | 3B | HR | RBI | BB | K | SB | CS | AVG/OBP/SLG | DRC+ | BABIP | BRR | DRP | WARP |
|---|---|---|---|---|---|---|---|---|---|---|---|---|---|---|---|---|---|---|---|
| 2021 | ANG | ROK | 18 | 116 | 21 | 8 | 1 | 4 | 24 | 23 | 28 | 1 | 1 | .253/.440/.506 | | .327 | | | |
| 2021 | IE | A | 18 | 42 | 2 | 2 | 0 | 1 | 6 | 5 | 16 | 1 | 0 | .206/.310/.353 | 84 | .316 | -0.8 | C(9) -0.5 | -0.1 |
| 2022 | IE | A | 19 | 515 | 86 | 35 | 2 | 17 | 75 | 73 | 91 | 12 | 5 | .312/.435/.530 | 139 | .360 | -2.5 | C(80) -8.8 | 3.2 |
| 2023 non-DC | LAA | MLB | 20 | 251 | 23 | 12 | 1 | 4 | 23 | 21 | 58 | 2 | 1 | .232/.306/.349 | 87 | .294 | -3.3 | C 0 | 0.3 |

*Comparables: Gary Sánchez, Travis d'Arnaud, Chase Vallot*

**The Report:** The Angels have found their own offensive-minded catcher to match the one they dealt for, and Quero has even more upside with the stick than O'Hoppe. He can rake from both sides of the plate, although the left-handed swing is a bit more advanced in terms of power actualization. He clears his hips early and whips the bat through the zone, looking to pull and lift, while his right-handed swing is a bit more level. It didn't really matter who he faced in the Cal League last year though—lefty or righty—all had to be wary. Like Neto, Quero simplifies things a bit with two strikes, and he's a tough out even behind in the count. He's a potential plus-hit/plus-power catcher, and that power should play from both sides of the plate in time. The dude can sting a baseball. A-ball is a ways off the majors, but I'm pretty confident in the bat, and I don't think he will be that far off Francisco Álvarez or Diego Cartaya in terms of bat-first catching prospects in due time.

Of course, Quero won't rank with them as catching prospects *in toto,* because the defensive side of his game needs some work. He's twitchy and throws well enough, so the fundamentals of his receiving should get there eventually, but at present he's snatchy and boxy at the edges. I also worry about his frame holding up over the long haul as a catcher. None of these are particularly worrisome for a 19-year-old low-minors catcher, but all catching prospects are worrisome.

**OFP:** 55 / First-division catcher

**Variance:** Extreme. Quero might not be a catcher in two years. He might be the best catching prospect in baseball in two years. This level of performance from any 19-year-old in A-ball would get our attention, but the heights of his current ranking are driven by a starting catcher projection. And catchers are worrisome, also weird.

**Jesse Roche's Fantasy Take:** Quero was the top qualified hitter in the California League at just 19 years old, and most of his production came after June 1 (.338/.465/.609). His size, performance and switch-hitting aptitude is reminiscent of Keibert Ruiz circa 2017. And there's the rub. Teenage catching prospects are a risky demographic, and their ETA is often equivalent to a shrug emoji. Still, Quero's recent performance and potential with the bat are tantalizing and place him on the edge of the dynasty top 100.

## 4  Chase Silseth  RHP          OFP: 50      ETA: Debuted in 2022

Born: 05/18/00   Age: 23   Bats: R   Throws: R   Height: 6'0"   Weight: 217 lb.   Origin: Round 11, 2021 Draft (#321 overall)

| YEAR | TEAM | LVL | AGE | W | L | SV | G | GS | IP | H | HR | BB/9 | K/9 | K | GB% | BABIP | WHIP | ERA | DRA- | WARP |
|------|------|-----|-----|---|---|----|----|----|-----|----|----|------|------|-----|-------|-------|------|------|------|------|
| 2022 | RCT | AA | 22 | 7 | 0 | 0 | 15 | 15 | 83 | 52 | 11 | 2.9 | 11.9 | 110 | 48.9% | .247 | 0.95 | 2.28 | 74 | 2.0 |
| 2022 | LAA | MLB | 22 | 1 | 3 | 0 | 7 | 7 | 28² | 33 | 7 | 3.8 | 7.5 | 24 | 44.6% | .310 | 1.57 | 6.59 | 110 | 0.1 |
| 2023 DC | LAA | MLB | 23 | 2 | 3 | 0 | 8 | 8 | 36.3 | 34 | 5 | 3.6 | 8.3 | 33 | 42.3% | .285 | 1.34 | 3.90 | 104 | 0.3 |

Comparables: Casey Kelly, Spencer Howard, Lucas Sims

**The Report:** Did you have Chase Silseth as the first 2021 draftee to debut in the majors? No? Neither did we. While the Angels' MLB pitching depth has often been a bit shallow, you'd have pegged Sam Bachman as the fastest-moving arm from that draft class, not Silseth. But while Bachman's velocity has faded in the pros, Silseth's jumped, and he used his mid-90s fastball and full suite of advanced secondaries to dominate Double-A hitters, earning a quick promotion to the Angels' rotation in May. He bounced back and forth between Madison (Alabama) and Anaheim, each successive major-league call-up looking a little bit worse.

As mentioned, Silseth now has plus fastball velocity, but it can play a bit below the radar readings. The pitch's movement is mostly unremarkable and his command is below-average. So it's not a huge surprise that he threw his fastball less than half the time in the majors, leaning more on three average-to-above secondaries. His mid-80s slider shows plus depth from his higher slot, and can be a swing-and-miss pitch at the highest level. Silseth's split-change is more change than split—you'd like a little more consistent late tumble—but it gets more whiffs than you'd expect from mere visual inspection. He also throws a slower curve which shows good depth when he gets it down under 80 mph or so, but it can be firm, slurvy and bleed into the slider. Silseth has a deep collection of average-ish major-league offerings, which will dispatch Double-A hitters, but he needs a little more command refinement and consistency with the slider and split to step into a big-league rotation permanently.

**OFP:** 50 / no. 4 starter

**Variance:** Low. Silseth's advanced repertoire and Double-A success make him a fairly safe bet for short- and long-term major league utility, but it's hard to conjure another jump that would get him beyond a 5% or 10% better-than-league-average starter. Granted, the Angels can always use that.

**Jesse Roche's Fantasy Take:** Silseth, a standout in May, experienced a rude awakening in MLB after his debut. The pieces are here for Silseth to be an impactful fantasy arm as soon as 2023, particularly if his command improves. It is unclear whether the Angels plan to continue to utilize a six-man rotation next year. If they do, Silseth will be in the running for that final spot in a lefty-heavy rotation. Given his proximity and quality secondaries, he is a top-200 dynasty prospect.

## 5  Ky Bush  LHP          OFP: 50      ETA: Late 2023

Born: 11/12/99   Age: 23   Bats: L   Throws: L   Height: 6'6"   Weight: 240 lb.   Origin: Round 2, 2021 Draft (#45 overall)

| YEAR | TEAM | LVL | AGE | W | L | SV | G | GS | IP | H | HR | BB/9 | K/9 | K | GB% | BABIP | WHIP | ERA | DRA- | WARP |
|------|------|-----|-----|---|---|----|----|----|-----|----|----|------|------|-----|-------|-------|------|------|------|------|
| 2021 | TRI | A+ | 21 | 0 | 2 | 0 | 5 | 5 | 12 | 14 | 0 | 3.8 | 15.0 | 20 | 46.4% | .500 | 1.58 | 4.50 | 103 | 0.1 |
| 2022 | RCT | AA | 22 | 7 | 4 | 0 | 21 | 21 | 103 | 93 | 14 | 2.5 | 8.8 | 101 | 44.7% | .282 | 1.18 | 3.67 | 93 | 1.4 |
| 2023 non-DC | LAA | MLB | 23 | 3 | 3 | 0 | 58 | 0 | 50 | 56 | 8 | 3.6 | 7.3 | 40 | 37.9% | .313 | 1.52 | 5.08 | 129 | -0.5 |

Comparables: Osvaldo Hernandez, Alex Wells, Nick Kingham

**The Report:** On paper, Ky Bush was also more likely to get to the majors faster than Silseth. A polished lefty who dominated the West Coast Conference in 2021 for the Gaels, he used that same advanced three-pitch mix to more than hold his own in the Southern League in 2022. Bush's fastball has settled down into the low-90s, but his herky-jerky southpaw delivery can keep hitters off balance, setting up his sweeping low-80s slider. It's a tough angle for his fellow lefties to deal with and can dive enough to give righties trouble as well. Bush rounds out his repertoire with a changeup with average fade, but he can guide it a bit too much to get swings and misses with any consistency. Like Silseth, Bush has a broadly average arsenal with some upper-minors pro success on his C.V. He's got less fastball, but a bit more command; choose your back-of-the-rotation fighter accordingly.

**OFP:** 50 / no. 4 starter

**Variance:** Medium. Bush has shown a bit more velocity in the past, if he can find those missing ticks, he'd be a bit more interesting as a starting pitching prospect. He also lacks the same kind of relief fallback as Silseth given the lack of a plus fastball or clear swing-and-miss secondary.

**Jesse Roche's Fantasy Take:** This profile typically does not make waves in fantasy. Even so, Bush should be rostered in leagues with up to 300 prospects due to his solid slider and likely long-term starting role.

## 6  Caden Dana  RHP      OFP: 50    ETA: 2026

Born: 12/17/03   Age: 19   Bats: L   Throws: R   Height: 6'4"   Weight: 215 lb.   Origin: Round 11, 2022 Draft (#328 overall)

| YEAR | TEAM | LVL | AGE | W | L | SV | G | GS | IP | H | HR | BB/9 | K/9 | K | GB% | BABIP | WHIP | ERA | DRA- | WARP |
|---|---|---|---|---|---|---|---|---|---|---|---|---|---|---|---|---|---|---|---|---|
| 2022 | ANG | ROK | 18 | 0 | 0 | 0 | 3 | 3 | 6² | 6 | 0 | 0.0 | 8.1 | 6 | 42.1% | .316 | 0.90 | 1.35 | | |
| 2023 non-DC | LAA | MLB | 19 | 3 | 3 | 0 | 58 | 0 | 50 | 58 | 9 | 5.1 | 7.0 | 39 | 35.4% | .316 | 1.73 | 6.30 | 153 | -1.1 |

Comparables: José Mujica, Jake Thompson, Nick Travieso

**The Report:** The Angels have not shied away from drafting cold weather prep players in recent years. They kicked off their Day 3 picks last summer with Dana and subsequently paid him like a second-rounder. And he is a very second-round prep pitching prospect: A tall, projectable righty who can pop a fastball up into the mid-90s and has some present feel for spin. The changeup is a bit better than you'd usually see from this type of prospect at this point in time too, flashing above-average. Dana's command and fastball shape are suboptimal at present and low-minors hitters were on it more than you'd expect. His delivery is pretty free and easy, so there's no mechanical reason he can't develop as a starter long-term, but the non-elite prep righty cohort does not have a lot of recent success in the prospect world.

**OFP:** 50 / no. 4 starter

**Variance:** Extreme. Dana is a 2022 prep arm with more upside then the pitchers ranked ahead of him, but a floor where he tops out as an upper-minors relief arm.

**Jesse Roche's Fantasy Take:** I'll repeat: "The non-elite prep righty cohort does not have a lot of recent success in the prospect world." Dana is a wait-and-see prospect avoided for now in even the deepest of leagues.

## 7  Adrian Placencia  MI      OFP: 50    ETA: 2025/2026

Born: 06/02/03   Age: 20   Bats: S   Throws: R   Height: 5'11"   Weight: 155 lb.   Origin: International Free Agent, 2019

| YEAR | TEAM | LVL | AGE | PA | R | 2B | 3B | HR | RBI | BB | K | SB | CS | AVG/OBP/SLG | DRC+ | BABIP | BRR | DRP | WARP |
|---|---|---|---|---|---|---|---|---|---|---|---|---|---|---|---|---|---|---|---|
| 2021 | ANG | ROK | 18 | 175 | 29 | 3 | 3 | 5 | 19 | 28 | 49 | 4 | 2 | .175/.326/.343 | | .225 | | | |
| 2022 | IE | A | 19 | 469 | 83 | 23 | 2 | 13 | 64 | 76 | 142 | 21 | 8 | .254/.387/.427 | 85 | .367 | -0.4 | 2B(67) 5.0, SS(32) 0.5 | 0.9 |
| 2023 non-DC | LAA | MLB | 20 | 251 | 22 | 11 | 2 | 3 | 22 | 23 | 96 | 5 | 3 | .220/.299/.325 | 79 | .368 | -1.5 | 2B 0, SS 0 | 0.0 |

Comparables: Luis Alejandro Basabe, Dilson Herrera, Esteury Ruiz

**The Report:** A seven-figure signing in 2019, Placencia struggled in his first taste of pro ball in 2021, finishing on the interstate at the Angels' complex in Tempe. Nevertheless, he was sent to full-season ball last year and showed marked improvement at the plate. The switch-hitting infielder has a very similar swing from both sides, and showed almost no platoon split, which is unusual for a switch-hitter with his limited amount of experience. Both swings are geared for power despite his rather narrow frame. Placencia employs a big leg kick and a bit of stomp-and-lift, but everything in his upper half is loose and he generates some real in-game pop already. The contact rate will have to improve as this level of swing-and-miss in the zone in A-ball portends hit tool issues further up the organizational ladder. Unlike most of the Angels' low-minors prospects from here on out on the list, though, Placencia can at least impact a baseball with some verve.

Like the rest of the Angels infield prospects on this list, Placencia moves around on the dirt. He played significantly more second than short in 2022, but is a slick fielder whose arm will play fine enough at shortstop, although he is a better fit for the keystone—also like the rest of the Angels' infield prospects.

**OFP:** 50 / Second-division middle infielder

**Variance:** High. Placencia is a projection bet who has some work to do in terms of both swing decisions and contact rate.

**Jesse Roche's Fantasy Take:** Like many Angels prospects below, Placencia has serious bat-to-ball issues, with a sub-65% contact rate and an unseemly 30.3% strikeout rate in the hitter-friendly California League. While his power is solid, it is not loud enough to outweigh the risk associated with his hit tool at present. As such, Placencia is at best an intriguing flier in leagues with up to 500 prospects.

## 8 Livan Soto  MI    OFP: 45    ETA: Debuted in 2022
Born: 06/22/00   Age: 23   Bats: L   Throws: R   Height: 6'0"   Weight: 160 lb.   Origin: International Free Agent, 2017

| YEAR | TEAM | LVL | AGE | PA | R | 2B | 3B | HR | RBI | BB | K | SB | CS | AVG/OBP/SLG | DRC+ | BABIP | BRR | DRP | WARP |
|---|---|---|---|---|---|---|---|---|---|---|---|---|---|---|---|---|---|---|---|
| 2021 | TRI | A+ | 21 | 406 | 49 | 14 | 8 | 7 | 36 | 39 | 99 | 14 | 5 | .217/.293/.358 | 91 | .274 | -0.9 | SS(69) -7.0, 2B(14) -2.7 | -0.2 |
| 2021 | RCT | AA | 21 | 44 | 3 | 1 | 0 | 0 | 4 | 3 | 11 | 0 | 0 | .225/.295/.250 | 80 | .310 | 0.1 | SS(10) 2.0, 2B(2) 0.1 | 0.2 |
| 2022 | RCT | AA | 22 | 543 | 69 | 17 | 1 | 6 | 57 | 71 | 102 | 18 | 8 | .281/.379/.362 | 98 | .345 | -0.6 | SS(68) 6.1, 2B(42) 2.9, 3B(7) -0.0 | 2.3 |
| 2022 | LAA | MLB | 22 | 59 | 9 | 5 | 1 | 1 | 9 | 2 | 13 | 1 | 1 | .400/.414/.582 | 80 | .500 | 0.2 | SS(18) -1.3, 3B(1) 0 | 0.0 |
| 2023 non-DC | LAA | MLB | 23 | 251 | 25 | 9 | 2 | 2 | 20 | 22 | 53 | 4 | 1 | .236/.307/.325 | 81 | .298 | -2.4 | SS -1, 3B 0 | -0.2 |

**The Report:** While the first line in Soto's SABR bio might inevitably be about his connection to Atlanta's IFA malfeasance, he has a chance to fill up the rest of the column inches with tales of his major-league performance. After a wretched 2021 at the plate, he bounced back in Rocket City, looking like the OBP-over-slugging version of Luis Rengifo. Soto's bat-to-ball skills are solid, despite a bit of a circuitous swing path that can make it appear a bit like a hammer toss. It's not the most physical of strokes, and there's commensurate well-below-average game power. There's also some risk that the hit tool falls apart again as Triple-A and MLB arms challenge him more, but Soto's eye is good enough and he moves the bat around well enough that there should be enough walks and base hits to keep the overall line within a shout of average despite the lack of game pop. Defensively, Soto can handle any of the infield spots, but his range plays a bit better at second or third.

**OFP:** 45 / Fringe starter or good fifth infielder

**Variance:** Medium. You'd prefer Soto to have a bit longer track record of pro production given the limited physical tools. He also doesn't project to have a ton of secondary offensive skills in the majors, so he's going to have to keep his contact rates where they've been in Double-A.

**Jesse Roche's Fantasy Take:** The acquisitions of Gio Urshela and Brandon Drury effectively close off a path to short-term playing time for Soto. Now, he is back to likely being upper-level infield depth with a contact-only profile that is not fantasy-friendly. Soto should be rostered in 30-team leagues as an occasionally useful bench piece, but that is it.

## 9 Werner Blakely  3B/DH    OFP: 45    ETA: 2025
Born: 02/21/02   Age: 21   Bats: L   Throws: R   Height: 6'3"   Weight: 185 lb.   Origin: Round 4, 2020 Draft (#111 overall)

| YEAR | TEAM | LVL | AGE | PA | R | 2B | 3B | HR | RBI | BB | K | SB | CS | AVG/OBP/SLG | DRC+ | BABIP | BRR | DRP | WARP |
|---|---|---|---|---|---|---|---|---|---|---|---|---|---|---|---|---|---|---|---|
| 2021 | ANG | ROK | 19 | 186 | 22 | 6 | 0 | 3 | 19 | 33 | 69 | 15 | 2 | .182/.339/.284 | | .308 | | | |
| 2022 | IE | A | 20 | 235 | 36 | 13 | 2 | 5 | 40 | 45 | 70 | 24 | 2 | .295/.447/.470 | 106 | .450 | 1.2 | 3B(34) -2.8 | 0.8 |
| 2023 non-DC | LAA | MLB | 21 | 251 | 21 | 10 | 2 | 2 | 20 | 25 | 88 | 11 | 2 | .220/.305/.313 | 78 | .352 | 0.7 | 2B 0, 3B 0 | 0.1 |

*Comparables: Nolan Jones, Juan Francisco, Josh Bell*

**The Report:** Blakely's pro career has had the kind of unevenness you'd expect from a cold-weather prep bat drafted in the middle of a pandemic. He's started to fill out his lean frame—adding some doubles pop—and I wouldn't be surprised if he gets to at least average game power eventually. Blakely has a very upright and stiff swing and is looking to lift the ball, which carries the usual swing-and-miss concerns, and he ran a near-30% K-rate in the California League.

In the field, Blakely has settled in at third base after playing some shortstop and second in 2021. He may grow off the infield, but should have the foot speed for either corner outfield spot, and adding defensive flexibility at all four corners will help carve out a major-league role for him down the line if the bat doesn't quite carry an everyday spot on its own.

**OFP:** 45 / Long-side platoon at all four corners

**Variance:** Extreme. Blakely has little pro experience above the complex, and there's a wide range of reasonable outcomes both at the plate and in the field.

**Jesse Roche's Fantasy Take:** Blakely's injury-riddled campaign in Low-A (.295/.447/.470) looks impressive at first blush, but his stint in the AFL was pretty ugly. There, he ran up a 41.1% strikeout rate and a 57.5% contact rate. Regardless, Blakely has intriguing fantasy upside with a tall, thin frame that promises on-paper projection (but may be too narrow) and a track record of base-stealing success.

## 10   Coleman Crow   RHP   OFP: 45   ETA: Late 2023/Early 2024

Born: 12/30/00   Age: 22   Bats: R   Throws: R   Height: 6'0"   Weight: 175 lb.   Origin: Round 28, 2019 Draft (#841 overall)

| YEAR | TEAM | LVL | AGE | W | L | SV | G | GS | IP | H | HR | BB/9 | K/9 | K | GB% | BABIP | WHIP | ERA | DRA- | WARP |
|------|------|-----|-----|---|---|----|---|----|-----|-----|----|------|-----|-----|-------|-------|------|------|------|------|
| 2021 | IE | A | 20 | 4 | 3 | 0 | 13 | 10 | 62¹ | 68 | 7 | 4.2 | 9.0 | 62 | 42.2% | .332 | 1.56 | 4.19 | 128 | -0.7 |
| 2022 | RCT | AA | 21 | 9 | 3 | 0 | 24 | 23 | 128 | 133 | 20 | 2.5 | 9.0 | 128 | 48.4% | .312 | 1.31 | 4.85 | 105 | 1.0 |
| 2023 non-DC | LAA | MLB | 22 | 3 | 3 | 0 | 58 | 0 | 50 | 58 | 8 | 3.6 | 6.6 | 36 | 38.3% | .312 | 1.56 | 5.46 | 137 | -0.7 |

**The Report:** The Angels went overslot for Crow on Day 3 of the 2019 draft. Then he didn't throw a pro pitch until 2021, because...well, you know. He flashed a fastball up to 94 and some useful secondaries in the Cal League and Fall ball that season, and Los Angeles responded by jumping him to Double-A in 2022. His fastball still sits mostly low-90s with some arm-side wiggle from his lower slot. He's got an uptempo and arm-heavy delivery—and Crow looks no more than his listed 6-foot-0 and 175 pounds—but he logged almost 130 innings last year and the stuff held deeper into games. It's not an overwhelming arsenal, although his mid-80s slider shows some effective sweep and both his curve and change are viable major-league offerings. The curve is more of a change-of-pace look, showing a bit more downer action as it rolls in 10 mph slower than the slider, while the change is usable, if fringe. Crow is willing to mix everything in and he will need to continue to use all four pitches and locate them well to keep hitters from getting the fat part of the bat on his offerings.

**OFP:** 45 / Back-end starter

**Variance:** Medium. There are more 45s than 50s here and Crow might end up a bit too hittable in the majors.

**Jesse Roche's Fantasy Take:** Even as an OFP 45, Crow is a better real-life than fantasy prospect. That should tell you something.

# Outside the Top Ten:

## 11   Jack Kochanowicz   RHP

Born: 12/22/00   Age: 22   Bats: L   Throws: R   Height: 6'6"   Weight: 220 lb.   Origin: Round 3, 2019 Draft (#92 overall)

| YEAR | TEAM | LVL | AGE | W | L | SV | G | GS | IP | H | HR | BB/9 | K/9 | K | GB% | BABIP | WHIP | ERA | DRA- | WARP |
|------|------|-----|-----|---|---|----|---|----|-----|-----|----|------|-----|----|-------|-------|------|------|------|------|
| 2021 | IE | A | 20 | 4 | 2 | 0 | 20 | 18 | 83¹ | 102 | 12 | 3.8 | 7.9 | 73 | 49.3% | .345 | 1.64 | 6.91 | 128 | -0.9 |
| 2022 | IE | A | 21 | 4 | 4 | 0 | 17 | 9 | 57² | 57 | 6 | 2.8 | 8.3 | 53 | 51.1% | .304 | 1.30 | 4.99 | 104 | -0.1 |
| 2023 non-DC | LAA | MLB | 22 | 3 | 3 | 0 | 58 | 0 | 50 | 60 | 8 | 4.0 | 6.2 | 35 | 37.4% | .318 | 1.64 | 5.81 | 144 | -0.9 |

An oblique issue cost Kochanowicz the first couple months of the 2022 season, and the 2020 draftee badly needed those missing reps. He continues to tantalize, flashing better stuff than any arm in the system other than Silseth. Kochanowicz can run the fastball up into the mid-90s and backs it with two potential above-average breakers. There's a developing split-change as well. His delivery features good arm speed and a bit of deception, but until the total package does more than flash, his OFP stays in the back-end starter or swingman range.

## 12   Kyren Paris   MI

Born: 11/11/01   Age: 21   Bats: R   Throws: R   Height: 6'0"   Weight: 180 lb.   Origin: Round 2, 2019 Draft (#55 overall)

| YEAR | TEAM | LVL | AGE | PA | R | 2B | 3B | HR | RBI | BB | K | SB | CS | AVG/OBP/SLG | DRC+ | BABIP | BRR | DRP | WARP |
|------|------|-----|-----|-----|----|----|----|----|-----|----|-----|----|----|-------------|------|-------|-----|-----|------|
| 2021 | IE | A | 19 | 136 | 29 | 5 | 6 | 2 | 18 | 27 | 41 | 16 | 4 | .274/.434/.491 | 98 | .429 | 0.7 | SS(17) 2.9, 2B(11) 1.2 | 0.8 |
| 2021 | TRI | A+ | 19 | 55 | 6 | 2 | 1 | 1 | 6 | 2 | 20 | 4 | 0 | .231/.273/.365 | 88 | .355 | -0.1 | SS(9) 0.6, 2B(2) -0.0 | 0.1 |
| 2022 | TRI | A+ | 20 | 392 | 58 | 18 | 5 | 8 | 32 | 49 | 117 | 28 | 4 | .229/.345/.387 | 104 | .330 | 3.7 | SS(60) -6.4, 2B(26) -0.1 | 1.2 |
| 2022 | RCT | AA | 20 | 51 | 11 | 2 | 0 | 3 | 8 | 10 | 14 | 5 | 0 | .359/.510/.641 | 109 | .500 | -0.2 | 2B(13) -0.5 | 0.1 |
| 2023 non-DC | LAA | MLB | 21 | 251 | 23 | 10 | 3 | 4 | 23 | 23 | 85 | 10 | 3 | .224/.305/.343 | 86 | .342 | 0.6 | 2B 0, SS 0 | 0.5 |

*Comparables: Javier Báez, Corey Seager, Jonathan Araúz*

Paris ranked fifth in this system last year, but his bat scuffled a bit in High-A. He strikes out a bit too much, given that he doesn't kill the ball when he does make contact. He does seem to be trying to create a little more torque and lift in his swing this year, loading his hands a bit later and swinging a bit harder. It did lead to a few more home runs, but it gives him less margin to adjust to breaking stuff. Paris is still a very good second baseman, but his arm strength is going to limit him to the right side of the infield, and despite an absolutely scorching couple weeks in Double-A to round out his 2022 campaign, I'm not confident that he will hit in the upper minors yet.

## 13   Ben Joyce   RHP

Born: 09/17/00   Age: 22   Bats: R   Throws: R   Height: 6'5"   Weight: 225 lb.   Origin: Round 3, 2022 Draft (#89 overall)

| YEAR | TEAM | LVL | AGE | W | L | SV | G | GS | IP | H | HR | BB/9 | K/9 | K | GB% | BABIP | WHIP | ERA | DRA- | WARP |
|------|------|-----|-----|---|---|----|----|----|-----|-----|-----|------|------|----|------|-------|------|------|------|------|
| 2022 | RCT | AA | 21 | 1 | 0 | 1 | 13 | 0 | 13 | 11 | 0 | 2.8 | 13.8 | 20 | 46.7% | .367 | 1.15 | 2.08 | 80 | 0.3 |
| 2023 non-DC | LAA | MLB | 22 | 3 | 3 | 0 | 58 | 0 | 50 | 49 | 8 | 4.3 | 8.6 | 48 | 37.9% | .295 | 1.45 | 4.71 | 120 | -0.3 |

*Comparables: Johnny Barbato, Sam Tuivailala, Jhan Mariñez*

No doubt Joyce's triple-digit heat was all over your Twitter feed last spring. You likely saw more video of him than any other college baseball player, assuming you weren't out there spending your Friday evenings binging NCAA games. And yep, he does sit 100+, which is impressive, but not *that* special once you get to the pros. Joyce's mechanics aren't ideal, and he's already had his share of injury issues. His slider has good spin, but not great shape. Triple-digit heat and a potentially-55 breaker is a major-league reliever, but it's not really late-inning stuff nowadays. Joyce can probably Hunter Strickland it up for a few years as long as he's healthy and would just be wasting bullets in the minors in 2023.

## 14   Denzer Guzman   SS

Born: 02/08/04   Age: 19   Bats: R   Throws: R   Height: 6'1"   Weight: 180 lb.   Origin: International Free Agent, 2021

| YEAR | TEAM | LVL | AGE | PA | R | 2B | 3B | HR | RBI | BB | K | SB | CS | AVG/OBP/SLG | DRC+ | BABIP | BRR | DRP | WARP |
|------|------|-----|-----|-----|----|----|----|----|-----|----|----|----|----|-------------|------|-------|-----|-----|------|
| 2021 | DSL ANG | ROK | 17 | 164 | 21 | 10 | 1 | 3 | 27 | 20 | 24 | 11 | 7 | .213/.311/.362 | | .233 | | | |
| 2022 | ANG | ROK | 18 | 211 | 38 | 11 | 3 | 3 | 33 | 15 | 44 | 3 | 1 | .286/.341/.422 | | .354 | | | |
| 2023 non-DC | LAA | MLB | 19 | 251 | 18 | 10 | 1 | 2 | 19 | 16 | 94 | 5 | 2 | .197/.255/.277 | 50 | .319 | -1.7 | SS 0 | -0.9 |

Guzman was a top IFA prospect in the 2021 class and received a commensurate seven-figure bonus from Los Angeles. He came stateside this year and performed well in the complex before looking horribly overmatched in his brief A-ball appearances. Guzman's swing starts almost wrapped and it's a bit on the longer side. There's enough bat speed that if he tones down his free-swinging ways and improves his swing decisions, the bat should be playable if not laden with impact potential. In the field he's capable of really picking it, but can get a little loose when he has too much time to wait on a grounder. There's an everyday shortstop projection here in the present defensive tools, but he may grow off the position as he's already filling out his lower half. Guzman is one to keep an eye on as he hits full-season ball full-time in 2023, but the Angels have had little out-and-out success with this kind of position player prospect in recent years.

## 15   Sam Bachman   RHP

Born: 09/30/99   Age: 23   Bats: R   Throws: R   Height: 6'1"   Weight: 235 lb.   Origin: Round 1, 2021 Draft (#9 overall)

| YEAR | TEAM | LVL | AGE | W | L | SV | G | GS | IP | H | HR | BB/9 | K/9 | K | GB% | BABIP | WHIP | ERA | DRA- | WARP |
|------|------|-----|-----|---|---|----|----|----|------|----|-----|------|------|----|------|-------|------|------|------|------|
| 2021 | TRI | A+ | 21 | 0 | 2 | 0 | 5 | 5 | 14¹ | 13 | 1 | 2.5 | 9.4 | 15 | 65.8% | .324 | 1.19 | 3.77 | 109 | 0.0 |
| 2022 | RCT | AA | 22 | 1 | 1 | 0 | 12 | 12 | 43² | 41 | 4 | 5.2 | 6.2 | 30 | 54.1% | .282 | 1.51 | 3.92 | 115 | 0.1 |
| 2023 non-DC | LAA | MLB | 23 | 3 | 3 | 0 | 58 | 0 | 50 | 57 | 7 | 5.0 | 6.9 | 38 | 42.0% | .318 | 1.70 | 5.75 | 141 | -0.8 |

*Comparables: Josh Sborz, Conner Greene, Justin Donatella*

The Angels' first-round pick in 2021, Bachman missed two months with biceps inflammation and was topping out more around 95 than the 100 he routinely flashed at Miami of Ohio. His slider will still get whiffs. Its shape and command are both above-average, but he throws it enough that there are diminishing returns and it works best when he's starting it glove-side and getting hitters to chase later in counts. Bachman does show an improving changeup, but given the injury issues and velocity dip, he might just be a 95-and-a-slider reliever now, as he really needs the extra few ticks on all his pitches.

## 16 Robinson Pina  RHP

Born: 11/26/98   Age: 24   Bats: R   Throws: R   Height: 6'4"   Weight: 224 lb.   Origin: International Free Agent, 2017

| YEAR | TEAM | LVL | AGE | W | L | SV | G | GS | IP | H | HR | BB/9 | K/9 | K | GB% | BABIP | WHIP | ERA | DRA- | WARP |
|---|---|---|---|---|---|---|---|---|---|---|---|---|---|---|---|---|---|---|---|---|
| 2021 | IE | A | 22 | 0 | 0 | 0 | 4 | 4 | 22² | 15 | 2 | 2.4 | 13.1 | 33 | 46.9% | .283 | 0.93 | 1.19 | 82 | 0.4 |
| 2021 | TRI | A+ | 22 | 2 | 7 | 0 | 13 | 13 | 57¹ | 38 | 4 | 6.4 | 13.3 | 85 | 40.5% | .309 | 1.38 | 4.40 | 83 | 1.0 |
| 2021 | RCT | AA | 22 | 0 | 3 | 0 | 4 | 4 | 15¹ | 19 | 7 | 5.3 | 12.9 | 22 | 33.3% | .343 | 1.83 | 9.39 | 87 | 0.3 |
| 2022 | TRI | A+ | 23 | 6 | 6 | 1 | 18 | 13 | 81² | 71 | 7 | 2.6 | 12.9 | 117 | 32.5% | .348 | 1.16 | 3.31 | 74 | 1.9 |
| 2023 non-DC | LAA | MLB | 24 | 3 | 3 | 0 | 58 | 0 | 50 | 48 | 8 | 5.0 | 9.7 | 54 | 33.0% | .302 | 1.51 | 4.85 | 122 | -0.3 |

*Comparables: Nick Nelson, Rogelio Armenteros, Matt Barnes*

Pina was a bit old for the Northwest League—where he spent most of his 2022 season—but he did throw more strikes there than he ever had anywhere else.  His split also continued to improve, giving him a real weapon against lefties. Pina's low-90s heater shows some sink and his slider continues to flash plus. The delivery and overall command profile still look like they will work better in the pen, but with two potential above-average secondaries, it might be worth it to give him another year in the rotation to see how it plays against upper-minors hitters.

## 17 David Calabrese  CF

Born: 09/26/02   Age: 20   Bats: L   Throws: R   Height: 5'11"   Weight: 160 lb.   Origin: Round 3, 2020 Draft (#82 overall)

| YEAR | TEAM | LVL | AGE | PA | R | 2B | 3B | HR | RBI | BB | K | SB | CS | AVG/OBP/SLG | DRC+ | BABIP | BRR | DRP | WARP |
|---|---|---|---|---|---|---|---|---|---|---|---|---|---|---|---|---|---|---|---|
| 2021 | ANG | ROK | 18 | 165 | 25 | 8 | 2 | 1 | 17 | 20 | 54 | 5 | 1 | .201/.303/.306 | | .315 | | | |
| 2022 | IE | A | 19 | 488 | 68 | 23 | 7 | 7 | 64 | 50 | 116 | 26 | 2 | .250/.326/.387 | 92 | .317 | 2.1 | CF(94) 2.0, LF(13) -0.3, RF(6) -0.7 | 0.8 |
| 2023 non-DC | LAA | MLB | 20 | 251 | 18 | 10 | 2 | 2 | 19 | 17 | 70 | 6 | 1 | .205/.264/.294 | 57 | .286 | -1.6 | LF 0, CF 0 | -0.7 |

Calabrese's speed and center field defense continue to keep him prospect-relevant even as he struggles to really do damage offensively. Calabrese is a plus runner and aggressive on the bases. In the outfield, he gets after fly balls like he's shot out of a cannon and adjusts his routes well on the fly. At the plate, Calabrese just kind of throws his wrists at the pitch. It's a very contact-oriented swing, and he doesn't even make as much contact as you'd like. The defensive tools will give him time to make adjustments offensively, but a speed-and-defense bench outfielder is a reasonable good outcome at present.

# Top Talents 25 and Under (as of 4/1/2023):

1.  Reid Detmers, LHP
2.  Zach Neto, SS
3.  José Suarez, LHP
4.  Logan O'Hoppe, C
5.  Edgar Quero, C
6.  Jo Adell, OF
7.  Chase Silseth, RHP
8.  Mickey Moniak, OF
9.  Ky Bush, LHP
10. Chris Rodriguez, RHP

The Angels don't exactly have an ancient roster, but it's remarkable to comb through their potential Opening Day 26 and see most of the club just entering or within a year of "Logan's Run" territory. That's hardly a catastrophe when you have a top-two like the pride of Orange County does, but Mike Trout and Shohei Ohtani have now had five years together and not a single one has brought Trout or the Halos to the playoffs, and much of that lies at the feet of a dearth of young talent produced by the farm over the past several seasons.

Detmers looks like he could be the most clear exception. The 10th pick of the 2020 draft was pegged as a fast-mover on draft day and seemed all but certain to be Anaheim-bound at pace. He debuted disappointingly in 2021, but tweaks to his mechanics and slider yielded promising returns in the back half of the season. The Angels will need to run a six-man rotation as they have for all of Ohtani's tenure, so they need depth as much as they require excellence. Detmers could provide a modicum of both, whereas Suarez seems more solidly the former. The squat southpaw ran a 102 DRA- in 109 innings, giving the Halos a chance to win if not typically being the reason they were in line for victory. The 25-year-old has ticked up command of his repertoire slightly, working in the zone more frequently to unremarkable, but untroubling results.

Neither of those terms could come to describe Adell's first three big-league seasons, which have totaled one full campaign of 161 games, 557 plate appearances and a ghastly .215/.259/.356 line. That's a 67 DRC+ and enough stagnation developmentally that even as Anaheim languished at the big-league level watching their red hot start slip away, Adell spent much of it in Triple-A Salt Lake. His numbers there were better, as he swatted homers with ease in the mountain air, but his 37.5%/3.9% K%/BB% in the bigs tells the tale for the talented 24-year-old-to-be. A breakout towards his top prospect ceiling alone could likely fly the rest of these Angels to the playoffs on their 50th-percentile outcomes, but at the moment he's looking less Kid Icarus and more Neon Yellow. Moniak's profile was always more limited than his 1-1 draft billing, and his challenge trade swap for Brandon Marsh in Philadelphia already looks suspect. It is more a commentary on the depth of the Angels' system that he is highlighted at all. A fourth outfielder without much power, Moniak needs a platoon partner to cover him against lefties but doesn't hit righties enough to justify the role. He's still just 25, and his defensive skill helps in an outfield that will need some support, particularly late for Hunter Renfroe.

Last is Rodriguez, whose catastrophic injury history includes the loss of the entire 2022 season and exactly one season with over 50 innings pitched as a pro (2017, when he was 18). It's reasonable to think that he does not merit inclusion at all here, but he was so brilliant in his flashes of health that I've extended this olive branch. His back and shoulder have utterly betrayed him, but if/when he finally gets on the mound again, hopefully healthy, he can be consolidated into a relief role that quickly would make him one of the top high-leverage options in Anaheim.

# Los Angeles Dodgers

## The State of the System:

The Dodgers have drafted, signed or acquired prospects with some of the best pitch characteristics and contact profiles around. They are now reaping the benefits with the deepest system in baseball and one of the best overall.

## The Top Ten:

**1** **Diego Cartaya  C**　　　OFP: 60　　ETA: 2024
Born: 09/07/01　Age: 21　Bats: R　Throws: R　Height: 6'3"　Weight: 219 lb.　Origin: International Free Agent, 2018

| YEAR | TEAM | LVL | AGE | PA | R | 2B | 3B | HR | RBI | BB | K | SB | CS | AVG/OBP/SLG | DRC+ | BABIP | BRR | DRP | WARP |
|------|------|-----|-----|-----|----|----|----|----|-----|----|----|----|----|-------------|------|-------|-----|-----|------|
| 2021 | RC | A | 19 | 137 | 31 | 6 | 0 | 10 | 31 | 18 | 37 | 0 | 0 | .298/.409/.614 | 119 | .353 | 0.5 | C(31) -4.0 | 0.4 |
| 2022 | RC | A | 20 | 163 | 31 | 9 | 1 | 9 | 31 | 23 | 44 | 0 | 0 | .260/.405/.550 | 118 | .321 | 0.1 | C(23) -1.2 | 0.8 |
| 2022 | GL | A+ | 20 | 282 | 43 | 13 | 0 | 13 | 41 | 40 | 75 | 1 | 0 | .251/.379/.476 | 109 | .310 | 0.6 | C(41) -3.2 | 0.9 |
| 2023 non-DC | LAD | MLB | 21 | 251 | 24 | 10 | 1 | 5 | 25 | 22 | 78 | 0 | 0 | .219/.302/.346 | 87 | .311 | -4.4 | C 0 | 0.2 |

*Comparables: Francisco Mejía, A.J. Jimenez, Jorge Alfaro*

**The Report:** At 6-foot-3 and 220-pounds, the 21-year-old catcher is equipped with a mature physique and natural power. While his batting average and OPS were both down from the previous season, Cartaya's 14% walk rate and reasonable 27% strikeout rate demonstrate quality at-bats and a formidable presence in the box. Cartaya's BABIP for the year was also 39 points lower than that of the previous season, suggesting his drop in production may be short-lived.

While there's little doubt about Cartaya's plus to plus-plus offensive potential, his ultimate defensive value is highly questionable. He's proven to be a capable receiver over three professional seasons, but his defensive abilities are not nearly as impressive as his offensive ones. His large physical stature can be detrimental as a backstop, placing limitations on his mobility and quickness. He's already dealt with multiple injuries over his young career, restricting him to just 95 games played at the catcher position since the start of the 2021 season. Despite Cartaya's solid arm strength, opposing basestealers have enjoyed an 80% success rate, signaling there's more work to be done.

**OFP:** 60 / Bat-first catcher

**Variance:** Medium. While his floor may be a right-handed hitting DH capable of launching plenty of dingers, there remains a lot of uncertainty in Cartaya's overall development going forward. His health is a significant concern, with those 95 games played last season being the most he's played in three seasons as a pro. If he's able to stay healthy, he then has to prove he can provide some value behind the plate, even if it's as a part-time catcher. Still just 21 years old, Cartaya has a high ceiling and plenty of time to reach it.

**Jesse Roche's Fantasy Take:** Cartaya has easy plus power that he maximizes in games due to an exaggerated lift-and-pull approach (50.6% pull and 48.3% fly-ball rates). Meanwhile, his contact rates sit comfortably on the wrong side of 70%, including just 64% in Low-A. Cartaya's underlying swing-and-miss and BABIP-draining approach limit his ability to hit for average. Yet, his power alone offers exciting fantasy possibilities, especially if he can hit .240+ with a solid OBP. Cartaya is a borderline top-50 dynasty prospect.

---

### Eyewitness Report: Diego Cartaya

**Evaluator:** Nathan Graham
**Report Date:** 07/20/2022
**Dates Seen:** Multiple June 2022

---

**Risk Factor:** High

**Physical/Health:** Extra-Large frame, physical and strong with a thick lower half; Mild projectable growth remaining.

| Tool | Future Grade | Report |
|---|---|---|
| Hit | 50 | Currently operates out of an upright, balanced, slightly open stance. The swing is quiet and features a mild load and leg kick. Has a feel for the barrel and makes plenty of hard contact with above-average bat speed and leveraged bat path. Length in the swing will create some swing and miss but he controls the zone well for a young player. |
| Power | 70 | Easy double-plus raw generated by above-average bat speed and physical strength. Ball jumps off the bat with his natural loft in the swing. A solid approach at the plate keeps the power playing in-game. Most of the current pop goes pull side but with more reps he'll learn to use the entire field. |
| Baserunning/Speed | 30 | Current below average foot speed and slow to accelerate. He will slow down even more as he matures becoming a base clogger. |
| Glove | 50 | Despite his lack of speed, Cartaya does show the ability to become a legitimate backstop. He's agile and shows an ability to block balls in the dirt. Continues to improve his receiving skills and game-calling ability. |
| Arm | 60 | Plus arm strength and he displays good carry and accuracy. Quick transfers make him tough to steal on. |

**Conclusion:** Cartaya's still pretty raw, especially behind the plate, but if it all comes together there is a chance he becomes an All-Star behind the plate. The power's the carrying tool, his strength and bat speed make for easy pop to all fields. He's made strides behind the plate but it's still not a lock he sticks as a backstop. If he does slide down the defensive spectrum, the bat will be strong enough to handle the move.

## 2 Bobby Miller RHP   OFP: 60   ETA: 2023

Born: 04/05/99   Age: 24   Bats: L   Throws: R   Height: 6'5"   Weight: 220 lb.   Origin: Round 1, 2020 Draft (#29 overall)

| YEAR | TEAM | LVL | AGE | W | L | SV | G | GS | IP | H | HR | BB/9 | K/9 | K | GB% | BABIP | WHIP | ERA | DRA- | WARP |
|---|---|---|---|---|---|---|---|---|---|---|---|---|---|---|---|---|---|---|---|---|
| 2021 | GL | A+ | 22 | 2 | 2 | 0 | 14 | 11 | 47 | 30 | 1 | 2.1 | 10.7 | 56 | 45.6% | .257 | 0.87 | 1.91 | 84 | 0.9 |
| 2021 | TUL | AA | 22 | 0 | 0 | 0 | 3 | 3 | 9¹ | 10 | 1 | 1.9 | 13.5 | 14 | 52.0% | .375 | 1.29 | 4.82 | 70 | 0.1 |
| 2022 | TUL | AA | 23 | 6 | 6 | 0 | 20 | 19 | 91 | 78 | 8 | 3.1 | 11.6 | 117 | 49.4% | .311 | 1.20 | 4.45 | 61 | 2.5 |
| 2022 | OKC | AAA | 23 | 1 | 1 | 0 | 4 | 4 | 21¹ | 17 | 4 | 2.5 | 11.8 | 28 | 56.0% | .283 | 1.08 | 3.38 | 75 | 0.4 |
| 2023 DC | LAD | MLB | 24 | 2 | 2 | 0 | 17 | 3 | 25.7 | 25 | 3 | 3.3 | 8.2 | 24 | 40.8% | .291 | 1.31 | 3.94 | 103 | 0.2 |

*Comparables: Andrew Heaney, Adam Warren, Daniel Gossett*

**The Report:** In the past, I've perhaps been a bit lower on Miller than the rest of the BP Prospect Team, but his 2022 campaign assuaged the lion's share of my doubts. Miller worked much deeper into games, topping 90 pitches regularly, and 100 on a couple occasions, with his power stuff still intact. His command profile remains on the wrong side of average, but it's good enough now that even upper-minors hitters struggled against his deep, plus arsenal.

Miller's fastball might legitimately be his fourth-best pitch, sitting in the upper-90s with decent ride, and he'll occasionally show you a power sinker wrinkle as well. The command and strike-throwing with the pitch still aren't quite sharp enough though and that can lead to a few too many walks or just general inefficiency. Both of Miller's breaking balls are easy plus. The curve is a low-80s, 12-5 breaker that he can dump at the back foot of lefties, but is equally effective when he drops it into the zone given how batters will give up on it. The slider is a smooth-shave electric razor of a pitch, upper-80s with less depth and run than the curve, but late, bat-missing action. Miller's changeup isn't as visually impressive, but the 10-15 mph gap off the fastball leads to plenty of whiffs despite less-than-impressive depth or fade.

So by my count, that's four plus-or-better pitches in the repertoire. Yeah, the command isn't great and he may be a frustrating starter at times, but Miller is going to be a starter, and a good one.

**OFP:** 60 / no. 3 starter

**Variance:** Medium. Would I be gobsmacked if Miller settles in as a high-leverage multi-inning monster? Not really; the Dodgers can get very creative with innings deployment and generally have a crowded rotation situation. His OFP would be in the same range in that role anyway, but 2022 has convinced me he's a good starter in the short, medium and long term, and he's a half-grade of fastball command away from a top-of-the-rotation profile. Conversely, he still hasn't really dominated the minors the way you'd want from a top-tier starting pitching prospect, so he hasn't assuaged *all* doubts from me.

**Jesse Roche's Fantasy Take:** Miller, a standout in August, checks so many boxes for a potential top fantasy arm. He throws absolute fire, *averaging* 98 mph. Check. His trio of distinct secondaries all miss bats. Check. Miller has a large 6-foot-5 frame often associated with a workhorse starter. Check. He generally throws plenty of strikes (7.2% career walk rate). Check. Miller's fastball too often plays below its elite velocity due to said command and inconsistent shape. Still, his stuff can go toe-to-toe with nearly any pitching prospect in baseball. Given his upside and proximity, Miller is on the edge of the dynasty top 50.

## 3  Miguel Vargas  3B/OF    OFP: 60    ETA: Debuted in 2022

Born: 11/17/99  Age: 23  Bats: R  Throws: R  Height: 6'3"  Weight: 205 lb.  Origin: International Free Agent, 2017

| YEAR | TEAM | LVL | AGE | PA | R | 2B | 3B | HR | RBI | BB | K | SB | CS | AVG/OBP/SLG | DRC+ | BABIP | BRR | DRP | WARP |
|------|------|-----|-----|-----|-----|-----|-----|-----|-----|-----|-----|-----|-----|-------------|------|-------|-----|-----|------|
| 2021 | GL | A+ | 21 | 172 | 31 | 11 | 1 | 7 | 16 | 9 | 32 | 4 | 0 | .314/.366/.532 | 121 | .353 | -1.1 | 3B(31) -1.9, 2B(2) -0.6, 1B(1) -0.0 | 0.6 |
| 2021 | TUL | AA | 21 | 370 | 67 | 16 | 1 | 16 | 60 | 36 | 57 | 7 | 1 | .321/.386/.523 | 125 | .344 | 1.0 | 3B(53) -0.4, 2B(15) -1.0, 1B(9) 0.1 | 2.2 |
| 2022 | OKC | AAA | 22 | 520 | 100 | 32 | 4 | 17 | 82 | 71 | 76 | 16 | 5 | .304/.404/.511 | 120 | .331 | 1.4 | 3B(74) -1.0, LF(23) -1.0, 2B(7) -0.5 | 2.7 |
| 2022 | LAD | MLB | 22 | 50 | 4 | 1 | 0 | 1 | 8 | 2 | 13 | 1 | 0 | .170/.200/.255 | 84 | .206 | 0.3 | 1B(8) 0, LF(7) -1.1 | -0.1 |
| 2023 DC | LAD | MLB | 23 | 381 | 43 | 18 | 2 | 8 | 40 | 33 | 67 | 9 | 1 | .240/.314/.370 | 94 | .279 | 1.0 | LF 0, 1B 0 | 0.9 |

*Comparables: Josh Vitters, Brandon Drury, Randal Grichuk*

**The Report:** The 23-year-old Cuban made his major-league debut last season after blazing through all six levels of the Dodgers' farm system in under four years. Along the way, he hit over .300 at every stop but one (.284 at High-A in 2019), earned the Dodgers' Minor League Player of the Year Award in 2021, was selected for the Futures Game and named PCL Top MLB Prospect in 2022 before finally capping last season with a call-up and a spot on the Dodgers' playoff roster. He did all this before his 23rd birthday thanks to an extremely high baseball IQ and an uncanny feel for the game.

In 113 games at Triple-A last season, Vargas slashed .304/.404/.511 with 53 extra-base hits, 17 home runs and 16 stolen bases. He did this while drawing 71 walks (14% walk rate) and striking out a mere 76 times (15% K-rate), demonstrating his plus feel for the strike zone and his professional offensive approach. Vargas uses the whole field with aplomb, driving the ball every which way and rarely over-swinging or compromising his swing decisions. Primarily a third baseman, Vargas expanded his defensive versatility last year, getting experience in left field, second base and first base, all positions that he may be asked to man for the Dodgers in 2023. Everywhere other than first base, he's fringe but playable with the glove.

**OFP:** 60 / The latest Dodgers Swiss Army knife

**Variance:** Low. Vargas is ready to find major-league success in 2023 and beyond.

**Jesse Roche's Fantasy Take:** As noted above, Vargas by most accounts thrived in Triple-A, flashing plus raw power and an advanced approach. While he went for a bunch of extra-base hits, it is reasonable to question how much over-the-fence power he'll get to—with just average EVs in Triple-A—denting his overall fantasy profile. There is a big difference between 30 and 20 home runs. Even still, Vargas can really hit. Plus, he has underrated speed (94th-percentile sprint speed), and he may provide some steals (17-for-22 last year). Vargas' proximity and well-rounded profile make him a top-20 dynasty prospect.

## 4  Gavin Stone  RHP    OFP: 60    ETA: 2023

Born: 10/15/98  Age: 24  Bats: R  Throws: R  Height: 6'1"  Weight: 175 lb.  Origin: Round 5, 2020 Draft (#159 overall)

| YEAR | TEAM | LVL | AGE | W | L | SV | G | GS | IP | H | HR | BB/9 | K/9 | K | GB% | BABIP | WHIP | ERA | DRA- | WARP |
|------|------|-----|-----|-----|-----|-----|-----|-----|-----|-----|-----|------|------|-----|------|-------|------|-----|------|------|
| 2021 | RC | A | 22 | 1 | 2 | 0 | 18 | 17 | 70 | 69 | 5 | 2.6 | 13.0 | 101 | 46.9% | .381 | 1.27 | 3.73 | 90 | 0.8 |
| 2021 | GL | A+ | 22 | 1 | 0 | 0 | 5 | 5 | 21 | 18 | 2 | 2.1 | 15.9 | 37 | 56.1% | .410 | 1.10 | 3.86 | 60 | 0.7 |
| 2022 | GL | A+ | 23 | 1 | 1 | 0 | 6 | 6 | 25 | 19 | 1 | 2.2 | 10.1 | 28 | 53.8% | .281 | 1.00 | 1.44 | 79 | 0.5 |
| 2022 | TUL | AA | 23 | 6 | 4 | 0 | 14 | 13 | 73¹ | 59 | 4 | 3.7 | 13.1 | 107 | 44.0% | .356 | 1.21 | 1.60 | 57 | 2.2 |
| 2022 | OKC | AAA | 23 | 2 | 1 | 0 | 6 | 6 | 23¹ | 14 | 1 | 3.1 | 12.7 | 33 | 46.0% | .265 | 0.94 | 1.16 | 71 | 0.5 |
| 2023 DC | LAD | MLB | 24 | 3 | 2 | 0 | 19 | 5 | 34 | 31 | 4 | 3.5 | 9.8 | 37 | 38.8% | .298 | 1.29 | 3.55 | 94 | 0.4 |

*Comparables: Erik Johnson, Rogelio Armenteros, Daniel Gossett*

**The Report:** Stone now has two seasons of minor-league dominance under his belt, and he was even better in the upper minors in 2022 than he was in A-ball the year before. His changeup might flat-out be the best in the minors. It tunnels well off the fastball with big sink and run, and when it isn't missing bats—which is a lot of the time—it induces weak groundball contact. It's an easy plus-plus for me visually, and if he can maintain the same kind of contact and contact suppression results with it in the majors, it would be hard to argue it isn't elite. Unsurprisingly, Stone throws the change almost as much as his fastball, which is mid-90s with excellent vertical action. His command of the fastball is less excellent, but he keeps it off the fat part of the barrel enough. He also has a pretty good slider which plays especially well off his change, showing similar depth, but taking a sharp left turn instead of fading off to the right.

There really isn't much to nitpick here. I will note that Stone was a small college reliever converted to the rotation. However, he threw 121 innings this year without issue, and the delivery is just fine for a starter. I suppose there's still a relatively short track record of this level of dominance, but it's not that short, and there's little reason to doubt the gains of the player and org are real. This will be a recurring theme throughout this list.

**OFP:** 60 / no. 3 starter

**Variance:** Low. Stone maybe doesn't have the pure upside in stuff that Miller has, but his change might be the single best pitch between the two of them. Both the fastball and slider should settle in as above-average, and he's close to the majors.

**Jesse Roche's Fantasy Take:** Despite heavy usage (40.2%), Stone's changeup still elicited 54.5% whiffs in Triple-A. Meanwhile, he is not dependent on his changeup, as his fastball and slider are both quality offerings. Stone is neck-and-neck with Miller as the top fantasy arm in this system, and they fall back-to-back in the dynasty rankings.

## 5  Nick Nastrini  RHP     OFP: 60     ETA: 2024

Born: 02/18/00   Age: 23   Bats: R   Throws: R   Height: 6'3"   Weight: 215 lb.   Origin: Round 4, 2021 Draft (#131 overall)

| YEAR | TEAM | LVL | AGE | W | L | SV | G | GS | IP | H | HR | BB/9 | K/9 | K | GB% | BABIP | WHIP | ERA | DRA- | WARP |
|---|---|---|---|---|---|---|---|---|---|---|---|---|---|---|---|---|---|---|---|---|
| 2021 | RC | A | 21 | 0 | 0 | 0 | 6 | 6 | 13 | 6 | 2 | 4.8 | 20.8 | 30 | 56.2% | .286 | 1.00 | 2.08 | 74 | 0.3 |
| 2022 | GL | A+ | 22 | 5 | 3 | 0 | 21 | 21 | 86¹ | 61 | 12 | 4.1 | 13.2 | 127 | 37.8% | .271 | 1.16 | 3.86 | 81 | 1.7 |
| 2022 | TUL | AA | 22 | 1 | 1 | 0 | 6 | 6 | 30¹ | 14 | 5 | 4.7 | 12.5 | 42 | 35.6% | .167 | 0.99 | 4.15 | 74 | 0.6 |
| 2023 non-DC | LAD | MLB | 23 | 3 | 3 | 0 | 58 | 0 | 50 | 44 | 8 | 5.0 | 10.9 | 61 | 34.4% | .297 | 1.44 | 4.54 | 116 | -0.1 |

*Comparables: Ryan Helsley, André Rienzo, Dylan Cease*

**The Report:** Yet another college arm who has seen big stuff gains with the Dodgers, Nastrini has a little less fastball than Miller, a little less present secondaries and similar command issues. But despite a bit more volatility than the arms ahead of him, he is yet another mid-rotation-or-better starting pitching prospect. Nastrini sits mid-90s, touching higher, with the fastball, and it has some decent ride up in the zone from his three-quarters slot. Like Stone, his changeup is his best secondary—although it's "merely" plus—it's a bit firmer, but has enough sink to get under bats and he sells it well with his arm speed. Both of Nastrini's breakers have above-average potential, with his mid-80s sweeping slider being the more advanced of the two.

There's a little bit more to nitpick here. Nastrini doesn't have the most fluid of deliveries, and there's some brute strength to it that impacts his command. He hasn't been all that hittable, but he walks a few too many guys, and when he's hit, he's hit hard. He's a higher variance arm than those above him and most of those below him as well. You'd rather have his upside than Ryan Pepiot's, but there's a decent-sized gap in terms of command and reliever risk between him and Stone.

**OFP:** 60 / no. 3 starter or first-division closer

**Variance:** High. Everything is a bit more volatile here. Nastrini gives up more dingers than you'd think given the stuff, throws fewer strikes than you'd like for a starter and thus is more likely to be a reliever than Stone or Miller. His OFP and upside are right there with them though, even if at this exact moment we are a bit less confident he gets there.

**Jesse Roche's Fantasy Take:** Nastrini had one of the highest whiff rates and the third-lowest batting average against (.178) of qualified starting pitchers in the minors last year. The upside is there for Nastrini to vault into the dynasty top 50 in short order should he show more command gains. However, the risk remains that his walk rate balloons further in the upper minors. That risk-reward tradeoff causes Nastrini to slot outside the dynasty top 100.

## 6  Dalton Rushing  C     OFP: 60     ETA: 2025

Born: 02/21/01   Age: 22   Bats: L   Throws: R   Height: 6'1"   Weight: 220 lb.   Origin: Round 2, 2022 Draft (#40 overall)

| YEAR | TEAM | LVL | AGE | PA | R | 2B | 3B | HR | RBI | BB | K | SB | CS | AVG/OBP/SLG | DRC+ | BABIP | BRR | DRP | WARP |
|---|---|---|---|---|---|---|---|---|---|---|---|---|---|---|---|---|---|---|---|
| 2022 | RC | A | 21 | 128 | 27 | 11 | 0 | 8 | 30 | 21 | 21 | 1 | 0 | .424/.539/.778 | 134 | .472 | 0.5 | C(17) 0.8, 1B(5) -0.5 | 1.0 |
| 2023 non-DC | LAD | MLB | 22 | 251 | 22 | 11 | 2 | 4 | 22 | 22 | 61 | 0 | 1 | .225/.302/.335 | 82 | .292 | -4.3 | C 0, 1B 0 | -0.1 |

*Comparables: Kyle Schwarber, Tim Federowicz, J.R. Towles*

**The Report:** Just what the Dodgers needed, another power-hitting catching prospect. Rushing destroyed the ball at Louisville his junior season, then was even better in his pro debut in the Cal League. He's able to consistently hit the ball hard in the air despite a pretty compact left-handed swing and is already making plus swing decisions in the minors. Rushing is out there trying to pull and lift, so there will be some in-zone holes that better pitchers can exploit—he's not going to hit .400 going forward, sorry—but he picks the right pitches to hack at generally, and I'd expect at least an average hit tool to go with plus or potentially plus-plus pop.

That kind of bat would make Rushing one of the best catching prospects in baseball if he was going to stick at catcher, and...well, he's one of the best catching prospects in baseball. He's not a plus defender by any means—although the arm strength certainly grades out there—but he's a perfectly fine, if a little stiff, with his receiving and is already built like the requisite fire hydrant. Rushing's track record is short, even considering his college years—he backed up Henry Davis and didn't play a ton his first two years with the Cardinals—but that's really the only thing keeping him from passing his former college teammate—among others—in the catching prospect ranks.

**OFP:** 60 / First-division backstop

**Variance:** High. Rushing hasn't caught much and 55/70 bats can become 45/55 bats over the long slog of a minor-league catching career. On the other hand, if we're more confident in those top-end offensive grades in a year or two, Rushing might look a lot like Will Smith—another recent Louisville catcher.

**Jesse Roche's Fantasy Take:** Normally, we recommend exercising caution approaching loud debuts of advanced college bats in late-season Low-A. Well, let's throw caution to the wind! Rushing absolutely ran roughshod over Low-A pitching, showcasing eye-opening exit velocities and an impeccable approach. It is the type of rare, meaningful small sample to which expectations should be adjusted. Overlook his second-round draft cost because Rushing is a first-round talent, a fast-rising borderline top-100 dynasty prospect and a top-15 option in FYPDs.

## 7 Michael Busch 2B OFP: 55 ETA: 2023

Born: 11/09/97   Age: 25   Bats: L   Throws: R   Height: 6'1"   Weight: 210 lb.   Origin: Round 1, 2019 Draft (#31 overall)

| YEAR | TEAM | LVL | AGE | PA | R | 2B | 3B | HR | RBI | BB | K | SB | CS | AVG/OBP/SLG | DRC+ | BABIP | BRR | DRP | WARP |
|------|------|-----|-----|-----|----|----|----|----|-----|----|-----|----|----|-------------|------|-------|------|-----|------|
| 2021 | TUL | AA | 23 | 495 | 84 | 27 | 1 | 20 | 67 | 70 | 129 | 2 | 3 | .267/.386/.484 | 112 | .337 | 0.4 | 2B(88) 7.2, 1B(11) -0.1 | 3.0 |
| 2022 | TUL | AA | 24 | 137 | 31 | 6 | 0 | 11 | 29 | 24 | 36 | 1 | 0 | .306/.445/.667 | 127 | .355 | 0.1 | 2B(26) -0.7, LF(2) 0.4 | 0.8 |
| 2022 | OKC | AAA | 24 | 504 | 87 | 32 | 0 | 21 | 79 | 50 | 131 | 3 | 2 | .266/.343/.480 | 98 | .327 | -2.4 | 2B(93) -3.6, LF(11) -0.2 | 0.7 |
| 2023 DC | LAD | MLB | 25 | 63 | 7 | 3 | 0 | 2 | 7 | 6 | 17 | 0 | 1 | .227/.307/.369 | 92 | .300 | -0.1 | 2B 0, LF 0 | 0.1 |

*Comparàbles: Mike Baxter, Kennys Vargas, Bruce Caldwell*

**The Report:** A 2019 first-rounder, Busch is now 25 years old and knocking on the major-league door. He spent the 2022 season at the two highest levels of the Dodgers' farm system, slashing a combined .274/.365/.516 with 70 extra-base hits—38 doubles and 32 homers. While he's prone to striking out, whiffing 167 times at a 26% clip last season, he also sees nearly four pitches per at-bat and posted a 12% walk rate. While he crowds the plate (nine HBPs in '22) and employs a slight pull bias in his approach, Busch is a well-rounded offensive contributor, capable of driving the ball to all fields and contributing from any spot in the lineup.

Busch's versatility also extends to the defensive side, where the second baseman by trade manned left field and first base at times last season. While he's not flashy with the leather, his athleticism and baseball IQ allow him to provide adequate defense at multiple positions. Busch may be most valuable as a super-utility player, capable of spelling teammates across the diamond while offering some firepower with the bat.

**OFP:** 55 / Above-average regular without a set position

**Variance:** Low. The 25-year-old Busch has 259 MiLB games under his belt, 249 of which were played at the Double-A and Triple-A levels. He plays the game with veteran savvy and has a strong grasp of who he is as a ballplayer.

**Jesse Roche's Fantasy Take:** I gushed about Busch in June, and much of what I wrote then remains true today. His age, defensive questions and uncertain role/opportunity this year add risk to a profile that may not have quite as much upside as other bat-first positionless players. However, Busch was quietly the Dodgers' minor-league leader in home runs, doing much of his damage in Triple-A. Indeed, he showcased above-average power—89.4-mph average exit velocity, 41% hard hit rate, and 104.1-mph, 90th-percentile exit velocity—with a leveraged swing to tap into it. Meanwhile, Busch makes enough contact (73%) to assuage concerns about his elevated strikeout rates. Ultimately, he may develop into a .260/25 bat with second-base eligibility. That'll do nicely. Busch remains a top-100 dynasty player regardless of what the naysayers say.

## 8 Nick Frasso RHP  OFP: 55  ETA: 2024

Born: 10/18/98  Age: 24  Bats: R  Throws: R  Height: 6'5"  Weight: 200 lb.  Origin: Round 4, 2020 Draft (#106 overall)

| YEAR | TEAM | LVL | AGE | W | L | SV | G | GS | IP | H | HR | BB/9 | K/9 | K | GB% | BABIP | WHIP | ERA | DRA- | WARP |
|------|------|-----|-----|---|---|----|----|----|------|----|----|------|------|----|-------|-------|------|------|------|------|
| 2022 | DUN | A | 23 | 0 | 0 | 0 | 7 | 7 | 25² | 13 | 0 | 2.8 | 14.7 | 42 | 40.4% | .277 | 0.82 | 0.70 | 75 | 0.7 |
| 2022 | VAN | A+ | 23 | 0 | 0 | 0 | 3 | 3 | 11 | 3 | 1 | 1.6 | 12.3 | 15 | 40.9% | .095 | 0.45 | 0.82 | 91 | 0.2 |
| 2022 | TUL | AA | 23 | 0 | 0 | 0 | 4 | 4 | 11² | 12 | 1 | 5.4 | 7.7 | 10 | 35.1% | .306 | 1.63 | 5.40 | 116 | -0.1 |
| 2023 non-DC | LAD | MLB | 24 | 3 | 3 | 0 | 58 | 0 | 50 | 46 | 6 | 3.9 | 9.2 | 51 | 37.4% | .297 | 1.36 | 3.97 | 105 | 0.1 |

*Comparables: Cale Coshow, Ryne Stanek, Brett Conine*

**The Report:** Not content with just developing their own Trackman-friendly arms, the Dodgers clearly targeted Frasso in the Mitch White/Alex de Jesus deal with the Jays. Frasso didn't pitch much in 2022 for either org—he was used very carefully coming off 2021 elbow surgery—but is yet another Dodgers pitching prospect with high-octane stuff. He's touched triple digits with the fastball this year, and it sits comfortably mid-to-upper-90s. Frasso's mechanics also make the heater difficult to pick up. He's tall and gangly, mostly legs, and his delivery features limbs flying every which way. The end result is that you think the fastball is going to come from a lower slot than it does, and the pitch shows good vertical angle as well. Frasso pairs the plus-plus fastball with a razorblade, upper-80s slider that isn't particularly much to look at, but just dives under bats at the last moment. His mid-80s change has plus potential as well.

He does have a fair bit of relief risk given that he's a 23-year-old with funky mechanics coming off elbow surgery. He does throw strikes despite the Ministry of Silly Walks delivery, but it's control over command. Like Stone, he was mostly a reliever in college, so there may be further gains to come if he can stay healthy and stick as a starter in 2023. That could make him one of the best pitching prospects in baseball this time next year. Or it just might make him the Dodgers' eighth-inning guy by August.

**OFP:** 55 / no. 3/4 starter or late-inning reliever

**Variance:** High. Frasso is even more likely to be a reliever than Nastrini, and he has a worrisome injury history as well. He also has the potential to be a Top 50 prospect in short order if he can throw 100 innings or so.

**Jesse Roche's Fantasy Take:** I love Frasso. I detailed his loud stuff in May. He ended his brief seven-start run in Low-A with a staggering 70% whiffs on his slider. Yes, Frasso was limited to just 54 innings coming off injury; yes, he never pitched more than four innings in a start; and, yes, he issued 10 walks in just 11 ⅔ innings in Double-A. All of this adds to his risk. But, man, his stuff "could make him one of the best pitching prospects in baseball this time next year," and I'm here for it. Frasso's high-upside/high-risk profile lands him in the dynasty top 200.

## 9 Andy Pages OF  OFP: 55  ETA: 2024

Born: 12/08/00  Age: 22  Bats: R  Throws: R  Height: 6'1"  Weight: 212 lb.  Origin: International Free Agent, 2018

| YEAR | TEAM | LVL | AGE | PA | R | 2B | 3B | HR | RBI | BB | K | SB | CS | AVG/OBP/SLG | DRC+ | BABIP | BRR | DRP | WARP |
|------|------|-----|-----|-----|----|----|----|----|-----|----|-----|----|----|----------------|------|-------|------|------------------------------|------|
| 2021 | GL | A+ | 20 | 538 | 96 | 25 | 1 | 31 | 88 | 77 | 132 | 6 | 3 | .265/.394/.539 | 139 | .305 | 1.4 | RF(83) 4.4, CF(27) -5.2 | 4.3 |
| 2022 | TUL | AA | 21 | 571 | 69 | 29 | 3 | 26 | 80 | 62 | 140 | 6 | 3 | .236/.336/.468 | 97 | .271 | 1.6 | RF(105) -0.3, CF(10) -0.6, LF(4) -0.3 | 2.7 |
| 2023 DC | LAD | MLB | 22 | 97 | 10 | 4 | 0 | 3 | 10 | 8 | 25 | 1 | 0 | .219/.301/.365 | 88 | .279 | -0.2 | CF 0, RF 0 | 0.1 |

*Comparables: Wladimir Balentien, Randal Grichuk, Franmil Reyes*

**The Report:** Pages' offensive profile was always going to be tested in Double-A, and the 2022 results were mixed. His extra-base hit rate fell a little bit, but he still smacked over 25 bombs with plenty of doubles, to boot. His K-rate was almost bang on the same, and while he hit a few more groundballs, he still has an elite fly-ball rate. However, staff reports on Pages questioned the strength of the swing decisions in Double-A and wondered whether he would stick in the outfield. He was an average runner on last year's report, but he's lost speed and gotten stiffer in his actions. If he's a first baseman or designated hitter, merely 25+ bombs might not be enough given the offensive bar at those spots.

**OFP:** 55 / Above-average slugger

**Variance:** Medium. Pages continues to tilt towards the three true outcomes, and he has the kind of raw power that will make that boom-or-bust profile play, but if he hits .240 and can't play right field, he's more of a second-division or fringe starter.

**Jesse Roche's Fantasy Take:** Pages' contact isn't always the prettiest, and he sure loves to see how high he can hit 'em at times. All those fly balls and pop-ups exact a heavy toll on his BABIP. Though, most importantly for our purposes, many do leave the yard. If he can tighten up his approach, Pages has similar offensive upside to Busch, with possibly a few more homers and a few less hits.

# 10    James Outman   OF     OFP: 55     ETA: Debuted in 2022

Born: 05/14/97   Age: 26   Bats: L   Throws: R   Height: 6'3"   Weight: 215 lb.   Origin: Round 7, 2018 Draft (#224 overall)

| YEAR | TEAM | LVL | AGE | PA | R | 2B | 3B | HR | RBI | BB | K | SB | CS | AVG/OBP/SLG | DRC+ | BABIP | BRR | DRP | WARP |
|------|------|-----|-----|-----|-----|-----|-----|-----|-----|-----|-----|-----|-----|-------------|------|-------|-----|-----|------|
| 2021 | GDD | WIN | 24 | 83 | 17 | 7 | 1 | 3 | 11 | 15 | 23 | 2 | 1 | .284/.422/.552 | | .390 | | | |
| 2021 | GL | A+ | 24 | 304 | 50 | 12 | 8 | 9 | 30 | 45 | 88 | 21 | 2 | .250/.385/.472 | 120 | .349 | 1.4 | CF(51) -6.5, RF(13) 1.6 | 1.4 |
| 2021 | TUL | AA | 24 | 187 | 40 | 9 | 1 | 9 | 24 | 18 | 51 | 2 | 2 | .289/.369/.518 | 98 | .368 | 0.7 | CF(36) 1.6, RF(3) -0.1 | 0.8 |
| 2022 | TUL | AA | 25 | 307 | 59 | 17 | 1 | 16 | 45 | 38 | 89 | 7 | 3 | .295/.394/.552 | 107 | .386 | 0.6 | CF(33) -0.1, LF(20) 0.2, RF(12) 1.4 | 1.4 |
| 2022 | OKC | AAA | 25 | 252 | 42 | 14 | 6 | 15 | 61 | 32 | 63 | 6 | 1 | .292/.390/.627 | 112 | .343 | -2.4 | RF(44) 2.9, CF(6) 1.1, LF(3) 0.5 | 1.2 |
| 2022 | LAD | MLB | 25 | 16 | 6 | 2 | 0 | 1 | 3 | 2 | 7 | 0 | 0 | .462/.563/.846 | 69 | 1.000 | 0.4 | LF(3) 0.2 | 0.0 |
| 2023 DC | LAD | MLB | 26 | 244 | 30 | 10 | 3 | 6 | 28 | 23 | 73 | 3 | 2 | .217/.302/.381 | 91 | .295 | -0.6 | LF 0, CF 0 | 0.4 |

Comparables: Brandon Boggs, Josh Rojas, Tyler Moore

**The Report:** Outman makes the Top 10 proper this year, although you could argue that he spiritually still fits the Factor on the Farm designation. It's a bit weird to have that two list cycles in a row, but the Dodgers are quietly one of the more conservative orgs in terms of player development tracks. Some of that is because there is rarely room in Chavez Ravine for anyone but the better prospects. And Los Angeles does not always give clear paths to everyday playing time for even their top guys—just ask Gavin Lux and Miguel Vargas—but Outman may be a Dodgers incumbent starting outfielder—at least as we go to press. He's certainly earned a look, crushing the upper minors to the tune of 31 home runs and a .978 OPS in 2022.

If the Dodgers' top 10 pitching prospects—and beyond—are united by analytically-friendly shape and spin profiles, the hitters are marked by hard contact in the air. Outman is no different. He's going to strike out more than you'd like—he swung over a lot of spin his late-season cup of coffee, but he's going to do enough damage when he does make contact to carry a corner outfield profile. That's the idea anyway.

**OFP:** 55 / Above-average outfielder

**Variance:** Medium. Outman has had upper-minors success with the stick. His swing decision and contact rates are good enough. His exit velocities are better than that, and his swing is optimized to hit the ball in the air. It should all work just fine, even if the swing-and-miss creeps up a bit more against major-league pitching, as you'd suspect it would.

**Jesse Roche's Fantasy Take:** Exit velocities, Outman! (A not-so-subtle Batman reference for those following along.) Indeed, he hits balls hard, including a 91.2-mph average exit velocity (POW!), a 45% hard-hit rate (BAM!), a 15% barrel rate (ZOK!), and a 106.9-mph, 90th-percentile exit velocity (CLUNK!). Outman does swing and miss plenty and struggles against lefties (.236/.325/.414), but he could immediately carve out a strong-side platoon role this year for the Dodgers. His potential short-term impact and power potential make him a top-200 dynasty prospect.

# Outside the Top Ten:

# 11   Ryan Pepiot   RHP

Born: 08/21/97   Age: 25   Bats: R   Throws: R   Height: 6'3"   Weight: 215 lb.   Origin: Round 3, 2019 Draft (#102 overall)

| YEAR | TEAM | LVL | AGE | W | L | SV | G | GS | IP | H | HR | BB/9 | K/9 | K | GB% | BABIP | WHIP | ERA | DRA- | WARP |
|------|------|-----|-----|-----|-----|-----|-----|-----|-----|-----|-----|------|-----|-----|------|-------|------|-----|------|------|
| 2021 | TUL | AA | 23 | 3 | 4 | 0 | 15 | 13 | 59² | 30 | 7 | 3.9 | 12.2 | 81 | 32.5% | .198 | 0.94 | 2.87 | 70 | 1.4 |
| 2021 | OKC | AAA | 23 | 2 | 5 | 0 | 11 | 9 | 41² | 54 | 12 | 4.5 | 9.9 | 46 | 40.6% | .350 | 1.80 | 7.13 | 99 | 0.2 |
| 2022 | OKC | AAA | 24 | 9 | 1 | 0 | 19 | 17 | 91¹ | 62 | 10 | 3.5 | 11.2 | 114 | 39.4% | .263 | 1.07 | 2.56 | 80 | 1.6 |
| 2022 | LAD | MLB | 24 | 3 | 0 | 0 | 9 | 7 | 36¹ | 26 | 6 | 6.7 | 10.4 | 42 | 26.1% | .244 | 1.46 | 3.47 | 110 | 0.2 |
| 2023 DC | LAD | MLB | 25 | 5 | 5 | 0 | 25 | 11 | 65.3 | 55 | 10 | 4.7 | 9.8 | 72 | 30.9% | .276 | 1.36 | 4.09 | 105 | 0.4 |

Comparables: Adbert Alzolay, John Gant, Alex Colomé

A couple years ago, Pepiot was a very similar prospect to the high-octane arms in the Top 10. A couple years later, he's made the majors, and his fastball/change combo still misses plenty of bats, yet his continued control and command issues make him feel like a 40th-percentile outcome for the current crop of top arms. In a way, this ranking isn't entirely fair. Pepiot is more likely to return major-league value in the short term, because he's already been in the majors. In another way, this ranking feels entirely fair. His stuff was never quite that loud. His fastball touches 95 with some regularity and has good spin and extension while riding up in the zone. It can miss bats up at the letters. But Pepiot's command wobbles means that it can be a bit too hittable when it drifts down towards batters' waists. The changeup is a plus, maybe even plus-plus pitch, no notes, but his slider got knocked around, and he doesn't really have the glove-side offering to complete the arsenal. Pepiot is going to continue to see major-league time, as even with the command and control issues, he's a potential above-average starter. However, he might find himself the odd man out in a year or two, or perhaps even in a different org by the time this Futures Guide goes to press.

## 12  Emmet Sheehan  RHP

Born: 11/15/99  Age: 23  Bats: R  Throws: R  Height: 6'5"  Weight: 220 lb.  Origin: Round 6, 2021 Draft (#192 overall)

| YEAR | TEAM | LVL | AGE | W | L | SV | G | GS | IP | H | HR | BB/9 | K/9 | K | GB% | BABIP | WHIP | ERA | DRA- | WARP |
|------|------|-----|-----|---|---|----|----|----|-----|----|----|------|------|-----|-------|-------|------|------|------|------|
| 2021 | RC | A | 21 | 3 | 0 | 0 | 5 | 0 | 13 | 10 | 2 | 3.5 | 18.7 | 27 | 50.0% | .400 | 1.15 | 4.15 | 77 | 0.3 |
| 2022 | GL | A+ | 22 | 7 | 2 | 0 | 18 | 12 | 63² | 41 | 2 | 4.0 | 14.3 | 101 | 41.1% | .310 | 1.08 | 2.83 | 71 | 1.6 |
| 2023 non-DC | LAD | MLB | 23 | 3 | 3 | 0 | 58 | 0 | 50 | 42 | 7 | 4.8 | 10.4 | 58 | 36.1% | .285 | 1.38 | 4.11 | 107 | 0.1 |

Comparables: Hector Perez, Mitch White, Jorge Alcala

At a certain point, I'm going to start to struggle to come up with new ways to describe this long list of Dodgers power arms. Sheehan was a sixth-round pick from Boston College who was not particularly dominant there and lost a chunk of his NCAA career to the pandemic. He fires mid-90s fastballs from a compact, deceptive arm action, and his three-quarters slot gives the pitch some uphill ride up in the zone. The sync and timing in his delivery can get out of sorts more often than you'd prefer, leading to issues with control and command. Further up this list, command issues have been a reasonable trade-off for the no-shit swing-and-miss stuff, but Sheehan's secondaries tend to land in the "above-average" range. It's an interesting and deep arsenal, no doubt. His change and slider both flash plus, but they are not quite as sharp or consistent as those you'll find from the Top 10 types. His 12-6 curve offers a different breaking ball look, but the mid-70s velocity can make it a bit of a lollipop at times. Overall, Sheehan is a little more likely to be a reliever and has a little less upside in the rotation, which makes him "only" one more OFP 55 in this staggeringly deep system.

## 13  Eddys Leonard  SS

Born: 11/10/00  Age: 22  Bats: R  Throws: R  Height: 5'11"  Weight: 195 lb.  Origin: International Free Agent, 2017

| YEAR | TEAM | LVL | AGE | PA | R | 2B | 3B | HR | RBI | BB | K | SB | CS | AVG/OBP/SLG | DRC+ | BABIP | BRR | DRP | WARP |
|------|------|-----|-----|-----|----|----|----|----|-----|----|-----|----|----|--------------|------|-------|------|-----|------|
| 2021 | RC | A | 20 | 308 | 59 | 19 | 2 | 14 | 57 | 34 | 74 | 6 | 2 | .295/.399/.544 | 122 | .362 | -0.1 | SS(32) -1.0, 2B(16) 1.2, 3B(9) 1.1 | 1.9 |
| 2021 | GL | A+ | 20 | 184 | 30 | 10 | 2 | 8 | 24 | 17 | 42 | 3 | 1 | .299/.375/.530 | 117 | .360 | -0.4 | 3B(15) -2.1, 2B(11) -1.1, CF(11) -1.1 | 0.4 |
| 2022 | GL | A+ | 21 | 566 | 80 | 32 | 4 | 15 | 61 | 45 | 119 | 4 | 4 | .264/.348/.435 | 109 | .317 | 1.3 | SS(104) -7.0, 2B(8) 0.9, 3B(7) -0.5 | 2.0 |
| 2023 non-DC | LAD | MLB | 22 | 251 | 21 | 12 | 2 | 4 | 23 | 16 | 65 | 2 | 1 | .222/.285/.336 | 77 | .294 | -3.2 | 2B 0, 3B 0 | -0.2 |

Comparables: Aderlin Rodríguez, Dawel Lugo, Aaron Cunningham

A 2017 IFA signing, the now 22-year-old Leonard slashed .264/.348/.435 with 51 extra-base hits and 15 home runs in the Midwest League last season. Primarily a shortstop, the 5-foot-11 and 195-pound Leonard is a quick-twitch athlete with pop to all fields. The free-swinger struck out at a 21% clip in 2022 while walking in just 8% of his plate appearances, revealing some work to do as he moves into the upper minors. Leonard's defensive versatility is a strength, as he played second base, third base and center field in addition to his natural shortstop position last season. His athleticism, range, receptive hands and above-average throwing arm make him a quality defender at any position on the field. Long-term, he profiles as a valuable super-utility player.

## 14  Jorbit Vivas  2B

Born: 03/09/01  Age: 22  Bats: L  Throws: R  Height: 5'10"  Weight: 171 lb.  Origin: International Free Agent, 2017

| YEAR | TEAM | LVL | AGE | PA | R | 2B | 3B | HR | RBI | BB | K | SB | CS | AVG/OBP/SLG | DRC+ | BABIP | BRR | DRP | WARP |
|------|------|-----|-----|-----|----|----|----|----|-----|----|----|----|----|--------------|------|-------|------|-----|------|
| 2021 | RC | A | 20 | 375 | 73 | 20 | 4 | 13 | 73 | 27 | 42 | 5 | 3 | .311/.389/.515 | 140 | .322 | -0.7 | 2B(38) -1.0, 3B(34) 2.6, SS(2) -0.1 | 3.0 |
| 2021 | GL | A+ | 20 | 102 | 12 | 6 | 0 | 1 | 14 | 13 | 13 | 3 | 1 | .318/.422/.424 | 121 | .361 | -0.7 | 3B(14) 0.0, 2B(9) -1.3 | 0.4 |
| 2022 | GL | A+ | 21 | 570 | 73 | 19 | 7 | 10 | 66 | 63 | 58 | 2 | 1 | .269/.374/.401 | 112 | .285 | -3.0 | 2B(91) 0.4, 3B(33) -1.9 | 2.0 |
| 2023 non-DC | LAD | MLB | 22 | 251 | 21 | 10 | 2 | 3 | 21 | 18 | 35 | 3 | 1 | .223/.293/.319 | 75 | .254 | -2.8 | 2B 0, 3B 0 | -0.3 |

Comparables: Travis Denker, Steve Lombardozzi, Jesmuel Valentín

Signed out of Venezuela in 2017, the now 21-year-old Vivas is a left-handed-hitting second baseman with an advanced hit tool and developing power. The 5-foot-10, 170-pound Vivas tallied 36 extra-base hits including 10 homers while walking more than he struck out last season (63 BB / 58 K). His BABIP (.285) dropped 45 points from the 2021 season's .330, suggesting he encountered some bad fortune among the vast amount of balls he puts in play. The athletically gifted Vivas can also play a nifty third base, providing valuable defensive versatility for a manager to utilize. While he's yet to play above the A-ball level, Vivas showcases an exciting all-around skill set and has a chance to develop into a quality infielder who can impact a game with his bat and glove.

## 15 Maddux Bruns   LHP
Born: 06/20/02   Age: 21   Bats: L   Throws: L   Height: 6'2"   Weight: 205 lb.   Origin: Round 1, 2021 Draft (#29 overall)

| YEAR | TEAM | LVL | AGE | W | L | SV | G | GS | IP | H | HR | BB/9 | K/9 | K | GB% | BABIP | WHIP | ERA | DRA- | WARP |
|---|---|---|---|---|---|---|---|---|---|---|---|---|---|---|---|---|---|---|---|---|
| 2022 | RC | A | 20 | 0 | 3 | 0 | 21 | 21 | 44¹ | 36 | 1 | 9.1 | 13.6 | 67 | 38.5% | .368 | 1.83 | 5.68 | 120 | -0.5 |
| 2023 non-DC | LAD | MLB | 21 | 3 | 3 | 0 | 58 | 0 | 50 | 47 | 8 | 7.6 | 10.4 | 58 | 34.3% | .305 | 1.79 | 6.05 | 144 | -0.9 |

*Comparables: William Woods, Kelvin Caceres, Ryan Wilson*

We've gotten through the pitching prospects who you might see in the bigs in 2023 or 2024, and now we move onto the next generation of "wicked stuff/not enough strikes yet" that dot all levels of this system.

We were aggressive in ranking Bruns last year despite notable control issues as an amateur. On one level, it was a bet that the Dodgers would get him to harness his stuff—which is every bit as good as those arms in the Top 10. Instead, he now ranks as the third-best pitching prospect from Los Angeles' 2021 draft class, as both Nastrini and Sheehan got their stuff jumps and threw "enough" strikes. So we weren't wrong about the Dodgers developmental prowess here; it just hasn't come together for Bruns yet. He has some devastating offerings when they're near the zone: mid-90s heat with ride and two potential plus breaking balls. They just haven't been near—or in—the zone enough.

The curve is the prettier of the two breakers, a lovely lefty 12-6 curve in the mid-70s, but Bruns can't really get it down and out of the zone as a swing-and-miss pitch. Although A-ball hitters will just give up on it as he drops it in for strikes, that may have less efficacy at higher levels. The slider may end up better in the end with its trendy 1-8 sweep. None of this matters if he can't throw strikes with the fastball, and he walked a batter per inning in the Cal League. It's not even the quantity of walks that would worry me as much as the quality, as Bruns can miss by so much that it would make Nuke LaLoosh blush. The stuff tantalizes and time is on his side for now, but there is a limit to how much stuff can cover for poor command and Bruns doesn't have the ratio quite right yet.

## 16 Jose Ramos   OF
Born: 01/01/01   Age: 22   Bats: R   Throws: R   Height: 6'1"   Weight: 200 lb.   Origin: International Free Agent, 2018

| YEAR | TEAM | LVL | AGE | PA | R | 2B | 3B | HR | RBI | BB | K | SB | CS | AVG/OBP/SLG | DRC+ | BABIP | BRR | DRP | WARP |
|---|---|---|---|---|---|---|---|---|---|---|---|---|---|---|---|---|---|---|---|
| 2021 | DOD | ROK | 20 | 68 | 13 | 6 | 0 | 3 | 15 | 7 | 14 | 1 | 0 | .383/.456/.633 | | .465 | | | |
| 2021 | RC | A | 20 | 220 | 30 | 18 | 3 | 8 | 44 | 16 | 57 | 1 | 4 | .313/.377/.559 | 108 | .398 | -1.6 | RF(44) 3.4 | 1.1 |
| 2022 | RC | A | 21 | 138 | 20 | 3 | 3 | 6 | 23 | 18 | 36 | 2 | 0 | .277/.391/.518 | 109 | .342 | 0.7 | RF(19) 0.4, CF(11) 0.2 | 0.8 |
| 2022 | GL | A+ | 21 | 407 | 63 | 19 | 3 | 19 | 74 | 39 | 133 | 2 | 0 | .240/.322/.467 | 102 | .322 | 0.1 | CF(43) -0.0, RF(41) 1.1 | 1.6 |
| 2023 non-DC | LAD | MLB | 22 | 251 | 22 | 11 | 2 | 4 | 24 | 17 | 88 | 2 | 1 | .225/.286/.346 | 79 | .342 | -3.5 | LF 0, CF 0 | -0.3 |

*Comparables: Marcell Ozuna, Eduardo Diaz, Jamie Romak*

Signed by the Dodgers as an international free agent in 2018, the now 21-year-old Panamanian outfielder slugged 25 homers across two levels of the Dodgers farm system last season. At 6-foot-1 and 200 pounds, Ramos' lean build and long limbs help him generate leverage and power to all fields. His 31% strikeout rate alludes to his aggressive, free-swinging approach at the plate. While he does profile as a power-hitting run producer, improved pitch selection would improve his quality of contact and place him in more favorable hitting counts. Defensively, Ramos is capable of playing all three outfield positions, although his strong throwing arm makes right field the likely destination.

## 17 Alex Freeland   MI
Born: 08/24/01   Age: 21   Bats: S   Throws: R   Height: 6'2"   Weight: 200 lb.   Origin: Round 3, 2022 Draft (#105 overall)

| YEAR | TEAM | LVL | AGE | PA | R | 2B | 3B | HR | RBI | BB | K | SB | CS | AVG/OBP/SLG | DRC+ | BABIP | BRR | DRP | WARP |
|---|---|---|---|---|---|---|---|---|---|---|---|---|---|---|---|---|---|---|---|
| 2022 | RC | A | 20 | 36 | 7 | 1 | 0 | 3 | 6 | 2 | 11 | 2 | 0 | .313/.389/.625 | 97 | .389 | 0.5 | SS(6) -0.1, 2B(2) 0.3, 3B(1) -0.0 | 0.2 |
| 2023 non-DC | LAD | MLB | 21 | 251 | 21 | 10 | 2 | 4 | 23 | 15 | 65 | 4 | 1 | .220/.273/.334 | 70 | .287 | -2.4 | 2B 0, 3B 0 | -0.4 |

Freeland was the Dodgers' third-round pick this year as a draft-eligible sophomore out of Central Florida. He has a well-balanced offensive skill set with a more fluid stroke than some of the optimized pull-side and lift hitters above, but flashes potential average pop nonetheless. Primarily a shortstop in college, he'll likely move around the infield a bit in the pros and is a better fit for second or third as his range and actions are a bit light for the six. I do think it's possible Freeland takes a step forward with the bat in 2023 because /gestures at the rest of the system/, but the OFP here is more average than above.

## 18 Ronan Kopp  LHP

Born: 07/29/02   Age: 20   Bats: L   Throws: L   Height: 6'7"   Weight: 250 lb.   Origin: Round 12, 2021 Draft (#372 overall)

| YEAR | TEAM | LVL | AGE | W | L | SV | G | GS | IP | H | HR | BB/9 | K/9 | K | GB% | BABIP | WHIP | ERA | DRA- | WARP |
|------|------|-----|-----|---|---|----|----|----|------|----|----|------|------|-----|------|-------|------|------|------|------|
| 2022 | RC | A | 19 | 5 | 2 | 1 | 24 | 9 | 57² | 36 | 3 | 5.8 | 15.9 | 102 | 49.1% | .308 | 1.27 | 2.81 | 71 | 1.1 |
| 2023 non-DC | LAD | MLB | 20 | 3 | 3 | 0 | 58 | 0 | 50 | 43 | 8 | 5.9 | 10.2 | 57 | 35.5% | .281 | 1.51 | 4.71 | 118 | -0.2 |

Comparables: Joe Ortiz, John Lamb, Melvin Jimenez

Kopp was a 12th-round JuCo pick in 2021 and only got slot, but this is not typical Day 3 stuff. The 6-foot-7 southpaw has a funky, two-stage delivery including a series of glove flutters, and consequently he can struggle to finish his pitches, especially the fastball. When he's not missing arm-side and up, the heater has average velocity and it's a rough angle/release point, especially for his fellow lefties. If Kopp can get ahead in the count, he unleashes two potential plus breakers. He's much more consistent finishing the curve and slider, both of which show 1-7 shape with the mid-80s slider showing a bit more depth and sharpness. The curve is 10 mph slower, but just keep running glove-side for what seems like hours. The command and control here is a real problem, as Kopp can just completely implode at any time, but the breaking stuff is good enough to keep him on our radar for a while. Hopefully, it will be long enough for him to get those BB/9 marks more in the 4-5 range like his compatriots in the Top 10.

## 19 Accimias Morales  RHP

Born: 09/13/04   Age: 18   Bats: R   Throws: R   Height: 6'5"   Weight: 190 lb.   Origin: International Free Agent, 2022

| YEAR | TEAM | LVL | AGE | W | L | SV | G | GS | IP | H | HR | BB/9 | K/9 | K | GB% | BABIP | WHIP | ERA | DRA- | WARP |
|------|------|-----|-----|---|---|----|----|----|------|----|----|------|------|-----|------|-------|------|------|------|------|
| 2022 | DSL LADB | ROK | 17 | 1 | 2 | 0 | 12 | 12 | 36² | 38 | 0 | 0.7 | 5.9 | 24 | 52.0% | .306 | 1.12 | 3.19 | | |

Signed last January out of Venezuela, Morales is a tall righty with a low release height and an analytically friendly spin axis on his low-90s fastball. He also has a feel for spin generally, although the arsenal doesn't miss bats yet. Unlike every other arm on this list, he does throw a lot of strikes. Yeah it's the DSL, but that's still gonna stand out here. Morales is a long-term project with some buzz and plenty of upside, but there is some chance the Dodgers have already optimized his stuff, and it's not on the level of the rest of these arms.

## 20 Andre Jackson  RHP

Born: 05/01/96   Age: 27   Bats: R   Throws: R   Height: 6'3"   Weight: 210 lb.   Origin: Round 12, 2017 Draft (#370 overall)

| YEAR | TEAM | LVL | AGE | W | L | SV | G | GS | IP | H | HR | BB/9 | K/9 | K | GB% | BABIP | WHIP | ERA | DRA- | WARP |
|------|------|-----|-----|---|---|----|----|----|------|----|----|------|------|-----|------|-------|------|------|------|------|
| 2021 | TUL | AA | 25 | 3 | 2 | 0 | 15 | 13 | 63¹ | 46 | 12 | 2.8 | 10.7 | 75 | 31.8% | .239 | 1.04 | 3.27 | 82 | 1.0 |
| 2021 | OKC | AAA | 25 | 2 | 3 | 0 | 6 | 5 | 26¹ | 26 | 6 | 3.1 | 7.9 | 23 | 35.4% | .263 | 1.33 | 5.13 | 99 | 0.1 |
| 2021 | LAD | MLB | 25 | 0 | 1 | 1 | 3 | 0 | 11² | 10 | 1 | 4.6 | 7.7 | 10 | 26.5% | .290 | 1.37 | 2.31 | 100 | 0.1 |
| 2022 | OKC | AAA | 26 | 2 | 7 | 1 | 21 | 19 | 75² | 68 | 10 | 7.3 | 9.0 | 76 | 47.0% | .280 | 1.70 | 5.00 | 86 | 1.0 |
| 2022 | LAD | MLB | 26 | 0 | 0 | 1 | 4 | 0 | 9² | 9 | 0 | 3.7 | 8.4 | 9 | 48.3% | .321 | 1.34 | 1.86 | 93 | 0.1 |
| 2023 DC | LAD | MLB | 27 | 2 | 3 | 0 | 24 | 3 | 24.7 | 25 | 4 | 5.1 | 8.5 | 24 | 37.7% | .306 | 1.59 | 5.29 | 129 | -0.2 |

Comparables: Jefry Rodriguez, Adam Plutko, Mike Clevinger

Jackson struggled as a starter in Triple-A last season, but once again looked like a solid multi-inning 'pen option during a September cameo. His plus change is a real weapon in relief, especially when he is landing his mid-90s fastball at the top of the zone to mess with the batter's eye level. Command and control have been an issue as a starter, and you can't just hand-wave those in the pen, but Jackson should get a shot to be a more significant part of the Dodgers' bullpen this season.

## 21  Peter Heubeck   RHP

Born: 07/22/02   Age: 20   Bats: R   Throws: R   Height: 6'3"   Weight: 170 lb.   Origin: Round 3, 2021 Draft (#101 overall)

| YEAR | TEAM | LVL | AGE | W | L | SV | G | GS | IP | H | HR | BB/9 | K/9 | K | GB% | BABIP | WHIP | ERA | DRA- | WARP |
|---|---|---|---|---|---|---|---|---|---|---|---|---|---|---|---|---|---|---|---|---|
| 2022 | RC | A | 19 | 0 | 1 | 0 | 15 | 13 | 31² | 22 | 7 | 7.1 | 11.9 | 42 | 36.1% | .231 | 1.48 | 7.39 | 104 | 0.0 |
| 2023 non-DC | LAD | MLB | 20 | 3 | 3 | 0 | 58 | 0 | 50 | 51 | 9 | 6.2 | 9.0 | 50 | 33.3% | .303 | 1.70 | 5.95 | 144 | -0.9 |

*Comparables: Henry Henry, Edgar García, Melvin Jimenez*

The Dodgers' second-rounder in 2021, Heubeck is the final Michael Keaton in the *Multiplicity* that is the Dodgers' top pitching prospects. His fastball is mostly low-90s coming from a higher slot with good ride. He has a big breaking curveball that he can get down and out of the zone, but because of the big shape, it's not always an effective chase pitch. Like Bruns, he can drop it in with more 12-6 shape and get A-ball hitters to freeze, but he has the longest way to go of the endless interesting arms we've covered thus far.

## 22  Yeiner Fernandez   C/2B

Born: 09/19/02   Age: 20   Bats: R   Throws: R   Height: 5'9"   Weight: 170 lb.   Origin: International Free Agent, 2019

| YEAR | TEAM | LVL | AGE | PA | R | 2B | 3B | HR | RBI | BB | K | SB | CS | AVG/OBP/SLG | DRC+ | BABIP | BRR | DRP | WARP |
|---|---|---|---|---|---|---|---|---|---|---|---|---|---|---|---|---|---|---|---|
| 2021 | DOD | ROK | 18 | 157 | 24 | 11 | 1 | 2 | 15 | 10 | 27 | 1 | 3 | .319/.382/.454 | | .381 | | | |
| 2021 | RC | A | 18 | 34 | 4 | 1 | 0 | 1 | 10 | 2 | 3 | 0 | 0 | .516/.559/.645 | 120 | .556 | 0.1 | C(5) -0.9 | 0.1 |
| 2022 | RC | A | 19 | 423 | 76 | 16 | 2 | 10 | 68 | 46 | 55 | 3 | 2 | .292/.383/.430 | 112 | .318 | -3.4 | C(62) -11.1, 2B(17) 0.6 | 0.6 |
| 2023 non-DC | LAD | MLB | 20 | 251 | 19 | 9 | 1 | 2 | 19 | 17 | 53 | 1 | 0 | .210/.274/.291 | 62 | .263 | -4.2 | C 0, 2B 0 | -0.6 |

Fernandez is a fun little prospect, but perhaps more fun than good. His catching game is raw, he's a stabby framer, especially lower in the zone, and he may be a bit undersized for regular work behind the plate. His arm strength is fine, but his actions and throwing aren't great and he will one-hop his 1.9 throws. Fernandez is fine at second base, if a bit mechanical there too. At the plate, he's an intriguing hitter with a knack for contact and a bit of sneaky pop that I'll want to see outside the friendly confines of the Cal League before he enters the Top 20 of a very deep system.

## 23  Carlos Duran   RHP

Born: 07/30/01   Age: 21   Bats: R   Throws: R   Height: 6'7"   Weight: 230 lb.   Origin: International Free Agent, 2018

| YEAR | TEAM | LVL | AGE | W | L | SV | G | GS | IP | H | HR | BB/9 | K/9 | K | GB% | BABIP | WHIP | ERA | DRA- | WARP |
|---|---|---|---|---|---|---|---|---|---|---|---|---|---|---|---|---|---|---|---|---|
| 2021 | RC | A | 19 | 2 | 4 | 0 | 20 | 18 | 73² | 81 | 9 | 2.9 | 13.3 | 109 | 48.2% | .383 | 1.43 | 5.25 | 97 | 0.5 |
| 2021 | GL | A+ | 19 | 0 | 1 | 0 | 2 | 2 | 7¹ | 10 | 0 | 7.4 | 7.4 | 6 | 38.5% | .400 | 2.18 | 8.59 | 119 | 0.0 |
| 2022 | GL | A+ | 20 | 1 | 3 | 0 | 14 | 13 | 48² | 43 | 6 | 4.4 | 12.6 | 68 | 41.0% | .336 | 1.38 | 4.25 | 90 | 0.7 |
| 2023 non-DC | LAD | MLB | 21 | 3 | 3 | 0 | 58 | 0 | 50 | 51 | 8 | 4.4 | 8.9 | 49 | 36.6% | .305 | 1.50 | 5.01 | 126 | -0.4 |

Offseason Tommy John surgery will put Duran on the shelf for all of 2023, and less importantly, cost him 10 spots or so on this list. When healthy, Duran showed three potential above-average pitches in his fastball, slider and change. The fastball can touch 95 with big run, while his low-80s slider flashes plus depth, and his changeup can show power fade. Duran dealt with arm issues in 2022 even before the TJ, and hopefully it gives him a clean start in 2024. He was a potential mid-rotation starter before the injury, but obviously we won't know much more for a while.

## Top Talents 25 and Under (as of 4/1/2023):

1. Dustin May, RHP
2. Gavin Lux, IF
3. Diego Cartaya, C
4. Bobby Miller, RHP
5. Miguel Vargas, IF
6. Gavin Stone, RHP
7. Nick Nastrini, RHP
8. Dalton Rushing, C
9. Michael Busch, 2B/OF
10. Nick Frasso, RHP

The Dodgers have one of the deepest systems in baseball and should get an influx of young talent in 2023, but their roster did tilt towards the veteran side in 2022. I don't have strong feelings about May versus Lux at the top. May was coming off Tommy John surgery and wasn't super sharp in his return, also dealing with some back tightness at the end of the season. Lux meanwhile didn't hit for any power last season—backed up by pedestrian exit velocities and a few too many groundballs—and his defensive acumen can vary a bit based on your metric of choice. May gets the nod here on upside, although he's the far more volatile player for the next few seasons.

Brusdar Graterol is the other eligible name of note, and he's carved out a nice little career as a useful reliever who doesn't miss as many bats as you'd think he would, given the 100-mph fastball and 90-mph slider. He's a close call with Frasso for the 10th spot, but let's give it to the guy who gets whiffs, even if he's still a bit away from the majors.

# Miami Marlins

## The State of the System:

Inside every Marlins org, there are two wolves: One wolf is a pitching prospect who has less-than-ideal fastball shape and is probably hurt at the moment. The other is a hitter who makes a lot of contact in the zone but has positional and power questions.

## The Top Ten:

**1** **Eury Pérez  RHP**          OFP: 70          ETA: Late 2023/Early 2024

Born: 04/15/03   Age: 20   Bats: R   Throws: R   Height: 6'8"   Weight: 220 lb.   Origin: International Free Agent, 2019

| YEAR | TEAM | LVL | AGE | W | L | SV | G | GS | IP | H | HR | BB/9 | K/9 | K | GB% | BABIP | WHIP | ERA | DRA- | WARP |
|------|------|-----|-----|---|---|----|----|----|-----|----|----|------|------|-----|-------|-------|------|------|------|------|
| 2021 | JUP | A | 18 | 2 | 3 | 0 | 15 | 15 | 56 | 32 | 2 | 3.4 | 13.2 | 82 | 36.0% | .268 | 0.95 | 1.61 | 78 | 1.4 |
| 2021 | BEL | A+ | 18 | 1 | 2 | 0 | 5 | 5 | 22 | 11 | 5 | 2.0 | 10.6 | 26 | 37.7% | .133 | 0.73 | 2.86 | 92 | 0.3 |
| 2022 | PNS | AA | 19 | 3 | 3 | 0 | 17 | 17 | 75 | 62 | 9 | 3.0 | 12.7 | 106 | 41.7% | .319 | 1.16 | 4.08 | 79 | 1.6 |
| 2023 DC | MIA | MLB | 20 | 1 | 2 | 0 | 5 | 5 | 21.7 | 21 | 3 | 3.7 | 9.1 | 22 | 33.8% | .297 | 1.36 | 4.31 | 113 | 0.1 |

*Comparables: Dylan Bundy, Julio Teheran, Francis Martes*

**The Report:** The 19-year-old Pérez has taken another step forward after his breakout in 2021 and is now one of the best pitching prospects in baseball. Listed at 6-foot-8, but likely a couple inches taller than that nowadays, he'd be one of the tallest starting pitchers in baseball history. And despite a telephone-pole frame that is 70% legs, he consistently keeps his full-windup delivery compact and on-line. Once the ball leaves his hand, Pérez has four different offerings that can all generate swings-and-misses.

Pérez's fastball is firm and steep, sitting mid-90s and touching higher. He's added a slider look to his potential plus slurvy—in a good way—curveball. The slide piece is still developing but flashes good depth. His changeup already flashes plus, and given the org he is in, you'd expect it to get there. Pérez spent his age-19 season in Double-A and struck out over a third of the batters he faced. He's about as perfect a pitching prospect as you could design, with four potential plus major-league offerings with advanced command for his age and experience level.

He's also a pitching prospect, so he missed time in 2022 with shoulder fatigue. And yeah, if you were designing a pitching prospect, they'd be built more like Gerrit Cole and less like Thurston Moore. So it's fair to quibble with how well Pérez will hold up under a more onerous workload on the mound. The stuff, however, leaves little room to quibble, only marvel.

**OFP:** 70 / Top-of-the-rotation starter

**Variance:** High. The Marlins already have a tall and somewhat slender ace at the top of their rotation, but we are a long ways away from seeing that kind of durability from Pérez. He's also coming off a shoulder issue, so...

**Jesse Roche's Fantasy Take:** The sky may not even be the limit for skyscraper Pérez. His high-spin fastball flashes elite, upper-90s velocity and elite, bat-missing shape. As the youngest pitcher in the Southern League, Pérez finished second in strikeout rate (34.1%) and first in K-BB% (26.0%). Despite a full season in Double-A, however, he may not arrive this year, especially given the Marlins' pitching depth. Another year building innings, maintaining health and sharpening his secondaries and command in the upper minors is the next step. Pérez is arguably the no. 2 fantasy pitching prospect and a top-20 dynasty prospect.

## 2   Max Meyer   RHP          OFP: 60        ETA: Debuted in 2022
Born: 03/12/99   Age: 24   Bats: L   Throws: R   Height: 6'0"   Weight: 196 lb.   Origin: Round 1, 2020 Draft (#3 overall)

| YEAR | TEAM | LVL | AGE | W | L | SV | G | GS | IP | H | HR | BB/9 | K/9 | K | GB% | BABIP | WHIP | ERA | DRA- | WARP |
|---|---|---|---|---|---|---|---|---|---|---|---|---|---|---|---|---|---|---|---|---|
| 2021 | PNS | AA | 22 | 6 | 3 | 0 | 20 | 20 | 101 | 84 | 7 | 3.6 | 10.1 | 113 | 52.7% | .304 | 1.23 | 2.41 | 91 | 1.5 |
| 2021 | JAX | AAA | 22 | 0 | 1 | 0 | 2 | 2 | 10 | 6 | 1 | 1.8 | 15.3 | 17 | 47.4% | .278 | 0.80 | 0.90 | 72 | 0.3 |
| 2022 | JAX | AAA | 23 | 3 | 4 | 0 | 12 | 12 | 58 | 39 | 5 | 2.9 | 10.1 | 65 | 51.0% | .246 | 1.00 | 3.72 | 67 | 1.8 |
| 2022 | MIA | MLB | 23 | 0 | 1 | 0 | 2 | 2 | 6 | 7 | 2 | 3.0 | 9.0 | 6 | 44.4% | .313 | 1.50 | 7.50 | 106 | 0.0 |
| 2023 DC | MIA | MLB | 24 | 2 | 2 | 0 | 8 | 8 | 32.3 | 31 | 4 | 3.5 | 8.5 | 30 | 42.2% | .296 | 1.34 | 3.90 | 104 | 0.2 |

*Comparables: Shane Bieber, Erik Johnson, Daniel Mengden*

**The Report:** Meyer's slider might have been the best single pitch in the 2020 draft. It's arguably been the best pitch in the minors the last two years. He can throw it almost as hard as Jacob deGrom's and it has almost a foot more vertical break. It's—to use the technical scouting term—disgusting. The Marlins, being the Marlins, have helped him to develop a plus change as well.

You'll have noted by now that we usually lead off pitcher blurbs with a discussion of the fastball. It's called "the old number one" for a reason after all. Meyer can certainly pop the catcher's mitt. He sits around 95, but the pitch is very pedestrian in both shape and command, and his short stature and traditional high-three-quarters slot gives him little added approach angle or extension. Major-league hitters—and even those in the upper minors—can square that and have a bit more than you'd like. The secondaries are good enough that Meyer can stay away from his fastball—he only threw it 40% of the time in his two major-league outings—but usually when we suggest throwing your best pitches the most, one of them is the heater.

You'll also have noted by now that we buried the lede: Meyer underwent Tommy John surgery last August and will miss all of the 2023 season. Given the elbow scar, fastball issues and shorter, slighter frame, he may be eventually ticketed for the bullpen, where he can throw the slider and change at even more of an outsized rate. He'd likely be a top-tier closer—that was not an uncommon thought coming out of the 2020 draft—but the top-of-the-rotation talent will hopefully still tantalize once he's back on the bump in 2024.

**OFP:** 60 / no. 3 starter or first-division closer

**Variance:** High. Any Tommy John surgery is going to significantly affect a pitcher's risk factors. While the surgery is common, every recovery is a bit different. And a healthy Meyer had some unanswered questions about how his fastball would play against a major-league lineup multiple times through the order.

**Jesse Roche's Fantasy Take:** Regardless of role, Meyer should be a solid fantasy performer. His slider lives up to the hype, and it is a true bat-missing out-pitch that he leans heavily on, including 46.1% over his two MLB starts. His fastball's shape, however, is akin to the natural cutting action of the fastballs of Andre Pallante, Garrett Richards or Antonio Senzatela, none of which miss bats. As such, Meyer may not rack up as many strikeouts as you'd expect. Still, his slider-centric arsenal should find success in the modern, slider-centric game. Meyer sits just outside the top-100 dynasty prospects, and likely will remain there for most of 2023 or until reports of the quality of his post-TJS stuff surface.

## 3   Jose Salas   IF          OFP: 55        ETA: 2025
Born: 04/26/03   Age: 20   Bats: S   Throws: R   Height: 6'2"   Weight: 191 lb.   Origin: International Free Agent, 2019

| YEAR | TEAM | LVL | AGE | PA | R | 2B | 3B | HR | RBI | BB | K | SB | CS | AVG/OBP/SLG | DRC+ | BABIP | BRR | DRP | WARP |
|---|---|---|---|---|---|---|---|---|---|---|---|---|---|---|---|---|---|---|---|
| 2021 | MRL | ROK | 18 | 107 | 14 | 10 | 0 | 1 | 11 | 11 | 23 | 8 | 5 | .370/.458/.511 | | .485 | | | |
| 2021 | JUP | A | 18 | 123 | 12 | 4 | 0 | 1 | 8 | 11 | 28 | 6 | 0 | .250/.333/.315 | 99 | .325 | 2.1 | SS(25) -2.6 | 0.3 |
| 2022 | JUP | A | 19 | 257 | 40 | 13 | 3 | 5 | 24 | 23 | 54 | 15 | 1 | .267/.355/.421 | 119 | .327 | -2.3 | SS(25) -0.3, 3B(16) 1.3, 2B(12) -0.8 | 1.1 |
| 2022 | BEL | A+ | 19 | 217 | 29 | 7 | 1 | 4 | 17 | 20 | 41 | 18 | 0 | .230/.319/.340 | 99 | .274 | 2.8 | SS(16) 0.7, 2B(14) -1.3, 3B(11) 0.2 | 0.8 |
| 2023 non-DC | MIN | MLB | 20 | 251 | 20 | 10 | 2 | 3 | 20 | 16 | 58 | 8 | 1 | .215/.274/.310 | 64 | .276 | -1.1 | 2B 0, 3B 0 | -0.4 |

*Comparables: Ketel Marte, Jonathan Araúz, Cole Tucker*

**The Report:** The Marlins' major signing of their 2019 IFA class, Salas has beaten an aggressive path through their system, making it to High-A in just his second pro season. The switch-hitting infielder has an easy, compact swing and good wrists. He's pretty level at present, but shows a bit more fluidity and loft from the left-handed batter's box—where most of his game power resides at present. Salas' raw power flashes here and there—every once in a while he will sting one despite the short stroke—but he should grow into average pop eventually.

In the field, he played a fair bit of second and third—often in deference to Nasim Nuñez's superior shortstop glove—and his hands and arm can be a bit more inconsistent than you'd prefer for a full-throated shortstop projection. He's also just an average runner so he's not the rangiest infielder. Salas will likely end up a better fit for second than short, but his actions and footwork around the bag are solid. The argument for him as an above-average regular is more on the broad base of skills than a loud tools projection, so you'd like to see the minor-league numbers start looking a little more garish on his player card. Salas will be more prospect-age appropriate for the Midwest League in 2023. It's time to see that potential plus hit tool shine.

**OFP:** 55 / Above-average infielder

**Variance:** High. Salas has gotten good on-field reports and held his own as one of the younger players in his leagues the last two seasons, but he may lack a carrying tool and will have to impact the ball a bit better in the upper minors.

**Jesse Roche's Fantasy Take:** Salas, a standout in June, earned a promotion to High-A in late June after a torrid stretch in Low-A at just 19 years old. Following a similarly hot first 10 games in High-A, he hit a wall, failing to make much impactful contact and hitting just .192/.292/.279 over his final 38 games. His late-season struggles can be forgiven due to a young bat adjusting to a new level. Generally, there is a lot to like. Salas has a "potential plus hit tool" with advanced bat-to-ball ability from both sides of the plate, an improving plate approach, and emerging power. Further, he has advanced base-stealing instincts despite average speed, evidenced by a 97.1% success rate stealing bases last year. How his power develops will determine his ultimate upside, and 20/20 potential is not out of reach. Salas is a top-200 dynasty prospect.

## 4 Dax Fulton LHP   OFP: 55   ETA: 2024

Born: 10/16/01   Age: 21   Bats: L   Throws: L   Height: 6'7"   Weight: 225 lb.   Origin: Round 2, 2020 Draft (#40 overall)

| YEAR | TEAM | LVL | AGE | W | L | SV | G | GS | IP | H | HR | BB/9 | K/9 | K | GB% | BABIP | WHIP | ERA | DRA- | WARP |
|---|---|---|---|---|---|---|---|---|---|---|---|---|---|---|---|---|---|---|---|---|
| 2021 | JUP | A | 19 | 2 | 4 | 0 | 15 | 14 | 58² | 50 | 3 | 4.6 | 10.1 | 66 | 51.6% | .313 | 1.36 | 4.30 | 109 | 0.3 |
| 2021 | BEL | A+ | 19 | 0 | 1 | 0 | 5 | 5 | 19² | 21 | 3 | 3.7 | 8.2 | 18 | 56.9% | .327 | 1.47 | 5.49 | 103 | 0.2 |
| 2022 | BEL | A+ | 20 | 5 | 6 | 0 | 20 | 20 | 97¹ | 104 | 6 | 3.2 | 11.1 | 120 | 47.7% | .384 | 1.43 | 4.07 | 83 | 1.8 |
| 2022 | PNS | AA | 20 | 1 | 1 | 0 | 4 | 3 | 21 | 9 | 2 | 3.0 | 12.9 | 30 | 66.7% | .175 | 0.76 | 2.57 | 76 | 0.5 |
| 2023 non-DC | MIA | MLB | 21 | 3 | 3 | 0 | 58 | 0 | 50 | 52 | 6 | 4.3 | 8.2 | 46 | 41.6% | .315 | 1.53 | 4.84 | 122 | -0.3 |

*Comparables: Arodys Vizcaíno, David Holmberg, Jacob Turner*

**The Report:** Fulton was one of the few healthy pitching prospects for Miami in 2022, but it was an uneven year despite the strikeout spike. He's another Marlins arm where we won't be leading with the fastball, because his big hook is the headline story here, a 1-7 breaker that he can move around the zone for strikes and also get whiffs with it boring down and under barrels. Fulton's curve comes out of his hand pretty similarly to his fastball, which can help the pitch elicit bad swings despite merely low-90s velocity. The shape and command negate some of that added effectiveness, though, and are perhaps the reason why he was a bit too hittable in High-A at times. Fulton has an average slider that plays up left-on-left when he gets it running away from southpaws with better tilt. His changeup is inconsistent at present, but flashes plus power sink, because he's, you know, a Marlins pitching prospect.

Fulton is almost as tall as Pérez and his delivery can be a little less fluid, which has led to issues throwing strikes in the recent past. He filled up the zone well enough in 2022 with command being more of the issue than control. Fulton has enough stuff in his locker that he won't need to split matchboxes on the plate, but he also doesn't have the plus-plus or better offering that will give him the same margin for error as a Max Meyer. Consequently, he also doesn't have the same upside.

**OFP:** 55 / no. 3/4 starter

**Variance:** Medium. We need to see how Fulton's fastball plays in the upper minors, but his secondaries are coming along well, and he reined in the control issues some in Beloit.

**Jesse Roche's Fantasy Take:** Fulton remains an under-the-radar arm due to his fastball, which, like Meyer above, also has a natural cutting action that limits its ability to miss bats. You know a left-handed starting pitcher with a similar fastball shape? Max Fried. This profile can work, especially when supported by strong secondaries. Indeed, Fulton managed to amass 150 strikeouts (29.8%) as a 20-year-old last year, including 30 strikeouts (37.5%) over four Double-A appearances. His profile may be non-traditional, but he has sneaky fantasy potential and he should be rostered in leagues with over 200 prospects.

---

## Eyewitness Report: Dax Fulton

**Evaluator:** Nathan Graham
**Report Date:** 05/15/2022
**Dates Seen:** 4/22/22
**Risk Factor:** High
**Delivery:** Extra large frame, tall with long limbs, average build. High 3/4 arm slot, average arm speed, works quickly from the far 3B side of the rubber. Repeats his easy effort delivery well.

| Pitch Type | Future Grade | Sitting Velocity | Peak Velocity | Report |
|---|---|---|---|---|
| FB | 50 | 90-91 | 93 | Straight and heavy offering, commands it well to all four quadrants, current low-90s velocity will play up a notch with physical maturity. |
| CH | 60 | 83-85 | 86 | Power change with above average fading action away from hitters, replicates arm action well, future bat missing offering. |
| CB | 50 | 77-79 | 80 | Best ones showed 12-6 shape and had some bite but got slurvy when the velocity dipped. Effective third offering but not a true swing and miss pitch. |

**Conclusion:** Drafted as a prep arm in the 2nd round of the 2020 draft, Fulton's size and solid mechanics from the left side give him a high prospect floor of a future back of the rotation starter. The command is better than I expected from someone his size and his easy delivery should make him a durable innings eater. He shows good feel for the secondaries but the fastball lacks life to help them play up and limiting his future ceiling.

---

## 5  Jake Eder  LHP      OFP: 55      ETA: 2024

Born: 10/09/98   Age: 24   Bats: L   Throws: L   Height: 6'4"   Weight: 215 lb.   Origin: Round 4, 2020 Draft (#104 overall)

| YEAR | TEAM | LVL | AGE | W | L | SV | G | GS | IP | H | HR | BB/9 | K/9 | K | GB% | BABIP | WHIP | ERA | DRA- | WARP |
|---|---|---|---|---|---|---|---|---|---|---|---|---|---|---|---|---|---|---|---|---|
| 2021 | PNS | AA | 22 | 3 | 5 | 0 | 15 | 15 | 71¹ | 43 | 3 | 3.4 | 12.5 | 99 | 50.3% | .261 | 0.98 | 1.77 | 82 | 1.4 |
| 2023 non-DC | MIA | MLB | 24 | 3 | 3 | 0 | 58 | 0 | 50 | 46 | 7 | 4.2 | 9.1 | 51 | 39.1% | .295 | 1.39 | 4.14 | 108 | 0.1 |

*Comparables: Drew Smyly, Matt Moore, Blake Snell*

**The Report:** Eder was one of the breakout arms of the 2021 season. His fastball jumped into the mid-90s, firming up his plus breaker as well, and he was well on his way to a potential major-league debut before a midseason UCL tear put him on the shelf. After Tommy John surgery in August, Eder missed all of the 2022 season, but will be over 18 months out from getting cut on Opening Day. That's a decent point in time to start gauging where the stuff is, but I imagine he will be on a fairly restricted workload even if it's possible he sees major-league time at some point in 2023.

**OFP:** 55 / no. 3/4 starter

**Variance:** High. Eder had a plausible relief fallback when healthy, but was also flashing the kind of changeup that would keep him in the rotation and perhaps even make him more of a 2/3 starter when considering the entire arsenal. He also won't have thrown a pitch since his Tommy John a year and a half ago, and again, while the surgery is common, every recovery is a bit different.

**Jesse Roche's Fantasy Take:** At his best, Eder was a bat-missing machine, including a 34.5% strikeout rate in Double-A in 2021. Let's see how his stuff and command looks before buying back in. For now, Eder remains a speculative stash in leagues with over 200 prospects.

## 6 Sixto Sánchez RHP OFP: 55 ETA: Debuted in 2020

Born: 07/29/98 Age: 24 Bats: R Throws: R Height: 6'0" Weight: 234 lb. Origin: International Free Agent, 2015

| YEAR | TEAM | LVL | AGE | W | L | SV | G | GS | IP | H | HR | BB/9 | K/9 | K | GB% | BABIP | WHIP | ERA | DRA- | WARP |
|------|------|-----|-----|---|---|----|----|----|------|----|----|------|-----|----|------|-------|------|------|------|------|
| 2020 | MIA | MLB | 21 | 3 | 2 | 0 | 7 | 7 | 39 | 36 | 3 | 2.5 | 7.6 | 33 | 58.0% | .303 | 1.21 | 3.46 | 78 | 0.9 |
| 2023 DC | MIA | MLB | 24 | 4 | 3 | 0 | 31 | 5 | 41.3 | 42 | 4 | 2.9 | 8.0 | 37 | 50.4% | .308 | 1.33 | 3.77 | 98 | 0.4 |

Comparables: Deivi García, Jacob Turner, Henderson Alvarez III

**The Report:** It's not often you'll see a debut date three years earlier than your prospect list publish date. Another three years before his debut was The Summer of Sixto for the BP Prospect Team. He established himself as one of the best pitching prospects in baseball, and it was an absolute joy to chart all the variations of his pitches at the park. But from 2017-22, he threw just a shade over 300 innings total. Granted 47 of those—including two playoff starts—came in the majors in 2020, when he looked like he was establishing himself as a top-of-the-rotation starter for a frisky, and possibly emergent, Marlins team.

Those were also the last pro innings that Sánchez tossed, as he missed all of 2021 and 2022 with various arm maladies, requiring two separate shoulder surgeries. You never want to get cut, but sometimes it can provide a clean reset for your arm. It hasn't yet for Sixto, who was never super durable even when healthy. But when healthy, he threw 100 with a suite of plus-or-better secondaries that moved a ton. Will that pitcher ever come back? It's unlikely, but man I miss him.

**OFP:** 55 / Well, at this point you'd take a good two-inning reliever

**Variance:** Extreme. It's possible that Sixto is done as a meaningful pitcher in professional baseball. It's possible that he steps back on a mound and pitches like it's 2020. There's no real middling or hedging this one, and at this point in the list, you might want to start chasing upside. You could also not rank him at all, and I'd just wistfully nod.

**Jesse Roche's Fantasy Take:** Sánchez's non-recovery saga continues. Will he return as anything close to what he was in 2020? Will he even return? I don't know. Let Sánchez be another dynasty manager's roster-spot eating stash.

## 7 Marco Vargas IF OFP: 55 ETA: 2027

Born: 05/14/05 Age: 18 Bats: L Throws: R Height: 6'0" Weight: 170 lb. Origin: International Free Agent, 2022

| YEAR | TEAM | LVL | AGE | PA | R | 2B | 3B | HR | RBI | BB | K | SB | CS | AVG/OBP/SLG | DRC+ | BABIP | BRR | DRP | WARP |
|------|------|-----|-----|-----|----|----|----|----|-----|----|----|----|----|-------------|------|-------|-----|-----|------|
| 2022 | DSL MIA | ROK | 17 | 221 | 30 | 13 | 3 | 2 | 38 | 35 | 32 | 14 | 6 | .319/.421/.456 | | .368 | | | |

**The Report:** The stats you find on a prospect's player card may or may not be representative of their projection, or even their current skill set, but as we say on the Prospect Team, "Statistical performance exists to be explained." Dominican Summer League stats can usually be explained with "Well, it's the Dominican Summer League." Normal important statistical markers like "hitting .300" or "having more walks than strikeouts"—both of which Vargas achieved in 2022—are often irrelevant in terms of future production or even present talent. The quality of the league is just too variable. However, Vargas' underlying metrics were downright great for a 17-year-old at that level. He picks the right pitches to swing at, makes oodles of contact when he does and hits the ball pretty hard already. So we've somehow come back fully around to those stats on that player card again. And well, we think it has a chance to be real.

**OFP:** 55 / Above-average infielder

**Variance:** Extreme. He signed a professional contract eight months ago, but at this point in the list, you might want to start chasing upside.

**Jesse Roche's Fantasy Take:** Chasing upside is what we do best! Vargas is a fun, very far away, prospect with intriguing traits that performed in, well, the DSL. If your league rosters up to 500 prospects, he should be rostered. Otherwise, Vargas should only be added to watch lists.

## 8  Jacob Amaya  SS    OFP: 50    ETA: 2023
Born: 09/03/98  Age: 24  Bats: R  Throws: R  Height: 6'0"  Weight: 180 lb.  Origin: Round 11, 2017 Draft (#340 overall)

| YEAR | TEAM | LVL | AGE | PA | R | 2B | 3B | HR | RBI | BB | K | SB | CS | AVG/OBP/SLG | DRC+ | BABIP | BRR | DRP | WARP |
|------|------|-----|-----|----|---|----|----|----|-----|----|---|----|----|-------------|------|-------|-----|-----|------|
| 2021 | GDD | WIN | 22 | 67 | 14 | 3 | 0 | 3 | 6 | 13 | 13 | 1 | 1 | .333/.463/.556 | | .395 | | | |
| 2021 | TUL | AA | 22 | 476 | 60 | 15 | 1 | 12 | 47 | 52 | 103 | 5 | 0 | .216/.303/.343 | 94 | .254 | -0.9 | SS(112) -3.8 | 0.7 |
| 2022 | TUL | AA | 23 | 216 | 39 | 10 | 3 | 9 | 26 | 32 | 29 | 3 | 1 | .264/.370/.500 | 120 | .267 | 1.4 | SS(49) -2.2 | 1.2 |
| 2022 | OKC | AAA | 23 | 351 | 46 | 10 | 1 | 8 | 45 | 49 | 83 | 3 | 1 | .259/.368/.381 | 102 | .329 | -0.3 | SS(80) 0.9, 2B(4) -0.4 | 1.1 |
| 2023 DC | MIA | MLB | 24 | 160 | 15 | 6 | 1 | 2 | 14 | 16 | 36 | 1 | 0 | .217/.300/.317 | 80 | .276 | -0.2 | 2B 0, SS 0 | 0.1 |

*Comparables: Orlando Calixte, Abiatal Avelino, Ehire Adrianza*

**The Report:** Amaya knocked the cover off the ball for a couple months repeating back in Tulsa, and then once he was promoted to Triple-A, settled back in as the sub-.400 slugger he's been for most of his pro career. He's never going to hit for a ton of power and he doesn't hit the ball all that hard nor in the air all that much—outside of those early-season Texas League at-bats. Amaya should put up a respectable batting average, get on base a bit and be a good defender up the middle. So not all that different from the infielder he's replacing in Miami. Amaya should have a bit more power than Miguel Rojas, mind you, as I'd expect him to knock 10-15 a year out of the park. But the calling card here is his ability to play the three primary infield spots well.

**OFP:** 50 / Second-division shortstop, et. al.

**Variance:** Low. Amaya may not be beating out Joey Wendle for the Opening Day shortstop job in Miami—there's a sentence—but he has little left to do in the minors and should be something between a useful fifth infielder and average regular for a number of years.

**Jesse Roche's Fantasy Take:** Amaya, also a standout in June, struggled to muster much offense after a blistering-hot first 30 games in Double-A, hitting just .236/.348/.337 over his final 103 games. This powerless performance is particularly concerning given that much of it occurred in the hitter-friendly Triple-A Pacific Coast League. That said, Amaya is not punchless, as noted above. In addition, he now has a clearer path to playing time in an org that has been content to provide regular jobs to the likes of Wendle, Rojas and Jon Berti. Amaya could receive meaningful MLB time as soon as 2023, and, as such, he should be rostered in leagues with up to 400 prospects.

## 9  Jacob Berry  3B    OFP: 50    ETA: Late 2024
Born: 05/05/01  Age: 22  Bats: S  Throws: R  Height: 6'0"  Weight: 212 lb.  Origin: Round 1, 2022 Draft (#6 overall)

| YEAR | TEAM | LVL | AGE | PA | R | 2B | 3B | HR | RBI | BB | K | SB | CS | AVG/OBP/SLG | DRC+ | BABIP | BRR | DRP | WARP |
|------|------|-----|-----|----|---|----|----|----|-----|----|---|----|----|-------------|------|-------|-----|-----|------|
| 2022 | JUP | A | 21 | 148 | 19 | 7 | 0 | 3 | 24 | 13 | 23 | 1 | 1 | .264/.358/.392 | 126 | .294 | -1.2 | 3B(24) -0.3 | 0.7 |
| 2023 non-DC | MIA | MLB | 22 | 251 | 20 | 11 | 1 | 3 | 20 | 16 | 56 | 1 | 0 | .215/.275/.308 | 64 | .272 | -4.1 | 3B 0 | -0.9 |

*Comparables: Jedd Gyorko, Spencer Steer, Jesus Lopez*

**The Report:** We don't even really bother to explain college performance. Berry also hit .300—well over, in fact—and walked more than he struck out for LSU. There's ping bats, wildly variable quality of pitching, etc. Berry can certainly hit a bit. He's short to the ball, doesn't miss often in the zone and doesn't chase too much, but is this really a plus hit tool in the pros? He doesn't use his lower half much, and a lot of his contact profile is medium-hit fly balls or fliners. He looks the part of a strong and burly corner slugger, but didn't hit the ball that hard in college and that has continued with wood in the pros. And Berry really needs at least an average power projection, as he's unlikely to stick as an everyday third baseman and may not have the foot speed for corner outfield.

**OFP:** 50 / Average regular at one (or more) of the four corners

**Variance:** Medium. It's possible a swing change could unlock a bit more power here, but Berry's hit tool is going to have to carry a profile that is likely to slip further down the defensive spectrum. That's a tall ask given it's not obviously plus barrel control and he doesn't make particularly impactful contact.

**Jesse Roche's Fantasy Take:** Berry lacks impact power or a defensive home, which puts a whole lot of pressure on his hitting ability to carry the load. His profile is one to generally avoid in fantasy, especially given the likely acquisition cost associated with the sixth overall pick.

## 10   Yiddi Cappe   SS    OFP: 50    ETA: 2026

Born: 09/17/02   Age: 20   Bats: R   Throws: R   Height: 6'3"   Weight: 175 lb.   Origin: International Free Agent, 2021

| YEAR | TEAM | LVL | AGE | PA | R | 2B | 3B | HR | RBI | BB | K | SB | CS | AVG/OBP/SLG | DRC+ | BABIP | BRR | DRP | WARP |
|------|------|-----|-----|----|---|----|----|----|-----|----|---|----|----|-------------|------|-------|-----|-----|------|
| 2021 | DSL MRL | ROK | 18 | 216 | 31 | 17 | 1 | 2 | 27 | 19 | 35 | 9 | 8 | .270/.329/.402 | | .308 | | | |
| 2022 | MRL | ROK | 19 | 132 | 23 | 7 | 0 | 6 | 25 | 9 | 19 | 6 | 4 | .305/.364/.517 | | .316 | | | |
| 2022 | JUP | A | 19 | 167 | 18 | 5 | 1 | 3 | 15 | 6 | 22 | 7 | 1 | .278/.299/.380 | 115 | .301 | 0.6 | SS(21) -0.7, 3B(9) -1.3 | 0.6 |
| 2023 non-DC | MIA | MLB | 20 | 251 | 18 | 10 | 1 | 2 | 20 | 11 | 52 | 5 | 2 | .215/.254/.297 | 54 | .266 | -1.6 | 3B 0, SS 0 | -0.8 |

*Comparables: José Peraza, Ketel Marte, Arquímedes Gamboa*

**The Report:** Cappe was the Marlins' big splash in the 2021 IFA class, and he came stateside this year. He had a strong debut at the Florida complex, but his free-swinging ways got exposed a bit after a promotion to Jupiter. He's very upright at the plate, with high hands that he drops into his swing before unleashing through the zone with a Piazza-esque, two-handed follow-through. Cappe doesn't have Piazza's bat speed or power—which is not a sentence I should even have to append, but just to be clear—but his swing does sweep up most of what he finds in the zone. Although he makes a lot of contact out of the zone too, it's rarely effective contact, and he will need to clean up his approach now that he's in full-season ball. Cappe is lean and projectable and looks like he could hit for at least average game power at some point, but at present he just doesn't lift the ball enough or make particularly emphatic contact. Defensively, Cappe is a better fit for second than short or third, and I wouldn't be shocked if he grows off the dirt entirely at some point.

**OFP:** 50 / Average regular, position TBD

**Variance:** Extreme. There are things to like in Cappe's swing, but without better swing decisions and/or more power, he's going to find full-season ball and/or the upper minors a tricky adjustment.

**Jesse Roche's Fantasy Take:** Cappe did one thing well in Low-A: he made tons of contact (80%). Otherwise, most of his contact was poor, including a 103.3-mph max exit velocity, 82.7-mph average exit velocity, and 23% hard-hit rate. Across 134 batted-ball events, Cappe had zero barrels. He also had more infield (23) than outfield (22) fly balls. Yikes! Cappe remains quite raw, though his bat-to-ball ability, frame and athleticism are promising. Given his potential (emphasis on potential), he is a top-200 dynasty prospect.

# Outside the Top Ten:

## 11   Kahlil Watson   IF

Born: 04/16/03   Age: 20   Bats: L   Throws: R   Height: 5'9"   Weight: 178 lb.   Origin: Round 1, 2021 Draft (#16 overall)

| YEAR | TEAM | LVL | AGE | PA | R | 2B | 3B | HR | RBI | BB | K | SB | CS | AVG/OBP/SLG | DRC+ | BABIP | BRR | DRP | WARP |
|------|------|-----|-----|----|---|----|----|----|-----|----|---|----|----|-------------|------|-------|-----|-----|------|
| 2021 | MRL | ROK | 18 | 42 | 13 | 3 | 2 | 0 | 5 | 8 | 7 | 4 | 1 | .394/.524/.606 | | .500 | | | |
| 2022 | JUP | A | 19 | 358 | 50 | 16 | 5 | 9 | 44 | 27 | 127 | 16 | 3 | .231/.296/.395 | 80 | .346 | 3.7 | SS(46) -1.1, 2B(23) 0.7 | 0.6 |
| 2023 non-DC | MIA | MLB | 20 | 251 | 19 | 10 | 2 | 3 | 20 | 14 | 99 | 6 | 2 | .208/.257/.307 | 56 | .346 | -1.3 | 2B 0, SS 0 | -0.7 |

*Comparables: Anderson Tejeda, Jonathan Araúz, Reid Brignac*

Last year, Keanan Lamb asked the question of Watson that you ask of any prep bat: "But as it always seems to be the question with young players: Can he actually hit?" Well, Watson struck out 35% of the time in 2022 due to an egregiously bad chase rate against Low-A pitching. He was capable of driving a ball when he did make contact, especially if he got a pitch up in the zone that he could extend on. He has plus bat speed that covers for some length in the swing, but will need to improve his swing decisions to make it all work. Watson is a fundamentally fine shortstop, but did seem to struggle at times with the jump in game speed in full-season ball. Unlike a lot of the other Marlins hitting prospects, Watson is able to make hard contact, but so far he hasn't made enough of it.

## 12 Karson Milbrandt   RHP

Born: 04/21/04   Age: 19   Bats: R   Throws: R   Height: 6'2"   Weight: 190 lb.   Origin: Round 3, 2022 Draft (#85 overall)

| YEAR | TEAM | LVL | AGE | W | L | SV | G | GS | IP | H | HR | BB/9 | K/9 | K | GB% | BABIP | WHIP | ERA | DRA- | WARP |
|------|------|-----|-----|---|---|----|----|----|----|----|----|------|-----|---|------|-------|------|-----|------|------|
| 2023 non-DC | MIA | MLB | 19 | 2 | 3 | 0 | 58 | 0 | 50 | 60 | 10 | 5.6 | 6.7 | 37 | 33.0% | .320 | 1.83 | 6.86 | 165 | -1.4 |

*Comparables: José Mujica, Jake Thompson, Nick Travieso*

The Marlins' third-round pick in the 2022 draft, Milbrandt can ramp his high-spin fastball up into the mid-90s—and ramp is technically appropriate here given the late-arm effort. The rest of the secondaries are in need of more significant development, and the mechanics could use a bit of smoothing out as well. Most third-round prep arms are going to carry significant reliever risk, but at this point in the list, you might want to start chasing the innate feel for spin.

## 13 Jordan Groshans   IF

Born: 11/10/99   Age: 23   Bats: R   Throws: R   Height: 6'3"   Weight: 200 lb.   Origin: Round 1, 2018 Draft (#12 overall)

| YEAR | TEAM | LVL | AGE | PA | R | 2B | 3B | HR | RBI | BB | K | SB | CS | AVG/OBP/SLG | DRC+ | BABIP | BRR | DRP | WARP |
|------|------|-----|-----|----|---|----|----|----|-----|----|---|----|----|-------------|------|-------|-----|-----|------|
| 2021 | NH | AA | 21 | 316 | 46 | 23 | 0 | 7 | 40 | 34 | 61 | 0 | 0 | .291/.367/.450 | 118 | .347 | -1.2 | SS(43) -1.9, 3B(21) -0.6, 1B(1) -0.1 | 1.3 |
| 2022 | BUF | AAA | 22 | 279 | 30 | 8 | 0 | 1 | 24 | 35 | 46 | 2 | 0 | .250/.348/.296 | 98 | .303 | -0.4 | SS(39) -0.8, 3B(14) -0.2, 1B(4) -0.2 | 0.6 |
| 2022 | JAX | AAA | 22 | 133 | 14 | 7 | 0 | 2 | 10 | 19 | 19 | 1 | 0 | .301/.398/.416 | 116 | .344 | -0.4 | 3B(12) -0.5, SS(10) 0.1, 2B(9) -0.7 | 0.6 |
| 2022 | MIA | MLB | 22 | 65 | 9 | 0 | 0 | 1 | 2 | 4 | 13 | 0 | 0 | .262/.308/.311 | 92 | .319 | -1.5 | 3B(17) 0 | 0.0 |
| 2023 DC | MIA | MLB | 23 | 59 | 6 | 2 | 0 | 1 | 5 | 5 | 11 | 0 | 0 | .243/.313/.336 | 89 | .294 | -0.1 | 3B 0 | 0.1 |

*Comparables: Richard Urena, Erick Aybar, Cristhian Adames*

Adding to their group of athletic infielders that make a lot of contact, but not necessarily hard, pull-side or in the air, the Marlins acquired Groshans from the Jays at the deadline for Anthony Bass and Zach Pop. A few years ago he looked like a breakout Top-50 prospect, but has never done more than flash average game power since and nowadays, it might not even project for fringe as he just doesn't lift the ball consistently. Groshans does make a lot of contact, albeit often of the medium-hard ground-ball type, but has grown off shortstop. He should play a solid third base, but it's hard to see much impact in a corner unless he finds a way to tap into his above-average raw power more often.

## 14 Jacob Miller   RHP

Born: 08/10/03   Age: 19   Bats: R   Throws: R   Height: 6'2"   Weight: 180 lb.   Origin: Round 2, 2022 Draft (#46 overall)

| YEAR | TEAM | LVL | AGE | W | L | SV | G | GS | IP | H | HR | BB/9 | K/9 | K | GB% | BABIP | WHIP | ERA | DRA- | WARP |
|------|------|-----|-----|---|---|----|----|----|----|----|----|------|-----|---|------|-------|------|-----|------|------|
| 2023 non-DC | MIA | MLB | 19 | 3 | 3 | 0 | 58 | 0 | 50 | 56 | 9 | 5.0 | 7.2 | 40 | 34.8% | .311 | 1.69 | 6.04 | 148 | -1.0 |

*Comparables: Alex Reyes, Luis Ortiz, Junior Fernández*

Drafted in the second round as an Ohio prep arm, Miller actually has two fairly advanced breaking balls despite his cold-weather background. His upper-70s curve has a big 11-5 shape and can show as a two power breaker, while his firmer slider flashes good depth as well. Miller can run his fastball up to 95, but it's not as overpowering as the velocity readings. His delivery has a bit of late effort as well, so the long-term home might be the pen, where he can let the breaking balls cook.

## 15 Joe Mack   C

Born: 12/27/02   Age: 20   Bats: L   Throws: R   Height: 6'1"   Weight: 210 lb.   Origin: Round 1, 2021 Draft (#31 overall)

| YEAR | TEAM | LVL | AGE | PA | R | 2B | 3B | HR | RBI | BB | K | SB | CS | AVG/OBP/SLG | DRC+ | BABIP | BRR | DRP | WARP |
|------|------|-----|-----|----|---|----|----|----|-----|----|---|----|----|-------------|------|-------|-----|-----|------|
| 2021 | MRL | ROK | 18 | 75 | 9 | 1 | 0 | 1 | 2 | 20 | 22 | 0 | 1 | .132/.373/.208 | | .194 | | | |
| 2022 | MRL | ROK | 19 | 31 | 2 | 0 | 0 | 2 | 3 | 4 | 7 | 0 | 0 | .296/.387/.519 | | .333 | | | |
| 2022 | JUP | A | 19 | 152 | 18 | 4 | 1 | 3 | 12 | 29 | 40 | 0 | 0 | .231/.382/.355 | 106 | .316 | -2.2 | C(30) 0.9 | 0.5 |
| 2023 non-DC | MIA | MLB | 20 | 251 | 21 | 9 | 2 | 3 | 20 | 24 | 89 | 0 | 1 | .215/.295/.308 | 74 | .342 | -4.3 | C 0 | -0.2 |

*Comparables: Francisco Mejía, Gabriel Lino, Kyle Skipworth*

Mack slides a bit from last year's ranking, as he missed time with a hamstring injury and showed a bit too much swing-and-miss in the Florida State League when he did play. Profiling as the rare Three-True-Outcomes catcher. Mack has a stiff swing and swings hard, generating impressively firm contact for his age. Despite not expanding the zone too much, there's swing-and-miss inside it, and he will swing over offspeed as his length-and-strength swing doesn't leave him much time to adjust. Defensively, Mack projects as likely to stick behind the plate, but broadly just average with the glove. When you draft a catcher from ~~Upstate~~ Western New York, you are committing to a fairly long development process, and there are no shortcuts to speak of after his full-season debut.

## 16 Xavier Edwards   IF
Born: 08/09/99   Age: 23   Bats: S   Throws: R   Height: 5'10"   Weight: 175 lb.   Origin: Round 1, 2018 Draft (#38 overall)

| YEAR | TEAM | LVL | AGE | PA | R | 2B | 3B | HR | RBI | BB | K | SB | CS | AVG/OBP/SLG | DRC+ | BABIP | BRR | DRP | WARP |
|---|---|---|---|---|---|---|---|---|---|---|---|---|---|---|---|---|---|---|---|
| 2021 | MTG | AA | 21 | 337 | 40 | 13 | 3 | 0 | 27 | 36 | 42 | 19 | 11 | .302/.377/.368 | 110 | .348 | -1.2 | 2B(55) -1.1, 3B(22) 1.7 | 1.3 |
| 2022 | DUR | AAA | 22 | 400 | 48 | 19 | 1 | 5 | 33 | 43 | 75 | 7 | 4 | .246/.328/.350 | 91 | .300 | -0.7 | 2B(49) -1.5, 3B(20) 0.1, SS(20) -0.5 | 0.5 |
| 2023 DC | MIA | MLB | 23 | 61 | 5 | 2 | 1 | 0 | 5 | 5 | 10 | 1 | 1 | .226/.291/.309 | 70 | .272 | -0.3 | 2B 0 | -0.1 |

*Comparables: Ronald Torreyes, Luis Arraez, Reegie Corona*

Edwards was sent to Miami in an offseason swap for the Fish's 2022 fourth-round pick, Marcus Johnson. Last season was the first year he failed to hit .300 in the pros, struggling badly in Triple-A. His profile is purely batting average and speed-driven, so a spike in both strikeouts and fly balls isn't ideal, despite sextupling his career home run total in 2022. Edwards isn't the elite runner he once was either, and while he can be a useful major leaguer without hitting .300, he's going to need to get back up into at least the .280 range to be a viable fifth infielder or second-division starter.

## 17 Sandro Bargallo   LHP
Born: 12/29/01   Age: 21   Bats: L   Throws: L   Height: 6'1"   Weight: 180 lb.   Origin: International Free Agent, 2019

| YEAR | TEAM | LVL | AGE | W | L | SV | G | GS | IP | H | HR | BB/9 | K/9 | K | GB% | BABIP | WHIP | ERA | DRA- | WARP |
|---|---|---|---|---|---|---|---|---|---|---|---|---|---|---|---|---|---|---|---|---|
| 2021 | MRL | ROK | 19 | 1 | 3 | 0 | 12 | 7 | 27² | 27 | 3 | 10.1 | 11.1 | 34 | 64.9% | .324 | 2.10 | 8.13 | | |
| 2022 | JUP | A | 20 | 2 | 3 | 0 | 22 | 20 | 82 | 60 | 3 | 7.7 | 10.5 | 96 | 63.1% | .292 | 1.59 | 3.51 | 111 | 0.9 |
| 2023 non-DC | MIA | MLB | 21 | 3 | 3 | 0 | 58 | 0 | 50 | 53 | 7 | 7.6 | 9.1 | 50 | 41.8% | .325 | 1.90 | 6.31 | 149 | -1.0 |

Signed in 2019 for low six figures, Bargallo remains a bit of a project, but at least he's in the right organization for pitching development. We'll round out our *leitmotif* for Marlins pitching prospect blurbs by starting once again with the breaking ball. Bargallo's is a high-spin, low-80s 1-7 curve, which shows very inconsistent command but can absolutely dominate Low-A hitters when he gets hard, late glove-side break. His change runs too close to his sinking fastball in both velocity and movement, but he does show the ability to pull the string on it at times and get more velocity separation and dive. The fastball is low-90s and gives up more fly balls than it should given the good vertical movement, but he really only can command it arm-side. That's a common problem with Bargallo's whole arsenal, as he has a stiff arm action and doesn't always finish across his body well. He struggled to throw strikes in the Florida State League, and might just be a lefty reliever in the end, but the secondaries flashed enough that he is worth keeping a close eye on despite the exorbitant walk rate.

## 18 Nasim Nuñez   SS
Born: 08/18/00   Age: 22   Bats: S   Throws: R   Height: 5'9"   Weight: 158 lb.   Origin: Round 2, 2019 Draft (#46 overall)

| YEAR | TEAM | LVL | AGE | PA | R | 2B | 3B | HR | RBI | BB | K | SB | CS | AVG/OBP/SLG | DRC+ | BABIP | BRR | DRP | WARP |
|---|---|---|---|---|---|---|---|---|---|---|---|---|---|---|---|---|---|---|---|---|
| 2021 | JUP | A | 20 | 228 | 33 | 2 | 1 | 0 | 10 | 35 | 46 | 33 | 10 | .243/.366/.265 | 105 | .319 | 2.2 | SS(48) 2.7 | 1.3 |
| 2022 | BEL | A+ | 21 | 378 | 53 | 11 | 3 | 2 | 27 | 71 | 103 | 49 | 11 | .247/.390/.323 | 99 | .365 | 8.1 | SS(84) -1.2 | 1.8 |
| 2022 | PNS | AA | 21 | 171 | 22 | 6 | 0 | 0 | 14 | 24 | 36 | 21 | 5 | .261/.371/.303 | 101 | .343 | -0.2 | SS(34) -1.7, 2B(4) -1.2 | 0.3 |
| 2023 non-DC | MIA | MLB | 22 | 251 | 22 | 9 | 2 | 1 | 19 | 29 | 61 | 17 | 5 | .228/.323/.303 | 84 | .310 | 4.4 | 2B 0, SS 0 | 0.8 |

*Comparables: Nate Samson, Jose Martinez, Pete Kozma*

Nuñez does everything well on a baseball field except make hard contact. He's a plus defender at the six, showing good range, actions and body control. His arm is strong and accurate, whether on the move or deep in the 5.5 hole. He's a speedster who is aggressive on the bases. He knows the strike zone very well, and is capable of defending himself with two strikes. He just isn't going to hit for any power, to the point that it's hard to see him maintaining the kind of walk rates or batting averages that would keep him in a major-league lineup. The glove and baserunning should get him shots at the end of your major-league bench, but it's the kind of 20 power that makes it difficult to find a much bigger role than that.

## Top Talents 25 and Under (as of 4/1/2023):

1. Eury Pérez, RHP
2. Jazz Chisholm Jr., 2B
3. Trevor Rogers, LHP
4. Jesús Luzardo, LHP
5. Max Meyer, RHP
6. Edward Cabrera, RHP
7. Jose Salas, SS
8. Braxton Garrett, LHP
9. Dax Fulton, LHP
10. Jesús Sánchez, OF

The conundrum in Miami is well-understood at this point, and well-illustrated in this list: pitchers with plenty of promise and even some strong performance, and a near-total dearth of position players who have delivered thus far. That indictment includes unlisted names like outfielders JJ Bleday and Peyton Burdick, who fell short of matching even Sánchez's middling campaign. Sánchez's 90 DRC+ was around par for the course in Miami's lineup of below-average swingers, but the big Dominican at least showed some power and defensive range worthy of platoon work or a bench role.

The other position player of consequence is the face of the lineup, and likely its best performer, though a broken back waylaid Chisholm for the final three months of the season and may have impacted him previously. It's a shame, as the exciting young second baseman was in the midst of a clear step forward at the dish, finishing with a 114 DRC+ that sets him still short of stardom but solidly as a player who Miami can build around (at least in theory).

The rest of the standouts make their money keeping hitters unhappy, with Luzardo as the most impressive in 2022. The fireballing lefty was every bit a rotation player in his 18 starts, though he managed to once again miss almost half the season with injury, in this case a forearm strain. He looked healthy upon return, but the potent Peruvian still faces the same knocks he has for years: Can upper-90s heat from a body that compact and a delivery that high effort be sustained for 30 starts each year? It hasn't been possible yet, though Luzardo was at least highly effective when on the mound in 2022.

When I was in middle school, there were triplets in my class—a pair of identical twins and a third brother who was taller and, though related-looking, was obviously far from identical. The third brother ended up attending a different high school and forging his own path, while the identical two other triplets remained close. This came to mind when considering whether Trevor Rogers was punished this year for his hubris and height by some deity or fey creature, who stripped the world of any record that he is the long-lost non-identical triplet of Taylor and Tyler Rogers. Instead, allegedly with only the MLB-familiar connection of being the cousin of Cody Ross, the 2021 All-Star saw his ERA jump nearly three runs in 2022 without one clear culprit to blame. Rogers' fastball command took a sizable step back, living over the heart of the plate too often, and his changeup drifted over the plate as well, but he otherwise did not see a downturn in velocity or spin. Back spasms and a lat strain robbed him of about two months, ending his season on the IL as well. Mechanical improvements are a must for Rogers to get his pitches back on the edges more consistently, and better fortune and defense would probably be welcomed to boot: out of 140 pitchers with at least 100 innings pitched in 2022, Rogers had the 10th-highest BABIP against (.330) and sixth-lowest strand rate (66.9%).

Both Cabrera and Garrett figure to start games for the Marlins in 2022, and each has a shot at opening the season in the rotation or the bullpen. Cabrera's health, much like almost every other pitcher named above, has been the biggest impediment to his performance, as elbow tendonitis cost him two months in the middle of last year. A lengthy rehab stint rounded out what was a fairly impressive sophomore attempt in Miami, with Cabrera averaging 96 on the heater and flashing a trio of potentially plus secondaries led by a firm changeup that sits hotter than plenty of fastballs. Southpawing his way into the conversation as well is Garrett, who is "now interesting" thanks to a particularly nasty sweeping slider that pairs well with his sinker and changeup and could easily make him one of Miami's top starters behind ace Sandy Alcantara as soon as April.

# Milwaukee Brewers

## The State of the System:

An improving Brewers system has produced their best Top 10 in recent memory—with a lot of that talent ready to help in the majors—but it's not particularly deep past that.

## The Top Ten:

**1** **Jackson Chourio  OF**       OFP: 70       ETA: Late 2024/2025

Born: 03/11/04   Age: 19   Bats: R   Throws: R   Height: 6'1"   Weight: 165 lb.   Origin: International Free Agent, 2021

| YEAR | TEAM | LVL | AGE | PA | R | 2B | 3B | HR | RBI | BB | K | SB | CS | AVG/OBP/SLG | DRC+ | BABIP | BRR | DRP | WARP |
|------|------|-----|-----|-----|----|----|----|----|-----|----|----|----|----|-------------|------|-------|------|--------|------|
| 2021 | DSL BRW2 | ROK | 17 | 189 | 31 | 7 | 1 | 5 | 25 | 23 | 28 | 8 | 3 | .296/.386/.447 | | .323 | | | |
| 2022 | ZUL | WIN | 18 | 87 | 9 | 5 | 0 | 1 | 4 | 4 | 16 | 1 | 2 | .256/.291/.354 | | .308 | | | |
| 2022 | CAR | A | 18 | 271 | 51 | 23 | 5 | 12 | 47 | 19 | 76 | 10 | 2 | .324/.373/.600 | 117 | .423 | 2.9 | CF(57) 7.5 | 2.3 |
| 2022 | WIS | A+ | 18 | 142 | 24 | 6 | 0 | 8 | 24 | 11 | 31 | 4 | 1 | .252/.317/.488 | 120 | .267 | 0.4 | CF(24) 2.3 | 1.0 |
| 2022 | BLX | AA | 18 | 26 | 0 | 1 | 0 | 0 | 4 | 2 | 11 | 2 | 1 | .087/.154/.130 | 71 | .154 | -0.1 | CF(5) -0.5 | -0.1 |
| 2023 non-DC | MIL | MLB | 19 | 251 | 22 | 12 | 2 | 6 | 25 | 13 | 82 | 5 | 1 | .225/.269/.361 | 76 | .319 | -2.1 | 2B 0, CF 0 | -0.1 |

*Comparables: Mike Trout, Jason Heyward, Estevan Florial*

**The Report:** We listed Chourio as a potential breakout candidate last year based on his strong batted-ball data in the Dominican complex. Well, his stock has risen so much in 2022 that he'd get booted off Bake Off due to over-proofing. The 18-year-old made it all the way to Double-A, socking 20 home runs in a hair under 100 games. He's not the biggest guy, but already has a sturdy frame and actualized some of the anticipated physical projection from last year. His plus game power is more real than mirage, he has an explosive swing with plenty of torque, even as a teenager, although his swing decisions aren't great even after adjusting for age and level. They'll likely be fine long-term—and he's got plenty of term to play with—but the hit tool will need further refinement. Defensively, Chourio should stick in center field given his plus speed and advanced route-running.

The underlying swing and contact metrics here don't really support this level of production, but Chourio was also 18 for the entire season. You'd expect him to improve in those areas, and he's already a very, very good prospect whose power/speed combo at a premium defensive position makes for some intriguing high-end outcomes.

**OFP:** 70 / All-Star outfielder

**Variance:** Very, very high. A lot of Chourio's case as one of the best prospects in baseball is predicated on age relative to league top-line stats rather than the underlying offensive traits. That said, he is not likely to go the way of Fernando Martinez, but I'd like to see sustained performance in the upper minors before he lands in the true S-Tier of prospects.

**Jesse Roche's Fantasy Take:** Chourio's blend of bat speed, power and athleticism is rare, and his performance is even more rare. Since 2006, only eleven 18-year-old prospects with at least 250 plate appearances in Low-A have had a 145 or higher wRC+ and an ISO over .101. This group includes a who's who of superstars: Mike Trout, Giancarlo Stanton, Bryce Harper, Jackson Chourio, Wander Franco, Fernando Tatis Jr., Vladimir Guerrero Jr., Freddie Freeman, Carlos Correa, Jon Singleton and Julio Rodríguez. Now that is illustrious company (other than, well, Singleton)! That said, Chourio does have work to do to clean up his swing decisions and contact rate. Regardless, he is a special, special talent with sky-high fantasy potential, and firmly within the dynasty top 10.

## 2  Sal Frelick  OF    OFP: 60    ETA: 2023

Born: 04/19/00   Age: 23   Bats: L   Throws: R   Height: 5'10"   Weight: 180 lb.   Origin: Round 1, 2021 Draft (#15 overall)

| YEAR | TEAM | LVL | AGE | PA | R | 2B | 3B | HR | RBI | BB | K | SB | CS | AVG/OBP/SLG | DRC+ | BABIP | BRR | DRP | WARP |
|------|------|-----|-----|-----|-----|-----|-----|-----|-----|-----|-----|-----|-----|-------------|------|-------|------|-----|------|
| 2021 | CAR | A | 21 | 81 | 17 | 6 | 1 | 1 | 12 | 9 | 10 | 6 | 2 | .437/.494/.592 | 128 | .492 | 0.3 | CF(14) 2.3 | 0.8 |
| 2021 | WIS | A+ | 21 | 71 | 7 | 1 | 1 | 1 | 5 | 10 | 13 | 3 | 0 | .167/.296/.267 | 110 | .196 | 0.1 | CF(13) 0.4 | 0.4 |
| 2022 | WIS | A+ | 22 | 92 | 12 | 5 | 1 | 2 | 9 | 13 | 14 | 6 | 3 | .291/.391/.456 | 128 | .333 | 0.3 | CF(17) 0.5 | 0.9 |
| 2022 | BLX | AA | 22 | 253 | 40 | 12 | 3 | 5 | 25 | 20 | 33 | 9 | 2 | .317/.380/.464 | 117 | .351 | -1.0 | CF(42) 3.2, LF(6) -0.6, RF(3) -0.3 | 1.5 |
| 2022 | NAS | AAA | 22 | 217 | 38 | 11 | 2 | 4 | 25 | 19 | 16 | 9 | 3 | .365/.435/.508 | 133 | .382 | 1.6 | LF(22) -1.4, CF(17) -1.2, RF(1) -0.2 | 1.4 |
| 2023 DC | MIL | MLB | 23 | 166 | 18 | 7 | 2 | 2 | 16 | 12 | 23 | 3 | 1 | .247/.309/.358 | 87 | .280 | -0.1 | LF 0, CF 0 | 0.3 |

Comparables: Raimel Tapia, Michael Hermosillo, Luis Barrera

**The Report:** We described Frelick as a "prove-it-at-every-level" prospect last year, and well, the preponderance of evidence is now pretty convincing that he's a top outfield prospect. He hit .331 across three levels in 2022 and saved the best for last, posting a .943 OPS with more walks than strikeouts in 200 PA for Nashville. The scouting report mostly backs up the performance, as Frelick is direct to the ball and covers the zone well. He has strong wrists and above-average barrel control. He's comfortable slapping the fastball away into left field and quick enough inside to sneak a dozen home runs or so over the right field fence. Power won't be a huge part of Frelick's game, mind you—and better defenses will pick off some of those soft liners and hard grounders—but he should be a plus hitter who gets on-base plenty and uses his plus wheels to cause havoc once he's there. Defensively, Frelick's foot speed covers for some deficiencies in reads and routes, but he should be more than fine in left field and playable in center.

**OFP:** 60 / First-division outfielder

**Variance:** Medium. Frelick doesn't really have impact tools on offense or defense, but the overall profile plays up given the approach and broad base of skills. But he will need to hit .280 or so to get his name in the lineup in permanent ink, and that's not nailed on even when you hit .300 in the minors.

**Jesse Roche's Fantasy Take:** How do you feel about Steven Kwan? Because Frelick has a similar profile as a left-handed, high-contact/high-average hitter with nominal power and enough speed to push 20 stolen bases. Granted, he likely comes up short of Kwan's otherworldly bat-to-ball skills, but he also likely offers a touch more thump (i.e., he may "sneak a dozen home runs or so over the right field fence"). That'll play in most formats. Frelick's proximity and average/speed game lands him just within the dynasty top 50.

## 3  Garrett Mitchell  OF    OFP: 55    ETA: Debuted in 2022

Born: 09/04/98   Age: 24   Bats: L   Throws: R   Height: 6'3"   Weight: 215 lb.   Origin: Round 1, 2020 Draft (#20 overall)

| YEAR | TEAM | LVL | AGE | PA | R | 2B | 3B | HR | RBI | BB | K | SB | CS | AVG/OBP/SLG | DRC+ | BABIP | BRR | DRP | WARP |
|------|------|-----|-----|-----|-----|-----|-----|-----|-----|-----|-----|-----|-----|-------------|------|-------|------|-----|------|
| 2021 | WIS | A+ | 22 | 120 | 33 | 5 | 2 | 5 | 20 | 28 | 30 | 12 | 1 | .359/.508/.620 | 126 | .491 | 0.8 | CF(13) -2.5, RF(2) 0.3 | 0.6 |
| 2021 | BLX | AA | 22 | 148 | 16 | 1 | 0 | 3 | 10 | 18 | 41 | 5 | 1 | .186/.291/.264 | 84 | .247 | -0.7 | CF(30) 0.9, RF(2) -0.0, LF(1) -0.1 | 0.2 |
| 2022 | BLX | AA | 23 | 187 | 29 | 9 | 2 | 4 | 25 | 16 | 52 | 7 | 1 | .277/.353/.428 | 93 | .378 | 1.0 | CF(26) -0.7, RF(12) 1.3, LF(3) -0.4 | 0.6 |
| 2022 | NAS | AAA | 23 | 85 | 15 | 6 | 0 | 1 | 9 | 10 | 18 | 9 | 0 | .342/.435/.466 | 106 | .444 | 1.7 | CF(9) -0.7, RF(5) -0.6, LF(3) -0.1 | 0.3 |
| 2022 | MIL | MLB | 23 | 68 | 9 | 3 | 0 | 2 | 9 | 6 | 28 | 8 | 0 | .311/.373/.459 | 56 | .548 | 0.9 | CF(28) 1.2 | 0.1 |
| 2023 DC | MIL | MLB | 24 | 427 | 46 | 18 | 3 | 7 | 40 | 38 | 124 | 19 | 4 | .206/.285/.326 | 71 | .285 | 3.1 | CF 0 | 0.3 |

Comparables: Jacoby Ellsbury, Adam Eaton, Stephen Drew

**The Report:** Two years and a bit after he was one of the more divisive 2020 draft prospects, Mitchell remains more of a projection bet than you'd like, especially given he spent the last month-plus of last season in the bigs. He's always looked the part of a perennial 20+ home run hitter, but his grand total after three seasons in college, a summer wood bat league and two seasons in the pros—covering over 1,300 plate appearances—stands at just 23 round-trippers. Mitchell did hit the ball pretty hard in his major-league cameo; he just didn't hit it consistently hard in the air. He just loves hitting line drives the other way.

Look, given the speed and defense profile—Mitchell is a top-of-the-scale runner who should be a plus glove in center—if he can shoot line drives into the left-center gap consistently, he'll have a nice, long career. You'd just hope for a bit more out of the bat. And there's no guarantee that the hit tool will hold up either. Mitchell was vulnerable to spin down-and-in in the majors, and there's no shortage of righties who will be happy to drop a slider or curve at his shoe tops. He's 24 now and should be in competition for a major-league job this spring, so Mitchell may just be what he's been: a speedy center fielder who hits at the top of the order. He may not look that part, but it's a major-league role.

**OFP:** 55 / Leadoff hitter, good glove in center

**Variance:** High. This one cuts both ways. Mitchell will need to adjust to MLB-quality breakers—and frankly swung and missed too much against fastballs too. He's also been a bit injury-prone so far in his pro career. Overall, there's not really a ton of floor here given the durability and hit tool concerns. On the other hand, if Mitchell ever does figure out how to lift and pull the ball a bit more often, he's a potential All-Star. I'm not betting on either extreme. I think he's mostly told us what he is.

**Jesse Roche's Fantasy Take:** Some fantasy managers may be salivating over Mitchell's brief debut in which he hit .311/.373/.459 with two home runs and *eight stolen bases* over 68 plate appearances. At the same time, he flashed real underlying power–92.9-mph average exit velocity and 109.9-mph max exit velocity–and elite speed–99th-percentile sprint speed. However, you may never see a disparity between production and underlying performance as striking. Mitchell's 58 DRC+, 41.2% strikeout rate and 76.9% zone-contact rate are frightening harbingers of things to come. Still, his loud tools paired with a likely Opening Day job demand attention just outside the dynasty top 100.

## 4  Joey Wiemer  OF    OFP: 55    ETA: 2023
Born: 02/11/99   Age: 24   Bats: R   Throws: R   Height: 6'5"   Weight: 215 lb.   Origin: Round 4, 2020 Draft (#121 overall)

| YEAR | TEAM | LVL | AGE | PA | R | 2B | 3B | HR | RBI | BB | K | SB | CS | AVG/OBP/SLG | DRC+ | BABIP | BRR | DRP | WARP |
|------|------|-----|-----|-----|----|----|----|----|-----|----|-----|----|----|-------------|------|-------|------|-----|------|
| 2021 | CAR | A | 22 | 320 | 53 | 11 | 2 | 13 | 44 | 45 | 69 | 22 | 4 | .276/.391/.478 | 126 | .326 | -0.4 | RF(50) 12.5, CF(23) 1.3, LF(5) 0.7 | 3.4 |
| 2021 | WIS | A+ | 22 | 152 | 33 | 7 | 0 | 14 | 33 | 18 | 36 | 8 | 2 | .336/.428/.719 | 155 | .363 | -0.1 | RF(22) -1.1, CF(4) -1.1 | 1.2 |
| 2022 | BLX | AA | 23 | 374 | 57 | 19 | 1 | 15 | 47 | 34 | 113 | 25 | 1 | .243/.321/.440 | 90 | .319 | 4.1 | RF(59) 5.8, CF(21) 0.9, LF(2) 0.2 | 2.5 |
| 2022 | NAS | AAA | 23 | 174 | 24 | 15 | 1 | 6 | 30 | 21 | 34 | 6 | 2 | .287/.368/.520 | 106 | .327 | -0.2 | RF(34) 2.5, CF(2) -0.2 | 1.0 |
| 2023 DC | MIL | MLB | 24 | 30 | 3 | 1 | 0 | 1 | 3 | 2 | 10 | 1 | 0 | .233/.302/.383 | 93 | .328 | 0.2 | RF 0 | 0.1 |

Comparables: Hunter Renfroe, Nick Torres, Johan Mieses

**The Report:** We suspected Wiemer wouldn't repeat his 2021 breakout campaign in the upper minors, but he consolidated enough of his power gains to remain a very good outfield prospect. His swing has a lot of moving parts, including a pretty handsy, hitchy load, and Wiemer follows that with a mighty, leveraged hack. Swing-and-miss in the zone will be a problem, but when he makes contact, he does damage. It's not pure pull-side pop either, as he's just as dangerous when he can get extended on pitches on the outer half and drive them to right field. Given the strikeout issues, it's hard to project more than an average hit tool, but the "swing hard in case you hit it" stratagem does mean Wiemer can muscle some hits into the outfield even with suboptimal contact. He just needs to make enough contact. Despite a tall and broad frame, Wiemer has retained a fair bit of quick-twitch athleticism into his mid-20s. He remains an above-average runner, and while he's not enough of a burner to play center, he should be plus in right field, and has plenty of arm strength for that corner spot as well.

**OFP:** 55 / Middle-of-the-order right fielder

**Variance:** Medium. The overall profile tilts towards Three-True-Outcomes, but Wiemer isn't merely a stiff corner slugger, despite those sorts of hit tool concerns. He will either have to make more contact in the zone in the majors or continue to get high-end batted ball outcomes when he does get the barrel on it.

**Jesse Roche's Fantasy Take:** It was an up-and-down season for Wiemer. On the one hand, he finished the season on fire in Triple-A and notched his second-straight 20/30 campaign. On the other, he generally continued to whiff *a lot*. Indeed, for most of the season, Wiemer hovered just above a 60% contact rate. Few players find success swinging and missing as much as he does. Wiemer could find that Adolis García sweet spot where he gets to his power and speed despite approach and whiff issues. And, to be frank, his small-sample Triple-A performance provides real hope that this is possible. As such, Wiemer falls squarely within the dynasty top 100.

## 5  Eric Brown Jr.  SS          OFP: 55     ETA: 2025

Born: 12/19/00   Age: 22   Bats: R   Throws: R   Height: 5'10"   Weight: 190 lb.   Origin: Round 1, 2022 Draft (#27 overall)

| YEAR | TEAM | LVL | AGE | PA | R | 2B | 3B | HR | RBI | BB | K | SB | CS | AVG/OBP/SLG | DRC+ | BABIP | BRR | DRP | WARP |
|------|------|-----|-----|-----|-----|-----|-----|-----|-----|-----|-----|-----|-----|-------------|------|-------|-----|-----|------|
| 2022 | CAR | A | 21 | 100 | 16 | 4 | 1 | 3 | 7 | 11 | 17 | 15 | 2 | .262/.370/.440 | 121 | .292 | 0.8 | SS(17) 1.0, 2B(3) 0.4 | 0.7 |
| 2023 non-DC | MIL | MLB | 22 | 251 | 20 | 10 | 1 | 3 | 20 | 17 | 57 | 16 | 4 | .210/.274/.304 | 65 | .267 | 3.4 | 2B 0, SS 0 | 0.1 |

*Comparables: Taylor Walls, Osvaldo Abreu, Justin Bohn*

**The Report:** Like the Orioles, the Brewers are unconcerned with how a hitter looks at the plate, and Brown's swing is downright wacky. The bat starts in front of his face, pointing up the third base line. He utilizes a big, hanging leg kick to kill time while the bat makes its loopy path to load. So when Brown chases out of the zone, the swing can look non-prospect-level bad. But the thing is, he doesn't chase much. He doesn't get fooled much. And he doesn't swing and miss much. Brown posted K:BB rates starting with a decimal point at Coastal Carolina, and continued to make good contact in the pros. It's not the most impactful contact profile, but he has the potential for average hit and power tools and his strong command of the zone should lead to solid OBPs. Defensively, he's rangy with a good first step. He throws well on the run, and has a zippy arm when he sets his feet. The hands and actions are fine, and while Brown is not a plus shortstop, he's a solid enough one. Once you get over the Busby Berkeley swing mechanics, you see an average hitter whose raw offensive tools play up due to the approach, and who can handle a premium defensive position. There are no showstopping numbers on the scouting sheet, but Brown is a well-rounded shortstop prospect.

**OFP:** 55 / Solid everyday shortstop

**Variance:** High. Brown has a triple-whammy of risk: A short pro track record, a swing with a lot of moving parts and not much wiggle room with the bat if his offensive tools don't play to full projection.

**Jesse Roche's Fantasy Take:** Brown should top double-digit home runs and stolen bases at peak. In his debut, Brown was 19-for-21 in steals across just 27 games! While that type of pace is unsustainable, he has legit wheels–he was also 13-for-15 across 33 games in the Cape Cod League in 2021. How much impact he'll have without a likely plus tool is the open question. Nevertheless, Brown is a borderline top-20 selection in FYPDs and a top-200 dynasty prospect.

## 6  Tyler Black  2B          OFP: 55     ETA: 2024

Born: 07/26/00   Age: 22   Bats: L   Throws: R   Height: 6'2"   Weight: 190 lb.   Origin: Round 1, 2021 Draft (#33 overall)

| YEAR | TEAM | LVL | AGE | PA | R | 2B | 3B | HR | RBI | BB | K | SB | CS | AVG/OBP/SLG | DRC+ | BABIP | BRR | DRP | WARP |
|------|------|-----|-----|-----|-----|-----|-----|-----|-----|-----|-----|-----|-----|-------------|------|-------|-----|-----|------|
| 2021 | CAR | A | 20 | 103 | 11 | 4 | 0 | 0 | 6 | 20 | 29 | 3 | 2 | .222/.388/.272 | 104 | .346 | -1.3 | 2B(15) -1.4 | 0.1 |
| 2022 | WIS | A+ | 21 | 283 | 45 | 13 | 4 | 4 | 35 | 45 | 44 | 13 | 6 | .281/.406/.424 | 120 | .330 | 0.5 | 2B(30) -2.2, CF(15) -1.4, 3B(6) -0.2 | 1.1 |
| 2023 non-DC | MIL | MLB | 22 | 251 | 21 | 10 | 2 | 2 | 20 | 27 | 50 | 5 | 2 | .220/.311/.310 | 81 | .275 | -1.7 | 2B 0, 3B 0 | 0.0 |

*Comparables: Jose Vallejo, Steve Lombardozzi, Emilio Bonifácio*

**The Report:** Like Brown, Black was a college superstar in a smaller Division I conference, showing a strong eye at the plate and sneaky pop. The power hasn't really shown up in the pros—despite a power hitter's leg kick, he's pretty level and looking to drive pitches into the gaps—but the approach sure has, and he makes very good swing decisions. The lack of pop is going to be a bit of a limiting factor offensively, but defensively his versatility will make him a useful player even if he's only swatting 10 homers a year. Drafted as a second baseman, Black has improved his foot speed and athleticism as a pro and is getting reps in the outfield as well. He should develop into a passable center fielder, perhaps above-average in a corner. It's not the highest-upside profile in the minors, but Black's approach and ability to tote around outfield and infield gloves makes him a high-probability major-leaguer.

**OFP:** 55 / What you imagine a 1980s no. 2 hitter was even though it was usually like Willie McGee

**Variance:** Medium. There's some risk of better velocity and defenses further up the ladder snuffing out some of these base hits, causing Black's batting average to settle more in the .250 range. That would make the profile merely a flexible bench piece.

**Jesse Roche's Fantasy Take:** How do you feel about Brendan Donovan?

## 7  Jeferson Quero   C/DH        OFP: 55      ETA: 2025

Born: 10/08/02   Age: 20   Bats: R   Throws: R   Height: 5'10"   Weight: 165 lb.   Origin: International Free Agent, 2019

| YEAR | TEAM | LVL | AGE | PA | R | 2B | 3B | HR | RBI | BB | K | SB | CS | AVG/OBP/SLG | DRC+ | BABIP | BRR | DRP | WARP |
|------|------|-----|-----|----|----|----|----|----|-----|----|----|----|----|-------------|------|-------|-----|-----|------|
| 2021 | BRWB | ROK | 18 | 83 | 15 | 5 | 1 | 2 | 8 | 12 | 10 | 4 | 3 | .309/.434/.500 | | .339 | | | |
| 2022 | CAR | A | 19 | 320 | 44 | 18 | 1 | 6 | 43 | 28 | 61 | 10 | 2 | .278/.345/.412 | 103 | .330 | 0.5 | C(53) 12.8 | 2.3 |
| 2022 | WIS | A+ | 19 | 85 | 10 | 4 | 1 | 4 | 14 | 2 | 15 | 0 | 0 | .313/.329/.530 | 106 | .344 | -0.1 | C(13) 1.0 | 0.4 |
| 2023 non-DC | MIL | MLB | 20 | 251 | 19 | 10 | 1 | 3 | 21 | 13 | 59 | 3 | 1 | .219/.265/.313 | 62 | .279 | -3.0 | C 0 | -0.4 |

*Comparables: Manuel Margot, Jesus Montero, Gary Sánchez*

**The Report:** Quero continues to progress through the Milwaukee system, and while he's still an A-ball catching prospect, that gives us a bit more to work with than the complex league catching prospect he was this time last year. And he's definitely a catcher, flashing above-average defensive tools behind the plate. At the plate, he shows good feel for the barrel, and puts some heft behind his swings, although the power is more gap than over-the-fence, and his projectability is limited. Reports from the Fall League were a little stronger than in-season—despite a much worse stat line—and Quero remains a breakout candidate once again headed into 2023. But all he really needs to do at this point is keep banking year-over-year gains to develop into an everyday catcher.

**OFP:** 55 / Above-average catcher

**Variance:** High. A-ball catchers are slightly less volatile than complex league catchers but still very volatile, and Quero hasn't really faced the full rigor of a starting catcher workload yet.

**Jesse Roche's Fantasy Take:** In the age of the catcher renaissance, Quero gets overlooked. (There is even another Quero catching prospect outperforming him in A-ball!) Yet, he quietly provided above-average offensive performance across Low- and High-A while flashing solid contact skills and some power. It may be a tired refrain, but catchers are risky fantasy investments, and, consequently, Quero likely should only be rostered in leagues with over 300 prospects.

## 8  Brice Turang   SS        OFP: 50      ETA: 2023

Born: 11/21/99   Age: 23   Bats: L   Throws: R   Height: 6'0"   Weight: 173 lb.   Origin: Round 1, 2018 Draft (#21 overall)

| YEAR | TEAM | LVL | AGE | PA | R | 2B | 3B | HR | RBI | BB | K | SB | CS | AVG/OBP/SLG | DRC+ | BABIP | BRR | DRP | WARP |
|------|------|-----|-----|----|----|----|----|----|-----|----|-----|----|----|-------------|------|-------|-----|-----|------|
| 2021 | BLX | AA | 21 | 320 | 40 | 14 | 3 | 5 | 39 | 28 | 48 | 11 | 7 | .264/.329/.385 | 107 | .300 | 0.4 | SS(71) 2.4 | 1.5 |
| 2021 | NAS | AAA | 21 | 176 | 19 | 7 | 0 | 1 | 14 | 32 | 35 | 9 | 2 | .245/.381/.315 | 100 | .315 | 0.1 | SS(44) 2.1 | 0.8 |
| 2022 | NAS | AAA | 22 | 603 | 89 | 24 | 2 | 13 | 78 | 65 | 118 | 34 | 2 | .286/.360/.412 | 109 | .342 | 1.6 | SS(104) 0.8, CF(14) -2.2, 3B(8) 0.3 | 2.6 |
| 2023 DC | MIL | MLB | 23 | 336 | 34 | 13 | 3 | 4 | 29 | 29 | 66 | 12 | 1 | .230/.301/.333 | 78 | .282 | 2.3 | 2B 0, SS 0 | 0.4 |

*Comparables: Tyler Pastornicky, J.P. Crawford, Asdrúbal Cabrera*

**The Report:** This is Turang's fifth entry in a Brewers Top 10. On the first one we wrote:

> The glove may have to be the carrying tool here, because it is tougher to see one at the plate. Turang steps in the bucket a bit, and his swing emphasizes contact with a slashy approach. None of this lends itself to consistently driving the ball. That—coupled with his smaller build—also limits any power projection, so he's going to have to find infield holes enough to hit .280 or so to be an above-average regular. Not impossible, but we are a long way off from that at present.

Let's see what's changed ... uh ... well, he's no longer a long way off, having spent all of 2022 in Triple-A, and he does drive the ball a little more nowadays, topping double-digit home runs for the first time in his pro career. Turang is never going to be a slugger, but if he can sting balls in the zone like he did last season, that should be enough to keep pitchers from overpowering him too often. His swing decisions are good but not spectacular, and he can struggle with spin, as his big leg kick means once things start going, it can be tricky to adjust.

Turang is still a solid defender at short and has seen some time at second, third and even center. He's a high-probability major-leaguer, but the defenses are going to close in on him in the bigs, and he'll need to prove he can hit MLB-caliber stuff over their heads.

**OFP:** 50 / Everyday shortstop, but maybe one who hits towards the bottom of the order

**Variance:** Medium. This was the first year that Turang's slugging percentage started with a 4. If it's not the last, he's a good regular, but there's some risk that better spin eats into his contact skills and the hit tool is more average.

**Jesse Roche's Fantasy Take:** If the offseason ended today, Turang may be the starting second baseman for the Brewers. He carries intriguing fantasy upside should he find his way into a regular role due to contact skills and, more importantly, his speed. Ultimately, he may look a lot like Isiah Kiner-Falefa at times, which has its fantasy uses.

## 9 Jacob Misiorowski  RHP    OFP: 55    ETA: 2025

Born: 04/03/02   Age: 21   Bats: R   Throws: R   Height: 6'7"   Weight: 190 lb.   Origin: Round 2, 2022 Draft (#63 overall)

| YEAR | TEAM | LVL | AGE | W | L | SV | G | GS | IP | H | HR | BB/9 | K/9 | K | GB% | BABIP | WHIP | ERA | DRA- | WARP |
|---|---|---|---|---|---|---|---|---|---|---|---|---|---|---|---|---|---|---|---|---|
| 2023 non-DC | MIL | MLB | 21 | 3 | 3 | 0 | 58 | 0 | 50 | 53 | 9 | 6.7 | 8.3 | 46 | 35.1% | .307 | 1.80 | 6.35 | 152 | -1.1 |

*Comparables: Riley Pint, Jheyson Manzueta, Trey Riley*

**The Report:** Misiorowski's Trackman gets passed around like early Guided By Voices pressings. That's how you get the biggest bonus in the Brewers' draft class after walking over five per nine at a Missouri JuCo. A 6-foot-7 string bean with an explosive upper-90s fastball and a sharp power slider, both pitches move this way and that, but rarely land all that close to where the catcher is set up. If his college season was effectively wild, his brief professional debut was downright Dalkowskian. The delivery is effortful with late torque, the stuff is elite and the control and command are a 10.

Misiorowski is one of the trickier profiles to rank and might be the highest-variance prospect in the minors despite being a Day 1, seven-figure junior college pick. Very few players are making a team Top 10 who might never get out of A-ball because they walk a batter per inning. Very few players are this low on a team Top 10 who could close with even 30 command. Misiorowski also has very little mound experience between the pandemic and a knee injury that cost him his freshman year at Crowder College. You can project whatever you like onto his projectable frame, but as good as his pitches are, the most important pitch is still strike one.

**OFP:** 55 / Second-division closer

**Variance:** Extreme. I get the pick and the bonus, I really do. Perhaps Misiorowski's stuff gets a bit more under control with a bit more physical development and a couple years of pro instruction. The upside here is tantalizing, but as a scout once said to me about this sort of prospect many years ago: "Let him be someone else's project."

**Jesse Roche's Fantasy Take:** Like Rick Vaughn before glasses, Misiorowski is indeed a Wild Thing. If somehow the Brewers discover Misiorowski's "glasses," we could have something special. Outside of deep fantasy formats, however, we must reiterate: "Let him be someone else's project."

## 10 Ethan Small  LHP    OFP: 50    ETA: Debuted in 2022

Born: 02/14/97   Age: 26   Bats: L   Throws: L   Height: 6'4"   Weight: 215 lb.   Origin: Round 1, 2019 Draft (#28 overall)

| YEAR | TEAM | LVL | AGE | W | L | SV | G | GS | IP | H | HR | BB/9 | K/9 | K | GB% | BABIP | WHIP | ERA | DRA- | WARP |
|---|---|---|---|---|---|---|---|---|---|---|---|---|---|---|---|---|---|---|---|---|
| 2021 | BLX | AA | 24 | 2 | 2 | 0 | 8 | 8 | 41¹ | 26 | 1 | 4.6 | 14.6 | 67 | 39.2% | .342 | 1.14 | 1.96 | 83 | 0.8 |
| 2021 | NAS | AAA | 24 | 2 | 0 | 0 | 9 | 9 | 35 | 27 | 3 | 5.4 | 6.2 | 24 | 43.6% | .245 | 1.37 | 2.06 | 117 | 0.2 |
| 2022 | NAS | AAA | 25 | 7 | 6 | 0 | 27 | 21 | 103 | 82 | 8 | 5.1 | 10.0 | 114 | 40.7% | .282 | 1.36 | 4.46 | 81 | 2.4 |
| 2022 | MIL | MLB | 25 | 0 | 0 | 0 | 2 | 2 | 6¹ | 8 | 1 | 11.4 | 9.9 | 7 | 33.3% | .412 | 2.53 | 7.11 | 154 | -0.1 |
| 2023 DC | MIL | MLB | 26 | 2 | 2 | 0 | 16 | 3 | 24.3 | 23 | 3 | 5.3 | 10.1 | 28 | 35.5% | .313 | 1.53 | 4.78 | 117 | 0.0 |

*Comparables: Matthew Boyd, Amir Garrett, Sam Howard*

**The Report:** Small was also an analytics darling as a draft prospect. He put up ludicrous strikeout rates in the SEC despite a merely low-90s fastball. His combination of extension, deception and ability to locate the pitch at the top of the zone makes it a swing-and-miss offering on its own. It's even more effective when paired with his change, which comes in 15 or so mph slower and drops in at the hitter's knees. The funky delivery and over-the-top slot which makes his stuff play up has also led to control and command issues at the upper levels (and majors). The fastball is effective at the top of the zone, but any higher and it's a ball, and any lower it can get squared. Small has run walk rates north of 10% the last two seasons and while he misses plenty of bats along with the free passes, he will have narrow margins to start in the majors.

**OFP:** 50 / Bulk/swing/multi-inning arm

**Variance:** Medium. Small's fastball/change combo will get whiffs, but he needs to throw more strikes and give up less hard contact when he's not missing bats.

**Jesse Roche's Fantasy Take:** A "bulk/swing/multi-inning arm" is not relevant in nearly any fantasy format.

## Outside the Top Ten:

### 11 Robert Gasser LHP

Born: 05/31/99   Age: 24   Bats: L   Throws: L   Height: 6'1"   Weight: 185 lb.   Origin: Round 2, 2021 Draft (#71 overall)

| YEAR | TEAM | LVL | AGE | W | L | SV | G | GS | IP | H | HR | BB/9 | K/9 | K | GB% | BABIP | WHIP | ERA | DRA- | WARP |
|---|---|---|---|---|---|---|---|---|---|---|---|---|---|---|---|---|---|---|---|---|
| 2021 | LE | A | 22 | 0 | 0 | 0 | 5 | 5 | 14 | 11 | 1 | 1.3 | 8.4 | 13 | 52.8% | .286 | 0.93 | 1.29 | 110 | 0.0 |
| 2022 | FW | A+ | 23 | 4 | 9 | 0 | 18 | 18 | 90¹ | 86 | 8 | 2.8 | 11.5 | 115 | 41.2% | .356 | 1.26 | 4.18 | 96 | 1.1 |
| 2022 | BLX | AA | 23 | 1 | 1 | 0 | 4 | 4 | 20¹ | 14 | 2 | 3.5 | 11.5 | 26 | 42.6% | .273 | 1.08 | 2.21 | 89 | 0.3 |
| 2022 | NAS | AAA | 23 | 2 | 2 | 0 | 5 | 5 | 26¹ | 26 | 1 | 5.5 | 10.6 | 31 | 31.0% | .357 | 1.59 | 4.44 | 109 | 0.2 |
| 2023 non-DC | MIL | MLB | 24 | 3 | 3 | 0 | 58 | 0 | 50 | 51 | 7 | 3.9 | 8.8 | 49 | 35.8% | .311 | 1.45 | 4.64 | 119 | -0.2 |

*Comparables: Daniel Mengden, Domingo Acevedo, Cody Reed*

Acquired at the deadline as part of the return for Josh Hader, Gasser is a fairly typical lefty fourth-starter type. He has a funky, almost undulating, delivery paired with a deceptive, compact arm action that slings low-90s fastballs from a low-three-quarters slot. It's a tough AB for fellow southpaws, especially when his sweeping slider is working for him. Gasser's changeup can come out a bit too flat and bump up a bit too close to his fastball velocity, but it's an effective pitch when it's more in the mid-80s, showing average sink and fade. He commands the change—like everything else—pretty well, and spots it down in the zone while also showing the ability to run it in to righties. Gasser might not have an above-average pitch in his arsenal—although the slider flashes there enough to keep a 55 in play—but everything is around major-league average. It's easy to get a bit jaded about how good average major-league stuff is, but it's really good. Case in point: Gasser struck out nearly 30% of the batters he faced in the minors last season.

### 12 Janson Junk RHP

Born: 01/15/96   Age: 27   Bats: R   Throws: R   Height: 6'1"   Weight: 177 lb.   Origin: Round 22, 2017 Draft (#662 overall)

| YEAR | TEAM | LVL | AGE | W | L | SV | G | GS | IP | H | HR | BB/9 | K/9 | K | GB% | BABIP | WHIP | ERA | DRA- | WARP |
|---|---|---|---|---|---|---|---|---|---|---|---|---|---|---|---|---|---|---|---|---|
| 2021 | RCT | AA | 25 | 2 | 2 | 0 | 5 | 5 | 27¹ | 32 | 5 | 2.3 | 9.5 | 29 | 43.5% | .338 | 1.43 | 5.27 | 100 | 0.2 |
| 2021 | SOM | AA | 25 | 4 | 1 | 1 | 14 | 12 | 65² | 43 | 6 | 2.7 | 9.3 | 68 | 43.6% | .233 | 0.96 | 1.78 | 99 | 0.4 |
| 2021 | LAA | MLB | 25 | 0 | 1 | 0 | 4 | 4 | 16¹ | 20 | 5 | 1.1 | 5.5 | 10 | 37.3% | .283 | 1.35 | 3.86 | 124 | -0.1 |
| 2022 | SL | AAA | 26 | 1 | 7 | 0 | 16 | 15 | 73² | 77 | 9 | 2.2 | 8.4 | 69 | 32.3% | .318 | 1.29 | 4.64 | 110 | 0.0 |
| 2022 | LAA | MLB | 26 | 1 | 1 | 0 | 3 | 2 | 8¹ | 10 | 1 | 3.2 | 11.9 | 11 | 65.2% | .409 | 1.56 | 6.48 | 86 | 0.1 |
| 2023 DC | MIL | MLB | 27 | 2 | 2 | 0 | 40 | 0 | 34.7 | 37 | 5 | 3.1 | 6.1 | 24 | 40.2% | .297 | 1.41 | 4.43 | 114 | 0.1 |

*Comparables: Tyler Cloyd, Brad Lincoln, Erick Fedde*

If you are a fan of nominative determinism, Junk's fastball is a shade below average on the radar gun, and he throws his two breaking balls more than half the time. He was the best prospect in the Hunter Renfroe trade, but none of his four pitches are what you'd call bat-missers. Junk relies on his pitch mix and command to keep hitters off balance, and that worked well enough in Triple-A, considering the unfriendly confines of the PCL. It hasn't really worked in the majors, save for one strong July outing against the Royals lineup. Junk will be 27 before the start of the 2023 season, and if he can tighten up and lean more heavily on his low-80s sweepy slider, he could take some starts for Milwaukee at the back of their rotation.

### 13 Victor Castaneda RHP

Born: 08/27/98   Age: 24   Bats: R   Throws: R   Height: 6'1"   Weight: 185 lb.   Origin: International Free Agent, 2017

| YEAR | TEAM | LVL | AGE | W | L | SV | G | GS | IP | H | HR | BB/9 | K/9 | K | GB% | BABIP | WHIP | ERA | DRA- | WARP |
|---|---|---|---|---|---|---|---|---|---|---|---|---|---|---|---|---|---|---|---|---|
| 2021 | WIS | A+ | 22 | 5 | 7 | 0 | 20 | 20 | 97 | 90 | 18 | 3.4 | 10.6 | 114 | 35.3% | .300 | 1.31 | 5.20 | 99 | 1.1 |
| 2021 | NAS | AAA | 22 | 1 | 1 | 0 | 3 | 2 | 12 | 9 | 0 | 6.0 | 12.8 | 17 | 33.3% | .333 | 1.42 | 2.25 | 75 | 0.2 |
| 2022 | BLX | AA | 23 | 4 | 6 | 0 | 23 | 22 | 106² | 97 | 16 | 4.0 | 9.3 | 110 | 35.7% | .286 | 1.35 | 3.97 | 115 | 0.2 |
| 2022 | NAS | AAA | 23 | 2 | 0 | 0 | 3 | 3 | 14 | 14 | 1 | 3.2 | 5.1 | 8 | 49.0% | .271 | 1.36 | 5.14 | 106 | 0.1 |
| 2023 non-DC | MIL | MLB | 24 | 3 | 3 | 0 | 58 | 0 | 50 | 55 | 8 | 4.3 | 7.9 | 44 | 35.1% | .316 | 1.57 | 5.28 | 133 | -0.6 |

We round out our post-Top-10 trio of back-end starters with Castaneda. He might have the best single pitch of the group, a low-80s splitter that he sells well and which shows good dive. The best just parachute off a cliff on hitters like an elementary-school egg-drop experiment. The rest of the arsenal is more pedestrian. His fastball sits in the low-90s, while a short slurvy breaker is a clear third-best offering. It does at least have some utility, even if just as a little glove-side chase pitch. Castaneda is major-league ready, and the splitty is good enough to offer some relief fallback—but like Junk and Gasser, he might be a more useful arm to a team a bit worse than Milwaukee that's looking to fill innings.

## 14 Carlos Rodriguez  RHP

Born: 11/27/01  Age: 21  Bats: R  Throws: R  Height: 6'0"  Weight: 180 lb.  Origin: Round 6, 2021 Draft (#177 overall)

| YEAR | TEAM | LVL | AGE | W | L | SV | G | GS | IP | H | HR | BB/9 | K/9 | K | GB% | BABIP | WHIP | ERA | DRA- | WARP |
|------|------|-----|-----|---|---|----|----|----|-----|----|----|------|------|----|------|-------|------|------|------|------|
| 2022 | CAR | A | 20 | 3 | 4 | 1 | 19 | 13 | 71¹ | 53 | 7 | 3.4 | 10.6 | 84 | 39.1% | .286 | 1.12 | 3.53 | 80 | 1.5 |
| 2022 | WIS | A+ | 20 | 3 | 1 | 0 | 7 | 7 | 36¹ | 21 | 0 | 3.2 | 11.1 | 45 | 38.3% | .259 | 0.94 | 1.98 | 75 | 0.8 |
| 2023 non-DC | MIL | MLB | 21 | 3 | 3 | 0 | 58 | 0 | 50 | 50 | 7 | 4.2 | 8.3 | 46 | 33.8% | .300 | 1.47 | 4.76 | 122 | -0.3 |

*Comparables: Matt Manning, Sean Reid-Foley, Drew Hutchison*

The Brewers' sixth-round pick in 2021—not to be confused with the outfielder also named Carlos Rodriguez who has made these lists in the past—the pitcher Carlos Rodriguez had a dominant season between two A-ball levels in 2022. He's a shorter, sturdy righty with some late arm effort in his uptempo delivery, and the whole aesthetic can look very relieverish. Rodriguez has a full four-pitch mix though, and throws enough strikes that it's not *fait accompli* he moves to the bullpen. His fastball sits mostly in an average velo band, but it is explosive up in the zone. His changeup is the best secondary offering and it flashes late twist and sink to get under bats. Rodriguez snaps off his breaker a bit too much and doesn't always get on top it, but the slider does show some promise. A 2023 campaign in the upper minors will bring some clarity to Rodruguez's ultimate role, but in a system lacking in impact arms, his potential upside as a starter is very intriguing.

## 15 Felix Valerio  2B

Born: 12/26/00  Age: 22  Bats: R  Throws: R  Height: 5'7"  Weight: 165 lb.  Origin: International Free Agent, 2018

| YEAR | TEAM | LVL | AGE | PA | R | 2B | 3B | HR | RBI | BB | K | SB | CS | AVG/OBP/SLG | DRC+ | BABIP | BRR | DRP | WARP |
|------|------|-----|-----|-----|----|----|----|----|-----|----|----|----|----|-------------|------|-------|------|-----|------|
| 2021 | CAR | A | 20 | 377 | 71 | 24 | 3 | 6 | 63 | 54 | 49 | 27 | 8 | .314/.430/.469 | 135 | .354 | 0.7 | 2B(40) -4.2, SS(18) -0.5, 3B(17) 2.4 | 2.5 |
| 2021 | WIS | A+ | 20 | 134 | 19 | 13 | 0 | 5 | 16 | 15 | 22 | 4 | 1 | .229/.321/.466 | 120 | .242 | -0.6 | 2B(27) -3.8 | 0.3 |
| 2022 | BLX | AA | 21 | 480 | 60 | 14 | 2 | 12 | 51 | 48 | 80 | 30 | 9 | .228/.313/.357 | 106 | .249 | -1.5 | 2B(82) 3.3, LF(8) 0.3, 3B(3) 0.1 | 1.8 |
| 2023 non-DC | MIL | MLB | 22 | 251 | 21 | 10 | 1 | 3 | 21 | 20 | 44 | 8 | 2 | .215/.288/.317 | 74 | .254 | -0.4 | 2B 0, 3B 0 | 0.0 |

*Comparables: Abiatal Avelino, Luis Valbuena, Vidal Bruján*

Valerio was the third piece in the 2019 Keon Broxton trade, but his 2021 performance made him the chalk pick to end up the best pro. Double-A was always going to be a strong test of his profile though and he struggled in the Southern League, especially in the second half. Valerio is patient, bordering on passive, and upper-minors arms were far more likely to challenge him in the zone—although he still drew his fair share of walks. His swing remains unorthodox: There's an early hand-load and big, hanging leg-kick that makes him look like he's striking the Heisman pose while he waits for his pitch. Valerio explodes forward from there, wringing everything he can out of his definitely, totally, absolutely, not-just-listed-at 5-foot-7 frame. It's impressive how much contact he can make with that swing, but it's not always good contact, and there are a lot of medium-depth fly balls and choppers to the left side in there.

Valerio is still primarily a second baseman—where he's a bit better than average—but he saw some time in the outfield as well. His foot speed is fine for the grass, and he's taken to the outfield, although he can kind of be a bit too gung-ho, especially when playing center. The athletic tools are a better fit for left, but the overall positional flexibility—he's spent time at third and short as well—will help him to carve out a bench role if he can figure out higher-level pitching.

## 16 Hendry Mendez  RF

Born: 11/07/03  Age: 19  Bats: L  Throws: L  Height: 6'2"  Weight: 175 lb.  Origin: International Free Agent, 2021

| YEAR | TEAM | LVL | AGE | PA | R | 2B | 3B | HR | RBI | BB | K | SB | CS | AVG/OBP/SLG | DRC+ | BABIP | BRR | DRP | WARP |
|------|------|-----|-----|-----|----|----|----|----|-----|----|----|----|----|-------------|------|-------|------|-----|------|
| 2021 | DSL BRW1 | ROK | 17 | 64 | 10 | 5 | 1 | 1 | 9 | 7 | 2 | 0 | 0 | .296/.391/.481 | | .288 | | | |
| 2021 | BRWB | ROK | 17 | 74 | 6 | 4 | 2 | 0 | 10 | 10 | 10 | 3 | 1 | .333/.425/.460 | | .396 | | | |
| 2022 | CAR | A | 18 | 446 | 47 | 11 | 1 | 5 | 39 | 62 | 70 | 7 | 8 | .244/.357/.318 | 115 | .286 | -4.4 | RF(85) -3.3, CF(2) -0.2 | 1.2 |
| 2023 non-DC | MIL | MLB | 19 | 251 | 19 | 9 | 2 | 2 | 18 | 21 | 42 | 2 | 1 | .207/.279/.283 | 61 | .247 | -3.2 | LF 0, CF 0 | -0.9 |

*Comparables: Agustin Ruiz, Zach Collier, Starling Heredia*

Inked during the 2021 IFA period for a high six-figure bonus, Mendez spent 2022 at a pretty aggressive full-season assignment and struggled to impact the ball against older and more experienced arms. There are things to like in his offensive game, but the bat can swing him a bit at present, as Mendez has a narrow, slender frame. If he can get a bit stronger, the swing does have some nice late torque to it and he can pull the odd ball with enough authority to project some power down the line. And I wouldn't even say he was overmatched despite some swing-and-miss issues in the zone in A-ball. This might have looked a bit better with another year in the Phoenix complex, but in a still-shallow system that can lack for upside, Mendez at least provides something to dream on.

## Top Talents 25 and Under (as of 4/1/2023):

1. Jackson Chourio, OF
2. Sal Frelick, OF
3. Aaron Ashby, LHP
4. Garrett Mitchell, OF
5. Joey Wiemer, OF
6. Eric Brown Jr., SS
7. Tyler Black, OF
8. Jeferson Quero, C
9. Brice Turang, SS
10. Jacob Misiorowski, RHP

The youngest position player who saw any significant playing time on the 2022 Brewers was Keston Hiura, who feels like he's already been around for a decade, but only turned 26 in season. Still, that makes him ineligible for this list, as is Elvis Peguero (acquired in the Renfroe trade). He misses by a week, but has similar command issues to Misiorowski without the high-end stuff. That leaves us with just Aaron Ashby. He had a bit of a roller-coaster season, but was more effective when used in short-burst relief work rather than starting. He might end up the Brewers' Josh Hader replacement, where he can lean more heavily on his power sinker and big-moving, bat-missing slide piece in fireman work.

# Minnesota Twins

## The State of the System:

Trades and graduations have diluted the top 10, and there are injury/durability concerns up and down the system again, but Minnesota still has a lot of depth, especially in pitching.

## The Top Ten:

### 1 Brooks Lee SS OFP: 60 ETA: 2024

Born: 02/14/01 Age: 22 Bats: S Throws: R Height: 6'2" Weight: 205 lb. Origin: Round 1, 2022 Draft (#8 overall)

| YEAR | TEAM | LVL | AGE | PA | R | 2B | 3B | HR | RBI | BB | K | SB | CS | AVG/OBP/SLG | DRC+ | BABIP | BRR | DRP | WARP |
|------|------|-----|-----|-----|----|----|----|----|-----|----|----|----|----|-------------|------|-------|------|------------|------|
| 2022 | CR | A+ | 21 | 114 | 14 | 4 | 0 | 4 | 12 | 16 | 18 | 0 | 2 | .289/.395/.454 | 114 | .320 | -1.9 | SS(20) -1.0 | 0.3 |
| 2023 non-DC | MIN | MLB | 22 | 251 | 22 | 10 | 1 | 4 | 22 | 20 | 61 | 1 | 0 | .225/.292/.332 | 77 | .290 | -4.0 | SS 0 | -0.3 |

*Comparables: C.J. Hinojosa, Luis Rengifo, Didi Gregorius*

**The Report:** Brooks Lee's swing looks like someone tried to draw Hunter Pence from memory with their off hand. The zoomers would call it "jank." You would not teach this, and if someone came to you with it, you might wonder if they ever watched baseball after 1983. All that said, it might produce plus hit and plus power in the end. That bat speed is quite good, as is the hand-eye. The barrel stays in the zone long enough to do damage line-to-line, and the ball rips off his bat at angles you just don't normally see. There's certainly risk in the long-term offensive profile as he sees better stuff, but that's true of basically every prospect in A-ball, and most don't have his underlying hard contact. Defensively, Lee shows off fine hands and footwork, but not the kind of range and actions that portend a future shortstop. That skill set works fine at third base, and he has enough arm for the hot corner. The bat should play just fine there as well.

**OFP:** 60 / First-division third baseman

**Variance:** Medium. If the swing was 20% less weird this would be low, but that's more a personal issue for me than a projection issue for Lee.

**Jesse Roche's Fantasy Take:** Regardless of Lee's unorthodox swing, he can really hit. In July, I wrote: "Many will label Lee as a 'better in real-life than fantasy' prospect. They'd be wrong." Indeed, as noted above, his bat drives his value, with potential plus hit and plus power upside. Lee has done nothing but hit and hit and hit over the past year plus, running up batting averages of .404, .357 and .303 across the Cape Cod League, his junior season, and his debut. His approach trends hit-over-power with tons of low-lying contact. Further, Lee is not a threat to steal bases. Nevertheless, he should profile as a high-average hitter with solid power and run production at peak. Lee is a borderline top-50 dynasty prospect.

### 2 Royce Lewis SS OFP: 60 ETA: Debuted in 2022

Born: 06/05/99 Age: 24 Bats: R Throws: R Height: 6'2" Weight: 200 lb. Origin: Round 1, 2017 Draft (#1 overall)

| YEAR | TEAM | LVL | AGE | PA | R | 2B | 3B | HR | RBI | BB | K | SB | CS | AVG/OBP/SLG | DRC+ | BABIP | BRR | DRP | WARP |
|------|------|-----|-----|-----|----|----|----|----|----|-----|----|----|----|-------------|------|-------|------|------------------------------|------|
| 2022 | STP | AAA | 23 | 153 | 30 | 12 | 1 | 5 | 14 | 18 | 32 | 12 | 2 | .313/.405/.534 | 116 | .379 | -0.3 | SS(26) -0.5, 3B(2) 0.1, LF(2) 0.2 | 0.7 |
| 2022 | MIN | MLB | 23 | 41 | 5 | 4 | 0 | 2 | 5 | 1 | 5 | 0 | 0 | .300/.317/.550 | 114 | .303 | 0.5 | SS(11) -0.7, CF(1) 0 | 0.2 |
| 2023 DC | MIN | MLB | 24 | 90 | 9 | 4 | 0 | 2 | 9 | 6 | 20 | 3 | 1 | .251/.303/.377 | 96 | .306 | 0.2 | SS 0, LF 0 | 0.3 |

*Comparables: Richard Urena, Wilmer Flores, Ketel Marte*

**The Report:** Royce Lewis' swing has been a concern of this publication's prospect team for the better part of three years now. In addition, two of those three years are null sets on his BP player page due to the pandemic and then an ACL surgery in 2021. Lewis emerged in 2022 with a much quieter setup and direct hand path, crushing Triple-A and hitting .300 with power in a major-league cameo. Then he tore the same ACL again, ending his season in June. If Lewis stayed healthy he would no doubt be ineligible for this list, and perhaps the Twins would have pushed the Yankees to five instead of the Guardians (okay, that part strains credulity).

Lewis looked once again like a top-10 prospect in baseball...for two months. This now makes two significant knee surgeries, and he will be 24 next season. The five-tool up-the-middle talent—with potential plus-plus offensive grades—was on display in 2022 for the first time in a while. Will he bounce back and carve out a big-league role despite Carlos Correa's unexpected return at shortstop? Can he still stick and thrive on the left end of the defensive spectrum after two ACL tears? There are a lot of open questions here. Another one, what—and how much—we see of Lewis in 2023 is anyone's guess, but he still has All-Star upside.

**OFP:** 60 / First-division starter somewhere in the middle of the diamond.

**Variance:** High. If you told me Lewis won 2023 AL Rookie of the Year running away, I'd believe you. If you told me he never got all the way back from a second knee surgery, I'd believe you.

**Jesse Roche's Fantasy Take:** Lewis made quite an impression last year, showcasing a revamped swing, power and speed in Triple-A and his brief, 12-game debut. Unfortunately, well, you know. Presuming he returns healthy next year, Lewis likely slots into the Twins lineup somewhere by midseason. A healthy Lewis is a power-speed dynamo with 20/20 or better upside. Of course, "health" is a necessary qualifier when discussing his short- and long-term potential. Absent that risk, he would be a clear top-10 dynasty prospect. Even accounting for "health," Lewis is the top dynasty prospect in this organization due to his five-category upside, recent upper-level performance and proximity.

## 3  Emmanuel Rodriguez  OF      OFP: 60      ETA: 2025
Born: 02/28/03   Age: 20   Bats: L   Throws: L   Height: 5'10"   Weight: 210 lb.   Origin: International Free Agent, 2019

| YEAR | TEAM | LVL | AGE | PA | R | 2B | 3B | HR | RBI | BB | K | SB | CS | AVG/OBP/SLG | DRC+ | BABIP | BRR | DRP | WARP |
|------|------|-----|-----|-----|----|----|----|----|-----|----|----|----|----|-------------|------|-------|-----|-----|------|
| 2021 | TWI | ROK | 18 | 153 | 31 | 5 | 2 | 10 | 23 | 23 | 56 | 9 | 4 | .214/.346/.524 | | .279 | | | |
| 2022 | FTM | A | 19 | 199 | 35 | 5 | 3 | 9 | 25 | 57 | 52 | 11 | 5 | .272/.492/.551 | 153 | .364 | 1.6 | CF(37) -0.2, RF(4) -0.4 | 1.7 |
| 2023 non-DC | MIN | MLB | 20 | 251 | 25 | 9 | 3 | 4 | 24 | 35 | 82 | 7 | 3 | .227/.342/.354 | 104 | .350 | -0.4 | LF 0, CF 0 | 0.9 |

Comparables: Khalil Lee, Akil Baddoo, Drew Waters

**The Report:** When a knee injury ended his season in June, Rodriguez was in the midst of a very loud breakout season in Fort Myers. He checks all the boxes for a future top offensive prospect. He knows the zone well, does not expand, and when he sees pitches over the plate, he punishes them.

Rodriguez generates plus-plus bat speed despite a fairly shallow load. It's a classic rotational lefty swing as imagined by Kenji Fukusaku—the violence feels gratuitous, but is intrinsic to the art. The best way to describe the contact is "wicked hard," and while there will no doubt be more whiffs further up the ladder given how hard he swings—and he will swing over stuff diving out of the zone—a plus-plus hit, plus-plus power outfielder is in play down the line. Rodriguez is a burner who plays a marauding center field with a bit of extra—but not gratuitous—flair. The normal course of filling out and slowing down in his 20s—plus the knee surgery—might eventually force him to a corner, but he has some speed to give back, and the bat will handle any of the outfield spots. You could even argue he has the highest realistic upside of the top three prospects here given he's still one significant lower body injury behind Lewis at this point.

**OFP:** 60 / First-division outfielder

**Variance:** High. The knee injury that cut off Rodriguez's season also means there's a fairly short track record of this level of performance.

**Jesse Roche's Fantasy Take:** A standout performer in Low-A Florida State League, Rodriguez displayed a leveraged swing with serious pop, including a max exit velocity of 111.6 mph and an average exit velocity of 90.2 mph. At the same time, he ran up a wild 28.6% walk rate due to a low 33% swing rate and superb plate discipline. As noted above, Rodriguez also can run (pre-injury) and likely provides some value on the bases as well. Rodriguez is a top-100 dynasty prospect that receives a substantial boost in on-base percentage formats.

## 4 Marco Raya   RHP     OFP: 60     ETA: Late 2025, maybe. Probably 2026

Born: 08/07/02   Age: 20   Bats: R   Throws: R   Height: 6'1"   Weight: 170 lb.   Origin: Round 4, 2020 Draft (#128 overall)

| YEAR | TEAM | LVL | AGE | W | L | SV | G | GS | IP | H | HR | BB/9 | K/9 | K | GB% | BABIP | WHIP | ERA | DRA- | WARP |
|------|------|-----|-----|---|---|----|----|----|----|----|----|------|-----|----|-----|-------|------|-----|------|------|
| 2022 | FTM | A | 19 | 3 | 2 | 0 | 19 | 17 | 65 | 47 | 8 | 3.2 | 10.5 | 76 | 43.5% | .255 | 1.08 | 3.05 | 96 | 1.2 |
| 2023 non-DC | MIN | MLB | 20 | 3 | 3 | 0 | 58 | 0 | 50 | 53 | 9 | 4.3 | 7.6 | 42 | 34.7% | .303 | 1.54 | 5.30 | 133 | -0.6 |

Comparables: Germán Márquez, Michael Kopech, Ian Anderson

**The Report:** I'll just repeat what I wrote in his Ten Pack from September: "When Marco Raya has a full, healthy season under his belt, he will be one of the top pitching prospects in baseball." He was mostly healthy in 2022, but tossed just 65 innings across 19 appearances. His fastball is merely above-average, sitting in the mid-90s with good analytic traits. Now let's talk about that offspeed stuff. Raya's slider is Charon, come to ferry batters back to the dugout. A plus-plus, big spin, mid-80s monster of a breaker. His upper-70s curveball is merely plus despite having five feet of vertical drop at times, as it doesn't always draw swings-and-misses in A-ball because what are you supposed to do with that exactly? (Just hope it's a ball.) There's even a reasonably useful change at present with power fade and sink in the upper-80s. Raya is on the shorter and slighter side. He missed most of 2021 with shoulder issues. There's extreme risk here—see below—but when I wrote that Rodriguez might have the most upside of the top three, well, I didn't write he has the most upside in the system.

**OFP:** 60 / no. 3 starter or first-division closer

**Variance:** Extreme. We might be a year away from calling Raya the best pitching prospect in the minors. We might be a year away from writing: "After missing most of 2023 with arm issues..."

**Jesse Roche's Fantasy Take:** Raya's injury history and size create extreme risk. Yet, his stuff is loud, as detailed above—most notably, his epic, sweeping slider which missed tons of bats and induced tons of swings out of the zone. Raya's upside is worth chasing in dynasty leagues, but he likely should be left only for formats that roster up to 300 prospects.

## 5 Simeon Woods Richardson   RHP     OFP: 55     ETA: Debuted in 2022

Born: 09/27/00   Age: 22   Bats: R   Throws: R   Height: 6'3"   Weight: 210 lb.   Origin: Round 2, 2018 Draft (#48 overall)

| YEAR | TEAM | LVL | AGE | W | L | SV | G | GS | IP | H | HR | BB/9 | K/9 | K | GB% | BABIP | WHIP | ERA | DRA- | WARP |
|------|------|-----|-----|---|---|----|----|----|-----|----|----|------|------|----|-------|-------|------|------|------|------|
| 2021 | NH | AA | 20 | 2 | 4 | 0 | 11 | 11 | 45$^1$ | 42 | 5 | 5.2 | 13.3 | 67 | 32.4% | .359 | 1.50 | 5.76 | 86 | 0.6 |
| 2021 | WCH | AA | 20 | 1 | 1 | 0 | 4 | 3 | 8 | 6 | 0 | 9.0 | 11.2 | 10 | 38.1% | .316 | 1.75 | 6.75 | 101 | 0.1 |
| 2022 | WCH | AA | 21 | 3 | 3 | 0 | 16 | 15 | 70$^2$ | 56 | 4 | 3.3 | 9.8 | 77 | 42.5% | .294 | 1.16 | 3.06 | 77 | 1.3 |
| 2022 | STP | AAA | 21 | 2 | 0 | 0 | 7 | 7 | 36$^2$ | 21 | 2 | 2.5 | 9.3 | 38 | 46.2% | .213 | 0.85 | 2.21 | 79 | 0.9 |
| 2022 | MIN | MLB | 21 | 0 | 1 | 0 | 1 | 1 | 5 | 3 | 1 | 3.6 | 5.4 | 3 | 20.0% | .143 | 1.00 | 3.60 | 120 | 0.0 |
| 2023 DC | MIN | MLB | 22 | 1 | 2 | 0 | 5 | 5 | 22.7 | 22 | 3 | 3.8 | 7.8 | 20 | 34.8% | .285 | 1.37 | 3.91 | 107 | 0.1 |

Comparables: Carlos Martinez, Jacob Turner, Deivi García

**The Report:** It's unfair to say that prospect fatigue has set in on Woods Richardson. He's only 21 and had a strong 2022 campaign across the upper minors. After an uneven 2021 marred by control issues and a lot of frequent flyer miles between New Hampshire, the Olympics in Tokyo, and Wichita, he struck out better than a batter per in 2022 while posting fairly nondescript walk rates. Woods Richardson had a reputation as a power pitcher given his velocity spike his senior year of high school, and big breaking curveball, but he's sat in the low-90s for a while now, and throws his slider and potential plus change more than the curve. His fastball has pretty good extension from a high slot and can get swings and misses up. It also can get punished lower in the zone.

His change has developed rapidly over the last couple seasons and now shows plus sink and fade with 10 mph of velocity separation off the fastball. His slider is more prominent but can be a bit slurvy. Both breakers have average projection as the curve can play well off the fastball up in the zone, but Woods Richardson isn't consistently on top of the pitch in a way that will get swing-and-miss down and out of the zone. His arm action is a bit stabby, his delivery uptempo, but outside of 2021, he's always thrown enough strikes. Whether he will get enough *swinging* strikes at the highest level is yet to be seen, but there's enough stuff here to see a mid-rotation starter if he can keep major-league hitters off his fastball.

**OFP:** 55 no. 3/4 starter

**Variance:** Medium. Woods Richardson has four usable major league offerings, but if his fastball plays down in the rotation, he's more of a back-end starter.

**Jesse Roche's Fantasy Take:** It may not be prospect fatigue–though, he has already been traded twice–but rather regressing raw stuff that has put many off of Woods Richardson. (He likely remains prominent in the minds of many for forcing a resizing of columns in Excel sheets.) Woods Richardson likely slots as a back-end starter, but one with a deep enough arsenal and proximity to make noise in the coming years, and he should be rostered in leagues with up to 300 prospects.

## 6 Louie Varland RHP    OFP: 55    ETA: Debuted in 2022

Born: 12/09/97   Age: 25   Bats: L   Throws: R   Height: 6'1"   Weight: 205 lb.   Origin: Round 15, 2019 Draft (#449 overall)

| YEAR | TEAM | LVL | AGE | W | L | SV | G | GS | IP | H | HR | BB/9 | K/9 | K | GB% | BABIP | WHIP | ERA | DRA- | WARP |
|------|------|-----|-----|---|---|----|----|----|-----|-----|----|------|------|-----|-------|-------|------|------|------|------|
| 2021 | FTM | A | 23 | 4 | 2 | 0 | 10 | 8 | 47¹ | 41 | 2 | 3.0 | 14.5 | 76 | 45.7% | .379 | 1.20 | 2.09 | 82 | 1.0 |
| 2021 | CR | A+ | 23 | 6 | 2 | 0 | 10 | 10 | 55² | 41 | 4 | 2.3 | 10.7 | 66 | 37.4% | .276 | 0.99 | 2.10 | 87 | 0.9 |
| 2022 | WCH | AA | 24 | 7 | 4 | 0 | 20 | 19 | 105 | 102 | 14 | 3.3 | 10.2 | 119 | 40.3% | .320 | 1.34 | 3.34 | 82 | 1.6 |
| 2022 | STP | AAA | 24 | 1 | 1 | 0 | 4 | 4 | 21¹ | 15 | 1 | 1.3 | 11.4 | 27 | 36.5% | .275 | 0.84 | 1.69 | 81 | 0.5 |
| 2022 | MIN | MLB | 24 | 1 | 2 | 0 | 5 | 5 | 26 | 26 | 4 | 2.1 | 7.3 | 21 | 38.5% | .297 | 1.23 | 3.81 | 111 | 0.1 |
| 2023 DC | MIN | MLB | 25 | 3 | 3 | 0 | 20 | 6 | 43.7 | 43 | 6 | 3.2 | 7.7 | 38 | 37.1% | .291 | 1.34 | 4.01 | 110 | 0.2 |

*Comparables: Tyler Duffey, Jimmy Nelson, Ben Lively*

**The Report:** Varland continued his 2021 low-minors breakout all the way up to Target Field in 2022. His mid-90s fastball comes in flat with good extension and jumps on hitters late, and a mid-80s slider with sharp 11-5 tilt complements the fastball well. His change looked pretty good in his major-league cameo although the pitch didn't consistently miss bats in the minors. Varland also will pop an occasional upper-80s cutter for another crossover option, although it's a below-average offering at present. Varland's delivery is a little quirky, with a glove tap and a short arm action. He's generally thrown strikes, but not always good strikes, and he's been susceptible to the long ball the higher up the ladder he's gone. He'll continue to cash major-league per diems off his above-average fastball/slider combo, but this profile might end up playing better in the pen.

**OFP:** 55 / no. 3/4 starter or setup arm

**Variance:** Low. Varland is likely to be on the Twins' staff in the short-term, although whether that role is back-end starter, reliever or something in between will depend on his ability to miss bats with his secondaries and work deeper into games.

**Jesse Roche's Fantasy Take:** Varland had a successful September cup of coffee, logging five solid outings with five scoreless innings against the White Sox to cap off his season. Much of his fantasy value is tied to his proximity rather than his true upside. Still, Varland likely makes an impact in 2023–even if it is only as a streamer–and should be rostered in leagues with up to 200 prospects.

## 7 Matt Canterino RHP    OFP: 55    ETA: 2024

Born: 12/14/97   Age: 25   Bats: R   Throws: R   Height: 6'2"   Weight: 222 lb.   Origin: Round 2, 2019 Draft (#54 overall)

| YEAR | TEAM | LVL | AGE | W | L | SV | G | GS | IP | H | HR | BB/9 | K/9 | K | GB% | BABIP | WHIP | ERA | DRA- | WARP |
|------|------|-----|-----|---|---|----|----|----|-----|----|----|------|------|-----|-------|-------|------|------|------|------|
| 2021 | CR | A+ | 23 | 1 | 0 | 0 | 5 | 5 | 21 | 10 | 1 | 1.7 | 18.4 | 43 | 41.9% | .300 | 0.67 | 0.86 | 54 | 0.7 |
| 2022 | WCH | AA | 24 | 0 | 1 | 0 | 11 | 10 | 34¹ | 17 | 1 | 5.8 | 13.1 | 50 | 26.4% | .229 | 1.14 | 1.83 | 73 | 0.7 |
| 2023 non-DC | MIN | MLB | 25 | 3 | 3 | 0 | 58 | 0 | 50 | 41 | 7 | 4.6 | 11.7 | 65 | 34.2% | .295 | 1.33 | 3.83 | 101 | 0.2 |

*Comparables: Yeiper Castillo, Mitch White, Scott Barlow*

**The Report:** As I did with Raya, I'll just repeat what I wrote in Canterino's 2022 Twins Prospect List blurb: "You might be surprised to hear me opine that Canterino has the best stuff of any Twins pitching prospect. You will be less surprised to hear that a former Rice pitcher had an injury-marred pro season." This year's injury was a torn UCL after just 37 innings, and it will likely cost him most if not all of the 2023 campaign. Perhaps this will get Canterino a clean, healthy restart in 2024. If the stuff comes all the way back, it's...well, arguably the best in the org: a mid-90s fastball that plays up from a high slot and funky stop-start delivery, a power change that just falls off the deck and a big-breaking mid-80s slider.

We've covered Canterino's injury issues the last couple years, and he still has the same high-effort delivery, so there are some blaring reliever markers in his profile at this point. And if we can say a pitcher is "effectively wild," you could say Canterino's offspeed is "effectively inconsistent." Sometimes the slider has razor-blade break, and sometimes it's more of a power slurve. The change can parachute in or have wiffle-ball run. Both pitcher and hitter might be guessing at times, but more often than not, Canterino wins.

**OFP:** 55 / Mid-rotation starter or late-inning reliever

**Variance:** High. Canterino won't step back on a mound until well into 2023. We don't know how the stuff will come back, and he might be better suited to just letting it loose in 1-2 inning bursts once he's healthy.

**Jesse Roche's Fantasy Take:** Canterino is at his best when he can air out his mid-90s fastball with borderline-elite shape and pair it with a devastating changeup with absurd depth. It likely will be in relief, though, which limits his fantasy upside, especially in an organization with Jhoan Duran.

## 8 Connor Prielipp LHP    OFP: 55    ETA: Late 2025
Born: 01/10/01   Age: 22   Bats: L   Throws: L   Height: 6'2"   Weight: 210 lb.   Origin: Round 2, 2022 Draft (#48 overall)

**The Report:** Prielipp fits right into the Twins' system as a high-upside pitcher with recent arm maladies, having missed almost all of 2021-22 after Tommy John surgery. He made all of seven starts in his three years at Bama, but has a potential mid-90s fastball and plus power slider in his holster when healthy. Normally a blurb for the eighth-best prospect in a system would be fleshed out a bit more, but there is little more to say about a pitcher who has been on a mound this little.

**OFP:** 55 / no. 3/4 starter or late-inning reliever

**Variance:** High. Prielipp was really only throwing in side sessions and workouts before the draft, and while the later ones wowed scouts, we will really only know if he's all the way back once he's on a pro mound next spring.

**Jesse Roche's Fantasy Take:** Don't get drawn too much into that pre-2021 hype. Prielipp never really faced top SEC competition in college. In upcoming first-year player drafts, Prielipp is a fine late-round flier–outside the top 40–but don't reach for him.

## 9 David Festa RHP    OFP: 50    ETA: 2024
Born: 03/08/00   Age: 23   Bats: R   Throws: R   Height: 6'6"   Weight: 185 lb.   Origin: Round 13, 2021 Draft (#399 overall)

| YEAR | TEAM | LVL | AGE | W | L | SV | G | GS | IP | H | HR | BB/9 | K/9 | K | GB% | BABIP | WHIP | ERA | DRA- | WARP |
|------|------|-----|-----|---|---|----|----|----|------|----|----|------|------|----|------|-------|------|------|------|------|
| 2021 | TWI | ROK | 21 | 1 | 0 | 0 | 2 | 0 | 5 | 1 | 0 | 0.0 | 14.4 | 8 | 37.5% | .125 | 0.20 | 0.00 | | |
| 2022 | FTM | A | 22 | 2 | 1 | 0 | 5 | 5 | 24 | 12 | 1 | 2.3 | 12.4 | 33 | 50.0% | .234 | 0.75 | 1.50 | 75 | 0.7 |
| 2022 | CR | A+ | 22 | 7 | 3 | 0 | 16 | 13 | 79² | 67 | 5 | 3.2 | 8.5 | 75 | 49.3% | .294 | 1.19 | 2.71 | 92 | 1.1 |
| 2023 non-DC | MIN | MLB | 23 | 3 | 3 | 0 | 58 | 0 | 50 | 54 | 7 | 4.1 | 7.7 | 43 | 39.3% | .313 | 1.53 | 5.02 | 127 | -0.4 |

*Comparables: Brody Koerner, Joe Colòn, Miller Díaz*

**The Report:** A rather anonymous Day 3 college pick from Seton Hall in the 2021 draft—who didn't even strike out a batter per inning his junior year—Festa had the kind of 2022 that puts your name near the top of the bill. A tall, wiry righty, Festa pops mid-90s heat and pairs it with a potential plus mid-80s slider with power 11-6 depth. The slide piece can roll a bit or back up on him, so it's not a consistent 6 yet, but it's likely to get there with further refinement and reps. Festa's change sits in the same velocity band as the slider and while it has rather unimpressive fade at present, there is some projection in the pitch and it may eventually settle in as an average arm-side offering.

Festa has one of the longer, narrower frames you'll see on a pitcher and is roughly 70% legs, but despite all that and a bit of twist and torque in the delivery, he keeps everything compact and on line to the plate. His stuff can fade a bit deeper in starts, so he might just be a 95-and-a-slider reliever two years from now, but he did throw 100 innings last season and the profile is certainly intriguing.

**OFP:** 50 / no. 4 starter or setup arm

**Variance:** High. Festa is a cold-weather college arm who dominated A-ball. The demographic means there could be a bit more upside, but the low-minors performance doesn't move the needle to mid-rotation starter on its own.

**Jesse Roche's Fantasy Take:** Festa was a dynasty standout way back in April after breezing through Low-A. Festa should be rostered in leagues with up to 300 prospects.

## 10 Matt Wallner RF    OFP: 50    ETA: Debuted in 2022
Born: 12/12/97   Age: 25   Bats: L   Throws: R   Height: 6'5"   Weight: 220 lb.   Origin: Round 1, 2019 Draft (#39 overall)

| YEAR | TEAM | LVL | AGE | PA | R | 2B | 3B | HR | RBI | BB | K | SB | CS | AVG/OBP/SLG | DRC+ | BABIP | BRR | DRP | WARP |
|------|------|-----|-----|-----|----|----|----|----|-----|----|-----|----|----|-------------|------|-------|------|-----|------|
| 2021 | SCO | WIN | 23 | 79 | 11 | 2 | 0 | 6 | 15 | 9 | 27 | 0 | 0 | .303/.405/.606 | | .412 | | | |
| 2021 | CR | A+ | 23 | 294 | 39 | 14 | 2 | 15 | 47 | 28 | 98 | 0 | 1 | .264/.350/.508 | 103 | .363 | -1.2 | RF(55) -7.1, LF(2) -0.2 | 0.2 |
| 2022 | WCH | AA | 24 | 342 | 61 | 15 | 1 | 21 | 64 | 62 | 107 | 8 | 5 | .299/.436/.597 | 111 | .407 | 1.3 | RF(66) 0.3, LF(1) -0.6 | 2.7 |
| 2022 | STP | AAA | 24 | 229 | 29 | 17 | 3 | 6 | 31 | 35 | 63 | 1 | 0 | .247/.376/.463 | 85 | .339 | -2.2 | RF(36) -0.2, LF(4) 0.3 | 0.2 |
| 2022 | MIN | MLB | 24 | 65 | 4 | 3 | 0 | 2 | 10 | 6 | 25 | 1 | 0 | .228/.323/.386 | 65 | .367 | 0.3 | RF(16) -0.3 | -0.1 |
| 2023 DC | MIN | MLB | 25 | 121 | 13 | 5 | 1 | 3 | 11 | 13 | 43 | 1 | 1 | .208/.306/.350 | 92 | .317 | -0.4 | RF 0 | 0.1 |

*Comparables: Billy McKinney, Brandon Allen, Matt Lawton*

**The Report:** Wallner was in consideration for last year's Twins list, but I wanted to see how the Three-True-Outcomes profile played in the upper minors. Well, he tripled down, walking, striking out, or homering in over half of his minor-league at-bats in 2022. Wallner utilizes a leveraged, long-and-strong stroke and is up at the plate to find a pitch he can elevate, and then commence to celebrate. He's pretty good at picking said pitches, but swing-and-miss in the zone is a significant concern going forward.

Wallner kept doing damage when he did make contact—all the way through to his cup of coffee with the Twins, but he will need to get the K-rate closer to 30% than 40%, if he wants to have any kind of sustained major-league success. He's a passable corner outfielder with a good enough arm for right field, but he does kind of plod out on the grass and may see some time at first base and DH. Wallner is a bat-first, second and third profile, and he's likely to have some platoon issues against major-league southpaws, so there are fine margins for him to stay afloat. But as long as he's launching 25 bombs into the right-field bleachers and getting on base, you will find a place for him in the the lineup.

**OFP:** 50 / Long-side platoon corner bat

**Variance:** Medium. Wallner's success is predicated on doing heavy damage on contact, but it remains to be seen if he can make enough contact in the majors to make that work.

**Jesse Roche's Fantasy Take:** Few hitters find sustained success in MLB making such little contact as Wallner did in his debut. Plus, he will be vying for playing time with fellow-lefty corner bats Max Kepler, Alex Kirilloff and Trevor Larnach. Still, he offers intriguing fantasy upside should he run into meaningful playing time. Wallner should be rostered in leagues with up to 300 prospects, particularly on-base percentage formats.

## Outside the Top Ten:

### 11  Jose Rodriguez   OF

Born: 06/10/05   Age: 18   Bats: R   Throws: R   Height: 6'2"   Weight: 196 lb.   Origin: International Free Agent, 2022

| YEAR | TEAM | LVL | AGE | PA | R | 2B | 3B | HR | RBI | BB | K | SB | CS | AVG/OBP/SLG | DRC+ | BABIP | BRR | DRP | WARP |
|------|------|-----|-----|-----|-----|-----|-----|-----|-----|-----|-----|-----|-----|-------------|------|-------|-----|-----|------|
| 2022 | DSL TWI | ROK | 17 | 219 | 39 | 15 | 3 | 13 | 49 | 21 | 52 | 5 | 0 | .289/.361/.605 | | .323 | | | |

I've long opined in these pages about the impracticality of ranking recent IFA signings with only Dominican complex reps. The reality is that sometimes it becomes hard to argue against them. The Twins system is pretty average, and I haven't run out of interesting bats yet, but Rodriguez is the most interesting bat in the next 10. It's a pure right field profile, but the hard-contact traits are elite for his age and level and already above major-league average. He's miles away from the majors, but his power upside makes him hard to ignore.

### 12  Tanner Schobel   2B/3B

Born: 06/04/01   Age: 22   Bats: R   Throws: R   Height: 5'10"   Weight: 170 lb.   Origin: Round 2, 2022 Draft (#68 overall)

| YEAR | TEAM | LVL | AGE | PA | R | 2B | 3B | HR | RBI | BB | K | SB | CS | AVG/OBP/SLG | DRC+ | BABIP | BRR | DRP | WARP |
|------|------|-----|-----|-----|-----|-----|-----|-----|-----|-----|-----|-----|-----|-------------|------|-------|-----|-----|------|
| 2022 | FTM | A | 21 | 120 | 11 | 3 | 0 | 1 | 10 | 18 | 23 | 6 | 1 | .242/.367/.303 | 118 | .303 | -1.4 | 2B(19) 1.8, 3B(6) -1.2, SS(3) 0.1 | 0.5 |
| 2023 non-DC | MIN | MLB | 22 | 251 | 20 | 10 | 1 | 2 | 19 | 19 | 49 | 5 | 1 | .211/.279/.293 | 64 | .259 | -2.0 | 2B 0, 3B 0 | -0.5 |

*Comparables: Alfredo Angarita, Kevyn Feiner, Cole Miles*

The Twins' second-round pick out of Va. Tech, Schoebel is a bat-first infielder—albeit a perfectly fine second baseman—with above-average bat speed and the ability to go with his pitch. He hit for a ton of power in the ACC last Spring, but has yet to translate that pop to wood bats. That certainly warrants keeping an eye on, as without average game power he's more of an extra infielder than everyday guy.

### 13  Austin Martin   SS

Born: 03/23/99   Age: 24   Bats: R   Throws: R   Height: 6'0"   Weight: 185 lb.   Origin: Round 1, 2020 Draft (#5 overall)

| YEAR | TEAM | LVL | AGE | PA | R | 2B | 3B | HR | RBI | BB | K | SB | CS | AVG/OBP/SLG | DRC+ | BABIP | BRR | DRP | WARP |
|------|------|-----|-----|-----|-----|-----|-----|-----|-----|-----|-----|-----|-----|-------------|------|-------|-----|-----|------|
| 2021 | NH | AA | 22 | 250 | 43 | 10 | 2 | 2 | 16 | 37 | 53 | 9 | 3 | .281/.424/.383 | 116 | .368 | 0.8 | SS(27) 1.1, CF(26) 4.5 | 1.9 |
| 2021 | WCH | AA | 22 | 168 | 24 | 8 | 0 | 3 | 19 | 23 | 30 | 5 | 1 | .254/.399/.381 | 112 | .304 | 1.6 | CF(20) 1.0, SS(16) -2.3 | 0.8 |
| 2022 | WCH | AA | 23 | 406 | 59 | 13 | 3 | 2 | 32 | 47 | 54 | 34 | 5 | .241/.367/.315 | 102 | .280 | 2.3 | SS(70) -4.0, 2B(7) 0.3, CF(7) 1.7 | 1.4 |
| 2023 non-DC | MIN | MLB | 24 | 251 | 21 | 10 | 2 | 2 | 19 | 23 | 44 | 7 | 1 | .220/.306/.303 | 78 | .267 | -1.3 | 2B 0, SS 0 | 0.0 |

*Comparables: Trevor Crowe, Nate Samson, Nick Ahmed*

The former top-five pick went back to the Texas League and saw his slugging percentage drop from .381 to .317. He continues to make a lot of contact, and the Twins have simplified his hand setup, but he really sells out for contact, feeling with the bat head and trying to keep in the barrel in the zone as long as possible. He just isn't able to do a ton of damage that way, posting concerning exit velocities in addition to the Belanger-ish slugging percentage.  And Martin isn't going to win eight Gold Gloves at shortstop—the arm strength makes him a better fit for center or second—but he does offer a fair bit of defensive flexibility and the ability to get on base and run once he's on. This doesn't really add up to an everyday guy at present unless he can sting better pitching a bit more than he's shown thus far.

## 14 Edouard Julien   2B

Born: 04/30/99   Age: 24   Bats: L   Throws: R   Height: 6'2"   Weight: 195 lb.   Origin: Round 18, 2019 Draft (#539 overall)

| YEAR | TEAM | LVL | AGE | PA | R | 2B | 3B | HR | RBI | BB | K | SB | CS | AVG/OBP/SLG | DRC+ | BABIP | BRR | DRP | WARP |
|------|------|-----|-----|----|----|----|----|----|-----|----|----|----|----|-------------|------|-------|-----|-----|------|
| 2021 | FTM | A | 22 | 204 | 41 | 12 | 1 | 3 | 24 | 50 | 54 | 21 | 2 | .299/.490/.456 | 128 | .451 | 0.1 | 3B(16) -2.5, 2B(13) -0.2, LF(6) -0.1 | 1.0 |
| 2021 | CR | A+ | 22 | 310 | 52 | 16 | 0 | 15 | 48 | 60 | 90 | 13 | 3 | .247/.397/.494 | 120 | .322 | -1.0 | 2B(26) -0.6, 1B(17) -2.3, LF(12) -1.2 | 1.1 |
| 2022 | WCH | AA | 23 | 508 | 77 | 19 | 3 | 17 | 67 | 98 | 125 | 19 | 7 | .300/.441/.490 | 128 | .393 | -2.0 | 2B(94) -8.2 | 2.2 |
| 2023 DC | MIN | MLB | 24 | 64 | 7 | 3 | 0 | 1 | 5 | 9 | 16 | 1 | 1 | .242/.353/.358 | 111 | .326 | 0.0 | 1B 0, 3B 0 | 0.2 |

*Comparables: David Adams, Devon Travis, Marvin Lowrance*

The former Auburn Tiger settled in as a full-time second baseman in Double-A, after bouncing between the infield and outfield in 2021. He's perfectly adequate at the keystone, but mostly just biding time there until he can step up to the plate. He hit .300 with decent pop in the Texas League and while I have concerns about the barrel control and contact profile against top level pitching, there's enough bat speed and strength to make him a useful three-days-a-week starter, especially if he puts an outfield glove back in his locker.

*Jesse's Fantasy Tidbit*: Julien hit just .210/.373/.276 against left-handed pitchers last year.

## 15 Jordan Balazovic   RHP

Born: 09/17/98   Age: 24   Bats: R   Throws: R   Height: 6'5"   Weight: 215 lb.   Origin: Round 5, 2016 Draft (#153 overall)

| YEAR | TEAM | LVL | AGE | W | L | SV | G | GS | IP | H | HR | BB/9 | K/9 | K | GB% | BABIP | WHIP | ERA | DRA- | WARP |
|------|------|-----|-----|---|---|----|----|----|----|---|----|------|-----|---|-----|-------|------|-----|------|------|
| 2021 | WCH | AA | 22 | 5 | 4 | 0 | 20 | 20 | 97 | 98 | 9 | 3.5 | 9.5 | 102 | 48.6% | .324 | 1.40 | 3.62 | 86 | 1.4 |
| 2022 | STP | AAA | 23 | 0 | 7 | 0 | 22 | 21 | 70² | 102 | 20 | 4.5 | 9.7 | 76 | 40.4% | .392 | 1.94 | 7.39 | 126 | 0.0 |
| 2023 DC | MIN | MLB | 24 | 1 | 1 | 0 | 14 | 0 | 11.7 | 13 | 2 | 4.0 | 7.9 | 10 | 38.9% | .311 | 1.53 | 5.07 | 132 | -0.1 |

*Comparables: Robert Gsellman, Jackson Stephens, Sal Romano*

Balazovic entered 2022 as a Top 101 prospect of the third starter or late-inning reliever varietal, who was pretty close to being in play for major-league rotation opportunities. A knee injury kept him off a Triple-A mound until May, and then...well a near-8.00 ERA and over 1.000 OPS against more or less speaks for itself. I'm not all the way out on him yet though. The stuff and performance improved towards the end of the season. He still has a mid-90s fastball with ride, a sharp upper-80s cutter and a power curve that should be at least average. Balazovic's velocity could be a bit variant, and the command still isn't all the way there for a mid-rotation arm, still I do wonder if I am fading him a bit too much. Then again, it's tough to hand-wave the performancem and the profile looks less like a starter than it did at this time last year.

## 16 Noah Miller   SS

Born: 11/12/02   Age: 20   Bats: S   Throws: R   Height: 6'1"   Weight: 190 lb.   Origin: Round 1, 2021 Draft (#36 overall)

| YEAR | TEAM | LVL | AGE | PA | R | 2B | 3B | HR | RBI | BB | K | SB | CS | AVG/OBP/SLG | DRC+ | BABIP | BRR | DRP | WARP |
|------|------|-----|-----|----|---|----|----|----|-----|----|---|----|----|-------------|------|-------|-----|-----|------|
| 2021 | TWI | ROK | 18 | 96 | 11 | 3 | 1 | 2 | 14 | 9 | 26 | 1 | 1 | .238/.316/.369 | | .316 | | | |
| 2022 | FTM | A | 19 | 469 | 62 | 12 | 4 | 2 | 24 | 76 | 110 | 23 | 7 | .211/.348/.279 | 110 | .287 | -1.6 | SS(98) 5.5 | 2.2 |
| 2023 non-DC | MIN | MLB | 20 | 251 | 20 | 9 | 2 | 1 | 18 | 25 | 62 | 6 | 2 | .209/.292/.288 | 68 | .282 | -1.4 | SS 0 | -0.3 |

*Comparables: Jesus Lopez, Cito Culver, Jio Mier*

A full-season assignment may have been a tad aggressive for Miller, a cold weather prep bat who went in the Comp A round in 2021. And the .212/.348/.279 line he put up sure points to an overmatched prospect. However, there are positives to take away. Miller controlled the zone well as a 19-year-old who only had 28 PA against pitchers younger than him. He played a smooth shortstop, and while he doesn't trumpet loud tools there, he's got a good chance to stick as an average glove. But he doesn't really drive the ball hard yet. It's a whippy, wristy, contact-oriented swing, and he will need to do more damage on said contact to end up an everyday player.

## 17  Cody Laweryson  RHP

Born: 05/10/98   Age: 25   Bats: L   Throws: R   Height: 6'4"   Weight: 205 lb.   Origin: Round 14, 2019 Draft (#419 overall)

| YEAR | TEAM | LVL | AGE | W | L | SV | G | GS | IP | H | HR | BB/9 | K/9 | K | GB% | BABIP | WHIP | ERA | DRA- | WARP |
|------|------|-----|-----|---|---|----|----|----|-----|----|----|------|------|----|-------|-------|------|------|------|------|
| 2021 | CR | A+ | 23 | 2 | 5 | 0 | 15 | 14 | 58² | 59 | 6 | 2.9 | 11.2 | 73 | 42.6% | .340 | 1.33 | 4.91 | 92 | 0.8 |
| 2022 | CR | A+ | 24 | 1 | 0 | 1 | 16 | 2 | 35 | 25 | 0 | 3.1 | 10.8 | 42 | 43.2% | .287 | 1.06 | 2.57 | 108 | 0.2 |
| 2022 | WCH | AA | 24 | 5 | 0 | 0 | 19 | 8 | 59² | 41 | 2 | 2.3 | 10.4 | 69 | 36.4% | .285 | 0.94 | 1.06 | 75 | 1.2 |
| 2023 non-DC | MIN | MLB | 25 | 3 | 3 | 0 | 58 | 0 | 50 | 49 | 6 | 3.5 | 7.9 | 44 | 35.8% | .293 | 1.36 | 4.07 | 108 | 0.1 |

Laweryson had an absolutely dominant 2022 between Cedar Rapids and Wichita. A Day 3 pick from the University of Maine, he doesn't have big stuff, but gets consistent swings and misses with a low-90s fastball up in the zone. His almost-shot-put delivery makes the pitch hard to pick up and it rides well at the letters. Laweryson also has a usable slider and change—which plays especially well off the fastball up in the zone, but you are mostly hoping both the secondaries scrape average. With a better breaking ball, this profile would be Joe Ryan-ish, but Ryan himself is a weird outlier as a pitching prospect. Laweryson's deception-based arsenal is likely better off one time through the order, but if he keeps missing bats at the upper levels, you'd be sorely tempted to keep him as a starter for a while longer.

## 18  Anthony Prato  UT

Born: 05/11/98   Age: 25   Bats: R   Throws: R   Height: 5'10"   Weight: 186 lb.   Origin: Round 7, 2019 Draft (#209 overall)

| YEAR | TEAM | LVL | AGE | PA | R | 2B | 3B | HR | RBI | BB | K | SB | CS | AVG/OBP/SLG | DRC+ | BABIP | BRR | DRP | WARP |
|------|------|-----|-----|-----|----|----|----|----|-----|----|----|----|----|-------------|------|-------|-----|-----|------|
| 2021 | FTM | A | 23 | 103 | 12 | 3 | 0 | 0 | 7 | 18 | 19 | 6 | 1 | .253/.398/.289 | 117 | .328 | 1.4 | 2B(15) 0.6, SS(7) 1.3, LF(6) 1.1 | 0.9 |
| 2021 | CR | A+ | 23 | 55 | 8 | 3 | 0 | 0 | 1 | 8 | 13 | 0 | 1 | .289/.418/.356 | 97 | .406 | -0.5 | 2B(5) 0.3, SS(5) 0.5, LF(4) -0.1 | 0.2 |
| 2022 | CR | A+ | 24 | 209 | 46 | 8 | 5 | 7 | 33 | 22 | 59 | 12 | 4 | .271/.349/.486 | 103 | .353 | 2.0 | 2B(28) 3.1, LF(15) -0.8, 3B(3) -0.2 | 1.0 |
| 2022 | WCH | AA | 24 | 356 | 51 | 22 | 3 | 3 | 31 | 45 | 71 | 10 | 2 | .294/.403/.419 | 103 | .373 | 0.5 | LF(45) 1.4, 3B(19) 0.0, SS(12) -0.2 | 1.6 |
| 2023 non-DC | MIN | MLB | 25 | 251 | 21 | 11 | 2 | 2 | 21 | 22 | 57 | 3 | 1 | .227/.306/.322 | 82 | .295 | -2.8 | 1B 0, 2B 0 | -0.1 |

Prato was a seventh-round pick the year before Austin Martin, but he isn't that far off from him as a prospect and fills a similar profile. His swing is funky—he drops his hands almost beneath his high leg kick, and it all can be a bit mechanical at times. However, he has good wrists and hand-eye despite the quirkiness, and is able to drive the ball to the gaps despite an overall below-average power projection. Prato played six different spots in 2022, and his defensive flexibility, feel to hit and ability to get on base makes him a useful bench piece who could start for you for a month—in any of six spots—without issue.

## 19  Yasser Mercedes  OF

Born: 11/16/04   Age: 18   Bats: R   Throws: R   Height: 6'2"   Weight: 175 lb.   Origin: International Free Agent, 2022

| YEAR | TEAM | LVL | AGE | PA | R | 2B | 3B | HR | RBI | BB | K | SB | CS | AVG/OBP/SLG | DRC+ | BABIP | BRR | DRP | WARP |
|------|------|-----|-----|-----|----|----|----|----|-----|----|----|----|----|-------------|------|-------|-----|-----|------|
| 2022 | DSL TWI | ROK | 17 | 176 | 34 | 13 | 3 | 4 | 20 | 18 | 35 | 30 | 5 | .355/.420/.555 | | .432 | | | |

Mercedes received the largest bonus—$1.7 million—of the Twins 2021-22 IFA class. The ordinal rankings here overstate the gap between him and Rodriguez, but the best information we have right now suggests that Rodriguez projects for more impact at the plate. Mercedes is more likely to stick up-the-middle though, and could certainly add more pop as he settles into professional baseball.

## 20  Ben Ross  UT

Born: 06/06/01   Age: 22   Bats: R   Throws: R   Height: 6'1"   Weight: 180 lb.   Origin: Round 5, 2022 Draft (#144 overall)

| YEAR | TEAM | LVL | AGE | PA | R | 2B | 3B | HR | RBI | BB | K | SB | CS | AVG/OBP/SLG | DRC+ | BABIP | BRR | DRP | WARP |
|------|------|-----|-----|-----|----|----|----|----|-----|----|----|----|----|-------------|------|-------|-----|-----|------|
| 2022 | FTM | A | 21 | 89 | 17 | 5 | 0 | 3 | 13 | 13 | 19 | 6 | 0 | .257/.371/.446 | 119 | .302 | 1.7 | SS(8) -1.1, LF(5) 0.8, 2B(4) -0.4 | 0.5 |
| 2023 non-DC | MIN | MLB | 22 | 251 | 20 | 10 | 1 | 3 | 21 | 19 | 61 | 6 | 1 | .210/.278/.308 | 67 | .273 | -1.5 | 1B 0, 2B 0 | -0.4 |

The Twins' fifth-round pick out of Notre Dame College in Ohio, Ross would fit well in past editions of these lists as a *Low Minors Sleeper*, or *Interesting Draft Follow*, but his pro debut was impressive enough that I want to get a bit of a stronger marker down on him in a pretty deep system. Ross has a strong approach, solid contact rates and the ball carries a bit more than you'd expect given his frame. Ross is also an aggressive baserunner with solid speed who can handle any of the infield or corner outfield spots, although second base is probably his best position. The Twins sure do have a type.

## Top Talents 25 and Under (as of 4/1/2023):

1. Luis Arraez, UT
2. Jhoan Duran, RHP
3. Brooks Lee, SS
4. Royce Lewis, SS/OF
5. Emmanuel Rodriguez, OF
6. Marco Raya, RHP
7. Ryan Jeffers, C
8. Jose Miranda, 1B/3B
9. Alex Kiriloff, 1B/OF
10. Simeon Woods Richardson, RHP

As Lyle Lovett once crooned, "It ought to be easier when you're in the AL Central." Okay, perhaps that's not the exact line, but the pride of Klein, TX may as well have been singing about the Twins' path forward in the AL Central. The snakebitten 2022 season saw Minnesota fall well short of their PECOTA projection of 86 wins, due in large part to injuries, poor cluster luck, and absolutely brutal showings from many of the young players they'd hoped would provide depth and take the next step. Even inexperienced players who don't quite make this age cutoff like Trevor Larnach struggled, as the hulking corner bat mustered just a 79 DRC+ when healthy.

The 78 wins that Minnesota did manage to scrape together were in no small part due to strong play from Arraez, who won the AL batting title while striking out less than he walked. The first-time All-Star was the only Twin to make at least 600 plate appearances, spending the majority of his time at first base for the first time in his career but still providing defensive versatility. Even after a surprising reunion with Carlos Correa, Minnesota will once again be searching for oomph in the heart of their order, but with Arraez at the top of the order with his 11th-ranked OBP among qualified MLB hitters, they can start games off better than most.

When they have a lead, Minnesota can close the door with authority as well. Duran's insanity did not dissipate with exposure, as he splinkered the American League to pieces. His 61 DRA- was sixth-best in all of MLB (min. 60 IP) in company with the best relievers and aces in the league. Few rookie relievers have had such an extraordinary debut, but there's nothing mysterious about it. He is set to either be the anchor of the next competitive Twins bullpen or a trade piece to address multiple key holes.

Jeffers, Miranda and Kiriloff all may still be solutions to some of those holes, but they all have their warts. For Jeffers, it's identifying how to take the next step offensively, going from "good enough for a catcher" with the bat to outright good as he seemed he might become in his minor-league journey. Similarly, judgment of Miranda's bat is tied to his defensive home. He didn't embarrass himself at the hot corner in his big-league debut, but rightly spent more time at first base. His bat deserves to be in the lineup, with a contact-laden approach that does not scrimp on power, and the short porch of left field is inviting indeed for his pull-heavy, elevating approach. The same could be true of Kiriloff, who once was as high as 39th on the pre-2019 Top-101 list here at BP. Injuries and ineffectiveness have wholly waylaid his development, but his decimation of Triple-A (a 1.145 OPS over the past two seasons) will continue to afford him chances. A lefty-swinging and throwing corner bat, Minnesota must decide if they are ready to let him and/or Larnach take the reins or find more stable alternatives.

Lastly, there are a couple role players on this youthful roster who could still have utility. Outfielder Gilberto Celestino could be to Byron Buxton what Manuel Margot was the past few years in Tampa to the excellent-but-oft-injured Kevin Kiermaier: a player capable of providing some of the defense and speed, without a complete hole in the lineup, affording the rest of the Twins' roster construction to not collapse without their singular star. It's a tall task, however, as a healthy Buxton is one of the league's superstars, while Celestino is going to be a 24-year-old with an 89 DRC+ in his 409 career plate appearances. It's likely that this is where Royce Lewis slots in in the dreamscape of Thad Levine, but given the tragically low number of knees that can be trusted between Buxton and Lewis, Celestino may be crucial. Lefty Jovani Moran also proved a surprise standout for Minnesota in 2022, as a ground-ball generator with a devastating changeup that helps him dominate righty bats, while still keeping lefties off balance.

# New York Mets

## The State of the System:

A trio of Day 1 draft picks in July have improved the top of the Mets' system, but organizational depth—especially at the upper levels—remains a notable weakness.

## The Top Ten:

### 1 Francisco Álvarez    C         OFP: 70         ETA: Debuted in 2022

Born: 11/19/01    Age: 21    Bats: R    Throws: R    Height: 5'10"    Weight: 233 lb.    Origin: International Free Agent, 2018

| YEAR | TEAM | LVL | AGE | PA | R | 2B | 3B | HR | RBI | BB | K | SB | CS | AVG/OBP/SLG | DRC+ | BABIP | BRR | DRP | WARP |
|------|------|-----|-----|-----|-----|-----|-----|-----|-----|-----|-----|-----|-----|---------------|------|-------|------|----------|------|
| 2021 | SLU | A | 19 | 67 | 12 | 5 | 0 | 2 | 12 | 15 | 7 | 2 | 2 | .417/.567/.646 | 143 | .450 | 0.1 | C(10) -1.7 | 0.4 |
| 2021 | BRK | A+ | 19 | 333 | 55 | 13 | 1 | 22 | 58 | 40 | 82 | 6 | 3 | .247/.351/.538 | 154 | .260 | 0.8 | C(49) -7.5 | 2.5 |
| 2022 | BNG | AA | 20 | 296 | 43 | 16 | 0 | 18 | 47 | 36 | 71 | 0 | 0 | .277/.368/.553 | 115 | .310 | -1.0 | C(46) 0.9 | 1.4 |
| 2022 | SYR | AAA | 20 | 199 | 31 | 6 | 0 | 9 | 31 | 34 | 52 | 0 | 0 | .234/.382/.443 | 109 | .283 | 0.1 | C(33) 0.6 | 0.8 |
| 2022 | NYM | MLB | 20 | 14 | 3 | 1 | 0 | 1 | 1 | 2 | 4 | 0 | 0 | .167/.286/.500 | 100 | .143 | -0.3 | C(2) -0.0 | 0.0 |
| 2023 DC | NYM | MLB | 21 | 304 | 38 | 13 | 1 | 10 | 39 | 30 | 88 | 0 | 1 | .227/.316/.389 | 102 | .301 | -1.7 | C 0 | 1.0 |

*Comparables: Xander Bogaerts, Marc Newfield, Carlos Correa*

**The Report:** Álvarez is the best offensive catching prospect in recent memory. He generates near-elite raw power from furious bat speed and plenty of loft. There's some length/wrap to his swing, but given the short arms and plus-plus barrel velocity, it's mostly a non-issue. His approach can also be overly aggressive in hitter's counts, although he knows the zone well. Álvarez can get pull-happy, something the better arms he faced were able to exploit, but he showed an ability to stay back on offspeed and drive the ball the opposite way when he stayed within himself. He'll get on base enough, and do enough damage on contact, that he will be a plus offensive force even if the batting average settles in at .240-.250 in the majors. And there's further upside in the bat beyond a 45/60 if he makes some approach adjustments—he is only 20 after all. Álvarez reminds me a little of Bo Bichette at this level, although Bichette had elite-level zone—and out-of-the-zone—coverage, and did make further refinements in his swing decisions. That gives you an idea of what the 90th-percentile outcome at the plate could be though, and that's a guy who could easily rank as the no. 1 prospect in baseball given that he's a catcher.

He's not a particularly good catcher, though. Even before a late-season ankle injury that cast further doubt on whether Álvarez will be able to handle 120 games behind the plate, the overall defensive profile was pushing the lower bounds of what you'd want as a major-league backstop. There are no out-and-out dispositive traits here, but Álvarez is fringy across the board. He's a snatchy framer who lacks the kind of twitchy athleticism to block balls or hold a quiet setup/receiving position. His overall arm strength is fine—and he'll pop the odd 1.9 here and there—but he can have a bit of a long trigger out of the crouch, and the ball doesn't always get to the right side of the base. Receiving is a teachable skill, and Álvarez has improved in that regard, but given his frame and recent lower-body injury, it's reasonable to wonder if he can handle the rigors of everyday catching. He'd be limited to DH if he has to shed the tools of ignorance, and while the bat will play there, he'd need that Bichette-level outcome to be an impact offensive player there.

**OFP:** 70 / All-Star catcher

**Variance:** High. There were significant questions about Álvarez's long-term defensive future, even before the ankle injury that functionally ended his season. He's not the twitchiest or most adroit defender, and if he continues having issues with his lower body, he might just be a DH.

**Jesse Roche's Fantasy Take:** In the briefest of showcases last September, Álvarez flashed the bat speed and power that make him the top dynasty catcher. A perfect world fantasy outcome is akin to Salvador Perez with a plate approach of sorts. Álvarez offers uncommon power upside at catcher with proximity and opportunity. That said, catchers often take time to fully adjust to the rigors of MLB. While Álvarez likely receives sizable playing time at some point this coming year, how that shakes out with free agent addition Omar Narváez now in the picture and Tomás Nido without options is unclear. Even when he arrives, he likely will experience his share of struggles. Patience will be necessary. Remember, Álvarez only turned 21 in November!

## 2  Brett Baty  3B/OF        OFP: 70      ETA: Debuted in 2022

Born: 11/13/99   Age: 23   Bats: L   Throws: R   Height: 6'3"   Weight: 210 lb.   Origin: Round 1, 2019 Draft (#12 overall)

| YEAR | TEAM | LVL | AGE | PA | R | 2B | 3B | HR | RBI | BB | K | SB | CS | AVG/OBP/SLG | DRC+ | BABIP | BRR | DRP | WARP |
|------|------|-----|-----|----|---|----|----|----|-----|----|---|----|----|-------------|------|-------|-----|-----|------|
| 2021 | SRR | WIN | 21 | 102 | 16 | 5 | 1 | 1 | 15 | 11 | 31 | 1 | 0 | .292/.373/.404 | | .431 | | | |
| 2021 | BRK | A+ | 21 | 209 | 27 | 14 | 1 | 7 | 34 | 24 | 53 | 4 | 3 | .309/.397/.514 | 118 | .402 | -0.3 | 3B(41) 6.7, LF(3) -0.4 | 1.6 |
| 2021 | BNG | AA | 21 | 176 | 16 | 8 | 0 | 5 | 22 | 22 | 45 | 2 | 0 | .272/.364/.424 | 91 | .350 | 0.0 | 3B(24) -0.8, LF(15) 1.4 | 0.4 |
| 2022 | BNG | AA | 22 | 394 | 73 | 22 | 0 | 19 | 59 | 46 | 98 | 2 | 3 | .312/.406/.544 | 128 | .390 | 0.0 | 3B(68) -1.4, LF(9) 0.8 | 2.2 |
| 2022 | SYR | AAA | 22 | 26 | 3 | 0 | 0 | 0 | 1 | 3 | 6 | 0 | 1 | .364/.462/.364 | 99 | .500 | -0.3 | 3B(4) -0.1, LF(2) 0.2 | 0.2 |
| 2022 | NYM | MLB | 22 | 42 | 4 | 0 | 0 | 2 | 5 | 2 | 8 | 0 | 0 | .184/.244/.342 | 90 | .179 | 0.0 | 3B(11) 0 | 0.1 |
| 2023 DC | NYM | MLB | 23 | 184 | 22 | 8 | 1 | 4 | 20 | 16 | 50 | 2 | 0 | .254/.330/.392 | 105 | .344 | -0.2 | 3B 0, LF 0 | 0.5 |

*Comparables: Abraham Toro, Mat Gamel, Juan Francisco*

**The Report:** Baty's 2021 breakout continued in fits and starts in 2022. A return engagement in the Eastern League stretched into the second half, and he still wasn't consistently lifting the ball for most of his tenure there...until he was. A scorching hot July got him promoted to Triple-A, and he was barely there a week before injuries to both the Mets' third basemen got him booked on a puddle jumper to La Guardia. He hit a home run in his first at-bat, then saw his ground-ball issues rear their head again—before a torn thumb ligament ended his season.

The two things we wanted to see from Baty in 2022 were more pull-side fly-ball contact and further refinement of his third base defense. He batted .500 in that regard. He's tapping into his plus, borderline plus-plus raw power more, without trading off too much additional swing-and-miss. It remains to be seen if that was just a good prospect adjusting to a level after 100 or so games, but signs are pointing up. However, Baty has regressed with the glove. He's a little bit bigger than he was in 2022, and while it's good weight, he was already on the larger side for a third baseman. His actions have gotten a little stiffer and more mechanical, and he would struggle with game speed at times on anything more complicated than a routine play. Baty is also capable of the spectacular given his arm strength, but you hold your breath on the typical 5-3 putouts a little more than you'd prefer. There's a difference between a 50 defender and a 40 defender, and Baty's 2021 and 2022 illustrate that well. He's seen some time in the outfield as well, and while it's not impossible his work at the hot corner smooths out to a playable 45 with more reps, right field might be the ultimate landing spot for him.

**OFP:** 70 / All-Star third baseman

**Variance:** Medium. We are pretty confident Baty will hit in the medium term; .280 and 25-30 home runs is a very plausible outcome. That looks a lot better at third base than corner outfield, though. There's also still some risk that he doesn't consistently tap into his raw power against major-league pitching, as his swing can get a little flat.

**Jesse Roche's Fantasy Take:** When ".280 and 25-30 home runs is a very plausible outcome" for any prospect, take notice. Baty has underrated fantasy upside with huge raw power, a swing that churns out hard, line-drive contact and solid plate discipline. As noted above, he has also begun to lift the ball more, decreasing his ground-ball rate by over 11% from 2021. Further, Baty likely sees substantial time in the majors this year. Whether he breaks in at third base, however, is unclear. The Mets have late-season dynamo Eduardo Escobar manning the hot corner in 2023. Nevertheless, Baty has serious four-category potential, especially if he can continue to tap into this power in games without sacrificing contact.

## 3 Kevin Parada   C          OFP: 60        ETA: Late 2024
Born: 08/03/01   Age: 21   Bats: R   Throws: R   Height: 6'1"   Weight: 197 lb.   Origin: Round 1, 2022 Draft (#11 overall)

| YEAR | TEAM | LVL | AGE | PA | R | 2B | 3B | HR | RBI | BB | K | SB | CS | AVG/OBP/SLG | DRC+ | BABIP | BRR | DRP | WARP |
|------|------|-----|-----|----|----|----|----|----|-----|----|----|----|----|-------------|------|-------|------|--------|------|
| 2022 | SLU | A | 20 | 41 | 5 | 1 | 0 | 1 | 5 | 10 | 12 | 0 | 1 | .276/.463/.414 | 109 | .412 | -0.3 | C(6) -0.2 | 0.1 |
| 2023 non-DC | NYM | MLB | 21 | 251 | 20 | 10 | 1 | 3 | 20 | 18 | 80 | 1 | 1 | .208/.276/.298 | 64 | .307 | -3.9 | C 0 | -0.5 |

**The Report:** The consensus best catcher in the draft, Parada slid to the Mets at the 11th pick as everyone's mock draft fell apart in the top 10. A draft-eligible sophomore who had a huge 2022 for Georgia Tech, he's a true two-way catching prospect, displaying above-average tools on both offense and defense.

Parada utilizes a fairly unorthodox setup at the plate, starting with the bat pointing almost directly to the ground behind his ear. He draws the bat up before loading and then lets it rip through the zone. You have to have really good wrists to pull this off, and he does, but I do wonder if he will run into quality-of-contact issues with wood bats against high-level professional stuff. Early returns in the minors were fine, and he has an advanced approach at the plate already, so a .270, 20+ home run outcome is in play, which would put Parada among the best-hitting catchers in the game.

Defensively, Parada sets a big target, receives well and is a solid catch-and-throw man. There's not a standout defensive tool here, and the overall profile hews closer to average than plus, but he should stick behind the plate all the way up the ladder. The usual risks for non-elite catching prospects all hold true, and we've seen plenty of Top-101 college catching prospects suffer offensive skill erosion as they inch closer to the majors, but Parada's two-way skill set means he can give back some of his tool grades and still be a useful regular.

**OFP:** 60 / Two-way catcher who makes a couple All-Star games

**Variance:** Medium. Catchers are weird, although there isn't anything concerning here yet.

**Jesse Roche's Fantasy Take:** "Catchers are weird." Yep. In fantasy, catching prospects are often a trap. They may offer exciting offensive tools and projection, but they're stifled–in both production and ETA–by the demands of the position. Parada is no different. His advanced approach and big power were on display in his brief debut. Yet, his development has only just begun and his ultimate upside–"a .270, 20+ home run outcome"—likely doesn't warrant the required investment in fantasy and upcoming FYPDs. That said, Parada is still a top-100 dynasty prospect with a chance to be an impact fantasy catcher.

## 4 Jett Williams   SS          OFP: 60        ETA: Late 2025
Born: 11/03/03   Age: 19   Bats: R   Throws: R   Height: 5'8"   Weight: 175 lb.   Origin: Round 1, 2022 Draft (#14 overall)

| YEAR | TEAM | LVL | AGE | PA | R | 2B | 3B | HR | RBI | BB | K | SB | CS | AVG/OBP/SLG | DRC+ | BABIP | BRR | DRP | WARP |
|------|------|-----|-----|----|----|----|----|----|-----|----|----|----|----|-------------|------|-------|-----|-----|------|
| 2022 | MET | ROK | 18 | 41 | 7 | 1 | 1 | 1 | 6 | 4 | 6 | 6 | 0 | .250/.366/.438 | | .259 | | | |

**The Report:** If Williams were 6-foot-2 instead of—listed at—5-foot-8, he would have likely been mentioned in the same breath as the top prep bats in the 2022 class. The Mets' once and future short King has everything else you'd want from a top hitting prospect. He makes a lot of high-quality contact and picks the correct pitches to try and drive. His bat stays in the zone a long time, and his leg kick generates a consistent tempo and weight transfer. Despite his shorter stature, he should develop at least average pop, and as we've seen recently, being compact to the ball with a good approach can be a positive marker for future power development. Williams has the foot speed for short, but his infield actions are a better fit for second, and the overall defensive package might be best suited to center. He should provide a good amount of defensive value wherever he lands—or offer flexibility to your big club—but the offensive tools will provide the real liftoff for his profile.

**OFP:** 60 / First-division regular, somewhere up the middle

**Variance:** Medium. There's a very limited pro track record for Williams, but that's the only real quibble here. We think he will hit. Conversely there might not be as much upside as you'd want in a prep bat, as the power may play more in the 40 range, and he's unlikely to be a significantly above-average defender wherever he ends up.

**Jesse Roche's Fantasy Take:** "Jett" is an apt moniker for the diminutive speedster. He has plus speed and acceleration with both aggression and instincts to be a consistent threat to steal bases. As noted above, his "power may play more in the 40 range" due to his short swing and limit his upside. The underlying power is there to unlock, though, providing Williams legitimate five-category potential. Don't overlook him in upcoming FYPDs!

## 5   Alex Ramirez   OF    OFP: 60    ETA: Late 2024

Born: 01/13/03   Age: 20   Bats: R   Throws: R   Height: 6'3"   Weight: 170 lb.   Origin: International Free Agent, 2019

| YEAR | TEAM | LVL | AGE | PA | R | 2B | 3B | HR | RBI | BB | K | SB | CS | AVG/OBP/SLG | DRC+ | BABIP | BRR | DRP | WARP |
|------|------|-----|-----|-----|----|----|----|----|-----|----|-----|----|----|-------------|------|-------|------|-----|------|
| 2021 | SLU | A | 18 | 334 | 41 | 15 | 4 | 5 | 35 | 23 | 104 | 16 | 7 | .258/.326/.384 | 84 | .376 | -3.4 | CF(46) 1.7, RF(22) 5.1, LF(5) -0.8 | 0.8 |
| 2022 | SLU | A | 19 | 306 | 40 | 13 | 6 | 6 | 37 | 28 | 68 | 17 | 9 | .284/.359/.443 | 116 | .357 | 0.9 | CF(56) -3.2, LF(3) -0.6, RF(1) 0.1 | 0.9 |
| 2022 | BRK | A+ | 19 | 246 | 22 | 17 | 1 | 5 | 34 | 16 | 54 | 4 | 7 | .278/.329/.427 | 97 | .343 | -2.5 | CF(34) -2.2, RF(17) -1.4 | 0.1 |
| *2023 non-DC* | *NYM* | *MLB* | *20* | *251* | *20* | *11* | *3* | *3* | *22* | *13* | *72* | *5* | *4* | *.233/.280/.340* | *75* | *.324* | *-0.9* | *LF 0, CF 0* | *-0.1* |

*Comparables: Jahmai Jones, Estevan Florial, Cristian Pache*

**The Report:** After holding his own as an 18-year-old in the Florida State League in 2021, Ramirez conquered the level in 2022, earning a promotion to the South Atlantic League—where he continued to show off intriguing tools at the plate. He can be a bit busy in his pre-swing, but with a flick of the wrist, he unleashes plus-plus bat speed with the kind of loft that portends 20+ home run totals. But Ramirez is already looking to launch pull side more often than not, which does create a bit of a hole down and away for spin or fade. The swing can be violent at times, too, sacrificing some barrel control and—as we often see with young, burgeoning power hitters—suboptimal contact. Now, he will absolutely punish anything you leave in the zone, but it's also an aggressive approach that is sure to be tested in Double-A and beyond. We are trying to move away from trite maxims like "he will grow into his power," but Ramirez is likely to add strength in his 20s. He's also likely to slow down some, and while he's an above-average runner at present, that's likely to end up average or perhaps a tick below as he ages. He's playing mostly center field, and has the foot speed for it for now, but takes some truly awkward and circuitous routes to balls. The offensive tools are loud enough to play in right or left—where the arm is a better fit—but you'd like to see him stick in center for a true impact outcome.

**OFP:** 60 / First-division outfielder

**Variance:** High. Double-A arms will test the swing decisions, and Ramirez might have to slide to a corner outfield spot sooner rather than later.

**Jesse Roche's Fantasy Take:** It is easy to become enamored with Ramirez given his electric bat speed and athletic frame. In addition, his production in A-ball at 19 years old mostly met and exceeded expectations. Indeed, Ramirez made more contact, put more balls in the air and churned out line drives. His power potential, however, remains theoretical, and, if anything, his contact quality regressed. Ramirez was also caught stealing 16 times–the fourth-most in the minors–on 37 attempts, a dreadful 56.7% success rate. Should his speed back up as he matures, he simply may not offer any value stealing bases. Ramirez still has significant upside, though, especially if "he grows into his power" and cleans up his swing decisions, and he is a back-end top-100 dynasty prospect.

## 6   Blade Tidwell   RHP    OFP: 55    ETA: Late 2024

Born: 06/08/01   Age: 22   Bats: R   Throws: R   Height: 6'4"   Weight: 207 lb.   Origin: Round 2, 2022 Draft (#52 overall)

| YEAR | TEAM | LVL | AGE | W | L | SV | G | GS | IP | H | HR | BB/9 | K/9 | K | GB% | BABIP | WHIP | ERA | DRA- | WARP |
|------|------|-----|-----|---|---|----|----|----|-----|----|----|------|-----|---|------|-------|------|------|------|------|
| 2022 | SLU | A | 21 | 0 | 1 | 0 | 4 | 4 | 8¹ | 4 | 0 | 6.5 | 9.7 | 9 | 40.0% | .200 | 1.20 | 2.16 | 114 | 0.1 |
| *2023 non-DC* | *NYM* | *MLB* | *22* | *3* | *3* | *0* | *58* | *0* | *50* | *54* | *8* | *5.4* | *7.8* | *43* | *36.0%* | *.309* | *1.68* | *5.88* | *144* | *-0.9* |

*Comparables: Alexander Vizcaíno, Denny Brady, Aaron Northcraft*

**The Report:** Tidwell has first-round stuff, but like most of this year's college pitching cohort, injury woes caused him to drop in the draft. While he wasn't in the midst of Tommy John surgery or recovery like many of the top NCAA arms, shoulder issues limited him to just 39 innings last spring. I don't usually care to draw a bold line between mechanics and injuries, but Tidwell does have an arm-heavy delivery that barely engages his lower half and relies mostly on pure arm speed to pump 95+ mph fastballs. That fastball can regularly touch the upper 90s and is a swing-and-miss pitch on its own. He also offers a potential above-average slider and average change, both in the mid-80s, and will pop a slower curve every once in a while. Broadly speaking, he's the kind of mid-rotation college arm who goes in the late first round every year, but given the recent track record of arm health, we'll want to see a full healthy 2023 from Tidwell before we wholeheartedly sign off on that projection. This will be a recurring theme with Mets pitching prospects this year.

**OFP:** 55 / no. 3/4 starter

**Variance:** Very High. Shoulder issues aren't weird, are concerning.

**Jesse Roche's Fantasy Take:** Tidwell is a rare post-draft college arm who received substantial work to end the season, helping lead St. Lucie to the Florida State League championship. During his run in Low-A, he flashed huge stuff. Health willing, Tidwell could be a quick mover with high-strikeout upside, and he is a recommended late-round target in upcoming FYPDs in formats that roster over 300 prospects.

## 7 Ronny Mauricio SS    OFP: 50    ETA: Late 2023

Born: 04/04/01   Age: 22   Bats: S   Throws: R   Height: 6'3"   Weight: 166 lb.   Origin: International Free Agent, 2017

| YEAR | TEAM | LVL | AGE | PA | R | 2B | 3B | HR | RBI | BB | K | SB | CS | AVG/OBP/SLG | DRC+ | BABIP | BRR | DRP | WARP |
|---|---|---|---|---|---|---|---|---|---|---|---|---|---|---|---|---|---|---|---|
| 2021 | LIC | WIN | 20 | 94 | 8 | 5 | 0 | 2 | 8 | 3 | 21 | 1 | 0 | .244/.277/.367 | | .299 | | | |
| 2021 | BRK | A+ | 20 | 420 | 55 | 14 | 5 | 19 | 63 | 24 | 101 | 9 | 7 | .242/.290/.449 | 115 | .278 | 0.1 | SS(87) 10.9 | 3.0 |
| 2021 | BNG | AA | 20 | 33 | 3 | 1 | 0 | 1 | 1 | 2 | 11 | 2 | 0 | .323/.364/.452 | 89 | .474 | -0.3 | SS(8) -0.4 | 0.0 |
| 2022 | LIC | WIN | 21 | 203 | 26 | 15 | 2 | 5 | 31 | 10 | 43 | 10 | 2 | .287/.335/.468 | | .348 | | | |
| 2022 | BNG | AA | 21 | 541 | 71 | 26 | 2 | 26 | 89 | 24 | 125 | 20 | 11 | .259/.296/.472 | 107 | .293 | 0.7 | SS(112) -7.5 | 1.5 |
| 2023 non-DC | NYM | MLB | 22 | 251 | 22 | 10 | 2 | 6 | 26 | 11 | 66 | 3 | 3 | .226/.264/.360 | 72 | .287 | -2.3 | SS 0 | -0.3 |

*Comparables: Domingo Leyba, Alen Hanson, J.P. Crawford*

**The Report:** Mauricio more or less xeroxed his 2021 line at Double-A, which is normally a positive marker, yet he has dropped four spots on the Mets' list and really isn't in Top 101 discussion. So what gives? Those preseason rankings baked in certain improvements in approach and swing decisions that just haven't shown up yet, and don't appear to be coming. For a prospect with plus raw power who already gets it into games, Mauricio takes some awkward hacks, and he struggles badly to recognize pitches with any significant vertical action, leading to subpar chase and zone-contact rates. He tracks east-west okay, but overall his approach is aggressive, and if he's not running OBPs that start with a 3 at these levels, the long-term prognosis is concerning.

Last year, Mauricio looked like he could stick at shortstop long-term, but he's added a bit more weight, and given back some range and fluidity in the field. His arm is above-average, so he might be able to slide over to third—although he'd be one of the bigger guys at that position as well. Beyond that, a corner outfield spot might beckon. Despite not having a ton of confidence in the hit tool at this point, Mauricio has shown enough ability to do damage on contact to keep him major-league relevant in the medium-term, but now the approach improvements have become a must-have, rather than a nice-to-have.

**OFP:** 50 / Slugging third baseman

**Variance:** Medium. There's hit tool risk and positional risk, but he did xerox his line at Double-A. So while he hasn't really put together the approach yet, it hasn't completely fallen apart either.

**Jesse Roche's Fantasy Take:** By most standards, Mauricio met the brief in Double-A, launching 26 home runs with a 107 DRC+ at 21 years old. Yet, his elevated, and worsening, swing rate–around 55%–and poor pitch recognition casts serious doubt on whether he'll ever actually hit enough. Regardless, powerful switch-hitting "shortstops" are afforded a long development, and dynasty, leash. Mauricio plummets in OBP formats, but retains intriguing upside in standard 5x5 due to his plus power and a batting average buoyed by his swing-happy approach.

## 8 Mark Vientos 3B    OFP: 50    ETA: Debuted in 2022

Born: 12/11/99   Age: 23   Bats: R   Throws: R   Height: 6'4"   Weight: 185 lb.   Origin: Round 2, 2017 Draft (#59 overall)

| YEAR | TEAM | LVL | AGE | PA | R | 2B | 3B | HR | RBI | BB | K | SB | CS | AVG/OBP/SLG | DRC+ | BABIP | BRR | DRP | WARP |
|---|---|---|---|---|---|---|---|---|---|---|---|---|---|---|---|---|---|---|---|
| 2021 | BNG | AA | 21 | 306 | 43 | 16 | 0 | 22 | 59 | 26 | 87 | 0 | 1 | .281/.346/.580 | 123 | .327 | -1.9 | 3B(41) -4.4, LF(12) -0.2, 1B(11) -0.1 | 1.1 |
| 2021 | SYR | AAA | 21 | 43 | 9 | 2 | 0 | 3 | 4 | 7 | 13 | 0 | 1 | .278/.395/.583 | 110 | .350 | -0.1 | 3B(9) 1.2, LF(1) -0.1 | 0.3 |
| 2022 | SYR | AAA | 22 | 427 | 66 | 16 | 1 | 24 | 72 | 44 | 122 | 0 | 2 | .280/.358/.519 | 112 | .350 | -0.7 | 3B(59) -2.9, 1B(27) -0.6 | 1.5 |
| 2022 | NYM | MLB | 22 | 41 | 3 | 1 | 0 | 1 | 3 | 5 | 12 | 0 | 0 | .167/.268/.278 | 91 | .217 | -0.1 | 3B(2) -0.2 | 0.0 |
| 2023 DC | NYM | MLB | 23 | 30 | 4 | 1 | 0 | 1 | 4 | 2 | 9 | 0 | 0 | .225/.288/.389 | 90 | .298 | -0.3 | 1B 0 | 0.0 |

*Comparables: Renato Núñez, Austin Riley, Jeimer Candelario*

**The Report:** In 2022, Vientos continued the three main trends of his prospect career: he hit for power, struck out a bit too much and slid further down the defensive spectrum. After an awful start to the season, his bat came alive and he hit .303/.378/.558 after the calendar turned to May. Much of that damage came against left-handed pitching; he does struggle against righties who can elevate plus fastballs, due to some stiffness in his swing. Vientos is capable of doing a lot of damage on contact though, and while his average bat speed makes for effortful plus power, it is plus power. He also knows when to unleash, and doesn't really expand, but his overall contact rates in the zone portend problematic swing-and-miss issues in the majors. It's a tricky balancing act for Vientos to get his power into games while carrying what's likely to be a below-average hit tool, and the profile would be a bit shinier if he offered a bit more defensive value.

Drafted as a shortstop, Vientos still plays mostly third base, but saw some time in left field in 2021, and spent almost as much time at first base and DH as the hot corner in 2022. Those last two spots are his best defensive "positions," as he lacks the foot speed for the outfield or the first step (and infield actions) for third. That puts a lot of pressure on the bat to produce, but if you leverage him against the right kind of pitchers—lefties, and sinkerballing righties—Vientos should provide some value as a Three-True-Outcomes slugger.

**OFP:** 50 / Mashing corner bat you sit against tougher righties

**Variance:** Medium. Vientos doesn't have much bench utility, and there is the broader issue that he might be more of a Quad-A type, given the in-zone contact issues in the upper minors. However, he is also young enough that a swing tweak could give him a little more zone control, and the power to be a useful corner bat is already present.

**Jesse Roche's Fantasy Take:** For context, Vientos hit .315/.401/.692 against lefties and .250/.326/.409 against righties last year. The risk, that he simply is a short-side platoon bat without a clear defensive home, is high. In the past, however, Vientos has held his own against same-sided pitching. Further, he has posted a staggering 28.5% HR/FB in the upper minors the last two years. In fantasy, his power and proximity is a worthwhile gamble outside the top 100, even if the probability that he develops into an impact everyday slugger is low. Expect Vientos to arrive in 2023 in, well, a short-side platoon role with Daniel Vogelbach.

## 9  Dominic Hamel  RHP          OFP: 50          ETA: Late 2023/Early 2024

Born: 03/02/99   Age: 24   Bats: R   Throws: R   Height: 6'2"   Weight: 206 lb.   Origin: Round 3, 2021 Draft (#81 overall)

| YEAR | TEAM | LVL | AGE | W | L | SV | G | GS | IP | H | HR | BB/9 | K/9 | K | GB% | BABIP | WHIP | ERA | DRA- | WARP |
|------|------|-----|-----|---|---|----|---|----|-----|-----|----|------|------|----|------|-------|------|------|------|------|
| 2022 | SLU | A | 23 | 5 | 2 | 0 | 14 | 13 | 63¹ | 48 | 5 | 4.1 | 10.1 | 71 | 44.1% | .276 | 1.22 | 3.84 | 102 | 1.0 |
| 2022 | BRK | A+ | 23 | 5 | 1 | 0 | 11 | 11 | 55² | 35 | 0 | 4.0 | 12.0 | 74 | 36.9% | .287 | 1.08 | 2.59 | 84 | 0.9 |
| 2023 non-DC | NYM | MLB | 24 | 3 | 3 | 0 | 58 | 0 | 50 | 51 | 7 | 5.0 | 8.2 | 46 | 35.6% | .305 | 1.58 | 5.14 | 128 | -0.5 |

*Comparables: Yefry Ramírez, Kyle Cody, Chris Vallimont*

**The Report:** The Mets' third-round pick in 2021 was on the older side on draft day, and he spent 2022 as an advanced college arm dominating A-ball hitters, but there is plenty of stuff to like in his analytics-friendly four-pitch mix. Hamel can crush Florida State and South Atlantic League lineups right now off his fastball alone. The heater sits low-90s, but it's high-spin and will explode with late ride and run to righties. It is a swing-and-miss offering on its own, but Hamel will inexplicably lose the zone with the pitch for a batter here and there. Well, it's not completely inexplicable. His delivery can be a bit stabby and stiff, with some slight crossfire that leaves him with fringy command even when he's throwing strikes.

Hamel throws a full suite of secondaries, all of which show at least average potential. His low-80s slider is clearly the best offering at present, flashing plus 11-5 tilt, although the shape is inconsistent and he doesn't always stuff it under barrels. His mid-70s curve is more of a true 12-6 downer, showing better command than the fastball or slider, but it's not a bat-missing power breaker. Hamel's change is the clear fourth option. He sells it well, and it occasionally shows some circle action, but too often merely floats into the zone. Hamel is a classic example of a potential mid-rotation starter who just needs a grade jump of command and changeup to get there. He probably won't, but the fastball/slider combo should play up in a setup role with a bit of refinement.

**OFP:** 50 / no. 4 starter or setup reliever

**Variance:** High. A nice fastball with fringe command is more than enough for the low minors, but Double-A will be a test of his secondaries and strike-throwing. Hamel's stuff is interesting enough that he should have some sort of major-league career out of the pen, even if the repertoire stagnates, but he's not an impact reliever without a more consistent slider.

**Jesse Roche's Fantasy Take:** Hamel has a narrow path to fantasy relevance in most formats. As a reliever risk with no late-inning fallback, he'll need to stick in the rotation. The necessary command and control gains to do so is a tall order for a prospect who will be 24 years old to begin the season. Hamel should only be rostered in leagues with up to 400 prospects.

## 10   Calvin Ziegler   RHP    OFP: 50    ETA: 2025

Born: 10/03/02   Age: 20   Bats: R   Throws: R   Height: 6'0"   Weight: 205 lb.   Origin: Round 2, 2021 Draft (#46 overall)

| YEAR | TEAM | LVL | AGE | W | L | SV | G | GS | IP | H | HR | BB/9 | K/9 | K | GB% | BABIP | WHIP | ERA | DRA- | WARP |
|---|---|---|---|---|---|---|---|---|---|---|---|---|---|---|---|---|---|---|---|---|
| 2022 | SLU | A | 19 | 0 | 6 | 0 | 16 | 16 | 46² | 26 | 3 | 6.8 | 13.5 | 70 | 31.9% | .261 | 1.31 | 4.44 | 83 | 1.1 |
| 2023 non-DC | NYM | MLB | 20 | 3 | 3 | 0 | 58 | 0 | 50 | 46 | 8 | 6.5 | 9.7 | 54 | 33.1% | .292 | 1.65 | 5.46 | 133 | -0.6 |

*Comparables: Matt Manning, Ben Brown, Aaron Sanchez*

**The Report:** Ziegler was intended to be the underslot signing who would free up pool money for the Mets to ink their first-round pick, Kumar Rocker. You are likely aware how that played out. Since draft day, though, Ziegler has flashed the kind of stuff you'd associate with seven-figure prep arms. However, the key word here is "flashed," as he has struggled with injuries and command in 2022. At his best, the Canadian prep could run his lively fastball up into the mid-90s and pair it with a potential plus downer curve. He has tweaked his no-spin change into more of a dead-fish split, which is inconsistent but has better projection as a third pitch. Ziegler looked like a breakout pitching prospect in his first few starts in St. Lucie, but came back from a pair of IL stints struggling to throw strikes with his fastball or breaker, and his command wasn't particularly fine before that. The heater lost a little oomph, he missed far fewer bats with it and all told, only threw 46 innings across 16 starts. As a shorter righty with some effort in his delivery, there was always going to be reliever risk, and nothing in Ziegler's 2022 season has dispelled those concerns. The charcoal sketch of a three-pitch, mid-rotation starter is present, but it remains firmly in the realm of abstract expressionism for now.

**OFP:** 50 / no. 4 starter or setup reliever

**Variance:** High. We really need to see a full, healthy season of Ziegler as a starter to really discern what the long-term profile is, and the fact that it didn't happen this year tweaks the risk upward.

**Jesse Roche's Fantasy Take:** Ziegler's stuff pops, and, as I wrote in May, he "has exciting upside should he maintain his health and improve his command." Neither has happened yet. Until then, he is better left as a flier in leagues with up to 500 prospects.

# Outside the Top Ten:

## 11   Jacob Reimer   3B

Born: 02/22/04   Age: 19   Bats: R   Throws: R   Height: 6'2"   Weight: 205 lb.   Origin: Round 4, 2022 Draft (#119 overall)

| YEAR | TEAM | LVL | AGE | PA | R | 2B | 3B | HR | RBI | BB | K | SB | CS | AVG/OBP/SLG | DRC+ | BABIP | BRR | DRP | WARP |
|---|---|---|---|---|---|---|---|---|---|---|---|---|---|---|---|---|---|---|---|
| 2022 | MET | ROK | 18 | 29 | 5 | 0 | 1 | 1 | 7 | 6 | 3 | 0 | 0 | .261/.414/.478 | | .263 | | | |

Reimer, a fourth-round prep infielder out of Southern California, might signal a bit of a sea change in the Mets' draft strategy. They started moving towards more analytically friendly pitchers in 2021, but didn't really dip their toes back into the pool of early-Day 2 prep bats. Reimer is a well-built, if a bit stocky, corner infielder with potential plus power. While his swing can be overly mechanical and features a near armbar, he's able to get the bat head to different parts of the zone and drive the ball. The power potential remains more raw than game at present, but the reports from early in his pro career suggest a 2023 breakout with the bat is a real possibility.

## 12   Joel Díaz   RHP

Born: 02/26/04   Age: 19   Bats: R   Throws: R   Height: 6'2"   Weight: 208 lb.   Origin: International Free Agent, 2021

| YEAR | TEAM | LVL | AGE | W | L | SV | G | GS | IP | H | HR | BB/9 | K/9 | K | GB% | BABIP | WHIP | ERA | DRA- | WARP |
|---|---|---|---|---|---|---|---|---|---|---|---|---|---|---|---|---|---|---|---|---|
| 2021 | DSL MET2 | ROK | 17 | 0 | 2 | 0 | 14 | 14 | 49¹ | 29 | 0 | 1.6 | 11.3 | 62 | 47.8% | .257 | 0.77 | 0.55 | | |
| 2022 | SLU | A | 18 | 3 | 2 | 0 | 16 | 10 | 55¹ | 62 | 7 | 4.1 | 8.3 | 51 | 42.0% | .340 | 1.57 | 5.86 | 119 | 0.4 |
| 2023 non-DC | NYM | MLB | 19 | 2 | 3 | 0 | 58 | 0 | 50 | 63 | 9 | 5.1 | 6.3 | 35 | 34.5% | .326 | 1.82 | 6.83 | 165 | -1.4 |

*Comparables: Lyon Richardson, Ludwin Jimenez, Scott Blewett*

Díaz has had some buzz since last offseason, but his stateside debut was a bit sputtering. Once he started leaning more heavily on his plus-flashing change later in the summer, better results followed. He sells the pitch well with his arm action/speed, and it shows power fade in the mid-80s. Díaz's curve has at least average potential, showing good 11-6 shape at its best, but riding high in the zone too often. His fastball sits mostly in the average velocity band, although he will run it up to 96 or so, but the present command is below-average, and it's a bit too hittable. A bit more velocity or command of the ol' number one will help here, as would a bit more consistent breaker. Díaz is only 18, so he has time to find those gains, but the overall profile looks more like a back-end starter at present.

## 13 Jesus Baez  SS

Born: 02/26/05   Age: 18   Bats: R   Throws: R   Height: 5'10"   Weight: 180 lb.   Origin: International Free Agent, 2022

| YEAR | TEAM | LVL | AGE | PA | R | 2B | 3B | HR | RBI | BB | K | SB | CS | AVG/OBP/SLG | DRC+ | BABIP | BRR | DRP | WARP |
|------|------|-----|-----|-----|-----|-----|-----|-----|-----|-----|-----|-----|-----|-------------|------|-------|-----|-----|------|
| 2022 | DSL MET1 | ROK | 17 | 118 | 23 | 6 | 0 | 2 | 12 | 17 | 24 | 3 | 3 | .255/.373/.378 | | .315 | | | |
| 2022 | DSL MET2 | ROK | 17 | 99 | 13 | 3 | 0 | 5 | 22 | 9 | 22 | 5 | 3 | .227/.303/.432 | | .242 | | | |

Baez signed for $275,000 out of the Dominican in January, but has already surpassed the higher bonus players (Willy Fañas and Simon Juan) from the class. We started hearing industry buzz that he had plus power potential with a feel to hit and a strong shot to stay on the dirt—albeit most likely at third base—as early as the spring. He put up a credible, if not overwhelming, offensive performance (.242/.341/.403) as a 17-year-old in the DSL, while continuing to receive plaudits for his future potential. The DSL is as far away from the majors as you can get in affiliated ball and performance there doesn't mean a whole lot, so all kinds of caveats about things like "swing-and-miss being exploited by better pitching" apply. But this system basically falls off a cliff once you get outside the top 10, and Baez is a name who should be on your radar as a potential significant prospect a year or two down the line.

## 14 Mike Vasil  RHP

Born: 03/19/00   Age: 23   Bats: L   Throws: R   Height: 6'5"   Weight: 225 lb.   Origin: Round 8, 2021 Draft (#232 overall)

| YEAR | TEAM | LVL | AGE | W | L | SV | G | GS | IP | H | HR | BB/9 | K/9 | K | GB% | BABIP | WHIP | ERA | DRA- | WARP |
|------|------|-----|-----|-----|-----|-----|-----|-----|-----|-----|-----|------|-----|-----|------|-------|------|-----|------|------|
| 2021 | MET | ROK | 21 | 0 | 0 | 0 | 3 | 3 | 7 | 3 | 0 | 0.0 | 12.9 | 10 | 57.1% | .214 | 0.43 | 1.29 | | |
| 2022 | SLU | A | 22 | 3 | 1 | 0 | 9 | 8 | 37 | 26 | 1 | 2.7 | 9.5 | 39 | 45.4% | .260 | 1.00 | 2.19 | 93 | 0.7 |
| 2022 | BRK | A+ | 22 | 1 | 1 | 0 | 8 | 8 | 33¹ | 24 | 3 | 4.1 | 11.9 | 44 | 46.8% | .276 | 1.17 | 5.13 | 93 | 0.4 |
| 2023 non-DC | NYM | MLB | 23 | 3 | 3 | 0 | 58 | 0 | 50 | 54 | 8 | 4.4 | 8.0 | 44 | 37.6% | .313 | 1.56 | 5.19 | 130 | -0.5 |

*Comparables: Nick Nelson, Matt Loosen, Spencer Turnbull*

Vasil isn't far off Hamel in both profile and projection, with a repertoire of Trackman-friendly stuff led by a high-spin fastball that he can run into the mid-90s and a big downer curve. He also has a slider/cutter-type thing and a changeup. All the secondaries have around average potential, but play best in short bursts, and Vasil dealt with injury issues in 2022. He also doesn't always hold the velocity deep into starts, or start-to-start, and while a full healthy 2023 might find him still a starter in the upper minors, signs point to the bullpen long-term.

## 15 Matt Allan  RHP

Born: 04/17/01   Age: 22   Bats: R   Throws: R   Height: 6'3"   Weight: 225 lb.   Origin: Round 3, 2019 Draft (#89 overall)

Allan missed all of 2022 after undergoing a second elbow surgery in January following his 2021 Tommy John. He's functionally missed three full seasons of baseball, given his limited alternate site and instructs reps in 2020. The stuff has shown as Top-101 quality in the past, but it's no longer the recent past. No one on this list needs a full, healthy 2023 more than Allan.

## 16 Layonel Ovalles  RHP

Born: 06/16/03   Age: 20   Bats: R   Throws: R   Height: 6'3"   Weight: 216 lb.   Origin: International Free Agent, 2019

| YEAR | TEAM | LVL | AGE | W | L | SV | G | GS | IP | H | HR | BB/9 | K/9 | K | GB% | BABIP | WHIP | ERA | DRA- | WARP |
|------|------|-----|-----|-----|-----|-----|-----|-----|-----|-----|-----|------|-----|-----|------|-------|------|-----|------|------|
| 2021 | DSL MET1 | ROK | 18 | 0 | 2 | 1 | 10 | 5 | 31¹ | 12 | 0 | 1.1 | 8.6 | 30 | 57.7% | .156 | 0.51 | 1.15 | | |
| 2022 | MET | ROK | 19 | 1 | 2 | 1 | 11 | 1 | 29¹ | 26 | 0 | 1.5 | 13.5 | 44 | 46.4% | .377 | 1.06 | 2.76 | | |
| 2022 | SLU | A | 19 | 0 | 1 | 1 | 5 | 3 | 17¹ | 15 | 3 | 6.2 | 11.4 | 22 | 31.1% | .286 | 1.56 | 6.23 | 110 | 0.2 |
| 2023 non-DC | NYM | MLB | 20 | 3 | 3 | 0 | 58 | 0 | 50 | 56 | 9 | 5.7 | 7.6 | 42 | 32.3% | .311 | 1.75 | 6.32 | 153 | -1.1 |

At 19, Ovalles is already a sturdy and stout right-hander, but he can dial the fastball up to 96 mph with elite spin from a fairly easy, old school delivery. The fastball gets late swings under it, which would tell you about the ride even if you didn't see RPM regularly topping 2,600. He has two occasionally distinct breaking balls plus a slower, loopy curve that he pops in for strikes but is fringy overall, and a power slider in the low-80s which has swing-and-miss projection, but is very raw. The changeup is a bit of a mess honestly, and Ovalles could probably benefit from a grip change. However, the fastball characteristics and feel for the slider are enough to dream on at present. He may just be a fastball/slider reliever—and beyond that, this is the kind of profile that can stall out as a Double-A fastball/slider reliever—but Ovalles has as much upside as any arm in the system.

## 17 Stanley Consuegra   OF

Born: 09/24/00   Age: 22   Bats: R   Throws: R   Height: 6'2"   Weight: 167 lb.   Origin: International Free Agent, 2017

| YEAR | TEAM | LVL | AGE | PA | R | 2B | 3B | HR | RBI | BB | K | SB | CS | AVG/OBP/SLG | DRC+ | BABIP | BRR | DRP | WARP |
|------|------|-----|-----|----|---|----|----|----|----|----|---|----|----|-------------|------|-------|-----|-----|------|
| 2021 | MET | ROK | 20 | 83 | 10 | 9 | 1 | 2 | 10 | 4 | 21 | 3 | 3 | .270/.325/.500 | | .340 | | | |
| 2022 | SLU | A | 21 | 287 | 38 | 14 | 4 | 8 | 32 | 26 | 77 | 8 | 8 | .251/.324/.431 | 100 | .324 | -1.8 | LF(43) 1.9, CF(16) -2.2, RF(2) -0.1 | 1.2 |
| 2022 | BRK | A+ | 21 | 249 | 33 | 13 | 2 | 5 | 27 | 18 | 62 | 4 | 2 | .239/.309/.381 | 90 | .308 | -1.9 | RF(37) 0.6, CF(15) -1.3 | 0.5 |
| 2023 non-DC | NYM | MLB | 22 | 251 | 20 | 11 | 2 | 3 | 21 | 15 | 83 | 3 | 3 | .212/.265/.317 | 64 | .312 | -2.3 | LF 0, CF 0 | -0.6 |

Signed for $500,000 in 2017, Consuegra has been buzzy for years, but on the field for only a fraction of that time. The 21-year-old had his first full, healthy season in 2021, showing off some classic right field tools with 70 raw power and a plus arm. Consuegra is also an above-average runner at present, although he should slow down a half-tick or so, and will be a fine defender in a corner. The question is: Will he hit? He has big bat speed and an okay approach for his experience level, but it's a hard uppercut that leaves him vulnerable to pitches below his waist. Consuegra is strong enough to do damage even when he doesn't make ideal contact, but he's going to need to make more contact. For now, he profiles as a high-variance bench bat.

## 18 Nick Morabito   SS

Born: 05/07/03   Age: 20   Bats: R   Throws: R   Height: 5'11"   Weight: 185 lb.   Origin: Round 2, 2022 Draft (#75 overall)

Morabito was a compensatory second-round pick in June, and that he's this far down as an overslot 75th-overall pick in a very thin system is not a good sign. He was an unusually old prep draftee, over 19 at the time of the draft, and he was a pop-up guy from the DC area without huge physical projection, so his pick was a bet on visual hit tool scouting over everything. That can work if you get it right—Jackson Merrill was an even deeper pop-up from Maryland last year and is now one of the better prospects in the game—but early signs are not promising; Morabito was completely overwhelmed by his first exposure to pro pitching, striking out 14 times in 24 complex PAs. No prospect should be written off from two weeks in the complex, so we'll summarize where we are thusly: "Overaged prep with severe contact concerns" is a player cohort which doesn't produce many great outcomes, the Mets aren't a particularly good hit-tool development organization, and we didn't hear much optimism about Morabito as we put together this list.

## 19 Bryce Montes de Oca   RHP

Born: 04/23/96   Age: 27   Bats: R   Throws: R   Height: 6'7"   Weight: 265 lb.   Origin: Round 9, 2018 Draft (#260 overall)

| YEAR | TEAM | LVL | AGE | W | L | SV | G | GS | IP | H | HR | BB/9 | K/9 | K | GB% | BABIP | WHIP | ERA | DRA- | WARP |
|------|------|-----|-----|---|---|----|----|----|----|---|----|------|-----|---|-----|-------|------|-----|------|------|
| 2021 | BRK | A+ | 25 | 1 | 3 | 6 | 26 | 0 | 32¹ | 22 | 1 | 7.5 | 11.7 | 42 | 42.1% | .280 | 1.52 | 4.73 | 107 | 0.1 |
| 2022 | BNG | AA | 26 | 1 | 1 | 3 | 14 | 1 | 17¹ | 11 | 0 | 7.3 | 12.5 | 24 | 65.8% | .289 | 1.44 | 3.12 | 87 | 0.3 |
| 2022 | SYR | AAA | 26 | 2 | 2 | 8 | 30 | 0 | 34 | 24 | 0 | 6.4 | 14.8 | 56 | 38.2% | .353 | 1.41 | 3.44 | 65 | 1.1 |
| 2022 | NYM | MLB | 26 | 0 | 0 | 0 | 3 | 0 | 3¹ | 7 | 0 | 5.4 | 16.2 | 6 | 54.5% | .636 | 2.70 | 10.80 | 84 | 0.1 |
| 2023 DC | NYM | MLB | 27 | 1 | 1 | 0 | 19 | 0 | 16.7 | 14 | 2 | 6.0 | 11.0 | 21 | 41.4% | .292 | 1.48 | 4.33 | 108 | 0.0 |

*Comparables: Juan Jaime, Jon Edwards, Tim Peterson*

Montes de Oca will be 27 shortly after Opening Day, has walked fewer than six per nine in exactly one season—his senior year at Mizzou—and missed three full years due to injury. He also throws 102-mph sinkers with elite extension and run, a mid-90s Dustin-May-style cutter and a big sweeping slider. He will likely never be healthy enough or throw enough strikes for this to matter, but if his command is even below-average for a year or two, he can close for you.

## 20 Dedniel Núñez   RHP

Born: 06/05/96   Age: 27   Bats: R   Throws: R   Height: 6'2"   Weight: 180 lb.   Origin: International Free Agent, 2016

| YEAR | TEAM | LVL | AGE | W | L | SV | G | GS | IP | H | HR | BB/9 | K/9 | K | GB% | BABIP | WHIP | ERA | DRA- | WARP |
|------|------|-----|-----|---|---|----|----|----|----|---|----|------|-----|---|-----|-------|------|-----|------|------|
| 2022 | BNG | AA | 26 | 1 | 0 | 2 | 23 | 0 | 28¹ | 36 | 4 | 4.1 | 13.7 | 43 | 34.6% | .432 | 1.73 | 3.49 | 73 | 0.8 |
| 2023 non-DC | NYM | MLB | 27 | 3 | 3 | 0 | 58 | 0 | 50 | 48 | 7 | 3.5 | 8.9 | 50 | 33.8% | .297 | 1.35 | 4.11 | 109 | 0.0 |

Popped by the Giants in the 2021 Rule 5 Draft and then returned after a UCL tear, Núñez returned from Tommy John rehab throwing a high-spin mid-90s fastball—touching higher—and a power mid-80s slider. Yes, we are ranking a 95-and-a-slider guy, but he has a really good fastball; while the stuff doesn't have the same upside as Montes de Oca, Núñez is far more likely to be a setup-level reliever for a few years—or a useful major-league reliever at all.

## Top Talents 25 and Under (as of 4/1/2023):

1. Francisco Álvarez, C
2. Brett Baty, 3B/OF
3. Kevin Parada, C
4. Jett Williams, SS
5. Alex Ramirez, OF
6. Blade Tidwell, RHP
7. Ronny Mauricio, SS
8. Mark Vientos, 3B/1B
9. Dominic Hamel, RHP
10. Calvin Ziegler, RHP

The impact youth of this latest wave for the Mets are either still on this list despite debuting in 2022, or in another organization's farm system. The 101-win NL Wild Card leaders were unceremoniously ejected from the first round of the playoffs. However, with a strong array of core veterans and (theoretically) oodles of cash, they will need to decide if the prospects listed above can best contribute directly or indirectly to their club's future.

# New York Yankees

## The State of the System:

While subpar at the moment, there are potential explosion spots littered throughout this system.

## The Top Ten:

### 1 Anthony Volpe  SS    OFP: 70    ETA: 2023

Born: 04/28/01  Age: 22  Bats: R  Throws: R  Height: 5'11"  Weight: 180 lb.  Origin: Round 1, 2019 Draft (#30 overall)

| YEAR | TEAM | LVL | AGE | PA | R | 2B | 3B | HR | RBI | BB | K | SB | CS | AVG/OBP/SLG | DRC+ | BABIP | BRR | DRP | WARP |
|------|------|-----|-----|-----|----|----|----|----|----|----|----|----|----|---------------|------|-------|------|------------------------------|------|
| 2021 | TAM | A | 20 | 257 | 56 | 18 | 5 | 12 | 49 | 51 | 43 | 21 | 5 | .302/.455/.623 | 153 | .331 | 0.4 | SS(40) -1.2, 3B(3) -0.3, 2B(1) 0.1 | 2.3 |
| 2021 | HV | A+ | 20 | 256 | 57 | 17 | 1 | 15 | 37 | 27 | 58 | 12 | 4 | .286/.391/.587 | 132 | .319 | 0.8 | SS(45) 0.8, 2B(1) -0.1 | 1.9 |
| 2022 | SOM | AA | 21 | 497 | 71 | 31 | 4 | 18 | 60 | 57 | 88 | 44 | 6 | .251/.348/.472 | 123 | .272 | -2.2 | SS(106) -1.7 | 2.5 |
| 2022 | SWB | AAA | 21 | 99 | 15 | 4 | 1 | 3 | 5 | 8 | 30 | 6 | 1 | .236/.313/.404 | 87 | .321 | 0.2 | SS(21) -1.1 | 0.1 |
| 2023 DC | NYY | MLB | 22 | 261 | 28 | 12 | 2 | 5 | 26 | 23 | 55 | 13 | 3 | .217/.296/.348 | 87 | .262 | 2.4 | 2B 0, SS 0 | 0.7 |

*Comparables: Brendan Rodgers, J.P. Crawford, Jorge Polanco*

**The Report:** We've talked ad nauseam about the jump in pitching quality from High-A to Double-A. And Volpe's season perfectly illustrates that point. Volpe had a miserable start to his season with Double-A Somerset, but he turned things around in a way befitting a top prospect. His slow start was a byproduct of his inability to lay off breaking pitches below the zone. This changed as the season progressed, as he began laying off breakers outside the zone and making contact with those in it. As noted in previous listings, his swing is more vertical than when he first entered pro ball. His hands during his load are quiet, allowing him to use his good hand-eye coordination to pull balls that most hitters can't. Thanks to his improved pitch recognition and demonstrated power, Volpe projects for above-average hit and power—a rare combo for an up-the-middle player.

Volpe is an incredibly instinctual baserunner who won't wow with his speed—it's above-average, at best—but should be able to tally 20 stolen bases a season. The same concept applies to his defense at short: His instincts have allowed him to be a serviceable defensive shortstop despite only moderate range. If he has to move off short, third might be a better destination than the keystone, as his strong arm can play better there. Volpe might not come to the table with all the tools you envision when you conjure up a top-tier prospect in your head, but the tools he does have pair with his instincts to make everything play up, and the result is one of the most well-rounded prospects in the game.

**OFP:** 70 / All-Star infielder who is better than the sum of his tools

**Variance:** Medium. He's not elite at any one thing, but 20/20 potential shortstops don't grow on trees. I have very little doubt that Volpe could make for an excellent plus-plus defensive third baseman, so a position change would have little effect on his outlook.

**Jesse Roche's Fantasy Take:** Boy, did Volpe turn his season around! Through mid-May, and noted by Jarrett Seidler at the time, Volpe was hitting just .165/.286/.321 with a 26.3% strikeout rate in Double-A. From then, he hit .271/.359/.498 with an 18% strikeout rate. Volpe is a disciplined hitter with strong bat-to-ball ability, but his extreme fly-ball rates (56.2%) place downward pressure on his batting average (.279 BABIP). Granted, his lift-heavy approach allows him to tap into all of his raw power and then some. As such, Volpe may not hit for as much average as you'd expect. Still, if he can reach his 20/20 potential or more–he was 50-for-57 in steals in the upper minors, no less–he'll be a fantasy star. Volpe is firmly within the dynasty top 10 and likely arrives at some point in 2023.

## 2  Oswald Peraza  SS    OFP: 60    ETA: Debuted in 2022
Born: 06/15/00  Age: 23  Bats: R  Throws: R  Height: 6'0"  Weight: 200 lb.  Origin: International Free Agent, 2016

| YEAR | TEAM | LVL | AGE | PA | R | 2B | 3B | HR | RBI | BB | K | SB | CS | AVG/OBP/SLG | DRC+ | BABIP | BRR | DRP | WARP |
|---|---|---|---|---|---|---|---|---|---|---|---|---|---|---|---|---|---|---|---|
| 2021 | HV | A+ | 21 | 127 | 20 | 10 | 0 | 5 | 16 | 12 | 24 | 16 | 1 | .306/.386/.532 | 127 | .349 | 1.0 | SS(25) 4.9 | 1.4 |
| 2021 | SOM | AA | 21 | 353 | 51 | 16 | 2 | 12 | 40 | 23 | 82 | 20 | 8 | .294/.348/.466 | 102 | .362 | -2.2 | SS(69) -2.7 | 0.7 |
| 2021 | SWB | AAA | 21 | 31 | 5 | 0 | 0 | 1 | 2 | 2 | 5 | 2 | 1 | .286/.323/.393 | 98 | .304 | -0.3 | SS(7) 1.5 | 0.2 |
| 2022 | SWB | AAA | 22 | 429 | 57 | 16 | 0 | 19 | 50 | 34 | 100 | 33 | 5 | .259/.329/.448 | 100 | .302 | 3.1 | SS(89) -1.3, 2B(10) -1.5 | 1.3 |
| 2022 | NYY | MLB | 22 | 57 | 8 | 3 | 0 | 1 | 2 | 6 | 9 | 2 | 0 | .306/.404/.429 | 111 | .359 | -1.0 | SS(12) 0.7, 2B(4) 0 | 0.2 |
| 2023 DC | NYY | MLB | 23 | 279 | 28 | 11 | 1 | 6 | 26 | 16 | 68 | 13 | 4 | .238/.294/.355 | 87 | .300 | 1.2 | SS -2 | 0.5 |

*Comparables: Willi Castro, Reid Brignac, Jorge Polanco*

**The Report:** The removal of extreme shifts in baseball is going to force evaluators to rethink how they value defense at certain positions, especially those up the middle. As such, Oswald Peraza will be a fascinating case study. I remember scouting Peraza in 2019 when he played for the now-defunct Staten Island Yankees and recall thinking how similar—both physically and stylistically—he looked to a younger Gleyber Torres. The 2018-19 version of Torres emphasized contact, had the potential to add game power (he did) and could potentially stick at short (he didn't). For his part, Peraza seems likely to stick at the six, showcasing plus or better defensive chops, especially in his ability to turn the double play. His instincts are double-plus and range is plus, whereas the arm grades out closer to above average—still more than enough given the rest of the defensive profile.

Peraza's swing is an aesthetically simple yet beautiful stroke that prioritizes contact and gap power over home run pop. I'm more cautious nowadays in assuming guys like Peraza can add game power without sacrificing some hit tool, especially when said hitter doesn't have good plate discipline (Peraza consistently walks at well-below-average clips). There's an argument that Peraza's ability to make contact in the zone at such a high level should be prioritized over increasing his currently average game power.

**OFP:** 60 / First-division shortstop, occasional All-Star

**Variance:** Low. Peraza's profile has been consistent in ways you'd like it to be for years now. We're highly confident he stays at short and can have a few nice offensive campaigns mixed in.

**Jesse Roche's Fantasy Take:** Like Volpe, Peraza got off to a sluggish start in Triple-A, hitting just .192/.267/.316 through mid-June. Thereafter, though, he caught fire, hitting .316/.382/.560 with 14 home runs and 22 stolen bases over his next 53 games. Then, Peraza impressed in his debut (108 DRC+), and he likely enters 2023 as the starting shortstop. He offers contact skills, sneaky pop and plus speed, and he should contribute across all five standard categories. In fact, he, like Volpe, may develop up to 20/20 potential, even if the power likely falls short. Peraza falls well within the dynasty top 50, with a boost in formats that favor proximity.

## 3  Spencer Jones  OF    OFP: 60    ETA: 2024
Born: 05/14/01  Age: 22  Bats: L  Throws: L  Height: 6'7"  Weight: 225 lb.  Origin: Round 1, 2022 Draft (#25 overall)

| YEAR | TEAM | LVL | AGE | PA | R | 2B | 3B | HR | RBI | BB | K | SB | CS | AVG/OBP/SLG | DRC+ | BABIP | BRR | DRP | WARP |
|---|---|---|---|---|---|---|---|---|---|---|---|---|---|---|---|---|---|---|---|
| 2022 | TAM | A | 21 | 95 | 18 | 5 | 0 | 3 | 8 | 10 | 18 | 10 | 0 | .325/.411/.494 | 113 | .387 | 0.5 | CF(18) -0.5 | 0.4 |
| 2023 non-DC | NYY | MLB | 22 | 251 | 20 | 10 | 2 | 2 | 20 | 17 | 70 | 10 | 2 | .215/.276/.306 | 65 | .297 | 0.1 | CF 0 | -0.2 |

*Comparables: Dominic Fletcher, Nathan Lukes, Andrew Toles*

**The Report:** The Yankees love their college bats in the first round, with Spencer Jones the third in as many years, following Austin Wells and Trey Sweeney. A slight adjustment to his swing before the 2022 collegiate season was the catalyst towards a seismic rise up draft boards.

Early in his college career, Jones' swing contained tons of moving parts, perhaps a byproduct of being a tall, svelte teenager. When he showed up bulkier this year, he exhibited a simplified, borderline effortless swing that allowed him to leverage his long levers and sensational bat speed: the results were 7 raw power and domination against SEC pitchers. The Yankees have a track record of maximizing this profile (Aaron Judge and Giancarlo Stanton have elite raw pop with effortless swings) and Jones is still relatively new to hitting full-time as a two-way prep, so there is genuine belief that Jones' still-underdeveloped skill set can improve with reps.

His swing decisions and z-contact rates aren't as bad as one might think given his inexperience and size, and he will become a mega producer if those decisions and contact rates improve to even below-average. Jones toyed with first base while at Vanderbilt, but there is optimism he will successfully man a corner outfield spot when all is said and done.

**OFP:** 60/ Power-hitting outfielder who could make a few All-Star games

**Variance:** High. We have a very small track record of success, but said success was in the most competitive college conference and carried over into his pro debut. You have permission to get excited.

**Jesse Roche's Fantasy Take:** I'M SO EXCITED! Jones, a standout in Low-A, has mammoth size to go with fantasy upside should he approach his ceiling. His top-end exit velocities led college baseball last year, and he regularly flashed his huge raw power in his debut. If he can learn to lift more often without sacrificing contact (like Judge), Jones could truly break out and fly up prospect rankings this year. Of course, he is not without his fair share of risk, especially given his 6-foot-7 frame and some underlying swing-and-miss issues. Yet, Jones has risen near the top of this college crop and is a borderline top-10 pick in upcoming FYPDs.

## 4  Jasson Domínguez  OF    OFP: 55    ETA: 2024

Born: 02/07/03   Age: 20   Bats: S   Throws: R   Height: 5'10"   Weight: 190 lb.   Origin: International Free Agent, 2019

| YEAR | TEAM | LVL | AGE | PA | R | 2B | 3B | HR | RBI | BB | K | SB | CS | AVG/OBP/SLG | DRC+ | BABIP | BRR | DRP | WARP |
|---|---|---|---|---|---|---|---|---|---|---|---|---|---|---|---|---|---|---|---|
| 2021 | YNK | ROK | 18 | 27 | 5 | 0 | 0 | 0 | 1 | 6 | 6 | 2 | 0 | .200/.407/.200 | | .286 | | | |
| 2021 | TAM | A | 18 | 214 | 26 | 9 | 1 | 5 | 18 | 21 | 67 | 7 | 3 | .258/.346/.398 | 88 | .371 | 0.2 | CF(38) -4.4 | 0.1 |
| 2022 | TAM | A | 19 | 324 | 54 | 17 | 2 | 9 | 36 | 46 | 89 | 19 | 6 | .265/.373/.440 | 104 | .360 | 0.1 | CF(65) -2.1 | 0.7 |
| 2022 | HV | A+ | 19 | 184 | 33 | 6 | 4 | 6 | 22 | 23 | 34 | 17 | 1 | .306/.397/.510 | 113 | .353 | 3.5 | CF(35) 1.1 | 1.7 |
| 2023 non-DC | NYY | MLB | 20 | 251 | 22 | 10 | 3 | 3 | 22 | 20 | 72 | 8 | 2 | .233/.301/.344 | 84 | .326 | -0.5 | CF 0 | 0.3 |

Comparables: Justin Upton, Jahmai Jones, Heliot Ramos

**The Report:** Boy, where do we start?

Domínguez's prospect hype has done him a tremendous disservice. I say this because, for all that hype, he could appear to be a letdown. In reality, he's turned into a nice prospect, one who many would look at differently had he not been *Jasson Domínguez*.

In simplest terms, Domínguez is a switch-hitting outfielder who shows a nice collection of tools, none of which have stood out as elite. He looks more comfortable as a left-handed hitter, though he was fine as a righty last season. Much of his 2022 offensive progress came in the form of far better plate discipline compared to 2021. Though he still swings over a concerning number of breaking pitches, his propensity for drawing walks does help to somewhat balance out his strikeout concerns.

Domínguez has hit the ball on the ground way too much to begin his pro career and is only posting above-average exit velos, but it's important to note that some teams place a premium on 90th-percentile exit velos as an indicator of what a prospect's power outcome could look like, and Domínguez fares quite well there. There's also the possibility, however, that he loses bat speed if he continues to beef up an already-yoked physique. His numbers in Low- and High-A in 2022 were quite good—especially age-adjusted—but bear in mind that 2022 was one of the worst seasons for pitching at those levels in a long time. Ultimately, there are a couple of things I'll be monitoring heading into '23: Does he maintain bat speed as he continues to fill out, and can he make contact with higher-quality breaking pitches in the upper minors?

As a result of filling out, Domínguez is nowhere near the 7-grade runner some expected him to be—he's barely a plus runner at this point—but he is an instinctual baserunner, which has allowed him to capitalize in the lower minors. Domínguez has played center field in his minor-league career, but I think he is ultimately destined to be a plus corner outfielder, where his arm teeters on the 55-6 border.

**OFP:** 55 / Above-average corner outfielder

**Variance:** High. 2022 was way more promising than 2021, but will his current style of play translate to the upper minors & majors?

**Jesse Roche's Fantasy Take:** Another Yankees' slow starter, Domínguez hit just .225/.247/.324 with a disastrous 25-to-2 strikeout-to-walk ratio in April in his repeat engagement in Low-A. Yikes! He quickly recovered, however, and hit .290/.405/.510 with a 22.6% strikeout rate and a 15.6% walk rate across three levels all at 19 years old. His batted-ball data truly pops, including a 112.7-mph max exit velocity and a juicy 107.2-mph, 90th-percentile exit velocity in Low-A. Power, speed, and an improving hit tool all point to a potential fantasy stud. That said, Domínguez's frame and continuing whiff issues are problematic and make him a riskier prospect than his pedigree or performance may indicate. Regardless, he is a top-20 dynasty prospect with huge power-speed upside if it all comes together.

## 5 Will Warren RHP  OFP: 55  ETA: Late 2023
Born: 06/16/99  Age: 24  Bats: R  Throws: R  Height: 6'2"  Weight: 175 lb.  Origin: Round 8, 2021 Draft (#243 overall)

| YEAR | TEAM | LVL | AGE | W | L | SV | G | GS | IP | H | HR | BB/9 | K/9 | K | GB% | BABIP | WHIP | ERA | DRA- | WARP |
|------|------|-----|-----|---|---|----|----|----|----|----|----|------|-----|----|------|-------|------|------|------|------|
| 2022 | HV | A+ | 23 | 2 | 3 | 0 | 8 | 8 | 35 | 30 | 2 | 2.3 | 10.8 | 42 | 57.0% | .333 | 1.11 | 3.60 | 95 | 0.3 |
| 2022 | SOM | AA | 23 | 7 | 6 | 0 | 18 | 18 | 94 | 89 | 8 | 3.2 | 7.9 | 83 | 52.5% | .302 | 1.30 | 4.02 | 110 | 0.8 |
| 2023 non-DC | NYY | MLB | 24 | 3 | 3 | 0 | 58 | 0 | 50 | 54 | 7 | 3.7 | 7.0 | 39 | 42.8% | .307 | 1.49 | 4.78 | 122 | -0.3 |

*Comparables: Zach Hedges, Luis Cessa, T.J. Zeuch*

**The Report:** Shortly after being drafted in 2021, the Yankees worked with Warren to optimize his arsenal: the early results in 2022 were promising. Warren is a similar pitching prospect to Randy Vasquez in that he began leveraging two versions of a fastball alongside a really good breaking pitch. I prefer Warren's two-seam/sinker to his four-seamer, and given that the Yankees taught him the pitch shortly after they drafted him, I think they agree. Both pitches can get up there—98 with arm-side run on the two-seamer—though they'll usually sit in the 93-94 range. The slider is a nasty, sword-inducing pitch that occasionally gets a couple of "wows" from scouts. The pitch has ridiculous horizontal bite, though he'll need to work on locating the pitch because he doesn't locate it glove-side as much as you'd like. I think that'll come with time, though there's a chance his command is just average at a 75th-percentile outcome.

Warren is sufficiently-built and athletic on the mound, with a medium-high effort delivery. Despite the effort involved, Warren throws enough strikes to stick as a starter if his pitch sequencing continues to develop, though he'll likely be more of a control-over-command guy. While his collection of pitches has improved leaps and bounds from draft day, it's not clear the arsenal is elite enough to be a top-end starter due to only average command. Regardless, Warren is already a huge developmental success.

**OFP:** 55/ no. 3/4 starter and @PitchingNinja favorite

**Variance:** Medium. Warren already reached Double-A during his first full season in pro ball, and there is further room for growth. With questions abound in the Yankees bullpen, perhaps Warren starts his MLB career there next season à la Clarke Schmidt.

**Jesse Roche's Fantasy Take:** Warren's ridiculous slider and solid two-seamer keep the ball on the ground and in the park. What they don't do enough of, unfortunately, is miss bats. Indeed, his 20.6% strikeout rate in Double-A was easily the lowest among the Yankees' Double-A starters. Warren's fantasy upside likely is limited and further complicated by the Yankees' recent usage of pitching prospects (again, à la Schmidt).

## 6 Randy Vásquez RHP  OFP: 55  ETA: 2023
Born: 11/03/98  Age: 24  Bats: R  Throws: R  Height: 6'0"  Weight: 165 lb.  Origin: International Free Agent, 2018

| YEAR | TEAM | LVL | AGE | W | L | SV | G | GS | IP | H | HR | BB/9 | K/9 | K | GB% | BABIP | WHIP | ERA | DRA- | WARP |
|------|------|-----|-----|---|---|----|----|----|------|----|----|------|------|-----|-------|-------|------|------|------|------|
| 2021 | TAM | A | 22 | 3 | 3 | 0 | 13 | 11 | 50 | 35 | 2 | 4.1 | 10.4 | 58 | 54.7% | .262 | 1.16 | 2.34 | 80 | 1.1 |
| 2021 | HV | A+ | 22 | 3 | 0 | 0 | 6 | 6 | 36 | 33 | 0 | 2.0 | 13.3 | 53 | 65.9% | .393 | 1.14 | 1.75 | 75 | 0.8 |
| 2021 | SOM | AA | 22 | 2 | 1 | 0 | 4 | 4 | 21¹ | 23 | 2 | 3.0 | 8.0 | 19 | 52.9% | .309 | 1.41 | 4.22 | 104 | 0.1 |
| 2022 | SOM | AA | 23 | 2 | 7 | 0 | 25 | 25 | 115¹ | 106 | 11 | 3.2 | 9.4 | 120 | 47.1% | .304 | 1.27 | 3.90 | 95 | 1.8 |
| 2023 DC | NYY | MLB | 24 | 1 | 1 | 0 | 3 | 3 | 13 | 14 | 2 | 3.8 | 7.7 | 11 | 42.4% | .304 | 1.45 | 4.43 | 115 | 0.0 |

*Comparables: Zach Hedges, Austin Voth, Jaron Long*

**The Report:** Vasquez was one of many Yankees prospects to take seismic leaps in 2021, much of which was attributed to a lower arm slot that led to added velocity and better two-seam shape. Though he wasn't as dominant in 2022, there is still a ton to like about Vasquez.

His four- and two-seamers both operate as primary pitches depending on the hitter's handedness. Although his velo was slightly down from 2021, Vasquez can still get both fastballs into the mid-90s as a starter and has shown a better understanding of how and when he should use each offering: They currently grade out as above-average, with the two-seamer a potential plus pitch. His arsenal's real standout, though, is the breaking ball—a hellish sweeping curve that easily passes both the eye and analytical tests. With two seasons of consistently missing bats with the pitch, it's now comfortably a double-plus offering. While he's worked on a change over the past few years, it's still far behind the other three pitches in his arsenal. I question whether he'll need it given the variation in fastball shape and the quality breaking pitch.

One could make the case that Vasquez's command regressed from the year prior, as he failed to establish his heaters for strikes in spurts last year. He gets very little of his lower half engaged, putting inordinate pressure on his upper half to generate his momentum toward the plate. If his command improves to 2021 levels, however, you could be looking at a nice mid-rotation guy.

**OFP:** 55 / no. 3 starter or excellent reliever

**Variance:** Medium. I wish we had a better idea of what Vasquez would be given his proximity to the majors, but he will be a major leaguer as soon as this upcoming year.

**Jesse Roche's Fantasy Take:** Take what you read about Warren above, add a few more strikeouts and remove a touch of command, and you have Vasquez.

## 7  Luis Gil  RHP    OFP: 55    ETA: Debuted in 2021

Born: 06/03/98  Age: 25  Bats: R  Throws: R  Height: 6'2"  Weight: 185 lb.  Origin: International Free Agent, 2015

| YEAR | TEAM | LVL | AGE | W | L | SV | G | GS | IP | H | HR | BB/9 | K/9 | K | GB% | BABIP | WHIP | ERA | DRA- | WARP |
|------|------|-----|-----|---|---|----|----|----|----|---|----|------|-----|---|-----|-------|------|-----|------|------|
| 2021 | SOM | AA | 23 | 1 | 1 | 0 | 7 | 7 | 30² | 24 | 2 | 3.8 | 14.7 | 50 | 29.9% | .338 | 1.21 | 2.64 | 80 | 0.6 |
| 2021 | SWB | AAA | 23 | 4 | 0 | 1 | 13 | 10 | 48² | 35 | 7 | 5.9 | 12.4 | 67 | 29.1% | .275 | 1.38 | 4.81 | 84 | 1.1 |
| 2021 | NYY | MLB | 23 | 1 | 1 | 0 | 6 | 6 | 29¹ | 20 | 4 | 5.8 | 11.7 | 38 | 32.4% | .239 | 1.33 | 3.07 | 100 | 0.3 |
| 2022 | SWB | AAA | 24 | 0 | 3 | 0 | 6 | 6 | 21² | 21 | 6 | 6.2 | 12.9 | 31 | 26.3% | .294 | 1.66 | 7.89 | 104 | 0.2 |
| 2022 | NYY | MLB | 24 | 0 | 0 | 0 | 1 | 1 | 4 | 5 | 0 | 4.5 | 11.3 | 5 | 41.7% | .417 | 1.75 | 9.00 | 99 | 0.0 |
| 2023 non-DC | NYY | MLB | 25 | 3 | 3 | 0 | 58 | 0 | 50 | 43 | 7 | 5.3 | 10.8 | 60 | 34.0% | .294 | 1.45 | 4.34 | 111 | 0.0 |

*Comparables: Jarred Cosart, Chris Archer, Jake Faria*

**The Report:** If you remove Tommy John surgery from Gil's profile, we are probably talking about the best pitching prospect the Yankees have developed since Luis Severino—though not *quite* that good. His fastball is a hellacious pitch that he can run into the upper 90s with ridiculous rising action. His changeup, though not a true change in a velocity separation sense, pairs well with his heater. The slurve has the movement profile of a slider and velocity of a curve and can occasionally get swords. All that's great, right? Well, Gil's issues commanding the ball continued into 2022 before he blew out his arm. He will likely not be available until around the All-Star break, and one has to imagine the Yankees ease him back into action as a reliever—which might be his ultimate destination anyway.

We are still bullish on his collection of pitches and acknowledge that any command improvement propels Gil into no. 2-3 starter territory, but we have no reason to believe that will come to pass given his extensive pro track record and non-ideal delivery.

**OFP:** 55 / Mid-rotation starter who you'll keep wanting more from, or a high-leverage reliever

**Variance:** Medium. It'd be high had he not performed in the majors, but tracking Gil's recovery from TJS will be crucial.

**Jesse Roche's Fantasy Take:** Gil has *never* had a walk rate under 10% at any level, and his career walk rate is 13.7%. He has walked 21 batters across 33 ⅓ MLB innings (14.2%). Oh, and he is recovering from Tommy John surgery, from which pitchers often take time to regain their command. All signs point to a future in relief, where Gil certainly could thrive given his loud stuff. Extreme role uncertainty, however, severely hinders his short- and long-term fantasy outlook.

## 8  Everson Pereira  CF    OFP: 55    ETA: Late 2023/early 2024

Born: 04/10/01  Age: 22  Bats: R  Throws: R  Height: 6'0"  Weight: 191 lb.  Origin: International Free Agent, 2017

| YEAR | TEAM | LVL | AGE | PA | R | 2B | 3B | HR | RBI | BB | K | SB | CS | AVG/OBP/SLG | DRC+ | BABIP | BRR | DRP | WARP |
|------|------|-----|-----|----|---|----|----|----|----|----|---|----|----|-------------|------|-------|-----|-----|------|
| 2021 | TAM | A | 20 | 83 | 17 | 5 | 1 | 5 | 22 | 10 | 21 | 4 | 1 | .361/.446/.667 | 110 | .457 | 0.5 | CF(9) -0.7, LF(4) -0.6, RF(2) -0.1 | 0.3 |
| 2021 | HV | A+ | 20 | 127 | 27 | 3 | 0 | 14 | 32 | 15 | 38 | 5 | 2 | .259/.354/.676 | 129 | .241 | -1.0 | CF(22) -2.4 | 0.5 |
| 2022 | HV | A+ | 21 | 325 | 55 | 13 | 6 | 9 | 43 | 34 | 87 | 19 | 5 | .274/.354/.455 | 96 | .363 | 1.0 | CF(58) -5.3, RF(7) 0.4, LF(1) 0.1 | 0.3 |
| 2022 | SOM | AA | 21 | 123 | 21 | 4 | 3 | 5 | 13 | 9 | 37 | 2 | 2 | .283/.341/.504 | 86 | .380 | -0.8 | CF(24) -0.1 | 0.0 |
| 2023 non-DC | NYY | MLB | 22 | 251 | 24 | 10 | 2 | 6 | 26 | 17 | 83 | 5 | 2 | .232/.292/.368 | 87 | .336 | -1.8 | LF 0, CF 0 | 0.2 |

**The Report:** Pereira is an aggressive hitter who will swing and miss a decent amount, and he hits the ball on the ground too much. But he has moments, sometimes months at a time, where he looks virtually unstoppable. Those moments led the Yankees to put Pereira on their 40-man roster to prevent a team from snagging him in the Rule 5 Draft. He features perhaps the best bat speed of any prospect in this system and has adjusted his swing to become more uphill. The idea is that if Pereira lifts the ball more, his exceptional bat speed will do the work on the power front, elevating his offensive profile. Though he chases *a lot*, he has shown an ability to make contact with pitches in the zone, which is enough given the rest of his profile.

Pereira takes good reads on balls, and he has plus range and an above-average arm. He would be higher on this list were it not for concerns over his lengthy injury record: He's dealt with several fairly significant injuries throughout his pro career. It doesn't help that his 40-man clock began last year, as he's lost and will lose option years despite not being particularly close to making an impact in the bigs.

**OFP:** 55 / Above-average-at-everything center fielder

**Variance:** High. This offensive profile could collapse in the bigs, but he's close enough to the majors and now has multiple years of impressive minor-league performance where we'll bet on the talent.

**Jesse Roche's Fantasy Take:** From April 13th to May 31st, the power-hitting Pereira failed to hit a home run. That lengthy drought saw his ISO sitting at just .082 through May. Eventually, he found his power stroke, hitting .278/.333/.533 with 13 home runs over his final 63 games. While his bat speed and power may not be in doubt, his hit tool is, and his sub-65% contact rate is concerning. If Pereira can make enough contact to get to his power, he could provide a tantalizing blend of power and speed. That is a big "if," though.

## 9 Drew Thorpe  RHP        OFP: 55        ETA: Late 2024/early 2025
Born: 10/01/00   Age: 22   Bats: L   Throws: R   Height: 6'4"   Weight: 190 lb.   Origin: Round 2, 2022 Draft (#61 overall)

**The Report:** The 6-foot-4 Thorpe went under the radar in the 2022 draft process due to his small school pedigree and his apparent command-over-stuff profile. In reality, though, Thorpe is a really interesting pitcher whose current weaknesses fit right into the areas the Yankees thrive at developing. He has excellent command of his arsenal thanks to a simple delivery with a short arm action featuring a high three-quarters arm slot. Though he features an above-average slider, his best secondary is a borderline double-plus *cambio* featuring nasty two-plane action. What's fascinating about Thorpe is his usage of a sinker as his primary pitch, which doesn't quite add up since he throws from a high arm slot. It's a low-90s offering that is surprisingly effective and pairs well with his change, but I wonder if the Yankees have plans to incorporate a four-seamer which he can get outs with up in the zone.

Thorpe didn't pitch after he signed, presumably to work with the Yankees on pitch design before he makes his debut this coming season. Watching him pitch, it's obvious he's projectable and very athletic, so there is potential for him to add velocity to whatever primary pitch he utilizes. If you're looking for a pitcher to have a potential Will Warren-type ascent from this draft class, it's Thorpe.

**OFP:** 55 / mid-rotation starter

**Variance:** Medium. The command profile and secondaries are so good that he's highly likely to have some role in a big-league rotation.

**Jesse Roche's Fantasy Take:** Right-handed pitchers with mediocre fastballs and command-and-changeup-first profiles generally are far better real-life than fantasy players.

## 10 Trey Sweeney  SS        OFP: 55        ETA: 2024
Born: 04/24/00   Age: 23   Bats: L   Throws: R   Height: 6'4"   Weight: 200 lb.   Origin: Round 1, 2021 Draft (#20 overall)

| YEAR | TEAM | LVL | AGE | PA | R | 2B | 3B | HR | RBI | BB | K | SB | CS | AVG/OBP/SLG | DRC+ | BABIP | BRR | DRP | WARP |
|---|---|---|---|---|---|---|---|---|---|---|---|---|---|---|---|---|---|---|---|
| 2021 | TAM | A | 21 | 129 | 26 | 4 | 4 | 6 | 13 | 18 | 29 | 3 | 1 | .245/.357/.518 | 119 | .280 | 1.3 | SS(25) 0.3 | 0.8 |
| 2022 | HV | A+ | 22 | 458 | 70 | 18 | 4 | 14 | 51 | 59 | 108 | 29 | 2 | .241/.350/.415 | 116 | .297 | -1.2 | SS(87) 5.2 | 2.7 |
| 2022 | SOM | AA | 22 | 50 | 6 | 1 | 0 | 2 | 5 | 7 | 10 | 2 | 1 | .233/.340/.395 | 105 | .258 | 0.0 | SS(10) 2.1 | 0.4 |
| 2023 non-DC | NYY | MLB | 23 | 251 | 23 | 10 | 3 | 4 | 23 | 23 | 61 | 6 | 2 | .219/.296/.341 | 81 | .280 | -1.4 | SS 0 | 0.1 |

*Comparables: Taylor Walls, Brad Miller, Nick Maton*

**The Report:** During the 2021 draft process, Sweeney was a darling in the Yankees' model which seems to prioritize swing decisions and quality of contact. Well, to nobody's surprise, Sweeney makes good swing decisions and hits the ball relatively hard, but he still manages to strike out at a higher clip than you'd think because he can be beaten in the zone. Much of what Jeffrey wrote up last year about his mechanics rings true today, and I have to wonder if a smaller leg kick will give him more time to adjust to pitches in the upper part of the zone. That's easier said than done, though. In totality, you're looking at a bat that's unlikely to be a true impact in the middle of a lineup, but one that any team would love to have on its roster.

Given the other infield prospects in this system and the new shifting rules, Sweeney is simply not a long-term shortstop. He could probably fill in a day or two a week there, but he could be an above-average third-baseman or below-average second-baseman. I will give Sweeney credit for being faster than I expected, as he's more of an average runner than below-average

**OFP:** 55 / Offensive-minded infielder

**Variance:** Medium. I don't think there's a star-level outcome here, but he is relatively close to making his major-league debut.

**Jesse Roche's Fantasy Take:** Sweeney makes contact, walks and is capable of generating hard contact. Nevertheless, he has yet to hit above .245 at any level due, in part, to a lot of weak contact. It is reasonable to question how much impact he'll ultimately have. Regardless, Sweeney has an intriguing fantasy starter kit, especially in OBP leagues, with a little hit, a little pop and a little speed (31-for-34 in stolen bases last year!).

## Outside the Top Ten:

### 11  Oswaldo Cabrera  UT

Born: 03/01/99   Age: 24   Bats: S   Throws: R   Height: 6'0"   Weight: 200 lb.   Origin: International Free Agent, 2015

| YEAR | TEAM | LVL | AGE | PA | R | 2B | 3B | HR | RBI | BB | K | SB | CS | AVG/OBP/SLG | DRC+ | BABIP | BRR | DRP | WARP |
|------|------|-----|-----|-----|----|----|----|----|-----|----|-----|----|----|-------------|------|-------|------|-----|------|
| 2021 | SOM | AA | 22 | 478 | 61 | 29 | 1 | 24 | 78 | 36 | 118 | 20 | 5 | .256/.311/.492 | 111 | .295 | 2.0 | 2B(43) -0.8, 3B(35) 4.9, SS(24) 3.9 | 3.1 |
| 2021 | SWB | AAA | 22 | 36 | 11 | 2 | 1 | 5 | 11 | 5 | 9 | 1 | 0 | .500/.583/1.133 | 134 | .625 | -0.2 | 2B(7) 0.0, 3B(1) -0.2, SS(1) -0.2 | 0.2 |
| 2022 | SWB | AAA | 23 | 208 | 29 | 12 | 3 | 8 | 29 | 19 | 55 | 10 | 3 | .262/.340/.492 | 97 | .331 | 0.2 | 2B(21) 4.4, SS(15) 0.5, 3B(6) 0.7 | 1.1 |
| 2022 | NYY | MLB | 23 | 171 | 21 | 8 | 1 | 6 | 19 | 15 | 44 | 3 | 2 | .247/.312/.429 | 94 | .305 | -0.6 | RF(27) 0.3, LF(9) -0.4, SS(4) 0.9 | 0.4 |
| 2023 DC | NYY | MLB | 24 | 422 | 44 | 19 | 2 | 11 | 44 | 31 | 109 | 13 | 4 | .217/.280/.362 | 80 | .273 | 0.8 | LF 0, RF 0 | 0.1 |

*Comparables: Avisaíl García, Starling Marte, Jorge Soler*

Cabrera was a surprising contributor to the Yankees down the stretch, but perhaps we should've seen this coming. After all, he was a versatile defender who provided sufficient offensive production from both sides of the plate in the high minors. Cabrera features an open stance and uses a fairly aggressive leg kick to time pitches. I was pleasantly surprised by his ability to combine contact in the zone with interesting batted-ball data: He put the ball in the air 13% more than league-average. Like Pereira, he's chased and missed out of the zone for several seasons now, thus limiting his overall offensive upside.

Cabrera played all over the field for the Yankees, though he looked quite raw at many positions. While he is a relatively athletic player, he isn't nimble enough to man short and is cutting it close at second, where his footwork will need to improve. He's still new to the outfield, but he made a few incredible plays where he tracked the ball well which suggests he could be a slightly above-average corner outfielder in time

### 12  Clayton Beeter  RHP

Born: 10/09/98   Age: 24   Bats: R   Throws: R   Height: 6'2"   Weight: 220 lb.   Origin: Round 2, 2020 Draft (#66 overall)

| YEAR | TEAM | LVL | AGE | W | L | SV | G | GS | IP | H | HR | BB/9 | K/9 | K | GB% | BABIP | WHIP | ERA | DRA- | WARP |
|------|------|-----|-----|---|---|----|----|----|----|----|----|------|------|----|------|-------|------|-----|------|------|
| 2021 | GL | A+ | 22 | 0 | 4 | 0 | 23 | 22 | 37¹ | 28 | 3 | 3.6 | 13.3 | 55 | 36.7% | .333 | 1.15 | 3.13 | 71 | 1.0 |
| 2021 | TUL | AA | 22 | 0 | 2 | 0 | 5 | 5 | 15 | 10 | 2 | 4.2 | 13.8 | 23 | 53.3% | .286 | 1.13 | 4.20 | 71 | 0.3 |
| 2022 | TUL | AA | 23 | 0 | 3 | 0 | 18 | 16 | 51² | 48 | 10 | 6.1 | 15.3 | 88 | 39.8% | .352 | 1.61 | 5.75 | 60 | 1.5 |
| 2022 | SOM | AA | 23 | 0 | 0 | 0 | 7 | 7 | 25¹ | 16 | 1 | 3.9 | 14.6 | 41 | 46.2% | .306 | 1.07 | 2.13 | 72 | 0.7 |
| 2023 non-DC | NYY | MLB | 24 | 3 | 3 | 0 | 58 | 0 | 50 | 42 | 8 | 5.0 | 10.6 | 59 | 36.0% | .284 | 1.41 | 4.21 | 109 | 0.0 |

*Comparables: Bryan Abreu, Ryan Searle, Vince Velasquez*

Beeter is a highly interesting, high-arm slot Dodgers draftee who was traded for Joey Gallo at the 2022 trade deadline. Beeter's three-pitch mix is arguably the most compelling in this system. It's headlined by a massive fastball that exhibits both elite spin and velocity and is supplemented by a slider and curve, both of which have serious bite sure to generate whiffs. Beeter would be way higher on this list had we not had significant concerns about his strike-throwing ability as a starter. The walk rates are already not ideal and could go higher as he faces tougher competition. While we have concerns about his starting ability, we are quite confident he will at least be a high-leverage reliever reminiscent of a healthy Nick Anderson. He is the best pure relief prospect in the system by a wide margin.

## 13  Austin Wells  C

Born: 07/12/99   Age: 23   Bats: L   Throws: R   Height: 6'2"   Weight: 220 lb.   Origin: Round 1, 2020 Draft (#28 overall)

| YEAR | TEAM | LVL | AGE | PA | R | 2B | 3B | HR | RBI | BB | K | SB | CS | AVG/OBP/SLG | DRC+ | BABIP | BRR | DRP | WARP |
|------|------|-----|-----|----|----|----|----|----|-----|----|----|----|----|-------------|------|-------|------|-----|------|
| 2021 | SUR | WIN | 21 | 79 | 14 | 5 | 2 | 2 | 18 | 13 | 16 | 1 | 0 | .344/.456/.578 | | .426 | | | |
| 2021 | TAM | A | 21 | 299 | 61 | 17 | 4 | 9 | 54 | 51 | 62 | 11 | 0 | .258/.398/.479 | 122 | .306 | -1.6 | C(47) -2.0 | 1.3 |
| 2021 | HV | A+ | 21 | 170 | 21 | 6 | 1 | 7 | 22 | 20 | 55 | 5 | 0 | .274/.376/.473 | 97 | .393 | 0.4 | C(23) 4.4 | 0.9 |
| 2022 | TAM | A | 22 | 34 | 5 | 2 | 0 | 2 | 6 | 8 | 5 | 0 | 0 | .231/.412/.538 | 127 | .211 | -0.4 | C(6) 0.7 | 0.2 |
| 2022 | HV | A+ | 22 | 121 | 21 | 7 | 0 | 6 | 16 | 19 | 27 | 9 | 0 | .323/.429/.576 | 131 | .388 | -0.5 | C(21) 6.1 | 1.4 |
| 2022 | SOM | AA | 22 | 247 | 34 | 8 | 1 | 12 | 43 | 29 | 58 | 7 | 0 | .261/.360/.479 | 103 | .301 | -0.8 | C(38) 4.7 | 1.2 |
| 2023 non-DC | NYY | MLB | 23 | 251 | 24 | 10 | 2 | 5 | 24 | 24 | 69 | 3 | 1 | .231/.315/.357 | 93 | .313 | -3.0 | C 0 | 0.5 |

*Comparables: Seth Beer, Carlos Santana, Luis Exposito*

Alright, "C" is not very nice, but Wells is simply not a catcher at this point. He is not fluid behind the plate, has struggled to frame even adequately at times, and doesn't have the arm to slow down a team's running game. So why is he 13th? Wells, for all his defensive warts, still has performed with the bat for multiple minor-league seasons. He has an excellent feel for the zone and is a strong dude who can pounce on mistake pitches. The bat speed isn't special and he swings and misses a lot, so he will be more of a 5/6 hitter in a lineup who either DHs a lot or is a bad catcher/corner outfielder.

## 14  Roderick Arias  SS

Born: 09/09/04   Age: 18   Bats: S   Throws: R   Height: 6'2"   Weight: 178 lb.   Origin: International Free Agent, 2022

| YEAR | TEAM | LVL | AGE | PA | R | 2B | 3B | HR | RBI | BB | K | SB | CS | AVG/OBP/SLG | DRC+ | BABIP | BRR | DRP | WARP |
|------|------|-----|-----|----|----|----|----|----|-----|----|----|----|----|-------------|------|-------|------|-----|------|
| 2022 | DSL NYY | ROK | 17 | 140 | 25 | 6 | 2 | 3 | 11 | 28 | 46 | 10 | 2 | .194/.379/.370 | | .305 | | | |

The most notable international amateur free agent from last year's class, Arias had a mixed bag in his pro debut, posting a DSL zone contact rate that was alarmingly bad. His age-adjusted batted-ball data was solid and the defense at short is good to very good, but we're simply not going to rate guys who struggle so mightily at making contact in the zone very highly. The physical tools are compelling and he wasn't chasing out of the zone a ton, so there is potential to improve his prospect status. Of anyone not in the top 10, Arias could be the candidate most likely to compete for a top-five spot on this list next year.

## 15  Elijah Dunham  OF

Born: 05/29/98   Age: 25   Bats: L   Throws: L   Height: 6'0"   Weight: 213 lb.   Origin: Round 40, 2019 Draft (#1204 overall)

| YEAR | TEAM | LVL | AGE | PA | R | 2B | 3B | HR | RBI | BB | K | SB | CS | AVG/OBP/SLG | DRC+ | BABIP | BRR | DRP | WARP |
|------|------|-----|-----|----|----|----|----|----|-----|----|----|----|----|-------------|------|-------|------|-----|------|
| 2021 | SUR | WIN | 23 | 101 | 15 | 6 | 3 | 2 | 14 | 14 | 10 | 11 | 1 | .357/.465/.571 | | .389 | | | |
| 2021 | TAM | A | 23 | 127 | 32 | 6 | 2 | 4 | 25 | 25 | 23 | 11 | 4 | .276/.441/.500 | 131 | .324 | -0.5 | LF(20) -0.4, RF(5) 1.2, CF(4) -0.2 | 0.9 |
| 2021 | HV | A+ | 23 | 268 | 40 | 19 | 0 | 9 | 32 | 22 | 62 | 17 | 1 | .257/.325/.448 | 98 | .308 | 1.0 | LF(36) 0.2, CF(15) -0.3, RF(7) -1.3 | 0.7 |
| 2022 | SOM | AA | 24 | 485 | 67 | 26 | 3 | 17 | 63 | 59 | 103 | 37 | 7 | .248/.348/.448 | 114 | .288 | 0.0 | LF(50) 1.2, RF(46) -2.2 | 2.0 |
| 2023 non-DC | NYY | MLB | 25 | 251 | 22 | 11 | 2 | 4 | 22 | 22 | 62 | 10 | 3 | .218/.294/.331 | 79 | .284 | 0.5 | 1B 0, LF 0 | 0.1 |

*Comparables: Jeff Corsaletti, Mike Yastrzemski, Deik Scram*

Dunham is a well-rounded, speed/power outfielder who could make an impact on the Yankees as soon as 2023. Undrafted in the shortened 2020 draft, the former Indiana Hoosier signed with the Yankees and has done nothing but produce. With a simple approach at the plate, Dunham began lifting the ball more without tanking his strong strikeout-to-walk ratios, resulting in a strong .248/.348/.448 Double-A line. He won't wow people with his exit velos, but he consistently hits the ball at above-average quality rates and could hit 15-20 homers in a 75th-80th percentile outcome season. He is also a menace on the basepaths, a plus runner with excellent instincts. He's more than capable of manning left but might be a bit challenged in center where his reads are fine at best. Dunham is my personal cheeseball.

# 16 Matt Sauer   RHP

Born: 01/21/99   Age: 24   Bats: R   Throws: R   Height: 6'4"   Weight: 195 lb.   Origin: Round 2, 2017 Draft (#54 overall)

| YEAR | TEAM | LVL | AGE | W | L | SV | G | GS | IP | H | HR | BB/9 | K/9 | K | GB% | BABIP | WHIP | ERA | DRA- | WARP |
|------|------|-----|-----|---|---|----|----|----|----|---|----|------|-----|---|-----|-------|------|-----|------|------|
| 2021 | TAM | A | 22 | 2 | 4 | 0 | 15 | 13 | 66¹ | 58 | 6 | 4.3 | 10.3 | 76 | 44.0% | .297 | 1.36 | 4.34 | 103 | 0.6 |
| 2021 | HV | A+ | 22 | 3 | 2 | 0 | 8 | 8 | 45 | 35 | 7 | 3.0 | 10.2 | 51 | 43.4% | .243 | 1.11 | 5.20 | 120 | -0.2 |
| 2022 | HV | A+ | 23 | 5 | 3 | 0 | 18 | 18 | 88¹ | 75 | 8 | 3.6 | 10.2 | 100 | 35.5% | .305 | 1.25 | 3.77 | 112 | 0.0 |
| 2022 | SOM | AA | 23 | 0 | 2 | 0 | 4 | 4 | 20² | 22 | 5 | 3.0 | 14.8 | 34 | 36.7% | .386 | 1.40 | 7.84 | 81 | 0.5 |
| 2023 non-DC | NYY | MLB | 24 | 3 | 3 | 0 | 58 | 0 | 50 | 50 | 8 | 4.2 | 7.8 | 43 | 35.2% | .294 | 1.48 | 4.90 | 125 | -0.4 |

*Comparables: Brody Koerner, Logan Verrett, Eli Morgan*

Sauer was drafted in the second round seemingly forever ago, way back in 2017. Interestingly enough, he received a bigger signing bonus than Schmidt, the pitcher selected in the round ahead of him. This season, we finally started to see the reasons why the Yankees were so high on him as a prep arm. A 2019 Tommy John recipient, Sauer got his fastball back to pre-injury levels and then some, topping 98 at times as a starter last year. The slider he features is eerily similar to the one Will Warren uses, a true frisbee offering that's going to be an out-pitch at the next level. The change is fringe-average to average, more likely to be the former than the latter at this point. Like Beeter, the command isn't conducive to starting long-term, but Sauer's stuff isn't nearly as good, which is why he's decently lower on this list. Sauer is a potential big-league bullpen piece for the Yankees this season if they don't add externally.

# 17 Antonio Gomez   C

Born: 11/13/01   Age: 21   Bats: R   Throws: R   Height: 6'2"   Weight: 210 lb.   Origin: International Free Agent, 2018

| YEAR | TEAM | LVL | AGE | PA | R | 2B | 3B | HR | RBI | BB | K | SB | CS | AVG/OBP/SLG | DRC+ | BABIP | BRR | DRP | WARP |
|------|------|-----|-----|----|---|----|----|----|-----|----|---|----|----|-------------|------|-------|-----|-----|------|
| 2021 | YNK | ROK | 19 | 113 | 18 | 8 | 1 | 2 | 16 | 16 | 31 | 4 | 0 | .305/.416/.474 | | .435 | | | |
| 2021 | TAM | A | 19 | 71 | 10 | 2 | 0 | 2 | 7 | 10 | 18 | 1 | 0 | .197/.310/.328 | 103 | .244 | -1.5 | C(15) 1.3 | 0.2 |
| 2022 | TAM | A | 20 | 370 | 36 | 10 | 2 | 8 | 48 | 35 | 100 | 1 | 3 | .252/.332/.369 | 91 | .335 | -5.4 | C(70) 12.6 | 1.5 |
| 2023 non-DC | NYY | MLB | 21 | 251 | 19 | 9 | 1 | 3 | 20 | 16 | 80 | 1 | 0 | .209/.268/.292 | 59 | .308 | -4.1 | C 0 | -0.7 |

*Comparables: Roberto Peña, Francisco Hernandez, Deivy Grullón*

We have been waiting for Gomez to break out seemingly forever. A very good defensive catcher with a hose for an arm, Gomez has the bat speed and a swing conducive to hitting for power, but he's hit the ball on the ground way too much for several seasons now. He's shown an ability to lay off pitches outside the strike zone, though, so there are enough offensive ingredients to have some optimism. What will determine whether we ever get to see the complete package is if he lifts the ball more. Given that offense at the catching position is optional these days, there is absolutely a scenario where Gomez is a defensive-minded backstop with an everyday role. We're less optimistic that happens than in recent years, though, and it's worth noting the Yankees elected not to protect him from the Rule 5 Draft.

# 18 Yoendrys Gómez   RHP

Born: 10/15/99   Age: 23   Bats: R   Throws: R   Height: 6'3"   Weight: 175 lb.   Origin: International Free Agent, 2016

| YEAR | TEAM | LVL | AGE | W | L | SV | G | GS | IP | H | HR | BB/9 | K/9 | K | GB% | BABIP | WHIP | ERA | DRA- | WARP |
|------|------|-----|-----|---|---|----|----|----|----|---|----|------|-----|---|-----|-------|------|-----|------|------|
| 2021 | TAM | A | 21 | 0 | 0 | 0 | 9 | 9 | 23² | 14 | 3 | 3.4 | 11.0 | 29 | 43.9% | .204 | 0.97 | 3.42 | 90 | 0.4 |
| 2022 | HV | A+ | 22 | 0 | 0 | 0 | 10 | 10 | 28 | 20 | 0 | 3.9 | 8.7 | 27 | 31.9% | .278 | 1.14 | 1.93 | 104 | 0.1 |
| 2022 | SOM | AA | 22 | 1 | 0 | 0 | 4 | 4 | 16¹ | 14 | 1 | 3.3 | 10.5 | 19 | 26.2% | .317 | 1.22 | 3.86 | 102 | 0.2 |
| 2023 non-DC | NYY | MLB | 23 | 3 | 3 | 0 | 58 | 0 | 50 | 52 | 8 | 4.4 | 7.7 | 43 | 33.1% | .302 | 1.53 | 5.09 | 128 | -0.5 |

Gómez is another promising Yankees arm who's missed extensive time with arm and/or shoulder woes. Initially selected onto the 40-man roster before the 2020 Rule 5 Draft, Gómez has pitched under 100 innings since then but has looked good when healthy. Gómez sits 92-4 with his analytical-friendly fastball. The interesting curveball that Ben Spanier wrote about a ways back is still present, but he's since added a cutter-ish pitch that acts as a complimentary, horizontal breaker. The changeup isn't anything special, but it's enough to act as a serviceable tertiary pitch. Despite the injuries, Gómez's mechanics are clean and simple, though he at times lost feel for the zone while building up his workload. That's to be expected and I think he could be a no. 5 starter/long reliever if he stays healthy.

## 19    Trystan Vrieling    RHP
Born: 10/02/00   Age: 22   Bats: R   Throws: R   Height: 6'4"   Weight: 200 lb.

It's pretty interesting to note the similarities between Thorpe and Vrieling: Both are tall, lean, athletic righties who utilize short arm action and don't overwhelm with velocity. Vrieling is way lower on this list because the command isn't hovering around double-plus as it is with Thorpe. The most interesting pitch in his arsenal is a slider that has monstrous spin rates, a true out-pitch that could be a double-plus offering. The curve also has some nice spin rates but isn't nearly as impressive as the slider. While he does use a change, it's a pretty distant fourth pitch. Like with any projectable Yankees draftee, there is potential that Vrieling adds velocity, but the biggest priority going into 2023 is to throw more strikes. If he does, he could be a back-end starter. If not, he's likely a long reliever.

## 20    Juan Carela    RHP
Born: 12/15/01   Age: 21   Bats: R   Throws: R   Height: 6'3"   Weight: 186 lb.

| YEAR | TEAM | LVL | AGE | W | L | SV | G | GS | IP | H | HR | BB/9 | K/9 | K | GB% | BABIP | WHIP | ERA | DRA- | WARP |
|------|------|-----|-----|---|---|----|----|----|-----|----|----|------|------|-----|-------|-------|------|-------|------|------|
| 2021 | YNK | ROK | 19 | 2 | 0 | 0 | 6 | 5 | 22 | 14 | 0 | 2.0 | 11.0 | 27 | 56.0% | .280 | 0.86 | 1.64 | | |
| 2021 | TAM | A | 19 | 0 | 2 | 0 | 6 | 6 | 20$^1$ | 32 | 3 | 8.0 | 9.7 | 22 | 39.4% | .460 | 2.46 | 11.51 | 175 | -0.6 |
| 2022 | TAM | A | 20 | 7 | 2 | 0 | 16 | 14 | 79 | 49 | 5 | 4.0 | 12.5 | 110 | 54.7% | .267 | 1.06 | 2.96 | 91 | 1.6 |
| 2022 | HV | A+ | 20 | 1 | 4 | 0 | 7 | 7 | 28 | 25 | 4 | 5.5 | 6.8 | 21 | 38.4% | .256 | 1.50 | 7.71 | 115 | 0.0 |
| 2023 non-DC | NYY | MLB | 21 | 3 | 3 | 0 | 58 | 0 | 50 | 51 | 8 | 5.4 | 8.3 | 46 | 38.2% | .302 | 1.62 | 5.67 | 139 | -0.7 |

The soon-to-be 21-year-old has emerged as an intriguing young arm after showing feel for three pitches, the best being a low-80s slurve that he does a good job locating to the glove side. The heater can get up to 95 but he sits in the 92-93 range, and the mechanics are fine but not amazing. He has a very short track record of throwing a sufficient amount of strikes, so there is collapse potential in the starting profile. He could still be an interesting middle reliever with a wipeout breaking pitch, though. It might be a stretch to include him as a top-20 guy right now, but he's close enough to the others and we wanted to put him on your radar as a potential breakout candidate.

# Top Talents 25 and Under (as of 4/1/2023):

1. Anthony Volpe, SS
2. Oswald Peraza, SS
3. Spencer Jones, OF
4. Jasson Dominguez, OF
5. Will Warren, RHP
6. Randy Vasquez, RHP
7. Luis Gil, RHP
8. Everson Pereira, OF
9. Drew Thorpe, RHP
10. Trey Sweeney, SS

The Yankees are the richest team in baseball; they *should* be re-signing their homegrown talent as they did with Aaron Judge. They should also be some of the biggest spenders in free agency every offseason. It does present a bit of a dilemma when trying to incorporate prospects onto the big-league roster, though, as we saw with Jackson Frazier and Miguel Andújar not that long ago. Notice how not a single non-prospect cracked the list above. As much as we love an owner willing to spend money, giving young players a shot like they did in 2017 will prove essential to the long-term viability of this club.

# Oakland Athletics

## The State of the System:

This farm system should be a lot better after trading Matt Chapman, Matt Olson, Frankie Montas and Sean Murphy. *A lot* better.

## The Top Ten:

**1 Tyler Soderstrom   1B/C**        OFP: 55        ETA: Late 2023/2024

Born: 11/24/01   Age: 21   Bats: L   Throws: R   Height: 6'2"   Weight: 200 lb.   Origin: Round 1, 2020 Draft (#26 overall)

| YEAR | TEAM | LVL | AGE | PA | R | 2B | 3B | HR | RBI | BB | K | SB | CS | AVG/OBP/SLG | DRC+ | BABIP | BRR | DRP | WARP |
|---|---|---|---|---|---|---|---|---|---|---|---|---|---|---|---|---|---|---|---|
| 2021 | STK | A | 19 | 254 | 39 | 20 | 1 | 12 | 49 | 27 | 61 | 2 | 1 | .306/.390/.568 | 125 | .373 | -1.2 | C(38) -4.1, 1B(9) -1.0 | 0.9 |
| 2022 | LAN | A+ | 20 | 371 | 47 | 19 | 3 | 20 | 71 | 29 | 99 | 0 | 0 | .260/.323/.513 | 123 | .306 | 0.1 | 1B(39) -0.2, C(31) 1.6 | 2.1 |
| 2022 | MID | AA | 20 | 147 | 17 | 1 | 2 | 8 | 28 | 10 | 33 | 0 | 1 | .278/.327/.496 | 118 | .305 | -0.3 | 1B(17) -0.1, C(16) -1.8 | 0.5 |
| 2022 | LV | AAA | 20 | 38 | 2 | 1 | 0 | 1 | 6 | 1 | 13 | 0 | 0 | .297/.316/.405 | 82 | .435 | 0.3 | C(5) -0.3, 1B(3) 0.4 | 0.1 |
| 2023 DC | OAK | MLB | 21 | 96 | 9 | 4 | 1 | 3 | 9 | 6 | 26 | 1 | 0 | .231/.282/.377 | 85 | .294 | -0.2 | C 0 | 0.1 |

*Comparables: Josh Naylor, Chris Marrero, Nick Williams*

**The Report:** Soderstrom has one of the prettiest swings in the minor leagues right now. Drafted out of high school as a hit-first catcher, Soderstrom has added power since turning pro to pair with his advanced feel at the plate. The A's have already begun conceding that he will not be an everyday catcher, having him split his time between first base and backstop last season, but with legit plus hit and power potential, that move should not preclude him from becoming an All-Star-caliber player.

Soderstrom struggled mightily at the start of 2022, hitting .159 with a 33% K-rate at High-A in April before improving to .283/.344/.559 with a 25.2% K-rate over the next three months. He cut his strikeouts even further after a promotion to Double-A, and hit .297 in a nine-game stint at Triple-A to end the year.

The aesthetics of Soderstrom's swing are a bit prettier than its results at this point. There remain some light concerns about his approach, walking in just 7.2% of his plate appearances last season, but he's always walked at decent rates when facing younger competition. Having just turned 21 in November, there's an expectation that his walk and strikeout rates will take noticeable steps forward when he repeats the upper minors in 2023.

**OFP:** 55 / First-division first baseman

**Variance:** Medium. Soderstrom seems ticketed for first base, but has the offensive potential to become an All-Star anyway.

**Jesse Roche's Fantasy Take:** Soderstrom did a lot right last year: He hit 29 home runs across three levels and finished the season in Triple-A all while seeing more time behind the plate (50 games started). But his once-lauded potential hit tool may no longer be a strength given his approach issues. His contact rates are mediocre largely due to chasing breaking balls outside the zone. Further, Soderstrom has serious platoon issues, hitting just .204/.281/.361 versus left-handed pitchers. The risk of his development stalling as a strong-side platoon first baseman is high. That said, Soderstrom still flashes serious offensive upside, including an impressive final three months, even if he arguably carries more risk than his peers.

## 2  Kyle Muller  LHP

OFP: 55    ETA: Debuted in 2021

Born: 10/07/97   Age: 25   Bats: R   Throws: L   Height: 6'7"   Weight: 250 lb.   Origin: Round 2, 2016 Draft (#44 overall)

| YEAR | TEAM | LVL | AGE | W | L | SV | G | GS | IP | H | HR | BB/9 | K/9 | K | GB% | BABIP | WHIP | ERA | DRA- | WARP |
|------|------|-----|-----|---|---|----|----|----|-----|-----|----|------|------|-----|-------|-------|------|------|------|------|
| 2021 | GWN | AAA | 23 | 5 | 4 | 0 | 17 | 17 | 79² | 66 | 9 | 4.7 | 10.5 | 93 | 41.6% | .286 | 1.36 | 3.39 | 78 | 2.0 |
| 2021 | ATL | MLB | 23 | 2 | 4 | 0 | 9 | 8 | 36² | 26 | 2 | 4.9 | 9.1 | 37 | 37.5% | .261 | 1.25 | 4.17 | 106 | 0.2 |
| 2022 | GWN | AAA | 24 | 6 | 8 | 0 | 23 | 23 | 134² | 119 | 14 | 2.7 | 10.6 | 159 | 46.6% | .325 | 1.18 | 3.41 | 79 | 3.3 |
| 2022 | ATL | MLB | 24 | 1 | 1 | 0 | 3 | 3 | 12¹ | 13 | 2 | 5.8 | 8.8 | 12 | 41.0% | .306 | 1.70 | 8.03 | 129 | -0.1 |
| 2023 DC | OAK | MLB | 25 | 6 | 6 | 0 | 19 | 19 | 93 | 88 | 11 | 4.2 | 9.0 | 94 | 39.2% | .298 | 1.41 | 4.08 | 109 | 0.5 |

Comparables: Danny Duffy, Mitch Keller, Travis Wood

**The Report:** Muller was the biggest piece the A's acquired from Atlanta in the Sean Murphy trade. He has always had an arsenal that could perform at the top of a rotation, but his command has prevented him from living up to that potential. Muller's fastball sits in the mid-90s and plays even better thanks to above-average spin and excellent extension from his 6-foot-7 frame. Big-league hitters have been unable to hit better than .211 with whiff rates in the 35-45% range against his slider and curveball over the past two seasons. He has experimented with a changeup, but it's been hit hard despite some promising whiff rates.

In 2022, Muller finally began pounding the strike zone with his fastball and it led to arguably the best minor-league season of his career, as he posted his best strikeout and walk rates in years. He reverted to nibbling in a brief big-league stint, however, and was knocked around across three starts. Already 25, Muller has yet to put it all together, but he's continued trending in the right direction. Now with the A's, Muller should be able to start the year in their rotation and with another step forward in his command, could be a Rookie of the Year candidate.

**OFP:** 55 / no. 3/4 starter

**Variance:** Low. Muller's command remains too far behind to bet on him living up to his potential, but he's not far away from being a solid mid-rotation arm.

**Jesse Roche's Fantasy Take:** Muller enters the 2023 season firmly on the cusp of a MLB rotation spot with just one option remaining and a group of oft-injured, underwhelming veteran arms ahead of him. PECOTA projects a sub-4 ERA, but despite recent Triple-A success, Muller's concerning traits—his command and lack of ideal fastball shape—make that more of an "I'll believe it when I see it" proposition, pending further gains.

## 3  Ken Waldichuk  LHP

OFP: 55    ETA: Debuted in 2022

Born: 01/08/98   Age: 25   Bats: L   Throws: L   Height: 6'4"   Weight: 220 lb.   Origin: Round 5, 2019 Draft (#165 overall)

| YEAR | TEAM | LVL | AGE | W | L | SV | G | GS | IP | H | HR | BB/9 | K/9 | K | GB% | BABIP | WHIP | ERA | DRA- | WARP |
|------|------|-----|-----|---|---|----|----|----|-----|-----|----|------|------|-----|-------|-------|------|------|------|------|
| 2021 | HV | A+ | 23 | 2 | 0 | 0 | 7 | 7 | 30² | 12 | 0 | 3.8 | 16.1 | 55 | 31.1% | .267 | 0.82 | 0.00 | 82 | 0.6 |
| 2021 | SOM | AA | 23 | 4 | 3 | 0 | 16 | 14 | 79¹ | 64 | 13 | 4.3 | 12.3 | 108 | 36.7% | .293 | 1.29 | 4.20 | 87 | 1.2 |
| 2022 | SOM | AA | 24 | 4 | 0 | 0 | 6 | 6 | 28² | 16 | 2 | 3.1 | 14.4 | 46 | 52.7% | .264 | 0.91 | 1.26 | 78 | 0.7 |
| 2022 | SWB | AAA | 24 | 2 | 3 | 0 | 11 | 11 | 47² | 38 | 5 | 4.3 | 13.2 | 70 | 40.7% | .333 | 1.28 | 3.59 | 75 | 1.3 |
| 2022 | LV | AAA | 24 | 0 | 1 | 0 | 4 | 4 | 18² | 20 | 3 | 1.4 | 10.1 | 21 | 38.9% | .333 | 1.23 | 3.38 | 95 | 0.2 |
| 2022 | OAK | MLB | 24 | 2 | 2 | 0 | 7 | 7 | 34² | 32 | 5 | 2.6 | 8.6 | 33 | 36.4% | .287 | 1.21 | 4.93 | 121 | 0.0 |
| 2023 DC | OAK | MLB | 25 | 7 | 7 | 0 | 34 | 19 | 106 | 92 | 14 | 3.9 | 9.5 | 112 | 36.4% | .280 | 1.30 | 3.76 | 103 | 0.9 |

Comparables: Matthew Boyd, Ben Lively, Wade Miley

**The Report:** Waldichuk has a deceptive left-handed delivery that has helped his four-pitch mix consistently generate strikeouts at elite rates despite lacking a plus offering. His four-seam fastball sits in the mid-90s but was consistently squared up at Triple-A and the majors. As with many pitchers, Waldichuk would probably benefit from decreasing his reliance on his fastball. His slider is easily his best pitch, with sharp 1-7 movement, and works well with a changeup that was rarely squared up in the minors and had some promising numbers in his big-league stint (30.2% whiff rate). Waldichuk's delivery is expected to make it hard for him to handle too heavy a workload, but he has held up well over the past two seasons.

**OFP:** 55 / no. 3/4 starter

**Variance:** Low. Waldichuk was already a solid back-end starter at the end of 2022.

**Jesse Roche's Fantasy Take:** Like Muller, Waldichuk likely sits on the outside looking in on a rotation spot entering the season, absent an injury. As noted above, his slider is the star of the show with huge two-plane movement, comparing favorably to other standout left-handed sliders from Brad Hand, Jake Diekman and Sam Moll. The risk, though, is that his slider bears similarities with, well, relievers, and he may be best utilized in the pen, particularly in the short term, where he can lean into slider/changeup usage. Waldichuk is a borderline top-100 dynasty prospect.

## 4  Mason Miller  RHP    OFP: 55    ETA: 2024

Born: 08/24/98   Age: 24   Bats: R   Throws: R   Height: 6'5"   Weight: 200 lb.   Origin: Round 3, 2021 Draft (#97 overall)

| YEAR | TEAM | LVL | AGE | W | L | SV | G | GS | IP | H | HR | BB/9 | K/9 | K | GB% | BABIP | WHIP | ERA | DRA- | WARP |
|------|------|-----|-----|---|---|----|----|----|----|----|----|------|------|----|------|-------|------|------|------|------|
| 2021 | ATH | ROK | 22 | 0 | 1 | 0 | 3 | 2 | 6 | 4 | 0 | 4.5 | 13.5 | 9 | 66.7% | .333 | 1.17 | 1.50 | | |
| 2022 | LAN | A+ | 23 | 0 | 1 | 0 | 3 | 3 | 7 | 3 | 1 | 2.6 | 16.7 | 13 | 45.5% | .200 | 0.71 | 3.86 | 78 | 0.1 |
| 2023 non-DC | OAK | MLB | 24 | 3 | 3 | 0 | 58 | 0 | 50 | 46 | 8 | 4.0 | 9.5 | 53 | 37.1% | .293 | 1.38 | 4.30 | 112 | 0.0 |

*Comparables: Stephen Strasburg, Matt Andriese, Jimmy Herget*

**The Report:** Miller has only completed 12 innings in the minors outside of the complex league because of injuries. Oakland fast-tracked him to Triple-A despite caution with his workload and he was one of the most dominant pitchers at the Arizona Fall League. Miller already has a plus fastball and slider, with a heater that sits in the high-90s and has reached 100 mph several times during the season, and a mid-80s slider that generates excellent horizontal movement. He has been developing a changeup, but that remains a work in progress.

Miller displayed above-average command, but it's a lot easier to show high-octane stuff with excellent control on such a tight pitch count. He has the repeatable mechanics necessary to stick in the rotation, but he has never thrown more than 100 innings in a year (including his college career from 2017-21). If he regresses with a heavier workload, Miller still has all the pieces to be an All-Star-caliber closer.

**OFP:** 55 / no. 3/4 starter or late-inning reliever

**Variance:** High. Miller has high-end upside but needs to show he can handle a far more significant workload.

**Jesse Roche's Fantasy Take:** Miller has yet to face more than 10 batters in a game in his career due to injuries. When he has toed the rubber, though, he has looked dominant. For example, in just five innings at Triple-A, his high-spin fastball *averaged* 99.6 mph with carry. Further, his slider and lesser-used changeup both flashed bat-missing utility. Miller's long-term role remains uncertain, but his stuff is arguably the best in the system and his upside is the type to chase in dynasty. He is a fast-rising, borderline top-200 dynasty prospect.

## 5  Jordan Diaz  DH    OFP: 50    ETA: Debuted in 2022

Born: 08/13/00   Age: 22   Bats: R   Throws: R   Height: 5'10"   Weight: 175 lb.   Origin: International Free Agent, 2016

| YEAR | TEAM | LVL | AGE | PA | R | 2B | 3B | HR | RBI | BB | K | SB | CS | AVG/OBP/SLG | DRC+ | BABIP | BRR | DRP | WARP |
|------|------|-----|-----|----|---|----|----|----|-----|----|----|----|----|-------------|------|-------|-----|-----|------|
| 2021 | LAN | A+ | 20 | 365 | 46 | 24 | 1 | 13 | 56 | 25 | 58 | 2 | 3 | .288/.337/.483 | 124 | .311 | 0.2 | 3B(52) -4.5, 1B(23) 1.9, LF(4) -0.7 | 1.8 |
| 2022 | MID | AA | 21 | 407 | 48 | 26 | 0 | 15 | 58 | 22 | 61 | 0 | 0 | .319/.361/.507 | 111 | .348 | 0.8 | 1B(41) -2.5, 3B(7) -1.4, LF(2) -0.3 | 1.3 |
| 2022 | LV | AAA | 21 | 120 | 19 | 8 | 1 | 4 | 25 | 6 | 15 | 0 | 0 | .348/.383/.545 | 109 | .372 | -0.8 | 1B(3) -0.1, 2B(3) -0.8, 3B(3) -0.2 | 0.3 |
| 2022 | OAK | MLB | 21 | 51 | 3 | 3 | 0 | 0 | 1 | 2 | 7 | 0 | 0 | .265/.294/.327 | 105 | .310 | -0.2 | 2B(12) -1.2, 1B(1) 0 | 0.0 |
| 2023 DC | OAK | MLB | 22 | 165 | 16 | 7 | 1 | 4 | 16 | 8 | 29 | 0 | 0 | .255/.294/.378 | 94 | .290 | -0.7 | 2B -1 | 0.2 |

*Comparables: Luis Sardinas, Jose Altuve, Mark Lewis*

**The Report:** The best pure hitter in the farm system, Diaz has never struck out in more than 15.9% of his plate appearances in a season, all while posting high-end exit-velocity numbers. He would be a consensus top-100 prospect if he had any semblance of a defensive home, but despite experiments all over the infield, many scouts still believe he will be limited to designated hitter.

Diaz recorded a .326/.366/.515 slash line with 54 extra-base hits in 120 games between Double and Triple-A in 2022 before making his big-league debut less than two months after his 22nd birthday. With the A's, Diaz continued putting the ball in play at an elite clip but struggled to impact the ball at the same level. His contact skills have potentially worked against him in his development, since he could benefit from greater selectivity. Even if he never walks at a close to league-average clip, though, Diaz has always hit for average despite facing much older competition and seems like one of the best bets in the minors to be a consistent .280+ hitter in the majors.

**OFP:** 50 / Average DH

**Variance:** Medium. Diaz should be a passable MLB hitter, but he is young enough where he could reach a high-end outcome with an unexpected defensive development.

**Jesse Roche's Fantasy Take:** While he has pop, Diaz is a hit-over-power bat who puts far too many balls on the ground to regularly get to his power in games. His abnormal profile carries a ton of risk and an extremely small margin for error. Diaz will need to hit, and hit a lot, to carve out a meaningful big-league role. For now, he is 2B-eligible, and he should receive a long MLB look at some point this year on the rebuilding Athletics. With .280+ average/15+ homer upside and proximity, Diaz is a top-200 dynasty prospect.

## 6  Max Muncy  SS        OFP: 50    ETA: 2025
Born: 08/25/02   Age: 20   Bats: R   Throws: R   Height: 6'1"   Weight: 180 lb.   Origin: Round 1, 2021 Draft (#25 overall)

| YEAR | TEAM | LVL | AGE | PA | R | 2B | 3B | HR | RBI | BB | K | SB | CS | AVG/OBP/SLG | DRC+ | BABIP | BRR | DRP | WARP |
|---|---|---|---|---|---|---|---|---|---|---|---|---|---|---|---|---|---|---|---|
| 2021 | ATH | ROK | 18 | 34 | 3 | 0 | 0 | 0 | 4 | 3 | 12 | 1 | 0 | .129/.206/.129 | | .211 | | | |
| 2022 | STK | A | 19 | 365 | 50 | 16 | 1 | 16 | 51 | 51 | 109 | 6 | 5 | .230/.352/.447 | 108 | .298 | 2.5 | SS(77) -1.1, 2B(2) 0.1 | 1.6 |
| 2022 | LAN | A+ | 19 | 190 | 19 | 12 | 2 | 3 | 19 | 18 | 60 | 13 | 1 | .226/.305/.375 | 84 | .327 | 1.7 | SS(35) 1.4 | 0.5 |
| 2023 non-DC | OAK | MLB | 20 | 251 | 21 | 10 | 1 | 4 | 22 | 19 | 84 | 5 | 1 | .209/.277/.315 | 69 | .312 | -2.0 | 2B 0, SS 0 | -0.3 |

*Comparables: Hanser Alberto, Ian Desmond, Lucius Fox*

**The Report:** Muncy quickly put an ugly pro debut at the complex in 2021 behind him, holding his own in his first full minor-league season in the California League by posting a .799 OPS in Low-A and receiving a promotion to High-A a month before his 20th birthday. Muncy struck out in roughly 30% of his plate appearances at both stops last season, and his long swing will likely always carry a good amount of swing-and-miss. Unlike most teenage power-first prospects, though, Muncy has an advanced approach and is very patient, walking in 12.4% of his trips last season.

Muncy faces a long-term trade-off between his offensive and defensive potential. He may have the ability to stick at shortstop if he can clean up his fundamentals defensively, but if he bulks up his thin 6-foot-1 frame to add more power, that will surely force him to third base. Since his bat is much further along in its development than his glove, it seems likely that maximizing his offensive firepower will drive his development.

**OFP:** 50 / Power-hitting second-division infielder

**Variance:** High. Muncy's approach should help him overcome his high strikeout rates, but he still faces legitimate questions surrounding his hit tool and defensive future.

**Jesse Roche's Fantasy Take:** Much like the older Max Muncy—with whom he shares a birthday—the younger is a patient power hitter. He also offers a bit of athleticism, and possibly even as much upside. His swing-and-miss is a concern, but it is important to remember that, at this same age, the elder Muncy was just entering his sophomore year. The younger Muncy should be rostered in leagues with up to 300 prospects.

## 7  Zack Gelof  2B/3B      OFP: 50     ETA: Late 2023/2024
Born: 10/19/99   Age: 23   Bats: R   Throws: R   Height: 6'3"   Weight: 205 lb.   Origin: Round 2, 2021 Draft (#60 overall)

| YEAR | TEAM | LVL | AGE | PA | R | 2B | 3B | HR | RBI | BB | K | SB | CS | AVG/OBP/SLG | DRC+ | BABIP | BRR | DRP | WARP |
|---|---|---|---|---|---|---|---|---|---|---|---|---|---|---|---|---|---|---|---|
| 2021 | STK | A | 21 | 145 | 26 | 8 | 1 | 7 | 22 | 19 | 36 | 11 | 2 | .298/.393/.548 | 120 | .366 | 1.5 | 3B(30) -6.8 | 0.3 |
| 2022 | MID | AA | 22 | 402 | 54 | 16 | 2 | 13 | 61 | 47 | 110 | 9 | 2 | .271/.356/.438 | 102 | .358 | -0.3 | 2B(53) -2.3, 3B(26) -1.9, CF(1) 0.5 | 0.8 |
| 2022 | LV | AAA | 22 | 38 | 7 | 1 | 0 | 5 | 5 | 3 | 11 | 1 | 0 | .257/.316/.714 | 103 | .211 | 0.5 | 2B(9) -1.1 | 0.1 |
| 2023 DC | OAK | MLB | 23 | 29 | 3 | 1 | 0 | 1 | 3 | 2 | 9 | 0 | 0 | .223/.292/.340 | 84 | .308 | 0.0 | 3B 0 | 0.0 |

*Comparables: Jimmy Paredes, Jesmuel Valentín, Aarom Baldiris*

**The Report:** Gelof flashed plus power potential in college at UVA, but the staff's archaic approach to hitting development kept him from tapping into it consistently until he reached pro ball. Gelof has a unique stride, and moves with some Hunter Pence-like stiffness, but has shown a quality approach and handled upper-minors breaking balls well. He hit 17 doubles and 18 home runs in 96 games between Double-A and Triple-A in 2022, and posted an average exit velocity north of 90 mph.

As with Soderstrom, the A's have already seemed to accept that Gelof will not stick at the more premium position he played as an amateur. Drafted as a third baseman, Gelof played the majority of his games at second base in 2022, and took to the keystone quite easily. There is some speculation that Oakland will let Gelof experiment with the outfield as well, but that's entirely unproven at this point. A right-hander, Gelof has hit .324/.400/.658 against southpaws as a pro, but his severe platoon splits (.253/.338/.393 against righties in 2022) raise further questions about his viability as an everyday player.

**OFP:** 50 / Second-division infielder with some positional flex who sits against tougher righties

**Variance:** Medium. Gelof won't have much room for error offensively unless he makes an Adam Duvall-like defensive jump to the outfield.

**Jesse Roche's Fantasy Take:** Gelof is a sum-of-his-parts, offensive-minded second baseman with impressive raw power that churns out line drives. His ability to generate hard contact allows him to hit for solid averages despite some underlying swing-and-miss issues. Gelof is a top-200 dynasty prospect.

## 8  Gunnar Hoglund  RHP    OFP: 50    ETA: 2024/2025
Born: 12/17/99  Age: 23  Bats: L  Throws: R  Height: 6'4"  Weight: 220 lb.  Origin: Round 1, 2021 Draft (#19 overall)

| YEAR | TEAM | LVL | AGE | W | L | SV | G | GS | IP | H | HR | BB/9 | K/9 | K | GB% | BABIP | WHIP | ERA | DRA- | WARP |
|---|---|---|---|---|---|---|---|---|---|---|---|---|---|---|---|---|---|---|---|---|
| 2023 non-DC | OAK | MLB | 23 | 3 | 3 | 0 | 58 | 0 | 50 | 56 | 8 | 4.5 | 7.2 | 40 | 37.5% | .312 | 1.63 | 5.62 | 139 | -0.8 |

Comparables: Yaya Chentouf, Harol González, Gabe Friese

**The Report:** One of the key parts of the return in the Chapman trade, Hoglund was a 2021 first-round pick who probably would have gone in the top 10 if he had not needed UCL surgery prior to the draft. Of course, that injury means he only made three late-season appearances between the complex and Low-A in 2022. Prior to the injury, Hoglund already flashed big-league ready command with a plus slider. He also has a low-90s fastball and changeup that have the potential to be above-average MLB offerings.

**OFP:** 50 / no. 4 starter

**Variance:** High. Hoglund was a dominant college pitcher with a broad repertoire, but hasn't seen significant mound action in almost two years now.

**Jesse Roche's Fantasy Take:** Hoglund remains in status quo as a borderline top-200 dynasty prospect on the strength of his pre-injury stuff and command.

## 9  Esteury Ruiz  OF    OFP: 45    ETA: Debuted in 2022
Born: 02/15/99  Age: 24  Bats: R  Throws: R  Height: 6'0"  Weight: 169 lb.  Origin: International Free Agent, 2015

| YEAR | TEAM | LVL | AGE | PA | R | 2B | 3B | HR | RBI | BB | K | SB | CS | AVG/OBP/SLG | DRC+ | BABIP | BRR | DRP | WARP |
|---|---|---|---|---|---|---|---|---|---|---|---|---|---|---|---|---|---|---|---|
| 2021 | SA | AA | 22 | 353 | 52 | 16 | 2 | 10 | 42 | 28 | 73 | 36 | 7 | .249/.328/.411 | 106 | .294 | 1.7 | LF(32) 6.0, CF(26) 0.6, RF(20) 0.7 | 2.2 |
| 2022 | SA | AA | 23 | 232 | 54 | 17 | 2 | 9 | 37 | 32 | 40 | 37 | 5 | .344/.474/.611 | 141 | .398 | 1.1 | CF(42) -1.8 | 2.0 |
| 2022 | NAS | AAA | 23 | 167 | 30 | 10 | 0 | 3 | 19 | 14 | 29 | 25 | 5 | .329/.402/.459 | 106 | .395 | 1.9 | LF(15) -0.1, CF(14) -0.0, RF(3) 0.5 | 0.7 |
| 2022 | ELP | AAA | 23 | 142 | 30 | 6 | 0 | 4 | 9 | 20 | 25 | 23 | 4 | .315/.457/.477 | 111 | .378 | 0.3 | CF(14) -0.6, RF(13) 2.3, LF(2) 0.1 | 0.6 |
| 2022 | SD | MLB | 23 | 27 | 1 | 1 | 1 | 0 | 2 | 0 | 5 | 1 | 2 | .222/.222/.333 | 92 | .273 | -0.5 | RF(6) 0.1, LF(5) -0.7, CF(5) -0.2 | -0.1 |
| 2022 | MIL | MLB | 23 | 9 | 2 | 0 | 0 | 0 | 0 | 1 | 2 | 0 | 0 | .000/.111/.000 | 94 | | 0.0 | LF(2) 0 | 0.0 |
| 2023 DC | OAK | MLB | 24 | 302 | 31 | 13 | 2 | 6 | 28 | 24 | 64 | 32 | 7 | .243/.314/.367 | 99 | .295 | 5.4 | CF 0, LF 0 | 1.5 |

Comparables: Junior Lake, Trayvon Robinson, Starling Marte

**The Report:** Ruiz was clearly the A's top priority in the Murphy package, with general manager David Forst immediately talking about him as the team's everyday center fielder after the deal. On paper, it's easy to see how a team could fall in love with his profile: He hit .332/.447/.526 with 85 stolen bases in 114 games between Double-A and Triple-A with just a 17.4% K-rate in 2022. He's also handled a move to the outfield well enough to profile as at least a 50-grade center fielder.

With that said, Ruiz had never managed a slugging percentage better than .411 at full-season ball prior to last season and has a .207 slugging in 95 plate appearances at LIDOM over the past two seasons. Most concerningly, the data backs up the inferior numbers. Ruiz routinely posts exit-velos in the mid-70s and 80s, generating triple-digit exit-velos at an extremely low rate. Moreover, the bulk of his damage last season was done at the launching pads in the Texas and Pacific Coast Leagues. Simply put, Ruiz could be one of the most exciting players in MLB if he can even manage a .450 slugging, but the numbers below the surface make it hard to envision.

**OFP:** 45 / Fourth outfielder

**Variance:** High. Ruiz's numbers would suggest he's a low-variance prospect, but the gap between his production and the peripherals adds a great deal of volatility.

**Jesse Roche's Fantasy Take:** Ruiz, a prospect standout in June, has truly elite speed that plays, and then some, on the bases. As such, his clear path to an everyday role with the Athletics—where he'll be set loose—is of great interest to fantasy managers. Even if Ruiz is another iteration of Jorge Mateo, he'll have substantial value in standard formats.

## 10    Freddy Tarnok   RHP     OFP: 45     ETA: Debuted in 2022

Born: 11/24/98   Age: 24   Bats: R   Throws: R   Height: 6'3"   Weight: 185 lb.   Origin: Round 3, 2017 Draft (#80 overall)

| YEAR | TEAM | LVL | AGE | W | L | SV | G | GS | IP | H | HR | BB/9 | K/9 | K | GB% | BABIP | WHIP | ERA | DRA- | WARP |
|------|------|-----|-----|---|---|----|----|----|-----|----|----|------|------|----|------|-------|------|------|------|------|
| 2021 | ROM | A+ | 22 | 3 | 2 | 0 | 7 | 5 | 28¹ | 21 | 6 | 4.1 | 15.2 | 48 | 34.5% | .306 | 1.20 | 4.76 | 74 | 0.6 |
| 2021 | MIS | AA | 22 | 3 | 2 | 0 | 9 | 9 | 45 | 35 | 2 | 3.0 | 12.2 | 61 | 33.3% | .324 | 1.11 | 2.60 | 81 | 0.9 |
| 2022 | MIS | AA | 23 | 2 | 2 | 0 | 15 | 15 | 62² | 54 | 8 | 3.9 | 10.8 | 75 | 32.7% | .293 | 1.29 | 4.31 | 106 | 0.4 |
| 2022 | GWN | AAA | 23 | 2 | 1 | 0 | 10 | 8 | 44 | 38 | 7 | 3.5 | 10.0 | 49 | 42.4% | .279 | 1.25 | 3.68 | 83 | 1.0 |
| 2022 | ATL | MLB | 23 | 0 | 0 | 0 | 1 | 0 | 0² | 1 | 0 | 0.0 | 13.5 | 1 | 50.0% | .500 | 1.50 | 0.00 | 98 | 0.0 |
| 2023 DC | OAK | MLB | 24 | 2 | 2 | 0 | 37 | 0 | 31.7 | 31 | 5 | 4.0 | 9.1 | 32 | 34.2% | .301 | 1.43 | 4.42 | 116 | -0.1 |

*Comparables: Touki Toussaint, Michael Fulmer, Rafael Montero*

**The Report:** A secondary piece of the Murphy deal, Tarnok made his big-league debut with Atlanta in 2022 after averaging more than 10 strikeouts per nine innings at Double- and Triple-A with a 4.05 ERA. The righty has a long arm action that tends to lag behind his delivery, but he can still throw a mid-90s fastball with excellent characteristics, sometimes reaching the high-90s as well. His true 12-6 curveball has been his best secondary pitch and a changeup showed some promise this past season. Paring down his arsenal and giving his fastball a chance to more routinely sit in the high-90s out of the pen seems like the best path for Tarnok going forward.

**OFP:** 45 / Swingman or setup

**Variance:** Medium. He's more likely to be a reliever, but the stuff should play well in relief.

**Jesse Roche's Fantasy Take:** Tarnok likely sits firmly behind Muller and Waldichuk in the pecking order for a rotation look. That doesn't mean his stuff is necessarily inferior. Yet, his slight frame and inconsistent secondaries have long placed him in a long-term relief bucket. Tarnok could surprise with the right opportunity, yet, even in Oakland, that opportunity may not come.

## Outside the Top Ten:

## 11    Lawrence Butler   RF

Born: 07/10/00   Age: 22   Bats: L   Throws: R   Height: 6'3"   Weight: 210 lb.   Origin: Round 6, 2018 Draft (#173 overall)

| YEAR | TEAM | LVL | AGE | PA | R | 2B | 3B | HR | RBI | BB | K | SB | CS | AVG/OBP/SLG | DRC+ | BABIP | BRR | DRP | WARP |
|------|------|-----|-----|-----|----|----|----|----|-----|----|-----|----|----|-------------|------|-------|------|-----|------|
| 2021 | STK | A | 20 | 396 | 62 | 20 | 4 | 17 | 67 | 55 | 131 | 26 | 4 | .263/.364/.499 | 104 | .370 | 0.6 | 1B(47) -2.3, LF(25) 0.1, CF(11) 0.2 | 1.2 |
| 2021 | LAN | A+ | 20 | 54 | 14 | 4 | 0 | 2 | 8 | 4 | 15 | 3 | 1 | .340/.389/.540 | 95 | .455 | -0.5 | 1B(6) 2.0, RF(6) -0.6, CF(1) 0.2 | 0.2 |
| 2022 | LAN | A+ | 21 | 333 | 52 | 19 | 3 | 11 | 41 | 40 | 105 | 13 | 5 | .270/.357/.468 | 104 | .384 | -0.9 | RF(40) -0.7, CF(13) 0.2, 1B(11) -0.8 | 1.7 |
| 2023 non-DC | OAK | MLB | 22 | 251 | 23 | 11 | 2 | 5 | 24 | 22 | 87 | 5 | 2 | .228/.299/.355 | 86 | .348 | -1.7 | 1B 0, LF 0 | 0.0 |

*Comparables: Ronald Guzmán, Casey Craig, Carlos Peguero*

The A's have been incredibly patient since they selected Butler out of high school in the sixth round of the 2018 draft, and he continued rewarding their patience in 2022. While injuries limited him to 84 games, Butler hit .270/.357/.468 with 11 home runs at High-A. Moreover, he walked as much as he struck out alongside an .833 OPS at the Arizona Fall League this offseason. An above-average athlete as well, Butler recorded eight assists in just 41 games in right field. Butler has big-time power potential and has made significant strides toward shortening his swing to make more contact, but his hit tool has a long way to go. He still had a 31.5% K-rate in 2022.

## 12    Denzel Clarke   CF

Born: 05/01/00   Age: 23   Bats: R   Throws: R   Height: 6'5"   Weight: 220 lb.   Origin: Round 4, 2021 Draft (#127 overall)

| YEAR | TEAM | LVL | AGE | PA | R | 2B | 3B | HR | RBI | BB | K | SB | CS | AVG/OBP/SLG | DRC+ | BABIP | BRR | DRP | WARP |
|------|------|-----|-----|-----|----|----|----|----|-----|----|----|----|----|-------------|------|-------|------|-----|------|
| 2022 | STK | A | 22 | 193 | 37 | 14 | 2 | 7 | 26 | 28 | 56 | 14 | 2 | .295/.420/.545 | 119 | .411 | -1.5 | CF(31) -0.2, RF(9) 0.5 | 0.8 |
| 2022 | LAN | A+ | 22 | 218 | 30 | 9 | 2 | 8 | 21 | 28 | 79 | 16 | 1 | .209/.317/.406 | 105 | .307 | 1.0 | CF(47) 5.0, RF(1) 0.3 | 1.2 |
| 2023 non-DC | OAK | MLB | 23 | 251 | 22 | 11 | 2 | 4 | 23 | 22 | 94 | 10 | 1 | .218/.295/.335 | 81 | .354 | -0.1 | LF 0, CF 0 | 0.2 |

*Comparables: Yusuf Carter, Brandon Downes, Jake Meyers*

Plus-plus power potential and plus speed make Clarke one of the highest-upside prospects in the A's system. As is often the case of prospects with this profile, though, Clarke also carries huge contact questions. Clarke crushed Low-A pitching, but was far more pedestrian at High-A. However, he capped his first year as a pro off with a solid stint at the Arizona Fall League. Clarke has consistently walked at above-average rates, but he's already striking out more than 30% of the time without maximizing his power.

## 13   Luis Medina   RHP

Born: 05/03/99   Age: 24   Bats: R   Throws: R   Height: 6'1"   Weight: 175 lb.   Origin: International Free Agent, 2015

| YEAR | TEAM | LVL | AGE | W | L | SV | G | GS | IP | H | HR | BB/9 | K/9 | K | GB% | BABIP | WHIP | ERA | DRA- | WARP |
|------|------|-----|-----|---|---|----|----|----|------|----|----|------|------|----|------|-------|------|-------|------|------|
| 2021 | HV | A+ | 22 | 2 | 1 | 0 | 7 | 7 | 32² | 18 | 4 | 5.2 | 13.8 | 50 | 50.0% | .241 | 1.13 | 2.76 | 79 | 0.6 |
| 2021 | SOM | AA | 22 | 4 | 3 | 0 | 15 | 14 | 73² | 65 | 7 | 5.0 | 10.1 | 83 | 50.5% | .314 | 1.44 | 3.67 | 84 | 1.1 |
| 2022 | TOR | WIN | 23 | 0 | 1 | 0 | 10 | 10 | 28 | 20 | 0 | 3.9 | 10.3 | 32 | 53.7% | .299 | 1.14 | 2.57 | | |
| 2022 | MID | AA | 23 | 1 | 4 | 0 | 7 | 7 | 20² | 35 | 3 | 9.6 | 11.3 | 26 | 46.2% | .516 | 2.76 | 11.76 | 114 | -0.1 |
| 2022 | SOM | AA | 23 | 4 | 3 | 0 | 17 | 17 | 72 | 46 | 4 | 5.0 | 10.1 | 81 | 51.4% | .240 | 1.19 | 3.38 | 80 | 1.7 |
| 2023 DC | OAK | MLB | 24 | 1 | 2 | 0 | 29 | 0 | 25.3 | 25 | 4 | 6.4 | 9.5 | 27 | 40.1% | .306 | 1.69 | 5.47 | 135 | -0.3 |

*Comparables: Alex Colomé, Jordan Yamamoto, Trey Supak*

Acquired in the Montas deal, Medina has one of the best fastballs in professional baseball with a potential 55 curveball and a developing changeup. However, Medina has never recorded a walk-rate below 13% in any of his professional seasons. At Double-A with the Yankees, Medina was showing the best command of his career (still probably well-below-average), but it immediately regressed after the move. In shorter, abbreviated outings at LIDOM this winter, Medina posted a 2.57 ERA with 32 strikeouts and a sub-10% walk rate in 28 innings pitched, suggesting that a move to the bullpen may be exactly what he needs to reach his true potential.

## 14   Royber Salinas   RHP

Born: 04/10/01   Age: 22   Bats: R   Throws: R   Height: 6'3"   Weight: 205 lb.

| YEAR | TEAM | LVL | AGE | W | L | SV | G | GS | IP | H | HR | BB/9 | K/9 | K | GB% | BABIP | WHIP | ERA | DRA- | WARP |
|------|------|-----|-----|---|---|----|----|----|------|----|----|------|------|-----|------|-------|------|------|------|------|
| 2021 | BRA | ROK | 20 | 1 | 3 | 1 | 10 | 6 | 25¹ | 19 | 4 | 5.7 | 17.4 | 49 | 52.2% | .357 | 1.38 | 3.20 | | |
| 2021 | AUG | A | 20 | 2 | 0 | 0 | 3 | 3 | 14 | 6 | 0 | 5.1 | 11.6 | 18 | 60.7% | .214 | 1.00 | 0.64 | 104 | 0.1 |
| 2022 | AUG | A | 21 | 0 | 1 | 0 | 5 | 5 | 23² | 10 | 1 | 4.6 | 19.8 | 52 | 40.7% | .346 | 0.93 | 1.52 | 56 | 0.8 |
| 2022 | ROM | A+ | 21 | 5 | 7 | 0 | 20 | 20 | 85¹ | 63 | 6 | 5.4 | 13.0 | 123 | 43.2% | .306 | 1.34 | 4.11 | 73 | 1.9 |
| 2023 non-DC | OAK | MLB | 22 | 3 | 3 | 0 | 58 | 0 | 50 | 42 | 7 | 5.6 | 10.9 | 60 | 36.9% | .288 | 1.47 | 4.44 | 113 | -0.1 |

Salinas is a powerful righty with a potential plus fastball, two exciting breaking balls and a changeup that has flashed above-average potential. Understandably, that arsenal helped Salinas rack up 175 strikeouts in 109 innings pitched in 2022 between Low- and High-A. However, he is a long way from big-league command, issuing 63 walks. Salinas will turn 22 in April and could return to High-A or face a challenge at Double-A. Repeating High-A probably would be best to give him a chance to gain better precision over his stuff. If that development never comes, though, Salinas should be able to hop on a fast track as a reliever.

## 15   Daniel Susac   DH/C

Born: 05/14/01   Age: 22   Bats: R   Throws: R   Height: 6'4"   Weight: 218 lb.   Origin: Round 1, 2022 Draft (#19 overall)

| YEAR | TEAM | LVL | AGE | PA | R | 2B | 3B | HR | RBI | BB | K | SB | CS | AVG/OBP/SLG | DRC+ | BABIP | BRR | DRP | WARP |
|------|------|-----|-----|-----|----|----|----|----|-----|----|----|----|----|-------------|------|-------|------|-------|------|
| 2022 | STK | A | 21 | 107 | 14 | 7 | 0 | 1 | 13 | 7 | 25 | 0 | 0 | .286/.346/.388 | 92 | .375 | -1.2 | C(11) -0.3 | 0.0 |
| 2023 non-DC | OAK | MLB | 22 | 251 | 18 | 11 | 1 | 2 | 19 | 14 | 59 | 0 | 0 | .210/.262/.290 | 56 | .272 | -4.4 | C 0 | -0.8 |

*Comparables: Henry Wrigley, Luken Baker, Manuel Rodriguez*

The 19th-overall pick in this year's draft, Susac was one of the more enigmatic first-round prospects from the collegiate ranks. A 6-foot-4 catcher, Susac faces the standard doubts that tall catchers face with the glove, but he has a strong defensive reputation. At the plate, he has at least plus power potential, but has a hit tool that will likely prevent him from ever fully tapping into it. While it's hard to make too much of pro debuts, Susac managed just a .286/.346/.388 line in 107 plate appearances at Low-A. If it all comes together, there's probably a Matt Wieters-type 90th percentile outcome, but first-round catchers have an unexceptional track record for a reason.

## 16  Ryan Noda  1B

Born: 03/30/96   Age: 27   Bats: L   Throws: L   Height: 6'3"   Weight: 217 lb.   Origin: Round 15, 2017 Draft (#459 overall)

| YEAR | TEAM | LVL | AGE | PA | R | 2B | 3B | HR | RBI | BB | K | SB | CS | AVG/OBP/SLG | DRC+ | BABIP | BRR | DRP | WARP |
|---|---|---|---|---|---|---|---|---|---|---|---|---|---|---|---|---|---|---|---|
| 2021 | TUL | AA | 25 | 475 | 73 | 15 | 1 | 29 | 78 | 74 | 127 | 3 | 1 | .250/.383/.521 | 120 | .288 | 0.4 | 1B(47) -0.6, LF(44) -2.1, RF(2) -0.2 | 2.3 |
| 2022 | OKC | AAA | 26 | 574 | 86 | 23 | 1 | 25 | 90 | 92 | 162 | 20 | 4 | .259/.395/.474 | 104 | .339 | 0.7 | 1B(104) -1.6, LF(16) -1.3, RF(5) -0.7 | 1.5 |
| 2023 DC | OAK | MLB | 27 | 197 | 21 | 8 | 1 | 5 | 18 | 23 | 57 | 4 | 1 | .228/.327/.376 | 103 | .308 | 0.6 | 1B 0 | 0.6 |

A Rule 5 selection away from the Dodgers, Noda is a former 15th-round selection who has consistently performed in the minors, but was too old and lacked a big-time tool to garner much prospect attention. Set to turn 27 in March, Noda hit .259/.396/.474 with 25 home runs at the Pacific Coast League in 2022, and performed even better at the Texas League the year prior. Noda has an elite approach, never walking in fewer than 15% of his plate appearances and doing a good job of maximizing his 55-grade power. He's a solid defender at first base and even stole a career-high 20 bases last season, although that's more a byproduct of his high baseball-IQ than athleticism.

## 17  J.T. Ginn  RHP

Born: 05/20/99   Age: 24   Bats: R   Throws: R   Height: 6'2"   Weight: 200 lb.   Origin: Round 2, 2020 Draft (#52 overall)

| YEAR | TEAM | LVL | AGE | W | L | SV | G | GS | IP | H | HR | BB/9 | K/9 | K | GB% | BABIP | WHIP | ERA | DRA- | WARP |
|---|---|---|---|---|---|---|---|---|---|---|---|---|---|---|---|---|---|---|---|---|
| 2021 | SLU | A | 22 | 2 | 1 | 0 | 8 | 8 | 38² | 26 | 3 | 2.3 | 8.1 | 35 | 57.4% | .237 | 0.93 | 2.56 | 78 | 0.9 |
| 2021 | BRK | A+ | 22 | 3 | 4 | 0 | 10 | 10 | 53¹ | 49 | 0 | 2.0 | 7.8 | 46 | 64.2% | .308 | 1.14 | 3.38 | 96 | 0.5 |
| 2022 | ATH | ROK | 23 | 0 | 0 | 0 | 2 | 2 | 7 | 4 | 0 | 0.0 | 6.4 | 5 | 84.2% | .211 | 0.57 | 0.00 | | |
| 2022 | MID | AA | 23 | 1 | 4 | 0 | 10 | 10 | 35¹ | 38 | 3 | 3.6 | 10.4 | 41 | 58.3% | .350 | 1.47 | 6.11 | 71 | 0.8 |
| 2023 non-DC | OAK | MLB | 24 | 3 | 3 | 0 | 58 | 0 | 50 | 52 | 6 | 3.5 | 6.9 | 38 | 45.0% | .303 | 1.43 | 4.42 | 114 | -0.1 |

*Comparables: David Peterson, Cy Sneed, Erick Fedde*

Ginn has had one of the most volatile careers of any prospect over the past few years. A two-time top-two round selection in the draft, he underwent UCL surgery before headlining the A's return for Chris Bassitt during spring training. Oakland was aggressive in 2022, assigning Ginn to the hitter-friendly Texas League (Double-A), and he recorded a 6.11 ERA across 10 starts. Granted, his strikeout, walk and home run rates were all roughly around league average and seemed to justify better numbers (a 4.07 FIP and 4.10 xFIP back that up). Ginn has become a soft-contact oriented pitcher, relying on a low-90s sinker that he locates well. He also utilizes a slider and changeup that have 50-grade potential. Ginn has the pieces to be a back-end starter, but questions about his ability to handle a starter's workload remain.

## 18  Brett Harris  3B

Born: 06/24/98   Age: 25   Bats: R   Throws: R   Height: 6'3"   Weight: 208 lb.   Origin: Round 7, 2021 Draft (#218 overall)

| YEAR | TEAM | LVL | AGE | PA | R | 2B | 3B | HR | RBI | BB | K | SB | CS | AVG/OBP/SLG | DRC+ | BABIP | BRR | DRP | WARP |
|---|---|---|---|---|---|---|---|---|---|---|---|---|---|---|---|---|---|---|---|---|
| 2021 | LAN | A+ | 23 | 94 | 14 | 3 | 0 | 3 | 11 | 8 | 20 | 3 | 1 | .222/.323/.370 | 109 | .259 | 0.6 | 3B(20) 0.4, SS(4) -0.0, 2B(3) 0.3 | 0.5 |
| 2022 | LAN | A+ | 24 | 123 | 22 | 7 | 0 | 7 | 18 | 19 | 21 | 0 | 0 | .304/.415/.578 | 157 | .320 | -0.1 | 3B(23) -0.9, 2B(4) -0.9 | 1.0 |
| 2022 | MID | AA | 24 | 360 | 51 | 15 | 2 | 10 | 45 | 31 | 62 | 11 | 5 | .286/.361/.441 | 112 | .327 | -0.2 | 3B(66) 0.2, 2B(17) -0.6 | 1.5 |
| 2023 non-DC | OAK | MLB | 25 | 251 | 23 | 10 | 1 | 5 | 24 | 19 | 48 | 3 | 1 | .222/.291/.340 | 80 | .259 | -2.8 | 2B 0, 3B 0 | -0.2 |

*Comparables: Marquez Smith, Patrick Kivlehan, Cody Overbeck*

Harris is arguably the best defensive infielder in Oakland's farm system, already a big-league ready defender at the hot corner and second base. He was a senior-sign in the A's 2021 class who crushed High-A pitching in his first full pro season and reached Double-A. In 84 games in the Texas League, Harris hit .286/.361/.441 with 10 homers and a 17.2% strikeout rate. Harris may not have any big-time tools, but he also lacks any obvious weaknesses. The biggest knock on his scouting report is that he's set to turn 25 in June, though he's performed well enough to justify a ranking despite his age. Harris could find his way to the majors by the end of 2023.

## 19 Henry Bolte   OF

Born: 08/04/03   Age: 19   Bats: R   Throws: R   Height: 6'3"   Weight: 195 lb.   Origin: Round 2, 2022 Draft (#56 overall)

| YEAR | TEAM | LVL | AGE | PA | R | 2B | 3B | HR | RBI | BB | K | SB | CS | AVG/OBP/SLG | DRC+ | BABIP | BRR | DRP | WARP |
|------|------|-----|-----|----|----|----|----|----|-----|----|----|----|----|-------------|------|-------|-----|-----|------|
| 2022 | ATH | ROK | 18 | 39 | 5 | 0 | 0 | 0 | 2 | 5 | 19 | 0 | 1 | .212/.333/.212 | | .500 | | | |

Once again, the A's turned to the best speed/power combinations among prep prospects, drafting Bolte with the 56th-overall pick in the 2022 draft. With plus speed and plus-plus power potential, Bolte has the potential to be a plus defender in center field who could also hit 25-30 home runs in a season. Of course, he also failed to record an extra-base hit and struck out 19 times in 39 plate appearances at the complex, so his big-league future is too far away to be having informative discussions at this point. Bolte will return to the complex in 2023, and if he begins squaring up pro pitching consistently, he could quickly become one of the best prospects in the farm system.

## 20 Brayan Buelvas   OF

Born: 06/08/02   Age: 21   Bats: R   Throws: R   Height: 5'11"   Weight: 155 lb.   Origin: International Free Agent, 2018

| YEAR | TEAM | LVL | AGE | PA | R | 2B | 3B | HR | RBI | BB | K | SB | CS | AVG/OBP/SLG | DRC+ | BABIP | BRR | DRP | WARP |
|------|------|-----|-----|-----|----|----|----|----|-----|----|----|----|----|----------------|------|-------|------|----------------------------------|------|
| 2021 | STK | A | 19 | 392 | 54 | 11 | 4 | 16 | 50 | 37 | 95 | 17 | 7 | .219/.306/.412 | 106 | .253 | -3.4 | LF(32) -1.8, CF(32) -2.4, RF(23) -1.0 | 0.9 |
| 2022 | LAN | A+ | 20 | 260 | 28 | 14 | 1 | 7 | 26 | 17 | 57 | 7 | 4 | .195/.265/.352 | 103 | .225 | -0.3 | CF(33) 0.0, RF(23) 0.8, LF(9) -0.7 | 0.8 |
| 2023 non-DC | OAK | MLB | 21 | 251 | 20 | 10 | 1 | 4 | 22 | 14 | 65 | 6 | 3 | .201/.256/.311 | 59 | .260 | -0.9 | LF 0, CF 0 | -0.6 |

*Comparables: Teodoro Martinez, Rashun Dixon, Sandro Fabian*

Buelvas has a baseball IQ well beyond his years and it's a huge part of the reason why Oakland has challenged him with aggressive assignments. The advanced competition finally caught up with him in 2022, when he recorded a .195/.265/.352 line at High-A. Still just 20, Buelvas can easily repeat the level and remain on track. He lacks a plus tool other than his general feel for the game, but he also has potential 50-grades across the board. He will probably have to move to an outfield corner down the line, forcing him to max out his offensive upside to become an everyday player, but most players with his profile end up with a 45/45 combination that is unable to justify a big-league spot.

# Top Talents 25 and Under (as of 4/1/2023):

1. Tyler Soderstrom, C/1B
2. Shea Langeliers, C
3. Kyle Muller, LHP
4. Ken Waldichuk, LHP
5. Mason Miller, RHP
6. Nick Allen, SS/2B
7. Jordan Diaz, 1B/DH
8. Max Muncy, IF
9. Zack Gelof, IF
10. Gunnar Hoglund, RHP

Only one returning player (30-year-old platoon OF/1B Seth Brown) with over 60 plate appearances on the 2022 Oakland Athletics had a DRC+ above 100, so it's fair to be deeply concerned about the lack of clear impact in the minors and among their young big leaguers. The A's best argument for themselves is that several of their most experienced youths are defensively adept, but it is cold comfort. Langeliers may not actually match his long-standing rep as a strong defensive backstop, as he's yet to post quality pitch-framing numbers in the minors and as long as that continues to matter with analog umpiring, it will be an issue. His second big-league season should at least offer more consistency, as the catching job is now fully his to master.

Both Allen and unranked outfielder Cristian Pache have the cachet of formerly reasonable prospect-dom, albeit Allen as a high-floor prep infielder and Pache as a one-time top prospect in baseball or close to it. The collective ability of the two youngsters to impact the game at the plate is borderline nonexistent, and Pache in particular had a catastrophic year at the dish. His 68 DRC+ was, if anything, rosier than his .166/.218/.241 traditional line in around half a year, before Oakland pulled the plug and put Pache back in Triple-A. The club has spoken about Ruiz as their everyday center fielder, meaning the 24-year-old has an uphill battle towards playing time and performing when it's earned. Allen's numbers were more mediocre than inconceivably awful, but the undersized infielder has always been expected to have to scrape for scraps at the plate. He immediately put the bat on the ball at a high rate in his first half-season or so despite a dearth of thump, but he should contend for a Gold Glove in a full season at shortstop now that Elvis Andrus seems unlikely to return.

# Philadelphia Phillies

## The State of the System:

The Phillies are well above-average at drafting and developing pitchers with big stuff, and well below-average at identifying and maximizing hit tools. That leaves a system with a lot of boom-or-bust potential, concentrated in big arms and (mostly lower-level) position players who have extreme hit tool variance.

## The Top Ten:

**1** **Andrew Painter   RHP**       OFP: 70       ETA: 2023

Born: 04/10/03   Age: 20   Bats: R   Throws: R   Height: 6'7"   Weight: 215 lb.   Origin: Round 1, 2021 Draft (#13 overall)

| YEAR | TEAM | LVL | AGE | W | L | SV | G | GS | IP | H | HR | BB/9 | K/9 | K | GB% | BABIP | WHIP | ERA | DRA- | WARP |
|------|------|-----|-----|---|---|----|----|----|----|----|----|------|-----|---|-----|-------|------|-----|------|------|
| 2021 | PHI | ROK | 18 | 0 | 0 | 0 | 4 | 4 | 6 | 4 | 0 | 0.0 | 18.0 | 12 | 88.9% | .444 | 0.67 | 0.00 | | |
| 2022 | CLR | A | 19 | 1 | 1 | 0 | 9 | 9 | 38² | 17 | 0 | 3.7 | 16.1 | 69 | 38.1% | .270 | 0.85 | 1.40 | 63 | 1.3 |
| 2022 | JS | A+ | 19 | 3 | 0 | 0 | 8 | 8 | 36² | 25 | 2 | 1.7 | 12.0 | 49 | 32.6% | .274 | 0.87 | 0.98 | 83 | 0.6 |
| 2022 | REA | AA | 19 | 2 | 1 | 0 | 5 | 5 | 28¹ | 25 | 3 | 0.6 | 11.8 | 37 | 35.3% | .338 | 0.95 | 2.54 | 82 | 0.6 |
| 2023 DC | PHI | MLB | 20 | 3 | 3 | 0 | 10 | 10 | 45.7 | 42 | 7 | 3.3 | 8.9 | 45 | 31.6% | .287 | 1.28 | 3.88 | 103 | 0.4 |

*Comparables: Francis Martes, Julio Teheran, Dylan Bundy*

**The Report:** Painter's report presents some Rorschach test qualities for modern prospect evaluation. Both Jeffrey Paternostro and I saw him live last year and thought he was very good but not great from an eye-scouting perspective. Jeffrey's live scouting report shows he consistently hit the upper-90s and scraped low-100s with his fastball but didn't have great command, threw a curve and a slider that had above-average-to-plus potential but were running together, and had a nascent changeup. My report was roughly the same.

A data-driven look at Painter will show him as a potential ace. His fastball velocity actually plays *up* due to carry and extension, and while he doesn't have great visual command, he fills up the top edges of the zone with pitches that batters cannot drive and often cannot even make contact on. The breaking balls work well in concert with each other as a diving curve and sweeping slider—two distinct breaking balls in the same velocity band is a feature, not a bug, and those are two good breaking ball shapes—and the changeup may not be used often but has good potential. He sliced and diced through Low-A, High-A and Double-A without any real challenge, and it's not impossible that he makes the MLB rotation out of spring training—as a 19-year-old.

**OFP:** 70 / Top-of-the-rotation starter

**Variance:** Medium. Even the eyeball scouting says he's like a no. 2 or no. 3 starter—it's whether or not there's something extra that gets him to an ace spot.

**Bret Sayre's Fantasy Take:** Were it not for Grayson Rodriguez's lat injury, Painter would be in discussion for the top fantasy pitching prospect in baseball. That is absolutely not a sentence I thought I'd be writing at the beginning of the 2022 season. You can quibble on ultimately how many bats those breakers will miss in the majors or have light nightmares about what his defense might look like with older versions of Kyle Schwarber, Nick Castellanos and Alec Bohm out there, but he's easy to project as an SP2 with strong ratios and there is definitely room for more.

### Eyewitness Report: Andrew Painter

**Evaluator:** Jeffrey Paternostro
**Report Date:** 06/30/2022

**Dates Seen:** 6/12/22

**Risk Factor:** High

**Delivery:** SWU, medium tempo, average arm stroke, three-quarters slot. Big man, but simple delivery that he repeats well enough for now.

| Pitch Type | Future Grade | Sitting Velocity | Peak Velocity | Report |
|---|---|---|---|---|
| FB | 70 | 96-98 | 100 | Cuts at times, shape and command below-average, but swing and miss pitch when he's getting it steep and down in the zone. |
| CU | 60 | 78-80 | 80 | Good 12-6 shape, but can snap it off at times, shows late downer action, confident enough to throw it 3-2 for a strikeout. Works it north-south well for his experience level. |
| SL | 55 | 81-83 | 83 | Slurvier action than the curveball, more 11-5, bores in/away, threw it more but the curve was presently ahead and showed more S+M shape. |
| CH | 40 | 89-90 | 90 | Firm with some fade, lacks arm speed. |

**Conclusion:** High upside 2021 prep arm that can beat A-ball hitters with his fastball, with enough breaking ball command to back it up. Raw and projectable arsenal/frame, could go in a number of directions and is currently on the IL for what the Phillies have termed "load management."

## 2  Mick Abel  RHP     OFP: 60     ETA: Late 2023/Early 2024

Born: 08/18/01   Age: 21   Bats: R   Throws: R   Height: 6'5"   Weight: 190 lb.   Origin: Round 1, 2020 Draft (#15 overall)

| YEAR | TEAM | LVL | AGE | W | L | SV | G | GS | IP | H | HR | BB/9 | K/9 | K | GB% | BABIP | WHIP | ERA | DRA- | WARP |
|---|---|---|---|---|---|---|---|---|---|---|---|---|---|---|---|---|---|---|---|---|
| 2021 | CLR | A | 19 | 1 | 3 | 0 | 14 | 14 | 44² | 27 | 5 | 5.4 | 13.3 | 66 | 40.0% | .259 | 1.21 | 4.43 | 78 | 1.0 |
| 2022 | JS | A+ | 20 | 7 | 8 | 0 | 18 | 18 | 85¹ | 75 | 6 | 4.0 | 10.9 | 103 | 39.1% | .315 | 1.32 | 4.01 | 101 | 0.5 |
| 2022 | REA | AA | 20 | 1 | 3 | 0 | 5 | 5 | 23 | 19 | 5 | 4.7 | 10.6 | 27 | 27.6% | .264 | 1.35 | 3.52 | 110 | 0.2 |
| 2023 non-DC | PHI | MLB | 21 | 3 | 3 | 0 | 58 | 0 | 50 | 50 | 8 | 5.2 | 8.7 | 48 | 33.4% | .300 | 1.56 | 5.16 | 129 | -0.5 |

*Comparables: Julio Rodriguez, Matt Manning, Grant Holmes*

**The Report:** Drafted a year ahead of Painter with a lot of the same general contours in his scouting report, Abel has "fallen behind" while also remaining on track as one of baseball's better right-handed pitching prospects. Abel also sits in the mid-to-upper-90s, but his fastball doesn't have the same elite traits and therefore doesn't get nearly as many whiffs. His slider is actually visually ahead of Painter's and flashes plus-plus, but it's not currently inducing enough chases to perform as such. His curveball and changeup both project to at least average, and he mostly hits his spots even if he nibbles a bit too much.

Because he spent much of the season in a rotation with Painter (and Griff McGarry and Ben Brown), Abel's success may seem a bit muted; he was more solid than dominant. But he's well on track for a very solid outcome.

**OFP:** 60 / Good mid-rotation starter

**Variance:** Medium. Abel's control does wander a bit, he did have some mysterious arm woes in 2021 and he does have enough stuff where if one thing jumps, he could exceed this outcome.

**Bret Sayre's Fantasy Take:** There's nothing absurdly special in Abel's fantasy profile, but there's also a strong chance that he becomes the kind of player who helps you a little everywhere. That might sound like damning with faint praise, but you wouldn't shake your head at a solid SP3 in the Logan Gilbert mold. That future is attainable, and could start as soon as the second half of 2023—just not soon enough to make him an NL-only sleeper just yet.

## 3 Griff McGarry  RHP      OFP: 60      ETA: 2023

Born: 06/08/99   Age: 24   Bats: R   Throws: R   Height: 6'2"   Weight: 190 lb.   Origin: Round 5, 2021 Draft (#145 overall)

| YEAR | TEAM | LVL | AGE | W | L | SV | G | GS | IP | H | HR | BB/9 | K/9 | K | GB% | BABIP | WHIP | ERA | DRA- | WARP |
|------|------|-----|-----|---|---|----|----|----|-----|----|----|------|------|----|------|-------|------|------|------|------|
| 2021 | CLR | A | 22 | 0 | 0 | 1 | 5 | 1 | 11 | 6 | 0 | 5.7 | 18.0 | 22 | 52.9% | .353 | 1.18 | 3.27 | 84 | 0.2 |
| 2021 | JS | A+ | 22 | 1 | 0 | 0 | 3 | 3 | 13¹ | 7 | 0 | 4.7 | 14.2 | 21 | 34.6% | .269 | 1.05 | 2.70 | 98 | 0.1 |
| 2022 | JS | A+ | 23 | 3 | 3 | 0 | 12 | 12 | 46² | 33 | 6 | 4.6 | 15.8 | 82 | 35.3% | .342 | 1.22 | 3.86 | 84 | 0.7 |
| 2022 | REA | AA | 23 | 1 | 3 | 0 | 8 | 7 | 32² | 13 | 1 | 5.5 | 10.7 | 39 | 44.9% | .176 | 1.01 | 2.20 | 95 | 0.5 |
| 2022 | LHV | AAA | 23 | 0 | 2 | 0 | 7 | 0 | 8 | 7 | 2 | 10.1 | 10.1 | 9 | 36.8% | .294 | 2.00 | 9.00 | 101 | 0.1 |
| 2023 DC | PHI | MLB | 24 | 1 | 2 | 0 | 5 | 5 | 20.3 | 17 | 3 | 5.9 | 11.1 | 25 | 36.4% | .287 | 1.48 | 4.52 | 113 | 0.1 |

*Comparables: Nick Nelson, Dellin Betances, Josh Staumont*

**The Report:** The post-draft breakout prospect from 2021 consolidated all his gains in 2022, and then some. McGarry throws both four-seam and two-seam fastballs in the mid-to-upper-90s, and he has two breaking balls that flash high outcomes. I preferred the curve to the slider in 2021, but the slider took a huge step forward in 2022 to the point that he had outings where he barely threw the curveball. He occasionally flashes a decent changeup but does not generally spot it well or induce many chases with it. While he usually throws enough strikes, he sometimes cannot put the ball where he wants on the edge inside or outside the zone, causing a few more cement-mixers and a few more uncompetitive balls than you'd like.

In the not-too-distant past, the lagging changeup and elevated walks would've consigned him to bullpen work. In the 2020s, he's got a real chance to start; his pitch arsenal is very well-suited to modern baseball.

**OFP:** 60 / Mid-rotation starter or first-division closer

**Variance:** High. McGarry had terrible command-and-control problems at Virginia, and they resurfaced when the Phillies challenged him late in the season in an attempt to get him ready for their 2022 pennant run. He has significantly more reliever risk than Painter or Abel.

**Bret Sayre's Fantasy Take:** This is generally the kind of pitcher I avoid in dynasty leagues given both the reliever risk and the elevated walk rate. Even if he's a starting pitcher, today's game is not kind to those who are inefficient, which could lead to fewer wins and strikeouts than a pitcher of similar IRL prospect value. Although he needs to be rostered in leagues with 200-plus prospect slots, he's probably not someone you'd hesitate to trade or cut for the next hot thing.

## 4 Hao-Yu Lee  IF      OFP: 55      ETA: 2025

Born: 02/03/03   Age: 20   Bats: R   Throws: R   Height: 5'10"   Weight: 190 lb.   Origin: International Free Agent, 2021

| YEAR | TEAM | LVL | AGE | PA | R | 2B | 3B | HR | RBI | BB | K | SB | CS | AVG/OBP/SLG | DRC+ | BABIP | BRR | DRP | WARP |
|------|------|-----|-----|-----|----|----|----|----|-----|----|----|----|----|-------------|------|-------|------|------|------|
| 2021 | PHI | ROK | 18 | 25 | 9 | 2 | 2 | 1 | 5 | 3 | 5 | 0 | 0 | .364/.440/.773 | | .438 | | | |
| 2022 | CLR | A | 19 | 302 | 37 | 11 | 1 | 7 | 50 | 36 | 57 | 10 | 7 | .283/.384/.415 | 133 | .338 | 1.3 | SS(23) 0.7, 3B(20) 1.2, 2B(15) 0.8 | 2.4 |
| 2022 | JS | A+ | 19 | 40 | 5 | 3 | 1 | 1 | 2 | 5 | 9 | 3 | 0 | .257/.350/.486 | 104 | .320 | -0.2 | 2B(6) -1.1, SS(3) 0.2 | 0.0 |
| 2023 non-DC | PHI | MLB | 20 | 251 | 20 | 10 | 1 | 3 | 21 | 18 | 61 | 4 | 3 | .217/.280/.310 | 68 | .283 | -1.9 | 2B 0, 3B 0 | -0.4 |

*Comparables: Juremi Profar, Cole Tucker, Xavier Edwards*

**The Report:** Lee was an accomplished amateur hitter when the Phillies signed him last summer for $500,000. Since signing, he has done nothing but hit, following a good nine-game sample in 2021 by putting up one of the better seasons by a 19-year-old in full-season ball in 2022 (despite missing a month and a half after a hit-by-pitch broke his hand). Lee is solidly built, with a simple right-handed swing, a good approach and strike zone awareness. Lee does not put up eye-popping 90th percentile exit velocities, but he consistently makes solid contact. On defense, the Phillies have played him all over the infield, but he lacks the range for shortstop and his arm is probably a bit light for third. He isn't a bad second baseman, but he also is unlikely to be a plus defender there.

Unlike most prospects in the Phillies system, Lee just hits and he always has hit. He is unlikely to have big-time power numbers, but it is at least a plus hit tool and he is likely to actualize a lot of his raw power.

**OFP:** 55 / Everyday bat-first second baseman

**Variance:** Medium. Second base has trended towards a higher offensive bar of late, though new shift rules could change the defensive needs, so Lee is going to need to show some power growth and hit near his offensive ceiling.

**Bret Sayre's Fantasy Take:** Teenage prospects who not only hit in full-season ball, but hit with strong plate discipline skills (like Lee's 43 walks to 67 strikeouts) are going to be popular targets among stat-driven dynasty players. The issue here is that there's a big question around what his secondary fantasy skills look like, although if he stays in Philly, the ballpark may be able to drag him to a 15-homer future. In the end, his ceiling may not be much different from the player who Phillies fans have been used to watching at the keystone: Jean Segura. (Not the speedy version, the 30-something version.)

## 5  Justin Crawford  CF    OFP: 55    ETA: 2026

Born: 01/13/04   Age: 19   Bats: L   Throws: R   Height: 6'3"   Weight: 175 lb.   Origin: Round 1, 2022 Draft (#17 overall)

| YEAR | TEAM | LVL | AGE | PA | R | 2B | 3B | HR | RBI | BB | K | SB | CS | AVG/OBP/SLG | DRC+ | BABIP | BRR | DRP | WARP |
|------|------|-----|-----|-----|----|----|----|----|-----|----|----|----|----|-------------|------|-------|-----|-----|------|
| 2022 | PHI | ROK | 18 | 43 | 6 | 0 | 1 | 0 | 5 | 5 | 6 | 8 | 3 | .297/.395/.351 | | .355 | | | |
| 2023 non-DC | PHI | MLB | 19 | 251 | 18 | 9 | 2 | 2 | 18 | 15 | 90 | 8 | 3 | .202/.256/.281 | 50 | .320 | -0.2 | CF 0 | -0.7 |

**The Report:** After experiencing success drafting college bats, the Phillies went back to their old ways in drafting Crawford, a prep outfielder without clear plus hit or power tools. Justin is the son of former All-Star Carl Crawford, and generally has the same broad outlines on his scouting report as his dad; it will not surprise you at all to learn that he is an absolute burner, for example. He projects to be a true center fielder and has a lot of the classic physical projection you might expect from a prep pick.

About the hitting attributes. Crawford has the visual attributes of a nice, quick lefty swing. But he doesn't do any of the things that we know tend to lead to hitting success as a professional; he doesn't hit the ball particularly hard, he doesn't hit the ball in the air much at all and he doesn't make a lot of contact yet. All of those things can come in time—he's an 18-year-old who has played only 16 professional games—but beyond aesthetic praise, that could be applied to *many* prospects' swings, we don't have much reason to tell you he's going to hit for much average or power.

**OFP:** 55 / Speed-first starting center fielder

**Variance:** Extreme. I have no idea if he'll hit or not, and it's been quite a while since we got from there to a regular with a solid bat in this organization.

**Bret Sayre's Fantasy Take:** You lost me at Phillies prospect with hit tool issues. I wouldn't take Crawford in the first 30 picks of a FYPD this year, bloodlines and all. He's fine as a third- or fourth-round flier given his speed potential in roto leagues, but I have no faith that this will go well.

## 6  Johan Rojas  CF    OFP: 55    ETA: 2024

Born: 08/14/00   Age: 22   Bats: R   Throws: R   Height: 6'1"   Weight: 165 lb.   Origin: International Free Agent, 2018

| YEAR | TEAM | LVL | AGE | PA | R | 2B | 3B | HR | RBI | BB | K | SB | CS | AVG/OBP/SLG | DRC+ | BABIP | BRR | DRP | WARP |
|------|------|-----|-----|-----|----|----|----|----|----|----|----|----|----|-------------|------|-------|-----|-----|------|
| 2021 | CLR | A | 20 | 351 | 51 | 15 | 3 | 7 | 38 | 26 | 69 | 25 | 6 | .240/.305/.374 | 100 | .283 | 3.4 | CF(66) 11.1, RF(10) -0.7, LF(1) 0.5 | 2.6 |
| 2021 | JS | A+ | 20 | 74 | 16 | 3 | 1 | 3 | 11 | 7 | 8 | 8 | 3 | .344/.419/.563 | 139 | .352 | 2.5 | CF(14) 2.8, LF(2) -0.3, RF(1) -0.0 | 1.1 |
| 2022 | JS | A+ | 21 | 292 | 40 | 12 | 2 | 3 | 22 | 21 | 55 | 33 | 1 | .230/.287/.325 | 111 | .278 | 2.9 | CF(63) 1.8 | 1.7 |
| 2022 | REA | AA | 21 | 264 | 42 | 8 | 5 | 4 | 16 | 21 | 44 | 29 | 4 | .260/.333/.387 | 112 | .305 | 5.1 | CF(51) 6.5, LF(6) -0.2, RF(1) -0.1 | 2.3 |
| 2023 non-DC | PHI | MLB | 22 | 251 | 19 | 10 | 2 | 3 | 21 | 14 | 49 | 11 | 3 | .217/.269/.312 | 64 | .264 | 1.2 | LF 0, CF 0 | -0.1 |

*Comparables: Greg Golson, Mason Williams, Che-Hsuan Lin*

**The Report:** A lot of what I wrote about Crawford also applies to Rojas, except he's way closer to the majors, so there's much more granular data showing what he does well and why that all adds up to mediocre hitting outcomes. Let's start with the good stuff: He's developed into a splendid defensive outfielder and one of the better runners in the entire minor leagues. If you watch him at 5 PM, he looks like he should hit for a lot of power; he has a lot of bat speed and even in games, if you watch him square one up, you'll think he has plus power potential. Like Crawford, the swing just looks right, but that also manifests with Rojas in plus barrel control and extremely positive swing-and-miss markers given his age and levels.

So why don't I think he can hit? Despite decent patience, his overall swing decisions collapse because his pitch *recognition* (especially on spin) is poor. Rojas takes a lot of hittable strikes and swings at a lot of pitcher's pitches, and it has reverberations down his entire hitting profile. When combined with his good contact ability and not-particularly-optimized swing path, that means a ton of soft-to-medium groundball contact—basically the worst possible outcome for a ball in play. And that's why his top-line stats have looked so mediocre even with everything else going for him.

**OFP:** 55 / Defense-and-speed starting center fielder

**Variance:** High. On the Prospect Team, we have some strong believers in Rojas' ability to figure out spin. Then again, name a Phillies prospect who has hit more than expected lately...

**Bret Sayre's Fantasy Take:** Far be it from me to shake my head at a 21-year-old who just stole 62 bases in 67 attempts this year, especially heading into the rule changes we're about to see. That said, he doesn't bring the wetness to the table that Brandon Marsh does and the Phillies have another $375 million or so locked up in corner outfielders, so opportunities to showcase that speed might be limited barring a trade. If he ends up hitting, he's an easy OF2.

## 7 William Bergolla  SS          OFP: 50     ETA: 2027

Born: 10/20/04   Age: 18   Bats: L   Throws: R   Height: 5'11"   Weight: 165 lb.   Origin: International Free Agent, 2022

| YEAR | TEAM | LVL | AGE | PA | R | 2B | 3B | HR | RBI | BB | K | SB | CS | AVG/OBP/SLG | DRC+ | BABIP | BRR | DRP | WARP |
|------|------|-----|-----|----|----|----|----|----|----|----|----|----|----|-------------|------|-------|-----|-----|------|
| 2022 | DSL PHW | ROK | 17 | 83 | 18 | 3 | 0 | 0 | 14 | 11 | 3 | 2 | 3 | .380/.470/.423 | | .397 | | | |

**The Report:** The Phillies made Bergolla their big international splash this January. An injury meant that he got a late start to the DSL season, only making it into 24 games, but he was instantly the DSL Phillies White's best hitter on their championship run. He has a simple left-handed swing that currently lacks impact, but there's good feel for solid contact. He is unlikely to grow into more than below-average to average power, but he should be a player who can pepper the gaps with doubles. He has an advanced approach, and great feel for the strike zone, including a bit of a mini-Juan Soto crouch and stare. In the field, he is a smooth defender at shortstop with plenty of range and arm for the position.

It is a bit of a sum-of-the-parts profile propped up by what should be plus defense at shortstop. The big question is how much power he will be able to add, because this will be the difference between a defense-first bench bat and an everyday regular.

**OFP:** 50 / Everyday shortstop

**Variance:** Extreme. Bergolla has 24 games of DSL action under his belt, and it has been a long time since a Phillies international hitter has not crashed and burned along the way to the majors. That said, Bergolla certainly looks as much the part as an 18-year-old can.

**Bret Sayre's Fantasy Take:** It's kind of a fun profile (11 walks to three strikeouts in his DSL debut), but someone with this long of an ETA needs to have a bigger fantasy carrying tool to his name. That leaves Bergolla on the watch list for right now unless you're in a league that rosters 300 prospects or more.

## 8 Alex McFarlane  RHP          OFP: 50     ETA: 2025

Born: 06/09/01   Age: 22   Bats: R   Throws: R   Height: 6'4"   Weight: 215 lb.   Origin: Round 4, 2022 Draft (#122 overall)

| YEAR | TEAM | LVL | AGE | W | L | SV | G | GS | IP | H | HR | BB/9 | K/9 | K | GB% | BABIP | WHIP | ERA | DRA- | WARP |
|------|------|-----|-----|----|----|----|----|----|----|----|----|------|------|----|------|-------|------|------|------|------|
| 2022 | CLR | A | 21 | 0 | 3 | 0 | 3 | 3 | 8 | 12 | 1 | 3.4 | 13.5 | 12 | 71.4% | .550 | 1.88 | 9.00 | 82 | 0.2 |
| 2023 non-DC | PHI | MLB | 22 | 3 | 3 | 0 | 58 | 0 | 50 | 54 | 8 | 4.6 | 8.0 | 44 | 39.6% | .312 | 1.59 | 5.38 | 134 | -0.6 |

*Comparables: Tony Santillan, Robert Broom, Freddy Pacheco*

**The Report:** When the Phillies selected McFarlane in the fourth round, it was easy to immediately jump to McGarry comparisons from their 2021 draft. Like McGarry, McFarlane's spin rates jump off the charts. In his nine-inning FSL audition, his fastball averaged nearly 96 mph and 2,700 RPM. His breaking balls both checked in over 2,800 RPM, and even his changeup comes in at 2,000 RPM. Once we get the raw numbers out of the way, the comparison does begin to break down, as McFarlane is primarily a sinker-heavy fastball user with his four-seam fastball not showing any of the bat-missing characteristics present in the Phillies top three prospects. He primarily throws a slider (he did show a curve), however his changeup might be his best secondary; that is less about fade and more just heavy arm-side bore. The pitch mix is not the idealized version that the top trio has, but it is one the Phillies are familiar with given Aaron Nola and Ranger Suárez in the majors.

Given their tinkering on other arms, it would not be surprising to see some amount of reworking. Particularly watch for a cutter to enter the chat, given the Phillies' trends. Despite all of this, the primary reason why McFarlane fell to the fourth round is that he simply has not had success as a starting pitcher and ended up mostly in the bullpen in college. His command, much like McGarry's, is not a strength, lending a significant risk that the bullpen is his long-term home.

**OFP:** 50 / Mid-rotation starter or late-inning reliever

**Variance:** Extreme. The Phillies have been decently good at turning questionable-command college arms into usable pitchers, but McFarlane wasn't even starting in college and unlike McGarry, who went on a 24-inning tour de force to cap his draft year, we don't have a similar display to put our minds at ease.

**Bret Sayre's Fantasy Take:** Another one for the watch list, in case it looks like he can hold up and miss bats as a starter. Not a consideration for a FYPD unless close to 100 players are being drafted from this recent signing class.

## 9 Símon Muzziotti OF     OFP: 45     ETA: Debuted in 2022

Born: 12/27/98   Age: 24   Bats: L   Throws: L   Height: 6'1"   Weight: 175 lb.   Origin: International Free Agent, 2015

| YEAR | TEAM | LVL | AGE | PA | R | 2B | 3B | HR | RBI | BB | K | SB | CS | AVG/OBP/SLG | DRC+ | BABIP | BRR | DRP | WARP |
|------|------|-----|-----|----|---|----|----|----|-----|----|----|----|----|-------------|------|-------|-----|-----|------|
| 2021 | PEJ | WIN | 22 | 83 | 10 | 1 | 0 | 0 | 13 | 15 | 13 | 3 | 3 | .254/.398/.269 | | .315 | | | |
| 2021 | LHV | AAA | 22 | 32 | 2 | 0 | 0 | 0 | 2 | 5 | 4 | 2 | 0 | .200/.333/.200 | 110 | .238 | 0.9 | LF(5) 0.4, CF(3) -0.1 | 0.3 |
| 2022 | REA | AA | 23 | 165 | 23 | 5 | 4 | 5 | 20 | 19 | 31 | 7 | 3 | .259/.339/.455 | 122 | .291 | 0.7 | CF(22) 2.3, LF(10) 0.2, RF(5) 1.2 | 1.5 |
| 2022 | PHI | MLB | 23 | 9 | 0 | 0 | 0 | 0 | 0 | 0 | 2 | 0 | 0 | .143/.250/.143 | 84 | .200 | -0.4 | CF(8) 0 | 0.0 |
| 2023 DC | PHI | MLB | 24 | 60 | 6 | 2 | 1 | 1 | 5 | 5 | 11 | 2 | 0 | .222/.288/.320 | 71 | .266 | 0.0 | CF 0 | -0.1 |

*Comparables: Cedric Hunter, Engel Beltre, Trayvon Robinson*

**The Report:** Muzziotti has barely played since 2019 between the pandemic, visa issues in 2021 and various leg injuries in 2022, but he has some of the same broad positives as Rojas. He's a solid defensive outfielder and has made a lot of contact whenever he's been on the field, albeit a bit too groundball-focused. In his abbreviated Double-A campaign this year, he showed significantly more pop than he had in the past, with the significant caveat that he only played about a third of the season and much of it was in Reading, a known launching pad. Muzziotti's most likely outcome is a nifty bench outfielder, but he's played little enough while showing enough intriguing traits that you can dream on some more.

**OFP:** 45 / Very good fourth outfielder

**Variance:** High. He's barely played lately, after all.

**Bret Sayre's Fantasy Take:** Other team lists will be deeper, I promise.

## 10 Carlos De La Cruz LF     OFP: 45     ETA: 2024

Born: 10/06/99   Age: 23   Bats: R   Throws: R   Height: 6'8"   Weight: 210 lb.   Origin: Undrafted Free Agent, 2017

| YEAR | TEAM | LVL | AGE | PA | R | 2B | 3B | HR | RBI | BB | K | SB | CS | AVG/OBP/SLG | DRC+ | BABIP | BRR | DRP | WARP |
|------|------|-----|-----|----|---|----|----|----|-----|----|----|----|----|-------------|------|-------|-----|-----|------|
| 2021 | PHI | ROK | 21 | 30 | 3 | 0 | 0 | 0 | 1 | 8 | 8 | 3 | 0 | .200/.467/.200 | | .333 | | | |
| 2021 | CLR | A | 21 | 139 | 10 | 5 | 0 | 2 | 11 | 13 | 56 | 2 | 0 | .148/.252/.238 | 65 | .250 | 0.2 | RF(24) 0.7, LF(6) -0.2, CF(4) 0.5 | 0.0 |
| 2021 | JS | A+ | 21 | 68 | 10 | 4 | 0 | 3 | 14 | 5 | 23 | 0 | 0 | .242/.294/.452 | 89 | .324 | 0.0 | RF(10) -1.8, LF(4) 0.3 | 0.0 |
| 2022 | JS | A+ | 22 | 241 | 29 | 10 | 1 | 10 | 24 | 19 | 75 | 5 | 2 | .266/.344/.463 | 103 | .362 | 0.7 | 1B(22) -0.6, LF(19) 0.6, RF(8) 0.3 | 0.8 |
| 2022 | REA | AA | 22 | 162 | 21 | 12 | 1 | 7 | 23 | 8 | 45 | 1 | 0 | .278/.315/.510 | 86 | .347 | -0.1 | LF(14) 2.3, RF(12) 1.3, 1B(4) 0.3 | 0.6 |
| 2023 non-DC | PHI | MLB | 23 | 251 | 21 | 11 | 1 | 5 | 23 | 13 | 91 | 2 | 1 | .222/.270/.337 | 71 | .340 | -3.5 | 1B 0, LF 0 | -0.6 |

*Comparables: Joe Benson, Bryan De La Cruz, Juan Silverio*

**The Report:** De La Cruz went from available in the Triple-A phase of the Rule 5 Draft to a top-10 prospect in just a year, which is both a testament to him making a huge leap as a prospect and the shallowness of this system. (Get ready for a bushel full of relief prospects in the next 10.) He's probably an inch or two *taller* than his 6-foot-8 listed height, and even that listing would tie him with Tony Clark and Nate Freiman as the tallest position players in MLB history.

De La Cruz generates incredible bat speed and some really impressive exit velocities with his fast twitch and long levers, albeit at the risk of tremendous swing-and-miss. He improved greatly over the course of 2022 in identifying and not swinging through non-fastballs, continuing through a promotion to Double-A and in the Arizona Fall League. He still does it too much, and therefore is still fairly likely to not have enough hit tool for a true major-league regular role; the Phillies also have a poor track record finishing off this profile. But given he has some of the highest power upside in the minors and that there's an improving chance, we're back in on the skinny giant.

**OFP:** 45 / Power-over-hit second-division regular in an outfield corner or first base

**Variance:** Very high. I think he's actually more likely to be a 3 or a 6 than exactly a 45 or 5. The left-tail outcomes encompass a wider range than most prospects, but the right-tail outcomes are better.

**Bret Sayre's Fantasy Take:** The history of interesting fantasy hitters taken in the Rule 5 Draft since the rules changed back in 2006 is mostly housed on Akil Baddoo's player page, and perhaps unsurprisingly, De La Cruz went untouched. I love a good "unusual physical profile player," but this one is more curiosity than anything else right now.

# Outside the Top Ten:

## 11 Andrew Baker   RHP

Born: 03/24/00   Age: 23   Bats: R   Throws: R   Height: 6'3"   Weight: 190 lb.   Origin: Round 11, 2021 Draft (#325 overall)

| YEAR | TEAM | LVL | AGE | W | L | SV | G | GS | IP | H | HR | BB/9 | K/9 | K | GB% | BABIP | WHIP | ERA | DRA- | WARP |
|---|---|---|---|---|---|---|---|---|---|---|---|---|---|---|---|---|---|---|---|---|
| 2021 | CLR | A | 21 | 1 | 2 | 0 | 7 | 1 | 10 | 4 | 1 | 15.3 | 14.4 | 16 | 44.4% | .176 | 2.10 | 11.70 | 98 | 0.1 |
| 2022 | JS | A+ | 22 | 3 | 1 | 0 | 40 | 0 | 43² | 41 | 5 | 4.9 | 12.6 | 61 | 51.8% | .336 | 1.49 | 4.74 | 92 | 0.5 |
| 2022 | REA | AA | 22 | 1 | 0 | 0 | 6 | 0 | 10² | 3 | 0 | 4.2 | 9.3 | 11 | 28.6% | .143 | 0.75 | 0.84 | 97 | 0.2 |
| 2023 non-DC | PHI | MLB | 23 | 3 | 3 | 0 | 58 | 0 | 50 | 51 | 8 | 6.6 | 10.2 | 57 | 36.9% | .320 | 1.74 | 5.88 | 142 | -0.8 |

Comparables: Matt Walker, Cam Hill, Robert Broom

The Phillies selected Baker in the 11th round of the 2021 draft, and went a bit overslot to bring in the JuCo right-hander. In his draft year, plus much of 2022, Baker looked like a project with a blazing fastball and good slider, and a walk rate just short of a batter per inning. In July, everything clicked for him, as he found delivery consistency and the strikes followed. Baker's arsenal is very much the modern reliever, his fastball has big spin and rise and sits 97-100 with some 101s sprinkled in. His breaking ball appears to now be labeled a slider, but is a high-80s pitch with more vertical break than sweep, playing more like a power curveball. Baker ended the year in Double-A and will likely return there to start the 2023 season, but he may be in the majors fairly early in the season, where he profiles as a late-inning arm.

## 12 Gabriel Rincones Jr.   OF

Born: 03/03/01   Age: 22   Bats: L   Throws: R   Height: 6'4"   Weight: 225 lb.   Origin: Round 3, 2022 Draft (#93 overall)

Rincones, a 2022 third-rounder, has one of the oddest backgrounds you'll ever see. Born in Venezuela, his family moved to Scotland when he was very young for his father's job, and then Rincones moved to Tampa to play high school baseball in the United States. He didn't sign as a late Padres JuCo pick in 2021 and lit up NCAA ball for Florida Atlantic in 2022, slashing .346/.451/.658 with 19 homers. He hits the ball extremely hard and has the resulting big power projection; on the flip side, he has a relatively light track record (only one season in Conference USA) and he's a big kid with a long swing and some chase. In sum, there's a lot of perceived risk in his hit tool, similar to De La Cruz, but we have no pro data to go on yet.

## 13 Francisco Morales   RHP

Born: 10/27/99   Age: 23   Bats: R   Throws: R   Height: 6'4"   Weight: 185 lb.   Origin: International Free Agent, 2016

| YEAR | TEAM | LVL | AGE | W | L | SV | G | GS | IP | H | HR | BB/9 | K/9 | K | GB% | BABIP | WHIP | ERA | DRA- | WARP |
|---|---|---|---|---|---|---|---|---|---|---|---|---|---|---|---|---|---|---|---|---|
| 2021 | REA | AA | 21 | 4 | 13 | 0 | 22 | 20 | 83 | 76 | 11 | 6.5 | 11.9 | 110 | 40.8% | .323 | 1.64 | 6.94 | 84 | 1.4 |
| 2021 | LHV | AAA | 21 | 0 | 1 | 0 | 2 | 2 | 8² | 6 | 0 | 7.3 | 7.3 | 7 | 44.0% | .240 | 1.50 | 0.00 | 114 | 0.1 |
| 2022 | REA | AA | 22 | 2 | 0 | 1 | 23 | 0 | 30¹ | 9 | 0 | 5.0 | 16.0 | 54 | 31.8% | .205 | 0.86 | 1.48 | 72 | 0.8 |
| 2022 | LHV | AAA | 22 | 3 | 3 | 2 | 22 | 0 | 20² | 24 | 1 | 12.2 | 7.0 | 16 | 47.1% | .343 | 2.52 | 9.58 | 147 | -0.2 |
| 2022 | PHI | MLB | 22 | 0 | 0 | 1 | 3 | 0 | 5 | 2 | 1 | 10.8 | 5.4 | 3 | 72.7% | .100 | 1.60 | 7.20 | 122 | 0.0 |
| 2023 non-DC | PHI | MLB | 23 | 3 | 3 | 0 | 58 | 0 | 50 | 42 | 6 | 6.9 | 10.4 | 58 | 42.2% | .293 | 1.61 | 4.77 | 116 | -0.2 |

Comparables: Arodys Vizcaíno, Phillippe Aumont, José Leclerc

Morales was close to a Top 101 prospect before the pandemic, but he was unable to even come close to throwing enough strikes in the upper minors to start. Reimagined as a slider-dominant righty reliever in 2022...well, he still didn't really throw strikes enough of the time, but you can see the contours of a dominant reliever nonetheless. Morales ran up huge whiff percentages, especially at Double-A, and made the majors at 22. His slider is a clear plus pitch and bordering on plus-plus, and he comfortably sits in the mid-90s with his fastball. He'll have plenty of individual outings (including much of the Arizona Fall League) where he looks like he's a few months away from being a first-division closer, and then he'll have runs like he had towards the end of last season at Triple-A where he walks 10 guys in four games. The Phillies have done sneakily well figuring these types of pitchers out lately.

## 14 Erik Miller LHP

Born: 02/13/98   Age: 25   Bats: L   Throws: L   Height: 6'5"   Weight: 240 lb.   Origin: Round 4, 2019 Draft (#120 overall)

| YEAR | TEAM | LVL | AGE | W | L | SV | G | GS | IP | H | HR | BB/9 | K/9 | K | GB% | BABIP | WHIP | ERA | DRA- | WARP |
|------|------|-----|-----|---|---|----|----|----|-----|-----|-----|------|------|-----|-------|-------|-------|------|------|------|
| 2022 | REA | AA | 24 | 1 | 0 | 0 | 22 | 7 | 36¹ | 25 | 0 | 4.2 | 10.9 | 44 | 38.6% | .301 | 1.16 | 2.23 | 79 | 0.9 |
| 2022 | LHV | AAA | 24 | 0 | 1 | 0 | 10 | 0 | 12 | 14 | 4 | 10.5 | 13.5 | 18 | 25.0% | .357 | 2.33 | 7.50 | 103 | 0.1 |
| 2023 DC | SF | MLB | 25 | 1 | 1 | 0 | 20 | 0 | 17.3 | 16 | 2 | 5.6 | 10.1 | 20 | 32.0% | .307 | 1.55 | 4.76 | 120 | -0.1 |

*Comparables: Nick Vespi, Nelvin Fuentes, Hunter Cervenka*

Speaking of 2022 bullpen conversions, Miller nominally started seven games at Double-A but was never truly stretched out; he maxed out at 11 batters faced and 47 pitches. His future is clearly in the bullpen at this point moving forward. Miller's profile reads a lot like Morales'—big kid, solid fastball velocity, extremely wandering command, leaning a good deal on the potential plus slider—but as a lefty, and less extreme in both command (which is good) and stuff (which is less good). Unlike Morales, he's still throwing a changeup, so he projects as another late-game leverage reliever instead of just a LOOGY type; he also has to start throwing more strikes soon.

## 15 Nikau Pouaka-Grego SS

Born: 09/13/04   Age: 18   Bats: L   Throws: R   Height: 5'10"   Weight: 175 lb.   Origin: International Free Agent, 2022

| YEAR | TEAM | LVL | AGE | PA | R | 2B | 3B | HR | RBI | BB | K | SB | CS | AVG/OBP/SLG | DRC+ | BABIP | BRR | DRP | WARP |
|------|------|-----|-----|-----|----|----|----|----|-----|----|----|----|----|-------------|------|-------|-----|-----|------|
| 2022 | PHI | ROK | 17 | 125 | 20 | 6 | 1 | 3 | 16 | 16 | 16 | 2 | 2 | .301/.424/.466 | | .333 | | | |

The Phillies signed Pouaka-Grego for $250,000 out of New Zealand in January and started him right off as a 17-year-old in the Florida Complex League. He showed feel for contact and a surprising amount of power, more than holding his own hitting .301/.424/.466 in 125 plate appearances. He is a solidly built infielder from the Pacific Rim without a set position who can hit, in what is becoming a bit of a surprising trend for the Phillies (joining Hao Yu Lee and now-Ray Curtis Mead in this club). Pouaka-Grego probably fits best as a second baseman in the long term, but expect the Phillies to try him in a bunch of different positions. He lacks some of the polish and track record of Lee, but should be getting some extra reps this winter with Adelaide before becoming one of the youngest hitters in full season ball next year.

## 16 Jaydenn Estanista RHP

Born: 10/03/01   Age: 21   Bats: R   Throws: R   Height: 6'3"   Weight: 180 lb.   Origin: International Free Agent, 2019

| YEAR | TEAM | LVL | AGE | W | L | SV | G | GS | IP | H | HR | BB/9 | K/9 | K | GB% | BABIP | WHIP | ERA | DRA- | WARP |
|------|------|-----|-----|---|---|----|----|----|-----|-----|-----|------|------|-----|-------|-------|-------|------|------|------|
| 2021 | DSL PHW | ROK | 19 | 1 | 1 | 1 | 10 | 6 | 30² | 19 | 1 | 5.6 | 9.7 | 33 | 39.1% | .265 | 1.24 | 3.23 | | |
| 2022 | PHI | ROK | 20 | 3 | 0 | 0 | 12 | 5 | 31¹ | 14 | 3 | 4.6 | 10.1 | 35 | 42.4% | .175 | 0.96 | 2.01 | | |

The Phillies used to have a pitcher pop up out of nowhere in their Florida complex every year, and recently that's gone dry. Enter Estanista, a now 21-year-old out of Curacao who signed just before the pandemic in November 2019 for $10,000. He looks the part with a tall, lanky frame that has room for further projection and a loose, easy delivery. His fastball is clearly his best pitch, sitting 93-96 and touching up to 97, with all the characteristics needed to miss bats in the zone. The secondary pitches are a much larger question; he has a mid-70s curve that does not look the worse, but he noticeably changes his delivery and can hang it. The Phillies have started to introduce a hard cutter/slider and he reportedly throws a changeup, albeit not in games yet. He has a lot of reliever traits and he is a long way off from the majors, but he has the pieces of a pitcher who could pop in the next few years.

## 17 Emaarion Boyd OF

Born: 08/22/03   Age: 19   Bats: R   Throws: R   Height: 6'1"   Weight: 177 lb.   Origin: Round 11, 2022 Draft (#332 overall)

| YEAR | TEAM | LVL | AGE | PA | R | 2B | 3B | HR | RBI | BB | K | SB | CS | AVG/OBP/SLG | DRC+ | BABIP | BRR | DRP | WARP |
|------|------|-----|-----|-----|----|----|----|----|-----|----|----|----|----|-------------|------|-------|-----|-----|------|
| 2022 | PHI | ROK | 18 | 36 | 6 | 1 | 0 | 0 | 2 | 5 | 5 | 7 | 2 | .345/.472/.379 | | .417 | | | |
| 2023 non-DC | PHI | MLB | 19 | 251 | 18 | 10 | 1 | 2 | 19 | 14 | 66 | | | .205/.258/.288 | 54 | .276 | | LF 0, RF 0 | -0.8 |

The Phillies selected Boyd in the 11th round of the 2022 draft and gave him the second-highest bonus in their draft class. Much of what was written above about Justin Crawford applies to Boyd, though Boyd is a right-handed hitter. There are similar questions about his ability to impact the ball. Boyd might be faster than Crawford and has more defensive upside, but lacks Crawford's frame and potential physicality. So it is hard to see him ever having more than poor power. Much like the center fielders ahead of him on this list, the glove and speed will give him plenty of chances for the bat to take a step forward.

## 18 Jordan Viars  DH

Born: 07/18/03  Age: 19  Bats: L  Throws: L  Height: 6'4"  Weight: 215 lb.  Origin: Round 3, 2021 Draft (#84 overall)

| YEAR | TEAM | LVL | AGE | PA | R | 2B | 3B | HR | RBI | BB | K | SB | CS | AVG/OBP/SLG | DRC+ | BABIP | BRR | DRP | WARP |
|------|------|-----|-----|----|---|----|----|----|-----|----|----|----|----|-------------|------|-------|-----|-----|------|
| 2021 | PHI | ROK | 17 | 64 | 13 | 1 | 0 | 3 | 18 | 11 | 12 | 2 | 0 | .255/.406/.468 | | .257 | | | |
| 2022 | PHI | ROK | 18 | 179 | 28 | 6 | 1 | 2 | 20 | 17 | 40 | 5 | 0 | .240/.330/.331 | | .304 | | | |
| 2022 | CLR | A | 18 | 28 | 2 | 0 | 0 | 0 | 3 | 2 | 9 | 0 | 0 | .208/.286/.208 | 91 | .313 | -0.7 | LF(1) -0.4 | -0.1 |
| 2023 non-DC | PHI | MLB | 19 | 251 | 18 | 10 | 2 | 2 | 19 | 16 | 92 | 2 | 0 | .207/.263/.289 | 55 | .331 | -3.6 | 1B 0, LF 0 | -1.2 |

Despite having a physically mature build, Viars was one of the youngest players in the 2021 draft when the Phillies took him in the third round. An injury in spring training meant that he started his season in late June in the FCL, and a poor showing meant that is where he stayed until the end of the year. Viars still showed big exit velocities, but he spent most of the season with his swing timing off, leading to a large number of ineffective fly balls. He began to show a bit more fluidity late in the season, but it was largely a lost year. He remains well down the defensive spectrum with corner outfield or first base being his likely defensive home. Despite all of the negatives, his raw tools are still all there and 2023 will be his age-19 season, so time has not yet run out.

## 19 Rickardo Perez  C

Born: 12/04/03  Age: 19  Bats: L  Throws: R  Height: 5'10"  Weight: 172 lb.  Origin: International Free Agent, 2021

| YEAR | TEAM | LVL | AGE | PA | R | 2B | 3B | HR | RBI | BB | K | SB | CS | AVG/OBP/SLG | DRC+ | BABIP | BRR | DRP | WARP |
|------|------|-----|-----|----|---|----|----|----|-----|----|----|----|----|-------------|------|-------|-----|-----|------|
| 2021 | DSL PHR | ROK | 17 | 146 | 15 | 3 | 0 | 0 | 9 | 22 | 15 | 3 | 1 | .256/.370/.281 | | .287 | | | |
| 2022 | PHI | ROK | 18 | 93 | 5 | 1 | 0 | 1 | 14 | 7 | 13 | 0 | 1 | .349/.387/.398 | | .389 | | | |

One of the Phillies' two large international signings in 2021, Perez missed all of extended spring training after an injury at the end of actual spring training. Perez is a solid defender behind the plate, but struggled to control the running game this season. He has a solid approach and feel for contact, and there is much more raw power than his five extra base hits in 73 career games would indicate. He might have just enough all-around upside to be a low-end starter, but more likely the path is as a solid second catcher. Either way, that is still a long way off.

## 20 Orion Kerkering  RHP

Born: 04/04/01  Age: 22  Bats: R  Throws: R  Height: 6'2"  Weight: 204 lb.  Origin: Round 5, 2022 Draft (#152 overall)

| YEAR | TEAM | LVL | AGE | W | L | SV | G | GS | IP | H | HR | BB/9 | K/9 | K | GB% | BABIP | WHIP | ERA | DRA- | WARP |
|------|------|-----|-----|---|---|----|---|----|----|---|----|------|-----|---|------|-------|------|-----|------|------|
| 2022 | CLR | A | 21 | 1 | 0 | 0 | 5 | 0 | 6 | 7 | 0 | 0.0 | 9.0 | 6 | 31.6% | .368 | 1.17 | 4.50 | 92 | 0.1 |
| 2023 non-DC | PHI | MLB | 22 | 3 | 3 | 0 | 58 | 0 | 50 | 57 | 8 | 4.2 | 6.7 | 37 | 34.8% | .311 | 1.61 | 5.70 | 142 | -0.8 |

Kerkering was a good reliever as a sophomore and was a mediocre starting pitcher as a junior, despite throwing more strikes. Given the Phillies' track record with college arms, it was a bit of a surprise that when they took Kerkering in the fifth round this year, they just left him in the bullpen. The reliever profile makes sense for him—he throws a pair of unremarkable fastballs that sat about 95 and touched 97 in his pro debut. His future upside in the bullpen is going to depend on his slider, an at-least-plus pitch with high spin (averaging just under 3,000 rpm with Clearwater) and big sweep. If the Phillies keep him in the bullpen role, there is a chance to move very quickly as a seventh- or eighth-inning type arm.

## Top Talents 25 and Under (as of 4/1/2023):

1. Andrew Painter, RHP
2. Bryson Stott, SS/2B
3. Mick Abel, RHP
4. Brandon Marsh, OF
5. Griff McGarry, RHP
6. Hao Yu Lee, IF
7. Justin Crawford, OF
8. Bailey Falte, LHP
9. Johan Rojas, OF
10. William Bergolla, SS

The National League pennant winners have earned their reputation for bucking the league-wide fixation with putting "cheaply" and "efficiently" as the 1a and 1b priorities in the concept of "winning as cheaply and efficiently as possible," with "winning" a distant runner-up. Still, Philly was able to mount their surprising run to the World Series by relying on some stabilizing performances from their young depth. Much of Philly's order was based on top picks from their own system or elsewhere, with over half of their lineup being drafted in the first round, including 26-year-old Alec Bohm.

That category also includes Stott, who was woeful in the postseason but put together a passable debut campaign nonetheless, with an 88 DRC+ and decent glovework at both shortstop and second base. One of those positions will be his in the coming season, though the Phils will likely look for more thump in free agency. Marsh cobbled together a similarly cromulent campaign, making some mechanical tweaks that may have accounted for a hot Philly finish upon joining the club. Still, his bat is a major liability moving forward without sustained strides, with just a 64 DRC+ on the year for the rangy defender.

The pitching staff is not in line to see great strides from its existing youth, though Painter and Abel in particular are cause for hope on the horizon. Falter has flashed capability in the bullpen but walked a tightrope in more extended rotation use in 2022, with a 3.86 ERA belied by his 5.29 DRA, though a 30.3% CSW% is promising that he can at least provide average length and depth behind Philadelphia's aces.

# Pittsburgh Pirates

## The State of the System:

Graduations, injuries and prospect stagnation have all taken their toll on last year's no. 1 system. It remains deep, but you have to squint a bit harder to see impact talent.

## The Top Ten:

### 1 Termarr Johnson 2B     OFP: 60     ETA: 2025

Born: 06/11/04   Age: 19   Bats: L   Throws: R   Height: 5'7"   Weight: 175 lb.   Origin: Round 1, 2022 Draft (#4 overall)

| YEAR | TEAM | LVL | AGE | PA | R | 2B | 3B | HR | RBI | BB | K | SB | CS | AVG/OBP/SLG | DRC+ | BABIP | BRR | DRP | WARP |
|------|------|-----|-----|-----|-----|-----|-----|-----|-----|-----|-----|-----|-----|-------------|------|-------|-----|-----|------|
| 2022 | PIR | ROK | 18 | 29 | 0 | 2 | 0 | 0 | 0 | 6 | 8 | 2 | 0 | .130/.310/.217 | | .200 | | | |
| 2022 | BRD | A | 18 | 53 | 7 | 4 | 0 | 1 | 6 | 10 | 13 | 4 | 1 | .275/.396/.450 | 114 | .345 | 0.0 | 2B(12) -1.6, SS(1) -0.4 | 0.0 |
| 2023 non-DC | PIT | MLB | 19 | 251 | 19 | 10 | 2 | 2 | 19 | 21 | 77 | 8 | 3 | .208/.279/.294 | 63 | .304 | -0.3 | 2B 0, SS 0 | -0.4 |

*Comparables: Rougned Odor, Omar Estévez, Wendell Rijo*

**The Report:** Johnson has long been seen as the best bet to hit among the prep bats in the 2022 class. Although it's not a classic, scout-friendly lefty stroke—there's a bit of a hitch, and a leg kick that has him closed off and diving in—he repeatedly gets to the point of contact on time and with intent of doing damage. Given the underlying metrics, I think Johnson is more likely to have a plus hit tool in the end, rather than competing for batting titles year in and year out, but will end up with 20-home run pop to round out the offensive profile.

It's a cliché that every good prospect gets drafted as a catcher, shortstop or center fielder, so if you are a prep bat further down the defensive spectrum, that can indicate issues with the glove. Johnson is fine at the keystone and sticks in well on the turn with fine hands and actions. The arm is clearly going to limit him to the right side of the infield, and he won't be obviously above-average there, but should be broadly fine enough to accrue some positional value along with the plus bat.

**OFP:** 60 / Offensive-minded second baseman

**Variance:** High. The "best hitter in the prep class" superlative is littered with prospects who didn't quite hit as much as you'd have thought, and Johnson had some underlying swing-and-miss issues as an amateur. All that said, we think he will hit enough to be a regular regardless.

**Jesse Roche's Fantasy Take:** Blessed with electric bat speed, Johnson churns out tons of hard contact despite his modest size. He also is adept at working counts and identifying hittable pitches with a precocious and patient plate approach. So while Johnson may not possess huge raw power or high-end bat-to-ball ability, he should hit and hit for surprising pop. Further, he has enough speed and baserunning acumen to contribute some steals. Johnson is a borderline top-20 fantasy prospect and a top-five pick in FYPDs.

### 2 Henry Davis C     OFP: 60     ETA: Late 2023

Born: 09/21/99   Age: 23   Bats: R   Throws: R   Height: 6'2"   Weight: 210 lb.   Origin: Round 1, 2021 Draft (#1 overall)

| YEAR | TEAM | LVL | AGE | PA | R | 2B | 3B | HR | RBI | BB | K | SB | CS | AVG/OBP/SLG | DRC+ | BABIP | BRR | DRP | WARP |
|------|------|-----|-----|-----|-----|-----|-----|-----|-----|-----|-----|-----|-----|-------------|------|-------|-----|-----|------|
| 2022 | GBO | A+ | 22 | 100 | 18 | 3 | 1 | 5 | 22 | 8 | 18 | 5 | 1 | .341/.450/.585 | 134 | .383 | 0.4 | C(13) -0.9 | 0.7 |
| 2022 | ALT | AA | 22 | 136 | 19 | 8 | 0 | 4 | 18 | 12 | 30 | 3 | 1 | .207/.324/.379 | 104 | .244 | 1.8 | C(20) -1.1, RF(2) -0.7 | 0.5 |
| 2023 non-DC | PIT | MLB | 23 | 251 | 23 | 10 | 2 | 5 | 24 | 16 | 62 | 3 | 1 | .222/.292/.341 | 81 | .285 | -2.8 | C 0, RF 0 | 0.1 |

*Comparables: David Rodríguez, Koby Clemens, Óscar Hernández*

**The Report:** 2021's no. 1 pick is beginning to cut a controversial figure among prospect analysts. Davis was promoted to High-A Greensboro to finish his pro debut, but was knocked out early with an injury. He began 2022 back in the (336) and spent exactly 100 plate appearances tearing through the Sally League before going down with wrist issues. He battled that malady for the remainder of the regular season as he scuffled at Double-A Altoona, though was evidently healthy enough to try and recoup some of those at-bats in the AFL. Davis has huge bat speed that should create plus game power, which is something for a catcher, but there is more swing-and-miss than you'd like, and the finer aspects of his defense are a work in progress. If he can be average behind the plate and make enough contact for the power to play, there is still star potential here. First he'll have to prove he can stay on the field for an entire season.

**OFP:** 60 / First-division offensively-minded catcher.

**Variance:** Medium. Davis has had trouble staying healthy and showed swing-and-miss issues when he was on the field.

**Jesse Roche's Fantasy Take:** Davis suffered a fractured left wrist in May due to a hit-by-pitch. Most of his time in Double-A occurred after his initial injury, in which he hit just .207/.323/.360. His injury is more concerning than other seemingly random maladies since he gets plunked, well, a lot. Specifically, Davis was drilled a staggering 27 times over 324 plate appearances (8.3%), which includes seven in the AFL. For context, his HBP rate was the second highest in all of baseball last year. While his power potential is undeniable, his risk is higher than you'd expect for a prospect with his pedigree, given his contact, defensive and, of course, health issues. As such, Davis is dropping down dynasty rankings, yet he remains a top-100 fantasy prospect.

## 3   Endy Rodriguez   C/IF/OF    OFP: 60    ETA: 2023

Born: 05/26/00   Age: 23   Bats: S   Throws: R   Height: 6'0"   Weight: 170 lb.   Origin: International Free Agent, 2018

| YEAR | TEAM | LVL | AGE | PA | R | 2B | 3B | HR | RBI | BB | K | SB | CS | AVG/OBP/SLG | DRC+ | BABIP | BRR | DRP | WARP |
|---|---|---|---|---|---|---|---|---|---|---|---|---|---|---|---|---|---|---|---|
| 2021 | BRD | A | 21 | 434 | 73 | 25 | 6 | 15 | 73 | 50 | 77 | 2 | 0 | .294/.380/.512 | 130 | .333 | -2.3 | C(54) -4.2, 1B(18) -1.7, LF(4) -1.2 | 1.9 |
| 2022 | GBO | A+ | 22 | 370 | 63 | 23 | 3 | 16 | 55 | 42 | 77 | 3 | 3 | .302/.392/.544 | 117 | .351 | -1.5 | C(51) -0.3, 2B(15) 0.9, LF(13) -0.5 | 1.8 |
| 2022 | ALT | AA | 22 | 138 | 27 | 14 | 0 | 8 | 32 | 18 | 21 | 1 | 0 | .356/.442/.678 | 135 | .378 | 0.7 | C(21) -0.5, 2B(2) -0.8 | 0.9 |
| 2023 DC | PIT | MLB | 23 | 257 | 28 | 14 | 3 | 5 | 29 | 21 | 52 | 0 | 2 | .248/.316/.395 | 100 | .302 | -2.9 | C 0 | 0.7 |

*Comparables: Devin Mesoraco, Nathaniel Lowe, Ji-Man Choi*

**The Report:** Rodríguez began the season as an interesting curiosity, but finished it hitting well enough that we're now forced to consider the possibility he's an impact major leaguer. He spent time at catcher, second base and in the outfield this past season, and in the abstract seems to possess the athleticism necessary to handle all three. In reality, he has some difficulty framing pitches, and once he sheds his catcher's gear is more corner outfielder than second baseman. The batter's box is where he does his best work, and it's where he seemed to unlock something at the end of the season.

Rodriguez has a quick, loose, pretty stroke that is angled to maximize power production, and when he gets into one, it really carries. He covers the plate well, but early on in the season was taking a lengthy path to the ball and making a fair amount of suboptimal contact on hittable pitches. A midseason adjustment—going from a wide stance when hitting left-handed to standing straight up—seems to have helped him simplify his approach and both get to a greater variety of pitches and drive mistakes with authority. He will likely have to consolidate his gains at Triple-A when next season opens, but should be a big-league contributor in the near future.

**OFP:** 60 / Run-producing corner outfielder who moonlights at catcher.

**Variance:** Medium. There's still a short track record of success and Rodriguez offers a wide range of potential outcomes in terms of positional/defensive value.

**Jesse Roche's Fantasy Take:** The hottest-hitting prospect in the minors in the second half, Rodriguez put up video-game numbers across three levels. For example, he hit .399/.477/.770 with 16 home runs and just 13.1% strikeouts over his final 49 games. Wowza! His uncertain defensive home is not really an issue in most fantasy formats. Indeed, there is a small hope he could go the route of Daulton Varsho and moonlight enough at catcher to retain eligibility year to year. Regardless, the Pirates will find a place for Rodriguez's bat in the lineup, and as he was just added to the 40-man roster, likely as soon as early 2023. For fantasy, he is a top-50 prospect and the no. 2 "catcher" behind only Francisco Álvarez.

## 4   Quinn Priester   RHP    OFP: 55    ETA: Late 2023

Born: 09/15/00   Age: 22   Bats: R   Throws: R   Height: 6'3"   Weight: 210 lb.   Origin: Round 1, 2019 Draft (#18 overall)

| YEAR | TEAM | LVL | AGE | W | L | SV | G | GS | IP | H | HR | BB/9 | K/9 | K | GB% | BABIP | WHIP | ERA | DRA- | WARP |
|------|------|-----|-----|---|---|----|----|----|-----|---|----|------|-----|---|------|-------|------|------|------|------|
| 2021 | GBO | A+ | 20 | 7 | 4 | 0 | 20 | 20 | 97² | 82 | 8 | 3.6 | 9.0 | 98 | 53.7% | .285 | 1.24 | 3.04 | 85 | 1.6 |
| 2022 | ALT | AA | 21 | 4 | 4 | 0 | 15 | 15 | 75¹ | 68 | 4 | 2.6 | 9.0 | 75 | 50.2% | .314 | 1.19 | 2.87 | 86 | 1.5 |
| 2022 | IND | AAA | 21 | 1 | 1 | 0 | 2 | 2 | 9¹ | 5 | 1 | 6.8 | 9.6 | 10 | 36.4% | .190 | 1.29 | 3.86 | 99 | 0.1 |
| 2023 DC | PIT | MLB | 22 | 1 | 1 | 0 | 3 | 3 | 13.3 | 15 | 2 | 4.0 | 7.2 | 11 | 40.3% | .312 | 1.52 | 4.87 | 123 | 0.0 |

*Comparables: Peter Lambert, Jonathan Pettibone, Jacob Turner*

**The Report:** Priester's profile has never really taken a leap over the past few years, but he should be on the doorstep of the majors roughly four years from his draft date. Very effective at High-A in 2021—despite featuring a different repertoire than advertised—he further consolidated his performance with Altoona in 2022. He won't be overpowering in the big leagues, but he has a feel for pitching and a true four-pitch mix: a four-seam/two-seam combo, a curve, a slider and a change. He'll touch as high as 96 with the four-seamer and go as low as 92 with the two-seamer, and both are useful when he commands them. The mid-to-upper-80s slider has short, almost cutter-like action and presents as a confounding change of pace from his sharp low-80s curve. Both breaking balls are above-average when executed and work well off of his fastballs. There will be days where his command lapses and he gets knocked around, but overall he should be a solid contributor.

**OFP:** 55 / Mid-rotation starter.

**Variance:** Low. It seems that he's just about reached his final form.

**Jesse Roche's Fantasy Take:** The key takeaway here is that Priester "won't be overpowering in the big leagues." His fastballs simply don't miss many bats. Further, his changeup is quite firm, with only 4-5 mph velocity separation from his fastballs. That is not to say Priester is without fantasy appeal. His breaking balls can carve through a lineup on good days. The problem is that those bad days may be quite bad. Priester likely will be a volatile arm with solid enough ratios to be rosterable in most fantasy formats.

## 5   Liover Peguero   SS    OFP: 55    ETA: Debuted in 2022

Born: 12/31/00   Age: 22   Bats: R   Throws: R   Height: 6'2"   Weight: 200 lb.   Origin: International Free Agent, 2017

| YEAR | TEAM | LVL | AGE | PA | R | 2B | 3B | HR | RBI | BB | K | SB | CS | AVG/OBP/SLG | DRC+ | BABIP | BRR | DRP | WARP |
|------|------|-----|-----|----|---|----|----|----|-----|----|----|----|----|-------------|------|-------|-----|-----|------|
| 2021 | GBO | A+ | 20 | 417 | 67 | 19 | 2 | 14 | 45 | 33 | 105 | 28 | 6 | .270/.332/.444 | 96 | .337 | -0.6 | SS(86) 8.1 | 1.7 |
| 2022 | ALT | AA | 21 | 521 | 65 | 22 | 5 | 10 | 58 | 29 | 111 | 28 | 6 | .259/.305/.387 | 97 | .316 | 0.4 | SS(94) -3.5, 2B(19) -1.2 | 1.0 |
| 2022 | PIT | MLB | 21 | 4 | 0 | 0 | 0 | 0 | 1 | 2 | 0 | 0 | .333/.500/.333 | 91 | 1.000 | 0.0 | SS(1) 0.1 | 0.0 |
| 2023 non-DC | PIT | MLB | 22 | 251 | 20 | 10 | 2 | 3 | 21 | 13 | 65 | 7 | 2 | .218/.265/.317 | 63 | .286 | -1.1 | SS -1, 2B 0 | -0.5 |

*Comparables: Richard Urena, Wilfredo Tovar, Jorge Polanco*

**The Report:** Aside from randomly making his big-league debut in mid-June, this past season was a step back for Peguero. He's still tooled-up and he's been relatively young for his levels, but his production over the past two years has not lived up to his abilities. Barrel control and feel for hitting are present, but he still hasn't developed a coherent plate approach and it seems to have hurt him against more advanced pitching. He has the skills necessary to play a good shortstop, but that position does seem to be occupied in Pittsburgh for the foreseeable future. He's been almost exclusively a shortstop thus far, but he should have the athletic ability to handle most of the infield or outfield if necessary. He'll have to lock in his strategy and execution at the plate for that question to become relevant, whether he begins 2023 back in Altoona or at Triple-A Indianapolis.

**OFP:** 55 / Solid regular at shortstop, or somewhere else.

**Variance:** High. His hit tool has yet to answer the questions offered by upper-level arms

**Jesse Roche's Fantasy Take:** Summer in the northeast can be brutal. It certainly was for Peguero, who hit just .176/.256/.241 across a 31-game stretch from late June to early August. His aggressive plate approach resulted in a boatload of weak contact. Yet, even during that time, he stole six bases. In fact, Peguero went 28-for-34 in stolen bases for the second year in a row. That speed, along with his solid bat-to-ball ability and power, provide intriguing fantasy upside should he put it all together.

## 6  Nick Gonzales  2B      OFP: 55      ETA: Late 2023
Born: 05/27/99   Age: 24   Bats: R   Throws: R   Height: 5'10"   Weight: 195 lb.   Origin: Round 1, 2020 Draft (#7 overall)

| YEAR | TEAM | LVL | AGE | PA | R | 2B | 3B | HR | RBI | BB | K | SB | CS | AVG/OBP/SLG | DRC+ | BABIP | BRR | DRP | WARP |
|---|---|---|---|---|---|---|---|---|---|---|---|---|---|---|---|---|---|---|---|
| 2021 | PEJ | WIN | 22 | 87 | 18 | 4 | 1 | 2 | 13 | 13 | 14 | 4 | 0 | .380/.483/.549 | | .446 | | | |
| 2021 | GBO | A+ | 22 | 369 | 53 | 23 | 4 | 18 | 54 | 40 | 101 | 7 | 2 | .302/.385/.565 | 112 | .388 | -3.4 | 2B(73) -0.8, SS(1) -0.0 | 1.2 |
| 2022 | ALT | AA | 23 | 316 | 47 | 20 | 1 | 7 | 33 | 43 | 90 | 5 | 3 | .263/.383/.429 | 85 | .367 | -0.5 | 2B(55) -1.5, SS(14) -1.4 | 0.0 |
| 2023 DC | PIT | MLB | 24 | 127 | 12 | 6 | 1 | 2 | 12 | 11 | 43 | 1 | 1 | .228/.307/.352 | 88 | .345 | -0.1 | 2B 0 | 0.2 |

*Comparables: Starlin Rodriguez, James Darnell, Stephen Bruno*

**The Report:** Gonzales is another top Pirates prospect and recent first-rounder who had his 2022 season truncated by injury, in addition to having some potential weaknesses exposed when he was on the field. He wasn't horrible at Double-A, but he did carry a strikeout percentage in the high 20s, and in-zone swing-and-miss issues were flagged in 2021 during an otherwise strong offensive season. As with Davis, the injuries may grant some leeway when interrogating his numbers, but persistent health issues cropping up at this age is also concerning on its own.

Gonzales has great bat speed and his swing is designed for lift, which has allowed him to maintain a 15-20 homer pace in the minors. He can get to fastballs, but his style of hitting can leave him susceptible to breaking stuff down in the zone, which limits his OBP potential despite a fairly robust minor-league walk rate. He's always struck me as tailor-made for second base, but he did play some short during the season and some third in the AFL. Gonzales bounced back well from a slow start this past season, and a strong beginning to next season would get him on the big-league radar.

**OFP:** 55 / Everyday bat-first second baseman

**Variance:** Medium. We need to see a full healthy season of production in the upper minors, but once that happens he won't be eligible for this list.

**Jesse Roche's Fantasy Take:** Those Keston Hiura comps that so many bandied about (including yours truly) before and after the 2020 MLB Draft are looking quite accurate, for better or worse. Gonzales continues to have serious whiff issues, including a dreadful 61% contact rate prior to landing on the IL with a heel injury on June 1. Yet, as noted above, he rebounded to the tune of a .287/.404/.513 line and made more contact over his final 31 games. Whether Gonzales will make enough contact is debatable; however, he offers a rare blend of potential power and speed at second base. (At least that last bit you can't really say anymore about Hiura.)

## 7  Luis Ortiz  RHP      OFP: 55      ETA: Debuted in 2022
Born: 01/27/99   Age: 24   Bats: R   Throws: R   Height: 6'2"   Weight: 240 lb.   Origin: International Free Agent, 2018

| YEAR | TEAM | LVL | AGE | W | L | SV | G | GS | IP | H | HR | BB/9 | K/9 | K | GB% | BABIP | WHIP | ERA | DRA- | WARP |
|---|---|---|---|---|---|---|---|---|---|---|---|---|---|---|---|---|---|---|---|---|
| 2021 | BRD | A | 22 | 5 | 3 | 0 | 22 | 19 | 87¹ | 82 | 5 | 2.9 | 11.6 | 113 | 51.3% | .344 | 1.26 | 3.09 | 89 | 1.5 |
| 2022 | ALT | AA | 23 | 5 | 9 | 0 | 24 | 23 | 114¹ | 100 | 19 | 2.7 | 9.9 | 126 | 46.5% | .288 | 1.17 | 4.64 | 86 | 2.3 |
| 2022 | IND | AAA | 23 | 0 | 0 | 0 | 2 | 2 | 10 | 4 | 1 | 3.6 | 10.8 | 12 | 56.0% | .125 | 0.80 | 3.60 | 81 | 0.2 |
| 2022 | PIT | MLB | 23 | 0 | 2 | 0 | 4 | 4 | 16 | 8 | 1 | 5.6 | 9.6 | 17 | 42.9% | .171 | 1.13 | 4.50 | 98 | 0.2 |
| 2023 DC | PIT | MLB | 24 | 4 | 4 | 0 | 29 | 6 | 46 | 47 | 6 | 3.6 | 8.3 | 43 | 41.4% | .307 | 1.42 | 4.44 | 114 | 0.1 |

*Comparables: Chris Archer, Vance Worley, Wily Peralta*

**The Report:** Ortiz continued his 2021 breakout all the way up to the majors in 2022. A sturdy righty with a triple-digit fastball and plus power slider, it's easy to project a late-inning reliever long-term—or I suppose short-term at this point, given that he's pitched in the majors. His fastball has top-of-the-scale velocity—with good spin and extension to boot—but his traditional three-quarters slot means the pitch mostly runs. That, along with Ortiz's below-average command of the offering, means it gets fewer whiffs than you'd expect from upper-90s and near-2,400 RPM. His slide piece will have no issues getting swings and misses though—it's a filthy upper-80s breaker that darts down and glove-side late. A little more consistency with the pitch should make it a plus weapon he can throw 40% of the time to make it harder for hitters to try and time the 100-mph heater. Ortiz's change was used pretty sparingly in his major-league debut—and it's a clear third pitch—but it has shown as a fringe, albeit useful offering in the minors. The demographics here—overaged, five-figure signee, physically maxed, fastball command issues and really only two pitches—suggest reliever, but I've always been intrigued by Ortiz as a potential bulk guy or five-and-dive starter, and would like to see him get a few more spins in the Pittsburgh rotation.

**OFP:** 55 / no. 3/4 starter or late-inning reliever

**Variance:** Medium. The variance here is ultimately starter versus reliever, which is not insignificant, but Ortiz is a major-league arm.

**Jesse Roche's Fantasy Take:** Ortiz throws very hard and his four- and two-seam fastballs share some similarities to Sandy Alcantara's fastballs. Indeed, Ortiz's 2022 season is somewhat reminiscent of Alcantara's 2017 season. Of course, Ortiz is not likely to be the next Alcantara, but he has unique, powerful stuff that is worth a flier in most fantasy formats.

## 8  Hunter Barco  LHP     OFP: 55     ETA: 2025
Born: 12/15/00  Age: 22  Bats: L  Throws: L  Height: 6'4"  Weight: 210 lb.  Origin: Round 2, 2022 Draft (#44 overall)

**The Report:** Barco had a dominant start to his junior season in the SEC before—like so many of the top college arms—undergoing Tommy John surgery. His plus slider is difficult to pick up given how much he throws across his body, and that slingy crossfire delivery helps his fastball—which plays mostly in an average velo band—as well. Once he's back on a mound in summer 2023, we will start to have a better idea if Barco can throw enough quality strikes to stick in a rotation long-term, but the fastball/slider combo is intriguing in short bursts as well.

**OFP:** 55 / no. 3/4 starter or late-inning reliever

**Variance:** High. He's coming off Tommy John surgery. It's common, but not routine.

**Jesse Roche's Fantasy Take:** A reliever-risk pitching prospect without big fastball velocity recovering from Tommy John surgery is not the type of prospect you target in fantasy outside the deepest of formats.

## 9  Mike Burrows  RHP     OFP: 50     ETA: 2023
Born: 11/08/99  Age: 23  Bats: R  Throws: R  Height: 6'2"  Weight: 195 lb.  Origin: Round 11, 2018 Draft (#324 overall)

| YEAR | TEAM | LVL | AGE | W | L | SV | G | GS | IP | H | HR | BB/9 | K/9 | K | GB% | BABIP | WHIP | ERA | DRA- | WARP |
|---|---|---|---|---|---|---|---|---|---|---|---|---|---|---|---|---|---|---|---|---|
| 2021 | GBO | A+ | 21 | 2 | 2 | 0 | 13 | 13 | 49 | 24 | 3 | 3.7 | 12.1 | 66 | 30.8% | .208 | 0.90 | 2.20 | 93 | 0.6 |
| 2022 | ALT | AA | 22 | 4 | 2 | 0 | 12 | 12 | 52 | 38 | 3 | 3.3 | 11.9 | 69 | 31.7% | .294 | 1.10 | 2.94 | 93 | 0.9 |
| 2022 | IND | AAA | 22 | 1 | 4 | 0 | 12 | 10 | 42¹ | 45 | 5 | 2.6 | 8.9 | 42 | 38.4% | .333 | 1.35 | 5.31 | 99 | 0.6 |
| 2023 DC | PIT | MLB | 23 | 1 | 1 | 0 | 23 | 0 | 19.3 | 19 | 3 | 3.8 | 8.4 | 18 | 33.0% | .301 | 1.40 | 4.31 | 112 | 0.0 |

*Comparables: Marco Gonzales, Luis Gil, Yency Almonte*

**The Report:** Burrows has missed large chunks of time the last two seasons, dealing with an oblique injury in 2021 and then a barking shoulder at the end of last season. However, when on the mound in 2022, he authored a breakout campaign in the upper minors. Burrows works off a three-pitch mix: a mid-90s fastball, a 12-6 curve pinned around 80 and an upper-80s change. The fastball plays at plus, and while the curve doesn't always have true bat-missing depth, the best ones flash solid-average and I'd expect the pitch to land there long-term. The change doesn't have a ton of movement or velocity separation—although Burrows sells the pitch well—and he can like trying to place it down-and-in to lefties a bit too much. Given the injuries, the 22-year-old has been used very conservatively as a pro, topping out at 90 pitches this year, and mostly working in the 4-5 inning, 60-80 pitch range. This isn't really out of line with modern starting pitching development, but we don't have a great idea how well the stuff plays deeper into games. Then again, there are plenty of roles nowadays for pitchers working exactly that deep.

**OFP:** 50 / no. 4 starter

**Variance:** Medium. The shoulder issue is concerning, but if Burrows breaks camp next year healthy, he'll likely be in contention for MLB innings in short order.

**Jesse Roche's Fantasy Take:** Burrows has spent 121 days on the IL over the last two years, succumbing to arm injuries in July and failing to pitch whatsoever in August. It may be that he is best-suited for short bursts in relief. Nevertheless, Burrows likely arrives early in 2023 and should be rostered in leagues with 200 prospects.

## 10  Bubba Chandler  DH

OFP: 50   ETA: 2025

Born: 09/14/02   Age: 20   Bats: S   Throws: R   Height: 6'2"   Weight: 200 lb.   Origin: Round 3, 2021 Draft (#72 overall)

| YEAR | TEAM | LVL | AGE | PA | R | 2B | 3B | HR | RBI | BB | K | SB | CS | AVG/OBP/SLG | DRC+ | BABIP | BRR | DRP | WARP |
|---|---|---|---|---|---|---|---|---|---|---|---|---|---|---|---|---|---|---|---|
| 2021 | PIRB | ROK | 18 | 37 | 3 | 1 | 0 | 1 | 2 | 5 | 16 | 0 | 0 | .167/.324/.300 | | .308 | | | |
| 2022 | PIR | ROK | 19 | 36 | 8 | 0 | 1 | 3 | 9 | 9 | 6 | 1 | 0 | .231/.444/.654 | | .176 | | | |
| 2022 | BRD | A | 19 | 88 | 8 | 3 | 1 | 1 | 8 | 11 | 35 | 3 | 0 | .184/.284/.289 | 73 | .317 | -0.1 | P(8) -0.1 | 0.0 |
| 2023 non-DC | PIT | MLB | 20 | 251 | 18 | 10 | 2 | 3 | 20 | 18 | 128 | | | .187/.251/.285 | 40 | .403 | | 1B 0, SS 0 | -1.3 |

Comparables: Mike McDade, Nellie Rodriguez, Chris Carter

**The Report:** Chandler split time as a two-way player in Bradenton, but at this point, his future clearly lies on the mound. At the plate, he has a noisy swing and is looking to launch, and while he can do damage on contact, his contact rates were so poor in A-ball that it's tough to see a way up the ladder as a hitter. Fortunately he's quite the prospect on the mound, working off a mid-90s fastball that can bump close to 100. He can overthrow the fastball at times and shows below-average control/command of the pitch more generally. Chandler has a full suite of three offspeeds, with slurvyish slider in the mid-80s showing the most present utility. He offers a shorter curve and a firm change with some two-seam action, but both those pitches will flash better than those rather-brusque descriptions. There's a fair bit to clean up on the mound for sure—Chandler has late-arm effort that causes issues finding his release point—but it's not hard to predict some gains as a pitcher as soon as that's his sole focus.

**OFP:** 50 / no. 4 starter

**Variance:** High. The two-way player work has cost him some development reps, and the secondaries require a fair bit of projection right now.

**Jesse Roche's Fantasy Take:** Chandler has special arm talent with a four-seam fastball that flashes elite, bat-missing carry. (It generated 40% whiffs in Low-A.) He has true breakout potential should the two-way experiment end and he improves his command and consistency with a focus on his work on the mound.

## Outside the Top Ten:

## 11  Thomas Harrington  RHP

Born: 07/12/01   Age: 21   Bats: R   Throws: R   Height: 6'2"   Weight: 185 lb.   Origin: Round 1, 2022 Draft (#36 overall)

A Comp Round Pick in last year's draft, Harrington found success at Campbell pounding the bottom of the zone with three major-league quality offerings. His low-90s fastball has some run from a three-quarters slot, and he has a potentially solid slider and change as well. There may not be a true consistent swing-and-miss pitch yet, but Harrington fits well into what the Pirates look for in pitchers, and he is an advanced strike-thrower with some physical projection remaining as well.

## 12  Jared Jones  RHP

Born: 08/06/01   Age: 21   Bats: L   Throws: R   Height: 6'1"   Weight: 180 lb.   Origin: Round 2, 2020 Draft (#44 overall)

| YEAR | TEAM | LVL | AGE | W | L | SV | G | GS | IP | H | HR | BB/9 | K/9 | K | GB% | BABIP | WHIP | ERA | DRA- | WARP |
|---|---|---|---|---|---|---|---|---|---|---|---|---|---|---|---|---|---|---|---|---|
| 2021 | BRD | A | 19 | 3 | 6 | 0 | 18 | 15 | 66 | 63 | 6 | 4.6 | 14.0 | 103 | 45.5% | .385 | 1.47 | 4.64 | 79 | 1.5 |
| 2022 | GBO | A+ | 20 | 5 | 7 | 0 | 26 | 26 | 122² | 115 | 19 | 3.7 | 10.4 | 142 | 38.9% | .310 | 1.35 | 4.62 | 94 | 1.3 |
| 2023 non-DC | PIT | MLB | 21 | 3 | 3 | 0 | 58 | 0 | 50 | 54 | 9 | 4.6 | 8.2 | 46 | 35.1% | .314 | 1.59 | 5.60 | 139 | -0.7 |

Comparables: Zach Davies, Robert Stephenson, Scott Blewett

Pittsburgh's second-round pick in 2020, Jones is an interesting enough talent that he would have made the top 10 in some weaker systems. Generally speaking however, the bad outweighed the good in 2022. A smallish 6-foot-1, Jones has a fast arm and generates a lot of ride with his mechanics. The fastball is excellent, maintaining 96-98 mph for innings at a time with great life and carry. Predictably, it plays well when located up in the zone. The issues here are with command and breaking stuff. The delivery has some effort to it and Jones will miss his spots at times, and when he misses his spots, he typically gets hit. He'll occasionally get hitters on the mid-80s slider due to change of speed, but it seldom shows a lot of oomph either vertically or horizontally. It's hard to make a starter projection at the moment, but he's just turned 21 and you don't give up on fastballs like this.

## 13   Anthony Solometo   LHP

Born: 12/02/02   Age: 20   Bats: L   Throws: L   Height: 6'5"   Weight: 220 lb.   Origin: Round 2, 2021 Draft (#37 overall)

| YEAR | TEAM | LVL | AGE | W | L | SV | G | GS | IP | H | HR | BB/9 | K/9 | K | GB% | BABIP | WHIP | ERA | DRA- | WARP |
|---|---|---|---|---|---|---|---|---|---|---|---|---|---|---|---|---|---|---|---|---|
| 2022 | BRD | A | 19 | 5 | 1 | 0 | 13 | 8 | 47² | 31 | 0 | 3.6 | 9.6 | 51 | 51.8% | .272 | 1.05 | 2.64 | 87 | 1.1 |
| 2023 non-DC | PIT | MLB | 20 | 3 | 3 | 0 | 58 | 0 | 50 | 54 | 7 | 4.7 | 7.6 | 42 | 36.8% | .311 | 1.60 | 5.35 | 133 | -0.6 |

Comparables: DL Hall, Robbie Ray, Stephen Gonsalves

Another piece of the Pirates' loaded 2021 draft class, Solometo dealt with a lat issue in 2022 and was limited to just 47 innings in Bradenton. They were very effective innings though, as his funky crossfire delivery was tough for Florida State League hitters to pick up, and his low-80s slider would get under their bats. His low-90s sinker has good vertical action, but he has limited command of it as present, and he would bleed some of that velocity later in outings. Solometo's changeup will flash at times, but it's a work in progress. The overall profile hasn't changed a ton since the draft, which in this case is a small net negative, but he still is a solid enough fourth starter prospect with some upside past that.

## 14   Lonnie White Jr.   OF

Born: 12/31/02   Age: 20   Bats: R   Throws: R   Height: 6'3"   Weight: 212 lb.   Origin: Round 2, 2021 Draft (#64 overall)

| YEAR | TEAM | LVL | AGE | PA | R | 2B | 3B | HR | RBI | BB | K | SB | CS | AVG/OBP/SLG | DRC+ | BABIP | BRR | DRP | WARP |
|---|---|---|---|---|---|---|---|---|---|---|---|---|---|---|---|---|---|---|---|
| 2021 | PIRB | ROK | 18 | 33 | 6 | 2 | 0 | 2 | 5 | 2 | 14 | 0 | 0 | .258/.303/.516 | | .400 | | | |

Another 2021 pick out of a Philly area prep school, White played just two games in 2022 before being sidelined by UCL and hamstring issues. He's a potential impact power bat, likely to end up in a corner in the long term. The questions about how his long and leveraged swing will play in the pros remain unanswered, and the most important thing for him will be to answer some of those during a healthy 2023 campaign.

## 15   Blake Sabol   C

Born: 01/07/98   Age: 25   Bats: L   Throws: R   Height: 6'4"   Weight: 225 lb.   Origin: Round 7, 2019 Draft (#214 overall)

| YEAR | TEAM | LVL | AGE | PA | R | 2B | 3B | HR | RBI | BB | K | SB | CS | AVG/OBP/SLG | DRC+ | BABIP | BRR | DRP | WARP |
|---|---|---|---|---|---|---|---|---|---|---|---|---|---|---|---|---|---|---|---|
| 2021 | BRD | A | 23 | 59 | 11 | 2 | 0 | 2 | 12 | 12 | 12 | 0 | 2 | .370/.508/.543 | 124 | .469 | 0.6 | C(3) -0.4, LF(3) -0.0, RF(1) -0.1 | 0.4 |
| 2021 | GBO | A+ | 23 | 229 | 39 | 12 | 3 | 11 | 33 | 27 | 72 | 6 | 0 | .296/.380/.553 | 104 | .407 | 0.1 | C(25) 1.8, LF(9) 1.3 | 1.1 |
| 2022 | ALT | AA | 24 | 412 | 61 | 23 | 5 | 14 | 60 | 38 | 107 | 9 | 2 | .281/.347/.486 | 102 | .355 | -0.3 | C(58) 2.7, LF(9) -0.1, RF(1) -0.0 | 1.5 |
| 2022 | IND | AAA | 24 | 101 | 13 | 3 | 1 | 5 | 15 | 17 | 22 | 1 | 0 | .296/.426/.543 | 118 | .345 | -0.7 | LF(12) -1.1, C(8) -0.6 | 0.3 |
| 2023 DC | SF | MLB | 25 | 127 | 13 | 6 | 2 | 2 | 13 | 11 | 37 | 1 | 1 | .238/.310/.371 | 91 | .333 | 0.0 | C 0 | 0.3 |

Sabol, a former seventh-rounder, began to pop onto radars last season as a somewhat overaged High-A guy with a neat lefty swing who could handle some catcher and some outfield. He's taken another step forward this season as a 24-year-old at Double- and Triple-A, putting up a very solid batting line and grading out fairly well behind the plate. He strikes out a bit but carries a healthy walk rate, and he's a big dude for whom the power increase should be sustainable. Sabol has an interesting collage of traits, and could turn out to be well worth a roster spot if he can get his barrel on enough pitches for his pop and versatility to play.

## 16   Dariel Lopez   IF

Born: 02/07/02   Age: 21   Bats: R   Throws: R   Height: 6'1"   Weight: 183 lb.   Origin: International Free Agent, 2018

| YEAR | TEAM | LVL | AGE | PA | R | 2B | 3B | HR | RBI | BB | K | SB | CS | AVG/OBP/SLG | DRC+ | BABIP | BRR | DRP | WARP |
|---|---|---|---|---|---|---|---|---|---|---|---|---|---|---|---|---|---|---|---|
| 2021 | BRD | A | 19 | 416 | 52 | 17 | 1 | 10 | 64 | 41 | 103 | 1 | 2 | .258/.341/.393 | 99 | .327 | -0.5 | 3B(45) -1.2, SS(35) -3.5, 2B(9) -0.6 | 0.6 |
| 2022 | GBO | A+ | 20 | 420 | 58 | 15 | 1 | 19 | 58 | 21 | 107 | 6 | 4 | .286/.329/.476 | 102 | .348 | -3.6 | 3B(55) -0.6, SS(25) -0.4, 2B(18) -0.1 | 0.8 |
| 2023 non-DC | PIT | MLB | 21 | 251 | 21 | 10 | 1 | 4 | 23 | 13 | 69 | 1 | 1 | .228/.274/.335 | 72 | .304 | -3.8 | 2B 0, 3B 0 | -0.5 |

This year's Pirates sleeper put together a very nice line at a very nice park for hitters—the power numbers in particular got a nice pop at the Greensboro confines—but it's a quick swing with loft and he can handle a high fastball. Good breaking stuff down gives him a bit more trouble and that will be something to watch Double-A, in addition to the park factor. Defensive versatility is an asset for Lopez—primarily a third baseman with a good glove and plus arm, he is also proficient at second and short. He'll have to adjust to Altoona if he's going to really break through, but if he's able to do it at age 21, we'll have a legitimate prospect here.

## 17 Tsung-Che Cheng  SS

Born: 07/26/01  Age: 21  Bats: L  Throws: R  Height: 5'7"  Weight: 154 lb.  Origin: International Free Agent, 2019

| YEAR | TEAM | LVL | AGE | PA | R | 2B | 3B | HR | RBI | BB | K | SB | CS | AVG/OBP/SLG | DRC+ | BABIP | BRR | DRP | WARP |
|------|------|-----|-----|-----|----|----|----|----|-----|----|----|----|----|-------------|------|-------|-----|-----|------|
| 2021 | PIRG | ROK | 19 | 157 | 32 | 8 | 1 | 4 | 31 | 30 | 14 | 16 | 6 | .311/.449/.492 | | .321 | | | |
| 2022 | CAR | WIN | 20 | 74 | 4 | 2 | 1 | 0 | 4 | 7 | 12 | 2 | 1 | .182/.270/.242 | | .222 | | | |
| 2022 | BRD | A | 20 | 458 | 79 | 25 | 7 | 6 | 52 | 63 | 95 | 33 | 6 | .270/.376/.418 | 120 | .340 | 2.0 | SS(84) 2.6, 2B(13) 0.9 | 2.8 |
| 2023 non-DC | PIT | MLB | 21 | 251 | 20 | 11 | 3 | 2 | 20 | 21 | 63 | 9 | 3 | .218/.291/.313 | 72 | .293 | 0.2 | 2B 0, 3B 0 | 0.0 |

Signed for $380,000 out of Taiwan, the 20-year-old Cheng had a strong full-season debut in 2022, displaying advanced baseball skills on both offense and defense. He's an aggressive hitter who stays back well on offspeed and makes a lot of contact—even on pitches he maybe shouldn't be swinging at. It's not always high-quality contact, although he has a little sneaky pop, and his ability to use the whole field is an asset. Defensively, he's played mostly shortstop and he's shown the first step, range and body control for the premium spot on the infield, but I suspect his arm will be a better fit at second, as he has a bit of a long trigger, a sidearm slot and only average arm strength. He's a high-probability major leaguer for a player in A-ball, but he will need to do a little more damage with the bat to project past a nice bench infielder.

## 18 Matt Gorski  CF

Born: 12/22/97  Age: 25  Bats: R  Throws: R  Height: 6'4"  Weight: 198 lb.  Origin: Round 2, 2019 Draft (#57 overall)

| YEAR | TEAM | LVL | AGE | PA | R | 2B | 3B | HR | RBI | BB | K | SB | CS | AVG/OBP/SLG | DRC+ | BABIP | BRR | DRP | WARP |
|------|------|-----|-----|-----|----|----|----|----|-----|----|----|----|----|-------------|------|-------|-----|-----|------|
| 2021 | GBO | A+ | 23 | 401 | 62 | 18 | 0 | 17 | 56 | 34 | 125 | 18 | 1 | .223/.294/.416 | 85 | .285 | 2.2 | CF(48) 4.8, RF(38) 6.7, 1B(3) -0.3 | 1.8 |
| 2022 | GBO | A+ | 24 | 146 | 34 | 3 | 2 | 17 | 37 | 17 | 39 | 9 | 1 | .294/.377/.754 | 153 | .278 | 3.4 | CF(25) 0.1, 1B(6) 0.5, RF(1) 0.1 | 2.0 |
| 2022 | ALT | AA | 24 | 159 | 27 | 8 | 2 | 6 | 28 | 15 | 47 | 10 | 2 | .277/.354/.489 | 100 | .375 | 0.7 | CF(16) 1.1, RF(10) -0.3, 1B(6) -0.2 | 0.7 |
| 2023 non-DC | PIT | MLB | 25 | 251 | 23 | 10 | 1 | 6 | 26 | 17 | 88 | 7 | 2 | .216/.278/.352 | 78 | .318 | -1.0 | 1B 0, LF 0 | 0.0 |

*Comparables: Brian Barton, Skye Bolt, Denis Phipps*

Gorski's power is for real—anybody who has ever seen him play live could tell you that. He's also a very good athlete who runs well and handles center field. Prior to 2022, none of that had any import thanks to the former second-rounder's debilitating swing-and-miss issues. He still strikes out quite a bit, it must be said, and the torrid homer streak that earned him his promotion to Double-A took place after his 24th birthday. Nevertheless, this is a guy who hit 24 homers in fewer than 300 plate appearances across two levels *and* has some positional utility. He's worth at least a mental note if he can bounce back from the quad injury that shortened his season.

## 19 Cody Bolton  RHP

Born: 06/19/98  Age: 25  Bats: R  Throws: R  Height: 6'3"  Weight: 230 lb.  Origin: Round 6, 2017 Draft (#178 overall)

| YEAR | TEAM | LVL | AGE | W | L | SV | G | GS | IP | H | HR | BB/9 | K/9 | K | GB% | BABIP | WHIP | ERA | DRA- | WARP |
|------|------|-----|-----|---|---|----|----|----|-----|----|----|------|-----|----|------|-------|------|------|------|------|
| 2022 | IND | AAA | 24 | 4 | 2 | 0 | 30 | 14 | 75² | 57 | 4 | 4.8 | 9.8 | 82 | 39.8% | .276 | 1.28 | 3.09 | 83 | 1.7 |
| 2023 non-DC | PIT | MLB | 25 | 3 | 3 | 0 | 58 | 0 | 50 | 48 | 6 | 4.3 | 8.3 | 46 | 36.4% | .293 | 1.43 | 4.29 | 111 | 0.0 |

After missing all of 2021 with a meniscus tear, the Pirates gave Bolton a rather unusual workload last season. He alternated longer rest periods with coming back on two or three days' rest to throw multiple innings, mostly out of the pen. All told, that led to 30 appearances, but only 75 innings. The stuff played well as a one-time-through pitcher. His slider still looked very sharp, and is a plus swing-and-miss offering at its best, with wicked two-plane break. His fastball velocity is a tick above average, but plays more in an average range due to command issues and a less-than-ideal shape. But that slide piece is good enough that Bolton should be able to help in the Pirates pen on Opening Day, if they are so inclined.

# 20 Carlos Jimenez  RHP

Born: 07/14/02   Age: 20   Bats: R   Throws: R   Height: 6'2"   Weight: 140 lb.   Origin: International Free Agent, 2018

| YEAR | TEAM | LVL | AGE | W | L | SV | G | GS | IP | H | HR | BB/9 | K/9 | K | GB% | BABIP | WHIP | ERA | DRA- | WARP |
|------|------|-----|-----|---|---|----|----|----|-----|-----|-----|------|-----|-----|------|-------|------|------|------|------|
| 2021 | PIRB | ROK | 18 | 3 | 2 | 0 | 10 | 8 | 34¹ | 25 | 2 | 3.9 | 11.5 | 44 | 46.2% | .288 | 1.17 | 3.15 | | |
| 2022 | BRD | A | 19 | 1 | 7 | 0 | 19 | 15 | 69² | 60 | 7 | 5.8 | 11.4 | 88 | 43.5% | .325 | 1.51 | 4.13 | 79 | 1.8 |
| 2023 non-DC | PIT | MLB | 20 | 3 | 3 | 0 | 58 | 0 | 50 | 53 | 9 | 5.9 | 8.4 | 46 | 35.9% | .306 | 1.71 | 5.95 | 145 | -0.9 |

Signed out of Venezuela as part of Pittsburgh's 2018 IFA class, Jimenez is an intriguing arm that—like a lot of Pirates pitching prospects—needs a command jump and fastball shape tweak. He sits in the mid-90s, but that dips into a more average velo band quickly, and the heater finds enough plate that even A-ball hitters could square it a bit too often. Both the secondaries are projectable though. Although Jimenez's 11-5 curve shows some interesting characteristics, the command of that offering isn't there yet either. His power change can flash good circle action, though he doesn't consistently pull the string on it. There's a wide range of future outcomes in play here, but you'd have hoped the present performance would have been a bit better given the stuff.

# Top Talents 25 and Under (as of 4/1/2023):

1. Oneil Cruz, SS
2. Termarr Johnson, 2B
3. Roansy Contreras
4. Henry Davis, C
5. Endy Rodriguez, C/UT
6. Quinn Priester, RHP
7. Liover Peguero, SS
8. Jack Suwinski, OF
9. Nick Gonzales, 2B
10. Rodolfo Castro, IF

The Buccos are born to be alive, specifically born around the turn of the new millennium. Prior to adding a few veterans in the offseason (including old friend Andrew McCutchen), they only had one player slated to reach age-30 by April of 2023: righty reliever Robert Stephenson. Their youth movement hinges on Cruz and Ke'Bryan Hayes (26 next year) joining Bryan Reynolds (28) in stardom. For Cruz, that seems easy to envision, though not quite guaranteed. Strikeouts still dog the towering wunderkind, but his azimuth laser rifle of an arm and titanic power are otherworldly delights for Pittsburgh to dream on and for the rest of the league to marvel upon his highlights. The most impressive young pitcher to debut in 2022 for Pittsburgh was Contreras, who sat in the upper-90s while mustering a respectable 106 DRA- as a 22-year-old. He has a gorgeous near-vertical dropping low-80s slider to pair with his heat that already looks like a plus pitch, though he'll need more distinction between it and his curveball to show he can stick in the rotation impactfully.

A few role players also emerged for the Pirates in an otherwise dark-as-expected 2022. Suwinski put up a 101 DRC+ and solid defensive numbers despite showing the expected need to be platooned for best results, while outfielder Cal Mitchell (just outside the top 10), well, had a more forgettable debut but made contact at a healthy clip and looking forward, should be able to get into his power as well. Castro will have a role on the 2023 club due to optionality and positional versatility, but Castro's manifestation of his pop was a pleasant surprise from a player whose contact profile seemed to be tenuous at times.

Pittsburgh's pitching staff also includes a bevy of young arms with a spark of intrigue but plenty of limitations, notably right-handers Johan Oviedo and Max Kranick. For Oviedo, pitching up into a rotation role will be the key, as he worked mid-to-upper 90s with his heater in between the bullpen and rotation this year after a shaky first couple seasons in St. Louis. Kranick will be rehabbing Tommy John surgery all of 2023, but, well, there will be innings to go around once again, it seems.

# San Diego Padres

## The State of the System:

Juan Soto is hitting third for the Padres. Remember that before you proceed.

## The Top Ten:

### 1 Jackson Merrill SS    OFP: 70    ETA: 2025

Born: 04/19/03   Age: 20   Bats: L   Throws: R   Height: 6'3"   Weight: 195 lb.   Origin: Round 1, 2021 Draft (#27 overall)

| YEAR | TEAM | LVL | AGE | PA | R | 2B | 3B | HR | RBI | BB | K | SB | CS | AVG/OBP/SLG | DRC+ | BABIP | BRR | DRP | WARP |
|------|------|-----|-----|-----|----|----|----|----|-----|----|----|----|----|--------------|------|-------|------|----------|------|
| 2021 | PAD | ROK | 18 | 120 | 19 | 7 | 2 | 0 | 10 | 10 | 27 | 5 | 1 | .280/.339/.383 | | .370 | | | |
| 2022 | PAD | ROK | 19 | 31 | 5 | 3 | 1 | 1 | 6 | 1 | 2 | 3 | 0 | .433/.452/.700 | | .444 | | | |
| 2022 | LE | A | 19 | 219 | 33 | 10 | 3 | 5 | 34 | 19 | 42 | 8 | 5 | .325/.387/.482 | 111 | .393 | 1.4 | SS(42) -1.3 | 0.9 |
| 2023 non-DC | SD | MLB | 20 | 251 | 19 | 10 | 2 | 2 | 20 | 15 | 50 | 4 | 2 | .217/.269/.310 | 62 | .265 | -1.9 | SS 0 | -0.5 |

Comparables: *Hanser Alberto, Royce Lewis, Alen Hanson*

**The Report:** Merrill was the biggest pre-draft pop-up prospect in 2021, going from unknown to most scouts to a late-first round pick in the span of a few months. So far, the Padres can feel good about gambling on his short track record. After holding his own at the complex last year, Merrill excelled as one of the youngest players in the California League. While a fractured wrist and hamstring injury limited him to 45 games, Merrill showed an advanced approach, excellent bat-to-ball skills, a knack for hard contact and all the fundamentals to stick at shortstop down the line.

Merrill's lanky frame has above-average power potential that should come as he learns to lift the ball with time, and given his advanced hit tool, he has a decent chance to hit .300 with 20+ homers if it all comes together. Even if his hit tool plateaus as he develops, he could still have an above-average offensive peak, and if he grows off shortstop he should excel at third base. Merrill is now one of the top handful of prospects in the game—and he doesn't turn 20 until April.

**OFP:** 70 / Star shortstop

**Variance:** High. He still hasn't played a lot and his current extremely groundball-heavy profile is a concern, but he has extremely high upside given his fast gains.

**Jesse Roche's Fantasy Take:** For a time, Merrill had a *contact* rate (not just zone-contact rate) around 90%! At the same time, he posted quality of contact metrics at or above MLB average (though, with a 59.6% ground-ball rate in Low-A). And, as noted above, the cement hasn't dried on his frame. Merrill is a fast-rising, top-50 dynasty prospect with substantial offensive upside—.300 with 20+ homers—and even some speed.

### 2 Samuel Zavala OF    OFP: 55    ETA: 2026

Born: 07/15/04   Age: 18   Bats: L   Throws: L   Height: 6'1"   Weight: 175 lb.   Origin: International Free Agent, 2021

| YEAR | TEAM | LVL | AGE | PA | R | 2B | 3B | HR | RBI | BB | K | SB | CS | AVG/OBP/SLG | DRC+ | BABIP | BRR | DRP | WARP |
|------|------|-----|-----|-----|----|----|----|----|-----|----|----|----|----|--------------|------|-------|------|----------------------|------|
| 2021 | DSL PAD | ROK | 16 | 235 | 44 | 16 | 6 | 3 | 40 | 32 | 36 | 11 | 7 | .297/.400/.487 | | .344 | | | |
| 2022 | PAD | ROK | 17 | 35 | 6 | 3 | 1 | 1 | 6 | 4 | 11 | 0 | 0 | .345/.412/.621 | | .500 | | | |
| 2022 | LE | A | 17 | 141 | 24 | 6 | 2 | 7 | 26 | 19 | 37 | 5 | 3 | .254/.355/.508 | 110 | .308 | -1.8 | CF(20) -0.2, RF(12) -0.6 | 0.2 |
| 2023 non-DC | SD | MLB | 18 | 251 | 20 | 10 | 2 | 3 | 21 | 18 | 81 | 5 | 3 | .209/.271/.312 | 64 | .308 | -1.2 | CF 0, RF 0 | -0.4 |

Comparables: *Fernando Martinez, Angel Villalona, Jose Tabata*

**The Report:** Zavala has proven to be one of the most pro-ready players from the 2020-21 international free agent class. He starred at the DSL in 2021 and continued putting up impressive numbers in the Complex League and in a late-season stint at Low-A. He's also nearly a year younger than the youngest player selected in the 2022 MLB Draft.

Zavala has an incredible feel for hitting at his age, never looking overmatched or out of place in his brief moments against full-season competition. He has a high leg kick that might need to be tamped down as he faces more advanced offspeed pitches, but he has a special ability to barrel up the ball. There's some hope he could develop league-average power, but his 6-foot-1 frame is closer to maxed out than the average prospect at his age. Still, Zavala is on a trajectory towards a plus-or-better hit tool.

He is not a standout athlete, but Zavala may be able to maintain enough of his range to stick in center field long-term. Either way, his bat, which hasn't even shown platoon splits yet, should be able to carry him to an everyday spot in a corner as well.

**OFP:** 55 / Starting outfielder

**Variance:** Extreme. Zavala was born in 2004 and has already held his own in full-season ball.

**Jesse Roche's Fantasy Take:** Over his final four weeks in Low-A, having just turned 18, Zavala hit .277/.368/.590 with six home runs in 22 games. Even with the caveat that late-season Low-A pitching is substandard, his performance was still impressive. While his power and speed may fall short of plus, his "trajectory towards a plus-or-better hit tool" and early returns are incredibly promising and bode well for his fantasy upside. Zavala is a top-200 dynasty prospect.

## 3 Dylan Lesko  RHP      OFP: 55      ETA: 2026

Born: 09/07/03   Age: 19   Bats: R   Throws: R   Height: 6'2"   Weight: 195 lb.   Origin: Round 1, 2022 Draft (#15 overall)

**The Report:** When you trade away nearly every top prospect in an already thin system, a high-variance first-round pick is going to rank a lot higher than you'd probably like. Lesko had been the consensus top prep pitching prospect in the 2022 MLB Draft for a long time. However, last spring, while he was making a case to be a top-five pick, he injured his elbow and underwent Tommy John surgery. With the 15th pick in the draft, the Padres were willing to gamble on Lesko's upside, signing him away from a Vanderbilt commitment.

When healthy, Lesko has showcased a mid-90s fastball with good carry at the top of the zone, one of the best changeups you'll see from a teenager and a true 12-6 curveball that has generated more than 3,000 rpm. The curveball was a new development in 2022, and will need the most work in his arsenal, but it has the potential to give him three plus pitches. Lesko has never struggled to throw strikes since popping up on scouts' radar, leaving some scouts optimistic that he could develop plus command as well.

It's easy to fall in love with a prospect you can write all that about, but it's also easier to talk about that potential when it has yet to be put to the test against college or professional hitters. The Padres will obviously be cautious with Lesko's rehab this season, and it's not out of the question that he'll stay in the complex until 2024.

**OFP:** 55 / no. 3/4 starter

**Variance:** Extreme. He is a high school arm coming off Tommy John surgery who has yet to appear in a professional game.

**Jesse Roche's Fantasy Take:** Although Lesko is recovering from Tommy John surgery, and he will likely miss the first half of the 2023 season, he still ranks as the top fantasy pitching prospect in this draft class. As noted above, he has dreamy potential with proponents envisioning three plus-or-better pitches with modern, analytically-friendly traits and plus command. Indeed, Lesko *could* develop one of the best stuff-command mixes in the minors. Of course, right-handed prep pitchers coming off TJS are far from a safe dynasty play, but his top-of-the-rotation upside is worth the risk. Lesko is a borderline top-150 dynasty prospect.

## 4 Victor Lizarraga  RHP      OFP: 50      ETA: 2025

Born: 11/30/03   Age: 19   Bats: R   Throws: R   Height: 6'3"   Weight: 180 lb.   Origin: Undrafted Free Agent, 2020

| YEAR | TEAM | LVL | AGE | W | L | SV | G | GS | IP | H | HR | BB/9 | K/9 | K | GB% | BABIP | WHIP | ERA | DRA- | WARP |
|---|---|---|---|---|---|---|---|---|---|---|---|---|---|---|---|---|---|---|---|---|
| 2021 | PAD | ROK | 17 | 0 | 4 | 0 | 11 | 11 | 30 | 25 | 5 | 4.5 | 10.5 | 35 | 32.5% | .274 | 1.33 | 5.10 | | |
| 2022 | LE | A | 18 | 8 | 3 | 0 | 20 | 19 | 94¹ | 87 | 5 | 3.2 | 9.1 | 95 | 48.1% | .313 | 1.28 | 3.43 | 97 | 0.3 |
| 2023 non-DC | SD | MLB | 19 | 3 | 3 | 0 | 58 | 0 | 50 | 58 | 8 | 4.3 | 6.4 | 35 | 36.2% | .312 | 1.63 | 5.78 | 143 | -0.9 |

*Comparables: Dustin May, Michael Soroka, Noe Toribio*

**The Report:** Lizarraga relied on his advanced feel for pitching and an above-average changeup to carry him through the California League as an 18-year-old. The 6-foot-3 righty is expected to gain weight as he matures, which should give his low-90s fastball a boost, and he throws a curveball with average potential as well. If his fastball becomes a consistent mid-90s offering, Lizarraga would probably jump into top-100 prospect conversations. However, even if his fastball doesn't develop further, his advanced ability to locate his pitches and changeup could still be good enough to stick in the rotation

**OFP:** 50 / no. 4 starter

**Variance:** High. Lizarraga had a promising full-season debut at Low-A, but remains far from the majors and in need of a velo jump.

**Jesse Roche's Fantasy Take:** Despite his success in Low-A as one of the youngest starting pitchers, Lizarraga lacks the type of upside to chase (absent hoped-for velocity gains) for an arm still years away. He should be left for watch lists outside the deepest formats.

## 5 Eguy Rosario IF — OFP: 50 — ETA: Debuted in 2022
Born: 08/25/99   Age: 23   Bats: R   Throws: R   Height: 5'9"   Weight: 150 lb.   Origin: International Free Agent, 2015

| YEAR | TEAM | LVL | AGE | PA | R | 2B | 3B | HR | RBI | BB | K | SB | CS | AVG/OBP/SLG | DRC+ | BABIP | BRR | DRP | WARP |
|---|---|---|---|---|---|---|---|---|---|---|---|---|---|---|---|---|---|---|---|
| 2020 | MAR | WIN | 20 | 112 | 18 | 6 | 2 | 0 | 14 | 7 | 13 | 8 | 0 | .327/.393/.429 | | .368 | | | |
| 2021 | PEJ | WIN | 21 | 73 | 9 | 3 | 0 | 1 | 12 | 8 | 13 | 2 | 2 | .250/.342/.344 | | .300 | | | |
| 2021 | SA | AA | 21 | 481 | 65 | 31 | 3 | 12 | 61 | 49 | 109 | 30 | 14 | .281/.360/.455 | 110 | .349 | -4.6 | SS(69) -3.3, 2B(38) 4.2, 3B(7) 0.6 | 1.7 |
| 2022 | ELP | AAA | 22 | 564 | 98 | 34 | 4 | 22 | 81 | 59 | 109 | 21 | 8 | .288/.368/.508 | 111 | .325 | 0.8 | 2B(54) -1.6, SS(37) 0.0, 3B(35) 1.6 | 2.6 |
| 2022 | SD | MLB | 22 | 6 | 0 | 0 | 0 | 0 | 0 | 1 | 2 | 0 | 0 | .200/.333/.200 | 91 | .333 | 0.0 | SS(2) -0.5 | 0.0 |
| 2023 DC | SD | MLB | 23 | 98 | 11 | 4 | 1 | 2 | 10 | 8 | 23 | 4 | 1 | .223/.290/.343 | 81 | .279 | -0.5 | SS 0, 2B 0 | 0.0 |

*Comparables: Josh Vitters, Asdrúbal Cabrera, Cheslor Cuthbert*

**The Report:** The Padres have aggressively pushed Rosario since he debuted in 2016, and he's been an upper-minors standout since the canceled 2020 season. Rosario has capitalized on the hitter-friendly environments in the Texas League and Pacific Coast League to post career-best power numbers. Last season, Rosario hit well in his first taste of Triple-A; however, in short stints in the bigs, LIDOM and the Puerto Rican Winter League, Rosario's power has been non-existent.

Rosario has average power potential, but has an aggressive, contact-oriented approach that limits his ability to tap into it. Defensively, Rosario is a fringy shortstop but has the arm strength and range to be a viable everyday player at second or third base if he can shore up his fundamentals. Granted, while his bat appears on the verge of big-league readiness, Rosario committed 20 errors, 11 of which came in his 54 games at second base.

Beyond Rosario's potential versatility, his .330/.397/.561 line against southpaws over the past two minor-league seasons also raises his floor quite a bit. Given his youth and track record of performance, I think he has a decent shot to become a borderline everyday player.

**OFP:** 50 / Platoon infielder

**Variance:** Medium. He's a sure-fire utility infielder, but will need to show his power gains were more than just a creation of the PCL.

**Jesse Roche's Fantasy Take:** You'd think I'd be extolling Rosario's 20/20 season in Triple-A at just 22/23 years old. Yet, he may not have a single average offensive tool. As noted above, he'll flash solid pop, but he makes loads of weak contact due. It is a bizarre batted-ball profile, to be sure, with a huge disparity between his 90th-percentile and average exit velocities. Rosario is still young, and likely will initially feature as a utility option, but he has displayed enough power-speed potential to warrant being rostered in leagues up to 250 prospects.

## 6 Robby Snelling LHP — OFP: 50 — ETA: 2026
Born: 12/19/03   Age: 19   Bats: R   Throws: L   Height: 6'3"   Weight: 210 lb.   Origin: Round 1, 2022 Draft (#39 overall)

**The Report:** The Padres signed Snelling for an above-slot $3 million signing bonus to forego his two-sport commitment (he was a four-star football recruit) to LSU. Snelling's stock rose as his fastball began sitting in the 90s during his senior year in high school. The southpaw has always generated excellent spin on his curveball, a pitch he has also shown the ability to adjust its velocity.

Snelling's motion utilizes a high leg kick and short arm action that has scouts skeptical about its repeatability. The Padres will likely focus on cleaning up his arm action early in his pro career, and he did consistently pound the strike zone throughout his high school career. Snelling played with a changeup in high school, but it remains his least-developed offering.

**OFP:** 50 / Back-end starter or reliever

**Variance:** Extreme. Snelling is mostly a two-pitch prep prospect with a violent delivery and a short track record of improved velocity.

**Jesse Roche's Fantasy Take:** He may lack the projection and upside of other prep arms, but his athleticism and present stuff portend further improvement with pro instruction. Snelling is a top-300 dynasty prospect.

## 7 Joshua Mears OF    OFP: 45    ETA: 2025

Born: 02/21/01    Age: 22    Bats: R    Throws: R    Height: 6'3"    Weight: 230 lb.    Origin: Round 2, 2019 Draft (#48 overall)

| YEAR | TEAM | LVL | AGE | PA | R | 2B | 3B | HR | RBI | BB | K | SB | CS | AVG/OBP/SLG | DRC+ | BABIP | BRR | DRP | WARP |
|---|---|---|---|---|---|---|---|---|---|---|---|---|---|---|---|---|---|---|---|
| 2021 | LE | A | 20 | 291 | 45 | 10 | 4 | 17 | 48 | 36 | 114 | 10 | 5 | .244/.368/.529 | 105 | .375 | -1.2 | RF(35) 0.8, CF(16) -1.5, LF(7) 1.1 | 1.1 |
| 2022 | PAD | ROK | 21 | 66 | 10 | 6 | 1 | 3 | 10 | 8 | 26 | 2 | 0 | .268/.364/.571 |  | .429 |  |  |  |
| 2022 | FW | A+ | 21 | 207 | 29 | 11 | 0 | 14 | 34 | 16 | 90 | 1 | 1 | .223/.304/.511 | 93 | .333 | 0.6 | RF(25) -1.4, CF(19) 2.3 | 0.6 |
| 2022 | SA | AA | 21 | 94 | 9 | 2 | 0 | 5 | 15 | 10 | 45 | 1 | 0 | .169/.266/.373 | 60 | .273 | -0.1 | CF(24) 0.1 | -0.2 |
| 2023 non-DC | SD | MLB | 22 | 251 | 25 | 10 | 1 | 8 | 29 | 17 | 115 | 4 | 1 | .217/.281/.379 | 86 | .389 | -2.6 | LF 0, CF 0 | 0.0 |

*Comparables: Johan Mieses, Greg Golson, Sean Henry*

**The Report:** Mears has the biggest power potential in the farm system and, unsurprisingly, some of the largest swing-and-miss in the organization to go with it. Mears hit .223/.304/.511 with a 43.5% strikeout rate at High-A before he was promoted to Double-A and continued striking out nearly half the time with a .169/.266/.373 line. Mears will turn 22 in February, and his youth leaves some room to dream that he can overcome his abysmal contact rates. Defensively, San Diego is hopeful that Mears can handle some center field, but his large frame will probably force him to a corner.

**OFP:** 45 / Fourth outfielder

**Variance:** Extreme. Mears' power gives him a ton of potential, but there's not a great track record for prospects with a 45% strikeout rate.

**Jesse Roche's Fantasy Take:** Is there such a thing as a two-true-outcomes player? Mears struck out or homered in 51.2% of plate appearances. It is difficult to imagine him developing into a MLB-caliber player with a sub-60% contact rate in High-A at 21 years old. The power is fun, though. Mears is, at most, a watch list option in deep leagues.

## 8 Jay Groome LHP    OFP: 45    ETA: 2023

Born: 08/23/98    Age: 24    Bats: L    Throws: L    Height: 6'6"    Weight: 262 lb.    Origin: Round 1, 2016 Draft (#12 overall)

| YEAR | TEAM | LVL | AGE | W | L | SV | G | GS | IP | H | HR | BB/9 | K/9 | K | GB% | BABIP | WHIP | ERA | DRA- | WARP |
|---|---|---|---|---|---|---|---|---|---|---|---|---|---|---|---|---|---|---|---|---|
| 2021 | GVL | A+ | 22 | 3 | 8 | 0 | 18 | 18 | 81² | 76 | 12 | 3.5 | 11.9 | 108 | 47.6% | .330 | 1.32 | 5.29 | 87 | 1.2 |
| 2021 | POR | AA | 22 | 2 | 0 | 0 | 3 | 3 | 15² | 12 | 0 | 2.3 | 14.9 | 26 | 27.3% | .375 | 1.02 | 2.30 | 87 | 0.2 |
| 2022 | POR | AA | 23 | 3 | 4 | 0 | 16 | 14 | 76² | 58 | 11 | 4.5 | 9.5 | 81 | 45.0% | .250 | 1.25 | 3.52 | 99 | 1.0 |
| 2022 | WOR | AAA | 23 | 1 | 1 | 0 | 3 | 3 | 16 | 17 | 2 | 3.9 | 8.4 | 15 | 35.4% | .326 | 1.50 | 3.94 | 99 | 0.2 |
| 2022 | ELP | AAA | 23 | 3 | 2 | 0 | 10 | 10 | 51¹ | 52 | 4 | 3.3 | 7.7 | 44 | 38.2% | .324 | 1.38 | 3.16 | 106 | 0.1 |
| 2023 DC | SD | MLB | 24 | 2 | 2 | 0 | 6 | 6 | 29 | 30 | 4 | 4.2 | 8.0 | 26 | 37.6% | .307 | 1.51 | 4.84 | 123 | -0.1 |

*Comparables: Yohander Méndez, TJ House, Luis Leroy Cruz*

**The Report:** A former first-round pick by the Red Sox, Groome has morphed from a high-upside prep prospect into a pitchability lefty without a clear carrying pitch. Groome's fastball sits in the low-90s, but he locates it well and uses different grips to try and induce soft contact. As for his secondary offerings, Groome's curveball has lost the sharpness it showed in his amateur days and joins a trio of 45/50 grade pitches (curveball, slider and changeup). Groome has had issues working deeper into games, but has the pitch mix and command to be a viable back-end starter. However, he seems best suited for a swingman role where he tosses 80-100 innings per year.

**OFP:** 45 / Swingman

**Variance:** Medium. Groome looks like a big-league ready bullpen piece, but he'll need to improve his ability to maintain his stuff to stick in the rotation.

**Jesse Roche's Fantasy Take:** To be honest, I'm shocked that Groome left the PCL unscathed. As noted above, he may not have a plus, let alone above-average, pitch in his arsenal. His once-lauded curve had just 4.5% usage in Triple-A. None of his pitches miss many bats or possess unique traits. Groome shouldn't be rostered in most dynasty formats.

## 9 Adam Mazur RHP    OFP: 45    ETA: 2026

Born: 04/20/01    Age: 22    Bats: R    Throws: R    Height: 6'2"    Weight: 180 lb.    Origin: Round 2, 2022 Draft (#53 overall)

**The Report:** After recording ERAs north of 5.00 in two seasons at South Dakota State, Mazur transferred to Iowa and began maximizing his physical projection just in time to become a top-rounds prospect. The Padres selected Mazur towards the end of the second round, and he has already added weight and velocity. Mazur's fastball sits in the mid-90s and pairs with a high-80s slider that has plus potential. He also has a changeup and 12-6 curveball that have flashed average potential, although he's never had to rely on them much before. Mazur has taken massive steps forward in his development over the past few years, and if that continues, he could turn into the next Padres steal. However, it's important to maintain some skepticism until he shows his development gains against professional competition.

**OFP:** 45 / Swingman

**Variance:** Extreme. Mazur had a 5.43 ERA at South Dakota State in 2021. He's also had incredible helium since.

**Jesse Roche's Fantasy Take:** Mazur's late-bloomer profile coupled with velocity gains makes him an intriguing late-round option in deep first-year player drafts. That said, he should only be rostered in leagues with over 400 prospects.

## 10 Nerwilian Cedeno 2B  OFP: 45  ETA: 2026
Born: 03/16/02  Age: 21  Bats: S  Throws: R  Height: 5'11"  Weight: 175 lb.  Origin: International Free Agent, 2018

| YEAR | TEAM | LVL | AGE | PA | R | 2B | 3B | HR | RBI | BB | K | SB | CS | AVG/OBP/SLG | DRC+ | BABIP | BRR | DRP | WARP |
|---|---|---|---|---|---|---|---|---|---|---|---|---|---|---|---|---|---|---|---|
| 2021 | PAD | ROK | 19 | 66 | 8 | 8 | 1 | 2 | 7 | 9 | 20 | 2 | 0 | .241/.354/.537 | | .333 | | | |
| 2022 | LE | A | 20 | 318 | 60 | 13 | 4 | 6 | 54 | 42 | 79 | 18 | 8 | .256/.362/.400 | 95 | .337 | 1.3 | 2B(59) -1.9, 1B(11) -0.0 | 0.7 |
| 2023 non-DC | SD | MLB | 21 | 251 | 20 | 10 | 2 | 3 | 21 | 20 | 79 | 5 | 2 | .219/.287/.318 | 72 | .323 | -1.7 | 1B 0, 2B 0 | -0.3 |

**The Report:** Cedeno held his own at Low-A, in his first full-season action, hitting .256/.362/.400 with a 13.2% walk-rate. Set to turn 21 in March, Cedeno is a switch-hitter with an advanced approach at the plate. His left-handed swing is further along in its development, but both swings are a bit stiff and have a tendency to get long. Cedeno is an average athlete with good defensive instincts, but probably will never be a viable shortstop. Some scouts believe he could develop 15-20 homer power, and that will probably have to happen for him to become an everyday player. However, despite his limited track record, he already has a good shot to find his way to the majors as a bench bat.

**OFP:** 45 / Bench infielder

**Variance:** High. Cedeno's path to the big leagues got a lot smaller once he stopped playing shortstop, but he's an advanced hitter with borderline everyday upside.

**Jesse Roche's Fantasy Take:** Cedeno carries some intrigue, with a disciplined approach and a bit of pop and a bit of speed, yet he lacks a standout tool. The juice (fantasy upside) is not worth the squeeze (lead time).

## Outside the Top Ten:

## 11 Jairo Iriarte RHP
Born: 12/15/01  Age: 21  Bats: R  Throws: R  Height: 6'2"  Weight: 160 lb.  Origin: International Free Agent, 2018

| YEAR | TEAM | LVL | AGE | W | L | SV | G | GS | IP | H | HR | BB/9 | K/9 | K | GB% | BABIP | WHIP | ERA | DRA- | WARP |
|---|---|---|---|---|---|---|---|---|---|---|---|---|---|---|---|---|---|---|---|---|
| 2021 | PAD | ROK | 19 | 0 | 1 | 0 | 8 | 3 | 21 | 18 | 1 | 3.0 | 10.7 | 25 | 51.9% | .333 | 1.19 | 4.71 | | |
| 2021 | LE | A | 19 | 0 | 4 | 0 | 4 | 3 | 9 | 25 | 5 | 6.0 | 9.0 | 9 | 31.0% | .541 | 3.44 | 27.00 | 145 | -0.2 |
| 2022 | LE | A | 20 | 4 | 7 | 0 | 21 | 18 | 91¹ | 83 | 13 | 4.1 | 10.7 | 109 | 39.2% | .304 | 1.37 | 5.12 | 96 | 0.4 |
| 2023 non-DC | SD | MLB | 21 | 3 | 3 | 0 | 58 | 0 | 50 | 55 | 9 | 4.7 | 7.7 | 43 | 34.6% | .308 | 1.62 | 5.83 | 144 | -0.9 |

*Comparables: Roman Mendez, Orlando Castro, Enmanuel De Jesus*

Iriarte has grown into his 6-foot-5, 200-pound frame since turning pro and has subsequently seen his fastball's velocity tick up. The right-hander's fastball already sits north of 95 mph, and he's able to hold his velocity fairly well. Granted, his fastball's shape leads it to play below its radar gun readings. Iriarte's changeup and slider have both flashed plus potential, although his changeup is closer to being a viable pitch. He has a smooth delivery with a high three-quarters release point that he tended to lose throughout his outings. Unsurprisingly, Iriarte is still trying to locate his pitches, issuing 42 walks in 91 ⅓ innings at Low-A last year with a 5.12 ERA. The Padres are clearly confident in Iriarte's ability to stick in the rotation, but given his limited command and fastball's unexceptional shape, most around the league expect him to be pushed to the bullpen.

## 12 Tirso Ornelas  LF

Born: 03/11/00   Age: 23   Bats: L   Throws: R   Height: 6'3"   Weight: 200 lb.   Origin: International Free Agent, 2017

| YEAR | TEAM | LVL | AGE | PA | R | 2B | 3B | HR | RBI | BB | K | SB | CS | AVG/OBP/SLG | DRC+ | BABIP | BRR | DRP | WARP |
|---|---|---|---|---|---|---|---|---|---|---|---|---|---|---|---|---|---|---|---|
| 2021 | NAV | WIN | 21 | 238 | 36 | 16 | 2 | 2 | 35 | 15 | 30 | 0 | 2 | .353/.397/.472 | | .399 | | | |
| 2021 | FW | A+ | 21 | 445 | 57 | 31 | 1 | 7 | 55 | 52 | 98 | 3 | 1 | .248/.344/.389 | 103 | .312 | 0.0 | RF(52) -2.5, LF(33) 0.6 | 1.4 |
| 2022 | SA | AA | 22 | 492 | 62 | 28 | 2 | 7 | 51 | 43 | 85 | 7 | 2 | .288/.355/.408 | 102 | .342 | 1.5 | LF(104) -0.6, 1B(1) 0.1, RF(1) -0.5 | 1.3 |
| 2023 non-DC | SD | MLB | 23 | 251 | 21 | 11 | 2 | 3 | 21 | 19 | 51 | 1 | 0 | .222/.286/.320 | 72 | .273 | -4.1 | 1B 0, LF 0 | -0.6 |

Comparables: John Drennen, Josh Bell, Domingo Leyba

Ornelas has an advanced feel for the strike zone, although he was more aggressive in 2022. He hit .288/.355/.408 at Double-A last year, which is far from an exceptional line in the Texas League. Ornelas has plus power potential, but he's never been able to show more than 45-grade game power over any prolonged period. Still just 22, Ornelas could probably benefit from some swing changes while in the Pacific Coast League. He lacks the range to handle center field, but is viable defensively in either corner.

## 13 Henry Williams  RHP

Born: 09/18/01   Age: 21   Bats: R   Throws: R   Height: 6'5"   Weight: 200 lb.   Origin: Round 3, 2022 Draft (#91 overall)

The Padres' third-round pick in this year's draft, Williams flashed a promising three-pitch mix during his sophomore season at Duke before undergoing UCL surgery in December of 2021. Williams has a lanky 6-foot-5 frame with space to fill out. Some scouts think his low-90s fastball could tick up if Williams focuses on bulking up during his rehab process. He also had a good feel for a changeup and slider. Williams looked like a potential mid-rotation arm at some points at Duke, but it's been more than a year since scouts have seen him pitch competitively.

## 14 Korry Howell  UT

Born: 09/01/98   Age: 24   Bats: R   Throws: R   Height: 6'3"   Weight: 180 lb.   Origin: Round 12, 2018 Draft (#365 overall)

| YEAR | TEAM | LVL | AGE | PA | R | 2B | 3B | HR | RBI | BB | K | SB | CS | AVG/OBP/SLG | DRC+ | BABIP | BRR | DRP | WARP |
|---|---|---|---|---|---|---|---|---|---|---|---|---|---|---|---|---|---|---|---|---|
| 2021 | WIS | A+ | 22 | 305 | 65 | 12 | 4 | 12 | 36 | 34 | 88 | 20 | 3 | .248/.361/.465 | 107 | .327 | 1.7 | CF(43) 7.6, 3B(9) -0.3, SS(9) -0.3 | 2.0 |
| 2021 | BLX | AA | 22 | 111 | 18 | 5 | 1 | 4 | 15 | 12 | 44 | 4 | 3 | .235/.318/.429 | 70 | .380 | 0.5 | CF(10) -1.5, 3B(7) 0.6, 2B(5) -0.3 | -0.1 |
| 2022 | SA | AA | 23 | 184 | 37 | 8 | 4 | 6 | 20 | 25 | 52 | 12 | 1 | .253/.390/.486 | 104 | .344 | 4.1 | CF(17) 0.5, LF(15) -0.5, 2B(10) 2.7 | 1.0 |
| 2023 non-DC | SD | MLB | 24 | 251 | 24 | 10 | 2 | 5 | 24 | 22 | 82 | 8 | 3 | .225/.306/.351 | 89 | .332 | -0.1 | 2B 0, 3B 0 | 0.5 |

Comparables: Jose Siri, Lorenzo Cain, Joe Benson

Acquired from the Brewers for Victor Caratini, Howell was drafted as an infielder who has taken well to center field over the past two years. He has plus-plus speed and 50-grade power potential, but has always struggled to put the ball in play. Injuries limited Howell to just 48 games last season, and likely led him to go unselected in the Rule 5 Draft, but he easily had his best offensive season as a pro. He hit .253/.390/.486 with a 28.3% strikeout rate (a significant improvement over years past) and only committed three errors while appearing in games at second base, shortstop and all three outfield positions. Howell has always struggled to handle offspeed pitches and will face a big challenge in 2023 when he presumably makes the jump to Triple-A, but his patience at the plate, power and defensive versatility give him a decent floor.

## 15 Brandon Valenzuela  C/DH

Born: 10/02/00   Age: 22   Bats: S   Throws: R   Height: 6'0"   Weight: 225 lb.   Origin: International Free Agent, 2017

| YEAR | TEAM | LVL | AGE | PA | R | 2B | 3B | HR | RBI | BB | K | SB | CS | AVG/OBP/SLG | DRC+ | BABIP | BRR | DRP | WARP |
|---|---|---|---|---|---|---|---|---|---|---|---|---|---|---|---|---|---|---|---|---|
| 2021 | LE | A | 20 | 378 | 50 | 21 | 3 | 6 | 62 | 44 | 80 | 3 | 2 | .307/.389/.444 | 114 | .386 | -0.8 | C(49) 11.5, 1B(19) 0.8 | 2.8 |
| 2021 | FW | A+ | 20 | 65 | 4 | 1 | 0 | 1 | 7 | 15 | 20 | 1 | 0 | .245/.415/.327 | 98 | .379 | -0.2 | C(14) -1.7 | 0.0 |
| 2022 | FW | A+ | 21 | 413 | 39 | 14 | 2 | 10 | 47 | 63 | 95 | 0 | 1 | .209/.334/.348 | 109 | .256 | -4.4 | C(65) 19.1 | 3.1 |
| 2023 non-DC | SD | MLB | 22 | 251 | 22 | 10 | 2 | 3 | 22 | 24 | 65 | 0 | 1 | .225/.304/.326 | 82 | .303 | -4.3 | C 0, 1B 0 | -0.1 |

Valenzuela is already a viable big-league defender behind the plate with plus blocking ability and an above-average arm, and he shows a veteran's ability to work with pitchers. At the plate, however, Valenzuela lacks bat speed and offensive potential. He has a decent approach, but probably tops out as a fringe big-league hitter. Still, that should be enough to be a major-league backup catcher.

## 16 Noel Vela  LHP

Born: 12/21/98  Age: 24  Bats: L  Throws: L  Height: 6'1"  Weight: 185 lb.  Origin: Round 28, 2017 Draft (#828 overall)

| YEAR | TEAM | LVL | AGE | W | L | SV | G | GS | IP | H | HR | BB/9 | K/9 | K | GB% | BABIP | WHIP | ERA | DRA- | WARP |
|------|------|-----|-----|---|---|----|----|----|-----|----|----|------|------|-----|------|-------|------|------|------|------|
| 2021 | LE | A | 22 | 1 | 8 | 0 | 13 | 13 | 54¹ | 42 | 5 | 5.0 | 10.4 | 63 | 42.8% | .264 | 1.33 | 3.98 | 92 | 0.6 |
| 2021 | FW | A+ | 22 | 0 | 3 | 0 | 8 | 8 | 33¹ | 31 | 2 | 4.3 | 11.9 | 44 | 50.0% | .354 | 1.41 | 3.78 | 81 | 0.7 |
| 2022 | FW | A+ | 23 | 6 | 7 | 0 | 20 | 20 | 87 | 74 | 6 | 4.9 | 10.4 | 101 | 44.2% | .312 | 1.39 | 3.83 | 88 | 1.4 |
| 2022 | SA | AA | 23 | 1 | 3 | 0 | 9 | 4 | 22² | 25 | 1 | 7.9 | 9.5 | 24 | 50.0% | .381 | 1.99 | 6.35 | 119 | -0.2 |
| 2023 non-DC | SD | MLB | 24 | 3 | 3 | 0 | 58 | 0 | 50 | 52 | 7 | 5.9 | 8.5 | 47 | 37.7% | .315 | 1.70 | 5.50 | 135 | -0.6 |

*Comparables: Garrett Williams, Daniel Tillo, Sugar Ray Marimon*

Vela has developed slowly since the Padres signed him out of high school back in 2017. Now 24, the southpaw has a low-90s fastball that has reached 95 mph with good carry, a nasty curveball and a changeup that flashes league-average potential. However, he lacks the command to utilize his arsenal. While he was solid in 2022 at High-A, Double-A hitters crushed him after a late-season call-up, recording him a 6.35 ERA in 22.2 innings pitched. Barring an unexpected development, Vela likely has a long-term role in a bullpen.

## 17 Ryan Bergert  RHP

Born: 03/08/00  Age: 23  Bats: R  Throws: R  Height: 6'1"  Weight: 210 lb.  Origin: Round 6, 2021 Draft (#190 overall)

| YEAR | TEAM | LVL | AGE | W | L | SV | G | GS | IP | H | HR | BB/9 | K/9 | K | GB% | BABIP | WHIP | ERA | DRA- | WARP |
|------|------|-----|-----|---|---|----|----|----|-----|-----|----|------|------|-----|------|-------|------|------|------|------|
| 2021 | PAD | ROK | 21 | 1 | 0 | 1 | 7 | 3 | 11 | 3 | 0 | 0.0 | 11.5 | 14 | 52.2% | .130 | 0.27 | 0.00 | | |
| 2022 | FW | A+ | 22 | 4 | 10 | 0 | 24 | 24 | 103¹ | 124 | 18 | 3.7 | 11.2 | 129 | 37.7% | .377 | 1.61 | 5.84 | 93 | 1.4 |
| 2023 non-DC | SD | MLB | 23 | 3 | 3 | 0 | 58 | 0 | 50 | 55 | 8 | 4.3 | 7.6 | 42 | 35.4% | .311 | 1.58 | 5.41 | 136 | -0.7 |

*Comparables: Justin Slaten, Jeremy Beasley, Taylor Williams*

A 2021 sixth-round pick out of West Virginia, Berger racked up strikeouts in his first pro season at High-A (129 in 103 ⅓ innings pitched), but was hit hard by opposing hitters (5.84 ERA with 18 home runs). Given that it was his first season back from Tommy John surgery, Bergert's ability to finish triple-digit innings while flashing an above-average changeup and average curveball garnered some attention. Berger's fastball sat in the mid-90s at times, and has the characteristics to be viable even as a low-90s offering. Bergert has always been more of a control over command pitcher, and that suggests his future will be in the pen.

## 18 Garrett Hawkins  RHP

Born: 02/10/00  Age: 23  Bats: R  Throws: R  Height: 6'5"  Weight: 230 lb.  Origin: Round 9, 2021 Draft (#280 overall)

| YEAR | TEAM | LVL | AGE | W | L | SV | G | GS | IP | H | HR | BB/9 | K/9 | K | GB% | BABIP | WHIP | ERA | DRA- | WARP |
|------|------|-----|-----|---|---|----|----|----|-----|----|----|------|------|-----|------|-------|------|------|------|------|
| 2021 | PAD | ROK | 21 | 3 | 1 | 0 | 7 | 0 | 15¹ | 15 | 1 | 1.2 | 15.8 | 27 | 43.8% | .452 | 1.11 | 2.35 | | |
| 2022 | LE | A | 22 | 5 | 0 | 0 | 17 | 17 | 77² | 73 | 9 | 2.3 | 12.5 | 108 | 31.6% | .348 | 1.20 | 3.94 | 81 | 1.0 |
| 2022 | FW | A+ | 22 | 0 | 3 | 0 | 4 | 4 | 15¹ | 22 | 6 | 5.9 | 7.0 | 12 | 26.8% | .320 | 2.09 | 8.80 | 162 | -0.3 |
| 2023 non-DC | SD | MLB | 23 | 3 | 3 | 0 | 58 | 0 | 50 | 53 | 8 | 3.8 | 7.2 | 40 | 30.7% | .299 | 1.49 | 4.97 | 127 | -0.4 |

*Comparables: Alex Romero, Michael Kelly, Chris Pike*

A 2021 ninth-round pick out of the University of British Columbia, Hawkins has a fastball that has reached the mid-90s, but primarily sits in the low-90s with a developing changeup and slider. Hawkins works from one of the most vertical arm slots you'll see and has dominated low-level hitters since he turned pro. However, after a 108:20 strikeout-to-walk ratio in 77 ⅔ innings pitched at Low-A, he struggled mightily at High-A. Hawkins showed unexpected command early in the year, but it faded as his first full-season workload built up on him.

## 19 Daniel Montesino  OF

Born: 02/12/04  Age: 19  Bats: L  Throws: L  Height: 6'0"  Weight: 180 lb.  Origin: International Free Agent, 2021

| YEAR | TEAM | LVL | AGE | PA | R | 2B | 3B | HR | RBI | BB | K | SB | CS | AVG/OBP/SLG | DRC+ | BABIP | BRR | DRP | WARP |
|------|------|-----|-----|----|---|----|----|----|-----|----|----|----|----|-------------|------|-------|-----|-----|------|
| 2021 | DSL PAD | ROK | 17 | 243 | 37 | 13 | 4 | 4 | 48 | 43 | 53 | 8 | 4 | .316/.444/.489 | | .406 | | | |

Montesino was a significant piece of the Padres' 2020-21 IFA cycle and had a promising pro debut in 2021. He hit .316/.444/.490 with 21 extra-base hits in 56 games at the Dominican Summer League before he missed all of last season after undergoing UCL surgery. Montesino is listed at 6-feet tall and does not seem to have the usual physical projection scouts generally expect from a teenager. With that said, he has flashed 50-grade pop and a good feel to hit.

# Top Talents 25 and Under (as of 4/1/2023):

1. Juan Soto, OF
2. Fernando Tatis Jr., SS/OF
3. Jackson Merrill, SS
4. Luis Campusano, C
5. Samuel Zavala, RHP
6. Adrian Morejon, LHP
7. Dylan Lesko, RHP
8. Victor Lizarraga, RHP
9. Eguy Rosario, IF
10. Robby Snelling, LHP

Well if there's a guy worth emptying the farm system for, it's Juan Soto. The eagle-eyed batsman assembled a solid 80% of his five-win season for the listless Nationals before experiencing a power outage upon arrival in the Gaslamp District. After never finishing a season with a SLG below .500, Soto registered a meek .390 figure in his time in the brown and gold, and a perfunctory .452 on the season as a whole. His walk rates continued to be pristine, and contributed to his solid 122 DRC+ as a Padre, but was a far cry from the 156 he was putting up as a National, much less the figures in the 160s from 2020 and 2021. We expect him to be back to business as usual with the tumult of the midseason trade behind him, which leaves us wanting for words. Soto is only entering his age-24 season and already has three five-WARP campaigns to his name. He is a present franchise cornerstone, and has all the markings of a generational hitter and future Hall of Famer. Can you imagine trading this guy away?

What do you do with Fernando Tatis Jr.? He's sublimely talented, producing jaw-dropping and breathtaking plays at an alarming rate. He also missed all of the 2022 season recovering from various injuries and serving out a PED suspension that will extend into the early portion of the 2023 season. What will we see when he returns? It's hard not to believe in the baseline superstar talent, but he'll have plenty of rust to shake off, a new position to learn (outside of 24 games in 2021) and a whole lot of weight on his shoulders. Not to mention avoiding further injury—the last time he was actually healthy included three separate stints on the IL for his shoulder, which he's since had surgery to address. If he proves to be whole, Tatis may well regain the title of "face of the franchise," as prior to his injury and suspension, he was one of the only players in baseball one could reasonably prefer to the guy ranked above him in terms of present and long-term value.

Campusano aged off this list due to active service days, but appears prepared to complement and perhaps supplant Austin Nola in the coming seasons. He posted improved strikeout and walk rates in Triple-A, though he did see his power regress a bit. Campusano still profiles as a potentially average glove/above-average bat as a catcher, which is quite the valuable package. He'll need to wrest playing time away from Nola to prove it, though. Morejon still brings the heat, averaging over 96 mph in 2022 but he did all of that in relief after starting at least two games in each of the three prior seasons. Somehow he's only managed to accrue 66 innings total in the majors despite appearing across four seasons. With only two starts in Triple-A last year, it's not clear if the Padres still envision Morejon as a starter anymore. They re-signed Nick Martinez and added Seth Lugo to fill out their rotation, but are thin enough that they could still be tempted to use him every fifth day rather than the bullpen. A light workload means even if he did start, it would take substantial time for him to build back up to a full-season workload, making the bullpen his likely home for the long-term.

# San Francisco Giants

## The State of the System:

Even after a down year for some higher-profile players, a couple shrewd draft classes and a handful of breakouts have the Giants on the precipice of graduating multiple potential everyday players for the first time in roughly a decade.

## The Top Ten:

### 1 Marco Luciano SS    OFP: 60    ETA: 2024
Born: 09/10/01   Age: 21   Bats: R   Throws: R   Height: 6'2"   Weight: 178 lb.   Origin: International Free Agent, 2018

| YEAR | TEAM | LVL | AGE | PA | R | 2B | 3B | HR | RBI | BB | K | SB | CS | AVG/OBP/SLG | DRC+ | BABIP | BRR | DRP | WARP |
|------|------|-----|-----|-----|----|----|----|----|-----|----|----|----|----|-------------|------|-------|------|---------|------|
| 2021 | SCO | WIN | 19 | 87 | 7 | 0 | 0 | 3 | 13 | 11 | 28 | 0 | 1 | .253/.356/.373 | | .364 | | | |
| 2021 | SJ | A | 19 | 308 | 52 | 14 | 3 | 18 | 57 | 38 | 68 | 5 | 5 | .278/.373/.556 | 129 | .309 | -0.9 | SS(60) -0.1 | 1.9 |
| 2021 | EUG | A+ | 19 | 145 | 16 | 3 | 2 | 1 | 14 | 10 | 54 | 1 | 0 | .217/.283/.295 | 69 | .351 | -0.1 | SS(29) -1.2 | -0.3 |
| 2022 | GNTB | ROK | 20 | 27 | 6 | 2 | 0 | 1 | 6 | 4 | 7 | 0 | 0 | .318/.444/.545 | | .429 | | | |
| 2022 | EUG | A+ | 20 | 230 | 27 | 10 | 0 | 10 | 30 | 22 | 51 | 0 | 0 | .263/.339/.459 | 112 | .303 | -0.1 | SS(51) 2.1 | 1.3 |
| 2023 non-DC | SF | MLB | 21 | 251 | 22 | 10 | 2 | 5 | 24 | 17 | 70 | 2 | 2 | .224/.282/.342 | 77 | .299 | -3.1 | SS 0 | -0.2 |

*Comparables: Cole Tucker, Richard Urena, Jonathan Araúz*

**The Report:** Luciano's career trajectory has followed a pretty consistent pattern so far: flash advanced hit and plus power tools at one level, struggle in a late-season cameo at the next rung on the minor-league ladder, conquer that level the following season. It seemed like that would be the case again in 2022, as Luciano mashed in Eugene for the first half of the year. A lower back strain in early June forced him to press pause for two months, however, and he never really regained his momentum after returning in August. When he was healthy, Luciano continued to show off his lightning-quick hands and huge power potential while cutting his strikeout rate and improving his pitch recognition in general. To wit, even with the two-month layoff, he bashed two grand slams in seven games after returning to Eugene's lineup. He also continues to show competence at short and has expressed a desire to play at the six in the majors, but his arm strength and athleticism will allow him to easily slide over to third if necessary.

**OFP:** 60 / Slugger on the left side of the infield with the occasional All-Star appearance

**Variance:** High. There's some inertia with Luciano's profile as it hasn't changed much in either direction over the last three years. That also means the bat still looks pretty special, but it would be nice to see Luciano truly pummel pitchers for a full season.

**Jesse Roche's Fantasy Take:** Last year, Luciano attracted many doomsayers after his strikeout rate ballooned upon his promotion to High-A (37.2%). His performance in the AFL that fall–including a 62% contact rate–only exacerbated those concerns. Yet, his approach remained sound, and his bat speed remained elite. In his return engagement in High-A, Luciano hit .288/.360/.507 with a 73% contact rate prior to his injury, and he generally appears back on track. Ultimately, his hit and power upside still rival nearly any shortstop prospect, but his performance wobbles, back injury and lack of upper-level experience add significant risk to his fantasy profile. Luciano is a volatile top-20 prospect who could quickly ascend into the top five or even drop out of the top 50 depending on how he adjusts to difficult Double-A Richmond next year.

## 2  Kyle Harrison  LHP          OFP: 60     ETA: Mid-2023

Born: 08/12/01   Age: 21   Bats: R   Throws: L   Height: 6'2"   Weight: 200 lb.   Origin: Round 3, 2020 Draft (#85 overall)

| YEAR | TEAM | LVL | AGE | W | L | SV | G | GS | IP | H | HR | BB/9 | K/9 | K | GB% | BABIP | WHIP | ERA | DRA- | WARP |
|------|------|-----|-----|---|---|----|---|----|----|---|----|------|-----|---|-----|-------|------|-----|------|------|
| 2021 | SJ | A | 19 | 4 | 3 | 0 | 23 | 23 | 98² | 86 | 3 | 4.7 | 14.3 | 157 | 49.1% | .393 | 1.40 | 3.19 | 82 | 1.6 |
| 2022 | EUG | A+ | 20 | 0 | 1 | 0 | 7 | 7 | 29 | 19 | 2 | 3.1 | 18.3 | 59 | 43.8% | .378 | 1.00 | 1.55 | 63 | 0.8 |
| 2022 | RIC | AA | 20 | 4 | 2 | 0 | 18 | 18 | 84 | 60 | 11 | 4.2 | 13.6 | 127 | 34.1% | .301 | 1.18 | 3.11 | 84 | 1.8 |
| 2023 DC | SF | MLB | 21 | 1 | 1 | 0 | 3 | 3 | 14.3 | 12 | 2 | 4.6 | 11.1 | 18 | 35.5% | .293 | 1.32 | 3.64 | 97 | 0.2 |

*Comparables: Henry Owens, Stephen Gonsalves, Jesse Biddle*

**The Report:** Few players—let alone pitchers—in the Giants' system improved their status as much as Harrison did in 2022, to the point that there was some brief internal discussion of whether he had overtaken Luciano as the organization's top prospect. Harrison flat-out bullied hitters in the Northwest League, striking out half of the batters he faced, and that performance backed up only slightly with Richmond.

Harrison's fastball sits 92-94, running up to 96, and is a weapon in its own right. The pitch explodes out of Harrison's compact delivery and low arm slot and gives the impression that it rises as it approaches the plate, which can generate some ugly emergency swings when he locates it at the top of the zone. Off the heater, Harrison's sweeping slider plays to both sides of the plate while his changeup has good fade. Fastball command continues to hinder Harrison's ceiling, however, as he can struggle to throw quality strikes or even enough strikes in general with the pitch. With just over 200 total innings as a pro, some of that command improvement could come with more time and more reps. Harrison maintains good balance in his delivery, pointing to the potential for a more accurate profile as he gets older.

**OFP:** 60 / no. 2/3 starter

**Variance:** High. Harrison is now the top left-handed pitching prospect in the league and has the stuff to front a rotation, but command may limit him as a frustrating arm that has flashes of greatness. That said, he wouldn't be the first pitcher to throw more strikes as he gets deeper into his 20s.

**Jesse Roche's Fantasy Take:** Harrison led the minors (among pitchers with over 70 innings pitched) with a staggering 39.8% strikeout rate. That elite bat-missing ability is fantasy gold. If his command improves, he could develop into one of the best pitchers in baseball. And as noted in August, "even if it never takes a big step forward, a Blake Snell-type outcome is well within the realm of possibility." For fantasy, those potential outcomes are fantastic, and Harrison is a clear top-50 fantasy prospect.

## 3  Luis Matos  CF          OFP: 60     ETA: Late 2024

Born: 01/28/02   Age: 21   Bats: R   Throws: R   Height: 5'11"   Weight: 160 lb.   Origin: International Free Agent, 2018

| YEAR | TEAM | LVL | AGE | PA | R | 2B | 3B | HR | RBI | BB | K | SB | CS | AVG/OBP/SLG | DRC+ | BABIP | BRR | DRP | WARP |
|------|------|-----|-----|-----|---|----|----|----|-----|----|---|----|----|-------------|------|-------|-----|-----|------|
| 2021 | SJ | A | 19 | 491 | 84 | 35 | 1 | 15 | 86 | 28 | 61 | 21 | 5 | .313/.358/.494 | 129 | .332 | 1.2 | CF(86) -4.7, RF(14) -2.9, LF(4) 0.0 | 3.0 |
| 2022 | EUG | A+ | 20 | 407 | 55 | 14 | 1 | 11 | 43 | 27 | 65 | 11 | 3 | .211/.275/.344 | 98 | .226 | 0.5 | CF(74) 3.1, RF(9) -0.1 | 1.3 |
| 2023 non-DC | SF | MLB | 21 | 251 | 19 | 11 | 1 | 4 | 21 | 12 | 49 | 5 | 1 | .205/.252/.302 | 55 | .245 | -2.1 | LF 0, CF 0 | -0.8 |

*Comparables: Angel Morales, John Drennen, Teodoro Martinez*

**The Report:** Matos had a huge breakout in 2021, looking like a future five-tool outfielder and vaulting himself into the top half of the Top 101. Then came 2022, a hellacious slump to start the season and a month-long injured list stint in May. Matos notched only 10 hits in his first 19 games with the Emeralds, none of them for extra bases, and still wasn't right when he returned in early June, posting a .590 OPS through the end of July with a .187 BABIP. Over the last six weeks of the season, he finally started to show flashes of the plus bat and power potential he had in San Jose, slashing .283/.312/.462 over his last 33 games. He also looked somewhat back to normal in the AFL and never lost his defensive ability, although he still might be more of a corner outfielder at higher levels. Some of his issues at the plate stemmed from his aggressive approach, as he couldn't extend much while pitchers kept him off-balance with offspeed and jammed him with fastballs. He hasn't lost any of the plus bat speed and rotation in his swing, though, and the tools are clearly still in there; it's just a matter of whether he can grasp them.

**OFP:** 60 / First-division outfielder

**Variance:** Very High. Matos got better as the season progressed, but he's just as likely to be atop this list a year from now as he is to fall off it completely.

**Jesse Roche's Fantasy Take:** Matos possesses so much you covet in a fantasy prospect. He makes plenty of contact with low strikeout rates. Meanwhile, his plus bat speed and torque generate plus raw power. To top it off, Matos has solid speed and utilizes it to steal bases. Unfortunately, he is arguably aggressive to a fault, with swing rates typically approaching 60% and walk rates under 4%. Players can still find success with aggressive approaches, and, if Matos can find the right balance and allow his tools to shine, he has high-end fantasy upside. Due to that upside, and despite his substantial risk, he is just outside the top 100 in fantasy.

## 4 Casey Schmitt 3B    OFP: 55    ETA: 2023
Born: 03/01/99   Age: 24   Bats: R   Throws: R   Height: 6'2"   Weight: 215 lb.   Origin: Round 2, 2020 Draft (#49 overall)

| YEAR | TEAM | LVL | AGE | PA | R | 2B | 3B | HR | RBI | BB | K | SB | CS | AVG/OBP/SLG | DRC+ | BABIP | BRR | DRP | WARP |
|---|---|---|---|---|---|---|---|---|---|---|---|---|---|---|---|---|---|---|---|
| 2021 | SJ | A | 22 | 280 | 36 | 14 | 1 | 8 | 29 | 22 | 44 | 2 | 2 | .247/.318/.406 | 110 | .269 | 0.4 | 3B(50) 6.0 | 1.7 |
| 2022 | EUG | A+ | 23 | 383 | 58 | 14 | 1 | 17 | 59 | 42 | 86 | 1 | 2 | .273/.363/.474 | 127 | .319 | 1.1 | 3B(50) -2.2, SS(40) -1.4 | 2.1 |
| 2022 | RIC | AA | 23 | 127 | 13 | 10 | 1 | 3 | 16 | 6 | 29 | 2 | 0 | .342/.378/.517 | 92 | .432 | 1.3 | 3B(29) -1.1 | 0.3 |
| 2023 DC | SF | MLB | 24 | 28 | 3 | 1 | 0 | 0 | 3 | 2 | 7 | 0 | 0 | .221/.280/.331 | 73 | .284 | 0.0 | 3B 0 | 0.0 |

Comparables: Chris Johnson, Danny Valencia, Michael Griffin

**The Report:** Schmitt was a two-way player in college, playing third and serving as the Aztecs' closer. The Giants put him on the dirt full time after the 2020 draft and a middling 2021 pro debut was almost immediately forgotten as Schmitt raced through the minors in 2022. Schmitt's defense at third is already plus, with excellent instincts and athleticism and the same cannon of an arm that had him in the mid-90s off the mound. Schmitt also filled in at shortstop in Eugene for 40 games while teammate Marco Luciano was hurt and didn't look out of place, but he's a sure-shot third baseman going forward and played there exclusively in Richmond and Sacramento.

Schmitt's bat is tougher to gauge, as he hasn't shown the usual power one would expect from the hot corner. His pop is almost entirely pull side and his swing does have some loft that could eventually be tuned to tap into more power, but could also be exploited by better pitching. There's also some room to add strength in his lower half, which could also bolster Schmitt's in-game power potential. He is a capable hitter for contact with above-average bat-to-ball skills and a patient approach, although his walk and strikeout totals diverged after each of his promotions. There's a lot to like about where Schmitt is now as a total package, but how much pop he can tap into day-to-day will make the decision of whether he's an everyday player or a fifth infielder in the majors.

**OFP:** 55 / Plus defensive third baseman with 15-20 homers

**Variance:** Medium. Schmitt can pick it clean at third and his strides at the plate may just be real, but more prototypical power would aid his future potential at the hot corner.

**Jesse Roche's Fantasy Take:** Schmitt may not sound like much from a fantasy perspective. Yet, his defense and strong upper-level performance put him on the fast track to a MLB debut this year. Further, Schmitt will still carry plenty of fantasy value in many formats even if he only tops out offensively similar to the likes of Jeimer Candelario or Brian Anderson. His greatest value, however, comes in deeper fantasy formats where his high floor–provided by his excellent defense–makes him nearly a lock for a meaningful extended look in the near future. Although Schmitt is not a top-200 fantasy prospect, he sits squarely in the next tier, and he should be on watch lists even in shallower formats for his potential early-season promotion.

## 5 Aeverson Arteaga SS    OFP: 55    ETA: 2025
Born: 03/16/03   Age: 20   Bats: R   Throws: R   Height: 6'1"   Weight: 170 lb.   Origin: International Free Agent, 2019

| YEAR | TEAM | LVL | AGE | PA | R | 2B | 3B | HR | RBI | BB | K | SB | CS | AVG/OBP/SLG | DRC+ | BABIP | BRR | DRP | WARP |
|---|---|---|---|---|---|---|---|---|---|---|---|---|---|---|---|---|---|---|---|
| 2021 | GNTO | ROK | 18 | 226 | 42 | 12 | 1 | 9 | 43 | 23 | 69 | 8 | 0 | .294/.367/.503 | | .398 | | | |
| 2022 | SJ | A | 19 | 565 | 87 | 35 | 2 | 14 | 84 | 49 | 155 | 11 | 6 | .270/.345/.431 | 91 | .362 | -1.3 | SS(118) 4.2 | 1.3 |
| 2023 non-DC | SF | MLB | 20 | 251 | 19 | 12 | 1 | 3 | 20 | 14 | 80 | 2 | 2 | .212/.263/.305 | 60 | .311 | -3.1 | 3B 0, SS 0 | -0.7 |

Comparables: Andrew Velazquez, Cole Tucker, Juremi Profar

**The Report:** Initially viewed as a glove-first player when he signed out of Venezuela, Arteaga showed legitimate two-way talent in his 2021 pro debut. He continued to show that the bat was real in the Cal League this past season. The counting stats weren't quite as explosive in 2022, but the 19-year-old Arteaga held his own at the plate and continued to show off a plus arm and excellent range at short.

As Eli said in a Ten Pack back in June, Arteaga loves to swing. That's not necessarily a bad thing when he makes contact, but so far it's also resulted in a strikeout rate that floats around 30%. He has some feel to manipulate the barrel, though, and the contact is loud when he connects and should get louder as his frame matures. Where Arteaga really shines is on the dirt. He's a legitimate shortstop, athletic and agile with plenty of arm strength for the left side of the infield. He's not much of a basestealer but has above-average speed that should stay at least average as he gets older. The defense is still going to be the carrying tool here, but he has a much higher chance of becoming a quality regular after his performance in San Jose.

**OFP:** 55 / Everyday shortstop

**Variance:** Very High. Arteaga's likely to be something of a slow burner, with the development of the bat trailing the glove. The strikeouts could limit him to a bench role at higher levels and he's not much of a power threat, but plus defense can carry you up the middle a long way.

**Jesse Roche's Fantasy Take:** Arteaga quietly had an impressive 19-year-old season in Low-A, capped off by a stellar final 18 games in which he hit .370/.466/.575 with a 13.6% walk rate. In fact, his walk rate jumped from 6.4% over his first 73 games to 11.8% over his final 49 games. With burgeoning power, improving contact and swing rates, and a touch of speed, Arteaga is a prospect on the rise with underrated fantasy potential.

## 6  Vaun Brown  OF          OFP: 55        ETA: Late 2023 / Early 2024

Born: 06/23/98   Age: 25   Bats: R   Throws: R   Height: 6'1"   Weight: 215 lb.   Origin: Round 10, 2021 Draft (#296 overall)

| YEAR | TEAM | LVL | AGE | PA | R | 2B | 3B | HR | RBI | BB | K | SB | CS | AVG/OBP/SLG | DRC+ | BABIP | BRR | DRP | WARP |
|---|---|---|---|---|---|---|---|---|---|---|---|---|---|---|---|---|---|---|---|
| 2021 | GNTO | ROK | 23 | 98 | 24 | 7 | 4 | 2 | 14 | 7 | 29 | 8 | 1 | .354/.480/.620 | | .542 | | | |
| 2022 | SJ | A | 24 | 262 | 50 | 14 | 5 | 14 | 41 | 25 | 67 | 23 | 3 | .346/.427/.636 | 116 | .439 | 0.6 | LF(35) 1.1, CF(11) 1.4, RF(3) -0.3 | 1.3 |
| 2022 | EUG | A+ | 24 | 194 | 50 | 10 | 2 | 9 | 34 | 22 | 52 | 21 | 3 | .350/.454/.611 | 115 | .460 | 4.5 | RF(25) 0.1, LF(8) -0.3, CF(3) -0.2 | 1.6 |
| 2023 non-DC | SF | MLB | 25 | 251 | 24 | 10 | 2 | 5 | 25 | 17 | 78 | 10 | 3 | .238/.304/.365 | 91 | .339 | 0.8 | LF 0, CF 0 | 0.5 |

*Comparables: Mitch Haniger, Jarrod Dyson, Terry Evans*

**The Report:** Making it to the majors as a 10th-round pick is an accomplishment in and of itself, and many of those who do are relievers or utility players. Becoming a bona fide prospect with everyday upside is another story, but Brown did just that with an electric first full season, punishing pitchers as an older player for both A-ball levels before an injury ended his season immediately after a promotion to Double-A.

Out of an upright and slightly hunched-over stance, Brown uses his strong, athletic frame and a short, direct swing to spray extra-base hits from gap to gap. He tends to keep his hands quite low before he loads and inside outs the ball fairly often because of it, but he's also vulnerable to good velocity on the inner half and breaking balls away. Brown was also a frequent base thief when he wasn't in a home run trot, and much like Grant McCray, he has plenty of speed to burn even if some of those bases were stolen off the minor-league pitch clock. That speed shows in the outfield as well as Brown can cover enough ground to play all three outfield positions, though he profiles best in a corner and his arm is just average. The overall dominance of his slash line is a bit of a mirage (check out his skyscraper BABIP across both A-ball levels) but Brown has the raw power and speed to be a 20/20 threat at his peak.

**OFP:** 55 / Slugging corner outfielder

**Variance:** High. It remains to be seen how Brown hits when he has league-average batted-ball luck and faces pitchers closer to his age, but his power/speed combo and defensive competence give him a floor as a fourth outfielder with pop. You take that every time from a 10th-rounder.

**Jesse Roche's Fantasy Take:** It is easy to dismiss a 23/24 year-old prospect dominating A-ball, but Brown is a special case due to his dynamic power and speed. Whether he'll continue to make enough contact and enough quality contact, though, is unclear. Still, Brown has legitimate 20/20 potential, and he should be rostered in leagues with up to 200 prospects.

## Eyewitness Report: Vaun Brown

**Evaluator:** Eli Walsh
**Report Date:** 07/10/2022
**Dates Seen:** 4/9/22, 5/15/22, 6/4/22
**Risk Factor:** Very high
**Physical/Health:** Strong lower half, muscular presence but remains athletic, mostly filled out, not much projection if any

| Tool | Future Grade | Report |
|---|---|---|
| Hit | 50 | Old-school stance, slightly open and upright with slightly bent knees and a bit of a hunch. Load is small and hands are short to the ball. Sprays it from line to line, shows good feel for going the other way. Takes his share of walks but won't appear on any rate leaderboards. Can be a little rigid at times and can get beat by good velocity, particularly high. |
| Power | 55 | Power is mostly to pull side, but loud contact is frequent. Punishes mistakes in any count. Uses legs well to get behind and drive the ball. Probably closer to a 20-homer bat than a 30-homer bat at peak with a whole lot of doubles. |
| Baserunning/ Speed | 60 | Easy above-average speed and fast for his size. Threat to steal 25-30 bases with high-efficiency. High motor and turns singles into doubles when fielders get lazy. |
| Glove | 50 | Quality corner outfielder who is stretched a little in center. Shows good range thanks to his above-average speed and takes smart routes. Unlikely to ever be best center fielder on a roster. |
| Arm | 50 | Strong but unspectacular. Slightly better fit in left but will work in either corner. |

**Conclusion:** One of the biggest pop-up bats in the system. Well-rounded corner outfielder, ideal as a lineup sparkplug with pop or just below the middle of the order. Even with performance considered, variance is higher than usual based on lack of track record, D-II pedigree, unsustainably high BABIPs. TBD on how he'll adjust in a slump. Old for his level, but also likely to move fast.

## 7 Reggie Crawford LHP    OFP: 55    ETA: 2024 as a reliever, 2025 as anything else

Born: 12/04/00  Age: 22  Bats: L  Throws: L  Height: 6'4"  Weight: 235 lb.  Origin: Round 1, 2022 Draft (#30 overall)

**The Report:** Crawford was a bit of a surprise pick at the end of the first round, announced as a two-way player and one recovering from Tommy John surgery at that. Crawford threw all of eight innings at UConn and punished Big East pitchers at the plate, but never posted walk and strikeout rates that were indicative of an ability to hit better pitching.

What we do know about Crawford is that he hits the ball very hard, throws it very hard and is built like a tight end. Those are very sturdy building blocks. Crawford's fastball has been clocked as high as 99 mph during his time with Team USA in the summer of 2021, but his delivery has some moderate effort and violence and a bit of a head whack. His secondaries are also well below the level of a typical college pitcher, with a fringy breaking ball and a changeup that he's been developing while rehabbing his elbow. At the plate, Crawford has an aesthetically pleasing swing but struggled with offspeed pitches both in college and across multiple summer wood bat leagues. It's loud when he does make contact though.

It's possible that facing professional pitching ultimately funnels Crawford toward the mound full time, at which point he would be a hard-throwing, one-pitch guy. With that in mind, Crawford's quickest path to the majors is probably in the bullpen, but there's a very wide variety of possible outcomes here.

**OFP:** 55 / Your guess is as good as mine

**Variance:** Extreme. This ranking is more about Crawford's lack of track record than a lack of ceiling relative to the guys above him. Until we see him face pro-level pitching and hitting every day, he's a bit of a mystery box.

**Jesse Roche's Fantasy Take:** Crawford's underlying issues and unclear future role create so much risk and uncertainty that he is better avoided outside of the deepest of fantasy leagues.

## 8 Grant McCray  CF    OFP: 55    ETA: 2024

Born: 12/07/00   Age: 22   Bats: L   Throws: R   Height: 6'2"   Weight: 190 lb.   Origin: Round 3, 2019 Draft (#87 overall)

| YEAR | TEAM | LVL | AGE | PA | R | 2B | 3B | HR | RBI | BB | K | SB | CS | AVG/OBP/SLG | DRC+ | BABIP | BRR | DRP | WARP |
|------|------|-----|-----|-----|-----|-----|-----|-----|-----|-----|-----|-----|-----|-------------|------|-------|------|-----|------|
| 2021 | GNTO | ROK | 20 | 65 | 16 | 3 | 1 | 1 | 6 | 9 | 20 | 3 | 1 | .309/.400/.455 | | .457 | | | |
| 2021 | SJ | A | 20 | 88 | 8 | 2 | 2 | 2 | 12 | 6 | 30 | 4 | 1 | .250/.299/.400 | 76 | .367 | -0.7 | CF(18) 1.8, LF(6) 0.2 | 0.2 |
| 2022 | SJ | A | 21 | 507 | 92 | 21 | 9 | 21 | 69 | 58 | 148 | 35 | 10 | .291/.383/.525 | 100 | .391 | 0.4 | CF(91) -0.6, RF(2) 0.2 | 1.4 |
| 2022 | EUG | A+ | 21 | 62 | 12 | 2 | 0 | 2 | 10 | 9 | 22 | 8 | 0 | .269/.387/.423 | 95 | .429 | 1.2 | CF(13) -1.0 | 0.1 |
| 2023 non-DC | SF | MLB | 22 | 251 | 22 | 9 | 3 | 4 | 23 | 19 | 89 | 9 | 4 | .226/.290/.342 | 78 | .351 | 0.7 | LF 0, CF 0 | 0.3 |

*Comparables: Luis Liberato, Steven Moya, Starling Marte*

**The Report:** The son of former outfielder Rodney McCray–yes, *that* Rodney McCray–was the sparkplug atop San Jose's lineup throughout 2022 and led the team in home runs and stolen bases, although some of his offensive performance, particularly the power, was surely helped by playing almost the entire season in the Cal League. He's a pure center fielder with plenty of speed and arm strength and may only get pushed to a corner by a player in the top echelon of outfield defensive talent. McCray has loose hands in the batter's box and a swing geared for pull power. While there's more raw here than you might expect, his size and swing plane lead him to profile as more of a line-drive doubles hitter at present, albeit one who can pop 10-15 homers a year. His approach leans toward patience, but it's to a fault at times as those deep counts lead to too many strikeouts to profile as a classic leadoff hitter. Keeping his strikeout rate below 30% going forward will be the best indicator of whether he's a major-league-caliber starter or a bench outfielder. So far, there are more signs pointing toward the former.

**OFP:** 55 / Everyday center fielder

**Variance:** High. The strikeouts are certainly a concern and could be exploited at upper levels, but there is an intriguing power/speed combo here.

**Jesse Roche's Fantasy Take:** Like Vaun Brown above, McCray has an exciting power/speed combo. Interestingly, Brown (23/44) and McCray (23/43) had nearly identical home run and stolen base totals last year. McCray is younger with a bit more swing-and-miss, but his loud tools similarly land him within the top-200 fantasy prospects.

## 9 Carson Whisenhunt  LHP    OFP: 55    ETA: 2024

Born: 10/20/00   Age: 22   Bats: L   Throws: L   Height: 6'3"   Weight: 209 lb.   Origin: Round 2, 2022 Draft (#66 overall)

| YEAR | TEAM | LVL | AGE | W | L | SV | G | GS | IP | H | HR | BB/9 | K/9 | K | GB% | BABIP | WHIP | ERA | DRA- | WARP |
|------|------|-----|-----|-----|-----|-----|-----|-----|-----|-----|-----|------|-----|-----|------|-------|------|------|------|------|
| 2023 non-DC | SF | MLB | 22 | 3 | 3 | 0 | 58 | 0 | 50 | 53 | 8 | 4.4 | 8.1 | 45 | 36.7% | .309 | 1.54 | 5.14 | 129 | -0.5 |

**The Report:** Whisenhunt lost the entirety of his junior year after testing positive for a banned substance, but he's the kind of college pitcher who teams usually take in the back half of the first round, with a trio of pitches that don't necessarily project as better than plus but aren't worse than average either. The southpaw has an ideal frame with room to add strength and a delivery that he repeats well without a ton of violence. The main event here is his plus-flashing changeup, which he uses on both sides of the plate and to steal strikes and generate chases. It's a legitimate bat-misser and plays well off his low- to mid-90s fastball. Whisenhunt also throws an 11-5 curveball that serves more as a setup pitch for the fastball and change than anything else. Whisenhunt has a ways to go to build up a foundation of innings—he's thrown under 100 between college and pro ball—but he has the look of a fast mover once he has more under his belt.

**OFP:** 55 / Mid-rotation starter

**Variance:** Medium. Whisenhunt is not completely bereft of risk—he is a pitcher, after all—but his current pitch mix and mechanical consistency point to a high floor.

**Jesse Roche's Fantasy Take:** Left-handed pitchers with advanced changeups and a solid fastball will always have a place on a real-life team. In fantasy, not so much. Without more velocity or an improved breaking ball, Whisenhunt lacks a ton of fantasy upside, even if his floor may be high.

## 10    Mason Black   RHP      OFP: 55     ETA: 2024

Born: 12/10/99   Age: 23   Bats: R   Throws: R   Height: 6'3"   Weight: 230 lb.   Origin: Round 3, 2021 Draft (#85 overall)

| YEAR | TEAM | LVL | AGE | W | L | SV | G | GS | IP | H | HR | BB/9 | K/9 | K | GB% | BABIP | WHIP | ERA | DRA- | WARP |
|------|------|-----|-----|---|---|----|---|----|----|---|----|------|-----|---|-----|-------|------|-----|------|------|
| 2022 | SJ | A | 22 | 1 | 1 | 0 | 8 | 8 | 34$^1$ | 25 | 1 | 2.1 | 11.5 | 44 | 60.2% | .293 | 0.96 | 1.57 | 81 | 0.5 |
| 2022 | EUG | A+ | 22 | 5 | 3 | 0 | 16 | 16 | 77$^2$ | 70 | 11 | 3.2 | 10.7 | 92 | 43.5% | .312 | 1.26 | 3.94 | 97 | 0.8 |
| 2023 non-DC | SF | MLB | 23 | 3 | 3 | 0 | 58 | 0 | 50 | 52 | 8 | 3.8 | 7.7 | 43 | 39.2% | .304 | 1.46 | 4.77 | 122 | -0.3 |

*Comparables: Domingo Acevedo, Scott Schneider, Daniel Wright*

**The Report:** Black put up video game numbers across eight starts in the Cal League and pretty handily had the best overall season of any of the 14 pitchers the Giants drafted in 2021. That production slowed a bit in Eugene as he allowed more homers and free passes and lost his command at times, particularly over a five-start stretch from late July through mid-August when he allowed 16 earned runs over 17 2/3 innings. Black's 112 innings were a career-high though, as he threw more than 33 innings just once while at Lehigh, so the fade wasn't entirely surprising.

Black sits in the mid-90s and can run it up to 97 out of a simple and repeatable delivery with an arm stroke that has a bit of loop to it. A plus-flashing slider is his best secondary and draws some ugly, lunging swings when he commands it while his changeup has average fade but is more of a pace-changing pitch than a strikeout one. It all comes together to enable Black to strike out more than a batter per inning. At the same time, he's kept his walk rate under 10%, where it hovered while he was in college—a good sign that he's on track to reach his no. 3 ceiling.

**OFP:** 55 / Mid-rotation starter

**Variance:** High. Black's fade down the stretch against improved competition slowed his rise up this list, but the stuff is legitimate and could carry him to a back-end starter role if his fringe-average command doesn't improve by another grade.

**Jesse Roche's Fantasy Take:** Pitchers like Black—with two plus-flashing pitches and so-so command—are increasingly in favor across MLB. Even if his long-term role may be best as a five-and-dive arm, that'll play in most fantasy formats if it comes with solid ratios and strikeouts.

## Outside the Top Ten:

### 11   Eric Silva   RHP

Born: 10/03/02   Age: 20   Bats: R   Throws: R   Height: 6'1"   Weight: 185 lb.   Origin: Round 4, 2021 Draft (#115 overall)

| YEAR | TEAM | LVL | AGE | W | L | SV | G | GS | IP | H | HR | BB/9 | K/9 | K | GB% | BABIP | WHIP | ERA | DRA- | WARP |
|------|------|-----|-----|---|---|----|---|----|----|---|----|------|-----|---|-----|-------|------|-----|------|------|
| 2022 | SJ | A | 19 | 3 | 7 | 0 | 22 | 22 | 85$^2$ | 77 | 11 | 4.1 | 10.4 | 99 | 37.8% | .313 | 1.35 | 5.88 | 104 | -0.1 |
| 2023 non-DC | SF | MLB | 20 | 3 | 3 | 0 | 58 | 0 | 50 | 54 | 8 | 4.8 | 7.7 | 43 | 33.5% | .307 | 1.62 | 5.60 | 139 | -0.7 |

Built like Roy Oswalt, Silva also has an intriguing fastball/breaking ball combination, but dealt with bouts of shaky command and allowed a few too many home runs. When he's right, Silva's fastball can run up to 97 but generally sits in the 92-94 range once he settles in. His two breaking balls—a power curveball with 1-7 shape and a slider with decent depth—are his best secondaries and, at times, his best pitches period. He also offers an inconsistent changeup, but it's well behind the other three pitches. Silva pitched all of 2022 at 19, so he has plenty of time to build his workload and get his command together, but he'd be a good bullpen candidate if the rotation doesn't work out.

### 12   Carson Seymour   RHP

Born: 12/16/98   Age: 24   Bats: R   Throws: R   Height: 6'6"   Weight: 260 lb.   Origin: Round 6, 2021 Draft (#172 overall)

| YEAR | TEAM | LVL | AGE | W | L | SV | G | GS | IP | H | HR | BB/9 | K/9 | K | GB% | BABIP | WHIP | ERA | DRA- | WARP |
|------|------|-----|-----|---|---|----|---|----|----|---|----|------|-----|---|-----|-------|------|-----|------|------|
| 2022 | SLU | A | 23 | 4 | 0 | 0 | 7 | 4 | 30$^1$ | 23 | 0 | 2.7 | 8.0 | 27 | 60.7% | .277 | 1.05 | 1.19 | 101 | 0.5 |
| 2022 | BRK | A+ | 23 | 1 | 5 | 0 | 11 | 9 | 51$^1$ | 45 | 8 | 2.1 | 11.4 | 65 | 55.3% | .298 | 1.11 | 3.68 | 82 | 0.9 |
| 2022 | EUG | A+ | 23 | 2 | 3 | 0 | 6 | 6 | 29$^1$ | 25 | 1 | 3.1 | 13.2 | 43 | 50.7% | .358 | 1.19 | 3.99 | 82 | 0.5 |
| 2023 non-DC | SF | MLB | 24 | 3 | 3 | 0 | 58 | 0 | 50 | 52 | 7 | 3.5 | 7.6 | 42 | 41.5% | .303 | 1.42 | 4.48 | 116 | -0.2 |

One of the players acquired in the Darin Ruf trade, Seymour has a massive frame at 6-foot-6 and 260 pounds but a repertoire that's more geared to generate groundballs than beat hitters with physicality, headlined by a mid-90s sinker and arcing vertical curveball. He looked better after the Giants' pitching development machine got its hands on him, but probably should have been feasting on A-ball hitters anyway as a 23-year-old originally drafted out of Kansas State. That said, there's a non-zero chance he ends up a decent back-end starter or multi-inning reliever down the line.

## 13 Jairo Pomares  LF

Born: 08/04/00   Age: 22   Bats: L   Throws: R   Height: 6'1"   Weight: 185 lb.   Origin: International Free Agent, 2018

| YEAR | TEAM | LVL | AGE | PA | R | 2B | 3B | HR | RBI | BB | K | SB | CS | AVG/OBP/SLG | DRC+ | BABIP | BRR | DRP | WARP |
|------|------|-----|-----|-----|----|----|----|----|-----|----|-----|----|----|-------------|------|-------|------|---------------------|------|
| 2021 | SJ | A | 20 | 224 | 45 | 22 | 0 | 14 | 44 | 15 | 54 | 0 | 0 | .372/.429/.693 | 138 | .448 | -0.7 | RF(26) -2.3, LF(3) -1.0 | 1.4 |
| 2021 | EUG | A+ | 20 | 104 | 13 | 5 | 1 | 6 | 15 | 1 | 33 | 1 | 0 | .262/.269/.505 | 107 | .328 | 0.4 | LF(22) -1.7 | 0.3 |
| 2022 | EUG | A+ | 21 | 386 | 49 | 20 | 0 | 14 | 59 | 36 | 127 | 0 | 0 | .254/.330/.438 | 88 | .362 | -1.1 | LF(80) -0.7 | 0.5 |
| 2023 non-DC | SF | MLB | 22 | 251 | 22 | 11 | 1 | 5 | 24 | 15 | 87 | 1 | 0 | .224/.276/.348 | 74 | .334 | -4.1 | LF 0, RF 0 | -0.6 |

Pomares crushed Cal League pitching in 2021 and showed enough promise for us to rank him fourth on this list a year ago with the caveats that he was limited to an outfield corner and his approach was overly aggressive. Those caveats still apply. Pomares struck out 33% of the time in 95 games at Eugene, a five-point increase over the strikeout rate he ran across both A-ball levels in 2021. Pomares still bludgeons the ball when he makes contact, still has the "this is what they look like" frame and looked much more like a top-five prospect again over the season's last 10 weeks, but the approach still needs a lot of refinement for the bat to carry him beyond the high minors.

## 14 Patrick Bailey  C

Born: 05/29/99   Age: 24   Bats: S   Throws: R   Height: 6'1"   Weight: 210 lb.   Origin: Round 1, 2020 Draft (#13 overall)

| YEAR | TEAM | LVL | AGE | PA | R | 2B | 3B | HR | RBI | BB | K | SB | CS | AVG/OBP/SLG | DRC+ | BABIP | BRR | DRP | WARP |
|------|------|-----|-----|-----|----|----|----|----|-----|----|-----|----|----|-------------|------|-------|------|------------------|------|
| 2021 | SJ | A | 22 | 207 | 45 | 16 | 0 | 7 | 24 | 28 | 47 | 1 | 1 | .322/.415/.531 | 122 | .403 | 0.8 | C(39) 19.5 | 3.1 |
| 2021 | EUG | A+ | 22 | 155 | 13 | 9 | 0 | 2 | 15 | 18 | 43 | 6 | 0 | .185/.290/.296 | 84 | .256 | 0.8 | C(25) 5.9, 1B(4) -0.0 | 0.8 |
| 2022 | EUG | A+ | 23 | 325 | 49 | 14 | 1 | 12 | 51 | 49 | 72 | 1 | 1 | .225/.342/.419 | 118 | .253 | -0.2 | C(72) 18.4, 1B(1) -0.1 | 3.5 |
| 2023 non-DC | SF | MLB | 24 | 251 | 22 | 11 | 1 | 4 | 22 | 24 | 65 | 1 | 1 | .220/.301/.331 | 81 | .294 | -3.8 | C 0, 1B 0 | 0.0 |

Here is where we start a run of underperforming former first-round picks. Bailey was playable in Eugene, but it's hard to have much confidence in a hitter that slashes .225/.342/.420 in High A and isn't the victim of some horrific amount of BABIP chicanery (Bailey's was .253). Bailey is still regarded as a good framer, and the acceptable offensive bar a catcher has to clear is more or less on the ground, but he's not regarded as a great athlete. There's still a decent catcher with pop in here, but Bailey's got a long way to go to get there.

## 15 Heliot Ramos  OF

Born: 09/07/99   Age: 23   Bats: R   Throws: R   Height: 6'1"   Weight: 188 lb.   Origin: Round 1, 2017 Draft (#19 overall)

| YEAR | TEAM | LVL | AGE | PA | R | 2B | 3B | HR | RBI | BB | K | SB | CS | AVG/OBP/SLG | DRC+ | BABIP | BRR | DRP | WARP |
|------|------|-----|-----|-----|----|----|----|----|-----|----|-----|----|----|-------------|------|-------|------|--------------------------------|------|
| 2021 | RIC | AA | 21 | 266 | 36 | 14 | 1 | 10 | 26 | 27 | 73 | 7 | 2 | .237/.323/.432 | 104 | .301 | 0.0 | CF(58) -3.2 | 0.7 |
| 2021 | SAC | AAA | 21 | 229 | 30 | 11 | 2 | 4 | 30 | 15 | 65 | 8 | 2 | .272/.323/.399 | 78 | .375 | 2.9 | CF(32) -2.4, RF(17) 1.2 | 0.3 |
| 2022 | SAC | AAA | 22 | 475 | 61 | 17 | 1 | 11 | 45 | 41 | 112 | 6 | 6 | .227/.305/.349 | 76 | .283 | 0.2 | CF(49) -4.5, RF(33) -2.6, LF(21) 1.6 | -0.5 |
| 2022 | SF | MLB | 22 | 22 | 4 | 0 | 0 | 0 | 0 | 2 | 6 | 0 | 0 | .100/.182/.100 | 99 | .143 | 0.2 | RF(6) -0.2, LF(3) -0.3 | 0.0 |
| 2023 DC | SF | MLB | 23 | 60 | 6 | 2 | 0 | 1 | 5 | 4 | 18 | 1 | 0 | .222/.285/.334 | 77 | .306 | -0.1 | RF 0, LF 0 | -0.1 |

*Comparables: Wil Myers, Carlos Tocci, Domingo Santana*

It's easy to forget that Ramos is just 23, but the dynamic everyday outfielder ceiling he once had is starting to look a little more distant now. Ramos has always hit the ball hard but his ground-ball rate hewed close to 50% over the last few seasons, prompting a swing change and, as a result, a massive collapse of his bat. It's worth noting that his strikeout and walk rates trended in the right direction in 2022, he's still a quality defender in a corner and making a swing change midseason is no small task. Out of anyone in the back half of this list, he might be the most likely to claw his way back into the top 10 by the middle of 2023 if the revamped swing mechanics start to click.

## 16 Will Bednar RHP

Born: 06/13/00   Age: 23   Bats: R   Throws: R   Height: 6'2"   Weight: 230 lb.   Origin: Round 1, 2021 Draft (#14 overall)

| YEAR | TEAM | LVL | AGE | W | L | SV | G | GS | IP | H | HR | BB/9 | K/9 | K | GB% | BABIP | WHIP | ERA | DRA- | WARP |
|---|---|---|---|---|---|---|---|---|---|---|---|---|---|---|---|---|---|---|---|---|
| 2022 | SJ | A | 22 | 1 | 3 | 0 | 12 | 12 | 43 | 25 | 7 | 4.6 | 10.7 | 51 | 43.4% | .196 | 1.09 | 4.19 | 104 | -0.1 |
| 2023 non-DC | SF | MLB | 23 | 3 | 3 | 0 | 58 | 0 | 50 | 51 | 8 | 4.8 | 8.6 | 48 | 36.3% | .305 | 1.56 | 5.51 | 136 | -0.7 |

Bednar's full-season debut was cut short as he didn't pitch after June 12 due to injury issues, but the 2021 first-rounder's 12 starts left something to be desired. Although there were times that he carved up Cal League lineups the way a credible SEC pitcher should, he also had bouts of wildness, allowed more homers than you'd like and still doesn't have much of a changeup. He probably has more leash as a starter, but the 95-and-a-slider repertoire makes him look like a future reliever from here.

## 17 Will Wilson MI

Born: 07/21/98   Age: 24   Bats: R   Throws: R   Height: 6'0"   Weight: 184 lb.   Origin: Round 1, 2019 Draft (#15 overall)

| YEAR | TEAM | LVL | AGE | PA | R | 2B | 3B | HR | RBI | BB | K | SB | CS | AVG/OBP/SLG | DRC+ | BABIP | BRR | DRP | WARP |
|---|---|---|---|---|---|---|---|---|---|---|---|---|---|---|---|---|---|---|---|
| 2021 | SCO | WIN | 22 | 74 | 9 | 3 | 0 | 2 | 8 | 6 | 19 | 0 | 0 | .164/.243/.299 | | .196 | | | |
| 2021 | EUG | A+ | 22 | 224 | 37 | 14 | 2 | 10 | 26 | 24 | 56 | 7 | 1 | .251/.339/.497 | 110 | .298 | 0.8 | SS(42) -2.0, 2B(4) -0.4 | 0.8 |
| 2021 | RIC | AA | 22 | 221 | 20 | 8 | 0 | 5 | 22 | 22 | 81 | 1 | 0 | .189/.281/.306 | 68 | .291 | -0.6 | SS(48) -6.8, 3B(3) -0.1 | -0.9 |
| 2022 | GNTO | ROK | 23 | 34 | 6 | 4 | 0 | 1 | 9 | 4 | 8 | 0 | 0 | .500/.588/.750 | | .684 | | | |
| 2022 | RIC | AA | 23 | 219 | 35 | 6 | 0 | 12 | 27 | 28 | 65 | 2 | 2 | .225/.324/.445 | 108 | .272 | 0.8 | SS(32) 0.6, 2B(16) 0.5, 3B(2) 0.2 | 1.0 |
| 2022 | SAC | AAA | 23 | 36 | 2 | 2 | 0 | 0 | 2 | 2 | 14 | 0 | 1 | .182/.250/.242 | 70 | .316 | 0.0 | SS(5) -0.7, 2B(3) -0.2, 3B(2) -0.0 | -0.1 |
| 2023 non-DC | SF | MLB | 24 | 251 | 23 | 10 | 1 | 6 | 25 | 20 | 85 | 1 | 0 | .214/.284/.340 | 77 | .314 | -3.9 | 2B 0, 3B 0 | -0.3 |

The former first-round pick for the Angels still hasn't recaptured the hit tool that he showed once upon a time at North Carolina State, but he did demonstrate more proclivity for power at Richmond and earned a brief promotion to Triple-A in mid-June before a hamate bone injury took him out of action for six weeks. As often follows with hamate injuries, that power was almost completely gone when he returned in August. Wilson can still play well all over the dirt, so there's still some utility upside, but it's unlikely to be pretty at the plate.

## 18 Cole Waites RHP

Born: 06/10/98   Age: 25   Bats: R   Throws: R   Height: 6'3"   Weight: 180 lb.   Origin: Round 18, 2019 Draft (#536 overall)

| YEAR | TEAM | LVL | AGE | W | L | SV | G | GS | IP | H | HR | BB/9 | K/9 | K | GB% | BABIP | WHIP | ERA | DRA- | WARP |
|---|---|---|---|---|---|---|---|---|---|---|---|---|---|---|---|---|---|---|---|---|
| 2021 | SJ | A | 23 | 1 | 0 | 2 | 10 | 0 | 10¹ | 1 | 0 | 3.5 | 20.9 | 24 | 62.5% | .125 | 0.48 | 0.87 | 75 | 0.2 |
| 2022 | EUG | A+ | 24 | 1 | 1 | 1 | 13 | 0 | 12² | 10 | 1 | 2.8 | 19.2 | 27 | 42.9% | .450 | 1.11 | 3.55 | 70 | 0.3 |
| 2022 | RIC | AA | 24 | 2 | 2 | 4 | 18 | 0 | 21 | 12 | 0 | 6.4 | 16.3 | 38 | 34.2% | .324 | 1.29 | 1.71 | 75 | 0.6 |
| 2022 | SAC | AAA | 24 | 1 | 0 | 1 | 7 | 0 | 8 | 3 | 0 | 3.4 | 12.4 | 11 | 50.0% | .214 | 0.75 | 0.00 | 84 | 0.1 |
| 2022 | SF | MLB | 24 | 0 | 0 | 0 | 7 | 0 | 5² | 6 | 1 | 6.4 | 6.4 | 4 | 41.2% | .313 | 1.76 | 3.18 | 107 | 0.0 |
| 2023 DC | SF | MLB | 25 | 2 | 2 | 0 | 41 | 0 | 35 | 27 | 4 | 4.8 | 11.0 | 43 | 38.2% | .270 | 1.29 | 3.38 | 92 | 0.3 |

Comparables: James Bourque, Chad Sobotka, Erik Hamren

Waites pitched at four different levels in 2022 and struck out 44% of the batters he faced, making it all the way to a brief tryout in the Giants' bullpen in September. You might think Waites is your standard 95-and-a-slider bullpen arm, but his fastball actually averaged 96 mph, so adjust your expectations accordingly. He does have some command concerns, as these types of bullpen arms do, and his delivery is definitely of the grip-it-and-rip-it variety. Not many pitchers are as dominant as Waites looked at times without doing something right, though. He probably won't be the go-to ninth inning option as long as Camilo Doval is on the team, but Waites looks like a plug-and-play seventh- or eighth-inning option to open 2023.

## 19 Landen Roupp   RHP

Born: 09/10/98   Age: 24   Bats: R   Throws: R   Height: 6'2"   Weight: 205 lb.   Origin: Round 12, 2021 Draft (#356 overall)

| YEAR | TEAM | LVL | AGE | W | L | SV | G | GS | IP | H | HR | BB/9 | K/9 | K | GB% | BABIP | WHIP | ERA | DRA- | WARP |
|---|---|---|---|---|---|---|---|---|---|---|---|---|---|---|---|---|---|---|---|---|
| 2021 | GNTB | ROK | 22 | 0 | 0 | 0 | 4 | 0 | 6 | 5 | 0 | 1.5 | 18.0 | 12 | 57.1% | .500 | 1.00 | 3.00 | | |
| 2022 | SJ | A | 23 | 5 | 2 | 0 | 14 | 2 | 48² | 33 | 2 | 3.1 | 12.8 | 69 | 49.5% | .295 | 1.03 | 2.59 | 80 | 0.7 |
| 2022 | EUG | A+ | 23 | 3 | 0 | 0 | 7 | 7 | 32¹ | 19 | 1 | 2.5 | 14.5 | 52 | 54.7% | .286 | 0.87 | 1.67 | 79 | 0.7 |
| 2022 | RIC | AA | 23 | 2 | 1 | 0 | 5 | 5 | 26¹ | 19 | 3 | 3.8 | 10.6 | 31 | 51.5% | .246 | 1.14 | 3.76 | 82 | 0.6 |
| 2023 non-DC | SF | MLB | 24 | 3 | 3 | 0 | 58 | 0 | 50 | 47 | 7 | 4.0 | 9.6 | 53 | 40.8% | .301 | 1.37 | 4.07 | 107 | 0.1 |

Roupp mowed through the low minors in his first full pro season, making it all the way to Richmond on the back of a fastball in the 92-94 range with tail and a big, high-spin curveball with two-plane movement. He also throws a decent slider and a mediocre changeup, but what places Roupp in this range on the list is that he already kind of pitches like a reliever, throwing the curveball more than any other pitch. His delivery is also a bit high tempo out of the windup and he's a little more controlled out of the stretch. Roupp started 14 of his 26 appearances in 2022, but he could be a fast-track bullpen candidate if the curveball keeps playing like it did last season.

## 20 Trevor McDonald   RHP

Born: 02/26/01   Age: 22   Bats: R   Throws: R   Height: 6'2"   Weight: 200 lb.   Origin: Round 11, 2019 Draft (#326 overall)

| YEAR | TEAM | LVL | AGE | W | L | SV | G | GS | IP | H | HR | BB/9 | K/9 | K | GB% | BABIP | WHIP | ERA | DRA- | WARP |
|---|---|---|---|---|---|---|---|---|---|---|---|---|---|---|---|---|---|---|---|---|
| 2021 | GNTO | ROK | 20 | 2 | 3 | 0 | 15 | 13 | 67² | 67 | 3 | 4.1 | 9.2 | 69 | 51.6% | .346 | 1.45 | 3.86 | | |
| 2022 | SJ | A | 21 | 6 | 3 | 2 | 27 | 10 | 90¹ | 74 | 2 | 4.0 | 10.2 | 102 | 56.2% | .310 | 1.26 | 2.39 | 86 | 0.9 |
| 2022 | EUG | A+ | 21 | 0 | 0 | 0 | 2 | 0 | 11 | 11 | 2 | 1.6 | 14.7 | 18 | 46.2% | .375 | 1.18 | 1.64 | 86 | 0.2 |
| 2023 non-DC | SF | MLB | 22 | 3 | 3 | 0 | 58 | 0 | 50 | 53 | 7 | 4.5 | 8.0 | 44 | 39.7% | .312 | 1.57 | 5.18 | 129 | -0.5 |

McDonald pitched out of the San Jose bullpen for the first half of 2022 before getting a shot to start when other pitchers were hurt or promoted. His 54 strikeouts and 10 walks in 42 ⅓ relief innings compared to his 48/30 K/BB ratio in 48 innings as a starter give you an idea of how that went. Much like Roupp, McDonald doesn't show much potential in his changeup but spins a pair of quality breaking balls, his fastball generally sits in the mid-90s or slightly below and could play up in short bursts and his delivery isn't particularly elegant. If that sounds like a reliever to you, well, yeah.

## Top Talents 25 and Under (as of 4/1/2023):

1. Marco Luciano, SS
2. Kyle Harrison, LHP
3. Luis Matos, OF
4. Casey Schmitt, 3B
5. Aeverson Arteaga, SS
6. Vaun Brown, OF
7. Reggie Crawford, LHP/1B
8. Grant McCray, OF
9. Carson Whisenhunt, LHP
10. Mason Black, RHP

Now that Logan Webb, Camilo Doval and Joey Bart have aged out of this section, we're left with just the prospects. This is a decent collection of talent, as well, and supports the Giants' braintrust's stated goal of getting younger and more athletic around the diamond as some of the legacy players age off the roster or out of the league altogether. Many of the same players who led us to rank the Giants' farm system second among all 30 organizations are still here and many still flashed at least glimpses of their respective upsides throughout 2022. It also doesn't hurt that they brought in Pete Putila, who has helped oversee the Astros' player development conveyor belt since 2015, as the organization's new general manager. Farhan Zaidi has spent the past four seasons rebuilding and retooling the organization for the modern game, and there have been some unquestionable development successes at the major-league level. The farm system may start graduating some of its own in 2023.

# Seattle Mariners

## The State of the System:

There's not much elite talent here anymore—graduating Julio Rodríguez and George Kirby while also trading Noelvi Marte will do that—but some intriguing second- and third-tier players still remain.

## The Top Ten:

### 1. Harry Ford  C  OFP: 55  ETA: 2025

Born: 02/21/03  Age: 20  Bats: R  Throws: R  Height: 5'10"  Weight: 200 lb.  Origin: Round 1, 2021 Draft (#12 overall)

| YEAR | TEAM | LVL | AGE | PA | R | 2B | 3B | HR | RBI | BB | K | SB | CS | AVG/OBP/SLG | DRC+ | BABIP | BRR | DRP | WARP |
|---|---|---|---|---|---|---|---|---|---|---|---|---|---|---|---|---|---|---|---|
| 2021 | MRN | ROK | 18 | 65 | 12 | 7 | 0 | 3 | 10 | 9 | 14 | 3 | 0 | .291/.400/.582 | | .342 | | | |
| 2022 | MOD | A | 19 | 499 | 89 | 23 | 4 | 11 | 65 | 88 | 115 | 23 | 5 | .274/.425/.438 | 116 | .358 | -0.6 | C(54) 8.2 | 3.3 |
| 2023 non-DC | SEA | MLB | 20 | 251 | 22 | 10 | 1 | 3 | 21 | 25 | 69 | 5 | 1 | .218/.305/.311 | 80 | .303 | -2.1 | C 0 | 0.2 |

*Comparables: Angel Salome, Bo Naylor, Iván Herrera*

**The Report:** God help us, we're still in on a prep catcher. Ford's full-season debut went about as well as it could have without a late-season promotion. He played roughly half of his 104 games behind the dish and DH'd for the other half while never catching more than two consecutive games. That's most likely a product of the Mariners trying not to grind the soon-to-be 20-year-old into the ground, because he posted excellent catching and framing metrics for a player his age and threw out just under a third of attempted base stealers. He's not a massive target for pitchers to throw to—in April, I described him as "sort of shaped like a fire hydrant"—but he has plenty of athleticism to work both sides of the plate and corral wild arms as he did through most of the summer.

There was less of a question coming out of the draft about Ford's bat, and he still looks like he can carry an above-average stick after walking nearly as often as he struck out while flashing some decent and promising in-game pop. Even with some loft in his swing, that power looks most likely to manifest itself in a lot of doubles at higher levels. That said, Ford can also motor around the bases as the rare catcher with plus speed and has the ability to stretch hits into extra bases.

**OFP:** 55 / Above-average catcher

**Variance:** High. As of this writing, Ford is still a teenager and hasn't faced any higher competition than Low-A, so there's still a long way to go. It also won't be surprising if he headlines this list for the next couple years.

**Jesse Roche's Fantasy Take:** A slow start—in which Ford hit just .196/.366/.280 with six extra base hits over his first 38 games—diminishes his otherwise exceptional season. He was truly electric over his final 66 games, hitting .320/*.459*/.530 with eight home runs and 16 stolen bases. Ford's blend of plate discipline, solid contact skills, emerging power and plus speed is uncommon, especially for a 19-year-old catcher. Yet, there's the rub. He remains very much a catcher (and a pretty good one), which will likely slow his ascent to the majors and dampen his loud tools due to the rigors of the position. Still, you can dream that Ford develops into a rare 20/20 catcher.

## 2  Emerson Hancock  RHP

OFP: 55   ETA: 2023

Born: 05/31/99   Age: 24   Bats: R   Throws: R   Height: 6'4"   Weight: 213 lb.   Origin: Round 1, 2020 Draft (#6 overall)

| YEAR | TEAM | LVL | AGE | W | L | SV | G | GS | IP | H | HR | BB/9 | K/9 | K | GB% | BABIP | WHIP | ERA | DRA- | WARP |
|---|---|---|---|---|---|---|---|---|---|---|---|---|---|---|---|---|---|---|---|---|
| 2021 | EVE | A+ | 22 | 2 | 0 | 0 | 9 | 9 | 31 | 19 | 1 | 3.8 | 8.7 | 30 | 57.0% | .231 | 1.03 | 2.32 | 100 | 0.2 |
| 2021 | ARK | AA | 22 | 1 | 1 | 0 | 3 | 3 | 13² | 10 | 0 | 2.6 | 8.6 | 13 | 36.8% | .263 | 1.02 | 3.29 | 95 | 0.1 |
| 2022 | ARK | AA | 23 | 7 | 4 | 0 | 21 | 21 | 98¹ | 80 | 16 | 3.5 | 8.4 | 92 | 34.5% | .245 | 1.20 | 3.75 | 91 | 1.0 |
| 2023 DC | SEA | MLB | 24 | 2 | 2 | 0 | 6 | 6 | 29 | 31 | 5 | 4.3 | 7.0 | 23 | 36.9% | .296 | 1.55 | 5.14 | 132 | -0.2 |

*Comparables: Drew Anderson, Brandon Bielak, Lay Batista*

**The Report:** Hancock didn't make his first start of 2022 until mid-May due to a lat strain, something of a concern for a pitcher a year removed from arm fatigue and one who had durability concerns as a Dawg as well. Once Hancock took the mound, though, he didn't miss a start for the rest of the season, throwing more innings than in any of his previous pro or college seasons and making a stirring appearance in the Futures Game.

Hancock's arsenal remains largely unchanged, with a heavy, tailing mid-90s fastball aided by his low-three-quarters arm slot and two secondaries that project as plus in a firm two-plane slider and a diving, fading changeup. Hancock also has a smooth, clean delivery that he repeats well and supports his above-average command that borders on plus when he's at his best. He has the frame of a workhorse starter if his body will cooperate with him, but even with his increased inning total in 2022, he still hasn't ever eclipsed 100 frames. He also hasn't proven to be much of a strikeout pitcher in pro ball, averaging just under a punchout an inning since he was drafted. He's near the top of this list in part because the Mariners have graduated some of their best young players or, in the case of Marte, dealt them away. But he's also leading the pitcher pack because the building blocks for him to be an impact starter are still very much intact, and he's not far from breaking through.

**OFP:** 55 / no. 3/4 starter

**Variance:** High. Hancock is still building toward a starter's workload and still hasn't shaken his durability concerns, but he hasn't had any major decline in the stuff or command that made him a top-10 pick two years ago.

**Jesse Roche's Fantasy Take:** On the surface, Hancock had a strong season, including the aforementioned impressive appearance at the Futures Game. However, his performance in Double-A was fairly pedestrian, including an elevated 5.31 FIP and a poor 13.1% K-BB%. Notably, his fastball shape causes it to miss few bats without generating many ground balls. So while Hancock can pump it up to the mid-90s, his fastball often plays down. As such, he lacks the type of fantasy upside to outweigh the ongoing health concerns, and he falls outside the top-100 dynasty prospects.

## 3  Cole Young  SS

OFP: 55   ETA: 2025

Born: 07/29/03   Age: 19   Bats: L   Throws: R   Height: 6'0"   Weight: 180 lb.   Origin: Round 1, 2022 Draft (#21 overall)

| YEAR | TEAM | LVL | AGE | PA | R | 2B | 3B | HR | RBI | BB | K | SB | CS | AVG/OBP/SLG | DRC+ | BABIP | BRR | DRP | WARP |
|---|---|---|---|---|---|---|---|---|---|---|---|---|---|---|---|---|---|---|---|
| 2022 | MRN | ROK | 18 | 26 | 6 | 1 | 1 | 0 | 5 | 4 | 4 | 3 | 0 | .333/.423/.476 | | .389 | | | |
| 2022 | MOD | A | 18 | 45 | 11 | 0 | 0 | 2 | 9 | 4 | 4 | 1 | 2 | .385/.422/.538 | 118 | .371 | -0.3 | SS(8) -0.3, 2B(2) 0.3 | 0.2 |
| 2023 non-DC | SEA | MLB | 19 | 251 | 20 | 10 | 2 | 3 | 21 | 16 | 50 | 3 | 3 | .219/.276/.312 | 65 | .268 | -2.2 | 2B 0, SS 0 | -0.5 |

**The Report:** Young is the kind of player who gets called a baseball rat. What he lacks in physicality or loud tools, he makes up for with an advanced feel to hit and control the barrel. He had one of the best hit tools among the 2022 prep draft class and showed it off immediately in a late-season assignment to Modesto. His bat path is relatively flat and he doesn't have a ton of physical projection left, so he may never get to more than average power at best, but he could also have a plus hit tool. Defensively, Young could fit as either a shortstop or a second baseman but profiles best at the keystone, as his range is stretched slightly at short. His arm will play at either position, however. Combined with his above-average speed, Young has a fairly high floor, particularly for a prep bat, and could move quickly as long as his bat keeps pace with upper-level arms.

**OFP:** 55 / Everyday middle infielder

**Variance:** Medium. Young isn't as sure a bet as he might be as a college bat with the same skill set, but at worst he's a light-hitting fifth infielder with speed. At his best, he looks like a future leadoff hitter.

**Jesse Roche's Fantasy Take:** It is rare to advocate for a high-floor, low-ceiling prep bat, but here we are. Young falls under the radar in this otherwise-stacked FYPD class. While he may lack much physicality, he can really hit, and he has enough pop and speed to be a non-zero contributor in home runs and stolen bases at peak. Don't overlook Young in FYPDs, especially if he falls outside the top 20.

## 4 Bryce Miller  RHP    OFP: 55    ETA: 2024
Born: 08/23/98   Age: 24   Bats: R   Throws: R   Height: 6'2"   Weight: 180 lb.   Origin: Round 4, 2021 Draft (#113 overall)

| YEAR | TEAM | LVL | AGE | W | L | SV | G | GS | IP | H | HR | BB/9 | K/9 | K | GB% | BABIP | WHIP | ERA | DRA- | WARP |
|------|------|-----|-----|---|---|----|---|----|----|---|----|------|-----|---|-----|-------|------|-----|------|------|
| 2021 | MOD | A | 22 | 0 | 0 | 0 | 5 | 3 | 9¹ | 15 | 0 | 1.9 | 14.5 | 15 | 53.6% | .556 | 1.82 | 4.82 | 81 | 0.1 |
| 2022 | EVE | A+ | 23 | 3 | 3 | 0 | 16 | 15 | 77² | 54 | 7 | 2.9 | 11.5 | 99 | 45.7% | .264 | 1.02 | 3.24 | 80 | 1.5 |
| 2022 | ARK | AA | 23 | 4 | 1 | 0 | 10 | 10 | 50² | 34 | 3 | 3.4 | 10.8 | 61 | 43.0% | .263 | 1.05 | 3.20 | 64 | 1.3 |
| 2023 non-DC | SEA | MLB | 24 | 3 | 3 | 0 | 58 | 0 | 50 | 48 | 7 | 3.8 | 8.1 | 45 | 37.8% | .291 | 1.38 | 4.25 | 111 | 0.0 |

Comparables: Erik Johnson, Bailey Ober, Logan Gilbert

**The Report:** Miller didn't start at College Station until his draft year, and even then he only started 10 of the 13 games in which he appeared, with a general lack of feel that contributed to a 14% walk rate, 13 HBP and six wild pitches. He looked like a completely different pitcher in 2022 after making some mechanical changes that, as our John Trupin noted in May, led to "flying open less frequently, fewer uncompetitive pitches, fewer walks and a greater chance of Miller seeing long-term development as a starter." Miller ultimately led the Mariners' farm in strikeouts while keeping his walk rate at a much more palatable level.

Miller has a very modern pitch mix with a mid-90s fastball, touching 98, that shreds hitters up in the zone and a 12-6 curve that sits in the upper-70s and low-80s, though the latter occasionally gets a little sweepy and can bleed into his firm mid-80s slider. His changeup is his fourth-best pitch and is mostly a pace-changer at present but still has some decent arm-side fade. He rotates well on the mound and, though his arm swing is a little long, is generally able to maximize his body and maintain his velocity well through his starts. His fastball-breaker combo also profiles well for late-inning relief work if his command backs up to where it was in college.

**OFP:** 55 / Mid-rotation starter or high-leverage reliever

**Variance:** Very High. Miller's size and command concerns could chase him for as long as he's a starter and will only really go away as he performs at every level. The clear relief fallback makes him an incrementally better bet than some of the arms behind him on this list.

**Jesse Roche's Fantasy Take:** Miller, not Hancock, may be the most interesting fantasy pitching prospect in the system. With a fastball-driven arsenal, he mowed down 163 opposing hitters (30%). Should his secondaries and/or command take another step forward, Miller could develop into a dynamic, high-strikeout starter.

## 5 Walter Ford  RHP    OFP: 55    ETA: 2027
Born: 12/28/04   Age: 18   Bats: R   Throws: R   Height: 6'3"   Weight: 198 lb.   Origin: Round 2, 2022 Draft (#74 overall)

**The Report:** The Vanilla Missile was one of the youngest players in the 2022 draft class after reclassifying out of 2023 and will pitch the entirety of next season as an 18-year-old. Ford's stuff is reflective of a pitcher a few years his senior, however, with a mid-90s fastball that's been up to 97, a low-80s slider that projects as plus and a developing changeup that could eventually get to average or slightly above. Ford's already-sturdy frame and huge arm speed also point to his heater eventually getting to plus or better as his body matures and he gains even more strength. He shows off his athleticism in his delivery with a sizable leg kick and some drop-and-drive in his arm and back leg as he moves down the mound, but he tends to control his body well for a pitcher his age. He'll be a very slow burn given his age and the general development curve for prep arms, but it's an intriguing set of tools for the Mariners' player development team to work with.

**OFP:** 55 / Mid-rotation starter

**Variance:** Extreme. Ford is about as far away from the majors as a prospect not playing in the Dominican Summer League can be. However, the stuff and frame point toward an eventual home in the rotation.

**Jesse Roche's Fantasy Take:** Prep pitching prospects that are light years away from MLB are very rarely recommended targets in dynasty. Ford offers palpable upside, however, and should be on the radar in deep leagues.

## 6  Taylor Dollard  RHP    OFP: 50    ETA: 2023
Born: 02/17/99  Age: 24  Bats: R  Throws: R  Height: 6'3"  Weight: 195 lb.  Origin: Round 5, 2020 Draft (#137 overall)

| YEAR | TEAM | LVL | AGE | W | L | SV | G | GS | IP | H | HR | BB/9 | K/9 | K | GB% | BABIP | WHIP | ERA | DRA- | WARP |
|---|---|---|---|---|---|---|---|---|---|---|---|---|---|---|---|---|---|---|---|---|
| 2021 | MOD | A | 22 | 3 | 2 | 0 | 7 | 7 | 37² | 40 | 2 | 2.4 | 14.1 | 59 | 40.2% | .422 | 1.33 | 3.35 | 93 | 0.4 |
| 2021 | EVE | A+ | 22 | 6 | 2 | 0 | 12 | 11 | 67¹ | 78 | 12 | 1.9 | 9.9 | 74 | 33.5% | .347 | 1.37 | 6.15 | 133 | -0.7 |
| 2022 | ARK | AA | 23 | 16 | 2 | 0 | 27 | 27 | 144 | 106 | 9 | 1.9 | 8.2 | 131 | 40.0% | .251 | 0.95 | 2.25 | 73 | 2.9 |
| 2023 DC | SEA | MLB | 24 | 1 | 1 | 0 | 3 | 3 | 13.3 | 14 | 2 | 2.7 | 7.0 | 11 | 34.2% | .290 | 1.33 | 4.19 | 114 | 0.0 |

*Comparables: Garrett Richards, Trevor Oaks, Walker Lockett*

**The Report:** The Mariners continued promoting Dollard aggressively even after he got knocked around in Everett in the second half of 2021. He responded by shoving against Texas League hitters throughout the summer with fairly average stuff and above-average command that borders on plus. Dollard sits in the low-90s, but his money pitch is a sweeping two-plane slider that he throws to righties and lefties alike and projects as a 60. His big looping curve and useful changeup are both fine offerings as well, although neither is likely to be too much more than average at peak. Dollard's mechanics are fairly simple, as he pitches out of the stretch full-time, but he's very consistent and doesn't try to overthrow his body. Dollard's arsenal ends up as more than the sum of its parts thanks to his command, generating a lot of weak contact even as he struck out fewer than you'd like in Double-A. This is a pretty polished profile overall and one you'd expect to slot in easily as a back-end starter, perhaps as soon as 2023.

**OFP:** 50 / no. 4 starter

**Variance:** Low. Barring a random velocity uptick or sudden change in his secondaries, Dollard is what he is: a quality back-of-rotation starter or depth arm.

**Jesse Roche's Fantasy Take:** A dynasty standout in June, Dollard lacks swing-and-miss stuff, but his strong command and viable slider should get him to the bigs soon, where he could provide decent ratios and a mediocre strikeout rate. If you like Chris Flexen, you might like Dollard.

## 7  Gabriel Gonzalez  LF    OFP: 50    ETA: 2026
Born: 01/04/04  Age: 19  Bats: R  Throws: R  Height: 5'10"  Weight: 165 lb.  Origin: International Free Agent, 2021

| YEAR | TEAM | LVL | AGE | PA | R | 2B | 3B | HR | RBI | BB | K | SB | CS | AVG/OBP/SLG | DRC+ | BABIP | BRR | DRP | WARP |
|---|---|---|---|---|---|---|---|---|---|---|---|---|---|---|---|---|---|---|---|
| 2021 | DSL SEA | ROK | 17 | 221 | 39 | 15 | 4 | 7 | 36 | 21 | 36 | 9 | 3 | .287/.371/.521 | | .313 | | | |
| 2022 | MRN | ROK | 18 | 140 | 20 | 9 | 0 | 5 | 17 | 8 | 21 | 5 | 3 | .357/.421/.548 | | .400 | | | |
| 2022 | MOD | A | 18 | 150 | 31 | 5 | 1 | 2 | 17 | 13 | 21 | 4 | 1 | .286/.400/.389 | 113 | .330 | 0.4 | LF(29) -0.5, RF(2) -0.1 | 0.7 |
| 2023 non-DC | SEA | MLB | 19 | 251 | 19 | 10 | 1 | 2 | 19 | 14 | 62 | 3 | 1 | .210/.268/.289 | 59 | .279 | -2.9 | LF 0, CF 0 | -0.9 |

*Comparables: Cole Tucker, Danry Vasquez, Paul Kelly*

**The Report:** Gonzalez bopped against inferior pitching in the DSL in 2021, with above-average hit and power tools despite his size and enough defensive ability to eventually profile in a corner. After splitting his first season stateside between the complex and Modesto, that report hasn't changed much.

Gonzalez is much stronger now and his listed weight seems out of date since he looks like he's added at least 10-15 pounds of good weight. That's allowed him to tap into his power to all fields with a much more balanced spray chart, going oppo about 40% of the time a year after pulling just over half of his batted balls in the DSL. His SLG in Modesto is also a little misleading, as nearly 54% of his batted balls were on the ground, a far higher rate than the batted-ball profile at either of his previous stops. Gonzalez's approach is fairly aggressive but he can still take a walk and has an above-average ability to get the bat to the ball and a well-balanced swing without much extraneous movement. He played nearly all of his games on the complex and in the Cal League in an outfield corner. That remains his likeliest defensive home going forward as his body matures, with right field possibly being the best fit for his arm strength. Gonzalez will play all of 2023 at 19 years old and will most likely start to climb this list quickly if he maintains this level of performance as the command and secondaries improve.

**OFP:** 50 / Average corner outfielder

**Variance:** Very High. This variance is down exactly one notch from our report on Gonzalez in last year's list cycle. The performance is certainly still there, but he also has just shy of three dozen games in full-season ball. While we still need to see him against proper competition, the very early returns remain promising.

**Jesse Roche's Fantasy Take:** Gonzalez's hit/power potential firmly places him as the second fantasy prospect in this system. In Low-A, he demonstrated precocious hitting ability, with a miniscule 14% strikeout rate, lowest among his 18-year-old peers. If he can more regularly get to his power in games, Gonzalez could quickly jump into the dynasty top 100.

## 8 Tyler Locklear 3B
**OFP:** 50    **ETA:** 2024

Born: 11/24/00   Age: 22   Bats: R   Throws: R   Height: 6'3"   Weight: 210 lb.   Origin: Round 2, 2022 Draft (#58 overall)

| YEAR | TEAM | LVL | AGE | PA | R | 2B | 3B | HR | RBI | BB | K | SB | CS | AVG/OBP/SLG | DRC+ | BABIP | BRR | DRP | WARP |
|------|------|-----|-----|-----|----|----|----|----|-----|----|----|----|----|-------------|------|-------|-----|-----|------|
| 2022 | MOD | A | 21 | 133 | 19 | 5 | 0 | 7 | 29 | 7 | 29 | 0 | 0 | .282/.353/.504 | 116 | .313 | -1.0 | 3B(22) -0.9, 1B(5) -0.3 | 0.5 |
| 2023 non-DC | SEA | MLB | 22 | 251 | 21 | 10 | 1 | 5 | 23 | 13 | 64 | 0 | 0 | .219/.271/.329 | 69 | .283 | -4.4 | 1B 0, 3B 0 | -0.8 |

Comparables: Emmanuel Rivera, Ramon Hernandez, Jermaine Curtis

**The Report:** Locklear has never really stopped hitting since becoming a starter at VCU and bludgeoned pitchers in the Atlantic 10 this year to the tune of a .799 slugging percentage across 62 games. Even considering opponent quality, it's hard to luck into that kind of production, although his numbers were a bit more pedestrian on the Cape in 2021. Locklear takes big swings and hits the ball as hard as you would expect looking at his filled-out frame, but he can be overmatched at times by better velocity. He also has a good sense of the strike zone and has a better feel for contact than your garden-variety TTO slugger. What will tamp down Locklear's value at higher levels is his defensive ability, or lack thereof. He was announced as a third baseman on draft day, but most likely will move across the diamond to first, as he doesn't have very soft hands or the footwork for the hot corner. Even more likely is that he's a DH and occasional backup first baseman. As such, he's going to have to keep hitting everywhere he goes.

**OFP:** 50 / Bat-first first baseman or DH

**Variance:** Medium. The hit and power tools here look legit even if he's unlikely to wear a glove every day in the majors.

**Jesse Roche's Fantasy Take:** Locklear's likely spot at the absolute bottom of the defensive spectrum certainly increases his risk moving forward. But, boy, his bat could be special, with advanced plate discipline, solid contact skills and big raw power.

## 9 Axel Sanchez MI
**OFP:** 50    **ETA:** 2026

Born: 12/10/02   Age: 20   Bats: R   Throws: R   Height: 6'0"   Weight: 170 lb.   Origin: International Free Agent, 2019

| YEAR | TEAM | LVL | AGE | PA | R | 2B | 3B | HR | RBI | BB | K | SB | CS | AVG/OBP/SLG | DRC+ | BABIP | BRR | DRP | WARP |
|------|------|-----|-----|-----|----|----|----|----|-----|----|----|----|----|-------------|------|-------|-----|-----|------|
| 2021 | DSL SEA | ROK | 18 | 191 | 33 | 7 | 0 | 1 | 29 | 20 | 46 | 15 | 4 | .259/.358/.321 | | .350 | | | |
| 2022 | MRN | ROK | 19 | 99 | 15 | 5 | 2 | 2 | 9 | 11 | 20 | 9 | 2 | .267/.354/.442 | | .323 | | | |
| 2022 | MOD | A | 19 | 152 | 27 | 13 | 2 | 8 | 37 | 15 | 42 | 4 | 1 | .305/.401/.618 | 104 | .395 | -0.2 | SS(28) 1.6, 2B(4) -0.8, 3B(1) 0.1 | 0.6 |
| 2022 | EVE | A+ | 19 | 34 | 0 | 1 | 0 | 0 | 1 | 0 | 9 | 0 | 0 | .235/.235/.265 | 76 | .320 | -0.6 | 2B(7) -0.0, 3B(1) -0.0 | -0.1 |
| 2023 non-DC | SEA | MLB | 20 | 251 | 21 | 11 | 2 | 4 | 23 | 14 | 79 | 5 | 1 | .216/.268/.330 | 68 | .308 | -2.1 | 1B 0, 2B 0 | -0.4 |

Comparables: Jonathan Schoop, Javier Báez, Travis Denker

**The Report:** An all-glove shortstop when he signed, Sanchez's bat started to show some life in his stateside debut. Lanky with a ton of physical projection left, Sanchez has loose and whippy hands in the box and can drive the ball when he really gets ahold of one. He has some raw to the pull side, but it's a swing that's more built for doubles at the moment. Like pretty much every other 19-year-old in pro ball, he still needs to refine his approach and his swing can get long when he tries to sell out and get his arms extended.

Sanchez played at all four infield spots throughout 2022, but his future is pretty clearly at the six, where his hands and footwork are both above average. He also has quality arm strength when he can set his feet, but his accuracy on the run can waver. His speed is only average and he'll likely slow a bit as he grows into his body, but his agility and instincts will allow him to stick at short for a while. Although it remains to be seen whether he'll keep hitting like this, he could pretty easily settle into a utility infielder role if he doesn't.

**OFP:** 50 / Glove-first shortstop

**Variance:** Very High. Sanchez only really started hitting in 2022, and the best portion of his season offensively with Modesto included some batted-ball luck. He has plenty of time left developmentally, however, and could be much further up this list next year with another strong season on both sides of the ball.

**Jesse Roche's Fantasy Take:** Sanchez looked like an entirely different player down the stretch, hitting an eye-opening .305/.401/.618 with eight home runs over his final 33 games in Low-A. That said, his offensive tools still are well short of plus. If they can get to average, Sanchez could surprise, especially with the long leash his glove provides.

## 10 Cade Marlowe CF     OFP: 50     ETA: 2023

Born: 06/24/97   Age: 26   Bats: L   Throws: R   Height: 6'1"   Weight: 210 lb.   Origin: Round 20, 2019 Draft (#606 overall)

| YEAR | TEAM | LVL | AGE | PA | R | 2B | 3B | HR | RBI | BB | K | SB | CS | AVG/OBP/SLG | DRC+ | BABIP | BRR | DRP | WARP |
|------|------|-----|-----|-----|----|----|----|----|-----|----|-----|----|----|-------------|------|-------|-----|-----|------|
| 2021 | PEJ | WIN | 24 | 92 | 18 | 5 | 0 | 0 | 7 | 17 | 23 | 7 | 0 | .233/.385/.301 | | .340 | | | |
| 2021 | MOD | A | 24 | 160 | 35 | 6 | 5 | 6 | 29 | 24 | 40 | 11 | 2 | .301/.406/.556 | 127 | .382 | 0.9 | LF(20) -2.7, CF(7) -1.3, RF(1) -0.2 | 0.8 |
| 2021 | EVE | A+ | 24 | 325 | 52 | 18 | 5 | 20 | 77 | 36 | 91 | 12 | 7 | .259/.345/.566 | 113 | .307 | -3.5 | RF(39) 0.4, CF(16) -0.4, LF(10) -0.9 | 1.2 |
| 2022 | ARK | AA | 25 | 518 | 75 | 18 | 4 | 20 | 86 | 55 | 133 | 36 | 10 | .291/.380/.483 | 101 | .369 | 2.0 | CF(113) 2.9, LF(1) -0.1 | 2.0 |
| 2022 | TAC | AAA | 25 | 60 | 8 | 3 | 1 | 3 | 16 | 7 | 23 | 6 | 0 | .250/.350/.519 | 79 | .385 | 0.7 | CF(5) 0.6, LF(4) 0.6, RF(4) 0.5 | 0.2 |
| 2023 DC | SEA | MLB | 26 | 29 | 3 | 1 | 0 | 1 | 3 | 2 | 9 | 1 | 1 | .227/.295/.373 | 92 | .305 | 0.2 | LF 0 | 0.1 |

**The Report:** Marlowe was a 20th-round senior sign in 2019 and enjoyed a brief-but-successful pro debut that year at then-Low-A Everett. He came out the other side of the canceled 2020 season as a bit too old for A-ball, but bashed his way through both levels anyway and did the same at Arkansas in 2022. Marlowe takes hearty but compact cuts and ropes line drives and fly balls to his pull side while using his above-average speed to both steal bases and flit around all three outfield spots, though he looks best at a corner. He's on the older side for a prospect at 25, and there are some swing-and-miss concern, but Marlowe has kept hitting at pretty much every stop since arriving in pro ball. Odds are that he'll find a place in the collection of outfielders who orbit around Planet J-Rod.

**OFP:** 50 / Average corner outfielder with speed

**Variance:** Medium. Marlowe looks like the type of player who starts around four days a week, spelling his fellow outfielders and crushing righties on the long side of a platoon. Of course, injuries and hot streaks often push those players into everyday roles, too.

**Jesse Roche's Fantasy Take:** Marlowe was a man possessed over the last month plus, hitting .390/.472/.764 with 11 home runs and 11 stolen bases over his final 32 games between Double- and Triple-A. If he can harness even a smidgen of that production and weather his contact issues in MLB, he'll be a very interesting power-speed option, as soon as 2023.

# Outside the Top Ten:

## 11 Robert Perez Jr. 1B

Born: 06/26/00   Age: 23   Bats: R   Throws: R   Height: 6'1"   Weight: 170 lb.   Origin: International Free Agent, 2016

| YEAR | TEAM | LVL | AGE | PA | R | 2B | 3B | HR | RBI | BB | K | SB | CS | AVG/OBP/SLG | DRC+ | BABIP | BRR | DRP | WARP |
|------|------|-----|-----|-----|----|----|----|----|-----|----|-----|----|----|-------------|------|-------|-----|-----|------|
| 2021 | MOD | A | 21 | 457 | 62 | 21 | 2 | 15 | 77 | 34 | 114 | 0 | 0 | .282/.359/.456 | 112 | .354 | -0.5 | 1B(66) 1.7, 3B(7) -1.0, RF(5) -0.1 | 1.8 |
| 2022 | MOD | A | 22 | 415 | 78 | 18 | 1 | 20 | 87 | 48 | 108 | 5 | 0 | .270/.369/.501 | 121 | .322 | 4.6 | 1B(83) 3.0, 3B(2) -0.1 | 3.3 |
| 2022 | EVE | A+ | 22 | 153 | 22 | 6 | 1 | 7 | 27 | 23 | 34 | 1 | 1 | .342/.477/.583 | 126 | .425 | -3.7 | 1B(15) 1.4, RF(7) -0.9 | 0.5 |
| 2023 non-DC | SEA | MLB | 23 | 251 | 24 | 10 | 1 | 6 | 25 | 18 | 82 | 1 | 0 | .225/.295/.353 | 85 | .325 | -4.2 | 1B 0, 3B 0 | -0.4 |

Perez crushed A-ball pitching in 2021 and then did it again in 2022, crushing even *more* after a promotion to Everett at the beginning of August. He's this far down the list, though, because the power is more or less his only tool that projects as anything more than average, he's limited defensively to first base and because he's the kind of aggressive hitter who usually gets shoved around by high-minors arms. The power potential is certainly huge, particularly to Perez's pull side, and he's a good athlete even with the defensive limitations, but he's going to have to hit and hit and hit some more to be anything more than a low-average DH or thumper off the bench.

## 12 Jonatan Clase CF

Born: 05/23/02   Age: 21   Bats: S   Throws: R   Height: 5'8"   Weight: 150 lb.   Origin: International Free Agent, 2018

| YEAR | TEAM | LVL | AGE | PA | R | 2B | 3B | HR | RBI | BB | K | SB | CS | AVG/OBP/SLG | DRC+ | BABIP | BRR | DRP | WARP |
|------|------|-----|-----|-----|----|----|----|----|-----|----|-----|----|----|-------------|------|-------|-----|-----|------|
| 2021 | MRN | ROK | 19 | 57 | 12 | 1 | 0 | 2 | 10 | 6 | 15 | 16 | 0 | .245/.333/.388 | | .303 | | | |
| 2022 | MOD | A | 20 | 499 | 91 | 22 | 11 | 13 | 49 | 65 | 133 | 55 | 10 | .267/.373/.463 | 101 | .358 | 3.6 | CF(95) -0.5, LF(5) 0.1 | 1.8 |
| 2023 non-DC | SEA | MLB | 21 | 251 | 21 | 10 | 3 | 3 | 22 | 21 | 79 | 14 | 4 | .226/.295/.336 | 79 | .331 | 2.6 | LF 0, CF 0 | 0.5 |

*Comparables: Sean Henry, Daz Cameron, Teoscar Hernández*

The switch-hitting Clase led the Mariners' entire minor-league system with 55 stolen bases and 11 triples, and he ranked second in runs scored. He was also only a league-average hitter by DRC+ in Low-A and, while he has decent instincts in the outfield, was just under league average by Fielding Runs Above Average. The end result is that Clase is quite fun to watch when he's cooking, with plus-plus speed and more pop than you might expect out of his 5-foot-8, 150-pound frame. He's a bit too aggressive to profile as a prototypical leadoff hitter, but he can still take a walk and could eventually get to average with the bat as a slash-and-burn type hitter.

## 13 Zach DeLoach   OF

Born: 08/18/98   Age: 24   Bats: L   Throws: R   Height: 6'1"   Weight: 205 lb.   Origin: Round 2, 2020 Draft (#43 overall)

| YEAR | TEAM | LVL | AGE | PA | R | 2B | 3B | HR | RBI | BB | K | SB | CS | AVG/OBP/SLG | DRC+ | BABIP | BRR | DRP | WARP |
|------|------|-----|-----|-----|-----|-----|-----|-----|-----|-----|-----|-----|-----|-------------|------|-------|------|-----|------|
| 2021 | EVE | A+ | 22 | 285 | 56 | 23 | 2 | 9 | 37 | 32 | 63 | 6 | 3 | .313/.400/.530 | 113 | .390 | 0.3 | RF(31) 0.7, LF(23) 1.4 | 1.6 |
| 2021 | ARK | AA | 22 | 216 | 28 | 10 | 2 | 5 | 22 | 28 | 58 | 1 | 2 | .227/.338/.384 | 98 | .303 | -0.1 | RF(26) 3.1, LF(17) 2.6 | 1.1 |
| 2022 | ARK | AA | 23 | 499 | 79 | 15 | 3 | 14 | 73 | 71 | 119 | 4 | 1 | .258/.369/.409 | 95 | .324 | -0.3 | RF(71) 1.4, LF(25) 0.4 | 1.9 |
| 2023 non-DC | SEA | MLB | 24 | 251 | 24 | 10 | 2 | 4 | 23 | 25 | 68 | 1 | 0 | .230/.313/.349 | 90 | .312 | -4.0 | LF 0, RF 0 | -0.1 |

*Comparables: Edgardo Baez, Elier Hernandez, Kyle Waldrop*

DeLoach flashed huge power potential at Texas A&M in the truncated 2020 college season, enough for the Mariners to call his name in the second round of that year's draft. While that pop and DeLoach's general quality approach showed up in 2021, he posted a much more pedestrian .258/.369/.409 line in Arkansas. The good news for DeLoach is his walk rate is still superlative, reaching all the way up to 14.2% in 2022, and he still hits the ball hard with his physical frame. The bad news is he hit like a long-side platoon player, with an .835 OPS against righties and just .630 against southpaws. Ultimately, that's probably his role in the majors as well.

## 14 Prelander Berroa   RHP

Born: 04/18/00   Age: 23   Bats: R   Throws: R   Height: 5'11"   Weight: 170 lb.   Origin: International Free Agent, 2016

| YEAR | TEAM | LVL | AGE | W | L | SV | G | GS | IP | H | HR | BB/9 | K/9 | K | GB% | BABIP | WHIP | ERA | DRA- | WARP |
|------|------|-----|-----|-----|-----|-----|-----|-----|-----|-----|-----|------|-----|-----|------|-------|------|------|------|------|
| 2021 | SJ | A | 21 | 5 | 6 | 0 | 24 | 24 | 98² | 79 | 13 | 4.8 | 12.3 | 135 | 39.2% | .310 | 1.34 | 3.56 | 94 | 0.9 |
| 2022 | EVE | A+ | 22 | 2 | 2 | 0 | 13 | 13 | 52¹ | 29 | 2 | 5.5 | 13.9 | 81 | 49.0% | .276 | 1.17 | 2.41 | 78 | 1.1 |
| 2022 | EUG | A+ | 22 | 0 | 0 | 0 | 4 | 4 | 13¹ | 5 | 0 | 4.0 | 10.8 | 16 | 32.0% | .200 | 0.83 | 0.67 | 88 | 0.2 |
| 2022 | ARK | AA | 22 | 2 | 1 | 0 | 9 | 9 | 35 | 20 | 3 | 6.4 | 13.6 | 53 | 46.4% | .262 | 1.29 | 4.37 | 69 | 0.8 |
| 2023 non-DC | SEA | MLB | 23 | 3 | 3 | 0 | 58 | 0 | 50 | 44 | 8 | 6.0 | 11.2 | 62 | 36.6% | .301 | 1.54 | 4.77 | 119 | -0.2 |

*Comparables: Cristian Javier, Enoli Paredes, Dellin Betances*

The Mariners acquired Berroa from the Giants in May and kept him in the rotation across High-A and Double-A, but make no mistake, this is a relief profile. Berroa attacks hitters with a mid-90s fastball, a sharp two-plane slider and below-average command, resulting in strikeout rates in the mid-30s as well as walk rates in the mid-teens. Berroa's changeup is below-average at best and he's thrown it sparingly in the low minors. While he has built up a solid foundation of innings so far, his stuff and ability to locate it both profile better in a one-inning setting where he can air it out.

## 15 Lazaro Montes   OF

Born: 10/22/04   Age: 18   Bats: L   Throws: R   Height: 6'3"   Weight: 210 lb.   Origin: International Free Agent, 2022

| YEAR | TEAM | LVL | AGE | PA | R | 2B | 3B | HR | RBI | BB | K | SB | CS | AVG/OBP/SLG | DRC+ | BABIP | BRR | DRP | WARP |
|------|------|-----|-----|-----|-----|-----|-----|-----|-----|-----|-----|-----|-----|-------------|------|-------|------|-----|------|
| 2022 | DSL SEA | ROK | 17 | 223 | 34 | 13 | 5 | 10 | 41 | 35 | 74 | 3 | 1 | .284/.422/.585 | | .421 | | | |

Part of Seattle's 2022 J2 class out of Cuba, Montes arguably has the most physical projection of any player on this list, having just turned 18 in October and already standing at a sturdy 6-foot-3 and 210 pounds. The Mariners started Montes in the DSL, as they tend to do with all international signees, where he dominated competition that was pretty clearly behind his level of proficiency with power and patience. We'll have a much better handle on who Montes is and can be once he debuts stateside.

## 16  Spencer Packard  LF

Born: 10/12/97  Age: 25  Bats: L  Throws: R  Height: 6'1"  Weight: 205 lb.  Origin: Round 9, 2021 Draft (#264 overall)

| YEAR | TEAM | LVL | AGE | PA | R | 2B | 3B | HR | RBI | BB | K | SB | CS | AVG/OBP/SLG | DRC+ | BABIP | BRR | DRP | WARP |
|------|------|-----|-----|----|----|----|----|----|----|----|----|----|----|-------------|------|-------|-----|-----|------|
| 2021 | MOD | A | 23 | 138 | 20 | 4 | 1 | 3 | 18 | 13 | 19 | 1 | 0 | .250/.348/.375 | 120 | .276 | 0.1 | LF(15) 0.1, RF(5) -1.2 | 0.7 |
| 2022 | EVE | A+ | 24 | 307 | 43 | 15 | 1 | 12 | 37 | 41 | 47 | 5 | 1 | .282/.397/.490 | 150 | .303 | -1.1 | LF(42) -2.2, RF(9) -0.9, CF(5) 1.1 | 2.3 |
| 2023 non-DC | SEA | MLB | 25 | 251 | 22 | 10 | 1 | 4 | 23 | 21 | 41 | 1 | 0 | .220/.297/.329 | 79 | .253 | -4.0 | 1B 0, 3B 0 | -0.4 |

*Comparables: Ben Ruta, Nick Banks, Brady Shoemaker*

A ninth-round pick in 2021 out of Campbell University (go Fighting Camels), Packard has walked nearly as much as he's punched out at both A-ball levels and posted quality contact and power numbers with Everett. Alas, given that he's this far down the list, caveats abound: He's already 25, hasn't played above A-ball, doesn't have more than an average power projection, doesn't run well and isn't a great defender, profiling best in left field or at first. He's also pretty much entirely maxed out physically; our John Trupin described him earlier this year as "(b)uilt like a spiral ham with short, muscular levers." So we're left with a relatively untested bat-first profile, but one that could find a home on the fringes of a 26-man roster in the near future.

## 17  Juan Then  RHP

Born: 02/07/00  Age: 23  Bats: R  Throws: R  Height: 6'1"  Weight: 200 lb.  Origin: International Free Agent, 2016

| YEAR | TEAM | LVL | AGE | W | L | SV | G | GS | IP | H | HR | BB/9 | K/9 | K | GB% | BABIP | WHIP | ERA | DRA- | WARP |
|------|------|-----|-----|---|---|----|----|----|----|----|----|------|-----|----|-----|-------|------|-----|------|------|
| 2021 | EVE | A+ | 21 | 2 | 5 | 0 | 14 | 14 | 54¹ | 68 | 12 | 3.1 | 9.8 | 59 | 47.1% | .354 | 1.60 | 6.46 | 100 | 0.4 |
| 2022 | ARK | AA | 22 | 0 | 1 | 0 | 10 | 0 | 10 | 11 | 2 | 2.7 | 12.6 | 14 | 25.9% | .360 | 1.40 | 5.40 | 88 | 0.1 |
| 2023 non-DC | SEA | MLB | 23 | 3 | 3 | 0 | 58 | 0 | 50 | 56 | 9 | 3.8 | 7.5 | 42 | 35.0% | .313 | 1.55 | 5.44 | 137 | -0.7 |

*Comparables: Matt Lollis, Arodys Vizcaíno, Drew Hutchison*

Then didn't appear in a game until August due to injury issues and pitched out of the Arkansas bullpen once he returned, with a couple blow-up outings obscuring his overall numbers. It's mid-90s heat—a lot of 95s and 96s with the occasional hump up into the upper-90s. Then throws the pitch out of a lower three-quarters slot, giving it effective tail that bores in on right-handers. Then's slider flashes plus when he puts it where he wants it, but it still has batters flailing at it even when he doesn't. His changeup is further behind the other two pitches, but they're high-octane enough that Then could find himself jogging out of a major-league bullpen in short order.

## 18  Bryan Woo  RHP

Born: 01/30/00  Age: 23  Bats: R  Throws: R  Height: 6'2"  Weight: 205 lb.  Origin: Round 6, 2021 Draft (#174 overall)

| YEAR | TEAM | LVL | AGE | W | L | SV | G | GS | IP | H | HR | BB/9 | K/9 | K | GB% | BABIP | WHIP | ERA | DRA- | WARP |
|------|------|-----|-----|---|---|----|---|----|----|----|----|------|-----|----|-------|-------|------|------|------|------|
| 2022 | MOD | A | 22 | 0 | 1 | 0 | 6 | 6 | 20¹ | 18 | 2 | 2.7 | 12.8 | 29 | 37.5% | .356 | 1.18 | 3.98 | 86 | 0.2 |
| 2022 | EVE | A+ | 22 | 1 | 3 | 0 | 7 | 7 | 32 | 32 | 2 | 4.5 | 12.9 | 46 | 35.4% | .375 | 1.50 | 4.78 | 92 | 0.4 |
| 2023 non-DC | SEA | MLB | 23 | 3 | 3 | 0 | 58 | 0 | 50 | 49 | 8 | 4.4 | 8.5 | 47 | 34.4% | .293 | 1.46 | 4.75 | 121 | -0.3 |

Woo was a sixth-round pick out of Cal Poly in 2021 but didn't debut until 2022 following his rehab from Tommy John surgery. He quickly shook off any rehab rust and is back to pumping mid-90s fastballs out of a delivery that he repeats well without much effort. His slider, changeup and command are all still improving as you'd expect for someone with just 57 pro innings and another 10 ⅔ in the AFL, but Woo looks like a candidate to jump up this list in a year's time.

## 19  Gabe Moncada  1B

Born: 12/17/01  Age: 21  Bats: L  Throws: L  Height: 6'2"  Weight: 175 lb.  Origin: International Free Agent, 2018

| YEAR | TEAM | LVL | AGE | PA | R | 2B | 3B | HR | RBI | BB | K | SB | CS | AVG/OBP/SLG | DRC+ | BABIP | BRR | DRP | WARP |
|------|------|-----|-----|----|----|----|----|----|----|----|----|----|----|-------------|------|-------|-----|-----|------|
| 2021 | DSL SEA | ROK | 19 | 206 | 29 | 16 | 2 | 4 | 30 | 37 | 46 | 2 | 5 | .358/.500/.560 | | .482 | | | |
| 2022 | MRN | ROK | 20 | 135 | 12 | 8 | 2 | 3 | 12 | 17 | 24 | 4 | 2 | .310/.400/.491 | | .367 | | | |
| 2022 | MOD | A | 20 | 91 | 13 | 2 | 0 | 2 | 10 | 11 | 28 | 0 | 0 | .154/.275/.256 | 87 | .208 | 0.4 | 1B(21) -0.6 | 0.1 |
| 2023 non-DC | SEA | MLB | 21 | 251 | 19 | 9 | 2 | 2 | 19 | 19 | 89 | 1 | 1 | .203/.271/.289 | 59 | .321 | -3.6 | 1B 0, RF 0 | -1.2 |

Moncada originally made his pro debut in the Dominican in 2019, but returned there in 2021 after the gap year and only made his stateside debut in 2022. The native of Caracas, Venezuela, doesn't hit for much more than gap power for now, but there's a good amount of room on his 6-foot-2, 175-pound frame to add muscle. He also has a good idea of the strike zone, generally keeping his walk and strikeout rates near each other outside of a short stint in the Cal League toward the end of the season. The bat is going to have to keep producing, as Moncada has been limited almost exclusively to first base, deploying to an outfield corner only a handful of times at each level.

## 20 Ashton Izzi  RHP
Born: 11/18/03   Age: 19   Bats: R   Throws: R   Height: 6'3"   Weight: 165 lb.   Origin: Round 4, 2022 Draft (#126 overall)

A fourth-round draft pick in 2022 out of Illinois, Izzi is dripping with projection at 6-foot-3 and 165 pounds. Despite the string-bean frame, Izzi can run his fastball into the mid-90s and has the early makings of a competent slider and changeup. Izzi should benefit greatly from the kind of offseason training and lifting program that a professional baseball organization can provide and could look like a completely different player, in a good way, once he fills out more.

## Top Talents 25 and Under (as of 4/1/2023):

1. Julio Rodríguez, OF
2. Logan Gilbert, RHP
3. George Kirby, RHP
4. Andrés Muñoz, RHP
5. Harry Ford, C
6. Emerson Hancock, RHP
7. Matt Brash, RHP
8. Jarred Kelenic, OF
9. Cole Young, SS
10. Bryce Miller, RHP

It's easy to feel better about a lean system when you have a half-dozen excellent young players who have already established their place in the majors. You would also imagine, though we haven't done any polling to this effect, that the vast, vast majority of Mariners fans don't give a rip about the depth of the farm system after the team reached the postseason for the first time since *Attack of the Clones* was in theaters.

I hate to spoil this for you, dear reader, but Rodríguez will almost assuredly be no. 1 with a bullet in this section until he ages out of it. The J-Rod Show provided everything the Mariners hoped for and more in his rookie season and became the best player on the team shortly after making the Opening Day roster, bashing 25-plus home runs and doubles, stealing 25 bases, nearly winning the Home Run Derby and providing one of the best catches of the entire postseason. That he was named the near-unanimous AL Rookie of the Year was almost an afterthought. Worst of all for the rest of the American League, this is only the beginning for the 21-year-old superstar.

Gilbert skipped any notion of a sophomore slump and took a significant step forward, throwing all of his pitches harder on average and cutting his home run rate while forcing more groundballs. He also dropped his fastball usage by a modest amount (61.5% in 2021, 53.9% in 2022) and struck out hitters at a slightly lower rate than in 2021, but still hasn't quite found a plus secondary pitch. Then again, he posted a better FIP and DRA than in his rookie year, so maybe he still doesn't need one for the time being.

Kirby was even better than Gilbert by some metrics after debuting in early May, posting the fifth-lowest walk rate among all starters with at least 130 innings and casually tossing the third-best fastball in the league by run value. Oh, and he simply added an excellent two-seamer, no big deal, to an arsenal that already plays up because of his plus command. It got lost in the 18 innings of it all, but Kirby ended the year by pitching one of his best games in the majors by Bill James' Game Score with the Mariners' backs against the wall.

Muñoz has looked like an impact reliever since he was a teenager in the Padres' farm system, blowing away minor-league hitters with a fastball that was clocked up to 104 mph. A few years and one elbow scar later, Muñoz still runs it up to and beyond the century mark consistently (he averaged 100.2 mph) but favored his slider roughly two-thirds of the time in his first full season since 2019. The most encouraging part for the young fireballer was his 6% walk rate, which previously sat in the 10-15% range when he was a prospect. Paul Sewald finished the most games for the Mariners in 2022, with Muñoz pitching mostly in the seventh and eighth innings, but you wouldn't begrudge Scott Servais for giving Muñoz more chances to slam the door going forward.

Brash graduated out of list consideration by the skin of his teeth, throwing 50 ⅔ innings between a handful of early-season starts and the bullpen, where he pitched most of the 2022 campaign. He generally pitched to his scouting report, with an electric fastball-breaker combination and not much command of it. Brash was much better out of the pen, however, lowering his walk rate from 17.9% to 12.6% and upping his strikeout rate from 20% as a starter to 33% as a reliever. He already had a lot of reliever risk as a prospect, but he seems to have found a home airing it out for an inning at a time.

What more is there to say about Kelenic and his struggles against non-fastballs? It prompted introspection from Jarrett Seidler about how we scout hit tools in the abstract and, more tangibly, it earned Kelenic a midseason demotion to Tacoma that lasted for the better part of four months. To his credit, he showed some slight—slight—improvement in September in his ability to at least avoid swinging and missing half the time against slow stuff, whiffing on 30.4% of his swings against breaking pitches and 34.8% of his swings on offspeed across both Triple-A and the majors. It didn't result in much success at the higher level, as Kelenic went 8-for-30 in his first eight games after re-emerging from the PCL, but just 3-for-37 across his final 11 games of the season, including the playoffs. There are some minor caveats—he's still 23 and was better defensively in 2022—but at this point, Kelenic has 500 major-league plate appearances under his belt. This is probably who he is.

# St. Louis Cardinals

## The State of the System:

The Cardinals have three potential impact talents at the top of their system, but less depth than recent years.

## The Top Ten:

### 1 Jordan Walker  OF/3B      OFP: 70      ETA: Late 2023/Early 2024

Born: 05/22/02   Age: 21   Bats: R   Throws: R   Height: 6'5"   Weight: 220 lb.   Origin: Round 1, 2020 Draft (#21 overall)

| YEAR | TEAM | LVL | AGE | PA | R | 2B | 3B | HR | RBI | BB | K | SB | CS | AVG/OBP/SLG | DRC+ | BABIP | BRR | DRP | WARP |
|------|------|-----|-----|----|----|----|----|----|-----|----|----|----|----|-------------|------|-------|-----|-----|------|
| 2021 | PMB | A | 19 | 122 | 24 | 11 | 1 | 6 | 21 | 18 | 21 | 1 | 0 | .374/.475/.687 | 145 | .419 | -0.3 | 3B(22) -3.6 | 0.6 |
| 2021 | PEO | A+ | 19 | 244 | 39 | 14 | 3 | 8 | 27 | 15 | 66 | 13 | 2 | .292/.344/.487 | 101 | .382 | -0.5 | 3B(54) -3.6 | 0.4 |
| 2022 | SPR | AA | 20 | 536 | 100 | 31 | 3 | 19 | 68 | 58 | 116 | 22 | 5 | .306/.388/.510 | 98 | .365 | -1.3 | 3B(70) -2.6, RF(25) -0.6, CF(4) -1.0 | 1.4 |
| 2023 DC | STL | MLB | 21 | 294 | 32 | 13 | 2 | 6 | 30 | 22 | 79 | 6 | 2 | .238/.302/.365 | 93 | .316 | -0.5 | 3B 0, RF 0 | 0.4 |

*Comparables: Rafael Devers, Josh Vitters, Bo Bichette*

**The Report:** Walker continued to redline every Trackman engine in Double-A despite not turning 20 years old until a month into the season. His batted-ball profile would have been among the best in the *major* leagues last year, and he routinely smacks baseballs 110 mph or more. His contact rates remain fine, although he did chase more against Double-A pitching. I think he's going to make enough contact and hit the ball very, very hard when he does. Walker does still hit the ball on the ground a little bit more than you'd like, and if he falls short of a true elite power outcome, that might be why. On the other hand, if he tweaks his approach enough and starts pulling the ball in the air more consistently, he's going to win home run titles, and he started to lift the ball more later in the year.

Walker is listed here at third base and outfield—because he did spend most of 2022 at the hot corner—but is clearly transitioning to a corner outfield spot. He runs well enough and throws more than well enough for right field, but he's going to take some time to develop into an average glove on the grass. The bat might be ready before the glove, and he's still not a lock to avoid first base in the long term, but once again this list cycle, the offensive upside here is so loud, that just doesn't move the needle much for me.

**OFP:** 70 / All-Star slugger, position TBD

**Variance:** High. Contrary to what I wrote about OFP 50s in the intro, you'd prefer your OFP 70s to be lower variance. Walker has true elite outcomes in the 90th percentile and up, but you also don't have to go too far below the 50th percentile to start seeing "better Nomar Mazara" in play.

**Jesse Roche's Fantasy Take:** In addition to the massive power, Walker has understated speed, and posts high-end sprint speed. Granted, it takes him a second to get up to speed, and stolen bases are not likely a big long-term part of his game. Still, his 22 steals last year are no fluke. How his contact rate holds up and whether he'll lift enough to get to his power in games are the biggest questions moving forward. Given his proximity, *loud* tools and performance, however, Walker is a clear cut top-five fantasy prospect.

## 2 Masyn Winn SS    OFP: 60    ETA: Late 2023/Early 2024

Born: 03/21/02   Age: 21   Bats: R   Throws: R   Height: 5'11"   Weight: 180 lb.   Origin: Round 2, 2020 Draft (#54 overall)

| YEAR | TEAM | LVL | AGE | PA | R | 2B | 3B | HR | RBI | BB | K | SB | CS | AVG/OBP/SLG | DRC+ | BABIP | BRR | DRP | WARP |
|------|------|-----|-----|-----|----|----|----|----|-----|----|----|----|----|-------------|------|-------|-----|------|------|
| 2021 | PMB | A | 19 | 284 | 50 | 15 | 3 | 3 | 34 | 40 | 60 | 16 | 2 | .262/.370/.388 | 108 | .331 | 3.8 | SS(55) 6.5 | 2.0 |
| 2021 | PEO | A+ | 19 | 154 | 26 | 4 | 2 | 2 | 10 | 6 | 40 | 16 | 3 | .209/.240/.304 | 87 | .274 | 0.7 | SS(31) 1.3 | 0.4 |
| 2022 | PEO | A+ | 20 | 147 | 22 | 11 | 7 | 1 | 15 | 13 | 29 | 15 | 0 | .349/.404/.566 | 132 | .431 | 0.8 | SS(28) -0.4 | 1.1 |
| 2022 | SPR | AA | 20 | 403 | 69 | 25 | 1 | 11 | 48 | 50 | 86 | 28 | 5 | .258/.349/.432 | 102 | .308 | 5.9 | SS(84) 4.5 | 2.4 |
| 2023 non-DC | STL | MLB | 21 | 251 | 21 | 11 | 3 | 3 | 21 | 19 | 55 | 10 | 2 | .222/.287/.329 | 76 | .280 | 0.2 | 1B 0, SS 0 | 0.1 |

Comparables: Jonathan Araúz, Cole Tucker, Domingo Leyba

**The Report:** Winn was an intriguing two-way prep in the 2020 draft, but it wasn't clear that the position player side alone would carry him, despite some offensive upside at a premium defensive spot. Two years on, he's ditched the pitching and developed into one of the better shortstop prospects in the game. Guess the Devil Magic isn't only limited to Day 2 college picks.

Winn's bat broke out in a big way in 2022 as he started to impact the ball more consistently. Despite a pretty average frame, he showed off above-average bat speed and the ability to drive pitches into the gaps where his plus-plus speed is often good for an extra base or two. The top-line exit velocities aren't close to Jordan Walker's, but indicate potential fringe-average pop which means Winn might end up at the top of your lineup rather than the bottom given an above-average hit tool.

Regardless, you'll want him in your lineup somewhere given the defensive skill set. Winn is a plus shortstop with possibly the best infield arm in organized baseball. He's rangy with good hands and actions, and his elite, accurate arm allows him a longer clock than most other infielders. The glove will absolutely get Winn to the majors, but he's now enough of an offensive threat that plus regular is in play, even without the mound work.

**OFP:** 60 / First-division shortstop

**Variance:** High. Winn's Double-A performance was more pedestrian with additional swing-and-miss, so he might settle in more as a good glove who bats eighth. But he's young enough and had enough of a breakout once his sole focus was on hitting that there might be a bit more in the tank at the plate too.

**Jesse Roche's Fantasy Take:** While his power may be fringe, his fantasy value is predicated on his impact speed and promising hit tool. Winn can truly fly and is more than willing to run, going 43-for-48 in steals last year. His solid plate discipline, bat-to-ball ability and, of course, speed should get him on base at a healthy clip. Even if he barely edges past double-digit home runs, Winn has potential to be a dynamic fantasy player.

## 3 Tink Hence RHP    OFP: 60    ETA: 2025

Born: 08/06/02   Age: 20   Bats: R   Throws: R   Height: 6'1"   Weight: 175 lb.   Origin: Round 2, 2020 Draft (#63 overall)

| YEAR | TEAM | LVL | AGE | W | L | SV | G | GS | IP | H | HR | BB/9 | K/9 | K | GB% | BABIP | WHIP | ERA | DRA- | WARP |
|------|------|-----|-----|---|---|----|----|----|-----|----|----|------|------|----|-----|-------|------|-----|------|------|
| 2021 | CAR | ROK | 18 | 0 | 1 | 1 | 8 | 1 | 8 | 11 | 1 | 3.4 | 15.7 | 14 | 31.8% | .476 | 1.75 | 9.00 | | |
| 2022 | PMB | A | 19 | 0 | 1 | 0 | 16 | 16 | 52¹ | 31 | 1 | 2.6 | 13.9 | 81 | 54.1% | .309 | 0.88 | 1.38 | 73 | 1.5 |
| 2023 non-DC | STL | MLB | 20 | 3 | 3 | 0 | 58 | 0 | 50 | 45 | 7 | 4.0 | 8.8 | 49 | 38.0% | .283 | 1.35 | 4.06 | 107 | 0.1 |

Comparables: Noah Syndergaard, A.J. Alexy, Marcos Diplán

**The Report:** Last year, we noted that the Cardinals were very cautious with Hence, and he had workload concerns going back to the draft. Sixteen starts and 52 innings—plus a handful in the AFL—won't assuage those entirely, but like Dave Wasserman, I've seen enough. Similarly to Marco Raya in the Twins system, Hence is just one full(er), healthy season away from being one of the top pitching prospects in baseball. His fastball sits mid-90s, touches higher, and is a heavy pitch. His low-spin curve flashes the kind of sheer drop you'll usually only find at Six Flags, and his mid-80s change is developing well, showing more consistent power sink and fade.

That description of the arsenal sure sounds like a top-of-the-rotation starter, but beyond having just thrown a tick under 70 professional innings, Hence has a narrow, slim frame and an effortful delivery. There's physical projection left, but I don't think he will ever look the part of a sturdy, 180-inning starter. He doesn't have to throw that many frames to be very good—it is the 2020s after all—but the delivery also leads to some overthrowing and fastball command issues, and I do wonder how it holds up when he's expected to go more than three innings per outing. This is a very, very high variance prospect profile, but the right-tail outcomes along that wide swath are quite tantalizing.

**OFP:** 60 / no. 3 starter or late-inning reliever

**Variance:** Well...very, very high. Hence could very easily break out next year once the training wheels come off, end the season in Double-A and be a top-25 prospect in the game. He could also throw another 50 innings...intermittently.

**Jesse Roche's Fantasy Take:** Hence, a standout in June, has three electric, bat-missing offerings that compare favorably to some of the top pitching prospects in baseball. Yet, as emphasized above, he is a high–borderline extreme–risk prospect given his frame and limited innings to date. Depending on how risk-averse you are, Hence could fall within the top 50 or outside the top 100 in fantasy.

## 4 Gordon Graceffo  RHP    OFP: 60    ETA: Late 2023/Early 2024

Born: 03/17/00   Age: 23   Bats: R   Throws: R   Height: 6'4"   Weight: 210 lb.   Origin: Round 5, 2021 Draft (#151 overall)

| YEAR | TEAM | LVL | AGE | W | L | SV | G | GS | IP | H | HR | BB/9 | K/9 | K | GB% | BABIP | WHIP | ERA | DRA- | WARP |
|------|------|-----|-----|---|---|----|----|----|-----|----|----|------|------|----|------|-------|------|------|------|------|
| 2021 | PMB | A | 21 | 1 | 0 | 1 | 11 | 1 | 26 | 28 | 1 | 3.1 | 12.8 | 37 | 63.2% | .403 | 1.42 | 1.73 | 87 | 0.4 |
| 2022 | PEO | A+ | 22 | 3 | 2 | 0 | 8 | 8 | 45² | 27 | 1 | 0.8 | 11.0 | 56 | 43.7% | .255 | 0.68 | 0.99 | 82 | 0.9 |
| 2022 | SPR | AA | 22 | 7 | 4 | 0 | 18 | 18 | 93² | 76 | 16 | 2.3 | 8.0 | 83 | 45.4% | .237 | 1.07 | 3.94 | 76 | 1.7 |
| 2023 non-DC | STL | MLB | 23 | 3 | 3 | 0 | 58 | 0 | 50 | 52 | 7 | 2.9 | 7.2 | 40 | 39.7% | .300 | 1.36 | 4.24 | 112 | -0.1 |

*Comparables: Trey Supak, Jordan Yamamoto, Dean Kremer*

**The Report:** Shortly after getting drafted by the Cardinals, Graceffo saw a significant velocity jump, and he maintained it in 2022, regularly sitting in the mid-90s with above-average sink and command. The now-plus fastball has helped his changeup, and his best offspeed ticks every box to be plus as well. He sells the *cambio* well, it shows good fade away from lefties and has 10 mph of velocity separation off the fastball. Both of Graceffo's breaking balls lag behind the rest of the arsenal. The slider is the primary glove-side offering and has average potential in the upper-80s, flashing solid two-plane action. His curve is used sparingly and has more of a 12-6 shape. Unlike Hence, Graceffo is already built like a mid-rotation starter, and while his stuff doesn't have the same upside, the plus fastball/change combo and advanced strikethrowing should have him contributing to the Cardinals' major-league rotation in short order.

**OFP:** 60 / no. 3 starter

**Variance:** Medium. Graceffo missed fewer bats and was a bit more homer-prone in Double-A, but those things can happen when you pitch your home games in Springfield. He does need to get one of those breaking balls to average to hit the mid-rotation outcome, but Graceffo is a fairly high-floor starter after maintaining his 2021 fastball gains.

**Jesse Roche's Fantasy Take:** Graceffo is a prototypical better-in-real-life-than-in-fantasy pitching prospect. His fastball, while effective, does not miss many bats, and his pound-the-zone approach is geared to forcing batters to put the ball in play and avoiding walks. That said, Graceffo should be good for strong ratios and eating innings, which always has a place in fantasy.

---

## Eyewitness Report: Gordon Graceffo

**Evaluator:** Nathan Graham

**Report Date:** 06/13/2022

**Dates Seen:** 5/8/22

**Risk Factor:** Medium

**Delivery:** Extra-large frame, average build, physically mature; Unique windup, steps straight back towards second base from the middle of the rubber. Very mechanical but repeats well.

| Pitch Type | Future Grade | Sitting Velocity | Peak Velocity | Report |
|------------|--------------|------------------|---------------|--------|
| Fastball | 60 | 94-95 | 96 | Heavy, sinking offering, has late life and generates plenty of weak ground balls; Excellent command to all four quadrants; Maintains velocity deep into games. |
| Changeup | 60 | 82-84 | 86 | True swing and miss offering, fades away from left handed hitters; Sells it well with good arm speed replication and velocity separation. |
| Slider | 50 | 86-87 | 87 | Currently a work in progress, still developing fell for both breaking pitches. Slider features some two plane movement, landed a couple backfoot to LHH in my look; Will become an average major league offering with more reps. |
| Curveball | 50 | 78-80 | 80 | Mixed in just a handful in my look; 12-6 shape, more vertical break than the slider; Showed potential as a future average offering. |

> **Conclusion:** During his time at Villanova, Graceffo worked to get into better shape and transformed himself from a non-prospect into a 2021 fifth round selection. The development has continued in the professional ranks with a jump in fastball velocity and improved secondaries making him now one of the top pitching prospects in the organization.

## 5    Cooper Hjerpe   LHP     OFP: 55     ETA: Late 2024/2025

Born: 03/16/01   Age: 22   Bats: L   Throws: L   Height: 6'3"   Weight: 200 lb.   Origin: Round 1, 2022 Draft (#22 overall)

**The Report:** Hjerpe throws in the low-90s from a near sidearm arm slot. Almost nobody can hit it. Even five years ago or so, the BP Prospect Team would have gathered around the virtual table like Clint Eastwood and John Goodman and pondered how Hjerpe could have gone in the first round. But he probably wouldn't have gone in the first round then, despite being a Golden Spikes finalist after a junior season of utter dominance in the Pac-12. His four-seam fastball from that low slot has elite vertical approach and despite righties getting a long look at it, they have been mostly helpless to hit it. Hjerpe also offers a trendy sweeping slider and a reasonably projectable change he hasn't needed much. He might not need it much in the pros either.

**OFP:** 55 / no. 3/4 starter

**Variance:** Medium. We'll see if pro hitters also hate Hjerpe's one weird trick, but there's a pair of decent secondaries backing the fastball, and he's always thrown strikes.

**Jesse Roche's Fantasy Take:** Hjerpe is a unicorn, "with a sub-4.5-foot vertical and -3.5-foot horizontal release point–lower and wider than any starting pitcher in MLB." The uniqueness of his release point causes all his offerings to play up. It also makes it difficult to project him. No one hit him in college. Hjerpe is a profile to gamble on after the top bats in upcoming FYPDs.

## 6    Leonardo Bernal   C     OFP: 55     ETA: 2026

Born: 02/13/04   Age: 19   Bats: S   Throws: R   Height: 6'0"   Weight: 200 lb.   Origin: International Free Agent, 2021

| YEAR | TEAM | LVL | AGE | PA | R | 2B | 3B | HR | RBI | BB | K | SB | CS | AVG/OBP/SLG | DRC+ | BABIP | BRR | DRP | WARP |
|------|------|-----|-----|----|----|----|----|----|-----|----|----|----|----|-------------|------|-------|-----|-----|------|
| 2021 | DSL CARB | ROK | 17 | 178 | 23 | 9 | 1 | 5 | 29 | 17 | 28 | 3 | 1 | .209/.298/.373 | | .224 | | | |
| 2022 | PMB | A | 18 | 171 | 22 | 8 | 1 | 7 | 29 | 12 | 32 | 1 | 1 | .256/.316/.455 | 120 | .280 | -0.5 | C(37) 3.5 | 1.2 |
| 2023 non-DC | STL | MLB | 19 | 251 | 20 | 11 | 2 | 4 | 22 | 14 | 73 | 1 | 1 | .218/.264/.324 | 64 | .299 | -3.7 | C 0 | -0.5 |

**The Report:** The Cardinals' highest-dollar signing in the 2021 IFA class, Bernal performed well in an aggressive assignment to the Florida State League as an 18-year-old. Already built like a major-league backstop, he sets a big, steady target, is a quiet, flexible receiver with good hands and is both twitchy and reactive on balls in the dirt. The only weakness in Bernal's defensive game is fringy arm strength and carry which he covers for to an extent with a quick transfer and release.

At the plate, the switch-hitting catcher is far more advanced from the left side, with above-average exits despite still being a teenager for another season. Bernal is compact inside, level against balls up in the zone, and able to turn and lift fastballs with his solid-average bat speed. There's a hair too much swing-and-miss in the zone—especially against offspeed—but some of that can be explained by seeing full-season spin for the first time in his life. The right-handed swing is a bit more of a work in progress, not uncommon for an inexperienced switch-hitter, but it's well, well behind the lefty stroke at this point—more tentative, less in sync with his lower half, and more prone to both strikeouts and weak contact.

It's a long path from an 18-year-old catcher in A-ball to the majors, and Bernal doesn't have much to give back at the plate if the usual offensive attrition takes hold as he makes his way through the minors. But he's an advanced prospect on both offense and defense already, and any gains with the hit tool, especially from the right side, could move him into the Top 101 conversation before he's legally able to drink.

**OFP:** 55 / Above-average catcher

**Variance:** Extreme. Despite being ranked ahead of Ivan Herrera on the 2023 version of this list, a perfectly reasonable outcome is Bernal slides down the Cardinals rankings like Herrera did, as the offensive tools get beaten back by the rigors of everyday catching. A 25th-percentile outcome here is something like a third catcher on your 40 for a few years. Bernal also does have the potential to be one of the five best backstops in the game, oh...six years or so from now. Catchers are weird, man.

**Jesse Roche's Fantasy Take:** Generally, it is not advised to target 18-year-old catchers absent extraordinary circumstances. Bernal nearly justifies it with his impressive pop, including a 110 mph max exit velocity and 87 mph average exit velocity in Low-A. His raw approach needs work, though. In deeper formats or two-catcher formats, he should be on your radar.

## 7  Alec Burleson  LF  OFP: 55  ETA: Debuted in 2022
Born: 11/25/98  Age: 24  Bats: L  Throws: L  Height: 6'2"  Weight: 212 lb.  Origin: Round 2, 2020 Draft (#70 overall)

| YEAR | TEAM | LVL | AGE | PA | R | 2B | 3B | HR | RBI | BB | K | SB | CS | AVG/OBP/SLG | DRC+ | BABIP | BRR | DRP | WARP |
|---|---|---|---|---|---|---|---|---|---|---|---|---|---|---|---|---|---|---|---|
| 2021 | PEO | A+ | 22 | 49 | 8 | 1 | 0 | 4 | 10 | 6 | 15 | 1 | 0 | .286/.367/.595 | 121 | .333 | -0.3 | LF(7) 0.1, RF(3) -0.4 | 0.2 |
| 2021 | SPR | AA | 22 | 282 | 34 | 10 | 0 | 14 | 44 | 19 | 59 | 2 | 0 | .288/.333/.488 | 113 | .321 | -0.7 | RF(54) -1.9, 1B(1) -0.1, LF(1) 0.0 | 1.0 |
| 2021 | MEM | AAA | 22 | 172 | 19 | 7 | 0 | 4 | 22 | 17 | 27 | 0 | 1 | .234/.310/.357 | 106 | .260 | -0.4 | LF(21) -4.2, RF(18) 3.0 | 0.5 |
| 2022 | MEM | AAA | 23 | 470 | 68 | 25 | 1 | 20 | 87 | 29 | 67 | 4 | 0 | .331/.372/.532 | 121 | .350 | 1.6 | LF(71) 0.2, RF(5) -0.8 | 2.8 |
| 2022 | STL | MLB | 23 | 53 | 4 | 1 | 0 | 1 | 3 | 5 | 9 | 1 | 0 | .188/.264/.271 | 94 | .211 | 0.0 | RF(9) -0.2, 1B(6) 0.3, LF(2) 0.1 | 0.2 |
| 2023 DC | STL | MLB | 24 | 94 | 11 | 4 | 0 | 2 | 10 | 6 | 17 | 1 | 0 | .242/.290/.376 | 88 | .275 | -0.1 | LF 0 | 0.1 |

**The Report:** Burleson continued to rake in the upper minors in 2022, leaving opposing pitchers singing the blues when they came through Memphis. He's steep but direct to the ball, and prioritizes contact with two strikes, making him capable of driving pitches early in counts, while being a pesky out later on. Burleson does like to swing, but he doesn't expand much. The two-strike approach has kept his strikeout rate low, but can limit his ability to impact the ball, so that bears watching in the majors, but given his ability to sting stuff in the zone generally, he feels like that classic Cardinals .270, 22-home run guy. Burleson will need to get all the way there though, as he's unlikely to run stellar OBPs and has limited defensive value. He's fringy in a corner outfield spot as he's, well, a burly dude, and his reads and routes aren't ideal, and first base—which he played a fair bit of in his major-league cameo—is occupied for the next couple seasons. St. Louis is as good as any team in baseball in terms of defensive positioning though, and if they can stand Burleson in good enough spots on the grass, you'll be more than fine seeing him standing in the batter's box day in and day out.

**OFP:** 55 / Three corners bat with just enough hit and power to play everyday

**Variance:** Medium. Burleson's first run in the majors was better than the top-line numbers, but he has very little margin for the offensive tools as this is a bat-first profile.

**Jesse Roche's Fantasy Take:** A "classic Cardinals .270, 22-home run guy" is useful in most fantasy formats. Whether the Cardinals will stomach Burleson's defense to get his bat in their crowded lineup, though, is a real concern. Regardless, he should receive a look this year at some point and either thrive or allow fantasy managers to move on. Burleson should be rostered in formats with up to 200 prospects.

## 8  Matthew Liberatore  LHP  OFP: 50  ETA: Debuted in 2022
Born: 11/06/99  Age: 23  Bats: L  Throws: L  Height: 6'4"  Weight: 200 lb.  Origin: Round 1, 2018 Draft (#16 overall)

| YEAR | TEAM | LVL | AGE | W | L | SV | G | GS | IP | H | HR | BB/9 | K/9 | K | GB% | BABIP | WHIP | ERA | DRA- | WARP |
|---|---|---|---|---|---|---|---|---|---|---|---|---|---|---|---|---|---|---|---|---|
| 2021 | MEM | AAA | 21 | 9 | 9 | 0 | 22 | 18 | 124² | 123 | 19 | 2.4 | 8.9 | 123 | 38.3% | .308 | 1.25 | 4.04 | 104 | 1.4 |
| 2022 | MEM | AAA | 22 | 7 | 9 | 0 | 22 | 22 | 115 | 118 | 16 | 3.2 | 9.1 | 116 | 41.8% | .328 | 1.38 | 5.17 | 111 | 0.9 |
| 2022 | STL | MLB | 22 | 2 | 2 | 0 | 9 | 7 | 34² | 42 | 5 | 4.7 | 7.3 | 28 | 37.7% | .346 | 1.73 | 5.97 | 144 | -0.5 |
| 2023 DC | STL | MLB | 23 | 4 | 6 | 0 | 16 | 16 | 74.3 | 78 | 10 | 3.5 | 7.4 | 61 | 38.7% | .302 | 1.44 | 4.49 | 118 | 0.0 |

*Comparables: Sean O'Sullivan, Bryse Wilson, Jacob Turner*

**The Report:** Liberatore has bounced around the middle of our Top 101 for several years now as a high-probability mid-rotation lefty. He never really dominated in the minors, but with the lost 2020 and a jump straight form A-ball to Triple-A, you could give him some leeway. But ultimately these reports are about projecting major-league performance, and neither Liberatore's Triple-A or MLB work suggest a clear-cut, above-average major-league starter anymore. There's still stuff to like, specifically the secondary stuff. Liberatore's high-spin, mid-70s curve has a nice shape and misses a fair amount of bats, and his upper-80s slider bores in on righties with enough run to make it a tricky left-on-left offering as well. The main problem is that Liberatore's fastball gets hit hard. Some of this is a control-and-command issue, some of it is a movement-and-spin issue. He's run fairly significant platoon splits in the upper minors and his sparingly-used change isn't going to mitigate that in the medium term. If Liberatore tightens up the command and gets some more groundballs—perhaps he could lean on his sinker a bit more than the four-seam—the offspeed might be above-average enough to make him a useful back-end starter.

**OFP:** 50 / no. 4 starter

**Variance:** Low. Liberatore is major-league-ready—and has major-league service time—but might not have a major-league swing-and-miss pitch.

**Jesse Roche's Fantasy Take:** A back-end starter without "a major-league swing-and-miss pitch" and a hittable fastball should not normally be rostered outside of deep formats. Liberatore's proximity and breaking balls provide enough intrigue to keep him on the fantasy radar in formats with up to 200 prospects.

## 9 Michael McGreevy RHP

OFP: 50    ETA: Late 2023

Born: 07/08/00    Age: 22    Bats: L    Throws: R    Height: 6'4"    Weight: 215 lb.    Origin: Round 1, 2021 Draft (#18 overall)

| YEAR | TEAM | LVL | AGE | W | L | SV | G | GS | IP | H | HR | BB/9 | K/9 | K | GB% | BABIP | WHIP | ERA | DRA- | WARP |
|---|---|---|---|---|---|---|---|---|---|---|---|---|---|---|---|---|---|---|---|---|
| 2021 | PMB | A | 20 | 0 | 0 | 0 | 5 | 5 | 6 | 10 | 1 | 1.5 | 6.0 | 4 | 75.0% | .391 | 1.83 | 9.00 | 111 | 0.0 |
| 2022 | PEO | A+ | 21 | 3 | 1 | 0 | 8 | 8 | 45¹ | 41 | 1 | 0.8 | 8.1 | 41 | 52.3% | .305 | 0.99 | 2.58 | 100 | 0.4 |
| 2022 | SPR | AA | 21 | 6 | 4 | 0 | 20 | 20 | 99 | 109 | 14 | 2.4 | 6.9 | 76 | 48.4% | .321 | 1.36 | 4.64 | 102 | 0.3 |
| 2023 non-DC | STL | MLB | 22 | 3 | 3 | 0 | 58 | 0 | 50 | 60 | 7 | 2.8 | 5.3 | 30 | 41.7% | .314 | 1.50 | 5.00 | 129 | -0.5 |

Comparables: Gabriel Ynoa, Tyler Phillips, Tyler Viza

**The Report:** Like Graceffo, McGreevy got a 2021 velocity bump, although his came during his junior season for UC-Santa Barbara. He also held his gains in 2022, but his fastball is more low-90s than 95. The pitch works in the zone though, due to being able to sink it down, ride it up and generally work around the margins with above-average command. McGreevy did start to run into issues in Double-A, and while some of that can be explained by park and league context, he may lack a swing-and-miss offering amongst his three secondaries. His mid-80s change is the best present option. It's an average-ish pitch that he can pull the string on now and again, but tends to twist it off a bit and it will firm up. His mid-80s slider has more cut than tilt, and is inconsistent in shape, while his low-80s curve has a more repeatable 11-6 break, but is short and not really a bat misser. McGreevy has an uptempo delivery, but repeats it well and his command profile is fine enough, but it's not a carrying tool to mid-rotation starter on its own.

**OFP:** 50 / no. 4 starter

**Variance:** Low. I think it's fair to pref McGreevy over Liberatore—I went back and forth—as he's more likely to have success throwing his fastball in the zone against major-league hitters, and his command is a bit finer. The lack of a clear swing-and-miss secondary is going to limit the ceiling at present though, and he struggled at his first run in Double-A.

**Jesse Roche's Fantasy Take:** Command-first profiles with mediocre stuff can develop into viable fantasy arms, but the margins are narrow, and narrower still without a bat-missing secondary offering like McGreevy.

## 10 Iván Herrera C

OFP: 50    ETA: 2023

Born: 06/01/00    Age: 23    Bats: R    Throws: R    Height: 5'11"    Weight: 220 lb.    Origin: International Free Agent, 2016

| YEAR | TEAM | LVL | AGE | PA | R | 2B | 3B | HR | RBI | BB | K | SB | CS | AVG/OBP/SLG | DRC+ | BABIP | BRR | DRP | WARP |
|---|---|---|---|---|---|---|---|---|---|---|---|---|---|---|---|---|---|---|---|
| 2021 | SPR | AA | 21 | 437 | 50 | 13 | 0 | 17 | 63 | 60 | 96 | 2 | 3 | .231/.346/.408 | 106 | .261 | -1.7 | C(71) 3.5 | 2.0 |
| 2022 | MEM | AAA | 22 | 278 | 41 | 10 | 1 | 6 | 34 | 38 | 52 | 5 | 1 | .268/.374/.396 | 119 | .318 | -1.3 | C(57) 4.0 | 1.7 |
| 2022 | STL | MLB | 22 | 22 | 0 | 0 | 0 | 0 | 1 | 2 | 8 | 0 | 0 | .111/.190/.111 | 80 | .182 | -0.1 | C(11) -0.1 | 0.0 |
| 2023 DC | STL | MLB | 23 | 60 | 6 | 2 | 0 | 1 | 5 | 6 | 12 | 1 | 0 | .208/.295/.322 | 80 | .249 | -0.1 | C 0 | 0.1 |

Comparables: Austin Romine, Wilson Ramos, Chance Sisco

**The Report:** After prospect writers spent well over a decade writing up Cardinals catching prospects blocked by Yadier Molina, Herrera looked to be in the right place at the right time to stake a claim as the next starting catcher at Busch Stadium prior to the Willson Contreras signing. He's improved behind the plate and is now a polished, above-average defender, a good receiver who sets a big, quiet target. The power he showed in 2021 didn't return, but the trade-off was a bit more bat-to-ball. The overall offensive tools are going to be fringy, as Herrera isn't very twitchy at the plate—and he can struggle to get to velocity on the outer half—but as a solid defensive backstop who could pop double-digit home runs, he'll at least be putting his name in the hat to replace St. Louis' long-tenured star backstop.

**OFP:** 50 / Average catcher, glove over bat

**Variance:** Low. Molina finally retired, opening up the Cardinals' starting catching role for the first time since the George W. Bush administration. Herrera appeared likely to be a candidate for the Opening Day job, as he has a strong glove and little left to prove in the minors. But he also doesn't have the kind of upside would keep you from, say, acquiring a 2022 All-Star to take the vast majority of reps behind the plate...which St. Louis did.

**Jesse Roche's Fantasy Take:** If Herrera ever runs into a regular role, he could surprise with plenty of contact and sneaky pop. That is one big "if," though.

# Outside the Top Ten:

## 11 Jonathan Mejia   SS

Born: 04/12/05   Age: 18   Bats: S   Throws: R   Height: 6'0"   Weight: 185 lb.   Origin: International Free Agent, 2022

| YEAR | TEAM | LVL | AGE | PA | R | 2B | 3B | HR | RBI | BB | K | SB | CS | AVG/OBP/SLG | DRC+ | BABIP | BRR | DRP | WARP |
|------|------|-----|-----|----|----|----|----|----|-----|----|----|----|----|-------------|------|-------|-----|-----|------|
| 2022 | DSL CAR | ROK | 17 | 208 | 33 | 14 | 3 | 5 | 34 | 33 | 48 | 3 | 2 | .267/.418/.479 | | .348 | | | |

The Cardinals' top international free agent out of the 2022 class, Mejia is already flashing the kind of tools that got him a seven-figure bonus. The prominent ones here are shortstop defense and bat speed, and if you have those two in your locker you get a long leash to develop the rest of the skill set. Mejia is still raw at the plate, with solid bat-to-ball skills covering for less than ideal swing decisions at present. The variance here is extreme, as Mejia hasn't come stateside yet, but the two-way shortstop potential gives him a much higher realistic upside than the names behind him (and a few of the names in front).

## 12 Jimmy Crooks III   C

Born: 07/19/01   Age: 21   Bats: L   Throws: R   Height: 6'1"   Weight: 210 lb.   Origin: Round 4, 2022 Draft (#127 overall)

| YEAR | TEAM | LVL | AGE | PA | R | 2B | 3B | HR | RBI | BB | K | SB | CS | AVG/OBP/SLG | DRC+ | BABIP | BRR | DRP | WARP |
|------|------|-----|-----|----|----|----|----|----|-----|----|----|----|----|-------------|------|-------|-----|-----|------|
| 2022 | PMB | A | 20 | 96 | 12 | 3 | 2 | 3 | 7 | 12 | 22 | 0 | 0 | .266/.396/.468 | 120 | .333 | -2.7 | C(17) 4.3 | 0.7 |
| 2023 non-DC | STL | MLB | 21 | 251 | 20 | 10 | 2 | 3 | 20 | 18 | 68 | 0 | 0 | .212/.279/.307 | 66 | .290 | -4.4 | C 0 | -0.5 |

*Comparables: Dom Nuñez, Juan Kelly, José Briceño*

Your centerfold for the December 2022 edition of *Cardinals Devil Magic*, Crooks is a fourth-rounder out of Oklahoma, where he put up nice, but not spectacular stats, so he broadly fits this org's usual type of college bat overperformance bullshit. Crooks is a catcher, which is a bit unusual for this genre of Cardinals hitting prospect, but his left-handed swing reminds me a bit of Burleson's and he's put up similarly loud contact in his brief pro debut. I do wonder if the barrel control will really play against better pitching—his swing can be a little stiff—but the potential for at least average offensive tools from a solid catch-and-throw guy is going to remain intriguing.

## 13 Brycen Mautz   LHP

Born: 07/17/01   Age: 21   Bats: L   Throws: L   Height: 6'3"   Weight: 190 lb.   Origin: Round 2, 2022 Draft (#59 overall)

St. Louis's second-round pick in last summer's draft, Mautz moved into the UCSD Tritons' rotation his junior year and showed an at-times dominant fastball/slider combo. Everything comes out of a funky, uptempo, deceptive delivery and he has a fairly short track record of throwing strikes. There's a fair bit of reliever risk here, but the Cards are the right org to turn Mautz into a solid back-end starter. The bullpen fallback isn't too bad either as he's been up to mid-90s in short bursts.

## 14 Moisés Gómez   RF

Born: 08/27/98   Age: 24   Bats: R   Throws: R   Height: 5'11"   Weight: 200 lb.   Origin: International Free Agent, 2015

| YEAR | TEAM | LVL | AGE | PA | R | 2B | 3B | HR | RBI | BB | K | SB | CS | AVG/OBP/SLG | DRC+ | BABIP | BRR | DRP | WARP |
|------|------|-----|-----|----|----|----|----|----|-----|----|----|----|----|-------------|------|-------|-----|-----|------|
| 2021 | MTG | AA | 22 | 301 | 34 | 13 | 0 | 8 | 23 | 27 | 115 | 5 | 3 | .171/.256/.309 | 68 | .259 | 0.8 | RF(51) 2.4, LF(10) -1.4, CF(8) -0.6 | -0.1 |
| 2022 | SPR | AA | 23 | 257 | 53 | 17 | 0 | 23 | 54 | 27 | 90 | 7 | 3 | .321/.401/.705 | 109 | .434 | -0.1 | RF(39) 4.5, LF(9) 0.8, CF(6) -1.1 | 1.5 |
| 2022 | MEM | AAA | 23 | 244 | 36 | 8 | 2 | 16 | 40 | 25 | 84 | 3 | 0 | .266/.340/.541 | 90 | .353 | 2.8 | RF(48) -0.7 | 1.1 |
| 2023 non-DC | STL | MLB | 24 | 251 | 26 | 11 | 1 | 8 | 30 | 19 | 92 | 1 | 1 | .231/.294/.401 | 96 | .344 | -3.7 | LF 0, CF 0 | 0.1 |

Gómez never got a ton of attention in the super-deep Rays systems of the late-2010s, and a disastrous post-pandemic season in Double-A dimmed much of his remaining prospect luster. The Rays released him after 2021, and the Cards picked him up. He promptly hit the most home runs in the minors, slugging over .600 between Springfield and Memphis. The power is legit, plus-plus potential, and Gómez doesn't need to get it right on the sweet spot to pull it out of the park. There's still a lot of swing-and-miss here, and he's not going to provide a ton of defensive value. Still, Gómez is at least ready to offer some right-handed platoon pop, and St. Louis must figure the same, as they added him to the 40-man after the season.

## 15   Pete Hansen   LHP

Born: 07/28/00   Age: 22   Bats: R   Throws: L   Height: 6'2"   Weight: 205 lb.   Origin: Round 3, 2022 Draft (#97 overall)

The Cards continued their run on left-handed pitching into Day 2 of the 2022 draft. Hansen has a more traditional lefty delivery and higher slot, but a bit less fastball than Mautz. His slider has a chance to be a plus swing-and-miss offering, and if he can get a little bit of a velo bump in a pro development program, he could settle in nicely as a back-end starter or lefty setup type.

## 16   Max Rajcic   RHP

Born: 08/03/01   Age: 21   Bats: R   Throws: R   Height: 6'0"   Weight: 210 lb.   Origin: Round 6, 2022 Draft (#187 overall)

A sturdy, sophomore-eligible righty out of UCLA, St. Louis went overslot to snag Rajcic in the sixth round of the draft. Rajcic works primarily off a low-90s fastball that can touch higher and a power slurve that can sometimes show a bit early. He arguably has the best shot to start of the three non-Hjerpe arms from the 2022 draft, but at least one of them is a good bet to take a leap in 2023.

## 17   Won-Bin Cho   OF

Born: 08/20/03   Age: 19   Bats: L   Throws: L   Height: 6'3"   Weight: 200 lb.   Origin: International Free Agent, 2022

| YEAR | TEAM | LVL | AGE | PA | R | 2B | 3B | HR | RBI | BB | K | SB | CS | AVG/OBP/SLG | DRC+ | BABIP | BRR | DRP | WARP |
|---|---|---|---|---|---|---|---|---|---|---|---|---|---|---|---|---|---|---|---|
| 2022 | CAR | ROK | 18 | 100 | 10 | 3 | 1 | 1 | 3 | 20 | 27 | 6 | 4 | .211/.400/.316 | | .313 | | | |

Signed out of Korea in January, Cho went right to the Florida Complex League, and displayed a strong batted-ball profile for an 18-year-old at that level, while almost never expanding the zone. There was a bit of swing-and-miss of course, and the approach could border on too passive at times. Whether this is merely an adjustment period or a larger pitch recognition issue remains to be seen. The potential for an everyday corner outfield bat is in play though.

## 18   Austin Love   RHP

Born: 01/26/99   Age: 24   Bats: R   Throws: R   Height: 6'3"   Weight: 232 lb.   Origin: Round 3, 2021 Draft (#90 overall)

| YEAR | TEAM | LVL | AGE | W | L | SV | G | GS | IP | H | HR | BB/9 | K/9 | K | GB% | BABIP | WHIP | ERA | DRA- | WARP |
|---|---|---|---|---|---|---|---|---|---|---|---|---|---|---|---|---|---|---|---|---|
| 2022 | PEO | A+ | 23 | 7 | 12 | 0 | 26 | 25 | 125² | 139 | 15 | 3.7 | 10.8 | 151 | 45.8% | .367 | 1.52 | 5.73 | 83 | 2.4 |
| 2023 non-DC | STL | MLB | 24 | 3 | 3 | 0 | 58 | 0 | 50 | 54 | 8 | 4.4 | 8.1 | 45 | 38.2% | .311 | 1.56 | 5.30 | 133 | -0.6 |

Love looked more like a future reliever than starter coming out of the 2021 draft, and after posting a 5.00+ ERA in the Peoria rotation, a move to the bullpen might be on the offer quite soon. The good news is that his stuff should play there as both the slider and change have improved and show above-average potential. If Love can get his mid-90s and better heat back in short bursts, he has a number of weapons that could play in the late innings of a major-league 'pen.

## 19   Joshua Baez   RF

Born: 06/28/03   Age: 20   Bats: R   Throws: R   Height: 6'4"   Weight: 220 lb.   Origin: Round 2, 2021 Draft (#54 overall)

| YEAR | TEAM | LVL | AGE | PA | R | 2B | 3B | HR | RBI | BB | K | SB | CS | AVG/OBP/SLG | DRC+ | BABIP | BRR | DRP | WARP |
|---|---|---|---|---|---|---|---|---|---|---|---|---|---|---|---|---|---|---|---|
| 2021 | CAR | ROK | 18 | 95 | 18 | 3 | 1 | 2 | 8 | 14 | 28 | 5 | 0 | .158/.305/.303 | | .208 | | | |
| 2022 | CAR | ROK | 19 | 43 | 4 | 3 | 0 | 1 | 5 | 5 | 14 | 6 | 1 | .237/.326/.395 | | .348 | | | |
| 2022 | PMB | A | 19 | 79 | 11 | 5 | 1 | 3 | 16 | 11 | 30 | 4 | 3 | .286/.418/.540 | 92 | .484 | -0.1 | RF(12) -1.4, CF(4) 0.4 | 0.3 |
| 2023 non-DC | STL | MLB | 20 | 251 | 20 | 10 | 2 | 3 | 21 | 18 | 105 | 6 | 3 | .206/.273/.308 | 65 | .362 | -1.1 | LF 0, CF 0 | -0.4 |

*Comparables: Jack Herman, Randal Grichuk, Abner Abreu*

The Cardinals' 2021 second-rounder dealt with a wrist injury early in the year, and while the top-line numbers look fine for a 19-year-old in A-ball—granted even that is only a month of games—there are some issues lurking in the profile. Baez's swing can get long and steep, and he uses strength over bat speed to generate his potential prodigious power. He can absolutely smoke the ball when he makes contact, but the K-rates here are concerning. More at issue is how those strikeouts happen. Baez misses too much in the zone, especially against offspeed, and while there were enough positive reports post-injury to keep him on the watch list (and the Cardinals list), this is the kind of profile we are souring on more quickly to the point that 2023 might be a make-or-break year. All in all, it's just too small a sample to generate broad conclusions, but a corner outfield prospect has to hit a lot, and that starts with consistent good contact in the zone.

## 20 Ryan Loutos RHP

Born: 01/29/99  Age: 24  Bats: R  Throws: R  Height: 6'5"  Weight: 215 lb.  Origin: Undrafted Free Agent, 2021

| YEAR | TEAM | LVL | AGE | W | L | SV | G | GS | IP | H | HR | BB/9 | K/9 | K | GB% | BABIP | WHIP | ERA | DRA- | WARP |
|---|---|---|---|---|---|---|---|---|---|---|---|---|---|---|---|---|---|---|---|---|
| 2021 | PMB | A | 22 | 1 | 2 | 0 | 12 | 1 | 22² | 28 | 0 | 2.4 | 10.3 | 26 | 40.8% | .394 | 1.50 | 5.56 | 100 | 0.2 |
| 2022 | PEO | A+ | 23 | 2 | 2 | 4 | 9 | 0 | 14¹ | 11 | 1 | 1.9 | 10.7 | 17 | 35.3% | .303 | 0.98 | 3.14 | 90 | 0.2 |
| 2022 | SPR | AA | 23 | 1 | 1 | 3 | 15 | 0 | 22¹ | 14 | 0 | 4.0 | 10.5 | 26 | 55.6% | .259 | 1.07 | 1.61 | 72 | 0.5 |
| 2022 | MEM | AAA | 23 | 0 | 3 | 2 | 22 | 2 | 27 | 44 | 4 | 4.0 | 9.7 | 29 | 52.8% | .471 | 2.07 | 6.33 | 104 | 0.3 |
| 2023 non-DC | STL | MLB | 24 | 3 | 3 | 0 | 58 | 0 | 50 | 53 | 7 | 3.8 | 7.8 | 43 | 39.3% | .311 | 1.49 | 4.79 | 122 | -0.3 |

An undrafted senior sign in 2021, Loutos made it all the way to Triple-A in his first full professional season, striking out well over a batter per inning on the strength of a mid-90s fastball that played even past those velocity readings due to a deceptive arm action. Lotus pairs his easy plus heater with a low-80s curve which can show good downer action, but is a bit too inconsistent to work in the late innings at present. The command profile wasn't all that fine once he hit the upper minors, and there's some effort in his uptempo delivery that will limit it to average at best, but the fastball/curve combo will play in a major-league 'pen as soon as 2023. Lotus is more "good middle reliever" than "leverage reliever" at present, but if he can tighten up his breaker, he might find his way into the setup innings.

## Top Talents 25 and Under (as of 4/1/2023):

1. Jordan Walker, 3B/OF
2. Dylan Carlson, OF
3. Nolan Gorman, 2B/3B
4. Masyn Winn, SS
5. Lars Nootbaar, OF
6. Tink Hence, RHP
7. Gordon Graceffo, RHP
8. Juan Yepez, UT
9. Cooper Hjerpe, RHP
10. Andre Pallante, RHP

The St. Louis sorcerers continue weaving their wicked ways, looking to prolong their trend of just a single last-place divisional finish in the past 105 years. The defending champs of the sad-sack NL Central were the first victims of the bludgeoning instrument that was the 2022 Philadelphia Phillies in the playoffs. Their organization is in excellent health, however, at least in regards to having young talent rolling in like the tides to abet their reigning MVP and runner-up.

Carlson's progression hasn't quite reached star status, though performing as around a league-average regular in all facets of the game at just age-23 is a rousing success for essentially any big leaguer. There isn't an obvious next gear of power in his frame, but his balanced success is a comfortable baseline. By contrast, Gorman looked every bit the potent slugger he has been since he was a prep, with 14 big flies in just 313 plate appearances suggesting the 30-homer seasons are on the horizon—at least if he can find somewhere on the field to get full-time reps. Gorman won't be unseating Paul Goldschmidt or Nolan Arenado, while 26-year-old surprise Rookie of the Year bronze medalist Brendan Donovan has earned a lion's share of reps at second base. That puts Gorman on utility duty, or perhaps the most yoked platoon in history with Tyler O'Neill or the similarly positionless Yepez.

Unlike Carlson and Gorman, Nootbaar had a more muted prospect pedigree, but has outperformed his fourth-outfielder billing thus far. Much of that can be credited to a patient approach that has continued bearing fruit against the best pitching in the world, albeit in predominantly platooned circumstances. As a more able defensive outfielder than the rest of his young compatriots, his path to playing time has many possible forks. Of note as well is Pallante, whose borderline meteoric rise through the Cardinals' system was a godsend for a St. Louis club that struggled with arm health for much of 2022. His fascinating pitch profile got him rightly dubbed a "unicorn" this season as a groundball-elicitation expert, and Pallante had the rare season of double-digit starts *and* bullpen appearances, with 108 innings in total over 47 appearances. His ability to offer length as well as performing as a stopper is a rare combo, albeit not yet with much bat-missing in the profile.

# Tampa Bay Rays

## The State of the System:

The Rays have achieved one of the most Rays systems possible, as they are now loaded with infielders with unclear defensive homes who can all really hit. Oh, there are a couple pretty good pitching prospects near the top of the list too, although this is presently a very bat-heavy organization.

## The Top Ten:

### 1 Curtis Mead  3B/2B    OFP: 60    ETA: 2023

Born: 10/26/00   Age: 22   Bats: R   Throws: R   Height: 6'2"   Weight: 171 lb.   Origin: International Free Agent, 2018

| YEAR | TEAM | LVL | AGE | PA | R | 2B | 3B | HR | RBI | BB | K | SB | CS | AVG/OBP/SLG | DRC+ | BABIP | BRR | DRP | WARP |
|---|---|---|---|---|---|---|---|---|---|---|---|---|---|---|---|---|---|---|---|
| 2020 | ADE | WIN | 19 | 76 | 11 | 7 | 0 | 3 | 12 | 3 | 13 | 2 | 0 | .347/.382/.569 | | .393 | | | |
| 2021 | SCO | WIN | 20 | 90 | 16 | 5 | 2 | 3 | 11 | 4 | 13 | 1 | 1 | .313/.360/.530 | | .343 | | | |
| 2021 | CSC | A | 20 | 211 | 36 | 21 | 1 | 7 | 35 | 15 | 30 | 9 | 2 | .356/.408/.586 | 134 | .391 | -1.0 | 3B(25) -0.6, 1B(15) 2.2 | 1.5 |
| 2021 | BG | A+ | 20 | 233 | 38 | 15 | 1 | 7 | 32 | 19 | 38 | 2 | 2 | .282/.348/.466 | 119 | .309 | 0.4 | 3B(43) 1.1, 1B(3) 0.1 | 1.4 |
| 2022 | MTG | AA | 21 | 246 | 35 | 21 | 0 | 10 | 36 | 25 | 45 | 6 | 2 | .305/.394/.548 | 133 | .342 | -0.3 | 3B(35) 0.6, 2B(16) -0.1, 1B(3) -0.4 | 1.6 |
| 2022 | DUR | AAA | 21 | 85 | 8 | 6 | 0 | 3 | 14 | 11 | 17 | 1 | 0 | .278/.376/.486 | 111 | .321 | 0.1 | 3B(11) -0.8, 2B(4) -0.4 | 0.3 |
| 2023 DC | TB | MLB | 22 | 96 | 10 | 5 | 0 | 2 | 9 | 7 | 20 | 1 | 0 | .229/.294/.354 | 86 | .277 | -0.1 | 3B 0 | 0.1 |

Comparables: Austin Riley, Evan Longoria, Mookie Betts

**The Report:** Mead does not have the most visually appealing swing. He starts upright, with high hands and a bit of a roundabout hand path. He ends with a short, stiff follow-through, almost Vogelbachian. In between, he just barrels baseballs. In 2018, we'd have nagging concerns about how the swing would play against major-league fastballs or adjust to down-and-away breaking stuff, but the upper-minors performance—both top-line and underlying—is all there to suggest Mead is one of the best hitting prospects in the minors. It's not terrifying bat speed, but the ball jumps when he barrels it, and he's usually on the good part of the lumber despite a visually stiff stroke. Overall, Mead has a well-rounded offensive profile with both plus hit and power tools, and bushels of walks and doubles that will make his stat line play up past "just" 6/6.

The bat will play anywhere in the field, but where he lands is still an open question. His hands and actions are fine for third, but the arm strength is short and his accuracy goes when he has to air it out. Mead is passable at second, rangier than you'd expect, although he's a big dude who can look awkward playing there. He has a first baseman's mitt hanging around his locker now too, but I'd expect him to move around depending on matchups, and for the Rays to lean heavily on positioning to keep his glove around average. That will be plenty good enough to land Mead in the middle of your lineup every day.

**OFP:** 60 / First-division infielder who hits his way to a couple All-Star games

**Variance:** Medium. Mead dealt with an elbow injury that eventually saw him shut down in August. Assuming no ongoing issues there, he should be ready to be an above-average major-league hitter as soon as this season. The ultimate variance here will come down to positional and defensive value, and the Rays are about as good at maximizing that as any org around.

**Jesse Roche's Fantasy Take:** Mead has been a model of consistency the past two years. If anything, he improved last year, exhibiting better plate discipline and cutting his swing rate by 7% while putting more balls in the air to tap into his plus raw power. Of course, Mead comes with positional questions and merely solid contact rates, but his bat is otherwise so sound that they shouldn't impact him. The Rays have little standing in his way at 1B/3B/DH, and he should arrive early in 2023 and immediately slot in the middle of the lineup. Mead falls in the middle of the top-50 dynasty prospects.

## 2 Taj Bradley   RHP     OFP: 60     ETA: 2023

Born: 03/20/01   Age: 22   Bats: R   Throws: R   Height: 6'2"   Weight: 190 lb.   Origin: Round 5, 2018 Draft (#150 overall)

| YEAR | TEAM | LVL | AGE | W | L | SV | G | GS | IP | H | HR | BB/9 | K/9 | K | GB% | BABIP | WHIP | ERA | DRA- | WARP |
|------|------|-----|-----|---|---|----|----|----|-----|----|----|------|------|----|------|-------|------|------|------|------|
| 2021 | CSC | A | 20 | 9 | 3 | 0 | 15 | 14 | 66² | 37 | 4 | 2.7 | 10.9 | 81 | 50.3% | .237 | 0.85 | 1.76 | 79 | 1.5 |
| 2021 | BG | A+ | 20 | 3 | 0 | 0 | 8 | 8 | 36² | 28 | 4 | 2.7 | 10.3 | 42 | 47.4% | .267 | 1.06 | 1.96 | 85 | 0.6 |
| 2022 | MTG | AA | 21 | 3 | 1 | 0 | 16 | 16 | 74¹ | 50 | 4 | 2.2 | 10.7 | 88 | 39.5% | .266 | 0.91 | 1.70 | 84 | 1.4 |
| 2022 | DUR | AAA | 21 | 4 | 3 | 0 | 12 | 12 | 59 | 55 | 10 | 2.3 | 8.1 | 53 | 34.1% | .271 | 1.19 | 3.66 | 93 | 1.0 |
| 2023 DC | TB | MLB | 22 | 2 | 2 | 0 | 6 | 6 | 30.3 | 31 | 4 | 3.1 | 7.7 | 26 | 36.1% | .294 | 1.35 | 4.24 | 112 | 0.1 |

*Comparables: Luis Severino, Brady Lail, Logan Allen*

**The Report:** A former overslot fifth-round selection who showed promising flashes but just mediocre results in his first two professional seasons, Bradley used 2020 to transform himself into an elite pitching prospect. He's been dominant in his march up the organizational ladder, posting a sub-2.00 ERA at every stop along the way until his late season stint at Triple-A Durham. He was challenged there for the first time, especially by experienced left-handed hitters, no longer able to blow them away with just pure stuff. Don't be mistaken, the pitch mix is electric with an easy mid-90s fastball, tight slider and plus curve but he'll need to continue to learn how to deploy it to get big-league hitters out. It's likely he gets another crack at International League hitters to start next season, but it shouldn't take long before Tampa finds a way to utilize him against rival AL East lineups.

**OFP:** 60 / Impact arm, occasional All-Star

**Variance:** Medium. Solid command and electric stuff for a pitcher with Triple-A experience gives Bradley a pretty high floor. However, there's still the concern that comes with every young pitching prospect.

**Jesse Roche's Fantasy Take:** Bradley has a legitimate arsenal to provide different looks for his imminent debut. Like Mead, Bradley should arrive early in 2023, though the Rays' rotation is far more daunting to break into. He is a top-50 dynasty prospect.

## 3 Kyle Manzardo   1B     OFP: 60     ETA: Late 2023/Early 2024

Born: 07/18/00   Age: 22   Bats: L   Throws: R   Height: 6'1"   Weight: 205 lb.   Origin: Round 2, 2021 Draft (#63 overall)

| YEAR | TEAM | LVL | AGE | PA | R | 2B | 3B | HR | RBI | BB | K | SB | CS | AVG/OBP/SLG | DRC+ | BABIP | BRR | DRP | WARP |
|------|------|-----|-----|-----|----|----|----|----|-----|----|----|----|----|-------------|------|-------|------|--------|------|
| 2021 | RAY | ROK | 20 | 50 | 10 | 5 | 0 | 2 | 8 | 4 | 6 | 0 | 0 | .349/.440/.605 | | .371 | | | |
| 2022 | BG | A+ | 21 | 275 | 53 | 16 | 1 | 17 | 55 | 45 | 46 | 0 | 0 | .329/.436/.636 | 155 | .343 | 2.8 | 1B(52) -0.6 | 2.7 |
| 2022 | MTG | AA | 21 | 122 | 18 | 10 | 0 | 5 | 26 | 14 | 19 | 1 | 1 | .323/.402/.576 | 131 | .333 | 0.2 | 1B(23) 1.3 | 0.9 |
| 2023 non-DC | TB | MLB | 22 | 251 | 26 | 12 | 1 | 6 | 27 | 26 | 50 | 0 | 1 | .241/.325/.386 | 104 | .285 | -4.3 | 1B 0 | 0.1 |

*Comparables: Sam Travis, Wes Bankston, Andrew Benintendi*

**The Report:** You could make the argument for Mazardo as the most complete hitter in the entire system. He's a former second-round selection who has done nothing but hit for power and average since being signed out of Washington State in 2021. It all starts with his advanced approach at the plate, where he's tough to strike out and makes intelligent swing decisions, punishing the ball to all fields. He's not a hulking slugger and doesn't produce elite exit velocities, but there's enough juice in the swing and he hits the ball at good enough angles to currently produce 20+ home runs and tons of doubles. There's also a chance that with continued physical growth, the over-the-fence pop ticks up even more. The bat will need to continue to be special due to his defensive liabilities. His lack of agility and arm strength limits him to first base, where he's currently inconsistent but should eventually develop into a capable defender.

**OFP:** 60 / First-division first baseman, occasional All-Star

**Variance:** Medium. There's always risk with a 1B-only prospect and we could see the bat come back to Earth against upper-minors left-handed pitching. However, there's also the outcome where we see Manzardo become a middle-of-the-order run producer in the very near future.

**Jesse Roche's Fantasy Take:** Finding flaws in Manzardo's performance and future outlook is picking nits at this point. While he won't light up Statcast, he churns out hard contact, often in the air (47.5% fly-ball rate) and to the pull side, to maximize and exceed his raw power in games. Manzardo managed an incredible .290 ISO in two largely pitcher-friendly leagues. Meanwhile, he has a nearly unmatched blend of plus bat-to-ball ability and plate discipline. A lot of what was said about Vinnie Pasquantino last year, can be said about Manzardo now (well, except the raw power). He is a top-20 dynasty prospect.

## 4 Mason Montgomery LHP   OFP: 55   ETA: Late 2023/Early 2024

Born: 06/17/00   Age: 23   Bats: L   Throws: L   Height: 6'2"   Weight: 195 lb.   Origin: Round 6, 2021 Draft (#191 overall)

| YEAR | TEAM | LVL | AGE | W | L | SV | G | GS | IP | H | HR | BB/9 | K/9 | K | GB% | BABIP | WHIP | ERA | DRA- | WARP |
|------|------|-----|-----|---|---|----|----|----|-----|---|----|------|------|-----|------|-------|------|------|------|------|
| 2021 | RAY | ROK | 21 | 1 | 0 | 0 | 5 | 4 | 10² | 4 | 0 | 0.8 | 16.9 | 20 | 12.5% | .250 | 0.47 | 0.84 | | |
| 2022 | BG | A+ | 22 | 3 | 2 | 0 | 16 | 16 | 69² | 49 | 6 | 3.5 | 15.2 | 118 | 43.7% | .333 | 1.09 | 1.81 | 73 | 1.6 |
| 2022 | MTG | AA | 22 | 3 | 1 | 0 | 11 | 11 | 54¹ | 40 | 5 | 2.7 | 8.8 | 53 | 45.6% | .245 | 1.03 | 2.48 | 90 | 0.8 |
| 2023 non-DC | TB | MLB | 23 | 3 | 3 | 0 | 58 | 0 | 50 | 48 | 7 | 4.0 | 9.1 | 50 | 36.7% | .297 | 1.40 | 4.29 | 112 | 0.0 |

Comparables: Brian Johnson, Steven Brault, Zac Lowther

**The Report:** The Rays haven't had great success with their early picks recently, but they are very good at getting Day 2 pitchers to pop in their system. It was Taj Bradley last year; this year it was Mason Montgomery. He threw well enough in college, pitching Texas Tech into the super regional—but was downright dominant in the pros last year, working off a three-pitch mix that baffled High- and Double-A batters. It's not the most visually impressive arsenal, and his mechanics might give you sympathy pangs in your rotator cuff, but he runs a boring, riding fastball up to 95 and moves it around the zone well enough that he could get outs even when he didn't have his slider and change working. Montgomery usually had the *cambio* though. It's a plus, borderline plus-plus pitch that disappears just enough at the end. He can cut it into righties and will use it left-on-left as well, although his slider is also effective against his fellow southpaws, coming from a tough angle. The two things keeping him from the Taj Bradley tier at the moment are his relatively short track record of this kind of performance, and the aforementioned mechanics. I'm never one to predict injury based on a delivery—there are lots of ways to get a ball 60 feet, 6 inches down the line—but I can't help but worry about him holding up with that arm action. Then again, he tossed 124 healthy innings for the notoriously conservative Rays last year, so how concerned do I really get to be here?

**OFP:** 55 / no. 3/4 starter

**Variance:** Medium. Montgomery has an advanced arsenal and could be in the Rays rotation by the second half of 2023. Also he's a pitcher (with a rough arm action).

**Jesse Roche's Fantasy Take:** Montgomery registered a bonkers 41.8% strikeout rate in High-A. LOL. (Good changeups are kryptonite to A-ball hitters.) He is unlikely to miss nearly as many bats as he continues to climb the ladder, and, in Double-A, his strikeout rate dropped by 17.5%. While he has remained effective, Montgomery will need to tighten up his slider or command to be fantasy-relevant at the MLB level. As such, he is still outside the top-100 dynasty prospects.

## 5 Junior Caminero 3B   OFP: 55   ETA: 2025

Born: 07/05/03   Age: 20   Bats: R   Throws: R   Height: 5'11"   Weight: 157 lb.   Origin: International Free Agent, 2019

| YEAR | TEAM | LVL | AGE | PA | R | 2B | 3B | HR | RBI | BB | K | SB | CS | AVG/OBP/SLG | DRC+ | BABIP | BRR | DRP | WARP |
|------|------|-----|-----|----|---|----|----|----|-----|----|---|----|----|-------------|------|-------|-----|-----|------|
| 2021 | DSL INDR | ROK | 17 | 171 | 26 | 8 | 0 | 9 | 33 | 20 | 28 | 2 | 0 | .295/.380/.534 | | .304 | | | |
| 2022 | RAY | ROK | 18 | 154 | 18 | 5 | 1 | 5 | 31 | 15 | 21 | 7 | 1 | .326/.403/.492 | | .349 | | | |
| 2022 | CSC | A | 18 | 117 | 19 | 2 | 1 | 6 | 20 | 8 | 22 | 5 | 0 | .299/.359/.505 | 117 | .329 | 1.3 | 3B(17) -0.4, 2B(2) -0.4 | 0.6 |
| 2023 non-DC | TB | MLB | 19 | 251 | 19 | 10 | 1 | 3 | 21 | 13 | 63 | 3 | 0 | .209/.258/.305 | 58 | .271 | -3.2 | 1B 0, 2B 0 | -1.0 |

Comparables: Vladimir Guerrero Jr., Josh Vitters, Matt Dominguez

**The Report:** The Rays plucked Caminero out of the Guardians' Dominican complex in a Rule 5 deadline deal after the 2021 season. He was not a particularly notable IFA signing but after his breakout 2022 season he's certainly a notable prospect. Like a lot of the top offensive prospects in the system, the swing is not classically pretty. Caminero's features a big leg kick, noisy hands and a late load, but once he decides to swing, everything is loose and whippy and he can cover all corners of the zone. He can look a bit out of control at the plate at times but he's always in control of the barrel. Caminero is not aggressively looking to lift, but there's enough loft and present strength in the swing that when he lets it go and can extend, the ball travels. The profile is hit over power for now, but I'd project both tools to end up in the above-average to plus range over the long haul.

Defensively the endpoint is a bit murkier. Caminero played mostly third this year, with a bit of second base and shortstop mixed in as well. He's a fine fit for the hot corner at present, showing a good first step, range and actions. I suspect he may end up the guy you move around between four or five different spots to get the bat in the lineup, with him being somewhere between fringe and solid at all of them.

**OFP:** 55 / Not actually Ben Zobrist, but

**Variance:** High. Caminero has a limited full-season track record and while there aren't any red flags in the bat at present, he's a long way from the majors.

**Jesse Roche's Fantasy Take:** Caminero laid waste to the Australian Baseball League, hitting .310/.375/.621 with 13 home runs (second-most) at just 18 years old. Did I mention that he is still just 18? This performance comes on the heels of an impressive campaign between the complex and Low-A. Indeed, Caminero was arguably the best hitter on a stacked Charleston team that repeated as Carolina League champions. His stout frame doesn't engender excitement, but his bat is real. Caminero is a fast-rising prospect well within the top-100 dynasty prospects and could quickly ascend to the top 50 with a strong start this year.

## 6 Carson Williams SS    OFP: 55    ETA: 2025

Born: 06/25/03   Age: 20   Bats: R   Throws: R   Height: 6'2"   Weight: 180 lb.   Origin: Round 1, 2021 Draft (#28 overall)

| YEAR | TEAM | LVL | AGE | PA | R | 2B | 3B | HR | RBI | BB | K | SB | CS | AVG/OBP/SLG | DRC+ | BABIP | BRR | DRP | WARP |
|---|---|---|---|---|---|---|---|---|---|---|---|---|---|---|---|---|---|---|---|
| 2021 | RAY | ROK | 18 | 47 | 8 | 4 | 1 | 0 | 8 | 6 | 13 | 2 | 2 | .282/.404/.436 | | .423 | | | |
| 2022 | CSC | A | 19 | 523 | 81 | 22 | 10 | 19 | 70 | 57 | 168 | 28 | 10 | .252/.347/.471 | 112 | .354 | -0.5 | SS(108) 0.8 | 2.3 |
| 2023 non-DC | TB | MLB | 20 | 251 | 21 | 10 | 3 | 4 | 23 | 17 | 92 | 7 | 3 | .217/.277/.334 | 73 | .341 | -0.4 | SS 0 | 0.0 |

*Comparables: Ronny Rodríguez, Richard Urena, Javy Guerra*

**The Report:** A two-way player in high school, Williams is just doing work with the lumber now, and his 2022 season was a bit of a mixed bag. He has a more optimized launch angle now, and the power projection we hoped would arrive eventually is already pulling into the station. It's a pretty standard modern swing—a bit of lift, quick inside and looking to pull, enough contact in the zone to make it all work. Williams should add more strength and eventually get to 20+ home run power. Despite the hard contact in the zone, Williams chased way too much, and swung and missed a whole lot when he chased. That's an overall approach issue more than a swing issue—still concerning, but potentially more fixable with more reps. It did dampen his overall line and does keep the hit tool projection a bit muted for now.

We expected Williams to eventually move off shortstop after the draft, and while he's not a lock to stick there at this point, the strong arm—he was a pitcher after all—and body control didn't look out of place at the six in Charleston. He does have a tendency to short his throws despite his arm strength, but I don't foresee that being a long-term issue. Williams may still slide over to third base in time, but the power jump—while he was still a teenager—mitigates that a bit, and if he can clean up the swing decisions, there may be a bigger offensive breakout to come.

**OFP:** 55 / Above-average left side infielder

**Variance:** High. There's plenty of positive variance here, as Williams looks more likely to stick at a premium defensive spot than I expected, and he's already started to tap into game power. If he can stop chasing out of the zone so much, he has clear first-division starter upside.

**Jesse Roche's Fantasy Take:** After a red-hot start in Low-A at just 18 years old, Williams hit a wall. Opposing pitchers began to double and triple up on breaking balls outside the zone, and he struggled to adjust. At his best, Williams flashed exciting power-speed upside with a patient, often disciplined, approach. His youth provides a mulligan for his swing-and-miss issues for now, but these same issues have sunk other tooled-up prospects before. Given his heightened hit tool variance, Williams has fallen outside the top-100 dynasty prospects.

## 7 Mason Auer OF    OFP: 55    ETA: 2024

Born: 03/01/01   Age: 22   Bats: R   Throws: R   Height: 6'1"   Weight: 210 lb.   Origin: Round 5, 2021 Draft (#161 overall)

| YEAR | TEAM | LVL | AGE | PA | R | 2B | 3B | HR | RBI | BB | K | SB | CS | AVG/OBP/SLG | DRC+ | BABIP | BRR | DRP | WARP |
|---|---|---|---|---|---|---|---|---|---|---|---|---|---|---|---|---|---|---|---|
| 2021 | RAY | ROK | 20 | 41 | 7 | 2 | 0 | 0 | 3 | 6 | 7 | 10 | 1 | .265/.390/.324 | | .333 | | | |
| 2022 | CSC | A | 21 | 270 | 46 | 13 | 9 | 4 | 31 | 31 | 48 | 24 | 3 | .293/.378/.478 | 127 | .348 | 4.7 | RF(40) 1.8, CF(13) 0.5, LF(1) -0.1 | 2.3 |
| 2022 | BG | A+ | 21 | 259 | 38 | 8 | 3 | 11 | 31 | 24 | 62 | 24 | 4 | .288/.367/.496 | 109 | .346 | 0.4 | CF(39) 2.6, RF(14) 1.3 | 1.8 |
| 2023 non-DC | TB | MLB | 22 | 251 | 21 | 10 | 3 | 3 | 22 | 17 | 64 | 12 | 2 | .226/.287/.340 | 78 | .298 | 1.1 | LF 0, CF 0 | 0.2 |

*Comparables: Eduardo Diaz, Daniel Johnson, Alexander Palma*

**The Report:** Another Day 2 pick from the Rays' 2021 draft class who popped last season, Auer is a well-rounded junior college outfielder who performed well across two A-ball levels while showing off at least average projection for all five tools. Calling him a five-tool center fielder is perhaps a little weird, but it would be technically correct (the best kind of correct). Auer is a better long-term fit in a corner, but he's fast enough now that an average defensive outcome at the premium outfield spot is possible. His arm is also just average, but fine enough.

The tools pop a little more at the plate. Auer has a sturdy frame and generates above-average bat speed and commensurate raw power. The swing can be a bit on the muscley side, and he did tend to chase a bit too much on breaking stuff, but he punished pitchers in the zone and his overall approach is pretty advanced for A-ball. Auer doesn't have a standout tool offensively, but both hit and power should land on the happy side of average, and he should add value with his approach and plus speed. If he can stick in center, he might be a full-fledged first-division regular. We're a little bearish on the long-term defensive outlook, but he should hit enough—and be a good enough defender in a corner that it won't push him out of an everyday role.

**OFP:** 55 / Above-average outfielder

**Variance:** High. Auer is the kind of prospect where the total is a bit better than the sum of the tools, so he might play more like a four-win player despite not having a clear plus tool projection. On the other hand, he also hasn't seen Double-A pitching yet, and there isn't an overwhelming tool on the offensive side, so there's a chance he falls into the dreaded tweener profile.

**Jesse Roche's Fantasy Take:** Whenever a prospect steals 48 bases, even in A-ball, it'll turn heads. Then, Auer added eight more stolen bases in the AFL. The speed is real. Further, his solid power–which didn't truly arrive until May–is also real. On the other hand, his contact rates and approach backed up in High-A and the AFL. If he can hit the ground running in Double-A, and assuage those concerns, Auer has top-100 upside. For now, he is just within the top-200 dynasty prospects.

## 8  Osleivis Basabe  IF        OFP: 55        ETA: Late 2023/Early 2024
Born: 09/13/00   Age: 22   Bats: R   Throws: R   Height: 6'1"   Weight: 188 lb.   Origin: International Free Agent, 2017

| YEAR | TEAM | LVL | AGE | PA | R | 2B | 3B | HR | RBI | BB | K | SB | CS | AVG/OBP/SLG | DRC+ | BABIP | BRR | DRP | WARP |
|---|---|---|---|---|---|---|---|---|---|---|---|---|---|---|---|---|---|---|---|
| 2020 | ZUL | WIN | 19 | 91 | 17 | 6 | 1 | 1 | 9 | 3 | 7 | 1 | 0 | .360/.385/.488 | | .380 | | | |
| 2021 | ZUL | WIN | 20 | 142 | 21 | 3 | 7 | 0 | 20 | 13 | 10 | 3 | 0 | .262/.336/.397 | | .284 | | | |
| 2021 | CSC | A | 20 | 309 | 51 | 10 | 6 | 2 | 35 | 26 | 39 | 18 | 4 | .284/.347/.385 | 120 | .322 | -1.6 | SS(39) 1.5, 2B(21) -1.2, 3B(6) 1.8 | 1.7 |
| 2022 | BG | A+ | 21 | 236 | 41 | 16 | 2 | 4 | 22 | 16 | 34 | 7 | 5 | .315/.370/.463 | 121 | .360 | 1.3 | 3B(20) 1.1, SS(16) 1.0, 2B(14) 0.7 | 1.7 |
| 2022 | MTG | AA | 21 | 259 | 39 | 23 | 3 | 0 | 25 | 24 | 25 | 14 | 0 | .333/.399/.461 | 122 | .369 | 2.2 | 3B(33) 0.5, SS(13) 0.9, 2B(12) -0.1 | 1.7 |
| 2023 DC | TB | MLB | 22 | 63 | 6 | 3 | 0 | 0 | 5 | 4 | 9 | 2 | 0 | .235/.287/.325 | 76 | .268 | 0.2 | 2B 0 | 0.0 |

*Comparables: Dawel Lugo, Henry Alejandro Rodriguez, Vidal Bruján*

**The Report:** We'll skip the few sentences of biographical introduction—all you really need to know is Basabe can flat-out hit. As is a recurring theme among Tampa Bay hitting prospects, his swing isn't going to hang in the Museum of the Moving Image. He utilizes a big leg kick, and he keeps his hands low throughout his setup and load before swatting at the baseball. Basabe makes oodles of hard contact without it looking pretty, and while he's too level to hit for much over-the-fence power, he's going to...well, just flat out hit. Basabe is a pretty smooth fielder despite a stocky physique. He's played all over the infield, but will fit best at third, although he has to ramp up for the left-side arm strength. Profile-wise this would make him the logical heir apparent to Yandy Díaz as a hit-tool driven corner infielder without a ton of game power. And Díaz must be getting a bit expensive for the Rays nowadays, as he's in his second arbitration season.

**OFP:** 55 / Above-average third baseman

**Variance:** Medium. Basabe hit boat loads of doubles last year, and the traditional scouting wisdom is that those will turn into home runs as he moves through his early-20s. We know a fair bit about what makes over the fence power though, and Basabe has an all-fields approach and makes a lot of hard ground-ball contact. He should keep swatting those doubles in the gaps, but the lack of over-the-fence power does limit his offensive upside. Conversely we're more confident at this point in time he will hit enough to be some sort of regular than Auer or Caminero.

**Jesse Roche's Fantasy Take:** Basabe does three things well: (1) make tons of contact, (2) hit tons of groundballs and (3) steal bases. His extreme hit-over-power approach limits his fantasy impact, as he likely will hit single-digit home runs (and he has only hit eight career homers over 1,220 plate appearances). Yet, Basabe should hit for average and provide 20+ steals. It is an uncommon fit for the hot corner, but, if anyone would try it, it's the Rays. Given his limitations, however, he should only be rostered in leagues with 300+ prospects.

## 9    Willy Vasquez   IF     OFP: 55     ETA: 2025

Born: 09/06/01   Age: 21   Bats: R   Throws: R   Height: 6'0"   Weight: 191 lb.   Origin: International Free Agent, 2019

| YEAR | TEAM | LVL | AGE | PA | R | 2B | 3B | HR | RBI | BB | K | SB | CS | AVG/OBP/SLG | DRC+ | BABIP | BRR | DRP | WARP |
|------|------|-----|-----|-----|----|----|----|----|-----|----|-----|----|----|-------------|------|-------|------|-----|------|
| 2021 | RAY | ROK | 19 | 173 | 26 | 6 | 3 | 2 | 31 | 20 | 27 | 14 | 6 | .288/.382/.411 | | .333 | | | |
| 2022 | CSC | A | 20 | 492 | 78 | 21 | 9 | 10 | 73 | 36 | 126 | 25 | 3 | .256/.313/.410 | 103 | .331 | 2.2 | 3B(72) 1.7, SS(17) -0.1, 2B(10) -0.8 | 2.0 |
| 2023 non-DC | TB | MLB | 21 | 251 | 18 | 10 | 2 | 3 | 20 | 13 | 74 | 6 | 2 | .211/.257/.307 | 57 | .296 | -1.4 | 2B 0, 3B 0 | -0.7 |

**The Report:** Vasquez has a major-league frame with some projection left, and a swing that is more traditionally orthodox—although he uses both a toe tap and leg kick which can make him look like he's shaking a spider out of his pants leg. The top-line stats are just okay for a 21-year-old in A-ball—mostly due to Vasquez chasing offspeed a bit too much—but he made good contact in the zone, and his top-end exit velocities suggest there will be more power to come than his ~.150 ISO might indicate. There's not an obvious plus offensive projection here, but average hit and above-average power are in play, and like every other Rays infield prospect, he has experience all over the dirt. His body control and actions should play fine up the middle, with second being a better fit that short. Vasquez is a bit more raw at the plate than the names ahead of him, and he needs to add some more physicality, but the upside here is intriguing and he might end up with the most pop of this tier of prospects.

**OFP:** 55 / Above-average infielder

**Variance:** High. If you chase too much as a 21-year-old in Low-A, the variance is going to be high. If your contact profile is this loud at any level, the upside is going to be there.

**Jesse Roche's Fantasy Take:** Vasquez is far bigger than his listed height and puts on shows in BP, though his power did not begin to translate in games until July. From then on, he hit .326/.386/.557 with nine home runs over 54 games. He certainly looks the part of a future big-leaguer and, if he can carry over his late-season gains into this year, he could truly break out. Vasquez should be rostered in leagues with up to 300 prospects.

## 10    Carlos Colmenarez   SS     OFP: 55     ETA: 2026/2027

Born: 11/15/03   Age: 19   Bats: L   Throws: R   Height: 5'10"   Weight: 170 lb.   Origin: International Free Agent, 2021

| YEAR | TEAM | LVL | AGE | PA | R | 2B | 3B | HR | RBI | BB | K | SB | CS | AVG/OBP/SLG | DRC+ | BABIP | BRR | DRP | WARP |
|------|------|-----|-----|-----|----|----|----|----|-----|----|----|----|----|-------------|------|-------|-----|-----|------|
| 2021 | DSL RAY1 | ROK | 17 | 114 | 7 | 2 | 1 | 0 | 12 | 8 | 30 | 7 | 6 | .247/.319/.289 | | .338 | | | |
| 2022 | RAY | ROK | 18 | 153 | 36 | 7 | 3 | 1 | 19 | 17 | 41 | 13 | 2 | .254/.379/.381 | | .365 | | | |

**The Report:** One of the more notable IFA prospects in the 2021 class, a hamate injury limited him in the Dominican complex in 2021. His 2022 was spent stateside, and more or less playing to the scouting report. He's an advanced defender with better batted-ball data than his top-line performance, but there's nothing in his profile yet that suggests a breakout at the plate. If Colmenarez does end up a future plus defender, the offensive performance won't have to be much better than fine, but there's a lot of unknowns in the projection until we see a longer pro track record of some sort.

**OFP:** 55 / Oh, let's go with glove-first everyday shortstop

**Variance:** Extreme. Colmenarez is an 18-year-old shortstop without notable present offensive tools. This could go in a lot of directions.

**Jesse Roche's Fantasy Take:** We are still waiting for Colmenarez to make good on his pedigree as a top international free agent in 2021. His performance at the complex was mostly promising, absent elevated swing-and-miss and limited power. Now 19, his anticipated arrival in full-season ball could make or break his prospect status. Colmenarez remains a boom-or-bust prospect who should be rostered in leagues with 250+ prospects.

# Outside the Top Ten:

## 11 Cole Wilcox RHP

Born: 07/14/99   Age: 23   Bats: R   Throws: R   Height: 6'5"   Weight: 232 lb.   Origin: Round 3, 2020 Draft (#80 overall)

| YEAR | TEAM | LVL | AGE | W | L | SV | G | GS | IP | H | HR | BB/9 | K/9 | K | GB% | BABIP | WHIP | ERA | DRA- | WARP |
|------|------|-----|-----|---|---|----|---|----|----|---|----|------|-----|---|-----|-------|------|-----|------|------|
| 2021 | CSC | A | 21 | 1 | 0 | 0 | 10 | 10 | 44¹ | 33 | 1 | 1.0 | 10.6 | 52 | 61.7% | .281 | 0.86 | 2.03 | 80 | 0.9 |
| 2022 | CSC | A | 22 | 0 | 1 | 0 | 4 | 4 | 11 | 8 | 1 | 1.6 | 12.3 | 15 | 66.7% | .269 | 0.91 | 2.45 | 66 | 0.3 |
| 2023 non-DC | TB | MLB | 23 | 3 | 3 | 0 | 58 | 0 | 50 | 52 | 6 | 3.0 | 7.3 | 41 | 41.8% | .301 | 1.36 | 4.21 | 111 | 0.0 |

Comparables: Wei-Chieh Huang, John Gant, Nick Green

Wilcox returned from Tommy John surgery late in the 2022 season. He was less than a year out from going under the knife during what was essentially a five-week rehab assignment, so evaluating the stuff at present seems a bit silly. For what it's worth, the slider looked sharp while the fastball was down a couple ticks from his dominant 2021 outings. Wilcox's command lagged as well, but again, that's typical for this point in TJ recovery. He'll enter 2023 18 months off surgery and with fewer restrictor plates on the mound. However, he's never thrown even 60 innings in a season, and between the elbow surgery and the stiffness in his delivery, he might be forced to the pen sooner rather than later. Wilcox would likely be quite good in relief, leaning on that sharp slider and perhaps getting a few extra ticks back on the fastball. He still has the potential to be a good mid-rotation arm if his return from surgery goes well, so I'd expect him to spend his 2023 time as starter.

## 12 Kameron Misner CF

Born: 01/08/98   Age: 25   Bats: L   Throws: L   Height: 6'4"   Weight: 218 lb.   Origin: Round 1, 2019 Draft (#35 overall)

| YEAR | TEAM | LVL | AGE | PA | R | 2B | 3B | HR | RBI | BB | K | SB | CS | AVG/OBP/SLG | DRC+ | BABIP | BRR | DRP | WARP |
|------|------|-----|-----|----|---|----|----|----|-----|----|---|----|----|-------------|------|-------|-----|-----|------|
| 2021 | MSS | WIN | 23 | 102 | 21 | 3 | 0 | 7 | 14 | 20 | 34 | 4 | 2 | .205/.373/.513 | | .231 | | | |
| 2021 | BEL | A+ | 23 | 400 | 58 | 22 | 3 | 11 | 56 | 50 | 119 | 24 | 2 | .244/.350/.424 | 95 | .338 | -0.1 | CF(38) -3.2, LF(36) -0.4, RF(7) 1.1 | 0.8 |
| 2021 | PNS | AA | 23 | 62 | 12 | 7 | 0 | 1 | 3 | 7 | 17 | 2 | 2 | .309/.387/.491 | 87 | .432 | -0.6 | CF(9) -1.0, LF(2) -0.0 | -0.1 |
| 2022 | MTG | AA | 24 | 510 | 80 | 25 | 1 | 16 | 62 | 86 | 155 | 32 | 7 | .251/.384/.431 | 110 | .356 | -2.2 | CF(99) -2.4, RF(11) 0.5, LF(2) -0.1 | 2.2 |
| 2023 non-DC | TB | MLB | 25 | 251 | 24 | 11 | 1 | 4 | 23 | 28 | 87 | 8 | 2 | .231/.324/.346 | 94 | .361 | -0.7 | LF 0, CF 0 | 0.6 |

Comparables: Ronnie Dawson, Cedric Mullins, Nelson Perez

Acquired from the Marlins for Joey Wendle, the cross-state organizational trek didn't change much more than the scenery for the former 35th-overall pick. Misner became even more Three-True-Outcomes-ish for the Biscuits, with a smidge over half his plate appearances ending in a home run, walk or strikeout. He looks the part of a Rob Deer Society Platinum Member at the plate, using the ol' stomp and lift to generate as many pull side fly balls as possible. Misner is a better defender than the Patron Saint of TTO, playing a rangy center field, where his long strides just eat up any ground between him and fly balls. There's no real floor for the hit tool here, but the Rays aren't averse to carrying a low batting average, platoonable player with some pop. So while nothing changed but the scenery, Misner may have found the right scene.

## 13 Cooper Kinney 2B

Born: 01/27/03   Age: 20   Bats: L   Throws: R   Height: 6'3"   Weight: 200 lb.   Origin: Round 1, 2021 Draft (#34 overall)

| YEAR | TEAM | LVL | AGE | PA | R | 2B | 3B | HR | RBI | BB | K | SB | CS | AVG/OBP/SLG | DRC+ | BABIP | BRR | DRP | WARP |
|------|------|-----|-----|----|---|----|----|----|-----|----|---|----|----|-------------|------|-------|-----|-----|------|
| 2021 | RAY | ROK | 18 | 47 | 9 | 1 | 1 | 0 | 5 | 10 | 9 | 2 | 0 | .286/.468/.371 | | .385 | | | |

There is an alternate timeline where we are writing about Kinney as another major prospect on that loaded 2022 RiverDogs team. Behind this sliding door, he's ranked in the same tier as Caminero and Williams, and is yet another Rays infield prospect with a potential plus bat, but no clear infield home yet. In our bubble universe though, he suffered a shoulder injury in spring training that necessitated surgery and cost him the entire 2022 season.

## 14 Brock Jones CF

Born: 03/28/01   Age: 22   Bats: L   Throws: L   Height: 6'0"   Weight: 197 lb.   Origin: Round 2, 2022 Draft (#65 overall)

| YEAR | TEAM | LVL | AGE | PA | R | 2B | 3B | HR | RBI | BB | K | SB | CS | AVG/OBP/SLG | DRC+ | BABIP | BRR | DRP | WARP |
|------|------|-----|-----|----|----|----|----|----|-----|----|----|----|----|-------------|------|-------|-----|-----|------|
| 2022 | CSC | A | 21 | 62 | 15 | 4 | 1 | 4 | 12 | 12 | 21 | 9 | 3 | .286/.419/.653 | 97 | .400 | 0.4 | CF(10) 0.6, LF(3) 1.0 | 0.3 |
| 2023 non-DC | TB | MLB | 22 | 251 | 21 | 10 | 2 | 3 | 20 | 23 | 93 | 16 | 6 | .211/.290/.307 | 71 | .345 | 4.2 | LF 0, CF 0 | 0.4 |

*Comparables: Brian Goodwin, Derek Fisher, Jonah Davis*

If you saw Brock Jones early in the college season, you might have wondered how the heck he went in the second round. If you saw him later on, you might have expected him to be one of the first college bats off the board. As you'd expect, the truth lies somewhere in the middle, but Jones' early-season swing-and-miss issues at Stanford did pop back up in his first taste of pro ball. He's looking to pull the ball in the air, and that opens some pretty big holes in the zone for pitchers to attack. Anything he hits will go far and the plus power/speed upside in the profile will tantalize until the K-rates stay over 30% for a bit too long. We're not there yet, so dream on.

## 15 Greg Jones SS

Born: 03/07/98   Age: 25   Bats: S   Throws: R   Height: 6'2"   Weight: 175 lb.   Origin: Round 1, 2019 Draft (#22 overall)

| YEAR | TEAM | LVL | AGE | PA | R | 2B | 3B | HR | RBI | BB | K | SB | CS | AVG/OBP/SLG | DRC+ | BABIP | BRR | DRP | WARP |
|------|------|-----|-----|----|----|----|----|----|-----|----|----|----|----|-------------|------|-------|-----|-----|------|
| 2021 | BG | A+ | 23 | 257 | 48 | 7 | 3 | 13 | 38 | 29 | 75 | 27 | 2 | .291/.389/.527 | 122 | .383 | 1.7 | SS(50) 1.4 | 1.8 |
| 2021 | MTG | AA | 23 | 60 | 8 | 1 | 1 | 1 | 2 | 4 | 21 | 7 | 0 | .185/.267/.296 | 70 | .281 | 0.3 | SS(15) -0.9 | -0.1 |
| 2022 | MTG | AA | 24 | 358 | 54 | 19 | 3 | 8 | 40 | 27 | 128 | 37 | 5 | .238/.318/.392 | 76 | .370 | 3.1 | SS(77) 7.8 | 1.2 |
| 2023 non-DC | TB | MLB | 25 | 251 | 22 | 10 | 2 | 4 | 23 | 17 | 91 | 13 | 3 | .225/.287/.336 | 77 | .354 | 1.9 | SS 0 | 0.3 |

*Comparables: Blake Davis, Pedro Florimón, Gift Ngoepe*

Jones dealt with injuries that limited him to just 79 games in 2022, but when he was on the field, his struggles in Double-A continued. The switch-hitter's swings look the part, smooth with good wrists, a bit more bat speed and loft as a righty, but his K-rate ballooned further, to over 35%. When he did make contact left-handed, there were too many weak groundballs. Jones will beat out his fair share of infield hits as he's still a plus-plus runner, but his legs can't impact the game when he's walking back to the bench as often as he was in 2022. Defensively, his hands and actions remain fine for the infield, but less than ideal for shortstop, so I wonder if a move to center field might be on offer soon, if for nothing else than a bit more positional flex. Jones will be 25 next season, and has yet to conquer the upper minors—although it's fair to grant a bit more developmental leeway to a 2019 draftee—so we are approaching a make-or-break season for the former first-round pick.

## 16 Xavier Isaac 1B

Born: 12/17/03   Age: 19   Bats: L   Throws: L   Height: 6'4"   Weight: 240 lb.   Origin: Round 1, 2022 Draft (#29 overall)

If the Rays had an overarching theme in their 2022 draft class it was betting on big raw power. Isaac might be able to put on a batting practice show on par with Elijah Green, but he's going to be limited to first base or designated hitter in the pros, and has similarly open questions about his ultimate hit tool projection. The recent track record of prep first baseman isn't much better than that of prep catchers, and a lot of things will have to break right for Isaac to turn into a plus regular at first. But given the true top-of-the-scale power potential, only a few things need to go right for him to be a useful long-side platoon bat.

## 17 Ben Peoples RHP

Born: 05/01/01   Age: 22   Bats: L   Throws: R   Height: 6'1"   Weight: 175 lb.   Origin: Round 22, 2019 Draft (#668 overall)

| YEAR | TEAM | LVL | AGE | W | L | SV | G | GS | IP | H | HR | BB/9 | K/9 | K | GB% | BABIP | WHIP | ERA | DRA- | WARP |
|------|------|-----|-----|---|---|----|----|----|----|----|----|------|-----|----|-----|-------|------|-----|------|------|
| 2021 | RAY | ROK | 20 | 2 | 1 | 0 | 9 | 4 | 19 | 16 | 0 | 6.2 | 13.7 | 29 | 47.6% | .381 | 1.53 | 2.84 | | |
| 2022 | CSC | A | 21 | 5 | 5 | 0 | 22 | 21 | 84 | 69 | 9 | 4.1 | 11.7 | 109 | 42.3% | .313 | 1.27 | 3.11 | 82 | 1.7 |
| 2022 | BG | A+ | 21 | 0 | 2 | 0 | 2 | 2 | 10 | 4 | 0 | 3.6 | 10.8 | 12 | 57.1% | .190 | 0.80 | 2.70 | 88 | 0.1 |
| 2023 non-DC | TB | MLB | 22 | 3 | 3 | 0 | 58 | 0 | 50 | 50 | 7 | 4.7 | 8.3 | 46 | 36.0% | .302 | 1.53 | 4.91 | 124 | -0.4 |

An overslot Day 3 prep arm from 2019, Peoples finally debuted in full-season ball last year and racked up the strikeouts across both A-ball levels. He can run his fastball up into the mid-90s, and his breaker can show good vertical action from his high arm slot. There is a rarely-used change as well. The top two pitches play better in short bursts, the command and control can be shaky, and Peoples isn't the biggest righty around, so he may end up a better fit in the bullpen where he can spam the breaking ball a bit more.

## 18 Tristan Peters  LF
Born: 02/29/00   Age: 23   Bats: L   Throws: R   Height: 6'0"   Weight: 180 lb.   Origin: Round 7, 2021 Draft (#207 overall)

| YEAR | TEAM | LVL | AGE | PA | R | 2B | 3B | HR | RBI | BB | K | SB | CS | AVG/OBP/SLG | DRC+ | BABIP | BRR | DRP | WARP |
|---|---|---|---|---|---|---|---|---|---|---|---|---|---|---|---|---|---|---|---|
| 2021 | BRWB | ROK | 21 | 55 | 9 | 0 | 2 | 1 | 6 | 8 | 14 | 6 | 1 | .239/.345/.391 | | .313 | | | |
| 2022 | WIS | A+ | 22 | 383 | 61 | 22 | 8 | 7 | 51 | 45 | 61 | 13 | 6 | .306/.386/.485 | 124 | .351 | 3.7 | LF(62) -1.6, RF(13) -0.8 | 2.2 |
| 2022 | RIC | AA | 22 | 149 | 16 | 7 | 1 | 1 | 17 | 15 | 31 | 5 | 2 | .212/.302/.303 | 94 | .270 | 0.8 | LF(28) 1.7, CF(3) 0.4, RF(2) 0.0 | 0.6 |
| 2023 non-DC | TB | MLB | 23 | 251 | 21 | 11 | 3 | 3 | 21 | 20 | 53 | 4 | 2 | .227/.294/.332 | 78 | .284 | -2.0 | LF 0, CF 0 | -0.2 |

The Rays were Peters' third organization of 2022. Tampa acquired him from San Francisco in a Rule 5 roster machination trade just a few months after the Giants got him from Milwaukee for Trevor Rosenthal. He struggled after his post-trade-deadline promotion to Double-A, but still projects as a contact-driven fourth outfielder who can play all three spots—although he fits best defensively in left.

## 19 Heriberto Hernandez  OF
Born: 12/16/99   Age: 23   Bats: R   Throws: R   Height: 6'1"   Weight: 195 lb.   Origin: International Free Agent, 2017

| YEAR | TEAM | LVL | AGE | PA | R | 2B | 3B | HR | RBI | BB | K | SB | CS | AVG/OBP/SLG | DRC+ | BABIP | BRR | DRP | WARP |
|---|---|---|---|---|---|---|---|---|---|---|---|---|---|---|---|---|---|---|---|
| 2021 | CSC | A | 21 | 320 | 57 | 15 | 0 | 12 | 44 | 49 | 90 | 7 | 4 | .252/.381/.453 | 113 | .325 | 0.2 | LF(54) -2.0, RF(12) -0.1 | 1.4 |
| 2022 | BG | A+ | 22 | 494 | 70 | 28 | 1 | 24 | 89 | 67 | 155 | 6 | 2 | .255/.368/.499 | 119 | .346 | -1.7 | LF(66) 2.4, RF(38) -1.1, 1B(6) -0.6 | 2.4 |
| 2023 non-DC | TB | MLB | 23 | 251 | 24 | 11 | 1 | 6 | 25 | 23 | 91 | 2 | 1 | .225/.305/.356 | 90 | .352 | -3.1 | 1B 0, LF 0 | 0.0 |

*Comparables: Chad Tracy, Kuo Hui Lo, Sergio Pedroza*

On Hernandez, last year we wrote: "We do kinda need to see him hit for average in a full-season league to really get the hype train rolling." Well, he followed up his 2021—where he hit .252 in Low-A—by hitting .255 in High-A. That rather unremarkable batting average did come with plenty of walks and pop, but the defensively limited Three-True-Outcomes slugger on the short side of the platoon—Hernandez slashed almost 200 points better against lefties in 2022—is a less-appealing proposition.

## 20 Blake Hunt  C
Born: 11/10/98   Age: 24   Bats: R   Throws: R   Height: 6'3"   Weight: 215 lb.   Origin: Round 2, 2017 Draft (#69 overall)

| YEAR | TEAM | LVL | AGE | PA | R | 2B | 3B | HR | RBI | BB | K | SB | CS | AVG/OBP/SLG | DRC+ | BABIP | BRR | DRP | WARP |
|---|---|---|---|---|---|---|---|---|---|---|---|---|---|---|---|---|---|---|---|
| 2021 | BG | A+ | 22 | 257 | 41 | 15 | 2 | 9 | 41 | 26 | 79 | 1 | 0 | .225/.307/.427 | 92 | .298 | -0.1 | C(50) 9.7 | 1.4 |
| 2021 | MTG | AA | 22 | 63 | 5 | 2 | 0 | 0 | 0 | 6 | 25 | 0 | 0 | .125/.210/.161 | 58 | .226 | 0.8 | C(17) -0.3 | 0.0 |
| 2022 | MTG | AA | 23 | 302 | 31 | 15 | 1 | 5 | 39 | 21 | 70 | 2 | 0 | .245/.315/.363 | 83 | .312 | -1.1 | C(72) -2.7 | 0.0 |
| 2023 non-DC | TB | MLB | 24 | 251 | 20 | 11 | 1 | 3 | 21 | 16 | 72 | 1 | 0 | .212/.271/.309 | 64 | .293 | -4.2 | C 0 | -0.5 |

We are now a few seasons removed from the "Blake Hunt is a secret super prospect" scuttlebutt after a strong instructs and subsequent trade to the Rays—the Sam Miller tweet will never die. In the Rays' organization, he has hit, well, a little worse than he did for the Padres, with his slash line hovering under a .700 OPS, the game power that was to come, mostly remaining theoretical. Hunt is a solid enough defender—although his framing hasn't graded out as well in the upper minors—and if he can get back to a .700 OPS, that can keep you employed as a major league backstop for a while.

## Top Talents 25 and Under (as of 4/1/2023):

1. Wander Franco, SS
2. Shane McClanahan, LHP
3. Isaac Paredes, IF
4. Curtis Mead, IF
5. Taj Bradley, RHP
6. Kyle Manzardo, 1B
7. Vidal Bruján, UT
8. Josh Lowe, OF
9. Jonathan Aranda, IF
10. Shane Baz, RHP

The Rays remain chock-a-block with 40-man talent, pushing several quality prospects out of this list. It would be easy enough to switch some of the back-end names out with prospects, and this even edges out fireballing young righty Luis Patiño, who has not yet put it all together in the bigs. The trio at the top, however, and in particular the top two are the foundation of a different sort of Rays roster than the more gimmicky variants of years past. The club's shift towards embracing the embodiment of rays of sunshine may finally be apt, as this group has multiple stars shining bright.

The nod goes to Franco over McClanahan despite the latter's brilliant 2022 in deference to the impending 22-year-old's youth and pedigree, but they could easily be flip-flopped. Franco underwhelmed somewhat in his sophomore campaign, missing half the season with a quad strain and later a broken hamate bone. Ideally the timing of his injury will allow him to heal over the winter and return to full form. Even in half a season, Franco looked sharp at the plate, with a 112 DRC+ and still every reason to expect him being a star-level performer in the near-immediate term. McClanahan was just that himself, falling in the "also-ran" category of the Cy Young voting behind the 39-year-old freak of nature that is Justin Verlander but stepping fully into the role of staff ace in his second season in Tyler Glasnow's absence. The southpaw's only clear path for further improvement is if he can gobble up even more innings, though it's unclear if Tampa Bay's pitching strategy will allow for too much more so long as MLB continues allowing 13-man bullpens.

The best-performing 25U member of the 2021 Detroit Tigers in the 2022 season was Paredes, whose breakout was a revelation for Tampa Bay and no doubt gutting for Detroit. The lefty-mashing infielder spread his time around the entire infield while running a 125 DRC+ in 381 plate appearances, and is essentially standing behind Yandy Díaz tapping his foot impatiently. If Tampa Bay takes their usual tack and deals Díaz lest they be forced to pay him more than a shade over league minimum, Paredes will have a chance to establish a full-time role. As it is, he's more than earned platoon work with Aranda at first base and rotating DH and pinch-hitting opportunities.

The rest of this list has a few more bruises but they're still good apples. Bruján's first couple cracks in the bigs haven't seen him establish any consistency at the plate, but he's athletic and versatile enough to help the club defensively. His track record of hitting in the minors still portends a productive big leaguer, especially with his ability to switch-hit. Lowe's basic numbers seem slightly better at the dish, but DRC+ is more dubious. The well-built Virginian is at least fifth in line for big-league reps however, and given the athleticism and versatility of many of Tampa Bay's infield prospects, it might take even more for Lowe to get a clear chance to play. His swing-and-miss issues have not done him any favors, but on most clubs he'd be given a chance to prove it full-time in a way he's not certain to at the Trop. Aranda's route to playing time is clearer given his ability to work on the dirt, and his numbers hold up well in Triple-A Durham, and the stocky lefty hit everything hard in his breakout 2022. Pairing with Paredes and Harold Ramírez will allow Aranda to hide against lefties as well.

Lastly, there is Baz, who is unlikely to pitch in 2023, but could feasibly return late in the season or perhaps work out of the bullpen. It's an absolute shame that Baz's age-24 season will be spent on the shelf, as every indication has been encouraging that he could be another exciting rotation arm. His electric stuff was highlighted by upper-90s heat and a dynamite slate of secondaries that he's shown increased control of over the past two seasons. Hopefully a return to full health is in store, though his role may look more creative upon his return to attempt to maximize his availability.

# Texas Rangers

## The State of the System:

With the big-league team finishing towards the bottom of the league and ownership finally buying into a rebuild, Texas' farm has taken major steps forward over the past couple of years. It's now one of the deeper systems in baseball, although there remains a lack of impact prospects.

## The Top Ten:

### 1 Evan Carter OF    OFP: 60    ETA: 2024

Born: 08/29/02   Age: 20   Bats: L   Throws: R   Height: 6'4"   Weight: 190 lb.   Origin: Round 2, 2020 Draft (#50 overall)

| YEAR | TEAM | LVL | AGE | PA | R | 2B | 3B | HR | RBI | BB | K | SB | CS | AVG/OBP/SLG | DRC+ | BABIP | BRR | DRP | WARP |
|---|---|---|---|---|---|---|---|---|---|---|---|---|---|---|---|---|---|---|---|
| 2021 | DE | A | 18 | 146 | 22 | 8 | 1 | 2 | 12 | 34 | 28 | 12 | 4 | .236/.438/.387 | 121 | .299 | -2.0 | CF(30) -4.0 | 0.4 |
| 2022 | HIC | A+ | 19 | 447 | 78 | 18 | 10 | 11 | 66 | 59 | 75 | 26 | 12 | .287/.388/.476 | 137 | .329 | -2.1 | CF(72) -0.2, LF(8) 1.1, RF(3) 0.0 | 3.1 |
| 2022 | FRI | AA | 19 | 28 | 8 | 3 | 0 | 1 | 7 | 5 | 6 | 2 | 1 | .429/.536/.714 | 104 | .533 | 0.2 | RF(3) 0.4, CF(2) 0.2 | 0.2 |
| 2023 non-DC | TEX | MLB | 20 | 251 | 22 | 11 | 3 | 3 | 22 | 26 | 52 | 8 | 4 | .232/.319/.344 | 91 | .291 | 0.2 | LF 0, CF 0 | 0.6 |

Comparables: Jason Heyward, Ronald Acuña Jr., Heliot Ramos

**The Report:** Carter was a head-scratcher when the Rangers popped him in the second round of the 2020 draft, totally off most public draft boards. Texas brass expressed confidence that, had the high school season not been suspended due to the pandemic, Carter would have rocketed toward the first round. As it turns out, they were likely right.

The profile here is a good mix of tools to dream on with advanced feel for the game. Maybe the best example for this is his feel for the zone and ability to pick up spin, both pretty extraordinary for a player who turned 20 towards the end of last season. When combined with a quality swing and quick bat, these abilities create both a projected plus hit tool, along with the soft skills for an even stronger OBP and the ability to avoid strikeouts even in deep counts.

Power numbers were decent enough, as well—21 doubles, 10 triples and 12 home runs, good enough for an ISO just short of .200—and project for growth as Carter fills out his body. The lefty hitter is currently shaped a little bit like Shaggy, a very narrow and skinny body. He's quick-twitch and can sting a ball, but the home run pop is somewhat restricted by his current size. A back injury limited his previous offseason, but Carter mentioned plans to hit the weight room hard. The shoulders here are narrow enough he will never be mistaken for Jose Canseco, but there remains room for additional muscle and resulting power.

Carter's strengths continue with the wheels and glove—he's a quick straight-line runner; the feet measure as plus and allow him to project as at least an above-average center fielder, even as he's a bit raw out there at present. The more you look at the profile, the more you like it—he's a good athlete with advanced soft skills, and little in the way of weaknesses.

**OFP:** 60 / First-division regular that makes a couple All-Star games

**Variance:** Medium. Back issues are always scary and add some variance—nothing has recurred yet but it's worth watching. On the flip side, if Carter can grow into 20+ home run power, there's star potential here.

**Jesse Roche's Fantasy Take:** Carter arguably broke out in the second half last year, hitting .343/.452/.490 with 15 stolen bases over his final 39 games between High- and Double-A, including the playoffs. His precocious hitting ability currently drives his future fantasy profile and there may be more to unlock in both his power and speed. As mentioned above, Carter's Shaggy-like frame is unlikely to add the type of mass you might expect on paper. However, he should maintain his speed, and he has shown a willingness to run, including 28-for-41 in steals last year. ("Run, Raggy, Run!" Scooby-Doo was a big hit with my three-year-old son this year). Even if his over-the-fence pop falls short of 20, Carter can have a fantasy impact with his on-base ability and stolen bases, placing him comfortably within the dynasty top 50.

## 2    Josh Jung   3B     OFP: 60     ETA: Debuted in 2022

Born: 02/12/98   Age: 25   Bats: R   Throws: R   Height: 6'2"   Weight: 214 lb.   Origin: Round 1, 2019 Draft (#8 overall)

| YEAR | TEAM | LVL | AGE | PA | R | 2B | 3B | HR | RBI | BB | K | SB | CS | AVG/OBP/SLG | DRC+ | BABIP | BRR | DRP | WARP |
|------|------|-----|-----|-----|----|----|----|----|-----|----|-----|----|----|-------------|------|-------|------|---------|------|
| 2021 | FRI | AA | 23 | 186 | 25 | 8 | 1 | 10 | 40 | 13 | 42 | 2 | 2 | .308/.366/.544 | 114 | .356 | -1.9 | 3B(32) 0.2 | 0.7 |
| 2021 | RR | AAA | 23 | 156 | 29 | 14 | 0 | 9 | 21 | 18 | 34 | 0 | 0 | .348/.436/.652 | 125 | .413 | -0.4 | 3B(24) 1.3 | 1.1 |
| 2022 | RAN | ROK | 24 | 29 | 4 | 0 | 0 | 3 | 5 | 3 | 5 | 0 | 0 | .240/.345/.600 | | .176 | | | |
| 2022 | RR | AAA | 24 | 106 | 15 | 7 | 0 | 6 | 24 | 4 | 30 | 1 | 0 | .273/.321/.525 | 97 | .333 | -0.2 | 3B(18) -0.2 | 0.2 |
| 2022 | TEX | MLB | 24 | 102 | 9 | 4 | 1 | 5 | 14 | 4 | 39 | 2 | 0 | .204/.235/.418 | 75 | .278 | 0.2 | 3B(25) 1.3 | 0.1 |
| 2023 DC | TEX | MLB | 25 | 507 | 48 | 22 | 2 | 14 | 49 | 30 | 135 | 4 | 1 | .213/.269/.359 | 77 | .266 | -0.3 | 3B 0 | -0.1 |

*Comparables: Matt Chapman, Brandon Laird, Chris Johnson*

**The Report:** A very different prospect from Carter—a strong-across-the-board, middle-of-the-field player—Jung is a promising piece of the present and future in his own right. He's more limited, and with more limitations comes more risk, but the bat has All-Star potential, a powerful thwack he can send to all fields. In his better years, a .270 average with 30 round trippers isn't out of the question. Now for the limitations. The glove is...fine. The arm is...fine, not a typical third baseman's arm, but not quite a disqualifier, either. He's not going to gain much value from that side of the ball; there may come a day when first base is the better option for him. The same goes for his baserunning: He's an intelligent runner, but not fleet-of-foot enough to do much more than break even in terms of value.

At the dish, 2022 numerically was a bit of a step back, although it's hard to tell whether that's the result of an injury which took several months of Jung's season or a regression in his approach. The best guess would be the former given his prior history and speedy progression, but if that best guess is wrong, the 4% BB-rate and 38% K-rate he sported in a short major-league debut would not be sustainable. Despite those contact and approach-based struggles, Jung's power did not wane–he knocked 11 home runs and 23 extra-base hits among his 128 balls in play across all levels.

Jung's bat has all the tools to be above-average or better in terms of both average and power, and prior to last year's shortened and delayed campaign, he picked up spin and controlled the zone well enough to access them. There's risk here in that if those tools don't come through to carry the profile, there's not much else to fall back on, but the makeup—an elite worker who has a blast on the baseball field in any capacity—is one to bet on.

**OFP:** 60 / First-division regular

**Variance:** High. There are a couple factors here. One is the lack of secondary value, should Jung's bat not develop as anticipated. The second is health—since being drafted, Jung has missed time with a variety of injuries; no soft-tissue or likely recurring problems, but enough quantity to question his ability to play 162 consistently.

**Jesse Roche's Fantasy Take:** Jung is the top fantasy prospect in this system because, well, defensive limitations are only issues if they jeopardize playing time. As of this writing, he is currently penciled in as the Opening Day third baseman for the Rangers. That isn't to say he isn't without more risk than you'd associate with a likely MLB starter, including the aforementioned approach concerns. Jung also lacks the type of elite power you'd normally associate with a potential 30-homer hitter. As such, his range of outcomes is larger than ideal. Regardless, Jung is a top-20 fantasy prospect who could help breathe life into an increasingly shallow third base.

## 3    Jack Leiter   RHP     OFP: 60     ETA: 2024

Born: 04/21/00   Age: 23   Bats: R   Throws: R   Height: 6'1"   Weight: 205 lb.   Origin: Round 1, 2021 Draft (#2 overall)

| YEAR | TEAM | LVL | AGE | W | L | SV | G | GS | IP | H | HR | BB/9 | K/9 | K | GB% | BABIP | WHIP | ERA | DRA- | WARP |
|------|------|-----|-----|---|----|----|----|----|------|----|----|------|------|-----|-------|-------|------|------|------|------|
| 2022 | FRI | AA | 22 | 3 | 10 | 0 | 23 | 22 | 92² | 88 | 11 | 5.4 | 10.6 | 109 | 36.0% | .322 | 1.55 | 5.54 | 88 | 1.1 |
| 2023 non-DC | TEX | MLB | 23 | 3 | 3 | 0 | 58 | 0 | 50 | 51 | 8 | 5.4 | 8.6 | 48 | 35.6% | .300 | 1.61 | 5.34 | 133 | -0.6 |

*Comparables: Chi Chi González, Anthony Ranaudo, Dan Cortes*

**The Report:** The ranking here is built more on pedigree, history and ceiling than on current looks. It was a rough professional debut for Leiter. The built-in rationale is Double-A being an extremely aggressive first-season assignment, and the excuse is a valid one. However, many of his biggest issues weren't problems which would be caused by the level of competition. Chief among the reasons for his 5.54 ERA/5.02 FIP were consistent glove-side misses that he was unable to fix mid-inning, allowing frames to spiral away from him; an inability to land his lauded curveball for strikes throughout the season; pure stuff which backed up throughout the year, namely the heater, which lost some of its jump. Control, command and mechanics generally aren't items affected by the prospect's level—certainly not for one with the self-confidence of Leiter.

That being said, there were some positives in 2022 and there's more than enough reason to believe in Leiter's future. The brightest spot in his season was the development of his slider, the big-league's current breaking ball of choice and a pitch which had been a distant third prior to the year. He also debuted a cutter late in the year, which Rangers officials believe has serious potential given the way Leiter releases his fastball. He's another one in this system whose makeup is a plus—an extreme competitor and worker with an obvious baseball background.

At his best, Leiter has three pitches which flash double-plus in his fastball, slider and curveball. That's simply not a tool set many minor-league arms can claim. The questions are whether he can A) return to throwing his best stuff, B) land them all for strikes and C) command them well enough to get the most out of them. His career dating back to college suggest the last of the three questions may be the hardest for him to achieve, but if he can answer the first two positively, he'll have plenty of margin for error.

**OFP:** 60 / no. 3 starter

**Variance:** Very High. Struggles in his debut put him further away from the big leagues than was initially expected and bring into focus control/command questions, on top of the natural risk of throwing a baseball 80+ times every fifth day.

**Jesse Roche's Fantasy Take:** Well, that didn't go well. Leiter crashed and burned for much of his debut, struggling *badly* with command and running up a 13.2% walk rate. Arguably more concerning was his regressing stuff. Still, Leiter flashed an electric arsenal, which, if consistently harnessed, would place him firmly in the conversation for the top pitching prospect in baseball. Those glimpses of greatness keep him in the top-100 dynasty picture. However, as strictly a word of warning, the same was said about Asa Lacy.

## 4  Owen White  RHP    OFP: 60    ETA: Late 2023/Early 2024

Born: 08/09/99  Age: 23  Bats: R  Throws: R  Height: 6'3"  Weight: 199 lb.  Origin: Round 2, 2018 Draft (#55 overall)

| YEAR | TEAM | LVL | AGE | W | L | SV | G | GS | IP | H | HR | BB/9 | K/9 | K | GB% | BABIP | WHIP | ERA | DRA- | WARP |
|------|------|-----|-----|---|---|----|----|----|----|---|----|------|-----|---|-----|-------|------|-----|------|------|
| 2021 | SUR | WIN | 21 | 5 | 0 | 0 | 6 | 6 | 28¹ | 20 | 1 | 4.1 | 9.2 | 29 | 39.4% | .271 | 1.16 | 1.91 | | |
| 2021 | DE | A | 21 | 3 | 1 | 0 | 8 | 8 | 33¹ | 25 | 2 | 3.2 | 14.6 | 54 | 41.2% | .348 | 1.11 | 3.24 | 68 | 0.7 |
| 2022 | HIC | A+ | 22 | 6 | 2 | 0 | 11 | 10 | 58² | 51 | 7 | 2.9 | 12.4 | 81 | 43.7% | .326 | 1.19 | 3.99 | 87 | 0.9 |
| 2022 | FRI | AA | 22 | 3 | 0 | 0 | 4 | 4 | 21² | 19 | 1 | 1.7 | 9.6 | 23 | 50.9% | .327 | 1.06 | 2.49 | 80 | 0.4 |
| 2023 non-DC | TEX | MLB | 23 | 3 | 3 | 0 | 58 | 0 | 50 | 48 | 7 | 3.7 | 8.9 | 50 | 38.0% | .298 | 1.36 | 4.10 | 108 | 0.0 |

*Comparables: Dan Straily, Aaron Blair, Chris Flexen*

**The Report:** It took three years for White to debut after the Rangers' disastrous de-load program with their 2018 draft arms (six of the 11 pitchers who went through the program needed Tommy John within a year, White among them) and he missed additional time in 2022 with "forearm fatigue" that lingered beyond expectations, but his time on the mound has been electric.

The profile starts as most power arms do, with the fastball, which sits 93-96 with whiff-inducing ride. White's mid-80s slider is his best offspeed offering, a late two-plane breaker which plays well off the heater. Beyond that, it's a full four-pitch repertoire, with his 12-6 curve and changeup each flashing above average. All four offerings have distinctly different shapes and velo bands, making for a tricky arsenal to square up. White finds the zone and locates within it, walking 35 in his 115 ⅔ career innings, living up with his heat and down with his offspeed. The makeup here is top-line competitor stuff, and a confident, mouthy and fiery mound presence. There are areas that prevent the ever-difficult top-of-the-rotation projection—a fastball a couple ticks higher would be nice, each of his pitches exceed average but none quite reach double-plus at present, though the slider is close, and he's liable to the longball in the rare outing his fastball control/command leaves him. But frankly, with less injury history, Barfight White would be the top-ranked arm in the system.

**OFP:** 60 / no. 3 starter

**Variance:** High. A copy-and-paste from last year should do the trick: "Injury history and the accompanying workload management required elevate the risk, but White looks the part of a strong mid-rotation starter."

**Jesse Roche's Fantasy Take:** White checks a lot of boxes for what you're looking for in a fantasy pitcher: repertoire depth, above-average stuff, solid command and Brady Singer-like "enthusiasm." Unfortunately, he has yet to check an important box: health. So it goes for so many young arms. If he can prove fully healthy next year, White could quickly push for a call-up, even in the increasingly crowded Rangers rotation. (Hello there, Jacob deGrom and Nathan Eovaldi!) His ongoing health issues, however, keep him outside of the fantasy top 100.

## 5   Luisangel Acuña   MI      OFP: 55      ETA: Late 2024

Born: 03/12/02    Age: 21    Bats: R    Throws: R    Height: 5'10"    Weight: 181 lb.    Origin: International Free Agent, 2018

| YEAR | TEAM | LVL | AGE | PA | R | 2B | 3B | HR | RBI | BB | K | SB | CS | AVG/OBP/SLG | DRC+ | BABIP | BRR | DRP | WARP |
|---|---|---|---|---|---|---|---|---|---|---|---|---|---|---|---|---|---|---|---|
| 2021 | DE | A | 19 | 473 | 77 | 15 | 3 | 12 | 74 | 49 | 110 | 44 | 11 | .266/.345/.404 | 106 | .329 | 1.9 | SS(42) 1.5, 2B(36) 1.0 | 2.1 |
| 2022 | HIC | A+ | 20 | 240 | 45 | 10 | 0 | 8 | 29 | 34 | 60 | 28 | 6 | .317/.417/.483 | 108 | .416 | 2.0 | SS(37) -1.9, 2B(9) -0.4 | 1.0 |
| 2022 | FRI | AA | 20 | 169 | 21 | 6 | 2 | 3 | 18 | 17 | 36 | 12 | 3 | .224/.302/.349 | 89 | .274 | 1.1 | SS(24) 0.5, 2B(13) 1.1 | 0.5 |
| 2023 non-DC | TEX | MLB | 21 | 251 | 22 | 10 | 1 | 4 | 22 | 20 | 69 | 11 | 3 | .227/.293/.327 | 78 | .309 | 1.2 | 2B 0, SS 0 | 0.3 |

*Comparables: Cole Tucker, Lucius Fox, Richard Urena*

**The Report:** At the basest level of his evaluation, Little Acuña is an interesting bat with loads of supplemental value.

The overall profile is very different from his big brother, but the swing itself is similar and one that's been proven to work. Listed very generously at 5-foot-10, Luisangel doesn't have the all-world pop of Ronald, but does have notable power of his own. Coupled with the raw ability to smack the ball, he'll go up to the plate aggressively looking to unleash his A-swing for big damage. Acuña jumps on pitches early in the count and takes some educated guesses to try and launch the ball, but without selling out to the point it dries up walks or strikeouts. There are problems here with hitting too many grounders and letting too many inner-third pitches get in on him to create pop-outs, but if you hit the ball hard and take your walks, there's wiggle room on some of the finer points of hitting. An OBP of around .325 with 15-plus round-trippers a year feels about right here.

Adding to that wiggle room is Acuña's other sources of value—he has plus- to double-plus wheels and isn't afraid of using them, with 84 steals over the past two seasons, and also sports an impressive glove. The hands are smooth, as he's a quick-twitch reactor and he's extremely athletic in his movements, both to get to balls and to get them from his glove to first base. As with many young infielders, there were a handful of botched plays on the easy side last year, but with a little more time and focus, Acuña should be an above-average defender at short or plus at second.

None of the tools on their own are overly exciting, but if you add up an above-average offensive profile, above-average defense at the six and an ability to create issues on the bases, that's a player who will accumulate value quickly.

**OFP:** 55 / Quality, up-the-middle regular

**Variance:** Medium. Acuña is still just 20 years old and despite flashing his tools and abilities did struggle upon his aggressive Double-A promotion. There's a chance the walks and Ks divert from each other and he settles in as a career utility guy.

**Jesse Roche's Fantasy Take:** While I was on field during batting practice at the AFL Fall Stars Game, Acuña hit a bomb midway up the grass in left-center. Team personnel ran to retrieve the ball. The hitting coach said, "They better keep their heads up." Then, Acuña proceeded to hit another bomb that narrowly missed them. Don't underestimate his pop because of his size. Meanwhile, his speed is his best tool, and steals are likely to be his most reliable fantasy contribution. Acuña does have hit tool risk, with some underlying swing-and-miss and too much low-quality contact. Yet, his 15-20+ fantasy upside is tantalizing enough to look past those issues: He's a borderline top-100 dynasty prospect.

## 6   Brock Porter   RHP      OFP: 55      ETA: 2026

Born: 06/03/03    Age: 20    Bats: R    Throws: R    Height: 6'4"    Weight: 208 lb.    Origin: Round 4, 2022 Draft (#109 overall)

**The Report:** The Rangers' fourth round-pick, but prize of the 2022 draft class, Porter was a projected mid-first rounder but fell due to his reported bonus demand, one which certainly lined up with his final signing number. Able to convince him to forego schooling at Clemson, Texas found a second first-round talent in a year they sacrificed their second- and third-round selections for Corey Seager and Marcus Semien.

Porter's a big kid, standing at 6-foot-4 with plenty of projection for good weight to come. His primary offering is the usual fastball, one capable of touching triple-digits but more commonly in the mid-to-upper-90s with run and life. The best pitch, though, is an absurd changeup that Porter calls a "helicopter" change. It comes out hard mirroring the fastball and then absolutely dies, floating to the plate with big dive-and-run. If all goes right, the offering projects as a 70-grade pitch and one of the premium *cambios* in the league. Porter's breaking balls are less developed and will be an area of focus, but there's some feel for spin there.

The determining factors, in his development and eventual major-league projection and role, will be his ability to develop one of his breakers into a plus pitch, getting his arm on time and how his control/command reacts as he continues to grow into his body.

**OFP:** 55 / no. 3/4 starter or back-of-the-bullpen arm

**Variance:** Very High. Despite his billing as an advanced high school pitcher, Porter is a northern righty prep arm who hasn't thrown a professional pitch yet.

**Jesse Roche's Fantasy Take:** The track record for prep right-handed pitching prospects is, well, checkered. Porter has exciting building blocks in his huge arm strength and advanced changeup. His breaking balls, command and mechanics are all works in progress, however. For those chasing upside in FYPDs, Porter rivals nearly any pitching prospect. He should be targeted outside the top 20.

## 7   Aaron Zavala   RF    OFP: 50    ETA: 2024

Born: 06/24/00   Age: 23   Bats: L   Throws: R   Height: 6'0"   Weight: 193 lb.   Origin: Round 2, 2021 Draft (#38 overall)

| YEAR | TEAM | LVL | AGE | PA | R | 2B | 3B | HR | RBI | BB | K | SB | CS | AVG/OBP/SLG | DRC+ | BABIP | BRR | DRP | WARP |
|---|---|---|---|---|---|---|---|---|---|---|---|---|---|---|---|---|---|---|---|
| 2021 | RAN | ROK | 21 | 26 | 5 | 1 | 0 | 0 | 2 | 3 | 7 | 2 | 0 | .273/.385/.318 | | .400 | | | |
| 2021 | DE | A | 21 | 67 | 13 | 4 | 0 | 1 | 7 | 10 | 13 | 7 | 0 | .302/.433/.434 | 122 | .375 | -0.2 | RF(10) -1.3, LF(1) 0.4 | 0.3 |
| 2022 | HIC | A+ | 22 | 375 | 61 | 10 | 3 | 11 | 41 | 68 | 79 | 10 | 5 | .278/.424/.441 | 133 | .344 | 1.2 | RF(67) -0.5, CF(6) -0.2 | 2.8 |
| 2022 | FRI | AA | 22 | 139 | 28 | 8 | 0 | 5 | 21 | 21 | 29 | 4 | 1 | .277/.410/.482 | 116 | .329 | 0.7 | RF(24) -0.5 | 0.9 |
| 2023 non-DC | TEX | MLB | 23 | 251 | 24 | 10 | 2 | 4 | 23 | 29 | 61 | 4 | 1 | .235/.333/.346 | 98 | .310 | -2.5 | LF 0, CF 0 | 0.3 |

*Comparables: Trevor Larnach, Kelly Dugan, Zoilo Almonte*

**The Report:** Zavala is a good example of the value of an elite eye and great swing decisions, skills which for most of baseball history have been overlooked and undervalued. He has a quick bat, which he utilizes in a compact swing to sting baseballs with consistency. His lower half is remarkably balanced, with the former Oregon Duck always on platform and between his shoulders. That's all important because it helps him clear the bar to punish grooved pitches, an ability which differentiates the 80-approach guys who stick and the 80-approach guys who can't handle the top level. And make no mistake, Zavala is an 80-approach guy. He sees spin and can hit breaking balls and changeups just as well as heaters, he has a feel for the zone in the Votto Realm and he'll jump on a mistake in any count but doesn't force the issue if that pitch never comes. His .277/.420/.453 line (notably .316/.465/.491 vs righties) and 17% walk rate in 2022 are pretty good indicators of his offensive projection. When Zavala wants to go for it, he has 60 raw power, but that's not so much his game at the moment: He's a line-drive hitter who fails to lift the ball consistently.

Defensively, the 22-year-old is limited to the corners and is a slightly better fit for left than right, though he is certainly capable of the latter. His quickness, athleticism and struggles against same-sided arms all limit Zavala's potential impact, but at the end of the day, he's just too good of a hitter to not make it in some capacity.

**OFP:** 50 / Strong-side platoon bat

**Variance:** Medium. This would have been low, but injuries have been an issue. A back issue nearly ended his professional career before it started, and next year will be delayed by a torn UCL.

**Jesse Roche's Fantasy Take:** A .420 OBP between High- and Double-A is not something to dismiss. Zavala gets on base like few other prospects. That said, it's reasonable to question what type of fantasy impact he'll make beyond OBP. While he crushed righties, he hit a dismal .183/.318/.269 against lefties, and he may be limited to a platoon role long-term. Regardless, Zavala is special, and, especially given emerging game power, he has intriguing fantasy upside, especially in OBP formats.

## 8   Anthony Gutierrez   OF    OFP: 50    ETA: 2026/2027

Born: 11/25/04   Age: 18   Bats: R   Throws: R   Height: 6'3"   Weight: 180 lb.   Origin: International Free Agent, 2022

| YEAR | TEAM | LVL | AGE | PA | R | 2B | 3B | HR | RBI | BB | K | SB | CS | AVG/OBP/SLG | DRC+ | BABIP | BRR | DRP | WARP |
|---|---|---|---|---|---|---|---|---|---|---|---|---|---|---|---|---|---|---|---|
| 2022 | DSL TEXR | ROK | 17 | 103 | 22 | 8 | 0 | 3 | 16 | 8 | 18 | 5 | 3 | .352/.408/.538 | | .403 | | | |
| 2022 | RAN | ROK | 17 | 87 | 13 | 5 | 2 | 1 | 8 | 3 | 16 | 6 | 3 | .259/.299/.407 | | .308 | | | |

**The Report:** It feels to me a little asinine to rank a 17-year-old who has never seen full-season ball, but such is the assignment and the Rangers really like their young center fielder. The team signed him as the biggest piece of their 2022 international class. There are a true five tools if the package clicks here—Gutierrez is billed as a legitimate center fielder with the speed for the position, an arm capable of right and a quick, powerful cut at the plate.

Gutierrez is a big kid at 6-foot-3 and, at 17 years of age, an understandably lanky one, leaving him as a good athlete currently with a big frame to grow into more. It's near impossible to know the soft skills from afar at this stage—his approach, ability to pick up spin, make adjustments, handle failure, etc. are all unknowns right now. Regardless, there's a big ceiling here to dream on with Gutierrez, and that the Rangers bringing him stateside in year one of professional ball is a good indication of what the organization thinks about him.

**OFP:** 50 / Heck if I know, he's 17

**Variance:** Extreme. There are just so many unknowns at this age, but early word is there is star potential at the top end of the profile.

**Jesse Roche's Fantasy Take:** Gutierrez was one of just three 17-year-old prospects signed during the 2021-22 international signing period who received significant run at the stateside complex level. His advanced performance, physical tools and projectable frame are worth the gamble in dynasty leagues that roster up to 200 prospects.

## 9 Kumar Rocker RHP    OFP: 50    ETA: 2024

Born: 11/22/99  Age: 23  Bats: R  Throws: R  Height: 6'5"  Weight: 245 lb.  Origin: Round 1, 2022 Draft (#3 overall)

**The Report:** There sure are a lot of questions here for a no. 3 overall selection just five months ago. Even with the understanding that Rocker was a below-slot selection who allowed the Rangers to grab Brock Porter later on, it's not exactly what you hope for from such an early pick. Going back to his high school and college days, there have always been questions surrounding whether his future would be as a starter or as a reliever, with the fastball/slider an electric duo but doubts about his other offerings. After the Mets failed to sign him last year, citing a mysterious shoulder issue for which Rocker would then go under the knife, health-related questions shaded any conversation around the big righty. Just to add another hot-button item, the Rangers shut Rocker down for the regular season, and his mechanics when he debuted in the Fall League were interesting to say the least—only increasing concerns about his long-term health.

All that being said, there is a reason why Rocker was a projected first-round pick out of high school, was popped 10th by the Mets in 2021 and then third by Texas a year later. He has a power sinking fastball he can run up to the high-90s that he pairs with a beast of a two-plane slider. These pitches, and in particular the latter, shredded the SEC during his time at Vanderbilt, and he also has a 12-6 curve that has shown some promise. Despite long-standing mechanical concerns, both with his college delivery and his newly-debuted one, Rocker has a history of strike-throwing, with just 68 in 236 ⅔ college innings and four in 20 indy-ball frames. Like much of this list, he's a bulldog of a competitor and a hard worker.

**OFP:** 50 / no. 3/4 starter or late-inning reliever

**Variance:** Extreme. If everything clicks, there's a front-of-the-line power arm here. There are an awful lot of ifs though—if he can stay healthy, if he can develop his tertiary offerings and if his control/command in a lower arm-slot will pass the test. Rocker's path could go anywhere.

**Jesse Roche's Fantasy Take:** Arguably the most divisive prospect in this draft class, Rocker still boasts a devastating fastball-slider combo. After that, there are so many questions. Even if his health limits his long-term viability, Rocker could arrive quickly and burn bright. If he turns into Dinelson Lamet 2.0, would fantasy managers be disappointed? Despite the extreme risk, Rocker is still a reasonable target outside the top 20 in FYPDs.

## 10 Dustin Harris LF/DH    OFP: 50    ETA: 2024

Born: 07/08/99  Age: 23  Bats: L  Throws: R  Height: 6'2"  Weight: 185 lb.  Origin: Round 11, 2019 Draft (#344 overall)

| YEAR | TEAM | LVL | AGE | PA | R | 2B | 3B | HR | RBI | BB | K | SB | CS | AVG/OBP/SLG | DRC+ | BABIP | BRR | DRP | WARP |
|---|---|---|---|---|---|---|---|---|---|---|---|---|---|---|---|---|---|---|---|
| 2021 | DE | A | 21 | 306 | 54 | 11 | 3 | 10 | 53 | 34 | 48 | 20 | 1 | .301/.389/.483 | 130 | .329 | 0.1 | 1B(50) 1.9, 3B(13) -0.9 | 1.9 |
| 2021 | HIC | A+ | 21 | 160 | 32 | 10 | 0 | 10 | 32 | 13 | 25 | 5 | 1 | .372/.425/.648 | 144 | .396 | -0.6 | 1B(24) -1.8, 3B(11) -0.2 | 1.0 |
| 2022 | FRI | AA | 22 | 382 | 58 | 16 | 2 | 17 | 66 | 42 | 74 | 19 | 5 | .257/.346/.471 | 112 | .279 | -1.1 | LF(58) -0.9, 1B(6) 0.8 | 1.3 |
| 2023 DC | TEX | MLB | 23 | 126 | 13 | 5 | 1 | 3 | 12 | 10 | 26 | 4 | 2 | .228/.293/.355 | 85 | .271 | -0.4 | LF 0 | 0.1 |

Comparables: Dwight Smith Jr., David Cooper, Thomas Neal

**The Report:** The second piece of the famed, oft-discussed Mike Minor trade (right up there with Babe Ruth, Tom Seaver and Roger Clemens), Harris' status has taken major strides in the past couple seasons.

His profile is a tough one to peg, one of peaks and valleys. He's an extremely good athlete with plus raw power, and is a strong runner once he gets going—traits demonstrated by a 20/20 season in 2021 and a pace to repeat in '22 prior to a season-ending wrist injury. At the dish, he generates loft to access his strength, and his walk and strikeout rates have always been above average—as has his performance on the whole. MLB banning the shift should be a positive for Harris as well, as he's a pull-happy lefty who muscles a lot of jam-shots into short right.

On the flip side, he has a massive hole both in his swing and his vision on offspeed in off the hands. Countless times last season, he would expand the zone and come up empty on breaking balls and changeups located middle-in from both lefties and righties. He also doesn't barrel the ball consistently, failing to reach his impressive top-end exit velocity numbers as frequently as others in the system. His top-of-the-line athleticism also has its faults—Harris is not a very twitchy or flexible player. His bereftness of those traits makes a big impact on his defensive work. A switch from first base to left field in 2022 was a bit of an adventure, with circular routes and a lack of comfort a theme from day one to the end of the year. There was growth, but not of the variety to provide any sort of confidence.

There are concerns and limitations here, and a high bar to clear with the bat to either make it at first or overcome his defense in left, but as always, a good athlete with consistently strong performances will always get a chance. The most likely outcome here is a slightly-above-league-average bat whose value comes in at the 1-2 win territory due to negative glovework, but there's more in the tank with some fine-tuning.

**OFP:** 50 / second-division starter

**Variance:** Medium. A hole in his swing and the athleticism to outstrip the expected defensive limitations lower the floor and raise the ceiling, respectively, but Harris is ultimately a reliably solid bat, giving him a big-league future somewhere.

**Jesse Roche's Fantasy Take:** Harris is a *much better* fantasy than real-life prospect. He makes plenty of contact with a solid approach. He is tapping more and more into his plus raw power. Oh, and he steals bases. All told, Harris has legitimate 20/20 upside if he can overcome the very real issues detailed above.

## Outside the Top Ten:

### 11 Justin Foscue 2B

Born: 03/02/99 Age: 24 Bats: R Throws: R Height: 6'0" Weight: 205 lb. Origin: Round 1, 2020 Draft (#14 overall)

| YEAR | TEAM | LVL | AGE | PA | R | 2B | 3B | HR | RBI | BB | K | SB | CS | AVG/OBP/SLG | DRC+ | BABIP | BRR | DRP | WARP |
|---|---|---|---|---|---|---|---|---|---|---|---|---|---|---|---|---|---|---|---|
| 2021 | SUR | WIN | 22 | 89 | 15 | 4 | 0 | 5 | 14 | 15 | 23 | 3 | 1 | .257/.416/.529 | | .310 | | | |
| 2021 | HIC | A+ | 22 | 150 | 34 | 11 | 1 | 14 | 35 | 16 | 39 | 1 | 1 | .296/.407/.736 | 127 | .315 | 0.7 | 2B(29) -0.2 | 1.0 |
| 2021 | FRI | AA | 22 | 104 | 14 | 7 | 0 | 2 | 13 | 8 | 29 | 0 | 1 | .247/.317/.387 | 84 | .333 | -1.6 | 2B(24) -0.7 | -0.1 |
| 2022 | FRI | AA | 23 | 460 | 60 | 31 | 1 | 15 | 81 | 45 | 66 | 3 | 4 | .288/.367/.483 | 118 | .308 | 0.3 | 2B(76) 1.7, 3B(12) 0.3 | 2.5 |
| 2023 non-DC | TEX | MLB | 24 | 251 | 23 | 12 | 1 | 5 | 24 | 18 | 46 | 1 | 0 | .220/.290/.349 | 82 | .256 | -4.1 | 2B 0, 3B 0 | -0.2 |

*Comparables: Nick Solak, Tony Kemp, Christopher Bostick*

Despite a solid enough offensive season (.288/.367/.483), Foscue drops from third last year to completely off the top 10. If that seems backwards, it shouldn't. This is a profile entirely dependent on the bat, to the point that a solid enough offensive season doesn't carry him. The feet will likely move him off second, the hands aren't a good fit for first and his 30-grade speed prevents him from left. That leaves either DH or defensive metrics in the extreme negatives at any position. He posted strong contact rates in 2022, but needs to access more home run power and lower his prolific infield flyball rates to post enough offensive value to carry an everyday role.

### 12 Cole Winn RHP

Born: 11/25/99 Age: 23 Bats: R Throws: R Height: 6'2" Weight: 190 lb. Origin: Round 1, 2018 Draft (#15 overall)

| YEAR | TEAM | LVL | AGE | W | L | SV | G | GS | IP | H | HR | BB/9 | K/9 | K | GB% | BABIP | WHIP | ERA | DRA- | WARP |
|---|---|---|---|---|---|---|---|---|---|---|---|---|---|---|---|---|---|---|---|---|
| 2021 | FRI | AA | 21 | 3 | 3 | 0 | 19 | 19 | 78 | 38 | 6 | 3.0 | 11.2 | 97 | 36.7% | .198 | 0.82 | 2.31 | 84 | 1.2 |
| 2021 | RR | AAA | 21 | 1 | 0 | 0 | 2 | 2 | 8 | 5 | 1 | 5.6 | 11.2 | 10 | 30.0% | .211 | 1.25 | 3.38 | 101 | 0.0 |
| 2022 | RR | AAA | 22 | 9 | 8 | 0 | 28 | 28 | 121² | 125 | 13 | 6.4 | 9.1 | 123 | 39.8% | .326 | 1.74 | 6.51 | 105 | 0.3 |
| 2023 DC | TEX | MLB | 23 | 1 | 1 | 0 | 3 | 3 | 14.3 | 14 | 2 | 5.3 | 8.4 | 14 | 35.5% | .289 | 1.54 | 4.80 | 121 | 0.0 |

*Comparables: Luis Severino, Michael Kopech, Matt Wisler*

Another big dropper, from no. 4 a season ago, Winn's 2022 was a disaster. His mid-rotation stuff—a mid-90s heater, a short-but-sharp slider, big curve, and above-average changeup—all maintained, but his control and command of it disappeared. He's been through this before, back in 2019, and was able to recoup his feel for pitching and re-establish himself, so hope is not lost, but he has to find himself next year and establish year-over-year consistency thereafter.

## 13    Yeison Morrobel   OF

Born: 12/08/03   Age: 19   Bats: L   Throws: L   Height: 6'2"   Weight: 170 lb.   Origin: International Free Agent, 2021

| YEAR | TEAM | LVL | AGE | PA | R | 2B | 3B | HR | RBI | BB | K | SB | CS | AVG/OBP/SLG | DRC+ | BABIP | BRR | DRP | WARP |
|------|------|-----|-----|-----|-----|-----|-----|-----|-----|-----|-----|-----|-----|-------------|------|-------|------|-----|------|
| 2021 | DSL RGR1 | ROK | 17 | 229 | 33 | 11 | 6 | 1 | 30 | 30 | 25 | 8 | 4 | .270/.395/.411 | | .302 | | | |
| 2022 | RAN | ROK | 18 | 173 | 31 | 13 | 1 | 3 | 21 | 17 | 34 | 5 | 5 | .329/.405/.487 | | .405 | | | |
| 2022 | DE | A | 18 | 29 | 3 | 1 | 0 | 0 | 3 | 3 | 6 | 2 | 1 | .231/.310/.269 | 102 | .300 | -0.3 | RF(5) 0.2, LF(2) -0.1 | 0.1 |
| 2023 non-DC | TEX | MLB | 19 | 251 | 18 | 10 | 2 | 2 | 19 | 17 | 69 | 5 | 2 | .209/.268/.291 | 57 | .290 | -1.8 | LF 0, CF 0 | -0.7 |

The Rangers have added a lot of interesting talent through international free agency in recent years, with Morrobel one of the bigger bonuses at $1.8MM. He possesses the sought-after combination of raw pop, above-average speed and blooming bat-to-ball skill. He's also the kind of quick-twitch athlete whose gifts translate best to the sport. At just 18, it's difficult to get too precise with a projection, but when you can turn and park high-90s up in the zone, have thus far made reasonable swing decisions and have a knack for barreling balls, you become one to follow pretty quickly. I'm expecting Morrobel will be a top-10 guy here next year.

## 14    Maximo Acosta   SS

Born: 10/29/02   Age: 20   Bats: R   Throws: R   Height: 6'1"   Weight: 187 lb.   Origin: International Free Agent, 2019

| YEAR | TEAM | LVL | AGE | PA | R | 2B | 3B | HR | RBI | BB | K | SB | CS | AVG/OBP/SLG | DRC+ | BABIP | BRR | DRP | WARP |
|------|------|-----|-----|-----|-----|-----|-----|-----|-----|-----|-----|-----|-----|-------------|------|-------|------|-----|------|
| 2021 | RAN | ROK | 18 | 68 | 11 | 2 | 2 | 1 | 5 | 3 | 15 | 7 | 2 | .246/.279/.393 | | .292 | | | |
| 2022 | DE | A | 19 | 456 | 62 | 26 | 1 | 4 | 35 | 40 | 87 | 44 | 17 | .262/.341/.361 | 100 | .325 | 4.0 | SS(76) 0.2, 2B(29) 1.6 | 1.9 |
| 2023 non-DC | TEX | MLB | 20 | 251 | 18 | 12 | 1 | 2 | 19 | 15 | 62 | 12 | 6 | .215/.268/.296 | 60 | .285 | 2.5 | 2B 0, SS 0 | -0.1 |

*Comparables: Luis Sardinas, Tyler Pastornicky, Malquin Canelo*

Acosta was a big-name, big-money signing out of Venezuela in 2019 who garnered only mixed reviews at the Arizona complex in 2021. Last year was something of a bounce-back season from the young shortstop, who hit at a league-average mark with solid enough walk and strikeout rates, and added 44 stolen bases—as a 19-year-old in full-season ball. Tools-wise, Acosta won't wow you with any one feat, but is the solid-across-the-board type that's rare within this system. If he can grow into more in-game power with age, he's got an interesting profile at a key position.

## 15    Thomas Saggese   IF

Born: 04/10/02   Age: 21   Bats: R   Throws: R   Height: 5'11"   Weight: 175 lb.   Origin: Round 5, 2020 Draft (#145 overall)

| YEAR | TEAM | LVL | AGE | PA | R | 2B | 3B | HR | RBI | BB | K | SB | CS | AVG/OBP/SLG | DRC+ | BABIP | BRR | DRP | WARP |
|------|------|-----|-----|-----|-----|-----|-----|-----|-----|-----|-----|-----|-----|-------------|------|-------|------|-----|------|
| 2021 | DE | A | 19 | 288 | 44 | 14 | 3 | 10 | 37 | 42 | 85 | 11 | 3 | .256/.372/.463 | 104 | .351 | 0.8 | 3B(24) 0.1, 2B(22) -0.8, SS(11) 0.2 | 1.0 |
| 2022 | HIC | A+ | 20 | 419 | 56 | 22 | 2 | 14 | 61 | 29 | 94 | 11 | 3 | .308/.359/.487 | 102 | .372 | -1.5 | 2B(48) 0.8, 3B(31) 1.3, SS(15) 1.2 | 1.5 |
| 2023 non-DC | TEX | MLB | 21 | 251 | 22 | 12 | 2 | 4 | 24 | 15 | 63 | 3 | 2 | .236/.288/.354 | 82 | .306 | -2.7 | 1B 0, 2B 0 | -0.1 |

Another in the Rangers' strong 2020 draft class, Saggese is a good hitter who would be first selection for an all-makeup team. Just 20 years old, he has already reached and succeeded in a short Double-A stint—last season on the whole saw a .312/.361/.506 slash line. He has strong bat-to-ball skills and accesses a surprising amount of power from his 5-foot-11, 175-pound frame, lifting the ball hard with consistency. Defensively, he has no perfect home, but should be capable at third, likely his best position, as well as second and first, with spot duty at shortstop a possibility. The likely outcome here is a quality utility player, but if he keeps hitting the way he has, he'll get a shot at more.

## 16  Gleider Figuereo  DH/3B

Born: 06/27/04   Age: 19   Bats: L   Throws: R   Height: 6'0"   Weight: 165 lb.   Origin: International Free Agent, 2021

| YEAR | TEAM | LVL | AGE | PA | R | 2B | 3B | HR | RBI | BB | K | SB | CS | AVG/OBP/SLG | DRC+ | BABIP | BRR | DRP | WARP |
|---|---|---|---|---|---|---|---|---|---|---|---|---|---|---|---|---|---|---|---|
| 2021 | DSL RGR1 | ROK | 17 | 190 | 23 | 6 | 4 | 2 | 28 | 28 | 31 | 3 | 2 | .231/.354/.359 | | .272 | | | |
| 2022 | RAN | ROK | 18 | 146 | 29 | 5 | 5 | 9 | 31 | 15 | 33 | 7 | 1 | .280/.363/.616 | | .302 | | | |
| 2022 | DE | A | 18 | 26 | 0 | 0 | 0 | 0 | 1 | 2 | 8 | 0 | 0 | .208/.269/.208 | 88 | .313 | 0.0 | 3B(2) 0.1 | 0.0 |
| 2023 non-DC | TEX | MLB | 19 | 251 | 18 | 10 | 2 | 2 | 18 | 15 | 96 | 2 | 1 | .202/.256/.281 | 50 | .334 | -3.4 | 3B 0 | -1.2 |

Another 18-year-old from Latin America, Gleider Figuereo was a relatively minor signing out of the Dominican Republic but quickly received aggressive assignments, seeing stateside spring training and complex ball before he reached college age. He's got a swing aimed for power and loft, and the frame to grow into plus raw (a tool that he has also accessed in what little gameplay he's had thus far). The Rangers gave him a bump to finish the 2022 season in Low-A, and that's where he's likely to start next season—as one of the youngest at the level.

## 17  Tekoah Roby  RHP

Born: 09/18/01   Age: 21   Bats: R   Throws: R   Height: 6'1"   Weight: 185 lb.   Origin: Round 3, 2020 Draft (#86 overall)

| YEAR | TEAM | LVL | AGE | W | L | SV | G | GS | IP | H | HR | BB/9 | K/9 | K | GB% | BABIP | WHIP | ERA | DRA- | WARP |
|---|---|---|---|---|---|---|---|---|---|---|---|---|---|---|---|---|---|---|---|---|
| 2021 | DE | A | 19 | 2 | 2 | 0 | 6 | 6 | 22 | 14 | 1 | 2.9 | 14.3 | 35 | 46.7% | .295 | 0.95 | 2.45 | 68 | 0.6 |
| 2022 | HIC | A+ | 20 | 3 | 11 | 0 | 22 | 21 | 104² | 95 | 19 | 3.0 | 10.8 | 126 | 38.5% | .298 | 1.24 | 4.64 | 96 | 1.0 |
| 2023 non-DC | TEX | MLB | 21 | 3 | 3 | 0 | 58 | 0 | 50 | 52 | 9 | 3.9 | 7.9 | 44 | 34.6% | .301 | 1.48 | 5.03 | 128 | -0.5 |

Comparables: A.J. Cole, Noah Syndergaard, Robert Stephenson

Selected in the third round of the 2020 COVID draft, Roby has impressed and progressed at a young age. Last season represented his age-20 season, and the 6-foot-1 righty handled himself well enough at High-A—a 4.64 ERA, 126 strikeouts and 35 walks in 104 ⅔ innings. He was home-run prone; not a surprise given that his heater, typically 93-95 mph, can be hittable when he doesn't get the pitch up. His best offering is his changeup, which features heavy drop and deception. Roby has already had injury issues and needed to reshape his arm path, but seems to have successfully done so and avoided the knife. There's still a ways to go in his development, but a big-league starter profile is within reach.

## 18  Mason Englert  RHP

Born: 11/01/99   Age: 23   Bats: S   Throws: R   Height: 6'4"   Weight: 206 lb.   Origin: Round 4, 2018 Draft (#119 overall)

| YEAR | TEAM | LVL | AGE | W | L | SV | G | GS | IP | H | HR | BB/9 | K/9 | K | GB% | BABIP | WHIP | ERA | DRA- | WARP |
|---|---|---|---|---|---|---|---|---|---|---|---|---|---|---|---|---|---|---|---|---|
| 2021 | DE | A | 21 | 6 | 3 | 0 | 19 | 19 | 80² | 73 | 4 | 2.9 | 10.0 | 90 | 36.7% | .325 | 1.23 | 4.35 | 113 | 0.2 |
| 2022 | HIC | A+ | 22 | 7 | 5 | 0 | 21 | 21 | 103¹ | 73 | 15 | 2.3 | 10.1 | 116 | 41.4% | .234 | 0.96 | 3.57 | 87 | 1.5 |
| 2022 | FRI | AA | 22 | 1 | 1 | 0 | 3 | 3 | 15¹ | 14 | 1 | 2.9 | 11.7 | 20 | 30.8% | .342 | 1.24 | 4.11 | 83 | 0.2 |
| 2023 DC | DET | MLB | 23 | 2 | 3 | 0 | 49 | 0 | 42.3 | 44 | 6 | 3.5 | 8.0 | 38 | 34.0% | .304 | 1.43 | 4.60 | 123 | -0.3 |

Englert doesn't have overpowering stuff, with all four of his offerings falling somewhere in the spectrum of 45 to 55 grades, but he makes it work. Those in the industry might even go so far as to call him a "pitcher" or a "ballplayer." The former Texas A&M commit will attack with the fastball, which a long stride and 6-foot-4 frame help play up—despite pedestrian velocity and shape, he gets heavy deception with the change, and is comfortable utilizing either the slider or sweeping two-plane curve at any time. He's a true four-pitch arm with strong pitchability and, most importantly, command that could come out of the developmental tunnel as plus. He's probably not a guy who can get through an order a third time through, but quality 18-batter outings carry a lot more value these days than a decade ago, so Englert projects perfectly fine as a back-of-the-rotation arm.

## 19 Jonathan Ornelas   SS/3B

Born: 05/26/00   Age: 23   Bats: R   Throws: R   Height: 6'0"   Weight: 196 lb.   Origin: Round 3, 2018 Draft (#91 overall)

| YEAR | TEAM | LVL | AGE | PA | R | 2B | 3B | HR | RBI | BB | K | SB | CS | AVG/OBP/SLG | DRC+ | BABIP | BRR | DRP | WARP |
|---|---|---|---|---|---|---|---|---|---|---|---|---|---|---|---|---|---|---|---|
| 2021 | HIC | A+ | 21 | 405 | 71 | 18 | 4 | 8 | 38 | 21 | 87 | 9 | 5 | .261/.310/.394 | 94 | .320 | 0.8 | SS(60) -1.7, CF(27) -0.6, 3B(7) -0.1 | 0.8 |
| 2022 | FRI | AA | 22 | 580 | 84 | 20 | 2 | 14 | 64 | 45 | 121 | 14 | 6 | .299/.360/.425 | 108 | .365 | -1.4 | SS(86) 7.6, 3B(29) 2.7, 2B(4) 0.7 | 3.3 |
| 2023 non-DC | TEX | MLB | 23 | 251 | 20 | 10 | 1 | 3 | 21 | 14 | 63 | 3 | 2 | .228/.280/.321 | 71 | .299 | -2.6 | 2B 0, 3B 0 | -0.4 |

*Comparables: Héctor Gómez, Junior Lake, Danny Santana*

The 22-year-old former third-round pick served a lot of roles in 2022 – shortstop, third baseman, second baseman, center fielder, de facto captain, team translator and I'm sure plenty more. He also solidified his status as a legitimate prospect and got himself a 40-man roster spot ahead of the Rule 5 Draft. The bat is solid, but unspectacular—a .299 average leading only to a 108 DRC+ feels about right. Ornelas has a strong hit tool and isn't devoid of power, but will likely strike out *juuust* often enough, and walk and slug *juuust* rarely enough, to prevent him from reaching league-average at the plate—even if he racks up hits. Regardless, the bat isn't the calling card here: Ornelas' glove projects as above-average to plus at each of the positions he manned a year ago, and he's a mouthy team-leader type. It's the exact type of profile constituting a valuable utility player, with room for more if more power or walks come.

## 20 Emiliano Teodo   RHP

Born: 02/14/01   Age: 22   Bats: R   Throws: R   Height: 6'1"   Weight: 165 lb.   Origin: International Free Agent, 2020

| YEAR | TEAM | LVL | AGE | W | L | SV | G | GS | IP | H | HR | BB/9 | K/9 | K | GB% | BABIP | WHIP | ERA | DRA- | WARP |
|---|---|---|---|---|---|---|---|---|---|---|---|---|---|---|---|---|---|---|---|---|
| 2021 | RAN | ROK | 20 | 4 | 2 | 0 | 19 | 0 | 29¹ | 24 | 0 | 5.5 | 14.7 | 48 | 68.8% | .375 | 1.43 | 3.38 | | |
| 2022 | DE | A | 21 | 3 | 6 | 0 | 22 | 17 | 84¹ | 51 | 7 | 4.7 | 12.3 | 115 | 59.1% | .249 | 1.13 | 3.09 | 64 | 2.5 |
| 2023 non-DC | TEX | MLB | 22 | 3 | 3 | 0 | 58 | 0 | 50 | 48 | 8 | 5.2 | 9.2 | 51 | 39.8% | .298 | 1.53 | 4.87 | 122 | -0.3 |

There are a number of closer-to-the-bigs arms in the upper levels of this system—Cole Ragans, Zak Kent and Cody Bradford, to name a few—who are more likely to make major-league impacts and will get there sooner. But Teodo is one of the more interesting rocket-arm-but-no-clue-where-it's-going genre pitching prospects. He pumps mega-gas, at and exceeding 100 mph with big spin, and pairs it with a curveball (a *curveball*) in the low 90s with 3,000+ RPM. An August 25 outing sums him up best: 12 outs, 11 strikeouts, no hits and a 51% strike rate. He's probably a reliever and he has a lot of development ahead, but if he becomes more successful at finding the zone, he more than has the stuff for the back of the pen.

# Top Talents 25 and Under (as of 4/1/2023):

1. Evan Carter, OF
2. Josh Jung, 3B
3. Ezequiel Duran, 3B
4. Jack Leiter, RHP
5. Leody Taveras, CF
6. Owen White, RHP
7. Luisangel Acuña, IF
8. Brock Porter, RHP
9. Aaron Zavala, OF
10. Anthony Gutierrez, OF

A handful of this wave of Ranger prospects graduated in 2022—Josh H. Smith, Bubba Thompson, Glenn Otto—but most notably Ezequiel Duran. He played mostly short and third a year ago, but is working in the outfield during winter ball and has a good chance to claim the organization's currently open left field spot in the spring. Leody Taveras graduated a year prior and has the inside track to the job next door in center, a plus defensive player who needs to hit just enough and took steps towards doing so. If those two plus Jung can take their respective leaps in 2023, it will make for a deep Texas lineup, as they look to make the jump into contention. At this stage, the utilityman Smith and C/1B Sam Huff look more likely to be depth contributors, but both have shown flashes on the big-league stage.

# Toronto Blue Jays

## The State of the System:

This Jays system might be the weirdest one I've dealt with in seven years. It's below-average overall, and specifically pretty shallow, but it also provides a difficult ordinal task as it involves comparing a lot of high-variance prospect profiles.

## The Top Ten:

### 1 Ricky Tiedemann LHP    OFP: 70    ETA: 2024

Born: 08/18/02   Age: 20   Bats: L   Throws: L   Height: 6'4"   Weight: 220 lb.   Origin: Round 3, 2021 Draft (#91 overall)

| YEAR | TEAM | LVL | AGE | W | L | SV | G | GS | IP | H | HR | BB/9 | K/9 | K | GB% | BABIP | WHIP | ERA | DRA- | WARP |
|------|------|-----|-----|---|---|----|----|----|------|----|----|------|------|----|-------|-------|------|------|------|------|
| 2022 | DUN | A | 19 | 3 | 1 | 0 | 6 | 6 | 30 | 11 | 1 | 3.9 | 14.7 | 49 | 46.8% | .217 | 0.80 | 1.80 | 68 | 1.0 |
| 2022 | VAN | A+ | 19 | 2 | 2 | 0 | 8 | 8 | 37² | 23 | 2 | 2.9 | 12.9 | 54 | 46.2% | .276 | 0.93 | 2.39 | 87 | 0.6 |
| 2022 | NH | AA | 19 | 0 | 1 | 0 | 4 | 4 | 11 | 5 | 0 | 3.3 | 11.5 | 14 | 63.6% | .227 | 0.82 | 2.45 | 90 | 0.2 |
| 2023 DC | TOR | MLB | 20 | 1 | 1 | 0 | 3 | 3 | 13.3 | 12 | 2 | 4.3 | 10.4 | 16 | 38.2% | .285 | 1.33 | 3.88 | 103 | 0.1 |

*Comparables: John Lamb, Deivi García, Francis Martes*

**The Report:** Tiedemann was a known prep prospect who might have been drafted higher than this with a full 2020 high school season. Instead he went to JuCo for a year, got his velocity jump there and then got popped in the third round by the Jays. Now another year on, he's one of the best pitching prospects in baseball.

Tiedemann's fastball still sits mid-90s—touching higher—with good life, but now his slider has jumped as well and is a wipeout, sweeping breaker. His changeup has improved as well, and projects as at least average. His delivery is uptempo, and he generates wicked arm speed, but has thrown strikes generally. Anyway, his command will never have to be too fine with this kind of arsenal (and it is fine enough). Tiedemann got all the way to Double-A in his age-19 season, but while he feels close to the majors, he has a lot of the same question marks you'd find with other good 19-year-old pitching prospects. Tiedemann was kept on a pretty strict throwing schedule in 2022, tossing only 78 innings and never working into the sixth. It remains to be seen how the stuff holds up in deeper outings and longer seasons. But this is just boilerplate for these blurbs nowadays. Tiedemann has two potential plus-plus pitches and top of the rotation upside that's far less common. And unlike most good 20-year-old pitching prospects, he could be in the majors as soon as this season.

**OFP:** 70 / no. 2 starter

**Variance:** Medium. Tiedemann has dominant stuff at times and overpowered even Double-A bats in his first pro season. If he consolidates his recent pitch gains and shoves for 100+ innings in 2023, he might just be the best pitching prospect in baseball. He also might throw a lot of those innings in the majors and not be eligible for next year's list. However, Tiedemann still has pretty much all the downside risks of a 20-year-old pitching prospect, no matter how good and how close to the bigs he is.

**Jesse Roche's Fantasy Take:** Way back in mid-April, I detailed Tiedemann's pitch data and predicted "he likely pushes the top 100 by midseason if not earlier." Well, that was an understatement! All three of his pitches miss tons of bats with wild movement. In fact, his changeup averaged more running action in Low-A than any left-handed pitcher in MLB. Tiedemann's absolute filth resulted in the second-highest strikeout rate (38.9%) in the minors last year. The next step is to build innings and improve command. Tiedemann is a top-five dynasty pitching prospect with as much upside as any arm in the minors.

## 2 Yosver Zulueta  RHP     OFP: 60     ETA: 2023
Born: 01/23/98  Age: 25  Bats: R  Throws: R  Height: 6'1"  Weight: 190 lb.  Origin: International Free Agent, 2019

| YEAR | TEAM | LVL | AGE | W | L | SV | G | GS | IP | H | HR | BB/9 | K/9 | K | GB% | BABIP | WHIP | ERA | DRA- | WARP |
|---|---|---|---|---|---|---|---|---|---|---|---|---|---|---|---|---|---|---|---|---|
| 2022 | DUN | A | 24 | 0 | 0 | 0 | 3 | 3 | 12 | 9 | 0 | 2.3 | 17.3 | 23 | 57.1% | .429 | 1.00 | 3.00 | 68 | 0.4 |
| 2022 | VAN | A+ | 24 | 1 | 3 | 0 | 6 | 6 | 23² | 18 | 1 | 4.2 | 11.8 | 31 | 52.6% | .304 | 1.23 | 3.80 | 87 | 0.4 |
| 2022 | NH | AA | 24 | 1 | 1 | 0 | 9 | 2 | 15¹ | 10 | 1 | 8.2 | 14.7 | 25 | 38.7% | .300 | 1.57 | 4.11 | 94 | 0.3 |
| 2023 DC | TOR | MLB | 25 | 2 | 2 | 0 | 16 | 3 | 25 | 22 | 4 | 5.1 | 10.2 | 29 | 38.2% | .294 | 1.46 | 4.58 | 117 | 0.0 |

*Comparables: Anyelo Gómez, Ariel Hernández, Drew Steckenrider*

**The Report:** Shortly after signing with the Jays, Zulueta had Tommy John surgery. He was then ready to go for the 2021 season and had a ton of buzz in spring, before promptly blowing out his knee covering first base against the very first batter he faced in the very first inning of his very first pro game. Nevertheless, Jarrett Seidler insisted on sneaking him on last year's Jays list as a "Factor on the Farm." I'm still not sure how a pitcher who faced exactly one A-ball batter makes sense in that category, but as it turns out about a calendar year later, you could in fact argue that Zulueta should have been in Toronto's pen for the stretch run and playoffs.

In 2022, he ascended all four full-season levels of the minors, striking out a third of batters along the way. Zulueta has a top of the scale fastball, sitting upper-90s and capable of flashing triple digits on the scoreboard, a steep bat-misser. Both his breaking balls have a chance to get to plus. I prefer the power curve a bit more at present. He even has off-and-on feel for an average changeup, although it tends to be too firm (and he rarely needs it).

Okay, so the stuff isn't that far off Tiedemann's, if at all, but after that some wider gaps start to open up. Obviously there's the injury history. Zulueta is also about to turn 25, and everything in his delivery feels a bit more relieverish (as does the command and control profile so far). Zulueta feels like a prospect you should give every chance to start, but realistically he could form a devastating 1-2 punch in the pen with Jordan Romano as soon as Opening Day 2023. That's going to be tempting even if a late-inning reliever wasn't the more likely outcome anyway.

**OFP:** 60 / First-division closer with a non-zero chance to start

**Variance:** Medium. I think the range of healthy outcomes here is reasonably low, but Zulueta has a checkered arm history, not a ton of pro reps, and not even fringy control and command.

**Jesse Roche's Fantasy Take:** The arm talent is undeniable, but, as a likely relief-only prospect with serious command issues, Zulueta carries a lot of fantasy risk. Still, his stuff and proximity is enough to put him on the edge of the dynasty top 200.

## 3 Brandon Barriera  LHP     OFP: 55     ETA: 2026
Born: 03/04/04  Age: 19  Bats: L  Throws: L  Height: 6'2"  Weight: 180 lb.  Origin: Round 1, 2022 Draft (#23 overall)

**The Report:** Barriera elicited a wide variety of opinions heading into the 2022 draft. The physical tools here are obvious and impressive. Despite checking in at a slight 6-foot-2, he has electric arm speed and can run his fastball into the mid-90s and higher. He can spin both a curveball and slider, with the latter showing above-average potential. You read those two sentences and naturally start dreaming of a top-of-the-rotation prep lefty prospect, but the fastball works more off velocity than shape, and "slight" doesn't necessarily mean projectable in this case. Barriera has a narrow frame and it remains to be seen if he can hold up to the rigors of a pro workload. It's also a reasonably advanced repertoire from a teenaged southpaw, but he's a long way from even major-league mid-rotation starter.

**OFP:** 55 / no. 3/4 starter or late-inning reliever

**Variance:** Extreme. Barriera could be ranked alongside 2022 breakout prep arms like Tink Hence and Marco Raya in a year, or he could be struggling with his command or hurt or you know, he's a pitcher.

**Jesse Roche's Fantasy Take:** Undersized but overstuffed, Barriera is not your typical prep pitching prospect—and he lacks the upside generally associated with prep arms worth gambling on in FYPDs. As such, Barriera is better left outside the top 20 in FYPDs and the dynasty top 200.

## 4 Dahian Santos  RHP    OFP: 55    ETA: 2025
Born: 02/26/03  Age: 20  Bats: R  Throws: R  Height: 5'11"  Weight: 160 lb.  Origin: International Free Agent, 2019

| YEAR | TEAM | LVL | AGE | W | L | SV | G | GS | IP | H | HR | BB/9 | K/9 | K | GB% | BABIP | WHIP | ERA | DRA- | WARP |
|---|---|---|---|---|---|---|---|---|---|---|---|---|---|---|---|---|---|---|---|---|
| 2021 | BLU | ROK | 18 | 1 | 2 | 0 | 10 | 7 | 35¹ | 30 | 5 | 3.1 | 13.5 | 53 | 47.0% | .321 | 1.19 | 4.58 | | |
| 2022 | DUN | A | 19 | 4 | 5 | 0 | 19 | 14 | 73¹ | 47 | 8 | 4.3 | 14.7 | 120 | 36.4% | .298 | 1.12 | 3.44 | 72 | 2.2 |
| 2022 | VAN | A+ | 19 | 0 | 2 | 0 | 4 | 4 | 12² | 17 | 3 | 6.4 | 15.6 | 22 | 37.5% | .483 | 2.05 | 10.66 | 74 | 0.3 |
| 2023 non-DC | TOR | MLB | 20 | 3 | 3 | 0 | 58 | 0 | 50 | 47 | 9 | 5.3 | 9.7 | 54 | 32.4% | .295 | 1.54 | 5.17 | 129 | -0.5 |

*Comparables: Marcos Diplán, Emilio Vargas, Sean Reid-Foley*

**The Report:** There are names further down this list with far more prospect pedigree than Santos. There are prospects closer to the majors who had breakout 2022 seasons. There are high-profile draftees. Dahian Santos on the other hand is a shorter, skinny righty who spent most of the season in Dunedin. All the prospects below him have some warts, as does Santos. Even if you are more willing to handwave concerns about the frame, his fastball command is below-average and both the secondaries are inconsistent. However, he has the potential for three above-average to plus pitches. Santos' low-90s fastball shows good sink and run, and I suspect he can find another tick or two with a bit of additional physical strength and a streamlined arm action. His slider can be a wicked pitch, just overmatching A-ball hitters with big sweep and enough depth to get it under bats. Santos commands it better glove-side than arm-side and can hang it when he tries to drop it front door to righties. Other times it will look slurvier than you'd like, but it has very obvious plus potential, and his best ones flash plus-plus.

His change can show power sink and he can also pop it away with a shorter circle action in the same velocity range as the breaker. Santos' delivery can be a bit effortful, uptempo and snatchy, and that has impacted his strike-throwing at times. There are a lot of relief markers here, but the arms below him have even more risk or lower upside, and I'm not sure any of the bats can actually hit yet. So sometimes you just see a guy and say "that's my guy here."

**OFP:** 55 / no. 3/4 starter or late-inning reliever

**Variance:** Very High. Santos is a smaller righty with profile/role risk who posted a 10 ERA in a High-A cameo. He also has a shot to be a 101 name at this time next year.

**Jesse Roche's Fantasy Take:** Santos may lack size, velocity or, at times, command, but his slider—which generated nearly 60% whiffs in Low-A—and his changeup are true out-pitches. Given what he lacks, however, he is best left only to the deepest of dynasty leagues.

## 5 Orelvis Martinez  SS/3B    OFP: 55    ETA: Late 2023/Early 2024
Born: 11/19/01  Age: 21  Bats: R  Throws: R  Height: 6'1"  Weight: 200 lb.  Origin: International Free Agent, 2018

| YEAR | TEAM | LVL | AGE | PA | R | 2B | 3B | HR | RBI | BB | K | SB | CS | AVG/OBP/SLG | DRC+ | BABIP | BRR | DRP | WARP |
|---|---|---|---|---|---|---|---|---|---|---|---|---|---|---|---|---|---|---|---|
| 2021 | DUN | A | 19 | 326 | 49 | 22 | 2 | 19 | 68 | 33 | 85 | 4 | 1 | .279/.369/.572 | 130 | .333 | -1.8 | SS(46) -5.2, 3B(12) 0.1 | 1.5 |
| 2021 | VAN | A+ | 19 | 125 | 17 | 4 | 0 | 9 | 19 | 10 | 28 | 0 | 1 | .214/.282/.491 | 125 | .197 | -0.4 | SS(19) -1.1, 3B(6) -0.5 | 0.6 |
| 2022 | NH | AA | 20 | 492 | 57 | 15 | 0 | 30 | 76 | 40 | 140 | 6 | 3 | .203/.286/.446 | 96 | .217 | -3.3 | SS(60) -1.3, 3B(43) -0.5 | 0.8 |
| 2023 DC | TOR | MLB | 21 | 29 | 3 | 1 | 0 | 1 | 3 | 2 | 9 | 0 | 0 | .214/.273/.374 | 84 | .283 | -0.1 | 3B 0 | 0.0 |

*Comparables: Bo Bichette, Javier Báez, J.P. Crawford*

**The Report:** The Eastern League might have been a slightly overzealous assignment for Martinez after he hit .214 in High-A for the last month of the 2021 season. To be fair, he didn't perform all that much worse in Double-A in 2022, hitting .203, but doing a heckuva lot of damage on those one out of five hits. Martinez's K-rate has continued to drift in the wrong direction, as his swing can be a little one-gear, and breaking stuff moving away from him—even if it stays in the zone—is an issue. That same swing creates a lot of hand-hip separation, and when he connects...well, over half his hits went for extra bases, the lion's share of which were his 30 home runs. Martinez's approach isn't hopeless—he tracks fastballs okay—just overly aggressive. Is he going to adjust enough to hit .220 or .230 in the majors? Maybe, but I'm not sure that's even enough.

I'd feel better about it being enough if he was a sure-shot shortstop, but everything is just a half-grade light, the first step a bit slow, the actions a little too mechanical. He should be a good third baseman, as his hands are fine and his arm is plus.

Power can be a carrying tool, and Martinez has plenty to spare. The only other players who hit 30 home runs in Double-A were 24-year-old Leandro Cedeno and 28-year-old Quincy Nierporte. There's the potential for game-changing power if he can consistently get it into games even further up the ladder. He may seem like a high-variance prospect, but really the whole profile comes down to a yes or no question. Do you think Martinez can hit? This ranking steadfastly dodges that inquiry and cowardly lands in the mushball middle.

**OFP:** 55 / Power-hitting third baseman

**Variance:** High. There is an outcome where Martinez is exactly an above-average regular. It might look a lot like his 2022 season with good defense at third, answering a different query: "What if Patrick Wisdom could pick it?" I don't know if that's a question anyone is asking.

**Jesse Roche's Fantasy Take:** Martinez turned 21 years old one month ago to the day. Yet, he toiled away in the ever-difficult Double-A Eastern League all year as one of the youngest position players. His ongoing swing-and-miss issues and extreme lift-and-pull approach are concerning. But, they can be somewhat forgiven due to his age, level and power output. The promise of a 30-homer slugger remains, and, even if his average is far closer to .200 than ideal, Martinez can return fantasy value.

## 6 Tucker Toman  SS     OFP: 55     ETA: 2026
Born: 11/12/03   Age: 19   Bats: S   Throws: R   Height: 6'1"   Weight: 190 lb.   Origin: Round 2, 2022 Draft (#77 overall)

| YEAR | TEAM | LVL | AGE | PA | R | 2B | 3B | HR | RBI | BB | K | SB | CS | AVG/OBP/SLG | DRC+ | BABIP | BRR | DRP | WARP |
|------|------|-----|-----|----|---|----|----|----|-----|----|---|----|----|-------------|------|-------|-----|-----|------|
| 2022 | BLU | ROK | 18 | 46 | 4 | 3 | 0 | 0 | 5 | 7 | 12 | 0 | 0 | .289/.391/.368 | | .407 | | | |

**The Report:** Toman had first-round buzz in last year's draft, but slipped to the Jays in the second. They paid him like a late first-rounder to get him to forgo three years in Baton Rouge, and the upside with the bat is well worth the investment. I don't know that I would call Toman's swing classically pretty, but it should be modernly effective with the right balance of leverage, bat speed and time in the zone. Both the hit and power tools should end up above-average, and there may be even more pop than that as he gains more strength in pro ball. Toman split time between third and short in the complex, although I'd lean towards him ending up at the hot corner long-term. The bat should play there without issue.

**OFP:** 55 / Above-average infielder

**Variance:** High. This one is pretty straightforward, he's only played in the complex league and may need his bat to carry a corner spot, but again, he also has a shot to be a 101 name at this time next year.

**Jesse Roche's Fantasy Take:** A switch-hitting infielder with hit-power potential? Yes, please.

## 7 Addison Barger  IF     OFP: 50     ETA: 2023
Born: 11/12/99   Age: 23   Bats: L   Throws: R   Height: 6'0"   Weight: 175 lb.   Origin: Round 6, 2018 Draft (#176 overall)

| YEAR | TEAM | LVL | AGE | PA | R | 2B | 3B | HR | RBI | BB | K | SB | CS | AVG/OBP/SLG | DRC+ | BABIP | BRR | DRP | WARP |
|------|------|-----|-----|-----|----|----|----|----|-----|----|-----|----|----|-------------|------|-------|------|-----|------|
| 2021 | DUN | A | 21 | 374 | 53 | 21 | 2 | 18 | 80 | 36 | 123 | 7 | 0 | .249/.334/.492 | 101 | .333 | -0.6 | SS(27) -0.1, 2B(24) -3.0, 3B(13) 0.5 | 0.7 |
| 2022 | VAN | A+ | 22 | 292 | 46 | 21 | 2 | 14 | 53 | 25 | 76 | 7 | 2 | .300/.366/.558 | 128 | .370 | 0.5 | SS(36) -3.4, 3B(19) -1.5 | 1.4 |
| 2022 | NH | AA | 22 | 198 | 26 | 11 | 0 | 9 | 29 | 18 | 50 | 2 | 2 | .313/.384/.528 | 104 | .390 | -1.7 | 3B(20) 0.1, SS(20) 0.7 | 0.6 |
| 2022 | BUF | AAA | 22 | 36 | 8 | 1 | 0 | 3 | 9 | 5 | 5 | 0 | 1 | .355/.444/.677 | 128 | .348 | 0.7 | SS(4) 1.0, 3B(3) -0.5 | 0.3 |
| 2023 DC | TOR | MLB | 23 | 96 | 11 | 4 | 1 | 3 | 11 | 6 | 28 | 1 | 0 | .233/.291/.382 | 89 | .313 | -0.2 | 2B 0, 3B 0 | 0.2 |

*Comparables: Zach Walters, Brad Miller, Chris Valaika*

**The Report:** Barger broke out in a big way in 2022, ending the season in Triple-A with 26 homers and 33 doubles on his ledger for the season. His left-handed swing is reminiscent of Cody Bellinger, starting very narrow and upright before utilizing a big leg kick, and whipping the bat through the zone. Granted, the bat speed and power projection here is more 2020s Belli than the MVP era, but Barger can punish you if you try to beat him inside and he moves the barrel around well enough that the K-rate should be manageable if not above-average. The bigger detriment to his hit tool is his barrel control. Barger swings very hard and is looking to lift everything, which can lead to a lot of pop-ups amongst his fly-ball-heavy profile. I'd expect major-league arms to exploit him enough to keep the hit tool on the fringy side of average—if maybe not to the level of 2021 Bellinger. Defensively Barger is fine at shortstop, but could be plus at third base where his 70-grade arm is a real weapon. It's not just pure arm strength either, as he throws accurately with good carry on the run and from a variety of angles.

**OFP:** 50 / Everyday, power-hitting third baseman

**Variance:** Medium. Barger doesn't have the longest track record of this kind of pro performance, and I do worry that top level pitching will find holes in his aggressive, high effort swing.

**Jesse Roche's Fantasy Take:** What a difference a year makes! In 2021, Barger spent most of the season in Low-A, running up a 32.9% strikeout rate behind a suspect 64.5% contact rate. This year, he torched three levels, cutting his strikeout rate by 8% and increasing his contact rate by over 5%. While Barger is unlikely to hit over .300—like he did at each level this year—he could settle around .250 with 20+ home runs. Meanwhile, the Blue Jays remain desperate for more left-handed bats in the lineup, and Barger arguably is their best immediate option to fill in across the infield. His impending arrival and power potential makes him a top-200 dynasty prospect.

## 8  Josh Kasevich  SS/3B    OFP: 50    ETA: Late 2024/2025

Born: 01/17/01  Age: 22  Bats: R  Throws: R  Height: 6'2"  Weight: 200 lb.  Origin: Round 2, 2022 Draft (#60 overall)

| YEAR | TEAM | LVL | AGE | PA | R | 2B | 3B | HR | RBI | BB | K | SB | CS | AVG/OBP/SLG | DRC+ | BABIP | BRR | DRP | WARP |
|------|------|-----|-----|-----|----|----|----|----|-----|----|----|----|----|-------------|------|-------|------|-----|------|
| 2022 | DUN | A | 21 | 122 | 18 | 8 | 0 | 0 | 7 | 11 | 9 | 0 | 2 | .262/.344/.336 | 130 | .283 | 1.7 | SS(16) 2.2, 3B(10) -1.0 | 1.0 |
| 2023 non-DC | TOR | MLB | 22 | 251 | 19 | 11 | 1 | 2 | 19 | 15 | 38 | 1 | 0 | .215/.274/.296 | 62 | .250 | -3.9 | 3B 0, SS 0 | -0.8 |

Comparables: Jeremy Rivera, Omar Luna, Juan Lucena

**The Report:** College stats can be a bit of a mirage, but if nothing else, Kasevich's time in Eugene describes the kind of hitter he's going to be. He's an absolute pest, short to the ball while covering every corner of the zone and rarely expanding, but also capable of fouling off your good two-strike pitch just off the plate. That carried over into his pro debut, as he didn't chase and put up elite contact rates in the zone. The main question that remains at the plate is can Kasevich impact the ball enough to keep this going into the upper minors. He isn't swinging a wet noodle, and can hit line drives to all fields, but he will need to develop some real game power to be an everyday infielder, as he's more of a once a week guy at shortstop in the majors.

**OFP:** 50 / Second-division starter or good fifth infielder

**Variance:** Medium. I think the hit tool and bat control are mostly real, and Kasevich should be able to draw walks and find gaps up to the majors, but I would worry that better stuff erodes enough of the batting average and OBP that he's more of a fun bench piece.

**Jesse Roche's Fantasy Take:** Unfortunately, far too many of Kasevich's hits are into the ground, and his hit-over-power approach saps his impact. As I've previously noted elsewhere, he projects as an empty-average hitter, much like Adam Frazier and his ilk. This profile can have fantasy utility, but it is not the type to roster in most dynasty formats.

## 9  Sem Robberse  RHP    OFP: 50    ETA: 2024

Born: 10/12/01  Age: 21  Bats: R  Throws: R  Height: 6'1"  Weight: 160 lb.  Origin: International Free Agent, 2019

| YEAR | TEAM | LVL | AGE | W | L | SV | G | GS | IP | H | HR | BB/9 | K/9 | K | GB% | BABIP | WHIP | ERA | DRA- | WARP |
|------|------|-----|-----|---|---|----|----|----|------|----|----|------|-----|----|------|-------|------|------|------|------|
| 2021 | DUN | A | 19 | 5 | 4 | 0 | 14 | 12 | 57² | 46 | 4 | 3.1 | 9.5 | 61 | 49.4% | .273 | 1.14 | 3.90 | 101 | 0.5 |
| 2021 | VAN | A+ | 19 | 0 | 3 | 0 | 7 | 7 | 31 | 39 | 3 | 5.2 | 8.4 | 29 | 52.0% | .367 | 1.84 | 5.23 | 114 | 0.0 |
| 2022 | VAN | A+ | 20 | 4 | 4 | 0 | 17 | 17 | 86² | 76 | 7 | 2.5 | 8.1 | 78 | 48.6% | .280 | 1.15 | 3.12 | 95 | 1.0 |
| 2022 | NH | AA | 20 | 0 | 3 | 0 | 5 | 5 | 24² | 19 | 4 | 3.6 | 6.9 | 19 | 47.9% | .217 | 1.18 | 3.65 | 104 | 0.3 |
| 2023 non-DC | TOR | MLB | 21 | 3 | 3 | 0 | 58 | 0 | 50 | 59 | 7 | 4.0 | 6.4 | 35 | 39.9% | .318 | 1.62 | 5.62 | 140 | -0.8 |

Comparables: Spencer Adams, Jacob Turner, Arodys Vizcaíno

**The Report:** Signed out of the Honkbal Hoofdklasse as a teenager, Robberse is a strike-throwing back-end starter type who fills up the zone with a low-90s fastball. He primarily uses the heater to set up his two breaking balls, the better of which is a tight 11-5 curveball, although his firmer slider has average utility as well. Robberse's stuff tends to get groundballs more than whiffs, but he's been able to keep minor-league hitters off balance well enough so far. He's on the shorter and slighter side for a starter, but he did throw over 100 innings last season, and while there is not a ton of upside, if he can wring out another tick or two on the fastball and refine his changeup a bit more, Robberse will be well on his way to being an effective, if not high-upside, major-league starter.

**OFP:** 50 / no. 4 starter

**Variance:** Medium. The stuff here is polished more than pops, and Robberse might not have a swing-and-miss pitch to the level you need in 2023 major-league baseball.

**Jesse Roche's Fantasy Take:** Robberse misses too few bats (21% strikeout rate) without the underlying stuff to engender excitement for fantasy managers outside of deep leagues.

## 10 Adam Macko  LHP     OFP: 50    ETA: 2024

Born: 12/30/00   Age: 22   Bats: L   Throws: L   Height: 6'0"   Weight: 170 lb.   Origin: Round 7, 2019 Draft (#216 overall)

| YEAR | TEAM | LVL | AGE | W | L | SV | G | GS | IP | H | HR | BB/9 | K/9 | K | GB% | BABIP | WHIP | ERA | DRA- | WARP |
|------|------|-----|-----|---|---|----|----|----|-----|----|----|------|------|----|------|-------|------|------|------|------|
| 2021 | MOD | A | 20 | 2 | 2 | 0 | 9 | 9 | 33¹ | 29 | 1 | 5.7 | 15.1 | 56 | 36.8% | .373 | 1.50 | 4.59 | 104 | 0.1 |
| 2022 | EVE | A+ | 21 | 0 | 2 | 0 | 8 | 8 | 38¹ | 33 | 4 | 4.7 | 14.1 | 60 | 43.4% | .372 | 1.38 | 3.99 | 83 | 0.7 |
| 2023 non-DC | TOR | MLB | 22 | 3 | 3 | 0 | 58 | 0 | 50 | 46 | 7 | 5.3 | 10.3 | 57 | 34.6% | .305 | 1.52 | 4.79 | 120 | -0.3 |

*Comparables: Vince Velasquez, Aliangel Lopez, Émilio Vargas*

**The Report:** On last year's list we tabbed Macko as "two healthy seasons away" from believing in his ability to start long-term. We're still waiting on the first of those two. The Slovakian-born southpaw by way of Canada went on the IL in late May and didn't return until the Fall League, where he both walked and struck out about a batter an inning. You might glean from his walk rates that Macko isn't much of a finesse pitcher, and you would be correct. He also has one of the better two-pitch combos in the system, with a double-plus, high-spin, two-plane curveball and a high-spin fastball he can run into the upper-90s, although he generally sits more in the mid-90s range in his starts. Macko also offers a below-average slider and changeup, but the two pitches could be scrapped with a move out of the rotation. Macko's delivery is not without effort, and likely led to some soft tissue shoulder issues in 2021—along with his relatively small size. He's also shortened his arm swing, to the point that he now keeps the ball well-hidden behind his hip. At one time Macko looked like he could eventually sneak into the back end of a rotation with improved command and another usable secondary. There's a non-zero chance that's still possible, and he still has time on his side as he pitched all of 2022 as a 21-year-old. That said, it looks more and more like a relief-only profile going forward, and a potential late-inning one at that.

**OFP:** 50 / Setup reliever

**Variance:** Very high. Macko's durability and command issues are legitimate concerns and he has yet to throw more than 52 innings in a calendar year. Given how dominant his fastball and curve can be, he's just as likely to move quickly as he is to stall out at Double-A.

**Jesse Roche's Fantasy Take:** "Setup reliever," you say? No, thank you.

# Outside the Top Ten:

## 11 Otto Lopez  UT

Born: 10/01/98   Age: 24   Bats: R   Throws: R   Height: 5'10"   Weight: 185 lb.   Origin: International Free Agent, 2016

| YEAR | TEAM | LVL | AGE | PA | R | 2B | 3B | HR | RBI | BB | K | SB | CS | AVG/OBP/SLG | DRC+ | BABIP | BRR | DRP | WARP |
|------|------|-----|-----|-----|----|----|----|----|-----|----|----|----|----|-------------|------|-------|------|-----|------|
| 2021 | NH | AA | 22 | 314 | 52 | 24 | 1 | 3 | 39 | 28 | 62 | 7 | 3 | .331/.398/.457 | 109 | .412 | 0.4 | 2B(43) -3.4, CF(17) 4.0, LF(3) 2.6 | 1.8 |
| 2021 | BUF | AAA | 22 | 194 | 36 | 8 | 3 | 2 | 25 | 13 | 26 | 15 | 1 | .289/.347/.405 | 101 | .324 | 3.3 | 2B(15) -0.3, LF(15) 3.0, SS(10) -0.5 | 1.1 |
| 2021 | TOR | MLB | 22 | 1 | 0 | 0 | 0 | 0 | 0 | 0 | 1 | 0 | 0 | .000/.000/.000 | 83 | | | | 0.0 |
| 2022 | ESC | WIN | 23 | 88 | 7 | 6 | 0 | 0 | 7 | 5 | 9 | 3 | 2 | .304/.353/.380 | | .343 | | | |
| 2022 | BUF | AAA | 23 | 391 | 53 | 19 | 6 | 3 | 34 | 41 | 61 | 14 | 5 | .297/.378/.415 | 117 | .351 | -1.5 | 2B(36) 0.6, LF(22) 0.6, CF(16) -0.6 | 1.6 |
| 2022 | TOR | MLB | 23 | 10 | 0 | 0 | 0 | 0 | 3 | 1 | 1 | 0 | 1 | .667/.700/.667 | 97 | .750 | -0.2 | SS(5) 0, 2B(1) 0, CF(1) 0 | 0.0 |
| 2023 DC | TOR | MLB | 24 | 172 | 20 | 7 | 1 | 2 | 14 | 12 | 29 | 4 | 1 | .229/.289/.315 | 76 | .270 | -0.8 | CF 0, SS 0 | -0.1 |

*Comparables: Hernán Pérez, Steve Lombardozzi, Dawel Lugo*

Lopez got a few more cameo appearances for the big club in 2022, going 6-for-9 (nice) across three separate call-ups. Back across the border in Buffalo, he added some OBP, but otherwise xeroxed his 2021 Triple-A line after missing the first bit of the season with an oblique injury. Lopez remains the same guy who clocked in one spot higher last year. He can hit a little bit, run more than a little bit, and play defense just about anywhere. You can reasonably worry if he will hit the ball hard enough to beat MLB-caliber pitching and defenses, and the Jays might not have room to carry his bat anyway, but Lopez should get a shot to be a useful 10th position player somewhere out there.

## 12  Cade Doughty  2B/3B

Born: 03/26/01   Age: 22   Bats: R   Throws: R   Height: 6'1"   Weight: 195 lb.   Origin: Round 2, 2022 Draft (#78 overall)

| YEAR | TEAM | LVL | AGE | PA | R | 2B | 3B | HR | RBI | BB | K | SB | CS | AVG/OBP/SLG | DRC+ | BABIP | BRR | DRP | WARP |
|------|------|-----|-----|-----|----|----|----|----|-----|----|----|----|----|-------------|------|-------|------|------------------------|------|
| 2022 | DUN | A | 21 | 119 | 21 | 5 | 0 | 6 | 24 | 10 | 29 | 3 | 2 | .272/.370/.495 | 114 | .324 | 1.0 | 2B(12) -1.9, 3B(11) 2.3 | 0.7 |
| 2023 non-DC | TOR | MLB | 22 | 251 | 20 | 10 | 1 | 4 | 22 | 15 | 69 | 3 | 1 | .211/.269/.313 | 65 | .284 | -2.8 | 2B 0, 3B 0 | -0.6 |

*Comparables: Jose Caballero, Claudio Bautista, Daniel Mayora*

The third of Toronto's three second-round picks last summer, Doughty mashed during his time at LSU. He has good bat-to-ball skills and a chance for average power, although his swing prioritizes contact at present. He's maxed out physically and kind of limited in the field. Doughty has played both second and third as a pro—as he did for the Tigers—but he's going to need to do it mostly in the batter's box to carve out a major-league career.

## 13  Gabriel Martinez  OF

Born: 07/24/02   Age: 20   Bats: R   Throws: R   Height: 6'0"   Weight: 170 lb.   Origin: International Free Agent, 2018

| YEAR | TEAM | LVL | AGE | PA | R | 2B | 3B | HR | RBI | BB | K | SB | CS | AVG/OBP/SLG | DRC+ | BABIP | BRR | DRP | WARP |
|------|------|-----|-----|-----|----|----|----|----|-----|----|----|----|----|-------------|------|-------|------|------------------------|------|
| 2021 | BLU | ROK | 18 | 125 | 16 | 8 | 0 | 0 | 14 | 21 | 18 | 7 | 2 | .330/.448/.410 | | .393 | | | |
| 2022 | DUN | A | 19 | 264 | 46 | 14 | 0 | 11 | 46 | 22 | 45 | 3 | 1 | .288/.348/.483 | 129 | .314 | -3.0 | LF(37) -1.9, RF(22) -1.4 | 0.9 |
| 2022 | VAN | A+ | 19 | 113 | 11 | 8 | 0 | 3 | 13 | 9 | 17 | 0 | 0 | .324/.381/.490 | 120 | .361 | -2.0 | LF(15) 0.5, RF(13) 0.4 | 0.6 |
| 2023 non-DC | TOR | MLB | 20 | 251 | 21 | 11 | 1 | 4 | 23 | 14 | 56 | 3 | 2 | .224/.273/.334 | 71 | .277 | -2.7 | LF 0, CF 0 | -0.5 |

*Comparables: Randal Grichuk, Manuel Margot, Carlos Correa*

Martinez provides a matched set with Doughty: outfield instead of infield, but covers the zone well and has a chance for average power. He's limited to a corner and only just fine there, but put together a strong 2022 campaign at the plate across two A-ball levels. Martinez is not super athletic at the plate, as there's some stiffness, and he's looking to lift. He can be pesky with two strikes, but will also show you some wild swings against offspeed out of the zone. I'd worry the K-rate will jump if he remains this aggressive in the upper minors, but he hits the ball reasonably hard for a 19-year-old and doesn't miss much in the zone. So despite the limited defensive/positional value, like Doughty, Martinez has a chance to hit his way to a major-league role.

## 14  Hayden Juenger  RHP

Born: 08/09/00   Age: 22   Bats: R   Throws: R   Height: 6'0"   Weight: 180 lb.   Origin: Round 6, 2021 Draft (#182 overall)

| YEAR | TEAM | LVL | AGE | W | L | SV | G | GS | IP | H | HR | BB/9 | K/9 | K | GB% | BABIP | WHIP | ERA | DRA- | WARP |
|------|------|-----|-----|---|---|----|----|----|-----|----|----|------|------|----|------|-------|------|------|------|------|
| 2021 | VAN | A+ | 20 | 2 | 0 | 0 | 11 | 0 | 20 | 11 | 0 | 1.8 | 15.3 | 34 | 37.1% | .314 | 0.75 | 2.70 | 80 | 0.4 |
| 2022 | NH | AA | 21 | 0 | 5 | 0 | 20 | 17 | 56 | 40 | 12 | 3.4 | 10.8 | 67 | 32.1% | .224 | 1.09 | 4.02 | 99 | 0.8 |
| 2022 | BUF | AAA | 21 | 3 | 2 | 2 | 18 | 2 | 32² | 23 | 6 | 4.4 | 9.1 | 33 | 42.4% | .215 | 1.19 | 3.31 | 91 | 0.6 |
| 2023 non-DC | TOR | MLB | 22 | 3 | 3 | 0 | 58 | 0 | 50 | 49 | 8 | 4.1 | 8.6 | 48 | 34.0% | .292 | 1.42 | 4.56 | 118 | -0.2 |

*Comparables: Kelvin Herrera, Joe Jiménez, Eduardo Sanchez*

It's 95-and-a-slider time, folks. This has become a catch-all for a wide swath of the relievers you see in the upper minors—and often a bit later on in the majors—so it can seem a little pejorative. However if you have a slider as good as Juenger's...well, you make the next 10 in a shallow system. His low-to-mid-80s sweeper might not be consistent enough for the highest of leverage work, but it's a bat-misser that you'd be fine seeing in the seventh or eighth inning. His fastball is also comfortably mid-90s—not just touch 95 like this profile sometimes is—and while the command isn't great it's fine for...well a setup-level reliever.

## 15 Alejandro Melean  RHP

Born: 10/11/00  Age: 22  Bats: R  Throws: R  Height: 6'0"  Weight: 175 lb.  Origin: International Free Agent, 2017

| YEAR | TEAM | LVL | AGE | W | L | SV | G | GS | IP | H | HR | BB/9 | K/9 | K | GB% | BABIP | WHIP | ERA | DRA- | WARP |
|---|---|---|---|---|---|---|---|---|---|---|---|---|---|---|---|---|---|---|---|---|
| 2021 | DUN | A | 20 | 3 | 5 | 1 | 19 | 10 | 63 | 69 | 10 | 4.3 | 10.7 | 75 | 40.4% | .341 | 1.57 | 5.29 | 87 | 1.1 |
| 2021 | VAN | A+ | 20 | 1 | 1 | 0 | 4 | 4 | 19 | 27 | 2 | 2.8 | 8.1 | 17 | 43.1% | .397 | 1.74 | 4.74 | 135 | -0.2 |
| 2022 | VAN | A+ | 21 | 2 | 1 | 1 | 9 | 5 | 32 | 20 | 2 | 2.3 | 9.8 | 35 | 38.8% | .231 | 0.88 | 1.69 | 92 | 0.4 |
| 2022 | NH | AA | 21 | 0 | 4 | 0 | 8 | 8 | 30 | 26 | 5 | 5.1 | 7.2 | 24 | 45.5% | .253 | 1.43 | 5.10 | 108 | 0.3 |
| 2023 non-DC | TOR | MLB | 22 | 3 | 3 | 0 | 58 | 0 | 50 | 57 | 8 | 4.4 | 7.4 | 41 | 36.9% | .318 | 1.64 | 5.79 | 143 | -0.9 |

Melean has bounced around Blue Jays full-season affiliates for a few years now as a swingman or piggyback starter, but didn't really put together a sustained run of success until his first couple months in Vancouver this past season. He got a late start to 2022 and then missed a month in the middle as well, but when on the mound found success spamming his big, sweeping slider. That didn't continue in Double-A, but despite having bounced around for a few years, Melean only just turned 22 this offseason. Now, he isn't a projection bet or anything, as he has an XL frame and already runs it up to—you guessed it—95 (not that you will see that fastball all that much, as Melean prefers to throw his slider first pitch, ahead, behind, whenever). He has a changeup as well, not a bad one either. It's got a little bit of fade and he will throw it inside to lefties or right-on-right when guys might be sitting on the sweeper. You'd prefer the slider to be a true plus pitch given how much he throws it—hitters can eventually time it the third or fourth time in the at-bat—but it's good enough that Melean might be able to keep on keeping on as a utility arm all the way up to the majors.

## 16 Leo Jimenez  SS/DH

Born: 05/17/01  Age: 22  Bats: R  Throws: R  Height: 5'11"  Weight: 215 lb.  Origin: International Free Agent, 2017

| YEAR | TEAM | LVL | AGE | PA | R | 2B | 3B | HR | RBI | BB | K | SB | CS | AVG/OBP/SLG | DRC+ | BABIP | BRR | DRP | WARP |
|---|---|---|---|---|---|---|---|---|---|---|---|---|---|---|---|---|---|---|---|
| 2021 | DUN | A | 20 | 242 | 35 | 8 | 0 | 1 | 19 | 51 | 35 | 4 | 1 | .315/.517/.381 | 145 | .388 | -0.7 | SS(37) -4.4, 2B(12) 0.6 | 1.6 |
| 2022 | VAN | A+ | 21 | 294 | 45 | 14 | 3 | 6 | 40 | 27 | 58 | 7 | 3 | .230/.340/.385 | 122 | .269 | -0.3 | SS(47) -0.3, 2B(3) -0.3 | 1.6 |
| 2023 non-DC | TOR | MLB | 22 | 251 | 21 | 10 | 1 | 2 | 20 | 22 | 48 | 1 | 1 | .216/.305/.307 | 79 | .265 | -3.9 | 2B 0, SS 0 | -0.2 |

*Comparables: Osvaldo Duarte, Jonathan Herrera, Emilio Guerrero*

Jimenez is an advanced infield defender who might be able to play shortstop in the majors right now. Well, I guess not right now. That would be weird, it's winter. Also he got hit in the hand in August and while I imagine he will be ready for camp, he might still be a bit sore. Anyway, Jimenez checks every box for a good middle infielder, rangy with good hands and actions, and a plus, left side arm. At the plate he shows a strong approach, and plus bat-to-ball skills. It's not likely there's enough power in his game to start—although he did post an ISO over .100 this year for the first time—but Jimenez projects as a useful bench infielder.

## 17 Chad Dallas  RHP

Born: 06/26/00  Age: 23  Bats: R  Throws: R  Height: 5'11"  Weight: 206 lb.  Origin: Round 4, 2021 Draft (#121 overall)

| YEAR | TEAM | LVL | AGE | W | L | SV | G | GS | IP | H | HR | BB/9 | K/9 | K | GB% | BABIP | WHIP | ERA | DRA- | WARP |
|---|---|---|---|---|---|---|---|---|---|---|---|---|---|---|---|---|---|---|---|---|
| 2022 | VAN | A+ | 22 | 1 | 7 | 0 | 21 | 21 | 88 | 85 | 13 | 5.2 | 8.8 | 86 | 45.8% | .287 | 1.55 | 4.60 | 115 | 0.1 |
| 2023 non-DC | TOR | MLB | 23 | 3 | 3 | 0 | 58 | 0 | 50 | 59 | 9 | 5.7 | 7.0 | 39 | 37.3% | .321 | 1.82 | 6.59 | 159 | -1.2 |

Dallas was a 2021 fourth-rounder out of the land of "Rocky Top." He struggled in the Canadians rotation last year, not throwing enough strikes, and getting hit too hard when he was in the zone. I don't know if a move to the pen will be a panacea, but his stuff should play better in short bursts. Dallas could run it up to 95 as a starter with good sink, and showed two different breaking ball looks, with his slider flashing plus. He doesn't have the major-league proximity of Juenger or the power stuff of Macko, but Dallas could move quickly with a shift to the pen, and the Jays have recently needed all the relief help they could get.

## 18 Davis Schneider    UT

Born: 01/26/99   Age: 24   Bats: R   Throws: R   Height: 5'10"   Weight: 190 lb.   Origin: Round 28, 2017 Draft (#849 overall)

| YEAR | TEAM | LVL | AGE | PA | R | 2B | 3B | HR | RBI | BB | K | SB | CS | AVG/OBP/SLG | DRC+ | BABIP | BRR | DRP | WARP |
|------|------|-----|-----|-----|----|----|----|----|-----|----|----|----|----|-------------|------|-------|-----|-----|------|
| 2021 | VAN | A+ | 22 | 179 | 26 | 7 | 1 | 9 | 22 | 26 | 59 | 0 | 1 | .231/.348/.476 | 110 | .305 | -2.2 | 2B(18) -0.0, 3B(5) -0.5 | 0.5 |
| 2022 | VAN | A+ | 23 | 189 | 26 | 10 | 1 | 8 | 25 | 29 | 50 | 6 | 1 | .229/.354/.459 | 122 | .280 | 0.2 | LF(31) -0.5, 2B(11) -0.4, RF(4) 0.3 | 1.4 |
| 2022 | NH | AA | 23 | 190 | 22 | 8 | 3 | 6 | 22 | 22 | 46 | 10 | 0 | .283/.368/.476 | 106 | .357 | 0.8 | 2B(28) 1.2, LF(7) -0.3 | 0.8 |
| 2022 | BUF | AAA | 23 | 75 | 18 | 4 | 0 | 2 | 9 | 14 | 20 | 1 | 1 | .233/.387/.400 | 100 | .316 | 0.3 | LF(8) 0.6, 2B(7) -0.5 | 0.3 |
| 2023 non-DC | TOR | MLB | 24 | 251 | 24 | 10 | 1 | 5 | 25 | 25 | 70 | 3 | 1 | .223/.306/.352 | 90 | .299 | -3.0 | 1B 0, 2B 0 | 0.1 |

A 2017 Day 3 cold weather prep bat, Schneider is yet another Jays prospect who racked up some travel rewards points in 2022. He started the year in Vancouver, ended it in Buffalo and in between showed a good approach and some sneaky pop. As has become a refrain in the 11-20 range of this list, there aren't really above-average tools in the profile. Schneider is direct to the ball and just seems like a dude who can handle the bat, but he also struck out about a quarter of the time and doesn't have the kind of pop that makes that palatable in your everyday lineup. Drafted as a third baseman, he plays mostly second and left field these days, but is still an average runner who goes hard down the line and likes to steal the occasional base. It's a rough bench profile in the modern game, but I can't help but think Schneider will hit just enough to carve out a major-league role for a while.

## 19 Adrian Hernandez    RHP

Born: 01/22/00   Age: 23   Bats: R   Throws: R   Height: 5'8"   Weight: 190 lb.   Origin: International Free Agent, 2017

| YEAR | TEAM | LVL | AGE | W | L | SV | G | GS | IP | H | HR | BB/9 | K/9 | K | GB% | BABIP | WHIP | ERA | DRA- | WARP |
|------|------|-----|-----|---|---|----|----|----|------|----|----|------|------|----|------|-------|------|------|------|------|
| 2020 | MOC | WIN | 20 | 1 | 0 | 0 | 20 | 0 | 25² | 14 | 0 | 7.0 | 11.9 | 34 | 39.2% | .275 | 1.32 | 2.45 | | |
| 2021 | DUN | A | 21 | 0 | 1 | 3 | 9 | 1 | 18 | 13 | 1 | 7.5 | 18.5 | 37 | 50.0% | .414 | 1.56 | 4.50 | 79 | 0.4 |
| 2021 | VAN | A+ | 21 | 3 | 1 | 0 | 12 | 0 | 28² | 12 | 2 | 2.5 | 13.8 | 44 | 28.3% | .196 | 0.70 | 1.88 | 84 | 0.5 |
| 2021 | NH | AA | 21 | 0 | 0 | 4 | 10 | 1 | 15² | 5 | 2 | 3.4 | 15.5 | 27 | 44.0% | .130 | 0.70 | 2.30 | 76 | 0.3 |
| 2022 | BUF | AAA | 22 | 3 | 0 | 7 | 31 | 0 | 32² | 25 | 6 | 4.4 | 12.1 | 44 | 43.4% | .271 | 1.26 | 4.96 | 76 | 0.8 |
| 2023 non-DC | TOR | MLB | 23 | 3 | 3 | 0 | 58 | 0 | 50 | 43 | 8 | 4.6 | 11.5 | 64 | 35.3% | .299 | 1.37 | 4.19 | 108 | 0.0 |

Comparables: Mark Montgomery, Evan Phillips, Wladimir Pinto

"Right shoulder soreness" is not what you want as a pitcher at any time, let alone when you are on the cusp of the majors. Hernandez dominated his three minor-league stops in 2021, and kept it going into Triple-A in 2022. Then he missed two months once his shoulder started barking and got knocked around once he came back. When healthy, he fires plus changeup after plus changeup and ties hitters in knots, like a live-action version of "Baseball Bugs." Hernandez will pop a low-90s fastball now and again, which probably looks like 95+ after watching the *cambio* float in every other pitch. Hernandez has never been too fine with his control even when healthy, and he lost the plate more often after coming back from his injury. Hopefully, he is 100% in spring and can compete for a spot in the Toronto 'pen in 2023. The world needs more changeup specialists.

## 20 Miguel Hiraldo    2B

Born: 09/05/00   Age: 22   Bats: R   Throws: R   Height: 5'11"   Weight: 197 lb.   Origin: International Free Agent, 2017

| YEAR | TEAM | LVL | AGE | PA | R | 2B | 3B | HR | RBI | BB | K | SB | CS | AVG/OBP/SLG | DRC+ | BABIP | BRR | DRP | WARP |
|------|------|-----|-----|-----|----|----|----|----|-----|----|-----|----|----|-------------|------|-------|-----|-----|------|
| 2021 | DUN | A | 20 | 453 | 66 | 26 | 4 | 7 | 52 | 51 | 111 | 29 | 5 | .249/.338/.390 | 102 | .323 | 0.2 | 2B(51) -7.5, 3B(37) -1.8 | 0.6 |
| 2022 | VAN | A+ | 21 | 428 | 47 | 19 | 4 | 11 | 55 | 27 | 126 | 28 | 5 | .231/.278/.382 | 71 | .307 | 0.1 | 2B(101) -4.0, 3B(4) -1.0 | -0.7 |
| 2023 non-DC | TOR | MLB | 22 | 251 | 19 | 10 | 2 | 3 | 21 | 15 | 82 | 8 | 2 | .208/.260/.308 | 60 | .304 | -0.5 | 2B 0, 3B 0 | -0.5 |

Comparables: Gilbert Lara, DJ LeMahieu, Emilio Guerrero

Four years ago I would have talked myself into Hiraldo 10 spots higher. Sure, he's a second baseman, but he's a solid enough second baseman. Yeah he hasn't slugged over .400 in full-season ball yet, but it's no-doubt plus raw power and plus bat speed and he can put it out to the deepest part of your local ballpark. He even runs okay too. What's that? You want to know if he can hit? Well one of the reasons Hiraldo has run those sub-.400 slugs is his low batting averages, the result of a max-effort swing coupled with an overly aggressive approach. He's aggressive broadly. He's aggressive against spin out of the zone. He's aggressive against spin in the zone. He doesn't make enough contact or enough quality contact to make this all work...yet. And maybe never, but four years after I should have known better, here we are.

## Top Talents 25 and Under (as of 4/1/2023):

1. Vladimir Guerrero Jr., 1B
2. Bo Bichette, SS
3. Alek Manoah, RHP
4. Alejandro Kirk, C/DH
5. Ricky Tiedemann, LHP
6. Yosver Zulueta, RHP
7. Brandon Barriera, LHP
8. Dahian Santos, RHP
9. Orelvis Martinez, IF
10. Tucker Toman, IF

Most clubs would be hard-pressed to find a collection of young talent like that which is the core of the Blue Jays' roster. Both Guerrero and Manoah were finalists for their preeminent awards within the past two seasons, with Vladito coming second in MVP voting for the monstrous realization of his potential only outshone by Shohei Ohtani, while Manoah saw a stellar Cy Young campaign nonetheless come up short behind Justin Verlander and Dylan Cease. Vladito's 2022 took a step backwards, which still saw him run a stellar offensive line of .274/.339/.480 in a year of a mostly-deadened ball. He'll be 24 in 2023 and seems every bit on track for a Hall of Fame career just like his dad.

Manoah's magnificent 2022 was a mastercraft in contact management, as he ran a 2.24 ERA in spite of a 3.87 DRA in 196 2/3 innings. The titanic northpaw had one of the most effective fastball combos in baseball, and leaned heavily on his four-pitch mix to keep hitters in the dark. His club needed his ace-hood as other rotation arms (besides Kevin Gausman) fell victim to ineffectiveness and injury, but Manoah should now co-anchor one of the more promising groups in the American League.

Defending behind him will be Bichette, the sparkplug second son of Canada's famed "Next Generation" trio of big-league kids. Bichette is nothing short of a star in his own right, with another strong year at the plate despite some miscues on the basepaths and a mixed bag in the field. He'll be 25 in 2023, and with the departure of Xander Bogaerts he can likely claim the title of the AL East's top shortstop—at least until Gunnar Henderson comes knocking (or moves to third).

Finally, there's the catcher who beautifully highlights what makes the sport of baseball brilliant and delightful. Kirk had a staggering campaign, with a 130 DRC+ and 4.3 WARP in 2022 despite huge limitations on the basepaths and mediocre work keeping runners in check behind the dish. His framing graded out brilliantly, a massive credit to a player whose size has always caused evaluators to expect a move away from behind the dish.

# Washington Nationals

## The State of the System:

This farm system should be a lot better after trading Juan Soto, Trea Turner and Max Scherzer, not to mention making the fifth overall pick. A *lot* better.

## The Top Ten:

### 1 James Wood OF — OFP: 70 — ETA: 2024

Born: 09/17/02   Age: 20   Bats: L   Throws: R   Height: 6'7"   Weight: 240 lb.   Origin: Round 2, 2021 Draft (#62 overall)

| YEAR | TEAM | LVL | AGE | PA | R | 2B | 3B | HR | RBI | BB | K | SB | CS | AVG/OBP/SLG | DRC+ | BABIP | BRR | DRP | WARP |
|------|------|-----|-----|-----|----|----|----|----|-----|----|----|----|----|-------------|------|-------|------|-----|------|
| 2021 | PAD | ROK | 18 | 101 | 18 | 5 | 0 | 3 | 22 | 13 | 32 | 10 | 0 | .372/.465/.535 | | .569 | | | |
| 2022 | FBG | A | 19 | 93 | 14 | 8 | 0 | 2 | 17 | 10 | 26 | 4 | 0 | .293/.366/.463 | 99 | .400 | 0.8 | CF(18) 0.9 | 0.3 |
| 2022 | LE | A | 19 | 236 | 55 | 19 | 1 | 10 | 45 | 37 | 42 | 15 | 5 | .337/.453/.601 | 138 | .387 | 1.9 | CF(43) 0.2, LF(2) 0.1 | 2.0 |
| 2023 non-DC | WAS | MLB | 20 | 251 | 22 | 12 | 1 | 4 | 23 | 22 | 61 | 7 | 2 | .221/.294/.335 | 79 | .285 | -0.9 | LF 0, CF 0 | 0.1 |

*Comparables: Drew Waters, Jarred Kelenic, Alek Thomas*

**The Report:** No prospect improved their stock over the course of the 2022 season more than Wood, who is now clearly one of the five best prospects in the game. As of summer 2020, Wood was one of the top prospects in the 2021 draft class, but he struggled in the year leading up to the draft and was perceived to have significant hit tool and swing-and-miss risk, partially due to his height. After getting first-round money in the late-second from San Diego, he was one of the most impressive players in the Arizona complex scene in summer and fall 2021, although the swing-and-miss concerns remained.

His 2022 campaign allayed a lot of that concern. Wood's feel for contact improved from his greatest concern to above-average—not above-average for a 6-foot-7 power hitter, just above-average. He maintained a patient approach at the plate, and he absolutely obliterated the ball on contact, posting some of the most impressive exit velocity numbers in the minors. He did miss about a month early in the season with a wrist injury and a few weeks late in the summer with a knee injury, but other than that, his season was a revelation. Given his size and the length of his levers, he's still not going to be a low-strikeout hitter, but his feel for contact at his age and size is unusually strong, and he's just straight-up as good a hitting prospect as any player in the minors now. If the Soto trade ends up working out, the most likely path is because Wood became a superstar.

**OFP:** 70 / All-Star outfielder

**Variance:** Medium. Given his size and past history of swing-and-miss, the hit tool is still going to be a mild potential long-term concern until he does it in the majors. But geez, this all looks good right now.

**Bret Sayre's Fantasy Take:** Even with the hype train in full motion, there's still time to get in at a value that you'll be pleased with in dynasty leagues. His height, exit velo and position are going to ultimately get him an unfair comp, but directionally it's not unreasonable. It's easy 30-homer power combined with the ability to actually help in batting average and double-digit steal potential thrown in for good measure. That's a clear-cut OF1.

## 2 Robert Hassell III  OF     OFP: 55     ETA: 2024
Born: 08/15/01   Age: 21   Bats: L   Throws: L   Height: 6'2"   Weight: 195 lb.   Origin: Round 1, 2020 Draft (#8 overall)

| YEAR | TEAM | LVL | AGE | PA | R | 2B | 3B | HR | RBI | BB | K | SB | CS | AVG/OBP/SLG | DRC+ | BABIP | BRR | DRP | WARP |
|---|---|---|---|---|---|---|---|---|---|---|---|---|---|---|---|---|---|---|---|
| 2021 | LE | A | 19 | 429 | 77 | 31 | 3 | 7 | 65 | 57 | 74 | 31 | 6 | .323/.415/.482 | 125 | .385 | 3.1 | CF(84) -3.8, RF(2) -0.1 | 2.9 |
| 2021 | FW | A+ | 19 | 87 | 10 | 2 | 1 | 4 | 11 | 9 | 25 | 3 | 0 | .205/.287/.410 | 102 | .245 | -0.3 | CF(16) -0.9 | 0.2 |
| 2022 | WIL | A+ | 20 | 45 | 9 | 1 | 0 | 0 | 3 | 6 | 12 | 3 | 0 | .211/.311/.237 | 86 | .296 | 0.5 | CF(7) 0.6, RF(2) 0.3 | 0.1 |
| 2022 | FW | A+ | 20 | 346 | 49 | 19 | 1 | 10 | 55 | 38 | 66 | 20 | 3 | .299/.379/.467 | 118 | .352 | 1.7 | CF(63) 1.6, LF(2) 0.5 | 2.1 |
| 2022 | HBG | AA | 20 | 122 | 9 | 5 | 0 | 1 | 12 | 13 | 35 | 1 | 0 | .222/.311/.296 | 82 | .319 | 0.6 | CF(27) -1.9 | 0.2 |
| 2023 non-DC | WAS | MLB | 21 | 251 | 22 | 11 | 1 | 3 | 22 | 20 | 59 | 7 | 1 | .234/.301/.335 | 82 | .302 | -1.4 | LF 0, CF 0 | 0.2 |

*Comparables: Engel Beltre, Manuel Margot, Victor Robles*

**The Report:** Hassell was nominally the lead prospect in the Soto deal, although Wood was overtaking him by the time of the trade. As recently as last year, we had been applying phrases like "plus-plus hit tool" and "potential .300 hitter" to Hassell, but some really bad late-season reports and a general refocus on what actually leads to good hit-tool outcomes now has us questioning that—and that was all before he broke his hamate bone in the Arizona Fall League.

Hassell has one of the most aesthetically pleasing swings in the minor leagues—a buttery smooth and balanced left-handed stroke that has wowed scouts since he was a high-school underclassman—but he does not do anything discrete that would lead you to believe that he's going to hit for a particularly high average in the majors. He does not hit the ball hard, really not at all; his median exit velos, 90th-percentile exit velos, and barrel-like rates (teams usually quantify this somewhat differently than MLB does) all range from average to pedestrian. He almost never lifts the ball, with ground-ball rates on the wrong side of 50% and, while he's a plus runner, he's not the type of burner where he's going to be legging out tons of infield hits. His swing decisions are perfectly fine, but to drive a profile like this, they need to be a lot better than fine—think of the Rangers' Evan Carter.

Although Hassell was good enough at the A-ball levels to hide a lot of this, the offensive profile caved in when he was promoted to Double-A shortly after the trade, and now all of a sudden he might be tracking as a defensive tweener without a carrying tool. There are evaluators who are still convinced that he'll hit for average as he advances, but he needs to show some sort of ability to point us in that direction, or the arrow is going to trend down quickly.

**OFP:** 55 / Starting outfielder

**Variance:** High. You can probably tell that we're becoming unconvinced by the hit tool, and hamate injuries can sometimes linger for years.

**Bret Sayre's Fantasy Take:** The arbitrage on Hassell is the polar opposite of his potential future teammate above. There's speed in the profile, but probably not more than 20 steals, ultimately, so the question is whether he can hit for enough average to both help in the category and allow him to tap into 20-homer power. If he's not a .280 hitter, he'll likely top out as an OF4. Skepticism is very much warranted here.

### Eyewitness Report: Robert Hassell III

**Evaluator:** Nathan Graham
**Report Date:** 06/01/2022
**Dates Seen:** Multiple 2021/2022
**Risk Factor:** High
**Physical/Health:** Extra-Large frame with a lean, athletic build. Smooth athleticism, mild projection for growth.

| Tool | Future Grade | Report |
|------|-------------|--------|
| Hit | 70 | Upright, slightly open, balanced stance; Simple load with toe tap for timing, classic left-handed swing. Plus bat speed allows the bat to stay in the zone; Elite barrel control with an excellent feel for the strike zone and pitch recognition, will rarely chase bad pitches. |
| Power | 50 | Plus raw power generated by bat speed; Hits the ball hard to all fields but swing is geared more for contact, producing plenty of doubles; Will produce average home run numbers with physical maturity. |
| Baserunning/ Speed | 60 | Smooth, athletic runner; 4.10 clock home to first; Average acceleration but has a second gear once he gets going; Physical build will allow him to keep speed for most of his career; smart baserunner who will steal a moderate amount of bags. |
| Glove | 60 | Improving routes and instincts in the outfield, has the raw foot speed to cover plenty of territory, will eventually settle into being an above-average centerfielder. |
| Arm | 50 | Average arm strength, accurate; Fine for center and left but would be stretched in right. |

**Conclusion:** One of the top young hitters in the game. His ability to find the barrel plus the speed and defense give him a high floor of a solid everyday major league outfielder. Continued development and physical growth will result in an occasional All-Star who contends for batting titles.

## 3 Elijah Green   OF        OFP: 55    ETA: 2027
Born: 12/04/03   Age: 19   Bats: R   Throws: R   Height: 6'3"   Weight: 225 lb.   Origin: Round 1, 2022 Draft (#5 overall)

| YEAR | TEAM | LVL | AGE | PA | R | 2B | 3B | HR | RBI | BB | K | SB | CS | AVG/OBP/SLG | DRC+ | BABIP | BRR | DRP | WARP |
|------|------|-----|-----|----|----|----|----|----|-----|----|----|----|----|-------------|------|-------|-----|-----|------|
| 2022 | NAT | ROK | 18 | 52 | 9 | 4 | 0 | 2 | 9 | 6 | 21 | 1 | 0 | .302/.404/.535 | | .524 | | | |

**The Report:** Green is among the most divisive prospects I can remember in the player evaluation world. I have had multiple scouts tell me he was one of the best prep hitting prospects in recent memory; I have had other scouts tell me they wouldn't have taken him in the first two rounds. It all depends on whether you think he projects for an average hit tool or a terrible one.

The reason for this dichotomy is unusually poor present in-zone contact ability for a top prospect. He swung and missed in the zone a catastrophically high amount in the prep showcase scene, and he swung and missed in the zone a lot against *high school* fastballs which, even granting that he played at IMG Academy, isn't something you see these days from guys who get drafted near where Green did. This disastrous level of in-zone swing-and-miss continued into his pro debut in the complex.

Because of the rest of his skill set, it hasn't actually mattered quite yet. Green has plus-plus (or better) power potential, explosive bat speed, plus-plus speed, good enough swing decisions for his age and a visually impressive swing. Basically, if you're watching him take swings in batting practice—outside of competition when the pitcher isn't trying to make him miss—you'd think he was the best prospect ever. But we've learned that in-zone contact rates are a lot of the secret sauce driving prospect busts during the pitch-tracking era. While this can improve—look no further than Wood—Green is starting out from an unusually low floor in this respect.

**OFP:** 55 / Power-driven starting outfielder

**Variance:** Extreme. If Green somehow gets to a 45 hit tool, he's going to win hardware. If he doesn't have massive improvements, he might not make it at all.

**Bret Sayre's Fantasy Take:** How you feel about Green should be tied to what size league you're in. He's the perfect shallow dynasty prospect because you can just move on if he can't overcome his contact issues. But if he does, he's one of the few prospects (maybe only) who can be a legitimate 30/30 guy. You may see him ranked inside the top-50 dynasty prospects, but use your league knowledge to know how to best evaluate him for your individual situation.

## 4 Cade Cavalli RHP

OFP: 55        ETA: Debuted in 2022

Born: 08/14/98   Age: 24   Bats: R   Throws: R   Height: 6'4"   Weight: 240 lb.   Origin: Round 1, 2020 Draft (#22 overall)

| YEAR | TEAM | LVL | AGE | W | L | SV | G | GS | IP | H | HR | BB/9 | K/9 | K | GB% | BABIP | WHIP | ERA | DRA- | WARP |
|------|------|-----|-----|---|---|----|---|----|----|----|----|------|-----|----|------|-------|------|------|------|------|
| 2021 | WIL | A+ | 22 | 3 | 1 | 0 | 7 | 7 | 40² | 24 | 1 | 2.7 | 15.7 | 71 | 49.3% | .329 | 0.89 | 1.77 | 63 | 1.2 |
| 2021 | HBG | AA | 22 | 3 | 3 | 0 | 11 | 11 | 58 | 39 | 2 | 5.4 | 12.4 | 80 | 38.3% | .296 | 1.28 | 2.79 | 80 | 1.1 |
| 2021 | ROC | AAA | 22 | 1 | 5 | 0 | 6 | 6 | 24² | 33 | 2 | 4.7 | 8.8 | 24 | 52.5% | .397 | 1.86 | 7.30 | 109 | 0.2 |
| 2022 | ROC | AAA | 23 | 6 | 4 | 0 | 20 | 20 | 97 | 75 | 3 | 3.6 | 9.6 | 104 | 42.6% | .293 | 1.18 | 3.71 | 85 | 2.0 |
| 2022 | WAS | MLB | 23 | 0 | 1 | 0 | 1 | 1 | 4¹ | 6 | 0 | 4.2 | 12.5 | 6 | 50.0% | .500 | 1.85 | 14.54 | 94 | 0.1 |
| 2023 DC | WAS | MLB | 24 | 6 | 7 | 0 | 21 | 21 | 96.7 | 92 | 11 | 4.2 | 9.3 | 100 | 40.5% | .305 | 1.42 | 4.23 | 109 | 0.5 |

*Comparables: Erik Johnson, Daniel Mengden, Dylan Cease*

**The Report:** The Nationals have collected an awful lot of pitchers who throw really hard without having pitch characteristics which whiff batters at a high frequency—often ones who have a checkered injury history. Cavalli is the best of them.

He sits in the mid-90s as a starter, touching the upper-90s or triple-digits, but the pitch has a very generic movement and spin profile even though it looks lively to the naked eye. In the 2020s, 96 mph with a little bit of sink at ~2,300 RPM doesn't even get past upper-minors hitters in great volume, let alone MLB hitters. Both his power curveball and hard slider have flashed plus without consistency, and his changeup might get to average. His command is decent enough, so this was all tracking towards something like a 55/60/55/45 arsenal with okay command despite a tough arm action. That would make him a mid-rotation starter who doesn't whiff nearly as many hitters as you think he should based on the visual quality of his stuff. He also would very likely hit triple-digits more regularly in relief, and that is enough to beat hitters, so the possibility looms that he'll wind up at the back end of a bullpen.

Of course, there's the injury history too. He's had red flags dating back to high school, and he was shut down in August just after making his MLB debut with shoulder inflammation. When he tried to start throwing after the prescribed two weeks off, he had additional discomfort that required a cortisone shot, and he never got back on a mound in 2022. Suffice to say that "recurring shoulder issues" are not what you want to hear attached to your young arm-strength pitching prospect.

**OFP:** 55 / Mid-rotation pitcher who flashes higher or closer

**Variance:** High. This goes both ways—the injuries are concerning, but it's plausible that Cavalli picks up another tick or two of velo, improves his fastball shape or one of the breaking balls advances to a true out-pitch.

**Bret Sayre's Fantasy Take:** The potential lack of strikeouts is going to be an issue, as there's not much more than SP4 upside here. But at least he'll get all the chances he can handle this year as the Nationals compete for the International League title. If we're honest, you'd forgive some upside for certainty and that is just not the case here either. He's a borderline top-100 prospect at best.

## 5 Brady House SS

OFP: 55        ETA: 2025

Born: 06/04/03   Age: 20   Bats: R   Throws: R   Height: 6'4"   Weight: 215 lb.   Origin: Round 1, 2021 Draft (#11 overall)

| YEAR | TEAM | LVL | AGE | PA | R | 2B | 3B | HR | RBI | BB | K | SB | CS | AVG/OBP/SLG | DRC+ | BABIP | BRR | DRP | WARP |
|------|------|-----|-----|----|---|----|----|----|-----|----|----|----|----|-------------|------|-------|-----|-----|------|
| 2021 | NAT | ROK | 18 | 66 | 14 | 3 | 0 | 4 | 12 | 7 | 13 | 0 | 0 | .322/.394/.576 | | .357 | | | |
| 2022 | FBG | A | 19 | 203 | 24 | 8 | 0 | 3 | 31 | 12 | 59 | 1 | 0 | .278/.356/.375 | 99 | .393 | 2.9 | SS(36) -1.1 | 0.7 |
| 2023 non-DC | WAS | MLB | 20 | 251 | 18 | 10 | 1 | 2 | 19 | 12 | 77 | 0 | 0 | .206/.255/.285 | 52 | .297 | -4.4 | SS 0 | -1.1 |

*Comparables: Adrian Marin, Nick Gordon, Ruddy Giron*

**The Report:** The Nationals getting House down to the 11th pick in the 2021 Draft was perceived as a coup; he looked like one of the top half-dozen or so prospects and made our 2022 Top 101. A year and change later, you can start to see the contours of why he might've fallen. Sandwiched around IL stints for recurring back problems, he struggled with both the bat and glove at Low-A.

House's power projection was purported to be the strong suit of his game. While his higher-end exit velocities still remain above-average for his age, they aren't in the league of Wood and Green, and he struggled to consistently hit the ball hard. He didn't lift the ball much, hitting it on the ground over half the time, and he struggled a bit with both chasing and swing-and-miss. Basically, he didn't do a whole lot of good underlying things on offense, and that led to underwhelming production in his full-season debut. Defensively, he fielded below .900 and, given his size and future growth, he already projected for a move off of shortstop.

It's possible that there was significant short-term skill degradation in all of these areas due to House's recurring back problems, and he might come back looking like the pre-draft player this year. Of course, given that he's a teenager with back problems, it's also possible if there was skill degradation, it might not be short-term. House will be one of the most important early-season 2023 follows, both to see if he's fully healthy and whether his skills will look more like the 2022 or 2021 vintage if so.

**OFP:** 55 / Starting infielder, likely at third base

**Variance:** Very high. He's a teenager with back problems and all sorts of concerns both offensively or defensively. He's also shown tremendous skills in the past.

**Bret Sayre's Fantasy Take:** Is it possible to have prospect fatigue with a teenager? If so, we're seeing it with House. Yes, the back stuff is concerning, but his performance in full-season ball was certainly good enough to avoid relegating him to future bust status given his age. There's still plenty of chance for him to develop into the .270-30 hitter that his raw skills suggest is in his wheelhouse. Be patient.

## 6 Jarlin Susana RHP    OFP: 55    ETA: 2026

Born: 03/23/04   Age: 19   Bats: R   Throws: R   Height: 6'6"   Weight: 235 lb.   Origin: International Free Agent, 2022

| YEAR | TEAM | LVL | AGE | W | L | SV | G | GS | IP | H | HR | BB/9 | K/9 | K | GB% | BABIP | WHIP | ERA | DRA- | WARP |
|------|------|-----|-----|---|---|----|----|----|----|----|----|------|-----|----|------|-------|------|------|------|------|
| 2022 | PAD | ROK | 18 | 0 | 0 | 0 | 8 | 7 | 29¹ | 15 | 1 | 3.4 | 13.5 | 44 | 56.6% | .269 | 0.89 | 2.45 | | |
| 2022 | FBG | A | 18 | 0 | 0 | 0 | 3 | 3 | 10¹ | 9 | 1 | 4.4 | 11.3 | 13 | 38.5% | .320 | 1.35 | 2.61 | 93 | 0.1 |
| 2023 non-DC | WAS | MLB | 19 | 3 | 3 | 0 | 58 | 0 | 50 | 56 | 9 | 5.4 | 7.8 | 43 | 34.1% | .314 | 1.72 | 6.19 | 151 | -1.0 |

Comparables: Carlos Calderon, Wilkel Hernandez, José Berríos

**The Report:** Susana was widely considered the top pitching prospect in the January 2022 IFA class, and his pro debut was nothing short of sensational. He skipped the Dominican complex and went straight to the States, dominated in the Arizona complex all spring and summer, was a key inclusion in the Soto trade (you'll be shocked to learn the Nationals prioritized a guy with huge arm strength), and made two flashy starts in full-season ball.

Susana is among the hardest-throwing teenagers in baseball history; he regularly clocks in as high as 102-103 mph. He pairs that with a very hard slider, as high as the low-to-mid-90s—Jacob deGrom (and pretty much nobody else) territory as a starter—and he has shown a feel for a changeup at times as well. On paper, this is ace stuff out of an 18-year-old.

There are a million caveats. though. Susana is a huge teenager with a fairly violent delivery he doesn't repeat well. His command comes and goes. The history of teenage pitchers who throw this hard with elite arm speed is poor; some pitchers who were once the hardest-throwing teenagers on the planet never even made it to the majors (whither Colt Griffin). Think of it this way—by age, he'd be a 2023 prep draftee, and he'd almost certainly be the best prep arm in the class. This track can go the way of Andrew Painter or Grayson Rodriguez, in which case Susana will be high up the Top 101 soon, or it can go the way of Riley Pint or Brady Aiken (or a million points in between).

**OFP:** 55 / Effective pitcher in some role

**Variance:** Extreme. He's a huge teenage pitcher whose entire profile is based on incredible arm speed. I would need a ouija board to tell you where he's at in two years.

**Bret Sayre's Fantasy Take:** This is the *clear* top pitching prospect for me in the Nationals' system and I'd have him squarely in the fantasy Top 101. His frame and raw stuff are what dynasty dreams are made of and with the minors slightly down as a whole, a big SP1 bet like Susana is one that's just too much fun not to make.

## 7 Cristhian Vaquero OF    OFP: 50    ETA: 2027

Born: 09/13/04   Age: 18   Bats: S   Throws: R   Height: 6'3"   Weight: 180 lb.   Origin: International Free Agent, 2022

| YEAR | TEAM | LVL | AGE | PA | R | 2B | 3B | HR | RBI | BB | K | SB | CS | AVG/OBP/SLG | DRC+ | BABIP | BRR | DRP | WARP |
|------|------|-----|-----|-----|----|----|----|----|-----|----|----|----|----|-------------|------|-------|-----|-----|------|
| 2022 | DSL NAT | ROK | 17 | 216 | 33 | 4 | 4 | 1 | 22 | 33 | 38 | 17 | 7 | .256/.379/.341 | | .317 | | | |

**The Report:** The Nationals spent nearly the entirety of last January's bonus pool on Vaquero, nicknamed "The Phenomenon" before he signed. A plus-plus runner with a projectable frame, two great looking swings and strong athletic bloodlines (both of his parents were national-level athletes in Cuba in other sports), Vaquero spent the summer playing in the DSL and was okay. He hit for almost no power and his exit velocities were surprisingly mediocre given the hype, so any power projection is going to come from future physical and swing development—there's not much right now. His contact and swing decisions were fine given his age and level, so the problem at present is that he's not hitting the ball that hard.

The DSL is just a slice of a fuller season of development, and Vaquero is likely to make his domestic debut in the Florida Complex League this year. Given prior hype and visual scouting, it's possible that he makes a big jump quickly; we wouldn't take small sample complex performance too seriously except it's all that we have.

**OFP:** 50 / Starting center fielder

**Variance:** Extreme. The history of extremely hyped international free agents is very mixed; just a few years ago, Erick Peña got a lot of similar but even greater hype, and he hasn't hit at *all* once he got stateside.

**Bret Sayre's Fantasy Take:** The combination of approach and projection here makes Vaquero a name worth keeping a very close eye on. Unfortunately he got too much hype as an international signee to be high watch list material, so you're going to have to commit a little to get in at this point. It's excusable though, as it's not too hard to dream on 20 homers and 30 steals if it all breaks right.

## 8  Zach Brzykcy  RHP       OFP: 50     ETA: 2023

Born: 07/12/99   Age: 23   Bats: R   Throws: R   Height: 6'2"   Weight: 230 lb.   Origin: Undrafted Free Agent, 2020

| YEAR | TEAM | LVL | AGE | W | L | SV | G | GS | IP | H | HR | BB/9 | K/9 | K | GB% | BABIP | WHIP | ERA | DRA- | WARP |
|------|------|-----|-----|---|---|----|----|----|-----|---|----|------|-----|----|------|-------|------|------|------|------|
| 2021 | WIL | A+ | 21 | 6 | 4 | 2 | 28 | 1 | 62¹ | 55 | 8 | 3.6 | 12.4 | 86 | 36.7% | .331 | 1.28 | 5.20 | 89 | 0.9 |
| 2022 | WIL | A+ | 22 | 6 | 1 | 4 | 17 | 0 | 21² | 10 | 2 | 4.2 | 16.2 | 39 | 38.2% | .250 | 0.92 | 1.66 | 81 | 0.4 |
| 2022 | HBG | AA | 22 | 2 | 1 | 9 | 32 | 0 | 38 | 21 | 3 | 4.5 | 12.8 | 54 | 39.7% | .243 | 1.05 | 1.89 | 65 | -1.2 |
| 2023 DC | WAS | MLB | 23 | 1 | 1 | 0 | 23 | 0 | 19.7 | 17 | 3 | 4.5 | 10.3 | 23 | 36.1% | .280 | 1.34 | 3.94 | 104 | 0.1 |

**The Report:** And here we have the one true data-friendly pitching prospect in the system (so of course he's an undrafted reliever). Brzykcy has some of the best fastball characteristics in the minors, with outlier vertical movement. Despite only having mid-90s fastball velocity, he's posted absurd whiff rates with old number one and can beat nearly any batter high in the zone with it. He's a three-pitch guy, with a flashing changeup and a slurvy breaking ball rounding out the arsenal. He reached Triple-A after completely dominating High-A and Double-A, and given the depleted state of Washington's bullpen, he could be in line for high-leverage MLB work very shortly.

**OFP:** 50 / High-leverage reliever

**Variance:** Medium. Relievers are volatile and he doesn't have an obvious plus offspeed, but Brzykcy has all the makings of a pitcher who can throw invisiballs past MLB hitters.

**Bret Sayre's Fantasy Take:** While a phenomenal story/profile, Brzykcy should not be on your radar in dynasty leagues.

## 9  Jeremy De La Rosa  CF      OFP: 50     ETA: 2025

Born: 01/16/02   Age: 21   Bats: L   Throws: L   Height: 6'0"   Weight: 199 lb.   Origin: International Free Agent, 2018

| YEAR | TEAM | LVL | AGE | PA | R | 2B | 3B | HR | RBI | BB | K | SB | CS | AVG/OBP/SLG | DRC+ | BABIP | BRR | DRP | WARP |
|------|------|-----|-----|-----|----|----|----|----|-----|----|-----|----|----|-------------|------|-------|------|-----|------|
| 2021 | FBG | A | 19 | 358 | 34 | 12 | 4 | 5 | 22 | 30 | 122 | 7 | 8 | .209/.279/.316 | 75 | .317 | -1.3 | CF(76) 1.1, LF(5) -0.7, RF(4) -0.2 | 0.1 |
| 2022 | FBG | A | 20 | 315 | 56 | 19 | 2 | 10 | 57 | 36 | 78 | 26 | 5 | .315/.394/.505 | 114 | .408 | -0.1 | CF(63) -3.0 | 0.7 |
| 2022 | WIL | A+ | 20 | 133 | 10 | 4 | 1 | 1 | 10 | 12 | 37 | 13 | 2 | .195/.273/.271 | 76 | .272 | 0.0 | CF(26) 0.5, RF(5) 0.6 | 0.3 |
| 2023 non-DC | WAS | MLB | 21 | 251 | 20 | 10 | 2 | 3 | 21 | 16 | 83 | 7 | 3 | .219/.275/.316 | 66 | .328 | -0.5 | LF 0, CF 0 | -0.2 |

Comparables: Lolo Sanchez, Kenny Wilson, D.J. Davis

**The Report:** De La Rosa has been pinging around the fringes of our Top 10 lists for four seasons because this system has been so bad and thin that, now, for the first time, he's being written up on his own merit. He skipped the DSL to play stateside as a 17-year-old and then skipped to Low-A after the pandemic as a 19-year-old, and was not ready for either assignment. Sent back to repeat Low-A in 2022, he dominated as a still-age-appropriate 20-year-old, hitting for tangible game power for the first time.

Like most of the rest of the top hitters in this system, it just looks right for De La Rosa in a baseball uniform; he's a strong-looking kid with a nice, smooth lefty swing, and he's now a plus runner who might stick in center. He's more barrel-control-over-bat speed at present, and he still swings and misses more than you'd like given the overall profile. The next step to conquer will be driving the ball in the air more often—like Hassell and House, his ground-ball rate is still on the wrong side of 50%. De La Rosa struggled after a promotion to High-A, and the Nationals had to add him to the 40-man to protect him from Rule 5, starting the clock on his developmental path.

**OFP:** 50 / Starting outfielder

**Variance:** Very high. De La Rosa has only hit for a few months last year out of his whole career.

**Bret Sayre's Fantasy Take:** If it works, it's roughly an OF4 profile who you're constantly looking to replace with someone better. He's likely worth rostering if your league holds 200 prospects, but his potential 20-steal profile will be the victim of that first watch list guy popping in April.

## 10 Jake Bennett LHP  OFP: 50  ETA: 2024
Born: 12/02/00  Age: 22  Bats: L  Throws: L  Height: 6'6"  Weight: 234 lb.  Origin: Round 2, 2022 Draft (#45 overall)

**The Report:** Bennett wasn't very high on the draft radar through his first two seasons at Oklahoma, but emerged in 2021 as one of the better arms on the Cape and pitched his way into a second-round pick during the 2022 college season. A high school and college teammate of Cavalli, Bennett looks right on the mound—a big, smooth, high-three-quarters slot lefty who throws the standard fastball/slider/changeup mix. The fastball comes in mostly in the low-90s, touching the mid-90s, but does not have big swing-and-miss characteristics. His best present secondary offering is his changeup, but his slider has flashed as well. His command improved greatly throughout his college career and even during his draft year, and all-in-all he's something of the classic second-round mid-rotation lefty starting prospect.

**OFP:** 50 / No. 4 starter

**Variance:** Medium. Bennett doesn't have a clear swing-and-miss offering yet, but he's a lefty and a strike thrower with three average-or-better pitches.

**Bret Sayre's Fantasy Take:** Deep leaguers can pay attention, but otherwise there's no good reason to keep an eye on Bennett until the point he gets to the majors and we get a sense of how he separates from the other back-end starters available on the waiver wire.

# Outside the Top Ten:

## 11 T.J. White LF
Born: 07/23/03  Age: 19  Bats: S  Throws: R  Height: 6'2"  Weight: 210 lb.  Origin: Round 5, 2021 Draft (#143 overall)

| YEAR | TEAM | LVL | AGE | PA | R | 2B | 3B | HR | RBI | BB | K | SB | CS | AVG/OBP/SLG | DRC+ | BABIP | BRR | DRP | WARP |
|---|---|---|---|---|---|---|---|---|---|---|---|---|---|---|---|---|---|---|---|
| 2021 | NAT | ROK | 17 | 59 | 11 | 2 | 0 | .4 | 12 | 5 | 14 | 1 | 0 | .283/.356/.547 | | .314 | | | |
| 2022 | FBG | A | 18 | 382 | 55 | 20 | 2 | 11 | 52 | 44 | 104 | 8 | 1 | .258/.353/.432 | 111 | .343 | -1.1 | LF(86) -3.2 | 0.9 |
| 2023 non-DC | WAS | MLB | 19 | 251 | 20 | 11 | 2 | 3 | 21 | 18 | 78 | 2 | 0 | .218/.279/.322 | 70 | .315 | -3.6 | LF 0, RF 0 | -0.6 |

A 2021 fifth-round pick who was young for both his draft class and to get a 2022 full-season assignment, White held his own with a credible .258/.353/.432 performance mostly as an 18-year-old at Low-A. He's another Washington hitting prospect who looks right in the uniform—a switch-hitter with great looking swings, speed, and power potential which shows up at 5 PM. Like most of the rest of the cohort, he hits it on the ground too much and doesn't quite make as much hard contact (or contact at all) as you'd like right now. His noisier setup and timing mechanism seems to be negatively affecting his barrel control at present. Given that he's only playing left field already, he's going to have to hit more than the guys who can carry center.

## 12 Jackson Rutledge RHP
Born: 04/01/99  Age: 24  Bats: R  Throws: R  Height: 6'8"  Weight: 243 lb.  Origin: Round 1, 2019 Draft (#17 overall)

| YEAR | TEAM | LVL | AGE | W | L | SV | G | GS | IP | H | HR | BB/9 | K/9 | K | GB% | BABIP | WHIP | ERA | DRA- | WARP |
|---|---|---|---|---|---|---|---|---|---|---|---|---|---|---|---|---|---|---|---|---|
| 2021 | FBG | A | 22 | 1 | 2 | 0 | 7 | 7 | 22 | 20 | 1 | 3.7 | 10.6 | 26 | 49.2% | .317 | 1.32 | 5.32 | 84 | 0.4 |
| 2021 | WIL | A+ | 22 | 0 | 3 | 0 | 4 | 4 | 10² | 17 | 0 | 7.6 | 8.4 | 10 | 39.5% | .447 | 2.44 | 12.66 | 107 | 0.0 |
| 2022 | FBG | A | 23 | 8 | 6 | 0 | 20 | 20 | 97¹ | 106 | 7 | 2.7 | 9.2 | 99 | 51.2% | .354 | 1.39 | 4.90 | 89 | 1.6 |
| 2023 non-DC | WAS | MLB | 24 | 3 | 3 | 0 | 58 | 0 | 50 | 58 | 7 | 4.0 | 6.5 | 36 | 38.6% | .317 | 1.61 | 5.50 | 137 | -0.7 |

*Comparables: Marco Camarena, Angel Sánchez, Justin Ferrell*

Entering 2022, Rutledge hadn't actually pitched much since he was drafted in the first round in 2019, between the pandemic and a combination of shoulder and blister issues in 2021. He made 20 starts at Low-A last year and while he generally threw strikes, he didn't miss all that many bats. His fastball is now mostly mid-90s with mediocre shape, although he did come on a bit late in the season. Like De La Rosa, the Nationals added him to the 40-man in advance of the Rule 5 Draft anyway—you don't find many 6-foot-8 former first-rounders who can scrape the upper-90s and show a plus slider, and it's not like they have a whole lot of premium talent to protect right now. The option clock is now ticking for him, although a relief fallback is quite plausible in the hopes that he'll show the upper-90s fastball with a plus slider more regularly—and perhaps not even far off.

## 13  Cole Henry  RHP

Born: 07/15/99   Age: 23   Bats: R   Throws: R   Height: 6'4"   Weight: 215 lb.   Origin: Round 2, 2020 Draft (#55 overall)

| YEAR | TEAM | LVL | AGE | W | L | SV | G | GS | IP | H | HR | BB/9 | K/9 | K | GB% | BABIP | WHIP | ERA | DRA- | WARP |
|------|------|-----|-----|---|---|----|----|----|----|----|----|------|-----|----|------|-------|------|------|------|------|
| 2021 | WIL | A+ | 21 | 3 | 3 | 0 | 9 | 8 | 43 | 23 | 3 | 2.3 | 13.2 | 63 | 46.4% | .247 | 0.79 | 1.88 | 74 | 1.0 |
| 2022 | HBG | AA | 22 | 0 | 0 | 0 | 7 | 7 | 23² | 5 | 1 | 3.4 | 10.6 | 28 | 42.6% | .087 | 0.59 | 0.76 | 92 | 0.4 |
| 2022 | ROC | AAA | 22 | 1 | 0 | 0 | 2 | 2 | 8 | 9 | 1 | 2.3 | 6.7 | 6 | 38.5% | .320 | 1.38 | 4.50 | 108 | 0.1 |
| 2023 non-DC | WAS | MLB | 23 | 3 | 3 | 0 | 58 | 0 | 50 | 46 | 6 | 3.8 | 9.0 | 50 | 37.3% | .293 | 1.34 | 3.96 | 105 | 0.1 |

*Comparables: Alex White, Sean Reid-Foley, Carl Edwards Jr.*

If Henry had any track record of health and durability, he'd be the top-ranked pitching prospect in the system. He throws an above-average four-seam and two-seam fastball in the mid-90s. He misses bats with a plus breaker. His changeup has taken steps forward and looks like it's going to get to above-average. His low release point creates strong deception and works well with his arsenal. Of course, he battled arm injuries in college, which was why he was available to the Nats in the second round in 2020 with this quality of arm talent, missed most of 2021 with an elbow issue and ultimately missed most of 2022 with a shoulder injury which turned out to be thoracic outlet syndrome—close to the worst diagnosis a pitcher can get, and one Nationals fans are very familiar with from Stephen Strasburg and Will Harris. Henry will try to make it back in 2023 after surgery, and we'll see if the stuff is still the same when he does.

## 14  Armando Cruz  SS

Born: 01/16/04   Age: 19   Bats: R   Throws: R   Height: 5'10"   Weight: 160 lb.   Origin: International Free Agent, 2021

| YEAR | TEAM | LVL | AGE | PA | R | 2B | 3B | HR | RBI | BB | K | SB | CS | AVG/OBP/SLG | DRC+ | BABIP | BRR | DRP | WARP |
|------|------|-----|-----|----|---|----|----|----|-----|----|----|----|----|-------------|------|-------|-----|-----|------|
| 2021 | DSL NAT | ROK | 17 | 197 | 22 | 8 | 1 | 1 | 17 | 16 | 27 | 11 | 4 | .232/.292/.305 | | .265 | | | |
| 2022 | NAT | ROK | 18 | 226 | 41 | 8 | 2 | 2 | 20 | 11 | 39 | 6 | 5 | .275/.320/.362 | | .329 | | | |
| 2023 non-DC | WAS | MLB | 19 | 251 | 18 | 10 | 1 | 2 | 19 | 14 | 85 | 6 | 2 | .203/.255/.285 | 52 | .310 | -1.4 | SS 0 | -0.8 |

The Nationals tend to swing big in international free agency like they do in the draft, and gave Cruz most of their pool in January 2021 as one of the top prospects on the market. He's only played a trio of games above the complex level, but in both the DSL and FCL he's made a very solid amount of contact without actually impacting the ball that hard. He's on the smaller side without obvious projectability, but he plays a good shortstop and perhaps there's physical growth coming which would enhance his power. For now, he's interesting because of his contact ability and defense, but we'd like to see either his power or swing decisions take a step forward as he moves to full-season ball.

## 15  Israel Pineda  C

Born: 04/03/00   Age: 23   Bats: R   Throws: R   Height: 5'11"   Weight: 188 lb.   Origin: International Free Agent, 2016

| YEAR | TEAM | LVL | AGE | PA | R | 2B | 3B | HR | RBI | BB | K | SB | CS | AVG/OBP/SLG | DRC+ | BABIP | BRR | DRP | WARP |
|------|------|-----|-----|----|---|----|----|----|-----|----|----|----|----|-------------|------|-------|-----|-----|------|
| 2021 | WIL | A+ | 21 | 315 | 35 | 11 | 0 | 14 | 48 | 18 | 83 | 0 | 0 | .208/.260/.389 | 106 | .239 | 0.7 | C(58) -2.6 | 1.0 |
| 2022 | WIL | A+ | 22 | 271 | 31 | 16 | 2 | 8 | 45 | 22 | 70 | 2 | 2 | .264/.325/.443 | 106 | .335 | -1.5 | C(55) -4.1 | 0.5 |
| 2022 | HBG | AA | 22 | 103 | 15 | 3 | 0 | 7 | 21 | 9 | 18 | 1 | 0 | .280/.340/.538 | 124 | .275 | 0.2 | C(22) -2.2 | 0.4 |
| 2022 | ROC | AAA | 22 | 26 | 3 | 1 | 0 | 1 | 5 | 5 | 7 | 0 | 0 | .095/.269/.286 | 96 | .077 | -0.8 | C(5) -0.9 | -0.1 |
| 2022 | WAS | MLB | 22 | 14 | 1 | 0 | 0 | 0 | 1 | 0 | 7 | 0 | 0 | .077/.143/.077 | 75 | .167 | -0.1 | C(4) -0.2 | 0.0 |
| 2023 DC | WAS | MLB | 23 | 89 | 8 | 4 | 0 | 2 | 8 | 5 | 23 | 1 | 0 | .200/.254/.329 | 63 | .251 | -0.1 | C 0 | 0.0 |

*Comparables: John Ryan Murphy, Rob Brantly, Miguel Gonzalez*

Still somehow only 22, Pineda's bat stagnated badly from 2019-21 due to poor swing decisions, and he slipped through last year's Rule 5 Draft. He pushed all the way up from High-A to a big-league cameo during the 2022 season—his plate approach improving from awful to mediocre unlocked the latent usable contact-and-power combination from four or five years ago, and he suddenly looks like a potentially useful offensive catcher. He has a strong arm behind the plate, but his minor-league framing metrics have been rough.

## 16  Matt Cronin  LHP
Born: 09/20/97   Age: 25   Bats: L   Throws: L   Height: 6'2"   Weight: 197 lb.   Origin: Round 4, 2019 Draft (#123 overall)

| YEAR | TEAM | LVL | AGE | W | L | SV | G | GS | IP | H | HR | BB/9 | K/9 | K | GB% | BABIP | WHIP | ERA | DRA- | WARP |
|---|---|---|---|---|---|---|---|---|---|---|---|---|---|---|---|---|---|---|---|---|
| 2021 | WIL | A+ | 23 | 2 | 0 | 4 | 10 | 0 | 14² | 8 | 0 | 3.1 | 17.2 | 28 | 28.6% | .381 | 0.89 | 1.23 | 79 | 0.3 |
| 2021 | HBG | AA | 23 | 0 | 1 | 0 | 10 | 0 | 11¹ | 9 | 2 | 7.9 | 14.3 | 18 | 21.7% | .333 | 1.68 | 5.56 | 84 | 0.2 |
| 2022 | HBG | AA | 24 | 1 | 0 | 0 | 14 | 0 | 16¹ | 5 | 0 | 3.9 | 12.1 | 22 | 26.7% | .167 | 0.73 | 0.00 | 92 | 0.3 |
| 2022 | ROC | AAA | 24 | 3 | 1 | 0 | 34 | 0 | 35² | 30 | 3 | 3.8 | 8.6 | 34 | 35.4% | .281 | 1.26 | 3.53 | 100 | 0.5 |
| 2023 DC | WAS | MLB | 25 | 2 | 2 | 0 | 46 | 0 | 39.7 | 36 | 5 | 4.8 | 9.7 | 43 | 30.6% | .298 | 1.45 | 4.35 | 112 | 0.0 |

Comparables: Donnie Joseph, Mitch Lambson, Kyle McGrath

I must admit, it's kind of puzzling that Cronin hasn't been up yet. We pegged him as a likely 2020 MLB debut as a highly-drafted, close-to-ready reliever on a team which at the time was in a contention cycle. He's not quite throwing as hard as he once did, more low-90s than mid-90s now, but he has two offerings with strong characteristics: a fastball with a strong movement and spin profile he can beat hitters up with, and a high-spin curve he can beat hitters down with. He pitched well in the high minors last year as the Nationals continued to take it slow with him, and should be a long-term bullpen contributor; this time it really should be the year he debuts.

## 17  Roismar Quintana  OF
Born: 02/06/03   Age: 20   Bats: R   Throws: R   Height: 6'1"   Weight: 175 lb.   Origin: International Free Agent, 2019

| YEAR | TEAM | LVL | AGE | PA | R | 2B | 3B | HR | RBI | BB | K | SB | CS | AVG/OBP/SLG | DRC+ | BABIP | BRR | DRP | WARP |
|---|---|---|---|---|---|---|---|---|---|---|---|---|---|---|---|---|---|---|---|
| 2022 | NAT | ROK | 19 | 199 | 41 | 10 | 1 | 5 | 28 | 9 | 46 | 3 | 1 | .289/.342/.439 | | .356 | | | |

Quintana had been impressing on the backfields and flashing a power/contact corner outfielder profile after signing in the 2019 IFA crop, but the pandemic pushed his debut back a year and then he missed all but a week of the 2021 season. He finally had a full go of it in 2022 in the FCL. He did indeed make a solid amount of contact, and he intermittently hit the ball pretty hard too. But chasing out of the zone was a pretty big problem—he only walked nine times in 199 plate appearances—and it's going to be a limitation on the rest of the profile until he gets things sorted out.

## 18  Jake Alu  3B
Born: 04/06/97   Age: 26   Bats: L   Throws: R   Height: 5'10"   Weight: 175 lb.   Origin: Round 24, 2019 Draft (#723 overall)

| YEAR | TEAM | LVL | AGE | PA | R | 2B | 3B | HR | RBI | BB | K | SB | CS | AVG/OBP/SLG | DRC+ | BABIP | BRR | DRP | WARP |
|---|---|---|---|---|---|---|---|---|---|---|---|---|---|---|---|---|---|---|---|
| 2021 | WIL | A+ | 24 | 157 | 22 | 10 | 1 | 5 | 19 | 8 | 32 | 8 | 0 | .303/.357/.490 | 111 | .361 | 0.4 | 2B(19) 0.6, 3B(11) -0.1 | 0.8 |
| 2021 | HBG | AA | 24 | 213 | 26 | 12 | 1 | 5 | 23 | 13 | 43 | 5 | 3 | .264/.315/.411 | 99 | .313 | -0.5 | 3B(33) -0.3, 2B(14) -2.4, 1B(1) 0.0 | 0.3 |
| 2022 | HBG | AA | 25 | 325 | 44 | 25 | 1 | 9 | 36 | 32 | 59 | 9 | 1 | .281/.360/.470 | 122 | .323 | 0.6 | 3B(64) 6.8, LF(4) -0.1, 2B(3) -0.3 | 2.3 |
| 2022 | ROC | AAA | 25 | 242 | 37 | 15 | 1 | 11 | 45 | 19 | 44 | 6 | 2 | .323/.372/.553 | 123 | .353 | 0.8 | 3B(50) 0.3, 2B(6) -0.6 | 1.4 |
| 2023 DC | WAS | MLB | 26 | 227 | 23 | 11 | 1 | 4 | 22 | 14 | 48 | 5 | 1 | .233/.290/.360 | 83 | .284 | 0.5 | 1B 0, 2B 0 | 0.1 |

Comparables: Josh Rojas, Marquez Smith, Freddy Sandoval

A 2019 24th-round senior sign out of Boston College, Alu mashed his way onto the 40-man by hitting .299 and bopping 20 homers in the upper minors last year, as his feel for contact maximized his limited physical power projection. He was mostly a third baseman in 2022 and is a pretty good one; he's played a significant amount of second base in the past as well. He looked to have a decent shot at beating out Carter Kieboom for the 2023 job at the hot corner, but Washington signed Jeimer Candelario, so they're suddenly both blocked.

## 19  Brenner Cox  OF
Born: 05/11/04   Age: 19   Bats: L   Throws: R   Height: 6'3"   Weight: 195 lb.   Origin: Round 4, 2022 Draft (#111 overall)

| YEAR | TEAM | LVL | AGE | PA | R | 2B | 3B | HR | RBI | BB | K | SB | CS | AVG/OBP/SLG | DRC+ | BABIP | BRR | DRP | WARP |
|---|---|---|---|---|---|---|---|---|---|---|---|---|---|---|---|---|---|---|---|
| 2022 | NAT | ROK | 18 | 42 | 4 | 1 | 0 | 1 | 5 | 5 | 14 | 2 | 0 | .286/.366/.400 | | .429 | | | |

A significant prospect in baseball as both a hitter and a pitcher, and football as a dual-threat quarterback, the Nationals enticed Cox out of going to Texas with a way-above-slot $1 million bonus after popping him in 2022's fourth round. He was fairly young for the draft class, runs very well and has a nice, smooth left-handed swing. He checks a lot of the "looks right and projectable" scouting boxes that Washington seems to love. He's basically all projection right now, with little game power or experience against decent pitching, so check back in a year or two to see if he can hit at all.

# 20 Daylen Lile OF

Born: 11/30/02   Age: 20   Bats: L   Throws: R   Height: 6'0"   Weight: 195 lb.   Origin: Round 2, 2021 Draft (#47 overall)

| YEAR | TEAM | LVL | AGE | PA | R | 2B | 3B | HR | RBI | BB | K | SB | CS | AVG/OBP/SLG | DRC+ | BABIP | BRR | DRP | WARP |
|------|------|-----|-----|----|---|----|----|----|-----|----|---|----|----|-------------|------|-------|-----|-----|------|
| 2021 | NAT | ROK | 18 | 80 | 16 | 2 | 0 | 0 | 10 | 15 | 20 | 2 | 1 | .219/.363/.250 | | .311 | | | |

Lile...wait for it...is another prep outfielder who has an aesthetically pleasing left-handed swing and questionable amounts of swing-and-miss in his game. After signing for $1.75 million as a 2021 second-rounder, he missed the entire 2022 season following March Tommy John surgery. We still don't really have any idea if he's going to make enough hard contact (or contact at all) to carry his offensive profile.

## Top Talents 25 and Under (as of 4/1/2023):

1. James Wood, OF
2. Keibert Ruiz, C
3. CJ Abrams, SS/2B
4. Robert Hassell III, OF
5. Elijah Green, OF
6. Cade Cavalli, RHP
7. MacKenzie Gore, LHP
8. Luis García, 2B/SS
9. Víctor Robles, OF
10. Josiah Gray, RHP

Much like the farm system, D.C.'s big-league club is not where you'd hope for it to be after three straight last-place finishes, albeit on the heels of almost a decade of high-level contention capped with the franchise's first World Series title. The second pick in the 2023 draft should be another impact talent, but as it stands, whoever that player may be will join an organization headlined at the big-league level by a solid-but-not-star-level backstop. Ruiz ran a 103 DRC+ and looked like a capable defender, rarely striking out but struggling to muster top-notch power to pair. The 24-year-old should be an above-average regular, and he cannot control who else may be joining him on the field.

That includes Abrams, García and Robles, a triumvirate of highly-touted prospects, two of whom (Abrams and Robles) are among the league's speediest players. Robles has the lengthiest resume of the three at the big-league level and is the unfortunate reigning benchmark for "this guy hits the ball almost as softly as _____" comparisons. Despite that, the 25-year-old center fielder is at least a reasonable big-leaguer, making up for a fair bit of his bat-based-anemia with stellar defense. His fleet-footedness hasn't quite manifested as a consistent base-stealer, but he's generally been a credit in all facets of the game outside of the batter's box. That's a bar Abrams failed to clear in his rookie campaign, as he racked up -9 Outs Above Average, primarily as an overextended shortstop. His range is such that he can often reach the ball, but mechanically he's struggled when delivering the ball accurately on throws. Across the second base bag from him is García, who has improved incrementally at the dish but was staggeringly *even worse* in the field. The upshot is a club with plenty of potential still up the middle but in need of striking mechanical improvements, particularly as shift limitations place more pressure back on infielders.

Gore and Gray will be rotation-mates in 2023, having both spent most of their development in the NL West. Neither has had the fluid onboarding into big-league ball they might've hoped for, but they're primed for extended opportunities in Washington. Of course, for Gore the issue hasn't been opportunity, but consistency and availability.

# The Top 101 Dynasty Prospects

## by Ben Carsley, Jesse Roche and Bret Sayre

The past year has been eventful! Our top-two prospects from 2022–Julio Rodríguez and Bobby Witt Jr.–did not disappoint in their MLB debuts. Both are now top-10 overall dynasty players, with Rodríguez sitting at the No. 1 spot. Yet, with the hits, come the misses. Notably, Spencer Torkelson, Riley Greene, CJ Abrams, Brennen Davis and Shane Baz each had forgettable seasons, due to poor performance, injury or some combination of the two. It is important to remember that prospect development isn't linear. As such, this list represents a snapshot in time. Prospect valuation can change quickly, and be sure to subscribe to Baseball Prospectus for updated rankings throughout the year.

As always, there are a few list-specific disclaimers to go over before we jump in. These rankings are for fantasy purposes only, and they do not directly take into account things like an outfielder's ability to stick in center or a catcher's pop time. That being said, these factors matter indirectly as they affect a player's ability to either stay in the lineup or maintain eligibility. Additionally, we factor in home parks and organizational strengths, just as when we are talking about a major-league player. We can't pretend that these prospects operate in a vacuum, unaffected by park factors. Of course, there's no guarantee that they will reach the majors with their current organization, so while it is reflected, it's not a heavy ranking factor. Most importantly, the intention of this list is to balance the upside, probability, and proximity of these players to an active fantasy lineup.

Within the list below, you'll find important information about each prospect, including their potential fantasy value (in dollars) at their peak and the risk factor associated with reaching their projected output. Also, you will find a fantasy overview, which summarizes the number of categories in which each player will be useful, along with any that carry impact. For this exercise, we defined "impact" as having the potential to be top-25 players in a given category. For instance, impact in home runs roughly equates to the potential to hit 30, impact in steals is 20 and impact for strikeouts is the potential to punch out 200. Then, you'll see a realistic ceiling and floor for each prospect, purely in terms of rotisserie value.

Each player's ceiling is labeled as "FTW" because, well, that's what it might look like if things go swimmingly for them. Each player's realistic floor is "FTX" for reasons you can likely guess. Just remember that these are prospects, so everyone's actual floor is someone you'll never roster in a fantasy league and get burned by over and over until you finally learn to stop touching the stove. The comments are brief because we've already written fantasy-specific comments on each of these players in the individual top-10 lists.

Previous Rank correlates to where repeat entrants placed on the 2022 version of the list. The "NR" key means the player was not ranked, while "N/A" means they were not eligible and "HM" indicates a previous honorable mention. Ages listed are as of 3/30/2023.

With all that said, and without further ado, please enjoy responsibly.

**1. Corbin Carroll, OF, Arizona Diamondbacks**

**Age:** 22.61, **Previous Rank:** 14

**Potential Earnings:** $35+

**Risk Factor:** Low

**Fantasy Overview:** Five-category contributor; impact potential in AVG, R, SB

**Fantasy Impact ETA:** Now

**FTW:** An OF1 you don't have to think much about

**FTX:** Halfway between younger Whit Merrifield and older Whit Merrifield

**2. Gunnar Henderson, 3B/SS, Baltimore Orioles**

**Age:** 21.75, **Previous Rank:** 65

**Potential Earnings:** $35+

**Risk Factor:** Low

**Fantasy Overview:** Five-category contributor; impact potential in HR, R, RBI

**Fantasy Impact ETA:** Now

**FTW:** Alex Bregman, banging and all

**FTX:** Still an easy top-10 third baseman

**3. Jordan Walker, 3B/OF, St. Louis Cardinals**

**Age:** 20.86, **Previous Rank:** 18

**Potential Earnings:** $35+

**Risk Factor:** Medium

**Fantasy Overview:** Five-category contributor; impact potential in HR, RBI

**Fantasy Impact ETA:** Early 2023

**FTW:** A .290/30/10 outfielder who anchors your offense

**FTX:** A properly appreciated Bryan Reynolds

**4. Elly De La Cruz, SS/3B, Cincinnati Reds**

Age: 21.22, **Previous Rank:** 87

**Potential Earnings:** $35+

**Risk Factor:** Medium

**Fantasy Overview:** Four-category contributor; impact potential in HR, SB

**Fantasy Impact ETA:** Late 2023

**FTW:** The prince who was promised

**FTX:** You know what they say about prophecies

**5. Anthony Volpe, SS, New York Yankees**

Age: 21.92, **Previous Rank:** 11

**Potential Earnings:** $25-30

**Risk Factor:** Medium

**Fantasy Overview:** Five-category contributor; impact potential in R, SB

**Fantasy Impact ETA:** Mid 2023

**FTW:** Yankees fans compare him to Derek Jeter

**FTX:** Yankees fans compare him to Gleyber Torres

**6. Jackson Chourio, OF, Milwaukee Brewers**

Age: 19.05, **Previous Rank:** NR

**Potential Earnings:** $30-35

**Risk Factor:** High

**Fantasy Overview:** Five-category contributor; impact potential in HR, R, RBI, SB

**Fantasy Impact ETA:** 2024

**FTW:** The best of the list of 18-year-olds with similar Low-A performance

**FTX:** The worst of the list of 18-year-olds with similar Low-A performance

**7. Jordan Lawlar, SS, Arizona Diamondbacks**

Age: 20.70, **Previous Rank:** 41

**Potential Earnings:** $25-30

**Risk Factor:** Medium

**Fantasy Overview:** Five-category contributor; impact potential in R, SB

**Fantasy Impact ETA:** 2024

**FTW:** Peak Ian Desmond

**FTX:** Are you talking about BP writer Adam Lawler's cousin?

**8. Grayson Rodriguez, RHP, Baltimore Orioles**

Age: 23.37, **Previous Rank:** 12

**Potential Earnings:** $25-30

**Risk Factor:** Medium

**Fantasy Overview:** Four-category contributor; impact potential in W, ERA, K

**Fantasy Impact ETA:** Early 2023

**FTW:** The best arm in Baltimore since Joe Flacco

**FTX:** Pro Bowler Tyler Huntley

**9. James Wood, OF, Washington Nationals**

Age: 20.54, **Previous Rank:** HM

**Potential Earnings:** $30-35

**Risk Factor:** High

**Fantasy Overview:** Four-category contributor; impact potential in HR, RBI

**Fantasy Impact ETA:** 2025

**FTW:** The top Google search result for James Wood

**FTX:** Showing results for James Woods

**10. Druw Jones, OF, Arizona Diamondbacks**

Age: 19.34, **Previous Rank:** N/A

**Potential Earnings:** $30-35

**Risk Factor:** High

**Fantasy Overview:** Four-category contributor; impact potential in HR, R, RBI, SB

**Fantasy Impact ETA:** 2026

**FTW:** Like father, like son

**FTX:** The apple fell far from the tree

**11. Jackson Holliday, SS, Baltimore Orioles**

Age: 19.32, **Previous Rank:** N/A

**Potential Earnings:** $30-35

**Risk Factor:** High

**Fantasy Overview:** Five-category contributor; impact potential in AVG, R, RBI, SB

**Fantasy Impact ETA:** 2026

**FTW:** Corey Seager with some speed

**FTX:** J.P. Crawford with more power but less glove

**12. Josh Jung, 3B, Texas Rangers**

Age: 25.13, **Previous Rank:** 19

**Potential Earnings:** $20-25

**Risk Factor:** Low

**Fantasy Overview:** Four-category contributor; impact potential in HR, RBI

**Fantasy Impact ETA:** Now

**FTW:** Healthy Hank Blalock

**FTX:** Injured Hank Blalock

**13. Ezequiel Tovar, SS, Colorado Rockies**

Age: 21.66, **Previous Rank:** HM

**Potential Earnings:** $20-25

**Risk Factor:** Low

**Fantasy Overview:** Five-category contributor; impact potential in R, SB

**Fantasy Impact ETA:** Now

**FTW:** Amed Rosario in Coors

**FTX:** Remember when we thought Rockies prospects were fun?

### 14. Miguel Vargas, 1B/3B/OF, Los Angeles Dodgers

**Age:** 23.37, **Previous Rank:** 45

**Potential Earnings:** $20-25

**Risk Factor:** Low

**Fantasy Overview:** Four-category contributor; impact potential in AVG, R

**Fantasy Impact ETA:** Early 2023

**FTW:** What we hoped Gavin Lux would become

**FTX:** A positionless version of Gavin Lux

### 15. Curtis Mead, 3B/2B/1B, Tampa Bay Rays

**Age:** 22.43, **Previous Rank:** 97

**Potential Earnings:** $20-25

**Risk Factor:** Medium

**Fantasy Overview:** Four-category contributor; impact potential in AVG, RBI

**Fantasy Impact ETA:** Mid 2023

**FTW:** Nectar of the gods

**FTX:** (Seth) Beer is better

### 16. Eury Pérez, RHP, Miami Marlins

**Age:** 19.96, **Previous Rank:** 74

**Potential Earnings:** $25-30

**Risk Factor:** Medium

**Fantasy Overview:** Four-category contributor; impact potential in W, ERA, K

**Fantasy Impact ETA:** 2024

**FTW:** Tyler Glasnow v 2.0

**FTX:** Just another tall pitcher

### 17. Francisco Álvarez, C, New York Mets

**Age:** 21.36, **Previous Rank:** 29

**Potential Earnings:** $20-25

**Risk Factor:** Medium

**Fantasy Overview:** Three-category contributor; impact potential in HR, RBI

**Fantasy Impact ETA:** Early 2023

**FTW:** A legit 30-homer catcher

**FTX:** Another reason not to trust catchers. Or Mets.

### 18. Andrew Painter, RHP, Philadelphia Phillies

**Age:** 19.97, **Previous Rank:** NR

**Potential Earnings:** $20-25

**Risk Factor:** Medium

**Fantasy Overview:** Four-category contributor; impact potential in W, ERA, K

**Fantasy Impact ETA:** Mid 2023

**FTW:** On display at the Louvre

**FTX:** Local art for sale

### 19. Ricky Tiedemann, LHP, Toronto Blue Jays

**Age:** 20.62, **Previous Rank:** NR

**Potential Earnings:** $20-25

**Risk Factor:** Medium

**Fantasy Overview:** Four-category contributor; impact potential in W, ERA, K

**Fantasy Impact ETA:** 2024

**FTW:** Livin' La Vida Loca

**FTX:** She Bangs

### 20. Triston Casas, 1B, Boston Red Sox

**Age:** 23.21, **Previous Rank:** 20

**Potential Earnings:** $15-20

**Risk Factor:** Low

**Fantasy Overview:** Three-category contributor; impact potential in HR, RBI

**Fantasy Impact ETA:** Now

**FTW:** Mo Vaughn in the modern era

**FTX:** At least they'll get power from their corner OF spots, right? Right?

### 21. Oswald Peraza, SS/2B, New York Yankees

**Age:** 22.79, **Previous Rank:** 34

**Potential Earnings:** $15-20

**Risk Factor:** Low

**Fantasy Overview:** Five-category contributor; impact potential in R, SB

**Fantasy Impact ETA:** Now

**FTW:** A Thairo Estrada you can believe in

**FTX:** The actual Thairo Estrada

### 22. Termarr Johnson, 2B/SS, Pittsburgh Pirates

**Age:** 18.80, **Previous Rank:** N/A

**Potential Earnings:** $25-30

**Risk Factor:** High

**Fantasy Overview:** Four-category contributor; impact potential in AVG, R, RBI

**Fantasy Impact ETA:** 2025

**FTW:** What we thought Willie Calhoun would be

**FTX:** Willie Calhoun

## 23. Jasson Domínguez, OF, New York Yankees
**Age:** 20.15, **Previous Rank:** 32
**Potential Earnings:** $25-30
**Risk Factor:** High
**Fantasy Overview:** Five-category contributor; impact potential in HR, R, RBI, SB
**Fantasy Impact ETA:** 2024
**FTW:** The Martian
**FTX:** Marvin The Martian

## 24. Brett Baty, 3B/OF, New York Mets
**Age:** 23.38, **Previous Rank:** 28
**Potential Earnings:** $20-25
**Risk Factor:** Medium
**Fantasy Overview:** Four-category contributor; impact potential in HR, RBI
**Fantasy Impact ETA:** Early 2023
**FTW:** "Bat" is in the name
**FTX:** Dominic Smith was a thing once, too

## 25. Royce Lewis, SS/OF, Minnesota Twins
**Age:** 23.82, **Previous Rank:** 59
**Potential Earnings:** $20-25
**Risk Factor:** Medium
**Fantasy Overview:** Five-category contributor; impact potential in R, SB
**Fantasy Impact ETA:** Mid 2023
**FTW:** Rolls-Royce
**FTX:** Broken down

## 26. Kyle Manzardo, 1B, Tampa Bay Rays
**Age:** 22.70, **Previous Rank:** NR
**Potential Earnings:** $25-30
**Risk Factor:** Medium
**Fantasy Overview:** Four-category contributor; impact potential in AVG, R, RBI
**Fantasy Impact ETA:** Mid 2023
**FTW:** Reminds people of Joey Votto
**FTX:** Reminds people of Ji-Man Choi

## 27. Emmanuel Rodriguez, OF, Minnesota Twins
**Age:** 20.09, **Previous Rank:** NR
**Potential Earnings:** $25-30
**Risk Factor:** High
**Fantasy Overview:** Five-category contributor; impact potential in HR, R, RBI, SB
**Fantasy Impact ETA:** 2025
**FTW:** Supplants Eduardo Rodriguez as "E-Rod"
**FTX:** George Valera lite

## 28. Marcelo Mayer, SS, Boston Red Sox
**Age:** 20.30, **Previous Rank:** 31
**Potential Earnings:** $20-25
**Risk Factor:** Medium
**Fantasy Overview:** Four-category contributor; impact potential in AVG, R, RBI
**Fantasy Impact ETA:** 2024
**FTW:** May-ya for May-ya
**FTX:** 2019 Andrew Benintendi

## 29. Daniel Espino, RHP, Cleveland Guardians
**Age:** 22.24, **Previous Rank:** 53
**Potential Earnings:** $25-30
**Risk Factor:** High
**Fantasy Overview:** Four-category contributor; impact potential in W, ERA, K
**Fantasy Impact ETA:** Mid 2023
**FTW:** Spencer Strider
**FTX:** We will always remember those four starts in 2022

## 30. Marco Luciano, SS, San Francisco Giants
**Age:** 21.56, **Previous Rank:** 8
**Potential Earnings:** $20-25
**Risk Factor:** Medium
**Fantasy Overview:** Four-category contributor; impact potential in HR, RBI
**Fantasy Impact ETA:** Late 2023
**FTW:** Aramis Ramirez
**FTX:** Heliot Ramos in a couple years

## 31. Evan Carter, OF, Texas Rangers
**Age:** 20.59, **Previous Rank:** NR
**Potential Earnings:** $20-25
**Risk Factor:** Medium
**Fantasy Overview:** Five-category contributor; impact potential in AVG, R, SB
**Fantasy Impact ETA:** 2024
**FTW:** A lot like 2016 Christian Yelich
**FTX:** A lot like 2022 Christian Yelich

## 32. Jackson Merrill, SS, San Diego Padres
**Age:** 19.95, **Previous Rank:** NR
**Potential Earnings:** $25-30
**Risk Factor:** Medium
**Fantasy Overview:** Four-category contributor; impact potential in AVG, R, RBI
**Fantasy Impact ETA:** 2025
**FTW:** .300/20+ shortstop
**FTX:** .270/10+ third baseman

### 33. Endy Rodriguez, C/UT, Pittsburgh Pirates

**Age:** 22.84, **Previous Rank:** NR

**Potential Earnings:** $20-25

**Risk Factor:** Low

**Fantasy Overview:** Four-category contributor; impact potential in AVG, R, RBI

**Fantasy Impact ETA:** Early 2023

**FTW:** An OF1 you don't have to think much about.

**FTX:** Ke'Bryan Hayes at the plate, Carlos Santana in the field

### 34. Noelvi Marte, SS, Cincinnati Reds

**Age:** 21.46, **Previous Rank:** 6

**Potential Earnings:** $20-25

**Risk Factor:** Medium

**Fantasy Overview:** Five-category contributor; impact potential in HR, RBI

**Fantasy Impact ETA:** Late 2023

**FTW:** A little like Manny Machado

**FTX:** The Reds traded Luis Castillo for who?

### 35. Pete Crow-Armstrong, OF, Chicago Cubs

**Age:** 21.01, **Previous Rank:** HM

**Potential Earnings:** $20-25

**Risk Factor:** Medium

**Fantasy Overview:** Five-category contributor; impact potential in R, SB

**Fantasy Impact ETA:** 2024

**FTW:** Starling Marte

**FTX:** Harrison Bader

### 36. Masyn Winn, SS, St. Louis Cardinals

**Age:** 21.03, **Previous Rank:** NR

**Potential Earnings:** $20-25

**Risk Factor:** Medium

**Fantasy Overview:** Five-category contributor; impact potential in R, SB

**Fantasy Impact ETA:** 2024

**FTW:** Trea Turner with just ~10 HR power

**FTX:** Only leaderboard he tops is Arm Strength

### 37. Colton Cowser, OF, Baltimore Orioles

**Age:** 23.03, **Previous Rank:** 76

**Potential Earnings:** $20-25

**Risk Factor:** Medium

**Fantasy Overview:** Five-category contributor; impact potential in AVG, R, RBI

**Fantasy Impact ETA:** Late 2023

**FTW:** Pre-2022 Jesse Winker with some speed

**FTX:** 2022 Jesse Winker with some speed

### 38. Hunter Brown, RHP, Houston Astros

**Age:** 24.59, **Previous Rank:** NR

**Potential Earnings:** $15-20

**Risk Factor:** Low

**Fantasy Overview:** Four-category contributor; impact potential in W, ERA, K

**Fantasy Impact ETA:** Now

**FTW:** The next Cristian Javier

**FTX:** Remember Forrest Whitley?

### 39. Kodai Senga, RHP, New York Mets

**Age:** 30.17, **Previous Rank:** N/A

**Potential Earnings:** $15-20

**Risk Factor:** Low

**Fantasy Overview:** Four-category contributor; impact potential in W, ERA

**Fantasy Impact ETA:** Now

**FTW:** A solid SP3

**FTX:** A solid SP3

### 40. Elijah Green, OF, Washington Nationals

**Age:** 19.32, **Previous Rank:** N/A

**Potential Earnings:** $25-30

**Risk Factor:** High

**Fantasy Overview:** Four-category contributor; impact potential in HR, R, RBI, SB

**Fantasy Impact ETA:** 2026

**FTW:** The next 40/40 superstar

**FTX:** Jo Adell

### 41. Matt Mervis, 1B, Chicago Cubs

**Age:** 24.96, **Previous Rank:** NR

**Potential Earnings:** $15-20

**Risk Factor:** Low

**Fantasy Overview:** Four-category contributor; impact potential in HR, RBI

**Fantasy Impact ETA:** Early 2023

**FTW:** Nathaniel Lowe

**FTX:** A.J. Reed

### 42. Esteury Ruiz, OF, Oakland Athletics

**Age:** 24.13, **Previous Rank:** NR

**Potential Earnings:** $15-20

**Risk Factor:** Low

**Fantasy Overview:** Five-category contributor; impact potential in R, SB

**Fantasy Impact ETA:** Now

**FTW:** 2016 Jonathan Villar

**FTX:** 2017 Jonathan Villar

**43. Zac Veen, OF, Colorado Rockies**
  **Age:** 21.30, **Previous Rank:** 21
  **Potential Earnings:** $20-25
  **Risk Factor:** Medium
  **Fantasy Overview:** Five-category contributor; impact potential in R, SB
  **Fantasy Impact ETA:** 2024
  **FTW:** A Trevor Story-like success story
  **FTX:** We're still waiting on that Brendan Rodgers breakout

**44. Kyle Harrison, LHP, San Francisco Giants**
  **Age:** 21.63, **Previous Rank:** HM
  **Potential Earnings:** $20-25
  **Risk Factor:** Medium
  **Fantasy Overview:** Four-category contributor; impact potential in W, ERA, K
  **Fantasy Impact ETA:** Mid 2023
  **FTW:** Blake Snell
  **FTX:** Sean Newcomb

**45. Gavin Williams, RHP, Cleveland Guardians**
  **Age:** 23.68, **Previous Rank:** NR
  **Potential Earnings:** $20-25
  **Risk Factor:** Medium
  **Fantasy Overview:** Four-category contributor; impact potential in W, ERA, K
  **Fantasy Impact ETA:** Mid 2023
  **FTW:** Early-career Gerrit Cole
  **FTX:** Robert Stephenson

**46. Sal Frelick, OF, Milwaukee Brewers**
  **Age:** 22.95, **Previous Rank:** 96
  **Potential Earnings:** $15-20
  **Risk Factor:** Low
  **Fantasy Overview:** Five-category contributor; impact potential in AVG, R, SB
  **Fantasy Impact ETA:** Early 2023
  **FTW:** A 10/20 Steven Kwan
  **FTX:** Tony Kemp

**47. Connor Norby, 2B/OF, Baltimore Orioles**
  **Age:** 22.81, **Previous Rank:** NR
  **Potential Earnings:** $20-25
  **Risk Factor:** Medium
  **Fantasy Overview:** Five-category contributor; impact potential in R, RBI
  **Fantasy Impact ETA:** Mid 2023
  **FTW:** 2021 Gleyber Torres
  **FTX:** 2021 Gleyber Torres

**48. Taj Bradley, RHP, Tampa Bay Rays**
  **Age:** 22.03, **Previous Rank:** HM
  **Potential Earnings:** $20-25
  **Risk Factor:** Medium
  **Fantasy Overview:** Four-category contributor; impact potential in W, ERA, K
  **Fantasy Impact ETA:** Early 2023
  **FTW:** Athletic Drew Rasmussen
  **FTX:** A Rays reliever

**49. Masataka Yoshida, OF, Boston Red Sox**
  **Age:** 29.71, **Previous Rank:** N/A
  **Potential Earnings:** $10-15
  **Risk Factor:** Low
  **Fantasy Overview:** Four-category contributor; impact potential in AVG, R
  **Fantasy Impact ETA:** Now
  **FTW:** The guy has 4 A's in his first name, he was born for Bah-ston
  **FTX:** Another Alex Verdugo

**50. Shane Baz, RHP, Tampa Bay Rays**
  **Age:** 23.79, **Previous Rank:** 10
  **Potential Earnings:** $25-30
  **Risk Factor:** Extreme
  **Fantasy Overview:** Four-category contributor; impact potential in W, ERA, K
  **Fantasy Impact ETA:** 2024
  **FTW:** The Wizard of Baz
  **FTX:** Baz the Great and Powerful

**51. Brooks Lee, SS, Minnesota Twins**
  **Age:** 22.13, **Previous Rank:** N/A
  **Potential Earnings:** $15-20
  **Risk Factor:** Medium
  **Fantasy Overview:** Four-category contributor; impact potential in AVG, R
  **Fantasy Impact ETA:** 2024
  **FTW:** Sort of like 2022 Carlos Correa
  **FTX:** Sort of like 2022 Nick Gordon

**52. Colson Montgomery, SS, Chicago White Sox**
  **Age:** 21.09, **Previous Rank:** HM
  **Potential Earnings:** $15-20
  **Risk Factor:** Medium
  **Fantasy Overview:** Four-category contributor; impact potential in R, RBI
  **Fantasy Impact ETA:** 2024
  **FTW:** Makes those Corey Seager comps look good
  **FTX:** Post-2019 Yoán Moncada

**53. Harry Ford, C, Seattle Mariners**
**Age:** 20.11, **Previous Rank:** HM
**Potential Earnings:** $20-25
**Risk Factor:** High
**Fantasy Overview:** Five-category contributor; impact potential in R, SB
**Fantasy Impact ETA:** 2025
**FTW:** The next 20/20 catcher
**FTX:** Bad Daulton Varsho

**54. Bobby Miller, RHP, Los Angeles Dodgers**
**Age:** 23.99, **Previous Rank:** 79
**Potential Earnings:** $15-20
**Risk Factor:** Medium
**Fantasy Overview:** Four-category contributor; impact potential in W, K
**Fantasy Impact ETA:** Early 2023
**FTW:** A version of Sandy Alcantara
**FTX:** A version of Brusdar Graterol

**55. Logan O'Hoppe, C, Los Angeles Angels**
**Age:** 23.16, **Previous Rank:** NR
**Potential Earnings:** $10-15
**Risk Factor:** Low
**Fantasy Overview:** Four-category contributor; impact potential in RBI
**Fantasy Impact ETA:** Now
**FTW:** Will Smith
**FTX:** Pre-2021 Danny Jansen

**56. Zach Neto, SS, Los Angeles Angels**
**Age:** 22.17, **Previous Rank:** N/A
**Potential Earnings:** $15-20
**Risk Factor:** Medium
**Fantasy Overview:** Five-category contributor; impact potential in AVG, R
**Fantasy Impact ETA:** Late 2023
**FTW:** Xander Bogaerts with a 20-homer governor
**FTX:** Joey Wendle isn't as bleak as it sounds

**57. Diego Cartaya, C, Los Angeles Dodgers**
**Age:** 21.56, **Previous Rank:** NR
**Potential Earnings:** $15-20
**Risk Factor:** Medium
**Fantasy Overview:** Three-category contributor; impact potential in HR, RBI
**Fantasy Impact ETA:** 2024
**FTW:** Cal Raleigh, in a good way
**FTX:** Gary Sánchez, in a bad way

**58. Gavin Stone, RHP, Los Angeles Dodgers**
**Age:** 24.46, **Previous Rank:** NR
**Potential Earnings:** $15-20
**Risk Factor:** Medium
**Fantasy Overview:** Four-category contributor; impact potential in W, ERA, K
**Fantasy Impact ETA:** Early 2023
**FTW:** They do seem to grow these guys on trees, don't they?
**FTX:** Jackson Kowar

**59. Tink Hence, RHP, St. Louis Cardinals**
**Age:** 20.65, **Previous Rank:** NR
**Potential Earnings:** $20-25
**Risk Factor:** High
**Fantasy Overview:** Four-category contributor; impact potential in W, ERA, K
**Fantasy Impact ETA:** 2025
**FTW:** What if Triston McKenzie threw 96 mph?
**FTX:** The reason we are worried about small frames

**60. Tyler Soderstrom, 1B/C, Oakland Athletics**
**Age:** 21.35, **Previous Rank:** 30
**Potential Earnings:** $15-20
**Risk Factor:** Medium
**Fantasy Overview:** Four-category contributor; impact potential in HR, RBI
**Fantasy Impact ETA:** Late 2023
**FTW:** Peak Wil Myers without speed
**FTX:** A run-of-the-mill 20-homer first baseman

**61. Spencer Jones, OF, New York Yankees**
**Age:** 21.88, **Previous Rank:** N/A
**Potential Earnings:** $20-25
**Risk Factor:** High
**Fantasy Overview:** Four-category contributor; impact potential in HR, RBI
**Fantasy Impact ETA:** 2024
**FTW:** What if Aaron Judge hit left-handed?
**FTX:** What if Gregory Polanco hit left-handed?

**62. Miguel Bleis, OF, Boston Red Sox**
**Age:** 19.08, **Previous Rank:** NR
**Potential Earnings:** $20-25
**Risk Factor:** High
**Fantasy Overview:** Five-category contributor; impact potential in HR, RBI, SB
**Fantasy Impact ETA:** 2026
**FTW:** The next Jackson Chourio
**FTX:** The next Hedbert Perez

**63. Robert Hassell III, OF, Washington Nationals**
  **Age:** 21.63, **Previous Rank:** 22
  **Potential Earnings:** $15-20
  **Risk Factor:** Medium
  **Fantasy Overview:** Five-category contributor; impact potential in AVG, R, SB
  **Fantasy Impact ETA:** 2024
  **FTW:** Peak Andrew Benintendi
  **FTX:** Adam Eaton with the Nationals

**64. Michael Busch, 2B/OF, Los Angeles Dodgers**
  **Age:** 25.15, **Previous Rank:** 64
  **Potential Earnings:** $10-15
  **Risk Factor:** Low
  **Fantasy Overview:** Four-category contributor; impact potential in HR, RBI
  **Fantasy Impact ETA:** Early 2023
  **FTW:** Max Muncy with just 25-30 HR power
  **FTX:** 2020 Max Muncy

**65. Joey Wiemer, OF, Milwaukee Brewers**
  **Age:** 24.14, **Previous Rank:** 85
  **Potential Earnings:** $15-20
  **Risk Factor:** Medium
  **Fantasy Overview:** Four-category contributor; impact potential in HR, RBI, SB
  **Fantasy Impact ETA:** Mid 2023
  **FTW:** Jayson Werth
  **FTX:** Junior Lake

**66. Cam Collier, 3B, Cincinnati Reds**
  **Age:** 18.36, **Previous Rank:** N/A
  **Potential Earnings:** $20-25
  **Risk Factor:** High
  **Fantasy Overview:** Four-category contributor; impact potential in AVG, R, RBI
  **Fantasy Impact ETA:** 2026
  **FTW:** Left-handed Justin Turner
  **FTX:** Ke'Bryan Hayes without speed

**67. Oscar Colas, OF, Chicago White Sox**
  **Age:** 24.54, **Previous Rank:** NR
  **Potential Earnings:** $15-20
  **Risk Factor:** Medium
  **Fantasy Overview:** Four-category contributor; impact potential in HR, RBI
  **Fantasy Impact ETA:** Early 2023
  **FTW:** Yoenis Céspedes
  **FTX:** Yoelqui Céspedes

**68. Tanner Bibee, RHP, Cleveland Guardians**
  **Age:** 24.07, **Previous Rank:** NR
  **Potential Earnings:** $15-20
  **Risk Factor:** Medium
  **Fantasy Overview:** Four-category contributor; impact potential in W, ERA, WHIP
  **Fantasy Impact ETA:** Mid 2023
  **FTW:** Bibee sounds a lot like Bieber
  **FTX:** Zach Plesac

**69. Ceddanne Rafaela, OF/SS, Boston Red Sox**
  **Age:** 22.53, **Previous Rank:** NR
  **Potential Earnings:** $15-20
  **Risk Factor:** Medium
  **Fantasy Overview:** Five-category contributor; impact potential in R, SB
  **Fantasy Impact ETA:** Mid 2023
  **FTW:** Mookie Betts with no plate discipline
  **FTX:** Gilberto Jimenez

**70. Coby Mayo, 3B/1B, Baltimore Orioles**
  **Age:** 21.31, **Previous Rank:** 71
  **Potential Earnings:** $15-20
  **Risk Factor:** Medium
  **Fantasy Overview:** Four-category contributor; impact potential in HR, RBI
  **Fantasy Impact ETA:** 2024
  **FTW:** Austin Riley
  **FTX:** Forever a condiment pun

**71. George Valera, OF, Cleveland Guardians**
  **Age:** 22.38, **Previous Rank:** 26
  **Potential Earnings:** $15-20
  **Risk Factor:** Medium
  **Fantasy Overview:** Three-category contributor; impact potential in HR, RBI
  **Fantasy Impact ETA:** Mid 2023
  **FTW:** Good Joc Pederson
  **FTX:** Bad Joc Pederson

**72. Brandon Pfaadt, RHP, Arizona Diamondbacks**
  **Age:** 24.46, **Previous Rank:** NR
  **Potential Earnings:** $15-20
  **Risk Factor:** Medium
  **Fantasy Overview:** Four-category contributor; impact potential in W, K
  **Fantasy Impact ETA:** Mid 2023
  **FTW:** Joe Musgrove
  **FTX:** Kris Bubic and Dean Kremer also once led the minors in strikeouts

**73. Jett Williams, SS, New York Mets**
**Age:** 19.41, **Previous Rank:** N/A
**Potential Earnings:** $20-25
**Risk Factor:** High
**Fantasy Overview:** Five-category contributor; impact potential in AVG, R, SB
**Fantasy Impact ETA:** 2026
**FTW:** Benny the Jet
**FTX:** Smalls

**74. Junior Caminero, 3B/SS/2B, Tampa Bay Rays**
**Age:** 19.74, **Previous Rank:** NR
**Potential Earnings:** $20-25
**Risk Factor:** High
**Fantasy Overview:** Four-category contributor; impact potential in HR, R, RBI
**Fantasy Impact ETA:** 2025
**FTW:** Eugenio Suárez with a more stable batting average
**FTX:** A reason not to get overly excited about Low-A exit velocities

**75. Gavin Cross, OF, Kansas City Royals**
**Age:** 22.13, **Previous Rank:** N/A
**Potential Earnings:** $15-20
**Risk Factor:** Medium
**Fantasy Overview:** Five-category contributor; impact potential in HR, RBI
**Fantasy Impact ETA:** 2024
**FTW:** Kyle Tucker with half the speed
**FTX:** with half the speed

**76. Gabriel Moreno, C, Arizona Diamondbacks**
**Age:** 23.13, **Previous Rank:** 54
**Potential Earnings:** $10-15
**Risk Factor:** Low
**Fantasy Overview:** Four-category contributor; impact potential in AVG
**Fantasy Impact ETA:** Now
**FTW:** A .290/15 catcher
**FTX:** Christian Vázquez

**77. Mick Abel, RHP, Philadelphia Phillies**
**Age:** 21.62, **Previous Rank:** HM
**Potential Earnings:** $15-20
**Risk Factor:** Medium
**Fantasy Overview:** Four-category contributor; impact potential in W, K
**Fantasy Impact ETA:** 2024
**FTW:** Matt Cain
**FTX:** Please don't use that language in Church, Patty

**78. Adael Amador, SS/2B, Colorado Rockies**
**Age:** 19.97, **Previous Rank:** NR
**Potential Earnings:** $15-20
**Risk Factor:** Medium
**Fantasy Overview:** Five-category contributor; impact potential in AVG, R
**Fantasy Impact ETA:** 2025
**FTW:** Remember when we got irrationally excited about Rockies prospects?
**FTX:** Yea, me neither.

**79. Chase DeLauter, OF, Cleveland Guardians**
**Age:** 21.48, **Previous Rank:** N/A
**Potential Earnings:** $20-25
**Risk Factor:** High
**Fantasy Overview:** Five-category contributor; impact potential in HR, RBI
**Fantasy Impact ETA:** 2024
**FTW:** George Springer
**FTX:** Take your pick of disappointing Guardians first-round outfielders

**80. Cade Cavalli, RHP, Washington Nationals**
**Age:** 24.63, **Previous Rank:** 46
**Potential Earnings:** $15-20
**Risk Factor:** Medium
**Fantasy Overview:** Four-category contributor; impact potential in W, K
**Fantasy Impact ETA:** Early 2023
**FTW:** Luis Garcia on a crappy team
**FTX:** Erick Fedde

**81. Jordan Westburg, SS/2B/3B, Baltimore Orioles**
**Age:** 24.12, **Previous Rank:** NR
**Potential Earnings:** $15-20
**Risk Factor:** Medium
**Fantasy Overview:** Five-category contributor; impact potential in RBI
**Fantasy Impact ETA:** Early 2023
**FTW:** 2019 Paul DeJong
**FTX:** Kevin Smith

**82. Hayden Wesneski, RHP, Chicago Cubs**
**Age:** 25.32, **Previous Rank:** NR
**Potential Earnings:** $10-15
**Risk Factor:** Low
**Fantasy Overview:** Four-category contributor
**Fantasy Impact ETA:** Early 2023
**FTW:** Sonny Gray
**FTX:** Scott Effross has a better career

**83. Bo Naylor, C, Cleveland Guardians**
  **Age:** 23.11, **Previous Rank:** NR
  **Potential Earnings:** $10-15
  **Risk Factor:** Low
  **Fantasy Overview:** Four-category contributor
  **Fantasy Impact ETA:** Early 2023
  **FTW:** 2022 Josh Naylor as a starting catcher
  **FTX:** Pre-2022 Josh Naylor as a backup catcher

**84. Nick Gonzales, 2B/SS, Pittsburgh Pirates**
  **Age:** 23.84, **Previous Rank:** 24
  **Potential Earnings:** $15-20
  **Risk Factor:** Medium
  **Fantasy Overview:** Five-category contributor
  **Fantasy Impact ETA:** Late 2023
  **FTW:** What we hoped Keston Hiura would be
  **FTX:** Keston Hiura

**85. Edwin Arroyo, SS, Cincinnati Reds**
  **Age:** 19.60, **Previous Rank:** NR
  **Potential Earnings:** $20-25
  **Risk Factor:** High
  **Fantasy Overview:** Five-category contributor; impact potential in R, SB
  **Fantasy Impact ETA:** 2025
  **FTW:** Dansby Swanson
  **FTX:** J.P. Crawford

**86. Kevin Parada, C, New York Mets**
  **Age:** 21.66, **Previous Rank:** N/A
  **Potential Earnings:** $20-25
  **Risk Factor:** High
  **Fantasy Overview:** Four-category contributor; impact potential in HR, RBI
  **Fantasy Impact ETA:** 2024
  **FTW:** Todd Hundley with the Mets
  **FTX:** Todd Hundley with the Cubs

**87. Drey Jameson, RHP, Arizona Diamondbacks**
  **Age:** 25.62, **Previous Rank:** HM
  **Potential Earnings:** $15-20
  **Risk Factor:** Medium
  **Fantasy Overview:** Four-category contributor; impact potential in W, K
  **Fantasy Impact ETA:** Now
  **FTW:** His 2022 debut over a full season (3.90 DRA)
  **FTX:** His 2022 Triple-A performance over a full season

**88. Brennen Davis, OF, Chicago Cubs**
  **Age:** 23.41, **Previous Rank:** 9
  **Potential Earnings:** $20-25
  **Risk Factor:** High
  **Fantasy Overview:** Five-category contributor; impact potential in HR, RBI
  **Fantasy Impact ETA:** Mid 2023
  **FTW:** The best version of Ian Happ
  **FTX:** Brett Jackson

**89. DL Hall, LHP, Baltimore Orioles**
  **Age:** 24.53, **Previous Rank:** HM
  **Potential Earnings:** $15-20
  **Risk Factor:** Medium
  **Fantasy Overview:** Four-category contributor; impact potential in K
  **Fantasy Impact ETA:** Now
  **FTW:** Robbie Ray
  **FTX:** Tanner Scott

**90. Henry Davis, C, Pittsburgh Pirates**
  **Age:** 23.53, **Previous Rank:** 56
  **Potential Earnings:** $15-20
  **Risk Factor:** Medium
  **Fantasy Overview:** Four-category contributor; impact potential in HR, RBI
  **Fantasy Impact ETA:** Late 2023
  **FTW:** .260/25 catcher
  **FTX:** Another first-overall bust

**91. Spencer Steer, 3B, Cincinnati Reds**
  **Age:** 25.31, **Previous Rank:** NR
  **Potential Earnings:** $5-10
  **Risk Factor:** Low
  **Fantasy Overview:** Four-category contributor
  **Fantasy Impact ETA:** Now
  **FTW:** 2021 Jonathan India without the steals
  **FTX:** Well, his 2022 debut

**92. Brayan Rocchio, SS/2B, Cleveland Guardians**
  **Age:** 22.21, **Previous Rank:** 47
  **Potential Earnings:** $15-20
  **Risk Factor:** Medium
  **Fantasy Overview:** Five-category contributor; impact potential in R, SB
  **Fantasy Impact ETA:** Late 2023
  **FTW:** Andrés Giménez
  **FTX:** Lost amid dozens of Guardians infield prospects

**93. Kevin Alcantara, OF, Chicago Cubs**

  **Age:** 20.72, **Previous Rank:** HM

  **Potential Earnings:** $20-25

  **Risk Factor:** High

  **Fantasy Overview:** Five-category contributor; impact potential in HR, RBI

  **Fantasy Impact ETA:** 2025

  **FTW:** Fills out and develops 30+ homer power

  **FTX:** All the limbs without the muscle

**94. Jonathan Aranda, 2B/UT, Tampa Bay Rays**

  **Age:** 24.85, **Previous Rank:** NR

  **Potential Earnings:** $10-15

  **Risk Factor:** Low

  **Fantasy Overview:** Four-category contributor; impact potential in AVG, R

  **Fantasy Impact ETA:** Now

  **FTW:** Reliable .290/15+ infielder

  **FTX:** Next Rays bench utility infielder

**95. Ken Waldichuk, LHP, Oakland Athletics**

  **Age:** 25.23, **Previous Rank:** NR

  **Potential Earnings:** $10-15

  **Risk Factor:** Low

  **Fantasy Overview:** Four-category contributor; impact potential in K

  **Fantasy Impact ETA:** Now

  **FTW:** Oakland pitcher in early '00s

  **FTX:** Oakland pitcher in early '20s

**96. Dustin Harris, OF/1B, Texas Rangers**

  **Age:** 23.73, **Previous Rank:** HM

  **Potential Earnings:** $15-20

  **Risk Factor:** Medium

  **Fantasy Overview:** Five-category contributor

  **Fantasy Impact ETA:** Late 2023

  **FTW:** A 20/20 1B

  **FTX:** Random PTBNL in forgotten Mike Minor trade

**97. Garrett Mitchell, OF, Milwaukee Brewers**

  **Age:** 24.57, **Previous Rank:** 89

  **Potential Earnings:** $5-10

  **Risk Factor:** Low

  **Fantasy Overview:** Five-category contributor; impact potential in SB

  **Fantasy Impact ETA:** Now

  **FTW:** Good Drew Stubbs

  **FTX:** Bad Drew Stubbs

**98. Dalton Rushing, C/1B, Los Angeles Dodgers**

  **Age:** 22.11, **Previous Rank:** N/A

  **Potential Earnings:** $15-20

  **Risk Factor:** High

  **Fantasy Overview:** Four-category contributor; impact potential in HR, RBI

  **Fantasy Impact ETA:** 2025

  **FTW:** Former Louisville catcher Will Smith

  **FTX:** Former Louisville catcher Colby Fitch

**99. Brady House, SS, Washington Nationals**

  **Age:** 19.82, **Previous Rank:** 51

  **Potential Earnings:** $15-20

  **Risk Factor:** High

  **Fantasy Overview:** Four-category contributor; impact potential in HR, RBI

  **Fantasy Impact ETA:** 2025

  **FTW:** 2011 J.J. Hardy without the glove

  **FTX:** Carter Kieboom

**100. Owen Caissie, OF, Chicago Cubs**

  **Age:** 20.73, **Previous Rank:** 75

  **Potential Earnings:** $15-20

  **Risk Factor:** High

  **Fantasy Overview:** Four-category contributor, impact potential in HR, RBI

  **Fantasy Impact ETA:** 2024

  **FTW:** O Canada

  **FTX:** Adam Loewen, the hitter (yes, he's Canadian)

**101. Christian Encarnacion-Strand, 3B/1B, Cincinnati Reds**

  **Age:** 23.33, **Previous Rank:** NR

  **Potential Earnings:** $15-20

  **Risk Factor:** Medium

  **Fantasy Overview:** Three-category contributor; impact potential in HR, RBI

  **Fantasy Impact ETA:** Late 2023

  **FTW:** Pre-2022 Franmil Reyes

  **FTX:** 2022 Franmil Reyes

# Top-100 First-Year Player Rankings for Dynasty Drafts

## by Jesse Roche and Bret Sayre

**B**efore we dive into the rankings, let's explore the landscape of first-year-player drafts (FYPDs) and how to approach this year's class. We last opined on the quality of the MLB draft class in July, stating, in part:

> For several years, this class received tons of hype. Phrases like "generational talent" have been bandied about for several prospects. Indeed, this class is replete with high-upside talent. In addition, strong bloodlines is a theme throughout this class, including the first two players selected. Most importantly, however, this is a deep, fantasy-friendly, hitter-heavy class.

These early observations hold true, and, since the draft, much has happened! Kodai Senga and Masataka Yoshida, two premier players from Nippon Professional Baseball (NPB), have signed substantial five-year contracts, and they are both poised to make an immediate MLB impact. The international signing period, and many high-upside prospects—such as Felnin Celesten, Brando Mayea and Ethan Salas—will officially enter this FYPD class. Finally, early-return debuts—positive and negative—have caused slight, and some drastic, movement within the MLB draft class.

## The State of the FYPD Class

Buckle up! Upcoming FYPDs are going to be a wild ride.

This class is loaded from top to bottom. Headlining the class, Druw Jones and Jackson Holliday are both arguably top-10 dynasty prospects with elite fantasy and real-life upside. Meanwhile, Elijah Green, aforementioned "generational talent," has plus-plus or better power and speed potential, and he is already cranking out 110-mph exit velocities with a wood bat. Then, Senga and Yoshida offer immediate production for competitive teams. And that just touches the tip of the iceberg of this FYPD class's fantasy goodness. Indeed, this class includes a staggering fifteen players in the top-100 dynasty prospects.

This FYPD class is not perfect, however. (Yes, the 2019 class is perfect.) Pitching throughout this class carries more risk than ever, with injuries attached to almost all the top arms. The following pitchers have undergone Tommy John surgery: Dylan Lesko, Cade Horton, Landon Sims, Connor Prielipp, Reggie Crawford and Peyton Pallette, among others. Kumar Rocker's shoulder appears to be a ticking bomb. Carson Whisenhunt was suspended for the 2022 season due to a failed drug test. The list goes on and on. Regardless, this class is not without some intriguing arms with big stuff.

Another likely common pitfall of this FYPD is trap picks. Several players selected early in the MLB Draft should rank far lower in FYPDs for dynasty, most notably, Rocker and Jacob Berry. As always, do not behold yourself to real-life draft order.

In sum, this FYPD class is exciting! If there is ever a year to hoard FYPD picks, it is this one.

## How to Approach FYPDs

It may go without saying, but before and during any draft, including a FYPD, you must:

- **Understand your league scoring.** Player values change across league formats. Most FYPD rankings are developed for standard 5×5 dynasty leagues. (We explicitly note that ours are.) For different formats, you should adjust your rankings.

- **Understand your league size and roster construction.** Meanwhile, how many prospects your league rosters should influence how you approach your draft. For example, you may choose to target high-ceiling prospects in shallow leagues and high-floor prospects in deep leagues. If your league rosters fewer than 200 prospects, you may not want to aggressively target players likely to debut at the complex in July with later picks. Back-end roster flexibility is often vital when you seek to burn and churn through pop-up prospects to find the next breakout. Borderline players unlikely to play until midseason should remain watchlist options in such leagues.

- **Understand your leaguemates and be flexible.** As with any draft, rankings are useful guides, but they are not gospel. Read the draft room, manager predilections and draft trends. It is all about squeezing the most value out of your selections. If it means slightly reaching for a coveted player that is likely to be taken before your next pick, do it. Get your guys! Be prepared and willing to deviate from rankings to account for your league.

- **Don't undervalue picks.** Picks provide flexibility, speculative uncertainty and, well, excitement until the selection is made. Many owners desire picks for this reason. Plus, drafting is part of the fun!

- **Don't undervalue Kodai Senga and Masataka Yoshida.** Both international prospects are established professionals with years of high-end performance in NPB. While they are not your typical first-year player, they should not be overlooked. Both should immediately contribute in meaningful ways in all fantasy formats.

- **Fade 16- and 17-year-old international signees.** As set forth below, selecting a "true J2 signee"–an untested, 16-year-old prospect–is a gamble. While some true J2 signees develop into stars, the track record of recent true J2 signees is poor. Further, the opportunity cost of rostering these prospects until their debut in the Dominican Summer League (DSL) in late June is often high. Meanwhile, true, unheralded J2 signees who break out are readily available on waivers in nearly all formats. It is best to bypass these prospects unless the acquisition cost is so reasonable that it easily offsets anticipated opportunity cost.

## Dynasty Valuation of MLB Draftees

The international signing period begins on January 15 (formerly, July 2). To be eligible, an international player must turn 17 years old before September 1. Typically, the vast majority of high-profile international signees are 16- and 17-year-old prospects. Meanwhile, each class often includes a handful of more established, under-25-year-old international players who are still subject to international signing pools (e.g., Yoán Moncada in 2015, Luis Robert in 2017).

The valuation of international free agents fluctuates year to year. Certainly, some years include the standout 16-year-old prospect who comes with unreasonable expectations (such as Jasson Domínguez and Kevin Maitan). However, most years, these extremely young, raw prospects receive inconsistent press and reports that understandably change dramatically over a short period. Further, these prospects do not debut until midseason–normally in the DSL–and likely do not arrive in the majors for five years or longer.

It is hard to wait.

Indeed, Bret Sayre once wrote about ranking Kevin Maitan at 13th overall in 2017 (notably lower than others in the industry): "Since I started making these lists, I haven't even had a true J2 signee inside the top-25, so putting one this high is a bit of a statement I guess." Bret learned a lesson that year.

Below is a table with first-year-player draft ranking of these players over the years:

| Year | Players (Rank) |
|------|---------------|
| 2022 | Roderick Arias (14), Cristhian Vaquero (16), Ricardo Cabrera (23), *Oscar Colas (29), Won-Bin Cho (31), Lazaro Montes (32), Diego Benitez (36), William Bergolla Jr. (40), Dyan Jorge (41), Anthony Gutierrez (43), Ryan Reckley (50) |
| 2021 | Wilman Diaz (14), Carlos Colmenarez (15), Cristian Hernandez (25), *Pedro Leon (30), *Yoelkis Céspedes (31) |
| 2020 | Jasson Domínguez (4), Erick Peña (13), Robert Puason (19), Luis Rodriguez (32), Bayron Lora (44) |
| 2019 | *Victor Victor Mesa (3), *J.P. Martinez (13), Marco Luciano (27), Noelvi Marte (43), Diego Cartaya (47) |
| 2018 | *Luis Robert (3), Wander Franco (27), *Adolis García (33), *Jose Barrero (34), Ronny Mauricio (47) |
| 2017 | *Lourdes Gurriel Jr. (8), *Yuli Gurriel (11), Kevin Maitan (13), *Adrian Morejon (17), *Jorge Oña (18), *Norge Ruiz (32), *Randy Arozarena (33) |
| 2016 | *Yoán Moncada (1), *Eddy Martinez (11), *Yusniel Díaz (15), *Yadier Álvarez (23), Vladimir Guerrero Jr. (27), Lucius Fox (36) |
| *Established international player | |

As gleaned from the table above, the track record of recent, well-regarded true J2 signees is poor. Of course, selecting a true J2 signee is a risk that some dynasty players simply will not take. Too often, dynasty players either get caught up in chasing the next big thing or scared away due to recent disappointing performances from such high-profile signees. Most dynasty players, and the industry at large, are now more firmly within the second group.

This ebb and flow of dynasty valuation is important to remember ahead of any first-year-player draft. It is vital to recall the successes of years past. The top-four players in the Top-500 Dynasty Rankings are all former true J2 signees. In fact, none of those players were even considered potential star fantasy players at the time of signing.

Below is a table illustrating the six most notable players in each international class since 2015:

| Signing Year | Notable Players |
|---|---|
| 1/15/2022 | Oscar Colas, Jarlin Susana, Josue De Paula, Anthony Gutierrez, Lazaro Montes, Cristhian Vaquero |
| 1/15/2021 | Jackson Chourio, Miguel Bleis, Edgar Quero, Gabriel Gonzalez, Yiddi Cappe, Pedro Leon |
| 7/2/2019 | Eury Pérez, Jasson Domínguez, Emmanuel Rodriguez, Junior Caminero, Adael Amador, Alex Ramirez |
| 7/2/2018 | Elly De La Cruz, Francisco Álvarez, Marco Luciano, Noelvi Marte, Endy Rodriguez, Diego Cartaya |
| 7/2/2017 | Julio Rodríguez, Wander Franco, Luis Robert, Ezequiel Tovar, Miguel Vargas, Brayan Bello |
| 7/2/2016 | Randy Arozarena, Alejandro Kirk, Oswald Peraza, Lourdes Gurriel Jr., Roansy Contreras, Luis García |
| 7/2/2015 | Juan Soto, Yordan Alvarez, Fernando Tatis Jr., Vladimir Guerrero Jr., Jazz Chisholm Jr., Andrés Giménez |

Some years have fallen flat. (Looking at you, Kevin Maitan and the 2016 class!) However, most years have included several big hits.

Even so, many of the above were not even considered top international prospects at signing. For example, dynasty managers likely scooped recent standout IFAs–Elly De La Cruz, Jackson Chourio and Eury Perez–off waivers during the season. Indeed, other than Oscar Colas, the top-two ranked IFAs from 2022–Jarlin Susana and Josue De Paula–likely were not drafted in most formats. (In fact, neither were drafted in one of my 30-team leagues.) As noted above, it is the best practice to avoid true J2 signees in FYPDs and be proactive in adding such prospects via waivers following positive reports or at a sign of a breakout in the DSL.

Most international free agents likely should be watchlist fodder in the vast majority of dynasty leagues (200 or less prospects). For deeper leagues, these prospects are solid mid-to-late round targets and stashes if–and only if–the price is very, very right.

## Concluding Thoughts

This FYPD class possesses the most potential since the epic 2019 class. The hype has been building for some time, and, by all means, it is justified. There is a prospect for every dynasty desire. At the same time, this class is deep with intriguing prospects well past the top 50. Even its weakest area–pitching–could develop into a strength as injured arms prove healthy and others emerge. The time to buy in on this class is now, via accumulation of picks or, for those who have already drafted, prospects before glowing reports are supported and/or gains are consolidated during the upcoming season.

With all that said, and without further ado, please enjoy responsibly.

(Ages listed as of 3/30/2023)

## Top 20

### 1. Druw Jones, OF, Arizona Diamondbacks, Age: 19.34

The son of superstar Andruw Jones, Druw is also a potential Gold Glove center fielder with plus speed and huge power potential. His high-waisted and broad-shouldered 6-foot-4 frame that oozes projection is a scout's dream. Jones has plus bat speed and already flashes above-average raw power to all fields with more likely to come as he continues to fill out his frame. However, Jones' present game power lags well behind where it may ultimately develop, as his flat swing and tendency to seek out contact over damage limit how much power he gets to in games. Meanwhile, he has solid bat-to-ball skills, especially for such a tall kid, with advanced pitch recognition, allowing projection on his hit tool. Yet, like all prep bats, he has hit tool variance, and his swing likely requires some work as he has had some issues making consistent contact and can struggle to pull the ball with authority. Even so, Jones possesses rare 30/20 potential with a solid foundation for his hit tool and, arguably, he has the most fantasy upside in this class.

### 2. Jackson Holliday, SS, Baltimore Orioles, Age: 19.32

The first-overall pick, Holliday is yet another son of a former MLB star, Matt Holliday. (Growing up around the game has its advantages.) An incredible spring season–which included breaking J.T. Realmuto's national high school record for hits–catapulted him to the top of the class. Unsurprisingly, Holliday has advanced bat-to-ball ability, makes solid swing decisions and runs up contact rates among the best in the prep class. Indeed, in his brief debut between the complex and Low-A (.297/.489/.422), he had an impeccable 12-to-27 strikeout-to-walk ratio. Holliday also has a sweet lefty swing with plus bat speed and excellent hip rotation and barrel feel that "should grow into 25+ home run power in time." All in all, he is a potential "plus-hit/plus-power shortstop" and a plus runner adept at stealing bases, including a perfect 30-for-30 last spring. Given his advanced, well-rounded skill set, Holliday is in play to be the first player selected in FYPDs, and a top-20 overall dynasty prospect.

## Top 21-50

### 3. Termarr Johnson, 2B, Pittsburgh Pirates, Age: 18.8

Johnson is not your prototypical top-five pick. He is short (5-foot-7) with little-to-no projection remaining and likely will only lose a step as he matures. His bat, though, is arguably the most advanced of all prep hitters. Johnson has elite bat speed, hand-eye coordination and barrel accuracy. His bat path is a dream, designed to create lift and damage. Indeed, Johnson flashes above-average raw power, and, arguably, his swing and quick hands allow him to tap into all of his power and then some in games. After settling into pro ball in his debut, he torched the Florida State League (FSL), averaging a robust 90.4-mph exit velocity with 9 of 30 balls in play over 100 mph. Finally, he has enough speed and baserunning acumen to contribute some steals, including four stolen bases in his debut. Despite such a lauded hit tool, however, his swing has a noticeable hitch, and he both whiffs and chases more often than ideal. Regardless, Johnson should still generate high averages and OBPs with "20-home run pop" and double-digit stolen bases. That is a pretty nifty fantasy player.

### 4. Kodai Senga, RHP, New York Mets, Age: 30.17

Senga has been among NPB's preeminent starting pitchers since 2016, and his eventual international free agency has been long awaited. Way back in 2020, we wrote:

> Senga has been one of the most dominant pitchers in NPB since 2016. This past year, he led NPB in strikeouts (227) by 39. His raw stuff matches his elite performance, with a mid- to upper-90s fastball; a double-plus, diving splitter; and a power cutter/slider. Indeed, many consider his forkball splitter to be one of the best splitters in the world. However, Senga has struggled with inconsistent command, at times, and elevated walk rates over the past two years. In addition, he is unlikely to be posted and not eligible for international free agency until 2022. With that said, Senga has legitimate frontline-starter upside, especially if he refines his command.

Much of that writeup remains true today. Senga's fastball averaged 96 mph last year in NPB, and touched as high as 102 mph, yet its mediocre shape causes it to play down and miss fewer bats than you'd expect. His "ghost fork" remains a lethal, bat-missing offering. There are concerns about his command (though, it has improved), the effectiveness of his cutter and slider, and his durability. Senga has a slight 6-foot-0 frame and has only pitched more than 148 innings once in his career. Further, the recent poor transition of Yusei Kikuchi, another hard-throwing arm from NPB, provides a fresh reminder for some caution. That said, Senga's track record compares more favorably to Kenta Maeda (though he throws much, much harder), and his splitter is a true game-changing offering.

Senga joins Justin Verlander and Max Scherzer in a stacked rotation on a hefty five-year deal. While he may not be a workhorse, he should provide strong ratios, plenty of strikeouts, and, of course, tons of @PitchingNinja GIFs. As of today, PECOTA projects Senga for 148 strikeouts, a sparkling 3.22 ERA and a 1.26 WHIP, while the depth charts team expects him to throw 132 innings.

### 5. Elijah Green, OF, Washington Nationals, Age: 19.32

Green sat atop this draft class for some time before scary swing-and-miss issues surfaced. Much like high-school teammate James Wood before him, though, Green rebounded last spring, nearly halving his whiff rate while somewhat easing concerns about his ability to handle fastballs up and breakers away. His raw power, which he routinely gets to in games due to a leveraged swing, is among the best in this prep class, already generates 110-plus mph exit velocities with a wood bat and comfortably projects to plus-plus. To top it off, Green has plus-plus or better speed and elite acceleration. In his brief debut, he showcased his power, speed and, well, his swing-and-miss (45.4% whiff rate). Yet, he just needs to make enough contact to allow his otherworldly combination of power and speed to shine. It is not hard to envision him developing into a 30/30 fantasy monster. If you're after pure, unadulterated upside, Green is the prospect for you.

# Top 51-100

### 6. Masataka Yoshida, OF, Boston Red Sox, Age: 29.71

Like Kodai Senga above, Yoshida has been a steady fixture in NPB since 2018. We last wrote about him in 2020, stating:

*Yoshida stands at just 5-foot-8, but he packs a punch, tallying 55 home runs over the last two years. He generates plus raw power from a lightning quick and leveraged swing. Meanwhile, he has a feel to hit with advanced plate discipline, resulting in a 64-to-79 strikeout-to-walk ratio last year. Due to injury-shortened seasons, Yoshida has only accrued approximately three years of service time. As such, he likely is not even eligible to be posted until after the 2022 season. Still, his bat should be worth the wait and a hold in open universe formats.*

Since then, Yoshida has continued to lay waste to NPB and even improved his spectacular plate discipline, inducing twice as many walks as strikeouts over the last three years. While he likely doesn't possess plus raw power as we once opined, he is far from punchless with an explosive swing capable of generating double-digit home runs and plenty of doubles. Where Yoshida truly stands out, however, is his elite bat-to-ball ability and selective approach. He immediately compares favorably with the best contact hitters in MLB while offering more pop. As of today, PECOTA projects Yoshida to hit .286/.383/.452 with 15 home runs over 557 plate appearances.

### 7. Brooks Lee, SS, Minnesota Twins, Age: 22.13

Many will label Lee as a prospect who is "better in real-life than fantasy." They'd be wrong. Lee is a physical, bat-first, switch-hitting shortstop at high risk of moving to third base long-term due to middling athleticism. Despite a "jank" swing, Lee has uncanny bat-to-ball ability, with in-zone contact rates around 90%, superb pitch recognition and solid plate discipline. While he can generate solid exit velocities and hard contact to all fields, his approach trends hit-over-power with tons of low-lying contact, as evidenced by a 56.9% ground-ball rate in his debut. Even so, he has done nothing but hit over the past year plus, including .404/.432/.667 in the Cape Cod League, .357/.462/.664 in his junior year and .303/.389/.451 in his debut. All told, Lee has underrated upside, and his offensive peak could look remarkably similar to former Twins shortstop Carlos Correa last year.

### 8. Zach Neto, SS, Los Angeles Angels, Age: 22.17

Neto, a small conference bat, hits and hits and hits. In his college career, he has hit .403/.500/.751 with 27 home runs and 31 stolen bases over 100 games, including an incredible 19-to-39 strikeout-to-walk ratio last year. While he has limited exposure against top arms, he stood out in the Cape Cod League (.304/.439/.587) and, more importantly, in Double-A (.313/.380/.508). His small-school background, only average raw power and unorthodox swing, including an exaggerated leg kick with less than two strikes, casts some doubt on the viability of his bat. Nevertheless, Neto has shown advanced contact skills and regularly puts the ball in the air to the pull side with backspin to maximize his game power. While he may lack a clear plus tool projection, he does everything well and could develop into a five-category producer capable of going .280/20/15. Plus, Neto is on a fast track to the majors, and the Angels have recently pushed draftees quickly, such as Chase Silseth last year.

### 9. Spencer Jones, OF, New York Yankees, Age: 21.88

Jones has and will inevitably receive left-handed Aaron Judge comps (even before the Yankees drafted him) due to his size (6-foot-7), gargantuan power, surprising athleticism and similar college performance. His college batted-ball data is truly wild, including a max exit velocity of 119 mph and a 90th-percentile exit velocity of 112 mph. For MLB context, only Giancarlo Stanton had a higher 90th-percentile exit velocity (114 mph). Of course, that data was aided by a metal bat, but he flashed big exit velocities with a wood bat in the FSL as well. Unfortunately, his flat swing (like Judge in college) generates tons of line drives and groundballs, which limits how much power he gets to in games. Indeed, Jones had a low, 5.7 degree average launch angle resulting in a 47.7% ground-ball rate in Low-A. Further, he does have some underlying swing-and-miss that likely will always be present due to his size. Regardless, his upside is sky high (see Judge) if it all comes together with a realistic shot at 80-grade raw power at maturity.

### 10. Cam Collier, 3B, Cincinnati Reds, Age: 18.36

Collier is another son of a former MLB player, Lou Collier. At just 17 years old, he acquitted himself well at Chipola Junior College (.333/.419/.537), showcasing elite bat-to-ball ability (89% zone contact rate) and plate discipline. In addition, he already flashes solid raw power with plus exit velocities for his age cohort and he "is likely to add significant physical strength." At present, however, his flat swing, hit-over-power approach and inconsistent quality of contact calls into question his ultimate game power potential. Yet, Collier has been aggressively pushed and has still excelled, including an impressive, albeit very brief, debut at the complex (.370/.514/.630). How he performs as likely one of the youngest prospects in the FSL next year will be telling. As Bret Sayre noted, "If 25-homer power comes, he could be a Justin Turner-type corner infielder with future .300 seasons sprinkled in."

### 11. Jett Williams, SS, New York Mets, Age: 19.41

"Jett" is an apt moniker for the 5-foot-8 speedster. He has plus speed and acceleration with both aggression and instincts to be a consistent threat to steal bases. Despite his size, Williams is an explosive hitter with a lightning-fast and compact swing, advanced bat-to-ball ability and sneaky power, including impressive exit velocities for his age. At present, his approach and short swing favors hit over power, and there is a risk "the power may play more in the 40 range" long term. The underlying power is there to unlock, though, providing Williams legitimate five-category potential.

### 12. Gavin Cross, OF, Kansas City Royals, Age: 22.13

Cross can mash with easy plus raw power, including a 90th-percentile exit velocity of 109 mph in college. His contact skills and swing decisions both took a step forward, and, together with solid bat control and hand-coordination, allow a potential-plus projection on his future hit tool. Ultimately, Cross offers a fantasy-friendly hit-power profile with even a little speed for good measure. His future home park is not ideal, but he has enough pop to overcome its power-suppressing environment.

### 13. Chase DeLauter, OF, Cleveland Guardians, Age: 21.48

DeLauter is the premier mystery box of FYPDs after a broken foot that cut his season short. On paper, he pops, with wild stats in college (.437/.576/.828) and in the Cape Cod League (.298/.397/.589). His dominant performance on the Cape juxtaposed against a poor, whiff-heavy showing against Florida State early last year and questionable competition at James Madison have many uncertain about his impact potential. While his swing is unconventional, he makes plenty of contact and has exceptional plate discipline. Additionally, DeLauter has a large 6-foot-4 frame that generates plus raw power that he gets to in games with a lofted swing. Oh, and he has present plus speed–evidenced by a 6.4-second 60-yard dash time at James Madison's pro day–that he aggressively uses on the bases. The outstanding question, though, as it often is for small conference players, is whether he will hit more advanced pitching. DeLauter's track record and tools do stand out and provide hope for a .270/25/15 long-term outcome.

### 14. Kevin Parada, C, New York Mets, Age: 21.66

Much like Henry Davis before him, Parada, an ACC catcher, was arguably the top college bat in this draft class after hitting .361/.453/.709 with 26 home runs and just 10.5% strikeouts. His unique blend of bat-to-ball ability, advanced plate approach and above-average power potentially project to "a .270, 20+ home run outcome." Such offensive upside at catcher is rare (well, maybe less so these days).

### 15. Dalton Rushing, C, Los Angeles Dodgers, Age: 22.11

Normally, we recommend exercising caution approaching loud debuts of advanced college bats in late-season Low-A. Well, let's throw caution to the wind! Rushing absolutely ran roughshod over Low-A pitching (.424/.539/.778), showcasing eye-opening exit velocities and an impeccable approach. It is the type of rare, meaningful small sample to which expectations should be adjusted. His loud debut lends further support to his late-college breakout–.310/.470/.686 with 23 home runs in his junior year and .314/.401/.542 in the Cape Cod League–after serving two years as the backup catcher to Henry Davis. Overlook his second-round draft cost, because Rushing is a first-round talent.

That said, catching prospects are often a trap. They may offer exciting offensive tools and projection, but they're stifled–in both production and ETA–by the demands of the position. Parada and Rushing are no different.

# Top 101-150

### 16. Drew Gilbert, OF, Houston Astros, Age: 22.51

Gilbert can do it all: make tons of contact (quality contact at that), exhibit strong plate discipline and flash plus raw power and plus speed. His college zone-contact rate (89%) and average exit velocity (94 mph) were among the best in the class. Yet, his flat bat path leads to a lot of that hard contact going into the ground. As a result, his present game power is a shade of his raw power. Gilbert flashed all his tools in his brief, injury-shortened debut (dislocated right elbow), hitting .313/.405/.531 with two home runs, six stolen bases and just two strikeouts (5.1%) in 10 games between the complex and Low-A. The whole package is slightly similar to Alek Thomas, who was also underrated coming out of his draft.

### 17. Cole Young, SS, Seattle Mariners, Age: 19.67

Young "had one of the best hit tools among the 2022 prep draft class" with exceptional plate discipline and advanced bat-to-ball skills, feel to hit and barrel control. Despite a lack of physicality, he has sneaky pop, which may get to average, but nonetheless plays down in games due to penchant for hard, low-lying contact, as evidenced by his 58.1% ground-ball rate in his debut. Regardless, Young can really hit, and he impressed in his aforementioned debut, hitting .367/.423/.517 with just 11.3% strikeouts between the complex and Low-A. It is likely not a high-upside profile, but he could provide high batting averages with mid-double-digit home runs and stolen bases at peak.

### 18. Jace Jung, 2B, Detroit Tigers, Age: 22.49

Jung, the younger brother of the Rangers' Josh Jung, had an underwhelming debut in High-A, struggling to impact the ball while mustering a paltry .101 ISO. As arguably one of the more advanced college bats, his pro performance, coming on the heels of struggles late in the college season, was particularly concerning. At his best, Jung has elite plate discipline–evidenced by an 18.6% walk rate in his debut–with solid contact skills and all-field power despite a setup reminiscent of Chuck Knoblauch. Given his defensive shortcomings, he'll really need to hit to carve out a big-league role.

### 19. Dylan Lesko, RHP, San Diego Padres, Age: 19.56

Lesko underwent Tommy John surgery (TJS) on April 26, 2022, and he will likely miss the first half of the 2023 season. Yet, he still ranks as the top fantasy pitching prospect in this draft class. He starts with a mid-90s fastball that generally sits 92-95 mph and touches 97 mph, with a ridiculous combination of carry and ride. At its best, it profiles as a potential plus offering, though it more regularly sits comfortably above-average. His best offering, however, is a low-80s changeup with elite separation, fading action and command. Finally, Lesko sports an improved high-spin, upper-70s curveball with above-average depth. Should he add a harder breaking ball, such as a slider in the mid-80s, to round out his repertoire, he would have one of the best stuff-command mixes in the minors. Of course, right-handed prep pitchers coming off TJS are far from a safe dynasty play, but Lesko's top-of-the-rotation upside is worth the risk.

### 20. Cooper Hjerpe, LHP, St. Louis Cardinals, Age: 22.04

Hjerpe is a funky lefty with a sub-4.5-foot vertical and -3.5-foot horizontal release point–lower and wider than any starting pitcher in MLB–and is coming off a dominant season in which he was named the National Pitcher of the Year. In addition to his unique release point, he has superb command of three solid offerings that miss bats. While his fastball only sits in the low-90s, his release point and plus extension allows it to play way up. His mid-to-upper-70s slider has huge two-plane movement that is even more lethal considering where he releases the ball. Finally, his upper-70s changeup has solid velocity separation, depth and running action. The whole profile is bizarre, and, frankly, unheard of in the modern game. It is easy to place Hjerpe in the future backend starter bucket based on his raw stuff, but his delivery truly separates him and provides sneaky mid-rotation or better upside.

# Top 151-200

### 21. Brock Porter, RHP, Texas Rangers, Age: 19.82

Don't let where Porter landed in the draft fool you. He received a massive over-slot deal ($3.7 million) commensurate with the slot value of a mid-first-rounder. His stuff rivals any pitching prospect in this class, with a fastball that sits in the mid-to-upper 90s with solid carry and run. Like Lesko above, Porter has an advanced, upper-70s "helicopter" changeup with strong arm speed and fading action. While his stuff pops, his breaking balls and command are works in progress, and his long arm action and borderline-violent delivery can cause inconsistency. Nonetheless, Porter has an exciting starter kit with a premium, projectable frame and a big fastball.

### 22. Eric Brown Jr., SS, Milwaukee Brewers, Age: 22.28

Brown has an unusual setup, akin to Julio Franco, with his bat positioned over his head and angled toward the pitcher, and then his bat actually drifts almost in front of his face as he begins a big leg kick before uncoiling at the ball. Naturally, his swing has its detractors. Incredibly, Brown has no issue making contact. In fact, his contact rates were among the best in the college class, including a 95% zone contact rate. Further, he rarely chases (13%) or, well, swings (34%) for that matter, and how his seemingly elite plate discipline holds up against pro pitching will be telling. Meanwhile, he generates above-average exit velocities, though his swing and hitting approach likely will result in less over-the-fence pop than you'd otherwise expect. Brown also offers above-average speed and should be a weapon on the bases. In his debut, Brown was 19-for-21 in steals across just 27 games! While that type of pace is unsustainable, he has legit wheels–he was also 13-for-15 across 33 games in the Cape Cod League in 2021.

### 23. Jacob Berry, 3B, Miami Marlins, Age: 21.9

On paper, Berry shines as one of the top college performers the last two years (.360/.450/.655 with 32 home runs) and a strictly bat-first prospect selected early in the MLB draft. While he certainly demonstrates advanced plate discipline, bat-to-ball skills and pitch recognition, he lacks impact raw power. His college average (85.2 mph) and 90th percentile (103.6 mph) exit velocities easily trailed all other first-round college hitters. Then, in his debut, which included a healthy sample of 104 batted-ball events, he maxed out at just 103 mph. That said, Berry is able to lift to his pull side regularly and generally taps into all of his raw power in games. In addition to his raw power concerns, he is without a defensive home, adding even more pressure to his bat. Ultimately, his profile may look awfully like Alec Burleson, though there remains hope for more.

### 24. Cade Horton, RHP, Chicago Cubs, Age: 21.61

Horton, a former two-sport star and excellent athlete, is a late bloomer who underwent TJS in 2021, struggled at times in his return to the mound this year and then absolutely dominated the College World Series. At his best, he showcases a high-spin, mid-to-upper-90s fastball and an upper-80s wipeout slider that often earns plus-plus grades. Given his limited track record, Horton is a bit riskier than other college arms, though he arguably has the highest ceiling.

### 25. Felnin Celesten, SS, Seattle Mariners, Age: 17.54

As noted in the Primer, the risk, necessary lead time and opportunity cost of drafting and rostering 16- and 17-year-old international free agents–especially given the recent poor track record of such well-regarded prospects–often outweighs the acquisition cost. As such, it is generally advisable to fade these prospects in FYPDs.

That said, Celesten offers substantial upside. A switch-hitter, he has a sweet swing from both sides of the plate, promising bat speed, burgeoning power and present plus speed.

### 26. Justin Crawford, OF, Philadelphia Phillies, Age: 19.21

Crawford is...wait for it...another legacy. The son of Carl likely will garner substantial fantasy buzz due to his bloodlines and elite speed, including an eye-popping 6.11-second 60-yard dash in 2021. However, the rest of his game is sushi raw. While he has strong bat-to-ball ability, he is hyper-aggressive at the plate and is basically a slap-and-dash hitter at the moment, including a 62.5% ground-ball rate in his debut. To make matters worse, his hitting style severely limits his present power output. Crawford offers a lot to dream on, but is far more of a project than you'd expect and may be another Johan Rojas in a few years. Of course, the upside is, well, do you remember what his father did?

### 27. Kumar Rocker, RHP, Texas Rangers, Age: 23.36

Arguably the most divisive prospect in this draft class, Rocker still boasts a devastating fastball-slider combo. After that, there are so many questions. His XL frame, inconsistent fastball velocity and command, and concerning shoulder health add more risk (including relief risk) than ideal. Even if his health limits his long-term viability, Rocker could arrive quickly and burn bright. If he turns into Dinelson Lamet 2.0, would fantasy managers be disappointed?

### 28. Ivan Melendez, 1B, Arizona Diamondbacks, Age: 23.18

Melendez is a right-handed hitting and throwing, first-base only prospect who is old for the draft class–not your typical fantasy darling. Yet, he arguably was the most impressive college hitter last year with a season for the ages, hitting .387/.508/.863 with 32 home runs and high-end batted-ball data, all in a major conference no less. His less-than-stellar debut (.207/.349/.368 in Low-A) has pumped the brakes on his hype. However, Melendez trails only Spencer Jones in raw power, makes consistent hard contact, regularly barrels up the ball, puts the ball in the air to all fields, makes plenty of contact and has strong plate discipline. The offensive bar for his profile is high, but much of the same was said about Pete Alonso (also a second-round pick) years ago.

### 29. Shintaro Fujinami, RHP, Oakland Athletics, Age: 28.97

In the shadow of more prominent NPB newcomers detailed above, Fujinami may go under the radar in FYPDs. The Athletics recently signed him for an one-year, $3.25 million deal and reportedly plan to use him in the rotation. An early-career phenom in NPB, Fujinami lost his command and reverted to a swingman for the last three years. Yet, his walk rate improved from a ghastly 15.0% in 2021 to 8.2% last year, and he eclipsed 100 innings for the first time since 2018. He's a 6-foot-6 flamethrower who sits over 95 mph with two solid secondaries in his slider and splitter. If he sticks in the rotation and if his command gains hold—both big ifs—he could provide surprising fantasy value in 2023 and beyond. If not, he may be an early roster-crunch casualty. Rebuilding dynasty teams need not target Fujinami. For all other teams, he is an intriguing back-of-the-roster flier with a likely acquisition cost much more reasonable than this ranking.

### 30. Brandon Barriera, LHP, Toronto Blue Jays, Age: 19.07

Barriera is not your typical prep pitching prospect. He has advanced command of a deep repertoire. How effective those pitches may become, however, is unclear. His four-seam fastball has good velocity, often sitting 93-96 mph and touching the upper-90s, but it lacks carry and generally has poor shape. Barriera's breaking balls–a mid-to-upper-70s curveball and a low-to-mid-80s slider–both flash bat-missing depth and sweeping action. His more seldom-used changeup displays solid separation and depth. All three secondaries are potential average or better offerings. The whole package may not sound exciting, and his slight frame is far from that of a typical starting pitcher, but, with more maturation and pro instruction, he could develop into a mid-rotation starter.

## Top 201-250

### 31. Dylan Beavers, OF, Baltimore Orioles, Age: 21.64

The Orioles seemingly have a type: college bats with unique traits. Beavers is no exception. Despite a prototypical 6-foot-4 corner outfield frame, he lacks true plus power, though his "power is more of the sneaky kind" as he is adept at putting the ball in the air and barreling the ball. Further, his contact skills are mediocre, particularly against breaking balls, but buoyed by a lot of hard contact and superb plate discipline. Beavers is also "a solid runner, but will settle into the kind of foot speed better suited for left field" long term. There is far more risk in his offensive profile than ideal, but he landed in a fantastic organization that may further unlock his potential.

### 32. Sal Stewart, 3B, Cincinnati Reds, Age: 19.31

"There's a shot for a plus hit, plus power bat here," you say? Stewart is a big, power-hitting corner bat with advanced contact skills who may ultimately call hitter-friendly Great American Ball Park his home park. Regardless where he lands defensively, his bat should play.

### 33. Mikey Romero, SS, Boston Red Sox, Age: 19.22

Romero feels awfully similar to Nick Yorke. Perceived as a low-upside hitter, he has superb bat-to-ball skills, a quick bat and sneaky pop, though his approach that favors all-field spray contact limits his game power. Jeffrey Paternostro loosely compared Romero's bat to Mets-era Daniel Murphy, who hit .288/.331/.424 over seven seasons.

### 34. Brando Mayea, OF, New York Yankees, Age: 17.55

Every year, the Yankees are attached to a high-profile international signee and dole out a hefty bonus. This year, that player is Mayea. While he lacks the size of others in the class, he has exceptional bat speed and a compact, powerful swing that portends solid future hit and power tools.

### 35. Tucker Toman, 3B, Toronto Blue Jays, Age: 19.38

Toman, a switch-hitter, is much better from the left side and flashes solid bat speed, bat-to-ball ability and pop, allowing above-average projection on both his hit and power tools.

### 36. Jacob Misiorowski, RHP, Milwaukee Brewers, Age: 20.99

For those chasing pure, unadulterated upside in FYPDs, Misiorowski is for you. His lanky 6-foot-7 frame promises further projection, yet his fastball already sits in the upper 90s with elite bat-missing carry and shape. In addition to his heater, his sharp power slider is another elite bat-missing weapon. The issue is that he has no command. Yet, if command comes, he is likely the best bet to skyrocket up rankings akin to Ricky Tiedemann last year.

### 37. Ethan Salas, C, San Diego Padres, Age: 16.83

Salas, the younger brother of Marlins prospect Jose, has an advanced feel to hit for his age with a picturesque swing that already generates solid power. As for any young prospect, and 16-year-old catchers in particular, Salas is light years away from his MLB debut.

### 38. Jordan Beck, OF, Colorado Rockies, Age: 21.95

The last time the Rockies successfully developed a hitting prospect was Ryan McMahon, drafted nearly 10 years ago. (The jury remains out on Brendan Rodgers and Ezequiel Tovar.) That atrocious track record must be taken into account in evaluating the potential fantasy impact of Beck (and later Sterlin Thompson). Coors Field can only help so much. With that important caveat out of the way, Beck has tangible offensive upside with plus-plus raw power and some speed. Like many college hitters in this range, however, he also has whiff- and approach-related issues that lead to questions about his future hit tool.

### 39. Peyton Graham, SS, Detroit Tigers, Age: 22.18

Graham offers tantalizing power-speed potential stemming from a highly projectable and athletic 6-foot-3 frame. Unfortunately, he has an aggressive approach with so-so bat-to-ball ability, pitch recognition and quality of contact. Graham's debut did not ease those concerns. His whiff (32.4%) and swinging-strike (15.1%) rates were borderline average for the FSL, which is particularly troubling for an advanced college bat. Meanwhile, the quality of his contact is not yet strong enough to buoy those contact issues. Graham may possess intriguing upside, but it is far more theoretical than ideal for a 22-year-old prospect entering next year.

### 40. Daniel Susac, C, Oakland Athletics, Age: 21.88

Last year, Susac outperformed fellow catching prospects Kevin Parada and Dalton Rushing in 90th-percentile max exit velocities and both contact and zone-contact rates. Unfortunately, he has no plate discipline. Among college hitters selected in the first two rounds, Susac easily had the highest swing and chase rates. More advanced pitchers likely will victimize his swing-happy approach. So while Susac arguably has plus contact skills and plus raw power, he may neither hit for much average or power due to his approach.

## Top 251-300

### 41. Owen Murphy, RHP, Atlanta Braves, Age: 19.51

Murphy may lack size (6-foot-1), velocity (low 90s), or much projection, but he offers intriguing upside due to his athleticism, advanced arsenal, solid command, and feel for spin. Further, his fastball plays up due to a low release height. Should he happen upon a bit more velocity, which is never a given, Murphy could explode up rankings.

### 42. Jud Fabian, OF, Baltimore Orioles, Age: 22.51

Fabian was an early contender to be selected first overall in 2021. Unfortunately, a junior season marred by strikeouts (29.4%) caused him to fall to the second round. Of course, he didn't sign, then proceeded to incrementally improve before being selected slightly later last year. Those improvements included a reduced strikeout rate (still high) and improved contact rate (still well below-average). Fabian will forever entice with his excellent plate discipline, plus power and solid speed, and it is possible that the Orioles will unlock his potential. So far, so good, after a strong debut in which he hit .333/.455/.615. (But, remember what we said about college bats crushing late-season Low-A pitching.)

### 43. Blade Tidwell, RHP, New York Mets, Age: 21.81

Considered a potential first-round pick entering this spring, Tidwell suffered shoulder soreness and missed the first six weeks of the college season. Given his missed time, he received extensive time in Low-A to end the season, where he was electric and helped lead St. Lucie to the FSL championship. Tidwell has an explosive fastball that averaged 95.7 mph, topping out at 97.7 mph, with bat-missing carry and run. His most intriguing pitch, however, may be his changeup, which possesses 11.5-mph separation from his fastball and excellent depth, particularly relative to his fastball. Tidwell's slider/cutter has inconsistent shape, and it can be flat, but it also flashes solid two-plane movement. As with most power arms, he has to develop better command and consistency with his secondaries. If he does, Tidwell could quickly put himself in the top-100 conversation.

### 44. Jacob Melton, OF, Houston Astros, Age: 22.56

Melton's college performance–.360/.424/.671 with 17 home runs and 21 stolen bases–is the type that fantasy managers salivate over. His raw power and speed both resoundingly support his production. Yet, will he be able to hit? He is a streaky, aggressive hitter with below-average contact rates and elevated ground-ball rates.

### 45. Landon Sims, RHP, Arizona Diamondbacks, Age: 22.24

Before undergoing Tommy John surgery in March, Sims was dominant, with an analytically-favored mid-90s fastball and lethal, mid-80s sweeping slider. Given his injury history and two-pitch arsenal, he has plenty of relief risk, but those two pitches and his command are strong enough to go five innings in the modern game.

### 46. Roman Anthony, OF, Boston Red Sox, Age: 18.88

Anthony has the type of huge physical tools that fantasy managers crave. Further, his contact skills have steadily improved, including an impressive 9.6% strikeout rate between the complex and Low-A in his debut. At the same time, however, Anthony put everything on the ground (60.6%) and failed to hit for much power. He'll need to marry his sizable raw power with his bat-to-ball ability to break out.

### 47. Tyler Locklear, 3B, Seattle Mariners, Age: 22.35

Locklear is a hulking slugger from a small conference and likely a right-right, 1B-only prospect. But, man, his power is something else. In addition to the thump, he has exhibited solid contact skills and plate discipline, albeit against inferior competition. Early pro returns are promising, though, including a .282/.353/.504 line with seven home runs and big exit velocities in Low-A. Locklear is effectively Ivan Melendez 20 spots later because he carries more risk.

### 48. Brock Jones, OF, Tampa Bay Rays, Age: 21.79

A standout at Stanford, Jones had a combined 39 home runs and 30 stolen bases over 121 games between 2021 and 2022. Yet, he also had a combined 137 strikeouts. In fact, his contact and in-zone contact rates were by far the worst among college hitters drafted in the first two rounds, including Jud Fabian. Jones continued to whiff in his debut and ran up a 33.9% strikeout rate in late-season Low-A. Yikes. When he makes contact, however, it is often hard and at good angles. Will he make enough contact, though?

### 49. Xavier Isaac, 1B, Tampa Bay Rays, Age: 19.29

Isaac is a rare prospect: a first-round prep first baseman. The last year that prep 1B-only prospects were selected on the first day of the draft was 2018 (Triston Casas and Grant Lavigne). They represent the high-risk/high-reward proposition of the profile. Isaac at least trends closer to Casas than Lavigne, with "true top-of-the-scale power potential." The risk: He develops into a one-tool player given concerns about his hit tool and generally poor quality of competition in high school. The reward: In four years, Isaac may be in a similar position that Casas is in now.

### 50. Robby Snelling, LHP, San Diego Padres, Age: 19.28

Snelling offers plus athleticism–he was also a four-star football recruit as a linebacker–with a physical, workhorse frame. While his fastball only sits in the low-90s, it plays up due to advanced command and solid carry and run. Meanwhile, his best pitch is an upper-70s curveball with bat-missing depth. Snelling lacks the projection of other prep arms, but his athleticism and present stuff portends further improvement with pro instruction.

## Top 301-350

**51. Joendry Vargas, SS, Los Angeles Dodgers, Age: 17.39**
**52. Noah Schultz, LHP, Chicago White Sox, Age: 19.65**
**53. Connor Prielipp, LHP, Minnesota Twins, Age: 22.22**
**54. Sterlin Thompson, OF, Colorado Rockies, Age: 21.76**
**55. Max Wagner, 3B, Baltimore Orioles, Age: 21.61**
**56. Cade Doughty, 2B, Toronto Blue Jays, Age: 22.01**
**57. Enmanuel Bonilla, OF, Toronto Blue Jays, Age: 17.19**
**58. Carson Whisenhunt, LHP, San Francisco Giants, Age: 22.44**
**59. Justin Campbell, RHP, Cleveland Guardians, Age: 22.13**
**60. Henry Bolte, OF, Oakland Athletics, Age: 19.66**

Schultz offers as much ceiling as height (6-foot-9). As projectable as they come, he already flashes mid-90s velocity from a unique release point with a bat-missing slider.

Wagner is a true pop-up prospect from the spring, as he went from a bench player to the ACC Player of the Year after hitting .370/.496/.852 with 27 home runs. How much of that performance is to be believed, given his short track record, pull-heavy approach and underlying swing-and-miss?

Doughty hit 21 home runs over 85 games between LSU and his debut in Low-A. Yet, his raw power is currently below average, including a weak 99.9-mph 90th-percentile exit velocity from him in college. That said, Doughty has strong bat-to-ball skills and advanced feel for the barrel, and a large portion of his hard contact falls in favorable launch angle buckets. As a bat-first second baseman, however, he will need to hit and it is unclear if his future hit or power tools will be anything more than average.

## Top 351-400

**61. Ryan Clifford, OF, Houston Astros, Age: 19.69**
**62. J.R. Ritchie, RHP, Atlanta Braves, Age: 19.76**
**63. Cayden Wallace, 3B, Kansas City Royals, Age: 21.65**
**64. Brailer Guerrero, OF, Tampa Bay Rays, Age: 16.76**
**65. Reggie Crawford, LHP, San Francisco Giants, Age: 22.32**
**66. Jackson Ferris, LHP, Chicago Cubs, Age: 19.21**
**67. Sebastian Walcott, SS, Texas Rangers, Age: 17.04**
**68. Walter Ford, RHP, Seattle Mariners, Age: 18.26**
**69. Drew Thorpe, RHP, New York Yankees, Age: 22.5**
**70. Luis Morales, RHP, Oakland Athletics, Age: 20.52**

Clifford, an 11th-round selection who signed for $1.26 million, possesses a beautiful left-handed swing and intriguing hit-power potential. Likely sitting at or near the bottom of the defensive spectrum, however, he'll really need to hit to eventually carve out a future MLB role.

Wallace flashed power-speed potential at Arkansas and in his debut. Yet, his swing and approach likely limits his game power to around average. Further, his inconsistent contact quality and some underlying swing-and-miss raises questions about his future hit tool. Regardless, Wallace could develop into a 20/15 bat that should stick at the hot corner.

Power defines Crawford at the plate and on the mound. Beyond that, he is a project with the common issues associated with great power–swing-and-miss as a hitter and command and control as a pitcher. Tommy John surgery further complicates matters. Crawford's underlying issues and unclear future role create a lot of risk, but he landed in a strong development organization that could unlock his massive upside.

## Top 401-450

**71. Jacob Miller, RHP, Miami Marlins, Age: 19.64**
**72. Colby Thomas, OF, Oakland Athletics, Age: 22.18**
**73. Derniche Valdez, SS, Chicago Cubs, Age: 17**
**74. Nick Morabito, OF, New York Mets, Age: 19.9**
**75. Danny Serretti, SS, Detroit Tigers, Age: 22.9**
**76. Adam Mazur, RHP, San Diego Padres, Age: 21.94**
**77. Ryan Cermak, OF, Tampa Bay Rays, Age: 21.83**
**78. Robert Moore, 2B, Milwaukee Brewers, Age: 21**
**79. Josh Kasevich, SS, Toronto Blue Jays, Age: 22.2**
**80. Chandler Pollard, 2B, Texas Rangers, Age: 18.91**

College senior signees are often overlooked within the industry and in first-year player drafts. Serretti, however, is not your typical senior sign. The switch-hitting infielder displays a patient, disciplined approach with promising contact skills buoyed by a hit-over-power, line-drive and gap-to-gap stroke. While he lacks big power, Serretti is not punchless, and has enough pop to clear the fence on occasion. Already, he closed the season as one of the only draft prospects in Double-A.

A disastrous 2022 season (.232/.374/.427) understandably caused Moore's draft stock to plummet. While he flashed solid power at times, he generally struggled to impact the ball, including a cringeworthy 23% hard-hit rate. There is reason for hope, though. Moore was on fire in the Australian Baseball League, hitting .279/.366/.490 with seven home runs and 14 stolen bases. His strong bat-to-ball ability, sneaky pop and plus speed at second base could be a nice fantasy-friendly package if his quality of contact returns to pre-2022 levels.

Kasevich may have one of the best hit tools in this draft class, pairing elite contact rates with superb plate discipline. Unfortunately, he offers little else. While he makes a ton of contact, most of his batted balls go into the ground (59.6%). His hit-over-power approach causes his below-average power to play down even further. To make (fantasy) matters worse, Kasevich also has little speed and is unlikely to be much of a threat on the bases. Effectively, he projects as an empty-average hitter, much like Adam Frazier and his ilk.

## Top 451-500

**81. Luis Guanipa, OF, Atlanta Braves, Age: 17.32**
**82. Thomas Harrington, RHP, Pittsburgh Pirates, Age: 21.72**
**83. Nathan Martorella, 1B, San Diego Padres, Age: 22.12**
**84. Peyton Pallette, RHP, Chicago White Sox, Age: 21.89**
**85. Tanner Schobel, 2B, Minnesota Twins, Age: 21.82**
**86. Clark Elliot, OF, Oakland Athletics, Age: 22.5**
**87. Jacob Reimer, 3B, New York Mets, Age: 19.11**
**88. Parker Messick, LHP, Cleveland Guardians, Age: 22.43**
**89. Chandler Simpson, OF, Tampa Bay Rays, Age: 22.37**
**90. Ben Joyce, RHP, Los Angeles Angels, Age: 22.54**

Martorella is a poor man's Kyle Manzardo. He is a smaller, 1B-only prospect with fringe power but strong bat-to-ball skills and plate discipline. Between the Cape Cod League and his junior season, he had a 40-to-53 strikeout-to-walk ratio, and he began tapping into more power last spring. Pro instruction might unlock another level, and Martorella had a solid debut (.322/.421/.511).

Schobel also has an advanced hit tool backed by strong bat-to-ball ability and a keen eye. Although he launched 19 home runs last spring (and hit .362/.445/.689), he lacks much raw power, and what power he does have mostly is limited to the pull side. Most importantly, however, he has solid speed, which he showcased in his debut (8-for-9 in stolen bases). Schobel likely has limited fantasy upside, but offers enough potential hitting ability, pop and speed to be a useful fantasy player down the line.

Simpson is Xavier Edwards 2.0. His true bottom-of-the-scale power resulted in a wild 6% hard-hit rate last year. What he does do, however, is make elite levels of contact (92%) with elite plate discipline while stealing all the bases. His top-of-the-scale speed amplifies his slap-and-dash approach and allows him to regularly hit for high averages despite his lack of any power. Simpson's profile has a poor track record (see Edwards), but, every once in a while, it hits (see Billy Hamilton).

## Honorable Mentions

**91. Alfredo Duno, C, Cincinnati Reds, Age: 17.23**
**92. Cole Phillips, RHP, Atlanta Braves, Age: 19.84**
**93. Jun-Seok Shim, RHP, Pittsburgh Pirates, Age: 18.98**
**94. Joe Lampe, OF, Cleveland Guardians, Age: 22.32**
**95. Logan Tanner, C, Cincinnati Reds, Age: 22.39**
**96. Jared McKenzie, OF, Washington Nationals, Age: 21.87**
**97. Jake Bennett, LHP, Washington Nationals, Age: 22.33**
**98. Jonathan Cannon, RHP, Chicago White Sox, Age: 22.7**
**99. Chase Meidroth, 2B, Boston Red Sox, Age: 21.69**
**100. Dominic Keegan, C, Tampa Bay Rays, Age: 22.66**

—*Jesse Roche and Bret Sayre are authors of Baseball Prospectus.*

# Team Codes

| CODE | TEAM | LG | AFF | NAME |
|---|---|---|---|---|
| ABD | Aberdeen | SAL | Orioles | IronBirds |
| ABQ | Albuquerque | PCL | Rockies | Isotopes |
| ADE | Adelaide | ABL | - | Giants |
| AGS | Aguascalientes | MEX | - | Rieleros |
| AGU | Aguilas | LIDOM | - | Aguilas |
| AKR | Akron | EAS | Guardians | RubberDucks |
| ALT | Altoona | EAS | Pirates | Curve |
| AMA | Amarillo | TEX | D-backs | Sod Poodles |
| ANG | ACL Angels | ACL | Angels | ACL Angels |
| ANG | AZL Angels | AZL | Angels | AZL Angels |
| ARA | Aragua | LVBP | Tigres | Tigres |
| ARK | Arkansas | TEX | Mariners | Travelers |
| ASB | FCL Astros Blue | | Astros | FCL Astros Blue |
| ASGO | AZL Athletics Gold | AZL | Athletics | AZL Athletics Gold |
| ASGR | AZL Athletics Green | AZL | Athletics | AZL Athletics Green |
| ASH | Asheville | SAL | Astros | Tourists |
| ASO | FCL Astros Orange | | Astros | FCL Astros Orange |
| AST | FCL Astros | FCL | Astros | FCL Astros |
| AST | GCL Astros | GCL | Astros | GCL Astros |
| ATH | ACL Athletics | ACL | Athletics | ACL Athletics |
| ATL | Atlanta | NL | - | Braves |
| AUG | Augusta | CAR | Braves | GreenJackets |
| AZ | Arizona | NL | - | D-backs |
| BAL | Baltimore | AL | - | Orioles |
| BEL | Beloit | MID | Marlins | Sky Carp |
| BEL | Beloit | A+ C | Marlins | Snappers |
| BG | Bowling Green | SAL | Rays | Hot Rods |
| BIR | Birmingham | SOU | White Sox | Barons |
| BLU | FCL Blue Jays | | Blue Jays | FCL Blue Jays |
| BLU | GCL Blue Jays | GCL | Blue Jays | GCL Blue Jays |
| BLX | Biloxi | SOU | Brewers | Shuckers |
| BNG | Binghamton | EAS | Mets | Rumble Ponies |
| BOS | Boston | AL | - | Red Sox |
| BOW | Bowie | EAS | Orioles | Baysox |
| BRA | FCL Braves | | Braves | FCL Braves |
| BRA | GCL Braves | GCL | Braves | GCL Braves |
| BRB | AZL Brewers Blue | AZL | Brewers | AZL Brewers Blue |
| BRD | Bradenton | FSL | Pirates | Marauders |
| BRG | AZL Brewers Gold | AZL | Brewers | AZL Brewers Gold |
| BRI | Brisbane | ABL | Bandits | Bandits |

| CODE | TEAM | LG | AFF | NAME |
|---|---|---|---|---|
| BRK | Brooklyn | SAL | Mets | Cyclones |
| BRWB | ACL Brewers Blue | ACL | Brewers | ACL Brewers Blue |
| BRWG | ACL Brewers Gold | ACL | Brewers | ACL Brewers Gold |
| BUF | Buffalo | INT | Blue Jays | Bisons |
| BUR | Burlington | MID | Angels | Bees |
| CAG | Caguas | PWL | Caguas | Caguas |
| CAM | Campeche | MEX | - | Piratas |
| CAN | Canberra | ABL | Cavalry | Cavalry |
| CAR | Carolina | CAR | Brewers | Mudcats |
| CAR | FCL Cardinals | | Cardinals | FCL Cardinals |
| CAR | GCL Cardinals | GCL | Cardinals | GCL Cardinals |
| CAR | Carolina | PWL | Carolina | Carolina |
| CAR | Caracas | LVBP | Leones | Leones |
| CC | Corpus Christi | TEX | Astros | Hooks |
| CHA | Charlotte | INT | White Sox | Knights |
| CHA | Charlotte | FSL | Rays | Stone Crabs |
| CHA | Chattanooga | SOU | Reds | Lookouts |
| CHC | Chi Cubs | NL | - | Cubs |
| CIN | Cincinnati | NL | - | Reds |
| CLE | Cleveland | AL | - | Guardians |
| CLE | Cleveland | AL | - | Guardians |
| CLI | Clinton | MID | Marlins | LumberKings |
| CLR | Clearwater | FSL | Phillies | Threshers |
| CLT | Charlotte | INT | White Sox | Knights |
| COL | Colombia | CS | - | Colombia |
| COL | Colorado | NL | - | Rockies |
| COL | Columbia | CAR | Royals | Fireflies |
| COL | Columbus | INT | Guardians | Clippers |
| CR | Cedar Rapids | MID | Twins | Kernels |
| CSC | Charleston | CAR | Rays | RiverDogs |
| CUB | ACL Cubs | ACL | Cubs | ACL Cubs |
| CUBB | AZL Cubs Blue | AZL | Cubs | AZL Cubs Blue |
| CUBR | AZL Cubs Red | AZL | Cubs | AZL Cubs Red |
| CUL | Culiacan | LMP | - | Culiacan |
| CHW | Chi White Sox | AL | - | White Sox |
| DAY | Dayton | MID | Reds | Dragons |
| DBT | Daytona | FSL | Reds | Tortugas |
| DE | Down East | CAR | Rangers | Wood Ducks |
| DEL | Delmarva | CAR | Orioles | Shorebirds |
| DET | Detroit | AL | - | Tigers |
| DIA | ACL D-backs | ACL | D-backs | ACL D-backs |
| DIA | AZL D-backs | AZL | D-backs | AZL D-backs |

| CODE | TEAM | LG | AFF | NAME |
|------|------|----|----|------|
| DIA2 | ACL D-backs 2 | ACL | D-backs | ACL D-backs 2 |
| DIAB | ACL D-backs Black | ACL | D-backs | ACL D-backs Black |
| DIAR | ACL D-backs Red | ACL | D-backs | ACL D-backs Red |
| DOD | ACL Dodgers | ACL | Dodgers | ACL Dodgers |
| DOD1 | AZL Dodgers 1 | AZL | Dodgers | AZL Dodgers 1 |
| DOD2 | AZL Dodgers 2 | AZL | Dodgers | AZL Dodgers 2 |
| DR | Dom. Rep. | CS | - | Dom. Rep. |
| DSL ANG | DSL Angels | DSL | Angels | DSL Angels |
| DSL AST | DSL Astros | DSL | Astros | DSL Astros |
| DSL ATH | DSL Athletics | DSL | Athletics | DSL Athletics |
| DSL BALB | DSL BAL Black | DSL | Orioles | DSL BAL Black |
| DSL BALO | DSL BAL Orange | DSL | Orioles | DSL BAL Orange |
| DSL BAU | DSL Dodgers Bautista | DSL | Dodgers | DSL Dodgers Bautista |
| DSL BLJ | DSL Blue Jays | DSL | Blue Jays | DSL Blue Jays |
| DSL BOSB | DSL BOS Blue | DSL | Red Sox | DSL BOS Blue |
| DSL BOSR | DSL BOS Red | DSL | Red Sox | DSL BOS Red |
| DSL BRA | DSL Braves | DSL | Braves | DSL Braves |
| DSL BRW | DSL Brewers | DSL | Brewers | DSL Brewers |
| DSL BRW1 | DSL Brewers1 | DSL | Brewers | DSL Brewers1 |
| DSL BRW1 | DSL Brewers 1 | DSL | Brewers | DSL Brewers 1 |
| DSL BRW2 | DSL Brewers2 | DSL | Brewers | DSL Brewers2 |
| DSL BRW2 | DSL Brewers 2 | DSL | Brewers | DSL Brewers 2 |
| DSL CAR | DSL Cardinals | DSL | Cardinals | DSL Cardinals |
| DSL CARB | DSL Cardinals Blue | DSL | Cardinals | DSL Cardinals Blue |
| DSL CARR | DSL Cardinals Red | DSL | Cardinals | DSL Cardinals Red |
| DSL CLEB | DSL CLE Blue | DSL | Guardians | DSL CLE Blue |
| DSL CLER | DSL CLE Red | DSL | Guardians | DSL CLE Red |
| DSL COL | DSL Colorado | DSL | Rockies | DSL Colorado |
| DSL COOP | DSL MIL/TOR | DSL | DSL MIL/TOR | DSL MIL/TOR |
| DSL CUBB | DSL Cubs Blue | DSL | Cubs | DSL Cubs Blue |
| DSL CUBR | DSL Cubs Red | DSL | Cubs | DSL Cubs Red |
| DSL DB1 | DSL D-backs1 | DSL | D-backs | DSL D-backs1 |
| DSL DB2 | DSL D-backs2 | DSL | D-backs | DSL D-backs2 |
| DSL | DSL D-backs Black | DSL | D-backs | DSL D-backs |

| CODE | TEAM | LG | AFF | NAME |
|------|------|----|----|------|
| DBB | | | | Black |
| DSL DBR | DSL D-backs Red | DSL | D-backs | DSL D-backs Red |
| DSL GIA | DSL Giants1 | DSL | Giants | DSL Giants1 |
| DSL GIB | DSL Giants Black | DSL | Giants | DSL Giants Black |
| DSL GIO | DSL Giants Orange | DSL | Giants | DSL Giants Orange |
| DSL GIT | DSL Giants2 | DSL | Giants | DSL Giants2 |
| DSL HOUB | DSL HOU Blue | DSL | Astros | DSL HOU Blue |
| DSL HOUO | DSL HOU Orange | DSL | Astros | DSL HOU Orange |
| DSL IND1 | DSL Guardians1 | DSL | Guardians | DSL Guardians1 |
| DSL IND2 | DSL Guardians2 | DSL | Guardians | DSL Guardians2 |
| DSL INDB | DSL Guardians Blue | DSL | Guardians | DSL Guardians Blue |
| DSL INDR | DSL Guardians Red | DSL | Guardians | DSL Guardians Red |
| DSL KCG | DSL KC Glass | DSL | Royals | DSL KC Glass |
| DSL KCS | DSL KC Stewart | DSL | Royals | DSL KC Stewart |
| DSL LADB | DSL LAD Bautista | DSL | Dodgers | DSL LAD Bautista |
| DSL LADM | DSL LAD Mega | DSL | Dodgers | DSL LAD Mega |
| DSL MET1 | DSL Mets1 | DSL | Mets | DSL Mets1 |
| DSL MET1 | DSL Mets 1 | DSL | Mets | DSL Mets 1 |
| DSL MET2 | DSL Mets2 | DSL | Mets | DSL Mets2 |
| DSL MET2 | DSL Mets 2 | DSL | Mets | DSL Mets 2 |
| DSL MIA | DSL Marlins | DSL | Marlins | DSL Marlins |
| DSL MIA | DSL Miami | DSL | Marlins | DSL Miami |
| DSL MRL | DSL Marlins | DSL | Marlins | DSL Marlins |
| DSL NAT | DSL Nationals | DSL | Nationals | DSL Nationals |
| DSL NYY | DSL NYY Yankees | DSL | Yankees | DSL NYY Yankees |
| DSL NYY | DSL Yankees | DSL | Yankees | DSL Yankees |
| DSL NYY1 | DSL Yankees1 | DSL | Yankees | DSL Yankees1 |
| DSL NYY2 | DSL Yankees2 | DSL | Yankees | DSL Yankees2 |
| DSL NYYB | DSL NYY Bombers | DSL | Yankees | DSL NYY Bombers |
| DSL OR1 | DSL Orioles1 | DSL | Orioles | DSL Orioles1 |
| DSL OR2 | DSL Orioles2 | DSL | Orioles | DSL Orioles2 |
| DSL PAD | DSL Padres | DSL | Padres | DSL Padres |
| DSL PHR | DSL Phillies Red | DSL | Phillies | DSL Phillies Red |

| CODE | TEAM | LG | AFF | NAME |
|---|---|---|---|---|
| DSL PHW | DSL Phillies White | DSL | Phillies | DSL Phillies White |
| DSL PIR1 | DSL Pirates1 | DSL | Pirates | DSL Pirates1 |
| DSL PIR2 | DSL Pirates2 | DSL | Pirates | DSL Pirates2 |
| DSL PIRB | DSL Pirates Black | DSL | Pirates | DSL Pirates Black |
| DSL PIRG | DSL Pirates Gold | DSL | Pirates | DSL Pirates Gold |
| DSL PITB | DSL PIT Black | DSL | Pirates | DSL PIT Black |
| DSL PITG | DSL PIT Gold | DSL | Pirates | DSL PIT Gold |
| DSL RAN2 | DSL Rangers2 | DSL | Rangers | DSL Rangers2 |
| DSL RAY | DSL Rays | DSL | Rays | DSL Rays |
| DSL RAY1 | DSL Rays1 | DSL | Rays | DSL Rays1 |
| DSL RAY2 | DSL Rays2 | DSL | Rays | DSL Rays2 |
| DSL REDS | DSL Reds | DSL | Reds | DSL Reds |
| DSL RGR1 | DSL Rangers1 | DSL | Rangers | DSL Rangers1 |
| DSL RGR2 | DSL Rangers2 | DSL | Rangers | DSL Rangers2 |
| DSL ROC | DSL Rockies | DSL | Rockies | DSL Rockies |
| DSL ROY1 | DSL Royals1 | DSL | Royals | DSL Royals1 |
| DSL ROY2 | DSL Royals2 | DSL | Royals | DSL Royals2 |
| DSL ROYB | DSL Royals Blue | DSL | Royals | DSL Royals Blue |
| DSL ROYW | DSL Royals White | DSL | Royals | DSL Royals White |
| DSL RSB | DSL Red Sox Blue | DSL | Red Sox | DSL Red Sox Blue |
| DSL RSR | DSL Red Sox Red | DSL | Red Sox | DSL Red Sox Red |
| DSL SEA | DSL Mariners | DSL | Mariners | DSL Mariners |
| DSL SHO | DSL Dodgers Shoemaker | DSL | Dodgers | Dodgers Shoemaker |
| DSL TB | DSL Tampa Bay | DSL | Rays | DSL Tampa Bay |
| DSL TB1 | DSL Rays1 | DSL | Rays | DSL Rays1 |
| DSL TB2 | DSL Rays2 | DSL | Rays | DSL Rays2 |
| DSL TEXB | DSL TEX Blue | DSL | Rangers | DSL TEX Blue |
| DSL TEXR | DSL TEX Red | DSL | Rangers | DSL TEX Red |
| DSL TIG | DSL Tigers | DSL | Tigers | DSL Tigers |
| DSL TIG1 | DSL Tigers1 | DSL | Tigers | DSL Tigers1 |
| DSL TIG1 | DSL Tigers 1 | DSL | Tigers | DSL Tigers 1 |
| DSL TIG2 | DSL Tigers2 | DSL | Tigers | DSL Tigers2 |

| CODE | TEAM | LG | AFF | NAME |
|---|---|---|---|---|
| DSL TIG2 | DSL Tigers 2 | DSL | Tigers | DSL Tigers 2 |
| DSL TWI | DSL Twins | DSL | Twins | DSL Twins |
| DSL WSX | DSL White Sox | DSL | White Sox | DSL White Sox |
| DUN | Dunedin | FSL | Blue Jays | Blue Jays |
| DUR | Durham | INT | Rays | Bulls |
| DUR | Durango | MEX | - | Generales |
| ELP | El Paso | PCL | Padres | Chihuahuas |
| ERI | Erie | EAS | Tigers | SeaWolves |
| ESC | Escogido | LIDOM | - | Leones |
| EST | Estrellas | LIDOM | - | Estrellas |
| EUG | Eugene | NWL | Giants | Emeralds |
| EVE | Everett | NWL | Mariners | AquaSox |
| FAY | Fayetteville | CAR | Astros | Woodpeckers |
| FBG | Fredericksburg | CAR | Nationals | Nationals |
| FLO | Florida | FSL | Braves | Fire Frogs |
| FRE | Frederick | CAR | Orioles | Keys |
| FRE | Fresno | CAL | Rockies | Grizzlies |
| FRI | Frisco | TEX | Rangers | RoughRiders |
| FTM | Fort Myers | FSL | Twins | Mighty Mussels |
| FW | Fort Wayne | MID | Padres | TinCaps |
| GBO | Greensboro | SAL | Pirates | Grasshoppers |
| GDD | Glendale | AFL | - | Desert Dogs |
| GIB | AZL Giants Black | AZL | Giants | AZL Giants Black |
| GIG | Gigantes | LIDOM | - | Gigantes |
| GIO | AZL Giants Orange | AZL | Giants | AZL Giants Orange |
| GL | Great Lakes | MID | Dodgers | Loons |
| GNTB | ACL Giants Black | ACL | Giants | ACL Giants Black |
| GNTO | ACL Giants Orange | ACL | Giants | ACL Giants Orange |
| GSV | Guasave | LMP | - | Guasave |
| GUA | ACL Guardians | ACL | Guardians | ACL Guardians |
| GVL | Greenville | SAL | Red Sox | Drive |
| GWN | Gwinnett | INT | Braves | Stripers |
| HAG | Hagerstown | SAL | Nationals | Suns |
| HBG | Harrisburg | EAS | Nationals | Senators |
| HER | Hermosillo | LMP | - | Hermosillo |
| HFD | Hartford | EAS | Rockies | Yard Goats |
| HIC | Hickory | SAL | Rangers | Crawdads |
| HIL | Hillsboro | NWL | D-backs | Hops |
| HOU | Houston | AL | - | Astros |
| HV | Hudson Valley | SAL | Yankees | Renegades |
| IE | Inland Empire | CAL | Angels | 66ers |
| IND | ACL Guardians | ACL | Guardians | ACL Guardians |
| IND | Indianapolis | INT | Pirates | Indianapolis |
| INDB | AZL Guardians Blue | AZL | Guardians | AZL Guardians Blue |
| INDR | AZL Guardians Red | AZL | Guardians | AZL Guardians Red |
| IOW | Iowa | INT | Cubs | Cubs |
| JAL | Jalisco | LMP | - | Jalisco |
| JAX | Jacksonville | INT | Marlins | Jumbo Shrimp |
| JS | Jersey Shore | SAL | Phillies | BlueClaws |
| JUP | Jupiter | FSL | Marlins | Hammerheads |
| JXN | Jackson | SOU | D-backs | Generals |

| CODE | TEAM | LG | AFF | NAME |
|---|---|---|---|---|
| KAN | Kannapolis | CAR | White Sox | Cannon Ballers |
| KC | Kane County | MID | D-backs | Cougars |
| KC | Kansas City | AL | - | Royals |
| LAA | LA Angels | AL | - | Angels |
| LAD | LA Dodgers | NL | - | Dodgers |
| LAG | Laguna | MEX | - | Algodoneros |
| LAG | La Guaira | LVBP | Tiburones | Tiburones |
| LAK | Lakeland | FSL | Tigers | Flying Tigers |
| LAN | Lancaster | CAL | Rockies | JetHawks |
| LAN | Lansing | MID | Athletics | Lugnuts |
| LAR | Lara | LVBP | Cardenales | Cardenales |
| LAR | Dos Laredos | MEX | - | Tecolotes |
| LC | Lake County | MID | Guardians | Captains |
| LE | Lake Elsinore | CAL | Padres | Storm |
| LEO | Leon | MEX | - | Bravos |
| LEX | Lexington | SAL | Royals | Legends |
| LHV | Lehigh Valley | INT | Phillies | IronPigs |
| LIC | Licey | LIDOM | - | Tigres |
| LOU | Louisville | INT | Reds | Bats |
| LV | Las Vegas | PCL | Athletics | Aviators |
| LWD | Lakewood | SAL | Phillies | BlueClaws |
| LYN | Lynchburg | CAR | Guardians | Hillcats |
| MAG | Magallanes | LVBP | Navegantes | Navegantes |
| MAN | Manati | PWL | Manati | Manati |
| MAR | AZL Mariners | AZL | Mariners | AZL Mariners |
| MAR | Margarita | LVBP | Bravos | Bravos |
| MAY | Mayaguez | PWL | Mayaguez | Mayaguez |
| MAZ | Mazatlan | LMP | - | Mazatlan |
| MB | Myrtle Beach | CAR | Cubs | Pelicans |
| MEL | Melbourne | ABL | Aces | Aces |
| MEM | Memphis | INT | Cardinals | Redbirds |
| MET | FCL Mets | | Mets | FCL Mets |
| MEX | Mexico | MEX | - | Diablos Rojos |
| MEX | Mexico | CS | - | Mexico |
| MIA | Miami | NL | - | Marlins |
| MID | Midland | TEX | Athletics | RockHounds |
| MIL | Milwaukee | NL | - | Brewers |
| MIN | Minnesota | AL | - | Twins |
| MIS | Mississippi | SOU | Braves | Braves |
| MOC | Los Mochis | LMP | - | Los Mochis |
| MOD | Modesto | CAL | Mariners | Nuts |
| MRL | FCL Marlins | | Marlins | FCL Marlins |
| MRL | GCL Marlins | GCL | Marlins | GCL Marlins |
| MRN | ACL Mariners | ACL | Mariners | ACL Mariners |
| MSS | Mesa | AFL | - | Solar Sox |
| MTG | Montgomery | SOU | Rays | Biscuits |
| MTS | GCL Mets | GCL | Mets | GCL Mets |
| MTY | Monterrey | LMP | - | Sultanes |
| MVA | Monclova | MEX | - | Acereros |
| MXC | Mexicali | LMP | - | Mexicali |
| NAS | Nashville | INT | Brewers | Sounds |
| NAT | FCL Nationals | | Nationals | FCL Nationals |
| NAT | GCL Nationals | GCL | Nationals | GCL Nationals |
| NAV | Navojoa | LMP | - | Navojoa |
| NH | New Hampshire | EAS | Blue Jays | Fisher Cats |
| NOR | Norfolk | INT | Orioles | Tides |

| CODE | TEAM | LG | AFF | NAME |
|---|---|---|---|---|
| NWA | NW Arkansas | TEX | Royals | Naturals |
| NYM | NY Mets | NL | - | Mets |
| NYY | NY Yankees | AL | - | Yankees |
| OAK | Oakland | AL | - | Athletics |
| OAX | Oaxaca | MEX | - | Guerreros |
| OBR | Obregon | LMP | - | Obregon |
| OKC | Okla. City | PCL | Dodgers | Dodgers |
| OMA | Omaha | INT | Royals | Storm Chasers |
| ORI | Caribes | LVBP | Caribes | Caribes |
| ORI | FCL Orioles | | Orioles | FCL Orioles |
| ORI | GCL Orioles | GCL | Orioles | GCL Orioles |
| ORIB | FCL Orioles Black | FCL | Orioles | FCL Orioles Black |
| ORIO | FCL Orioles Orange | FCL | Orioles | FCL Orioles Orange |
| PAD | ACL Padres | ACL | Padres | ACL Padres |
| PAN | Panama | CS | - | Panama |
| PAW | Pawtucket | INT | Red Sox | Red Sox |
| PEJ | Peoria | AFL | - | Javelinas |
| PEO | Peoria | MID | Cardinals | Chiefs |
| PER | Perth | ABL | Heat | Heat |
| PHE | GCL Phillies East | GCL | Phillies | GCL Phillies East |
| PHI | FCL Phillies | | Phillies | FCL Phillies |
| PHI | Philadelphia | NL | - | Phillies |
| PHW | GCL Phillies West | GCL | Phillies | GCL Phillies West |
| PIR | FCL Pirates | | Pirates | FCL Pirates |
| PIR | GCL Pirates | GCL | Pirates | GCL Pirates |
| PIRB | FCL Pirates Black | FCL | Pirates | FCL Pirates Black |
| PIRG | FCL Pirates Gold | FCL | Pirates | FCL Pirates Gold |
| PIT | Pittsburgh | NL | - | Pirates |
| PMB | Palm Beach | FSL | Cardinals | Cardinals |
| PNS | Pensacola | SOU | Marlins | Blue Wahoos |
| POR | Portland | EAS | Red Sox | Sea Dogs |
| PUE | Puebla | MEX | - | Pericos |
| PUR | Puerto Rico | CS | - | Puerto Rico |
| QC | Quad Cities | MID | Royals | River Bandits |
| RA12 | RA12 | PWL | - | RA12 |
| RAN | ACL Rangers | ACL | Rangers | ACL Rangers |
| RAN | AZL Rangers | AZL | Rangers | AZL Rangers |
| RAY | FCL Rays | | Rays | FCL Rays |
| RAY | GCL Rays | GCL | Rays | GCL Rays |
| RC | Rancho Cuca. | CAL | Dodgers | Quakes |
| RCK | ACL Rockies | ACL | Rockies | ACL Rockies |
| RCT | Rocket City | SOU | Angels | Trash Pandas |
| REA | Reading | EAS | Phillies | Fightin Phils |
| RED | ACL Reds | ACL | Reds | ACL Reds |
| RED | AZL Reds | AZL | Reds | AZL Reds |
| RIC | Richmond | EAS | Giants | Flying Squirrels |
| RNO | Reno | PCL | D-backs | Aces |
| ROC | Rochester | INT | Nationals | Red Wings |
| ROM | Rome | SAL | Braves | Braves |
| ROY | ACL Royals | ACL | Royals | ACL Royals |
| ROY | AZL Royals | AZL | Royals | AZL Royals |
| ROYB | ACL Royals Blue | ACL | Royals | ACL Royals Blue |
| ROYG | ACL Royals Gold | ACL | Royals | ACL Royals Gold |

| CODE | TEAM | LG | AFF | NAME |
|------|------|-----|------|------|
| RR | Round Rock | PCL | Rangers | Express |
| RSX | FCL Red Sox | | Red Sox | FCL Red Sox |
| RSX | GCL Red Sox | GCL | Red Sox | GCL Red Sox |
| SA | San Antonio | TEX | Padres | Missions |
| SAC | Sacramento | PCL | Giants | River Cats |
| SAL | Salem | CAR | Red Sox | Red Sox |
| SAL | Saltillo | MEX | - | Saraperos |
| SAN | Santurce | PWL | Santurce | Santurce |
| SB | South Bend | MID | Cubs | Cubs |
| SCO | Scottsdale | AFL | - | Scorpions |
| SD | San Diego | NL | - | Padres |
| SD1 | AZL Padres 1 | AZL | Padres | AZL Padres 1 |
| SD2 | AZL Padres 2 | AZL | Padres | AZL Padres 2 |
| SEA | Seattle | AL | - | Mariners |
| SF | San Francisco | NL | - | Giants |
| SJ | San Jose | CAL | Giants | Giants |
| SL | Salt Lake | PCL | Angels | Bees |
| SLU | St. Lucie | FSL | Mets | Mets |
| SOM | Somerset | EAS | Yankees | Patriots |
| SPO | Spokane | NWL | Rockies | Spokane |
| SPR | Springfield | TEX | Cardinals | Cardinals |
| SRR | Salt River | AFL | - | Rafters |
| STK | Stockton | CAL | Athletics | Ports |
| STL | St. Louis | NL | - | Cardinals |
| STL | St. Lucie | FSL | Mets | Mets |
| STP | St. Paul | INT | Twins | Saints |
| SUG | Sugar Land | AAA W | Astros | Skeeters |
| SUG | Sugar Land | PCL | Astros | Space Cowboys |
| SUR | Surprise | AFL | - | Saguaros |
| SWB | Scranton/WB | INT | Yankees | RailRiders |
| SYD | Sydney | ABL | Blue Sox | Blue Sox |
| SYR | Syracuse | INT | Mets | Mets |
| TAB | Tabasco | MEX | - | Olmecas |
| TAC | Tacoma | PCL | Mariners | Rainiers |
| TAM | Tampa | FSL | Yankees | Tarpons |
| TB | Tampa Bay | AL | - | Rays |
| TDN | Tren del Norte | | - | Tren del Norte |
| TEX | Texas | AL | - | Rangers |
| TIG | FCL Tigers | | Tigers | FCL Tigers |
| TIG | GCL Tigers East | GCL | Tigers | GCL Tigers East |
| TIG | Quintana Roo | MEX | - | Tigres |
| TIGE | FCL Tigers East | FCL | Tigers | FCL Tigers East |
| TIGW | FCL Tigers West | FCL | Tigers | FCL Tigers West |
| TIJ | Tijuana | MEX | - | Toros |
| TIW | GCL Tigers West | GCL | Tigers | GCL Tigers West |
| TNS | Tennessee | SOU | Cubs | Smokies |
| TOL | Toledo | INT | Tigers | Mud Hens |
| TOR | Toronto | AL | - | Blue Jays |
| TOR | Toros | LIDOM | | Toros |
| TRI | Tri-City | NWL | Angels | Dust Devils |
| TRN | Trenton | EAS | Yankees | Thunder |
| TUL | Tulsa | TEX | Dodgers | Drillers |
| TWI | FCL Twins | | Twins | FCL Twins |
| TWI | GCL Twins | GCL | Twins | GCL Twins |
| VAN | Vancouver | NWL | Blue Jays | Canadians |
| VEN | Venezuela | CS | - | Venezuela |

| CODE | TEAM | LG | AFF | NAME |
|------|------|-----|------|------|
| VIS | Visalia | CAL | D-backs | Rawhide |
| WCH | Wichita | TEX | Twins | Wind Surge |
| WIL | Wilmington | SAL | Nationals | Blue Rocks |
| WIS | Wisconsin | MID | Brewers | Timber Rattlers |
| WM | West Michigan | MID | Tigers | Whitecaps |
| WOR | Worcester | INT | Red Sox | Red Sox |
| WS | Winston-Salem | SAL | White Sox | Dash |
| WAS | Washington | NL | - | Nationals |
| WSX | ACL White Sox | ACL | White Sox | ACL White Sox |
| WSX | AZL White Sox | AZL | White Sox | AZL White Sox |
| WV | West Virginia | SAL | Mariners | Power |
| YAE | GCL Yankees East | GCL | Yankees | GCL Yankees East |
| YAW | GCL Yankees West | GCL | Yankees | GCL Yankees West |
| YNK | FCL Yankees | | Yankees | FCL Yankees |
| YUC | Yucatan | MEX | - | Leones |
| ZUL | Zulia | LVBP | Aguilas | Aguilas |

# Index of Names